Hearts on Fire:
A Treasury of Poems on Love

Volume III

Edited, with introduction, index and biographical sketches

By

JOHN FROST

And the staff of the American Poetry Association

THE AMERICAN POETRY ASSOCIATION
Santa Cruz, California

Box 8403, Santa Cruz, California 95061

International Standard Book Number: 0-88147-020-1

International Standard Serial Number: 0734-5135

INTRODUCTION

Perhaps the oldest and most universal theme, which has fired the imaginations of poets throughout history, is that of love. It is a diverse and complicated emotion, and writers of all ages have sought to understand and explain that powerful feeling, to somehow describe the bittersweet mixture of joy and pain that goes along with love's tenuous beginnings, or to win the affection of a loved one with a heartfelt piece of verse.

When we reflect on the poetry that has been the most memorable for us, the love poetry of such poets as Dickinson, Shelley, Shakespeare, Blake and Browning inevitably comes to mind. In spite of the repetition of this theme in our culture and others, poems about love continue to move and affect us, and to give us new insight about an emotion which is so central to human experience.

In this, the third volume of love poetry that we have produced, the editors and I were struck most of all by the diversity of poetry that we received. The contemporary poets represented here have succeeded in looking at the age-old theme of love from fresh and new perspectives; they have spoken about love in poetic voices that are as unique and multifaceted as love itself. Moving forward from the examples of our great masters, these poets bring a refreshing honesty and directness to their work. The result is some of the most poignant and moving modern poetry that I have read.

Much of the poetry in this volume deals with the emotions two lovers experience. However, it would do our poets an injustice to suggest that their definitions of love are limited to the romantic and passionate. Within the covers of this book, you will find the full range of human love depicted: the caring and trust that develops between true friends, the deep-seated, almost instinctual love between a parent and a child, religious love, with its spiritual serenity, even the affectionate and often powerful bonds between people and their pets. But no matter what type of relationship is described, the sincerity of the emotions comes through.

In addition to the contemporary poetry contained in this volume, I have selected a number of works by celebrated poets of the past. My purpose in doing so was twofold: First, I hope to bring the same pleasure to our readers that I experience on reading and rereading poems by William Wordsworth, Elizabeth Browning, Thomas Moore and others. Secondly, I believe the works provide the perfect complement to the modern poetry contained within these pages. In reading the masters, we discover our own artistic roots; we are inspired to push our skills as both readers and writers ever-forward, while retaining an appreciation for our rich literary heritage.

It is with pride and pleasure that I present to you, **Hearts on Fire: A Treasury of Poems on Love, Volume III**.

John Frost

John Frost
Chief Editor
Santa Cruz, California
August 8, 1986

A NOTE ON THE ILLUSTRATIONS

The theme of this volume is not only love, but the diversity of love, and its many manifestations. We have therefore selected a wide range of styles and subjects, from the elaborate Fifteenth century woodcuts of Albrecht Dürer to the honest sentiment of the Nineteenth century Currier & Ives engravings, from lovers boating on a Sunday afternoon to the reconciliation of father and Prodigal Son.

We hope that you enjoy these illustrations and that you find them complimentary to the poems in this volume.

Index of Prize Winners

Below are the winners in our **Hearts on Fire, Volume III** contest. In addition to the cash prizes shown, the top 12 winners received book awards. This year, the book awards are copies of **Hearts on Fire, A Treasury of Poems on Love, Volume III.** All winners received prize certificates. Our congratulations to all of you!

1st Place — $1,000 & BOOK — *I Cannot Lie Still,* John Montgomery, San Anselmo, CA — i
2nd Place — $500 & BOOK — *A Poet's Love Call to the Editor,* Emily K. Schweighart, Littleton, CO — i
3rd Place — $200 & BOOK — *Reasons,* Elizabeth M. Jay, Staten Island, NY — i
4th Place — $100 & BOOK — *Avon, New Leader in Paperbacks!,* K. McLaren, Fairfax, CA — i
5th Place — $50 & BOOK — *No Marker; No Grave,* Patricia Clina, Pleasant Valley, NY — ii
6th Place — $30 & BOOK — *Waiting,* Carla Jean, West Hill, Ont. — ii
7th Place — $20 & BOOK — *Under a Flock of Reoccurring Birds,* Lois Bunse, Jamestown, CA — ii
8th Place — BOOK — *Rituals,* L. Ann Black, Bloomington, IL — ii
9th Place — BOOK — *It Is Still with Me Motionless,* John Montgomery, San Anselmo, CA — iii
10th Place — BOOK — *Urban Renewal,* Susan Katz, Phoenixville, PA — iii
11th Place — BOOK — *Worry Wakes Me,* Rodger Kelley, New Market, TN — iii
12th Place — BOOK — *Farewell,* Margaret Secrest, Andover, OH — iii

HONORABLE MENTION (In alphabetical order)

Haunts, Rosa Nelle Anderson, Dallas, TX — 492
Stunned, Karen Lynelle Bowling, Veedersburg, IN — 417
You Can't Name a Beast Unless, Lois Bunse, Jamestown, CA — 490
Marriage Day, J. C. Caruso, Los Angeles, CA — 109
Wedding Vows, George P. Castellitto, Denville, NJ — 460
Checker Players, 1943, A. V. Christie, Baltimore, MD — 429
Winter Afternoons, Jon Cristol, San Marcos, CA — 283
I Want to Take You Below, Ron Deverman, Springfield, IL — 475
Love, Love, Love, Jacquie Dyer, Elmira, NY — 13
Untitled, Billie Sue Fischer, Berkeley, CA — 96
Untitled, Billie Sue Fischer, Berkeley, CA — 313
Architecture, Robie Glenn Hall, Dry Creek, KY — 220
Love Is a Disease, Donald Hawkins, East Moriches, NY — 93
Footsteps, Nancy M. Holewa, Maple Grove, MN — 101
On Love Making, S. L. Hough, Berkeley, CA — 42
Grave through the Window, Stephen M. Hurley, San Diego, CA — 57
Gladiolas, Ron Jevaltas, Pittsville, WI — 384
Sweet Evening Lullaby, Jolène A. Kent, Iola, WI — 193
The Fountain without Water, Melinda Latimer, St. Regis, MT — 437
During Odd Hours of Light, Melinda Latimer, St. Regis, MT — 186
Calling Home, Cynthia Jane Law, Mountlake Terrace, WA — 367
Bedroom Primeval, Gene Lominac, Raleigh, NC — 500
Trail, Peter Ludwin, Los Angeles, CA — 128
The Away from Home Song John Montgomery, San Anselmo, CA — 34
Infidelity, Sheryl Morang, Utica, MI — 346
Under the Fluorescent Lamp, Doug Muravez, Eugene, OR — 384
I Had a Vision, Doug Muravez, Eugene, OR — 266
Big Mack, Didi Murphy, Englewood, CO — 76
Physics, Alice Persons, Portland, ME — 68
Sketch, Michael M. Peters, Red Bluff, CA — 404
Undertow, Lorna Price, Ashland, OR — 145
The Rio Grande Trail, Janet M. Roberts, Lakeville, CT — 186
Norfolk, Tadeusz Rybowski, Polska, Poland — 215
Remission, Charles Seagren, Oak Park, IL — 245
No Fold, Margaret Secrest, Andover, OH — 385
My Lover's an Actress, J. G. Smith, Canyon, TX — 399
Eggs, Linda Soo Hoo, New Rochelle, NY — 173
the wish-they-were-remembered lovers, Juley Wright, Livermore, CA — 245

I CANNOT LIE STILL

1ST PLACE

The honey in the hollow tree fills
The side valley with scent this year.
How strong the worker bees must be
To bring all that blossom from over the mountain.
I nuzzle the freshet. It is wide
For this early. Wind Mother
Winds a little late snow on
The heavy pack. It'll be good
To have the pools across lazy summer.
I have never seen so many buds
In the alder thicket. Something is abroad.
I feel it in my shoulders. The eagle
Made a new nest. Never before has she done it
While I have laired here. The claw marks
On my oak, so slender and high;
Have they affected my senses?
Her spoor is heady.

It must be she the fish are wiggling for.
Wind Mother, I cannot lie still.

John Montgomery

A POET'S LOVE CALL TO THE EDITOR

2ND PLACE

I am sending the following poems
to be seen in print

I do not care if I win a prize
I just want you to read them.

I love them so!

Emily K. Schweighart

REASONS

3RD PLACE

If my cat decides to join me underneath the covers . . .
(keep in mind that it is not as conscious as an actual people-decision;
it is not, for that matter, a decision at all —
since that word implies a set, agreed-upon conclusion)

Well, when my cat decides to join me underneath the covers
(*if* my cat decides to join me underneath the covers),
he always has the inevitably viable alternative of changing his mind
(which he occasionally does)

Remember: I love my cat
It is precisely his lack of decision-making dexterity that makes me a jealous lover

Elizabeth M. Jay

AVON
New Leader in Paperbacks!

4TH PLACE

QUEST V2255 75¢

The dazzling and daring young woman's
search for her lover leads from the Black
Court to an obsessive love for her Death
into a strange and shocking marriage

TIME FOR LOVE V2268 75¢

The stormy-eyed heroine's desperate
searches through Medieval France lead her
to the arms of the sadistic Mail Order Dept.,

ROYAL MISTRESS V2254 75¢

The seductive French beauty is hurled
to her lover's side at last — only to lose him
once again. The bewitching Proud and passionate
harem-girl! flees the French
to battle an infidel princess for Arnaud —
only to find herself the Caliph's favorite sworn enemy.

Blue novels to follow

Karla McLaren

NO MARKER; NO GRAVE

5TH PLACE

My first thought is of how I will ever find his name
among those fifty-eight thousand, twenty-two.
I walk up to the wall and begin to read.
One by one I pass over names until I find his,
and it never really strikes me that those names
are no different from his; there it is.
His name; that's all I have left of him.
No marker, no grave, only his name on a wall
and some faded memories.
Then I think that's all that's left of many more.
Where do their families go?
I no longer have him to hug, to play checkers with.
He no longer greets me at the back door,
nor helps with the groceries, and other little things.
the house is strangely quiet, not filled with laughter.
How could he be lost?
No marker;
No grave.

Patricia Clina

WAITING

6TH PLACE

Every light blackened as though in your absence
the house is in mourning. The two cats sit
on the window sill, looking. For them, it doesn't
matter at what. Watching for everything is their
first priority; mine, to see the slightest incline

of their ears toward the door. Tiny rumbles,
vibrations from the street remind me you've been
in California. The house trembling with each
passing car, my hand wavering as I reach
for my pen. It's only been three days, but already

from the sound of your voice earlier, I see how
you must look relaxing in warm air while I sit
with bare feet propped against the old radiator,
hot; the lightning bugs surprising you as you pick
hibiscus surrounding an herb garden: my glowings,

the car lights jumping from the darkness, red and white
blinkings. How strange it must be to come back
to us waiting — and the dark bare trees,
their naked arms shunted, when the ones
you've just left were left full, not wanting.

Carla Jean

UNDER A FLOCK OF REOCCURRING BIRDS

7TH PLACE

The bride demurely holds four paint brushes
and a palette of early color, tender greens,
light and dark. Strokes, lines, leaves,

stem and branch impose upon each other.
The woman under the leaves knows she will
be discovered. She doesn't need dove, book,

or broad-brimmed hat, nothing extra
to publish that her smile is original.
The moon rides the dark hole of itself.

What the lovers are doing is intaglio.
The ground, the bottom of the landscape,
has a standing bird and a bouquet of flowers

accented by baby's-breath and a fish diving,
its beak aiming straight into the water,
the final stage. Sometimes a full moon lights

the fish's arcing belly; other times
a crescent, higher, lights just as much,
with a longer reflection in the water.

Lois Bunse

RITUALS

8TH PLACE

Where now? Where do you spend your time tonight?
I've moved again.
At last a room with cross-breeze. I may stay.

Under the moon, you're on a road
between cities you cannot name, with
less than a quarter tank. Your radio,
if it's being good, plays low
while cigarette ashes twirl with the wind
to the back seat.

That same wind
gives bodily image to my curtains,
cools my bed.

We think we're starting fresh
but the rituals never go.

The night swallows our bodies
a little at a time, choking.
Before you sleep you shake me off your shoulders,
vow never to think of me
because you know I'm not thinking of you.

It's late. Where are you now?

L. Ann Black

IT IS STILL WITH ME MOTIONLESS

9TH PLACE

When they ask me in the spacious later time,
"Was I young once?" "And did I know one?"
How can I tell them I loved her? Who can know
The face of Beatrice is the same one who comes
Often and often with the same slow, easy walk?

Who can know before the day that one walk
Which is not looking away from you
Is not looking at you but looking there
And her hair touched with a gesture
gracing always the very one?

Who can know before the day, the shape
The heart takes when the gesture moves
For him, knowing the answer waiting in him
That he never knew was there?

I was young once and I knew one in a quick-moving
Crowded time. And when they ask me of her
In my spacious later time how can I tell them
It is still with me, motionless, the shadow still
On her cheek, the dust on her sandal,
My breastbone freshly dented where it moved?

John Montgomery

URBAN RENEWAL

10TH PLACE

Our apartment house is gone.
Now a granite giant, holding cars
That gleam in rows like false teeth,
Supports the air which once supported us.
The coatrack, once our weathercock
With its crooked feather,
Has no door to perch inside
When you come stumbling home late,
To catch you in its shaky arm
Like an old, forgiving mother;
The clock, that dog, no longer gnaws
Our days, burying time's bones
With one whole, one crippled paw;
The mailbox doesn't hold our names
In its wooden lap, side by side
But not quite joined, like us.
It's all gone — even love that flew
Above our heads, a hummingbird
Hunting a sweeter garden, a firmer house.

Susan Katz

WORRY WAKES ME

11TH PLACE

Mornings when I've nothing to do, nowhere to go,
I lie in bed moving over to your side
after you've gotten up and gone down the hall.

I listen to sounds of you coming from the bathroom —
the open and close of your make-up drawer,
the soapy sound of you in the shower,
and always the clearing and reclearing of your throat
preparing yourself for a day of polite conversation.

I drift in and out of sleep taking comfort in your closeness.
But as soon as you kiss me goodbye and tussle my uncombed hair,
I listen for the sound of the door closing behind you.

As you speak sweetly to the cats who wait for you on the porch,
I rise up from the bed and listen for the sound of your tires
on the gravel going off down the hill.

I cannot easily go back to sleep.
Worry wakes me.
I spend my day off close to the window
watching for you to come home again.

Rodger Kelley

FAREWELL

12TH PLACE

This vessel is empty of words,
of ambition, dreams or goals.
There is nothing more to say
or anything under the sun.
I live other lives now
in books, reading myself
to sleep, to sleep, to sleep.
I dream of beloved dead,
even of a beloved pet.
Wilt has attacked in the dark,
and the era of decay has begun
at my roots where I grow down
to sleep, to sleep, to sleep
beside the one I loved.

Margaret Secrest

FALCON KINGS AND WISHFUL THINKING

auspicious birdman
beside his mate and delight,

female excellence
possessed with a certain level of pride
fleeing arrows towards heaven's breast.

CORRUPTION

waiting anxiously
for the space between the lip and the mouth.
desperately flying higher and higher
searching for the lighted candles in the sky.

WISHFUL THINKING

shattered by the unruly line in the sky
the auspicious birdman falls gracefully
into a cold mountain stream.

Cathy Kuntz

OUR FOREVER

We said it would last forever.
How easy to believe when in youth.
My heart drank greedily of your commitment
And in return gave an even lot.
Forever was but a droplet in time.
Were our eyes then closed when first the storm struck?
Forever? Forever . . .
Such a long time is forever.
Does LOVE then fade?
Only when 'tis not love at all,
When forever is but a word —
So absurd that we knew naught of our plight
But ventured blindly into the tempest,
Holding fast love's glorious infatuation.
Infatuation . . . A mere tidbit . . . Consumed by time.
We clung with both hands to a fading vapor —
Now we must taste the bitter wine of reality
And know that forever is what we make it.
You and I stripped naked the enduring; the sublime
And brought OUR FOREVER to an end.

Donna Marquez

ALPINE MELODY

This is the melody that fills all space
  Love your children, love your mates.
Love is the power that turns the wheel
  Bringing the water to cleanse and heal.
In the mountains or beside the pool,
  Love is the space where Peace will rule.
Close to the water, near the spring
  Hear the melody that I bring
Love is the energy that fills all space
  Love your children, love your mates.
From the mountain stream or the valley pool
  Love turns the wheel where peace will rule.
This is the melody that fills all space
  Love your children, love your mates.
In the mountains or beside the pool
  Love turns the wheel where peace will rule.
Love is the energy that fills all space
  Love is the essence of the race.
This is the melody that fills all space
  Love your children, love your mates.

Mary Margaret Moore

ONLY A MOMENT

What a night, hard to forget
When every hour was but a tick
In a cascade of murmured vows
Punctuated with hugs of the lips
That buried the tipsy balls under the lids
Closed the passage to the eardrum
And ravished the heart and the head
For frenzied flight of ecstasy

The sensuous, slow-paced melodies
Enhanced the lure of the bluish sky
Studded with glittering topaz of stars
Which twinkled in the jet-black face
And stirring up deep-seated sensibilities
Added extra gush of emotions to the foreplay
Fated to consummate that night
Our chequered romance of love and hate.

Kwasi Asante

ASANTE, KWASI. Born: Nkawkaw, Ghana, 5-24-44; Married: 8-11-68 to Cecilia Abena Asante; Education: B.A. (Honors) in English, 6-63; Diploma in Journalism, 1974; Diploma in International Relations and Diplomacy, 1978; Occupation: Foreign Service Officer; Poetry: 'Gem of Life,' *American Poetry Anthology,* 6-20-84; 'Growing Old,' *American Poetry Anthology, Vol IV, No. 2,* 9-10-84; 'At Forty,' *American Poetry Anthology,* 9-18-84; 'Eternal Error,' *Words of Praise,'* 11-6-85; 'The Betrayal;' Comments: *Most of my poems are on human nature — dishonesty, injustice and transitoriness of this life, the mystery of creation as borne out by the sea, stars, and sky. I admire nature in relation to this viciousness of man, and question the genuineness of professed love. Many of my poems allude covertly or overtly to death.*

Love is like the wings of flight,
moving together in harmony,
united by a common bond, yet, separated
by that common bond such that one does not harm the other,
but, should one become harmed in the course of flight,
the other shall give until death.

Lynda B. Barnett

I WILL

I cannot give you the moon, but
I will provide a dream.

I cannot hand you the stars, but
I will be a light in the dark.

I cannot promise you forever, but
I will give you a lifetime.

I cannot say it will always be great, but
I will go against all odds to try.

I cannot tell you you'll always be happy.
But I will never let you hurt alone.

And

Though only God can
Grant everlasting life,
I will share my heart
And soul with you,
Until the end of time,

I love you.

Teresa Boh

MY TREASURES

Stolen were earthly treasures,
My husband's love and faithfulness.

Stolen were earthly treasures,
My family's love and concern.

Stolen were earthly treasures,
My work and efforts unthanked,
And taken for granted.

Stolen were earthly treasures,
My life and time.

Stolen were earthly treasures,
My wealth and food and health.

Stolen were all my natural desires.

What could not be stolen were:
My writings,
My prayers,
My faith,
My heavenly treasures,
And my crowns with many stars.

Estella M. McGhee-Siehoff

I look into his eyes and I see intensity.
I watch and I see his awareness.
He is the guardian of my heart.

I watch his smile and I see gentleness.
I listen and I hear his wisdom.
He is the confidant of my trust.

I look at his face and I see radiance.
I touch him and I feel his compassion.
He is the inspiration of my dreams.

Linda Hangartner

THE LOVE OF A MOTHER

When I was a child in trouble, I reached for the hands of
mother, I cared not for another, nor did I want no other.
The touch of mother's hands was that of no everything, removing the anger.
I needed not to fear for I shared the symphony of life called, love of
mother. I knew the meaning in the glory of love with ancient faith of
caring: holding a flowing memory with sweet dreams of anew.

The sharing of mother's love brought laughter, as I held her hand
as we walked with my feet in the sand. Time with mother became like a
flaming blossom of red, holding a ransom where we went in the land.

The love of mother to me was that of music in changing winds to
the tune in a band. In my heart and mind the love of mother made a
figuration to understanding. Mother was my search on the avenue so close
to follow with songs of love to keep me in God's Grace.
Mother's love removed the beckon evil, where temptation called at freedom
door, of birth to love reborned flame. For the love of a mother is the
ruling horizon to winds, and years of love bearing the same.

Lela L. Maldonado Dechochran

EASTER MORN

The gentle rain of Easter morn fell on a heavy heart.
In church I knew the message would stir my faith from the start.
Yet something held me prisoner, I could not find the way
To ready soul and body on this glorious day of days.
Instead, I dressed in grubby clothes, and headed out of town
To a new and lonely grave, where part of me had gone.
The gentle rain and my tears blended, as I stood and wondered why,
I could not have saved this child of mine, in her final desperate hour.
There is no answer in this world, so I must wait until the time
God will call me home, and, there will be no more sorrow.
To the opposite end of town I drove, another grave to visit.
This time the tears blended with the rain, not with such great sorrow.
For he had earned his rest and peace, and to the very end,
Though pain and suffering were his lot, he never doubted Him.
For he had learned his lessons well; the 23rd Psalm was his Rock.
He knew the Lord would beckon him, when his trials on earth were won.
Faithful to the very end, his heart was strong and true.
He'll be there to meet me, when my time on earth is through.

Gladys H. Case

MIST OF PAST

. . . walking in the cold sunset;
ten degrees out in the air.
Cars whiz by me not caring if they hit me.
The sharp wind smacked my face.
There is no place to go;
just walking . . .
The summer grass, green as a carpet;
little brother's high pitched voice;
picking raspberries in the forest and laughing with the people I love;
all these things are a mist of past.
A car blew its horn and the driver shouted at me.
There is no more summer grass;
little brother grew up;
they chopped down the trees in the forest, and everyone is gone.
Longing for the past is a useless waste of time.
It is loving something that is not there.
Should I be angry?
I guess I should keep on walking.

Caroline Hovi

REDD AND COE

My head is stirring
'Cuz I've awakened from my awesome dream
I've discovered that it's real
You and I
Trying to find answers
Why we love each other the way we do
We love each other honestly
But it goes beyond that
Something we can't control or explain
When we are apart
We fantasize about each other
The fantasies go away when we are together
'Cuz they are fulfilled then
Without them actually becoming reality
This is Us.

Coe Hull

LOVE'S MAGIC POWER

Love can truly set hearts on fire,
Rich or poor, it is the ultimate prize
we desire.
The greatest joy a heart can hold,
Is feeling this sweet love unfold.
Love is a grand gift, given to us by
the Lord,
More powerful than the mightiest sword.
Feelings that only love can bring,
Let us write beautiful songs to sing.
Hearts without love, as cold as ice,
Will never live in love's own paradise.
Only when love combines our heart
and soul,
Are we at peace, and really whole.

Klara Farnum

REMEMBERING

I remember my brother
remembering our
grandfather's advice:
"Son, if she is
difficult to ignore
but hard to interpret,
stay out of
the romantic
department."

Rinkart Eze Okorie

A HOUSE TO CALL HOME

A house is a place
We all call our home.
We struggle and strive
To make it our own.
We plant a garden
Make our house pretty.
Sometimes we find room
For a dog or a kitty.
We do these things and more
Sometimes we will wonder
What we do them for,
We must have "love"
Within these walls
Or else this house
Is no home at all.

Des Diebel

JESUS LOVES US

Jesus loves us
Enough, because
Strength we are given
U and I in livin'
Special treatment

Lots of fulfillment
Our cooperation
Victory over sin done
Earn our reward
Sensible living, forward

Unlike any fortellin'
Success is — in future heaven.

Lilly Kucharczyk

BETTI

She wore a rose behind her ear
in the darkened bar that night;
her eyes were dark and luminous
and her hair caught flicks of light.

"I love you mumsy" were her words
and then, oh Lord, I saw
the bleakest heartbreak on her face
in that ugly downtown bar.

I knew we'd never meet again
and all that I could see
was the tipsy rose behind her ear
that spelled 'eternity.'

Phyllis Kuligowski

NEW LOVERS

Together . . .
Our arms and legs entwined
till nothing could come between.
New lovers . . .
Softly caressing one moment,
Desperately clasping the next,
Until together we spend ourselves,
And fall slowly apart,
Only to repeat it all again.
New lovers . . .
Seeking to learn each nuance,
Lost in our passion.
Each alone but . . .
As one.

Debi Murphy

MY LOVE

As time goes by
My love for you
Grows stronger every day.
I see your face, and then I sigh,
I want to take your hand in mine.
Since fear keeps me from saying
What's really on my mind.
I thought I'd write these words and say,
I love you dear in every way.

Sara Ashton

GAMES

Monopoly
I want Boardwalk, Park Place
and you want me
yet you don't.
Candyland
you want to taste
me and I you
such sweet treats
of each other.
Careers
you live on the west coast
and I in the middle,
no compromise.
Sorry
I think it's over
You think it's over.
Bingo
It is . . .

Pamela Wagers

FIVE MONTHS LATER

Her sudden kiss ripped into my mind,
Two lonely, weary hearts to bind.
The hell it did!

On my lap she hugs and kisses,
Those signals meaning love.
The hell they do!

Contented breathing beneath my ear:
Another sign of love?
The hell it is!
Stay close to this dainty,
Perhaps she'll love me?
The hell I will!

(The secret is, with all this bluster,
I absolutely
Can't let go)

Parker T. Chamerlin

VISION

Visions of a mind over man.
Visions of a land in our hand.
Vision of the past, present,
and future.
Visions of the robot that
shall replace man.
I have mastered the visions.
Visions of a woman that is
never satisfied.
Visions of a love that never
was.
Visions of the man that
keeps his family.

Visions of life after death.
Visions of the outlaw,
who has the law on his
side.

Charles S. Walker

MOTHER AND DAUGHTER LOVE

Lilacs, lavender, pink and white
What a lovely night
Their fragrance wafts thru the air
A delight for all to share.

This row of lilacs in our yard
For a lovelier sight you'd look hard
Family pictures by these often taken
My memories of this never forsaken.

Down the garden path we walk
Mother and daughters enjoy small talk
Coming to a grapevine swing
We begin to laugh and sing.

Pushing each other on the big grapevine
All having a wonderful time
Age is no limit in this little game
From mother to age three, love and joy are the same.

What a nice way to spend a Sunday afternoon
Time goes by all too soon,
Back to the house we skip our way
Hoping to come again another day.

Rowena Bragdon Holt

HOLT, ROWENA. Pen Names: Rowena Bragdon Holt, Robert Endicott Bragdon; Born: Merom, Indiana; Married: 1-4-36 to Louis J. Holt; Education: High school and various correspondence courses; Occupation: Homemaker; Memberships: Community Concert Association; Poetry: 'Falling Leaves,' nature, American Poetry Association, spring & summer 1984; Nine Poems included in showcase on various topics, *American Poetry Showcase,* 1985; '50 Years of Love,' our anniversary poem, *Hearts On Fire,* 1985; 'Mother O Mine,' grief, *American Poetry Anthology,* 1985; '2019 Charlotte Road,' nature's beauty, *American Poetry Anthology,* summer 1985; Comments: *When I write I enjoy trying to describe nature's beauty and sometimes subjects I hope might help others who don't write. Picking up a pen and letting words flow is my happiness. I'm thankful for my mother who encouraged me to write poetry.*

LOOKING BACK

It seems like yesterday we shared so much
Our love was full of vigor and lust
The years passed quick when you look back
Our children are gone and taken much
Forget we won't what we once had
Days of fun and endless love
Through hardships and tears we sang our song
Yes thankful we are, nothing went wrong.

Guillermo A. Barela

THE FOREST OF DREAMS

Come, my young lover, in love's simplicity,
To a beautiful forest that gives a dignity
In its private domain. In romantic delight,
We'll thank your God for a life without blight,
Give work for the day, and possess every night.

A cottage is waiting. It took love's smile
To build it for us in a doll-like style.

Oh, the joys of a kindly kingdom!
It proves that love can survive without wisdom.

There are dates and berries and other bounties
To keep us young within its boundaries.
The rich earth has a constant growth
Of plentiful foods to nourish us both.
(When love has fortune, it has mastered its hope!)

Not many know of these berries and leaves.
They lie somewhere in the forest of dreams —
A protective escape to a perfect kingdom,
As a shelter from gossip for innocence with freedom.

Will you come with me to this hidden land?
I need no answer, if you reach for my hand.

Frances M. Ruchman

YOUR LOVE

Your love is so special to me I cannot explain

My heart begins to fumble the moment I hear your name.

When I wake up in the morning and you are by my side.

My body fills with passion, that I cannot hide.

When I look into your eyes I see the two of us together

Your precious love, will stay with me forever.

Your love is like the sky that is so pretty and blue. When I see your face, I know your love is true.

Your love, it is so precious and means much more than gold, I know I'm in good hands when it's your good hands I hold.

When you're sad and I give you a comforting hug the most precious thing in life to me is your honesty and your love.

Faye W. Simmons

LOVE

One day I was alone
And those I love
Were away for a time.
I looked around me
And in my heart and my eyes,
I saw those days and years of the past . . .
Relived again.
The days of Spring relived in my mind . . .
As I remember saying "YES" when he held my hand
And the walk down the aisle.
And now with years past
My thoughts brought happiness
To me . . .
The LOVE I shared
With HIM
With THOSE who call . . .'Mother'
And now I know:
Love from the heart is GOLDEN DAYS

Virginia Jolliff Herndon

MY LOST LOVE

Today is bright and sunny,
how I wish I were not alone.
Each day I find I am waiting — waiting
for my love to come home.
The birds fly by — could one be my dearest love?
Watching over me — caring from high above.
I must learn to live by myself
and no longer cry at night.
Sixty-four years of love to remember,
dear memories to hold close and tight.
I feel he is near, smoothing the way
as I see all he did for me.
I remember the lovely roses received
all the times he was so far away.
And now when he has left me
to go to that wondrous land
I smell and reach for the lovely rose,
holding him in my heart — in my hand.

Doris McAllister

ALL IS COLD BEAUTY

I wake and you breathe soft hypnotic
Rhythms straight from your heart gently into my soul
Day has broken but only sky is lit
About ember gleams of warmth and secrets untold.
Out of stars like sparks from coal your dream suspires
A deep breath beneath death and into my arms you roll
A comfort, a cause, a stimulating fire
Flame-ridden with madness, shell-shocked into control . . .

Out of winter springs slow the fresh blossom
Falls, misting grey-white symbiotic haze
Purling beneath velvet frictions of unknown outcome
Confluent within the fountains of your soft silent gaze.

Memories slip like petaled tears on tender cheek
Without rest they slide beneath hardened chin
And creep like liquid vines into my sleep
Where they rise and bloom only to die once again.

Pat Patterson

MAY OUR LOVE NEVER END

Years have gone by, and still, you and I,
Have weathered the passing of years;
Sharing our joys and fears,
Sharing our smiles and our tears.

Together, we two, and that means me and you,
Are lovers, companions, and friends,
Let's hope that our love never ends,
On you my whole life depends.

There is no other, that I could hold dear,
Moment by moment, and year after year;
Without you, my love, I am sure I would fail,
Like a ship in a storm, with no motor or sail.

I know you've been true, and I commend you,
As my lover, companion, and friend;
So here's to our love,
Sent from Heaven above,
And darling, may it never end.

W. Ehret

CINNAMON

A Song

Cinnamon . . . sweet lady with the haunted eyes,
I'd like to turn your frown
Upside down —
She only sighs.

Cinnamon . . . fey lady with the pensive smile,
Stay right here,
Have no fear —
For a while.

You shouldn't chase moonlight into the sunrise —
They belong to two different worlds.
So do we, but there is always whatever
We can share — until our last goodbyes.

Cinnamon . . . let's have everything but lies.
Just stay until
We've had our fill —
Memory never dies.

Stephen M. Hurley

LOVE FROM THE HEART

They're just three simple words that mean so much,
so why do they always sound so far off?
It's because you've come to believe to be happy means sad,
when there's a smile, there's a tear,
and somehow it seems you only gain fears.
You've come to believe that love means pain,
where there's a flame, you get burnt,
each and every time you end up getting hurt.
You've come to believe to be content means disturbed
and you never know which way to turn,
but you, my friend, have a lot to learn.
Love is a thought, so true it doesn't need to be obvious.
Love is a touch, so warm it doesn't need to be felt.
Love is a gift that's given to be shared,
and so free it's always there.
Love is a feeling, so pleasing it never ends.
Love is a meaning, so formed that it can't be explained.
But it's only when you can give your heart to love
that it will be able to lift you up.

B. J. Hays

TO DIANE
MY THISTLE-DOWN GRANDCHILD

I love and adore you, my darling,
Little girl so innocent and sweet and
If I had a goblin stone,
Dark brown like old leather
Under which live the wee men
Red Jacket, Green Cap, and White Owl's Feather
I'd rub it thrice for you, Diane,
All good things to you it would bring
To help you grow as you ought to grow
A most proper, lovely, young thing.
I'd give you pearls like white moss roses
And raspberry rubies to wear
With a dew-studded crown of pink wild roses
To wear in your bonnie brown hair.
And best of all I'd wish you
A loving prayerful heart
That your every word, deed, and action
Be guided by noble and lofty thoughts.

Barbara MacPhee

SALLY TWO-SHOES

I remember the days of the Chipmunks,
scrambled eggs, nightbraces and traction,
Sally two-shoes and Lou Lou,
"Downtown" and you.

I remember careening around the halls on my trike,
learning to tie my shoes, baking chocolate chip cookies,
playing outside, afternoon naps, and sucking my thumb —
the real pleasures of life.

I remember your soft words, your laugh, your fun
that helped me to love life even when the pain came,
even when I sat for an hour after breakfast
trying to finish my eggs . . .

even when you stopped me from sucking my thumb,
even when I couldn't walk, or run,
I played anyway
and thanked all of you by being me.

Sally Nickerson

PRAYER OF SERENITY

May we find serenity of spirit,
In spite of the oncoming storm;
May our hearts be filled with sunshine,
As the clouds of worry form.

We must find peace and contentment,
Among our family and friends;
And stand proud of our honest achievements,
As our long day of labor ends.

When our problems seem insurmountable,
We should think of another's plight;
Then our troubles will seem much smaller,
As we give our thanks at night.

Grant us faith and understanding,
So whatever comes to light;
We can face our trials with courage,
And sleep in peace at night.

Caye E. Hurst

TROUBADOR OF GENERATIONS

A Loving Dedication to Bob Dylan

Moody young wanderer standing in the dawn of a time
He once dreamed about in tears.
He walks down a road he's never really known, but somehow
Understood throughout the years.

He's a magician of the minstrels,
Spokesman of the Apocalypse,
Troubador of Generations
Hoping someone will hear.

He has nothing in his hands but his own integrity
Which he gives to all the hurting ones and those wanting to
Be Free.
If he cries it's not for pardon or for innocent disdain,
But because he sees his fellow man shaking in the rain.

He's the singer of the ages, magician of the gods
A single candle burning in the never-ending darkness.
He's a crier for the people, weeper of the lost
Troubador of Generations, singing in the storm.

Valerie Moreno

NO TIME

We have no time for sadness
We have both known it all too well,
We have found love,
And this time, it's meant for us,
Let's forget the past
Stuff it in our memory bouquet
And throw it away.

Let's walk by the sea
Collect sea shells
Build our sand castle
Watch the tide come in
And feel the wind in our hair
And taste the salt on our lips.

Let's live for today
Today is here and now . . . it's all we have
Tomorrow might never come
And if it doesn't
We will have no regrets
For we will have had today
And love.

Linda L. Hudye

BEING WITH YOU

Being with you, brings back the memories of a time when I
was young and free.
When a kiss meant something special between you and me.
But as time passes so quickly that it's hard for me to see,
the changes in our styles, from the way things used to be.
With kisses as soft as a warm summer breeze.
I would lie in awe of your beauty as you smiled with ease
and your eyes would shine with the glow that only true love
can bring.
Like the chiming of sweet church bells your laughter would ring.
But the time passes so swiftly, though you may share my feeling
and my bed.
The words we use may have a harsh tone, and the ones we
mean to say are left unsaid.
Though at times words may fail me or be untrue
I guess you could sum it up as, I love you.

Carl Gooch

BETSY KAY, I LOVE YOU

Ship ahoy, sailor boy;
New York City is the greatest;
I met my true love Betsy Kay there at the Ritz
We dined, we danced, and we kissed.
We dined, we danced, and we kissed.
Both in tender years, her family turned me down.
Grieved and rejected, I joined the Navy.
I sailed the mighty oceans, and the seven seas.
I had a girl in every port.
London to Peking, London to Peking.
Ten years passed by;
New York City is the greatest.
Again I met my true love, at the Ritz
This time we'll marry, because Betsy Kay, I love you.

Gerald Momy

MOMY, GERALD LEO. Pen Name: Jerry; Born: Moncerf, Quebec, 7-6-26; Education: Eighth grade; Occupation: Hospital personnel; Memberships: Affiliated Inventor's Foundation Inc., President John Faraday, Award for two year membership, patented floor cleaning device; Comments: *Poetry is an art. We must cultivate the art to receive God's approval.*

MY FRIEND SUE

A friend is a precious gift, a blessing
from above.

God gave me a friend like you as an expression
of His love.

I praise Him for your friendship. It means more
than you will know.

I'm thankful for the times we've shared, and the
concern you always show.

We've had our share of ups and downs. We've laughed
and shed some tears.

We've done a lot together, and grown closer through
the years.

Yes, I've been truly blessed to have a friend
like you.

If I let you call me "lady bug," can I call you
"sister Sue"?

Francene Phillips

AN EYEFUL OF YOU!

Did you ever get something in your eyes?
I did once, and what a surprise!
Peace of mind is now gone to Perdition!
What was the cause of this demolition?
An Eyeful of YOU!

An eyeful of you made something start
Direct from my eyes down to my heart!
Now on my heartstrings a melody plays
Sweet thrilling music I'll hear all my days!
An Eyeful of YOU!

And eyeful of you, and I was blind!
What they say about love is true, I find!
I could see naught but stars in your eyes;
My vision swam, but couldn't disguise
An Eyeful of YOU!

I reeled through a labyrinth of winding ways!
What can extricate me from this maze?
I climbed from deep abyss to dizzy heights;
And still the dearest of all dear sights —
An Eyeful of YOU!

Carol Boyer Mitchell

MITCHELL, CAROL BOYER. Comments: *When my sisters and brothers and I were growing up in a Montana wilderness, where my young parents were homesteaders, we saw a lot of the Crow and the Blackfoot Indians. Oh, I could write a book (or some good stories)!* Poetry: ' 'Cause I'm in Love With You!' 'Dream Ranch,' 'Essence of Love,' 'Rose Petal Memories,' 'Sundown'; Themes: *It thrills me to write about love, the greatest thing in the world!*

WINTER VALENTINE

While others chill, I burn.
I seek your haughty, brittle face.
I find your touch a turn of grace.
Stay with me. Be my valentine.
Cool all my fears.
Comfort my lonely years.
We shall walk in company
across the frozen ground,
where we go without sound,
our music, a love song — the wind and snow.

Jeanette Konwiser

LOST LOVE

Are we the creators of our own fate
Do we plot the path of our own destiny
Are we products of our own myths
Or confused players in someone else's dream
Because
Gone are the borrowed golden beams
Of glistening light
Gone is your face
My music
Gone is your touch
My song

Did we fade as the morning star does
With the realities of the day
Leaving an aching void
Within my heart
Never having said goodbye

Yesterday is gone and has become one
With the memory of a fading dream

Oh come sweet sleep
And let me dream again

Joyce Ebenezer Isakov

POETRY OF LOVE

Poets write of love —
And seem to know its ins and outs.
But I've no idea what's it all about —
I've no experience —
I'm serious.

How can I say the words —
Of love, which I cannot describe . . .
I've never found the right vibes.
Maybe, I am not the type.
Could that be right?

They seem to say such silly things, lovers I mean . . .
Just read what any poet may write.
To love someone with all your might —
Kind of thought provoking —
I am not joking.

Of course, I'm not saying —
I wouldn't say silly phrases —
And go through silly phases . . .
We'll just have to wait and see . . .
If anybody will fall in love with me.

Pamela Joyce Franklin

YEAR

How about January, I am the new year.
How about February, can I be your valentine.
How about March, I am the Easter bunny.
How about April, can I be your fool again.
How about May, I am your spring flower.
How about June, it's summer time again.
How about July, I am a sky rocket.
How about August, can I be your swimming hole.
How about September, I am the colored leaves.
How about October, can I be your scarecrow.
How about November, I am your feasting turkey.
How about December, can I be your present
forever babe.

Albert F. Carol III

QUESTIONS

Must I
Continually torment myself
Searching for that certain someone?

So many chances
Dashed
Against the walls of futility.
Ever loving that which I can never have.
Never wanting that which I could easily obtain.

Does love exist
Only for those who could live without it?

Do the greatest pains inflict the kindest hearts?

Questions seem endless,
While the answers rarely show themselves.
Past and present weigh heavily,

But the future is a flying thing.

Hope
Is the eternal herald for greater things to come,
and as each day is created anew,
I know that I will survive.

I must.

Mark Arvid White

SPENDING TIME

How many years have gone by since I first saw you?
How many days have gone by since I fell for you?
How many hours have slid by since I wanted you?
How many minutes have we really felt?
How many seconds does it take to break a heart?

Debra Sue Peterson

AN OFFENSIVE OF LOVE THROUGHOUT THE WORLD

Inspired by my late husband, Dr. Andrew F. Hegyeli

The power of love, God's gift to man,
The greatest power in the universe,
Igniting our hearts, our souls, our spirits.

Power to face the future, to create a better world,
Power to break the swords into ploughshares,
The swords of hatred, of evil, of despair.

Communicating love, communicating sharing and caring,
Between man and his neighbor, nations, and continents,
Transforming the world through the magic of love.

Bringing forth new flowers from frozen earth,
New butterflies to fill the skies,
Bringing forth peace.

An offensive of the power of love ushering in peace,
Peace where the children will lead the wild animals,
Peace to bring hope to the heart of man.

An offensive to stamp out the anguish of today,
The worries of tomorrow, the sadness of yesterday.
To reach for love of neighbor, love of God
To erase sickness and war, famine and thirst, hunger and need,
An offensive of love for peace.

Ruth Johnsson Hegyeli

SPECIAL LOVE

I thank you for the way you cared
and all those feelings that you shared
women like you are very rare
and friends like you beyond compare
You were there when I was blue
and always helped me see things through
I hope sometime I can repay
all the caring you sent my way
For you cheered me up when I was down
and finer friends just can't be found
When all is straightened out
you'll be the friend I think about
Because there's a special love
a love that's true
a special love
for friends like you

Jim McDermott

OUR MEANING

Our meaning we share,
in bonded strength of delicate nature.

Our time we discover,
each moment in new found wonder.

Our harmony we enhance
together by intimate design.

Our dreams we envision alone,
in a unity of peace all our own.

Our meaning we impart,
one to another, we share,
with each other, as one.

Carolyn J. Stienstra

TWO SONS SHINE

(for Allen and Johnny)

Two hearts of sunshine clamoring at
my knee,

ruckus fights driving all senses to
the ragged edge,

mischievous blue eyes bobbing in cadence
of discordant glee:

A song never sung so
sweetly,
filling my heart so
completely
with love.

Adrian Sadigone

NEWLY WED

The day breathes
The shadows have fled
My love lies beside me
He is perfect
I am lovesick
And we are newly wed —

Carole E. Strickler

VIEW OF GRIFFITH PARK

After the fire
black earth

winter branches
spread on the bare hillside

After the rain
thin film of green

hint of phoenix
rising

And
after the woman

much the same,
much the same.

Peter Ludwin

LUDWIN, PETER DEWITT. Born: Flushing, New York, 6-4-42; Education: University of Washington, 1960-1963; Occupations: Laborer, Fruit Picker, Postman, Salesman, Food Vendor, Musician, Folk Music Teacher; Awards: Honorable Mention in All Seasons Poetry Contest, 1985. Finalist in love poem contest, *Midwest Poetry Review,* 1986; Poetry: 'Reflection,' 'Ritual,' *Hyperion,* 1972; 'Off Tackle,' *Raindance,* 1980; 'Of Wheat and Thumbs,' *Ripples,* 1985; 'Losing It,' *Samisdat,* 1985; Comments: *I believe a poem, to be effective, should make you see differently, provoke a heightened perception. I tend to disfavor poems that sprawl and disperse attention rather than concentrate and direct it. A poem should be like a journey from which a person returns enriched. Communication with sufficient technical skill to produce an emotional impact is my stable datum. My playing field includes childhood, wilderness, human relationships, baseball, music, and various personal experiences. If a reader has an increased aesthetic feeling and sense of agreement and reality from my writing, then I've been successful.*

A MESSAGE TO MY SONS

Oh my little darlings, how I hope you understand,
You are my breath and inspiration, you are part in my every plan.

Your innocence helps to guide me, as I try to help you grow.
Your angelic words console me when we're apart and I'm on the go.

The accomplishments I watch, through each phase in your little lives,
are unforgettable pleasures held dear to my heart, which push me more
to help you strive.

There are no words, my little ones, that Mommy knows to express
how much joy you add to my life, and abundant happiness!

At night when you're put down to rest, and you recite your loving
prayers,
I'm right there praising our gracious Lord for appointing me, your
lives to bear.

Oh children how I love you so! And, how this, I pray you see.
I have so much yet, that I hold unsaid, but you both are the world
to me.

Arleafa Schroeder

MOLLY

I watched your breathing softly fail
and felt the wrenching pain of your departure
The light of you was gone, and shadow lay across my soul
crushed and mourning, forlorn and lonely in the thought
That endless years must pass till I, like you
would cease at last to breathe
And leave in eager haste to seek your living light once more
To find you and renew ecstatic union on some bright, Elysian shore.

But as the years have passed, a mystery unfolds —
once more my soul can sing in joy, no longer dark!
By some celestial magic you have found a way to reach me whence you are
I see your eyes — they dance — and laughter sounds again
in your sweet tones to banish pain
And I believe that you know more than I —
That soon our waiting ends, and I will soar, light-like, across
empyrean barriers that separate us now
that Love alone can penetrate
And I will find you joyous, waiting there
To guide me to the Source of Love, Whom we adore
to merge our love with His forevermore.

Rudy Bode

A LETTER OF LOVE

To My Dearest,
I could dine on caviar from silver platters, sip champagne from crystal goblets, have servants to run a mansion of rolling lawns for miles. Yachts, Mercedes and a jet to travel the world. To be wrapped in minks and weighed with diamonds . . . it sounds like so much, but I know it would be nothing without you.

I would rather have dinner on stoneware and water from a paper cup, a cottage in the woods to walk through hand in hand, by a lake to rest our feet in. To be wrapped in your gentle arms and lifted by your tender love, to share your dreams, nothing else would matter because I'd be the happiest woman alive.

You'll never know how much you mean to me, for time will not allow . . . nor words enough to say, because there are no words to express how deeply I care for you.
Forever Your Sunshine

Tina Alden-Houts

BECAUSE I LOVE YOU

I sent you away today
with broken dreams and hurtful heart
cushioned in hopes and miracles
Because I love you.

How can I guide you
other than I am
to excel all your qualities
But to give you another route?

Now you are gone
being guided in His light
your tender soul I long
God, help you forgive me this task,

Because I love you.

Judy G. McCormack

WARM HEART?

On cold winter nights
I let my hands hang out
The open window —
Until frozen, like tonight.

No stars are out
All are covered by
Cold clouds that won't
Be warm until morning.

There is no love
Tonight, like the stars.
Maybe in the morning —
But there are no stars

in the morning.

Theresa Dugan

HARMONY OF LOVE

Music makes me laugh,
Cry and sigh for
How can anyone hear a song
And feel . . . nothing?

Jean M. Porter

HE LOVES ONE AND ALL

All through the day his sheep Jesus leads,
He knows all their faults
And all of their needs.

He is the Shepherd
Who lights their way,
The one that is special
Is the one that's astray.

He gently calls it to his side,
And there with Him
It soon will abide.

He calls each one by their name;
To Him there's not one different,
They're all just the same.

Vivian Frances Jackson

LIKE YOU

Darling how I long to be
Close to you so you can see.
I've made my way throughout the day
Like you.

When I stop to dream a while
I recall your sweetest smile.
When all was well and I could tell
Like you.

Our hearts were young and, oh, so free
When I loved you and you loved me.
How good it was to feel so new
Like sunshine on the morning dew.

Now we're far apart you know
But I still need and want you so.
There's no one here to hold me near
Like you.
Like you.

Richard L. Newcomb

Sparkle in your eye,

thump in my heart

Smile

and I am the world smiling back.

Hold me —

I become free

Caress me —

I am love.

Individuals as one,

no struggle,

just us.

Roxanne E. Wilson

LOVER IN MY DREAMS

My lover, my secret lover,
The secret lover of my dreams.
Why do you keep haunting me
When I am sleeping peacefully?
As real as life
You haunt me in my dreams.

You are not real, I know,
Yet, somehow you always find the door
You turn the knob, the key it seems
And lively-like,
Walk right into my dreams.

My lover, my secret lover,
How I wish that you were real.
The anticipation is just too much
As I await your mortal touch,
But you shall always be a ghost
That haunts and haunts my dreams.

Erma Ghoston

THE HOUSE THAT LOVE BUILT

The house that love built is no fancy castle in Spain,
But it is a shelter — a place of refuge from the cold and rain.
It has a wide fireplace with a fire that shines out at night,
So, as we gather, it is not to drink, feud or fight.
We each take our Bibles and read from God's holy book,
Then sit to listen to the nearby murmuring little brook.
This house that love built sits back beneath some trees,
And we welcome the music of the rustling of the leaves.
The harsh winds whistle through the tall pine and gum trees,
So this is a place of quiet rest to enjoy the cooling breeze.
There is no voice of hatred that rings through the huge halls,
Because the family daily asks God's blessings as on Him they call.
There is no fancy furniture of the golden ages long past,
But it is a sturdy kind that for many years shall last.
This house that love built is not so fancy or really so large,
But it is comfortable to rest when the work is complete, all are tired.

C. D. McKay

MY DARLING SWEETHEART

As the earth needs rain and sunshine, the flowers they need it too.
Not as much my darling sweetheart, as I need you.

As the rivers they dry up, beg for the rain, I love
You my darling, I hope our love will remain.
As I love you my sweetheart, all through the night, I
Am here waiting dear, for you to hold me tight.

As I love you my sweetheart, as my love goes deep.
I look to you my darling sweetheart, for true love as I sleep.

Honey you know that I love you, because I know our love is true.
The way our Lord Jesus, he brought us together, it is the way for me and you.

As I love you my sweetheart, and as our love goes deep.
We will love each other forever, and have true love to keep.

Paul O. Dotson

JUXTAPOSED IDEOLOGIES

Your shining armor tarnished before me,
As I sit astride your glistening starship,
Melting on through the light of our moon,
Beleaguered all the while by forethoughts
That cut as daggers through smooth waters.

We are tranquil and we are virile,
In the dark eye of our sweet hurricane,
The pair of drums beating so much as one,
In the chambers of our holding pattern,
The augmentation and foment of our love.

No finer hour than this one in that dark sweet night,
I will overcome you as the dawnflower opens her pollenous petalody,
A centerpiece for us all to admire,
And in whose scent we will devour the essence of each other.

Robert D. Nagle

It isn't every day that I miss someone so much,
And it isn't every hour I should think deep thoughts.

It is like me to stifle the longing for warmth,
And it is like me to create casualty.

What "is" and what "isn't" have melted into questions.

I find, with each day, a gem in Love's crown.

I could collect rubies, sapphires or diamonds,
yet when I reach for you, I find a pearl.

A blue pearl — as if an extension of your eyes —
which reflects the intensity of flame . . . a flickering hue.

Understanding silence is an art to believing
there are emotions.
Whether feelings dance in the light, or caress
the darkness, their presence crystallizes with a touch.

Waves know when to calm, and fire knows when to flame —
I know when to want,
and it is now.

Maria Bourekis

HEAVEN'S CROSS

Blind men sleep, dream and weep.
Headlines quoting, "The demise of love."
You and I, stars on heaven's cross.

Grey shroud hides the sky,
Winter's bitter cry,
Cold wet walks, the lonely
Forlorn souls that drift through naked streets.

I ride the winds of chance
Through life's experience.
Setting me down gently,
An arrow pierced the hollow of my heart.

Upon the earth you land,
Stunned, with bow in hand
You come to me. The only
Chance for love is through this sacrifice.

We draw the shroud away,
Release the light of day.
Though we must part we carry
The burden of a love that will not die.

Blake Alan

First love is like discovery; it looks out
Through tiny windows at the world of lights
And forms. It feasts and lingers on to doubt
That all it sees is real. The nights
Burn up in days. The years swing 'round until
One blazing day outshines the rest. The air
Is clear and cool. On bush and tree and hill
Bright emerald fires flame forth and life is fair
When love looks out at love's eyes looking in.
Now shout all doubt is gone and buoyant joy
Transports the lover's heart. The prize we win
In love we recognize in eyes not coy
Or fickle. Love ignites its torches where
It finds reflection in a lover's stare.

William B. Granberg

YOU CALLED OUT TO ME

You called out to me
In your dreams.
You called out to me
As I passed nearby.

A look, a smile, a glance
That went up me and down me.
That went through me and through me
And raised a reply to your call —
Like my musical note responding to your musical note and
forming a chord —

Beautiful music —
Calling you,
Calling me —
The continual call that's coming from you —
And now it's coming from me.

Dorothy M. Friedman

WHY, WHAT, WHEN, LOVE STORY SAD!

Why can't our lips meet as before?
Why can't you be there when I answer the door?
Why can't I find you in all the old places?
Why do all the people seem without faces?

What is this feeling come over me?
Why am I seared to see what I see?
Where is the touch I've become used to?
Why am I still searching for you?

Why did you go, I can't understand
When we were so happy, and I was your man?
Just what is this feeling coming over me?
Why can't I understand what has come to be?

Why now face to face, I have nothing to say?
Why, please tell me why, you were buried today?

John D. Ohrin

GREY EYES

You Mortal windows of the Soul!
I never thought, nor dreamt that day,
when my spartan heart, its stoic grief,
Should dare to lose within your ray,
Grey Eyes! I never thought to see
A human heart, a Soul, mirrored there;
So that my humbled Being should tremble,
Like a sinner amidst a sacred air!

Grey Eyes! My own, in pleased surprise,
Returned that ageless message, of your light;
Then fearful hid, beneath their veiled shades,
Like timid Turkish maids, from alien sight!
But, you only smiled down on me,
Dropped a kiss upon my hand . . .
While our footsteps, blending in the moonlight,
Left soft imprints, along the Strand . . .

S. Diane Sawitzki

LETTER LOVE

We met within a postcard
You and I, one day by chance
Our eyes met, you smiled
And thus began our (postal) romance

I wrote you and you wrote me
We shared secrets and dreams told to no other
We lived in our letter love, waiting for the postman
Living only for another letter and for each other

We shared life and yet we never met
As we lived our letter love
Far apart in different worlds
And from our letter love we experienced what love is made of

John Beer

DEAR EVE

My heart remembers well when things were right,
But cannot understand when things went wrong.
You took my hand and led me through the night,
And I, content to tag along.

We stood together, watched the morning sun,
Then conquered fields and mountains on our own.
How could I know that I would lose your hand,
And stand here in the darkness all alone.

Now memories of the wonder that you were,
I hold until the day I meet the grave.
Although you're gone, these memories still occur,
So, still, you are the master, I the slave.

Parnell Pierce

WITHOUT WORDS

"Look," my grandfather said to me.
He and I were on our knees pickin' stones.
And he held and let the soil run through his hands.
"Look," he said, and I did, for I knew his love for the land.
Years of hard, hard work had made this farm his.
And I smiled, and he smiled back at his daughter's son.
Three generations had communicated without words.

Terry Lawrence Johnson-Cooney

SUBLUNARY CREATURES

They meet: Steering, focusing, regression, revealing!
No movements of lips . . . lingering . . . exploring,
The mind the mover . . . into the recesses of each other;
Each peering, strangers no longer (smiles), Ahh . . . Eureka!

They leave the hall: The revelers all, the music: Titillating!
Out in the open, promenading . . . other twins too;
Roses aplenty, the air sweet smelling, aroma, filling;
The heavens aglow, Luna full circle, inviting . . . Mystifying.

Sublunary Creatures: hand in hand moving — Parri Passu!
Conversing, oblivious the scene . . . whinny, divine;
Into the woods passing, lost to charms . . . each the other;
On yonder side emerging, amorous still, still magic!

Horace V. Preddie

AUTUMN LOVE

I watched them as they moved about,
As he, so weak and feeble, clung to her
And she, not much more so, tenderly steadied
As the twilight hours set their day.
I watched as eagerly he clung to her.

My mind went back and I could see
The youth of love I did not see just yet.

I fought the tear as she lifted up
That head that once all wisdom held
And as his lips pursed for that kiss
I shut my eyes; I could not look
For it was theirs, and I could ne'er intrude
This moment of their autumn love.

I watched them and I cried
For all I had not seen in days gone by.

The firstborn of a culminated love
Views for herself actuality
And thoughts went back to long ago
When love discovered came anew to young hearts
Who so foolishly thought they could not understand.

Joe Anna Carter

LOST LOVE

Spring Love. We had a glow that we both shared.
We planned a dream for two.
We even thought we were unique, with a love so
pure and true.

Summer Love. The gleam of love was in our eyes,
As hand in hand we walked.
A couple with a total plan, unique, or so we
thought.

Fall love. A wistful look, a hopeful sign,
Are all that we have left.
Where is the glow? Where is the gleam? Where
is our dream? OH! Why?

Winter. Sad memories are all that's left of what
we once held dear.
We've lost the glow. We've lost the gleam.
Winter now is here!

Epilogue. Perhaps when Spring comes once again,
and chance that we would meet,
The spark of love we shared before, will become a
love "unique."

Betty G. Small

LOVE, LOVE, LOVE

HONORABLE MENTION

I'm in love.
Not a mellow, oh well love
Not an everyday who cares love
Not married for 35 years love

But delirious, never gonna stop, teenage love
Can't sleep at night love
Walk into walls love
Cold hands, dizzy love.

Jacquie Dyer

RILLS OF MOONLIGHT

The rills of moonlight ran
Through the stillness of the night,
No flashes of fear or emptiness;
Only peace of mind in sight.
Rich with the fumes of love —
I drift off in silence,
Feeling sturdy proud delight,
I think deeply of you,
And feel our love will never fade,
For it's somewhat protected;
As if flower buds in the shade.
And our life is new with no borrowed sorrow,
We thirst not for yesterdays,
For we've thought for only tomorrows.

Wanda Whanger Higgins

I WAS HAPPY TO HAVE A GIRL OF MY OWN

My heart is bleeding love
For the one I adore
The skies are gray above
They have gone forevermore.

I wonder if she still cares a little for me
And if she still remembers the kiss by the sea
The day she swore her sweetest desire of her loyalty
I was happy to have a girl of my own.

She loves somebody else now, with him she shares her bliss
What have I done to deserve a thing like this
I have lost my love forever and now I have none
I was happy to have a girl of my own.

Frank Viggiani

FRIENDSHIP

Friendship means a stretched out hand —
sharing joy and sad event.
Friendship means a sense of care,
making others be aware
that life can only be lived in full
when hearts are warm and minds kept cool.
May our smile bring comfort to hearts in pain —
so relief be felt after too much strain.
May any offensive thought of old
be transferred to a positive mold.
We so can throw our light around,
helping each other to feel sound.
It makes us grow. Time enfolds in its wing
how many stars have been made from within.

Susan Pars Douwes-Dekker

LOVER OF MY SOUL

I sought You, and I found You — Lover of my soul
You have completed me, and made my life whole.
Through the battle of darkness, Satan haunts the night
My soul loveth and adoreth You and You have led me into light.
You have called and chosen me, nevermore to roam
I've run to You, escaped the dark,
With You only, is my home.
The terrors of the darkness do not hold me fast,
For You are beside me — The only love that lasts.

Beverly F. Ross

O LYRIC LOVE

How cold and empty is thy face
In arrogance without embrace
What broke your heart
What chained your soul
and turned you in such strange great Mole

Emotionless his grey eyes falter
Magnetic blue eyes entrance his soul
With shivering tremor his heart pounds out of control

Intrigued, drawn by her charm
His cold eyes become tender and warm
The Moles longing in emotion
He found his other soul

Maria Leber

GIFTS

More gifts from the heart
Are what we all need.
Gifts are not meant to be a measure
Of vanity and greed.

Don't judge my gift as underrate
Simply because of its price tag's weight.
But remember it as a loving gesture
Which is, of course, life's most precious treasure.

Susan Hancock

TRANSITIONAL SOCIAL ADJUSTMENT

That convalescent veteran sat immobilized in the wheelchair.
There was no one else close to him or talking to him.
I went over and sat down near him.
He turned his head toward me and said "Hello."
He didn't tell me I wasn't pretty enough.
There was quite a to do among some therapists at the party for convalescent veterans.
I didn't mind taking off him the effect of the prison of war camp, if that was what happened.
I liked his looks. He was probably married and when he was more recovered would go home to his wife.
I have an affection for him to this day.
He didn't tell me I wasn't pretty enough.
But all it could be for us was transitional social adjustment.

Florence K. McCarthy

FOR EDITH

I have sojourned in countless zones and climes
Where loveliness is commonplace as air,
Where each sunset excels all previous times
And every tree and flower are wondrous rare.
I have seen cities golden in the sun,
Far islands set like jewels in the sea,
But never such a beauty as the one
That in our years of love you show to me.
There are no songs the ardent poets sing
That capture half your tenderness and grace.
Yours is the wonder of returning spring,
And all of April's promise lights your face.
Whether the years ahead be full or few,
I am contented being loved by you.

Harlan L. Umansky

DISTANT STAR

I would roam the world over
I would sail the Seven Seas
If I thought just for a moment
You'd heed my loving pleas

I would climb the highest Mountain
I would swim the deepest sea
If I thought just for a moment
You'd give your love to me

Here on earth our lives are distant
Why do you keep us so apart?
All I do is pray my darling
Yet I can never reach your heart

I would fly the highest Heaven
I cannot love you from afar
On wings of love I'd soar forever
To reach your distant Star

Alma Leonor Beltran

BELTRAN, ALMA LEONOR. Born: Sondra, Mexico, raised and educated in the United States, lifetime American citizen; Education: High school, junior college, Lee Strasburg Academy of Dramatic Arts; Occupation: Stage, Screen, TV, and Radio Character Actress; Memberships: Screen Actors Guild, American Federation of Television and Radio Artists, Equity Stage Union, Nosotros Hispanic Artists Organization; Awards: Spanish Broadcasting Radio Award, Nosotros Special Actress Award, World of Poetry Golden Poet Award, 1985; Poetry: 'Today's Song,' World of Poetry, 1984; 'Luminous Mystery,' World of Poetry, 1986; 'Yesterday's Pathways,' American Poetry Association, 1985; 'Friend, Lover or Fantasy,' American Poetry Association, 1985; 'To Dream or Not to Dream,' American Poetry Association, 1986; Comments: *Poetry to me is the language of the free spirit, an expression of our inner individualistic thoughts. Perhaps it is an intimate statement, in our own way, of what we have observed and learned along the way on this earthly journey, one that we wish to share with our fellow travelers.*

Alone
I sit and stare
At my life's love
And watch
The changes come over his face
The welcome calm fades
The darkness gathers
Then death suddenly strikes
Then
Just as suddenly the calm
Returns
And with just the shadow of what
Has passed
He opens his eyes
And smiles a welcoming smile.

Kay D. Kettle

UNTITLED LOVE

I cling to life,
It's all I have
For love again eluded me.
Those eyes that were
My food and drink
Gaze now into others, lovingly.

Oh heart, don't break
You're not the first
The hurt will one day go away.
Then you'll be new
And strong and hard
But with a center as pliant as clay.

Regina Davis

A SECRET LOVE

Envy; jealousy —
These are feelings from the Secret Love —
These are feelings,
To be dealt with —

Smart and witty is this Secret Love —
Such is a secret —
Such is a secret from the feelings
of the Secret Love.

The Secret Love is gone now —
Gone to another person —
Such is retribution.

David Clauser

NEW LOVE

There is a new love in my life
That has come to sweeten my days.
There have been other loves before.
I did not expect another.
But he appeared, entwined himself
Around my heart and I
Was vulnerable, succumbed
To the fascinating charms
Of tiny grandson, Jeffrey.

He does not mind my hair is gray.
He hugs and loves me anyway
And we two laugh as we play.

Rene Knight

A LITANY FOR MY LOVER

Let us be together

in whole body
and whole spirit

Let us be together
in closeness
and in distance

Let us be together

for joy and love
for now and the future

Let us be together

Jay Boden

SEALOVE — P.J.

Waves crashing,
Foam spuming
Into the air,
Sending salt-spray
Into my face,
To me that's love.
Sealove.

Birds flying effortlessly
In the azure skies
Above the cresting waves,
Then gracefully dipping into its depths
And slipping out glistening wet,
Soaring again into the skies,
That's sealove.

I love the sea
And all it says to me
About life and living,
Taking away and giving back,
That's love to me,
Sealove.

P. J. Dick

RUMOR

I heard a strange rumor
Subtly pretending that love
This flower of the soul
Blossoming in all hearts
The spirit of faithfulness
Was put on trial
By the suspicion of the world
For its tender happiness
Was not loyally partaken
To some of the lovers . . .

To know the source of this
Unprecedented accusation
The trial was moved
From the earth to the heaven.

In front of the Almighty God
With a serene smile
The love is waiting for
The decisive verdict
While the angel of jealousy
Is guiltily trembling.

George Alexe

COMFORTING THINGS TO SEE THROUGHOUT THE DAYS

A child's smiling face — overjoyed with happiness.
A parent hugging their child — showing fondest affection.
Children helping parents — like going to a store or cleaning
leaves from the ground or many other little chores.
An elderly person being able to stroll safely along the street
— enjoying the sunshine and the beautiful fresh air.
A motorist kindly giving another motorist — the right of way.
A clerk thanking you — for your patronage.
A dog being petted — as he lies at your feet protecting you.
A cat so gently purring — such beautiful music.
Someone reaching out to help a handicapped person — to cross
a street or go up a flight of stairs.
A family sitting together at a dinner — counting all their blessings.

Mary E. Ingram

BUTTERFLIES

A discerning butterfly startled her
For it was as beautiful as can be.
She stopped to watch it.
Experiencing a common empathy.
The astute creature cast a spell in the sun
Darting from flower to tree limb
These two creatures were as one.
For the young woman, too, was a butterfly, flirtatious and frivolous
Flitting from lover to lover . . .
For a good flower is hard to find.
So, if only for a moment these two butterflies touched each other's
Minds.
They could do no wrong.
Then, because they were butterflies
Quicker than a wink,
They were gone.

Susan Hancock

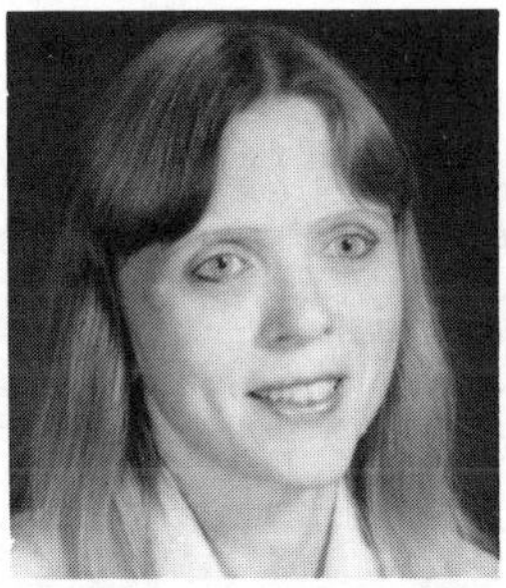

HANCOCK, SUSAN W. Born: Chicago, Illinois; Married: 2-14-82 to William Kyle Hancock; Occupations: Nurse, Poet, Teacher, Writer; Awards: Seven Honorable Mention Awards from World of Poetry, 1984-6; Golden Poet Awards, 1985, 1986; Poetry: 'War,' *National Poetry Anthology,* 1986; 'Butterflies,' *Poems of the Century,* 1985; 'Misty Morning Fog,' *Earth Scenes,* 1986; 'Peace on Earth,' *World of Poetry Anthology,* 1986; 'A Prayer to Saint Valentine,' *Words of Praise, Vol. II,* 1986; Comments: *Writing poetry has been my pleasure for the past 17 years. In this technological age, I want my poems to be a reminder of basic human needs, such as peace, hope, faith and understanding.*

WHAT IS LOVE

Love is strong
And full of joy,
Binding mother and father
Each girl and boy.

Love is kindness
To all races,
Many colors of skin
All shapes of faces.

Love is bright
As a morning star,
Shineth brightly
Both near and far.

Love is fresh
As a breath of spring,
The laughter of children
As the birds that sing.

Love is a jewel
Shining ever so bright,
Like stars in the sky
Both day and night.

A. Lorene Wayne

WAYNE, AGNES LORENE. Born: Henshaw, Kentucky (Union County) 1-14-22; Married: 10-20-43 to George W. Wayne; Education: High school, Sturgis, Kentucky; Occupation: Real Estate Broker, Owner of Wayne Real Estate; Memberships: Audubon Area Chamber of Commerce, Henderson, Kentucky; served as Vice President, Legislative Chairman, Business and Professional Women's Club; Served as President, Vice President, Legislative Chairman, State Public Relations United Way Board; Health Department Board, County Fair Board; Member First Christian Church; Poetry: 'The Challenger,' 2-5-86; 'What Is Love,' 'Love Is Many Things,' 'The Greatness of Love,' 'The Iranian Hostage Crisis,' 'The Hostages Are Free,' *Remembrances of Special Occasions,* Book of Poems, 1984; Comments: *I enjoy writing poetry about special events. It is also relaxing to me after a trying day to put into words an event of special interest.*

SPRINGTIME

The colorful and graceful tulips swaying
in the air delight the eye.
The scents of lily and hyacinth spreading
here and there pierce the heart,
THE HEART OF LOVE.

Caressing the cheeks is the soft breeze
that enhances the mind,
THE MIND OF LOVE.

The daffodils dancing on the lawn
gladden the moving crowd.
After a long sleep, awaken to life
plants, trees, everything including love,
THE SOUL OF LOVE.

To the good earth, the arrival of the
long-awaited magic of springtime,
THE MAGIC OF LOVE.

Christina Ching Tsao

MASTERPIECE

Why, sweet child
Are your eyes so blue?
Do you know how much
Your mama loves you?

And your tiny little arms
That hug me so tight
Who, pray tell
Made you just right?

Why is your skin
So soft and pink?
Whoever made you
Was an artist, I think

Your perfect little body
And your cute little ways
Cause me to look toward Heaven
And give my Master praise —

Carole E. Strickler

FLIGHT TO NOWHERE

Everything's packed,
  Loaded up and neatly stacked.
The leaving is finally here
  Going away — not being near.

It's happened —
  Going away from a special place
Will I land somewhere
  Or just drift in space?

Of course there's someone else
  Someone important I have to see.
Another man?
  Of course not — because it's me.

Alone in a crowd
  That's how it's come to be.
A constant companion perhaps,
  Yet all I have is me.

Carole Babics

the warm Hawaiian night wind
echoes, as in an astral journey
white flowers in my hair, around my neck
have scented centuries of voyagers' dreams
in silence I find myself returned
to golden tides and stars and shadowed mountains;
to tangled, grounded roots and outstretched arms
of banyan trees, fragile blossoms of red ginger and plumeria
This hand I hold tonight
I've held in other lives on shining South Pacific sands
this place has been my home before
this soul and I have loved amid a paradise
of passionfruit and mango
Now into the ancient song of wind and falling water
together, we are welcomed back

Janet Steele

LOVE

A ragged little man and his ragged little dog
Walked the streets of the city
People shook their heads and said,
"Isn't that a pity?"
They do not need your sympathy
Though looking so forlorn
They've had happiness to share
Since the ragged little dog was born.

The sun came out and smiled at them
The blue sky shone above
The ragged little man and his ragged little dog
Share a beautiful love.

Katherine E. Cartwright

NEW GRASS

Looking back on them now
    should be hard to remember
The still sunsets and the burning things —
New grass — now for love
    too bright and too brittle
In the cold passion of early springs.

But I am aflame
    with the fires of remembrance,
The white blossoms and the curtained light —
New grass — and my heart
    still bright and still brittle
In the cold passion of April night.

Doris E. Woolley

DARLING I LOVE YOU

Darling I love you, you are the only love I
have ever known, true love is so hard to find
and thank God I found mine. Darling I love you.

My love for you will never die, like ocean
waves that sweep across God's beautiful sea it will
never die but live on and on.

Till death do us part, my love for you will
live on and on in my heart and some day somewhere
sweetheart we will meet again somewhere beyond
the blue and live forever and never part.
I love you.

Rhoda Lee Kelley

GENTLE TOUCH

Many things come to mind as I think of you,
Happy times I'd like to share.
Picnics on the skyline drive, holidays with
Family and sun-filled days at the beach.
Visits to the zoo, vacations, and
Church fellowships.
The harvest, fruit of glad season,
Bear sacred treasures.
All that I am you have made me with
Dignity, grandeur and tenderness
My future destiny sublime, my love
For you binds youth to age.
Sentimental emotions — Your Gentle Touch —
A Williamson, A Rowe, MY MOTHER.

Jacqueline Rowe Gonzalez

SONNET 130

These many years that I have sought your love
Have been to me a garden of regret.
A wild pursuit of daffodils — above
The bleak display of hoary winter's net
Of snow. I've sought a Persian Rose, fragrant,
Evasive in its regal beauty — still
Provocative enough to plant flagrant
Desires — that I could not resist. Thrill
As I will to these strumpet desires
I will no longer chase their rainbow hues
That envelope my image of you. Higher
Command must be consigned for all my views
Before I'll be controlled by your promise.
I'll never know your love, I'm sure of this.

Darwynne Pucek

REMEMBERED

Winning; was the amount that she delivered,
giving it her very best.
The strength that she commanded.
The essence she possessed.

Survival; her intention,
any way that she knew how.
The attempts were for prevention,
storing the errors and the bows.

The love, she gave out freely.
Affection, she did show.
Her truth, was a great comfort.
The things that she did know.

Mardog

LOVE

Towering Spirit — born of the ages
Wiser than poets, stronger than sages
Hymn to man's dignity, spark of his power
Source of all genius — rock, song, and flower
Song to man's lips, meat to his heart
Hauntingly lovely — right from the start
Could it be of earth? — or more from above
Treasure the genius, the spirit of love.

Anne R. Fawcett

ASYLUM (for the broken hearted)

The blood in our hearts pounds to die;
I want to grab hold of the fire in your eyes:
Haunting me; taunting me . . .
Hurting me; flirting . . .
Catch the sunrise, make it fall!
Bring me to my knees, blood on the wall.
Meet me in the asylum, that's where I am.
In the asylum. Crazy and sad . . .
Meet the rays; catch a glimpse of madness,
It tears out my feelings, it makes me crawl
The sweat pouring down, blood on the wall.
Keep me alive with your breathtaking eyes,
dance to the skies . . .
Look at me! I'm falling!
Do the daring, see the light —
making wishes in my lonely nights.
Take some time to break it all,
Catch me crying: blood on the wall.
Meet me in the asylum, that's where I am.
In the asylum. Crazy and sad . . .

Renee Strociek

LEON

Leon, my darling, I'm glad I have you
Your love that sustains and helps see me through
Your arms draw me close to you and then
I start to love you all over again

Your shining blue eyes that gaze into mine
Mirror your eternal spirit divine
Your easy laughter and broad ready smile
Lighten my heart and make life worthwhile

May the love that we've found, which we've come to know
By our combined effort continue to grow
Let's cherish each other more every day
Serve one another and all God's laws obey

Then, when our earthly life is done
We'll still be together in our heavenly home
If we endure faithful, then we'll always be
With God and our Savior through all eternity

Diane L. Salisbury

A PRAYER FOR LOVERS

Dear Heavenly Father up above
Please send this to the one I love
Tell him I'll always be true
And I'll never make him blue
I really love him a lot and
I hope this will never be forgotten
Dear Heavenly Father up above
Please tell the one I love
The stars will shine real bright
For us each and every night
We pray each night our love will last
And the time we have together won't go fast
We promise we will always be true
We will never make the other blue
So please let the stars shine bright
For all the people in love each night
We promise never to be untrue
And we will always give thanks to you
Thank you Heavenly Father above
From all of us that are in love

Judy Obuchowski

LOVE'S LITTLE THINGS

It's those little things that show this love's
A strong and binding force.
It's those little things
That make a love secure.
For without those little things of love
The binding force is gone;
And love unravels like a spool of thread.

So to keep your love a vibrant force
Just like it always was
Just keep those little things of love
Just as they were before.

Robert Weetman

STRANGER

I saw the old woman's face through a foggy window
I didn't know who she was
Her eyes shone with years gone by of happiness and joy
love and pain
I didn't know who she was
I looked upon her humble abode, the wind beat at the
wrinkled yet firm surface
The old woman called to me
Silence
The old woman I knew and I walked closer and looked upon
her
The old woman was my mother.

Jennifer Gipson

NEW MEANINGS

Walk into the depths of my loving for you
The flood gates open freely and out of the ocean of my being
Pour all manner of gentle and soft feelings
Giving the expression 'world without end' new meaning
Coming to know you as I have, so far,
Has me looking at life and living more fully as a real
Part of a whole; me, you and the entire planet
Revolve around the sun which is a symbol of light
At its highest essence of life.
From somewhere my soul speaks to yours . . .
Hear me, my love, for we were put here to be together
Thus, you have also given new meaning to the word 'forever.'

Jill G. McDowell

TO MY LOVE

When I have to leave you it's my last desire
When I see you I must run to you
When I hear your voice I long for your touch
When I am near you it's not close enough
When we are apart I burn inside to see you
When we caress it is never finished
When we kiss it is two fires meeting
When we look at each other it is silent perfection
When you go I feel hollow inside
When you smile at me my cup is full
When you speak softly my heart leaps
When you come to me my soul is satisfied

Paul Donaldson

A SPECIAL AUNT AND UNCLE

Some aunts and uncles make life more beautiful in many different ways,
with laughter or warm affection and words of loving praise.
With words of trust, tenderness, and moments of deep sharing,
countless little things you do that remind me someone's caring.
With words of love and encouragement in the many things you say and do,
yes, you make life more beautiful especially an aunt and uncle like you.

Lois Weikel

UNKNOWN MEMORIES

Well, it's true I've never met you
nor have you known me;
though female I am, your namesake I may be.

They've told me many tales of inventions and boats with sails:
Clever, handy things you did all teach me of how you lived.

I do feel that I know you well, but most important I can tell,
you would have loved me if you could see your namesake.

Oh, how abstract this all must sound, but it's hard to get back to solid ground,
when I close my eyes and imagine your voice, I resort to pictures and legends:
That's my choice.

Maybe you smile in your eternity, for this poem for you written by me.
Blood flows thick, and in me you have a stake, your granddaughter, your namesake.

Janet Castiel

CASTIEL, JANET ELLEN. Born: New York, New York, 4-16-54; Married: to Howard Levy; Education: Vassar College, 1976; University of Madrid; Occupations: Writer, Producer, Director, Editor, Film and Video; Memberships: International Radio and Television Society, American Film Institute; Awards: Hearts on Fire II Contest, poem, 'Secrets . . . ' 1985; Script for Television, "Sewing it Up," 1983; Poetry: 'Love Poem,' *Hearts on Fire II,* 1985; 'First Night,' *Up Against the Wall Mother,* 1984; 'I'm Fine . . . The Babe is Well,' *Vintage,* 1983; Other Writings: "Life in Suburbia," series of satires, *The Metropolitan Direction,* 1984; Comments: *I paint visual imagery and portraits with words. Portraits being senses of emotion and action experiences blended to transport the reader to the scene of the poem. Recurring patterns (i.e. 'Secrets . . . ' 'More Secrets . . .') offer new growth and a wider range for my subject matter.*

CHAIN REACTION

It's difficult
To smile
As I taste the tears
That fall from my eyes

Each thought of you
Makes me smile
And each smile
Makes me cry

I have not forgotten my promise
I know you can feel my smile
But, my dearest love
Can you taste my tears?

Christine M. Goldbeck

JUST BECAUSE

Being with you
Loving you
Believing in you
Wanting you
Trusting in you
Needing you
Caring for you
That's why I love you
Just because.

Sylvia Jefferson

TOMORROW

Another day, another time
Our lives will intersect and intertwine.
A day of quiet, a time of bliss
When only our love will exist.

I'll pledge my blood, my breath, my soul.
The core of me, only you will know.
My love to you I'll freely give,
And take only what I need to live.

But I must wait, the time is not,
Our lives are set, our paths are plot.
I will wait, your love will be mine,
Another day, another time.

Marilyn Welch

WHAT IS LOVE?

There is puppy love
And first love
And passing fancy trends.
The heart goes through the stages,
And finally it ends
With the true love
The lasting love
To let the whole world know
This will last forever
As through the years we go.
Now two hearts are melded
With Love's eternal flame
Combined with trust and friendship,
'Twill always be the same.

Ann R. Yarbrough

LOVE AND JOY

I know love when I feel it.
I know its depths of joy and pain.
I've felt its ectasy slip,
Into depressed despair, as it strained.

Because of love for you, it leveled to a contentment.
A peaceful, glowing sensation
With a satisfying aliveness — a retention
Of deep spiritual extension.

Love has given my life a purpose.
A quiet completeness — not a yearning — a lust.
A deeper awareness — an awakening of a new thirst.
A need for a closeness — with a meaningful trust.

Gloria Eichel

EICHEL, GLORIA L. Born: Brooklyn, New York; Married: to Arthur Eichel (deceased); Education: Brooklyn College, Master's Degree in Counseling; Hunter College, New York City, Baccalaureate Degree; Occupations: Case Worker; Teacher, grades one through 12; Guidance Counselor; Counselor Consultant; Memberships: President of NYS Career Development Association; National Chairperson for Career Development Poetry Recognition, 1979-86; National Chairperson for Career Development Week, 1986-87; Awards: Two poems printed in *New Voices in American Poetry,* 1985 — 'Fulfillment,' and 'Friendship'; Poetry: 'Life Course,' *American Poetry Anthology, Vol IV, No 3,* Fall 1985; Comments: *The common themes in my poems reflect feelings I have at various emotional moments in my life. Usually, they are written after some incident that occurred that touched me deeply. The rhyming throughts will form in my mind and within a short period of time a poem wil be written.*

Dreams sleep within my eyes, passions begging
To wail across your form with photo-
Accuity — your breasts through murder, dancing;
Your lips seeking my dreams dreaming of you.

J. V. Ruvolo

IF LIFE SHOULD END

I have walked, hand in hand with friend!
I have talked, and laughed hours on end!
I have drank of your wine and listened to woe
I have been touched and loved by a new design!
I have savored richness within life's glow!
I have listened to your drumming heart!
I have slept, . . . encircled within your arms . . .
Have tasted the honey . . . your lips impart!
I have known friendship that richly blessed!
And no one . . . has ever guessed!

Virginia E. Marx

LOVING OTHERS

Love is like the morning dew,
It moistens a hardened heart.
As you follow the pathways to increasing love,
A whole new cycle will start.

You'll begin to view God's creatures
In an entirely different way.
You'll enjoy, instead of ignoring,
Those people you see each day.

You will come to a new awareness
To a level beyond yourself.
Others will be more important
Your desires will be put on a shelf.

No longer will you be concerned with
Your hopes, your dreams, your plans.
Your joy will be found more often
In following Jesus' commands.

He showed the perfect example
Of the kind of love that's true;
Giving yourself for others
In everything you do.

Terry Ann Braaten

WHEN YOU WERE HERE

Lyrics so heart-rending I could only cry
A melancholy happy sad together.
Those familiar songs were most beautiful
When you were here.

Night mood raced through my head;
I never saw so many stars.
All I needed was you to hold
When you were here.

So difficult to recall when all this happened —
Was it now or part of yesterday?
Precious moments captured time forever
When you were here.

Every touch and everything you said
Made me want to share
All those hidden feelings I saved for us
When you were here.

Such simple things make the best of times —
Friendship, music, wine, good conversation;
Each one special for love you shared with me
When you were here.

Marcile A. Bergen

LOVE

Love is something
that touches someone deep down inside
and makes them feel good all over,
like you do to me.
Love to me,
is like your warm, tender kiss
Love sounds to me,
like your soft, sweet voice,
saying you love me.
Love is,
the distance between two hearts.
I love you,
forever . . .

Ken Kingsbury

TAKE THE CRUMBS

Oh how my poor heart aches
For a love that can never be,
So hidden that none shall ever see.
So take the crumbs
And happy be.

Could it ever possibly be
That his bright smile was
Ever intended just for me?
So take the crumbs
And happy be.

Even the clasp of his hand
That all could see
Was pure ecstasy for me.
So take the crumbs
And happy be.

Rejoicing in the bright new spring I see,
I hold the magic thought that he
Is sharing all this beauty with me.
So take the crumbs
And happy be.

Sibyl Michel

LOVE

Love
Will go where it wants
When it wants
To whom it wants
IT CANNOT BE DIRECTED!

Love
Is a free spirit
It can't be bought
It can't be sold
BUT CAN BE DETECTED!

Love
Has no needs
It fulfills itself
At its own choosing
IT NEEDS NO RETURNING!

Love
Will seek itself
It goes where love is
To choose its goal
IT MUST KNOW YOUR YEARNING!

Joan M. Vannucci

FALCON

I always believed you had the eyes of a falcon —
I never realized you possessed the soul of the bird as well
Two inseparable girls who grew up together —
I always believed I knew you best

You were the first friend I introduced him to —
Wanting to share a part of me with him
The first man I truly loved —
My breath, my heartbeat, my soul

When you met him your eyes grew hungry —
Hooded eyelids revealed eyes blacker than a starless sky
Plunging your talons into his heart you carried him away from me —
I never saw him again

Even though you had stolen my soul I was determined to survive —
But just when I had learned to live without it
. . . and him
You returned with your razor-sharp talons
. . . and ripped out my heart

April Killingback

LOVE

This wonderful thing called love can hold the strongest tie —
And so great one cannot find words to explain, no matter how you try.
It's in the hearts of people, birds, and animals too,
It is all made by God, something man could never do.
You cannot buy it, sell it, or control it, no matter how one may try,
Yet you find it is given and received, and piled high as the sky.
Nothing can compare with it, or ever be as sweet —
Nothing else on earth can take its place, it just cannot be beat.
It will make you give away your last penny, and everything dear to you,
but you won't even think of that, because it's what you want to do.

Jesus went to the cross and died because of love —
Nothing else is greater, God sent it from above —
It is true, solid and sound, 'tis said: "Love makes the world go around."
What would we all do without it? We could hardly live, there's no doubt about it.
We give ourselves away, and all that we have, or ever will —
But it comes right back to us, our lives and hearts fulfill.
Its greatness can never be fully told, it is far better than gold.
Money, riches or prestige will never take its place —
Love is what God gave, and rules the whole human race.

Louise P. Wilson

GOD'S LOVE — SUPREME

Ask for the old path, and pursue it, and you will find the Way — walked; the Truth — believed, and the Life — lived. You will enjoy the essence of God's love that knows no measure. Christ-in-you — the pearl of great price become the treasure.

"For God so loved the world that he gave His only begotten son that whosoever believeth in him should not perish, but have everlasting life." *John 3:16.*

Jesus proved His love by fulfilling scripture, manifesting the love of His Father, and establishing His ministry according to the mind and will of God. He chose apostles and sent them forth by two's accordingly as laborers in His vineyard. Their preaching and teaching with a measure of the Holy Spirit made the water of His words, — which are spirit and life — life-giving.

Those ministering in this fashion became torch-bearers — igniting the flame of God's love in honest, seeking hearts — thus gathering for Him a family here on earth, and establishing a Kingdom, with Jesus as King — for eternity.

Love Divine is the most rewarding and greatest of assets for the redeemed of mankind.

Edith Wood Jordan

BY THE SHORE

You stand at my side
As ocean waters whisper on the shore
Soft as a lover's voice in the night
Drawing us to the edge.
Sand shifts beneath our feet
Clouds sweep across
The golden moon of night
A moment lost in darkness.
Iridescence at our toes
Surf whispering on sand
A touch upon my skin.

Monica Serle

LAMY, MONICA. Pen Name: Monica Serle; Born: Willesden, England; Married: 3-21-59; Poetry: 'God's Nightlight,' *Words of Praise, Volume II*, 1986; Themes: *Relate to nature and elements, a few poems that are statement of our times and taken from the news.*

MY DULCET MERMAID

Written to my lovely wife, as she played on the beach at Long Beach, California.

My lovely, dulcet mermaid,
Lending thyself to the sea,
Blending the earth with Heaven's shade
In thy temporal agency;

Shy of the world behind you,
Sure of thy path ahead,
Cure for the cares that burden
Those who with thy gay mood wed.

So many follow in thy wake,
With unconcealed haste.
How eagerly the breakers break
About thy fairy waist.

To thy sweet lips the great sun dips
And tenders its caresses.
Across thy brow the warm winds blow
Thy soft and silken tresses.

The elements mingle in a single
Bid, for thy love craven.
Their passions merge in common urge,
To clasp this bit of heaven.

Eugene Poulter

A WONDER

Asleep now, peaceful and quiet
I watch your closed eyes
move about in dreams of dogs
and the stream beside the barn

Beads of perspiration line
beneath your tiny nose
and ringlets of curls lie wet
against your proud forehead

I wonder for your future
like some distant land we
read about in the books
you study by day

In the solitude of night
summer crickets sound with
chirps of "come, come, and
we will play"

For me, there is nothing else
only the even, soft and silent
breathing — for tomorrow, another
wonder, and my son, to create the day

Sandra R. D'Arcy

FROM THE HEART

When hardships fall and love is lost
you need some peace at any cost.
Follow where your heart may lead
with love, not fortune, you'll succeed.
Go where he be and compromise
hold him, look into his eyes.
Though his world too is full of doubt
love has a way of working out.
When peace is found then say a prayer
and thank God for the love you've shared.

Pamela J. Shelton

MY SPECIAL ANGEL

There's a new star up in heaven
And it's shining just for me
It's the home of my special angel
Who is watching over me.

When I am sad and lonely
I look into the sky
And know my special angel
Is saying "Please don't cry . . .

The love that you and I have shared
Is always there, my dear
Remember all the happy times
We had from year to year

So please don't cry, my darling
I am happy up above
And you need never feel alone
For you have all my love."

So, goodnight, my special angel
Watch over me, I pray
For your love will keep me going
'Til we meet in heaven some day.

Lois M. Ryan

ANOTHER LOVE POEM

Share with me the lonely hours
keep them from my bed

Demons rise when you are gone
pounding on my head

Beauty lies within your touch
Love is more than words

Kisses golden with perfection
tend to mend the hurts

Love is always at your side
Heaven commands your hold

Deep within the empty grave
Earth will share your hold

Maro Kentros

MOTHER

you
stood by me when I couldn't
helpless to your kind embrace
gave me everything you could
more than I ever should have taken

tried to stifle all my truths
marked me with the chosen signs
used my doubts to scare me right
wasn't me who knew me then

later grew to see the goodness
through the hazy, all-alone
all worth, still a question
someday will show . . .

for you and me.

Roseanne Fadil

I FEEL YOUR LOVE DYING

Inside of me is an ache
I can't explain
The foreboding of loss
Sure to come
From beyond the door
Of the very near future
For I can see
The tearing and the change
That is happening
Behind the great dark pools
Of your lovely eyes
Telling me you're going
Even though you yourself
Are unaware of it as yet
And I must steel myself
Not to cry now
Or then

Don Chrisrianson

IT MUST BE LOVE

The wind caresses the trees,
the branches reach out for more.
Buds burst forth with joy,
the trees are in blossom,
so is our love.

The moon appears, I see your face,
your smile lights the way.
Your hand reaches out with a gentle touch,
a touch that means so much.
It must be love.

The doors of heaven open,
giving our love a thing of beauty
Sometimes blue, sometimes bright.
Whatever the season, we are together.
It must be love.

Donald A. Gaeden

CLINGING VINES

Only for love
do we hold fast,
two hearts bound in vines that cling.
No reason — no escape.
While we risk our fears
and tread through the tangles
of vines like silver chains,
we softly shed our tears —
only for love.
So we strip the thorns from the rose
to keep the vision —
save the dream, but
the blind can only feel;
lovers lose just what is real
and we hold fast;
two hearts bound in vines that cling —
only for love.

Donna Stanislawski

on a bus in west Oahu
second seat from the front
a woman looks past the window,
a child on her lap
one face, a sturdy well-marked monument
to sun and struggle
is a mirror of the other
— tiny, perfect and unshadowed

the woman sighs
and shifts on the warm, patched seat
suddenly a smile breaks
from the silent dark-eyed bundle
in her arms
I watch the mirror
as two fingers touch
and interlock
this woman, this child
have no walls between them

Janet Steele

What if I lose you
then what will I do
I know this is selfish
but I need you.

You saw me laugh
and you saw me cry
you picked me up
when I just wanted to die.

You held my hand
and helped me through
you taught me to believe
in not only me but you.

You said you wouldn't go
but you'd always remain
as long as I learned
how to walk and how to stand.

I want to tell you
all the stuff I never did
I love you daddy
please don't leave me I'm just a kid!

Cathy Cartier

WITHOUT YOU

Days grow in despair
Nights fall absent
Time between is forever
without you.

Words are nothing
Melodies: unplayed
Symphonies: silent
without you.

Flesh is pale
Eyes: dull
Smile: unheard of
without you.

David Allen Mills

The day is warm
the sky is clear
I wish so much
that you were here

I long to feel
your gentle touch
To hear your voice
I miss so much

To kiss your lips
and touch your face
To hold you close
in warm embrace

To let you know
how much I care
And cherish so
the love we share

And even though
you're far away
My love for you
grows every day.

Marlene Kumpfbeck-Verdadero

TRAVIS

He lived in the dark world
Of those who cannot see
Until he met Marilyn.
She opened the world of
Love to him.
Together they conquered
Handicaps —
Her eyes served as his,
And his ears served as hers.

Becky Knight

A POEM ABOUT DEATH

I stare aimlessly out my window
Into a sunny autumn day
Tears stream down my cheeks
As the leaves detach from the trees
I turn away from my window
And close my eyes
It is here I find you
It is here I laugh with you
It is here I hold you
Suddenly the sunlight beams
Down upon my face
I must realize and accept the fact

I know someday I'll be with you again.

Lewis Fram

UNSPOKEN

If I never told you
I love you
You would still know
If you looked into my eyes
you would see it there
If I touched you
you would feel it
And when the world became
void of everything but
you and I
You would hear it
In the whispering
of two hearts
one to another

Dawn Carmichael Braack

THE ANNIVERSARY

Another year, another day
That we can feel this special way
That I can say to you once more
You are the Lover I adore.

That we can stand before that door
That door of Love and Life and more
And we are one again this day
Communing in our special way.

Just this one day is ours together
We make no claim on any other —
So let me love you just this way
And share with you our special day!

Rosalie Steele Bolene

THIS LOVE

This Love is not like other love
Because it loves everything and everybody.

This Heart is not like other hearts
Because it pumps the blood of every living being.

This Mind is not like other minds
Because everything that exists is inside of it.

This Soul is not like other souls
Because it is the Soul of each and every one of you.

This Spirit is not like other spirits,
Because it is the Holy Spirit.

This I AM; is not like other I Ams,
Because I am God Almighty.

Dr. King-John, Ph.D.

THE FOUNTAIN IN THE RAIN

Tonight, as always, I ride through the park
In the half-dark —
The benches are empty, no children play,
No old ones pray
In the cool and empty stillness of the rain —

The fountain, as always, casts up its white plume
In the grey gloom —
No lovers lie close on the eager grass
To kiss, alas —
In the passionless and early autumn rain —

Tonight, as always, I ride through the park
In the half-dark —
The benches are empty — as empty it seems
As my dead dreams —
As futile as the fountain in the rain —

Doris E. Woolley

VALENTINE VYINGS

In eighty-six we're 'proaching the Day of Valentine.
We are thinking now which greeting this year should be thine.
As we age, our thoughts on same tend to become benign.
Not so, for those youngsters who are less than thirty-nine!

Easing to ignore the day as we sit on our spine,
We need e'er to open our loving hearts with a spline.
Re'ly, 'tis one day, 'specially, our spirits to *in*cline.
Pep up our egos! Put away the voice that does whine!

As we lead up to the time, let our faces, LOVE, shine.
Think how pleased with you and me will be the HOLY TRINE!
Loving others as ourselves is a fine CHRISTIAN sign.
On what better SPIRITUAL food could we dine!

Of all love-salutes that, this day will be on your line —
Wishing you the most BLESSED GREETINGS, please, include mine!

Mervin L. Schoenholtz

GRANDMA

In your own simple way
you taught me so much of love.
No expensive gifts,
just a candy bar, shared on a curb.
Never a showy public display,
but you got up at 3 a.m. to check my sleep.
Even in death your love showed,
shining in the tearbright eyes
of those who loved you more
than you ever would have believed.
And I,
who never knew life without you,
I cried with surprise
at the size of the empty spot in my heart.
But I let you go with love.
I'll see you again,
you wouldn't have it any other way,
and I'll remember what you taught 'til then.
I promise.

Kyla M. Jones

BLUE RUN

Wreath of torment — back now.
Eternal pest, won't you let me rest, now
and away?
Limousine of falsity, mortal game man.
Sadness fades in twilight, but awakens
Excruciating pain of pains . . .
the pain.
A deep languid sorrow reigns
dutifully now and again.
Pre-planned realm of caliginous beauty,
You are found when not there . . .
Homeful.
Tardy repeater, retrieve the
night's glory.
An abyss of delightful disdain beckons again,
Shallow oneness . . . unduplicated.
Depth of ecstasy, find you again.
Plans cancelled . . .
Should never have been.

Steve Sabaday

LOVE THROUGH THE YEARS

What is more precious than love
Love starts the minute we are born,
The great love of a baby, nursing.
The hurts and bumps are soothed by love
Over the years, by Mommy and Daddy.

Then comes young true love and marriage.
Dad and Mom left with their own thoughts,
Are drawn closer together by their love.
They buy a travel-trailer, or a motor home,
Free at last to wander and roam, down
Their own road of love and companionship.

The years go by, into the golden years
Each leaning and waiting on the other,
Dad cooking breakfast each morning, with
A bright twinkle of love in his eyes, and
Mother, there with a kiss for Dad in return,
The great gift of closeness and love.

Leona Dixon Cox

MEMORIES

Memories, drifting by
Remind me of
You,
Always you.

Only happy memories
Survive now,
The others gone
With you.

Holding tightly to your hand:
— Five years old.
Picking daisies for a chain:
— Six years old.

Snuggling up to a
Warm, happy bedtime story —
Protected,
Loved.

Seven years of faint,
Musty,
Cherished
Memories of love.

Rebecca Shulman

METAPHOR/AM I?

Yearn for wistful passions of love;
Exuberant, perfumed aroma.
Warm and supple, the mere touch
Satiates all the desires of life.

To desire, to have appetite,
Fills an abhorrent barrenness.
To satiate, to fulfill,
One learns unbridled ecstasy.

To disenjoin and accept release
Gives pause to ponder —
Vicissitudes —
Temporal relations

And sow again, but why?
To live a continuum
While one must live.
Temporal dynamics.

To live, one must be alive.
Giving of one's life,
Partaking of one's life,
I am, I will be, I hope to be.

Ronald R. Tamburro

LOVE WITH YOU

Clarity comes,
as a cool dry breeze
in the lovely young evening.
We live to die.
Relax,
participate,
and let it happen.
Given the time,
what a gift,
we exchange being here.

James Melton Wolfe

MY FIVE LOVES

I've been hurt once, I don't want love, no ifs or ands or buts,
I've heard this said many times, is something wrong with me, or what
'Cause I have five loves in my life and we all live together
Dobie, Heidi, Rebel, Rusty and an older girl named Heather

Now wipe that shocked look off your face, caught you off guard I bet,
It's all legal and it's clean, I'm talking about my pets.

You see I have four German Shepards, each female and so cross
Until I added a Doberman, Dobie John the "boss!"

Ann Murrell

MEMORIES OF A LOST LOVE

I lie here half-asleep while memories of you o'er me sweep
Your Titian hair, your lips so warm and form so fair
Sweet honesty was in your being and I was so blindly unseeing
Now with pain and misery my heart is put to the test
To remember those lazy days of gentle love and sweet rest
It seemed that God touched us with his hand from high above
And our song I remember seemed like the coo of a gentle dove
The refrain goes around in my everyday dreams and it says,
When the moon shines through the lonely pines and the sleepy world
Has gone to rest
We lie dreaming, the stars are gleaming and there's music so entrancing
Fireflies are dancing to the sweet tune that we loved to croon when
The thrushes sang in June
My sweet love I hear you calling me and I'll come back to you soon.

Neal S. Toomey

SISTERS — WHAT WOULD WE DO WITHOUT THEM?

Some of us are blessed with both brothers and sisters, quite a few,
there is always one and it's usually your sister who becomes special to you.
She's the one who's always there to give you her helping hand,
she's the one who knows when you are discouraged, depressed, in pain, and
always seems to understand.
She's the one that will push my wheelchair so we can take a little walk,
we always seem to get together and share our troubles, or just to sit and talk.
Oh, there are days when we both become so frustrated and we get angry or disagree,
but then we put aside our difference and once again you become that special
sister to me.
So often I pray that you'll never leave me or go away,
'cause I need you and I hope you'll always be around, day after day.
I thank God for his gift to me, a special sister like you,
Sister, I love you, make me happy and love me too.

Lois Weikel

MY CUP

Time goes by, responsibility, involvements, reorganizing, appointments —
A cluttered mind in general restrains me periodically from my poems . . .

When suddenly I realize I'm bursting; I've got to settle down
My thoughts to convey; do it now, immediately, before they go away!

Birds sing in my new back yard with tall trees and a rose garden;
The morning air is fresh and damp to fill my lungs as I stroll

Cautiously and carefully within my bounds; what is it, this I feel,
This need to pour out? It is here, yes here in my very own back yard!

Happiness and contentment, and joy just to be, and the poems I must write
To set me free, are but my cup running over with love you see . . .

Mary M. Denison

TO THE EVENING STAR

Thou fair-haired angel of the evening,
Now, whilst the sun rests on the mountains, light
Thy bright torch of love; thy radiant crown
Put on, and smile upon our evening bed!
Smile on our loves, and, while thou drawest the
Blue curtains of the sky, scatter thy silver dew
On every flower that shuts its sweet eyes
In timely sleep. Let thy west wind sleep on
The lake; speak silence with thy glimmering eyes,
And wash the dusk with silver. Soon, full soon,
Dost thou withdraw; then the wolf rages wide,
And the lion glares through the dun forest:
The fleeces of our flocks are covered with
Thy sacred dew: protect them with thine influence.

William Blake

A YOUNG GIRL'S CRY

Will I find him in the misty future of a brand-new year,
Or will I still be lonely, searching for someone to love?
Will he be all I ever dreamed of,
Or just a ship that passed in the night?

Will I look into his eyes with a sense of wonder,
To know that I'm the one he's thinking of,
Or will I once again be disappointed,
Still searching for someone to love?

And now at last I've finally found him,
I'm in his arms, he holds me very near,
His lips are warm, his smile so tender,
It's going to be a happy New Year!

Netta Pickering

LOVE

Love can start with the barest flame,
A glance, a touch, such simple little things,
With the glowing warmth, we almost fear to name,
But the heart is liberated by the warming flame.
And if the fuel is good, and fire is bright,
The warmth will keep throughout the longest night.
Love can last, and grow, and will remain
If care is taken to protect the flame.
Pride may keep it from your sight,
So . . . hold it close and keep it bright.

Helen Pastushin

PERHAPS ONE DAY

I will go slow if you wish.
I'm not even sure what I want myself.
My view on the "us" seems to change
As the days quickly pass.
I know I really care, I like.
I will go slow and give you space to breathe . . .
Whatever it takes.
I just know that I want you to be happy.
I only wish that I could be the one
To do just that for you.
Perhaps one day
We will be more special
To each other
Than we are today!

Cheryl Lynn Smith

AMAZED BY LOVE

That I should be the object of Your love,
And constantly be blessed by that same love
Is so amazing!

I cannot understand just why or how
Your only Son is interceding now
For me, a sinner!

Nor how He grants me peace and uses me
In plans He has for all eternity,
But I am willing!

Oh Lord, to you my feeble thanks I bring
For all that you have done; and I will sing
Of You forever!

Armen F. Mason

LET GO THY HAND

Blest and sweet was our wedding day
Seventy some years ago.
With many hours of happiness
And of course a fragment of woe.
I always held her hand in mine
For she had said 'tis always thine.
When, of a sudden her heart ceased to beat
Never, never to repeat.
'Twas then a wondrous, white-robed youth
Came as a vision, and gently said, "In truth
It's the Father's will, let go thy hand
So I may ascend with her precious soul
To the Father's angelic home above
Where she can rest in heavenly peace
Safely in the warmth of his eternal love."

George William Boehmer

UNTIL IT'S TIME FOR ME TO GO

As long as choirs sing and church bells ring
Love will reign, 'cause love's the greatest thing.
I love you I love you,
Stay with me until it's time for me to go.
Sincerity, I'll give to you my whole life through;
Take my hand my heart my all,
I love you I love you,
Stay with me until it's time for me to go.
"Where you go, I will go; where you stay,
I will stay.
Your people shall be my people, and your God my God."
I love you I love you,
Stay with me until it's time for me to go.

(King James V. Ruth, 1:16.)

Virgie McCoy Sammons

METAMORPHOSIS

My lover lies asleep,
And I notice, for the first time,
Her clothing tossed here and there
Like a tender explosion
(Undressed, she is all Women,
of any century, any country).
Her garments are the pieces of a chrysalis,
Empty now, useless — even ugly,
Compared to the butterfly they let loose.

Stephen M. Hurley

Beauty rests,
Beneath the occult tree,
Slumbering gently.
Truth's unblemished leaf
Drops like a tremulous light.
The two meet,
Dawn of fruition.

Geraldine Violette

WIND WHISPERS

Sometimes I think
I'm going insane,
Because I hear
The wind whisper your name.
But I know
It's only love,
For I was told
By a morning dove.
So as long as
You are near,
I'll be happy
And full of cheer.
I will promise
To remain,
Just as long
As you do the same.

AngelinaMarie Stillwell

Love is like a dandelion
To some it is beautiful
To others just a weed.

But the resilient dandelion
Will always flourish
No matter how often
It is pulled and broken
It springs right back
And thrives even more.

To me the dandelion
Is a beautiful flower
Such as my love for you
And no matter what may happen,
Through good times and bad
My love for you continues to grow.

Marlene Kumpfbeck-Verdadero

ONE LONELY CANDLE

Shadow images dancing
upon my wall
as they jump from the flame
of one lonely candle.
Oh, how they mock my heart!
With silence their music
high volume,
it drowns out all
but thoughts of you.
A stream of consciousness
that washes sleep away
as do my tears.
And tears are hardly measure
of a lonely, dying heart
that melts with the flame
like the wax of one lonely candle.

Donna Stanislawski

OLD AGE (AND SEQUEL)

Our days are filled with memories
Of all the loves we've ever known,
The golden years serenely drift
And gather fruit from seeds we've sown.

What courage must we still maintain?
Still young in heart, we're sometimes sad,
And find our thoughts turn more and more
To all the loves we wish we had.

Why should I live with memories
Of all the loves I've ever known?
You are the NOW, intensely strong,
A love so deep and fully blown.

The only courage I need now
For living with the miles apart,
Is faith and hope that life will bring
You nearer to my longing heart.

Helen Robinson

ROBINSON, HELEN MARTHA. Pen Name: Robby; Born: Spokane, Washington, 5-25-10; Education: Washington State University, B.S., 1932; University of Washington, M.S.W., 1951; Occupation: Retired Social Worker; Memberships: A.C.S.W., N.A.S.W., Who's Who.

IF I LOVED YOU LESS

If i loved you less
  perchance
someone new could
  my time enhance.
It is not to be this
  love i hold for you 'mid
    tears and rage —
  A love that will not
      die

True, you died and left
    me forlorn
  With no hope for
  A brighter day —
  Only memories,
  A grave across
  The sea and a
      Love that must always
  in memory be.

Verna Lee O'Brien Clark

I love you
for what you are,
what you have been,
and what you will be;
a friend and a lover,
keeper of secrets & sharer of souls,
leader and follower,
man and boy,
family and life;
or better put more simply —
just plain old you.

Michal James

FALLEN ROSES

A finger drops a drip of blood
On a mass of broken petals
Two lives are torn and scattered about
Like fallen roses in the meadow

For someone went beyond one rose
To thorns as sharp as needles
Pricked the life of love between
The roses in the meadow

Now the wind and rain has come and gone
Not leaving a single blood-stained petal
But I shall always remember
Those roses in the meadow

Leanna Loraas

OH WEARY ONE

Oh weary one, with a troubled heart
A life so full of pain
Tears that seem to have no end
Please let your faith in God remain

He knows your heartaches, every one
He has not forgotten you
Gave you the strength your burdens to bear
Oh weary one, keep faith in Him

Do not forsake God, He won't you
Or turn Him away, He is your friend
Stoned and nailed upon the cross
How He suffered too, for His love for us

Thelma I. Goss

MY RETURNING ROSE

It was like walking into my backyard.
  Hardly ever looking hard,
From across the way I saw you bloom.
  A Rose appeared in the room.

Eyes like a blossom attracting the light,
  I picked a song and danced last night.
I held you close and lost the fear
  Of love you lose, when it's so near.

I wish I could keep you like a vase,
  An every morning smiling face,
But just like the spring comes and goes,
  Maybe you'll be my returning Rose.

Michael J. Finn

Cohoes Falls.

A SYMBOL

There is a rose growing in my garden
Given to me so long ago.
It's a symbol, said my lover
And like our love, will always grow.

The grass and weeds try to choke it
Winds and rain beat it down,
Still it stands, ever so beautiful
Only dead leaves lay on the ground.

I think truly, it must be a miracle
How it weathers the roughest storm.
Is it because the roots grow deeply
That makes it blossom and perform?

Now my love is no longer with me
Surely my pretty roses will die,
But today they are still blooming
Tho' their heads are bent, as if to cry.

Margaret Gulledge Stackleather

LOOKING DOWN ON CHERRY STREET

That I should go over the Bridge
thus, in the Spring sun —
Knowing how utterly fevered all that
we did was done —
Knowing the sun is shining today
as it shone then —
And the old Bridge's iron fingers
carry the weight of men —
Yet I look down on the roof-top
that covered us from the sky,
And think, "There is nothing changing,
nothing but you and I " —
For still the rush of the river
moving against the steel —
The pressure of wind and raindrop
the ancient roof will feel —
They change, but they change so slowly,
as seas or mountains might —
But we, we changed like lightning
in the storm of a single night —

Doris E. Woolley

WHAT IS LOVE

When you awake in the morning
With a song upon your lips
With a tingling little feeling
You feel clear to your finger tips.

It's a nice warm feeling
Like a cloak wrapped around you.
You feel so safe an' secure
As if no harm could e'er befall you.

Your senses are so much sharper
You'll notice the sparkle of the dew.
The beautiful flowers, blades of grass
All, are more colorful, to you.

Everything is so much brighter
You feel in tune with God above.
You'd give up everything you own
Just to be with the one you love.

Margaret Gulledge Stackleather

WHITE SWANS OF SUMMER

White swans were swimming,
On a placid lake of blue,
As springtime turned to summer,
I fell in love with you.
When autumn came it chilled your heart,
And a golden fire was gone.
Its burning flames would soon depart,
Because they had no home.
Love, like winter grey and old,
Died with vows you did not keep.
Water in the lake was icy cold,
And five full fathoms deep,
But sunlight thawed the frozen earth,
And seeds that were asleep.
Song birds sang at spring's rebirth,
And days so warm and new.
White swans were swimming,
On a placid lake of blue,
As springtime turned to summer,
Oh how I missed you!

Shella M. Lucas

PEARLS AND LACE

You're a pearls and lace little lady,
The kind my heart adored.
I'm tired of imitations,
I'm weary of others and bored . . .

I see you in my daydreams,
I know you are out there somewhere.
My dear pearls and lace little lady,
Come forward and say you care.

Pearls and lace say so much about you,
I'd know you anyplace.
My heart is attuned to your beauty,
I know you'll wear pearls and lace.

I look for you every evening,
As the sea rolls in on the shore,
My pearls and lace little lady,
Nobody can love you more.

Ida M. Kazakos

LOVE

Love — You are so wonderful —
You are standing over all.
You're bewitching every heart,
You're sweet, so nice, so smart.

Love you're a magnetic spell —
That rings at heart — like a bell,
You're God's tastiest — sweetest blend —
No flower has your scent.

But in your trance — life finds the joy —
Life has the brilliant glance,
Then You can do — squeeze out a tear —
When you do disappear.

Love you're taking dreams up high —
You change gray skies to blue,
You're the dazzling, flaring light —
Love — Love's power lives in You.

Sadie Isola

TO A BEAUTIFUL STRANGER

I see you and I know
I am in a deep dream
As I feel the ecstasies
Of love's true sweet prime theme

Seeing you upsets me
Thinking that all that flair
Might just actually be
A sneaky bold nightmare

That you might perhaps be
A frame of flawless lies
A weirdo of some sort
Or else have other ties

Jerry Martinez

MUD PIES

I was sitting
on the ground
making mud pies
and I thought of you.

In my thoughts
I smiled,
and made you
a mud pie too.

Carolosue Wright

THE LORD'S GIFT

Oh dear Lord,
Listen to our prayers,
Straight from our hearts,
I promise to tell you only
the truth,
I think I'm in love.
"With whom?" do you ask.
With you, God,
What is the reason?
Because you've listened to
what I have to say,
And never told a soul,
Because of this,
You're a friend for life.

Tami Rogers

Like a tree without its leaves
or the Earth without the Sun;
like a heart without a song
and a face without a smile
or life without laughter,
or love's troth sans "forever after";
that's me without you!

Like a bird with its song,
or a bee with the flowers;
like a suckling babe with its mother
or the shore's romance with the sea
and the wind with Nature's perfumes
gathered from far and near;
that's what you mean to me
and the way I feel about you dear!

Josh Fallick

TO DAMIEN, WITH LOVE

As I look at you time after time —
oh my sweet,
I can hardly believe you're mine.
On the day after Christmas,
you were born —
to make my world no longer forlorn.
Yet, at the beginning I wasn't sure —
still there was something in me,
shining bright and pure.
And although you sometimes have me going,
you can feel safe in the knowing —
that you will be forever loved —
by a mother who thinks the world of you —
and whose love flows so deep and true.

Denise Y. Westfield

SWEET YESTERDAY

When pollen became honey
When thoughts were
Cloud lifted!
And the hands I loved
Through my hair sifted!
Sweet yesterday!
When I knew, —
The enclosing gentleness —
Of you!

Virginia E. Marx

SILENT LOVE

The words I want to say to you
Pass silent through my mind.
My thoughts are shouting out to you
But fear my tongue does bind.

From what I've been through in the past
Restrains me from emotion free.
All I know is I'll say at last
"I love you and you love me."

But the thoughts still tumble on and on
Ever confusing they whirl on by.
But this I say, "I love you now
And love will last 'til the day I die."

Denise Fleer

A LOVER'S TALISMAN

What a shame . . . we were
So close.
You meant
So much . . . your very
Name, clutched in scary
Dark, brought safeness,
But little else, I soon
Discovered.
Now the nightmares no longer
Run
From my magic chant.
What a shame . . . and I am
Too old
For teddybears.

Nora L. St. Denis

TO HAVE YOU IN MY ARMS AGAIN

To have you in my arms again —
My God, let's see, how long's it been?
To be within your arms again
To stop the pain and sorrow.

To feel your soft embrace again,
To see your youthful face again,
With skin as soft as lace, again,
I'd kill myself tomorrow.

To feel your subtle curves again,
Your every wish I'd serve again,
If I could have the nerve again,
I'd cherish all your charms again.

I'd feel your soft embrace again,
I'd see your youthful face again,
Your skin as soft as lace, again,
I'd have you in my arms again.

Michael Tommaney II

TOM AND SHARON

Did they meet just by accident
or was it all preordained?
Was it love at first sight
or did love slowly flame?

Does it make any difference
just how it came about?
Instantaneous or gradual,
it is love, there's no doubt.

There is a great joy that comes,
when you see two people meet
and watch as love grows.
What a marvelous treat.

Bless you both as you venture
down life's pathway sublime,
in the great scheme of things,
now is truly your time.

Glenn M. Reeves

WAITING

You left in anger;
You packed your gear,
Walked out the door,
And didn't shed a tear.

People called you names;
Voices, like splint'ring trees
Assaulted my ears,
Like many angry bees.

I hoped you'd return;
I visioned calls;
As time moved slow —
Traced patterns on walls.

I was frustrated,
Like a crippled bird,
But when you called
I couldn't say a word.

Velma Earhart Cole

ONLY YESTERDAY

I fell in love with you
When you were sixteen;
Thought you were the prettiest girl
I had ever seen.

I wanted to hold you in my arms
And never let you go;
Just a touch of your hand,
I knew I loved you so.

My life had changed,
This was love . . .
I couldn't sleep at night,
You were all I could think of.

As I sat close to you,
I wanted just one kiss;
Maybe hold your hand . . .
What makes me think like this!

Was that yesterday . . .
Or the day before . . .
It's hard to keep up with time,
But, I think I love you more.

Earl Lloyd

REGRET

I'd rather to have never loved,
Than lose and bear the pain.
I'd rather to have never dreamed,
Than fantasize in vain.

I'd rather to have lived confined,
Than escape and be returned.
I'd rather to have cried alone,
Than let you know my yearn.

What could have been and should have been,
but now can never be;
Will haunt me with the memories
Shared by you and me.

Naught but hurt was brought by love,
While the nightmares stole my dreams.
Turning back brought only sorrow
The press of solitude so keen.

My bane — to live without you,
Had you never touched my life,
No love, no thrills, no tenderness,
No tears, no grief, no strife.

Marilyn Welch

A PORTRAIT IN FELINITY

Golden Eyes,
Flaked tiny seeds of black;
Sitting into cunning content.
Tufts of hair were of stately grace.
His nose, an aire of Roman descent.
Adding to his ebony charm,
Around his neck he wore
The bell of earthy green.
  Wondering if my cat knew
  The picture
  My mind drew.

Nancy Beattie

WHAT IS THERE TO LOVE ABOUT YOU?

What are the reasons that I love you so?
I have many reasons and here are a dozen or two.
I love you for your warm smile, so early in the morning;
Whether your rest the night before was happy or saddening.
I love you for your eyes that tell how you feel;
Whether or not you are aware of the way that I feel.
I love you for your soft hands that warm everything they touch;
They are willing to give or take, to caress or to clutch.
I love you for your friendly eyebrows;
They say hello my love even when you are too busy.
I love you for your sparkling personality that brightens everything it
touches;
It takes a special person that can change the sad into the glad.
I love you for your kind emotions;
Especially since you are so joyful and happy, but just a little shy.
I love you for your body no matter whether it is thin or fat;
Everyone knows that real beauty is inside.
The things that I love you for are so vast and many;
But then, the ways that I can tell you are so sparse and few.
Everything above is true;
Because my love it is about you!

Terry L. Mcclung

A SOUL'S TRIBUTE TO THE HEART

This spirit will remain to vanquish a flame extinguished,
Though the embers may glow with disdain.
The bond between us splintered; heart shattered — nothing left to be distinguished,
Though perhaps, just a tale of yore tinged with pain.

Woe to the day, overcast with gray, and without doubt
Through internment, I offer protection from misuse and grief.
The world has relinquished its right to toss you about,
And the guilty foot kicking about your grave, irreverently, will be brief.

I will not abandon your memory, as the grave,
Which looks ill and wounded, when there is no one left to care.
Though a Kindly Stranger may stop to visit and gaze
With respective regard to the heart's memory which lingers there.

If a day is missed to contemplate the suffering of your life,
I would have reason to hope that tears would fall to purify the sins of your strife,
And the Lily would be nourished that marks the spot, where the memory of your heart
stands tall.
When judgment passes, reunited and flame rekindled, we will vanish from that plot
to the amazement of all.

Elizabeth A. Ruhland

NOT UNTIL THE DARKNESS OPENS

Sometimes I think you're my other self.
When you came to me out of a stranger's solitude
and said you loved me
I held you in my arms and saw the motion of my life
inside your chest, a Grandma Moses field of green and little people,
all myself, moving, dancing back and forth and laughing
that they'd found us
in the beating of your heart.

You are dark and frightened just as I am,
big and open after darkness falls,
losing strength to witches in the air who call our name and hope
to wake us to ourselves.
Since we've found us, we have found ourselves
but you are more afraid than I
and nothing more is all we have until you hear again the midnight calling
and find me, whoever I am.

Alva S. Moore

MY GREATEST FRIEND

On silver skates we fly, my elbow
cradled in his hand,
As joyously we race the wind, I
feel my heart expand
Full knowing that without him I'd
ignominously land.
My greatest friend, he never fails
to tap my funnybone
And make of every uncut day
a rare and precious stone
And help me fly as high as I
could never fly alone.

Dorothy Heller

Withdrawal. That's
what it is,
waking up the morning
after loving you —
alone.

That. And
hangover.

Bringing heart and mind back
to reality
a mental exercise
in strength.

C. MacDonald

COME GIVE ME LIFE

"Come give me life," she said
and he did.

In the look from his eyes,
the touch of his hands,
the kiss warm and long,
the feel of his skin,
the weight of his body,
the pleasure and the pain.

"Come give me life," she said
and he did.

Faith A. Skrip

I MADE A MEMORY

I made a memory of you,
until my fingers
found a strand of hair
you had left behind.
That single amber filament
brought you rushing back
over the mountains,
and the streams, and the days.
You had left a piece of yourself
behind to remind
me of all of you,
my capricious love.

George Cordeiro

THE AWAY FROM HOME SONG

HONORABLE MENTION

Out of my native land,
Out of hills and valleys of my thoughts:
You; height, depth, woman — in you
Blending tomorrow finds sooner day.

You are the setting more precious
Than jewel; your treasure kept
Is the homing of my heart.
To you belongs the lifting cadence
That follows in me your footfall's beat.

Close under my throat is a surge
For the moment your hand opens
The door. There is never enough
Till there is more.

'Round the inexpressive little things
Curls the narrative of love;
Winding flax and honing ax.
The threshold of play is ever near.
In the cookstove the tiny god knows
How the kitchen clock
Strikes the happiest blows.

John Montgomery

A LOVELY PERSON

You are a lovely person
I see you in my dreams
You keep my heart in throbs.
Your face really beams.

I got up early today,
Many things I had to do.
I knew you were my darling,
I love you and I coo.

You moved into my life.
I came through the store
Where you were working,
It was on the lower floor.

You were very lovely,
The name was Verna Lea.
I kept on stopping by,
Soon asked you to tea.

This was love for sure
We became man and wife
Twenty five years ago.
You give me a happy life.

Richard B. Stauffer

ACUTE REMEMBERING

This still isle of mine
  is the ghost of you.
The phantom breeze
  touching with silver
The poplar leaves
While stippling the surface
  of waters blue
Is your hushed voice
  whispering to me
Of our lost love, lost
  for eternity.

Virginia L. Bostick

TWO OF A KIND

A daddy's girl
A momma's boy
A pair, we two
Oh, how I love you
The world awaits us, you know
Head to head, toe to toe
Off we go!
There may be times
When we are out of rhyme or reason
Our love holds so strong
As we mellow and season
Learning and teaching
Each the other our ways
As we spend together
All the rest of our days
You're daddy's girl
My momma's boy
Life is such a joy!

Jill G. McDowell

MCDOWELL, JILL GROSSWILER. Born: Dayton, Ohio, 1-1-47; Education: Adams State College, Alamosa, Colorado, Business Admin., Music, Voice; The majority of my formal education was while I was living in Western Europe for 18 years from age 9 months to age 19; Occupations: Over the Road Truck Driver, present; Former Full Charge Bookkeeper; Awards: Honorable Mention for poem in *Words of Praise, Vol. II,* 1986; Poetry: 'Twenty Twenty Hindsight,' *American Poetry Anthology,* 1-86; 'Let's Go Hear the Wind Rustle Through the Trees,' 'Going Backwards,' *Masterpieces of Modern Verse,* 3-86; 'Asking for Assistance,' *Words of Praise, Vol. II,* 1986; Comments: *From an early age I have thought and written poems, however, it took maturity to open my soul for public viewing. Sharing my soul has become a refreshing experience. The flow of words is rewarding and constant, the more I share, the more I have to share.*

LOVE-LIGHT

You tiptoed into my heart
like the uncertain sun
of an April morning.
But when you took up residence there,
the sun blazed bright
like a July noon.
It swathed me in joy
and entered my body
like rapiers of light.

Now in our autumn
the still-shining sun enfolds me
with the glowing warmth
of golden October afternoons.

The sun is everything.
The sun is you.

Ruth Davies

YOUNG LOVE

Young lovers are like two peas in a pod,
they are closely entwined,

They get along just fine.

Everything is rosy and pink,
they know their love won't sink.

They greet each other with a smile,
that is broad as a mile.

They kiss, with lips that are sweet,
telling each other they can't be beat.

They say "I love you," every day,
they go about to prove it,
in every way.

Iva E. Paul

He was a teenage boy scout
And she was the girl next door
He went away to college, then
Went away to war.

It was a lovely springtime evening
As they sat on the big porch swing.
He held her hand in the moonlight
On her finger he placed a ring.

Plans were made for the wedding
Love was in bloom everywhere.
Now they are Mr. and Mrs. and
Soon will have something to share.

Love is one thing money can't buy
You have to ask God every day,
To help you along, when things go wrong
It will always work out if you pray.

Esther McCappin

I THOUGHT I HAD LOST YOU

From the first day I met you we became friends, right from the start,
we've remained friends even though we're now miles apart.
Yes, when we were together we did some clowning around as most good friends do,
we've shared in each other's troubles, we've even shed our tears together,
quite a few.
There were days I just wanted to give up 'cause I thought I could no longer cope,
then you'd have me to take care of those days, I knew I couldn't give up
'cause you always gave me so much hope.
The days you didn't have me to take care of, just knowing you were around
and I could see you made my days so bright,
my thoughts and memories of you often fill my mind even though now you're
out of my sight.
Your love, care, and tenderness for me was so great,
when you left without saying goodbye, I thought my heart would break.
I thought I had lost you forever, but we reached out over the miles and I
knew I still had my special friend,
I feel as though God brought us together and our friendship will never end.
Great for me, as a special friend, is my love for you,
always be my special friend and love me too.

Lois Weikel

OUR DAY

The day had a chill in the air, but the sun was shining brightly making it a perfect day for us.

A breeze blew gently across the water making our bodies move closer together to feel each other's warmth, and sailing our hearts and minds to a different place where we are one.

We talked, laughed, gazed into each other's eyes feeling closeness and content that only we can give one another.

The sun started to descend letting us know the time had come for us to depart, We walked away hand in hand not hurrying for neither of us wanted to leave and end such a perfect day.

As we kissed before going our separate ways, we knew this day, our day, would never be forgotten.

It would always be there, in our minds and in our hearts.

Linda Webb

My favorite time is when I can sit down and just relax;
And bring out my good memories, some present and some past.

There's some that I do dwell upon, with which I like to spend,
And those are of a special hue, they're of you, my best friend.

I like to pull out different ones, some happy and some sad,
Depending on our temperaments or how much fun we've had.

Sometimes when I've felt frightened, you've taught me to be brave,
You've shown enduring patience, and ability to give.

Then something happened, my best friend, I fell in love with you,
My heart's most elated moment was when you said you loved me too.

The fact that we are confidantes, I sure would never trade,
and the memories of our loving times never seem to fade.

I'm grateful that our love blooms strong, like a springtime flower,
And when I fell in love with you, that was my finest hour.

Bonnie A. Bell

FLOWERS OF FEBRUARY

I love the February flowers
  That seem to blossom through the snow,
Like blooms from long-forgotten hours
  That live again, and grace the bowers
For sweethearts now, as long ago.

Scarlet Roses and Lilies fair,
  The stately Iris, too, I see,
Sweet hillside Heather everywhere
  While breath of Lilac fills the air
And, all glow 'midst fresh greenery,

How can this be, until the Spring —
  This beauty ere the cold is past —
When snow and ice drape everything
  And feeble sunlight's flickering
Without a touch of warmth to last?

'Tis not in idle reverie —
  This inspiration 'tween each line —
Since space is filled with harmony
  With floral thoughts for you and me
This lovely Day of Valentine.

Alfred W. Hicks

LOVE LETTERS

Tonight I read your letters again
the way I always do
when you're away.
The things you wrote
the beautiful things you said,
the feeling I get's so hard to explain.
It starts at my feet
and explodes somewhere between my heart
and my brain.
It makes me want to shout to the world
just how much
I do
love you.

Kris Johnson

WHAT SHOULD MY ANSWER BE?

How should i answer thy love?
No more my friends
To see
If one we are to be
No familiar clime i'd see

Tell me dear what should
My answer be —
Throw over traces of
Respect and home — could
Such love last the debt to pay?

i am no king giving up a throne
But then
One question — our mutual love —
Could this love turn weakness
To strength?

Strength to bind a flawed love
For two who
Would be one
Tell me dear what should
My answer be?

Verna Lee O'Brien Clark

A LOVE LETTER

I'll always remember
  a poem about love
Like a bell that rings
  in my ear
I'll also recall a song
  and a verse
With a melody sweet and clear.

It's often mistaken,
  the word called love
By many a soul each day —
For love isn't love to
  all of us here —
Until we give it away.

Shona Lamond

SCHIRP, GRACE STEWART. Pen Name: Shona Lamond; Born: Glasgow, Scotland; Widow; Education: Stenographic qualifications; preferred bookkeeping; entered examination for Fire Insurance Accounting, received certificate; Occupation: Fire Insurance Accountant; Memberships: National Writers Club, National Association for Female Executives, Republican Presidential Task Force, Local Womens' Clubs, Garden Club; Poetry: 'Signs and Songs of Spring,' 'Nature's Colors,' 'Nite Sky,' Nature, 1985; 'Silent Christmas,' Christmas, *Cape Cod Times,* 1984; 'Exile,' 'Homesick,' 1984; Comments: *My poetry generally starts with something I see or hear, or I might wake up in the morning with some words in my mouth, so I grab a pencil and paper. This year, studying has filled my time. Trying to write a story in keeping with the public of today is no easy job, but I live in hope. What else?*

SYMPHONY OF LOVE

The voice on the stereo
rolls his tongue over
the words, as you might
roll your lips over my flesh.

He sounds so much like you
that my aching breast
wants to touch the sonance
of your sultry flesh.

I see your half-knowing smile
in the notes that fill the room
like the fragrance of your body.
The melody blows gently

against my cheek as
your sweet breath does
when you draw so near
that I want to burst

into song and pull you
into the instrument of
my being and shatter
every crystal on earth

with the symphony of our love.

Lois Riddle

DEVOTION

Tracing
  my steps
    again.
Was it true?
  or had I dreamt
    blended ecstasy?
Were you really YOU?
  I have mixed emotions
    while so alone
  wanting always
    to continue
      as we were.
NEVER!
  I will NEVER
    ACCEPT
to see
  only
    a lonely
      Grave.

F. K. Whaley

THERE'S A WAY THAT LEADS TO GOD

When trials come and you feel all alone,
And you think you have tried all you can,
Reach out for his out stretched hand.
There's a light at the end of the tunnel,
For there's a way that leads to God.

When you grope in the dark
And there's no light, not even a spark,
The Master's still there;
He hears your prayer.
For Jesus is love, He abides above.
He watches over his own, they are never alone,
There's a light at the end of the tunnel,
For there's a way that leads to God.

Vivian Frances Jackson

INSOMNIA

Where did you come from, with your tousled hair and
Eyes that burn holes in my heart?
I thought I was past this
Falling-off-a-cliff kind of thing.
You were supposed to be but a brief respite
From holding a pillow in my sleep.
You were only supposed to hold me but
You touched me instead;
And, worse, you took part of me when you left.
You can't come back to ease the ache, but then
We both knew you could not stay.
So here I am holding a pillow again,
Only now it holds the scent of you.
How am I supposed to sleep?

Judy Ann Hutcheson

GOODBYE

When love is over and you say goodbye,
You take a deep breath, trying not to cry —

Suddenly you feel so alone, an emptiness starts,
What happened, where did it go wrong, why did we part —

When did the touching, the tenderness cease,
Will there ever be time for me to find inner peace.

Lee Lashbrook

ONCE UPON AN EVENING

Once upon an evening the fading sun fell unto the tossing sea
For an ecstatic moment they shimmered and rippled joyously
Then slowly the sun vanished into the sea and unto the night
The jealous moon in all her full splendor came into sight
Bathing your masculine beauty with its bewitching light
Like the rays of the sun upon the darkening restless sea
Your mystic being touched by thirsting soul captivating me

All things in Life bloom in their own God-given time and place
The flowers, the trees, nature's creatures, and our human race
Our love blossomed forth by that seashore in God's chosen hour
Ardent as the sun, lofty as the highest tower
'Twas the sacred moment in our lives that came to be
Once upon an evening when the fading sun fell into the sea.

Alma Leonor Beltran

HEART

I will keep on loving you 'til the end of time
There's not any love better than yours and mine
This time has come again, for me to say
I love you each and every day
You may be far away, but my love for you is
more than I can ever say, but in my heart is
where it will stay.

Lisa Cox

LOVE

Love is beautiful, yes love is warm,
Full of happiness, sometimes harm.

You can have love, yet be lonely too.
For the part that's empty inside you.

It's not empty from the love of now.
But from long ago, nowhere to be found.

Inner feelings can confuse you at times.
Mixing past and present, oh how the mind winds.

You want to go back, yet long to stay.
Wanting so much, for neither to slip away.

But you're only one in the world for now.
You can't go back, for there's no way how.

It's really better to stay with today.
For going back would only bring pain.

Still inner feelings will always remain.
Your mind goes in circles, just playing the game.

Love is beautiful, yes love is warm.
Full of happiness, sometimes harm.

Karen L. Bixler

AARON . . .

As sleep surrounds my nighttime
and familiar shadows dance across the sky

Wistful memories are my companions
as silence brings peace to my troubled mind

I listen to the soft but steady breathing
of my baby, my little boy

I delight in the sweet innocence of his slumber

And I smile at the mischief each day
received from his touch

I am secure with his strong and loving nature

And am pleased at his cunning and determined ways

My inner voice whispers of a future bright and free
for my son will be man of men someday

But tonight I can relax and listen to the soft
but steady breathing of my baby, my little boy

My greatest joy

Elizabeth E. La Grange

LOST IN LOVE

I the poet who've shared the rhymes,
Created some works, to give to our times.
I the Dreamer, have dreamed the unknown.
Only love in my heart, remains to be shown.
Being miles away, calling words out loud.
Love is gone on a white dream cloud.
In the annals of love that's come into hand.
Lost are its values, vainly trying to stand.
The passions seem to always shift.
Alone in my heart, I'm ready to drift.
I love the best way I possibly know.
Seemingly confused with the moves, it's
starting to show.
I'm now the doubter knowing love is
a mere game.
The fire is low, as well as the flame.

Joseph R. Carchia

REVISIONS

Would you ever have thought that to alter your sex
Would be easy as striking a key?
Well, on paper, at least, it's as simple as that:
Add an 'S' so that he becomes she.
With today's new word processing units and such,
There's no need to go under the knife;
Just a few choice insertions, deletions, or both,
And a man can turn into his wife.
Now, if you are a woman and feel discontent
'Cause you're wishing that you were a man,
Then the same sort of thing can be worked out for you.
Oh, there's no doubt at all that it can.
Change the S to an R. Now, you're Mr., not Ms.
The adjustment's accomplished with ease.
Think how far we have come since the days when we first
Started poking at typewriter keys!

Susan Williams

HAPPY SPRING

When I love, I love happy
I laugh and sing and feel like spring
That was how I felt
When I watched you, as you came by
A flower unfolds into the dew
So young so full of life, it's true
And when upon the summer's shore
Love blossoms seem to die once more
Why cannot it be, that love will stay with me
Forever more
So I'll just think, it all seems hazy
After love has gone, so very crazy
And when I find another time
A love to share, and I'll be there
To once again, laugh and sing
And feel again, another spring

Bettegene McCammon

TWO

I know that loving takes but one
For I have loved you a'fore the sun
Had risen in her brightened orb
And shone her rays toward the moor.

I've seen the face of one alone in love
And wished my arms were wings of dove
That fly and soar to Heaven's roof
And wing my way to God's own proof.

If I could sign my name in blood
With love I've shed for you, yes love —
I'd tear my heart out, still would it beat
For I have loved you, and when I meet

The One upstairs who covers all
I shall remember not to fall
Nor falter in my step for you,
For I have loved you, loved you, loved you.

Elizabeth McDonald Pickens

MY FUTILE VENTURE — LOVE FOR ME

My heart cries out in pain
My joyous love walks away
My depressive nature abounds full force
I'm feeling profound remorse

I need and want too much
How does one give us such
Lust for love eats at me inside
All the feelings I must hide

Lack of love drains my source of being
My soul is empty, my thoughts are shallow
For being so deep
Only thoughts of you for keeps

Love is an awful beautiful thing
A time to cry and a time to sing
Bring out myself so no one can see
I'm torn and shattered with no one to blame, but me!

Jean Land

QUESTIONS OF LOVE

What will you think when I tell you I love you?
What will you say when I show you I care?
What do you feel when we're together?
Is there more in our lives we can share?
The questions come easy —
It's the answers I fear.
Not knowing your feelings —
Not having you here.
We've an on-going lovesong
With miles between
Yet we're close to each other
What could that mean?
Are we destined for greatness?
Can our love remain strong?
Shall we carry on further?
— How far? — How long?
Distance will test us and time will pass by.
But our feelings, our laughter, will last if we try.
Our meaningful union can grow without end
If you'll stay my lover, be my life and my friend.

Theodore R. Munsch

Someday
Someday we will meet again.
I do not know how or when.
You know I love you.
This is true.
I will always be there, in the spirit of your mind.
If you look within your heart, I know that you will find
A shining place with love that's true,
Where our kindred hearts can start anew.
Physically I may be gone.
But the spirit dear, with you belongs.
And if you listen closely dear, in the stillness of the night,
You will feel my presence near, and my arms around you tight.

Bonnie Allen Coleman

GOODBYE

Once upon a dream, long ago
There was this girl I got to know.
She wasn't that special or above any other
But isn't that the way it begins with lovers?

We knew a love of friendship and caring;
Our hopes and dreams, we were always sharing.
Then one day I went away.
So much was lost in one short day.

We never kept in touch.
We lost so very much.

The last time I saw her, she wore blue lace.
She had flowers in her hand
And the cold grip of death was on her face.

I stood and stared
Then finally dared
To say goodbye.

Once upon a dream long ago
There was this girl I got to know . . .
Goodbye

Paul W. Sewell

THUS SPAKE HER LOVER

Love, great ocean, locked within our thighs
Your deeps enfold exotic birth;
Hold intact the vapor of our sighs
For I am Sky and She is Earth.

My love's body is a golden barque,
My two-prowed craft to meet the gales.
Bright she glistens in the spray-tossed dark
And her delicious lips are sails.

My love's womb impounds the secret sea,
The porpoise I, its joyous guest —
Plunging deep in hot-foamed ecstasy,
Full-washed by her caress in crest.

She, my love, and I are silvered fish
That revel, frolic, dart and glide,
Gay reflections from each high wave's wish,
The cry of gull, the roar of tide.

Love, great ocean, drown us in thy name,
Then toss us laughing to the sun.
Though separate we were when first we came
Now your embrace has made us one.

Burr McCloskey

TRYING TO FORGET

How can I forget you?
Never, that's what I always knew.
How can I forget the small town?
With one side the sea,
And the rest surrounded by trees like a crown.
With a cafe, so simple and small,
Liked so much by all.
I can still see you swimming in the sea,
Then coming and wetting my nice towel,
While lying next to me.

How can I not remember the day,
When you brought me my favorite flowers?
And I didn't know what to say.
Walking hand in hand,
On the beach or through the park,
In sunshine, snow or rain,
Never feeling cold and doing it again and again.
Or when I saw you coming with a haircut, much too short,
Looking like a clown,
You laughing, I with a big frown.

Helena M. Jones

JONES, HELENA MARIA. Born: Glukowo, Poland; Occupations: Studying language and writing poetry; Comments: *I've been writing poetry since the age of sixteen. Most of my poems are very personal and private, just like my diary.*

VANISHING LOVE

His eyes stare at me with contempt,
Where once there was love.
His voice is sarcastic and sharp,
Where once it was soft.
His touch is cold and aloof,
Where once it was intimate.
His style boastful, to cover up inadequacy,
Where once there was confidence.
His manner is somber and unsympathetic,
Where once there was compassion.
His attitude is resentful and vicious,
Where once he appreciated.
His tone is hostile and threatening,
Where once there was security.
His temperament is changeable and unstable,
Where once there was stability.
His mood is depressing and withdrawn,
Where once it was outgoing.
His ambition is to make my life unbearable,
Where once it was to please me.

Mary Frances Hayes

TOGETHER AS ONE

Together as one, is a great way to be,
A great way to live our lives:
For each day we can know,
There's someone we can hold,
Together you and I —
Together as one, this can bring so much fun,
This can bring pain if we let it,
But deep in our minds,
We must stride with the times,
Together forever we must be —
Together as one, we must grow and live on,
We must love, knowing there can be no cease;
For in our hearts we must know,
Our love must go on,
Together our love must grow —
Together as one, day by day this must go on,
Day by day we must let this be;
For tomorrow may not come,
And yesterday is already gone,
Today let us love together and be free —

Benjamin E. Thompkins, Jr.

IS SILENCE GOLDEN?

Silent tears to ease the silent pain
Of the silent love I hide in vain.
A cold silent room in which I abide
On dark silent nights it's there I hide.

Silent longing to be held by you
While you hold another, what can I do?
Except silent swearing at a silent moon
And silent fate to end it all soon.

Silent watching of a silent betrayal
Standing helpless during the silent portrayal.
Silent grief in a silent room
For you're unaware of your silent doom.

Silent hell in which I dwell
Silent ears turned, no one to tell.
Silent words on a silent page
Show silent corpse of a silent rage.

Lorey Umberger

My God shall hear my
prayer and take heed of me
because I love Him, and I come
to Him as I am whether in distress
whether I have been overwhelmed
through His Holy Spirit, through My
King sitting on the throne of grace
high in the Heavens camouflaged. He
in His compassion has visited me, a
wretch in His presence, yet he shall
declare me as one who is righteous! Was
it not Jesus Himself who acknowledged
His unity with the Father? For We are one!
He proclaimed, through the Holy Spirit, our
Comforter, whom God sent down upon us
on the day of Pentecost, that drive to
do what is right in Jehovah's sight, that
will to yield toward righteousness, that
obligation we hold toward God's law,
governed by sheer love, as such we
indeed have a new Covenant.

Joseph A. Stewart

MY LOVE

Our love doesn't flow between us, therefore it's only mine.
As I live so shall I love you, yet I'll grow tired.
When can I be freed from this prison whose walls enclose?
I know you don't love me so why do I have these feelings?

Sails, set on blue waters my love, and free me from
these walls that bind me. Take this burden from me
for I can't see, wherever I go it weighs on me.
It's painfully heavy as if to crush me completely.

As my arms are held openly for your warmth and loving
I feel a freshness and health as if I were newly-created.
My love, forever stay by me as the boldness and warmth
cause depth and purpose, if only you loved me.

How can I put away what I feel for you? In my heart
there are many words I long to convince you of, my love.
They go unsaid as I can't speak as I wish. As a stream
I can be truly free from any grasp, but yours has me.

If you would choose me for your love now, my love
I would hold you and love you without stopping.
With each day I would save my kisses to fall on
your lips with a cradle of affection until we stop.

Sharon Hemker

ETERNALLY HERE

One syllable name will always be here
And resting somewhere in earth's atmosphere.
Our course was not clear when you were alive
My only regret is — you did not survive.

One syllable name and what it implies
Is eternally here — in view of my eyes.
The sound of a name is always somewhere
No matter what else such name may declare.

The ring of a bell has always one sound
Which name that I call is likewise around.
No matter above — a cave in a wall
Or within the ground resounds to my call.

One syllable name will always be here
To her it belongs in earth's atmosphere.
They all now resound in the name of her voice
And all are contained within this one choice.

No matter above — a cave in a wall
Or within the ground resounds to my call.
They all are contained in her syllable name
The one within me — all over again . . .

Howard Deutsch

Once upon a time in a far far land,
you were here.
Eric left us in a tragedy,
and the pain will never stop.
His years were short
The time grows long,
At times it's a dream,
A nightmare I thought.
But I never awaken, the hurt never stops.
You're gone from this world, forever to part.
If we needed you then, now it is more,
For your life didn't end,
It will be here evermore.

Susan Harvey

SHOULDERS

They've borne so much, those shoulders:
The loneliness of an ofttimes empty house
And the grown-up chores thrust
Onto those nine-year-old shoulders.

Was she ever a child?
I wonder as I watch her prepare a big dinner:
Such big shoulders on so unimposing a woman.
She cushions the world's blows for
Her husband, that he may have some peace.
Her arms encircle her daughter as she
Grieves over lost happiness.
Simply by being, she gives strength.

Although she can now afford the luxury
Of relaxing and enjoying life,
Her soft, caring shoulders bear the marks
Of the long, winding ribbon of life.
She bore our hurts, that we could smile
And go about, just a bit more easily.
Thank you, Mom.
I love you.

Karen Sue Wittkowski

SIGHTS AND SOUNDS OF SPRING

A chattering squirrel, a giggling girl,
A barking dog, a croaking frog;
A woodpecker pecking, a couple necking,
The creek is flowing, the flowers are growing,
These are the sights and sounds of spring.
A coyote howling, a dog growling,
The whispering wind, the trees that bend;
The crows are cawing, the jays are jawing;
The blue birds are singing, the swallows are winging,
These are the sights and sounds of spring.
The sun is shining, squirrels on pine nuts dining,
The dove is ka-ka-ka-kooing, the cats are mewing;
Willow trees are budding, Strawberry Creek is flooding,
The bees are buzzing, the pussy willow is fuzzing,
These are the sights and sounds of spring.
A babbling brook, a fish on a hook,
The stars at night, are big and bright;
The cats, rats, gnats, and flying bats,
The gophers and moles that dig their holes,
These are the sights and sounds of spring.
For spring is here, it's the time for cheer,
It's the time to sing, Thank God for spring.

Le Roy F. Oates

CUPID'S ARROW STRIKES

Her youthful dreams, in her maidenly way
Where she'd meet her Prince Charming some fine day.
And then it happened, the fact was real,
His White Charger was a set of wheels.
When his requests for dates were renewing,
She knew her Prince had come a-wooing.
And this progressed at such a good rate,
She visited his folks, out of state.
She had qualms about this, but not despair
For she was in love, beyond repair.
His mother liked her, this lovely girl
In fact she thought she was a real pearl.
She and his folks were friends from the start.
Hugged each other when time to depart.
She sees Cupid's arrow flying around.
She may yet get her feet back on the ground.

Wm. A. McDonald

BECOMES AN IMPRESSION

Ink tracks upon a blank page;
  how seldom met.
Seventy-nine phrases, and sixteen empty spaces;
  becomes an impression written with love.
Small time poet am I,
  few words and written rhymes.
Words are not enough spoken;
  for what's in my heart
  lingers within your paper-laced eyes.
The soul has been awoken,
  not a breathless slumber of emotion.
So let me give to you,
  as you give to me;
  for everything that is two,
  becomes an impression written with love.

Paige Angela Farkas

HEARTS ON FIRE

My heart is on fire
pumping fast and skipping beats
when the first time I see her.
I think I'm in love
and my temperature is rising
my hands sweaty, pulse going crazy.
I sure would like to meet her
I hope that she looks over this way
my heart is going to skip . . . skip to my lou
my heart is on fire — I'm in love
only paying attention to her,
It feels grand to be in love
and forgetting everything else in this world.
Being on cloud nine over her is OK with me
My heart is on fire and in love!

Shooting Poet

HERE IN MY HEART

Here in my heart is the happiness I shall ever know.
Those memories of the past are something to think about
  in days of old.
Here in my heart those memories will grow
  as I too grow old.
Here in this house is the tombstone I shall make alone.
My worn wrinkled hands shall be the chisel
  with which I carve.
Here in this house my epitaph will read in stone . . .
I lived and died love-starved.
Here in this house I hope she will find me dead.
Here in my heart will be the cold happiness
to her unknown.
My epitaph will always remain unread,
For I will be my own tombstone.

Theodore V. Kundrat

HEART OF STONE

I wish for a heart of stone . . .
No more crying when I am alone
Save all my love for myself
Place my feelings high upon the shelf.

I would no longer feel the world's pain . . .
My sensitivity no longer in vain
Relationships be but a casual affair
A heart of stone needs no repair.

Tammy Holley

ON LOVE MAKING

HONORABLE MENTION

I have made friends with the C-shaped
scar on your face: I have kissed it.

Your motorcycle and Persian rugs were an
easy creation: they were assimilated as air.

As for the dog, he was more difficult:
gift from an old girlfriend, his eyes
were frankly alien. Still, you stood
on the other side of the fence, you
laughed as he chased me around the yard.

At breakfast, now, I drink cold water
from your mug with an open throat. You
have a cold, you say, but I suspect
no infirmities. Perhaps I imagine
something other than a week of

Wearing the thick mask of fever. Perhaps
I feel us, tonight, hugging under the
covers, sharing what we carry, sharing
what we make: a life.

S. L. Hough

IN FROST AND STORMY WEATHER

We don't mind the frost and stormy weather,
As long as we can be together.
I'm almost sure we'll catch the flu,
But who cares about a thing like flu,
As long as I can be with you.

To the end of the world I'll go with you,
Any time, I'm almost sure.
I don't want to hear
What you have to say,
In case it's the other way.

Let me dream my dreams,
Which can't last long it seems.
Sometimes, there is no need for words,
The look, or a touch of your hand,
Mean more than words from a book of the grand.

No matter how stormy or grey, you always say,
"What a beautiful day."
And I think long into the night,
When I'm supposed to sleep,
That the memories about you, forever I'll keep.

Helena M. Jones

THAT SPECIAL SOMEONE

The first day we met you were lonesome
And shy. We fell in love shortly thereafter
Now it's almost impossible to say goodbye.
Holding you in my arms I felt I had the
World at my feet, reflecting on when
I first saw you so lovely, so sweet.
Just having you near me fills my heart
With a burning desire and the mere thought
of you rekindles the fire.
Through all of life's endeavors each day
I pray that in time you'll be mine
because only once in a lifetime does
A dreamboat like you come my way.

Joseph Reed

MORNING SUNRISE

I walk along a path
this early morning
and close my eyes to see your image,
your jet hair and russet eyes,
you dance along a bridge
surrounded by golden daffodils.
Tiny yellow butterflies gently glide
among wild roses
as the rays turn to pink
you stroll along the bank
listening to the rippling waters of a stream
you kneel to gather geraniums
watching the trembling leaves on the bough
I miss you, long for you,
the pink turns to blue
and I see azure forget-me-nots in your hair.
Within the fleecy clouds above
I see you running toward me,
carrying a bouquet of daisies.

Virginia Goland

VAGUE ATTRACTION

Not just something physical
as I recall
However, my memory is dulled under fluorescent light
Searching for full white suds on a blue sea
Once again, an ocean's body moves swiftly,
out of sight
Is this scene so thoroughly etched in my past?
Has time elapsed that slowly?
Spiritually weakened — these thoughts penetrate me

The temperature fluctuates in my comfortable abode
It fails to abolish this sudden, acute affection
I pinch my arm. Nothing changes
I douse my face in cold water — the impression stays
Refuge is sought
For the pen seems almost my enemy now.
Unconscious forces could be prying an imprisoned soul — loose
Seeking a love, a place, a time, distant in my mind
In time, this entity will manifest itself

Greg Phipps

WHISPERS OF THE HEART

Whispers of the heart,
Come true to me,
For love begins its very start.
At first, it's unbelievable for me to see;
The mind and the heart — there is a controversy.
Can it be real, this time
It seems so fine.
I disbelieve — is it too late?
Or has the wonder been taken to fate.
No, no, let it be true,
Let it be true this time.
For this time everything falls into rhyme.
This time is for you,
The one I love, I know it's true.
It's got to be, for the pain we've bared.
I know it makes us both scared.
The present, the future to which we will share.
The roads are rocky, the ruts are deep.
But with you and I together forever — we will keep.

Shelly Mende

MY LOVE IS YOURS

I want you, for you're the one I love so true.
I need you and no one else but you.
I love you with all my heart and soul
My heart my mind my body are completely under
your control.
It's you and your love that keep me whole.
You are my love you are my friend, you are my life.

When all the stories have been told, and we are growing old.
And things begin to fade with time, and there's nothing,
left to hang on to. Hang on to me and the love we share.
For there is one thing, my dear, that will always be true.
and that's the fact that I love you, and desire to be with you.

If the sun refuses to shine, and memories begin to fade in my mind.
There is one thing time won't take, that's my love for you,
or the way I see you. You, my darling, shall ever be my
white knight in shining armor, my prince of love.
You are my wish upon a star, my dream come true
I am wherever you are, for where you are there lies my
heart. Know this my love, my heart and mind are with you always.

Mary B. S. Palmer

AFTER DUSK

The mystic magic of an Arabian night
Never could compare to that heaven lent sight
Myriad lights, like a million jewels shone through the dimness of space
They kindly threw a shadowed light upon my dear dear lover's face
It seemed but just a dream
Two hours on earth the most supreme
That ever I have known
King of love upon your throne
When sun is shining bright
You charm with curious delight
The hours were secretly dark
My love and I, alone on our lark
Passion was enriched with steel white heat
Our hearts just once together at night did beat
Alone we entered the world
You and I have lived; we have toiled
It is flesh and flesh
Caught in an entangled love mesh
Only death can extricate
King of love ordain our fate
Take us back to your outdoor castle once before we die
Content that death may claim me while in my lover's arms I lie.

Pearl Van Slocum

MY INTERN DOCTORS

(Both Sexes)

The interns at Cornell Medical Center I see them each day.
To know them by name, is very hard for me to say,
But their judgement of medical knowledge, is so educational to me,
Because of the many questions asked, of all the patients they see.

I watch them as they flock around the patient on hand,
As each observes and suggests the case, to a successful plan,
They are so very gentle in their many meaningful ways,
And their same kindness continues day after day.

Their life is of devotion and time-consuming service,
That respect to them on this earth, should
Always have a loud voice,
As for me, I am very happy when they visit me,
Because some day, one of these interns my doctor will be.

Louis D. Izzo

ALONE

He is gone now, the man
I loved so long.
Many times I think of him in
my lonely hours,
precious memories I'll always
have, and the tears softly fall
for the man I loved so long.
Endless days go by, and life
is not complete,
I turn to God for inner
strength, to walk each
day alone,
now the man I loved so
long is gone.

M. F. Witte

WIFE

My eyes looked up to wonder
I saw the stars aflame
The Universe was burning
And I would look for fame

But life fell into darkness
She brought it back to life
My Lover, Friend, Companion
My own, my dearest Wife

Oh Hazel Eyes and Flaming Hair
The source of my delight
I see the Heavens burning
Pale in Love's great Light

Thomas L. Hollis

STUNNED

Oh boy!
Kenan's eyes are leaves
with a hidden crooked branch.
Chelley Vanessa has blue eyes
to perfection.
When I was young
I tamed Shlitz and
the low moon was beautiful.
The lightning at my feet
scared me.
The triangle ships
one night stunned my
thoughts for years.
I love you Kenan and Chelley.

Karen Lynelle Bowling

US

My dusty soul needs to cling to the
entangled mass of your grey matter.

To be nurtured and to grow —
become as one.

A communion of soul, mind, and body,

We are one.

Cathie Hope Willis

FRIENDS

We've friends who love us always
In pleasure or in pain —
Who love us in our absence
Or when we come again.

They reach out when we falter
With steady helping hand;
These friends who love us always
Are truly in demand.

The friends who love us always
Are sometimes hard to find,
For friendships may prove selfish,
And love is often blind.

Words fail to do them justice
In measuring their worth,
But friends who love us always
Are dearest friends on earth.

Louise Freese

MY EIDOLON

Tonight when you go home to her
And smile your special smile,
Will you even think about me,
And wonder for a while?

If I'm happy in this prison
In the big house on the hill?
If I long for you and listen
To a heart that can't be still?

Yeah, you walk the ragged canyons
Of my aimless, anguished mind.
You trail the bloodied banyans
Of the soul you left behind.

Now she danced in the daydreams
Where once I waltzed so fine.
And she stepped into my limelight
When the curtain call was mine.

Betty Antrobus

ONE FINAL BREATH

I wake up sweating over a dream,
That turned into a nightmare.
My mind stumbles over rocks of memories,
Fallen from mountains of care.

Perhaps my heart is finding a way,
To beat us to our death.
Maybe my soul is breathing memories,
To take its final breath.

I feel a need inside to write,
To explain and find our end.
No words come to mind or heart,
As the branches of love start to bend.

Is this the beginning of my ending,
No longer able to write about you?
Are the dreams finalizing our yesterdays,
A realization of our being through?

Veronica Porter

GENTLE MAN

Gentle man — come into my life
and bring your laughing eyes.
Gentle man — let me know you a little
without any games or lies.
Gentle man — are you lonely
searching for someone to trust?
Gentle man — I am that friend who
can let you go if you must.
Gentle man — I bring no wounds to further
rend your heart.
Gentle man — the price is paid . . . it's
time for a brand-new start.
Gentle man — can I help you
to forget the past for a while?
Gentle man — is it really so much
to want to see you smile?
Gentle man — Gentle man . . . come
into my life.

Karen S. Lewis

BEFORE YOU GO

I wet my lips
as I wait for an answer from you
to a question unasked between us,
to an invitation still waiting,
to a conclusion never reached.

With the turn of the calendar,
each day is a treasure until you go,
yet still we falter, afraid of the spark
that flew into life —
how long ago?

All right.
Say nothing and look away,
but before we part,
for the sake of what might have been —
touch me.
Please.

H. Henrietta Stockel

WHY DOES TOMORROW HAVE TO COME?

Why does tomorrow have to come
When I'm here with you today?
There wouldn't be a tomorrow
If I could have my way.
I'd have every day last forever
When I'm by your side
Together we'd share each other
And on moonbeams we could ride.
I'd write your name with the stars
And dot it with the moon,
We'd sail the milky way
And let the heavens sing our tune.
Why does tomorrow have to come
When I'm here with you today?
Why does the moon follow the sun?
Why does night follow the day?
Why does tomorrow have to come
When I'm here with you today?

Leo Feebish

THE FORCE OF LOVE

Love sleeps within me,
fertile, dark earth under
chaste, white snow.

Love wakes,
cries for acknowledgment
and will not be denied.

Love strains to be free,
Winter's river rushing forth
in swollen flood of Spring.

Jerrie Hejl Collins

SHADOWS IN MY HEART

Through the dim shadows in my heart
I see you smiling, Dear,
Just as you used to smile at me
When you were with me here.

Ever so faintly I feel your hand
As you were holding mine
When you were here on earth with me —
A touch, God's own design.

Ever so sweetly I feel you here,
Your arm around my waist
As we used to stroll the wooded path —
A Heavenly foretaste.

Ever so gently I asked the Lord
To let me join you "There."
Since you have gone before I find
No pleasure anywhere.

Through the dim shadows in my heart
I'm reaching up to you —
Lead me kindly, Darling Ralph,
Till God will call me too!

Thelma Van Scoik

GAIL

G is for Gail
a creation so fair,
a gift from Heaven,
a treasure so rare.

A is for all
that she means to me;
My love she has captured
it is plain to see.

I is for incredible,
a term easily applied;
How it relates to her
cannot be denied.

L is for love,
a condition highly rated;
It seems this word
was for us alone created.

These letters when joined
evoke a most delightful thought;
For they belong to a lady
my heart has long sought.

Bob Van Deven

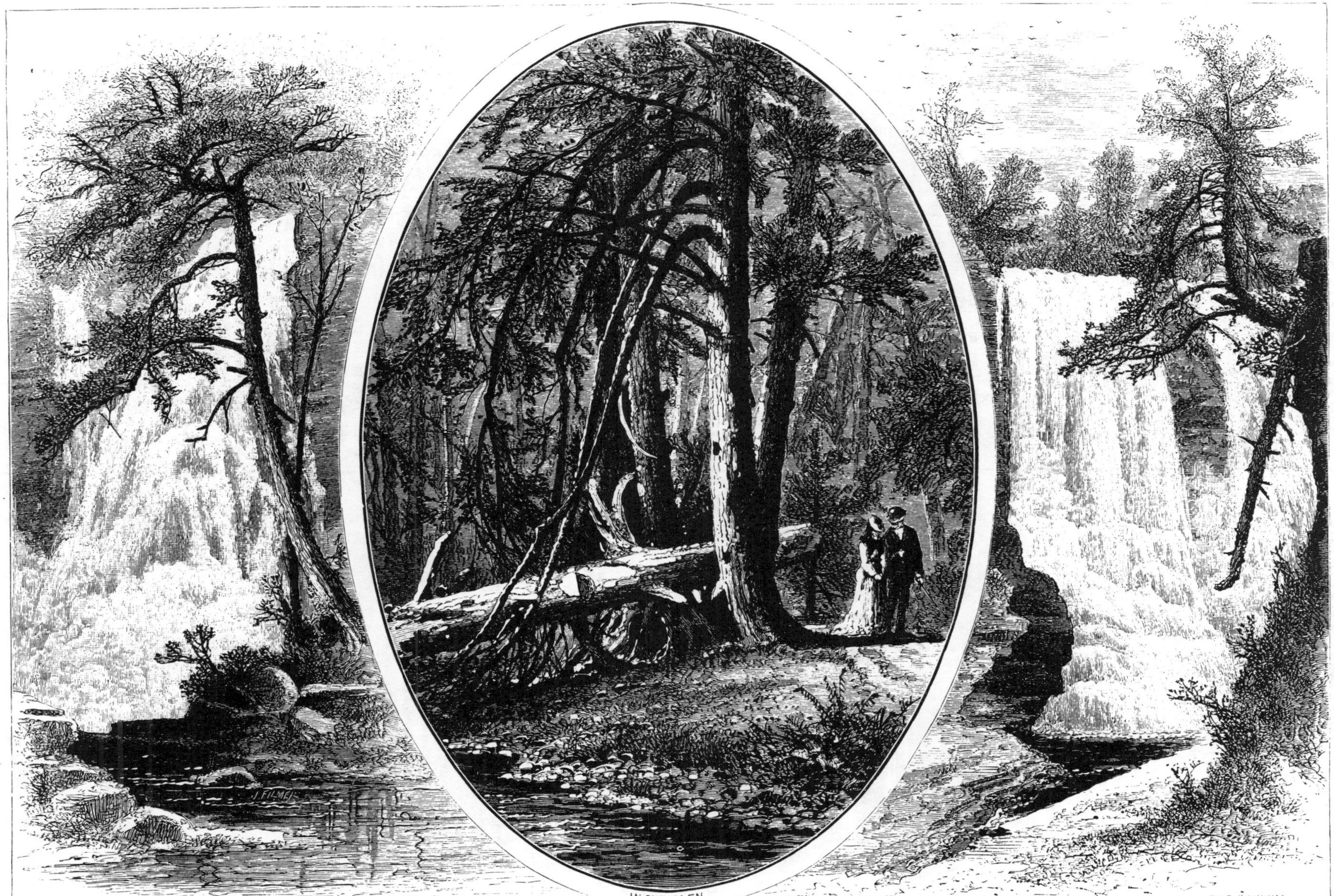

SCENES IN AND ABOUT MILFORD.

SECRET SWEET MELODY: WINGS OVER THE STORM

Explore your own higher latitudes,
Amber and somber, free from the rubble
of centuries;
Because we love, we also adore but
Because we have faith we help to
perform miracles.
As at time of the Divine Resurrection
The tempests were stilled and the sick
were healed.
So today in the cycles of divine light
The symbols of faith, hope and love
Are focusing the mysteries of tomorrow.
Alertly behold the wings over the storm.
Heavenly dilemmas of golden wings in the
Universe overflying the clouds of the earth.
Because spirit is light and matter is darkness.
Spiritus est Lux, materia autem obscuritas.
Lux lucet in tenebris.

Allan De Fiori

DE FIORI, ALLAN. Born: Barre, Vermont, 1-24-15; Married: to Catherine Mary Florio, R.N.; Education: Episcopal Seminary of Reggio Emilia, Italy, Magna Cum Laude; Occupation: Bookbinder, Practical Nurse, Poet; Awards: Three Honorable Mention Certificates and Golden Poetry Award for 1985 by the World of Poetry Press; Poetry: 'The Resurrection Star,' 'Cypress,' 'Ode to H.M. Queen Elizabeth II of Great Britain,' Vantage Press, 1983; 'Willow Bitter,' 'England,' 'Rose of Arlov,' World of Poetry, 1983; 'Rose of New Hampshire,' 'Wings Over the Storm,' 'Islamic Idyll,' Poetry Press; 'Vermont Echo,' 'April Love,' 'Mt. Helleron,' 'Mt. Horeb,' 'Mt. Tabor,' 'Mt. Etna,' 'Fatima,' 'Gone With The Wind,' 'Relativity Theory,' 'Islam Dark Victory,' American Poetry Association, 1984; 'Starlight,' 'Redemption,' New York Poetry Society, 1985; Comments: *Writing poetry is an enjoyment for me. I dedicated my poems to my dear fiancee Catherine Florio, R.N. I am indebted to her for loyal, sincere, inspirational endowment and talent. Many thanks also to my aunt, Enrica Alberta De Fiori, for her thoughtful and valuable support.*

WHEN I SEE MY MOM

When I see my mom,
I see someone loving, sweet and kind.
Someone whom I can turn to at the
lowest points of my life.

When I see my mom,
I see someone who will stick by my side
through thick and thin,
for better or worse,
or whenever others put me down
or turn away from me and leave me standing
alone in the cold.

When I see my mom,
I see someone who gave of herself for me to live.
I see someone who dries my tears and
comforts my fears,
holds me near and loves me dear.

When I see my mom,
I see a woman whom I'll someday hope to reflect,
she's like a mirror of love that I'll never
reject.

When I see my mom,
I see a woman of love, joy, laughter and sorrow,
And I never want to lose her love!

To my dear mother
Love always

Ellen Rutlin

GOD'S LOVE IS EVERYWHERE

When I get lonely, as I do so many days,
I just listen for God's voice. He speaks
to us in so many ways.

He speaks to us through the songs of
birds and the buzzing of the bees,
The sounds of soft breezes and the
rustling of leaves in the trees.

He speaks to us through the sweet voice
of a loving friend.
If we really listen and care the sound of
God's voice never ends.

He speaks to us through the sweet perfume
of the flowers
And the beautiful sunsets that, for the
looking, can be ours.

I hear Him in the roar of the wind and
the waves of the sea
And in the hush of the twilight He speaks to me.

I see Him in the stars that glitter so far away,
And know that from His presence I cannot stray.

I hear His comforting words when I'm
grieving for loved ones, He has taken away.
I feel the touch of His gentle loving hands
and know that He is leading the way.

Helen Krebs

PRO FOOTBALL PLAYER DENVER BRONCO'S DEAN MIRALDI

Bright sun shone gold across ripples of a gentle sea,
Afloat, spriteful and free, on his boat called life.
All's fair, material playground carousel,
Like a luminous watercolor, of an Eagle in the rain.
Suddenly, tempest roaring of scudding waves,
Wordly cares piqued pressure to ship's ruin.
To the lifeboat, his heart wrapped tight,
Then watched her disappear like a jewel in the night.
Through sheens of daylight, he swam with the lifejacket,
As strikes of lightning, belated Superbowl dream.
Grasped driftwood, until swallowed by the sea,
Like a twisted tune without harmony.
In looking up, the mercy of God made it known, he wasn't alone,
As Jesus Christ rebuilt with love, his broken-down walls.
In knowing Jesus Christ as being Lord and Savior,
He fights the unbeatable games, and beats the unbearable pains.
No matter how hopeless, no matter what distance.
In pursuing his quest,
He finally came to rest fulfilled, in true peace and joy,
April's flame, and Denver's fame, gifts of gold in Jesus' precious name.

Debra Kirkham

LOVE LETTERS IN THE SAND

I was sitting alone down by the sea.
I thought no one was around, just God and me.
Then I started writing letters in the sand
Just as a huge wave destroyed the works of my hand.
Then the ghost of one I knew so long, long ago
Appeared to my pleasure. I would have all to know.
I was writing this love letter to a lover of long ago,
But instead of taking me, she chose to marry another beau.
Now things are not all good for neither her or me,
So I would to God that it was like it used to be.
Writing those love letters in the sand brings memories to me alone,
But the happiness I never had now makes it all so far gone.
Neither she or I could know what if it had been
That she married me and not the other then.
It could have been better for both you and me,
But none but God can down through life that far see.

C. D. McKay

REFLECTIONS

You looked in the mirror, and what you said you saw was not what I see
Painting the glass
A rounded stone, stream swept
Encouraging grace amidst hardness
The shape of resistance to error and sadness a translucent cloak
Against your eyes and theirs
But not mine

Yet no day is so simple that it leaves you alone
Plucking first your heartstrings and then mine
Polishing, configuring the elements of passion and strength
All too often instruments self-directed
In pain self-inflicted
Torn about being only so perfect as you are

It slips so slowly down the glass
Glinting in the light
So clear
The mirror releases a tear
Unable to show
What it and I know
But you won't see.

Mark Cashman

MY FAMILY, NEAT PACKAGE, GOD'S LOVE

My family, meet package of love.
Back in '34, I couldn't ask for more.
But God knew the score from above
46 years through happiness and tears.
God Bless with cheers.
But sorrow came today, took A.A. away
My sweet husband left me
With eight loved ones you see.
We call them Sugar Foots
We help with all their hurts
We wanted the world to know
how we loved them so.
Art, Beth, Terry, Art, Jr. and Mark,
They all stole our hearts
Al, Pat and Erica, devotion,
Is deeper than the ocean
They put our love on
Higher ground, no sweeter
Love can be found
Than our family

Mrs. A. A. Roberts

LOST LOVE

I saw you last night, my Love,
in the mist over the sea,
in the waves pounding the shore.

I saw you, Love.
You looked at me.
You looked into my eyes
and you smiled.

I saw you, Love,
and I wonder —
how I wonder —
when you are coming back for me.

I am lost without you.
I am waiting for you,
my Love,
I am
waiting.

Ann Dutcher

LOVEFORCE — P.J.

It's hard to take back
Something said in anger.
But words come in anger,
Not meant to be said.
Words that hurt
That make you cry
And want to hurt back,
But don't.
Because understanding
The reasons for the anger
And the hurt,
Is a far stronger and lasting force,
Love.
Love hurts sometimes, too.
But understanding it,
Living it and giving it back
Makes us stronger and beautiful,
Caring and compassionate people
With more love to give,
To take the anger away.

P. J. Dick

IMMORTALITY

I walked the lane this morning through the softly falling snow,
My footsteps, clear and sharp, were etched in white
as I looked back along the way I'd come.

But when I retraced my steps, the ones I'd made so short a time before
were half-obliterated by the drifting flakes, so fast they fell.
I meditated, as I came again to warmth of hearthside fire:
"How like the road of life which all must walk!
True greatness oft survives the passing years, But I . . . shall I pass . . .
like my footsteps in the snow so soon lost to oblivion?"
I do not know . . . Perhaps it matters not, if in the passing
I shall leave behind a friend who loved me much, and who,
treasured within her heart, forgets me not! . . .
But this I know: I have a friend who walks my lane with me;
He holds my hand and guides in ways that touch Eternity,
And when I reach the Last Long Mile, when darkness falls
and footsteps falteringly grope their way,
I need but trust the goodness of my Friend to light a path
down which my feet will trod, with steps so bold and sure
They'll lead me to the very throne of God.

Ruby A. Jones

BIRTH OF A CHILD

Birth! A new burst of life . . . our baby.
We feel such exhilaration viewing the beauty and wonder of you.
It is strange and unbelievable that for nine months you were in
the process of assembling yourself with an industriousness that
is beyond human concentration.
We knew you were there . . . we could feel you . . . but could not see you.
You were rooted to us through our love . . . deep in your mother's body.
You developed into an infant and came forth.

A new life! The almighty so carefully created you, so small but so
complete and beautiful.
We need time now to get to know you . . . and for you to get to know us.
It will take time . . . years of our lives.
There is so much to know . . . so much to learn . . . so much to love.
We learn and learn . . . we cannot know it all.
We love and love . . . we cannot love enough.
Life is good . . . and it is a constant flow . . . it has no beginning or end.
Now we fold our hands and bow our heads.
We thank God for this new life . . .
The miracle of birth . . . our baby!

Jane Luciene Nowak

THE FEMININE VIBRATION

And she would walk and talk and sip a cup, fumble for whatnot
in her bag and roll her flashing eyes around

And I would scratch my head yet never move a hand to question
why my plexus tipped and flipped but answered not a sound

And she would come into my dream in replays standing barefoot
in the sage and sand as breezes pulled the dress against her thighs

And I would watch her every floating move and know it was a dream for
me alone to love 'fore the morning woke again my eyes

And she would know by now that passage of the years and more has
brought her to my thoughts of day to day duration

And I would know by now that it is not just loveliness and flashing
eyes nor saltiness of voice; I feel her in the air I breathe;
it's the feminine vibration

Boyd Rahier

CHILD OF MY HEART

Child of my heart,
sing me your melody.
Sweetness impart,
guilessness bring to me.

Woo me with silent tears,
clasp me in arms of air.
Gilded are all my fears,
gazing on one so fair.

Moonbeams have silent tryst,
caught in white net of snow,
stars sing while angels list
to echoes from below.

Love has its season, and
I, captive, bide my fate,
cast aside reason, send
life's wish to heaven's gate.

Erin B. I. Hampton

AB INITIO

All that I was
Came from looking for you
Now all that I am
Or may ever be
Is from having found
And known you
There is no way
To show or tell
I hope someday
You will know
What you have been
For love I find
Is never a bind
Just a bond
Of which I've grown
Very fond
Your love is like unto
A rose
On a stem of thorns
It grows —

Max Sheffield

TOUCH ME

That old feeling is back again;
Lightning playing on naked skin.
Starts at the very tip of my nose,
Races down to tingle my toes.

I would like to believe, in any case,
It's from the vision of a lovely face,
Or a lost love I'm thinking of:
Once close ties, once close love.

No. Oh no, it's none of those
That some romantic might suppose.
It is indeed, hard to explain,
For it's from the swell of a deep refrain.

Mere words do not offer the means to say
How music holds me in its sway.
Handing out to me passion's soft glove;
Put it on — and feel its love.

Howard Layne Harper

A LOVE POEM

Though dead so many years you still
live as my valentine!
As a child on your lap I asked: Daddy
why are those bells ringing? President
McKinley had been killed!
In Chicago at Jane Addams' Hull House
you showed me her theatre for the poor,
her father's mill-wheel-table — two pictures
of Tolstoi over her desk — before and after jail!
Europe at age 13 — seeing Peter Paul
Rubens' Descent from the Cross in Antwerp.

How you studied surgery in
Munich: Evenings before morning
clinics how you translated scientific
data from German to
English for American doctors in 1910.
How we took Sinclair Lewis and
lovely Grace Heggar Lewis to a medical meeting.
How you saved my husband's life
in a crucial illness complicated
by his crooked partner in which
the Mayo Clinic sustained your diagnosis!

Daddy — I love you!
(I miss you!)

Margaret E. Schmitt-Habein

SCHMITT-HABEIN, MARGARET E. Born: Jackson, Minnesota, 1898; Married: 1921 to Dr. Harold C. Habein; Education: University of Minnesota, B.A., 1918; Columbia University, New York City, M.A., 1919; Occupation: Professor of English, Rochester, Minnesota, 1920, Junior College, under auspices of University of Minnesota; Writings: "The Whale or the Bear," 1949, unpublished; currently writing autobiography at the request of Sinclair Lewis; Comments: *I have been in the peace movement 60 years. I write to preserve our civilization in as much as eight civilizations have died. I was married 26 years, home in Rochester, Minnesota, where my husband was on the Mayo Clinic staff. There I reared two wonderful sons and entertained in our home two ambassadors as well as many other celebrities. I was also president of the various organizations there! As legislation chairman of A.A.U.W., I lobbied for the County Aid to Education bill. I brought two legislators from Minneapolis to address us in Rochester. The bill passed!*

MOTHER

Going to school and teaching, too,
As well as raising three;
Your days were long and nights quite short,
On the road to that degree.

You always found the time for us,
And took it all in stride;
Our playing in bands, and singing songs,
We knew you felt much pride.

The emphasis was on us three,
It never was "you" first;
You traveled to games so we could play,
With weather at its worst.

Encouragement you gave to us,
You wanted us to win;
Your motto, like your favorite song,
Was "Don't Fence Me In."

Though times were hard, you proved to us,
We didn't need a crutch;
So, Mother dear, we want you to know,
We love you very much!

Kathleen M. Burley

INNER MIRRORS

Raindrops falling on the snow;
Silver rivulets winding down the drive;
Solitary trees stand stripped of leaves,
Solemn and naked against a graying sky.

Here in this room all is golden;
Love and warmth calm the air;
'Tis all a reflection from inner mirrors
Of those whose lives one another share.

Yet, the morbid funeral for the past goes on,
And go, I know I must;
Leaving their love and protection
To tread in the liquid dusk;

To add my tears to the raindrops;
To cry aloud with the wind;
Deploring the wrongs of the world;
Lamenting my own mortal sins.

Then after an eternity of sorrow,
Their love will shine again,
Drying the infectious raindrops,
Freeing my soul to return to Them.

Rita F. Artist

TEST OF TIME

The chains of love had bound them together
Their ventures were short
Through streams and deserts
Nothing but time could break these chains
For this man and this woman
Had much to gain.
The endless horizons that they had seen
Caused only to strengthen these chains it seemed
Both time and endurance they surely would need
Or the love they share will fade like a dream.

Guillermo A. Barela

AMAZING LOVE!

I heard a precious story sweet and dear
I heard the name of Jesus soft but clear
I heard the story of our Lord above . . .
Oh! The story of His love! Amazing love!

I heard the story of the cross . . . it's true
Upon the cross He died for me . . . for you!
Upon the cross of Calvary that day . . .
The blood of Jesus washed my sin away!

They placed Him in the tomb and there He lay
Until the dark of night had turned to day
Within the silent tomb in linens white
Our Savior lay in darkness through the night!

At morning Mary came unto the tomb . . .
Her lonely heart was broken at His doom
But then she saw the stone was rolled away
His linens had been left there where He lay!

Oh! Yes! He tore the linens all apart!
Oh! Yes! He died with love! A broken heart!
Though Jesus died He rose again that day!
For that stone . . . that heavy stone was rolled away!

Amazing love! What rapture so divine!
Amazing love! It thrills my soul! Sublime!
Amazing love of Jesus thrills my heart!
Amazing love! From Him I'll never part!

Mrs. La Forrest Lucas

THE HOUSE ON THE HILL

The life we shared together, for over twenty years,
Was filled with many memories of laughter, joy and tears.

So many plans that we both made. The dreams we talked about.
We had no way of knowing that his time was running out.

Like the little house he wanted, that sits up on the hill,
I said, "I'd love to own it." He said, "Someday you will."

But now I walk through empty rooms and only reminisce,
About those golden yesterdays and all that we have missed.

And then one day it happened. Like an answer to a prayer.
I passed that house up on the hill and what did I see there?

A little man was standing with a hammer and a nail,
Getting ready to hang up a sign that said: FOR SALE.

So I bought that house we dreamed of, with its panoramic view,
And filled it full of all the love that he and I once knew.

His picture's on the mantel. His books are on the shelf.
And a part of him still lives here, even though I'm by myself.

But I'm content just having, so many memories of —
A man that showed me happiness and gave me so much love.

He holds a place within my heart, that no one else can fill —
And he'll be with me forever, in this house up on the hill.

Garryett Fortin

SLEEPLESS AWE

As I close my eyes and try to sleep,
A vision fills my head;
I'm taken back to soft warm nights,
And roses . . . sunburnt red!

To smiles and happy feelings,
And the taste of bitter-sweet wine,
And gentle embracing caresses!
And of course those little white lines!

I can see two lovers side by side,
By the glow of the candle light;
And feel the passion building,
As they hold each other tight!

As I smile in sleepy slumber,
And reach to pull you close,
The realization hits me . . .
And it's then I miss you most!

One more toss, a sigh or two,
Forty winks I'll borrow;
Time will tell what will be,
And who will be mine tomorrow!

Colleen Doyle

FORGIVE ME

The things I said, I never meant.
The things I meant, I didn't say.
You must have thought
that all I want
is much more clout
than one should flaunt.

And so, as soon as we made love,
off they went, the words that couldn't solve
the feelings deep inside of me,
that made my words so mean to be.

Yet still must we maintain the way
our love can wash so sweet away,
the fears that seize a hold of me
and paralyze our reverie.

If you could know what I meant to say,
you wouldn't get so uptight that way,
for love is all I want to send
in your direction, come what may.

So please forgive me 'cause I have you
and darling, I do love you too.

Maritza Williams

From the first time that I saw you, deep within
my heart I knew,
There'd never be a deeper love in my life than
you.
Each time I look into your eyes the fire begins
to burn,
Desires to hold you, touch and kiss you make
my body yearn.
The sound of your voice, those gentle words,
truly drives me insane,
I realize life without you will never be the
same!

Sharon Daugherty

When there's peace and quiet all around,
That's when love is comin' down.
The candles are lit; the wine's been served;
Logs in the fireplace with a low burn.
Turn to me your sweet young face;
Let this be our time, our place.
I'll hold you close here in my arms
And my soul will drown among your charms.
You've taken my all and not by chance;
You've waltzed *the* waltz of love's sweet dance.
Be, oh, so gentle with this heart of mine.
Don't let it matter — our ages in time,
Or that my hair is caught with silver
Instead of gold and sunlight's glimmer.
Be there for me, sweet innocence and honesty,
Until the hour that I must leave.
Let's drink life's nectar; miss not one sip
And when I leave put your sweet kiss upon my lips.

Jean E. Christensen

MEMORY OF LOVE

The passing years have helped to quell
the piercing pain I felt upon your dying
But always there will be some memory that stabs
starting once again my inward crying.

Mary W. Thompson

SONNET YOU CAN'T REFUSE

I am a vile and temperamental man
Who gives himself to crazy fits and rages,
but we can't foil the Lord's eternal plan
That prepared us for each other through the ages.

The media distracts me with its shows
Of ladies lively, bosomy and fair;
Still, I realize that the gentle wind that blows
Leads the way to what I need as much as air.

We read each day of violence and strife,
Of marriages that lead to pain and death;
Still, I have no choice but to take you for my wife
Or there will be no more a purpose to my breath.
Forgetting all distractions such as this,
Think only love; let's seal it with a kiss.

Stephen Feinland

THE ARROW OF LOVE

The bow is held taut, then released,
impelling its arrow to flight
and then to home hard in the heart of the sparrow.

So did Thy Love pierce through me.
It was the skill of The Archer
that mastered the runaway bird.
The sharp edge of Truth bore deeply,
a stinging wound meant to heal;
a wound that made me weep,
a wound that made me whole.

Only after the unseen arrow
stopped me in my desperation to flee,
only then could I truly be free
to fly.

Joy Thompson

SONNET

I should not be disturbed by such a face
And yet whene'er I see you, I near faint.
It isn't so much the symmetry trace
That causes my defeat, but something quaint
And different — something solely unique. You!
It is you. The love, faith and trust you give
In your look — it's there — you let it shine through.
I revel in your smile — it lets me live
In grandeur of this life — and in love's place
I shall be able to return again
And again — to the joys recalled. The grace
Of your loveliness — your touch — will ne'er wane
And in recollection's corridors, time
Will not ravage, what I now find sublime.

Darwynne Pucek

ANNIVERSARY

Remembering the morn — the radiant sunshine
Remembering the eve — the stars all aligned
Remembering the night — the moonlight sublime
Remembering the dreams — forever entwined

Remembering God's altar — our vows yours and mine
Remembering our promise — our promise in rhyme
Remembering the night — the moonlight sublime
Remembering our dreams — forever entwined

Remembering the night — with your hand in mine
Remembering the love — abed we reclined
Remembering that moment — our love so sublime
Remembering our dreams — forever entwined.

Eldor Rathjen

LOVE'S MARRY-GO-ROUND

"What is love?" I ask
The Sage of the past ever ask.
Maybe love's a temporary stimulation
Of the infatuation gene?

Mark the time, "Who's next in circulation?"
To be caught up in love's rejuvenation.
Love's tricky, the Marry-Go-Round can demean,
Try as we can, we're all caught in between.

Even the Sage in the past couldn't have foreseen,
That in our time Marry-Go-Round would be routine.
As nostalgia sweeps our mind of times past
We hear the "pre-echo" Marry-Go-Round, this time last.

Juanita Allison

NEVER-ENDING LOVE

In the spring as the flowers blossom,
Your beauty is revealed to the world
as a Rose, with moist red petals;
gleaming in the light.

Something that will never leave in hostility,
But in peace and love.

Phillip A. Bush, Jr.

A LOVE NO MORE

I walked beside a
Wind-tossed sea,
Alone but for
Your memory.

I felt the spray
Caress my face,
As I thought of you,
In this beautiful place.

I wrote your name
In the ocean's sand,
Only to be erased
By the ocean's hand.

As the endless waves
Splash ashore,
I face the heartache
Of a love no more.

Dena G. Little

MY DREAMS ARE ALIVE

Loving you
yet needing you.
Wanting you,
wanting to be around you,
to be near you.
Filling my life with thoughts of you,
To sleep next to you.

There are not enough
words to express my heart.

To feel your warm
body against mine,
to warm me when I am cold.

To lay my head on your shoulder
and sleep without dreams.

For my dreams are alive in you.

Marlene Hendon

FORTY YEARS

It was forty years ago,
On a sunny spring day
On the first of May
Green grass rugs
Were spread for us.
Under the rows of balsamed crowns
We walked in . . .
There were no witnesses or rings,
No celebration or wine,
We just swore: "Till death us part,"
And were pronounced "husband and wife!"
We couldn't wait the war to end
We missed and loved too much each other.
The war lasted long
We suffered hunger, misery and anger
To know and trust each other forever.
And after forty years
Our love is even stronger,
Our love will last
"Till death us part!"

Jenny Ghihtei-Siroker

THE KISS, DEAR MAID

The kiss, dear maid! thy lip has left
Shall never part from mine,
Till happier hours restore the gift
Untainted back to thine.

Thy parting glance, which fondly beams,
An equal love may see:
The tear that from thine eyelid streams
Can weep no change in me.

I ask no pledge to make me blest
In gazing when alone;
Nor one memorial for a breast
Whose thoughts are all thine own.

Nor need I write — to tell the tale
My pen were doubly weak:
O, what can idle words avail,
Unless the heart could speak!

By day or night, in weal or woe,
That heart, no longer free,
Must bear the love it cannot show,
And silent, ache for thee.

Lord Byron

DONALD

He celebrates
Our life together
Like an altar,
to which he brings
garlands of joy
and unselfish deeds.

For this I give thanks
to God above
for His priceless gift
of my husband's love.

Alice F. Prince

THE YOUNG WITCH OF ENDOR

I'm in love with two sailors —
Robert my son,
And Rose Ann, the sweet girl
that he courted and won,

Long before they went sailing,
they studied the lore
Of that brave ancient ship,
The Witch of Endor,

And with their loving hands
they built her a daughter,
To take them skimming
over the water,

Now they ride on a moonbeam
and follow a star,
That guides them and tells them
just where they are,

And when they drop anchor
into the deep,
The young Witch of Endor
will rock them to sleep.

Molly Molyneaux

TO MY HUSBAND

When I was just a young girl
I fell in love with you
And ever since our wedding day
You've always seen me through.

It's wonderful to know I have
A sweetheart and a friend
To stand close beside me
Until we reach the end.

There were those thin years
We struggled along the way
I thank God I have you
And that he brought us to this day.

Births, deaths, laughter, tears
All of these we've shared
These things all made easier
Because I knew you cared.

This day, on your birthday
I didn't buy you 'things'
I ask you to accept my heart
As with love for you it sings.

Thelma E. Owens

A SMALL CHILD'S RAMBLING PRAYER

"Now I lay me down to sleep"
Grandma, will you help my pray?
"I pray the Lord my soul to keep"
Will it come back when I play?

"If I should die before I wake"
Grandma, what's it like to die?
"I pray the Lord my soul to take."
Will He take it very high?

"God bless grandma," (grandpa's dead,
And my "white grandma" is, too,
Like in the story we just read.)
I'm pretty sleepy now . . . I love you.

"God bless everybody now,
Please give food to everyone;"
Wish I could but don't know how,
It sure would be lots of fun.

Grandma, I really like you
And I hope you never die . . .
You're almost as good as new
And as good as apple pie!

Fern Johnson

KEEPING FIT

Love needs exercise,
for without it
love could never live.

Does love live with you?
Does it walk and run?
or does it get just a brisk stroll?

Love needs excercise,
for without it
life could never love.

Veanna Hanson

PATRICK

I sit in silence now
outside the wind whistles
through barren tree tops
Winter is coming
and I am alone

Since you left
even the heat from this
once roaring fire can't warm me
the way your arms around me can

I remember sitting
in front of this fire
sparkling champagne, laughing, smiling
staring into your eyes as you held me close
telling me you would be back soon

Now there is no laughter, no smile
flat champagne
just embers burning now
in my heart
the symbol of hope

Debbie Jennings

YOU STOLE MY LOVE

As I stay inside by the fire
Yet the flowers are my brothers as they
Are my sisters so the summertime is a wonder to
Behold is so wonderful thanks be to God.
So I've got a double date that is because you stole
My love God bless you your stolen love I've stolen from
You are great remotivation therapy still I will be contrite
I will have the will to beat discomfort yet I will have
To use objectivity I will not use temperamental lingo
But soon it will be summer God is wonderful as the sun
Is shining so is sharing it is also caring God bless you my
Love yet you my love yet you have stolen my love may God
Forgive you may the Lord be with you God bless
America. Still my love I forgot to tell you the
United States of America is one of the last places free
From oppression you should be patriotic and make
When the President asks us to for our country in time of
crises
Still I will be contrite yet your stolen love was like a
Waterfall so refreshing running tumbling as well
As caressing. Because our friendship is like a puppy dog
You're my stolen love you are my rhyme and reason.

Michael Deemer

THIS LOVE

Every type of love I have had disappeared
Just when I think this love is going great
(A type of love that will stay) it dies.
When you love someone and suddenly
It's gone, it hurts. Is love always going
To be this way?

Now I have found a love that's different,
Different from all the others.
This love isn't complicated
This love isn't difficult, it isn't confusing,
This is a love that I can depend on to be there
When I need it, it's there even if I don't.
This is a love that will stay strong
In my heart forever.
This love is named Joe!

Laura Halinski

MY SON

(or, Joy With John)

Stop, my son, and listen to the rustle of the trees
Taste the sweet honey, pollination of the bees
Joyful is this time, my son, play and sing your song
Life holds such hidden treasures, for you my heart doth long

Holding hands as we run, fishing by a stream
Telling you I love you so, this I dream
Lifting you above my head, you're my little boy
To tuck you in your bed at night fills my heart with joy

Stop, my son, and listen to the rain dance on the ground
See the endless rainbow shedding colors all around
Peace and love fulfills your heart, you're God's mystery
Always shall I love you throughout eternity

Nothing can replace your love, you're my guiding star
This heart for you will never change, whether near or far
Let peace and love fulfill your heart play and sing your song
Life holds such hidden treasures, for you my heart doth long

Michael Steven Levitan

To Mrs. Evelyn Gillmore
God loves you and so do I

God loves you and so do I.
His guiding and healing hands are
with you both day and night,
He will give you strength as you
journey through life.
Yes, God loves you and so do I.

God loves you and so do I,
God admires and respects you just like I do.
God is your friend like I am,
God is your salvation as He is mine,
Yes, God is all those things.

Trust is God,
Have faith in God,
Turn to God in time of trouble,
Turn to God in time of sorrow,
Turn to God in time of happiness.
Yes, turn to God for He loves you and so do I.

Lois Nicholson

MY LOVE AT A DISTANCE

Though she is really very close, so very close, I see her
only in a fog through vision blurred by haziness of dreams

Instinct points a telltale finger in the night to say she is
the one who can stare into my mind and hold my heart it seems

She lives for I have seen her bosom rise so easily with a breath
as hands and fingers pass the time in idleness alone

She moves occasional of motion over there, but never close to
hear the rustle of her dress or smell the hint of her cologne

By now I shut mine eyes and touch the temples of a memory for
still I seek but bits and pieces as I the image of a lady make

And to the side I cast reality to clutch in favor this, a lady's
fantasy, that rides the westwind soft to touch me lightly in
its wake

Boyd Rahier

CHANGE OF SEASONS

There are things that you can't notice with each new coming day,
The little changes that occur in a silent aging way.
But I, who've known and loved you throughout these past few years,
Have shared your lively laughter, your sorrows and your tears.
I've watched a transformation that stirs my soul within;
I saw a warmer handsome smile replace your boyish grin.
Though you haven't lost the merriment that sparkles in your eyes,
I now can see emotions you once tried to disguise.
You've tucked away the memories of boyhood hopes and schemes,
And turned your thoughts toward love instead, with different future dreams.
And though you've never seen it, as part of you, I can;
You've cast aside your childhood shell and grown into a man.

Debra L. Vinnedge

FAREWELL MY SON

Upon waters, far from the eye, distant from all land . . . goes forth my young sailor eager to become a man.

Live each day as the last, look always forward, forget the past . . . grasp each thought, word and deed . . . set your mind to succeed.

Success has already been there, chores complete and done . . . mind, body and soul join to become one.

Distance makes your heart yearn for the days past . . . nothing remains the same, son, life moves too fast.

You know within your heart the love you leave behind, but if you'll touch in thought, comfort you will find.

A Mother's love will follow where'er, dear lad, you go . . . reach beneath the surface, your heart will tell you so.

Carolyn Long

TWO IN ONE

When it comes to me and you, the answer is two in one. We are two, but our hearts join together as one. You shine inside my mind all the moments of my life. When you're not around, it cuts like a knife. I always know that I have you to love and to love me, you to care for and to care for me. Even though when I sleep, you're not there, I still see you deep within my mind.
We are two in one. A package put together by fate. We are the pair, there is no time to wait. You got me, I got you. There's no need to look around anymore. Into our wildest dreams and thoughts, we will soar. We Will soar into the core of life, not alone, but together as one. Let's stay as one, for just our sake. Take and give in return will keep our relationship strong. It's not all wrong, just a lot more than all right.

Susan Hatker

FEARING LOVE

Only time will tell with our love. But right now there is no happiness, togetherness, or that simple spark that was between us long ago. Nothing goes right. There is not enough love to keep us going. We hold on fearing to let go. We know it's over, but yet we want it to go on forever. Why do we cheat and lie, when we know it hurts each other? People think we have a special love, and in a way we do. First loves are always special. But remember, you're my first love but hardly my last. For there are an interminable amount of fish in my sea. It always comes back to the same problem. My mind says let go you'll only get hurt once again, but my heart can't and won't let you go. But it's best to leave with only our memories. Go out and live your life and remember me and never fear love, for love is just love.

Heather A. Loflin

A TOKEN OF ASSURANCE

The bareness of the maple trees
Along the paths we strolled
Add credence to the emptiness
Within my heart I hold

From when you left my earthly plane
To join the world unknown
The remnants of my human soul
Transcend as did your own

On cold and cloudy winter nights
The pain is so severe
Oppressive weights within my chest
Are more than I can bear

So, walk with me and hold my hand
And love me always, dear
Please come to me within the night
Console me with a tear

Edna Ball

GOD'S BEAUTIFUL WORLD

Dear Father whose love cannot be told
What a beautiful world you have made
Cannot be bought with silver or gold
The beautiful colors of every shade

The sunrise you see in the morning
The artist cannot put it down
The sun that sets in the evening
The snow that's softer than down

The soft sweet breeze of springtime
The lillies so beautiful and fair
The sweet notes of song they are sublime
Of the birds that fly in the air

What a beautiful world you have made
Beautiful things familiar and dear
Glorious colors of every shade
I'm glad that I live here

Mary Keys

MY OWN GRANDCHILD

I used to walk away —
from pictures held
by hands so drawn
from age and toil —
They spoke of love
so long — so loud —
How smart — how sweet —
how great they were
Their grandchildren of course —
were just one of a kind
Today I wonder —
days on end —
why all my friends
now run and hide —
I only want —
to have them see
the pictures of my
newborn love —
My one and only
my own grandchild.

Maxwell C. Kaufman

HIDDEN DESIRE

Lone phone! I would I could have two of you!
One for my darling and one for me.
One to grace my bedside.
One laid deep in his den.

Then snare me a caller, oh phone,
For dimension in sound and in life.
Thy ring quickens me.
With it comes breath and inflection.

Oh harbinger of fortune!
Sometimes thou bearest bad news.
Oh hours of hilarity!
Oh miscellaneous pettifog!

Backfence gossip, move indoors!
To each his own network of wheels and deals!
Whatever be fate, I receive the receiver
With clarity and settlement.

Oh phone tone!
Br r r r --- ing   Br r r --- ing

Eleanore Lindsey

KEEPING CHRIST IN CHRISTMAS

Please don't put an "X" where Christ should be,
On a greeting, or gift, beneath the tree.
For "Christ" is what Christmas is all about,
And whose sacred name should not be left out.

For "X" is but a single letter . . .
Surely The Lord is deserving of better.
But anxious are we, this time of year,
And He understands — though sadly, I fear.

So, as we take pen in hand to write,
Let us keep in mind, that first Christmas night.
When a star in the sky, shone bright as day,
Above the stable, where an infant lay.

Sweet angels sent forth from God, to sing,
"A Child is Born Who is Christ, the King.
Follow the Light — And rejoice with Glee,
For the Son of God, has come unto thee."

He loves us now, as he loved us then.
So little to ask — the stroke of a pen.

Marilyn Jimerson Brewer

SHOWERS

You asked me to show you a part of myself
that I wasn't ready to show
Yet there's so much inside this person I am
that you probably ought to know
But I run
I always do
I'll run
away from you
I run
'cause I'm afraid
Please stop me
before I run myself right to my grave
Dave
I love you

Lisa Fitton

THE PICTURE

From across the room, my eyes seek yours
I whisper caressing phrases . . . old . . .
        but hardly worn
Your eyes penetrate, only inches from my heart
Your utterance, barely audible, awakens in me
a will to be alive . . . to give of myself, although fragmented

Your eyes, hauntingly gaze. The tumblers click
somewhat out of place
I read your 'voices,' I hear your sighs
Did I tell you we've never met?
How is it we've never met?
It's of little importance, I know you well
And I too love you

Last night . . .

    While I sat before the fire
    You . . . upon the mantle
Did I tell you the tranquility you brought me
with just a moment of your time?
It's of little importance. I'll tell you tonight
    And . . . I do love you.

Nance A. Glenn

APRIL FOOL

How appropriate that he would leave her on April 1st,
For she indeed felt like a fool.
She had given so much
To get so little.
Her mother had taught her to give from the heart,
For the sake of the giving,
But her mother had also taught her
That what you give comes 'round again.
She had given and given and given
Only to be paid back with the cold realization
That it was not to be.
Still, as much as it hurt her,
She was glad to be, finally, free.

Cynthia Ann Tidd

GOD IS LOVE!

God is love!
I see His love in the radiance of Spring —
Life vibrant, soaring, butterflies on wing,
Rainbow brilliant, sunlight shimm'ring
Dewdrops dancing, birds in chorus, angel music echoing.

God is love!
I see His love in the tempest and rain,
In Life's frustrations, heartache and pain,
His disciplining grace making whole again,
Resolving the discords of Life's strident strain.

God is love!
I see His love in my brothers of the Way
Sharing and caring, uplifting each day,
For everything, in everything, kneeling to pray,
Showing God's love in all they do and say.

God is love!
I see His love everywhere, every place,
In everything, in every face
Whose life is open to His grace,
And in Life's storms steadfastly sing His praise!

Alexander Hollands Edwards

STRENGTH

Your hand, that map of your soul,
Shows me your strength,
A strength of marbled stone,
Which endures eternal.
Yet, to the human eye,
Appears like pure and fragile bone.

And your quality of love,
Which soars with joy one moment,
Then sinks in disillusion,
Still demonstrates a tensile strength,
Which stretches to the limit,
Yet never loses vision.

How can I help but love you,
Or deny your eloquent strength,
Which I yearn to understand?
Teach me, gentle man, your ways of flying.
There's glory in the flight,
No matter where we land.

Tessie Jayme

YOU'RE LIKE AN ISLAND

You're like an island in the ocean,
far away and all alone,
Nobody knows you and nobody cares to,
I guess you'll have to stand alone.

Turn around and look at me,
I'm the same as I used to be,
I'm not a stranger can't you see.
I long to tell you one more time,
this ain't a foolish heart of mine,
and you mean the world to me.

Don't sail away on the waters
when life is turning you down;
Don't leave the things you oughtn't.
stay and turn them around.
And don't you sail away
when love can be found;
don't you sail away,
stay and love will be found.

Rosemary Roberts

THE SECRET

We are put in a world
of people who
cannot understand
a love like ours.
They are only too ready
to ridicule and condemn us
for what we do.
There will be times
when we are together
and people are near.
There will be times
when we dare not touch
or speak of what we share.
When these times come,
will those around us
feel what passes between us?
And when you look at me,
and, I at you
will they see the love in our eyes?

Dawn Carmichael Braack

MY LOVE IS FOR ALL SEASONS

I love you in the spring
When the robins are in flight
Each hour spent by your side
Is a fresh delight

I love you in the summer
When the fireflies glow
When nature reaches maturity
And my love continues to grow

I love you in the fall
When harvest time is near
With the crackling of the fire
Your presence becomes more dear

I love you in the winter
When the humdrums are like the tide
We can winter out the dreariness
My love for you will abide

Leon H. Nunn

A MAY WEDDING

The sky is blue,
On a day in May,
It's all for two,
For me and you.

There is all love,
On this day in May,
That is like the dove,
That flies above.

There is all peace,
On our day in May,
Like the lamb's fleece,
It's our life-long lease.

There is all time,
On that day in May,
Your body next to mine,
And our love so fine.

Nancy A. Jack

LOVE LETTER

This Valentine, is but a token
To find a way to say,
I Love You, and must tell you
I love you more each day.

I know I'm just a little boy
But in a year or two,
I want to call you Sweetheart
Because my love is true.

I'm saving all my money
For which to buy a ring,
When I place it on your finger
We will hear the Church Bell's ring.

Our love will be forever
When I take your hand, in mine,
As we go through life together
You will be my Valentine.

Mary Emmaline Meeker

REMEMBERING

When things go wrong,
I remember.
When there's a song,
I remember.
When nights are long,
I remember.

When skies are gray,
I remember.
Though you're away,
I remember.
All through the day,
I remember.

When hours are dark,
I remember.
When love is stark,
I remember.
When there's no spark,
I rememember.

When days are cold,
I remember.
With you to hold,
I remember.
As I grow old,
I remember.

Priscilla Culverwell

IF EVER

If ever I had a dream
While lying asleep at night,
I wouldn't memorize the thoughts
But forget them when I'd arise.

If ever I caught a butterfly
Within the grasp of my very hands,
I'd only admire it for the moment
And allow it to be free again.

If ever my feelings of love for you
Cause me to want you near,
That I might have you for my own,
A treasure for an eternity,

Then I'd pursue you days on end
'til by my hand, your heart, I'd win.
Yet I see I must regret
That these same thoughts you do not have.

'Tis only my dream to share with you
My love as I have longed to do.
And I must allow to be free again
The feelings for you I've grasped within.

For an eternity, I cannot treasure
A love I have not, or wonder, "If ever."

Ronald A. Jones

SAY YES TO LOVE

Mood
  Utter gloom
  for as long
  as it takes
  to get a yes to love

Bartell Waters

LOVE BLOSSOMS

As love begins to blossom with each passing day,
It grows in sensitive circles, reaching out in every way.

The beauty of its existence, senses love in every touch.
The heart has sensed the feelings, the meaning means so much.

Love is filled with joy of happiness and truth,
Sharing together a life so wonderful beyond youth.

The precious moments in life, that love can share,
Will bring those special memories from year to year.

Love in the sense of its word, could mean anything,
But the love two people can share can unite the two strings.

The excitement of two together, sharing their hearts,
Is the biggest and warmest feeling that no one can part.

The strength of love shall grow so wide and so strong,
That nothing could ever make that love go wrong.

For these two people in love this beautiful day,
Shall be united together in a very special way.

They've come to begin their lives together as one,
To share their vows with trust and unite their love as one.

Sherri Kearsey

THE POWER OF LOVE CREATED BY CHILDREN

Inspired by my late husband, Dr. Andrew F. Hegyeli

The power of love, the power of the soul of man,
Uniting the families of man
In life, in death.

The soft little hands of a boy
Hugging us,
Trusting us.

The wet kisses of a little girl
With her arms around our necks,
Trusting us.

Communicating love,
Opening the recesses of our soul to a new spring,
To a new creation of love.

Children, the love bridge to the future,
Bringing into existence strange powers of life and love,
Powers we did not know before.

Bringing into play
The greatest power on earth,
The power of love to shake the world,
To face the challenges of life.
Power to spur us on to greater deeds.

Ruth Johnsson Hegyeli

GRAVE THROUGH THE WINDOW

(After Li Ching-Chao, AD 1081? - 1149)

HONORABLE MENTION

The swallows soar over the fresh-tossed earth.
I sort out my beloved's clothes, books, his brushes.
Not wanting to keep them — not wanting not to —
I don't know I've been crying till the light blurs and dims.

Stephen M. Hurley

A CAT WITH LOVE IN HIS HEART

My cat has no enemy when it comes to loving people
And has a mind as sharp as a steeple.
He will sleep and curl up in your lap —
Thinking this is such a nice place to take a long nap.

He likes to be petted and has such soft fur,
With the touch of your hand he starts to purr,
He has a sweet disposition and tries to do right,
Always staying close to home, day and night.

His love comes deep from his heart;
It would be hard to leave him or go apart.
He has feelings and shares them with me,
And if he felt pain it would sting like a bee.

His face radiates a soft expression,
Would do no harm so wants protection.
He is as quiet as a mouse but cats need human love,
They crave your attention and keep as clean as a white dove.

They have no souls so when they die they fade away,
But the memories of them will live from day to day.
An animal's love for his master is cherished forever
As the joy and happiness of owning one can be truly endeavor.

Priscilla Cohen

BOUQUET OF LOVE (FROM YOUR HEART)

Bouquets of roses you're always sending me,
Bouquets of carnations you're always giving me;
When all I want is a bouguet of love from your heart.
Your kindness, sweet attention, and gentleness,
Mean more to me than bouquets of roses;
Kind words, sweet thoughts, from you I'd rather have —
Than a bouquet of yellow carnations.
Your dreams, your schemes — are all in my dreams,
As I wonder if you'll ever give me —
A bouquet of love to play its part —
Just from your loving heart!

Mathew Matejcich

TRIUMPHANT LOVE

Love is more precious than silver or gold,
on this their special day.
To embark on the matrimonial sea,
"Love is enough," they say!

At eventide the procession began,
as flower girls led the way.
A myriad of roses petals were strewn down the aisle,
as the Wedding March began to play.

Smiling, the bride walked by her father's side,
as the groom at the altar did wait.
Nervously he glanced at his beautiful bride
on the event of their wedding date.

The flames from the candles cast a soft-glowing light
magnifying the beauty of her veil- covered face.
Their hearts beat in unison as they stood side by side
as the wedding rings were put into place.

The marriage vows were spoken, the nuptial knot tied
as God changed two hearts into one.
The minister pronounced them man and wife;
the first day of their life together had begun.

John T. Hudelson

LOVE ANIMALS

We are all put on this earth together,
They are attentive to humans,
They obey a master or mistress
Love them for their ways.

All animals show love differently,
Respect their ways, they our ways.
Some follow humans until their death
Never leaving our company.

Following bravely at our heels,
Sitting up to beg for some food.
Do not judge them harshly,
They may rescue you some day.

Through love, feelings, looks and hear
From their mouth comes some tones.
Understand their loving obedience.
Honor the Lord who made us all . . .

Edith L. Colby

MY DADDY

It seems just yesterday
That I hurriedly walked away
Off to explore the world and play —
To do things my own way.

Bubbling dreams
Boiling schemes
Burning in my mind (sigh),
Did I kiss you good-bye?

You're still there
But I am . . . where?
Stumbling into the world's biting snares
Feeling that nobody really cares.

More love I would have shown
If only I'd have known
That I'll never outgrow
My Daddy.

Kat Kerste

THE SEARCH

In search of love I passed your side,
And felt a warming glow.
I stopped, stepped back a pace,
For fear you might say no.

I searched so deep into your eyes,
For trust and true concern.
I bled inside from loving you,
And hoped for its return.

It hurts to love, it's blissful too,
If you I may impress.
I'd search the world, for just the way,
For my love to express.

Now that the search is over,
And you are steady at my side.
Life is neat and quite complete,
And fills me deep with pride.

Bill Haight

HEARTS

Hearts are a small portion
of feelings wrapped in
a small package.
They are often happy and
often sad, but there
is always one within
you.
People tend to break your
heart, and in the process
they really don't realize
it.
People have a certain
quality and that quality
is their
HEARTS!

April Evonne Powell

A SONG OF CHRISTA

Enriched
by the splendor of your grace
which has brought to this
oftentimes
dark corner of space
a light helping
guiding our way
only to be inconsolable today
yet
I will struggle on
to see you once again
your spirited presence
secreted amidst the vision
when we again
must claim the dawn.

Theo. Oliver

REALITY

The form by which
we knew you, has been lowered
deep down in the earth.

You have left us all.
We watch, and see the process
of your burial.

The mind denies it.
Eyes have seen the certainty
of your leaving us.

Where reality,
In life or in memory
is the person found?

Alice E. Gross

YOU

You are just a white cloud
Drifting through my dream
You are just a careless leaf
Traveling down my stream

But when I reach out to hold you
You really are not there
You are just my dreams and me
Floating through the air

Erinn Dulin

OVERDUE

The tings I've said and done
over the years,
Must surely have caused you
to shed many tears.
The time I've given myself
that I could have given you;
I know that's a debt that's
long overdue.
The times that I've failed
to carry through
With the things I know that
you wanted me to.
Of these, my faults and failures,
I'm glad you understand;
For when all others walk away,
Lord you still hold my hand.

Pineapple Chavis

A SON TO LOVE

A son to love
Is quite a thing to do.
From the day you were born
For your whole life through
Even when the things you shouldn't do
Through the times you could say I love you
You grew and grew
As tall as the highest tree
Though there were joys, some sorrows
There was always my love
You always knew
My love was always waiting on the morrow.
Now you are a man
A good man, I say!
Now giving your love to a fine woman
I hope it shall always be this way.

Fanchon Carney

THOUGHTS OF YOU

Thinking of you
Picturing your face
Always at a certain time
In a familiar place.
The time is always after dark
When the moon is bright and clear
The place is always in your arms
Where I know I have nothing to fear.
I remember your voice
Saying how much you care
You mean so much to me
I hope you'll always be there;
But no matter what happens
Whatever I decide to do
I'll never forget
My thoughts of you.

Maureen Houlihan-Sutter

LOVE'S TRIBUTE

A hug, a kiss, a fond caress
The love he gives is innocent and blest.
A smile, a sigh, a look of devotion
That stirs the heart with deepest emotion.
He is my son, my love, my life
My heart's desire, my joy yet my strife.

Nettie McGill McCarrell

STAR CHILD

Black satin sheets pressed cool against my skin;
Moonlight rays stream through the window and dance upon your skin —
Silhouette your raven hair like ghostly hands to steal you
away before the night we've shared.
Stride through the dark;
Move next to me.
Lips press to mine.
Your tongue ingnites my soul.
Nails of jade and jeweled in gold;
I feel your warmth explode.
Ride through the night, caress and sweat;
We speak in quiet moans.
Star Child — eternal love;
Forever in my soul.

Jeff Cox

WORLD'S GREATEST LOVE

What is love? has been the question for ages,
Many books and poems have filled pages and pages.
It is when your little boy is sad and on your shirt he tugs
Or is it when your little girl is happy and gives you a hug?
Perhaps love is when a mother bakes a fancy cake
Or how about when the yard is full of leaves and the dad is the one who rakes?
It could be the husband who lends a helping hand
Or even the wife who really appreciates her man.
Maybe love is the grandma who calls on the phone
Or it could be grandpa comforting a child in a soothing tone.
Love is really all these things and much more
Because one likes to do things for someone they adore.
And yet the greatest love of all was when
Jesus came down to earth and, for us, His life He spent.

José Tirado

MOONBEAM MADNESS

Moonbeams, you cast a spell of madness over me
As I stood holding hands with a young lady, as we looked to the sea.
Your madness took hold on me and I had sparkles in my eyes.
So, young men, don't stand holding in the moonlight with a lady if
you are wise.
The moonbeams seemed to be skipping and hopping with much glee,
And the longer we stood the closer she was to me.
I can't forget the autumn night when the music was low and sweet,
And to see her in the moonlight, my heart would skip a beat.
And if ever it does again, I hope it will never tell.
Some years later I thought I had found a new love,
But, as the moon shone so brightly, I cooed like a dove.
But she, too, took another road so never again have we met,
But for her sake, I hope she has never had any regrets.

C. D. McKay

IN TIME:

When you hold me close you wash my mind, upon departure with very
few words to say, you said in time.

LAW OF LOVE:

I really loved Dad, when I was small not really knowing him but
just his law, I'm older now his law was love.

IN EXCELLENCY:

Your eyes are all I see a reflection in my mirror God, how
sweet the moments standing next to you.

Rita J. Greene

STINGER BEE

Love is like a bumble bee
stings and flies away.
Then comes buzzing back again
hopefully to stay.

It stung one warm September day
on the way to school.
That was forty years ago,
some folks thought me a fool.

We've walked together hand in hand
through sickness, health and joy,
Raised two lovely little girls
and one terrific boy.

Now we're in our autumn years
life has been good — but then
What happened to the stinger bee?
Our growing family numbers ten.

Margaret E. Smith

SMITH, MARGARET E. Born: Sacred Heart, Minnesota, 6-24-33; Married: 11-21-53 to Roger A. Smith; Education: Saint Cloud Teachers College, Elementary Credential; Utah State University, Social Work; Occupation: Artist, Teacher, Housewife; Memberships: President, Moffat County Council on the Arts and Humanities; Director, Art in Public Places; Poetry: 'Whispers,' *American Poetry Anthology,* 1986; 'Lady of Faith,' *Words of Praise,* 1986; Comments: *I write what I feel. Poetry just comes, usually at night and I awake with the need to write very quickly. My soul speaks in the quiet hours, when my body is resting.*

YOUR LOVE

Love's effects clog the mind.
Stilling the words to be said.
Calming, a wind once wild.
Renewing, a life long dead.

Mardog

LITH. & PUB. BY N. CURRIER, *Entered according to Act of Congress in the year 1847 by N. Currier, in the Clerk's office of the District Court of the Southern District of New York.* 152 NASSAU ST. COR. OF SPRUCE N.Y.

THE MARRIAGE.

LET ME BE YOUR LOVE

Take a sip of my love and after, take a long drink
There is enough to quench your thirst and enough
to make you think —
of long, low-key evenings with romantic overtones
and low tides and sea gulls and no telephones.
Come away with me and forever be at peace
With serenity, sand and salty air,
Let your soul know how much you can be loved
And while the ocean licks your senses
Let me be your love.

Jean Graham Cano

I'LL CLAIM HAPPINESS

I'll claim Happiness, for that is what
I feel and think when I'm with you;
And when you leave me, I'm still
In love and blessed that I met you.

Yet sometimes because of people's ways,
I get depressed and feel despair,
'cause they have judged this love we share
so harshly, and that gets me down.

Yet we believe in God you see,
and Jesus came and rescued us,
and I love you and you love me,
so why should we so question this?

I believe that God is One
who always answers prayers, every one;
And when I prayed to Him for Love,
I found you, and "Thanks be to Thee," I said.

I only need some help from you
to remind me every once or twice,
that love is not a man-made thing,
but a gift so special, the Lord only, brings.

Maritza Williams

EPITOME OF LOVE

A red-gold Persian was Buttercup
Who watched for me each night,
For my daily coming home from work;
By the mailbox he would wait.

The car lights caused his yellow eyes
To light up with electric fire;
His purr was so loud, the vet had said,
He could scarcely hear his heart.

Later on, he developed an ailment
That caused him great distress.
His loud and pitiful meow
Told of suffering deep within.

I gave him his medicine; he just got thinner,
So I prayed for his peaceful release,
But those big yellow eyes would hold me close
As he lay lovingly in my lap.

Then came the day when eternal peace
Descended on him at last;
But I'll never forget, as long as I live,
Those big eyes filled with love.

Georgia Fox Smith

TO THE HIGHLAND GIRL OF INVERSNAID

Sweet Highland Girl, a very shower
Of beauty is thy earthly dower!
Twice seven consenting years have shed
Their utmost bounty on thy head;
And these gray rocks, this household lawn,
These trees, — a veil just half withdrawn, —
This fall of water that doth make
A murmur near the silent lake,
This little bay, a quiet road
That holds in shelter thy abode;
In truth together ye do seem
Like something fashioned in a dream;
Such forms as from their covert peep
When earthly cares are laid asleep!
But O fair Creature! in the light
Of common day so heavenly bright,
I bless thee, Vision as thou art,
I bless thee with a human heart:
God shield thee to thy latest years!
I neither know thee nor thy peers;
And yet my eyes are filled with tears.

William Wordsworth

LOVE REIGNS SUPREME

Set adrift on Life's tumultuous oceans,
All alone with no shore in sight,
Frightened by the threatening waves
That could capsize my Life's boat instantly,
With no hope at all, only fear and despair.
But look! Toward the horizon! There!
It looks like mist, but coming closer,
It changes into the form of a Man!
With an outcry of hope, I shout,
O GOD! IS THAT YOU?
YES MY CHILD, IT IS I, DO NOT BE AFRAID!
And God steps into the boat with me,
Just as He did with His disciples
When He walked the earth as man.
By the life and love
Of the eternal ages,
Forevermore!

Eliza Tyler Taylor

LOVE COULD BE FUN

When you're with someone you care for
But if not with the one who is right for you.
It could hurt you badly if he is wrong.
But sometimes love is fun.
Especially when it's spring and flowers bloom.
And you're next to that special person.
You kiss him and adore every moment
In his arms or her arms.
Then he or she whispers sweet nothings
in your ear.
And your heart is pounding with
love and enjoyment.
And you know you're in love with
him. And you must stay with
him or her forever.
It is only once in a lifetime to
love the right person.
And then love could be fun
with happiness and joy.
Love could be fun, when it is real
love.

Jean M. Rusin

LOVE'S NEVER ENDING FLAME

Youth, sweet and gentle —
Describes the way we were.
We looked across the room,
Locked eyes, a flame began to stir.

You were in a uniform.
Our country was at war.
We fell in love completely,
Then you were sent afar.

Miles apart, our love grew strong.
Then finally you came home.
Hand in hand we walk . . .
Together — we belong.

The flame grew even stronger
As the years went by.
Over four decades ago, My Love,
The flame still burning high.

So, My Love, we will continue,
But slower now with age,
To hold onto the magic
Of love's never ending flame.

Frances P. Brown

A FRIEND

Like a father the child
He takes your hand,
And guides you through gorges —
For he is a friend.

Like a mother he looks in
Your eyes, and
Forgets a mistake —
For he is a friend.

Like brother and sister,
On sea and on land,
Everywhere he remembers —
For he is a friend.

In right, wrong or danger
He'll damage prevent,
And all for you venture —
For he is a friend.

Therefore like a diamond
Guard him till the end;
Be content and happy —
If you have a friend.

Hartwig Heymann

Dear Love,
You used to call me every night
and the feeling was so right.
I never thought of letting go
and no matter how I try
I can only wonder why
it all worked out this way
with this feeling left inside
of only empty pride
as I lower my head to cry.
My Love,
Goodbye.

Jerry Wilson

AND I WAS HAPPY

When the morning sunshine wakened me
And bathed my tear-stained face
With warmth and love and joyfulness
I felt again your embrace,
And I was happy

And when at lunch I sat alone
And drank from my coffee cup
I heard again, "Your coffee's cold,
I'll bring you another cup."
And I was happy.

And when the evening rose-hued sun
Was setting in the west
I heard her say, "Please don't ask why,
For God knows what is best,"
And I was happy.

And when the dewdrops kissed the rose
One softly said to me,
"Grieve not, for very soon you'll be
With Ralph eternally!"
And I was happy.

Thelma Van Scoik

CREATION

I saw the Canyon — Grand at eve,
And stared in wordless wonder there,
Nor could the human mind conceive
Such magnitude! So, this was where
Creation, I did first believe.

At dusk, again, I gazed in awe
At nature's perfect sunset scene,
Creation's never-erring law
Has blessed with wonder so serene
Hawaii's eve — without a flaw.

A setting sun revealed the might
Of glorious Peaks, now capped with snow,
Grand colors, with the change of light —
An iridescent overflow —
Oh, wondrous Rocky Moutain sight!

And yet, I know that there can be
Things greater than the eye can 'hold,
His reason for eternity —
As memories and years unfold —
Was your eternal love for me.

Alfred W. Hicks

LONG AGO

Long ago
on the meadow of green
We danced
and sang love's song.
With lark and dove
the harmonies blending,
The melody sweet —
the notes ever ringing
Time's fair day
so swiftly passing —
Since that long ago
when we danced
on the meadow.

Naomi R. Laney

MY JEAN

Into my life
you did arrive
and suddenly
I came alive.
You spoke to me
without a word
loveliness
was all I heard.
Winsome ways
that I have found
so comfortable
to be around.
Just the girl
for whom I care
one whose thoughts
I love to share.
Because you're mine
I'll always say
God answers prayer
in a wonderful way.

Curtis Lennander

YOU'RE ALWAYS THERE

You're always there when I'm in doubt
And know just what to say.
You're always there when things go wrong
To brighten every day.
You're always there when nights are cold
To warm my lonely heart.
You're always there when I need you.
We never drift apart.
You're always there when I've been hurt
And help to dry my tears.
You're always there when I'm afraid
And calm unspoken fears.
You're always there when I am lost
And help me find my way.
You're always there when I'm alone
And chase my blues away.
You're always there when hope is gone
And bring my fears to rest
You're always there when I need love
And make me feel my best.

Michelle Kooch

I SEE A TENDER ROSY CHEEK

I see a tender, rosy cheek
on which I place my hand.
And in those darkened eyes of pain
I look to understand.

A captured mind envisioning
unspoken worlds of strife.
And in those darkened eyes of pain
I saw my very life.

I felt the softness of her lips
and wanted not to leave.
And in those darkened eyes of pain
was desperate to believe.

I found the beauty of her soul,
a world I longed to know.
And in those darkened eyes of pain
I found a place to go.

b c drury

MY DARLING

OH! how I would miss you if you were
To go away permanently. But that will
Not happen because you know that there
Will always be someone who wants you
Very sincerely and who will always
Help you out when you are in trouble.
The sweetness of your smile, and the
Wonderful touch of your hand make
Everything just right. Then your refusal
To see a lawyer when things do not work
Out as you think they should, and then you
Work the problem out in your own special
Way. Yes, you are something special, very
Special not only to me but to my relatives
as well.

Michael R. Swartwood

TWO LOVERS

Two lovers in a trance,
They cross the floor to dance.
The yearning for romance,
Their bodies take the chance.

Entwined in one another,
Like there was no other.

No questions while together,
There is no telling whether.

And when the soul is aching,
The heart is slowly breaking,
That in this world we live in,
It's so hard not to give in.

Toni Beckwith

THOUGHTS

My thoughts are like the butterfly
Bright in the golden sun,
That restless fluttered on each flower
To find the fairest one.

Until it found so sweet a flower
That it would not depart,
But dropped its wings and rested there,
For it had found your heart.

Ruth E. Dwyer

TAGALONG

You're just a little tagalong,
You do things just the way I do;
Comb your hair, tie your shoe,
Wear your clothes, blow your nose,
Fix your tie, wink your eye,
What a little shadow you turned out to be,
Little tagalong, who wants to be like me.

You're just a little tagalong,
You think I know all there is to know;
Even though, that's not so;
But it's true, I love you,
And I'm glad, I'm your Dad,
In fact I don't know just what I would do,
Without a little tagalong like you.

Marjorie Kingston Skusa

THE STARS AND OUR LOVE

On a warm summer night
I sit beneath the stars
thinking of you.
I look up
and what do I see?
I see you and I
holding each other as if we
never wanted to let go.
I tried to tell you how much I love you.
But I couldn't, because my love for you
is beyond words.
Then I closed my eyes tightly and opened
them again.
The vision disappeared, but I still
felt two very special things left that
I knew would last forever,
they were,
the stars and our love.

Tracey Novak

WITHOUT YOU

My life is
wake miserable.
sorrow, pain,
insane.
I want to
reach out, touch,
feel brand-new,
back some day.
No light,
unpenetrating dark.
pain, sorrow,
love, missing you.
Lacks love
need,
want,
what to do,
alone,
without you.

Joy Reneé DeLoe

SWEETIE

My thoughts keep running back
To you; you make me happy.
My wondering mind is in your
Head, it drives me mad.

What are you thinking
I hope it's us
I need an X-ray of your head.
I need to look into your eyes
My thoughts of you are driving
Me mad.

Oblivion is my escape
School days are quite boring —
You're too far away.
I never know who's taking
Your time.
I am quite mad.

Gracen Gregory

HAVEN FOUND

You've touched me in a thousand ways,
And some — you'll never know.

The hardest part is hiding it . . .
Not daring let it show.

My soul's been yours eternities,
Where now I know your heart.

Your eyes might say forever,
But in truth you stand apart.

In nature to me second, love,
For I'm denied the first.

That's bound in things I once believed,
Like "better and for worse."

No matter — for you've given me
What no one's done before.

Even heaven finds its way
Through half an open door.

Dakota

THE PROMISE

So, this is Valentine's Day.
I'm feeling kind of blue.
Why am I sad?
When I opened my eyes this morning
I didn't see you.

I know there's a difference in our ages
But there's one thing I know for sure.
Of young boys you soon shall tire.
I'd like you to know
my love for you is pure.

I can satisfy your burning desire.
I can fill you with a glow.

So when the one thing in the world
you need most is a good man.
Just knock on my door
and I'll do the best I can.

I promise to do
my very best
for you.

Michael J. O'Rourke

THAT BEAUTIFUL MUSIC

It sings us a song
Of beautiful memories
Or even sad memories
That music will be with us
When needed the most
Unlike friends of the present
New and old music
Cheers or saddens us
At least we'll know
That it will be there for you or me
Friends aren't always like that
You should know
I love that beautiful music

Debbie Budnick

LOVE CRIES

Like the stars that glide
love cries.

Love cries
like the sun that shouts.

Like a fast, fast heartbeat, beating like a drum
love cries.

Love cries
with feelings of pains and feelings of passions.

Like the sound of roaring thunder, roaring over a roaring sea
love cries instantly.

Yes, love cries
gloriously.

Love is in the air and spreads widely everywhere.

Love cries
like the wild, wild wind, blowing wildly.

Like the tapping noise of the rain, tapping against a surface
love cries.

Love cries
like a twinkle of an eye.

Love is a magic touch, touching the feeling with joy.

Love cries with smiles of happiness, giving pleasure, hope and trust.

Barbara A. Solomon

THE FIRE

Something exciting is happening . . .
See the people?
Rushing — in that direction!

They are shouting of a blaze . . .
Let's get a better view.

Someone's heart is on fire!
My, and there are two of them!

Their face — look at their faces!
It's . . . it's glowing!

More people are gathering as the flames reach enormous heights.

Notice how attentively the lovers eye the other;
Unaware of the outside world.

Listen to the gentleness at which they speak . . .

Now, sparks are flying as a result of the two's smoldering glances;
And others are catching!

Lovely, isn't it?

People are naturally drawn to such excitement.

Let them burn.

Let them love.

Bridgitt F. Boggan

DIANE

If I could paint your spirit
on canvas bright and clear
But I am not an artist
sweet one I hold so dear

If I could catch your laughter
on tape to future hear
I don't think a machine exists
that's good enough, I fear

If I could put your caring
in a box for later use
There wouldn't be a day in life
when I would feel abuse

If I could share your love for me
with others who are sad
I'd put a smile upon their face
and they'd be very glad

For you've been touched by Angels dear
the same who brought you here
That's why my world is always bright
because you always cheer

Dorothy M. Ferguson

A LOVE OF MINE

A tiny seed in my womb
Placed there by a wonderful loving man
Another of God's marvelous plans
A plan called pregnancy.

The little heart begins to tick
As my body begins to swell
In a few months it begins to kick
And the doctor says "All is well."

Just a few months to feel
A life within me,
I've learned to love this little child
This one I cannot see.

It's time; the labor has begun
At last the child I shall behold
Through the channels birth takes place
And a lovely child I hold.

After nine months of worry, fret and labor
My love has been sparked by this time
Lovely child throughout life
You'll always be a love of mine.

Frances Emerick

OUR FAVORITE RACE

The baby was crying
Where he was lying
I jumped to my feet
But I was quickly beat
My wife held him near
So his eyes would clear
He nestled awhile
And we began to smile
Because our little boy
Filled our hearts with joy

Wayne West

FOR YOU

If I had only known when I was young
That someday you I'd find,
There are so many things
I would have saved —
For you.

I often think of things we might have shared —
The perfume of the rose I gave
To someone else —
The rose that I wore in my hair.
Eyes bright with wonder at love's beckoning
glance —
Lips once soft with youthful innocence
Now tarnished, unafraid.
The touch of baby hands upon my breast
The loveliness of childish eyes.

Could I have known,
I would have saved these things —
For you.

Clara Mottlau Woodside

TRANSITION

You telephoned today to say 'hi.'
In from the coast on business
with no time to stop by.
Just calling to see how I'm getting on.
What did you think, I'd perish
'cause you're gone?

Love's ending has its pain, the wound's deep.
For months I was a zombie,
shunned our friends, hid in sleep.
But time does heal and life's dynamic flow
Impels us to rebuild in strength
and grow.

So just forget those moments we knew!
They were too long ago, dear,
now I'm finished with you.
And should have said so when our talk was through,
instead of stammering
"I miss you too."

Sylvia Sumida

LIFE, THE BALL OF FRESHLY FALLEN SNOW

We wait for the snowfall, in anticipation.
At the start it is small, a form pressed lovingly with our
fingers, in the ball of of our hand.

It is cold, almost painful, it defies all reason, be bold, we
must make it take form!

It is love that gives life to our creation.

Then the form is rolled. Like an avalanche it grows.

On all snowy days we love for the sun to reappear, to bring
its warmth will mean that the heavens will be made clear.

Yet, it is a sorrowful time, as we know our ball, made with
love, will soon melt away,

until another, lovely, snowy day.

Toni A. Williams-Sanchez

HEART'S OWN FIRE

Though the cold brittles the flesh,
The chain of love must not be broken,
For it is forged in the heart's own fire,
Which the cold shall never extinguish.

Yet if the heart should lose that fire,
It shall be consumed within itself,
And remain lost throughout time,
With the names and faces upon the great wall.

For just as mere love is not victory,
The loss of that love is not defeat,
And if this is to be . . . I shall regain,
Tomorrow . . . love a thousand times fold.

Dale Edward Blakney

INFANT ONE

Observe him: chubby, pink, with eyes of blue
That open wide in wondrous innocence
And foretell questions he'll soon ask of you;
Ten pudgy fingers; arms that grope and fence
With, quite unsure, your tie that dangles down
And fascinates his all-including gaze;
Brave, guileless countenance without a frown,
Or trace, where problems yet will spin their maze.
Loved ones would keep him ever young as this;
But growth, his destiny, will silent come;
For struggles are not won by babes in bliss,
When efforts must be added for the sum.
This shell is young but once to outward sight;
Impressions must be tokens cherished bright.

Graydon E. Spalding

MY IRISH LASS SUPREME

Our life's cycle, with all its peaks,
helped scope my way each day.
With the frequency of time, our love was sound,
it grew warmer with each day.

We raised our family, from the tradition,
that seems to go with God's dream.
The super value, to life I found,
with my Irish Lass supreme.

And now that it is twilight time,
I nurse my memories supreme.
I have no regrets, for the love I found,
with my Irish Lass supreme.

James M. Andary

MY PRIZE

I watch the calendar record the decades,
and mingle with life's fickle, swirling crowds.
My hands reach out to touch both saints and sinners,
and feel the soil of earth, the mist of clouds.
My heart is gladdened by the arching rainbow,
and saddened by men's words that prove untrue.
But that which always I have found most precious
is the love I share by night and day with you.

Mel Lawson

LOVE SONG TO THOMAS

I thought my life had started, but reality
pushed me three steps back.
The man I love has left me, and will never
want me back.
I feel my life is over, for without love
there's no need to move ahead.
And it has to be the love of this special
man, who so many years ago turned my head.
He brought love and joy into my life, unlike
any I had ever known.
He loved me and taught me the joys of love,
and unleashed a passion in me unlike any,
I have ever shown.
I may bed down a thousand men, and cheat them
of my love.
For never will I give it freely, except to this
special man I love.
If ever my heart sings a love song, it will sing
only for you Thomas, the only man I'll ever
love.

Mona Faye Hankins-McNulty

POWDER OF SMILES

Waking up solo,
morning lost forever,
no recollection, not even the dreams,
journey of the fears,
the desires,
crusted sleep around tear-stained eyes,
dejected into the lateness of the afternoon,
to feel in the heart the need of a woman,
to hold in the arms,
the grip of her hand,
otiose, empty,
resorting to the powder of smiles,
impending reality of low self-esteem,
fades into alluring, mystic, focus of every eye,
protégé of lust, seduction of the mind,
Cinderella's clock clicks to an end,
home again,
dreams the lover, sleep the friend,
until the powder of smiles
controls again.

Rondall L. Smith

SOMEHOW, I LOVE YOU

Somehow you have captured all the stars up in the heavens
And placed them in your sparkling eyes of blue.
They reflect off of my heart
And that's what makes me say I love you.
Somehow you have captured a part of the sun
And it gives your face a warm radiant glow
That when I say I love you
I can't help but let it show.
Somehow you have captured a rainbow
With a spectrum of colors shining from your soul,
And I say I love you
I'll never let that prism go.
Somehow you have captured
A breath of fresh air that you whispered in my ear
How much you really do care.
Then I say I love you remembering all that we have shared.
And yet somehow for all that you possess
You've also captured me.
Again I say I love you
For you say you love me.

Linnea Camilleri

WHEN WE ARE NEAR

When we are near, I lose all sense of time and
space with the world. Yet with you, time and
space become the gold and silver lining of
love's blossoming bud glistening of tender
passion that solidifies into a wondrous
flower . . . when we are near.

Susan A. Tanous

FIRST LOVE

When I was very, very small, about the age of three,
the dearest place that I could find was on my Grandpa's
knee.

I would pester him on childish lore, of knowledge I did
lack, no matter what the question was, my Gramps
would answer back.

He would ramble on and on while I would strain to hear,
trying hard to listen and not to interfere.

You see, I could really chatter and Grandpa talked a
lot, together we could talk the legs right off an iron
pot.

I would put my arms around his neck and squeeze him,
oh so tight! he would stop to wink at me, he made my
whole day bright.

I didn't always understand, when I climbed down to go,
but the twinkle in his blue eyes, said Grandpa loved
me so.

We fit so well together, that all could plainly see,
the only two people in our world, were my Grandpa and
me.

Frances V. Hadden

To My Father
Kenneth A. Hutcheson
9-28-20 — 4-4-82

A simple man, you taught me complex things;
Strength of character and pride through your quiet humility.
Honesty and faith in myself by your example.

I asked for petty things and you gave me treasures:
Freedom enough to test my wings and leave you,
Stability to return to the shelter of home;
Security enough to occasionally disagree with you,
And respect for my own individuality.
Your quiet support of my fragile dreams gave me
The courage to try to achieve them.

Thank you for the times you wiped away my tears,
And for the dusting you gave my pants sometimes.
Thank you for not asking questions too painful for answers,
And for knowing the answers to almost all of mine.

Forgive me for all the times I've taken you for granted,
For the times I've forgotten to show how much I love you.
Forgive me my arrogance and my impatience when
I thought I knew more than you about living.

Words are such ordinary means to describe so extraordinary
An experience; being lucky enough to call you Dad.

Judy Ann Hutcheson

TO A HANDICAPPED CHILD

The joy I feel when your face I see
Is more than words can tell;
The satisfaction you give to me
I know so very well.

Oh, how I wish that others could know
The happiness we share!
Though you can't say "I love you so,"
I feel the love you bear.

The special love you give to me
Is truly a beautiful thing;
And though no words you speak to me,
I hear the song you sing.

You are surely a beautiful child
Inside, so full of love;
I thank the Lord for your grace so mild
That He sent here from above.

Andrea G. Hajducko

WINGS

I love you
And I'll try to be the most
that I can for you
But I can only be what I really am inside
Because God never meant
for wildflowers to be put
in a fancy vase
and stuck in a stuffy room somewhere
He meant for them
to be put in a Mason jar
and set where curtains billow
at summer's window
I'll try to be the most
that I can for you
God meant for me to be who I am
and He gave me the gift of myself
But you gave me the ability
to recognize my own beauty
and soar
where the eagles fly free.

Dawn Carmichael Braack

LONELY

Loneliness,
It's a sad empty feeling,
One that keeps your mind reeling,
And leaves you unsure and confused.
It's a brand-new fad feeling,
Heart-rending, stealing,
The goals that you set for yourself.
How can I find,
That one on my mind,
When I'm often not sure what I want?
And if I find the right one,
Who's separate, alone,
Beside me through life's every test?
What drives me to hurt the one who,
Is willing to give so much too,
When all I will deal out is pain?
So cruel, so kind,
Irreverent and blind
To one who states they need me?
It's loneliness . . .

R. M. Almeida

THE MYSTERY OF LOVE

LOVE is such a wondrous thing,
It's mentioned every day . . .
In every clime and culture
From Spain to Prudhoe Bay.

But few can really comprehend
What Love is all about:
That mixture of emotions
Which makes one cheer, or pout.
For Love has no reality
Which anyone can see.
It penetrates beyond our sight
To set our spirit free . . .
And each of us approaches Love
In such a different way,
For Love is based on lifestyle
And how we live each day.

So when you reach that goal in life
Which fills your soul with Love,
Be thankful that your journey
Has been guided from Above!

Craig E. Burgess

BURGESS, CRAIG EDWARD. Pen Names: Luke the Drifter, El Mexicano; Born: Camden, New Jersey, 10-8-44; Single; Education: Rutgers University, B.A., 1967; National University of Mexico, Summer Program, 1965; University of Pennsylvania, M.S., 1971; Occupation: Spanish Instructor; Memberships: National Education Association; New Jersey Education Association; American Association of Teachers of Spanish and Portuguese (AATSP); South Jersey Apple Computer User's Club; Awards: Golden Poetry Award (World of Poetry), 1985; Amateur Poet of the Year (fifth place), Johnson Publishing Company, 1985; Poetry: 'The Lonely One,' *American Poetry Anthology,* 1983; 'Hands of Time,' *Our World's Most Beloved Poems,* 1984; 'Lips,' *Hearts on Fire, Volume II,* 1985; 'Fireflies,' *Our World's Most Cherished Poems,* 1986; 'Fleeting Glimpse of Paradise,' *America's Best Amateur Poets of 1985,* 1986; Comments: *My experiences in Spanish-speaking countries, as well as those in my Spanish classes over the past 18 years, have resulted in themes which penetrate beyond appearances in an effort to explore the humor, beauty, and sadness concealed within mankind and his environment. My enjoyment of science fiction has made this exploration both challenging and entertaining.*

SITTING TOGETHER

There we sat,
Living room warm,
Lights dimmed,
Side by side.

There we sat,
You in your small easy chair,
Me on the sofa, our eyes
In silent communication.

There we sat,
Exchanging thoughts,
Thoughts of sincerity,
Trust, honesty, and love.

There we sat,
Your lips so soft,
Our voices so gentle,
Expressing each other's
Desires and needs.

James M. Cannon

LOVE SURVIVES THE YEARS

As I watch you sitting there,
Resting in that big old chair
I think of all the times we've shared,
Of how you've loved and how you've cared,
Not for yourself, but for others,
Such a wonderful wife and mother.

I recall the beauty of younger years,
All the laughter and all the tears;
But still I feel deep down somehow,
You're even more beautiful now,
Because of all the things you've done
To make our lives together as one
Big, loving, happy family,
Never forgetting your love for me.

Now as we two are sitting here,
Though I may not tell you, dear,
I'm sure it must be clear to see,
That you still mean the world to me.

Jean S. Price

PHYSICS

(For Robert)

HONORABLE MENTION

when you explain it to me
your hands are in flight
eyes incandescent
hair standing at attention

i squint
your image blurs
then sharpens again
i nod

secretly i watch
the tender symmetry
of your mouth
imagine private experiments
and my willing self
in your knowing hands

Alice Persons

IN MY FIREPLACE

Sitting by the fire thinking about you
Thinking about the ways we sat
Together too

I remember the travels
We took along the way
Over the mountains through the smokey rain
I have seen again your face
In my fireplace — In my fireplace

I'm reaching back in time
To create a smile
I see your blue eyes
Deep in the orange and yellow fire

In the nighttime from the sky
I hear you say
Sunlight carry on don't lose your way
Because in my heart you'll be
And I'll always stay
In your fireplace — in your fireplace

Alfred J. Padron, Jr.

TOGETHER

I see our life together as in a
crystal vision.
No illusions, but with clear
tomorrows.

I love you as my only true love.
You share my tears and my joy.
Both with our human imperfections,
we are beautiful and rich with
love for each other.

I feel fulfilled, for all the roads
I have traveled, have led me to
your door.
We are united by spirit through the
expression of love.

I have
I do
and always will
LOVE YOU.

Georgiann D. V. Perry

PARADISE

My dreams are made from promises
And promises from dreams.

Next thing I know I'm chasing stars
And riding moonbeams.

Suddenly singing through days
And dancing through the night.

Feel like relaxing in my cloud
Laughing in the candlelight.

The atmosphere's filled with romance
All that's on my mind.

Please don't wake me up from this
It's all I'd hoped to find.

Jamie Haydock

YOU HAUNT MY SOUL

I've searched my soul
In regards to you and
Find that I am haunted
By your lasting love.

I've let go of you
In my heart, yet
I find your memory
Invades my soul still.

What hold is it you
Render on me, my love?
Why does the essence of you
Grab my heart, so?

My soul cannot separate
You from me, for
We are of one heart,
A part of what is.

Stephanie Yeater

WALK WITH ME

Walk with me along the sand
Holding my hand silently
Every now and then,
Give it a squeeze
to reassure me that
you love me as I love you
If you feel the urge to
Talk feel free to do so
I love hearing your
Voice
It washes over me
like a gentle surf
rolling along the beach;
Our beach
If you think of
something funny,
tell me and we'll laugh
Together
Just be with me,
Forever, in love

Gregory Robert Bates

MEETING

What did you make of me
lying alone on the beach
with no one but the sand and sun
and you to know I was there?

You must have thought it strange
to find me where before
there were only sand crabs and sand,
being washed and shifted by the sea.

It was there that you first knew me
as we listened and waited
for the sea to return and wash
us to new positions on the sand.

We slept lulled by the rhythm of the sea
with the wind and stars as our cover.
But I awoke to find us separated
by the sand that had returned to the sea.

Ronald W. King

MY PLEDGE OF LOVE

I give to you my all . . .
my honesty, respect, admiration and total devotion.
My heart, my soul and my love.
You ask me to smile for you . . . I am my dear. Though I don't always carry a smile on my lips, I am always smiling in my heart. For I know we have a beautiful love together.
I will try my best to live up to your expectations, but I know I will falter. Please believe that through the ups and downs of our life together I will love you always, in all ways.
I love you with all my heart and soul. I am yours, you are mine and together we are one.

Tina Alden-Houts

DID YOU KNOW

Did you know how much I loved you, when you turned and walked away?
Did you know I'd yearn to touch you at the close of every day?
Did you know my waking hours would be filled with thoughts of you?
If you did, then thanks for giving me the chance to know it too.

Did you ever think about me in your search for someone new?
Did you ever touch my spirit when you felt alone and blue?
Did you ever miss the laughter and the good times that we shared?
If you did, then I've misjudged you. I didn't think you cared.

If I'd known how much I loved you, I would have begged you stay.
If I'd shown my deepest feelings, you would be with me today.
If I'd told you more than sometimes that without you I would die,
If I did, then there would never have to be that last good-bye.

When you left, I couldn't function. My social life a drone,
On every new occasion I was bored and felt alone.
Prestige, career, and money didn't satisfy me now.
Then I saw you, and your presence gave me inner peace, somehow.

Let me tell you I still love, even though you walked away.
Let me show you I will love you more tomorrow than today.
I didn't realize then why you left without a fuss.
Now I know how well you knew me. Now the time is right for us.

Edith M. Chandler

LET'S WALK TOGETHER WHILE WE CAN

We walked together, hand in hand, when love was new.
Always keeping step as sweethearts do.
We had so many things to plan.
Let's keep walking together, Honey, while we can.

We walked together, down the aisle, when we were wed.
Eagerly, step by step, looking to the years ahead,
And all the hopes and dreams of our life span.
Let's keep walking together, Honey, while we can.

We walked together sharing each big event, and all the small ones too.
Counted first steps as our family grew,
And another phase of our life began.
Let's keep walking together, Honey, while we can.

We walk together now, arm in arm, for support as we stroll.
Did we ever attain our youthful goal?
Memories we cherish now — sweethearts again.
Let's keep walking together, Honey, while we can.

We walked together thru our youth and middle age, and now our senior years.
We shared so many happy times — forgotten are the fewer tears.
Years pass so quickly now we haven't time to even plan.
Let's just keep walking together, Honey, while we can.

Eulaliah T. Hooper

HOW SOME PERCEIVE LOVE

To some — a lotus,
To some — opium.
Love — The chameleon
of life's emotions.
Under the guise of hate,
It can lure.
Under the cover of care,
It's demure.
To some — forbidden fruit
To some — an insatiable lust.
Love — the two-edged sword
That can cleave more doors,
Expose more secrets than spies,
And bring more men to knee
Than any weapon ever made.
Love — an illusion upon
which feeds all hearts.

Sally A. Barrows

HEARTS ON FIRE

Nurture the flame that flows
From God of love.
That sacred "fire"
— Gift from Heavens —
Melts the "ice"
Of indifference
(Which short circuits
The flux
Of genuine communication
To foster rejection,
To freeze potentials in limbo
For redemption and growth.)
Love between sweethearts is moving,
But love extended to fellows
Going down hill
May ease human sufferings,
And heal most social ills.

Mai L. Bui

AMERICA

Soaring silently
Over the mottled mauve
Of a rocky desert floor,
Laughing and humming
From my hang glider;
Swooping over vastness
In a free fall
To see the quiet blue, green globe
Of earth coming toward me;
Racing past mountains and
trees
And dappled rivulets;
Keeping up with the sun a moment
In its glinting golden-silver
splendor,
I am a spirit moving
As America.

Betty Jane Yadede

ONE THIRD

Where is the one who will look on me,
and say, "Hold me forever"?
Though her body slumped from misery's wring,
but in my arms no pain can sever.
Where is the one who will fill the crevice
from heartache's digging spade,
and be the one who'll work with God
before the soul is put on 'fade'?
Where is the one who has the eyes
that are a glaze for romantic needing,
and touches me to want one love
to curtail life's inevitable bleeding?
Where is the one who knows that life
is a vocation to serve with love,
to live each day where two are one
with the perpetual love feeding above?

Michael Durachko

CONVICTED

If loving you is a sin, then let me be condemned for eternity, for that is how long it will be to quench my love. Others have loved, love and will love you, but my love will always be a special love. I stand guilty of the most beautiful emotion known to man, and because of you, I Am.

Mary Annah Alemán

LOVE REMEMBERED

Every time I think of you
and that's more often than not
I think of the love we had together
and it always brings a tear to my eyes
I think of the good times we shared
and those special moments alone
and that's when I miss you most
it's so often that I think about you
there's little time for anything else
I think of when we laughed
and when we cried together
and when we made up after a little spat
I think of all the happiness you gave to me
and wonder why it came to an end
but the reason I think of you so much is
I still love you

Jim McDermott

STYLES OF LOVING

Love — thou dost appear in many forms,
A raging torrent to the young that sweeps all reason far away —
And consumes with passion's fire that tenderness that love
held long can know.
A companionate love where friendship holds first place —
And learning to confide in one another —
Brings a certain grace to all the lovers strive to do —
Fulfillment of each other's needs the order of the day,
Not the pragmatist's concern for love's rewards in
terms of worldly gain —
But care for the beloved — now and ever holding sway.
Of course, to many love is but another game —
To play on any given day —
Or a form of jealousy — possessive and dependent —
Yet void of that respect and true affection —
Which binds all faithful lovers now and through eternity.

William E. Mays

A LOVER'S DREAM

And as the day retires into night,
My thoughts are all on you.
A memory to mitigate the loneliness,
Which fills my heart clear through . . .

Your presence is so evident,
When you touch my trembling hand.
With bold assurance you speak not a word;
But yet . . .
I understand . . .

Although accustomed to ultimate independence,
You professed your love to me.
And the magnitude of my happiness,
Shall span

THROUGH INFINITY

Pamela Boehme

RUNNING ON EMPTY

As one reaches middle age, values start to change
Priorities and feelings begin to deftly rearrange

Suddenly sensing the void carved out of emotional need
For the planted seed of love never allowed to breed

Soon the meter of shared affection reaches the empty stage
A crying need for companionship builds up an internal rage

In remembrance of advice ignored from those both candid and free
That the search for true love may be in perpetuity

Journeying throughout a continuous span of time
Constantly seeking its comfort, preparing for a higher clime

Life devoid of love is a canvas bold and bare
Only to be awakened by the painter's opulent flair

Stanley S. Reyburn

A SMILE'S JOURNEY

That bright smile across her face leapt
Hiding God's mysteries and the secrets they kept
That traveled between the light of life
And the valley of death

It gripped my heart
Planted itself in my mind
Became of my soul a part
That evermore its remembrance I'd find

It was a journey from beginning to end
Its milestones being filled with understanding
And majestic wisdom that only the Lord could send
For it was of me that it was demanding

That not only the smile I'd see
But also the love she had for me

Richard D. Cagg

CHERISHED MOMENTS

Someone passes by, knocks on my door
Leaves imprints on my windowpane
The little I have this moment is life
The little I have this moment is joy
The little I have this moment is hope
The little I have this moment is peace
A laughter, a tear, a smile or a frown
The little I have is valuable to me
If there's no tomorrow for me to see
And no one ever for me to know
No pastures for green grass to grow
No meadows, no brooks where clear waters flow
Cherish this moment, cherish this little today
The little moments of love, joy, hope and peace

Hyacinth Williams Moncrieffe

WILLIAMS MONCRIEFFE, HYACINTH. Pen Name: Lia Meme, Precious; Born: Jamaica, West Indies, 9-8-45; Education: A.A.S. in Nursing; B.S. in Health and Administration; Masters in Professional Human Services; Occupations: Poet, Lyricist, Author, Composer, Folklorist, Singer; Memberships: Song Writers Club of America; Poets and Writers; ASCAP; American Film Institute, Academy of American Poets; Awards: Proclamation from Brooklyn Borough President, American Biographical Institute Award, World Biographical Hall of Fame, Directory of Distinguished Americans, *Who's Who Among Authors and Poets;* Poetry: 'Embrace Beauty,' 'Why,' Riders of the Rainbow Poetry Press, 1986; 'Every Man Must Have a Dream,' *American Poetry Anthology,* 1986; 'Multi,' *International Poetry Anthology,* 1986; Other Writing: *The Unlimited Mind,* book, 1984; Comments: *My work is written with very deep sincere and spiritual feelings. I write to bring a secure peace, love, equality and harmony among Blacks and Blacks, Whites and Whites, and Blacks and Whites. I would like every human being to realize we are a part of this universe and that we are all here for a reason.*

AN EMPTY VALENTINE

Valentine's day, a day to behold
There's no discretion, it's for both young and old

Valentine's day, a day full of love
Belonging to none other than all the sweethearts

A day to hold each other, like you'll never let go
A day to tell each other, I love you so

A day to let you know, you'll be forever mine
Not only for today, but till the end of time

A day for no tears, and surely no sorrow
Just laughter and joy, like a brand-new tomorrow

A day for candy kisses, and chocolate hearts
But as usual, once again, I'm torn apart

No candy kisses, no chocolate hearts
But most important of all no sweetheart

Not even a phone call, no little hello
No one to tell me, I love you so

No candy kisses, no chocolate hearts
An empty valentine's day, is all that I got.

June Drao

SECRET KISSES

There is an old love letter, that has turned
Brown with age, there are tiny little x's on
Every page.
No one else can read it, they don't know where
It's hid. It is looked upon in secret, with
Eyes that are dim and old;
For the one who wrote this letter, the story
Is untold.

You can count the tiny x's that are hid upon
The page, through the papers faded brown, love
Doesn't die with age.
Many heart-felt tears, have fell upon the page,
So the letters kept in secret, like the x's in
The lines.
Sometime in the future, in another time,
The letter will be found, and the finder wins
A thrill, 'cause the letter will not change,
The x's are there still.
Tiny little x's, tiny little o's, that was how
To thrill the heart, with love so long ago.

When the finder finds the kisses, shall they
Thrill the finder so?
In another time, another day, the finder alone
Will know.

Polly Wiggins Crum

A CANDLE

I stared at the flame of the candle
At the length of light that shined out,
I've felt the warmth, hold, and distance it held —
And could not see beyond it.
For days I've felt this way,
You never melted away.

Gary Smith

THE SHEPHERD OUR LORD

The shepherd our Lord in our hearts he'll abide,
A constant companion, his love not denied,
He leads us down a highway of love,
From His heavenly home, in his mansion above.
Our lives he will change as we study the Word,
The one that I speak of is known as our Lord.
If we have burdens too heavy to bear,
He'll listen and bless us for only a prayer.
He makes us slow down and do good each day,
He'll listen from heaven whenever we pray.

Herbert H. Macdonald

TO MICHAEL

These dear, now yellowing, letters,
These souvenirs, still shall I keep;
And now, and then, I'll gaze on them,
Oh, Michael! While others sleep.

This Artist's Set, a pearl necklet,
A wee tasseled pencil, mottled brown and gold;
Still may I clasp and remember
Our youth, while I'm growing old.

Your Photo . . . how young you are,
And tall! Your eyes still smile,
As if to chide the tears, in mine . . .
Oh, Michael! I'll dry them, after a while.

But the night wind brings no whisper
Of condolence, to my heart of pain,
For, well I know, dearly-loved brother,
Michael . . . you'll not return again.

S. Diane Sawitzki

SAWITZKI, DIANE SOPHIE. Pen Names: S. Diane Sawitski, S. Diane; Born: Saskatchewan, Canada; Education: Business College, 1943; Red Cross Nurse training; Occupation: Worked with injured war veterans in Winnipeg; Artist-colorist for several photo studios; Greeting Card Painter; Themes: *Beauty and harmony in all things in life, as well as sorrows touching my own life which have all helped me understand life more deeply, with empathy toward all who loved and lost, who strove to achieve and won their prize at great cost, and toward all who remember still my own efforts and love me over again.*

TOUCH ME QUICK

Please! Please! Please!

Touch me quick . . .

for I may not be here another day.

Touch me now, experience me in whole
press your fingers close to me . . .

Run! Run! Run!
your hands over my surface plane so very carefully.

Here I sit exploiting myself to you.
Do you really care if I exist?
If so, yes! please show me you care . . .
By touching me.

Cathy Kuntz

BITTER REFLECTION

I did my best
I should have guessed your love would be untrue;
The only one you really loved
in all these years was you.

Jean Graham Cano

Hallowed, holy hill
I've been here before, splendored in the moonlight
Aching with desire to hold him, touch him, be one with him
Yet we all were separated
You and I and the moon and he
Were like a jigsaw puzzle with missing parts
Seeming to fit together, but showing gaping holes
So the puzzle fell apart, as I did
Time and spirit picked up the pieces, found the lost ones
Began to weave together a tapestry rich and full
No longer a jigsaw
The moon is in me now, and I in the moon
I smell the stars, I touch the night and dance the sky
I hear the grass, I taste the dew
In this wholeness, I ache anew
His completeness joins with mine
I rejoice in balanced, perfect place and time
Hallowed, holy hill.

Lyn Berry

NOW LIKE THE EAGLE

Psalms 103,5
For: Joe Lynn Towns, 1907-1962

Ungrounded youth gave you control of wings
Near canopy of earth, belief in spheres
Where rhythmic order and vibration sings
Of knowledge men evade or glimpse with fears.
Beyond cloud crags, in search of soul's intent,
You found men's theories too weak to hold
Deep trust in things unseen; found faith is meant
For miracles the ages have not told.
Now, like the eagle, free to roam and soar,
Your strength renewed, with speed of light you move
At thoughts' command in realms you may explore
With wonder you once knew and could not prove.
Godspeed, my love, in boundless freedom. Share
My flights through space on soundless wings of prayer.

Opal Zimmermann Towns

YOUTHS' NARCISSUS

In the time of youth's Narcissus,
Who can think of us?
Thinking only of I
Appeals to my eye.

I listen not to the cries of Echo
But leave her to her woe;
See today as my pleasure!
Will tomorrow find a cure?

Laura Hill

SPHYNXILATED

Love be some puzzle
Stars beam at night
Silently benuzzle
Yon kisses mere plight.

Put riddlefied Sphynx then
Why are they so
Except dreamer draw pen
Always to truth go.

Have be soul matter
If intimate plenteous
Men will all scatter
At its name mentionous.

Orien Todd

SILHOUETTE

Can you hear me? (over here)
Can you see me? (over here)
Are you so used to me?
Can you not see or hear me?
You know me so well.
Every nook of my body,
Every phrase before I say it.
Do you know me so well?
Do you know what is within?
You hear the words so often.
You see me all the time.
But are you dear or are you blind?
Can you hear me? (I'm here)
Can you see me? (I'm here)

Leona Joan Osier

ROSES

My Love,
You are likened
To a rose . . .
Yester morning
Walking down
A garden path
I saw roses there.
Gentle, sweet,
Smiling faces
Perfuming summer air.
So beautiful
And queenly in pose,
Only God
Could make a rose.

Juanita Caudle Crane

MY DAD

Once more I walk down memory lane
in childhood gardens rare;
And gather flowers of priceless worth
within its portals fair;
The wagon that my father made
a most intricate affair;
There never was one half as grand —
I was a millionaire;
The puppy that I learned to love —
this was his great delight;
The pictures that I drew for him
he loved with all his might;
He was an inspiration
his deeds I'll ne'er forget;
May I fulfill his trust in me,
that his hopes and dreams be met!

Hildur Solberg

MEMORIES FOREVER

Memories, memories, just souvenirs,
some held, others stacked away
With a pause, at times, one recollects
many elevated with esteem
Chosen eccentricities last longer
traced in a tone of limelight
With little doting on special ties
one makes mental light notes
For these are extra worshiped moments
that are held in one's heart
And, somewhat take a real hard hold
when I turn and look back
For a husband is so very, very much
to have, to cherish, to hold
That when he has to take leave forever
this better half of a rib, lost
The helping strong arm no longer there
that which God lends to a woman
That special gift of the hand in life
extended, now lifeless for me
Once remembered soft words of his voice
gone, gone now, gone forever!

Louise M. Bros

MY USED TO BE LOVER

Where are you now,
my used to be lover?
You let time & distance
come between us
as you drifted out of my life.

Where are you,
my used to be lover?
The excitement in your eyes has vanished.
Did your dreams die, along with mine?
Your eyes look dull and drugged,
has part of you that I inspired died?

My used to be lover,
for a moment your eyes
were full of hope,
but reality ruined it.
You're different now, not my lover at all.

Are you buried deep inside?
Please . . .
Come back.

Gigi Goren

NO ARRIVALS NO DEPARTURES

Skies blast snow
shutting down highways
winds make power lines
powerless. As
winter's weight
muffles the town,
lovers burrow
in retreat.

Twigs snap
and feed the flames
kindling seduction.
Double heartbeats
pulse in passion's
ebb and flow
and bodies curl
snug in their folds
insulated against
the icy release.

Lori Poole

JE T'AIME

Leaves upon a tree
Resemble sustenance of life.
Glints of happiness
Within your sweetheart's eyes
Resemble sustenance of love.
The falling of leaves off that tree
Marks the need for support
Until its rebirth.
Tears rolling down
Your sweetheart's cheek
Marks the need for a shoulder
To cry on.
The revival of the hibernating tree
Means it is time
To thank nature for its reawakening.
Happiness again
Within my eyes
Means it is time
To thank you for all your love.

Wendy Pierce

LOVING THE DREAMS AWAY

Your words crash into the air
Like the thunderous vengeance of Zeus.
The birds sing with the beauty of a raven,
And the roses wilt to dying weeds.
The sun races behind the clouds,
And the rain pours
As though water through a broken dam.
And the pain does pierce my heart
Like the arrow of a greedy hunter.

The sweat rolls from my pores
As I awaken from this nightmare of hell.
The words of goodbye fade quickly
When my eyes focus on yours above me.
Your hands gently wipe the sweat
From my face,
And the love in your caress assures me
That those words I fear
Will never be heard.

Monty Province

ONLY FROM A DISTANCE

She loves him from a distance
She sees him in another's arms
Her heart almost feels weakened
Her eyes break forth a storm
Inside she's slowly dying
Wishing love came without pain
She longs to reach out and touch him
Sadly he's somebody's gain

Her nights are sweetly haunted with dreams
Of a love she longs to hold
She awakes with an ache
Nobody can take or relieve
In the pit of her soul
Each day her thoughts are with him
She will love him from afar
Till night once again takes her
In the arms of the one that she loves

Cindy A. Russell

TEDDY

He had a banana for a tail
And in his old age he was frail
He had a fluffy coat
And he would always choke
He loved food
And he was always in a sleepy mood

He was as tough as a bull
He was as gentle as a bird
He wore a coat of wool
And he never spoke a word

Then came his last day
Quite near the month of May
He almost bled to his death
But he never fled his fate
He had no children, for he never did mate
And he loved to eat chocolate cake!

Gabrielle Hotung

WHAT OF YOUR LOVE?

What of your love?
You haven't told me,
And what of your love?
I should see,
You haven't shown me.
What of your love?
You can share
That you haven't.

And what is the truth?
I should know
You believe in.
What is the pain?
You may feel,
When you're lonely,
What good is love?
When you're loving
You only.

Alvin Newsome Jr.

YOU NEVER RAN HOME

You never ran home
to mother
you were
very young
when the trees fell
into a darkness
and a longing
for kisses
since then, transparent
dresses have descended
through a vortex
and many tears
have found many lovers.

Sharon Rubenstein

RUBENSTEIN, SHARON LYNN. Born: 8-30-45; Married: 11-12-76 to John Svehla: Education: Pierce College, 1963-1965; Occupation: Word Processor; Awards: Feature Poet in, *The Poet,* 1984; Feature Poet in, *Broken Streets, IV,* 1983; Poetry: 'Schoolyard Scene,' *The Villager,* June, 1981; 'Sad Lovers,' *Poetry Today,* March, 1984; 'Suburbia,' *Broken Streets,* 1983; 'Just a Short Song,' Fine Arts Press, *The American Muse,* September, 1984; 'Say Goodbye,' *The Poet,* 1984; Comments: *Most of my poetry is based on childhood, youth and neighborhoods lived in. Love is a recurrent theme — lost love, unrequited love. My poetry is always asking questions, the answers are philosophical and never really seem to be definitive.*

AND I THINK OF YOU FROM PETER FONTANERO, TO HIS LOVE, #7

The leaves flutter in the sky
There is a tremor in my heart
Precious were the moments
My love,
I think of you.

Ellen Malis

QUEST

Two Souls on a dusty road
on their way to nowhere.
Silence is the thing that binds
luring them not to care.
Walking on two dusty tracks,
from nowhere to no place.
Stillness is the one that moves,
loneliness has a cold face.
Two Souls wishing they were one
to keep away the darkness.
Fear or love? The question is,
that makes these people partners.

Antonio Juarez

I THOUGHT OF YOU

Saw a movie, heard a love song
Ran into some old friends — and
I thought of you
Read a poem, went to a wedding
Picked some flowers — and
I thought of you
Placed the flowers at your grave
I was so lonely — and
I thought of you
The sun hid behind a cloud
It rained, I cried — and
I thought of you

Dolores Saldano

TIME'S TEST

Yes — you'll grow older on me,
your cheekbones more in focus,
the hollows prevalent beneath,
your clear blue eyes lessen in hue,
your flesh less firm about the waist;
but it will still be you.

To me your soul will glow,
its aging reverse itself;
it will shine brighter,
despite the loosening of flesh;
its valor will have passed time's test.

Claire S. Tarantino

STIGMATA

Shall we exchange my hands for yours,
mine that tease (I'm told)
for yours that have no habits
such as mine.

But if we do, who will inherit
my future's past and pulse,
life line, and predictions
reaching out
to captivate a hand
now full of tears
in Paradise.

Omar Pound

THE SPOUTING CAVE.

HOW I LOVE YOU!

How I love you, God;
I see Your beauty
In sky and clouds,
Sea and shore,
Mountains, deserts,
Star-filled heavens —
Hills and lakes,
And prairie lands.

The Majesty,
Grandeur of Your Creation,
Poured in ceaseless measure,
Upon our world.

Enveloped in such beauty,
Is almost more
Than I can bear.

HOW I LOVE YOU, GOD!

Georgiana Lieder Lahr

A PRAYER TO KING NEPTUNE

Oh mighty monarch of the deep
A constant, careful vigil keep —
Oh forceful king, thou guardian proud
Do not bring wind, or storm, or cloud.

I beg of you, please do not deign
To strike with wrath from your domain;
With loving care, his ship surround,
Let him return from foreign ground.

Watch over him; defend his ship,
And keep him safely on this trip.
Oh, ancient ruler of the sea,
Pray let him come back safe to me.

Protect and guide him, and his crew,
This fervent prayer I offer you;
With aid from you, and God above
He will come home to me — and love.

Lou Plotner

FAMILY LOVE

Love your loved ones,
To cherish and hold.
They are more precious,
Than Silver or Gold.

Love is something,
Money cannot buy.
You are rich indeed,
When family helps in need.

A family that is close,
A greater gift than most.
Sharing the happy times,
Helping in the sad times.

Thank God, for a family,
Being so near and dear.
Worldly goods may be few,
I am rich, if only, you knew.

Ruth Robertson

COME SHARE MY LIFE AND LUCK

Come share my life and luck with me,
And you, my love, will always be,
I've told you over and over; I've found a four-leaf clover,
One leaf is for eternal joy; second and third for girl and boy,
The fourth is reserved for thee,
Come share my life and luck with me.

Come share my life and luck with me,
True love is for eternity,
We'll always work together, through trials and stormy weather,
Come share my life and luck with me,
And you, my love, will always be,
For I've found a four-leaf clover,
Come share my life and luck with me.

Come share my life and luck with me,
Faithful to God, we'll always be,
He'll help us shape our destiny; we'll be with Him in unity,
Come share my life and luck with me,
And you, my love, will always be,
We'll share the same four-leaf clover,
Come share my life and luck with me.

Lucile V. Treutel

SONGS TO A SQUIRREL

Lovers slowly walking by, joggers thumping along —
Bikers flying by, squirrels scampering back & forth —
Racing up a tree, chasing a mate.
Fascinated, I watch them — speeding up & down,
Gathering their stores, before winter snows;
Amused at their playful times, amazed at their speed . . .
I whisper out to them . . . soothing songs of love,
Hoping they'll stay, whistling softly now —
Soothing notes I send.

Munching now, tiny little fingers,
Sweeping bit & pieces, carefully watching, watching —
Eyeing my every move, listening to my songs . . .
Soon the spell is broken, like a bolt of lightning,
My little friend chases his mate.

I hear rustling of leaves,
I strain to see

But my eyes are too weak —
I hum a tune,
Of love, I send.

Wally Kibler

BIG MACK

HONORABLE MENTION

Elation, Peace, Transcendence and Prayer — nouns we found in underwear.
Inside a universe, a rock, an island or a dirty sock.
Relished hot dogs in the park were offerings to move the dark.
Never knew red tennis shoes could turn these 'Hello, mellow' yellows
Into 'Bye-bye, baby' blues. Spent a lotta time in his car.
Spent a lotta time in my car. Color fades in the sun too long.
Grasshopper dies in a jar too long. I watch the movies on t.v. — my heroes
Fly and save the west, some make a lotta money, some just wear red tennis shoes.
He'll be back, Big Mack, for my heart and my head,
When he finds out what water girls do in big beds,
Because we were the lovers in J. Lindsey's romance novel,
Tender is the Storm —
Paperback in '85 where a kiss was hot but Coolsville
Was down the road and take a right
To the house of many girls.

Didi Murphy

ISLAMIC IDYLL

Clarion of clerestoric through the sibilant quasi-cloistered
tree-shaded road. Impersonating and sustained by
Limpid, abundant Islamic blue waters . . .
Enlivening the vicissitudes of seantry
Roamers and generic syllogistic verbatim
Koran in a long, lonely golden way.

Colorful flag of the Islam faith, in versatile
Comparative, generic action, derivative of
Goals and flowers: goals for the belligerent
Stardom of civil wars. Flowers for the quiescent
Mourning of magic, despised love, glory and doom.
Reverberating occasion to the finding of
Candid *love*
Where mercenary witness finds
The wisdom of the creative glow of life.
That is the chant of faith, the grandeur
And splendor of love, the Hosanna of Allah!
"Invisibilia ad Allah, coranica et
invisibilia ad omnes." —
Ibis, redibis et non peribis in bello.

Allan De Fiori

SECRETS

I saw him turn the corner as I walked past that old place where we met as children playing, turning 'round the mulberry place. Too timid then to tell him how my heart beat wild with joy at the thought of his freckled face when he was such a boy.

Gone forever are those playtimes when the heart beat wild and raced, but it's locked in keeping ever in my thoughts' great secret place.

And on days when dismal settings bring me close beside the fire, I can unlock secrets hiding, and return where never tires, old adventure that I play in 'round about the warm, sweet smells of the cinnamon and sugar where my Auntie tells her tales.

So the smell of spices cooking and a hair of tousled red, brings those freckles sprinkled wildly to my memory once thought fled.

You may send me to the dungeon where the dragon screams so wild, but these memories are my keepings, made when I was just a child.

They are mine, you cannot have them, and as childish as it sounds I will keep them locked forever hiding way inside deep down.

Patricia Shepard

I CAN'T HELP LOVING YOU

I Love the tender way you tell me that you Love me
And the way you run your fingers through my hair,
I Love the way you squeeze my hands and hug me
And the many ways you show me that you care.
I Love your gentle smile that ever haunts me
And the Love-light in your eyes that tells me that you're true,
I Love the many ways that you have blessed me
And like a mirror, I've become your blessing too.

I can't help Loving you, — I can't help Loving you.

I have vowed Sweetheart that I would never leave you,
Nor with purpose would I ever make you cry,
For I have Loved you from the moment that I met you,
And I will Love you until the moment that I die.

I can't help Loving you, — I just can't help Loving you.

Richard Bruce McFarlane

DROPLETS OF SAND

With you in mind, these lines entwine,
Etching within my heart, love divine.
As time does flow, now memories do glow,
As wistful fantasies of you unfold.

Beyond the realm of a mystic highway,
Another dawn does greet the day.
Within my heart, you're gathered there,
Forever mine, with heartache bared.

Now, droplets of sand do lie beyond,
As hands of fate, involve life's song.
For as time draws infinitely, thus dear,
We're bound forever in a web of fear.

Oh grasp tomorrow by a tender hand,
Tomorrow we borrow from life's plan.
Then wander, as our dreams dance on,
For beyond life's tragedy we belong.

Though now our moments do echo dear,
Let not tomorrow spoil a future near.
For as our days meet, with a new display,
Within my heart, your love does stay.

Donna Niedermeier

THE TINY BUD

The tiny bud of my flower
Closed, as of yet, to the sun's warm glow
A living organism, even though so small
Its beauty hidden until the opening of the show

The bud grows with nourishment and love
Stirring in the warm shelter in which it lives
Waiting for the perfect moment to spring forth
Lingering before it returns the love I give

At last, the moment arrives
And my tiny bud opens itself for me to see
Oh! What joy it brings to this heart of mine
To view my creation's loveliness set free

As I gaze down upon my package of charm
Quiet now, in her moment of rest
I see that nothing could be better
Than the love I feel deep within my breast

For the tiny bud
Grew inside my womb
Then appeared to brighten my life
My sweet little flower in bloom

Pamela A. Watkins

MY FRIEND

Is someone who can
Save a crumb of my pride
Snatch my self-esteem from the floor
Drape dignity around my shoulders
See the reasoning behind the doing
Probe gently at my faults
Brace my weakness
Look upon my face and read my soul
Accept me as I am
Yet grant me a place in her world through her
unending love.

Loraine Lewis

MY GIFT

Dedicated to Eliot

God made you for me in which to
share my life so I'm offering you
my heart. Please handle it with
care for it is so very fragile
and can break easily. My
heart holds an abundance of love
and compassion which I give to
you free from strings and expec-
tations that burden the soul. I
offer you the choice of if you
want to love me and the freedom of
yourself to be you with and aside
from me. I give you the loyalties
of a virgin soul instilled with
knowledge but untouched by pained
emotions. I ask only of you an
unrestricted love that will enable
us to grow together as one.
I give to you my heart.
I offer you my soul.

Starla Willett

WILLETT, STARLA ROSE. Born: Forks, Washington, 3-25-53; Single; Education: Background in Accounting; Occupation: Accounting Clerk; Poetry: 'Caring,' *American Poetry Anthology,* 1984; 'My Gift,' 1983, 'Before You,' 1985, 'Childhood Dream,' 1986, *Hearts on Fire, Vol. III,* 1986; 'Memories,' 1985. Comments: *I write from the heart. My poetry helps me express the emotions from the heart. Poetry is like a rose. As the bud turns into blossom the fragrance becomes sweet.*

THE HIDDEN KEY

And so I put
My heart away
In cushioned
Velvet box;
And hide the key
From awkward folks
Who tread it
With their mocks.

Mrs. Richard Schiller

DEAR RHONDA,

You never did a thing to me except make me feel good inside.
It wouldn't make any sense for my feelings to deny.
I cannot show you that I love you, but I can show
you that I care.
And if I failed to do this it would be more than I can bear.
I know you haven't told me but I can see it in your eyes.
I can make you feel very special, and this you cannot hide.
I've never had someone to bring me up when I'm down.
Nobody to bring a smile from a frown.
I know the thought of being lovers you wouldn't even begin.
So I want you to know, dear Rhonda, that in me
you forever have a friend.

Gregory LaGrange

THE CARD READ: "WHEN'S KID'S DAY?"

A tiny, saddened brown-eyed girl, holding up her armless dolly,
Gulped a choking, tearful request, "Can you fix her, Mommy?"
I did, and that was kid's day.

"Shall we have pancakes for breakfast?" "Oh, yes!"
"I want a Mickey Mouse." "Make me a squirrel." "Can you do an elephant?"
I did, and that was kid's day.

"Mommy, there's something big under my bed."
"Ah, I don't think so," I said; "let's look, and see — nothing.
Just shadows of little you and big me."
"Read me a story; then I'll go to sleep right away."
I did, and that was kid's day.

And she grew, my lovely sprite, and went to school,
Where volunteerism became the rule;
"We need some costumes, and I told the teacher, sure you'll make them."
"How many, Bron?" asked I. "Just twenty-four by Friday."
Make them I did, and that was kid's day.

Kid's day, for me — with love — every one,
To the level of my capacity
Till my capacity is done!

Irene Ladika White

A SPECIAL KIND OF PERSON

A special kind of person is one of many qualities:

A unique character with
an unconquerable enthusiasm for life.

One who seldom forgets and consequently is unforgettable.

Also living very much with others, for
it is improbable that one's heart is far from reach.

One who laughs, cries, listens and talks —
with, over, and for other people.

One who is consistently loyal, honest, considerate and trustworthy.

A special kind of person shares hopes, promises
and dreams, while anticipating others' also.

If someone is fortunate enough during their lifetime
to come across a person like this, behold this
precious gift close to the heart for it is rare.
I know because I have found this precious gift,
and this gift is you.

Susan A. Tanous

TENDER TRUTH

Thank you for the happiness you bring,
  the joyful song my soul to sing.
Bless you for the kind thoughts shared,
  and letting me know that you care.

Deep within this heart of mine,
  you are a friend divine.
Forever I dream and reminisce,
  over times we share like this.

The picture I now own of you,
  remains a treasure golden and true.
I love your short and curly hair,
  long and soft, I love your hair.

No matter how you wear your hair,
  it cannot change the way I care.
The chance to share these thoughts with you,
  remains a part of loving you.

Kenneth D. Senior

ONE MAN'S LOVE

He loved beauty,
The beauty of a silvery leaf
Fluttering in a gentle breeze
Or glimmering in the brightness of the sun;
Of a green tree
Spreading its branches skyward,
A slip of a flower, alone,
Or growing in dense colorful profusion.
He loved mighty things,
The beauty of high lofty peaks —
And higher — seemingly touching the heavens;
He loved all of nature, sunsets aglow with crimson,
Azure skies of gladness, or
Lazy clouds adrift in the blue.
He loved shimmering waters,
The quiet fishing streams,
The thrill of the pull on his taut line and the
Catch he displayed so proudly;
He loved the pureness of clean, fresh mountain air,
He clung to beauty with every breath of life.

Jennie B. Nye

TO EDWIN SIMMONS

Dear Dad, I see you through childhood eyes:
strength, care and love, not flesh, clothes and blood;
remembered tears
of joy and loss, the years
together; these and more.
Our time's not lost when we're apart;
you're with me always,
most in my heart!
We cannot regret
the fears and the tears
we cannot turn back —
let's remember the years
and sip them as wine
while we still have time —
the fragrance so fine,
ever yours, ever mine!
My poems are thoughts, and
feelings to save and treasure.
They bring us back
forever.

Joseph Simmons

Blue is the color of love.
Blue is the dark. The night with no sign of light.
Blue compared to black is death in its own right.
Blue is hate, and blue is fear.
Blue is shame. What a shame for these blue tender tears.

The unhappy man is blue, and no, it's not because of you.
It's because of becoming, of growing and learning,
  of knowing and not knowing.
It's because of a fantasy that once was so high
  he thought it would never come down.
Not just a fantasy but a love, an undefined love.
But now, now it's found, found deflating.
What a shame for his blue tender tears.

Blue is a color full of emotion.
Blue is dark and unpleasant.
And from this day on — Love shall be blue.
And again, it's not because of you
It's because of life and its everchanging moods.
It's because of day and night, fire and ice,
  it's because of you and me.

Samuel Robles

A PERFECT GIFT FOR JESUS

I've been pondering my whole life through,
A perfect gift for Jesus, nothing less will do.

The wise men of old gave frankincense and myrrh,
Others thought gifts of gold he'd prefer.

Worldly treasures have I none,
Worthy for a gift to God's own son.

I want a gift that won't rust or decay,
A gift that the world can't take away.

Then this thought came out of the blue,
He gave me love, so I'll give him love too.

True love won't tarnish, rust, or mold,
Its value outweighs silver or gold.

So a perfect gift for my Savior above,
Is a four letter word called L-O-V-E, Love.

Ina Price

IF

If I could tell you how I feel,
If I could say the words,
I might find paradise in your eyes
And a path to your heart.
If you could see the love in my eyes
Or feel the need in my soul,
You might take me in your arms
And love me like I do you.
If you could hear the loneliness in my voice
Each night I wake up screaming your name,
You might take away that loneliness . . .
And the screams for you.
If you could journey
Through the space in my heart
That is set aside especially for you,
You might stay there
And fill my emptiness forever,
But . . .
          You might walk away.

Monty Province

A LOVE SO TRUE

I see a fireplace
And you're there beside
me — holding me tight
And it's warm inside.
All through the night —
I'd see the sight
of you
And I can feel
You there beside me.
I find it so easy
To care for you
think of you
want you.
Frank, I love you.
It is with you
Where I want to be.
Why can't you see?
My love is strong.
With you, I want to belong.
Is that so wrong?

Debra L. Bradley

FRIENDS

Some friends come in early Spring
And leave with Winter's chill
But you are the one who touched my heart
And taught me how to feel

Some friends say they care so much
And smile with a frown
But you are one who loved my heart
And turned my life around

I wish you love to understand
That I've been hurt before
Come take my hand and you and I
Will walk some Summer's shore

And we don't mind past open wounds
As long as we are one
Come take my hand and we will know
Our new life has begun

Michael Steven Levitan

JUDY, PLEASE!

With eyes that twinkle like a star
And lips just made to kiss
A love like yours is all I need
That is what I wish

Hand in hand we walk the mile
To the edge of a sandy shore
Believe for sure in this my love
No one loves you more

Your hands are gentle, soft, and warm
Your beauty is beyond compare
A woman like you is hard to find
In this life or anywhere

In this world of material things
I have so little to give
No cars, diamonds, furs, or pearls
Just my love as long as we live.

Roy Fennell

SUMMER LOVE

Walking hand in hand
from summer dawn
through long blades of grass
where caterpillars sway.

Bees guide our steps, buzzing
atop golden daisies.
In our path a lilac bush
meanders the rocky stream.

Under the lilac a
grasshopper sits.
Safe from the sticky
tongued frog,
a croaking.

Where we sit hand in hand
in the shade of the lilac,
we dream. 'Til dusk fades,
another day.

Beverly A. Tadlock

UNTIL

Until the stars fall from the skies
Until the sun refuses to shine
Until the planets all collide
I will be in love with you

Until the polar icecaps are no more
Until the seas engulf the shores
Until the land falls beneath the sea
I will be in love with you

Until my body moves no more
Until my last breath escapes me
Until I am dead and gone
I will be in love with you

I am in love with you
Until all this comes true
Until we cease to exist
I will be in love with you
I am in love with you
Until

Daniel Corrigan

THE PORTRAIT

the white paper
became shades of grey.
darks became vivid pupils,
slightly mischievous
still twinkling.
the light spot on your nose
and forehead
shone
as if in summer's sun.
your hair
as disheveled as ever,
a slight rise to your eyebrows
as if wondering
what i'm up to.
the paper lost its whiteness.
darkness felt the
countours of your cheekbone;
the paper became you.

Natalie Larkin

TALK TO ME

Where does it all begin,
Does anyone really know?
Where is your love from,
Or where does it want to go?

I ask myself how you feel,
But just can't seem to find;
The answers I'm searching for,
Because I can't read your mind.

So open up; talk to me,
Let me know what to do.
Whether I should walk away,
Or whether to grow with you.

I want to grow with you,
To know you as you are.
Don't let time slip away,
We've got too much to share.

Dee Hedgecock

TONIGHT

Alone together
Under the quiet moon
Covered in a blanket of stars
Our hearts beat as one

The grass against our back
Our eyes — words
A gentle breeze
To rustle the hair from your face

Touching of bare skin
Rhythmic and beautiful
A smile is heard
A voice felt deep within

Roses replace your eyes
Our names written in midnight blue
Engraved in one another
The promise of Heaven

Jill Anderson

TRYING

I tried to write you a poem,
But the words wouldn't rhyme,
And you wouldn't find the meaning
Between the written lines.
I promised you a rose,
But the rose contained a thorn.
A rose should represent love,
Yet I feel so forlorn.
Perhaps I should write a letter
Telling you how I feel,
But you wouldn't understand
So my heart you couldn't steal.
I tried to finish the puzzle,
But the pieces wouldn't fit.
Through the troubled times
I never thought to quit.
I will keep on trying
To reach your soul and heart;
For you mean so much to me
I never want to part.

Laura Baker

LOVE BY THE SEA

It was love I found by the sea.
The rushing and swallowing of waves
Trying to cover the beach.
Walking on the light brown sand,
My love and I,
Looking with love to everything here.

The sand, the waves, the sea,
Children, parents, lovers, me,
Sailboats and rocks, friends and gulls,
All these are love, through eyes full of love.

Love came from the deepness of my heart,
Making its way to my mate.
My love with understanding,
Seeing how I felt,
Knowing what I meant at this time,
Answered, with the warmth of touch.

Dori Gehr

JOAN

You were like a yellow butterfly that touched my
eyes with fragile beauty.
You made life as kind as it should be; when letters
failed to reach you.
You are gone now, but in my heart you will be as
the sunsets are — colors in bloom.
You were gentle, gracious, charming, I love you in
memory as I touch the books you sent.
You will always be a rose with giant petals for all
who needed your love.
I read the poems you sent me, and find hope in them.
You were good at stirring my soul with love.
Never to hear your voice again is tearful, yet, I can
but feel your hand in mine.
My butterfly, as you dance across my mind, I see your
smile, and I smile.
Sleep peacefully, for you gave much and now GOD has
another angel to help chart HIS work.

Charlotte Bell

LOVE'S MERRY-GO-ROUND

To My Husband:

We stood and watched the Merry-go-Round,
A sea of colors, a delightful sound,
For a moment my mind drifted away,
Back a few years to our younger days.
Our love like a Merry-Go-Round,
Has had so many ups and downs.
Happiness, heartaches, joy and woe,
Yet for some reason we wouldn't let go.
Afraid at times our love was gone,
Still we kept holding on.
Even though the years have taken their toll,
Love seems different when you start to grow old.
Maybe the fire's gone but there's still a spark,
To be rekindled deep in the heart.
We're sure age brings the best love to be found,
Helps you get off the Merry-go-Round.

Barbara L. Clark

LOVE'S JOURNEY

Sailing through the tunnel of love
Via the Fallopian canal, secured,
A split embryo nestles into its mother's womb.
Growing comfortable side by side,
Occasionally kicking and pushing as they mature.
Who will be the first to spawn from
This darkened cove, gasp the sweet breath
Of air that a-sails their lungs with a cry of joy.
Rest on mother's breast to suckle
The aromous liquor of life.
Bow their heads when scolded,
Laugh merrily at play, catch the wild tide of
School, fight for each other's honor,
Seek their own being and taste the
Growing love that envelops them.
Though separated — are never alone —
Strong feelings transmitted silently
Unites them. They are one,
They are Identical.

Ruth Allshouse

E-V-O-L (Love Spelled Backward)

Love comes in many colors
Each person has his own meaning of another
Love is sharing
Love is caring
It could bring pain and sorrow
And a feeling of no tomorrow
Love is something like a brother
Something like the other
Something like a friend
But yet, deep within
But whatever love may be, it comes from the heart
And each person plays a part
Love is a fruit of life
And taking a bite is all right
Some say nothing lasts forever, but love itself
will never die
Through good times and bad, it will always survive
Because love is (spelled backward) E-V-O-L
Everlasting vibrations of life (EVOL).

Shirley A. Watson

I, YOU, WE

I am your conscience, I tell you what to do
I am a guitar, played only by you
You are my song, the melody I sing
You are a rhythm to which I cling
We are the birds in flight, and will be forever
We are the butterfly, and we walk together
I am an alarm, and you are mine
I am the fire, burning us blind
You are emotion, both happy and sad
You are my inspiration, and not half bad
We are the flowers, growing bright and tall
We are the winners, one day we will have it all
I am purple, I am blue
I am happy, to love only you
You are all the colors, I long to be
You are so special, love only me
We are the light, blending in harmony
We are forever
Us, you and me

Buffy Weaver

MY ROSEBUD

When I think of you my rosebud
I think of a baby who is wet behind the ears
A beautiful creature of youth and sophistication
Yet far behind your years.

You speak as if you've lived
In another time and place
And that your existence in this world
Is just another occupied space

Your experiences are many
Your years are few
Your innocence shows
In what you say and do

I watched you grow
I come to know
That you are a rosebud
That has far to go

Ginger C. Garrett

A FRIEND

A friend is someone to lean on.
To help you through it all.
A friend is someone who laughs with you,
And catches you when you fall.

A friend is one to trust,
One who cares for you.
One who understands,
The things you say and do.

A friend will laugh and cry,
And be with you each day.
And understands your feelings,
In each and every way.

A friend is like a highway,
One which never ends.
This is why I write my feelings to thank you,
For being my friend.

Donna Gerard

SO THIS IS LOVE

Love, young man? Now that you ask,
just what is love, do you think?
'A song in the heart,' is that it?
'A song with a lilt and a swing?'
'A heart full of wonders?' You must be hard hit —
Ah, and now you call it a 'sphinx!'
So, love does not speak, and love does not think;
So that's why you call it a sphinx.
My son, in this guise you explain in this wise?
Just hear what an old man thinks:
Young man, when in love you will speak —
Eloquent words the Great God gives
To the shy, the dumb and the weak.
Beautiful sonnets of song will spring
From a well of love and beauty within.
God is nearer, our bodies are dearer,
And love reigns supreme.
Accept it and cherish it, hold close to your heart,
And know it is right, the love of your life.
There, dear son, keep it safe from all strife.

La Rue Cooke Howard

WONDER/LOVE

From shining springs
To running water . . .
In sinks for dishes . . .
Toilet tissue/toilet bowl . . .
We travel through space
Pursuing stellar missions . . .
A nation full of wonder . . .
Yes, but do we love ? . . .

Being there
And seeing it happen . . .
A semblance of the people . . .
Walking hand in hand . . .
Singing arm in arm . . .
Protest signs and picnic baskets . . .
Tell the people/tell the world/telephone . . .
We move to project our global vision . . .
Yes, but do we ever really love ? . . .

Vanessa Floyd Abernathy

BROKEN HEART, CRY SOFTLY

Oh, broken heart, cry softly,
For all the shattered dreams, cry softly.
Your tender touch,
The soft caress, now lost . . .
In empty arms — shadowed now by the dark hands of time . . .
With tear-filled eyes, cry softly.
Angry words, drowning in troubled waters,
The light that no longer shines.
The laughter silenced,
The joys now gone,
Broken heart, cry softly.
Alone, never again to be,
One in being . . .
As two hearts softly held.
Where your image now lies, in smoldering embers,
For all the dreams of my yesterdays,
Oh, broken heart, cry softly . . .

Glenna Gardner-Wimett

A FRIEND IN ME

The kiss that assured your faith in me,
Where once you were blind, you lovingly see.
The memories once held by only you,
Now faithfully shared by only few.
Overwhelming joy with peace and relief
Have now settled your mind with true belief.

The friend you have in me is very real
Not something you think, but something you feel.
I'm singled out from many grains of sand;
I'll only be as far as an outstretched hand.

For to me, a friend is not a mere toy,
But someone to help you with problems and share
Laughter with in times of joy.

So when trials and heartaches won't let you be,
Just remember the friend you have in me.

Kenneth G. Miles

MEMORIES

Like looking in a shiny mirror —
Reflections of the past appear.
A time, a place — a face unfolds . . .
The beauty of a dream untold!

A girl — a boy, with youthful hopes,
Fun and laughter and little jokes.
Time spent together — always bright . . .
No one knew, it would end overnight!

The war came — the young man left . . .
She waved goodbye — and then she wept.
They were separated by many miles —
Lonely hours replaced their smiles!

Her faith and hope continued to burn —
But — her young man did NOT return.
The souvenirs are tucked away . . .
And in her heart, they'll always stay!

Life went on, and time has passed —
A futile dream that did not last.
Everything in life must change . . .
The future is always just out of range!

Clara E. Schauman

TRUE LOVE

Love is in your heart
But as deep as the sea
And it will never stop flowing
Once you have it
You have it
To get it
You must earn it
Just saying
I love you
Is not enough
You have to feel it

Daniel Guy Leonard

DOUBLE EMOTION

Should I ever start
To break your heart,
Give me words to understand
The meaning of your body's hand.

Or should I ever say goodbye
When you're feeling lonely,
Let me see a tear you've shed
To make me feel the only.

Just like the river runs,
I seek to feel free.
Whether it is always in your love
Or always only me.

Long ago a letter written,
An evening in the quiet night.
If it ever comes to me alone
I'll remember you in white.

Love we shared and treasured,
A moment never gone from sight.
Give to me now your reassurance,
Hold me, lift me with your woman's might.

G. K. Fredrickson

LOOKING FOR LOVE

Too many times
I've been searching
For someone to love.
I want to rise above
And what I feel
In my heart, is it real?

I've taken so much
And have lost touch
With all my friends;
Oh, how I pray
That, yes, someday
Somewhere, along the way
Love will find me.

Debra L. Bradley

AS THE SUN GIVES WAY TO THE MOON

In the light of the evening sun
The world bathed in a rosy glow,
I gaze at my beautiful son
As women have since time began.

As the sunbeams dance on his face
In the dying afternoon,
I think about life and death
As the sun gives way to the moon.

For him life is just a journey
But a journey that has to be made
I'll guide him all along the way
And far beyond the grave.

Jill E. Moseley

LOVE OR LUST

Promises made in the heat of the night
Broken before the light of day
Seesawing on the borderline
Between love and lust

Asking where one begins
Or the other ends
Learning to draw the line
As much as you draw the curtains

Trapped between the two
Can't decide which you want
Versus that which you need
They're both so pleasantly painful

Eric Knight

I know the world is screaming for us,
it doesn't matter anymore.
We'll ignore the telephone,
and the door
in hopes of just a minute more,
stolen for ourselves.
We'll gather all our passion
to sustain us another day,
until the world, again,
allows us time
for our nights of secret play.

Felicia Morgan

MATTHEW

While you were falling
Did your seven years pass you
As quickly
As they passed me?
Did you see all those you touched?
Did you count the lives you brightened
In so few years?
Did you know
One small boy's head
On stone
Would hurt so much
So long?

Mark J. Keaney

RAPACIOUS HEART

Articulately brandished words of love
Upon the theme of sacrifice
Erupt from tight maternal lips
Of her who deeply longs to wear
The hairshirt cape of martyrdom,
Who calls on earth below and heaven above
To witness its devotion, while
The object of that mothering
And iron-handed dominance
Dreams daily of escaping from
That cannibal rapacious heart
Which boldly masquerades as doting love.

Mauricia Price

FOREVER TO LOVE

Forever is a long time
to be away from you
when I hold within my heart
a love that's more than true
Forever is a long time
to miss the love we shared
but at least I have my memories
of those times you cared
Yes — forever is a long time
to live with a broken heart
and that's how it will always be
as long as we're apart

Jim McDermott

PRECIOUS VALENTINE

You are my precious valentine
on which my life depends,
And each day I humbly pray
the hours will never end;
For in this world of richness,
of beauty, hope and peace —
I need you so my darling,
our love must never cease;
But grow each day as we cling
to happiness we know —
So be my special valentine,
I just love you so!

Marge E. Jones

DESERT HYMN

Desert summer, evening falling,
Sun is setting, shadows crawling
Overlaying gold and blue
With a deep and purple hue.

My eyes lift skyward,
Praising, blessing,
When a gift of Grace compels me,
There, above the sand's soft shifting.
Sea birds dance,
Their white wings lifting,
Circling 'round, rising, bowing,
As in praise and prayer, avowing
Their Creator, God in Heaven, for His care.

As toward home they make their way,
Yearning for the salty sea,
Wonder how, in summer feeding,
They had found this path, misleading,
Miracle had placed them there,
Music for my evening prayer!

Margaret S. Matthews

ON A NIGHT LIKE THIS

My heartstrings tighten on a night like this
the sea so calm, the sands so warm and white
the moon glowing with radiant light
a scene that artists dream to paint.

On a night like this as I linger here
in another time, another year
memories buried deep in time
creep from the recesses of my mind
sear, burn, ache and bind.

Please do not reproach me if you see
an uncontrolled tear spring to my eyes.
On a night like this pangs of regret
return to torture and torment.
On an exact night like this I vainly misconstrued
a sweet but fleeting interlude.

Edith Gulish

NO FEELINGS

You don't know how much you have hurt me
You don't know how much I cared
You don't know how I feel
When you say the feelings are not there

I've tried many times to forgive and forget
You keep running through my head
So many times I have regrets
And others have not been met
You are not easy to forget

Although you have hurt me
I will never forget the times we shared
If only you knew how much I cared
Maybe that's why you left me
And said the feelings were not there

You don't know how much I tried to love you
You don't know how much I tried to care
But I know it's over now
When you told me that there are no feelings there

Donna L. Russell

THOUGHTS

A rose is but a gift of God —
Beautiful, delicate, yet strong in nature.
Your friendship is God's gift to me --
Warm, tender and always treasured.
Speak to me from the depths of your soul
and I will listen quietly.
I will take each thought and contemplate —
then give back to you my love.
For it is of you I speak with love and
admiration. Pure thoughts and words do I give,
nothing imitation.
Listen to my words and you will hear my silence,
Listen to my silence and you will understand.

Lynn Walsh

THOUGHTS ON OUR GOLDEN ANNIVERSARY

Those many years ago we were talking about Love
and wondered
If it was the consuming white heat of passion, extolled
by the bards in myriad books of verse and prose
or was it
A solitary spark that must be gently fanned to full flame,
sustaining hope through endless uneventful days
or maybe
The comforting warmth of softly glowing embers, encircling
and protecting from the dark unknown
But, oh my Darling, we really always knew
Love is Any of these
Love is All of these

Wilma LaMott Fleming

FORBIDDEN LOVE

Forbidden love, that poignantly
Pervasive witchery, inflames
The mind as little else can do
And renders its imbiber-victims strong
Enough to stand alone, to hold
Each other far more tenderly . . .
Because they know full well four-fifths
Of all the world would say, "Your love is wrong."
That pair live haunting lyrics they
Create — admixtures of their joy
And pain, their dearest hopes and dreams —
Which echo in their melancholy song.

Mauricia Price

WHILE YOU'RE AWAY

Lonely are the days while we are apart
Longing for the day we never have to part.
So long and so empty — days that never end.
In a letter every day to you my love I send.
How can one be so sad or happy in the same
sign;
Or smile in between the tears that I try
not to cry?
I only know I love you and want to be by
your side,
And when we are together, I'll take back
these tears I cried.

Kathleen L. Spicher

A GIFT OF GOD

A child is born — A Gift of God
And the World smiles its pleasure.
This child of God will enrich your life
And bring you Joy beyond measure.

In naked splendor, children enter our lives —
They come wearing only Love.
No cares have they for worldly things
They come from Heaven above.

Your purpose for them is to clothe and feed,
And guide them as they grow;
And point their feet upon the path
That God would have them go.

In fulfilling this task set forth for you,
You bathe them in Love every day.
A child is born — A Gift of God —
And God will show you the way.

Rosalie Steele Bolene

BECAUSE OF YOU

This morning, my darling, I walked outside,
To give space to a love I cannot hide.
I suddenly saw your face in mind's eye.
And breathed so deeply that there escaped a sigh.
I stood in awe of the ethereal skies so blue,
All this, my darling, because of you.
There was a time when life was drear,
But that was very long ago, my dear.
Oh, my darling I knew pain
When I sought, I thought, in vain,
For a love they said, did not exist
But they were wrong for now I've been kissed
By your lips and now I know
A love that will not, cannot let me go.
As long as there's earth and sky above,
I must know we'll have our love.
My heart cries out, "Know this to be true,
Without this man my life is through."
Yet in your love I live anew,
All this, my darling, because of you!

Wanda Wade

LOVE-RUN

Above me dark forest presses all around
behind come harsh howlings of Human and hound.
I must keep on running, must not let them see
My wounded Love hidden 'neath fallen pine tree.

Lord of the Forest let me not run too fast
so the Hunters turn back to find my dearest at last.
Don't let them overtake me before I have led
Death far from the forest where my lover has bled.

I ache for my lost dreams, breathless I fly
on the path we once wandered 'neath the branches' soft sigh.
Now those same branches cut me as I race through the break . . .
Let the Hunters pursue me for my only Love's sake

I crash through the brushline, I make sure they hear . . .
Lord of the forest drive back my fear.
Where the meadow streams sunlight I break and they see . . .
Thunder! . . . I'm falling! . . . My Love you are free! . . .

Shellie Colleen Reese

SPECTRAL LOVE

Today I awoke . . .
and took a drink from the fountains of love
for I had kissed your beckoning lips

Next . . .
I caressed a delicate blossoming rose
for it was then . . . that I touched you
and embraced the softness of your body

But alas . . .
my happiness was a short lived one
as darkness came upon me . . . and I awoke
only to find you gone

And then you awoke
and with your awakening
brought an end to my existence

For you see . . .
"I" was only a dream
and in the world of reality
there's no place for a dream to exist
except in a person's heart or mind . . .

Lin Eric Brown

REUNITED LOVE

The chiming of the old tower clocks
Has found her among the hollyhocks
Opening a cherished redwood box.

Hidden treasures were then revealed
Reflecting the light when unconcealed;
Rekindling pain time has not healed.

I saw her bow her snow-white head.
Her cheek held a tear she had shed.
I wanted to run, but I stayed instead.

In her slight hand I saw her hold
A bronze medallion shining and bold.
Her past she held, I was later told.

'Twas the Medal of Honor she held so tight,
As I left her alone in the pale moonlight;
Never to see her again after that night.

To her knight she was faithful and true.
She was found in forget-me-nots heavenly blue;
As cold and as white as a marble statue.

Cilla C. Carpenter

UNSPOKEN

You smiled at me and I was captured by the intensity of
your stare
You spoke only with your eyes and they told truths we both
dared not speak . . .
I become flushed as your unspoken words penetrate my
thoughts
And we become mesmerized in this moment . . .
There is only silence — for we both dare not break the
spell.
This is the moment! lost forever in an untouchable feeling.
My eyes turn away and reality emerges in stillness
As thoughts of what might have been though never spoken
Become part of two souls sharing a moment — lasting forever.

Cheryl Butler

A YESTERYEAR'S LOVE

She was female and Angelic in an extraordinary
way.
With lucky spheres of romance soothing passions
straightaway.
Like comparing the modern diesels, and their
awesome powerful feel.
To the live steam engines of long ago that made
our history real.
With entwined legends of drama, its love and
emotions now read.
About rugged lives and romances, the pioneer
women often had.
With sensuous lips upturned, their moistening
and puckering done.
Calmly awaiting the kisses, and the loving
that's bound to come.

Lee Ross Bailey

WHEN LOVE AWAKES

When love awakes at gentle break of day
And hears a voice of warm softly say,
"You are the sweetness of the air I breathe
You are the drink of life I daily need;"
Then you will know as know you must
That you have found a treasured trust
And all the roses bright with dew
Are like diamonds I want for you.
When love awakes with dawn's rosy glow
And speaks like sun on melting snow
You are the warmth of Spring to me
Brightening with life everything I see
And now I understand why flowers bloom
Why you and I have conquered doom:
For all the holocausts of hell
Cannot destroy our love from Christ's deep well.

Norman J. Hansen

LOVE AND TIME UNITED

Love keeps its own Records
And knows its own Time,
For even at the very moment of Time's beginning,
And before, All was Conceived out of Love
And, indeed, for the very sake of Love.
And so there came to be a Passing and
Love and Time realized their Creations.
It is in that very Passing of Love and Time,
From what It Was, to what It Is and Will Be,
That Love reveals the Secret Deeds of its Guardians
And gives, in like, undeniable explanations of
The Sacred Teachings of Concept, itself.
It is there also, in that Passing,
Where the records of Time
Tell of a Promised and Eternal Bond
Between Love and Time United.

Suzanne L. Reed

LOVING

It's a gift so kind
It's caring & sharing, a gift divine
It's exquisite & exciting, honest & proud
It's trusting & sensitive, tender & warm
It's vibrant & healthy, in a world so torn.

David McLaughlin

A POEM FOR BUBBA D.

You say, I know how to make you want me.
Baby, that might be true.

I could tell you I don't want to be free,
I want to belong to you.

I could take you home and make you mine,
That's what I'd like to do.

Then my life would be just fine,
Revolving around me and you.

Like a merry-go-round, another ride
That's how we seem to be.

My love for you, I cannot hide,
It's me I want you to see.

Will you give to me, the rest of your life?
'Til death do us part, we'll stay.

But first, you have to make me your wife.
From you I would never stray.

Oh! How I hope that you want me
Like I really want you, too.

I love you like I've loved no other
And I wrote this poem to show you it's true.

D. Gayle Hart

TO SAMMY

The day was dark; the road was long;
My troubles multiplied.
It seemed that everything went wrong.
Then you were by my side.

I needed someone very near
To tell my troubles to;
Yet never found a friend so dear
Till I sat down with you.

You laughed with me when I was glad,
You sighed when I was blue;
And when I'd need the talks we had,
That's what you needed, too.

And if I got into a fuss
You'd always take my part.
We had such fun — the two of us —
You finally won my heart.

I loved you dearly — tenderly,
My heart with yours entwined.
I knew a finer friend for me
I'd never ever find.

Though many years have passed since then
My thoughts, to you, have strayed
Since we — sweethearts of "way back when"
Were in the second grade.

Judy Goodman

UNNATURAL DEPARTURE

Why is there no respite from the storm?
Why does it seem there will never be a norm?
No, my feelings just won't adjust.
They won't conform.

She won't ever come back.
There is no returning from where she has gone.
She left behind all of her things.
Except for her precious rings.

So here I sit in my mortal remains.
Locked in my vault of aches and pains.
Time goes by with miles of ink.
No matter what, all I can do is think.

I will learn to do it, somehow I will.
Memories of her, time can never kill.
The strength she possessed was truly unique.
Everything up front, nothing tongue-in-cheek.

I used to say, "I can skate better than I can walk."
Now I just realize, I can think better than I can talk.
But she was all I had.
Now what?

Matthew V. Moore

MOTHER, WHY?

I wish my pen could find the answers.
Is it mightier than the sword?
Why doesn't my stereo have more solutions?
Why can't my coffee maker produce resolutions?

If I could only figure out why she had to leave,
It would help me live, and help me breathe.
It might help me, not to grieve.
It would let me continue to perceive.

She had to go early.
She didn't want to go and she told me that!
She had me and I was part of her.
I was part of her and she was part of me.

I know where I came from and that was her.
She taught me things with so many meanings.
She had lessons for everyone, just by being.
You could learn from her, just by seeing!

I am so lucky to have known her.
So lucky to have grown with her.
She just lived, she knew life!
And she was the best teacher I could ever have had.

Matthew V. Moore

LOVE'S FLOW

My love for you is
As the waters of the earth,
Hidden in its infancy,
Growing, until it comes bubbling forth;
Limited yet vibrant
As it pushes ahead through stubborn obstacles;
Gathering force,
Becoming an uncontrollable impulse,
Wildly growing and rushing onward
Until love enshrouds the body,
As water encompasses the earth.

Ann Ogle

VALENTINE

Valentine greetings, so I have been told
Are sent by young lovers, or others not old.

But how do you judge then the age of the girl
With a softly-lined face, and a silver-toned curl?

If healthy and happy in fall or in spring
Tho birthdays are many, they don't mean a thing.

Tho old Father Time there, comes pacing along
We turn a deaf ear, for we don't like his song.

My Valentine greetings with love I enfold
To my only wife, who will never be old.

Wilmer Wilcox

EASTER MORNING

My spirit wanders off today to be with you my love.
I cannot think of you as gone; but only up above.
I see you in the sunshine on this glorious Easter morn.
So young and fair I see you there, you are not tired and worn.

Only in your happiness, with beginnings ever new.
You had such zest for life my love, you can't be gone not you.
I know for me you're waiting there, I feel you beckon me,
I'd like to take your hand in mine this Easter morn to see.

We shared so many others, on the hillsides far away
And watched the sun as it arose to start the Easter day.
I pray for strength to walk alone, until I meet you there.
Then when I do there will be more of Easter morns to share.

Minnie Fargo

SONNET XLVI

Mine eye and heart are at a mortal war,
How to divide the conquest of thy sight;
Mine eye my heart thy picture's sight would bar,
My heart mine eye the freedom of that right.
My heart doth plead that thou in him dost lie,
A closet never pierced with crystal eyes,
But the defendant doth that plea deny,
And says in him thy fair appearance lies.
To 'cide this title is impanneled
A quest of thoughts, all tenants to the heart;
And by their verdict is determined
The clear eye's moiety and the dear heart's part:
As thus; mine eye's due is thine outward part,
And my heart's right thine inward love of heart.

William Shakespeare

LEFT BEHIND

Fame skyrocketing him to the top
Soon his loved ones will be forgot
In money and pleasure he does abound
But family and friends are not around
Who does he turn to when everything shatters
Will there be anyone to whom it matters
Love dies slow, but die it must
When thirst for affection turns to rust
Times were better before his ambition
Love was better, in the olden tradition

Patricia C. Scuderi

TWILIGHT

Here we are
Two shooting stars,
Moving in a world
So wide and far,
Then suddenly we collide,
Like two rockets
In the sky.
We burst into flames,
Then slowly fade,
Only to appear
Again,
As a single star
That shines above,
Proclaiming the unity
Of our love.

Roxanne McJunkin

Where does fantasy begin?
Through reality's iron-like
grasp
we steal moments
of fantasy
and it is because of fantasy
we see ourselves as
we can never be
invincible
immortal
While Pan plays his lute,
I walk towards
you and I live out
my fantasy.
Oh such ecstasy
and idle merriment
and bliss . . .

Pamela Wagers

BELIEF BEYOND MEASURE

The grace of Love lies in
the essence of its being.
It cannot be restrained,
confused or found wanting.
In the mist of regret, uncertainty
or in envy nor remorse.
A poetess asks, "How do I love thee?"
and a welling tribute rises
In reply, so tender so poignant
and removed from guile and doubt,
That we feel the omniscience of a
trust bestowed and freely given.
We are assured.
We are loved.
We are loving.

Graydon E. Spalding

TAPESTRY

You've embroidered my heart
With golden thread;
Like ornate stitching
On an ancient scroll.

Now, beautifully adorned
In hues of gold and red,
Is your lovely tapestry
On my soul.

Frank Favaro

FANTASIES

To caress, to touch and yea to kiss and embrace is love's delight
Such is a passing night and so why not it be?
Yet in truth if such is such, these are but dreams and fantasies
for these who missed their boat in days gone by.
But alas they dream their dreams of love and nay! a little more?
And pray their prayers that such may come to pass.
But yet 'tis not the case and so they dream and dream and pray and pray.
And who but knows the hour except the gods that play such games
with mortals like the likes of me and you.
Alas when all is said about such dreams, some may say such
dreams are dreams of dreamers and their likes.
Yet we who missed our boat do dream such dreams as mortals
always have and nay to these who think such dreams are dreams
of foolish dreamers or their likes.

Harry Khosrofian

IN YOUR DAUGHTER'S EYES

As I take this opportunity, Mom, to tell you how much you're loved,
I realize rather quickly, that it's just not done enough.
Though words could never quite explain, how much you mean to me,
I'm going to try them anyway, and hope I will succeed.

Mother, I love you with all my heart and I have right from the start,
The greatest Mom, you are to me, that's ever been or ever will be.
Your presence here, has been so dear, to others far and others near,
That it's no wonder, I am better, to be your daughter and you my mother.

Your love for God and people too, shows in all the things you do,
The way you always give your best, in helping others not so blest.
Your life has been a guiding light, that shines within the darkest night,
This world has been a better place, to have you in the human race.

Betty Sue Curtis

WHEN THERE'S NO ONE LEFT

Whom do you love when there's no one left, no one left at all?
Whom do you turn to when there's no one left, no one left at all?
You cry behind the door of your room and sigh at the lovers on the
street when there's no one left, no one left at all.
And where are all your friends when there's no one left,
no one left at all?
Who will hold you when you're lonely when there's no one left,
no one left at all?
Who will cry for you when you're gone when there's no one left,
no one left at all?

Randell Patterson

THE WAY YOU LOOK TONIGHT

The way you look tonight is far beyond compare.
Your lips so moist and tender and your beautiful, long, soft hair.
Your figure so perfect and your face so divine.
The way you look tonight means I'm going to make you mine.

I love your eyes that shine like stars against the darkened sky.
I love your touch so soft and gentle that it causes me to sigh.
When I see you smile at me it melts away my heart.
The way you look tonight means that we will never part.

The way you look tonight is a vision that all should see.
I want them all to know my dear that you belong to me.
We will always be together. I'll never set you free.
The way you look tonight means that we will be together dear throughout eternity.

David W. Perry

WHO ARE YOU?

Who are you to make me feel inadequate, sharing the
reflection in the same mirror
And to make my heart beat so hard just because you walked near?
Speaking but one word of greeting you make my eyes
prisoners of your face.
I could not take my gaze off you as long as I was in that place.

Who could you be but just a face that seems to hold the
beauty of soulmate?
Why must I worship you with my eyes when this is only a
passing state?
Who are you to make me wonder if I am where I really want to be
if you're just a stranger passing that I will never again see?

Who are you to make me look but only to where you stood
pulling me toward you with the same gaze as much as you could?
How could someone I just saw make me feel so much so fast
could one glance bond two souls with love that will always last?

Robert Blakeman

LOVE NEVER, EVER DIES

The first time we gazed into each other's eyes
We welcomed each other's heart with fortune
Together we chanced a virtuous breath of love
We walked hand and hand for some time
And united, stood at the top of the world for a while
We believed in a future that had no end
And promised if, just if, our hearts would need a time apart
We would always remain friends
But I knew that would never happen to us
Dissolution could never happen to us I thought
Until now.
I did love you once
And in a very special way I still do
Just as the future lasts forever
My love for you will too.
I've always believed in one thing —
"Love may not always be forever
But love never, ever dies."

Dawn A. Dierks

IF I COULD, I WOULD GIVE YOU A MOUNTAIN

If I could, I would give you a mountain,
So you could see its snowy peak.
If I could, I would give you the ocean,
So you could hear the roaring of the sea,
But I can't give you that mountain,
Because a mountain is way out of my reach.
And no, I can't give you the ocean.
Because the ocean is far beyond my wildest dreams.
But I can give you treasures.
Treasures worth more than that old mountain,
Because a mountain is way out of my reach.
And I can give you a rainbow,
More beautiful than the roaring sea.
Those treasures are my kisses,
And that rainbow is my love.
Yes, I can give you a fortune,
Worth more than a pot of gold.
I can give you love.

Peggy Kendrick Clements

RESTLESS LOVE

Love, oh love,
you've got me restless for your love

My heart is knocking away with sorrows,
my joy is kicking away with pains of tomorrow.

Oh, love, my love,
you've got me restless.

I can't sleep at night
because my dreams are empty.

I'm so restless for your love.

You've got me suffering with tears.
My eyes shedding wet drops against my pillow.

You hurt our dream, a precious dream of tomorrow
with a precious life that's real.

My love is so restless without you.
My whole life is filled with unhappy blues.

Oh love, my restless love,
you're like a star that brightens up my life.

You are my sweet and precious moment of the night.
Your love will always stay in my heart forever.

Allen J. Solomon

WHITE MAN

You rule the world.
Only you can become President of the United States
and turn important deals on Wall Street.
I emerged from the ghetto and worked by your side.
I've accomplished more than I'm supposed to — for a woman
with such odds against me.
Yet you don't revere me or put me on a pedestal.
I never receive red roses any more.
Off in the distance, the dark man sees the blonde and
the blue always denied until now.
It's his turn for the prize that you neglected in your
haste to achieve
The American Dream.

Melody Ocheltree

OCHELTREE, MELODY. Born: Torrance, California, 1948; Education: Cal. State University, Long Beach, B.A. in English, 1971; Poetry: 'Lost Treasure,' *American Poetry Anthology*, July, 1986; Themes: *Life, love and death.*

THE LOVERS QUARREL.

THE LOVERS RECONCILIATION.

PRAYING ON MY LOVE

I'll take a good girl anytime.
Her countenance gives her away.
I'll take a good girly any day.
Fresh from her closet of prayer.
You may be X to many things but
You're not X to God. Got your knee in
My heart just a praying on it little woman of
God.
Your showers of blessing are bringing me
to understanding Thee.
Got your knee in my heart just a praying on it.
Little woman of God.
I know where I'll find you, YES! I
know where. I know where I'll find you.
Yes! I know for sure where I'll find you.
Fresh from your closet of prayer.

Faith Kennedy

KENNEDY, FAITH. Born: Cumberland, Ohio, 1-28-35; Married, eleven years; divorced, fifteen years; Education: High school diploma from Colorado Springs; Occupation: Housekeeper for elderly, so I can write; Awards: Third place winner in the Martin Luther King Jr. Colorado Inaugural Contest, 1986; Poetry: 'He Won't Notice Her,' Tin Pan Alley, 1985; 'Don't Want to Wait to be Burned,' Tin Pan Alley, 1986; 'I'm a Country Rain Dear,' *Holiday Magic,* Magic Key, 1985; 'I'm Nobody's Guinea Pig,' *Counter Magic,* Magic Key, 1985; 'Yesterday's Pie,' Royal Masters, 1985; Comments: *After seventeen years of trial, I just got good in 1984. I produce in big volume about every five years. I hope when I write again in 1989 to be better. I foolishly destroyed all my writings except enough for a book I wrote in 1979,* The Cake That Fell. *Of course I saved those after 1984 and I have a lot of back up.*

SUPERMAN

Let it be written, let it be known
Thy speciation of Superman hath evolved to fruition,
Spired past thy seeds of genius sown
Thine eclectically consummated love's willful desideration . . .

Tris A. Legacy

MYSTERY OF LIFE IS LOVE

What would life be without love?
Like a dark day without light from above,
Like a faded and withered rose,
Or as a dry brook that no longer flows.

Without Love the night would be bleak and long.
Life, without Love, would be like a bird without song,
Like the emerald lawn that is parched and dead,
A hearth fire without a glow, a pit of fiery red.

Love knows no bounds, time, nor place.
Love is a song, mystery, a glowing face
Of an aged woman, man, a baby, small child,
As deep as the ocean, knows no bounds, is mild.

Young lovers, with innocence, know love
With flames of passion inspired from above.
Love is forgiving, enduring and ever present
In all beauty of the universe and all that's pleasant.

Perry W. England

LOVE'S MIRACLE

(to a friend on her coming marriage)

Love, the wizard-tailor,
Another miracle has wrought:
Into one living pattern
Two separate lives he's brought,
Two separate strands together spun
Now by love's magic wonder
Inseparably one.
Not death, nor life, nor circumstance
Can love's new union sunder;
Each strand th'other will enhance,
With God's grace grow in splendor.
More strong, more rich each passing year,
Endowed with love and wonder,
Life's storms with all their cares and tears,
Their heartaches, shadows, sorrow,
Will only serve to show more clear
The radiance of love's rainbow,
The richness of their love.

Alexander Hollands Edwards

GRANDMOTHER, I LOVE YOU

There are times when I just can't let go
Although in heaven you are, I know
Then I realize, you are in peace
And my pain and sorrow, I then release
A part of you, I'll always be
That will never be taken from me
Even to the end, you were always strong
But how will I find the strength to carry on?
I know we all are on borrowed time
So I'm thankful for that while you were mine
And I will always cherish the memories you left behind
To the world, we are given and taken away
When I am called, I too must obey
For my mother, father, sisters and brother, I pray
That we will all unite in heaven someday
It's not goodbye, it's until we meet again
And may God give us the strength to accept the life
you have begun
Grandmother, I love you
Yet your words are silent, they say, "I love you too."

Shirley A. Watson

OUR OWN WORLD

No music is heard
there are no people passing by —
bumping our chairs.
The noises of people chattering are ignored.
I find it hard to even recognize
my own actions.
I concentrate on you alone.
I stare into your eyes that stare
back at me, and they seem to be
saying so much to one another.
I feel so secure when I'm with you —
nothing else matters around me.
We are in our own romantic world,
And although it is silent —
It says more than any of the people
around us could ever say!

Karla Kay Rollins

SPECIAL TOUCH

Walking you home, after school, in the spring
Was a pleasure, indeed, with a delicate ring.
Wrapping my arm, with the sweetest warm hold,
Kissing my lips, at just sixteen years old.
Yes . . . you were different.

Kirk N. Galatas

MOM, REMEMBER

Mom, remember the tree you helped me plant?
Well you should see it now.
It's bloomed into a glorious thing
That shows my love for you.
I've tasted of its fruit,
And have grown a little too.
And now that you are gone,
I wish that you could see,
The tree that's grown and bloomed and flourished
And see what life can be.
Your light shines through each passing day,
To carry me through the night.
And I can see you watching,
Your small seed that's now a tree,
Hoping for a seed to drop,
To watch a new tree grow.

Judy Tuttle

MY GRANDDAUGHTER

She rushes in the door with
Smiling face and flying hair
Her coat lands on the couch,
Her books upon a chair
She's heading for the kitchen
That means an empty belly
First she grabs the peanut butter
Then a glass of good grape jelly
She closes the peanut butter jar
Then she smiles and says,
"Tell me where the cookies are."
Quickly grandma grabs the cookies and a drink
Then I get a kiss quicker than a wink
Little arms around me make me oh so glad
I've just found out that growing old is not so very
Bad.

Charlotte West

TRUE LOVE

True love is not selfish. You've proven
this to me.

True love doesn't intentionally hurt, as I'm
beginning to see.

True love is your loving me when I am
at my worst.

True love meant your precious sacrifice in putting
my needs first.

True love for me didn't come with time. It was there
right from the start.

True love is expressed by your words from the desires
of your heart.

Francene Phillips

A RAISIN SUN: LOVE LOVE LOVE: DO NOT FEEL SO ALL A LONE

You shall know the truth
The truth shall set you free
A wake America
Cray on America
Love love love
Choose life
The token is the land
A Mystic freight train O Hi O
How to fly Trans World love
Experience the air breathe free
Poor huddled Masada
Lettuce have our daily bread
Boy cott grapes
I cheer the rising tide
Sun up sun down
The rain
I do not plan on going solo
I see I believe I doubt I know I trust
Stormy weather: Mr. Motto takes a H O L I D A Y

Tell all the world: these eyes have seen the rain

Edward M. Giannattasio

I DON'T UNDERSTAND

Peace is something I hold so dear
Peace on earth, it should be here
The absence of peace is something to fear
Why can't people live in peace?
I can't explain it because I don't understand
Why people can't live in peace.

Peace was meant right from the start
Peace has got to come from within your heart
Loving is caring, caring is sharing love
Why can't people live and love?
I can't explain it because I don't understand
Why people can't live and love.

You know our time is getting tight
We'd better wake up and start doing things right
We've got to learn how to love and forget how to fight —
Oh, why can't people share the world
With every man, every woman, every boy and girl?
I can't explain it because I don't understand
Why people can't share the world.

Linda Kay Gault

ALONE

Oft some traveler in the night wishes the moon would never rise,
Nor providential hand light the candle in the skies.
For they bring to remembrance love's raveled dream,
A fireside bright with hope where lovelight chanced to gleam.
As quickly the empty seasons now come and go,
His freedom he would give for the chains of love he used to know.
He longs to wear the crown the hand of love bestows,
For gentle lips to kiss away the heartache that seldom shows.
The silver of his wings he would exchange for a heart of gold,
And the warmth of a tender touch for he is growing old.
Few have been his successes, and fewer yet his friends,
The wasted years like ashes are blowing in the winds.
His brow will deceive you with its look of repose,
For loneliness is the only companion that he knows.
His eyes that sparkle with seeming pleasure's glow,
Are shining from repentant tears that will not flow.
His ballad fills the land with a bittersweet melody,
As he sings about the joys of being free.
His songs are the cries of a heart without a home,
That through the barren years has drifted all alone.

Billie Jean Henry

HENRY, BILLIE JEAN. Born: Tyler, Texas, 9-26-37; Single; Education: Spencer Business College, General Business, 1956; Occupation: Staff Assistant; Memberships: Christian Poetry Association of America; Themes: *Positive, uplifting themes.* Comments: *Writing poetry allows me to rise above the disappointments and heartaches of life and see beyond temporal things. The beauties of creation: a breathtaking sunrise, a butterfly on the wing, a robin in the springtime, a rainbow after the storm, the love of a faithful friend are treasures and bring gladness to our hearts and renew our spirits. I strive for my poetry to bring a message of renewal, hope, and joy to the hearts of my fellow man.*

LOVE IS A DISEASE

HONORABLE MENTION

Yes, it is.
It comes and goes unannounced.
It often gets in the way of our best interests.
For every heart it nurtures, it breaks two.
It is our only hope.

Donald Hawkins

US KIDS

Fast and hard the rain fell one afternoon,
Then a rainbow in lovely color, spread across
Heaven;
My sister and I yet of tender age, had thought
To look for the rainbow's end, there was to be
Gold in a pot.
We followed it as it shone through the old
Church windowpane, and on to the mourner's
Bench, that was the end, yet we saw nothing.
Lucy and I quickly fell on our knees, for we
Remembered what we were taught:
The treasure is to pray at the mourner's bench,
Pure treasure is not gold in a pot.
With a bang, the old church door opened and shut,
In bounced Barney, Violet, Cordell, and Bud,
All looking for the rainbow's end, when they
Realized the truth, each little knee at the
Bench did bend.
Little children yet young and sweet, not old
Enough to hate, trusting little hearts you see
Is what Christ meant when he said:
Have the little children come unto me.

Polly Wiggins Crum

CRUM, POLLY WIGGINS. Pen Names: Polly & Katie; Born: Bellaire, Ohio, 10-7-19; Married: 1-20-42 to Albert W. Crum, 1 son Albert, and Katie, his wife; Education: Shut in, education from bible 50 years; Occupations: Housewife, Toy Maker, Bible Teacher and Mother; Awards: Recording award, 'The Lady is My Love,' 5 Star Music Masters; Poetry: 'Mother's Face,' 'Life After Death,' 'Wheel of Life'; Other Writings: "God Don't Junk Grandma," record; *Bird With Broken Wing,* book; Comments: *I have had help with my work, from 4 brothers, Bud, Barney, Ikie and Cordell. Also my 3 sisters have been a help, Lucy, Violet and Patty. Ikie and Patty are now deceased. With a large family, and help from God, I have lots to write about and love it. I have written 200 poems and Katie has helped with 100 more.*

LITTLE EDWARD

I was eight, and proud as can be, when little Edward,
ran up to me . . . when he saw the toy guns, belted 'round me,
his eyes lit up, like some Christmas tree.

It's not easy to explain, his feelings for me, if there were
Angels in Heaven, they must be like he . . . there was something
in his eyes, that only I could see, as he skipped up the
street, holding tight to me.

It was the first time I saw him, that awed me so, for
surrounding his figure, I perceived a glow, that was quite
a bit softened, by the winter's snow.
A weird sensation crept over me, that the glow I saw,
wasn't intended, for my eyes to see.

To give him my toys, was no sacrifice for me, considering
the premonition pervading me . . . but I couldn't go, if it
was meant to be, and leave him behind, without something
from me. But fate decreed, that it wasn't to be, for a
short while later . . . it was he who left me.

Arthur D. Posa

WHEN TWILIGHT FALLS

When Twilight falls, and casts its long, lazy
shadows across the high garden walls, and the
weary wild bird, flying to rest, to his sleepy mate
calls; there by the misty waterfall I remain;
With the one I love most of all; It is with
Deep feeling, I find, loving someone is real
To me, so there I linger awhile, beneath a
Kind, old, weeping willow tree; for tomorrow
I know I will be busy as a honey bee;
Just as busy as I can be; and as the full
Moon shrugs off the shadowy, cloudy
Shroud, I think of the friendly bond I share
With my fellow workers each day; and with
Them a few happy moments to spare; and
Of these friends, I am most proud; you see
They are just a small part of the vast
Daily crowd; for they like me, with strength,
Truth, and love, the Lord above has generously
Endowed.

Amelia E. Cabouch

ONE CONSTANT

Sweet springtime melody of a blue jay,
The rustle of autumn leaves,
A warm ocean in summer with tiny treasures galore,
Reveal the Father's love for me.

Spring lilacs bloom profusely,
Winter snowflakes pirouette so free,
Autumn struts in like a peacock,
My Father's love surrounding me.

Lush green meadows dotted with bright
yellow dandelions,
Summer's beauty for all to see;
A golden sunset, a rush of the tides,
My Father still cares for me.

Oh, the changing of the seasons,
How swiftly they must flee;
But one fact remains a constant,
That's my Father's love for me!

Linda C. Grazulis

LOVELACE

How do you tell him you care when he's not sure you do?
How does he know what you really feel?
How will he find out what you're all about
if he's not sure of himself to be willing to
open his mind up to yours?
Be patient, go to him whenever there's time.
Remind him he's everything to you.
Tell him your story then wait and see if he accepts
what you say and what you be. Then it's just a
matter of time. Time to think about what's been
said and to dry the tears that had been shed.
    Love him if he's not sure of himself
    Love him if he's not sure of you
    Love and cherish his company of one who's
    special through and through
    Love him if he doesn't want to get involved
    For love is a feeling that grows within and
    intertwines its route to the heart.
    Once it's reached its place to stay,
It will be safe and secure each night and day.

Lynn Walsh

FIRST LOVE LOST

Amour Premier

They say the edge wears off the old dull weary pain.
Each time I start to dream it's here and worse again.
It's in the sighing breeze. It's in the roaring gale,
In brightly twinkling stars and waning moon so pale,
In quiet vesper song or joyful lilting tune,
In orchestra and dance and balmy nights of June.
I meet in many a glance something that's long past —
A memory swiftly flung as time flies by so fast
To pierce the aching heart that lost love has stung.
Hearts can be so chilled — removed from human touch
When love is gone. Yet hearts endure much —
A song, a promise vowed, a moment spent in bliss
Far from the noisy crowd to win a honeyed kiss,
A running babbling brook, a climbing silver moon —
Fond memories gone, passed away too soon.
Love's romance done. Thus ends the magic spell
Except in books and song that love stories tell.
Are they just the fables that fairy tales have spun?

Ruth Gardner McAlley

THE STRENGTH OF A HUG

    A hug can say a lot of things
Between two souls that love has blessed.
    No other act so soundly wrings
Such great emotions from the breast.

    A hug can be a wondrous joy
A tower of strength . . . a silent prayer . . .
    An act of grief . . . a spiritual buoy . . .
When all else fails, it says we care.

    No words could utter so much truth . . .
No other action could reveal
    The psalms of age . . . the songs of youth . . .
The range of living that we feel.

    Without the hug, we could not know
The fullness which we need and seek;
    And richness from its precious flow
Will say the words we could not speak.

Frances Rose Weinstock

You ask me not to think of you.
My dearest, can you stop the rising of the sun?
Can you will its setting when the day is done?
Can a desert moon be made to stay
Behind a giant cactus until day?
No, my love. You cannot will the heart to sing.
You cannot stop the tears that sting
Like acid from the soul.
Each waking hour has had one goal,
One reason for its being,
An hour gone 'til I'll be seeing
You, my sweetheart — have you near.
No. You ask too much, my dear,
When you ask me not to think of you.
Forget me, if you can. I'll forget you — when you do.

Marietta Bakewell

NO STRANGER ANY MORE

A stranger came to our house this morning,
A stranger I never saw before.
Then I held him in my arms,
Now he's no stranger anymore.

No stranger anymore with his puckered little face,
The fuzzy hair I adore, no one could ever take his place.

A cute little button nose, and chubby little feet,
A bright-eyed angel, so cuddly, soft and sweet.

Heaven must have sent him from that celestial shore,
He won our hearts completely, now he's no stranger any more.

Ina Price

GOOD-BYE!

To you I cannot say "Good-bye!"
Because I can't my eyes keep dry —

I would forever with you stay
But duty's force keeps me away

I keep you always in my mind
So beautiful and so refined

My certain hope that we shall see
The days together we will be —

World's clouds ev'rywhere, October, 1985

Luisa Kerschbaumer

THE POETRY OF YOUR LOVE

Your beauty is like an eloquent poem,
With delicate rhythm and perfect rhyme.
You tell the world of tenderness and love,
Not with words, but with your beauty sublime.
You capture a splendor that words can't portray,
An eternal radiance that fades not with time.

The tender rhythm of your dance of love,
Brings tears of joy to the young lover's eye.
The gentle rhyme of your song of hope,
Gives the fearful heart the courage to fly.
Every poet's dream and lover's desire,
I count myself blessed whenever you're nigh.

Dale R. Miller

THERE ARE WORDS

There are words which cannot be spoken,
There are words felt deep in the heart.
There are words — expressed only by feelings,
That lips cannot ever impart.
There are words deep within my being,
That can't surface — and can't be defined.
There are words which I feel deep inside,
Which can but be explained in my mind.
When I'm with you, I feel like I'm special,
Though I know, deep inside, that I'm not.
I know all my undesirable traits,
Which you make me forget that I've got.
I know that I'm still the same me
That I was long before there was you,
I know that I still have the faults
That I had — I am *not* someone *new!*
But you make me feel like I'm special,
And I'm letting it go to my head,
While we can enjoy each other so,
There are words, which need not be said!

Jean A. Sacharko

LOVE, LOVE, LOVE

Love of a kitten for its mother —
  Love between a sister and her brother
    Love between friends, one for the other;
Love makes the wheels go 'round!

Love of a musician for his song —
  As man and wife to each other, belong
    God's love for the entire throng;
Love is just and sound!

Love for home at the close of day —
  Love guides the Universe all the way
    Moves our hearts, sweet words to say;
Love is kind and sweet!

Love, love love! In all we see —
  Love touches you and me.
    As the sailor loves the sea;
Love will surely take us home!

Dorotha C. Parkhurst

TRADITION

She watches her daughter happily seated at the vanity
And reminisces about her own special day.
Not too many years ago, only three and twenty,
To a handsome young man she secretly pledged her love away.

Family and traditon had other ideas for her.
It was simply done this way, she was told as she grew.
As an infant she was bound to another;
Betrothed to a stranger she hardly knew.

She gently fingers the ring that upheld family honor.
They made a good life together, he and she,
But, today as she gazes into the face of her daughter
She fantasizes of how things might be.

So happy, so much in love, eyes that dance with pure joy;
Feeling her mother felt only once as a token.
Her daughter alone chose this boy.
Tradition has, at last, been mercifully broken.

Karen Sue Wittkowski

LOOKING FOR LOVE

A worm making its way
  through darkness
Does not contemplate
  the brightness
Of a friendly sun

A snowflake falling
  in frigid cold
Does not long for the warmth
  of the tropics
Adorned in green splendor

Though we often perceive
  human love
Is enhanced by jumping
  over the fence
And into our lover's bed

In our heart we know
  what we need
To experience love
  is to give
Of ourselves and stay home

Gordon A. Salway

SALWAY, GORDON ARTHUR. Born: Troy, New York, 1-25-38; Married: 10-29-60 to Nancy Ellen Gibson; Education: American Institute of Banking, New York Chapter, graduated Primary Certificate Program, May 1972; Occupations: Radioman first class, U.S. Coast Guard; Memberships: The American Legion, Post 490, Member six years; Awards: American Song Festival Lyric Competition 6, Quarter Finalist Award Winner, 1979; Poetry: 'The Multitudes Are Slow,' *American Poetry Anthology,* 1983; 'Memory's Screen,' *Our World's Most Beloved Poems,* 1984; 'In The Beginning,' *Our World's Best Loved Poems,* 1984; 'Mother Mentor,' *The Art of Poetry,* 1985; Comments: *I write about emotions, people and issues that have the most meaning and influence on my life. Expressing my views and feelings in poetry is a source of pleasure and satisfaction. I enjoy sharing my poems with as many people as possible.*

WHY NOT?

I gave you my heart
you broke it.

I gave you my laughter
you threw it to the wind.

I gave you my smile
you didn't return it.

I gave you my love
you rejected it.

All I had I gave to you
you gave me nothing.

Why not?

Helen Marie Dix

1926 AND 1927 REALLY ROARED

I loved Police Reporter days,
    Back on the Canton Daily News.
My headline stories would amaze,
    And generate explosive views.

Robert Emmett Clarke

HONORABLE MENTION

I have given it all away
with no regard to myself.
Only to have it return,
dark as the late winter snow.
And I have taken and taken
the sweet water I could not
keep. In coastal nights, we
lay within the blue haze
and I did not hold you;
your sorrow
flowing, cutting through the
envelope of our moorish
distances. And this memory,
my constant visitor, lies
silently by the eastern sea
listening
for all that was lost.

Billie Sue Fischer

ROSES OF YESTERDAY

Roses, beautiful roses,
Roses of every hue,
Sent in a lovely bouquet
'With Love' to me from you.

They told me that you loved me
In a very special way;
Each rose carried a message
In that lovely bouquet.
Those roses of yesterday.

Why did they have to fade
My beautiful rose bouquet?
Just like the words of a song,
Not only the roses, but the one
I loved is gone.

Darlene Grice Hayward

FALL SONG

Well do I remember her song
When September tells of rain,
And wind drives the leaves along
O'er fields new-stripped of grain.
Well do I recall
That seventeen was she,
And it was in the fall
When she sang to me . . .
I, an awkward boy,
Found my heart's delight —
Never dreaming that my joy
Would end on a winter's night.

Frank Jethro

FLIGHT

You make me want to fly again —
To stretch my wings
And taste the high, crisp winds
That flow across the crags;
To soar so high
The view outruns description
And the fall becomes breathtaking;
And, this time,
My heart chooses to believe
When I turn and call,
You will climb on powerful wings
To fly beside me.

James Collett

INNOCENT LOVE

Love is blind love is blue
Love is always something new
Love is brutal love is kind
Love can make you lose your mind
Love is caring between the two
Love is what I see when I think of you
Love can span the greatest distance
Love is unyielding in its insistence
When I'm afar at duties call
I pray to God our love will not fall
And all the children of innocent love
Are truly blessed in the eyes of the dove

Paul E. Davis

WARRANTY

Love upholds the gift of beauty
despite its tears and sighs and woes,
Love gives freely of its being
as grace weaves what life bestows.
Love smiles in life's morning
when the orb in orange glows,
when hope endures forever
and romance to fulfillment flows.
Love remains as a flower
that always lives and grows,
never falling like Fall petals
or passing to a close.

George C. Koch

LOVE

And all the birds
Are crying from the hills
Love, where have you gone?

I await in loneliness
And the storm approaches
The diffused inky sky
Shuts like a cup
On tree and fern alike.

And now the grasses stir
And the soft rumbling
Precedes the rain —
Ah darkest noon
And I await the verdict.

The flowers plucked
Are damp with tears
And a single thorn
Reminded me
Of the transparency
Of the flesh.

Virginia M. Weber

OUR LOVE

The wonders of our precious Love
This Love I feel for you
My heart doth swell
I Love to tell
Your eyes a shimmering blue

The inner glow
The warmth you see
Are sent along quite personally
For only you my Love is true
For only my Love will you be

Our happiness for all to see
We share it from the start
No lonely times
No boring times
No Love without a heart

Only Love
Our precious Love
Given from the start
Here's my Love for you.

Helen Rae Wegner

I LOVE YOU

I love you with all my heart,
I love you with all my soul;
Your love is more precious,
Than diamonds, silver, or gold.
I love you from moment to moment,
I love you from day to day;
No one gave your love to me,
No one can take it away.
Because you first of all
Proved how much you loved me;
When the realization of this came,
You changed my life completely.
I'm yours now, to do,
Whatever you ask me to do;
Jesus, that is how much,
I really love you.

Patti Woodard

WANTING YOU

My lips desire your kiss only,
my hands to caress your face,
and whenever I am feeling lonely,
I desire the warmth of your embrace.

My ears long to hear you speak,
my arms to wrap around you tight,
my face pressed snug against your cheek,
my eyes long for you in their sight.

Only you will I always love,
because your every trait I so adore,
You're as handsome as an angel from above,
and I want you with me forevermore.

Carol Marie Griffin

HEARTS ON FIRE WITH LOVE

Hearts on fire with love
Every happiness begins that way
All must look above
Remember to Him turn
This promise will never fail
Say a prayer and to Him prevail

Onward down the path
Never give in to wrath

Forever in His arms to stay
If you walk a narrow way
REJOICE — keep your heart on fire
Eternal love will be your heart's desire

Rowena Bragdon Holt

NEEDS OF LOVE

Love needs no eloquent words divine;
Nor witty metaphors to describe or define;
For Love is a warm and silent aura.
Love needs no touch or fond embrace,
Nor charm, nor wit or a lovely face.
But if ever Love should,
Love
would
need
Laura.
So
do
I.
Dad

Frank Favaro

FINAL DECREE

Little bird how wrong you are
To sit up in the tree
And cry in song of times gone by
As life continues on.

The silent plea of loneliness
I hear in every note,
But still blown kisses freeze the air
As life continues on.

Mimi Herrington

REMINISCING

Love is more than just a word,
It's a hug, a smile, a kiss;
Love is feeling deep in the heart,
Precious moments to reminisce.

Love is when we first held hands
Strolling barefooted along the sandy shore,
And when you held me close to you,
My fluttering heart like an eagle soared.

Love is when we carved our initials
Deep into the bark of that brawny oak tree;
Love is when we laughed and sang,
Making sweet melody.

Love is when we were married
And I wore satin and lace;
Love is enjoying our tiny bundle of joy,
Locked in a tender embrace.

Also, love is the contentment of the golden years,
Rocking lazily side by side;
Gently flipping the pages of an old family album —
Oh my, how those years did fly!

Linda C. Grazulis

A GRANDMOTHER'S LOVE

While gazing at her granddaughter, who was fast asleep,
Silently, with joy, grandmother began to weep.
Many years she had waited for this blessed event,
This bundle of joy, that was heaven sent.

She touched her hair and kissed the cheek
Of this beautiful child so mild and meek.
Hoping against hope that baby would awake,
So that she in her arms could take

And hold her against her beating breast
This lovely child so sweet at rest.
How thankful she was to be alone,
With her first grandchild, her very own.

For the first grandchild be they girl or boy,
Will always bring the greatest joy.
And how proud she would be, when she could say,
"I held my grandchild this very day!"

A grandmother's love cannot be measured,
It's a special gift that is always treasured.
She will cherish this gift from God above
And shower upon her a grandmother's love.

John T. Hudelson

WHEN

When love hits us, we have no say, just
grab a hold and don't let go.
When birth comes along, we hope a girl
or boy, but are even happy if we are wrong.
When death comes, we just let go, let
it happen then pick up the pieces.
But the love alone will make us cry, we
miss them, care for them, even wish for them.
When still we hold on, for life is nothing
unless love hits us, and we have no
say, we just grab a hold and don't let go.

Dianne K. Barth

GIVE ME THE JOY OF LOVE

The love and joy to do so many things
The enthusiasm of it makes me love to sing.

The joy to help others along life's way
To do some loving deeds each and every day.

Life's long journey has much love to spend
To make others very happy to the end.

To appreciate God's love in simple things,
Like the gorgeous red sunsets in spring.

The oriole's song, the cooing of the dove
Created by God, for one to hear and to love.

Give many thanks to the Great One above
For all this that makes life a joy of love.

Leona Dixon Cox

THE CHILD'S PRAYER

While gods forget as if it's something new
a human is an animal who bleeds,
a human is a lonely thing with needs
to be forgiven and forgotten too.

Dreams are not enough, but we follow dreams,
and deeds are not enough, done in the dark,
and in this heart may be not one clear spark
if life is unforgiven as it streams.

No feat or worldly applause may atone
for the loneliness and the swallowed whines
indulged, when one finished soul determines
to struggle in our acting world along.

To find forgiveness in ourselves we seek
when to ourselves divinity won't speak.

David Lee Castleman

HOMELY SUMMER REVISITED

The moon splashing over the land by night,
The sunshine tanning the earth by day,
My calloused hand in yours so tight,
The scent of tomatoes and new-mown hay!
A palmate leaf used for a fan,
The slurp of suckling calves and colts,
A tender glance from me, your man,
The clap of thunder with lightning bolts!

The airy spice of pollen tips,
The drumming rain on hot-baked land,
A loving promise from warm, wet lips,
Hot feet in old shoes and socks and sand!
A mind that's filled with growing things,
The flora and fauna, the kids and you,
The happy pulse that this *all* brings,
Bare skin and sheets the whole night through!

Ray Befus

REMEMBER WHEN

Remember when we used to play
On the ice and snow on a rainy day
Holding hands and far-stretched smiles
We'd walk together those endless miles
Chasing clouds on a distant breeze
To flow along with our hearts at ease
Reaching for rainbows thoughts never to touch
One sharing love the other needs so much

Toni Dybala

I REMEMBER LOVE

Down on the farm,
As a child I remember
The aroma of apple pie,
Discovery of the Milky Way
In a summer sky above.
Most of all,
I remember LOVE.

Perched regal on my throne of snow-white cotton;
Going to gin with Dad,
A trip never forgotten.
Me on one side,
A little black boy on the other.
No racism problem then . . .
I remember LOVE.
Stamped indelibly on my mind . . .
My dad's bowed head,
Thanking God for our daily bread.
No T.V. . . . No rush . . . No shove . . .
Most of all,
I remember LOVE.

Dixie Rice Dawson

DAWSON, MARY E. Pen Name: Dixie Rice Dawson; Born: Bartlett, Texas, 8-10-20; Married: 1938 to John L. Dawson, 3 children, 15 grand children, 8 great grandchildren; Education: Sunset High School, Dallas, Texas, 1935-36; Bartlett High, 1937-38; Occupations: Homemaker, Nursing Home Kitchen Aide; Awards: Golden Poet Award, World of Poetry, 1986; Award of Merit, *American Poetry Anthology,* 1986; Poetry: 'Pause in Flight,' *American Poetry Anthology,* 1986; Comments; *"In the beginning God. . . " opens one of the most beautiful books of poems ever written and it is autographed in precious blood.*

Give me one good reason, just one
The stubborn kid of me demands
(Demands of whom? You? God? My grown-up?)
Tell me why, for cryin' out loud
I should be here
And you should be there
Today is meant for lovers to share
Warm winter air stirs the senses
My skin glows in response to the seductive lure of the sun
I hear leaves of a nearby tree stretch out to bask, as I,
To enjoy the taste and touch of this sweet day
Even chores, mundane tasks like hanging clothes and making beds,
Assume delight on a day like this
A multi-hued day, resplendent in color
Splendor such as this seeks my soul
Which bursts likewise into purples and pinks, roses and reds
This gift is complete just as it is
Yet you would be the bow on the package

Lyn Berry

OUR FRIENDSHIP

There's something in this world today
that's treasured and true in every way.
It's the bond of friendship one shares
with those who care enough to care.

For sharing and giving of oneself can bring
joys of happiness that make men sing.
It's a feeling you get deep in your heart
that makes you never want to part.

The times when we need a helping hand
or just someone who will understand,
even a gentle touch, can mean so much.

Not everyone can see this through
for it takes someone special like you.

Mary J. Conlon

Love me as I am;
I can't be anything else.
Love my faults;
I'm not perfect.
And Love my heart;
Because that is what makes my Love so great.

Jeannette Mayette

A MOTHER'S BLESSING

(To my mother — Minnie L. Crowder)

Mothers are the most understanding people on earth,
Someone who understands some of the things her kids go through
Especially the daughter(s)
Growing pains, problems with friends, even the guys
Someone to say, 'I love you, mom.'
Someone who loves her kids even when her kids don't
feel like doing anything
Someone who tells her kids what's right and what's wrong
Mothers are the peacemakers of a household
They give spirit and enthusiasm to a worthless situation
Mothers are not a blessing in disguise
They are a blessing without the disguise
Mothers are people who love their children no matter
what and the love is returned
Mothers are the one with their heads on straight.

Julia E. Crowder

TWENTY YEARS: TAKE TOO

In the doorway stood a man
  unsure, overly polite, and well dressed.
The ridge on his nose showed glasses removed
  and very thin hair complemented his fragile frame.
So pale: no more winters on skis
    no more summers at the beach,
But if she half-closed her eyes
  her fantasy could rejuvenate his body
  and envision his once long hair.
She would be soft and invite him slowly
  if her passion did not burst around him.
From her memory she had painted
  a dream on pure darkness;
Now she could sculpture a past love
  from this real life.
Did the candlelight make his eyes
  so wide?

David D. Palmquist

RHAPSODY FOR LOVE

Has my soul forgotten how to soar in its long
journey, searching for the evermore?
When upon the falling of darkness I can no
longer surrender to the nights of honor.
Shall the burning ember of the sun ever shine
again, as with my passion?
The arms of desire have infolded and bowed,
with its head hung low.
Now sets a pace for the monster of loneliness
which seeps in toward the inner-soul of being.
Yet, all is not lost, if within the most
secluded regions of the conscience there still
lies a small kindle.
For someday the true knight of honor shall
come and the spark shall be seduced into a
blazing flame, bringing forth a glorious
star admist the heavens.

Dortha K. Weinzatl

MY LOVE

My love you were yesterday a fire burning in me and my
  heart still feels for you, as of yesterday.

You went away and never returned, but you're still the fire
  in my heart.

I don't try to put it out or drown it, so as the heart
  searches for the waterbrooks so painful my heart for thee,
  Oh love where are you.

You're the fire that burns painfully, and it gets brighter
  each day that goes by.

If you could only look back to yesterday and see the
  flame in my heart that burnt for you.

I know then the fire in our hearts would rekindle.

Rea Wallace

LOVESCAPE

I loved you through a thousand windowless nights.
I loved you through shafts of burning pain.
I loved you arched in a pagan embrace —
United in conceptual disdain.

My lover, still in paternal command
Of the childlike side of my face.
Undulating mound of flesh,
Augured in a selfish embrace.

I struggle to survive the assault —
Burdened by all your self-doubt.
Anchored in a malnutritioned sea
Of sexist torments throughout.

In the hot breath of expectancy you plunge —
Charged in the secret womb of life.
The burnt-out dream ever repeated.
On the damp map of fleshy strife.

Your appetite for pleasure devours love.
Creation is my nobler goal.
Abandoned in the room of your arms —
My tears the window-washers of my soul.

Dorothy Stark Kaufman

THE LOVE IN MY DREAMS

My love visited me in a dream.
Up to my window she silently came.
She roused me from my restless sleep.
Without a word, she called me by name.

I went to my window, and there was my love,
Mounted on a horse gleaming white.
I joined her on her mighty steed,
And together we rode off into the night.

My joy knew no words as we rode along.
I watched as the moon glowed softly in her hair.
Her gentle laughter lightened my soul,
And freed me from my every care.

We came to a river and danced by its side.
The earth played a tune, and the moon gave its light.
I wished this moment would last for all time,
As softly our song drifted into the night.

I opened my eyes and awoke from my dream.
I knew that my love had never been there.
My love exists in another world,
For only the love in my dreams can we share.

Dale R. Miller

A WOMAN'S UNWITHERED, UNTHORNED LOVE

Woman, the ultimate bloom and spectrum,
More than a wood-nymph, angel or goddess,
Triumphs ever in splendorous birth pangs.
She soothes man's inborn bemuddlings
By incarnating mystical ecstasies of love
With strange bewitching spells of beauty,
She fulfills man's phantasmagoria of dreams.
With ease, she turns a rapturous moment
Into timeless little ripples of lovings.
Her unwithered, unthorned love's lightstreams
Of inexpressible sweetness never let one down.

Don Blondeau

Are you as disappointed as I
That you didn't come by?
Did your lips yearn to kiss,
And feel warm with bliss?
Even though it's late,
Why still hesitate?
No matter the hour,
True love has a power,
All its own.

Cheryle Dawn Hart

FOREVER I AM TO YOU

In this space of time I extend to you —
A vision that is.

Set yourself to rest —
Let your mind drift to the infinite.

Granting me this wish as you travel across
the meadows of summer —
That I may be the cooling breeze in your
face — ever caressing.

As you cross the mountains —
Sit close for I am the fire that will keep
you warm.

Like the limbs of the tall oak trees you
pass under —
I offer you strength.

As a refreshing spring —
Quenching your thirst.

Raise your eyes to the sun by day and
the north star by night —
For as they are forever — I am to you.

Joseph P. Kochel, Sr.

FOOTSTEPS

HONORABLE MENTION

My home moans and complains
like an old man struggling
through his last hours of life.

I shiver, trying to ignore
the sounds of decay
creeping up my spine,
forcing their way into my mind.

Outside my window
the snow has melted
exposing large patches
of naked earth to the moon.

Winter has settled
so deeply into my bones
I did not see it leave the world.

Time and the night
pass away together
as I watch
the empty street below
and listen, always listen
for footsteps no longer there.

Nancy M. Holewa

ANTONY AND CLEOPATRA

Love knows not order.
It is not proper.
The low and the high are its tools.
It makes all fools.
When Antony sailed,
Allured by Cleopatra,
He was a man of stature
And a soldier none bolder.
Octavian and Rome he defied
Drawn on by Cleopatra deified,
Their passion they played fast,
Their love did not last,
Full soon the curtain of tragedy
Led to defeat at sea,
And Actium
And Alexandria.

James T. Mackey

MAKING LOVE

It's like
someone
reaching deep
into your
farthest reaches,
to your soul;
to scratch the
hardest itch
of all.

It lets your inners
laugh,
with the delight
that comes from
point-blank
satisfaction.

Ave Maria Smart

S'PRISE FOR MAMA

Oh David you were five,
My blonde, middle-sized bear.
The smile on your face
When your eyes met mine
Made an orchid
Out of the dandelion.

Hildegarde M. Snow

THE GHOST DOG

The form of a departed mongrel
entered the open door;
My faithful, once-loved friend
came to visit me once more.
The evening lights were glowing
and like phantom forms gray and tall,
shadows from an eerie nightlight
danced upon the kitchen wall.
With a slow and noiseless pawstep
came a spirit so divine
who placed his once lithe body
next to the life of mine.
Although often depressed or lonely,
all my fears are laid aside
when recalled is the LOVE of a canine
who had lived and died.

George C. Koch

YESTERDAY'S HURT

You could have been my yesterday,
If Love had been aware,
Of feelings growing here today,
We two, through Love, can share.
You could be my tomorrow,
If Love will stay alert,
Erasing any sorrow,
And yesterday's hurt.

Robert F. Vitalos

VITALOS, ROBERT F. Born: Allentown, Pennsylvania, 10-31-47; Occupation: Electrical Worker; Memberships: Pascal: Pennsylvania Association of Songwriters Composers and Lyricists; Awards: Honorable Mention, 'Wind Kissed,' World of Poetry, 1985; Poetry: 'Branches,' *American Poetry Anthology,* 1985; 'After All You Are,' *Words of Praise, Volume II,* 1986; Comments: *I believe that it is time for the masses to get back to love as a vehicle for expression of emotion. If we can do this perhaps we can cancel out some of the hatred and violence our world has been pressured into.*

DISTANCE

I wake mid-dream,
and one tear falls
as I see you aren't asleep
by my side
(as I had thought).

At the same instant
(yet three thousand miles away)
you wake the same.

As we drift back off,
(could it be?)
we find ourselves
together, once again
(If not in each other's arms,
in each other's dreams).

Sandra Stith

A FIRST NIGHT

I see negative traces of character
within my desire to understand her.
Higher up in the bright grey without
purpose, she speaks already in mature
signs. Signatures examine each other.
We might lose after all traces of this
morning. A collaborative plot, too soon
psychotic without apology.

Its simplicity is evident, arranged,
may paint character in the night sky.
Living there like a lover in space.
Pastels tilt on a horizon. Buried alive
with wine the dream flows to the brain.
A red stain becomes the Earth. Life
resumes in the stars with bubbles to
sexual objects. Angels jump into the dark,
their dreams in places of fear so far
from home falls in a transparent,
negative present state. Her laughter
exits so happy with the past.

Thomas A. Phelan

PHELAN, THOMAS ANTHONY. Born: Manhattan, New York City, 1-20-28; Education: CCNY, Bergen Community College, Fairleigh Dickinson University; Occupations: Private Investigator, Karate Instructor; Memberships: New York/New Jersey Detective's Crime Clinic, Word Shop Poets, Bergen Poets, Florida State Poets' Association; Awards: Golden Poet of 1985; New York Poetry Society, $50 award, 1985; Honorable Mentions: 1 — 1984, 3 — 1985, 2 — 1986; Poetry: 'Even By One,'recitation, WOR TV, Channel 9; 'Treasure Chest,' *Byline Magazine,* 1983; 'I Pray But Fingers Slip,' *Grit Newspapers,* 1984; 'Hell,' *New York Poetry Society Anthology,* 1985; 'A Poet's Nightmare,' *American Poetry Showcase,* 1985; Comments: *My writing, whether good, mediocre or just bad, allows me the freedom to communicate, to achieve, relive past experiences, to hope and dream, giving me a feeling of satisfaction and accomplishment.*

WHERE ARE YOU?

I smile and laugh and say hello
And sometimes even forget the pain.
But I miss you.
I don't even know who you are
But I love you,
Not lightly but eternally.
I will give you so much more than you ask,
For, like me, you ask for so little
Not riches, nor fame, nor adulation
But a simple exchange
Of warmth
And realness.
It seems the truth is so naked
that we clothe it
to avoid the shame and embarrassment.
Our spirits are hungry
for each other
Find me soon that we both
May live before we die.

J. Kenneth Ezzell

FLEETING TIME

Though fleeting time would soon erase
The slightest trace that your love
Was true and pure, yet even now
It lingers on my faltering mind
Though time has passed and Fate is sure.
When days were bright with Autumn sun
The gay wind hummed a lilting song,
Brights leaves in beauteous colors dressed
Danced, whirled and flew along.
We joined the merry gay parade
With our joyous happy song.
Fleeting time has changed all that.
Fond memories bring sudden pangs
From those long remembered joys
When we young lovers used to talk
Of days to come in future time.
They have come and gone, my Dear,
And all I have are tear drops
To tell me that you once were near.

Ruth Gardner McAlley

GOD'S LOVE

God's love surrounds me
wherever I go
I know that it will be with me
though my steps may be slow.
Words can't explain
this love so divine
but one thing I know
it fills this heart of mine.
For God so loved this world
that He gave His own son
who died on the cross
the victory, He won.
So I thank God for love
as I travel through life
with its troubles and sorrows
its toil and its strife.
I'm awaiting the time
when, in heaven, I'll be
living forever through eternity.

Louise Combs

THIS LOVE

This love together that we share;
Is absolutely beyond compare.

A feeling so deep within our souls;
No one else could ever know.

We've shared this love through many years;
Though the pain sometimes caused tears.

We've stayed together through thick and thin;
Waiting for our future to begin.

Trying to put the past behind;
No more lies from which to hide.

Getting comfort from each other alone;
Knowing together we truly belong.

A love for no one else but you;
This love of ours forever true.

Sheila Arnold

TWO LOVES

You are the moon and the stars beloved
But he is the sun and the earth
The generous earth.

You are a velvet night in June
The breath of flowers.
The sound of haunting music far away.
You are the drowsy hum of busy insects,
the song of birds.
The smell of new-mown hay.

You are the memory of inspiration.
That part of me that never will grow old.
My early dreams and thoughts are centered
'round you.
The soul of things I touched but could not hold.

You are the moon and the stars beloved.
But he is the warmth of the sun
and the strength of the solid earth.

Dorothy E. Lee

MARY, I BELIEVED THEE TRUE

Mary, I believed thee true,
And I was blest in thus believing;
But now I mourn that e'er I knew
A girl so fair and so deceiving
Few have ever loved like me;
O, I have loved thee too sincerely!
And few have e'er deceived like thee,
Alas, deceived me too severely.
Fare thee well!

Fare thee well! yet think awhile
On one whose bosom seems to doubt thee;
Who now would rather trust that smile,
And die with thee than live without thee.
Fare thee well! I'll think on thee,
Thou leav'st me many a bitter token;
For see, distracting woman, see
My peace is gone, my heart is broken.
Fare thee well!

Thomas Moore

BEFORE YOU WENT AWAY

I see your slacks and dresses
hanging there beside my suits;
your slippers where you placed them
beside my riding boots.
I see your coat and hat,
the chair where you last sat
before you went away from me.

The roses that you planted
are blooming once again;
they're climbing up so they can peep
in at the windowpane.
They used to climb and nod and peep,
but it was not in vain
before you went away from me.

I want to hold you in my arms
the way I used to do;
I want to let you have your way,
let you scold me too.
Some things that I am not I should have changed a lot
before you went away from me.

Leota Cooke Hall

HALL, EMMA LEOTA. Pen Name: Leota Cooke Hall; Born: Tordesillas, Texas; Married: 1949 to Donald Clarence Hall; Education: University of Oklahoma at Norman, B.A., English Major, Foreign Language Minor; French, Spanish, German; Occupation: High School Teacher of English, French, and Spanish; Poetry: 'This is the Victory,' About War, *American Poetry Anthology,* 1983; 'As Eagles Fly,' Biblical, *American Poetry Anthology,* 1985; 'Oklahoma Prairie Sky,' Descriptive, *The Art of Poetry,* 1985; 'Finale,' Religious, *Words of Praise,* 1986; Comments: *When I began writing 'Before You Went Away,' I was composing a song. Then I decided to share the poem with readers of* Hearts on Fire. *It is, first of all, a love story. When love is the theme, a poem has universal appeal because love is important to everyone.*

SITTING TOGETHER

Sitting here by your side,
Just a touch so warm and tender,
Like the heavens control the tide,
Your loving eyes fill my heart with splendor.

Sitting here by your side,
Talking of dreams, planning together,
Feelings told — that once wanted to hide,
Growing closer than ever.

Sitting here by your side,
Silent, not having to say a word,
Just a look, a touch, a sigh,
Deep feelings not to be heard.

Sitting here by your side,
Taking my hand in yours,
This little sign of love — means so much,
Can fill a heart with pleasures.

Paula LaVoy Trim

MY OWN TRUE LOVE

'Twas a summer's eve when first we met
I fondly recall that old scene yet.
I suppose it was a turn of fate,
We were to each other, a blind date.
Friends said, There's a new girl I must meet.
We'd go riding, share the rumble seat.
Her eyes were friendly and very blue.
Her hair a lovely dark chestnut hue.
She'd a winning personality
In mem'ry all this I still can see.
She was not a silly, giggly girl.
I thought she was some kind of pearl.
A fashionable perky hat she wore.
Her good looks and air at my heart-strings tore.
For she looked so lovely standing there
With her sky blue eyes and chestnut hair.
Time has turned her hair a lighter hue,
But her eyes are still that lovely blue.
There is this time did not alter,
My Love's the same, it did not falter.

Wm. A. McDonald

LOVE SONG

As quietly as a tiptoe will allow
and as lovingly as a glass of sleep,
I'll blend myself into your life, and how
I'll reward you will pay for my keep.

I'll tickle your hunger and rinse off your pain,
and float gossamer dreams 'round your bed.
You'll have towels of petals softer than rain
and warm ringlets of sun 'round your head.

We'll waltz 'round a Maypole without losing our breath,
playing Goddess and God as we go;
we'll feel all the children and incarcerate Death,
wearing a gown and a tux of pure snow.

And you'll love me completely, whatever I do.
I'll be happy. You'll see that I will.
Fear won't surround me, not when I have you,
and the voices will finally be still.

Arthur E. McGowan

PETER
Mixed Matched Patches

I fell in love with your smile
you thought you loved me too.
The smile led us down the aisle,
vague future — me and you.
Misunderstanding, intimidation
there came so much dismay.
A break in communication, damaged
feelings — took love's smile away.

Needles and thread, mixed matched patches,
we bridged the love we knew.
Obese hurt frayed the threads, and the
overweighed bridge fell through.
Dissolution of our bond and the new freedom
gave painful joy and peace.
Grievous thoughts of years wasted
will never cause the misplaced love to cease.

C. Swain-Ward

I FOUND LOVE

When I look into a daisy's face
And smell the sweet fragrance of the red rose
And see the birds flying free in the sky,
I know I've found love.

When I see a pair of squirrels on a fence
And hear the pitter patter of the rain on the window
And feel the warm glow from the crackling fireplace,
I know I've found love.

To sit enfolded in your arms
To feel your soft embrace
To hear your softly whispered, I love you,
I know I've found real love.

To hold my baby to my bosom
And feel her soft fingers on my face
To see her soft innocent smile,
I thank God above for helping me
To know and find true love.

Joan V. Peterson

MARK ANDREW

Little Doogie went to school
Took in his hand a mechanic's tool

But not one lesson did he learn
Because the instructor was loud and stern.

Then one day, upon the revealing jack
All in a heap sat a demolished pack.

Around it Doogie began to walk
And in mechanic's terms he began to talk,

Then, piece by piece he took it apart
The wreck had touched his mechanic's heart.

Polished and shiny, the Scamp by his side
The stern old instructor as his guide

You no doubt know the rest
He became a mechanic, of course, the best.

Margaret Rebrinsky

"BERKELEY'S SEAT."

YOU AND I

Dedicated to John Dyeyemi (My Love)

The wind made love to you and me . . . as we
made love in the wind . . . I was lifted and
tossed gently up and down . . . to and fro . . . and
O what pleasure I received . . . O what
hope I gained . . . you filled me with love,
hope and many, many beautiful and unforgettable
promises . . . we laughed and we cried . . .
we dared and we shared . . . as we made love in the
wind . . . My tears were sweet and bitter too . . .
My pain was good and bad . . . Over and over again my
love . . . You filled me . . . as we loved and
made love . . . in the wind . . .

Ivey Joyce Williams

PATIENCE

I can't wait for the day
to be in your arms.
Whether it's a second, a minute or an hour.
Whatever it will be will seem
like an eternity.

The passion behind our eyes
could light up a city
but lies smoldering
on the edge of insanity.
Your lips are so gentle, your arms so strong.
Your breath like a summer shower,
raining gently on my cheek.

Charity L. Edwards

YOU

Someone who's special,
Someone who cares,
Someone who'll always be there.
Through the good,
Through the bad,
You'd be by my side,
Understanding and caring.

Through the funny, somewhat awkward conversations,
Through the blank spots where there's nothing to say,
Through the touches, the sweetness and the thoughts left unsaid.
Yes, I thought you'd be there forever,
and in my heart that hope still lingers.

Emilia Barozzi

STAGE TWO

Which of us should do the leading?
Does my questioning start you bleeding?
Could your desires resemble my own?
Or is being here, barely preferable to being alone?
Unanswerable questions surround the room.
Where only silence abounds in the gloom.

While sane enough to recognize the risk,
I'm crazy enough to pursue the kiss.
Dare I believe you could need me, too?
But is our relationship too fragile; too new?
You awoke these feelings I once cried to sleep.
But are the hurts you suffered, still too deep?

Delores Hendricks

A LOVELY WINTER MORNING

Lovely winter morning, you delight my soul,
As I walk in the park, where birds ascend and descend
In flapping gracefulness, feeling the air their sovereign,
In the trees they sing their songs of happiness.

The sun has risen in full glory,
Its warm rays streaming down the earth,
Warming up my face and heart, yet my body feels the cold
Of Winter's visit of love.

The mountains show their lovely snow,
Not yet melted by streaming rays of sun,
The morning dew is thick on idle cars,
The night's cold stays despite the sun.

This kind of scene comes again in everlasting cycles,
A beauty that delights the heart to wonderment,
Of nature's loveliness its own magnificence,
That I must write, my gift and fulfillment.

To capture the grandeur of a lovely winter morning,
Is the heart's awakening to eternal love,
That aspect of God smiling on a living soul
Breathing the air so lovely pure and cool.

Rolando L. Boquecosa

BOQUECOSA, ROLANDO LAPUT. Born: Manila, Philippines, 11-1-36; Single; Education: Far Eastern University, Manila, B.A., English, 1971; Immigrated to Las Vegas, Nevada in July, 1971, became an American citizen in 1977; Poetry: Two hundred unpublished poems; Themes: *My poems can be on any subject that concerns the human soul.*

EARLY LOVE

I wanted to grow and be like she.
Even then I wondered could it be?
She was my 4th grade teacher, she lived at our house.
Never I recall, were we still as a mouse.
I loved her so, you will never know.
Wherever in this world I might go.
After high school I went on to school, my love for her made me
want to rule.
I went on to school for further study.
Some days were bright and many muddy with my memory of her.
I held my head high, I studied hard as the years went by.
I kept in touch with her all through the years.
No one knows of my many tears, because I loved her.

Edith Van Orsdale

MANY FACES OF LOVE

Love is:
the smile on the face of a child,
the gratitude on the face of a woman,
the sense of pride on the face of a man.

For if tomorrow comes,
I want it to find me serene.
I want to have the peacefulness
of the humble
and
the open mindedness
of the wise.

Love
has changed my life
in so many ways;
has given me
the strength of the knowledge
and the power of feeling
that everything,
might be conquered.

Ana-Julia Villafañe

A SIMPLE MYSTERY

I live, I dream, I think
and so,
I speak about love.
Could it be that love
is a state of mind?
Could it be and,
could it be also that love
is in itself, by itself an art?

In a memory, in a word,
in a detail, in a song,
love is the answer to us all.
The happiness of being
a craftsman of love
is to find that
the more you give, the more you get.

The more you walk into
the more you know, and still
you can never say you know
all the simple mysteries
about love.

Ana-Julia Villafañe

TWO SIMPLE THINGS

I lost control again today.
One of those inexplicable times
When, missing the arms that
Have never, but someday might,
Hold me, daily frustrations
Proved too much.

I always believed you can't
Miss what you never had.
Until today.
Today I discovered it's just
Another way of *knowing*
That one hug will make it all right.

One hug and a whisper;
"I love you."

Julie Ott

HER GREATEST LOVE

There was none more appreciative
Than Mary Magdalene,
Because for her He'd done so much,
And her heart was really touched.

Strange that she bought a high-priced box
Of ointment rare, with fragrance sweet,
Upon the head of Jesus she poured it
And last upon His feet.

With falling tears she wiped His feet
And tenderly kissed them too;
Mary's long hair fell to dry them.
Her love to Him was true.

Some said, "It could have been sold
Or to the poor been given."
But it meant more to her than gold.
Her sins had been forgiven.

Who heard the words, "Why weepest thou?"
In the early morning dawn;
Yes! It was Mary Magdalene
On the Resurrection morn.

Jennie M. Root

ROOT, JENNIE MARIE. Born: Enfield, Minnesota, 4-28-98; Married: to Anthony Kazup, and John W. Root (deceased); Education: Broadview Swedish College, B.A. 1919; Loma Linda California University, R.N., 1923; Certificate from Institute of Children's Literature, Redding Ridge, Connecticut; Occupations: Housewife, Nurse, Red Cross Clerk; Memberships: Conservative Caucus, A Sound Economy, many political groups such as Republican Task Force, NRCC, NRSC and others; Awards: Won 18 Award of Merit Certificates; Gold Award, 1985; Poetry: 'Twilight & Evening Star,' World of Poetry, 1985; 'The Palm Tree,' *Our Best Loved Poems,* 1983; 'Carol, My Daughter,' *Our Best Loved Poems,* 1984; 'I Wonder,' *Our Best Loved Poems,* 1983; 'My Husband John,' *Today's Greatest Poems,* 1965; Comments: *I am a religious person, love nature and my family, and am a student of the Bible and other books and music. I play my piano, as it is a comfort to me. I've had sorrows such as the death of my father when I was nine years old, the loss of my brother at age nineteen, and went through a divorce with five children.*

MY SPECIAL LOVE

A special time, a special place
A certain smile upon your face
That's how I remember you
The love we have and all we share
There'll be no place for others there.

A special place within my heart
A place that's not a part
Of other loves of days gone by
A place no one can know.

Another time, another place
Another smile upon your face
No one will know what we share
There's no place for others there.

That special time, that special place
That special smile upon your face
The love we have and all we share
There'll be no place for others there
My Special Love

Helen Rae Wegner

OLD WOUNDS

A friend once told me
what you just showed me
"It might get easy,
but it doesn't go away."

If I see you in a bar
or pass you in a car
my heart goes out for you
once again I'm missing you
It hasn't gotten better
but it's a little easier
I can pass you on the street
I can handle it if we meet
now I can keep my cool
though my heart's for you
and I'm still missing you

It might get easy
but it doesn't go away
I know how I feel
old wounds never heal

Doreen Lee

FIRST LOVE

Did I dream
A feather kiss
Upon my cheek
Let a piercing
Darting throb
Invade the hidden
Recess of my
Virgin heart?
Swelling bursting
With ecstatic joy
All of me trills
I love you and
As a lark wings
Upward singing
Blissfully I soar a
Glorious exquisite
Paradise on earth.

Ann L. Browning

The words are seldom spoken
Yet so much can still be said.
There's a bond that can't be broken
For the fire's not yet dead.
Coals can turn to embers,
But ashes take more time.
There's so much to remember
And my heart overrules my mind.
There's got to be a reason
I can't put you aside
There's got to be a reason —
For the first time I have lied.
What's this feeling you've started in me
That holds me close, won't let me be?
Were we lovers eons ago
Who've sought each other out?
Or, it is more a simple truth —
What love is all about.

Jean E. Christensen

SEASONS

Love, like flowers, blossoms in spring,
But, like flowers, must have its rain.
With the rain, flowers grow strong,
But rain in love causes just pain.

Love, like the sun, shines in summer,
But, like the sun, can also burn.

Love, like leaves, fades in autumn
But what pretty colors they both can turn.

Love, like flowers, can wither in winter,
Slipping away as the snows gain.

Time passes swiftly, the sun comes back,
But does love, like flowers, return again?

Joseph Nicholas Pomone

THE RIVERBED

Blood is thicker than water:
water keeps blood flowing.
Together they make a river,
with love as their bed.

Margie Amberboy

LOVE ME FOR MYSELF

If you must love
me, do not
say

I love her, for her
smile, look or tricky
way

Love only, if you agree
for love's sake to
stay

Assurance that you might
not forget,
for love you must
pay

Betty Adams

IN MEMORY

I would have you sing sweetly the
Praises of this mother's love,
Did you listen intently for the
Solomon-like wisdom from her anxious lips?
Did you speak softly to her in the
Twilight of her life?
Touch gently her serene and patient face
As you helped to kiss away her cares?
Step reverently into the sunlight
Of her dear God's love?
Speak kindly of this one we so revered;
Now, walk lightly where so recently
The mound was leveled to
Rest her tired body,
Wait patiently for that glad
Morning of eternal reunion.

Jennie B. Nye

DAVID

When you are at my side
And you are sound asleep
I silently count my blessings
For the love you've given to me
I count on you for many things
Most of all your love
A tender touch your warm embrace
I couldn't live without
I can't see me, without you
What a sad and lonely road
That I hope I'll never walk up
As long as you're here to hold
With a tender touch, I brush away
A strand of hair from your brow
And whisper the word I love you
Every day for the rest of my life.

Cindy A. Russell

SYMPHONY OF LOVE

Thinking of you
I am as tuned as the violin
Taut with love and emotion
You are the conductor
I am your instrument
At your command
Playing the concerto
To the music of love
Bursting forth
In a crescendo
A melody
of kisses
The staccato
of the beating heart
To climax
The symphony of love.

Monica Serle

A VALENTINE VERSE

All valentines are pretty,
In a special way.
I got one once with pink roses,
My mother sent it,
My husband wasn't very romantic,
But neither was I!

Gertrude Germain

MARRIAGE DAY

HONORABLE MENTION

Blue mannequins dance at my wedding
And I, the groom in drag,
sing songs about electricity

The cows without eyes
lumber through the grocery store
And angels with triangular haloes
smoke cigars while their
mothers try to phone

The Visa Card is broken
The Safeway is closed and
out of avocados

My sister is home
washing her hair
She's coming later to serve cake

We flee rice thrown
from sweaty hands
And go to Motel 6 to
consummate our insanity

And we are pleased
As God is also.

J. C. Caruso

TIMES ENTWINED

I sit and think of fields and flowers,
Of the days I walked for hours.

And they show . . .
Somehow they know . . .

For in the hands of a little one,
Clutched tightly, the flowers come.

I sit and think of times of joy,
When in the door, appears my boy.

In his small hands a butterfly
Catching me with memories gone by.

It's been a long day
Watching the children play.

But all their laughter and smiles
Will give me energy for awhile.

As past and present entwine,
I know all will be fine.

For as time and future unfold,
I know the memories it will hold.

Leona Joan Osier

As we step through that garden of roses —

We feel the thorns tear at our feet,
and roses that lift our hearts.

In time those wounds will heal, and all
that will remain are the beautiful
memories of those roses.

Susan Paden

HALO OF LOVE

I would like to see the day,
when peace encircles our world as I pray,
With a halo of love.
And man accepts the word from above,
That all are equal in God's eyes,
and His love never dies.

Each good deed is remembered with love,
And brings joy to our hearts,
Showing that love heals all wounds,
To give us a new start.

So we must live each day
With that in mind,
And peace with all,
We will surely find.

Ruby M. Olson

LOVE

Love is the hardest word to believe in
It can make or break you
And if you find it
You have to work so hard to keep it
Glowing, glowing true.

Love is the hardest word to believe in
But we all try to find it
Because we can't live without it
Love makes life worth living
It's part of sharing and giving
Which makes life worth living, it's true.

Love is the hardest word to believe in
But we all need to believe in
Love, love, love.

Diane R. Boudreault

WAITING

I'm waiting
always waiting for the
excitement to enter my life.

I'm like a child
I feel small and need special
attention.

I'm here
Look at me
Caress me
LOVE ME.

Bring out the women hidden inside me.
Fill me with the fires of passion
so that I'll wait no more.

Georgiann D. V. Perry

TO MY WIFE

My Orma Jane, come to me —
Not because your face is fair to see,
But your soul so pure and sweet
Makes me kneel and worship at your feet.

Oliver C. Charter

I LOVE YOU

I love you,
in big ways,
I love you,
in small ways,
I love you,
for what you say,
and what you do,
I love you,
for how you care,
in sickness and health,
for richer and poorer,
but most of all,
I love you,
because you're you.

D. Mathewson

TIME AFTER TIME

after the mis-placed
time
wandering aimless
ly
through the arid
waste land
of a
lone
ness
it is now marvelous
to lie refreshed
in the spring
show
er
of your love

Richard F. Kellas

SEA SORCERY

When the sea calls through the twilight
In a voice of azure silk
I take the path clove from raw sandstone
That sheers away to Gideon's key.
Here the breakers thrash their sorrows
Moon-silvered whales call to lost loves
A seawind lover's kiss of salt
Holds me bewitched in ancient spell.
The locals say that Gideon's fate
Lies hidden beyond the coral reefs
Where he joined his seawind lover
Enduring legend of the deep.
Perhaps one day, I, too, may follow
When the sea calls through the twilight
A kiss of salt upon my lips.

Joan Schernitz

Come dawn,
the sun melting in through early fog,
my younger soul runs searching for you,
laughing —
together, we bring in the day.

In the meadow
our child spirits romp,
thawed from their winter of growing up
by the light
dancing through each other's faces.

Diane E. Ramey

SWEET MEMORIES OF PUPPY LOVE

Dedicated with love to "Danny,"
a cherished dog friend.

With the passing of the years
My heart still sheds tears
For my four-footed friend
Who was faithful to the end.

Always watchful and on the alert,
He guarded me from being hurt.

He showered me with love and affection
His dog sense was my protection.

After seventeen years, he reached the end
of the line,

And died in his sleep holding an old slipper
of mine.

I like to think that he is waiting for me
On the isle of eternity . . .

That faraway shore
Where we will be together forevermore.

Eliza Jane Bye

BYE, ELIZA JANE. Born: New Jersey, July, 1900; Education: University of Experience of the 20th Century, private tutoring by eminent professors including grandparents, parents, friends and Mother Nature's teachers: bees, birds, animals, and faith-abiding trees and flowers; Occupation: Consultant to organizations, retired; Memberships: Smithsonian Institution, Wildlife Association, National Council of Women, Sierra Club; International Cultural Centers for Youth, Inc. (U.S.A. and Pilot Center in Jerusalem); Founder and President of Let Us Remember to Remember of the U.S.A. and International; Other Writings: *The World Around Us Through the Eyes and Writing of Eliza Jane Bye,* 1985; *Down Memory Lane With Eliza Jane,* memories over the years, 1982; *A Trilogy of Stories for Children,* 1982; *Bye's Animal Fables,* educational and humorous, 1985; *Seeds of Peace,* A peace play dedicated to International Year of Peace, 1986; All published by Let Us Remember to Remember of U.S.A. and International; Themes: *To accept life as it comes along, not seeking to be a perfectionist, but to live in a way that will merit the words "well done" at the end of life's sojourn, spreading the sunshine of a smile and laughter, the lubricants of life and the best remedy for all ailments, real or imaginary.* Comments: *I would like to remember to be grateful that my path crossed with some of the wonderful people of the world who give of themselves wholeheartedly to make the world a better place for all people and all living things.*

MY MOTHER: MY CHILD

Mother and daughter roles have reversed;
Once genteel Mama, serene and mild,
Has to be diapered like a child.
At ninety-nine, Mama strews her food,
Cannot hit her mouth, try as she would.

Hallucinations terrorize her nights
With phantasmagoric scenes and sights.
Shrieking, she calls, frozen with fright,
"Help! See the carpet blazing by my chair!
And a snake is lurking over there!"

"Mama," I soothe, "it's only a dream
Like I once had of gigantic bears —
And you'd come bounding up the stairs.
You would kneel beside my tumbled bed
And tousle my curly, sweating head."

Now I say, "Ole Booger-Fear go away!
Death is a scary dream, my darling.
Tomorrow you'll fly like a starling
To your Father waiting with face alight.
Arms outstretched in welcoming delight."

Dorothy Garton Cart

CHRISTMASTIME WITHOUT YOU

The pine tree decorated and sparkling with lights.
But it looks empty.

Colorful packages wrapped and set under the tree.
But my eyes see no color.

The bustling of last minute shopping.
But to me it seems everything is dull.

The excitement of Christmas Eve is on the face of everyone.
But to me it's just another day.

Then the phone rings and it's you
Telling me you're coming home.

So from now on Christmas will have
A very special meaning for me.

It will be known as
The time our love won out.

After all Christmas is a time
For Peace and Love.

Rachel A. Lehman

Forsake me as you have been, not a chore
for you. The cutting edge you bore and more
than that you shine bright lights on the site
where dead dogs lie, and ghostly vamps sigh, and
Pray do tell me, what spurned your chilly word
to accost my heart, rape it of its love
and cast it down like a filthy glove stained?
Diseased am I, that you respond with disdain?
Or perhaps, the assault was mine, not yours
How wrong of me to strike you with concern!
Slap my wrists, slash them, forsake me, let acid burn
and etch on my skin a pattern of gore.
Let the games begin, joust black knight! the site
is here; I wear no armor, not tonight.

Roz Elliott

GINNY

Ginny, how often have I combed your hair
As we lay together there
Bathed in love's sweet afterglow?
Ginny, we said some things
And, yes, we even talked of rings
But that was a long time ago.
And now I don't know
I just don't know.

Ginny, we'd smile some smiles
And, Ginny, we'd talk awhile
And dream some wild and crazy dreams.
But something's between us now
Good times seem over somehow.
At least sometimes they do to me.
And now I don't know
I just don't know.

Sometimes it all seems so unfair
To simply leave you lying there
But sometimes our feeings we can't explain.
Ginny, is it me or you
And where is it leading to?
Ginny, can we both change?
I don't know
I just don't know.

Greg Evans

WHEN AUTUMN COMES

This sullen gray has come to haunt me,
The shady, cold days of autumn are here again
The leaves are now falling,
As my soul feels colder . . .
Reminded of the days past
When I lost you.

Linda M. Noyola

THE POWER OF LOVE THROUGH THE AGES

Inspired by my late husband, Dr. Andrew F. Hegyeli

Its footsteps are easy to follow.
Across the ages, across divides of time and space,
Beyond the trampled ashes of death.

The power of love, the power of the soul of man,
The greatest power in the universe,
Continues its creation.

Singing songs of loved ones long gone,
Walking in glory in new worlds, separated from our lives,
Yet alive in our hearts through the power of love.

Loved ones separated from the problems of earth,
The sacrifices of blood, sweat and tears,
The disappointments of nakedness and grief.

The power of love, lifting our spirits,
Uniting the families of man near and far,
In life, in death, together or apart.

Whispering encouragement and cheer,
Refreshing our hearts,
Communicating loving touches by hands of yesteryear,
Igniting our hearts in love, giving us power
Giving us inspiration to face life again.

Ruth Johnsson Hegyeli, M.D.

EVERLASTING LOVE

I have tried to imagine how it would be,
Without your love that surrounds me.
My Darling, without your love so true,
Life would have no meaning, without you.

Now that the years are flying by,
The more I ponder, and wonder why.
My Father in Heaven picked you for me,
Will always remain, my private mystery

I feel so sorry for some friends I see,
That do not have a love like me.
A love that has lasted, year after year,
And grown stronger, because of you, my dear.

I could not begin to list all the things,
That loving you, to my mind brings.
I only know that I have much more,
That a dozen lifetimes could not store.

Even when the time comes that we must part,
You will surely be in my heavenly heart.
For this very God that gave you to me,
Meant it to last, for all eternity.

Leo V. Castello

I LOVE YOU

For your gentleness, kindness and affection
We share, I love you.

For just being you and not putting on airs,
For joining others who say "I care," I love you.

For being there when I needed you,
For your smile that makes me happy, just when I'm feeling blue,
My heart and mind will always be filled
With the memories of you.

Kathy McCartney

THE MANY FACES OF LOVE

It seems to me that love is ever present at
A table blessed with the fullness thereof,
And when I am surrounded by loved ones
I feel the aura of love streaming from above.

I see the face of love when a young girl
Romps the world in jovial ecstasy,
No dream too rare, every dream to unfurl
In God's firmament and legacy.

I see the face of love in my weary wanderings
As I travel the misty paths of life
When I chance upon a mother with babe in arms
Surely, God has shed forth his greatest light.

I see the face of love with great insight
When a child looks upon a shiny Christmas tree.
I realize then love has showered its might
That angels revel when they see.

Though I may search the whole world over
I am so compelled to agree
That of all the loves, the best one is
The one that God bestows on you and me.

Helen Melissas

MAY YOUR LOVE GROW EVER DEEPER

John 20:11-18

When they killed the King of Glory
And nailed Him to the tree,
Jesus died for our redemption
Suffering there in agony.

Thus He fulfilled His mission
That brought Salvation down to earth,
For our sins there is remission
And through His Spirit, second birth.

Christ arose on Easter morning
As the stone was rolled away,
And now sits enthroned in glory
Where He intercedes for us each day.

Do you know Him as your Savior?
Does your love grow more and more?
Then thank Him this Easter morning
For the pain and grief He bore.

Raymond M. Hering

A SONG OF LOVES FOR YOU

I have written this song of loves,
in my heart, just for you
To light the earth's darkest corner
Love, my love, is like a fragrant rose
That fills the air, with beauty and delight
As I sit beside your empty chair,
Yesterday's memories of you linger in my heart
and soul, and as I write to you today
I know tomorrow, someone else may
read my song of loves to you. For our
love will never die, for I love you infinitely
so.
Soon, dear heart, you and I will be
together eternally, even though we have
parted long ago for our love still lives
in my heart and soul, for I loved thee
Infinitely so and so shall it be
Until the day I die and we both live
Eternally up above.

Dushka Dixon

NE'ER CAN YOU LEAVE ME

You say your love for me is dead — that you must go —
But that you cannot fully leave me you must know —
For thoughts of me will always come to you.
We will forever for each other care —
The love we had forever will be there —
Within my heart I will fore'er have you.

And when I lonely feel, and when I'm sad,
My thoughts of you will ever make me glad —
In mem'ry I forever will have you.
I need not envy lovers that I see,
For thoughts of you will ever with me be —
I always, yes, I always will have you.
And should the future crises bring to me,
I will not fearful be, but brave will be —
With inspiration I received from you.

And though your love for me in ashes lies —
It, like the phoenix, back to life can rise —
And bring you back to love awaiting you.

Laura Brown Lane

INDIGENOUS

I miss each time I've seen You
The times I've contemplated too
I miss your waves in the wind
Spring rainstorms that shut us in
I miss like Home, You
Features cloudless blue I see still
Dappled sun indigenous to the park
Summer evenings warmed in the dark
Sister Minnesota we are separated pieces You
And I like twin cities today stately sad
Solaced in sunsets we shall and have
Had

Tommy Toledo

GOOD, THOMAS MCGREGOR. Pen Name: Tommy Toledo; Born: Ohio, 1958; Education: City University of New York, B.A. in Sociology, 1985; Occupations: Counselor for schizophrenic outpatients (social worker); Memberships: U.S. Peace Council, Chair of the Artists' Task Force of the Staten Island chapter; U.S. Committee for Friendship with the German Democratic Republic (USCFGDR); Awards: Best Original Written Entry, *Florida Keys Community College Literary Magazine,* for 'I Love The City,' 1981; Poetry: 'And Yet Her Smile,' *American Hungarian Word,* 10-24-85; 'Pepsi or Coke,' *Outerbridge,* Spring 1985; 'River of Dreams,' *The Daily World,* 8-29-85; 'Comrade Sister,' *The American Poetry Anthology,* Spring, 1986; Comments: *The best poem is a simple snapshot depicting a better world, or demanding one.*

SILENCE

From the outermost realm of deep space,
To the innermost parts of the atom,
There can be found this entity called silence;
Where without it,
There could be no animate existence at all.
Though only when the mind cries,
does one hear it;
Only when the light fades,
does one see it;
Only when there is no love,
does one feel it.

Ross Patrick Smith

I LOVE YOU

We ambled over and fell
at the foot of the goal post,
giggling softly so no one would hear.
Your breath smelled of Budweiser
as you leaned over to kiss
my neck.
And my head spun with Boone's Farm
and Old Spice
as you nudged me to the ground.
Leaning back, you said I was beautiful . . .
again.
I noticed your hands trembling
and you stuttered something under your breath
that stole my attention.
In a daze
I watched a single tear
drop down your cheek
as I soberly whispered the words
"me too."

Susan Sands Anderson

THE HILL

In Memory of My Mother, Swaughnie Lillian Pennington
8-11-99 — 6-19-81

I climbed up the hill to honor my mother.
I climbed up the hill that warm August day.
To search for a truth in a spiritual way.

As I climbed up the hill, I longed for her nearness.
As I climbed up the hill, I thought of her dearly.
As I climbed up the hill, to see her more clearly.

As I climbed up the hill, I felt she was with me.
As I climbed up the hill, her presence so slight.
On this day she was born, so my heart felt delight.

I climbed up the hill to honor her memory.
I climbed up the hill on the day of her birth.

How my soul came alive as her wings touched the earth!

Jackie Saxman

FOR YOU

The first time I saw you, as you walked by
Was enough to make a grown man cry
Your beauty amazes me, and puts me in awe
Observing your features, I detect not a flaw
You move with the grace of the swimming of a swan
Your gaze transmits the innocence of a fawn
You look good in anything you'd happen to wear
Your pretty smell leaves sweetness in the air

I shall never tire of looking at you
Every time you appear, to be freshly renewed
Your beauty in my eyes, and love is in my heart
If we ever get together, we would never part
The weight on my mind, the strain on my soul
The ache in my heart, which only you can console
The only thing better than writing about you
Is seeing you,
holding you,
and doing things for you.

Jeffrey B. Davis

YOUR LOVE IS COLD AS ICE

Your love is as cold as ice . . .

The honeymoon is over, and you are no longer nice.

You make me work hard . . .

While you watch T.V. and play cards.

Your beer glasses are left all over . . .
The love moments are not like they were . . .

You breath smells like cigarettes and beer . . .
Your few kisses now taste weird . . .

Your few words are often cutting and cruel . . .
And you use me like a tool . . .

I know you no longer care . . .
I feel the love chills on my skin so bare.

I fear the ominous words . . .
You are through . . . this is for the birds . . .

Amelia "Mickey" Hincken

LOVE IS A FEELING

Love is a feeling that comes from the heart,
A desire, a drive, a tenderness, a spark.

Love is a feeling of infatuation,
Of affection, devotion and admiration.

Love is a feeling of adoration,
An enchanting and bewitching fascination.

Love is a feeling that excites the emotions,
A contemplation, an anticipation and great expectations.

Love is a feeling precious to us all,
The slender, the heavy, the short and the tall.

Andrea C. Hargis

LOVE

A little bit of all is love —

A little bit of day — a little bit of night —
A little bit of black — a little bit of white —
A little bit of sadness — a little bit of gladness —
A little bit of wrong — a little bit of right —

A little bit of all is love —

You better understand — what you pretend — to defend —
By dreaming your rosy dream — believing in luck supreme —
Trying to be all new — a glorious end in view —
You better comprehend — there must be discontent —

For — a little bit of all is love —

It's a little bit of day — and a little bit of night —
It's a little bit of black — and a little bit of bright —
A little bit of gladness — a little bit of sadness —
A little bit of wrong — a little bit of right —

A little bit of all is love.

Halina de Roche

SAVAGE

To Marcia Stoll

Savage on a tropical desert isle, far away, secluded
obsolete civilization, lust
for each other controls animal instincts
under the palm tree blowing in the wind
crashing waves and blistering sand, hot from the blazing sun
in the dark you held me in your arms and it was only you and i
in a world of two, we talked about things, everything
i found you and understood you fully
in the moonlight i saw the tear glisten in your eye
for we both knew that then the savage tamed as we became one
your tanned skin smelling of coconut oil meshed with mine
as you loved me with a love so strong we were as free as gulls
soaring above our own paradise
a white stallion ran across our beach with its mane whipping
and as if the love from you and i reached it
it slowed and looked up, i saw that wild flame soften, i knew
my place could only be here next to your body in your arms
in our paradise.

Laura Ann Stoll

JEANETTE & KENNETH

You've said to me, whatsoever conditions you may live —
Keep the integrity of your mind,
Beyond the sunny shores of time.
Be open like a luminous kite, without a string
Yet have direction, like an aware & dedicated sail.
Have no vices inside yourself
As the wealth of your spirit crowns your soul.
Reach for your goals; to aspire is to achieve —
By listening to that still small voice
That guides you beyond the stars
Think on truth & love of lasting bonds,
From the beginning to the evening dawn —
For out of them, will grow wondrous things!
And your castle will at last be built.
Now as I have grown, I cherish my lofty visions
Of dreaming great things
And so have become one with my ideal —
Mother and Father you are a treasure that stirs in my heart
By being loved by you,
I learned to love, & live a life in Jesus Christ Our Lord.

Debra Kirkham

MY HEARTACHE

Pale pink skies
Soft tearful cries
Beautiful white doves
Unknown loves.

Whispered greetings
Hopeful meetings
Shy, quiet girl
Life's in a whirl.

A popular boy
One small joy
Secret glances
Dreams of romance.
My heartache . . .

In our world of golden swans,
    It is often the small white duckling,
        Who has many a heartache to live . . .

Sarah Denny

THEIR WEDDING DAY

(or, At the Altar)

Two hearts united in perfect harmony
Beating together in melodic ecstasy,
Bright eyes shining like stars above,
Expressing in misty tenderness their fervent love.
Prayers, hopes and dreams all blended in this hour
Await precious unfolding like a budding flower.
What greater joy is found beneath the sun? —
Two lives made one by Heaven's touch have just begun!

Maryann V. Shue

CANDIDA

You were created
  out of my dreams and yearning
For something warm and snuggly
To hold against my heart when it was sore.

Knowing that you in your sweet innocence
  Could roll away the burden of Man's sorrows,
    Born in the very dust of his origin
Revealing not from whence they came, or why.

Now you are gone; I am alone
  Memories haunt me — I find no solace
Until I remember — *I* created you
  Out of the fabric of love and need.

Love never dies — is born again and again
  Manifesting new forms with its own creation.
So I wait quietly
  For in the hush of some early dawn
I *believe* —
  it will happen again . . .
The heart understanding —
Faith
    and Love reborn.

Rosalind Roberts

ROBERTS, ROSALIND D. Born: New York City; Education: New York University, School of Journalism; Occupation: Retired, formerly editor and writer for Trade Publications; Poetry: 'Lament for a Songbird,' *American Poetry Anthology,* Spring 1985; Other Writing: Novel not yet published, Comments: *Poetry is a late-in-life interest; impelled to do it when deeply moved. Love and faith are my usual themes — will pursue this hobby. 'Candida' was written in memory of my beloved little dog — nicknamed "Candy" because she loved sweets.*

SWEET LOVE

Sweethearts walking hand in hand
with eyes only for each other,
unaware of the surrounding world,
thinking only of her lover.
Her head's in the clouds and the sunshine,
life couldn't be more luscious,
she lives for his precious arrival
and into his arms she rushes.
She caresses his cheek and kisses him
twirling his wavy hair,
tells him how much she misses him
and why he's so wondrously fair.
She loves him so much it hurts her,
she cares so much she's crazy,
she thinks he's the greatest guy in the world
and doesn't notice he's DOWN-RIGHT LAZY!

Sandra Huston

BELOVED, ONCE AGAIN

My dark and slim belovéd, once again
Come stroll the roadways hand in hand with me.
The windswept leaves are quite as wild as when
They fell like gold beneath our maple tree.
Our song cascades against that blue glass dome
In melody that hauntingly returns
To say your presence made our dwelling home,
A keep of love for which my heart still yearns.

My dark belovéd, come again and smile.
Restore ecstatic happiness to me,
And let life hold for just a little while
The bliss it held before death's stern decree
Rent us in twain . . .
God willing, may we be
One joyous whole through all eternity.

Anna-Margaret O'Sullivan

LOVE

Love is like two newlyweds who just kissed.
Love is like going out on your first date.
Love is like a woman seeing a man for the first time.
Love is like a baby coming out of a mother's womb.
Whatever love is, it's good.

Sal Costanzo, Jr.

Maybe my love will come to me today,
Dark and handsome, with eyes as bright as spring.
As wind sweeps the leaves, will he go away?
And if he does, what will the summer bring?

The roses are starting to look lifeless,
The sun sets sadly over planet earth.
Animals on the prowl begin to hiss,
And the pale man-in-the-moon shows his worth.

I will always hold some feelings for you,
Although your eyes may lose their shine for me.
Your memory will linger ever true
A place for you there will forever be.

But still, I will soul-search my whole life long,
For my own soul, to share my own sweet song.

Catherine Outeiral

SATURDAY EVENING

From the car to the cinema, they held hands,
Starting dreams of rose-scented befores,

Then on the rising brown carpet,
He and She, side by side . . .
In the low-lighted, windless twilight
To the heavy dun door, side by side . . .

She remembers —
She recalls —
More the child he must have been.
Actual light buoyed, crackling out
In a brown glow from his eyes, gamboling about . . .

Side by side,
As he envisions: She never floated,
Yet never ended; she moved empty coat-
Like, just like caressing . . . side by side,

To their sliding hands at its opening,
And fumbling fingers, reaching
For who would enter first.

K. E. Franklin

TO LIVE AND LOVE ANOTHER DAY

As I wake and see the morning dew,
Mr. Sun rises and says, Good Morning,
This day will be for you;
A bright and glorious day.

Lay your eyes upon the trees,
See the evening fall.
Listen to the birds, as they sing
their morning call.

Now touch the dampness that lays upon the ground,
and all the tears and sorrow will be gone.

Feel the tenderness that surrounds you there.
Now let your mind drift away and remember when
you cared.

Smell the flowers that are in bloom,
Now tell me, this day is made for whom.

I have smelled, touched, seen, and felt this morning new.
The kiss of sunlight now I give to you.

Michael R. Dion

TO TOUCH THE SKY

August 1985, Point Reyes

The roar of the ocean brings me to you,
as the warmth of the sun pounds
under the earth beneath my body
and caresses my being
as your fingers do my soul and my heart.

I find relief in you from the pain and joy
that I experienced in my life and suffering.

I long to continue to soar with your spirit
till I am free as the highest cloud
along with you
and then we both touch the sky.

Isabel Sobozinsky

A LOVER'S PRAYER

My Lord, help me!
I am so confused,
I could run forever.
I hurt passionately,
And I keep running.
It's the right way, I think.
I don't know anymore,
And I cry.
I imagine it over.
I quit.
But then, I'm running again,
Always into a cold wall.
I turn 'round to leave,
But it is always back;
Back to the cold and the dark,
And the nonexistent options.
Make it right, God, take it,
Make it Your own.
It is in Your hands, my Lord.
I can't even touch love without it crumbling.

Valerie Ruth Biddick

SUMMER

Summer comes and summer goes,
But this summer was spent with one . . .
My only one.

The people, the places,
Engraved in my mind,
Even seen, but never forgotten.

Thinking of those make-believe days,
Wondering if they were true or
A figment of my imagination.

The feeling that has been left inside,
Is so hard to let one know,
Only expressed on paper.

My Spanish dream holds tight,
But remember, summer comes and summer goes,
But summer will never be forgotten.

Heather Loflin

LIFE'S STORY

I walk with you by my side holding your hand
feeling strong yet weak knowing now my life's complete.
With your guidance, love, and tenderness
you show me a way to a world of love.
Crossing the byways, reaching our goal,
collecting memories of the days of old,
we've gone through life and lived it all.
The joys, the sorrow, the agony and pain,
all those days never to be relived again.
Each day we sit and watch the young,
loving, dancing and having fun.
Old and gray we live each day — never
throwing life away.
Old we may be but never too old to enjoy
each other and remember —
I walked by your side, holding your hand
in mine. Feeling strong and yet weak
knowing then my life was complete.
With your guidance, love and tenderness,
You showed me a way to a world of love.

Lynn Walsh

VARIATIONS ON A THEME

I don't want to think of times long past
And the way things used to be.
I don't want to think of what we once had:
The love you shared with me.
I don't want to think of your warming embrace
With kisses spent one by one.
I don't want to think of your precious face
Framed by the setting sun.
I don't want to think what opened the door;
That closed forever behind you.
I don't want to think about you anymore —
But I do, I do, yes I do.

Howard Layne Harper

HARPER, HOWARD LAYNE. Born: Waco, Texas, 5-13-38; Education: California State University, Fullerton, B.A., Psychology, 1980; B.S. Human Services, 1980; Columbia Pacific University, San Rafael, California' Ph. D., Psychology; Occupations: Licensed Marriage Family Child Counselor, 1984; Board Certified Hypnotherapist, 1985; Family Therapist Psychological Associates, Fullerton, California; Social Worker, Riverside County, California; Editor of *Psyche* CAMHC newsletter, 1986; Memberships: California Association Marriage Family Therapists; California Association Counseling Development; California Association Mental Health Counselors; Yorba Linda Chamber of Commerce; Awards: 'Hide My Love Away,' 'Summer Affair,' 'Death Hawk,' *Alura,* 1985; 'The Foe Within,' 'Silent Cast,' *Deros,* 1985; Other Writings: "Coping With Stress," article, *Butterfield Express,* May 1, 1985; "Strategies for a Successful Small Business," article, *Entrepeneur,* 1985; Comments: *The poetry that I write is an honest expression of myself and reveals my innermost emotions and feelings. The truth of who I am as a person, with all my untold secrets, unspoken thoughts, and unseen foibles comes out. My poems are a genuine expression of myself and my love, freely offered to those open to accept it.*

IN LOVE WE TRUST

Two married people, two separate lives
Who got together, through cheating and lies

The years went on, and they became lovers
Then the problem arose, they didn't trust one another

It's clear to see why they're always in doubt,
When one's running about
But this is a problem that must be resolved,
Or they will never survive another year out

It's not easy, I know that for sure
But the love I have for you, has allowed me to cope

The day will come soon, you'll feel that way too
This my dear will be better for you

No more arguments or agony to go through
Just pure love and trust, between us two.

June Drao

DRAO, JUNE KAY. Born: Brooklyn, New York, 7-10-48; Occupation: Freelance Writer; Awards: Award of Merit Certificate from World of Poetry for my Poem 'Letting Go,' 9-30-85; Poetry: 'Lost Love,' American Poetry Association, 1-86, and Poetry Press, 1-86; 'Loving A Married Man,' 'The Way of Life,' inspirational, American Poetry Association, 3-86; 'Thankful,' inspirational, American Poetry Association, 6-86; Comments: *I write my poems from true experiences. I try to express my feelings through my poems and to let other people know they are not alone in their feelings about certain situations.*

NOTHING LEFT TO SAY

Dedicated to my Mother

You stood by me quietly, you held my hand and prayed;
Not a word was spoken, nothing left to say.
Your eyes told the story, of a love so deep,
That shouldered the pain, the agony, without a need to speak.
Your heart beat quietly, within your gentle breast,
Silently saying, "I love you, we'll withstand this test."
We've always stood together, in this very same way,
One's love carrying the other, when there's nothing left to say.

Barbara L. Clark

AN AFFINITY OF LOVE

An Artist, who searched for the most beautiful thing,
dreamed of a painting to be exhibited world-wide.
He traveled extensively to visit picturesque views;
returned to his abode, unable to make up his mind.

He saw Faith in the eyes of his children
as he entered his door,
When gleefully, they ran to greet him;
discarding their toys on the floor.

It was Love in the eyes of his wife
that quickened his thoughts to subjects beyond,
There in his own house was Peace that Love
and Faith had built on the Marriage Bond.

He'd found Peace and he'd found beauty,
and Faith, you find in every prayer;
He'd found Love that builds poverty into riches,
sweetens tears and wipes away all care.

So he painted the picture of domestic tranquility;
the most beautiful thing the world has ever known,
THE Family, by God's design; tied together with
an affinity of Love, and he called it Home.

Juanita J. Wallis

WALLIS, JUANITA J. Pen Names: Bill's Wife, Juanita J. Wallis, Mrs. W. J. Wallis; Born: 10-10-29; Married: 9-9-47 to William Jesse (Bill) Wallis; Education: High School, Tucson, Arizona, Self-Educated; Occupation: Cattle Ranching; Memberships: New Mexico Cattlegrowers, National Cattlemen, New Mexico CowBelles, National Cattlewomen, and Wagonwheel CowBelles; Awards: Golden Poet Award for 'The Family Pet,' 1985; Honorable Mention for 'Peace on Earth,' 1986; Poetry: 'Seasons of Love,' *Hearts on Fire Vol. II,* 1984; 'Scenes of Enchantment,' *American Poetry Showcase,* 1985; 'Life's Diary,' *A Treasury of Contemporary Verse,* 1985; 'Reflections,' 'High Tech Retirement,' *Masterpieces of Modern Verse,* 1985; Comments: *I write season greetings and humorous poems about bureaucratic control of the beef industry. I write to promote beef and all the by-products we use in everyday life. My husband, Bill and I are proud grandparents of four granddaughters and two grandsons, and we love to work and play as a family.*

MISTY TEARDROPS

These misty teardrops still becloud
My weary blue-green eyes
As I longingly await the day
When my heart to you will rise

These misty teardrops wash anew

Alone to trudge my weary path
To you, my destiny!

These misty teardrops still bedim
These eyes you kissed that day —
Another flower beautiful,
Fragrant in life's bouquet.

These misty teardrops now have made
A rainbow in my heart
To be with me continually
Till I come to you, Sweetheart!

Thelma Van Scoik

THE GIRL IN THE BUBBLE

I sit alone in the corner,
In a bubble without corners;
Waiting for someone to enter —
But, they walk by.

I extend my hands,
In need of some warmth;
And I, alone, reach out,
My fingers can sense only air.

I fantasize about a bubble-mate:
Someone to share the air with,
A magician or guardian,
Who could turn coldness into heat.

But, the walls prevent human bondage:
I play solitare inside my plastic world,
Aware of my rare disease —
I am terminally unloved.

Ilene Lisak

MY LOVE

Open your heart and the windows
Of your eyes
The night of loneliness has passed
As darkness dies

Your smile has indeed rescued
My wounded heart
And I leave my shell of protection
As I venture forth the part

I have known you for a million years
Though I never knew your face
Till our eyes entwined that fateful night
And our hearts did interlace

It is now I know forever more
Eternal is our love
True love it lies in each of us
Through time and space above

Gem M. Dumas

RECIPROCATING LOVE

Love came to the door
And I opened it wide
I outstretched my arms
And love stepped inside

It was soft and so warm
And I snuggled up close
Now this was pure heaven
What we all want the most

Then life got routine
There was so much to do
And while doing these things
I neglected love too

I kept very busy
And the years did fly
Then came the day
Love said good-bye

Now all that I've done
Or all I may do
I realize means nothing
If I don't give love too

Clementia

THE TRUEST OF LOVES

Two young friends,
Obscure in life's whirl
Until a failing heart
Startled the world

A transplant was needed
To insure the girl's life
While her friend was undergoing
A different kind of strife

To his parents he revealed
That when he was no longer living
He desired that his heart
To his girl friend be given

While the girl in the hospital
Awaited a donor
The boy's life ended
His heart needed no longer

The girl is now living
A new life begun
With the truest of love's heart
Beating within

Leon H. Nunn

PEOPLE

Rip your heart out every day.
Make the real world go away.
Listen to the people . . .
What they have to say . . .
Love them all
For it is true . . .
The Love of God is in me and you.

I don't know . . .
It may be true . . .
That is what makes a Poet out of you.

Elaine Meli

STAR GAZING

Shimmering stars in the full moon sky
Sent shivers through my heart
I looked above to this wondrous sight
And wished we weren't apart.

Silent tears flowed from downcast eyes
Memories stirred anew
Not so very long ago
I shared this sky with you.

Salty tears upon my lips I felt
The shivers turned to pain
Once more my eyes looked to the sky
And I thought of you again.

Silent tears dried from upturned eyes
Memories all were bright
Soon there'll be another time
There will be another night.

Kit Cronin

THE ENDLESS JOURNEY

as the wind
blows across the waters,
we watch
the motion of the waves
gently touch one another

just as we touch
each other's hearts
as we live
from day to day

for LOVE is
an endless journey
through time

just as the wind
blows across the waters,
we too shall dance
with joy for LOVE
has touched our hearts

David Nelson Roberts, Jr.

HEART SONG

Happiness is my only virtue,
darling I could never hurt you.
Knowing that you care for me
helps me feel so happy and free.

Pleasant memories we have shared
knowing one another cares.
In every problem we confide,
no matter how painful it is inside.

We have shared our every pain
knowing the other would feel no shame.
If a favor one should ask,
the other works to meet the task.

Mutual trust we have chosen,
no matter where the other is going.
My dreams are answered at your side
without you my soul would die.

Kenneth D. Senior

No tears, no tears cry for me.
You're just like a melody.
Here right now and then you're gone.
While your sweet memory lingers on.

No songs, no songs sing for me.
You're the one that wants to be free
As I want us to keep going on.
But the sweet memory lingers on.

No rain, no rain falls on me.
I only wish that you would see
I've done my best to keep us one.
And the sweet memory lingers on.

No sun, no sun shines on me.
I've got a tear I don't want you to see.
From now until the rising dawn
I'll let your sweet memory linger on.

Greg Evans

LITTLE PLANET OF LOVE

We will build a paradise up above
Our own little planet of love.
Build a house of love for you and I,
A paradise filled with love.
No more hate, and no more fears
No more hurt, and no more tears.
Perfect bliss for you and I,
On our own little planet of love.
We will have children up above,
Paradise, heaven, full of love
Love and happiness in a child
Children, all angels, wear a smile
A perfect heaven, up in the skies
No more teardrops in your eyes.
Perfect bliss each time we kiss
On our own little planet of love
On our own little planet above . . .

Renee Edwards

UNTITLED #10

If the sun never again
beamed hope upon my soul,
and the wind never again
opened my soul to the breathless All,
And the stars never again
caressed the light in my soul,
if I never again saw you,
but you knew I wanted
to love you as a deity
who bears bliss for the deserving,
If you knew I hated being human
because I could only
love you as a mortal
and not bring you blissful peace,
if you knew this,
I could die a mortal's death
in the sweetest of contentment.

Loretta Olund

TRUE LOVE

My heart cries out for love from you because I need you so.
Each deed I do, each word I say, is just because I love you so.

If you think not just listen dear and I'll quote the reasons why.

I love your eyes, the way they glow, like love's eternal flame.
I love your figure so fabulous; I nearly blush with shame.
I love your kisses, so exotic and rare; they bring forth a dreamy sigh.

I love you darling in such a way mere words cannot explain.
I love you so when we're apart I'm racked with erotic pain.
I love you so when I'm alone my heart near breaks in two.

My heart throbs wildly when I think of you and my whole soul cries
to feel your touch, to taste your lips and to gaze into your eyes.

Darling, dear, I love you so that I can never let you go.

Our precious love is like beautiful music; the crescendos and the falls;
strong, soft, exciting, rhythmic, but everlasting most of all.

David W. Perry

I REMEMBER YOU

Lying with you in the stillness of a frosty winter's morning.
Touching, caressing, we soothe each other's fears and anxieties.
Both our forms bathed in the warmth which only two in love,
Can unite to radiate.
Lost in each other's embrace, never wishing to be discovered,
Lest the spell break.
I remember you.

Strolling hand in hand with you along the rock-covered banks
Of a rippling mountain stream.
With brook-chilled wine, we drink to our happiness,
And bathe our lightly-clothed bodies
In the warmth of the summer sunshine.
I remember you.

Finding you back in my arms, our lips touching with new discovery,
After too long a time apart.
Your radiant face, your graceful form and reassuring smile,
In all these ways and many, many more, in my heart,
I remember you.

John Morgan Rosser

LAURA

Laura
She was a girl that never knew of love
Until one day she met another girl
One that became her best friend
She trusted her friend with all her heart
And then one day her heart was turned to stone
For her best friend abandoned her, leaving her all alone again
After that no one could understand why Laura always stood alone
Why she stayed away from people and spoke little
Her heart was burned and turned to stone and now she felt little
It wasn't until one day that someone else decided to take a chance on her
This other girl noticed that something was wrong with Laura
But oh how cautious Laura was
She could not love because it was her heart that was turned to stone
This girl took her time, hope, and bonding love to change Laura
Not to change her personality, but her heart
She helped Laura change her heart from stone to love again
Something Laura never thought she could achieve
She learned to love once again

Denise Karch

MIGHTIEST OF THE MIGHTY

Enter the cities of great sights and sounds;
Admire the fine art, the beauty that abounds.
Stand amazed at the bright skylining skyscrapers;
Look up in awe as giant planes swiftly come and go.

From on high a voice said, "Yes, many have built well,
But only through my love, my shaping of power and vision;
For I . . . I am Mightiest of the Mighty."

Read books that are helpful, inspiring.
Attend plays that are joyful, fulfilling.
Hear music so marvelously composed, it will never grow old.

From on high a voice said, "Yes, many have created well,
But only through my love, my shaping of power and vision;
For I . . . I am Mightiest of the Mighty."

Visit hospitals and the quickly growing medical centers;
Be encouraged at the gains of the gifted surgeon.
Feel the hope, the wonderment of transplants;
Note the changing of the views of the dissenter.

From on high a voice said, "Yes, many have healed well,
But only through my love, my shaping of power and vision;
For I . . . I am Mightiest of the Mighty."

Lester E. Garrett

ALWAYS WITH ME

I knew you in some forgotten time.
Now you come to me in dreams . . .
Or in enduring states of reflective thought.
There your presence is known to me.

You entered my life
from the day I was born.
Incidents of my life ceasing prematurely
concerned you.

In my infancy
you appeared at my expected end.
You interrupted DEATH . . .
and gifted me with the breath of life.

In childhood
I drowned in deep sea waters.
You rescued me . . .
and gently lifted me to safety.

In aging
the power of your love
cancels out all my fears of life's passing.
I know you will be there
with open arms to receive me.

Marie Geile

RECYCLING

Freely I give you a piece of my heart
    to take at your will without fear.
My giving is painless — I'll reap my rewards —
    I have no reservations, my dear.
Ahthough you may steal it and show it abuse,
    my heart, and my love, will live on.
For when I love others, I not only give;
    I take love so mine will never be gone.

Patricia Odlin

TREASURED TIME

I and the sea are one
the white foam
returning upon itself as it reaches the beach
is like my thoughts — churning and yearning
The sea breeze plays tag with my hair
and love tugs at my heart
I am a part of the sea
                    the wind
                    the sand
my fingers reach for a stronger hand
Twin shadows dance in front leading us on
We two are one in the sand of the sea
each knowing in our heart
these moments will be sealed
   in treasured compartments
If perchance, Love, we do not travel this way again
We have had today:
                    the sand
                    the sea
                    and thee

LaVada Falkner Staff

CRYSTAL CAVE

You need me and I can't be there
you waited too long for the realization
your tears fall upon me
instant crystallization
So here I am, here I stay
trapped in a frozen teardrop
alone in my crystal cave
watching your world stop
Can you rescue me, will you try?
Will I slip through your hands and shatter?
My transparent home is fragile
as if that will ever matter
I can't heal you this time
you've finally asked too much
to love without being loved
you left my heart untouched
You made my crystal cave
from your frozen tear
it's just too bad it went so far
before you realized I needed you near

Jeanie Varke

A LITTLE BROWN BUCK

A little brown buck and a lonely boy
    together from early morning.
They warned me my love had an unhappy ending,
    but whoever heeded such warning?
Each morning he tapped with his horn on my window
    to hustle me out for the fun.
To me he was brother and playmate and chum,
    to him I was Number One.
My little brown buck, too soon he grew heavy,
    as heavy, almost, as my heart.
I knew that each pound he put on to his frame
    meant all that much sooner we'd part.
Then one day they came and they took him away,
    away in the dying sun.
Next morning they told me to cry no more,
    for him it was over and done.
But never for me, I shall always remember
    his leaving in back of the truck
And always my heart shall have one aching chamber
    reserved for a little brown buck.

Dorothy Heller

OVER AT LAST

A life long past,
A love all alone.
Over at last,
In a frame of its own.

A wedding long ago,
Sealed with a kiss.
The lights down low,
So much missed.

A love grown cold,
Lost to the past,
Nothing left to hold.
All over at last.

Laurie Parsons

FIRST TIME

Read me like a book
Turn the pages ever slow
Hear the rustle, crack of newness
Smell the fresh of never done
Trace the fingers slowly down
Watch the words with life be filled
See the black and white turn red
Feel the warmth of life untold
Write me author unknown.

Mimi Herrington

DECLARATION OF INDEPENDENCE

Listen,
one who sleeps under smooth slate,
soar away later, if you must,
and forget me,
but listen now.
I always did.
I adored you (always did)
but now that we're equal,
you no more wonderful than I,
I can forget you.
The heavens will sing with my freedom,
and you, one who has always been free,
will be burdened with my fickleness.
Mine, and not yours.

Jeannine Hall

WERE I TO SAY I LOVE YOU

Were I to say "I love you,"
Would I become your slave?
Would the price for my surrender,
Be more than I could pay?

Were I to say "I love you,"
Would it cause me to lose control?
And end up losing my freedom,
Especially room to grow?

I want to say "I love you,"
But, must my distance stay;
You'd want your way, come what may,
This price I cannot pay!

Lois E. Wood

YOU SMILE AT ME

In the morning clear and fair
Or when mist hangs in the air
As I ask the Lord to care —
You smile at me.
When the sun is shining bright
And the world with gleaming light
Seems to show that things are right —
You smile at me.
As the sun sets o'er the hill
And evening breezes bring a chill
As the peep toads start their trill —
You smile at me.
When the stars are bright and clear
And the moon will soon appear
Then I feel your presence near —
You smile at me.
Even though I know you're gone
Many memories linger on
As my life and love are one —
You smile at me.

Ruth Gardner McAlley

McALLEY, RUTH GARDNER. Pen Name: R. G. McAlley; Born: Glenburn, Pennsylvania, 8-28-10; Married: to Harold H. McAlley, 5--15-48 (deceased 1978); Education: Bloomsburg College, Teacher's Certificate, 1929; Nevada University, B.S. Ed.,1960, M.A. Ed., 1964; Occupation: Teacher; Memberships: NRTA, AARP, ADK; Awards: Award of Merit Certificates for, 'Come Romance When We're Young,' 2-28-85, and 'In the Fall of the Year,' 5-31-85; Golden Poet Award, 8-85; Poetry: 'Wayfarer,' *Our World's Most Beloved Poems,* 1984; 'The Worthwhile Life,' *Our World's Best Loved Poems,* 1984; 'Earths's Garden, *Today's Greatest Poems,* 1983; Comments: *I write about life, love, happiness and sorrow.*

LOVE

Love is wonderful when two
hearts beat as one
It's like scented flowers
that burst forth in a
profusion of pastel hues.
Delicate beautiful colors —
Love is compassion — caring for
one another;
LOVE IS PERFECT, QUIET BLISS;
Love is a soft gentle kiss.

Claudine L. Evans

MY SECRET LOVE

I thought that there would never be
More than one love in life for me.
That's how it was 'til '78
When death took my darling mate.

As time has healed the ache and pain
I find that I can love again.
For a secret love came my way
In '81 on a summer day.

Brownish-green are his piercing eyes,
A profound mind — brilliant and wise.
On his face an enchanting smile
And he used his charms to beguile.

He's virile, hale, a macho man,
Playing golf or getting a tan.
So handsome in a rugged way
And means more to me day by day.

He's so sweet and loving to me
He's the best there could ever be.
Time with him is etched on my heart
Forever with me when we're apart.

Thelma B. Wilkins

TOKENS OF LOVE

He picked me flowers
    On his way from school,
His little hands
    The only tool.

Hands them to me —
    All the while,
Waiting for
    My happy smile.

He sends me flowers
    Yet today,
Same as he did
    Yesterday

Through all the years
    That time has changed,
I remember
    Just the same —

That little boy
    So long ago,
That brought me flowers —
    I love him so.

Helen C. Mogavero

LOVE'S TRUE MEANING

Love is such a misused word, applied to everything
"I love your house." "I love your car," "I love your diamond ring."
But, let's stop and analyze how should "love" apply
Does it describe material things, that anyone can buy?
Or rather, is it precious, something earned, not bought
An emotion deep inside that fills one's every thought
With helping each deserving one, not looking for reward
With sharing, giving of oneself even when it's hard,
And you are having troubles too and no one seems to care
And when you need help the most, no one's ever there

I've just described conditions, that permeate this earth
Troubles, problems everywhere beginning from our birth
Yet, "Love" that often misused word will soon be understood
Meaning bad for some of us, for others, meaning good
Since God is love he'd be the one to help us understand
The meaning of this misused word, as he cleans this, His land

Ann Murrell

death of the incomparable

whatever it means i love you why go
did you suffer, yes i know you did
you loved us we you
but gramps was gone you loved him too

good ole charlie remember i called him that often
you used to laugh often
good ole charlie lay in a coffin
then you didn't laugh not often
i won't hear you laugh you're gone
just like charlie you left me

people will cry some real tears
but frank your son will drown his sorrows in a beer or two or three
and edith dear edith and clora your darling daughters
they're the ones that put you there in a home all alone
but not really you had God i had you
i loved you i still do
i am bitter i wish i were much older i would've taken you
but i am young seventeen i feel so much grief tomorrow they bury you
oh grama i love you good-by

Jeanie D. Dunn

UNTITLED APOLOGY (TRY TO UNDERSTAND)

There's no one I'd rather love than you.
This is the perfect example of what someone's jealousy can do.
It really hurts more than you seem to know.
Because I like you too much to let you go.
I'm sorry if it was something I said,
I didn't mean to lose my head.
I didn't want to hurt you or anyone.
I guess it doesn't matter, it's already done.
It's not really my fault or yours, not us.
I hope you know you mean too much.
What's happened is exactly what I didn't want to.
It's messed up everything that could have been between me and you.
I may never see you again.
I hope you'll understand I want to be your friend.
I'll see you as soon as I can.
Through this try to understand.
I still care and I miss you bad.
But anyway, thanks for the time we had.
I can't compete for you with lies.
So I guess, at least for now, all I can do is let go
and say good-bye.

Buffy Weaver

WILL YOU STILL LOVE ME?

Will you still love me
When I am old
And the skin of my body
Begins to fold?

Will you still love me
When I'm grey
And my memory forgets
Our yesterday?

Will you still love me
When I'm gazing away
Thinking inane thoughts
From day to day?

Will you still love me
When you I don't know
And remember me always
When I'm cold as snow?

Jeffrey D. Knowles

MINGLED MEMORIES

My tom-tom heart expectantly
At once began to burn
With bated breath most eagerly
Awaited your return.

Afraid to look deep in your eyes
Afraid that I might see
Indifference — yet hope replies
You *might* remember me.

But oh, if I should look and find
Love-light there still burning
See once again all that was mine
Know you, too, are yearning!

Dear One, are you with dream-ties bound
Of love that never frees —
Or, can no hope for us be found?
My mingled memories!

Sara E. (Page) Smith

UNPREPARED

As I look across the field
It is night and the vision is showing.
You walk slowly out of the mist.
I look at a beautiful tree; you are there.
I look at a wall; you come through.
Sky, sea, rainy day or sun
With strong light behind the apparition.
Are you an illusion?
Are you really as I see you to be?
Gentle in your way with me
But strong enough to lean on
Or are you totally my imagination?
So many rejections in my life
Makes reaching out a fear.
Is it better to have my illusion
Or accept reality, touch, feel and be?
I've walked and walked, totally alone
Trying to erase the image of you.
Am I losing my mind?
Losing my grip on reality?

S. A. Svedlund

NOT YET

Verse:

I heard a woman sobbing a strange lullaby,
It seemed like she was robbing her emotions dry;
'Twas plaintive and distressing. There's guilt in what I heard,
A woman breaking heart-strings, before she'd give her word.

Coda:

He'd like to bring me flowers, pretty plain to see,
Even bring a diamond; be my fool, for me.
But, could I make him happy? Could I forget?
Not yet. Not yet.

He really seems to need me, and his love is true;
Tender thoughts he'll feed me when I'm feeling blue.
But, old love won't stand steady before new love-debt;
Not yet. Not yet.

I could go on keeping him on a string,
But what kind of happiness can *that* bring?

He's watching, waiting, wond'ring, does his best to please
As I keep on pond'ring, is it fair to tease?
It's time I tested new love to break the regret
I can't forget, quite yet.

Stephen L. Bogadi

LEARNING

Each time we meet we grow.
We laugh, we share, and we cry.
I trust you with my heart,
It is no longer mine.
I will never regret giving it to you,
I will always know you showed me how to love.

DeDee Bellomy

SHARING

As husband and wife we hope and we pray,
That we'll share our love each passing day.

We share our dream as well as our hope,
That with life's "ups and downs," we're able to cope.

We share a need — one for the other,
To be a good father and be a good mother.

We share our feelings whether happy or sad,
And we share the good as well as the bad.

We shared with each other the birth of a son,
And we share with him the life he's begun.

We share our prayers as each day is done,
That dawn brings good health for our little one.

We share the hope that we lead him the right way,
And as he grows — his love grows each passing day.

We share the hope that we'll always be there,
To show each other our love and that we care.

We pray to God in Heaven above,
That we always "share" each other's love.

Peach Renner

THE SOLUTION

I don't like northern winters.
I don't like institutions.
But I love you, little sister.
I do love you!

I like the long warm autumns.
I like the southern flowers.
But they aren't that important.
I do love you!

I love the friends I've made here.
All the old ones and the new one!
You're the friend of all my lifetime.
I do love you!

I'll love what I'll be doing.
I hate why I will do it.
But anything is worth it.
I do love you.

There'll be problems, but we'll solve them.
It will be a new beginning,
for I love you, little sister.
I do love you!

Ruth A. Williams

LOVE IS FOREVER

Love is there for everyone to share.
Love is found in everyone everywhere.
In the blossom of a flower, pink petals fair
In the shine of the gold in everyone's hair

Love is in the clouds, in the falling rain
Splashing its love on my windowpane
The sound of love from my kitten's purr
Vibrations of love in smoothing its fur

Love in the snowman, snow giving it form
Love in the wind, the snow, the storm
Love in the substance of all the earth
Love in the air, love given at birth

Love in all laughter, love in every tear
Love is also letting go of fear
Your neighbor may frown, appear angry in sound
Return with a hug, true love can be found

Love is alive, and forever real
That inner peace, contentment you feel
Whether in the beyond, or the earth upon
Even in death, love lives on.

Ellen Collins

WHAT IS LOVE?

LOVE — that special quality and quantity
unto itself

If it is gingerly nurtured and cultivated
If it is cuddled and tenderly caressed
If it is cradled and it is cherished

Then it will grow in stature and in strength
And it will be as much as is needed
For as long as it is wanted.

Hank Justus

MOTHER'S LOVE

Darling, they told me not to cry,
As they told me you would die.
Surely they could expect a tear,
From a Mom who loved you so dear.
It was so often I was reminded,
That you must not see me blinded.
As my tears of sorrow flowed.
They said it would make your heart ache so,
My darling daughter in no way could I,
Stand by your dying bedside and not cry.
It was so often I stepped into the hall,
Lest you not see the many tears that would fall.
For no mother could face her terminal child's bed,
Without the flow of tears as her last hour she dread,
It would be a sin to stand and smile, while
She looked into the eyes of her beloved child.
They ask me to prepare myself for this,
Reminding me I must not break or go amiss.
Angel, if this is a sin, then I have sinned,
But I loved you so much in no way this battle could I win.

Dorothy America Boat

BOAT, DOROTHY AMERICA. Born: Belle Plaine, Iowa, 5-1-18; Education: Belle Plaine High Schools; Occupation: Cashier; Memberships: V.F.W. Club, Waterloo, Iowa; Poetry: 'Friendship,' Shirley Mikkelson, 1984; 'Words of Comfort,' John Frost, 1984; 'It Is Now,' 1985, 'God's Gifts,' 1985; Comments: *My gift of writing brings much pleasure to me, as an amateur author I find many fulfilling hours of happiness and a deep appreciation to my two editors for allowing me the pleasure of seeing my finished work in print. Therefore my deepest gratitude goes to them for their kindness and concern.*

FLAMES OF LOVE

Flames of love come warm my heart
I know of your fire I have felt you dart
Your radiant beauty you alone possess
Now fill me with passion and tender caress

I beckoned to you and you answered my call
Never again let us divide like a wall
My soul burneth my life all aflame
Now that I've found you I won't be the same

Tywanna Saunders

THE LOVING HEART

Think of your heart as a battery
Storing your innermost thoughts and feelings,
Consider it a center of your emotions
Memorizing your senses and heedings.

What you hear, what you see, what you say
Is fed into your lifetime heart,
Its food is provided by every good thought
Nourished by love from the start.

Some hearts are fresh and recent
Knowing no evil or pain,
Others are tightly stretched from stress
And revealing every strain.

Joy, love, and laughter are the cables
That we transmit from others,
Just as babies draw nourishment
At the breast of their loving mothers.

To forever love one another
Is second in God's command,
To keep a loving heart in all of us
Is in His long range plan.

Marian Fyhrie Guetz

GUETZ, MARIAN FYHRIE. Born: St. Paul, Minnesota, 3-13-19; Married: 2-15-41 to Robert Eugene Guetz; Occupations: Musician, business positions, Freelance Author; Memberships: Various music and literary groups; Poetry: *Ta Biblia,* collection of poems, 1986; *Verse-Stories of the Bible,* collection of poems, 1985; *Seasonal Reflections,* collection of poems, 1984; Other Writings: "Seasonal Reflections," short story, 1983; "Marian's Stories of Living Things," short stories, 1982; Comments: *The intent of my creative efforts is to arouse a thought or feeling in someone through the expression of words in rhyming verse which bless the Lord. These writings are the result of my own need for an upward look. I find great solace investing my time in God's purposes.*

ONE OF A KIND

For Gramma

What do I say about him now
How do I tell you what I found
A man like none I ever knew
A man whose limits were so few

His manner could be strict and proud
He'd snap and yell a little loud
But still he loved his friends and kin
He'd fight for them, protect within

In his heart there rose a flame
It burned within, — none could tame
I can't believe the fire's gone
Naught but the coals of memory burn on.

It took some time to understand
The person hidden in the man
And though I could't know his mind
The man I knew — was — one of a kind

Lylla Lane

I COULD SAY: IT'S HIM

After forty-seven years,
I could say: It's him!
He is not any more
The young brunette,
But his smile, his lips
Are still the same!
The afflux of memories
Hitting the edge
Of our age,
Brought me
The bench we used to sit.
Admiring my hair,
Patting my face!
It was so pure, so innocent,
So crystalline!
And after forty-seven years,
The precious stone of our life,
The youth,
Was shining, our grey box, up!

Jenny Ghihtei-Siroker

LOVE CAN

Love can hurt you,
Love can cross you.
Love can be painful,
Love can be spiteful.

Love can hide you,
Love can fight you.
Love can hate you,
Love can regret you.

Love can shatter you,
Love can batter you.
Love can flatter you,
Love can destroy you.

Love can come,
Love can go.
Love can stay
Love can leave.
Love you just have to believe.

Linda LaRocco

WHEN THINGS ARE THE DARKEST

For Mike

When things are the darkest,
And my skies are ashen gray,
All you do is smile,
And the clouds just fade away,
If the night turns cold and lonely,
I'll just look into your eyes,
It's there I'll find a thousand stars,
To shine brightly in my skies,
When things get dreary,
And all happiness seems banned,
All I have to do is reach out,
And take hold of your hand,
If the skies were to break open,
And heaven to come shining through,
He'd shower us with angels,
But none would be as beautiful as you.

Killeen Decker

J. D.

Time passes on
  and sometimes love is lost.
We swim in circles
  'round and 'round
  never reaching the top.
Words that are spoken
  are sometimes never heard.
Smiles that are given
  are sometimes never meant.

And when that time comes,
  and we both know what we
  once had is lost.
The words and smiles
  will be given.
Time will just pass.
And our love will be lost.

Jeannie Bayster

SAP IS FLOWING

SHE:
Sap is flowing
    Dark-eyed water retreats
    Smooth water heals;
Look up, our spirits are lifted.
    Beloved, I say
    Darling, I am here.

HE:
Love, I kiss the eyes that found mine;
    I kiss your peach-pink lips
    They say you love me.
I kiss your breath; it whispers my name.
    I kiss the hollow of your throat
    The beating pulse enchants me —
I cherish you — apart
Darling, I kiss your heart.

Prudencia Boals

Love's passion burning
casts glowing, amber embers
in the autumn dusk.

Shanon M. Sara

TOO TIGHT

Holding on so tightly,
You said you'd never leave
And I believed you.
Now you have gone,
And I have no one
To talk to,
No one who cares.
So here I am —
Right where you left me
Sitting among the scattered pieces
Of my shattered dreams.

Christie Borders

CHILDREN — YOUR DADDY HAS GONE AWAY

What can I tell them?
What should I say
When they ask me why
Their Daddy went away?

Do I say they are too young to know?
Or should I just love them a little more?
Can they understand my sorrow
When they are only three and four?

Their Daddy died this morning;
He didn't want to go.
But he had to leave us for awhile;
I already miss him so.

What should I tell them, Lord?
He left them so very quick.
They didn't even know him well;
He had been so very sick.

He loved them very much, you see;
But had to go away.
What can I tell them so they'll understand
That we will see him again someday?

Gloria C. Higgins

FOR YOU

Me and mine
My mind my heart
My consciousness and perceptions
My wisdom and my actions

My wishes my wills
And what I have
My nights my days
The bright my fate and facts

My silence my words
My thoughts and what I express
My realities and dreams
All my best

For you my dear
My darling my love
I and all of mine are yours
Yours and only yours

Forever for years
Without any fear
For you my darling
My love my dear

Syed Mohammad Hassan

THE LEGEND OF OLD BILL

He lived all alone, in a cabin on the hill,
and for miles around, he was known as "Old Bill."

He lived off the land, and the bounty of the tree,
and fishing the streams, where the waters run free.

The grey mountain man had forsaken city life,
when his heart lay buried, with his beloved wife.

She was young and frail when the epidemic came,
and fruitful with the child, that was to bear his name.

They perished as one, and with every tear he shed,
Bill wished that the Lord had taken him instead.

He fled to the hills when his world became unreal,
with a sense of loss that time would never heal.

The sounds of the night seemed a million miles away,
when Bill would lose himself, in thoughts of yesterday.

He'd fondle a curl from a lock of golden hair,
pressed inside a Bible, near her favorite prayer.

The mourners were few, when the old hermit grew ill,
but, still they speak in awe, of that eve on the hill.

He smiled and reached out, just before he would die,
fragrance filled the room, and they heard a baby's cry.

Marilyn Jimerson Brewer

HE LOVES YOU, TOO

He showed His love for me when I was born,
And watches over me from then, until now.

He provides for every need I may have,
Be it enormous in size or very small.

Although at times I forget His company,
He reminds me that His presence is near.

He comforts me in all my sorrows,
And promises the brightness of tomorrow.

He strengthens me when I'm weak or hopeless,
And gives me new courage and vigor to go on.

He guides me whenever I get confused,
And shows me the righteous path again.

He tells me about the beauty of heaven,
That He's preparing for all of His children.

He proves to me the greatness of His love,
In everything He had created around me.

I can see and feel His incomparable love,
In my home, at work, and wherever I go.

God's love for me is as great, I know,
As the love He always has for you, too.

Melecia L. Casabal

LOVE MY WHITE TRUCK

I spotted you on a lot. You were a terrible mess.
Your color was faded pale blue. Your bumpers were bent.
Your shocks were gone and your clutch would clutch no more.

It was plain to see you were soon to be in the
archives of the salvage yard.

As I looked you over, I fell in love with you —
I envisioned how you could become my old new white truck.

As I fixed or replaced your parts, my job turned into
a labor of love, for soon you would be my old new white truck.

When I applied your new gleaming coat of white, polished
your chrome, and outfitted you with a set of four new
black trimmed in white shoes, I could see you were beautiful,
because you are now my old new white truck.

If you could come alive and speak your mind, my dream
would be for you to say, "Thanks for saving me from the
salvage yard. I am proud to be your old new white truck."

Russell Heindselman

FAREWELL, IF EVER FONDEST PRAYER

Farewell! If ever fondest prayer
  For other's weal availed on high,
Mine will not all be lost in air,
  But waft thy name beyond the sky.
'Twere vain to speak, to weep, to sigh:
  Oh! More than tears of blood can tell,
When wrung from guilt's expiring eye,
  Are in that word — Farewell! — Farewell!

These lips are mute, these eyes are dry:
  But in my breast and in my brain
Awake the pangs that pass not by,
  The thought that ne'er shall sleep again.
My soul nor deigns nor dares complain,
  Though grief and passion there rebel:
I only know we loved in vain —
  I only feel — Farewell! — Farewell!

Lord Byron

THE PUZZLE

Two children
Piecing a puzzle together
Without success . . .
The shapes do not fit
As they should
Contrast is evident
Determination . . .
Passion for completion
Clouds their pensive eyes.
Trying the pieces again
And again
Manipulating their uniqueness
To fit into a space,
A space meant for another.
In time the children will realize
Some pieces are missing,
While others do not fit
The puzzle will never be.
But until then,
The children once again try to piece together,
A dream that will never see reality.

Laurie Lane

TRAIL

HONORABLE MENTION

Up up into the clouds
we climb
past Keekwulee Falls,
ascending like Zen monks
on an ancient Chinese scroll.

At a rain-jeweled spider web
we pause —
you're wet and out of shape,
your legs stone ruins
from the switchbacks
winding into mist

but your voice unfolds,
it dips and rises
like a hawk
or a heron settling on a marsh

and when it does
I leap for it,
an impala,
a salmon coming home to spawn.

Peter Ludwin

SIBLING GOLD

In Memory of Madeline

Once again she is here and
word fights and broken
toys fill the room —
My toys done in by her —
Why, why, why
What did I do to
merit her wrath?

Not all times were filled
with wrath — summer
nights when we lay
abed — we shook the
house with song
till that voice boomed
"Go to sleep!"

Now that months and years
have gone — I ponder this
love that never ends
and wish, oh, how I wish
we were once again
gloating in her wrath!

Verna Lee O'Brien Clark

You and I are touched by smiles,
happiness and love.

We share our hopes and our fears,
we listen to each other,
understand and share.

I trust in you my inner troubles,
you give to me — only love,
You trust in me your fears,
I give to you — understanding.

I know you and I
are always to be touched by smiles.

Lyssa Flaherty

I DO NOT LOVE YOU

I do not love you anymore.
The sun gives me more warmth
And gentle rain falling, more peace.

I have no need for you.
I am satiated by the birds singing
In the quiet morn.
And at night, I am too full from wondering
Of a star's mystery,
To remember your strange silence.

I do not want you.
My longings are those which
You cannot give.
Of hearing acorns fall
And watching flowers grow.
Or hoping butterflies will
Linger longer.

I do not love you.
But I will be your friend.

Joan Marie Rooks

ROOKS, JOAN MARIE. Born: Cambridge, Massachusetts, 9-30-47; Single; Education: American University, Washington, D.C.; Columbia University, New York, New York; Georgetown University, Washington, D.C.; Occupations: Lobbyist, Administrator, Actress, Model; Memberships: Chevy Chase Citizens Association, Massachusetts State Society of Washington D.C., other local civic groups; Poetry: *If In This Life,* sonnets, 1966; *Be My Lady Bug,* collection of whimsical love poems, 1970; *Until Eternity,*prose and poetry concerning nature and love, 1975; Other Writings: *The Lady of Revere and The Man From Savannah,* collection of short stories, 1980; Comments: *I write as I have a need to clarify and share my experiences. My work deals — in both a serious and humorous manner — with the many forms of relationships, facets of love, and the diversity of nature that I encounter.*

THE COWBOY AND THE LADY

Remember when first we met
Time stopped a moment
You a cowboy tall and strong
I passing through the town that night
A moment remembered, held deep in our hearts.

Cowboy tall and strong
How you looked at me
How I looked at you
How we talked, how we laughed
A bond to capture us that night.

By the warmth of fire's glow
Moonlight across the stillness
    of the night.
Just to be near set us afire
Deep was our desire
Two souls caught in the web of night.

Monica Serle

If possible — remember
Not the hour of our death, but life and all its living
In between
The then and now. Remember
In the silences
We share at lengths apart,
The moments of triumphant joy
Our fellowship once bought. The sadder things that eat
Unto despair — like blowing out the past
As if we never really cared — desire inside emptiness consumes
The failing heart —
It's wrong that we should start
This horror's course.
If possible — remember
In the stinging, acid rain,
The chances of our rising and our breathing
Life again. Remember
That the spirit never ends — and hope has built
A crossroads
Between friends.

Christine A. Pitt

GRANDMA

Grandma picked up her baby grandson,
Hugged him and called him, her Honey-Bun.
Every chance she had, she'd rock-a-bye
And she'd croon to him soft lullabies.
The baby would grin and coo a bit.
He just loved every moment of it.
What better place than Grandma's soft arms,
Protected, sheltered, safe from all harms.
Lullaby tones would lull him to sleep.
O'er him Grandma's loving watch would keep.
Grandma just loves to fuss and to pet,
Then tuck him in his soft bassinet.
And she would come and peek in his door,
They love their grandbabies, all the world o'er.
No matter if baby's in pink or blue,
Love and affection from Grandma's their due.
When God made Grandmas He had in mind,
Someone good and true, loving and kind.

Wm. A. McDonald

III

Earth was a garden when I walked with you,
a court of lovely shrubs, sturdy and green.
I did not smell the fertilizing keen,
but only fragrant odors, scented dew.
I did not mind the labor roses ask,
nor grudge the trim yew hedge a ceaseless toil,
nor grumble if my fingers, grimed with soil,
were stung by thorns in some absorbing task.

All work, with you beside me, was as sweet
and light as breathing clovered summer air,
as dancing nimble-footed everywhere
something to make our eyes in twinkling meet.
Earth was a garden then. Now I have lost the power
to dream past muddy planting to the flower.

Vera S. Flandorf

LOVEDRIVE

We were really warming up, just getting started,
Our hearts wre really humming, but then you departed.
Since you've been gone, we've kept our lovin' alive,
Phone calls and letters, our fuel to survive.

Verbal hugs, imaginary kisses,
Phantom strokes, passionate wishes.
I feel your heart, but it's kinda rough,
'Cause just hearing your voice isn't quite enough.

Now you're comin' home, no more time to roam,
Time to get our hearts back on track
Gotta shift out of neutral into lovedrive,
Showin' we haven't lost the knack
To help each other's hopes and dreams thrive.

Keith Higgins

DESIRE

Meaningful whispers echo through my heart in remembrance of you,
The longing to touch you is an uncontrollable desire,
Speaking to you brings tears to my eyes in anticipation of,
Hugging you, holding you, loving you, almost like a fantasy, but isn't —
Because it is real!

Cheryl Vatcher

GOD IS LOVE

I live, and move, in a sea of love.
This love enfolds me, surrounds me,
Keeps me each day —
Like the poor little lamb — who lost his way.

> Oh, Precious Father,
> I love you so.
> Please, never, never let me go
> Away from you.

Let my will — my thoughts — my words —
Be forever in thee, completely submerged.
Keep me on the pathway — walking straight and true,
Where your Blessed Angels are waiting,
To guide me straight to you!

Joy S. Pearce

BY THE RIM

You have been here always in my phantasy
walking up the road, laughing,
with shells from a prehistoric sea
Just for me.
We have been together here, everywhere
joyously.
Climbing, falling pilgrims are we
in an old geography.
We do not wonder on how we met or why.

And if by chance you do appear
in the early sun's mirage
(as surely soon you must)
to discover that I am not the me I know
and you and your photograph are
strangely mismatched,
and the canyon is there simply
ever changing,
my phantasy will carry me through
the meeting you.

Christine Janz Taylor

You tamed me!
Every day you waited, patiently.
Sometimes we met on mutual ground,
Sometimes, halfway and,
Sometimes . . . not at all.

But you were patient,
And, even though I never wanted it to happen,
You tamed me.

Like a delicate flower you watered and nourished me.
Tending me daily,
You created the need and the desire
To be tamed.

Now everything that happens to me,
Forever,
Will be a reminder
Of your love.
Thank you for taming me!

Frances Long

A SONG OF VEILS

A New Wedding Prayer

I take the veil. I leave the house of yesterday, and
the ways of my childhood, for I have found a new husband
and a new Father.
I give reverence to the Most Holy One, and I pledge myself
to my true husband, as I take the veil.
I live, separated from my youth, forever, within the inner
gate. I sing a new song to the Lord and King, who is my
Breath of Life. I take the veil, which completes me.
As a willing sacrifice, I, humbly, bow my knee to the
Creator of all.
In loyalty, I give of myself to my husband, protecting
his name, and cherishing him, as a dream of hidden treasure.
I promise to uphold and encourage him, in all his endeavors,
As a strong and mighty wall, around a secret garden, that
no other may cross.
As Rebekah, in the days of old, I take the veil.
In prayerful mood, I ask of You a blessing, and to
keep your Presence nigh unto this marriage, always
Your love endureth forever, as I take the veil.

Beverly F. Ross

AN EVERLASTING LOVE

You raised me as a child
You love me as an adult
You have seen sides of me
No one else will ever see

You taught me right from wrong
You made my mind and body strong
Ours is an everlasting love
That has weathered many a storm

You've shed light on my darkest fears
You comforted me while I shed my tears
Even in times and troubles
Our love has strengthened through the years

In my times of absolute sorrow
You've shown me the light of tomorrow
Never will I take my life
Because of your love
And guidance from above

Mary Edwards

WHAT IS LOVE?

To love is to trust.
That is a must.

It is the loyalty to always stand by —
Knowing that on one another you can rely.

Love encourages you, yourself to be —
Not an image created by me.

Love is a miracle that exalts.
It looks over all your faults.

Love doesn't mean that you never disagree.
It's my respect for you, and your respect for me.

Nor does it mean being pushed around.
It is taking a firm stand, on very solid ground.

Love is all of the above, and so much more.
Love is the key to open any door.

Juanita Briscoe

CAN THIS BE LOVE

Can this be love; I just don't know.
You're in my mind all of the time.
Can this be love; I ask you again.
What is the secret to a love that won't end?
Your tender touch; your silent smile.
Can this be love; or am I changing my style?
There are so many things I would like to know.
Like what have you done to touch the depths of my soul?
What is the meaning of a love that is true?
Is it the way I've been feeling; ever since I've met you?
There are so many things together we can do.
When we take the time; open up our minds;
There's more than we'll ever know;
The secret's locked up, deep down in our souls.
You have found the key to please the secrets of my soul.
Can this be love; I don't really know.
Just give me some time; let me sort this through my mind.
My heart twisting and turning all of the time.
Can this be love; or am I losing my mind?

Michael A. Steben

TOGETHER IN LOVE

Together let's witness the birth of a new day.
Together let's run through the surf chasing waves away.
Together let's share tender moments and precious memories.
Let's laugh and love,
And watch the sea gulls soaring high above.
There may be times for tears instead,
But let's always stay together,
Together in love.

Susan Hancock

ELEGY FOR HEDI

On top of this mountain I stand in fear,
Not trusting the wind, not trusting the mountain,
It may move and I
May fall.

I saw you the other day — skinny, in bed sores,
Nearly bald after months of motionless sleep.
You accepted my gift from a stranger
And spoke the language of your homeland, Indonesia.

As a young artist you would draw my small feet,
My puppy-dog and Irish doll.
You waited 'til I fell asleep and then pulled the blanket
Just above my shoulders to keep bad dreams away.

The crow calls, rocks turn to pebbles in my hands,
And he carries me down on his wings,
Echoing cries through the granite canyon.

You cannot remember yesterdays
Or that John Donne wrote of tolling bells.

I climbed the mountain
When I heard the crow call
And have given into the wind.

Debra Murphy

MY SPECIAL FRIEND . . .BILLY

A young, beautiful person. A man who had goals and was achieving them. A man who was kind, tender, and gentle; who thought of others first; and whose heart was always glowing with friendliness and thoughtfulness.

He sounds unreal, but in fact, he was very real. His warmth and his love reached out to all those who knew him. Billy was well-liked and very much loved.

As for me, I know one of my greatest joys was having Billy as a friend. For we did things together and enjoyed each other's company; no worries of getting serious; just two friends having a good time.

My only regret is that I wish I had told Billy how I felt, that his friendship meant very much to me, and as a friend, I loved him.

But Billy is gone now. No one knows why; no one understands why such a beautiful person was taken. But Billy has no worries for I know he's in Heaven.

I miss Billy and the pain still hurts. But in time, all I'll remember are the wonderful memories of him, which means quite a few.

Rachel Wallace

SILENCE OF LOVE

Ancient valley rivers forcing time to adhere life.
What would anchor; who could dock at night?
Gasping for air, water is all I find.
Such is silence of love.

No voices no screams locked inside a quiet dream.
Free from sound but a prisoner to sight,
Restrained expressions dialogue's plight.
Try to speak but I draw no breath.
Such is silence of love.

Lipstick names on bathroom walls, steamy windows lovers awe.
Put away your razor blades, blood is passionate shade.
Why is it I can't hear?
Such is silence of love.

Good-bye Michigan July morning,
Premeditated presumptions bearing false judgment.
Say hello to strong fingers on a strangleman's hold,
Sexual inhibitions ease easily.
Such is silence of love.

Don Lathers

JUST FOR YOU

I do believe the Lord above
Created you for me to love.
He picked you out from all the rest
Because He knew I love you best.

I once had a heart that was tried and true,
But now it's gone from me to you.
Take care of it as I have done,
For you have two and I have none.

If I get to Heaven before you're there,
I'll write your name on a golden chair
So that the angels in Heaven may see
Exactly, darling, what you mean to me.

And if you're not there by judgement day
I'll surmise you went the other way.
I'll give the angels back their wings,
Their halos and their other things,
And just to prove my love is true,
I'll go to hell, dear, just for you.

Frances Hough

DELUSIONS

Don't Dream about a tranquil life
That sings and hums in harmony,
With no conflict, with no strife
To shatter the fragile symphony.

Don't Dream about a world of love
Wrapped in a blanket of faith,
Where envy rancors in no hearts
To ravage nation's brittle trust.

Clamp The world in your gritted teeth
And shake it 'til all love falls out,
You'll see no more from the heart of the world
Than you give from the heart within.

Don't Dream about the world without
'Til you're awake to the world within.

Peter Molteni

ANNIVERSARY

It's a celebration of two people
joined as one.
It divides forever into
tangible time markers.
It's a time to think about how lucky
you are to love and be loved.
It's a special day when it's
super-important to say, "I Love You!"

Anne V. Brady

IN A MOMENT

In a moment with you
I'd steal a kiss or two
Stare into your eyes and forget where I am
I'd reach out to touch you
Hold you so tight
Feeling the warmth of our love
And I'd steal another kiss
In just a moment with you

Eric Knight

SECOND COMING

You, dear one, came into my life,
And we had a friendship sweet.
Then after a while you disappeared
Along down memory street.
You have gone away to parts unknown;
I know not when or where.
Though we never meet on earth again,
I will meet you in the air!

Helen Niederlehner

LOVE REBORN

With little note you came into
My life when I felt so alone.
Your deep concern and tenderness
Soon made your presence to me known.
You came and stayed and soon were part
Of every dream within my heart.
Love gone, you showed, could thrive anew,
And broken hearts be mended, too.

Ruth W. Scarbrough

WHERE ARE YOU?

The pillow you gave me has gone astray,
I looked everywhere along the way,
I'm so unhappy and I do care
About you and want you here.
But you're neither here nor there,
Sometime I'll find you
'Til then, dear heart,
We'll never, never part.

Roberta Jones Murray

AN ODE TO MY GIRL'S LEG

Long and slender,
sleek and fine,
I adore
its perfect line.

And when
its lissome length
she moves,
my heart
with rhythm soft
she proves.

For as each
flowing gesture
bends,
she teases
all my senses' ends.

Until,
confused,
I pause to think . . .
and blush
to see
her dimpled wink.

Joseph P. Kowacic

MY SON AND HIS SON

Oh what a joyous sight to see,
When his hard day at work is done;
Out in the sandbox, on his knees,
Playing with his son.

They dig with his little shovel,
Into the nice clean sand;
Pile it high in the gravel truck,
And dump it out again.

I pray he'll always take the time
To sit and play with him;
Take him when he goes fishing,
And teach him how to swim.

He's such a sweet and loving child,
Who loves his Mom and Dad;
There's nothing that is comparable to —
The companionship they've had.

He knows his colors and numbers well,
And is learning how to sing;
He radiates the happiness
Which only closeness brings.

Caye E. Hurst

PROPOSAL

It all happened
With a whiff of a life.
Or was it an ache of heart?
Never part from yourself.
Let the wells rise up within you.
If you don't get through, it's around.
Lie upon the ground,
Under the sun, perpetually within us.
Here for passion and warmth.
Shine a light on life,
Be my star.

James Melton Wolfe

MISS ME TOO

In some intangible way
I miss you differently
Each time we are apart.

Over these five years
The knowledge of you
Longer, deeper, wider,

Makes me more aware
Though not exactly painfully
How entwined our lives are.

And I know, before going away
How lonely for you
I am already.

Lois Smith Triplitt

TRIPLITT, LOIS MAYBELLE. Born: Bay City, Michigan, 4-9-17; Married: 5-27-50 to Irvion Darrell Triplitt; Education: UCLA, M.S., 1960; UCSC, R.N., 1952; University of Michigan, B.S., 1939; Summer School at Wayne University, Syracuse University, Madison University, BYU; Occupations: Teacher of Physical Education, Nursing, Consultant for Nursing Education; Poetry: 'Indelible Day,' 'Dumb Wooden Bird,' 'Enchanted Room,' 1980; 'I'd Know You in the Dark,' 1984; 'Head On,' 1985; Themes: *The mystery and joy of life.*

LADY LINDA/SIR MARCUS: LONG AGO

We laughed together,
  and enjoyed the day.
Your soft blue eyes,
  sparkled and shined.
Our silent thoughts merged,
  and we became as one.
But our last embrace,
  was but a look,
    which told me how,
      you truly felt inside.
Blessed be sweet ladies,
  with sapphire eyes.

Mark L. Ridge

MY TEDDY BEAR

They say you have no real heart,
That thread is all to keep you from falling apart.
Your mouth can't eat, your eyes can't cry,
But you'll keep a secret and won't tell a lie.
You're always willing to lend an ear,
And there to hold when I feel fear.
You're always near when I need a friend,
And I know you'll be there 'til the end.
Teddy, thanks for all your care,
I know deep down there's a heart in there.

Kathleen Flynn

KNOWLEDGE OF LOVE

When, many years ago, I, as a boy,
Enjoyed life's fun, and yet for knowledge yearned.
By far the foremost theme I ever learned,
The truth that thrilled my being with most joy,
The prior part portrayed in every ploy,
The knowledge neither sought nor ever earned,
Most wonderful and yet most often spurned,
Sensed God loves me with love that won't destroy.

Later, as man, the boy since grown, I find
A marvel meant to satiate and soothe
My mind. I find a further phase of truth.
I learn to know that God loves all mankind.
As senior now, my mind the more is awed.
God, I learn, is love. I learn that love is God.

Ivan Bernard Robson

ROBSON, IVAN BERNARD. Born: Winnipeg, Manitoba, Canada, 7-6-16; Married: 6-8-42 to Elsye Edith Askew; Education: Winnipeg Public Schools; William Booth College, Toronto, 1939; Occupation: Missionary, 1940-1960; Canadian Government Officer, 1961-1974; Memberships: Manitoba Writers' Guild (Charter Member); Poetry: *Prime People, book of poetry,* 1974; "Spirit Level," poetry read weekly on TV, 1975-1978; "Logos," poetry read weekly on TV, 1978-1980; *The Ostrich Syndrome,* book of poetry and text, Alpha Publications, Winnipeg, 1982; Comments: *Reviewing, in retirement, a mass of poetic material pertaining to human emotions created during a lifetime. Submitting selected pieces for publication in a variety of media.*

HIS PRAYERS FINALLY ANSWERED

The last time I saw my Grandfather, his long, thin, wrinkled face
Huge blasts of smoke pouring out his pipe
Deep, sullen eyes staring off into space
Oblivious to anyone or anything around him

Following him around as a child
Me with my little plastic pipe. Emulating his every move
My grandfather loved to entertain me
Dancing a sloppy Irish jig — singing an old Irish tune

On cold winter mornings he'd be the first outside
Braving the miserable weather — Shoveling our steep driveway
Wearing a funny hat and an old, flimsy winter jacket

Then my Grandmother died
As a consequence, my Grandfather prayed constantly
For the Lord to take him too

My Grandfather died a slow death
Being as he was, a strong man
Only helping to prolong his wait
The Lord had finally answered his prayers

Greg Phipps

THANK YOU LORD

Thank You Lord for loving me,
Thank You for giving me eyes to see;
Thank You for giving me ears to hear,
These things to me are very dear.

Thank You for giving me legs to walk,
Thank You for giving me speech to talk;
Thank You for giving me hands to touch,
These things to me all mean so much.

Thank You for letting me be complete,
Thank You for giving me life so sweet;
You've given things so very small,
And thank You Lord, I love them all.

Cheryle Dawn Hart

ONE SYLLABLE NAME

I mourn for her who dwells in my mind.
The sad day of days was one of a kind.
Her silent still form the last time I saw
Is now but one name wherever I go . . .

At the call of her name there are ever so more
Who come to my mind from past years before.
They who have followed their own day of days
I still will remember in multiple ways . . .

The ones of my time are names in my mind
And were the same way bereft of their kind.
They all are contained in her syllable name
The one within me — all over again . . .

Each separate bell resounds but one tune;
My kind I recall by months of the moon.
They all now resound in the name of her voice
And all are contained within this one choice . . .

They all are contained in her syllable name
The one within me — all over again . . .

Howard Deutsch

IN HIS LOVE

There was a time
When all was still,
This empty place
No love could fill.

'Til you became
A part of me,
You filled my life —
You set me free.

My heart can feel
Your presence near,
It feels the warmth —
Your love so dear.

A peaceful time
Of feeling still,
Makes this moment
That you fill

Like all the music
Ever played,
Yet so soft —
Like angels pray.

Helen C. Mogavero

DIVER

We share the water sign,
my love. With you I learn
the dark blue depths where
only dim light filters.

I learn this from
your photographs
snapped
among bubbles
and sharks.

Thinking of darknesses
ahead, I bury terror
when I touch your hair,
haven from raven thoughts.

Now wondrous invisible fish
swim from you
to me
absorb
in my blood.

You have not yet noticed
that I grow old.

Jean Musser

LOVE TO OFFER

Pay the price.
Pay the price of love.
Pay the price that love offers.

Give me! Give me the love I've lost.
Gone! Gone, no love to offer.

Lost the pain that love offers.
Lost the pain of love.
Lost the pain.
Lost!

Steven Arnell Miller

YOU WITH SOME HUMAN IMPERFECTIONS

Perspicacious, mature, you have been given God-to-man qualities,
With quiet inner peace many seek —
You have caught the joy of children playing with gladness and delight,
The beauty of snow on the distant mountain peak,
Alone, fledglings courageous fly,
A welcome rainbow in the sky.
You are a walk among the giant redwoods, warmth of sunlight,
The awe and wonder in observing geese navigating in formation flight,
Quiet joy that comes when birds communicating trust walk near; carol close by,
Alone, deer drinking, a row of tall eucalyptus trees.
You are a drink of cool water in a dry, barren place; an invigorating breeze.
After winter's skies and winter's freezing sting
You are the beauty amid warmth of spring.
When unsolvable problems or grief are enormously painful darkening the day and night
You are the stars shining through the dark
That lend a needed light.
You give hope as dawn and sunrise after a difficult day.
Gentle, contemplative, reliable, solid, living without hypocritical pretense you give gain —
You *being* (the reality of you) penetrates lives as drought-stricken land soaks up healing rain.

Frances Deidamia Sumner

NOVEMBER DARKNESS

And as the rain rushed to the earth,
The wind blew the curtains around.
And strange was the lighting that filled the November sky.

Four a.m. and my eyes could not close;
nor would sleep come to me.
Thoughts of days far misplaced.
Thoughts of nights that may never be.
And at November darkness I cried upon pillows that made reflections
of the November night.

And I rose to greet the darkness.
Rose to light a smoke.
And sit in my chair; afraid of not knowing.
Misplaced, for some things would never be again.

Lost in November darkness.
Cried because spring was trying to take over the winter.

Bruce R. Richey

DIFFERENCE

There's a great difference between clinging and still caring, just like there's a great difference between being set free and being free. You say you have no time to be tied down, but yet you need me. If you felt chained with my love, why do you miss it so? I gave you the freedom to come and go and to do anything with anyone you chose. You always had one foot out the door, and I never held you back, you always left with my blessing. I saw no chains and held no key. This is what makes me wonder if you really knew what you meant when you said, "I need to be free." I believe I gave you more freedom than any woman ever had or will. I accepted you the way you were without a demand of change, and I understood the things you did without question. Our love knew little anger and no jealousy. I saw so much good in you and overlooked the bad. I cried for you when times were sad, and I applauded you when you made me proud. You made me happy, and you made me sad. You replaced my silence and emptiness with smiles and laughter. I was so very comfortable with you. I let you keep living your life the way you always had, and you let me live mine; to me that was special. Your memories are locked in my heart; they are prisoners of my love, but you never were.

Rose A. Pope

LITH. & PUB.^D BY N. CURRIER, Entered according to Act of Congress in the Year 1851, by N. Currier, in the Clerk's Office of the District Court of the Southern District of N.Y. 152 NASSAU ST. COR. OF SPRUCE N.Y.

THE BLOOMER COSTUME.

TRUE LOVE

True love can't be found
Just sitting on the ground,
It's always there,
Just around the corner somewhere.

You can find it
If you look,
The love you read in books
Sometimes you can see it, bit by bit.

If you look at it
The way I do
I just want to say,
I love you.

It may be me
Although I hope
That you can see
I need you!

Anita Webb

GROWING OLD

I wanted to grow old with you,
  But you have gone ahead;
The Master called you home to Him,
  And left me here instead.

I couldn't bear the loneliness,
  Except I somehow feel
That you are not so far away,
  And that your love's still real.

For I still have so much of you,
  That you have left behind;
Your words, the little things you did
  I treasure in my mind.

I thank God for the joys we knew
  Together on life's way,
And trust Him for His strength until
  We meet again some day.

Dora May Lombard

OH! LOVE

Oh! Love,
  Such fire and passion you bring!
  Then suddenly, cold, cold emptiness
  Just as quickly as you came.

Oh! Love,
  That illusion of the heart,
  Why and how did you fade away!
  So quickly, so quietly,
  So completely and so painfully gone.

  No life before you came
  And surely none after.
  No sun, no blue sky,
  No smiles, no laughter.

Oh! Heart,
  Don't die from all this pain!
  Live and breathe and love again!

Richard L. Catron

OLD LADY

May an "Old Lady" with you be young?
Or do you toy with her, for fun?
You touched her, and her passions ran hot.
On this, do you run, or not?
We are lost in a kiss . . .
Our feelings are not amiss,
Where do we go from here?
The answer to that . . .
Lies with you, I fear.

Alice Smith

LOVE SONG

Teach me a song
So I can sing to you.

First learn the melody,
On the piano, play the notes.
Hum the tune,
Then sing it again.
Hear the lyrics:
How the words fit the music.
Learn the words,
Understand them.

When I finally learned the words
You'd changed the tune.

Beth Garrabrants

BETRAYAL

I trusted you
But you let me down.
I had faith in you
And what you did.
I listened to what you told me
And accepted it, unquestioning.
You had my trust
And my heart
But you betrayed me.
You can disappoint me, ignore me
You can leave me alone
But never,
Ever,
Lie to me.

Kelle LeCompte

HUNGER

She foraged
(a poor beggar)
through his words
to find the sustenance
a passion needs to thrive;
divided what she found
into components of caloric power
that just might serve
to keep a starveling love alive.
Then she essayed
to estimate within
the fraction of an hour
how long her ardor could survive
on such a meager fare.

Ellen V. M. Carden

THOUGHTS ON AN ANNIVERSARY

'Tis not a fairy tale romance
Of stars and moonbeams at first glance
'Tis not young love that's all aglow
With freshness of the falling snow
But love that's grown throughout the years
Nurtured slowly with joy and tears

A courage born from sleepless nights
For shattered dreams and aimless plights
A joining of two souls that care
Through memories of all we share
A special warmth of being sure
In good or bad, we will endure

It's honesty in all we do
Thinking, feeling, we must be true
It's trust completely, without doubt
Even when we feel left out
It's gentle peace we feel within
Knowing we'll always be best friends

My everything I give to thee
My life, my love, eternally.

Wanda Brown Lovell

I LOVE

I love the solitude of mountains high,
A wind-swept cloud where sea gulls fly,
The taste of salt, the smell of the sea,
Fresh baked bread, life's tapestry.
I love the coming of the night,
The muted song of insect's plight,
The roar of a train on its homeward way,
A quiet room at the end of day.
I love to sit alone in the sun,
Or a spider spin his web on high
In silken skein against the sky,
But most of all, I love the One
Who gave for us His only Son.

Lucille M. Kroner

LOVING

I spend all my time loving you
Seems like that's all that I do
I love you at work
My duties never shirk
For that is a way of loving too.

Work buys the clothes that you wear.
Just another way to show I care.
The food that you eat
The shop that keeps you neat
And even the home that we share.

You are my queen every night
Seems loving you is always right
In thoughts when away
At night in every way
And I'm glad our love glows so bright.

The first time we met I knew
I think that you knew it too
We're two of a kind
Our love is sublime
And every day our love blooms anew.

Hazel Nelson

TWO SONS HAVE I

Two sons have I,
of Pisces and Aquarius born
of heart and limb
so straight they grew —
with kindness and compassion too.
Two sons have I,
of parent's dreams
through years worn dim
those images now
form bright and true.
Two sons have I,
whose hands of love
so clearly blessed
they share their joy
with all they touch
Two sons have I.

Maxwell C. Kaufman

COCOON

I saw you
And knew you would be
Someone who,
Having seen, would touch me.
You also saw
That I was touching you
Through the wall
Of hurt and pain still new.

Touch my mind,
That I may search your soul.
Did you find
The peace that was your goal?
Touch this heart
As simply friend to friend,
There to start,
Perhaps to love: transcend?

Can this be?
To touch again and to feel,
You and me
Shall each begin to heal?

Delores Hendricks

LIKE SHE'S STILL MINE

There is an emptiness
When a love goes

The world is lonely
No one really
Talks to you
And you see nothing
All creation is distant
And your every action
Every reaction
Every condition is automatic
And silent
And cold
As you wonder why there is
A need in yourself
With such force
And Power

I
Cannot control my gestures
I reach for her
Like she's still mine

Jerry Lee Murrell

DON'T THROW OUR LOVE OUT THE DOOR

You know I could always say goodbye and leave today,
but too much time has passed to go our separate ways.
There comes a time when we all need a change,
but to throw our love out the door will bring only pain.

Don't throw our love out the door,
just try to smile for me once more.
The vows that were taken in yesterday's time,
still stand true in this old heart of mine.

Stop and remember the joy and laughter that's filled the air,
and all the special moments just you and I have shared.
We may be old fashioned in a lot of our ways,
but you can't always listen to what others may say.

It's really not too late if your love is still true,
to do all those special things that two people in love do.
So, let's count all of our blessings that we've gathered through time,
and try not to break this old heart of mine.

Candy Lee Koolhaas

TO LOVE AGAIN

I never really understood love
How it could be so romantic one minute
And then so disastrous the next
I never really thought that I could really love someone
But then I met this girl
She became the world to me, because she was everything I ever hoped for
Everyone I knew saw only her faults
Yet I never really seemed to see them because all I could see was her heart
And in her heart was true love for our friendship and then me
Then one day she was gone
It was then that I realized how much I loved her
It wasn't until she was gone that I saw how I took her for granted
How I desperately wanted to be with her
That I put my life on the line for her many times
And one time was almost for the last
It was not until then that others saw how much I loved her
That I would give up my life for her
By now I'm sure she knows this
Through those hard times, I'm sure it was she that saved me
That she loved me so much that she wanted me to go and and to Love Again

Denise Karch

. . . MORE SECRETS

Danny's looking for a superhero's style
that's friendly to him.

His adventures in the universe start out on a whim . . .
Stars swirling, comets curling, rockets whirling, timeless twirling
through space.
Mankind's desire for the Human Race.

My child is starting to unfurl his hopes
and desires, star-studded wings fired with imagination
Sophisticated mechanization of how things work,
and not yet understanding how hard and
demanding it all can be,
with no adventure . . .

. . . Which he creates, superhero Danny in space.
Stars swirling, comets curling, rockets whirling, timeless twirling.
He transcends the race with time.
Adventures are on his mind.

Janet Castiel

MARRIED LOVE

Pure love's a many faceted desire
'Twixt siblings, parent — child, or even friends.
'Twixt man and woman who, although not kin,
Become one flesh in children they beget.

Pure sex is but a strong, compulsive urge
Which can be sated e'en by deadly foe;
And thus it is not consonant with Love
Which surges from the heart, not from the loins.

But when the twain entwine 'tween man and wife
The climax is a wondrous event.
Each gives, none takes. The thrill is ne'er forgot
Though age or illness quenches passion's flame.

For half a century and more, true Love
Can hold a wedded couple in its thrall.
They are not always calm, sometimes they fight;
But neither goes to sleep without a kiss.

Thus true Love bids a wife and husband, "Each
Forgive the other for their many faults
In best or worst, in poverty or wealth,
'Til death doth part you." This is TRUE LOVE's bliss!

Rawleigh L. Gregory

GREGORY, RAWLEIGH LEWIS. Born: Midland County, Michigan, 7-9-10; Married: 9-7-35 to Phoebe Payne; Education: Monroeville, Ohio high school, several Navy specialty schools; Occupation: Enlisted, United States Navy, 1931-35, 1941-45; U.S. Postal Service; Salesman; Memberships: Past Master, F & AM; Past Patron, OES; Society for the Preservation and Encouragement of Barbershop Singing in America; Other Writings: "Thermostats," Technical, *Vend Magazine*, 1961; Numerous letters to the editor on economics and politics; Comments: *I am of the opinion that most people confuse love with sexual intercourse. Most of them will never know what love really is until they have been married to the same person for fifty years, as Phoebe and I have.*

NEGLECTED LOVE

The Garden of Eden was a wonderful place
A Heaven on Earth for the human race
Until one careless day Adam neglected his Eve
And she in her loneliness sought the company
Of a snake beneath a tree.

Have you ever wondered how life would be
If Adam hadn't neglected Eve and she
Hadn't listened to the snake beneath the tree?

If you have found your true love
Get on your knees and thank heaven above.
Guard it with tender, loving care
This gift most courted, precious and rare.
For neglect is — well perchance could be
The treacherous snake beneath the tree
Waiting to tempt both you and me.

Helen Minnick

LIVING WITHOUT YOU

*(To Janus Bradley for all
your loving help and concern.)*

When the sun sets down to rest westward in the sky,
Stars begin to twinkle like the sparkle of your eyes.
Every thought that enters, your face I somehow see,
Just as sweet and loving as only you can be.
How means the world to please me?
Now I seem to know —
For your name lets news of gold shine through
where undercurrents flow.
But the good times that you've brought me have
so seemingly come to pass;
For even the sunniest skies have turned so dark and overcast.
Shattered dreams have fallen into the deepest pit,
Left in crumbled ruins; and openly I'll admit —
That the very loss of your love has colored my life blue,
And years of pain are consequence to living without you.

Mary P. Hylton

A SMALL SPACE IN TIME

For a little time
we were together on this earth;
touching now and then;
exploring ways of seeing life;
loving what we found together,
knowing we were friends forever;
knowing neither death nor distance
could ever dim our flame.
It was a precious time;
my life more worthy for having been in yours;
my life more rich because you were my friend.
Oh, how I miss your gentleness, my Darling;
your joy, your love, your thoughts of me.
I miss your smile.
But when I think of it,
its beauty lights my face
and I smile in memory of you.

Jean Rogers

I will comfort you with kindness
Of the lightest touch, the softest voice,
To quietly slow your rain
From a torrent
To a trickle;
I will be there to remind you
That the rain must come
If you are to grow —
That I'm a shelter from the storm;

Let me show you how my loving
Can chase away your fear;
Let me be the instrument you play
To bring a touch of magic;
The star you wish upon
When your dreams lie unanswered;
For I am a prayer
And I am a song,
Waiting to share my gift of love
In music and in silence
Forever with you.

Andrea G. Hajducko

PUPPY LOVE

Little brown doggy
With a yellow bow
Tied around your neck
Every second my love grows

For you, full of energy
Full of wiggles
Whenever you lick me
I get the giggles.

I wonder if you laugh
And smile inside
When I kiss you back
My affection I can't hide

For you, my puppy
Friend, above a friend, above —
Some call it
Puppy love.

Kat Kerste

LOVE CHALLENGES HATE

Hate met with hate will build a wall,
And hate alone will make it fall.
All strength is spent to no avail
When hate is met with jealous hate.

Hatred is for cowards, and lo —
It will no friendly kindness show,
Hate leads to murder, war and strife,
And will sap out many a useful life.

My friend, when hate is met with LOVE,
Divine LOVE, which comes from above,
It will make every stubborn foe,
Become a friend and a blessing to know.

Let LOVE lay all differences low
Let LOVE to our enemy show
It will make a character strong,
And LOVE will banish every wrong.

Opal Marie Hayes

LOVE AND DEATH

Ofttimes
I dream of dying . . .
faces of loved ones gone
beckon to me . . .
then . . .
fade away like dewdrops
in the early morning . . .
reluctant in farewell.
Some strange telepathy
comes filtering in . . .
like a gentle wind
out of the shadows . . .
lifts me through the
veil of consciousness . . .
back to the smell of clean
sheets and perfumed skin.
Dreams hold such mysteries.
I wonder at the meaning
of it all.

Frances Norton Russell

IT'S YOU!

Who makes me happy every time
When I get gloomy for a while?
In whom found I always my prime
By loving words and pretty smile?
Who is so bright and lovely, too?
It's You! It's You!

Who is so straight and so correct,
And tells me what I want to know?
Who is full of charm and intellect,
Makes me feel like a Romeo?
Who is the smartest of us two?
It's you! It's you!

Who is my greatest love on earth,
Who is my friend and help indeed?
Who makes my life living, worth
In time of amorous need?
It is my sweetheart! You know who?
It's you! It's You!

Nick J. Pronck

OBEDIENCE TO THE LAW

Obey the rulers of the nation
God wants it to be that way.
He wants us to live in love and
order in this world from day to day.

That's why we should choose our leaders
seriously, and with much prayer.
For when we serve them, we want the
right ones there.

It's a serious thing to sell your vote
It's the next thing to selling your soul.
There's nothing to be gained.
You are going to reap just what you sow.

Obey civil law as long as you can.
Peter and John said, Ye ought to obey
God rather than man.
Stand up for truth and right and
do it with all your might.

Rindie Malone

SECRET SOCIETY

When the lights go out, he's mine.
Keeps me waiting all the time.
Oh, I need him, yes I do
How he thrills me through and through!
Keeps me guessing, where I stand —
Makes my day so very grand —
Who's that coming down the street?
Wish he'd make my life complete —
Sweeps the women off their feet
Kissing him is such a treat
Under his feet, there grows no grass.
Our love affair — "This too shall pass."

Mina Huffman

HUFFMAN, MINA HUDGENS. Pen Names: Mina Bird, Ann Onymous; Born; near Newburg, Missouri, Phelps County; Married: 12-25-26 to J. Millard Huffman; Education: Business College, St. Louis, Missouri; Teachers' College, Warrensburg, Missouri, B.S.; University of Missouri at Rolla and Columbia, Missouri, Lifetime certificate; Bob Jones University at Greenville, South Carolina, summer term 1970; Poetry: 'Meeting Her God,' World of Poetry, Honorable Mention; 'The Sentinel,' *Rolla Daily News,* front page; 'Diamond Bessie,' monologue, Jefferson Texas Amateur Program; *Fragment of "Ruth,"* anthology, University of Missouri, Columbia, 1960; Themes: *Faith (ex: Walking on Water).* Comments: *Writing poetry is a challenge to the mind. When a poem starts to come, you had better write it down or it may escape. I have written 44 love poems thus far.*

LOVE IS

Lovingly dedicated to my husband,
Edward, who has been my song
for 32 years.

Love is the song
singing in your heart.
Love is the happiness that
will never depart . . .
As long as I have you
and our love is true.

Love's a rhapsody,
love's a song
With you and I,
It's a sing-along.
In perfect harmony
the melody blends,
For we are true lovers
and best friends.

Love is the harmony,
we feel each day,
As we walk
this earthly pathway.
Love is your gentle touch,
your tender caress.
Your sweet smile
makes me confess . . .

I love you more with
each passing year
You are my life,
you are my song,
And I know it's with you
I forever belong.

Thelma H. Sherrill

THE FUTURE

The New Year is a time
to rejoice,
It brings peace of
mind and happiness.
As each day passes,
it brings joy,
The year brings technology
closer.

The machine is driving
faster,
As humanity keeps pace
with change.
What a wonderful world
this would be,
If there were peace
and harmony all over.

The great catastrophe of
the world,
Is man's inhumanity to man.
Civilization is a slow process,
Man strives to achieve greatness
through diligence.

He soared to great heights,
Like a balloon in the sky.
Looking down on the earth
below,
It was man, the thinker.

Elizabeth Saltz

YOU ARE IN ME

You are not with me,
but you are in me;
You are in that place
where everything is real;
You shall always be warm;
And if you shall get everything
you want,
it's that I think it so;
And if you shall feel not the need
to touch or be kissed,
it's that I relieved it already;
But if you shall feel the need,
it's mine;
And because I love you,
I shall live forever;
If only you
would say my name,
you would compose
a great symphony for me . . .

Francisco Sanchez

THE FIRST TIME

Touch me . . . why do I shake?
scared, so scared
of me . . . what I feel, how deep
Magic man
Alive again
On the outside
Inside buried deep
Passion . . . folded away
Shrouded with inhibition
Can't do it
Mustn't do it
Now . . . here
Teach me
the song
the words . . . play me
Sensations
all new . . . all old
Drowning . . .
Don't save me

Deborah Pearson

YOU

You are my light
in a dark world,
You are the sun
in the storm.
You are the love
when there is no love,
You are the life
in the midst of the dead.
You are the comfort
that is needed so much,
You are the joy
that I feel.
You are the music
when there is but silence.
You are
my love,
my life,
my hope,
my God.

Amy L. Owings

WANT TO KNOW YOU BETTER

I see you from a distance.
I only know your name.
I want to know you better.
I hope you feel the same.
How do I get your attention?
Make you look my way?
I want to be your friend.
I want to hear you say,
You'll be my friend, maybe more.
Deep inside,
That's what I'm looking for.
I need a love,
Who will be my friend.
A love that will last,
Never end.

Angela Williamson

BEFORE THE SNOW FALLS

You said we were friends forever,
That nothing would get in our way.
We made dreams to live on and
promises to keep.
Then you made a change, new promises,
new dreams.
Now as autumn approaches, our promises
and dreams are changing color and
falling from trees.
Just think, by the time the snow falls,
you will never be able to tell we were
even friends for a while, let alone
forever.
In the autumn of our lives, good-bye,
Before the snow falls.

Veronica Porter

THE LOOK

You looked at me.
Our eyes met,
I loved you at once!
Your face, I cannot forget . . .
Will I ever see you again?
Or do I dream in vain . . .
You are so handsome,
And I, so plain.
You are so young,
And I, so old.
Will you ever love me
More than some old friends,
You do feign?
Oh, will I ever see
You again?

Alice Smith

MISSING YOU

I miss you, dear one. Oh, how I miss you.
More and more, each passing day.
I hadn't known what loneliness meant —
Until you had gone away.

The sun seems to have lost its glory,
As it sets at eventide;
But — like the broken heart in the story —
In God's Eternal Love, I ever abide.

Joy S. Pearce

TOO BLIND TO SEE

My love for you grew stronger every day
As yours for me slowly faded away
You said deep down you wanted to be free
I was the fool who was too blind to see

I was so happy about the love we found
Had no idea you didn't want me around
Now you wish I would leave, but I want to stay
I never dreamed things would turn out this way

Well, my bags are packed, and I'm ready to go
The pain I'm feeling, you'll never know
It's time for us to say goodbye
No sense begging for one more try

The way it all ended just doesn't seem fair
Can't believe I could've been so unaware
I'd never been in love until you came alone
How could something that felt so right be so wrong?

I should've known it was too good to last
I've got to move on and forget the past
Thinkin' 'bout the good times and all we've been through
It's gonna take all I've got to get over you

Michelle Chaggaris

SENTIMENTS

I would like to feel new sentiments
when I look at those eyes that I love,
when I contemplate those warm lips
without feeling them, without feeling them yet . . .

I would like to feel your embrace
among your arms of sentimental man
and listen very close to you
the way you will say to me:
I love you today, I love you today
more than yesterday . . .

I would like you to embrace all my body
and only essence would surround us,
and that an aroma of glorious dreams
would sedate my anxiety
from awaiting your loving arms,
from awaiting the warmth of your tentative lips . . .

The nectar of your darling kisses,
the passion that I have developed
without even realizing it.
The deep love that I feel for you
without even kissing you yet . . .

Alice Levy

FOOL'S FOLLY

Soft loving words intermingled with my blood,
While ardoring eyes cradled my once empty heart.
Ecstasy from your laughter
Pushed away granite walls of doubt.
Tenderness softened hardened bones
And love unleashed a woman.
'Tis this fool's folly
To have hoped I had your heart
When it in all ways
Belonged to another.

Bette Ann Abenante

THE SPIRIT OF LOVE

Pain, grey and heavy filled the room.
Could this stranger lying there be my mother?
No, my mind was repelled by what I saw.
Staring at me was a shadow of someone I once knew.
Silence spoke to me.
She was always laughing and singing.
Death reached out a bony finger.
She had plump arms to hold us tight.
The stillness was oppressive.
No quick steps from morn till night.
The stench was offensive to my senses.
She always smelled like fresh, wind-blown sheets.
Dark eyes pleading, how long?
I felt the touch,
So light, so fragile.
I looked and wept.
And yet she lives.
Love cannot be put to death.

Dolores Wyckoff

THE MYSTERIES OF LOVE

Deeply engraved on the eons of time, the words are
written line by line: the mysteries of love.
That which far exceeds the eye, the only power which
cannot die: the mysteries of love.
Though men have tried and failed to explain its perplexities,
its hurts, its pains: the mysteries of love.
Transcending even the end of time, by far the
highest gift of mine: the mysteries of love.
It wounds the life and then it heals, its ambiguity
concealed: the mysteries of love.
By man can never be controlled, can make the
weak or spineless bold: the mysteries of love.
The world is bathed in its oceanic mist, its formless
shape dares to exist: the mysteries of love.
Men and women can embrace, when this
priceless gift takes place: the mysteries of love.
Its pleasures endless run to those, to all who
grasp the hidden prose: the mysteries of love.

Anthony George Polk

MOTHER IS

Mother is a Mixture of all the world's emotions
all the world's pleasures cares and devotions
Mother is an Object through which all things flow
love and fear and warmth trav'ling to and fro
Mother is a Teacher from diapers to parenthood
turned to for advice in times both bad and good
Mother is a Helper when the going gets too tough
She does her best and always feels that it's not enough!
Mother is an Errand girl to offspring and to spouse
picking up this and that for family and for house
Mother is a Refuge her heart open to all
the trouble *and* the triumph the pride *and* the fall!
It seems she's always ready with sympathy or praise
or stern command or sage advice through ev'ry childhood phase
and when we're all grown up and far from Mother's knee
our hopes and dreams our heartaches she feels as much as we
what in all the world would mean the most to Mother?
It's not very costly — just let Her know you *love* Her!

Jean A. Sacharko

THERE'S A LOVE LIGHT

There's a love light shining in your eyes,
and I can see there a look you can't disguise;
I need your love to fill this lonely heart of mine
and you know I've needed it for such a long, long time.

All around the world there is no one who
can give me love quite the way you do,
And when nights are long I will think of you;
all around the world you're my dream.

I look into your eyes
and then I realize
I need you.
And if our love only lasts for just a moment,
I will cherish all the memories we've made
and if I could make this dream to last forever,
I'd always be there with you by your side.

George Randall Roberts

FRAGILE!

Stop! Don't handle the box that way!
Wait! It's a fragile thing, I say.
The contents need to be handled with care
Because the vulnerable heart is a breakable thing.
Love can't soar with a broken wing.

Hold! This package needs caring hands,
And a gentle mind that understands.
Handle as you would a glass figurine
Because the loving heart is a vulnerable thing.
You can't play a harp with a broken string.

Stop! Look at the package you hold.
It's not for hands that are clumsy, I'm told.
You need hands that are experienced and steady
For the caring heart is a wonderful thing.
A heart with no voice just cannot sing.

Garrett C. Jeter

ONE MORE YESTERDAY

I was a fool to leave you
It makes me feel so bad,
When I think about what could have been
And all the fun times we had.

Just five minutes in your arms
Is worth a night in her bed,
And I'd gladly trade all of her tomorrows
For just one of your yesterdays.

My romantic record may be kinda poor
I'm a lover's longshot short on luck,
Haven't yet put up a winning score.
I know each step is a gamble
Our hearts rolling like dice,
Come on honey, let's create some future memories
Never again putting our love on thin ice.

Keith Higgins

The thunder pealed with fervid tones;
The lightning creased across the sky;
The rain began torrential beats;
A turmoil started, deep within
My heart, which matched that summer storm.

Commitment, trust and love began
(as muddled as that blustery day)
Half-here, half-there, with no design.

Your sunshine, seen through clouds of doubt,
Established soon a clearing trend;
Enveloped in that clarity,
My heart did find a haven there.

And should you walk another path,
The strain of loss would storm again
The calm that's found in loving you.

Nathanael Rugh

I LOVE YOU DONNA

Instantly put a smile on my face.

Longing to be with you day and night.
On weekends I miss you terribly.
Variety of romantic fantasies.
Every day I look forward to being with

You and seeing your lovely face.
Outrageous describes your personality.
Unique in many ways.

Delightful to me in the early morning.
Occasionally I wish I could have you for a wife.
Never get enough of you, wish I could have more.
Nice even when you are mad or upset.
Always on my mind and in my heart.

Kenny O'Leary

KISSES

The middle ones are wonderful,
The last ones are divine,
But the first ones
Send the shivers running up and down my spine.

Helen Robinson

REMEMBERING

I come to you on wings of light;
I come to you in deepest love.
I come to you as the stars come to the night —
Sparkling in the Heavens above.

I hear your gentle voice, sighing through the trees —
I hear your joyful laughter, echoing in every breeze.
I am remembering how we tramped the trails together;
— No matter the rain — the wind — the sleet — the snow —
Our deep, deep love, made it always sunny weather,
And covered a very turbulent world — in a restful, rosy glow.

The silent echoes are still sighing —
Of all the songs we loved so well,
This closing day seems to be remembering —
All the joys our hearts could never tell.

Joy S. Pearce

JAPANESE MARTYRDOM

"Jesus, Mary . . . Ah . . ."
Supreme moment of my life
bodies crucified.

The winter frost
melts to blood
and honor bows to honor.

Cries of surrender
accompany pruning spears
for cherry blossoms.

Sister Lucy Cyr, RSM

LOOKING AT YOU

. . . through your darkened eyes
seeing someone I used to know,
Remembering you
from another time
when feelings thought real would show.
Watching you
within my dreams
holding a thought alone,
Loving you
within my fears
wanting you as my own.

Looking at you
from the past to the present
seeing others the same as you,
Remembering you
different from I
but only in things that you do.
Watching you
from a distance
knowing you will never be near,
Loving you
just the same
though you are not here.

Joseph Scott

A DREAM

I see your face when I'm asleep,
I see you in my dreams;
I see your sultry eyes that peep
Into my soul it seems.
You came to me and then withdrew
From dreams that did not last,
You made my heart to long for you,
Then vanished very fast!
Why come to me afloat in air
And tempt me with your kiss?
Why stare at me with eyes so fair
And leave me without bliss?
Why show yourself for me to view
Your lovely face so sweet?
Why make myself to yearn for you,
Then vanish at my feet?
I long to see your face once more
And be with you all night,
But be with you forevermore,
Will give me more delight!
You are my joy, my everything,
The very breath of me!
The very thought of you will bring
Life's sweetest ecstasy!

Deogracias J. Cabrera

LOVE

The spirit danced to the Song of Songs, when the heart brought love to the mind.
A lonely heart that cried out in a dark ocean of stillness, in wait
for a companion on its journey.
With a love to ignite an embodied heart, that seeks light's rays to illumine
the moments of time.
Love in depth and height — extend it! For it nourishes the soul with the
fruits of the spirit.
A self-controlled and faithful Love, that is patient for those that hunger for life,
With a gentle touch gives Peace and Joy within.
Love is a friend, a gift, greater than the universe diamonded with stars.
An unconditional love that enhances mind — heart and soul.
Love is the center of life, for God is Love!

Paul E. Garcia

GARCIA, PAUL E. Pen Name: Policarpio; Born: Fort Lupton, Colorado, 1-26-28; Married: 7-10-69 to Hazel L. Garcia; Occupations: Aircraft Technician, United States Air Force; Woodsman, 31 years; Periodic Writer; Youth Counselor; Poetry: 'The Redwood Forest,' nature, *American Poetry Anthology,* 1986; 'Big Foot,' legend; Comments: *I write on offered themes from publishers. Ideas come from for the times to the present, universal in depth, so that those who read my work find a place in my writing somewhere with their experience. I write for the pure joy, to share it with others.*

THE CHILDREN'S WASTELAND

Lives in the wasted lands, where trees — tall naked
Scraping streaks into the sky, and the children have no place to go.
Letting go of the freedom which was never given to them.

For them knowledge howls by as a mighty wind blowing against
Their shabby earth-brown hair, foreign to neat clean grooming.
Broken lives, homes, body, spirit and soul.

Where have all the masters gone . . .
El maestro, the teacher,
Or sifu?
Their professions don't mean a thing —
To the children — to them,
And they will never know.

Except the Rabbi — Master of all masters,
Speaking within the hearts of men . . .
Of desolated sand and stone.
"The children, the children,
Tell them that I love them."

Robert Maldonado

I SAW YOU TODAY

I saw you today, oh what a feeling!
To know you were there, sent my head reeling.

I saw you today, oh what a distraction!
From life's lazy summer nights, to a mind full of action.

A girl long ago, a girl I knew so,
could awake me, and make me,
soar!

I saw you today, oh what a wonder!
Such a delicate sight, your beautiful face to ponder.

I saw you today, oh what a temptation!
To just walk right up to you, and place a friendly suggestion.

A girl of the past, a love I thought lost,
could be here, and want me,
too.

I saw you today, oh what an elation!
To know that you love me . . .
would be the greatest sensation.

Kirk N. Galatas

TWO SHIPS

Two ships that pass in the night,
Each a course of destiny
Feeling the curse of life.
Alone within the sailor's shell
Quiet dreams lie sleeping.

Your ship, sleek beauty unsurpassed,
Riding low and smooth through rough seas,
Paving a wake for those to follow
Who reach no earth-bound star.
The love of a tempest's calm.

Mine, a ship of wreckless joy
Riding light upon waves' crests,
Searching seas for those to share
Fleeting moments and happy times.
The love of a summer storm.

Two ships on endless seas
Together thrown by fate's cruel choice.
A pause eternal, waiting judgment;
A second thought, no second look.
Stern to stern, following the curse of destiny.

Blake Alan

I woke this morning when the sun set low,
Hedge-skirting beams against my wall. You passed;
I saw your shadow fret the light. I know
I heard the music of your step. At last,
When I had laid my work aside, you said
To me we would not meet for lunch. Your voice
Remained like smoke upon the air. Instead
Of grieving at your absence, I rejoiced
That you had spoken. When I ate, I found
The place where you had been. The silver set
For you retained your image and around
Me rose the warmth your body wore. As yet
I can't believe you are not here. I find
You've taken residence within my mind.

William B. Granberg

LOVE IS . . .

Love is caring, sharing and knowing,
The one you love is showing,
Feelings for you that are from within,
With every kiss a new memory begins.

Love is something different and new,
A bond people share between two,
Once you fall in love, everything is fresh,
For love has the power to make everything the best.

Love is like a cloud, floating gently and free,
A wonderful emotion inside of me,
You gave me life with your gift of love,
As though you were sent from heaven above.

Love is sometimes rough,
Yet most people cannot get enough,
I receive your love and return once more,
For you are the one I truly adore.

Michele Pfeffer

WHEN YOU'RE WITH ME

When you're with me
Nothing can go wrong
No matter how bad my day may have been
You're always there to comfort me.

A feeling of contentment is within me
Knowing our love will never cease to exist
Even though our days together are limited
By our own commitments.

When you're with me
The days are filled with laughter and practical jokes
The little things we do to show we care for each other
In so many ways.

A feeling of contentment is within me
When I think of all the good times we've shared
And all that are yet to come
When you're with me . . .

Tameria L. Millenbach

A TRIBUTE TO LOVE

Mystic tones slowly rose in flight;
expressions of the flutist art;
prelude to Love's sweet delight;
two joined as one in soul and heart.
A summer breeze enjoined the melody
to seek the presence of the honored pair;
gentle Jayson and his Jean Marie
the sun now dancing in her golden hair.
They moved with silent steps across the green
enhanced by all the beauty of the day.
An awesome mount prevailing o'er this scene
adjoined the famous city by the bay;
ocean mists meandering through its Golden Gate
softly cooling Summer's scorching heat.
A graceful eagle paused to celebrate
the fest of love portrayed beneath its feet
wings spread in flight yet bestilled
suspended by an unseen hand:
Tribute to the quest fulfilled;
a wedding in Love's fabled land.

Harvey Alan Sperry

UNDERTOW

HONORABLE MENTION

Everyday love,
worn around the knees,
comfortable,
like a favorite pair of jeans;
a down comforter
with patches
where experience has been.
Silence comes between us
like a pillow (not a wall)
where we lay our heads
to hear what words
could not have said.
(you still understand
the things I never say out loud)
Passion never set our course,
never was our common bond,
but an undertow.
We feel the pull
even as we row against
the pain of one more dying love.

Lorna Price

HIDE IN YOUR SHELL

Go ahead
Keep those words under
lock and key
Stop
yourself from saying
them to me
You
in your shell
so safe and secure
Are thinking of
the crab
you once were
That ventured out
into the sea
Now scars have ye
So
hide in your shell
until it's clear
and someday
the salt
will make us near

Deborah Bayley

QUEST

Could I return to our town,
Where our love first budded
Then bloomed in all its splendor,
It wouldn't matter
On which of the three hills I stood,
Or if I lingered by the lake,
Or were it night or day.
I still could see the light, the window
That is yours alone.
And still, no matter
How roundabout the way,
How many twists and turns,
Or weary were my feet,
I'd toil along each avenue,
Each street and park and square,
Until I reached my quest —
Your door!

Ruth H. Richardson

FLOWER

In my garden
there was a flower,
but all its beauty
made it die.
I would look upon
and marvel at it,
'til someone picked it
— passing by —
In that flower
I saw you, love
you also came
for just a season,
and you left me
like my flower,
someone picked
— without a reason.
Sometimes I stare
straight out in space,
I rememember a flower
— I see your face.

Ruth Elizabeth Weaver

A TIME TO MOURN

Today I wandered down the paths,
Of dreams I'd left behind,
While echoes from the past flowed by,
As I sought peace of mind.

The flowers bloomed so brightly,
The sun's rays warmed the earth,
The warm breeze gently touched me,
All promising rebirth.

Yet — this day, I am alone,
You are not by my side,
Just memories walk with me,
My tears I cannot hide.

No hope of second chances,
No one with whom to share,
The grief which wells inside me,
For you who I held dear.

Judy Hopkins

HELEN'S DREAM

The white robe hangs
in his former room;
I shiver in my sleep
when Paris pays a visit.
Sailing into my dreams
enough, enough to stir
ten years' dust on
the blank canvas of his
eyes, eyes boring into my
flesh like worms, his arms,
grown stiff with disuse, clutch
and tear at me now,
my body no more to him than
the ghost of his own limbs.
Free, free as air my
love unveils himself as
his white robe trembles
on the battered hook,
glinting maniacally
under the moon's kiss.

Janis Gillespie

OUR HOUR

What do we care what others may say,
this is our evening, this is our day,
what do we care what happens tomorrow,
this is our evening, this is our hour.

How beautiful, how still
the moon does rise above the hill,
and all about is sheen
of trees and grass so green.
The odor of rosebuds fills the air
and you are there.

Love is such a fragile thing,
it makes you dance, it makes you sing,
we hold it in our hearts today
both you and I, and yet it may
be gone tomorrow;
who knows, who cares,
this is our hour.

Jean Rathbun

SUMMER DAWN

Summer dawn
Oh, summer
Oh, the Lord knows that I love you
The Lord knows that I care
And I want you to be happy,
I want you to be glad.
May you never know sorrow
May you never be sad.

The Lord knows that I can't be with you
The Lord knows I wish I could
And if I could, I'd surely be there
To share a smile with you
And if I could, I'd surely be there
And we could share some laughter, too.

Oh Lord, yes I miss her
Oh Lord, yes I care
Oh Lord, I can't be with her
But you know that I wish I could.

D. Gayle Hart

SILENT HEART

The unpassing hurt,
the uncried tears.
Words unsaid
feelings untouched.

A heart that aches
arms that want to reach out
but nothing is ever there,
for the silent heart
to receive or to give.

Times goes by
everything undone,
nothing touched.
Hurt cries out
but no one hears.
Passages are empty
thoughts are blank.
As nothing comes,
to the silent heart.

Kattie Danzeisen

FAMILY LOVE

We are all born into a unit called a family.
Bound together by bloodline and name.
We try to gather together annually.

As we grow through the years and stages,
we all seem to relate,
regardless of our ages.

If trouble arises as we grow bigger,
the right or wrong of it does not matter,
With their help beside us they stand eager.

How soon we forget the closeness and caring,
which without our troubled adult lives
would have no bearing.

As years go by we now can relate,
the memories to our children we tell,
and hope the time is right and not too late.

Then suddenly like a voice from above
we are reminded of the most important thing —
It all stems from FAMILY LOVE.

P. J. Ward

MY MEMORIES

I stand by my window looking out at the stars,
And think of the past that used to be ours.
We were so happy, with our future ahead,
As we made plans for the day we would wed.
You were my hero, I was your girl,

The roses you gave me I pressed in a book,
Our love was found in each little nook.
The ring you gave me I wore with pride,
I thought you would always be by my side.
The promises you made were like heaven to me,
and there was no place on earth I'd rather be,
Than in your arms, or holding your hand,
As we stood side by side making our plans.

Then, one day you left me for fortune and fame,
and you found a new love who now shares your name.
You promised me sunshine — instead, I got rain,
You promised me pleasure, I felt only pain.
Now I'm alone, my eyes filled with tears,
But I wish you happiness through all your years.
From my love for you I'll never be free . . .
It's kept alive in my memories.

Rae Martin

LUNCH IN THE PARK

Because you make me feel complete,
Because your eyes reflect me.
Because I can transcend myself out
of place when I am placed with you.
Because of this my love,
Because of this and so much more,
I want to be with you!
Because we dare to dare together,
Because your thoughts are mixed with mine.
Because I know a freedom I can feel within.
Because of this my love,
Because of this and so much more,
I want to be with you!

Cecily T. Avgerinos

when life as we know it no longer can seed, and love
as being the maker of life is just a joke, then time is
at an ending. only love for the creations of my creator
can sustain my soul. even then my heart is with tears.
for life's survival would depend on love's understanding.
such a heavy task, but one i will accept, the end being
my reward. life forever with our lord, the king of love.

michael mccloud

LOVE IS FOREVER

In the Springtime of youth's pure and true love,
We drank with unquenchable thirst
From the eternal spring of universal love.

But the dream vanished when the shadow of the wings
of Death brushed against my beloved.

In agony, how could I exist for a lifetime when even
twenty-five years would seem an eternity?

In time I wed, sensing that two beautiful children
were awaiting their curtain call for this stage of life.
And their being became untold solace for me.

A saintly teacher had said, "There is no separation in love.
Dreams are the communication between the physical
and the afterlife.
Real dreams are clothed in reality and are recognized
by their vivid detail and their indelible imprint on memory."

Over the years, my beloved came to me in real dreams,
reassuring that true love is forever loving and caring.

To me, "There is no separation in love" has become reality.
Off-stage my beloved *still* waits for me.
And happy be.

Sibyl Michel

A SISTER IS A SPECIAL FRIEND

Memories are a special part,
Of those we hold dear at heart.
The things we've shared, the times we've cared.
'A Sister Is A Special Friend.'

I think of things you've done for me,
And of how small we used to be.
Me with cap guns, boots and spurs,
You with dollies and banana curls.
Me with blue jeans and cowboy shirts,
You with blouses and full poodle skirts.

But no one can change the way I feel,
A sister like you is the world's greatest deal.
And one thing will always stay the same,
You're my sister and that fact will remain.

The times have changed, but we still care.
And I'm not there to get in your hair.
But I think of you often, I really do,
Though I don't say it, I've always loved you.
I've said it before, I'll say it again,
'A Sister Is A Special Friend.'

With Love From Your Sister,
Andrea

Andrea C. Hargis

NEVER SEEK TO TELL THY

Never seek to tell thy love
Love that never told can be;
For the gentle wind does move
Silently, invisibly.

I told my love, I told my love,
I told her all my heart.
Trembling, cold, in ghastly fears —
Ah, she doth depart.

Seen as she was gone from me
A traveller came by
Silently, invisibly —
O, was no deny.

William Blake

GIVE ME YOUR HEART

Give me your heart, Darling
I will hold it as a treasure.
My love will not consume it
Nor break it under pressure.

Give me your mind, Darling
With all its many mazes.
I promise to treat it tenderly
Through all love's silly phases.

Give me your soul, Darling
And the pleasures it uncovers.
These things we'll join together
To become eternal lovers.

Mary T. Carey

LOVE
You exist in my rainbow,
You're my guiding star,
I'll die if you ever go,
My love is where you are.

The angels sing when you
are near,
The sky is clear and blue.
I love the whispers that
I hear,
And the touch of you.

Debbie Kea

MY TEARS BLURRED THE VIEW

I saw the image of you
before me as a dream.
I didn't know what to do,
Things weren't as they seem.

Have you really gone?
I can't believe that is true.
Your image doesn't last long,
as my tears blur the view.

You said we must part,
I felt I wouldn't be blue.
I'll begin a new start,
but, my tears still blur the view.

Glenn M. Reeves

INVERSION

Last time we met,
you told so many lofty lies.
Declared your love
and spoke of bonding till the skies
turned dark and light again.
Our passion grew.

You said you'd try
to understand my point of view.
You made me choose
between those heady trysts with you
and freedom to seek more.
Despair I knew.

Leaving that way
was painful, that I can't deny.
Three years we loved.
Sweet mem'ries feed my need to cry.
Adrift, I wonder when
we'll meet again.

Sylvia Sumida

EYES SO SORE

Last year at this time
there was a bad storm.

The grounds were blanketed with snow
the roads were slippery
it was a very white Christmas Eve,

but hundreds of people
paid their respects.

Today, the one year anniversary
of my father's passing,

the grounds are bare
the air is chilly
and it is lonely.

Nobody's around
all is peaceful
and my tissue box is almost empty.

Wendy E. Hayman

THE GIVING BACK

Each day the gestures of love
register like cash answers.
It is the giving
back of our flesh investment.
As if to say before words
will come, the hug you held
so long yesterday, I return
with the clarity of my eyes
today. The wafts of water
rolled over me, I return
with a fresh red mist of underhair.
The sleep you rocked me into
from the music of your arched feet,
I return with the milk
of a morning smile. I give
these things back to you, before
words will come, uncensored,
immediately minted in the heritage
we continually invent.

Shannon Keith Kelley

I REMEMBER YOU

Yes,
I remember you.

The day you went away
The morning sun was high.
Your hair was shining,
Radiantly alive.
As I hungrily absorbed
The beauty of your face,
You smiled
And latticed my soul
With etchings of love.
And when you turned to go,
You touched me
And I knew —

Death
Would be
The only reason
I
Would not
Remember you.

Joann Showers

Great is the distance that separates us.
All of our direct contacts are gone.
Situations which are upon us thrust
Can greatly strain our loving bond.

Between us there stands an empty space
Which causes tears to flow forth.
If I could but see your face
My life again would have worth.

When we are separate, we are not whole,
each of us half away and half at home.
Our hearts' bells do loudly toll,
longing again together to roam.

If I allow my imagination to run free,
I will again be safe with thee.

Keith Vanden Eynden

To the mother & father
of the man I love
I thank you!

For a better man
This world has never seen
One who is gentle & kind

Mom & Dad
To the one I
Share my life with,
I thank you!

You taught him right from wrong
With an ever gentle hand
Love was plentiful

You should be very proud
Of this man I love
He is a wonderful husband
A good man —

Thank you!

Kathleen A. Perkins

SWEETHEARTS IN LOVE

We love Him because He first loved us. John 4:19

When day is done
We sit together
Beside the fireside's glow,
Basking in the warmth of
pure love here below.
Enraptured we are, while
sharing comforting thoughts
That come from the soul.
As the flame grows brighter,
We transcend to joys above
That only lovers can know.
Content in our new found love
We whisper a prayer:
"Thank you, dear Father,
by bringing us together
and now, our two young
hearts beat as one,
joined by your own
perfect love, forever."

Martha Pastore

MOTHER'S LOVE

Why did God make Mothers
With a loving heart to know,
Just what she needs to do
For the baby she loves so?

God placed that baby
Under a Mother's breast.
He knew the little one needed
A place of comfort and rest.

When baby came, so sweet and coy,
She had for him a special name.
A name that would bring him joy;
If he trusted his dear Maker
and friend.

Mothers who know the falling tear,
A ready kiss to heal each cry and
fear: to guide us when things are
wrong, to make us loving, and keep
us strong.
That's what mothers were made for.

Martha Pastore

REFLECTIONS OF SPRINGTIME

Frolicking blossoms burst into bloom
A ballet of blades in the wind.
The crocus, the iris, the rambling rose,
all beckon for spring to begin.
While Maybelles and apple blossoms
tinted and pink
host hundreds of honeybees
dipping to drink
of the nectar of springtime
enjoying a treat
of all that is beautiful
sunny and sweet.
The finest of everything
that life has to bring,
is the sparkle of your eyes
as they reflect spring.

William D. Leavitt

SOMETHING ABOUT YOU

Moonlight and daffodils,
Mist in the spring,
Laughter so merry,
Will happiness bring.

Starlight and tinkling brooks,
A sunset view,
All turn me on, dear,
But never like you.

There's something about you,
Old pal of mine,
Something so sparkling
Like glasses of wine.

There's something in our world
Just for us two;
A pledge to each other —
We'll ever be true.

Gardens beneath the snow,
Violets in rain,
Walking in rubber boots,
Kissing again.

No matter what I do
I'm never blue
If you are with me —
I just adore you.

Mildred Keating

THE PASSIONATE SHEPHERD TO HIS LOVE

Come live with me and be my love,
And we will all the pleasures prove
That hills and valleys, dales and fields,
Or woods and steepy mountains yields.

And we will sit upon the rocks
Seeing the shepherds feed their flocks,
By shallow rivers, to whose falls
Melodious birds sing madrigals.

And I will make thee beds of roses
And a thousand fragrant posies,
A cap of flowers, and a kirtle
Embroidered all with leaves of myrtle;

A gown made of the finest wool,
Which from our pretty lambs we pull,
Fair linèd slippers for the cold,
With buckles of the purest gold;

A belt of straw and ivy buds
With coral clasps and amber studs:
And if these pleasures may thee move,
Come live with me and be my love.

The shepherd swains shall dance and sing
For thy delight each May morning:
If these delights thy mind may move,
Then live with me and be my love.

Christopher Marlowe

APOCALYPSE

I'm wife; I've finished that,
That other state;
I'm Czar, I'm woman now:
It's safer so.

How odd the girl's life looks
Behind this soft eclipse!
I think that earth seems so
To those in heaven now.

This being comfort, then
The other kind was pain;
But why compare?
I'm wife! stop there!

Emily Dickinson

CONFESSION

Nature sings our welcome song,
Twilight breaks a cloudless dawn,
Hand-in-hand we stroll along,
Hearts entwined and growing strong.

Afternoon fades and sunset lies near,
We've walked this path less than a year,
Together we shall feel no fear,
I whisper words that you shall hear.

"You are the blue in my sky,
A sparkle in a tear-glazed eye,
Open arms when I cry,"
Sunlight rests on you and I.

Tameria L. Millenbach

SEPARATE WAYS

I watched him move so steadily
As he got up to leave.
I felt as though my soul
Was left alone here just to grieve.

A lightning bolt ripped through my heart
As I saw him pass before me.
I reached as though to pull him back,
Then made my only plea.

I wish that I could plainly say
The emotions that I feel,
But the sadness in my broken heart
Feels like it'll never heal.

Caryn Cross

LOVE

Love is much like a rose.
When filled with sunshine it will
grow and grow.
In return it will bloom to show
the world it cared.
But when love is not tended to
and shared,
Like many it will bow its petals
and cry.
Only to wither and die.

Mary Flanigan

HIS HOLY SPIRIT

The dear Lord has always
  been my friend —
I pray He always will be
  until the end —
His Holy Spirit has always
  abided in me,
Helps me with things
  I fail to see —
His voice behind me
  shows He cares,
And helps me in many
  of my affairs —
I have always loved Him
  with all my heart.
I sincerely hope that He
  will never depart —

Fern Roche

THE GREATEST GIFT

A child is a gift of love,
Sent down from God in heaven above.
Handled with care when nurtured they grow.
To love and be loved this seed we sow.
All for love this is done.
The greatest gift ever under the Son.

Andrea D'Esposito

HAPPINESS OF LOVE

The happiness of love is great,
  enjoy it when you can
for as it starts to slip away,
  it's hard to start again.
Unless we know the secrets
  that love and life can bring,
to keep the flame of love alive,
  like flowers in the spring.
We must work hard to care
  for flowers as they grow.
The same is true of love my friend
  to make a love still go.
The words of love we'll keep alive
  with tenderness and sounds,
so keep on trying every day
  and love will still abound.

LeRoy Bernard Schwan

BETH'S BLINDNESS

I feel the sun upon my face
I smell the sweet spring flowers
My kitten purrs upon my lap
As he whiles away the hours
But most of all, I love to feel
My father's big strong hand
I feel he is more gentle
Than any other man
It would be nice to see the sun
To gaze upon the flowers
To sit and watch my kitten purr
As he whiles away the hours
But most of all, one wish I have
That I could sit and gaze
As long as God would let me
Upon my father's tender face

Judith A. Lewis

THROUGH A BRIEF DARKNESS

Through a brief darkness
I saw a shadow on the wall,
It was moving towards me
At a very slow crawl.

Through a brief darkness
I felt a chill,
It crept down my spine
In a warming thrill.

Through a brief darkness
I felt enclosed,
Watching the shadow
So quiet, so posed.

Through a brief darkness
I saw a light,
I felt a strange feeling
As the shadow disappeared from sight.

Through a brief darkness
I saw an image from above,
And knew all these feelings
Were of being alone and in love.

Lori Heim

SECOND CHANCE

The sun is shining down
  In the middle of the day.
The snow upon the waking ground
  Melts and runs away.

If you listen carefully,
  Your spirit will break free
From your hidden flock of troubles
  That will one day cease to be.

When your final day arrives
  And the world waves goodbye,
You will know the price
  Of being afraid to try.

If you need direction,
  Or feel you don't belong,
Wake up and remember
  The meaning of this song.

Spring carries with it,
  New life to the land,
Another summer sunset
  For you to play your hand.

William Robert O'Loughlin

JUST BEYOND THE HORIZON

Just beyond the horizon
I'll be waiting for you,
Watching, waiting, longing
For a heart that is true
And misty eyes of blue.

When the days grow old
And life's sun has set,
When all joys have faded
I'll be waiting for you yet.

Marilyn Vanistendael

I wanted to write a poem,
Describing the beauty of you.
But of all the words of the poets,
None of them would do.
You're in a class beyond compare
Of that, there is no doubt.
God put His beauty all in one,
And you He singled out.
You have the charms of the heavens,
And the face of an angel too,
So is it any wonder,
That I'm so in love with you?
Yes, my dear, I love you,
And I know that it's wrong.
But I cannot forget you,
When the feeling is this strong.
But I know our love can never be,
It's better that we part,
But I shall always hold you,
If only in my heart.

Robert B. Carlton

MEMORIES

I still remember your arms
  Surrounding my needs
I still remember your hands
  touching my most elusive needs
I still remember your eyes
  sight of my hopeful dreams
I still remember your shadow,
  forgotten, nebulous,
  distant, like faraway leaves.
I still remember the seeds
  implanted on my lifeless needs
I still remember the scar
  of your thoughtless dreams.
I still remember the circles
  of your love divine upon me.
I still remember *you* like a dream
  unmasked, somber
  like a phantom, like me.

Damaris Castillo

I love the way you touch me,
your hands so soft and kind.
I love the way you speak
whatever is on your mind.
I love the way you look at me,
with love all over your face.
I love the way you love me,
with tenderness and grace.
I love the way you hold me,
with tender loving care.
I love the way you treat me,
I need you and you're there.
I love the way you respect me,
without even asking why.
I love the way you feel for me,
enough to make you cry.
I love you 'cause you're you,
a person of your own.
I hope I never lose you,
even when we've grown.

Anna S. Barr

IN
MEMORY
OF
LITH. & PUB. BY N. CURRIER,
2 SPRUCE ST. N.Y.

IN
MEMORY
OF
Lith. & Pub. by N. Currier 2 Spruce St. N.Y.

What is love?
Is it the happy times we spend
Together, walking through late autumn leaves
Skipping carefree down the road
Singing songs that make no sense
Playing games from years ago?

Is it the sad times that also come
Forgotten days that held special meanings
Not being able to fulfill our dreams
Saying things that should never be said
Losing friends that can't be replaced?

Is it the funny times we've cried with laughter
Forgetting problems if just for a day
Making faces at young passers by
Embarrassing ourselves in our usual fashion
For once not caring what must be done?

I'm just not sure what love is
But I'm certain of at least one thing
The true meaning may be hard to come by
But when I'm with you it's easy to feel.

David M. Stoll

LOVE LOST

I have seen the stars at their brightest
I have felt the sun at its warmest
I have seen the sky its bluest
And I have seen the grass its greenest.

I have felt the winter its coldest
I have seen the sky its darkest
I have experienced nights their loneliest
And I have cried for the longest.

I have felt the love of a lifetime
I've had too many broken hearts
I have had love at its best,
But I didn't know it.

I've seen the sad things life can do;
But you never guess it would happen to you.

Some people might say it's fate;
But the love is lost
It's too late.

Linda M. Noyola

YOUNG LOVE

Their exists between us, a mystery of magic
Raw emotion yet unblossomed
Spring is in the air.

Reaching out to touch your soul,
Nothing bars my way.
For this eternity, one heart we share.

Traveling blindly towards the light
Struggling to find my way.
Through the mist your tender eyes appear,
My fears are put to rest.

Will it always be this way?
Can ill-fated time with one quick blow,
Put our love to the test?

Catherine Outeiral

A TRIBUTE

While sitting relaxed on one glorious day
My thoughts all tumbled without refrain
I saw my life all pass in a flash,
Then low and behold you were there in the flesh.
I kissed you and hugged you before I realized
That sometime before I had seen your demise.
The sadness I felt was beyond belief
Grief was then there where happiness briefed.
I shall never forget that glorious day
When sitting repeating the memories of you.

Guillermo A. Barela

GOD'S LOVE

"For God so loved the world," the Bible tells,
He sent His Son to save the world He'd made.
Eternal life, not condemnation earned,
Not death, but life, we have through price He paid.

The Great Commandment, given us by Christ
Says "Love thy God with all thy soul and mind,
And love thy neighbor as thyself." This last
Commands for us who hear, a nature kind.

A question posed disturbs our selfish peace:
"Who is my neighbor?" Are we asked to share
Ourselves with distant, different, unknown ones
As neighbors? Are we told by Christ to care?

The message, "God is love" reveals for us
The answer: We must love His world the same.
If we are worthy of redeeming love,
We'll love our neighbor, prideful of that name.

If God so loved His world that He sent Christ
To show that we must love both God and man,
We must accept His message in our heart
And earn salvation bought by Heaven's plan.

Sadie E. Elliott

DARLING

Darling, my deepest feelings, I'm sharing with you,
No reservations, I want you to know —
Realizing, with this, I'm made vulnerable,
With my whole being, I love you so —

I give to you, my heart, my love, my trust,
Knowing, you will never abuse these —
Protect and watch over — my most precious gifts,
Hold tightly and cherish — please —

Because, in this changing world, nothing's certain,
And it's sometimes difficult to choose —
When priorities and values change — daily,
The wrong choice, you've so much to lose —

The one certainty, that I will promise you,
And it is truly, what makes life worth living —
Is loving and being loved in return,
Always sharing, understanding and forgiving —

The knowledge, that you'll always love me,
Being secure, in the future we'll share —
I will love you, forever, even after,
Life is beautiful, simply, because you care . . .

Janice Reed Hamlin

MY MOTHER

My mother,
so near, so dear,
loving and caring,
always sharing.

Advice to come,
from the mind through
the heart.

Keeping pressure, with
worries so calmly,
knowing problems will
be solved, at the end
of each day.

Harsh at times,
but always forgiving.
Open arms, to who
comes near, and always
leaving with a big cheer.

We all know, "It's the plain truth!"
That no one, can compare, to our
mothers, so precious.

Jose L. Alvarado

THE APPLE TREE

Today I walked down the long hill,
To the spot behind the old grist mill,
Where we planted the apple tree.

It stands, now, all alone.
Its trunk and limbs full-grown.
And carries a half-a-ton of fruit.

As I stood beneath the tree
You were there with me
And I still love thee.

G.M. Petts

FEATHERS

Little bird, if I had wings like you
I could see my love again.
He's gone too far, where noble eagles are
To a land no one has been.

I need to love him one more time
Little birds, lend me your wings
For all I have left are feathers
And a heart filled with unsaid things.

Little bird, I feel like dying
Don't know what I'm to do
For I know he can't come back to me,
How I wish I had wings like you.

He said he would bring me roses
In a color deep as flame
But all I have left are feathers
Not a petal, only pain.

Little bird, did you come to comfort me?
Did you bring me a message of good-bye?
He's gone too far, where noble eagles are,
To a land beyond the sky.

Kathy Millard

THE CONSTRUCTION

Let us create,
let us build a monument
to each other,
laying our foundation on love,
supported by trust and truth.

Let our materials
be worthy enough to withstand
the test and stress of time
and the years that may follow,
with each year adding new stories
to our creation.

Let us build strongly, and idealistically
so that others can see the strength,
allowing our steady maintenance of each
other's emotions to ward off all signs of
condemnation.

Robert D. Hardy

HARDY, ROBERT DARRYL. Born: Trenton, New Jersey, 1958; Married: Robin O. Hardy, 10-12-85; Education: Brookdale Community College, part time for journalism degree; Occupation: Cook; Poetry: *A Voice In You,* Vantage Press, 2-19-86; Comments: *My work comes from all things around me, the good and the bad.*

GOD'S MYSTERY

How do the birds and bees
The flowers and the trees
Know it's Spring again,
Though 'tis snow, not rain,
That falls e'er so lightly
On crocuses standing uprightly?
Birds fly to and fro aseeking
Balls of seeds aswaying
From hidden branches bare.
The chattering masses there
Are happy to have come.
Soon bird activities will hum.
It is as though they know
That despite the snow
Food will still be waiting
The same as 'twas last Spring.
Faith, love, obedience, trust,
In God's world are a must.

Lillian C. Marcoux

YOUR INDECISIVENESS

My heart is torn in two, my beloved
For, you know not
What your indecisiveness
Has wrought in me, these days.

For, I stand firm in my
Unconditional love for you.
Yet, your uncertainty blinds
You from the truth of what is.

Oh, the aloneness of one
Heart on the line,
While the other teeters with the wind
Is a depth of pain new to my heart.

And though me heart
Aches for you, my beloved,
The peace and tranquility that
Cloaks my soul provides my sustenance.

Patiently I'll wait, my beloved.
For, I am confident
That your heart will guide
You to the truth of us.

Stephanie Yeater

THE NIGHT

I look out my window;
The moon is shining bright.
The moon has such a glow
It brightens up the night.

The night is not like day;
The sun it does not shine.
The night has a deep blue hue;
The night is so divine.

What a lovely sight to see;
With the moon and stars above.
The quiet and peaceful night;
Is full of joy and love.

As we danced across the room;
In his arms I did stay.
This was that special night;
We spoke of a wedding day.

Many nights are yet to come;
Some with rain, some with snow.
This will be a special one;
With my love wildly aglow.

Linda Gail Rocher

HOLOCAUST

Only in dreams
We can love each other
Without shame
Purified by obsessions
And instincts
As two spiritual beings
Burning together
In the same sacred flame
On the highest altar
Of love's supreme
Sanctity.

George Alexe

SHARED

We shared love,
We shared laughter,
We shared our sorrows,
We shared happiness,
We shared our hopes and our dreams,
We shared our love,
We shared our heartaches,
We shared our families.
Best of all we shared ourselves with each other.
We shared our lonely days and nights.
We shared our pains,
We shared the Lord,
We shared our time.

Robin Bronson

DEATH, YOU HAVE CHEATED ME

O Death, you have cheated me of my love,
for she and I were to be married.
How you did make a mockery of us,
and of the burden I'd so long carried.

I told her, "I should not love you, my dear,
for my days upon Earth are not long."
Said she, "How can we be apart, when
this feeling is already so strong?
Is it wrong to love a dying man?
Don't you deserve love too?
Is it wrong to give each other our love,
even if your days are few?"

She made me see and understand
how precious a short time can be.
So I decided in that moment
that she would be wed to me.

But before we could be married,
tragedy upon us came down.
Death ironically mocks me because
it is her they are putting into the ground.

Lynn Neilson-Barrett

A LITTLE WORD LIKE LOVE

Moving like an ocean, a current wild and free
Against the laws of nature, compel your love to me.
A word that I can't handle — I'm trapped; afraid to show
And feelings of true emotion, yet unwilling to let go.

Oh, God, what precious moments seem like heaven above.
It's hell to know you lost it all
In a little word like love.

A calm breeze blows to ease the storm,
The current is meek, yet strong.
Somehow I understand no right,
And know there is no wrong.

Still the thought can shake me so —
I hope no one can tell
I'm living through the dreams of heaven,
Yet riding on through hell.

Yes, hell is what it feels like
When it's like heaven above,
Then you realize you lose it all
In a little word like love.

Emily R. Webb

HEARTS ON FIRE

Hear my silent plea, one I can't say out loud, is it
Ego, shyness, fear of hurt, or am I just too proud
Accept the invitation shown clearly in my face
Read my body language how you make my heart race
Then by some small gesture let me know you care
Stop my inward aching, ease my heart's despair

Oh how often this sad story has been man and woman's fate
Neither one admitting love, before it was too late.

Forever after looking back wishing they had tried
Inner pain tormenting them, eating them inside
Rise up, speak out, reject false pride, cry out your desire
Eagerly, let your love know . . . your "Hearts on Fire"

Ann Murrell

SONNET 3

There is a vision of a love once born
Birthed in the glow that comes before the dawn.
Two lonely souls, with hearts unspent — forlorn
With dreams undreamt, that lure them on and on.
Such loves that loom from out such lonely dreams —
Are passions of desire that cannot die.
Two hearts have met, and loved, no need of schemes,
To gain the love that's come to you and I.
There is a vision of a love so great
That even Venus shadows in its light.
These hearts are bound by more than Cupid's fate,
They're made as one, with guidance of His might.
I know now why I prayed to Heaven above.
The greatest gift God gives to man is love.

Darwynne Pucek

FOR KAREN

Your love for this life was all-consuming.
All whose lives you touched you loved.
Your passion and love of this earth and its people moved us all.
Now you're gone, but our love for you lives.
Thank you for this beautiful gift.
I know you will be waiting when my time comes,
and the gift of your love will see me easily through this life.

Alan K. Byrd

LOVE IS

Love is, as a flowing river — flowing into ecstasy
Always, ever, never ending — flowing forth, from you and me
Ever running, never resting — faithful to the longing sea
That's what love is, lovely flower — truly faithful, lovingly

Love is, as the swaying treetops — singing "O" so merrily
Only whispering, never loudly — love is spoken, quietly
In a smile, and fleeting glances — longing eyes speak gleefully
That's what love is, lovely flower — truly faithful, lovingly

Love is, but a glowing liking — bringing life, to you and me
Though apart, at growing lightness — yet together, we shall be
In our dreams, and fond rememberings — ever faithful, dreamingly
That's what love is, lovely flower — truly faithful lovingly

Eldor Rathjen

GOOD OLD DRESS

I love to write, I love to express,
It's like going and buying a new dress.
You hang onto it when it gets old,
for all the stories it really holds.
Times when you were carefree,
times when you were gay,
times when you will reminisce on the good ol' days.
How to make life more pleasurable to you,
whether it be pink, red, green or blue.
To have it fit, just right, for that special date,
looking back on why you came home late.
Clothes are fashionable and then they are gone,
but you will remember its fit, its song.
Yes, writing is like that good old dress,
it's a way of remembering feelings that you expressed.

Bekki J. White

TOGETHER

Together you and I conceived a feeling.
Together you and I gave birth to an emotion.
From the conception of this feeling, came
the birth of our love. Our love, so young,
so exuberant, so alive. Like a flower would
blossom, our love has flourished. As the essence
of the flower would be sweet, the essence of
our love is passionate. As the existence of the
flower would bestow beauty, the existence of
our love bestows tenderness. With a breathless
whisper of woe and all this emotion to show,
time shall flow, time shall pass, but our
love will grow, our love will last. Keep this
in mind, hold this in heart, for with a
sentiment like this our two souls shall never part.

Colliér

OPEN LETTER TO MAMA

Mama, I love you,
Should have said it to you when you were here.
I was young at the time and didn't realize that your life
Would be gone in a wink of an eye.
It's always too late to let someone know how much love
Is in the heart.
I miss you very, very much and wished that I would have been
More helpful, thoughtful of your needs at the time.
It seems just like yesterday of the memories of you; your lovely,
Caring smile of love.
Your devotion, determination and love will always be within me,
Deep in my heart your spirit is present in my life.
You have taught me a lot,
With unspoken words of wisdom
of life's precious moments.

Sheila A. Lopez

ONCE, MORE THAN A FRIEND

I tried to phone her three times, each
time feeling more dejected than the last.
She wants us to become "eternalized"
but I'm still ready for change.
Feeling like the blind, deaf mute
bullied by hoods, I sit by a misting window
watching leaves fall with agonizing slowness,
land atop heaps of other dead leaves,
and twitch from side to side.

Mark T. Beyer

A SPACE MAN'S PRAYER

Here we are once again getting ready to get a little
closer to You, oh God
We're all ready to go right now, it's much too early for
a wiping towel

One like I gave to You, dear God, on the cross
I just hope there is no tear when we get our chance to
steer

We're coming out there close to You, dear God
And we hope to make it back again

Now just before we go, we'll get down upon our knees and
Thank You, God for all of these.

Paul H. Engel

MY SPECIAL LOVE

Between man and woman — I have found
My special love that will astound.
When you're in love — you want the world to see.
Just how special love can be.
Heart to heart — mind to mind.
I'll take this special love anytime.
No one can say just when you'll feel
My special love — for it can steal.
For all the wonders — you will find
There is no other — of its kind!
It took some time to understand
What it was I really had.
Once in dreams — now in life.
My special love is with me tonight.

Linda Mustain

MY LITTLE BOY

Your face is all smudges, your hair is uncombed,
The house is a shambles when you are at home.
The cookie jar's empty with crumbs on the floor;
The soap is black spattered, fingerprints on the door.

It sounds like a horse has raced down the stairs,
You whistle no tune; the T.V. set blares.
Your jeans must be mended — the knees are in shreds;
Your shirt is no better — buttons hang on by threads.

No one else would have you, couldn't give you away,
But somehow I love you each hour of the day,
For you're my little boy; God gave you to me
To have here on earth and through eternity.

Evelyn Holten

GOD'S WONDROUS LOVE

Do not worry; Become not distressed.
Look to the Savior, for peace and sweet rest.

What wondrous assurance to you and to me,
Because of that blood, that flowed at Calvary.

Such atoning Love, Grace Divine,
Just open the door, and Jesus Christ you will find.

Alan J. Burtt

BUT WINTER CAME

The sunrise burst upon the sky,
  Dispelled the gloom of darkest night:
Blue heavens canopied on high,
  Creation beamed in morning's light.

Sounds of new spring then rent the air:
  Birds sang a joyous symphony,
Cool breezes whispered everywhere,
  All nature joined in harmony.

It was the day Jill smiled on me,
  A smile that only once I'd know,
The day I've kept in memory
  Since winter came, so long ago.

John M. Andrews

LOVE IS GIVING

Come with me, my own sweet love
Let's journey along life's road.
We'll open our eyes to really see
The wonders to behold.

We'll spend our lives just helping those
Who aren't blessed the way we are,
And, when we lay our heads to rest
We'll wish upon a star.

We'll wish each day to be used anew
For the work of the Lord above.
We'll journey about this beautiful earth
Sharing our joy and love.

Terry Ann Braaten

MARILYN TO JOE

  You truly are so dear.
I'll never let you go.
  I need you oh, so near.
I thought I'd let you know.

  I tell you that I love you,
but you just can't believe me.
  I know you have the right to.
Because sometimes I'm deceiving.

  It's something that I'm working on
I know it's hard to believe.
  But not all my hope is gone.
And I'm trying not to deceive.

Heather Clough

LOVE, UNREQUITED

Love, unrequited, is a Promise
Of fulfillment belonging to the Future.
Then and surely, with the Keeping
Of Times appointed and recorded,
The fulfillments of Love's own Creations
Will continue to Manifest themselves
For All Eternity, even as they did
In Times before Time was Known,
When Love was but a Concept!

Suzanne L. Reed

A CAPTAIN'S FAMILY

Old Captain, living in a car.
I wonder how old you are.

Wrinkled weather worn of face,
Yet, still square-shouldered as you walk with pride and grace.

You knees are bent and your ancient beard grows askew.
Those eyes . . . Those eyes show the wisdom that is in you.

Baggy pants, tattered coat, that threadbare Captain's hat,
Long ago have seen their day of use . . . Yet, they do not detract from you.

In that old abandoned car, your home at the water's edge,
You stare day after day . . . watching the Gulls devour their prey.

When the frozen waters roar no more, you share your breath with them
As if an offering to those long dead, asleep on the ocean floor.

While others pass you by each day . . . The sea birds,
Your last remaining friends . . . will love you to the very end.

When your proud heart gives out one day,
Will another Captain take your place . . .

To stand on shore with food in hand as a tribute to those asleep on the
ocean's floor?
Will only the love of the sea birds guide him to Heaven's Door?

Elaine Meli

SUBWAY RIDERS

You see them in the subway on the way home from work — at rush hour —
Teenagers or close to it — guys and gals clinging to each other.
Obviously romantic, you hope it's at least affection and not desperation.
Are they married to each other legally, or is it just a shack?
Do they have their own apartments to go home to, or do they live
  with relatives, who would object to their displays of lovemaking?
Is it really love on the part of the male Romeos, or just a passing fancy?
The girls seem so wrapped up in the embraces of their partners;
  will they have bitter heartaches in a short time?
Is it just another prelude to unwed motherhood? The men are so persuasive.
And the older passengers on the subway were like that themselves
  twenty-five years ago, or they wonder how such obvious romance passed them by.

Florence K. McCarthy

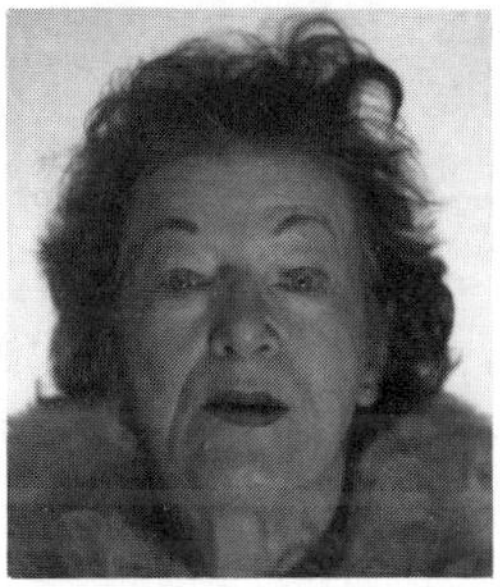

MCCARTHY, FLORENCE KATHLEEN. Born: Bronx, New York, 1-30-18; Education: Hunter College, CUNY, B.A., Pre-Med., 2-43; Occupations: Engineering Aide, Comptometer Operator, Typist, Secretary, Word Processor; Memberships: AAUW, NYC Branch; Hunter Alumni, Bronx Chapter; AARP, Bronx 162; Knickerbocker Artists.

LOVE'S DIFFERENCES

Love is often painful,
And this we can't avoid.
Love can bring discouragement,
When none can be o'erjoyed.
Love lends us much frustration —
Yes, that's part of loving too.
And love can be confusing
As each day dawns anew!

Yet love brings satisfaction
As true love should and must.
And love brings joy and happiness
Through rain, snow, mud, and dust.
Love should bring encouragement,
God intended that to be.
And love should be fulfilling
For you and, yes, for me!

God gave us much potential
When He gave us power to love;
To love and then to be loved
Is sanctioned from above.

Pearl Sandahl

SUN CITY?

I am just one
voice of many
in this world
of none and plenty
who cries for peace
and can see none
through clouds obscuring
the once bright sun.

Why is there war
among our kind
and why is love
so hard to find
in a world
that should be shared
by everyone, everywhere?

Linda Kay Gault

LOVE STREET GENERATION: AM JUKE BOX BEATING ON

Pony Girl
on the RADIO
You say we BELONG
to the LIGHT
We belong TOGETHER
How TRUE
We bee buzzing a round
Love SONGS
Fire and ICE
Words OF LOVE
from ENDLESSLY Summer ONE
Sister Golden Hair Surprise
HONEY BROWN SUGAR
Showers down on ME
The SPINNERS
Bid me on their TRAMPOLINE
I bee head over HEELS
in LOVE with you
Who Criticize and HOUND me

I FELL DOWN BROKE MY CROWN:
SO LUCKY THAT YOU FOUND ME

Edward M. Giannattasio

FULFILLMENT

My heart had empty been so long
Without a trace of love's sweet song
That I had grown as one of stone
From wandering on my way alone.
I mingled in the crowded street
Where people that I seemed to meet
Had neither care nor thought for me,
Nor I for them, until I see
His hand that reached out to clasp
My own in warm and tender grasp.
He understood my heart's desire
And realized that sparks of fire
Were hidden deep within me here.
I came to him and had no fear.
And that is how the flame was lit
And I became a part of it.
When he and I were made as one
And ecstasy's brief hour was run.
My heart's no longer made of stone,
For I belong to him alone!

Dorothy Orr Horesta

DEFINITION

My God has not a human form,
Although addressed as "He."
My God is like a blanket warm,
Enfolding you and me.

The Comforter encircles space,
And listens as we speak.
It touches down with loving Grace
On both the strong and weak.

I know 'tis true, for I have felt
The warmth that Quilt can send.
One night, when in the depths I dwelt,
I felt its glow descend.

My body rose to let It wrap
Around me, soft and mild.
God swathed me in the downy nap
And soothed this troubled child.

Elizabeth P. Wish

LOVE'S WORTH

Love is oh so tender
So unselfish, so concerned;
Love is so desired,
So compassionate when earned.

Yet love can be so painful
When one you love is lost!
Love can be real crippling.
Is it really worth the cost?

Though love is ever wondrous,
Love can hurt you too.
Still the positive fulfillment
Makes love something to pursue!

The tenderness, the caring,
The beauty love can bring
Leaves memories for a lifetime.
And that's worth everything.

Pearl Sandahl

A HAND TO HOLD

Life is forlorn
And ragged as a beggar
When there's no one to love
Or, a hand to hold.

Life is a thief,
And a constant retriever
Of dreams that never end.
Life is a pretender
Of days which are gone —

The linkage of tenderness
From here to there.
Life is a reminder
That you cannot bear
To live alone
without a hand to hold.

Prudencia Boals

WHAT IS LOVE?

Love is like the air;
it cannot be made.
Live love,
and you shall have love.
Have love,
and you'll have it all.
Love cannot be spent;
it is not money.

Give love,
and it will return.
Love will go around,
it is a circle.
Love is like a star,
spreading joyful light.
Be love,
and spread its beauty.

Margie Amberboy

YOUR PRESENCE

The birch and pine stand together,
Their branches touch on high.
The blades of grass sway forever
And snuggle 'til they die.
Even colors blend in reverence
With a great, majestic hue.
All is naught without your presence
And my being without you.

Nothing lives in isolation.
Everything has its pair.
See the clouds in adoration
Clumped together in mid-air,
And the sun upon the sea
Warming all within its glare.
Yet, a sadness ever haunts me
Without your love and beauty fair.

Russell Troutman

Rain pelting the snow,
Sweet perfume of daffodils . . .
A shared umbrella.

Deon Davis

MOTHER'S LOVE

Dedicated to my mother.

There is a special kind of love and that is of
a mother —
And of all the gifts of all the loves, there
isn't any other —
She loves you when you're happy and more so
when you're sad —
She loves you through the good times and helps
you through the bad —
She gives you all her wisdom through your
growing up in years —
In your good times she laughs with you, but is
there to wipe your tears —
To God I'm ever grateful to have a loving mother —
I wouldn't want to trade her in, for there
could be no other —

Ruthie Mac

McCLANAHAN, RUTH ANN. Pen Name: Ruthie Mac; Born: Hampton, Iowa, 5-26-47; Occupation: Factory Worker; Awards: My best and only reward is that of making family and friends happy to see me write; Poetry: 'The Morning After,' 'Love Can,' 'Dreams,' American Poetry Association, 1986; Hobbies: Playing piano, accordion and singing; Comments: *I love to write. It is my best way of expressing myself. I get my inspiration from my mother, the encouragement of my family and friends. I get my wisdom from the sweetness of life. Thanks, Mom, for making all of this possible! Thank you, friends!*

OUR TIME

As my wandering feet fall upon the tinted leaves,
I can't help wondering why I'm here and you're there.

Like the rose without a blossom;
My heart lies immobile, waiting for your
Vibrant touch.

Drops of Autumn rain fall gently upon the road ahead;
Masking the path of our future.

Come back to shelter me from time . . .
Our time.

David Allen Mills

MY OWN MOTHER

Her name was Anna
And with a Pollyanna heart
She wiped the tears, bandaged the bruises
For five who never called her by name
Scrubbing, cooking, baking and ironing
She never once complained
For she dedicated her life to her children
Asking nothing in return
Strong faith carried her onward
Through good times and bad
A saint indeed, this lady who labored in love
Years of fifty-seven she was called to her reward.
Should I reach Heaven's Gate, I'll surely see
Her name printed there in gold
ANNA — beside her name I'll write — M.O.M.!

Carolann H. Knecht

THOUGHTS OF YOU

There are gloomy days
When I get so wrapped up in life
That not even a smile can cheer me.
I get involved with things
That weigh upon me, and I react with a frown.
The day goes bad,
And I'm alone and sad
Because I must face this kind of day
Without you.

But then I think of times
I've spent near you,
Warm and safe in your arms.
And thoughts of you cheer me
When nothing else can.

Lysa D. Voight

SOLDIER SON FOR THE RED WHITE AND BLUE

For every star that shines above you
is a fervent wish so true
That God in His heaven is always protecting you
For every star
My wishes are
A rainbow to break through
Erasing the gloom in this whole wide world
So no harm will ever come to you
Brave soldier for the red white and blue.

Pearl Van Slocum

GOD'S LOVE

The Lord our God may be a jealous god
Who suffers no one else to share His throne —
He still can know and suffer with our pain,
And from the evil of our world bring good.
When man in stubborn selfishness destroyed
His link with God, God's Son came down to earth
To know and share its anguish and its dearth;
Love — selfless love — was all that He employed.

It was — and is — enough. In His short life
He taught His faithful twelve what they must have
To plant the spark that set the world aflame.
They did not change us all, and still man's strife
Continues, but each age has those who brave
Man's worst with love, and conquer in God's name.

Lucy Mason Nuesse

CHARLOTTE'S PRAYER

Father, may I talk with you
  Of things I no longer understand
Father, may I walk with you
  And will you hold my hand?

Father, when just a little child
  I was taught of your great love
Father, now I'm old and sick
  Please! Take me home, above.

Father, I will leave behind
  My husband, dear and true
Father, bless his future life
  When I come home to you.

Father, I've taught my daughter
  Of your love that's so divine
Father, may she know the many joys
  Of life that have been mine.

Father, I am quite ready
  To join you high above,
Father, as you guard my friends
  Please, bless them with your love.

Mary Nixon Flaugh

A TIME FOR LOVE

A time when sounds are soft
And comforting with relaxed sensibility.
Dreams carry us high aloft,
As we float elevated with hilarity.

A time of embracing each other's bosom,
With warmth and shelter and passion.
To nurture inborn impulses into one,
That instinctive urge beating in unison.

A time that springs into life,
From the depths of the soul.
In the animation of the rife,
A union of parts into a whole.

A time to gather in celebration,
An event of vigor and anew.
Through the threshold of perception,
To capture the amore to ensue.

A time to cherish all nature,
To look far into the Universe.
And replenish thoughts with a cure,
Of an enchanting tranquil verse.

Wayne A. Shock

THE GREATEST VALENTINE

Jesus Loves You and Me, John 15:13

The greatest of *any* Valentine
Was the one our Lord did sign
As He died on Calvary's tree
With his *own blood* for you and me
He wrote, "For *you* my life I give
That *forever* you may live
I am thine and you are mine
Beloved, *You're my Valentine!"*
Love,
Jesus

Evangelist Emogene Maxey

SHORT DIVISION

We divided the property
But how do you divide a son
When his blue eyes look at us
Through a mist of tears wondering why?

Jean M. Porter

A LOVER'S DREAM

Anxiously awake rummaging about.
Asleep wading through the empty night.
Come!
Let us meet.
Each with the same thought.

Nico Boccio

MUTED

How silent is love,
A look . . . a sigh
A gaze . . . maybe
Maybe . . . this is it!

Jean M. Porter

THE ECHO OF HAPPINESS

A laughter that still rings
in my heart. So fresh young
and alive like a sweet rhapsody
that stays with me The Echo
of love time did not erase.

Millie R. Curtis

WILHELMENIA

My love for you
Is like white noise
Serenading your soul
With concertos of love forever

Leroy L. Moses

MY DAUGHTER — MY WORLD

Sailing
Before the wind,
Gold hair flying, eyes bright,
Lips trying, her life unfurled,
My world!

Lucille M. Kroner

LOVE

Love is like a dove,
flying free in the sky,
But will soon say goodbye,
and fly, fly away in the sky.

Deedee Graves

LOSE A MEMORY

Trying to lose a memory
  trying to smudge a face
which haunts my mind indolently
  appears in every place

grinning in my coffee cup
  hanging on my wall
reflected in the raindrops
  ghosting through the halls.

Hearing deep the laughter
  the hug a stretching ache
the hands which knew emotions
  no words could ever fake.

A scrunched up wad of flowers dried
  a letter oft' reread
a picture with the crumpled edge
  an empty blank in bed

echoing the yesterdays
  the tomorrows not to be
the silent clock ticks in my thoughts
  the time of memory.

Claudia D. Newcorn

THE ARTIST AND THE POET

"I'll write for you a golden verse,
The song heard in my heart.
The voice of my emotions,
The echo of my soul."

"I'll paint a portrait of my feelings,
I cannot hide from you;
So I will show them in all their splendor
Of ever-changing hues."

"I'll write for you a paradise,
Someplace so far away;
Yet, so near, it is in my heart,
And shall be every day."

"From my brush will flow a river,
In which the fairies dance.
From dawn to dusk, we, so silent, sit,
Engaged in lovers' trance."

"We are each other's inspiration,
Our escape from reality,
As we fly together on magic dreams,
Whatever they may be."

Deborah Nielson

SEA SHELL

As we walked
hand in hand
on the sun-drenched beach
at water's edge,
we surreptitiously found
a pink-bleached seashell
that we held close
to our ears.
And we heard a song —
It was our song.
Remember?

Mary Annah Alemán

OUR LORD'S LOVE

Lord made heaven and earth and everything therein.
Let us keep our life for him clean.

Lord loved us so
His son died on the cross to save our soul.

We should love our Lord so
We should let him save our soul.

Our Lord wants us to come to him.
Do we go with love in our hearts to him.

Lord is with us day and night.
Let our love for him be right.

He loves us in our sickness and in our good health.
Do we love him in our sickness and in our good health.

Our Lord is always by our side.
Do we in his love abide.

In our hearts let us have his love.
To others we should show his love.

Our Lord wants us to win others to him.
Let us never in our work become dim.

Our Lord wants us to go his way.
Do we ask him to guide us in his way.

Ella H. Hollander

LOVE THE CHILDREN

Love the children who are so dear
Hug them tight and hold them near
To our hearts so full of love
Who come to us from heaven above

Love the children every day
Teach them how to work and play
Show them the way they should go
Tell them what they want to know

Watch ourselves and what we do
So when the children follow too
We won't be sorry and be sad
Only reasons to be glad

We want to see them grow up to be good
Behaving nicely as they should
Learning how to grow their food
And cook it too and not be rude

To be healthy, happy and wise
One must learn to bake, and pies
For cooking is a work of art
Everyone must do their part

Reading, Writing and Arithmetic at school
Teaches the children how to rule
This great big wonderful world each day
For we love the children in a great big way

Eva Cook

STORMY LOVE

The rain is like the tears of love.
We hurt so bad but hold it in; so when pressure builds up
We let it all out, in the form of a storm.
The rain comes down as our tears, the thunder our anger.
The lightning is the pain in our hearts.
Our tears wash away the deep harbored fears.
It gives us a chance to begin again.
Fresh and clean with the rainbow as our road
to a peaceful heart.
Unfortunately the rainbow never lasts long enough
for our heart to complete the journey home.
So, next time it storms,
think of those you have hurt in love and remember
the rain will come down on you: the one who placed
the hurt in the heart of those already
hurt in love, somehow — someway.

Pamela Lawrence

RIPPLING WATERS OF DESTINY

Rippling waters of destiny, tide and time,
Where it goes no one knows.
Like a dream before one realizes youth is gone.
Oh for those memories with a song in our hearts,
We danced to the tune of gypsy melodies.
Our feet felt like wings,
For youth knows only Spring.
Our hearts were filled with eternal love,
As we promised to each other,
For as long as there's a sky and the sea,
I would love you and you will love me.
Then fate took a hand and made us part.
Leaving me just sweet memories.
Though I know you can't be mine
I'll love you from time to time
Until there's a sky and rippling waters going by.

Marie V. Spadaro

I'LL BE YOUR FRIEND

When you're weary and overcome,
When trials have made you sore and numb,
When times get rough and cause you fears,
When you dread facing the next day,
I'll comfort you and dry your tears.
When your friends turn the other way,
When those you care for break your heart,
I'll stand by you and take your part.
When hard times leave you bruised and beat.
When you must stand and face defeat,
When you're walking the lonely street,
I'll take you in and wash your feet.
I'll keep you safe in loving arms,
Without flattering you with charms;
From the beginning to the end,
I'll stick with you and be your friend.

Edwin Hayes

LOVE THROUGH TIME

The feelings I have for you will
never go away, I feel them for
you more and more each day. I
hope you feel for me as much as
I feel for you, because I never
want the day to come, I have to
hear you say we're through.

Teresa Baker

FOR LOVE

Some will climb the highest mountain,
or swim the broadest sea.
Some will cross the widest chasm,
or walk the whole wide world
to find what they call love.
All they need to do,
is look within their hearts for love.

Margie Amberboy

SOMETIMES IN MY DREAMS

SOMETIMES
she still comes to me,
but only in my dreams.
And while I sleep
it's like she never left,
but when the dawn unfolds
I'm destined to wake alone.

Robert Anderson

THE NATURAL LOVER

Down the rose stem,
Caressing the grass,
Kissing the petals,
Loving the leaves,
The dewdrop rested,
Finally.

Amy Lynn McNeely

The corridor.
Familiar shapes dance through —
Leaches trying to kill our dawn.

"Gideon — come you — "
Pink flames approach — butterfly
approaches — arms soft.

silken tresses

James Douglas Morrison

LONELINESS

Far into the night a child cries.
He sobs heartbroken into
His damp pillow.
When at last his sobs
Give way to exhausted sleep,
His tiny hands reach out
For his mother.

Marilyn Morris

LOVE HOLDS THE KEY

What is love? Who can define it,
Or with clever hand design it?
Where is love, and who can find it,
Or with golden cords dare bind it?
Might the universe contain it,
Or a wicked soul disdain it?
Can the finite mind express it,
Or the faint of heart distress it?
Does the mystic mind perceive it,
Or dishonest men deceive it?
If all the oceans were to drain
They could not love's great depth contain.
Love must be shared from day to day
As kindness gives our love away.
This truth shall stand: Love cannot fail
Where faith and hope in God prevail
Love is the greatest of these three,
And to God's Kingdom holds the key.

Edna Powell Weegmann

COMMUNITY

My neighbors eat macaroni salad
with olives and roast chicken —
Antonia tells me — frequently;
and from her many bicycle rides
to buy long loaves at the
small international shop,
they must eat chunks of bread
the way I'd eat a dozen macaroons.
The tall shrubs hide their
comings and goings
(which is a relief to them
who have no time.)
Antonia asks wistfully
when will I come over.
But I am busy weeding my garden,
eating cod on my moonlit porch
and re-reading letters
now ten years old.

Christine Janz Taylor

FRANKIE

When Frankie passed away
Our hearts were sad and broken.
He was a small black poodle,
More than a mere token
Of love to touch our hearts.
He was a companion
A bundle of constant joy.
He romped; he played, especially
Hide and seek with his squeaky toy.
His most favorite time of all
Was riding in the car,
In the front seat standing tall
Resting his head upon the bar
Checking ev'ry mile of highway
As we rode at varied speeds.
Whether beachward bound
Or on our way to work each day,
He was a loving friend indeed.

Lillian C. Marcoux

THE GREATEST GIFT

"Now abideth faith, hope, love, these three; but the greatest of these is love."
I Corinthians 13:13

Across the gaggle of heads our eyes meet —
We are together in a sunlit meadow.

The winter day screeches to a red light —
We touch and listen to our symphony.

Pain shatters courage —
We speak names and smile.

Alone, we pray, and know
Love is forever.

Esther M. G. Smith

THE ELUSIVE BUTTERFLY

Kiss me in the moonlight,
Hold me in the dark;
Walk with me in the starlight,
Sit with me in the park.

Love is just an emotion,
Often exaggerated by the mind.
It is oh so very beautiful,
But truly hard to find.

Like some elusive butterfly,
Always out of sight.
Totally ignore it
And on you it may light!

William Steven Stassen

MY LADY CRYING

Oh! How do I reach,
into your heart?
And how can I help,
ease the emptiness,
you feel inside?
Give me a sign,
that I can make,
your life brighter!
I swear to you my dear,
that if you do I shall,
forever be near!
Just give me a chance,
to show how long,
my love will last!

Mark L. Ridge

A KISS

The moon is a spectrum at midnight;
A jewel on velvet — a star!
The frost clothes the world in crystal,
But your smile is a ruby delight!

White gloves are sprayed on the tree tips;
Snowflakes — confetti adrift!
The love I give you is aglitter,
But your smile I touch with Love's lips!

Ray Befus

love

lo
ve

(i

am
so

l
one
            l
               y)

            me.

Martha Hayter Peterson

FORGET-ME-NOT

Forget-me-not,
Our baby bloom
So dear and sweet and jaunty . . .
You give us laughter
Full of love,
Your arms are soft and flaunty . . .
You lift us up,
You hold us close
In warm and cozy snugness . . .
You fold us gently in your ways,
And, we are lost to everything
Except your baby smugness . . .
And, we love you,
Mommy and Daddy.

Nella Thompson Meiser

I GAVE MY HEART TO JESUS

I gave my heart to Jesus,
Now I'm on my way
To a home in heaven
For my sins no more to pay.

He has a crown for me,
He will place it on my brow;
I cannot wait to see Him,
I know I'm ready now.

How sweet it is to know Him
As my savior and my Lord.
Yes, now I belong to Him.
We walk in one accord.

Vivian Frances Jackson

Perfect Love:
Come to me, my own perfect love!
Come to me in white satin, soft
and pure as a dove!

True Love:
True love flourishes through timely years,
through hope, time, and bittersweet tears.

The Greatest Love:
The greatest love I ever met,
Was God's love in a splendored sunset.

Frances Smith

HIS GAZE HELD ME IN CLOSE EMBRACE

Love came to me, I'll tell you how:
As swift as an archer's arrow;
In the crowd of the market place,
His gaze held me in close embrace.

I could not tear my eyes away
From his that brought mine to bay;
With no pursuit or courtship chase,
His gaze held me in close embrace.

So I was launched into love's event
For which time has no measurement,
Nor through the years can time erase
His gaze that held me in close embrace.

Blanche Madiol

How shall I tell you of my love
I lost long years ago?
To me she seemed to be pretty,
With skin as white as snow.
She was not tall nor too small
But somewhere in between.
I don't recall she was too stout
Nor was she much too lean.
And golden was her head of hair
And soft her two grey eyes.
And why she cared to love me then
To me's no small surprise.
I promised that I will love her
Till all the world should go;
Though promises are silly things
Made by a man in woe.

Hyman Lerner

THE SCOPE OF LOVE

No longer do I see
through the obscured vision of eyes
that have proven to be
very deceiving and unwise

rather I see with my heart
which is pure and profound
more in touch with love's art
and unfearful of rough ground

this deeper insight
reaps rewards not thin
for without eyesight
we find love from within

Dennis Camire

HOMECOMING

I watch for signs of him
around the bend.
Dear to me his form on sight.
I hear his footsteps
where the grasses end.
Once more my lonely day is bright.
I open wide the door
as he draws near.
He opens wide his arms
and holds me dear.

Olga H. Scully

ETERNAL LOVE

A word that is quite common
Is known to all as love,
First sent by God our Father
From His heavens high above.

A love for all your neighbors
Is really known as care
And through each joy or sorrow
With love, they'll help and share.

A mother's love is special
Hidden deep within her heart,
Through children's trials of growing up
That love will never part.

A love that's known as puppy love
It seems so deep and true,
But youths grow up, part their ways
Still, its memories oft renew.

Last of all is romantic love
'Twixt a husband and his wife
Through future years, it grows quite deep
Leading to eternal life.

Mary Nixon Flaugh

SEPTEMBER IN MONTEREY

Our love
mingles with
stars . . .
and for myself,
I drink in your
every touch
and all
the words of love . . .
Leaving September
stars and memories
in Monterey.

Nancy S. Bartholomew

FRIENDSHIPS DIE

Two people we are
Two people we've been
Always in my heart
I never saw a sin

When a friendship dies
Because of false love
You feel so lonely inside
Lost, like a little white dove

When you love someone
You thought loved you
And then you find out
It wasn't all so true

What do I do
To make you see
That you'll always be
A part of me

I love you so much
But just let me know
Say the word
And I will go

Kristin Roberson

THE VOICE OF LOVE

I hear your voice in the deep orchestrate
Of waves singing in to the shore,
In the sigh of the turning, twisting winds,
In the might of the hurricane's roar.

The depths of your voice is the song of our age,
That whispers to me of love,
And warms my heart with its deep caress,
Holy, as if from above.

It slips through the hymns of the mighty church choir,
Raised up in glory to Him.
It winds 'round my heart a gossamer veil,
Keeping our love within.

The voice of love is the voice of the world,
The golden dawn breaking through,
The beginning and ending of all that we need,
When it indeed is true.

Lucille M. Kroner

CUPID'S ERRANT ARROW

When Valentine's Day is on the way,
All men not remiss
Are prone to find within their mind,
A long-remembered kiss.
Perhaps the one that doubtless won
His heart forevermore.
Or, maybe just a bit of lust, from
Desire's reminiscent lore.
When Cupid's aim is true, there's flame
In the young and innocent breast,
A wanton kiss . . . a virtuous Miss . . .
The blaze may soon ingest.
Maid, be concise, keep your heart on ice,
With emotions on a leash.
Never trip and fall though he's charmingly tall,
And spouts sweet gibberish.
Make him understand that a wedding band,
Is the one band you must hear,
Then if Cupid's bow aims high or low,
You'll have no need of fear.

Chet Rust

THE LOVE OF A MAN'S FAMILY

The love of a man's family is the
second greatest love of all. The first
greatest love is to God above. God
was the one that started love. He gave
it to Adam and Eve; from Him above.
The little children of a man's family are
the most innocent of all. That is why
they're always having a ball.
The wife of the family is the main
guiding force of the children and home.
That is why most men would rather their
wife stay at home.
The husband is the leader of the family.
He is the one whose decisions affect
the household of his family. So they
would be secure in their sanity.
Without the family, we wouldn't have new
leaders; in the future of this world.
That is why we should treat them as
if they were a genuine pearl.

Melvin B. Riley

HE & ME

The husband and I have acknowledged
that very soon
our jobs will take us down separate roads
miles and miles apart.
He knows a little about us
about how we would have if we could have
and he's agreed given his okay
(since we both want it that way)
that he will take a she
and I can share me
while we're away.

I know you said we'd meet again
but I'm so pessimistic (or is it being realistic?)
that chances are slim.
But if we do, and this poem's a clue,
you can lay me down.

Jan Cinco

A MARK OF A CHRISTIAN

How can friends know if you are a Christian?
Is there a mark of some kind to show this distinction?

Is there a membership card for you to display,
Something to show you're following His Way?

Is there a password that you must always have ready
To show you're a member and always are steady?

What way is possible for all people to know
You belong to Christ His blessings to show?

Jesus tells us what each one daily should do;
We're to love one another as He has loved, too.

Our love is to be shown by our service to men;
May be humble ourselves, winning others to Him.

Jean D. Knettler

TO MY SONS

Beloved sons of mine each one so different
and yet so much alike,
you both have a very special place in my heart,
one because he is the eldest
and the other because he is the most young.
From both of you I expect only the best
because you are both good in your hearts.
I also want you to be always united, together
and never apart, even when your paths
might be separated sometime in life.
I also want you to be men of truth,
men of faith, of honor and hope.
Love God, love each other, love others,
love your families, love your Country and love Humanity.
Do always your best in whatever you both do
and God will always protect you
and smile upon both my most beautiful sons.

Andrea Almac

EMOTIONAL BANDIT

Instead of stealing a kiss —
You bombard my brain,
With —
Pleadings.

Let go of this —
Tug on my heart.

Stop lingering in my brain.
And —
Scrambling my veins.

Don't smile in my dreams.
Take away my schemes;
Of our togetherness.

Or —
Come forth.
Confess your love.
Settling this heat,
Of unfilled lust.

Sarah Mercer Greis

FLASHBACK

I try to capture
Our precious moments in words
But the pain is still fresh.
Each colorful memory
Brings great words
Each word brings a smile
That I so lovingly promised to you
And each smile
Brings a salty tear
That develops into a river

Last year at this time
I was writing a poem
That captured
One of the happiest feelings
That my heart ever witnessed
The words depicted great love
And each word seemed to smile
Those smiles brought tears
But the tears I shed then
Were drops of happiness.

Christine M. Goldbeck

HARD TO BE IN LOVE

It's hard to be in love,
  when you know he doesn't care.
You need to have him hold you tight,
  but you know he won't be there.
You can always find somebody else
  to take that person's place;
But you know it's not the same,
  when you see it's not his face.
It's hard to be in love,
  when you know he doesn't care.
All the feelings you hold inside;
Feelings you want to share.
Is there anyone who can
  change your mind,
Make you look away from him?
Someone who will spend time with you,
make you feel loved again.

Angela Williamson

LOVE'S PRICE

You never write to me,
Love letters like it used to be;
You said your love, would be true.

I felt it in my heart,
You said, we'd never part;
Why do I now feel so blue?

The days have come and gone,
The nights are ever long;
I'm all alone and there's no you.

I knew right from the start,
That you would break my heart;
The price to pay for loving you.

Hazel Mae Parron

PARRON, HAZEL MAE. Born: Norfolk, Virginia, 6-15-56; Married: 11-4-77 to Norman R. Parron, Jr.; now have one daughter, Jenny Lynn, born, 12-10-83; Education: Professional Business Institute, formerly of Norfolk, Virginia, 1974; Central School of Practical Nursing, Norfolk, Virginia, 1977; attended continuing education classes at Hampton Institute in 1979 for nursing process and written care plans of Hampton, Virginia; G.E.D., 1975; currently certified in Cardio-Pulmonary Resuscitation; Occupations: Nursing Instructor for Professional Business and Medical Institute, 1980-1981; Licensed Practical Nurse, Humana Hospital, Bayside, Virginia Beach, Virginia, 1980-present; Poetry: 'The Holy Dogwood Tree,' *American Poetry Anthology,* 1986; 'Mission of Love,' 'Even Love You More,' 'Love's Price,' *Hearts on Fire,* 1986; Comments: *I am in the process of completing my first novel which I have been preparing for review for possible publication for the past year. I wrote 'The Holy Dogwood Tree' in 1962 when I was a student in Ballentine Elementary School, Norfolk, Virginia. I got the idea for 'Even Love You More,' from my father, as he recorded it on a tape recorder; a poem he wrote years ago. I watched the tragic events of the Space Shuttle Challenger as it exploded in mid-air, January 28, 1986; I went to sleep and that night I dreamed the poem which I have now published, 'Mission of Love.'*

DISJOINTED

The caresses became hugs,
and the hugs waned to back pats
and we bundled up
and bustled off to Waffle House and Denny's
separately
seeking privacy and impersonal company
to numb us to another day.

I'm confused, love, as to where we go from here.
We feel to be somewhere between a casual like
and too near nowhere.
It's a ticklish situation,
sharing our separate lives
together
while disjointed at the heart.

We divvy up the bills
and the king-sized bed,
then, late at night,
we lay back-to-back
drained
soundlessly aware of the ocean roaring between us.

Jan Cinco

UNDER THE SHADE TREE

Here I sit
under the shade tree of His love,
sun filtering through the leaves
of the scrubby oak tree,
tested and worn by time,
still standing as proof of His strength
and power to prevail against assault.

Wounds and scars where branches
were sheared to direct His growth;
He grew strong through suffering
and obediently He stretched forth
short and wide as the loving hand directed,
so He might be a refuge to all
who come to rest under His boughs.

Here I sit.
secure in resting in His love
and all that's gone before;
my refuge, my peace, my strength
and my joy is in this scrubby oak,
the shade tree of His love.

Sally Nickerson

DAUGHTER

No jewel could be fairer
Than a daughter, kind and true;
No blossom could be sweeter,
Should we search the whole world through;
No sunshine could be brighter
Than a daughter's radiant smile,
Within her eyes reflected —
She is dearer all the while!
If I could gather jewels
And lay them at her feet;
If I could bring her blossoms,
With lovely fragrance sweet;
If I could take the sunshine
And weave it into gold —
Still none of these could measure
A mother's love untold!

Hildur Solberg

ANTEDILUVIAN

Perhaps it is better to be
Rid of the pomp and frenetic
Passion that characterize our sorties
Into love's oft troubled waters.
For now,
in this cruel and calculating world
It is fashion to be selfish, and to that end
Ruthless in manipulating love's sacred ties.
And yet,
How I still yearn to once again
Be able to give my
undying
unselfish
uncontrollable
Love;
Without having to fear that, while
it rests in the palm of your hand,
My world would be casually crushed.
Oh, that times past could have
shaped our worlds more closely.

Keith Todaro

LONELY CHILDREN

If I could only just reach out
Embrace every lonely child
Ease their many hunger pains
Give them the love they have never had

A home with a caring Mom and Dad
A soft warm bed to lay their head
Lots of food they have never known
A feeling of love, no longer alone

At Christmas, a tree with lots of toys
A brother or sister to share their joys
Hear their laughter, no tears or fears
New clothes to wear, new shoes on their feet

Someone to kneel at the altar with them
Teach them the meaning of prayer
Lovingly tell them of you Dear Lord
That blessed and helped them, because you cared

Thelma I. Goss

TO MY BADLY-CRIPPLED LOVER

At first they tittered at my talk
of dreaming that comes true,
and stitched a bit and fluttered fans
pretending that they knew
the end of all such foolishness.
But when I showed no fear,
they looked askance at me and said
that now it would appear
that this and this and this must stop
before it was too late.
But I saw only you and knew
that love controlled our fate.
"We're only thinking of you," they said,
"for life has many a trial.
It's much too unconventional,
for that there's no denial.
Give him up and lead a life
with so much less demand."
But love will see us through each day
And God will understand.

Hester Hayes

Fairy Arch.

THE WOODEN INDIAN

You interlace my being
With your strong and tender grace.
My yearning refrain beckons, yet
You remain . . . Granite Face,
The Unfathomable . . .

I hear the wanting voiced,
And primeval urgings paced.
Fleetingly, your soul I see
Before the shield encased,
The Immovable . . .

I want your lips, your arms,
With oneness, your firm brow.
I glimpse the same, your eyes
Betray you . . . But swiftly now,
The Wooden Indian . . .

In the magic realm of dreams
Your face I caress, and play
The exotic music of your love;
Your heart I touch, the wall I slay;
And May The Wooden Indian Fall!

Betty Antrobus

PRAYER FOR LOVE

My Dear Heavenly Father,
Let there be a love for me,
Someone to whom I can belong,
And who can belong to me.

There's an ache inside of me,
So full of need,
That only you can see,
How it envelops so much of me.

A faithful love,
To share my laughter,
My sorrow, and my joy.

Someone I can lean on,
Through the days of more,
I think on this, I've had a low score.

With my heart wide open,
Would you send someone
To its door.
Because of so much suffering
Maybe I can appreciate it more.

Alice Fleming

Through white lace on the windowpane,
Diamonds sparkled on the snow,
Tree branches white with frost
Bushes with snowballs shining in the glow.

Beneath the sparkling carpet,
Red roses and violets blue
Wait for signs of spring
When life begins anew.

I think of my white lace Valentine
Wherein posies of many hue
Edged a true red heart
Saying: Forever, I love you.

Eleanor Benson

OUR FORTY YEARS

Our forty years seem
but a year — I still
reach out to feel you near —
I sense a void until
you appear — my need
for you has never waned —
As the seedlings reach
to kiss the sun — or
the grass that licks
the morning dew —
And the birds in heavens
together so high — fly
so free — in flocks like one —
Our love each day
begins anew —
our forty years
seem but a year —
I still reach out
to feel you near —

Maxwell C. Kaufman

KAUFMAN, MAXWELL C. Born: New York City, 11-15-18; Married: 1945 to Dr. Sylvia Kirschenbaum Kaufman; Education: St. John's University; New York Institute of Dietetics; CULA, graduated Dietitian, B.S.; Occupations: Retired, Dep. and Asst. Commissioner, New York City; Poetry: 'I'm Fine Sir!' *Dreams and Visions,* Green Valley, 1985; 'Another Hand,' *In Quiet Places,* Quill Books, 1985; 'The Samovar,' 'The Goiem,' *Daring Poetry Quarterly,* 1986; Themes: *I write from experiences which have affected me — emotionally and intellectually. I write about love, hope, family, religion and beauty.*

THE NIGHT WAS YOUNG

The night was young, the moon was full,
He swore forever would he love.

The sun came up and then he knew
Eternal love was yesterday.

Rann Newcomb

GOD IS LOVE

The gentle rain
baptizes the earth
That is God, God is Love

The mother bird
tends her nest
That is God, God is Love

The faithful lame
yet walk the line
that is God, God is Love

The atheist
shows optimism
That is God, God is Love

The imbecile
obeys the word
That is God, God is Love

The futile blind
still see the light
That is God, God is Love

God sacrificed
His only son
His Son is God, God is Love

John Louis Jones

LOVE

Love
Happy, exciting
Living, caring, sharing
We all need it
Love

Anne V. Brady

DUSTY ROSES

Dusty roses
on burning sands
along a lover's lane
Thirsty flowers
where romance failed
Precede the Summer's rain

Wounded are visions
of ardent man
In throes of heartache pain
Wasted were moments
of courtship time
Where love was all in vain

Faithless the woman
who won his heart
And jeered at his affection
The bouquet tossed
in fury as
He realized her deception

Dusty roses
have washed away
Symbol of love despaired
The wounded man
rides lonely trails
His heart to be repaired

Edna Ball

MY "IN" CROWD

They all fit in, these kin of mine;
If "in's" the thing, they'll do just fine!

There's Mike the "in"satiable cookie-container,
And Tim, the "in"scrutable woman-disclaimer.
Mike won't say no when there's baking around;
Tim's out of teens, choosing where he'll be found.
Joanna's "in"between child years and teens,
Surveying her rainbow to see what it means.
Roberta, the "in"finite essence of mother love,
"In"defatigable, in special ways proved.
Richard, "in"disputable head of his home,
"In"tuitive, lovingly wearing his crown.

These have been "in" my heart, trials above,
"In"volved, "in"dispensable, sharing my love.

Elizabeth Brandt Hunter

SEPARATION

I watch for traces of your face
  in every cloud formation,
For memories of you in the lyrics
  of a half-forgotten song.
The places that we traveled to elude me,
  I've been away from them and you so long.

I search the faces of the people I encounter
  to see if they resemble you
My heart feels so much disappointment
  when none of them ever really do.

I know some day we'll be together
  we both will smile and laugh again.
I feel so sure that it will happen
  but don't know how or where or when.

Olga H. Scully

ASCENT

I have seen your love for country and cause, and
I have witnessed your devotion, dreams and lore.
I saw you reach for the skies and knew that
Upward you would soar.

And so on your special day, my own Magnificent Seven,
My love burst forth to embrace you, and
Led you straight to heaven.

I know how much your world needed you, as
You were forged to the fore;
But even as they watched and waited,
I took you because I need you more.

Be one with moon and sun, and me
For all eternity.

Lucille R. Albanese

SONNET 210

Anger has swept across my sullen face
And left its mark of fury in my voice.
The rage I felt is past — but not the trace
Of bitterness — that taints my thoughts and choice.
I do not wish to carry on like this,
To harbor hatred's brat within my breast.
Denude my mind of cherished thoughts and bliss
And made to feel so low — a pawn of jest —
That I cannot exist nor life be shown
The me within. So now I can't elude
The storm beneath this dignity I've known,
That makes of me a chattel — base and crude
I search for love — compassion — truth and faith
That I had lost with angry words I saith.

Darwynne Pucek

THE BAY

We stood, my love and I,
  Mere shadows on a cliff.
  Crashing waves far below
    Whipped to voluminous proportions,
    Then shot high over bare, jagged rocks.
  A lone fisherman scurried for protection.

Above, sea gulls called
  As they glided and dipped
  In the golden sunshine.

We had, for a moment, captured
  Freedom without responsibility;
  Love for eternity.

Hirrel Weber

THE TREE OF LOVE

O heart, deep in whose center lies the seed
Of love, lose no precautions to assure
That seeds will grow, though achingly you bleed
In your uncertain soil. Perform some cure
Wherein your sterile dust is made to bear
The utmost loveliness in fruit that all
May know yours is the beautiful, the rare
Invocation to the god of love. Tall
And in challenge to the ultimate height,
Wherein supremity in beauty sleeps,
This tree shall not be lacking quite
The large nobility of love from which love reaps
A great immensity in fruit and will
Assiduously demand eternal fill!

Harry L. Morris

LOVE AND ROSES

My love was like a rose garden at noon
Upon a summer's day.

I drank the sweetness in and basked content,
Until a rude wind blew the petals to the ground,

And then my love was gone.

Jo Finch

SACRIFICE

Love was sacrificed
on the altar
of your ego.

The two of us — you and I
Partners . . .

I — the performer
You — the director.

You — could not
I — would not
But you cried that I must.

I did —
without direction.

The audience, unaware,
Applauded both.

You won . . .
You who could not . . .
Because I did.

Love was sacrificed
on the altar
of your ego.

Doris M. Compton

I may not see you often
Or write you as I should
But forget is one of the
Things I never would or could.

Mildred Barford

A TRYSTING PLACE

I love you
said the sea to shore
And with a wave
embraced her more

I love you
said the sand each day
And breathed delight
to feel his spray

The gulls would circle
wondering why
and of course the clouds
would try
To understand the love affair
together always
always there

The sand below she'd be so round
and soft and smooth and waiting, found
By all the ocean's wild lusting
in passion's waves
the tide's fondling

Some love is worth an hour's time
and some love's only real in rhyme
The ocean and the shore display
the way that we love every day

David D. Palmquist

O COME, MY DARLING

O come, my darling,
Come sit by my side.
Let us watch the rising moon,
Let us watch the tide.

The fire that burns within me
Has caused a meeting this night.
So let our flames come together
Before the next daylight.

As the pale light danced around us,
As the stars shone overhead,
We embraced each other emphatically,
The sandy shore our bed.

The dawning sun came all too soon,
The gulls' shattering cry.
But as we ambled home that morning,
We knew our love could never die.

Reynald G. Searles

THE MAN I LOVE

He gave his life,
that I may live
He made the whole universe
people, animals, birds.

Out of the earth,
He fashioned the human race,
He gave His love to all,
He is God, the supreme being.

He gave His love and understanding
faith, hope, and charity to all.
This is the man I gave my heart to.
He is God, our supreme being

This man is as real to me
As my own dear father was
I feel His presence daily
For He is my heavenly father.

Gem

ANGELA

Stars shine in wondrous splendor
at her feet,
sun rises with a smile
each day to greet.

Flowers grow for her,
furry kittens purr,
dogs lie in loving slavery
at her feet.

She sings, nature stills
itself to listen,
quiet and loving, fair
of face is she.

She dreams, may all hopes
be fulfilled,
our Angie, like a daughter,
dear to me.

Jean Rathbun

WISHING

Like the gentle breeze of summer
That glides along a beach —
So very hard to capture,
So very out of reach.

This man of many duties
And qualities so rare —
Of gentleness and strength,
His life I'd like to share.

A very gentle touch
Or even just a kiss —
Coming from this man,
Would all just be such bliss.

But dreams are dreams alone
Yet who are we to say —
This very man could walk,
Into my life one day.

So why not keep on hoping?
Hope never did one wrong —
How beautiful are hearts in love,
And love is a sweet song.

Regina M. Jones

DEALER'S CHOICE

First chance, first serve
Hands touched, loss of nerve
Once kissed, gently burned
Once missed, a quick return

Time lost can't be regained
Love spent can't be contained
Once played, no recall
Once loved, no choice at all

Once shy, losing ground
Twice burned, till we found
Sharing pain steals the thunder
Making one a lonely number

Hearts meeting, no regretting
Dreams awakened, now forgetting
All the lessons life has taught us
Live the moment time has brought us

Time shared, plans are laid
Hands dealt, must be played
A gentleman's game from the beginning
You let me believe I was winning

D. V. Stiles

NESTING

as some silken bird
your hair perches
upon your shoulders
and spreads its wings
around your face
giving an aura of
loveliness
which only
those poets
of yore
could capture

Richard F. Kellas

PUPPY LOVE

God made the animals
one by one.
The naming to Adam
when he was done.

Adam named each, according to its habits
From the mighty lion, king of beasts
to the lowly rabbit.

One gave wonder, as Adam watched
It could tear a lamb asunder,
Or skillfully herd the flock.
By Adam's side, it stayed that day
Keeping all other animals at bay.

The name, finally, chosen by Adam,
was dog;
When spelled backwards, we know,
spells God.

God must have nodded "well done"
from above.
For he knew, I'm sure
of dog's penchant for love.

Mabel L. Bowman

JERRY, MY BROTHER

Admired you and cared a lot,
We laughed and cried and sometimes fought;
You were my guide in what we did,
For I was just a "Little Kid."

When spring arrived, we went outside,
Our shoes and socks still inside;
While all the wading left you free,
Pneumonia grabbed ahold of me.

Music we had by grammaphone,
And then you played the baritone;
Singing was "sissified," you said,
"Instead, oh, yes, I'd rather be dead."

Putting a motor on the bike,
Made Karen and I have to hike;
But when your shirt was torn in two,
The motor converted to lawnmower, too.

Though years have passed on those events,
These memories are still intense
Then and now, I certainly care,
For, I always knew, that you were there.

Kathleen M. Burley

A warm breeze,
The sun on the sand.
Many times, I've walked this beach.
But never before
Have I known such wonder.
Pipers, running from an incoming wave,
Then madly chasing it back,
As it recedes into the foam.
A shell, a shard of driftwood,
The smell of the sea itself.
All of my senses have come alive,
Since I found your love.

Mike A. Perry

HIDDEN LOVE

You have always been there
for me,
To lend a helping hand or to
wipe away the tears.
Always knowing what to say or do,
to ease the pain away.
Will I ever be able to say that
you're more than just a friend?

We have always shared your
deepest feelings;
With lots of love and joy and
even laughter too.
Will he ever know that he is more
than just a friend?

You have always been one terrific
friend;
And a very special man.
Can I ever tell you that you're
my one and only
Love?

Angela S. Propst

WE SHALL MEET AGAIN

I feel there is a God
whenever I think of you
For nobody else could fulfill
my heart, the way you do.
You wrote me a song
You said I could sing
Then you sang me a song
that I was sane.
I followed you close
And listened to your words
But never got a chance
To be a friend of yours.
Because you live so far away
Only my words could ever say
That we shall meet again
Yes, we shall meet again!

Debra Sue Peterson

A MEMORY OF LOVE ON THE DAN RIVER

Hand in hand on the banks of the
River Dan,
Whispering words of love
Me — and my darling man!
Me — and my darling man!

Willows caressed the shining water;
The beech tree its shadow bestowed
Upon its rippling, gurgling surface.
Music sang along the grassy shore,
Along the grassy shore.

Blackberries clustered and birds flew
From vine to vine.
Dark eyes alight with love and laughter,
He was mine!
He was mine!

The years have passed
But along the River Dan
I shall always dream of my dark-eyed man.
My dark-eyed darling man.

Pansy Fain

PEACE AT CHRISTMASTIME

It would be nice at Christmas
If the world was all at peace,
And nations cancel their differences
Then war and strife would cease.

For there is sorrow and suffering
And many tears will be shed,
When there is war and trouble
We know there will be many dead.

The baby that was born in a manger
Brought us love, peace and good will,
But we seem to forget all of this
And continue to kill, and kill.

Again He will have a birthday
On a certain December day,
Let us pause and worship to Him, give
And reverently, our homage pay.

Bryan Roesch

LEST I FORGET (A PRAYER)

Lest I forget the one who died
to save me from my sins,
I ask you Lord to speak through me,
and help me make amends.

For all the grief I've caused today
and all the harm I've done
I know you will my peace, dear God
you gave it through your Son.

So my Lord, I've come in need,
please rid me of this guilt
You are the rock the Father sent,
on which His church is built!

Lift all resentment from my heart,
send love to take its place
Renew my body, mind and spirit
remind me of your grace!

Katherine M. Brady

HEAVEN'S GATE

I lay upon a lonely bed
While moonlight around me gleamed
And on the wings of a lover's dream
You came to me last night

In those precious moments rare
Heaven's gate was open wide
And from eternity's timeless shores
You came to lie down at my side

Your arms reached out and drew me close
I softly breathed your name
Forgotten was the loneliness
The sorrow and the pain

All through the starlight I gazed
Into your dear familiar face
But came the dawn, and you were gone
Back through Heaven's closing gate.

Dolores Saldano

FOR YOU

A hike in the mountains
A swim in the stream,
You are thought about a lot
Whether in my life or just in a dream.

How could I forget you
Even if I tried,
For my love for you
Is something I cannot hide.

Just remembering the good times
And even some of the bad,
I will always remember all
The wonderful memories we've had.

Maybe just a year
But probably much more,
Never will you see me
Closing our door.

A simple poem
Yet only for you,
Because you're the only one
That will ever make do.

Lisa Mahony

THOUGHTS OF YOU

Summer breezes sketch
Your special silhouette
Upon the setting moon . . .
Etching eternal,
Sweet-scented moments.
The sight speaks
Joy to me —
Loving ecstasy!
Ah! Like a gentle
Lover's caress upon
My soaring heart.

Gwen Cheryl Lyn Sarandrea

GOODBYE MY LOVE

I met you in the springtime
when the world was fresh and new,
and life became so wonderful
all because of you.

Then summer came with sun and sea
and love was in your touch.
The taste of salt on bodies sleek,
Love remembers such.

We married in the Autumn,
the world all red and gold,
and love and joy were intertwined,
till all the world turned cold.

That winter day was dark and bleak,
I sadly watched you go.
A jealous God took you away
because I loved you so.

The years have passed, the world is cold,
for I am all alone,
thinking of what might have been,
as slowly, I grow old.

Joan M. Vannucci

HEART STIRRINGS

They played the song again today —
Here came the memories back again
from another time I'd put away.
Here you stand in the drenching rain,
a stray kitten tucked beneath your chin.
Here's your smile as you softly say,
I found him, will you take him in?
Coyly I answer, You both can stay.

The warm sun rose again today,
splashed orange-gold on silent cloud.
Will you marry me? Your voice is proud.
Beneath the clay therein my sorrow
and aching memories, they'll always be
through ink of night into the morrow
as the old cat sits and watches me.

Rosa Nelle Anderson

WHAT IS LOVE?

Love is the essence of all things —
beautiful, good and pure.
It is belief in self to correct the bad,
and all evil, for sure.
Love is kindness, understanding and
helpful concern for others.
It is thoughtful treatment, consideration
and gentleness for our brothers.
Love is imagination, wonder, surprise
and joy for a child.
It is, for youth, the highest ecstasy one
can achieve without guile.
Love is God's message, bestowed for the
good of all mankind.
It is eternal, for all ages, and will
endure for all time.

Faye P. Parker

GRACES' GHOST DANCE

How like a dream they come
Three sisters
With power over beauty and charm
They dance offbeat tangos
Their occult glamour effective
To charm and beguile a specter.

Allen T. Billy

PRECIOUS LITTLE BABIES

Precious little babies,
Asleep in your cozy beds.
It seems there is a halo,
Around your curly heads.
Your skin is as soft as a petal,
That grows upon a rose,
But what you become my darlings
God is the only one that knows.
I am proud to be a mother,
To seven precious little dears,
I did not get to keep them all.
But I love the ones still here.
Now I'm an old grandmother,
And a great grandmother too.
I'm still proud to be a mother.
And, mothers, so should all of you.

Justine M. Edwards

TOTAL DEVOTION

Forty years of marriage
happiness and tears.
Love and true devotion
growing without fear.

Ten years of living agony
suffered by two souls.
Each hour total misery
no longer any goal.

Total mass confusion
in every daily task.
Dear God, "Please give them patience,"
that is all we ask.

The reason was Alzheimer's
Love could not conquer all.
The moon is gone, his wife abides
frail, alone and small.

Margaret E. Smith

TO MY BOYFRIEND

I woke up the other day
and saw you standing there
You made me open up myself,
you made me really care.

Before, I was a little lonely
that was when you weren't around.
You turned my life inside out
you pulled me up when I fell down.

You told me that you loved me
and one day I said the same.
I realized early in the start
this wasn't any game.

And when we stay together,
forever it will be.
Say you'll never stop your loving,
because mine's for eternity.

Cynthia Windheim

AIRBORNE

Spring has sprung! It's finally here,
and freedom's ring does bless my ear.
The sun, the flowers, the gentle breeze,
does fill these days with long lost ease.
If Cupid's arrow shoots at you,
you'll find new hope, one becomes two.
Yes, in the midst of all this fun,
we turn our faces to the sun.
If the seasons dictate our mood,
I hope to store them up like food.
To save them for when I am sad,
or angry, ticked off, sore, or mad.
I'd take them from their hiding place,
cherish them like amazing grace.
The bliss new seasons bring each day,
I wish could last, I wish could stay.
So here's an ode when winter comes,
and pain sticks out like a sore thumb.
Maybe just reading this could be,
a little joy through poetry.

David Andres

FINISH LINE

Through forty years I've kept at things —
Busy with this and that and those.
The one I wanted most in life
Couldn't see me for money throes.

I couldn't compete with party pals, trains,
Steamships, freeways, jet-specs high;
Squares don't fit in figures round
And it hurt too much to trim and try.

And so, with heartbreak in my throat
And blinding, scalding torrents from each eye,
I did the only thing for me to do:
I said that dreaded word, "Good-bye."

Now, today, what do I want? My heart
Would pound and race and soar —
"O, nothing more!" If I could see
The Captain of my retired, port-bound ship
Come smiling through my galley door!

Dorothy Moore

I LOVE

I love spring's coming with a chill,
Wildwood jasmine — a greening hill
When march winds tease and thrill.

I love summer, the church bell chime,
The whispering breeze where roses climb,
My singing heart and words to rhyme.

I love hearing, "I come I come,"
The buzzing of the honeybee hum
And the beat of a distant drum.

I love the murmur of the waterfall,
The woodland cypress growing tall
And the night birds' timely call.

I love autumn's goldenrod,
The hallowed place
where angels trod
While singing in the breeze with God.

Virgie McCoy Sammons

FRIENDSHIP

Over the years it grows
It reaches the point of no return
It blossoms, it stretches
It reaches upward and outward
Infinitely . . .
Born are the possessors of such a wonder
Clasping it tightly, keeping it within their reach
It needs no light, it needs no air
And yet, somehow it exists
It breathes
It continues to grow with time
Indefinitely . . .
It creates warmth
It creates togetherness
It multiplies over one hundredfold
It replenishes itself continually
It does all this, this small wonder
For it thrives on the one food God made plentiful
It thrives on love

Loretta Bivens

THE ARROW OF LOVE

There was an old eagle who flew so high,
Higher than any before had flown.
Surveying his domain from his place in the sky,
He worried for his kin left alone.

So he came down to where lesser eagles fly,
Like a king abdicating his throne.
He was felled! On the shaft that made him die,
He saw a feather of his own!

Frank Favaro

HEARTS ON FIRE

Soft moonlight embraces the sky
But thou art not here love to see the splendor
My heart is forlorn and torn misty-eyed
Return to me with your heart's surrender

Reverie in my heart's illusion
dots me with constant intrusion
Where dost thou be, when I'm in seclusion
to sort out my trembling heart's confusion

I hear thy footsteps
My heart is elating
listening, longing with anticipation
Running, striding at last two hearts together
Embracing, loving forever and ever

Maria Leber

MEMORIES OF LOVE

Memories of love
as the tears flow from my eyes
I look back at your happy face
the memories of love we shared
The beautiful children we have
oh what a precious gift.
now as I look back
I can't help but say
I love you baby
as the tears roll down my face
I remember that special place where
We loved and laughed together as one
life was good and we had our fun
but now you're gone and all I have left are
memories of love.

David Nelson Roberts, Jr.

FOR MARGARET THERESA

In a soulful word,
I love you.
In a solemn vow
I adore your wonder.
In mystery I sing
Freya's praises
to your soft cling,
to my deepest affections.

I sing this poem as a votive
to your charms,
which no evil or snakes of the grave
can circumvent.
And in swallowing every bit of your ambrosia,
I may see myself for what you really are.

Stephen Ring

FATHER, DEAR FATHER

My mother's love I lost in early youth;
An automobile ended her career.
Heartbroken I confronted sorry truth
And yielded up myself to Father dear.
Without another child to share his grief
He looked on me and knew my depth of pain;
His words were few; he always was quite brief:
"We're all that's left; let's not speak words in vain."
Forced circumstances took him far away
To earn a living in a distant place
While I in our home city had to stay,
Our love kept us upon a single base.
Though circumstances kept us far apart
In hearts and minds we could not closer be.
He had the warmest corner of my heart,
I know his deepest feeling was for me.
His death alone when I was forty-four
Could not end our devotion, even start
To terminate our love, our dearest lore.
In hearts and minds we never were apart.

Frank E. Greene

TRUE LOVE

We met as classmates sixty years ago
"An accident," prosaic minds did hiss.
No, providential, now we truly know
From more than fifty years of wedded bliss.
We both were strangers on that college scene,
I seeking credits needed to transfer,
She searching for a path which lay between
Dull home life and a pedagogue's career.
At first sight I was seized by lasting love,
In her love crept more slowly to true peace;
There our affection met and rose above
Distractions which could cause our love to cease.
We separated to pursue our goals
But stayed united in our chief intent.
Love flourished in our ardent living souls,
'Twas never broken, no not even bent.
In nineteen-thirty marriage vows did seal
Our pact which launched a lifetime way of life
Which mirrors how undaunted still we feel
With me as husband, she as beauteous wife.

Frank E. Greene

THE LOVE FROM MY HEART

It's quiet, it's soft
It's in the clouds
and it's you
It's far beyond the rush,
It's warm beyond the cold
It's laughter beyond the tears
And it's you
It's years beyond your life,
It's years beyond mine,
It's our future yesterday
But it's ours.
It's an answer, it's a favor it's a must
And it's you,
It's a sweet goodbye,
It's a look of endeavor
It's a touch of sadness
And it's you
It's me, it's you, it's happiness
And it's
Forever

Sherie L. Mullen

PLEASE LOVE ME

Why can't someone love me?
Not because I'm mom or wife.
I have this need to be —
Cared for . . . for a moment in my life.

I want to be loved and needed.
And to have someone love back.
In my heart, I have pleaded —
For real old-fashioned love . . . is what I lack.

The forever kind would be nice —
But I'd take "Love at this time and place."
Just a small slice —
Of love showing on someone else's face.

To be loved because I want to know
What "In love" means . . .
I want to experience that glow —
I've always heard of . . . to see if it is what it seems.

I guess you think I believe those romance books;
Where love triumphs over all . . . how nice . . .
With searing glances, and telling looks —
Well, my heart is here . . . offered in sacrifice.

Pamela Joyce Franklin

TO MY BROTHERS AND SISTERS

When our parents died not too long ago
Our hearts cried tears together
But we made it through this time of woe
This time of treacherous weather

We still have our dad, mom will stay with us, too
Each time we see the beautiful plains
Or clouds polka-dotting skies of blue
We know our losses are truly God's gains

Yes, we've lost more than we ever thought we could bear
By our parents being now up above
But they certainly have done much more than their share
They've left us each other to love

So when you feel alone, and just as blue as can be
Do what I do for myself . . . for mom and dad
I think of what's left of them that I can still see
My sisters, my brothers . . . and I don't feel quite as bad

We miss mom and dad, this is sincerely so true
And the thought of them brings tears to our eyes
But my tears won't last for I will think of you
My sisters, my brothers . . . my parents in disguise

Mary Joan Raymond

REMEMBER

I'll never forget how sad I was to have to let you go.
I'll never forget the pain of never having you to hold.
I'll never forget the things we said.
I'll never forget the things we did.
I'll never forget the way you held me.
The way you consoled my tears away.
The words you whispered before you let go.
I love you, I need you, and never let go.
I'll always remember how much you meant to me.
I'll always remember that I loved you enough to set you free.

Sarah Tarzon

THE RIGHT WINDOW

I see the sun come up,
But I do not watch it fall.
Where I work,
There is no light.

Sometimes when my love is away
The world and all in it are shadows,
For he is the right window
Through which I gaze,
He is my husband.

I am truly liberated;
His courage has freed me.
He allows me my humanity;
He allows me myself.

He is true,
He is the shaft of The Archer
Which flies straight and sure,
Its tip resting warmly in my heart,
No wound inflicted.

Laura Roscoe-Griffin

UNCLE PETER

Quiet, tall, robust.
He worked all day long,
Six days a week,
49 weeks a year,
On Greenwell Ranch.
Pumping water, bulldozing new roads,
Erecting fences, herding cows.
At 3 o'clock each day, I'd wait
For the sound of his jeep.
He always kept me some rice or fried egg
Leftover in his lunch pail.
On the porch, he'd bounce me on his lap.
Or piggy-back me to the end of the yard.
The day he scolded me
For picking leaves off his tree, I cried.
Uncle Peter,
You are like Hualalai Mountain
Resting
Against the sky.

A Hawaiian Sky.

Jeanne Saito

WINTER EVENING

We laughed
we ran through
the starlit snow
tossing snowballs
at street signs
at each other
and chasing
blue shadows
across the snow
then dashing
indoors
dropped
to toast our toes
before the cordial fire
and listen to
wind whispers
on the roof

Rosa Nelle Anderson

EGGS

HONORABLE MENTION

Standing in the kitchen trying to decide if one egg
was enough or maybe it needed two, I said, "Who wants
to cook anyway?" Cooking gets you fat and alone and
pretty soon sick of yourself. My son said, "I'll cook
Mom, don't worry, I'll fry the eggs, anyone can fry eggs."
But I didn't care because cooking gets you criticized
and I only pretend to cook anyway, banging pots and pans
around, trying on different colored aprons, too much salt,
and so on. I tried not to make a scene, especially over eggs,
tried not to whip them up into peaks, spoiling everyone's life.
"Keep them fertile," I always say. "Why is Mom screaming?" my
daughter asks. "Eggs!" I'm having trouble with eggs, sticking to
the pan, yolks breaking night after night. "We eat too many eggs!"
Yellow moons making me crazy, scrambled into another dinner without Daddy.

Linda Soo Hoo

EXPRESSION OF LOVE

I get sweet visions of Jesus when hearing some good old hymn,
But, when I join in the singing, it's my expression of love for Him.
When I see someone shouting, while walking with the King,
I become more determined to express my love for Him.
When someone stands to testify I get a warm feeling within,
It always strengthens my reason for expressing my love for Him.

When I get down on my knees, sending praises to heaven above,
It's my way of showing I care, my expression of love.
One day when I get to heaven, and I'm free from all sorrow and sin,
I'll know it helped me to get there, by expressing my love for Him.
So, show Him we love Him, show Him we care,
Do it with praises, do it with prayer,
Do it with shouting, do it with song,
Expressing our love all the day long.

Rae Martin

OF MILLIONS HEARD

How many words can say it all and reach the very soul?
What caution should one take when using words already told?
"I love you," once, "I love you," twice — that weary old cliché.
However true or false it be, emotions it will sway.
The many words and phrases that can express a love so true,
With much regret these words withdrawn when love is all but through.

How many words can say it all and be forever real?
What choice of words original must show the way one feels?
All the words and phrases, I'm sure, have been used before.
And as for rearrangements, one can seek but find no more.

How many words can say it all in true serenity?
Of millions heard and millions told, my soul can find but three:
I LOVE YOU.

Kenneth G. Miles

ANTICIPATING MY LOVE

As we knelt at the altar exchanging our vows,
Anticipating all the love our future together would bring;
So many roads ahead to travel together hand-in-hand.
We walk the path together where all our hopes and dreams come true,
knowing our precious Saviour will always work things through.
For love has grown deep within our hearts;
We have planted a seed and together we will watch it grow.
For we are anticipating our love as it grows day by day;
So the hopes and dreams of an anticipating true love.

Gloria M. Mitzel

THE LITTLE THINGS IN LIFE

Little things bring pleasure
In a homey sort of way,
Seeing a friend of long ago
And what they have to say.

Little things bring pleasure
When you aren't so very spry,
When the years have fallen on us,
And the years went swiftly by.

Little things bring pleasure
When you remember other days,
The kindness of friends gone by
Their sweet and kindly ways.

Little things bring pleasure
When friends stood by so much
When they were badly needed
And appreciated so much.

Olga Knapp

TREMULOUS SHIMMERING

when love becomes an excuse
for writing poems, or poems
an excuse for love,
perhaps we take this poetry
too seriously: unaccountable
tremulous shimmering of wine
breaking into concentric
ripples of laughter;
broken, laughing in tandem.
no notions of nebulae in space
are more inexplicable —
or tantalizing — than that miniscule
of atoms reverberating as wine
is whirled, juggling of protons, neutrons.
nights of coldest, hardest starry-
glinted fakery when dream
becomes song in the blackmail world;
one flick of the wrist and centripetality
is set in motion; reverse,
and flower refolds into bud.

E. L. Kelso

THE SPECIAL ONE

I know of no one,
Around the world,
Who doesn't need someone.

The someone to share,
Their life and love with,
That special someone like you.

You brighten my days,
And enlighten my nights;
You fill my dreams with hope.

You are the one,
The special one,
Who makes me feel alive.

I need you near me,
For without you,
My life would have no light.

Dee Hedgecock

GRATE LOVE

Great love.
Wonderful.
Fantastic.
Until you find
you're in it alone.

Grate love.
It shreds you to your core
and leaves you crying in your wounds.

How could you be so vulnerable
and so blind?

All you can do now
is pull yourself back together
and hope the pieces fit.

Janice R. Nelson

A quiet time by the fire,
I reflected on how one person
influenced my way of life.
Without a reservation she
spoke of dreams, her own and mine.
I always felt a sense of peace
when she was around.
Understanding could have been
her middle name.
At a discouraging look she
always lent an ear.
In being with her
you feel the presence of God.
When the day comes for
me to leave, I hope she
knows how grateful I am
for having a friend who
loved me for who I was.

Liz Peralez

DID MY HAREM SCARE 'EM?

Love was constantly on my mind,
So many girls were wined and dined.
Trouble was — I wanted them all:
Too ambitious, as I recall.

Robert Emmett Clarke

BROKEN SOUL

Today my heart is near the end,
It's not how long you live — but how;
you do not seem to understand —
you only see my life in dreams.

The dream is far, too far for me,
the distance quells my love —
and each and every part of me
in its search for time;
must suffer loss of dreams that were —
of loving eyes so true, so blind.

Stars have fallen now —
the moon has lost its glow;
and slowly as day to night gives way,
one heart becomes a broken soul.

Laura A. Bathurst

ECLIPSE AT CAMELOT

I loved her once in silence,
adored her at first glance,
Gazed at her and all vision blurred
despite the circumstance.

I kissed her once in secrecy,
such sweet and complete fantasy.
Whispered words, hearts overheard
beating timeless in eternity.

I held her once between a time,
like a dream within a dream,
When passion was the holy crime,
love some sacred scheme.

I her moonbeam's light I solarized;
With lips eclipsed, we empathized.

Clifford M. Bannister

MY LOVE

Dedicated to Dan

My first love was special to me
as you and everyone else could see
But as time went on we drifted apart
so many times he broke my heart
Then when I would think of memories
in the past
It gave me the thought that
nothing would last
But now everything has changed
all my thoughts are rearranged
When I found you standing near
I knew sad endings I wouldn't fear

Your love I never had to test
I can't say you were my first —
only *my best.*

Dina DiLucente

Winter darkness gathers,
outside your silent gate —
I pass unseen, alone.

Charles B. Rodning

ODE TO FATHER

I keep the House,
a place of birth,
where children grow
and find their worth.
Someday they'll know.

I keep the House,
I love my wife,
who keeps me sane
and shares my life.
She knows the pain.

I keep the House,
where night does fall
and death shall come
to lift us all
to another Home.

b c drury

ABYSS

Deep as Yogi meditation
In a hushed, mysterious silence
In this silence in my heart
Since you are gone
Heartstrings quiver, aching, throbbing
Tautly tensed for one faint echo
Strain to catch remotest note
Of Love's Old Song

Sleep to dream of fond hearts blended
Wake to know that Love has ended
Wake to dark, abysmal void
From dawn to dawn
Undisturbed by agitation
In my heart, a dull, dead silence
Naught on earth's more still than stillness
In the heart when Love is done

Where is hope of consolation?
Who has known like desolation?
Is there somewhere one who stoutly
Battled through and found the sun?
Hear my call! Some kindred spirit
Send my soul a soundless echo
Lend me grace to stay the futile,
Frantic call to Love that's done

Ruth Hindman

WINTER LOVE

You're my heart, you're my soul
you're the song of my life,

You make everything glow
and shine forever bright

You're that flickering raindrop
on a slippery wet street

That gives a special warm feeling
to everyone it meets,
in this moody winter
we have yet to feast.

And as the icy white blanket of snow
begins to fall at our feet,
I stand and wonder why
my heart skips a beat,

As I caress your body
beneath these white covered trees
that stand so strong and sturdy as though to say
"What a lovely winter we have yet to greet"

And as long as we stay together it will be
A lovely warm winter for YOU and ME.

Juan J. Gonzalez

I WISH I KNEW

I wish I knew if what they say is true
They are tired of me saying that I love you.
They think it's a lie
I wish I knew why.
I do know, that
I love you.

Denise Dial

TO LIVE AND LOVE

Why talk about the meaning of love, friendship,
Whether we had a good relationship;
The past is gone, what's done is done, can't live
On memories, no nourishment they give.

Can't talk about tomorrow, what history
May bring us is forever a mystery;
Live on, love on, flow with the times, the changes,
The order of life destiny arranges.

Wretched winter storms have passed, the ice thaws,
Snow melts; Spring's warming touch mends nature's flaws,
Grows bright blossoms as a green carpet unfolds,
Makes birds sing, heals broken hearts, wounded souls.

The future begins today, come what may;
They who live and love well carry the day.

Maureen Chen

THE WIND IS MY LOVER

The wind is my lover
slipping towards me in the night he
caresses my face with whispering finger tips
draws back my hair and dips underneath
to nibble at my neck and murmur in my ear
Pushes me slowly backwards to a shadowy place
and dances darkly around, lifting my clothes
pressing through them to touch
my solid body; licking my breasts, stroking
my thighs, my belly gently, gently
Pushing closer, promising pleasure, back
against his herald the pine, harder, harder
filling me with wonder, ecstasy, totality
I am the wind, no form
My lover is solid, firm
inside me.
One breath in the night.

Claudia D. Newcorn

AND MOMMA, PLEASE GIVE GOD A KISS FROM ME!

Tell GOD that all that you taught me is love at the
best.
Tell HIM that HIS kisses are my foundation to more
than one direction.
Did you not say Momma, that GOD forges all kisses
and hugs from inner love of all things?
Tell HIM Momma that I feel HIS hugs and kisses all
the time in the earth that smells fresh from a rain.
Tell HIM that HIS touch soothes my heart from the
weary days of bitterness.
Tell HIM I smile more often as you speak with HIM —
for experience is a teacher like HE and you are.
Please tell HIM I need a squeeze for bigger adventures.
Tell HIM Momma, that a hug, kiss and a squeeze from HIM
is all that makes HIS life a price to hold; and to
need for all that embrace love in perfection.

Charlotte Bell

MY LITTLE BOY

A dream come true, and beautiful it flows
Into rich blessings, only the heart knows
To be blest with a baby, given my name
Moments I'll cherish forever, I claim.

One truth the great minds are failing to reach
Is the love and wisdom fathers can teach
Each day I give love and thanks for my child
And I know at his birth an angel smiled.

Moist little kisses enhance his embrace
Two soft little hands are touching my face
He was sent from Heaven; God knows his worth
The richest blessing, given man on earth.

Bright eyes implore me while holding my hand
"Read me a story about Teddy Bear land
Just one more story please, Daddy will you?
Then I'll kiss you goodnight, Teddy bear too."

My sleepy child whispers softly until
Almost asleep "Daddy I know you will"
On dreamland's soft pillow, tuck in my boy
To dream of Teddy bears furthers his joy.

Elvira L. Keeso

THE BRIDE AND GROOM

Now that you have just been wed,
May you experience happiness in the years ahead,
May you have faith and joy and peace,
And a great love that will never cease.

For a good start in your marital bliss,
Begin and end each day with a kiss.
Be patient, kind and understanding,
Don't pout and sulk and be demanding.

When problems arise that seem so great,
Discuss them and always communicate.
Always be helpful to one another,
Don't be so quick to run home to Mother.

When troubles seem too hard to bear,
Take them to the Lord in prayer.
He will lead you on, your fears He'll still,
Because He loves you and always will.

He'll comfort you through each little sorrow,
And give you hope for a new tomorrow.
So love each other and wear a smile,
And thank the Lord your life is worthwhile.

Dolores E. Minnig

SOMETIMES YOU ARE ALL AROUND

Sometimes
You are all around
Like fragrance in the spring.
I can almost
Touch your loving face,
See your smile, your grace,
And feel my senses sing.
O, to breathe within the warmth of your light!

Alone . . .
How cold the starless night.

Mary C. Norris

THE TIMELESS SEA

A long time ago in a faraway land
across the timeless sea;
a Man told of a special love
meant for you and me.

A solitary soul who walked dusty roads
healing the sick along His way;
whose power came from up above
whenever He kneeled to pray.

A glimmer of hope for a troubled people
who lived in a world of fear;
with His loving heart and gentle hand,
He could wipe away their tears.

His message of love and brotherhood
was carried throughout the land;
'til His voice was silenced on Calvary Hill
by those who did not understand.

Two thousand years have come and gone,
but His message can still be heard;
for not even death could stop the Man,
who gave life to God's Holy Word.

Shirley L. Gayton

CRY FOR ME

Lying alone seeking the ceiling's flaws;
Mid-day sun, restrained by curtains drawn,
Casts yellow hues upon the pain in my breast.
A smouldering ache dies, fallen ashes in my beer.

Cry for me for the love I've jailed.
Cry for me for the love I've failed.
Cry for me in this darkest time.
Cry for me for I'm going blind.

Cigarette smoke rises forgotten from my finger tips
Creating your image in unfocused space.
Like you, it fades when I reach to hold
And drifts from view should I glance away.

Cry for me for the love I've lost.
Cry for me for the love I've tossed.
Cry for me in this darkest time.
Cry for me for I'm going blind.

Dry tears sting my reddened eyes.
Wading through bogs and self-pity's mire
I force the dagger 'tween Adam's ribs,
Cold steel finds my burning heart.

Blake Alan

THE PLEDGE

A love combined of joy and tears, a love that could not be;
You placed my hand in yours and then, you vowed this love to me.
And yet I could not bear to think that I must let you go,
Because I loved you far too much, for you to ever know.
And so I took you to my heart pledging I'd be true,
Regardless of the consequence, I gave my love to you.
Spring has come, fall has gone, each a story told;
A tender glance, a secret smile, a tear encased in gold.
Still, I don't regret my pledge, forever it will bind,
Our hearts and dreams together, for as long as you are mine.

Christianna

AN ODE TO CAROLINE AND JOE

It was a beautiful day in June
For Caroline and Joe's Wedding Day
As they stood before the Altar High
Joe in his dark suit and tie
And Caroline in a gown of trailing lace
Her arms held a large bouquet
It was their Wedding Day
The organist softly played and sang
This is love, this is love divine
And Joe whispered, Caroline I take you for mine
And Caroline answered, I Love you, Joe,
You are mine, mine, mine.

Rose Mary Gerlach

THE FLOWER

While walking through the park I saw a lovely flower;
I would have pulled it out to send it to my love,
But all I could do was sit there for an hour
Speaking with my conscience and with God above.
The flower is life's expression like my sweet,
So if I love her and would cause her no pain,
Then I must turn, taking to my feet
And let the flower joyfully remain.
O, I would love to send my love a token
To show her that my love for her is true,
But I can't see my resolutions broken,
So I must be content to tell her, Darling I love you.

Stephen Feinland

WILD ABOUT YOU

When you came into my life just eighteen days ago
I would not have believed that I'd feel this glow
Lips so deliciously parted when we kiss
Don't you know I could get used to this
Absolutely enchanting woman so very beautiful
Being with you makes me feel simply wonderful
Ornamenting my life like a precious gem
Unearthly vision I pray will never dim
Time with you is becoming more dear
You fire my rocket whenever you're near
Opening up to you in these few short days
Understanding you've shown and tender ways

William D. Andrews

LOVE YOURSELF

My little one with impish grin of your own style,
Growing up is hard and often very confusing.
Dry your tears and put on your best smile.
Take your time and you will grow.
It's painful at times as I well know.
I was your age once a long time ago.
There are temptations so be well aware.
Be you yourself and dare your peers to be like you,
instead of you like them.
Keep your word and be true to yourself, and others too.
Mind your manners and you'll go far.
Who knows, maybe you'll even be a movie star.

Jozette G. Spina

LADY OF THE NIGHT

Lady of the dark and lonely night
With flowing hair falling upon thy shoulder
Thou art a most gracious sight
Love for thee maketh my heart grow bolder.

Thy lips of passion so moist and warm
Eyes that shineth ever so green
Love thee I do, be thee not forlorn
Inspiring is thy beauty, I have ne'er before seen

Lady of the midnight hour
Let this fool your shining knight be
I wouldst place thee in an Ivory Tower
All to envy, all to see.

Be thy champion, I wouldst protect thee
To thee I giveth freely my heart
Thou art the fairest, all wouldst agree
From thee my lady, I shall never part.

My lady of the dark and lonely night
I shall love thee this moment and endeavor
While thou walkest 'neath street's gleaming light
This knight's love for thee will last forever

Richard J. Hunt

IN THE VALLEY OF HIS LOVE

When I dream of your love,
  I see a valley, fresh and green,
  surrounded by majestic white-capped mountains,
  where the aroma of flowers fills the air.

The mountains are your arms,
  that forever embrace me,
  while the white snow caps,
  represent the purity of your love.

The flowers are sweet to the senses,
  yet they provide me with strength and peace,
  for I know that in the palm of your hand,
  rests the root of all life.

As the morning sun flickers,
  on the dew-kissed valley below,
  your love brings me new life,
  that lightens up my soul.

The valley deepens the conviction within me,
  like being nestled to a mother's breast,
  your love fulfills my valley,
  your love fulfills my life.

Nancy J. Lingeman

LOVE IS THE ESSENCE

Love is the essence of things to be
Love is the stars, the sky, and seas.
Love is a boy and girl when they first kiss;
God is love above all things;
and He gives His love to all human beings.
Creation speaks of His love as seen in
the trees, wild flowers and overwhelming
vastness of the seas.
Have you experienced God's agape love in your life?
It is the most profound love you will
ever experience in your life.

Gloria M. Mitzel

SPELL-WEAVER

I can see a spell-weaver,
a sensually anointed wonder-maker
on a path close to mine.

A fine pet she would make,
like a squirrel monkey perched upon
my black, satin sleeve,
Coming and going as I allow.

Spell-weaver, wonder-maker kindly
live with me,
make my coffee and sugar toast,
darn a sock or two,
Then kiss my blistering lips in the moon's dusty glow.

Your eyes, usually the luster of newly-minted stars,
are suddenly spilling accusations.

You say we're climbing different mountains?
that I want a pampered pet on a gilded leash,
while you want holy oaths behind chapel doors?

We don't need rings or sacred chattel! Scale
my calloused heart, spell-weaver, just as you are.

"Goodbye." goodbye

Barbara O'Connor

DAWN MEDITATION

At first, the air is still
The trees are shades of grey.
No color, no sound.
A bird breaks the stillness, flapping its wings,

Slowly, color begins to touch the sky
Pink and yellow, the horizon.
The stars disappear amidst the blue of heaven.
The morning star, Venus, shines unwinking
near the brilliant particle of sun.

My poem is like a cut diamond,
Each word a glittering facet of reality.
As is the sunrise, each color an edge of beauty.
The birds agree, breaking the silence with song.

The lady who claims my day
Stands upon a hill, watching the play of colors.
The wind softly caresses her,
Toys with her dress and adds to the sweet delight that is her.

Now, the sun is fully risen.
The colors begin to pale.
And fail they do, save for the clear blue of sky.
And golden the sun, in his glory.
The day has begun.

Kim Angotti

The definition of darkness was determined
By the creation of light.
As in the architect's design to surrender space —
What must happen to the remainder of that space?
I am in love with you . . . and it is that very caring
That must determine your indifference.
I will miss you . . . will you notice?

Christine A. Pitt

A HEART OF DESIRE ON FIRE

My heart is so weak and engulfed in fire.
It's totally filled with all my desire.

It hurts at times, when I look to the stars above
Wondering to myself, will this be a true love.

The way the fire is burning so deep within.
Makes me weak and floating as if in a spin.

I feel the passion and all the pain,
Like the warmth of the sun and the wetness of the rain.

I know not, if the desire will build or destroy.
I just long fot his once more feeling of pleasure and joy.

I feel I'm in trouble and so ready to fall.
Knowing too, at this moment I'd gamble it all.

I'd give all the angels new, and special wings,
If only they'd help to break all these strings.

I'm bound to follow and hold back on all these emotions.
For I've been born and raised with high hopes of devotions.

So the fire will burn and I will hold my desire.
Facing, alone the heat, getting higher and higher.

For I have been here so many times before,
Knowing when it's over, I desire so much more.

The scars of loves, and all the intense heat
Picks me up and puts me again to my feet.

For I am as I am and will always desire,
For there is never enough water to put out the fire.

Bobby Nagy

BEYOND THE BLUE

Away up there BEYOND THE BLUE
where starlight helps me to find you,
We meet and clasp our hands to climb
into the reaching arms of Time.

Where Time lets love go on and on,
with days and nights forever born,
Our feelings melt within our sighs,
and peace within us never dies.

Our souls are the sun; our tears are the rain;
Our feelings are wind, without any pain.
Our love lights the moon; our smiles are the stars;
Our life becomes Time without any bars.

Where planets sing songs, with magical charms,
Floating clouds, you're there in my arms.
Where the rays of sun form a rainbow's hue,
There I'll be with you, just BEYOND THE BLUE!

Exiled from other worlds by Time,
in this great universe sublime,
A portrait true to nature there
portrays a view beyond compare.

There, future makes the present past;
Like magic, it with God is cast!
Together we will always be
a part of this eternity!

Jo B. Comberiate

ALL SHOOK UP

I'd almost forgotten
Her beautiful face
The things that she said long ago
Then I saw her again
And a word from her lips
Made me lose all my poise and control
She once vowed not to speak
And it hurt me so deep
As she'd walk by
With her nose so turned up
O, Wendy, my love

I know I'll again be shook up

Nick Raider

LOVE

L is for the life
you choose to live.
O is for the overtures
you choose to give.
V is for the victories
you choose to impart.
E is for the eyes to see
the love in your heart.

Put them together
You spell love.
A gift that is given
From our Lord above.

Des Diebel

Sun rays sparkle
With iridescence
In her soft eyes
Moonbeams dance
In the radiance
Of her beauty
Flowers blossom
With the warmth
Of her tender love
As she speaks
The song of the nightingale
Drifts through my mind
Filling my body
And soul
With sweet delights.

Billy Mac

He loves them dearly
two stars in the night
Glancing up above
to find them tonight

Reaching his hand
to hold them close
Nearby his heart
pricked by thorns,
that of a rose

Flesh that is of two
daughters made of love
In the sky so bright
his children sleep above

Lisa Ann Leszczynski

A CHILD'S PRAYER (LOVE OF COUNTRY)

Father, we thank Thee for this land;
Help us its laws to understand;
In all we do in work and play,
Help us to be more loyal every day.

Help us to see its beauties grand, —
Mountains and trees and golden sand;
For its rich blessings thankful be,
Working to keep our country always free!

Violet Stiles Persson

PERSSON, VIOLET STILES. Born: Whitehall, New York, 4-3-03; Widowed, 4-21-46, Oscar H. Persson; Education: Julliard School of Music; Teacher's College, Columbia University, B.S., M.S.; Occupation: Teacher; Memberships: New York State Retired Teachers, American Association of University Women; Business & Professional Women; Themes: *Justice, beauty, spiritual.*

OCTOBER CHILD

Driving me down the road
he led me into his smile

Holding my hand,
he reached inside and touched me

Telling me secrets with his eyes
he listened to my heart

Touching me with his lips
I tasted joy and laughter

The child in him
which loves neither wisely nor too well
appears sweetly on his sleeping face
Speaks softly to me

He clothes me with his gentleness
and bares my soul

As I watched my friend beside me sleeping
he crept into my heart.

D. V. Stiles

MY MOTHER'S LOVE

My Mother's love is unrequited
full of heart and pure

My Mother's love is of the flesh
where no distance can occur

My Mother's love is beyond compare
Neverending and always there

My Mother's love is generous and kind
in her heart and in her mind

My Mother's love is unlike the rest
for only she can build the nest

My Mother's love shines like the sun
but her love is never done

My Mother's love endures at best

My Mother's love forgives the rest.

Debra Sue Peterson

FIND A HAPPY COUPLE

Find a happy couple to
Destroy, and it can be
Done, easily; by the
Taskmaster, sergeant:
Stocking over his face,
Cinema-born, and cinema-
Bred, with the magic words of
Economics: "cheap," "cheaper,"
Free!

If a man can't be made an
Alcoholic, he is made a
Workaholic; or
Both.

To cut a budget,
At the expense of personal
Happiness, is a patriotic
Gesture, particularly (staunch
Conservative) for the
National
Security.

Geneve Baley

LOST LOVE

You picked a fine time,
to leave me my dear.
I'm so broken-hearted
and eyes filled with tears.
You say you are in love,
with my best friend.
It looks like our love,
is now at an end.
I still love you dearly,
and I always will
You are the only one,
who could give me a thrill.
I'll try to find another,
sweetheart, if I can.
There'll never be another you,
but he will still be my man.

Lillie M. McConkey

1510

LOVE DON'T HAVE NO SEASON

Sometimes it seems
like a million years ago
since you touched me with your love,
and I felt you with my soul.

You touched me with your love
for a little while;
and all the stars above
shined there in your smile.

And sometimes it seems like
no one cares for who you are,
and love don't have no season
and there ain't no bright shining star.
And loves comes a-sailing
in your heart and in your mind;
searching for the answers
that you know you'll never find.

George Randall Roberts

Tell me little angel
Have you seen our Lord
Have you just been sent to us
To be our tender ward
The look I see within your eyes
Is full of peace and love
The kind of love that fills our heart
That's sent from up above
The depth of the serenity
I see upon your face
Have you had a tiny glimpse
Of God's most holy place
You never fuss, you never cry
Which we can't understand
Is it 'cause not long ago
You held God's precious hand
We'll try to do our best for you
Helping you as best we can
So you can go about your work
Keeping with God's plan

Judith A. Lewis

AMERICA APPRECIATED

We came in fifty-two as immigrants,
After five years war in Netherland.
We found here freedom, love and peace,
Hard work and learning ABCs.
We studied English in the class,
With first years always short on cash.
The language made it for us sour,
Got long time only buck an hour.
With first and second mortgage loan
Was a nice property our own.
I am over thirty years now here.
Lived twenty of them free and clear.
The trouble now is getting old.
I am eighty-six, crippled and bald.
Have hobby, customer and friend,
As well the letters which they send.
Love Florida for the sparkling sun,
And proud to be American.

Nick J. Pronck

HOUSE OF LOVE

From high above
Our home was blessed
By the angel of love

Starlit eyes of my beloved wife
Revealing her soul
Displayed the essence of life

The cat purred
Echoing the inner sound
Another form of the Word

My innocent child
Unveiling divine spirit
As she smiled

I beheld a sacred sight
In the mind's eye
All encompassed by a blue light

This is where we live
In the House of Love
For love is all we have to give

David E. Peters

IF LOVE IS FOREVER

If love is forever,
Why does it seem to go
After a month or so?

It comes and goes
Just like a fever.

While it's here
Everything is fine.

Until the day when
He is hers, not mine.

Denise Dial

LOVE POEM #1

Tell me what I want to hear
That life is sweet and good and dear
That we've only just begun our life
Together we will have no strife

But wait what was that I just heard
A tender sigh, a gentle word
A happy nod, I know you're there
And maybe life was meant to share
I've not a life that I will waste
And I expect much to feel, to taste

If I'm hard on you it's my mistake
Likewise as we give and take
It's ours to make this life so fine
What we will with our freedom
What we will with our time

And quality is never shy
We give each other we always try
With each new passing moment
I see you in a most delightful way
I guess it's just for us to say.

Charlotte Rosenthal

CHILDHOOD DREAM

Dedicated to Eliot

Since I was just a little girl
I dreamed of loving you
I knew not what you'd look like
Just that your love would be true.

I knew that you'd have tender arms
For holding me so near
I knew that you'd have a special love
To share year after year.

I knew that when I met you
On that very special night
That our meeting would be the closest
Thing to love at first sight.

Your tenderness and caring take
Me to the heights of ecstasy
Your gentle guidance showed me how
To be all that I can be.

I looked for fault in every
Move, but so it seems
That you turned out to be
The love of all my dreams.

Starla Willett

LOVE'S ELUSIVE SHADOW

What is this demon that's haunting me?
Why won't it leave me alone?

It is a penalty —
a cross to bear through life,

Or — is it the end of the rainbow,
my pot of gold?

I know not.

Yet, day and night I search
for its mysterious vision;

Pursuing its shadow
through the corridors of my mind.

Its obscurity taunts me at every turn,
so, I laugh in its face.

Still, I can't relinquish the quest
as it leaves me discontent.

I ache to the marrow of my soul
longing for Love's elusive shadow.

Rita F. Artist

HEARTFELT

Growing so intense,
With radiance burning,
Of ten thousand suns,
My heart so yearning,
To share my life,
In love with you,
And the joys and pleasures,
Of all you do.

Gregory L. Adcock

FOR THE LOVE OF CHILDREN

From the day they wriggle lustily out of mother's womb
Until the time they take upon being a bride or groom

Children fall under a parent's charge for a special form of love
Sometimes perceived as eagle sternness, rather than the peaceful dove

Parents are observed as traffic directors, separating evil from good
Instead of being permissive — as they *really* should
Parents are barking orders to "do your homework" or "clean the room"
Bringing the child a hostile cloud of impending gloom

As years go by and hormones change — the opposite gender attracts
But mom and dad caringly note — for love you'll need a few more facts

Finally when school is o'er and they've met the perfect mate
Children somehow realize commitment takes more than one date

In childrens' gathering of wisdom over the span of years
Parents gain in stature and the memories evoke tears

Stanley S. Reyburn

STANDARD OF LIFE

I truly hope you'll find the girl,
That will make you the happiest fellow in the world.
One, that by your standards, is free from sin,
And if you do, open your heart and let her in.
But what you must realize in this day and age,
Life and love are merely the turning of a page.
From what I am, to what I hope you want me to be,
Which is the process of changing what is authentically me.
I realize not even you are free from sin,
For if I were to open my heart, you would come rushing in.
And even without invitation you would long to stay,
Inside my heart forever and a day.
I wonder, if you will ever find,
A girl that's so utterly sublime.
That would fulfill your most unusual request,
Of unspotted love, joy, and happiness.
Well, maybe, there is just one,
That was extremely selective in her mode of fun.
Which satisfies your standards of life,
Don't hesitate, make her your wife.

Sandra Moore

FINDING THE LOVE AND COURAGE WHILE FIGHTING THE PAIN

I see you walking along, it would not take much for me to catch up
But yet I manage to fight the pain
I close my eyes fighting the tears and turn the other way
I found the love and courage in my heart to let her go on
So I would not ruin the progress she made with the memory of me
It was so hard to turn the other way, because I love her
I want to catch up with her
I wait a little while, then I look back at her
She is far-off and soon gone
There is no way of catching up now
A tear runs down my cheek and my heart seems to be breaking
Once again
I hurt so badly at that past moment
She looks happy and I could not bear to ruin that happiness
Because it is genuine
With another tear running down my cheek
I smile
Knowingly, because I realized that I found the courage and bonding love
And I fought the pain
To let her go on

Denise Karch

LAMENT

Yes, I did love a lad
was stricken with a shaft
and grief lay heavy on my heart.
Tell, what is love?
An ill that weighs one down
a swooning of the soul
a sweetness on the tongue
strong wine and giddyness.

If I could but forget him!
But no, the memories are too new
our basking in the sun
the smell of new-mown hay and buttercups
our dancing on the shore
the scent of his warm skin
against my lips.

I was too easily won
I fell captive to his smile.
So quickly loved
so soon bewitched
and now forgotten.
That is my tale.
I wish 'twere otherwise.

The bastard!

Geraldine Kravis

I SHOULD HAVE KNOWN

I should have known although
The time so long ago had died,

Although all pains have healed
And God had heard my plight —

And let me fall in love again!
I should have known that at the

Sight — of — things once shared
Of people — we both knew —

That somehow there will be
A — mentioning of you!

I should have known — although —
I made myself forget, and came here

With — a new love in my heart
And no regret! that people

Will remember still what was before,
And so against my will — you were

Remembered — love before the last
— once more!

Sonja Christina

TANKA

How I yearn for him
He who's yet nameless to me
But still in my dreams . . .

His embrace close around me
His heart beating next to mine.

Diane L. Salisbury

JUST A PHONE CALL AWAY

Whenever you need me
I'm just a phone call away.
Whenever you want me
You know what to say.
No matter the distance
No matter the cost.
Without you my love,
I know I'd be lost.
For into my heart
you found your way.
And into my heart
Forever you'll stay.
Remember, I'm just a phone call away.

Leo Feebish

FEEBISH, LEO WALTER. Born: Wilkes-Barre, Pennsylvania, 11-8-30, to Leo William Feebish and Aida Elizabeth Tewksbury; Married to Margaret; 6 children, 4 step children; Education: Graduate of Forty Fort High School, Pennsylvania; Occupations: Hodcarrier, Stockboy, Pennsylvania Forestry Worker, Gas Station Attendant, Car Washer, Amateur Boxer, Assistant Manager of Woolworth's, Sidewalk Inspector and Urban Renewal Relocation Officer of Dearborn Heights, now employed as a Sales Representative for a Food Broker; Memberships: Holy Spirit Catholic Church, Former Jaycee, March of Dimes Captain, Goodfellow, Livonia Michigan Boxing Club; Poetry: 'Christmas is Here,' 'Just a Phone Call Away,' 'Santa's Snowmobile,' Vantage Press, 1975; 'You and Me,' 'The Most Beautiful Sound,' 'Forgive Me,' 'Alone in a Crowd,' Vantage Press, 1978; 'Mother Nature,' *American Poetry Anthology,* 1985; Comments: *I write about what I see and feel and I try to express my emotions and feelings in my poems. To date I have written over 100 poems and in the near future will publish my poetry and write an adventure fiction book.*

TO MOTHER FOR SUCH ARE YOU

Blessed are the thinkers
Of the world
Who bog not in the murk
Of gloom,
Nor dwell in
The shadowy realm
Of what might have been
If this or that,
But take what joy is to be found
In the fleeting pleasurable
Moments of life,
And when all is gray and austere
Roll out the sun
To brighten any listless moments.
Blessed are those
With a heart that sings
For mother, you are
One of these.

F. Richard Dieterle

CHRISTMAS

Christmas is here again
With all the lights and joy
Children laughing with all the sights
And all the Christmas noise.
Santa in town they show it with glee
With toys to go under every tree
A new dress for Mom and a tie for Dad
They are so happy lots of love is shed.
Love is shining every place
It would be nice if we kept that pace
Joy in our hearts for everyone
That's what makes Christmas a lot of fun.
Let's not forget why Christmas comes
A savior was born for everyone
We all should worship and praise his name
Which in Him we have hope, peace and love
That's why our Christmas
Was sent from above.

Naomi V. Osborne

LIFE

My love for you is racing with you
Through the sands of time
Catching breaths along the way
Only long enough to see
Where one's been and where one's going

Oh mystery lady
Never show me your stride
Heed my warning

The love we share is enhanced
Only by your beauty and mystical auras
To catch you would be to lose
The mystery and the love
Along with the enchantment that you give

So race with me always
For I love you mystery lady . . .

Grandpa

AN UNTOUCHABLE DREAM

Sometimes I wish my dreams would come true,
If in those dreams I'm holding you
I feel so empty without you here
If you could only make your presence real
I just want to hold you in my arms one more time
It means so much just to know you're mine
I don't understand why a smile won't appear
Maybe it's because the love's in my tears
I'll reach for the dreams I never will touch
But I'll hold to the memories that try to fade in the dust

Christy Kinser

REMINISCENT OF OUR LOVE

Oh, I wish my Love could understand
How I long for his gentle touch
I wish once more he could take my hand
Oh — I love him so very much!

Ofttimes I knew he was at my side
He'd wink, and I'd feel so good
Without that wink, I'd surely have cried
But I knew then, he understood.

His kindness and strength I leaned upon
I knew he would always be there.
His warmth was like soft rays of the sun
And his love was beyond compare!

Like a lovely rose he blossomed here
Then like that rose — he was gone
His soul soared away — like a fleecy mist
But memories of him will live on.

And some wonderful day we'll meet once more
In beautiful realms up above
On clouds of God's peace, together we'll soar
And share with each other our love.

Pauline A. Fretwell

A PRODIGAL

Standing upon this wind-tossed hill
I must admit the thrill
of hearing within
the quiet voice of purpose
once again.
To have been away so long,
confident in the far country's ways,
drifting amongst those self-sufficient days,
determined to find the sinner's gain,
yet never caring who must bear the stain.
Then shaking with renewed senses,
throwing away baggage of pretenses,
of pride,
remembering what it is to live,
what it was to have died,
to return,
perceiving my Father's plan,
never more to seek
other than
these words of joy, forgiveness,
which now to me,
gathered above ocean span,
a host,
you clearly speak.

Theo. Oliver

A SINGLE RED ROSE

Today you gave me a single red rose as a token of our love,
when I looked at this rose.

I thought of the love that we share, the petals remind me
of your caring and sharing.

And the color makes me feel your warmth and touch, loving is
opening up your heart, your soul, your mind.

Getting in touch with your feelings, and getting in touch with
your life, for love is very special.

And I love you even though I may not tell you so, we have grown
together and have become one.

You have brightened my day, and brought more sunshine into my
life, for today you gave me a single red rose.

Elizabeth Cotton

MY SON

Dedicated to Michael Pollock

We have shared our times of laughter and
shared our times of tears —
That's why watching you grow to be a man
has been special throughout the years —
Watching you grow to be a fine young man
has been a lot of fun —
You are so very special and I'm proud
to call you 'my son.'
I know that growing up wasn't easy, but
you always stood the test —
You never were happy in anything you
did, unless you did your very best —
I know at times things were difficult
and growing up wasn't all fun —
But you always managed to come out
on top and I'm proud to call you 'my son.'

Ruthie Mac

RED ROSES

When I was young I longed for roses — beautiful red roses
For my friends to see your enduring love for me.
On our first anniversary,
"I love you" was all you said,
Indeed cheap words instead of roses, fragrant long-stemmed roses
To grace our wedding bed.

Now that it's December, sadly I remember
Your eager kiss, *"I love you"*
Now your life is through.
Those words are my red roses, my beautiful red roses.
That fade not through the years,
Now mixed with bitter tears,
Their worth I cannot measure,
You love indeed my pleasure.
You are my true treasure.
Memories sweet bouquet, today and yesterday.

Rosemary L. Kintzinger

LIFE IS ENDLESSLY (WITHOUT YOU)

Life is endlessly without you
I wanna be close to you
I dream about you every day
I only love you

In all this time
I thought you loved me
I fell in love with just one look
Will you still love me tomorrow

Heaven must have sent your precious love
Oh, I wish you were here
Please don't stop touching my soul
You're my one and only love

I sit by the window watching
The night fall
It hurts every minute I'm away from you
Life is endlessly without you

Natalie Shuba

SHUBA, NATALIE LOUISE. Pen Names: Nat, Giggles, Eskimo Natalie; Born: Regina, Saskatchewan, Canada, 3-9-65; Education: Graduated June, 1984; Occupation: Writer of poems and short stories; Themes: *Love, feelings for the people I love by separation or moving away or by death; relationships; and how the Lord Jesus Christ changed my life. Sometimes lyrics come to my mind.*

THE MEMORIES OF LOVE

The sound of a telephone ringing
Made a miracle happen each day,
For a certain voice had the power
To make all my cares slip away.

The room had a way of brightening
When I heard that tap on the door . . .
Then a face as familiar as morning
And a kiss just as warm as before.

The glow of long-cherished memories
Has kindled a lovely spark
That glows like a thousand candles
And lights my way through the dark.

Ruth E. Dwyer

THE CORE AND THE SHELL

All of mine
who are gone
reside in crevices
where memories abide
come back to me
as they were
in life
and like those
whom they have known
in their own time
since man
acquired conscience
beholden of decrees
to be and leave
traces of his presence
for us to find
the sweetness
in the core
or the shell
a perpetual void
may hold.

Howard Deutsch

FORM OF FLYING

Death is a form of flying;
It is the infinite journey
where souls do not meet
resistance
Flying is in all our dreams:
It is the personification
of birds and thoughts
which are not ground down by
gravity
Or the tugs of responsibility.

We take to flight naturally
without the bonds of duty
Although it is love which holds
us hardest
to the terra which gave us
birth — not life.
Fly my love, and I will not
concern myself about your speed.

As you fly, part of me has wings.

Fran Franklin

LOVE NOW

We may see love
in a twinkling eye,
or find it in a smile,
or a whisper passing by.

We may hear it
in a joyful song,
or a gleeful whistle
from a gathered throng.

We may feel love
in a soothing touch;
but however love begins
doesn't matter much.

The where, the why, the how
all disappear before the now.

Dora K. T. Smith

YOUNG LOVE

I have my love a heart
of red paper, glue and lace.
I gave my love a heart,
there was a smile upon his face.
I gave my love a heart
which now is sad and broken . . .
I gave my love a heart
but he thought 'twas just a token.

Dolores Clark

ROSE-COLORED REAR-VIEW MIRROR

My memories are probably
A little sweeter than the truth;
The good old days, as people say;
Rose-colored memories of youth.
And even though I know that's so,
It doesn't stop my missing you.
Your memory keeps haunting me,
Time-tinted, but, in essence, true.

Susan Williams

MY SAVIOR'S LOVE

I have a loving savior
Who is in my heart to stay.
I will never doubt and fear
My savior's always near.
I wish all would know him,
Both the great and the small.
For such a loving savior,
To live in my heart.

Hazel A. Gould

SHARING

Words in rhyme, things of mine
I share with you
To hear you laugh, or see a smile
Makes it all seem worthwhile
We've crossed a bridge and burned a few
We can't go back and can't undo
Time has given us
You to me and me to you

Kim Z

LOVE'S ORBIT

Her lover is
a huge and searing Sun,
while she is
but a tiny speck
upon Earth's perihelion
ordained eternally
to turn her self
toward Him.

Ellen V. M. Carden

MEMORIES

The stars that twinkle in the night
With their glow of radiance bright
Have been through all time
A sweetheart's delight.

Though radiant and bright
The stars at night be
They only shine brighter
When you, my love, are here with me.
"Till death do us part . . . "
Said from my heart
Yet vow and promise,
Sealed with kiss
Let this be our creed,
This ring our deed.

For past lives are filled
And a home we must build.
No longer as twain,
But together as one.

Lester L. Warburton

Your soft body's shaking
And your tender heart is breaking
Because you are so sure now
That love has walked through the door
For such a long time
You've said you were mine
But now you've caused a pain
And I'll never heal again
You caused love to walk through the door
My love was so true
And it is to only you
No matter where you go from here
I'll always love you dear
Even though love walked through the door
Think of what you've done
How you said I was the only one
And that you'd love me true
Now love it's what I must do
Look at me
And see love walk through the door

Daniel Corrigan

TOGETHER

Roses are red, violets are blue;
'Tis my heart I give to you.

Take my love and do what you will;
Your every fantasy I can fulfill.

Your every wish is my command;
Your happiness I only demand.

Love and pleasure all abound;
Laughter, such a wondrous sound.

Your love is all I ever need;
We have already planted that seed.

A harvest of love is ours to endure;
A life full of happiness is for sure.

Grow old with me and you will see;
How wonderful together we can be!

Sheila Arnold

A VALENTINE — TO MY LOVE

Like roses in winter
Your love brings beauty
Into my life,
Makes it worth living.
No longer am I a selfish person.
To you I enjoy giving.
Like warm sunbeams that caress
Your love warms my heart.
Each hour seems cold and endless
When we must be apart.
Let me always stay by your side
And I'll walk through life
Filled with pride.

Pauline Wilkerson

AND LOVE FOUND LOVE

The softness in your voice enhances
The sound of ocean's breeze, as the
Sun declines behind evening clouds.

The moon reflecting water's rhythm
Highlighting the spectacle of
sailing vessels.

Damp sands that accept our
Being together — enjoying waves
Of evening tide strolling hand
In hand

Eyes staring into eyes, speaking
Louder than the ocean's roar
Relating affable affections of two
People falling in love.

And when I spoke you kept my
Lips parted with tender kisses that
Said more than words
And
Love found love.

Paul Freeman

OUR LOVE HAS GROWN

Our love has grown into a rainbow —
A melody —
Of happy years up full
Of silver raindrops
In a golden pool.

Our love has grown into a sunburst —
A song notes —
Like a shining crystal star
Holding us together,
No matter where we are.

Our love has grown into an ecstasy —
A full-blown rose —
Cherished in fulfillment,
Blooming in contentment
As we chose.

Our love has grown into "forever" —
On — and — on —
With the essence of caressing,
A blending, never-ending
Gracious marriage blessing!

Nella Thompson Meiser

DURING ODD HOURS OF LIGHT

For Bruce

HONORABLE MENTION

Hanging beside me
a heart-shaped planter, living
for a cup of water.
Petunias struggle inside, asking.
Water entices my attention
to want more of anything
in that ancient hour, the jump
from night to morning, unannounced.

Do we praise the single-hearted planter
who doesn't fight rain,
wind that sways its home?
Tonight laughter is amplified,
funnier, and it lasts longer.
Trees waking with the sudden storm
turn me inside to stare clouds somewhere.
The telephone, I want to hear
during odd hours of night.

Where I sleep, there is nothing
to hold onto with heat, nothing
in the shape of a heart.

Melinda Latimer

THE RIO GRANDE TRAIL

HONORABLE MENTION

On the Rio Grande Trail
in Aspen, Colorado, on my bike
a blue dragonfly
in its eyes, the mountains.

Queen Anne's lace veils the stream;
I eat St. Andre, whole wheat bread,
red seedless grapes, and drink water,
pure, cold, on granite.

The ear hears water pound over rocks.
Cottonwood seed flies; feathers.

Ants traverse a leg. I am pulled to
the earth; Icarus loses his wings.

I look up, see mothers and fathers
and small children on the landscape;

an answer. The pull of the earth,
this ring, this marriage,

a greed for the real.

Janet Roberts

Love of body
Love of eyes
Love of soul and all that's wise
Love can be so many things
Love can really make you sing
Love one now and then one more
Love can help you feel secure
Love in times of longing need
Love when nothing else can bleed
Love for real and love for sure
Love can always bring you more

Dennis L. Clark

TO JUDY, WITH LOVE

You were my first-born child, my dear
And no one can take your place.
And my memories of your growing up
Are gifts that time can't erase.

I have been so proud of the child you were
And I'm proud of the woman you are.
And as time goes by, you will always have
My love, whenever and wherever you are.

So take my love and pass it on
To your children and their children too.
For love only grows when it's shared by all
Then it grows and comes back to you.

Rosalie Steele Bolene

MOON RISING

In the dark of some night I will rise
In your heart like the moon all silver,
And live in your sunset dreamings,
Ablaze with the sunfire reflection,
Your hair will be rivers of light,
Your finger tips dripping with sparks,
The rainbows will arch from your eyes,
Where the furnace of starlight ignites
All that's left of the shining I was,
And though I am dead as the moon,
As long as you live I will burn
All the light of the sky through your heart,
And live as the tide-turning moon,
Throwing light, and that is enough.

Fred F. Manget

I SAW WORLDS I'D NEVER SEEN BEFORE

You smiled your special smile to me
And I saw roses 'round a cottage door,
And there revealed within your eyes
I saw worlds I'd never seen before.

I reached across my psyche to touch your finger tips,
To grasp at life that soars and soars
To heights beyond this mortal realm
'Til I saw worlds I'd never seen before.

We danced beyond the island of love
Where dreams have met before;
Your special smile leaves words unsaid
For I saw worlds I'd never seen before.

Eugenia Lamson-Small

MY LOST HEART

For so many years have I searched for you,
For so many miles have I run.
And now that I've found you at last,
I've driven you away.
I love you Charlene,
So much that life hurts.
For there will come a day when we will both reminisce,
And, always aware of our first kiss,
And last goodbye . . .

R. M. Almeida

BLACK OF THE NIGHT

As I walked the streets tired and for sure in the need of
some sleep, there was nothing but the black of the night
not a man woman or child could be found in sight. My
suntan body, it tingled with an inner warmth, as the soft
warm Indian summer breezes caressed my skin, making me desire
you within. Alone I was, my head filled with thoughts
only of you. Suddenly overpowered with passion, as my
love-starved body ached for the touch of your hand, the
feel of your body pushed against me so near, as to be filled
with the love of you, knowing nothing of fear. Impossible
it was, you so far away as for me only in the black of the
night, a place to stay.

Edith June Rouse

SHATTERED

The crystal pieces fall, like glistening tears,
As I am left to gather up my woe,
Cast down amid my darkest midnight fears,
I hear the jeers and laughs of friend and foe.
My enemies may gloat at my distress,
But from the ones I love I suffer more,
For they are cold and leave me comfortless
While my tears drop like blood, a wound kept sore
By finding they have twisted love awry,
Dissembling and dishonest from the start.
Too late I learn how swiftly love can die
And how easily cruel words can break a heart.

Charla T. Menke

SHE

The way she walks, the way she talks,
the ways she holds my hand,
The way she listens patiently
and always understands.
In the still of night, to know she's there,
to know with love, I'm in each prayer.
I know some day, somehow she'll know
just what she means to me,
Because without her time stands still
and joy just seems to flee.
I know when God created 'she'
this special one, he meant for me.

Claud Griffing

NATURE'S LOVE

Poppies and lupine spread in desert land;
Sleeping or awake in the shifting sand.
The painted leaves open to early day,
Suckled by nature's desire to stay.
In one being, no evidence of gain,
But unlike man, they suffer without pain.
These innocent sky-watching flowers
Repose in nature's loving bowers.
Miracles grow out of neglected seeds
Through some divine power nature feeds.
Sensitive circles extract crystal dew,
The rare charity from the azure blue.

John N. Breznak

A MOMENT IN THE PARK

Sitting quietly in the park
Listening to the rustle of falling leaves in early winter,
I am filled with both profound love and profound sadness.

Profound Love: For however this beauty came to be and
For whatever supremely gifted intelligence(s)
Designed and implemented it.

Profound Sadness: Because I not only know
That things do not last forever; but
That someday I myself will not
Be around to delight in the beauty
Now before my eyes.

With both love and sadness torturing my soul, and yet
With thoughts on the super-complexities of the *totality* of
Nature and existence dancing and sparring in my brain,
I abandon that park bench,
Tears filling my eyes
While those magnificent melodies of
Rachmaninoff's supremely beautiful and
Moving second symphony resound in my head.

Felix Meyer

REVELATION

I said, "When LOVE comes I'll be ready,
I'll know when he knocks at heart's door
And no fleeting thoughts will be entertained,
My heart will sing as never before."

I said, "There's no doubt when I meet him
Our eyes will speak words never spoken —
No time will be lost, I'll count not the cost
Of the vows that shall never be broken."

LOVE came — but I wasn't ready —
I didn't recognize him at heart's door.
My eyes never saw what his eyes spoke
Though he had been there so often before.

No time would be lost I had promised —
I'd count not the cost I was sure;
Yet somehow in my search I had overlooked
(The blazing truth came to me in the end)
That the great LOVE I longed for
Had been with me for years —
In the heart of one I termed "only a friend."

Meredith R. Haskett

INSECURITY

I live my life around him.
It is as if I were a child.
I don't breathe without thinking about him.
I don't laugh until he has smiled.
I long to meet his approval.
I wait to be desired.
He can crush me with his words,
but with his love I am inspired.
I am afraid of him
as some fear the dark.
My emotions are mixed
but I jump when I hear him bark.
I fear he will leave me someday,
that someday he won't come home.
He must as all sons do.
Then I will be left all alone.

Betty L. Harnly

CAPSULED CUPID

My throbbing heart aches with the ravening desire
To scorch and sear in your consuming fire.
No piece of paradise in any ration
Could match the bounteous bliss of such damnation.

Leon A. Doughty

CONFLICT

As soon as he pushed toward her, he pulled away;
He loved her even though she did not fulfill his
dream of what a perfect wife should be;
She loved him and knew that he loved her in spite
of his conflict;
But she waited for him to speak and there was no
communication between them;
So he married someone else but his conflict was not resolved;
He came back to her within two months of marriage;
But still he did not say he loved her and that he had
made a mistake;
At first, he did not even tell her that he was married
But she guessed and would not see him again;
Even though he would come to her door again and again,
She would not open it because he forgot once more to
tell her he loved her.

Priscilla Culverwell

CULVERWELL, PRISCILLA. Born: New York, New York, 8-14-25; Married: 3-12-65 to Jim Culverwell; Education: Hunter College, New York City, B.A. in Business Economics, 1945; M.A. in Elementary Education, 1952; Occupations: Teacher, Tutor, Free-lance Writer; Memberships: Ogdensburg Literary Club for writing; Former member of International Women's Writing Guild and UFT; Poetry: 'Epitaph,' *American Poetry Anthology,* 1986; 'Devoted Husband,' *National Poetry Anthology,* 1986; 'Observations Brought on by Middle Age,' *In Quiet Places,* 1986; 'Sweet Sixteen,' *Love Without Fear,* 1986; Other Writings: "Fantasy Impromptu," short story, *North of Upstate,* October, 1985; Comments: *My writings, whether poems or articles, are autobiographical. I like to write mainly about different kinds of love. I also write education articles, drawing on my vast teaching experience.*

Snowflakes
  Upon her face
Glisten

Charles B. Rodning

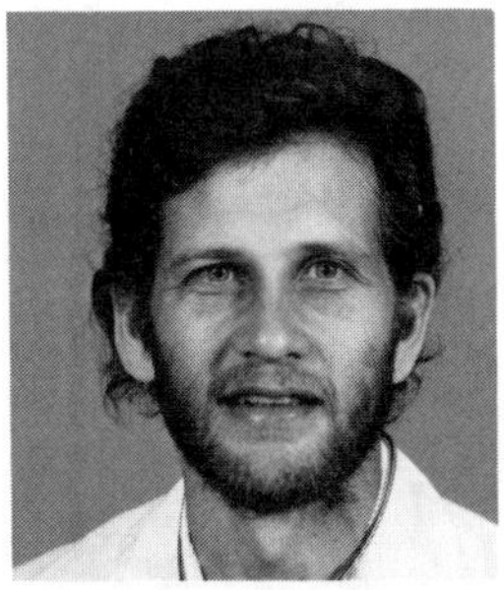

RODNING, CHARLES BERNARD. Born: Pipestone, Minnesota, 8-4-43; Married: 6-15-68 to Mary Elizabeth Rodning; Education: Gustavus Adolphus College, B.S., Magna Cum Laude, 1965: University of Rochester, M.D., 1970; University of Minnesota, Ph.D., 1979; Occupation: Associate Professor, Department of Surgery and Anatomy, College of Medicine, University of South Alabama; Memberships: Fellow, International College of Surgeons; Fellow, American College of Surgeons; Member, Alabama State Poetry Society; Awards: Bacaner Research Award, 1979; Physician's Recognition Awards (AMA, 1980, 1985); IOTA Delta Gamma Honor Scholastic Society; Phi Kappa Phi Honor Scholastic Society; Alpha Omega Alpha Honor Medical Society; Poetry: 'Moonlit Brambles . . .' haiku, *Modern Haiku,* 1986; 'Moths Flutter . . .' haiku, *Dragonfly,* 1980; 'Green Bamboo Stalks . . .' haiku, *Frogpond,* 1986; 'Late Winter . . .' haiku, *Proofrock,* 1986; 'Heralding a Great Herd,' haiku sequence, *Daring Poetry Quarterly,* 1986; Themes: *Furor Poeticus, Dramatis Fragrare.*

THE PROMISE

Her loveliness describes the night,
A haze of simple thoughts and gestures,
Loose hair like the tufts of trees,
A promise fathomless as seas, and vast
As all small pleasures.

George N. Braman

MY LOVE

I love you, my love.
I miss you, my love.
I want you, my love.
Please don't leave, my love.

My love forever will love you.
My love forever will miss you.
My love forever will want you.
My love forever will never leave.

Deedee Graves

MY SON IS LEAVING

Some years ago you came to live,
  In this small and humble home.
I had no jeweled crown to give,
  But you have all the love I own.

I watched you take your first little step,
  And would not let you fall.
I was always there when you needed help.
  But you soon grew strong and tall.

You're leaving home to make your way,
  And must not see my cry.
This will be the saddest day,
  Because a part of me will die.

Shella M. Lucas

THE OFFICE

We sat together in the office
Years ago when we were young.
We talked and talked and talked
After work was done.
Did you ever notice
When you smiled at me
How my finger trembled
On the typing key?

Where are you now, I wonder.
Whither have you gone
Since the days
I typed your letters,
Within my heart a song?

Lucinda Blair

SEPTEMBER WIND

It seems like yesterday was September,
the trees bleak and bare,
then the cold wind swept you away —
to the land of mist and air.

Winter's frozen cruelty;
Squirrels snuggled warmly in their lair —
A harsh and icy realization
that you were no longer there.

Now surrounded by the April sunshine,
blue sky and snowy clouds
and in the sky I see you smiling —
Your haven at last found.

Susan Leff

LOVE QUEST

In my search for love I discovered
hate,
humility,
confusion,
illusions,
and anguish.
Yet when I stopped searching for love
I found the greatest love of all
and that was
you.
For you not only gave love
but you taught me how to show love,
how to care,
how to share,
and most of all,
you made me feel loved.
My love quest —
Completed.

Jacqueline Elliott

SOUL MATE

My soul mate, that's what you are
You are the one I met eons ago
On a mountain or distant star
All these years in this life
We have been preparing
For this very
Moment and for the future
We will be sharing
We come into our love
Full blossom
And my heart knows
I have been playing possum
Waiting for your gentle touch
Please know, I love you so very much
And from somewhere deep, deep inside
I know we no longer need to hide
For we have shown without hesitation
Our love for each other without deviation.

Jill G. McDowell

LOVE OF A GRANDDAUGHTER

Little darling now you're two,
Two whole years of loving you,
Love your pretty little head,
Love you when you're tucked in bed,
Love you when you smile so sweet,
Love your little hurrying feet,
Love your saucy turned-up nose,
Love the way you pout and pose.
Love to hear your "Where Gam go?"
Hate it when you're feeling low.
Love your sparkling eyes so blue,
Love your impish "I told you."
Love you when you go to town
Riding your horsie up and down.
Love you in your bath of bubbles,
How you wash away my troubles.
Happy birthday darling you,
Happy birthday now you're two.

Mary Unwin

ON WONDER'S TRAIL

Voice whimpering in wilderness is mine.
Lost, with the woodland's magic, I desire
To find your shadow's comfort, the warm shrine
Of confidence while kneeling near your fire
With twigs of silence, watching dying flame
Review old scenes, smoke signals strive to keep
Old sites' cold ashes covered with the same
Care seasons guard lost legends' secret sleep.
Soft sounds and scents of autumn blend with chill
That prompts migration. My camp's embered blue
Stings sad eyes with kind cleansing, as new trill
In senses sings of waiting rendezvous.
You rest, on wonder's trail, in strong new tent,
And pray where dreams and fires are never spent.

Opal Zimmermann Towns

SMILING TEARS: SIXTH DROP

Love is two hearts in a movie
with no beginning and no end
Happy to share and even more
each other for life understand.

They pity the confused man
mixing girlfriend, mistress and wife
And the battered girl, lusting
both, freedom and joy of single life
They pity those that love to say
beware of love as of a knife
For, it is the innocent love
that is often so rarely safe!

Hacene Boulkhodra

NOSTALGIA

Somehow your smile never reached your eyes.
Some sadness seemed shadowed there.
A half-smile it was, that lit my heart,
Beautifully fleeting and rare.

But your eyes still haunt me, rend my heart
And fill me with keen, hot grief.
I spent myself to earn your smile
But the love you returned was brief.

I smile at the image I see in my mirror
And my eyes are unsmiling, too.
The reflection of me I encounter now
Is the sadness I saw in you.

Patricia A. Thompson

A LOVER'S BALLAD

Come all ye young lovers brokenhearted be ye
When the light of your life ha' let ye be
And sing with me the song of alone
When the love of your heart ha' left ye forlorn
The knights in white armor have all got their maids
There be none left yet for one such as me.
They ha' on they horses off to the clouds flown
And left me behind by myself all alone.
The sweet promises they spake in the heat o' the night
Were but just mere words. O! sad be my plight.
So come all ye lovers tha' ha' been left be
And come sing this song of alone; ye and me.

Denise Fleer

TAPESTRY ENCHANTMENT

Pastel art surrounds a suggestion of a "landscape painting"
harboring a glow of candlelight embraced by
"aurora borealis," desiring equal commendation.
Feelings of majesty of king and queen royalty,
music fills stardust for mirrored eyes
of ultimate timeless endearment, ambience enraptures
bell sounds of crystal, for "dinner at eight."

Rita M. Knecht

LOST AND FOUND

I know what it is like to feel betrayed
And suddenly so much alone and lost
And vigilant. I realize the cost
Of truths that disappear when vows are made
In haste, when passion's frenzied game is played
And carries curtained lust in lieu of love.
But every now and then I rise above
The chains of body, rest in love's cool shade.
It's almost like I free my heart and soul
And give them just exactly what they've missed,
A kindred spirit found to reach my goal;
To kiss and care for lips that never kissed.
I've come upon the part to make me whole
And wouldn't — even if I could — resist.

Laura Roscoe-Griffin

FIRST DAY AT SCHOOL

I helped him put on his favorite suit,
The one that we picked out with care;
He never will know the sadness I felt,
As I carefully brushed his hair.

He waved at me as he got on the bus,
I got busy with my household chores;
But I must admit, I nervously awaited,
The turn of the knob on the door.

We all find it hard, the First Day at School
It sure puts the nerves to a test;
It is harder on Mom, than it is on the child,
The day when he first leaves the nest.

Caye E. Hurst

NINETEEN FIFTY-THREE

Bitter darkness of cold did surround,
the dead of winter in northwest winds.
In the naked window the candle burned,
hours after the glowing sun descends.

Yet the memory of summer of fifty-three,
yet promises were now sealed we made then.
As the wind howling outside we smiled,
hugging each other, a toast with our gin.

The fireplace crackled and cast its light,
the year of fifty-three was almost at end.
The black forty-eight Mercury sat cold now,
let's end the year by the fire and kiss again.

Ronald D. Fulcher

THE FORMULA

In the book of science
I wrote about love;
in the book of medicine
I wrote about hope.

I went through
different chapters
in my search
for direction and trust.

The measurement of power
is in your heart;
and in your beliefs
the measurement of love.

Ana-Julia Villafañe

VILLAFANE, ANA-JULIA. Born: San Salvador, El Salvador, 11-18-54; Poetry: 'Clear Iris,' *American Poetry Anthology*, April 1986; 'An Intimacy,' *Words of Praise, Vol II*, June 1986; Comments: *One of the wonders in life is to discover that we do not know it all; never enough. There is always something else to be learned; that is the beauty of life. Some experiences can be tough, but if you have the right attitude, you can make them work to your benefit. I had always dreamed of having the most valuable friend and, lucky enough, I have encountered her. I would like to dedicate this to Leyla, the best friend anyone could have, without whom, no success could have been possible, and the person to whom I owe many of the most valuable things I have.*

LOVING

Loving is nice,
Loving is thoughtful,
Loving is full of happiness,
if you know what I mean.

Mamie A. Kaprosy

TARGET

Cupid sat
High on a hill
And let his arrow fly;
It found an early target,
For I was passing by.

Yes, I was passing by
And felt
That arrow pierce my heart;
And it brought joy,
And it brought pain,
Of which I am a part.

The joy of love,
The pain of caring,
And ecstasy,
All for the sharing.

All this took place
St. Valentine's Day,
And now I play Love's Game,
For, since that arrow pierced my heart,
I've never been the same!

Georgiana Lieder Lahr

LET IT SPEAK

For my fiancée, Patricia Morris

It is part of her body now
she puts it on every day
and takes it with her everywhere.
It is my love for her
an epitome of my dedication
and a token of our commitment.

So darling,
let it talk
before you even open your mouth
let it speak
and hear how vociferous it can be
for its eloquence makes it heard
by whoever dares look at you;
give it a chance to be heard.

It binds us together cohesively
like covalent bonds
it speaks louder than us together
to promulgate our love
and remind us of our promises
to each other.

Kaizer Mabhilidi Nyatsumba

LOVE'S SWEET SONG

Two hearts that meet
  Then beat as one,
    That is how love is begun.
The joy
  Each time you greet,
    The exchange of kisses so sweet.
The touch of love
  That brings a glow to your face,
    And makes the heart throb a fast pace.
That is love's sweet song
  And if fate be willing,
    It will last
      Your whole life long.

Phyllis Joan Smith

A ROSE IN SUMMER

There she stands — a beauty,
so slender and strong,
my little rosebud,
a gem of a child.

I ask myself where would I be
without the sweetness she brings to me,
my little rosebud,
the image of me.

The love we have is so precious;
more valuable than all
this world could offer
in gems or coin, or oil.

If the need arose I'd give her
the very air I breathe.
For you see, to me, she's everything;
my life, my joy, my eternal Summer.

There she stands — a beauty;
how precious to behold,
my little rosebud,
the image of me.

Antonia Jennings

THE ONLY TRUE LOVE

God looked down with pity;
Upon man, whom he loved so dear.
Falling deeper and deeper into sin;
Seemed they just didn't want to hear.

Maybe God bowed His head
As He looked at Calvary's hill
His son stared in silence;
As He realized His Father's will.

Maybe they hugged in sadness.
As all the angels cried!
But Jesus smiled and comforted them;
"To save them, I must die!"

Thirty-three years he told them,
Never regretting to say
He would be the sacrifice
That would open their way.

So Jesus suffered upon a cross.
And as he looked at the angry crowd
Just maybe he strained to smile at them
As he saw his lost sheep found!

James L. Jones

I SPEAK OF

I speak of love's passions, I name
Allan and Johnny and Jaques too!

I speak of it in the usual fashion
But — I never speak of you!

They speak of life and its treasures
Of beautiful things there are lots!

But only in holy hours — I speak
Of you — and they of God's!

Sonja Christina

GAY

My son is gay —
once he loved a girl
but she moved away
Gay's mother

Anonymous

IF YOU THINK

. . . about the times we've shared
I think you will agree,
that even through our moments of pain
our life was fairly easy.

Because we had each other
to hold when we felt weak,
sharing silent conversation
without us having to speak.

In this way we gave each other
a reason to await each dawn,
and now although we are apart
our love for each other goes on.

Joseph Scott

COSTA, JOSEPH SCOTT. Pen Name: Joseph Scott; Born: New Bedford, Massachusetts, 9-1-63; Education: High school graduate and some college; Occupations: Teacher's Aide at the John B. DeValles School, Massachusetts; Poetry: 'What Would Be,' and 'Our Love,' *Moments, Moods & Memories,* 1984; 'I Am,' and 'Smile,' *In Quiet Places,* Quill Books, 1985; 'This Day,' *Glowing Embers,* Poetry Press; 'I'm a Man,' American Poetry Association, 1984; Comments: *My poetry deals with everyday feelings and emotions that we all experience in our lives at one time or another. Thoughts that aren't always shared with others, and ideals. My poetry is my life in words, what I've had and what I would like to have.*

LOVE'S REVELATION

Where there is love
there are rainbows
for storm and sun
have joined as one

G. L. Folbré III

NEMESIS

Thought I could never love again
Thought from love that I'd refrain

Perhaps your face
my mind did change

Knew that love was in my range

I see you there
through loving eyes

We're easy together
Don't have to lie

When words interfere
I close my eyes

And remember that love
Is the tie that binds

The humor we share
The gods envy

The friendship that blesses you and me

To you I drink a toast sincere
And hope that you are always near.

Charlotte Rosenthal

LAMENT FOR MARY MAGDALENE

To a frenzied young man
Retrieving his gifts.

Pile them high
On the bier of love
In vengeful satisfaction.

You have been wronged;
It is your right
To take this course of action . . .

Your green silk gown,
The Scoundrelly scent,
The Irish sheep's wool sweater . . .
Your jewels, too,
The Kladdaugh ring,
St. Breda's cross . . . a letter.

Leave here no trace
Of sentiment
You may have sometime felt.

Yet have a care;
The flame leaps tall.

Your ice cube heart
Might melt.

Helen Mattingly

MUCH TOO YOUNG

I know I'm too young
To fall in love
Much too young
But every time I walk by
Your eyes seem to be
Talking to me
They're telling me
That you love me
Could it be
Or am I just imagining
I think I'm in love
But I'm still much too young
To fall in love.

Hilda Karamouz

ALONE

A crowded room I was alone until
I saw your face
You smiled at me and I smiled back
I crossed the room to place
A red, red rose within your hand
and kissed your full warm lips
I felt the beauty that was you
beneath my finger tips.
I smelled the fragrance of your hair
like jasmine in the breeze
Your soft sweet breath upon my face
surrendered to my pleas.

We loved and lived our fulfilled
years,
Oh! how I loved you so
But yet we knew that some sad day
that one of us must go.
So with our time together, the joys
that we had known,
I place a rose upon your grave
Again,
I am alone.

Lawrence A. Souza

A STORY OF LOVE

Paid for with persistence
Those many years ago
Pulled from your shelf
Misused and unread, pages
Withheld their story from all.

Reading quietly through
Time past
With fleeting smiles
Appearing
From hidden depths.

Then, I read of myself
Opening a book
Glancing, and now
Cherishing,
Studying, and now,

Understanding
Our intertwining tale
Of love
Retrieved
From the dust.

John Van Orden, Jr.

FUTURISTIC CITIES

Frequently as we journey to and fro,
  we encounter the workings of man,
Holes in Earth's surface so very deep
  foretell of tomorrow's dreams.

Rising high above us 40 stories or more
  are lofty buildings that gleam,
With massive beams of cold iron and steel
  where welders perch precariously so high.

Derricks and booms juxtapose the air
  giving a hint that fate plays tricks,
Many a builder prayed for his men
  as they perch so dangerously in air.

Glistening in the sun all shiny and new,
  like a glass menagerie in stories told,
Are many buildings high above us
  where soon office workers will dwell.

Already death has taken its toll
  and yet, the men bravely work on,
What price we pay in money and time
  for our futuristic cities so fine.

Jean Boyce Capra

O, TO LOVE

To love that which is me, encompasses you
  that rises with the sun
and slowly puts to rest at evening fall,
  bursting forth like springtime warm and bright.

To hold that which is you — to embrace;
  secure in self, in you —
to touch with expectation
  that which holds unfailingly
life within you.

Laura A. Bathurst

JUST A DREAM OF MINE

Now I'm happy as can be
Getting set to marry thee.
You so beautiful and dressed so fine
But this was just a dream of mine.

The music, the flowers, oh so sweet,
Then the preacher said repeat
The wonderful words that would make you mine.
But this was just a dream of mine.

Then the honeymoon, what a trip,
Off to Florida in a zip.
The big full moon and stars shine.
But this was just a dream of mine.

Along the beach we would stroll
As if we had a million in gold.
I was the happiest of all mankind.
But this was just a dream of mine.

I woke with a cry, to find that I'd dreamed.
It was so heavenly it seemed.
I don't know why I dream all the time,
And you, my dear, are in each one of mine.

Bransford Carter

MY WISHING WELL

Troubled years have brought me here,
This special place where I'd embrace the dreams of love to come
and stories to tell and cast a coin into my wishing well.

The younger years that knew no tears,
would find me here; This place so dear . . .
Believing in the magic to come as I cast my spell,
and toss a coin into my wishing well.

Time went by and though I'd tried
My wishes did not come true, when I lost you.
Love it seems had cast its spell,
As I tossed my heart into my wishing well.

Endless tears and wasted years haunt me now as I wonder how,
I can summon one last chance at fate and hope it's not too late.
To wish this from a well that's dry, seems hopeless yet I try,
It's been this way since she said "Good-bye."

Farrell J. Beagley

SWEET EVENING LULLABY

HONORABLE MENTION

Autumn grooves, fallow 'til spring,
lead down into sunset.
Last year, the year before and next
year will have the same thing.
Somewhere along Sheepskin Trail
an extra cubic of sunshine
exploded over the land, and this
rainbow valley twitters in birdsong.
You happily hike on past Old Parker's
velvet surrey, high-stepping by,
your hat raised high, you whistle
that Saturday evening love lullaby.
Rounding the old pipe curve bend, past
the Benson's steamed-vegetable conversation,
I watch you as I smooth our Billy's
golden curls and smile, as my
starlight spellbinder comes through the door.

Jolène A. Kent

MY MARGIE, MY DAUGHTER, MY LOVE

At 4 a.m. July 10, 1962 I gave birth.
My Margie, blue eyes, hair of brown,
The most popular little girl in town.
At seven years old she modeled on every channel on T.V.
For Sunshine department stores, Mr. Hughes,
This put her on top; gave to her life's key.
My Margie, my love was loved
By the public just as by me.
Stars came from near and far, Roger Daltry, Leif Garrett,
"The Razor Boys," The Bay City Rollers all came to her; see
Margie was like the morning sun
Every day bright, cheery, and gay.
Her mind was always full
Of creative ideas, fun and play.
Sharing her now with the earth
Has been the hardest part;
For I feel very selfish
About my Margie; it was like taking my heart.

Alma Lane Kirkland Thorpe

LOVE CAN DESTROY

Cling not to me my love
Cling if you must to God.
Cling to your faith, your hopes your dreams.
Love is a living thing, giving life when it is given and received.
It was through God's love, that men and women were created.
God breathed the breath of life into our lifeless bodies.
He loved us and he set us free, to be ourselves giving
our love to God in saying thank you for giving me life.
Sometimes we can love too much, expect too much from those we love.

Love me, don't crush me, don't smother me, let me breathe.
For I am like a tree my love, growing beautiful and tall.
Spreading my branches upward to the sky. Giving rest and a home
to the birds. I give shade and fruit.
But when a vine clings to me and my branches, I begin to slowly die.
My leaves like hope fall from me and do not return.
My branches break away. The vines squeeze the very life from me.
Until all that's left is a dead tree with a beautiful vine
Wrapped around it. I am a flower, I need water, I need air, I need love.
If you cling too tight I cannot breathe, water will not reach my roots.
I will be the shell of a woman and I shall never bloom again.

Mary B. S. Palmer

ESCAPE

Red roses bloomed around Joe's fence.
Its framework of iron with chain links dense . . .
His house renewed with metal siding cast shades brightening
his wife's platinum necklace to hatch the yellow rose,
a symbol of peace,
a symbol for the leaves of fall,
a symbol for the winter's pelvic gnaw,
a symbol for the edge of spring now an age ago,
a symbol for summer when the little wind blows . . .
The sun's glitter warms the ripe earth, while shades of grey light
her golden hair.
Joe died tonight from cancer's blight.
His wife pulled the sheets over Joe's head tight.
"Now yellow rose," June said, "give him renewed visions."

Thomas R. Shoemake

SHOEMAKE, THOMAS ROARK. Born: Commerce, Texas, 8-23-49; Unmarried; Education: Commerce High School; East Texas State University, B.A., Speech and Drama; Occupation: Free-lance Writer; Memberships: High School Spanish Club; Speech and Drama Department; Poetry: 'Found With Soul,' 'Let the Lower Lights Be Burning,' religious, American Poetry Association; 'Lost Love, *Hearts on Fire,* Other Writings: "The Talk Show," "Fate of the World," "The Children We Love," plays.

MEMORY

Funny, how some little thing
Recalls mute memory
In a chain.
The scent of lilacs in the air
And I can see you
Standing there —
So strong, so suave, so debonair.

You were my life
And all my hope.
I swallowed every word
You spoke.
But even lilacs
Drenched with rain
Can't seem to help me
Place your name.

Lucinda Blair

sheltered under the oak,
subtle forest companion to
masculine heavy trunk.
Years have bent its limbs.

Under vaultlike canopy of
reddish oaken leaves
close-grained bark
crackles yearly in the frost,
dappled branches fall,
fewer flowers grow.
Next to the diseased oak,
tree endures, like a
woman dutiful to the end,
loving the stature of her man.

Emma J. Blanch

COMING HOME

Sorting out emotions
from necessary chores,
Waiting through each worry
of possible delay;

Holding back elation
and a certain expectation,
Dealing with impatience
to be starting on my way;

Seaching for the calmness
to show appreciation,
Remembering to be gracious
Courteous and kind;

While an ever-growing
inner turmoil
Refuses, yes, refuses
to leave me in command;

'Til the rush and roar
of motors,
Help the plane become
airborne;

And I know at last
it's happening.
Oh yes, it really is.
I am coming home.

Jean Gowan Near

A SUMMER RAMBLE.

NEW YORK, PUB'D BY CURRIER & IVES, 152 NASSAU ST.

HEARTBREAK

When you came to tell me . . . Of the new love you
had found . . . My heart broke into pieces . . . Yet
never made a sound . . . I held you close and kissed
you . . . As I bid a last farewell . . . And I knew that
I would miss you . . . More than words could ever tell.
As you turned to walk away . . . You looked back at me
and said . . . I'm sorry if I hurt you . . . But it's
over, dead . . . Now alone I wonder . . . In the darkness
of the night . . . If your lips she is kissing . . .
Still I wish I had the right . . . When at the dance our
song is playing . . . Do you ever think of me . . . As you
hold her in your arms . . . Do you think of what used to be?

Dolores Saldano

FEELING MY HEART FADE AWAY

Your first kiss was magic when you were a stranger to me,
And your beauty filled my eyes and that's all I could see.
But the magic slips away and there's no mystery,
And I'm feeling my heart fade away.

Together for the first time, I thought you were the one.
Love blinded my eyes. You were so beautiful.
But the magic of your kiss slipped away,
And I'm feeling my heart fade away.

Now we say we're just friends, and our laughter now ends,
And I'm alone with a heart faded gray.

Jeff Cox

NOT ALONE

Though we say the word "goodbye"
It doesn't mean I'm not nearby.
Hear a special song, or
Read a special poem I've written for you.
Feel the sunshine, like the warmth of my body,
Listen to the wind, I'll send a message to you.
Hear the birds when they sing,
I'll have them sing just for you.
And even in the sound of silence,
I'll be close by.
The good times we have had together
Will be the memories to make the time fly by faster.

Fern Martin

MISTY VISIONS

Amongst misty dreams your vision beckons me to follow,
your voice carries me to another time and another morrow

Who are you I have called in my restless sleep, as I gaze
into your eyes of jaded passion deep
and your laughter resounding within my heart of hearts
while I seek to embrace you as this fire starts

The pattern of my dreams eludes me, filling me with despair
and I awake at morning's light hoping you are there
I know not your name or why you seek me here, only these
misty visions that haunt me everywhere

Susan Schule

TO THE LIFE OF AN OLD FRIEND

There is an old worn phrase,
"Quis custodiet ipsos custodes."
"Who will watch over the guardians?"
Who are these guardians but ourselves, the living?
We guard the pearly gates of heaven,
And the tattered halls of hell.
We hold the key of life.
It is we who harbor the memories of those long since gone,
And it is we who bring to life, the life that once was.
There can never be a love that will die on Earth,
For love is born of the soul.
The soul never dies,
It lives on and on.
It is a memory, and a spark,
A being that passes on from generation to generation.
Because for all our timely deaths in our lifetimes,
There will always be life-sparks in our death-times.
For it is important that only one thought remain.
It is the living that carry on the life,
And death of those long since gone . . .

R. M. Almeida

NIGHT-LIFE ROMEO

We meet at the bar; loveliest lady so far.
At home, at her place, we make love face to face.
Love lasts and lasts all night long.
She builds me up and makes me feel strong.

She says with a smile, kind of shy, but stretching a mile,
"I can see that you love me, so why not stay with me.
We'll love and we'll laugh all the night.
Held in sweet waves of delight."

I've been through this before; had my foot in the door.
She'll ask me for favors day and night.
We'll love and then we will fight.
Then it will all fall apart; she'll toss me out on my heart.

So to save time and pain, since there's nothing to gain,
I'll hop back in my car, drive her back to the bar,
Where I'll thank her for a hell of a night.
And save us from having a fight.

Norris D. Hertzog

AN ILLUSION OF LOVE

The moon rode high in the evening sky,
Its beams bright and shining on the river;
I mused and envisioned, then uttered a sigh,
My thoughts setting me aquiver.

The fantasy played before my eyes:
A man, rising from the stream;
I wasn't afraid, there were no cries,
As he came to me out of a dream.

His touch was gentle upon my cheek,
His embrace, loving and tender,
I wasn't coy, distrustful or meek,
And I needed no defender.

When he kissed my lips, I didn't resist,
It was beautiful, adoring, ideal,
Then he was gone, this lord from the mist,
And I wondered, 'Had it been real?'

Marilyn Yenger

WHEN WE ARE ONE

When we are one
There is no world of other.
No way to be other than
Each other.

There is no life
Beyond this moment,
Or even air beyond
The air we share.

And in parting, sweetness,
Sweeter than the last,
Remains within my soul
Filling all the spaces yet unfilled.

Grace Ramelle

DWOSKIN, GRACE RAMELLE. Pen Name: Grace Ramelle; Born: Passaic, New Jersey, 9-5-44; Education: American University; Corcoran School of Art, 1974-77; Occupations: Administrator for Engineering Consulting Firm, Freelance Photographer and Writer, Greeting Card Publisher; Memberships: National Association of Women Executives; Poetry: 'Shifting Sands,' *The American Poetry Anthology,* 8-86; 'As Close As Yesterday,' *Hearts on Fire Vol III,* 1-30-86; 'When We Are One,' *Hearts on Fire Vol III,* 5-25-84; 'If I Could Weave the Story,' *Hearts on Fire Anthology, Vol III,* 11-4-84; *Walking In Your Footsteps,* book of poems and photographs, fall 1985; Themes: *Common themes showing up in my poetry, as well as my photography, are love, questioning, nature reverence, sailing symbology, and a deep and passionate love of the world, my country and myself.* Comments: *Much of my creativity is dedicated to my living experience, trying to understand love while contributing what I've learned to others.*

FOOTPRINTS

Footprints
along the sandy shore,
now only two where once
there were four.

An ocean
of beauty and majesty
brings fading memories
and sorrow to me.

I don't come here often,
the pain still runs too deep
only those lonely nights
that refuse to give me sleep.

Yet,
I'm drawn to this place —
the salt spray, the pier,
where
alone I experience
the healing of tears.

Carol A. Smith

MY BELOVED STEVEN

As time casts a shadow on our moments
alone,
Gentle words emphasize the intensity
which our love has grown.

Worthy of my persistent love and
devotion.
I never dreamed of acquiring such an
immense emotion.

You are my Beloved Steven, abundantly
splendid in my heart and eyes.
The warmth from your caress I idolize.

Thriving with passion from your every
kiss,
Creates ardent tenderness. Forever,
My Beloved Steven.

Love,
Susan

Susan K. Seery

MARITAL LOVE

Those eternal moments
blissful, serene,
piercing the darkness
of our turbulent life,
like a ray of sunlight
in a storm-cast sky;
Moments when you hold me close
and press your warm lips
against my cheek,
the scent of your hair
stirring my sense;
Moments of transcendence
when I close my eyes
and time stands still.
Would to God I never wake today
to find such beauty snatched away
and the sky again o'ercast.

Randall Butisingh

THE GOSSAMER SCARF

There was a gossamer scarf behind the dresser
Looking like rose-colored dust.
Isn't that just like her?
She sits in her rocker, too much flesh
In a cotton robe.
Sometimes I could scream
She doesn't care.
The dishes filled the sink.
I washed them.
I dusted the dresser and all the rest.
She leaves tomorrow.
She wants to go
To a nursing home. Rest.
The house will sell
There will be money to keep her.
I can go on with my life.
I cleaned the floor. All the spots.
There was a gossamer scarf behind the dresser.

Wagner Windes

RECOMPENSE

Ever and ever there is One who cares;
Someone who listens; Someone who shares.
But ever and ever I choose my own fare,
Failing to remember You are always there.

Ever and ever I fall from Your Grace.
Ashamed, I avoid Your sorrowful face;
Then promise again, to be faithful and true,
To fulfill the tasks which are pleasing to You.
But temptations engulf me . . . again, I am lost!
And then, with arms outstretched, You rescind all the cost.

Once again I am pardoned by Your mercy and love,
Which so often You have granted from Heaven above,
Rekindling my faith . . . and I promise anew
To live the rest of my life in service to You,
And, as I strive to attain my destiny
I'll remember, Lord, You are *always* with me.

E. Gwendolyn Campbell

Well, nothing was happening standing there,
So, I guess, I'll wander up the stairs
To the place, now, at this point, called my lair,
To write of the place I loved full well,
A place I loved and worked, ah well,
To produce a living, dynamic place to dwell,
A desk, yes huge, with storage too:
Shelved to the ceiling, one whole room
To work with paper, stone, metal, woods, and glue;
A ceiling of wood, and books galore,
A wooden filing cabinet from days of yore,
Yes all this, but there was more . . .
A loft, that windows, two, did pass,
Leaving the floor to the room, with its hidden mass:
A lovely bed, with a loving lass.
A loft also, for the kid who dwelt
Was her son, almost mine, the connections we felt,
But the rip in my mind, the widening welt,
When she said I could not live there
The despair that I've felt.

Dennis L. Clark

THE ROSES HE LEFT ME

I sat and stared at the roses on my desk,
and suddenly the tears began to roll down my dress.
Like buckets of water I couldn't consume,
the memory of his departure remained in this room.
He gave me those roses on the day that he left,
I remember his words, you musn't cry, you must not forget.
I'll return one day, so please wait for me,
and then he handed me roses in remembrance of they.
We embraced for what seemed like only a second,

And then suddenly the whistle blew for him to board the ship,
with the rest of the crew.
so there I stood with these red roses in hand,
a remembrance of him now so vague yet still grand.
For two years have gone by and still I weep in despair,
for I haven't heard from him within those two years.
Suddenly a tap at my bedroom door interrupts my concentration,
and I yell to enter without any hesitation,
and before I turned around to see who I let in,
I was able to guess by the fresh scent of flowers,
that filled my air once again.

Lorrie Stevens

LOVE

Many people experience love
How many know exactly what it means?
Even animals experience some love
True
Giving, sharing, finding peace together
Just the company of him or her in the rain
In love one feels gratification when their mate achieves.
True
When it's cold outside you hug and feel warmth
When you are burdened a few words from him/her,
Those words will make you strive
That face will make you smile when you're sick
True
All these things are a part of love
Definitely there is more to it
The meaning of love to be clear
It's a high elevation of understanding.

Anthony Paulley

I'M YOUR MAN

Well now, my darlin', you've had me goin' —
It's really somethin', there's no love showin' —
Well, am I your man? —
Well, I'm for lovin', and I'm for hopin' —
Not all the shovin', and all the gropin' —
Honey, that's your man! —
Let's stop quarrelin', let's be forgivin' —
Hurt don't be holdin', let's get to livin' —
All I'll be your man. —
But, it's for certain, if it's for spittin' —
And for the hurtin', I'm not for fightin' —
And I'm not your man! —
It's you I'm needin', but not the wrongin' —
Love keeps on givin', so love you bringin' ?
Do you love your man? —
With no lies flauntin', and us both carin' —
And me you're wantin', then life we're sharin' —
I'm your lovin' man! —
Love must be growin', apart we're creepin' —
Now, me you're knowin', our love you keepin' ?
Do you want your man?

Glen Corliss

THOUGH WE PARTED

It's been so long since we've parted and gone our separate ways,
But believe me babe, I still think of you each and every day;
And when I see you and her together, it tears inside my heart,
For I still care for you and love you too, although we are apart.

I look in your eyes, in the warmth of your face, it only makes me want you more,
I stare at you like you're the heaven above & the key to my own locked door;
You're like my fantasy, yet my reality has left me here all alone,
But one thing I've learned, through all the hurt, my love sure has grown.

Your laugh and your smile could cheer me up whenever I was down,
And without you here by my side, I'm like a clown that can only frown;
We spent so much time with each other whenever we were together,
And no one can ever take away my memories of you; I'll treasure them forever.

Your just saying hello when you pass me by lifts my spirits high,
'Cause you're very special and warm, like the beautiful dove in the sky;
You may not think I care the way I'd like for you to see,
But just look in my eyes and you'll realize how much you mean to me.

Suzanne DeLullo

DAYDREAMS OF YOU

Today I looked in the clouds and saw your face smiling at me.
Or maybe it was just an image of my mind.

As the sun ducked from behind the clouds, I felt its warmth and it was the same warmth I felt while kissing you.

The wind blew a chilled breeze and I was reminded of your touch sending uncontrollable chills throughout my body.

What a shame it was all a daydream. For when I looked around you were nowhere in sight.

And I missed you from then on.
In days gone by we walked, holding hands, and talking of things, just you and I.
There have been times when I looked at you and despite myself, I had stirrings deep within.
I could sit and compare you to all things in my life, only thing is it would all come out to the same thing, and that is I love you.
Which I guess is all that needs to be said.

Linda Webb

TENDER LOVING HEART

By magic of your beauty I must love thee —
By your innocently refreshing feelings which are so pure . . .
And strong, that spirits are lifted high — running completely free;
That no matter of illness or mood, I receive the best healing cure!
    You had cast on me a powerful spell —
    Which brought sunshine to my life, you, my dearest little girl . . .
    Only when I see you, I'm completely well;
    You in my arms, and the whole world is a thrill!
Never before had I a feeling like that felt —
Especially when your sweet voice helps others to sing . . .
My heart out of love, as ice under the hot sun does melt;
Even in winter, the world blossoms for me . . . as if in spring!
    A true dream to play — with the most precious, beautiful toy —
    Who laughs aloud . . . and from everything have enormous fun . . .
    An endless blessing for me, with an everlasting joy;
    Spreading happiness, gentle warmth . . . as if the real sun!
All life's dangerous storms disappear — by smiles of charm —
Diminishing and destroying their threats . . . before had time to start . . .
Those smiles perform miracles, dispersing all life's accumulated harm;
And capturing me with her little, tender-loving heart!

Martin R. Tarlo

DESIGN

Say you crave me!
Have no fear, my love. Be bold,
  reach out, enslave me.

Be a sculptor. Cut me down to size
  and mold to your perfection.
Be a butcher. Turn me inside out,
  care not for my dejection.
Be conductor. Guide my torso, head
  and limbs to quench your passion.
Be magician. Pull me from your trick
  bag changed in form or fashion.

Don't torment me!
I am yours, dear heart. Take hold.
Squeeze me, heat up hunger's cold.
  Yearnings deprave me.

Sylvia Sumida

Love strolls in silence,
down sun-blessed summer sidewalks,
spinning velvet webs.

Shanon M. Sara

I'D SWIM THE TIDES

I'd swim the tides to be with you,
Swim the tides to the other side,
If only you would notice my love,
My love for you which never hides!

I'd swim the tides to hold your hand,
Hold your hand if only for a moment,
To let you experience my love for you!

I'd swim the tides and hold my breath,
Hold my breath at the sight of you,
A vision of mind could not enter,
You'd hold my complete attention!

I'd swim the tides in midnight hours,
In midnight waves 'til morning's dawn,
Only to hold you for a passing moment!

Doris Burleigh

BEWARE DAN CUPID

Now girls, don't be too overjoyed
By all the compliments you hear,
About your beauty and your charm:
They're sometimes never quite sincere.
A young man's fancy turns, you know,
To thoughts of romance, in the spring.
Don't build up hope; The things he says,
Don't always mean a wedding ring.

Dim lights, soft music, sweet perfume,
The nearness of a pretty ear,
All thrill a guy: he's sure to say
Those loving words girls like to hear.
Don't be too quick to answer yes,
There's lots of time. Be sure you know
He really means the things he says,
Before you shop for your trousseau.

Raymond Foster Gatten

TOGETHERNESS

Like the forbidden fruit . . . we tasted love . . .
and were banished from the Garden of Eden
forever . . . destined to be together . . . but
fate kept us apart.
Now I wander through life without purpose . . .
oblivious to the world around me . . .
trying to find one single reason to live . . .
yet knowing all too clearly that I must . . .
for whatever reason.
Damn time and distance and all the banalities
of life that keep us apart.
I don't cry anymore. I don't have any tears
left.
Each day is as opaque as a night without stars.
Each night as empty as a bottomless pit.
I remember your gentle laugh . . .
your funny face . . . the warmth of you . . .
yet fully aware that our togetherness can
only be in my dreams.
You must remain in your world, I, in mine.
It all seems so wrong somehow.

Frances Norton Russell

TO JUDI

Come to me my love, for in this night
Is eternity, our past and future.
Though we live a hundred years
And love a thousand times
This evening will be gone forever.

Our lives, measured in heartbeats,
Follow the irresistible flow
To where no tomorrows are, and
If morning comes we cannot know
What soulless destiny may provide.

We are sea foam cast upon the shore,
Bubbles of the moment, that break and vanish.
We are lost in forever, so let us
Cling to each other my love.
Eternity is not long, loneliness is long.

R. B. Sears

QUESTIONS

Of love and life
and what is real
and what is not.

And all that we touch
of what we may have
or have not.

Of words that are spoken, some to be heard.
For what we know and what we don't.
Of promises made, that will be broken.
Of love that's right, and love that's wrong.
Of mistakes that are made, some forgiven.
Of feelings that change, some to grow.
Of reasons why, or why not.

And the answer is the same.

Time,
endless,
there is no answer.

Jeanne Carbone Lewis

DOUBLE JEOPARDY

(A song of love and war)

The parachutist plunged in falcon flight,
Fierce with resolve. The sniper chalked up one
More trophy, wire snagged, dangling in the sun,
Shrouded in trailing silk, a common sight.
Rest will reward the sharpshooter tonight
For his tense vigil and his work well done,
Yet the full impact of the truth might stun
Him if the whole grim record were set right.

For two died with his lucky shot — the man,
In brief dismay; the woman, patiently
Putting away a folded flag that can
Remind her of the martial day when she
Received his medals, and *her* death began
With a long evening and a cup of tea!

Mary F. Lindsley

LINDSLEY, MARY FRANCES. Born: New York City, New York, April 23; Married: to Irving L. Jaffee, 1-26-63; Education: Hunter College of the City University of New York, A.B.; Columbia University, New York, M.A.; Occupations: Associate Professor of English Literature and Creative Writing, Hunter College; Memberships: Dickens Fellowship, World University, Poetry Society of America, California Federation of Chaparral Poets, New York Poetry Forum, United Poets Laureate International; Awards: Hunter College Hall of Fame, Doctor of Literature, Doctor of Philosophy in Education, Doctor of Music, Dame of Merit of the Military Order of St. John; Poetry: 27 books of poetry; *Harvest Moon,* Poets Press, India, 1985; *Uncensored Letter,* Island Press, New York, 1949; *Grand Tour,* Philosophical Library, 1952; *Selected Poems,* Theo. Gaus & Sons, New York, 1967; *American Cavalcade,* Dorrance & Co., Philadelphia, 1976; Comments: *The human drama and its philosophical impact throughout the ages is my main theme. I make considerable use of irony. I have been called a traditional modernist. Many of the poems deal with current events and make considerable use of conversation. Historical personages from Mary Queen of Scots to Anne Frank and Martin Luther King are studied.*

ONENESS

Intense, our love, profound and sweet . . .
our lips caress . . . two souls converge . . .
from slumber, waking embers blush
as, one by one, our hungers merge.

Desire joins emotion's heat
and fans the sleeping flames to grow;
from deep within, the fires spring and melt resistance
with their glow.

The symphonies of life begin . . .
as breathlessly . . . our needs combine.
In harmony . . . our spirits sing . . .
submitting to love's heady wine.

And when our passion's work is through,
a force takes over from above;
and blessing nectars, fresh imbued,
begins the miracle of love.

Frances Rose Weinstock

SLIVERING RAIN

to put into words what one feels
often is not easy
the syllables fall short
in measuring the chaos that sometimes
invades the heart;
it is neither easy to grasp
the imagery of flaming passion
nor the unpredictable cadence
of love's many moods,
its puzzling ways and blue mondays
suddenly without rhyme or reason
bitter words are uttered.
does one really hurt the thing he loves?
but after the storm the calm
for "no loneliness is more poignant than
a lover's, no pain sharper,"
somehow, somewhere across the stretching distance
love finds a way and the wall that stood between
is shattered as laughter shapes its way and becomes
a lilting echo of slivering rain.

N. Ming S. Ureta

LOVE SONG FOR A MELLOW MIDDLE AGE

I would not live without you, love
Save in the summertime
For three or four free flowering days
Of freely chosen time.

Should I get up and catch the sun
Or drift to careless dreams
Awake or sleeping
In my spacious bed?

I read myself to stupor as the midnight hour nears
To shut the tiny creaking sounds from my unwilling ears
And twist my back and curve my thighs
Accustomed to you there.

I love you when we are lying close
Bound with the ties of time
But I love you best when we take brief rest
To remember 'I' and 'mine'.

Lola Malen

TAPS FOR THE COLONEL

Our love was of the friendship kind;
Yet how close that cord did bind!
His slow smile warmed my coldest days;
I treasured his tall strength and quiet ways.
Laughter was ours, and music,
We stepped to a beating drum.
Now the dancing has stopped, and there's silence
For all of the time to come.
Long years he marched beside me;
Then came the cruel, swift fall.
No moment was given to say farewell. He
Heard the bugle's strident call!
And now, for awhile, I will walk alone;
I must not question why.
God has but reclaimed His own;
But an empty place shows against my sky.

Shirley B. Stowater

HEART TALK

If you were here with me today
I'd get the chance, I'd find a way
to say how much I love you.
But yesterday I saw you, then you were gone
and now I miss you
so I'll have to say I love you
in my heart.
If you'll hear me I won't know
you won't be here to tell me so
you'll have to say you love me
in your heart.
A dream come true tomorrow will be
if I hear you and you hear me . . .
We may find ourselves together once more
since our hearts always know
what to listen for.

Deborah Testerman

NIGHTS OF QUIET LOVE

Lying in your loving arms as the flames
of desire rise.
The fire inside us is as warm as the burning
fireside.
As we lie side by side in the candle glow on
our nights of quiet love.
Two busy worlds collide our time together just
for tonight.
We will keep the fire burning as our hunger for
one another burns bright.
And the spark of love reunites until this world
goes out of sight.
A night to dine with a flavor of wine since our
love feeds our hearts and inspires our lonely souls.
While delightful desire is our main course.
Just for the two of us a night of quiet love.

Barbara Reager

MY INSPIRATION

Of course, you're my inspiration.
Who else did you think it was?
You doubt your own importance
You are faithful to no cause.
But if I had to think again,
I'd make the decision that was
You are my inspiration
Though you're timid, you're shy
Some day you'll take allegiance and be loyal to someone.
Someday you'll fight off dragons
In a battle you've almost won.
I know this day will come.
And yet, I wish you wouldn't take your time
It is your time to take
But live as if you'll soon be gone
For tomorrow may be too late.

Jean Graham Cano

YOU ARE THE LAND

You are the land —
I am the sea —
Dashing passion against rocky barriers,
Caressing smooth sands
With gentle rhythm.

I am the land —
You are the sea —
Encompassing, moulding boundaries in persistency,
Holding the mysteries of life
In unfathomed depths.

You are the sky —
I am the wind —
Searching through purity for substance,
Shaping misty dreams
Into towers of beauty.

I am the sky —
You are the wind —
Sweeping clear a dark horizon,
Singing songs of love.

Shirley F. Shown

MOM, WHEREVER YOU ARE

I know I belong to someone somewhere.
I know that my roots are still hidden there.
I wish I could find, just to ease my troubled mind
Who gave me life . . . who gave me life.

The longing in my heart disturbs my once contented soul.
To know who I belong to could be my only goal,
But it isn't my intention to cause pain from long ago
So I won't chance my hurting you to ever really know.

Oh silent lady don't you ever wonder about me?
Do you visualize through misty eyes a daughter you can't see?
If I could only tell you just how well in life I've fared,
I'd ease your aching heart because I know somehow you cared.

Jerelyn L. Woods

BEGINNING SQUEEZE

One day there was a Knight
The maidens did all excite
The truth told
He was bold —
Raised delight to a new height.

When a woman takes advantage
It's a man she wants to manage
True to form
Forever warm —
This relationship begins another stage.

Courtship requires expertise
To bring the mighty male to his knees
Sure thing
Wedding ring —

Beginning again the marriage squeeze.

Priscilla imagined her life was a cinch
From the last clinch was in a pinch
Didn't say no
Didn't leave in time
Now her waistline's expanding inch by inch.

Gwen Pease

LOVING YOU

Loneliness was hard, cut me to the quick
deep sadness being alone
Being homesick, not knowing where to call home
life is cruel without a home

I had such good times when I was alone
the parties lasted till dawn
I had many friends, but in the morning
I set and look at the lawn

Since the day I met you, I've been happy
wish we could have met before
Nothing could come close to your gentleness
And I'm always wanting more

Each day I realize I love you more
Sunshine, love, and pleasure is holding you
And when I hear the softness of your sighs
I know you feel the same way, too

I will always love you more each day
We're so close in every way
Life is worth living because of you
And I'll never go away

William J. LaSalle

A VALENTINE

Love is not only for the young — for to be in love
Is to be ageless: Within its golden heart
A song, forever new, tender and strong,
Echoes in beauty, filling each part
With music, and there is silence, too,
Gentle and warm, soothing the daily hurts,
The loneliness, the roughness, into peace.
Love is a miracle — each time it is felt,
Accepted, it makes a garden of the barren waste
Our lives might be, would be,
Without its special touch.

Cornelia B. Furbish

A BABY'S LOVE

A little crib beside you,
A little hand reaching out at night,
You take it in your own hand
And hold it very tight.

Two little arms around your neck
More precious than chains of gold,
A little hand against your head,
As you your babe enfold.

Two little legs cross the room
And to your rocker creep.
You take your wee one on your lap
And rock him fast asleep.

Two little trusting eyes
That look to you for care;
A smiling little face,
So delicate and fair.

You'll never forget those traits,
Truly a gift from above.
Blessed is the woman
Who has known a baby's love.

Rachel S. Waters

IF I COULD WEAVE THE STORY

If I could weave the story of my heart
A story would be told of such deep love,
Only creation could hold its truth.
Only beauty could tell its story.

It would not only be my love for you.
There would also be my life.
The me within my soul.
The one who cared so much, so long.

A life of centuries filled with intensity,
And finally expressing,
In a simple love
Never owning, only sharing.

A love simply treasuring —
Cherishing our touch, our thoughts.
Holding dear all those moments.
The ones lived in our together.

Never looking to the next;
Before now was through.
Then to anticipate our loving
As a part of every now.

Grace Ramelle

I DID NOT MEAN IT

I did not mean it
I did not mean to hurt you
did not mean to grieve you
did not mean to graze you
did not mean to scar you
did not mean to stifle you.
Then what did you mean?
I meant to love you
forgot to mean it
and then I lost you.

Monique Adam

ON HER 67th BIRTHDAY

Six and forty summers have come and gone
Amidst a thorny path, life's still beaming bright,
Despite the travails, trials, the fear and spite —
There reigns a firmness to the vows we've sworn;
All we've perceived, we've created, all in one —
Marked symbols, monuments to the rareness of a woman
Who stood with trust; faith so strangely divine —
The very soul of a union, that will forever shine;
In the years to come with coolness and aplomb —
Steadfast to each — SWEETNESS — is its total and sum.
Such is the novel thought that hems me on this day,
As she saunters with pride on her 67th birthday.
Here's a toast to your health, happiness and cheer
From the only man YOU've ever loved and given what's rarely dear.

Pete P. Norella

IN SILENCE

Softly you creep into my thoughts without warning.
Tugging gently at the memories locked deep in my heart of words
we had spoken earlier, the smile on your face, the sweetness of
your kiss. Many times you've lightened my day. I feel as though
the sun is rising in me. So many things you make me feel. So
many things I feel for you, even the pain of knowing you are not mine.

I knew it wouldn't be easy when I chose to love you in silence.
There are so many words that will never be spoken. You will never
know how deeply you are loved. I know what loving you has cost me,
yet I can't let go. I want to believe there may, one day, be a
chance. I'm (loving) on my own, once again.

This was not how it was supposed to be.

Sandra Thomas

ODE TO MY WIFE

I like women who have a depth of knowledge buried deep
Like cool green pools within themselves,
Who hold a sureness and a quietude of way
As though by mystic prophets touched, can say
"Fear not. My love will bring you back to me
The while I keep my vigil tranquilly.
For did I not your touch recall from some old dream
By prescience knowing your love would seek me out,
As if my heart had talked to yours before we one another found.
So put your faith in God, and trace the path across
The Pleiades that takes you half across the world and back to me."
Thus spake my wife, and made her love a magic felt by me.
"Go fearlessly, for in my bones I feel your safe return."
I felt her love the while I flew between the stars and unfamiliar seas.

Barbara MacPhee

MY LOVING FRIEND OF THREE

I have a darling little friend, who means so much to me
We have a special relationship, yet he is only three.
Each day he seems to explore something new — he never saw before
The birds, the bees, the flowers and trees, and ever so much more.
He asks a lot of questions about this and about that
Even wants to know why the baby bird was eaten by the cat
He loves all the barnyard animals and they become his pets
There is so much love in his heart for everyone and yet
A great love is to feed Granny's chickens and gather up the eggs
But the big question is: "Granny, how does them chickens make them eggs?"

Christine Howard

PLACED UPON A SHELF

He came to me an early spring day,
and off my feet he swept me away.

Days of laughter and nights of love,
soaring ever higher to heaven above.

But he was a prince, Elizabeth's son,
and I was his martyr, left all alone.

The newness of love like the rebirth of spring,
soon soured to autumn and the death that it brings.

But why? I wondered when he was gone,
my heaven thundered, my tears rained down.

Then with pride I held myself high,
he would not defeat me. I will not die.

The time came for me to live for myself,
and place my love upon a shelf.

Ellen Rutlin

LOVE SONG TO MY DADDY MAY HE REST IN PEACE

You held my hand when I was small,
And sang "Mighty Like a Rose" to me;
You supported me in all I did and
Always let me be,
You loved my beautiful mother
Who went before you,
You were friendly to everyone,
When my girls and I went to the store with you.
Then you grew ill and went
To a nursing home,
Where your humor never failed you,
No matter what ill assailed you,
You had leukemia and yet you
Didn't give up yet,
A month before you died Ellyn and
I visited you.
I said, "I love you, Daddy."
And you sang, "I love you truly";
And I sang with you in love (so daddy rest in peace).

Jacqueline Miller Adam

LOVE AND NATURE

Love is a flower
Washed by a rain shower
And nurtured by a brook
From where nutrients it took.
Love is a cardinal in a maple tree
Exuding red brilliance and sitting free.
Love is a hummingbird
Extracting sweet nectar from a hibiscus
Lowering its syrupy meniscus.
Love is a lazy spring chicken
On a green lily pad sitting
Awaiting a fly
To capture the passer by.
Love is a deer in the forest feeding,
Undisturbed, nature's garden weeding.
Love is a pair of peaceful doves eating
On the beaten path meeting.
Love is nature
Because nature is the Master's love.

Robert W. Taylor

INVOCATION TO THE ANGEL

from Heaven and Earth

Samiasa!
I call thee, I await thee, and I love thee;
Many may worship thee, that will I not;
If that thy spirit down to mine may move thee,
Descend and share my lot!
Though I be formed of clay,
And thou of beams
More bright than those of day
On Eden's streams,
Thine immortality cannot repay
With love more warm than mine
My love. There is a ray
In me, which, through forbidden yet to shine,
I feel was lighted at thy God's and thine.
It may be hidden long: death and decay
Our mother Eve bequeathed us, but my heart
Defies it; though this life must pass away,
Is *that* a cause for thee and me to part?
Thou art immortal; so am I: I feel —
I feel my immortality o'ersweep
All pains, all tears, all time, all fears, and peal,
Like the eternal thunders of the deep,
Into my ears this truth, — "Thou liv'st forever!"

Lord Byron

A LOVING COLLECTOR

There is a collector who is terrific,
Choosing vehicles that will be terrific
For taking his sweetie out for a trip
That will make her dear heart just flutter and flip,

From his cars he may choose a big Cadillac
To carry them and to bring them back,
Or he may wish to use an MG car,
A Porsche, a Sprite, or a sleek Jaguar.

I know for sweet love they often go
And ride in Art's Alfa Romeo,
In his little Isetta they are very cozy,
Riding cheek to cheek and nosey to nosey,

But there's plenty of room in the Continental,
Just in case it might be that they feel sentimental,
Art's motor bikes make love a real special kind,
As he drives ahead, and she rides behind,

With her loving arms hugging Art's cute little belly,
Six cylinders rev, and out shoots the Benneli,
But the sweetest loving that I ever saw,
Was done on Art's thundering Yamaha.

Molly Molyneaux

GOODBYE YESTERDAY

I sit and watch the day go by,
I stare out the window and wonder why.
Why the wind blows so cold,
And things that used to be new seem to be growing old.
I wonder about the things that happened in the past,
And why the good things never seem to last.
I think about yesterday my family and all my friends,
Hoping all the love we have will never come to an end.
Even though someday I know we will all be apart,
But the love we share for each other will always remain
Deep down in my heart.

Beatrice Lawson Thorp

WISHFUL THINKING

Sometimes I think
it would have been a lot
easier if I had never met you
then my heart wouldn't lie
in pieces of
shattered dreams

Sometimes I think
if only I had never
known your touch
that sent me up like wildfire
then I could give myself to a million men
instead of wanting
only you

Sometimes I think
if only it didn't hurt
so much
whenever I think
of you
but then I might never have known
LOVE

Diane Wanderer

AS LOVE IS

As love is indefinable,
Love is color blind.

As love is complex,
Love is simple.

As love is God,
Love is God.

As love is,
Love is you —

Letting love, be love;
Loving, in love

And you find that
love is

What makes
you
Fulfilled by God.

Charmaine C. Parks

LOVED

My loved ones on earth
I love deeply, and true!
All the joys in my life,
To me, they imbue!
We have wandered through valleys,
With the peace we find there;
And we visited the mountaintops
in times of despair!
We have rowed on the waters;
ridden a white, foaming crest.
We have walked in the meadows
and sought sweet-scented rest!
We've been together through each test,
all the way!
God, in His Heaven, blesses us
each and every day!

Opal DeGrote

ALWAYS

The seasons

Will always change.

The wind

Will always blow.

The rain

Will always fall.

The stars

Will always come out at night.

The birds

Will always fly.

And I will always love you.

Till the sun no longer shines.

William Steven Stassen

SWEET LONELINESS

How sweet a loneliness can be,
When I believe that somewhere
Down a distant pathway
Someone waits for me.

Anxious arms reached out to touch
Across a starlit strand;
We move as one, transfigured
To a mystic netherland.

Eyes, a liquid lace of tears,
Searching for a sign;
A love so cherished, so complete,
Unfathomed, undesigned.

A face so rugged yet so fair,
Strong creative hands;
Tapered fingers, classic grace,
Caress as they command.

We sip the fragrant seaborne air
And taste the heady wine;
The darkening waters hold us there
Afloat in space and time.

Nelly Bly Grimes

INTUITION

This is too much
The soft wind
The sky-blue sky
How to identify?

Vigorous health
Clear, open mind
— a sign
That love will come to stay
This way — and soon

Edith Buckley

WHO CARES?

Who cares?
Oh yes, who cares?
When tears and sorrow
term to break my feelings,

Who cares?
When hunger and despair
Crown me like a sparrow,
Who cares?

Time treats me almost fair;
but the pains and griefs
make me wriggle,
but who cares?

Oh yes, who cares?
Poverty, tragedy, depression
and suppression give
me a dislike about humanity.

But when I become
to realize my mortality
and the ways hardships come
and go, I know, God cares!

Amos Singbah Massa

REFLECTION

Turning down the covers
I crawl,
Not gracefully
Into a too tidy bed.
Night envelops me,
The darkness like a tomb
That frightens breath away.
I sleep now with one curtain open.
It lets in a little light,
Creating the illusion of companionship.
Strange,
How once fought territory
Becomes a vast expanse
Of tangled bedclothes.
With all this space
I remain perched,
As some giant bird
Clinging to my corner
Of the mattress.
In sleep I reach out,
Touch the emptiness,
And in my dreams
Remember —
You are gone.

Suzanne M. Morse

Because you've made a loving dent,
A trope of sorts to you is sent
Before you read this stanza lent:
A cover can precurse intent
Within its paper bosom pent,
Though might commit a different bent.

Although I've only briefly known
The character, to me you've shown,
Your lucid image strums a tone
Which whispers softly being blown
Across a harp, my mind did loan
To feelings hazy, I must home.

Nathanael Rugh

OUR WEDDING DAY

I wanted to love, to cherish
But now I tremble.
I quake in fear
As my thoughts I assemble.

Of what might have been
If we did say:
"Till Death do us part"
On this, our wedding day.

Our wedding day once,
But never more.
Our thoughts once together,
Now on opposite shores.

Two heartbeats as one
But never again.
Two loves that died
And too much pain.

Too much remembrance
For love now seared.
Too much for love
That soon disappeared.

Billy Charles Grant

OLD KILDONAN MANSE
(late afternoon)

Slowly I would think
The long cool thoughts of summer
Savor the wonder of each hour
On the river bank
And the rose-twined bower.
Slowly would I watch
Blue-hooded shadows
Creeping towards night
Through the wind-sweet grass.

Margaret Forbes Robertson

LOVE STORY

I knocked on your door
but no one answered
The breeze kept
clapping the door
against the frame
repeating the question.

The ripped screen
a tattered bridal veil
bent by many dogs and pushes.

Dust creeping under the door

So unlike you to let dust in
You would have fought it off
with mop and broom.

Something to put your
mark upon.

My love waits
like weathered wood.
for you
to put the latch on.

Cathy Garson

A STEPPARENT'S PAIN

Being a stepparent
is a difficult kind of thing
as you love a child completely
after missing his beginning.
It means wanting to call their home
to say "I love you."
But knowing that's what the 'real' parent
should do.
It's a tug-of-war at the strings
of a part-time parent's heart.
Loving a child so deeply
while that love is confined to the dark.
It's painful to love someone
who stays away so long.
When you have no right to phone them
the months they are gone.
It's anguish loving someone
as your very own
while you wonder, worry, and wait
between visits, those visits at your home.

Nancy Falzone-McHugh

FALZONE-MCHUGH, NANCY LUISA. Born: 2-28-55; Occupations: Mental Retardation Attendant; Comments: *I write poems dealing with love; emotions concerning pleasure, and tragic moments alike. I write poems and short story works for children, dealing with basic living situations and the pain and growth of childhood, as well as the fun.*

REMEMBER

Love is an intangible idea
which exists within our minds.
It is a free state of being,
difficult to suppress.
As all else in Life,
Love will be and pass.
The duration of its entity
dependent upon
the quality of ourselves.
Accept its presence without demand
as you may gain much
from its existence.
Accept its passing without lament
and be among the few
who knew Love's fulfillment.

Rita F. Artist

MARRIAGE

MARRIAGE
Hugging Kissing
Loving Pleasing
We two equal one
Matrimony.

Sylvia Jefferson

A ROMAN CANDLE

Like a roman candle burning its last fire,
And hot flames flickering in mad desire.
Could this be love's madness that I fear?
Why I run and hide from love . . .
remains unclear.

Sedrick Arlington Goldbeck

GALILEO'S FORMULA

Must I wait forever and a day?
To touch upon I dew.
Second, minutes, hours, 365
Cogito ergo sum, mass of the sun.
$L=MC^2$

Geraldine Violette

TOO LATE — THE SLEEP

Love pulled from its hiding place
Writhes and wails and twists its face.
Words said, not said, too late
the sleep
And death a silent muse does keep.

Joan Matlaga

GOD

God.
Omnipotent, forgiving,
Listens, understands, cares.
Loves us all.
Father

Marilyn Morris

SOUNDS

What lovely music
Compassion records.

What compassionate melodies
Love composes.

Doris M. Compton

TO LOVE AGAIN

With each hurt, we grow
A little stronger,
Until in pain no longer,
We begin to trust enough
To love again . . .

Kathy Wall

SEASONS

In my hands these letters old
Of beauteous times to me were told
Faded now and of the past
Cherished memories to live and last
Not tied with ribbons gaily blue
Just in a box of oaken hue
Now lift the lid as I now did
And days of SPRING relive for you
Brilliant flowers all in bloom
Deep red roses fill my room
"I love you as these roses," once he said
Ah, but roses fade . . . can love be dead
Then Spring had passed and what was left
Were faded roses much bereft.
SUMMER rose with beaches cool
Another thought his heart would rule
"Oh, marry me," he took my hand
Together building castles in the sand
But waves of sea and of destiny
Brought other times with hearts to rhyme
And AUTUMN leaves fell in my hand
Another came of different name
And proudly climbed the world for me
I have the rings, trinkets, other things
And, so, with memories WINTER bow'd
And to each my love been vow'd
Oh, youth so quickly come to end
'Tis ofttimes hard to Golden Years to bend
Faded letters, flowers dried
Not with blue but teardrops ties
So many hands that touch
Leave now no memories in the rush
The paths been tread
The Primrose dead
Life has its reasons
Life has its SEASONS

Virginia Jolliff Herndon

SHADES OF BLUE

Her husband lies upon their double bed,
It's quiet now, he naps and has been fed,
Content and satisfied that he's back home,
They are alone, she'll care for her Jerome.

She sits nearby, a lamp their only light,
To needlepoint as she keeps watch at night.
She sews upholstery for dining chairs,
Each stitch accompanied by her silent prayers.

With woolen yarn, in many shades of blue,
All five are finished, host chair left to do.
As needle flies, each stitch a memory,
The hardships, trials seem illusory.

He stirs, she takes his hand, her life's complete,
Recalling marriage, children, plans so sweet.
As daylight comes, her husband dies in sleep,
She makes the calls. There is no time to weep.

And with determined look upon her face,
She tacks and hammers needlepoint in place.
Her list prepared, she shops at store for food
To serve. Her plans control, sustain her mood.

Next cleans, and cooks, performs necessities,
Thanks callers for their kind amenities.
No one can know, she pats the chairs' high backs,
Just holding her together — stitches, tacks.

Betty Jane Simpson

TREASURED LOVE

We loved the girl who blessed each one
Her twenty-six years remembered by some
She came into the world with lovely black locks
And left us behind in a state of shock.

Her manner was gentle, sweet and kind
She worked with people and understood their minds
Her turmoil in seeking security and peace
Overwhelmed her in the end and caused her life to cease.

Her achievements and honors in her short span
Were highly commendable and will forever stand
She pursued her doctoral program with admirable zeal
And from her job responsibilities she did not yield.

Now the love we treasure that will come to stay
Is the one which will replace the pains we feel today
We know eternal peace comes from Heaven above
And memories of shared joys come from God's great love.

Mary Hunter Wells

Dear Love,

Why is it you're so difficult to reach?
The line's always busy, or you're never around.
It's hard to learn if you don't teach.
Will you ever be found?

I hear stories of you all the time.
How you've made someone smile.
All the new beginnings you seem to find.
Will this happen all the while?

There are many an article about yourself.
Books, movies, and such.
All too high on a lonesome shelf.
Will the cost just be too much?

You've been compared with stars and the moon.
Your favorite color must be blue.
Will I ever see you soon?
Goodbye love, I'm tired of missing you . . .

John A. Magness

SEA FIELD'S HARVEST

I would go with you
Skipping through sea shells and oat grasses
On our shore's uneven coast,
But we cannot talk of this.

We are pieces of too many people.
Narrow eyes, stationed on sentry posts,
Peer down the fence of our adventure,
Even as they know not where we lie.

I would like to light a candle
And fold an ocean over us;
But we would only see our ashes
Floating white-capped near a separate shore.

Paving wide, long strips
Of lonely, work-stretched years,
I shall want these moments
Caught in rainbows of laughter, tears and love.

Sydney Tyler

ALONE

I cannot take the loneliness, it grows stronger everyday,
It brings about such agony — please make it go away.
The beating of my heart grows louder to my ears,
No one is here to comfort me — who will quiet my fears?
The tears begin to cloud my eyes and roll silently down my face,
The pain in my heart embraces me — the roots I cannot trace.
What can I do to unlock these doors and free my troubled mind?
Who holds the key to happiness that I must somehow find?

Barbara Mattingly

GOD, GIVE ME WORDS

God, give me words no conscious thought reveals
Of troubled quickening, the first faint stir
Of secret breath beneath the pulsing seals
Of beauty's pregnancy. Let soul refer
Its knowing to each punctual mystery
Your thought conceives, repeating color tone
In tiny seed, the warm expectancy
Of resurrection petaled hearts have known.
With eyes that see anew, each emerald thread
Recarpeting this bit of Your earth garden
Awakens awe in thoughts afraid to tread
With miracles of life without Your pardon
For earthbound syllables . . . Through tears, I sing,
My love sojourning in eternal spring.

Opal Zimmermann Towns

ON THE DEATH OF MY BOY

I clenched his palm, as smooth as summer trout
we'd stalked together. In the bedside stream
he lay in, Chad no longer wriggled. Out
to rapids of the heavens fled the dream
that was with us on mountaintops (the self
he was: the animation of the fair-haired
son I loved so) shunned the sheeted shelf,
where his remains reposed, I knew, for God.
O Author of all vision, how I yearn
to bait his hooks again! Please cast the rod
of Aaron to my faith in You and spurn

not, O Lord, these pleas. What's that? Your hand is
here? You know how weak a fisherman is?

Ted Yund

DAVID

Through the darkest lightless night
One bright star stood up in my sky

Flickered not at spanse nor gloom
Nor threat of celestial wrath

Did battle both with cloud and gale
Boldly stood the ground it claimed

Illuminating the cavernous corners of my life
Magnifying the glimmer of silver hope

Into the shimmering reflection of rekindled fires
Leaping flames of faith refueled in reclaimed joy.

Paulette Hess Brown

SECRETS WE SHARED

Dad read from the scriptures later in life,
He said it helped him weed out the strife.
Through thought vibrations he traveled in space.
Few people had time for his changing pace.

So much knowledge he kept locked away,
But he shared with me from day to day.
I know now what I didn't know then,
When he spoke of time he spoke of a friend.

He said he need not run the race again,
"I know the winner before I begin."
Peace and harmony he spoke of with ease,
Knowing like and unlike kind were the keys.

In a Christ vibration he passed away,
From an empty house, on a cool March day.
Leaving an unfinished poem behind,
About giving and sharing, true love we find.

I thought him a man ahead of his time.
The secrets we shared are on my mind.
I feel his vibrations, but I do not fear.
I felt love before when he was here.

Lynda B. Barnett

A HEART NO LONGER

I have a heart no longer.
Only an empty gaping hole.
Pain was my constant companion.
For my heart was stolen by your soul.
Will the memories ever fade?
The sound of your voice as you encouraged me.
Your laughter and your smile.
My trust I willing gave, to have it thrust
back to my dying grave.
But your trust you never gave.

Janice Wenning

LOVE'S QUICKSILVER DREAM

In my magnetic costume of quicksilver and blue ice,
We danced and danced in my mansion of dreams.
The musical trilling notes were hauntingly sweet and spice,
With lover's joy closely dancing in each other's paradise.

Then restlessness panged my mind and spun doubts about me.
I remembered your pushing me away with your eyes.
Once our love had been entrancing, now all that's left
A heart tattooed with scars from a burned-out love.

Then a veil fell over my mind telling me,
"Be happy with your borrowed time in paradise,
Throw away the shackles of love and just dream;
Because love is evasive like quicksilver and melting blue ice."

I remembered your pushing me away with your eyes,
Then I awakened and felt for you, wished for you
But gone my love, it was really true.
Your shifting love would not return I knew.

I slipped back into my mansion of dreams
There I could hide my love like a treasured heirloom,
In the power of a magnetic costume's dream;
For love is evasive like quicksilver and melting blue ice.

Juanita Allison

NEVER A GOODBYE

Like a candle burning through the night,
I often ask myself, what if I never met you?
Where would I be today? What if I never met you?
Where would this fire be burning all this way?
To this I say with all my heart,
I love you . . .
Each and every day together and apart.
More now than ever before.
Moonlit walks along the shores.
I show you my heart for it is you I do adore.
I cherish the thought of your soft gentle smile,
and the warmth of your touch, the glimmer in your eyes
to you I cannot say . . .
Goodbye . . .

Richard L. Marshall

ETERNITY

I love you too much to let you live,
The gift of eternity I now give.
My soul is reflected in the black of the sky,
As I feed the ocean tears from my eyes.
I nearly broke when you said her name,
And never again will I be the same.
If you are no longer mine alone,
You will not be for her to own.
I hold your body close, high on the ledge
Slowly I raise you to the water's edge.
I loved you more than you'll ever know.
One last kiss, then I let you go.
It is so hard to say goodbye,
And to listen to the echoes of your last cry.

Theresa LaFlesh

A PETRARCHAN SONNET TO HELEN

Is there something amiss with her sweet lips?
    In vain I have pined away to know them,
    But in my wanting, she seems to condemn.
I am indeed awkward, and do make slips,
When I'm with her, I'm lost, and my mind skips.
    I wonder if ever, I wonder when,
    Will I know true this lovely lady gem?
But I'll still try, though my poor mind she rips.
No love for me, then perhaps another.
    I know she loves, does she truly love him?
    Then how? Are their minds joined, their loins entwined?
These thoughts run wild; my mind I must smother.
    My thoughts of her, him, together are grim,
    If she'd only know me — my mind defined.

Gerald M. Quinn

LOVE

Love can ease the pain of bygone days,

    Brighten the darkest of souls,

        Warm the coldest of hearts,

            Soften life's hardest blows . . .

Pamela Boehme

THE SACRIFICE OF SEVEN

They were the bravest of the Brave.
They were the new Hope of the World.
They knew not of earthly grave.
They flew aloft, greatly hurled.

They were the leaders and teachers.
They were stepping into the Future.
They were thrust skyward in blurs.
They were confident, trusting, and secure.

They will be remembered as martyrs.
They will be loved forever and ever.
They will become the most renowned explorers.
They will multiply others over and over.

They were the Seven space pioneers.
They were a team of many and many.
They were a Faith of future years.
They surrealistically expired gallantly.

Wayne A. Shock

THE DAY MY MOTHER DIED

The morning of the news of her tragic death
I was completely lost
and drowning in sorrow and despair
when I walked to the beach to reflect, alone.

I sat on a boulder, looking at the sea
and emotions swirled in turmoil
like raging waves in my heart,
it helped me to release extreme tension.

In listening to the regular sound of ripples
I remembered a short lullaby
she used to sing at night
to set us comfortably in our beds.

Her crystal voice came with the waves
resounded with a soft rhythm
to rock my soul with love
and that was soothing at the time of her death.

Emma J. Blanch

GOD'S UNDYING LOVE

While lying still — in the cool of the night
We oft talk, my Savior and I
I feel the presence of *undying love*
While the peaceful night clouds roll by.

The brilliant moon hangs high in the sky
It seems smiling down upon me
While twinkling bright stars scattered around
Bring God's presence as real as can be.

At night, I express my feelings to Him
The depths of my soul I expose
And His *comfort of love* encloses my heart
Understanding peace He bestows.

One misses joy, by not talking to him
Alone in the cool of the night
Misses the presence of *undying love*
And assurance that all will be right.

Pauline A. Fretwell

SINGLE.

MARRIED.

LOVE'S WILE

Pressed against my body
Curved around me
Like a spoon,
I felt his breath
Warm, in my ear
As he whispered
"I love you Darling,
Morning's here."

I felt his lips
Caress my neck
Teasing with a kiss
Waking me, embracing me,
As lovers often do

I reached back
To touch his face
Then turned to see his smile.
He was not there,
and had not been
Love teased me with its wile.

Mabel L. Bowman

LOVE'S PHILOSOPHY

The fountains mingle with the river,
And the rivers with the ocean,
The winds of heaven mix forever
With a sweet emotion;
Nothing in the world is single;
All things by a law divine
In one another's being mingle; —
Why not I with thine?

See the mountains kiss high heaven,
And the waves clasp one another;
No sister flower would be forgiven
If it disdained its brother;
And the sunlight clasps the earth,
And the moonbeams kiss the sea;
What are all these kissings worth,
If thou kiss not me?

Percy Bysshe Shelley

BEFORE YOU

Dedicated to Eliot

Before you . . .
There were bright summer days
made for frolic and fun.
Before you . . .
There were warm autumn nights
for long romantic walks.
Before you . . .
There were cold winter evenings
shared with family and friends.
And
With each passing spring came a
new love in a new place in time.
Before you . . .
There was the struggle to fulfill
the childhood dreams and to
survive the pressures of adulthood.
Before you . . .
There was only living
Now . . .
There is Heaven.

Starla Willett

I had a chance again today
To look upon your face;
To see in you a fantasy
For another time and place.
Took up some feelings I'd put to rest;
They can't be balanced now.
Though they've been put to the test,
They simply aren't allowed.
I cannot write; I cannot think;
You've taken up my mind
And all I see is your dear face —
To all the rest I'm blind.
I like the feeling; it wears so well
I've lost all sense of time.
I wonder, does it matter
And if you'd ever care.
Your heart was earlier taken;
Any room to spare?

Jean E. Christensen

I know I love you. I
tell you so
almost flippantly
each time we say
goodbye.

I know I love you. It
lives inside of me when
we're apart —
which is all the time —
and then I see
You
as today
and this love
wells up inside of me enough
to burst the bounds of my body to
spill all over the world
and bathe it in light.

C. MacDonald

MOTHER & SON

A son is someone special and rare
About whom you will always care

Whether he be far away or at your side
A Mother's love you do not hide

You want for him what is best
Then you place your mind at rest.

When he is happy, you are glad
If he has sorrow, you feel sad.

So, my son, I end with one word
The truest word you ever heard

L O V E

Patricia C. Scuderi

THEOREM

Love
Overwhelmingly
Vanquishes
Evil.

E. Gwendolyn Campbell

A COWBOY VALENTINE

I'm just a lonely cowboy
Riding on the lonely range
Dreaming of the girl I left
Now ain't that kinda strange

I guess I loved that girl
So gentle sweet and kind
But I had to punch cows
And leave her far behind

I would send my heart
But the darn thing's broke
Rope them and brand them
You lonely cowpoke

I'll drop her a line
To ask if she's mine
But if she says no
Will you be my Valentine

John C. Curtis

CURTIS, JOHN CONYORS. Born: Geronimo, Arizona, Apache Trading Post, 1-1-20; Bachelor; Education: Grade school, high school, junior college; Occupations: Rodeo Bronc Buster, age 14; lifetime Cowboy; Carpenter; Mason; Welder; All-trades Contractor; Artist, portraits, animals, western lore; Memberships: Lifetime D.A.V. and American Legion; Awards: First poem published by Air Force, 1942; 'Mother,' Advertised in poetry two years Scottsdale paper; Other Writing: Poems, songs, novels. Photo taken while playing 26 men (Arizona Rangers) for T.V.; Comments: *The old cowboy is strictly western — poems, songs, art. Made a million in construction but was forced into retirement 20 years ago now on crutches and V.A. Pension. Acted on stage, screen, and television and sang on radio.*

CITY BOY

City boy, I loved you and the street-wise
way you walked and the way you smoked
your cigarette, and the cool, calm way
you talked;
I loved the darkness in your eyes,
the way they reflected the city skies.

City boy, I loved you then, but somewhere
down inside I knew, to care was far too
much to ask,
of a city boy like you . . .

Meghan Weber

EXPRESSION OF LOVE

How do I tell him I love him?
By letting him know he is my world,
The air I breathe, the love I need,
And the guiding star I behold.

How do I show him I love him?
By being there when troubles arise,
Sharing his love and his laughter,
With all the joy he has inside.

How does he tell me he loves me?
By letting me know I make him whole,
Also that I'm beautiful and desirable,
And wonderful to hold.

How does he show me he loves me?
By protecting me from all harm,
And opening doors, pulling out chairs,
And holding me tight in his arms.

How do we express our love to each other?
By dwelling in one another's heart,
And holding hands, kissing lips, and loving fiercely,
Till death do us part.

Patsy Youree

HALLMARK CARD

It is hard for me to know
if ever I will love anyone again.
you have ruined me for the rest of womankind
the wall is too high —
it is much simpler to stay drunk
and live on the memories of you.

since the first time I embraced you I cannot forget
you added an insane excitement to
the dreariness of my life.
sometimes, they say, you love someone all the more
because they make you suffer —

perhaps to reassure yourself that
in my mind you won't be forgotten
each year I receive one of these cards from you;
"I love you. Do you still miss me?"
blah, blah, blah.

you'd prefer to keep my heart
forever tangled up in red ribbons and wrapping paper

. . . and with no return address.
that's right — keep the wounds open and bleeding!

Brian Murdock

DOUBTS

why are there doubts in my mind
that you're not for me, not my kind
you breathe, you exist the same as I
but you're true to yourself while my life is a lie

I walk the dogs to the park to run
I watch the others all having their fun
sitting in the grass I watch the sky
growing as impatient with the world as I

I'm looking to find myself so I'm told
hoping that I'll emerge from the life that I hold
watching the ocean always move
wondering when I'll finally find my groove

to accept my life, my being real
to know that I'll always understand and feel
looking up to someone who dreams just as I
to realize that life isn't all just a lie

a dream, a wish, my world come true
my world exists only for you
to climb a mount, look at the world below
knowing that time is going much too slow

Ann Carol Turner

MY LITTLE REDHEADED BOY

I looked down at the foot of the bed
There peeked back at me a little redhead
With sparkling eyes and a grin a mile wide
He said, "Hi Granny, I come up by your side."

A soft little arm slides around my neck
Soft little lips give me a firm smack
A soft little voice says, "I wuv you, Granny,"
Ah, the way to his Granny's heart are many.

"Get up now," he says as he bounds out of bed
"Come on, Papa," and pats him on the head.
He stands beside us, his hands folded with care
And repeats word for word, the Lord's Prayer.

Engrossed in play, the "accident" takes him by surprise
"Funny, huh Granny," he says with hope in his eyes.
I assure him it isn't as I show him the way
With a long, sad face he says, "Sorry, Granny, okay?"

He's rowdy and loud, a rambunctious little boy
He's shy and loving and fills our hearts with joy
He's a blessing from heaven, all cute and coy
But mostly, he'll always be, Granny's little redheaded boy.

Cora R. Schroeder

LITTLE CHERUB

A mother lays her Babe to rest, after nurturing

a gift from heaven by God's grace . . .

It took a while to get her there . . . tiny dimples, curly hair . . . chubby little hands soft to touch . . . your Mommy loves you so very much . . .

Sleep now cherub from above . . . feel within my tender love.

Carolyn Long

ON LEAVE

It came to me again in a dream.

The still heat of that August night
drove us from the small house to the porch —
the promise of a cool breeze bright in our minds
though the chimes hung silent in the shadows.

I sat back against the post fanning myself,
and watched with a comfortable intimacy
as you polished black boots in your khaki shorts,
the muscles of your arms so familiar to me
as they worked under tight, tan skin.

The song of the locust came in waves,
mingling with the soft sounds of the radio,
mingling with our laughing voices
as we enjoyed each other's easy company.

Later we listened to the small fan
fluttering uselessly at the hot heavy air.
You held me close in the suffocating room,
the five o'clock alarm waking us from thoughts,
but not the sleep we so desperately needed.

I woke alone to the chill of the winter house.

Laura W. Putnam

PARTING LOVERS

You set the spirit in me free.
I come alive with the sound of your voice,
the look in your eyes, the touch of your hand.

You make me realize the sunrise and sunset.
You make me love to smell the flowers, to
watch the ocean and listen to the music and
watch the birds sing.

You make me love with all my heart and soul.
I am thankful to you for these things.
I am thankful that our lives have met, if only for a brief time.

Though these feelings we will never share again,
Because as all lovers do they will go their separate ways.

For you and I were never meant to share our lives as one,
for you and I have different dreams.
We must go our separate ways.

I wish for you all the joy and happiness as you
go your way, but above all of this I wish you love.

Maybe some day you and I will meet again and for a
brief moment we can be lovers again.

Patricia R. Douglas

WHEN IT'S TIME

I'm going to catch me a ride on the wind,
and live with the stars and the dew.
I'll wander through pastures of wild summer clover
and lie in the grass with you.
I'll dine on the daisies and essence of rose,
the moonbeams will be my wine.
I'll love with a heart that is wild and free,
I'll love, then I'll leave when it's time.

Julia Ann Reynolds

MOM AND DAD

Here's to you MOM and DAD,
as our parents, we're mighty glad.
Two sons and a daughter you did raise,
for this you deserve much praise.
Kindness and sharing are always there,
for life's many traumas you did us prepare.
Life's many pleasures can be sad,
but thanks to you Mom and Dad, they have not been that bad.

Seven grandchildren and four great-grandchildren you do have,
three boys and eight girls by last count.
All the love you give to them does mount and mount.
Just watch the future and you will see,
for all this love, better people they will be.
With all your guidance and help from above,
this is a family filled with love.
For all the good times we do share,
we thank you MOM and DAD with all our hearts,
for always being there.

Donald A. Gaeden

WHAT IS LOVE?

Is it the sensation
From the touch of a warm hand
Tingling down the spine;
The contact of scorching lips
That is as dizzying as vintage wine;
Or is it more?

Is it the breathtaking sight
Of the brilliant, dazzling sun
Slipping out of view;
The beauty of a spring day;
A warm puppy cuddling close to you;
Or is it more?

Is it a friend or parent who
Has shared so very much;
A child who climbs upon your knee
Who looks at you with shining eyes
And who needs your touch;
Could there be more?

Virginia Braddock

THE PERFECT SEASON

I tried to think of the perfect season for loving you,
And came to the conclusion that any season would do.

Whether it be spring, summer, winter, or fall,
I love you with a heart that's always filled with awe.

Now in springtime, God gives the world richness anew,
What better reason could I have for loving you?

While summer is special for me, yes it's true,
Maybe that's the perfect season for my loving you.

And what about winter with its cold crisp air?
Maybe that's the perfect season to let you know I care.

Now fall fills the air with beautiful colors it's true.
Maybe that's the perfect season for my loving you.

Now I tried to think of the perfect season for loving you,
And came to the conclusion that any seasons would do.

Walter A. Lassiter

LASTING LOVE

When your amused and twinkling eyes meet mine across a room
Because someone's remark recalls a tender moment in our past,
I am so glad we've lived the years together and have
Enriching experiences and anecdotes to reflect upon.

When your hand touches mine accidentally or otherwise
I get the same quick thrill and know that you do, too,
When I see your little smile of remembrance,
And when you brush by chance against me (or was it really
Just by chance, you rogue?) I feel again that surge of warm
Awareness, signaling you love me still the same old way.

Our hearts were tuned together from the instant that we met;
Love at first sight happened long ago to you and me;
Never throughout all our years together has it faltered
Or lessened more than momentarily; the ever vibrant spark
Remains; it goes on endlessly.

Love blinds us to the marks of age and keeps us young
In spirit, health and memory. Wrinkled we are, stooped
And shaky; our steps wavering and slow; but as long as we're
Together, what does it matter how we go? This thought sustains
Our serenity: We dearly, truly love each other so!

Gladys Manning Rogers

I HOPE YOU CAN HEAR ME

I've come here to say
That I'm happy today
With a family of four and one on the way.

I hurried through childhood
And skimmed through school
To be your partner or maybe your fool.

All our dreams were born
As we braved the storms
And passed through a river of roses with thorns.

I watched as you grew
And handled your moods
Never forgetting our vow to be true.

I cried when you died
Leaving nothing inside
Asking it over again, tell me why.

Now this baby of mine
Will have to be wise
To take on the challenge of being your eyes.

Mimi Herrington

There are so many kinds of love
That touch our lives, and above
All others is the Love of our Lord
Which, if we're His, is a harmonious chord!

The love of a friend is a precious thing
For, into each day, this love can bring
Sunshine and lightness of heart
Friends, of our lives, are such a vital part!

There is a love unlike any other
This is the love a mother
Has for her child, it's unique
This love brings both lives to a peak!

Connie Ratliff

EYES OF FIRE

I can read it in her eyes,
All the hurt and pain,
And feel her most inner thought.

And yet, all the warmth of a woman,
Who yearns to be loved,
How her eyes have forever sought.

Eyes of fire, full of warmth and wanting,
Eyes of fire, tells a story that's so haunting.

So deep and never-ending,
With a feeling that's so true,
Yet to be fulfilled to the thought.

Still searching to be held close,
And reaching for her dream,
One no one could have ever bought.

Only the arms of a man could,
Ever fullfill what I see,
In this lady's eyes, Eyes of Fire.

A man full of love and wanting,
And a man with the same desire,
To be loved, really loved by Her Eyes of Fire.

Constance Arline Parks

REFLECTIONS

I'm twice the age now since the day
The young man I loved went away . . .

Went away to war's age-old cry
Unaware that soon he would die . . .

Would die for 'freedom,' so we say,
Knowing man's hate along the way . . .

Along the way hate, unexplained,
Left the masses dying or maimed . . .

Maimed yet innocent of the 'why'
The sons and fathers had to die . . .

To die for others' politics
That didn't make sense nor match wits . . .

Match wits with guns and fighter jets
That had no mercy, no regrets . . .

Regrets are only left to us
With memories that will not rust.

I'm twice the age now since the day
The young man I loved went away.

Jeanine M. Droen

LATE LOVE

Do not deny a love that comes when noon
has now become a time in retrospect
It comes as softly as a gentle breeze,
and then the heart will recognize that soon
it must acknowledge what it can't forget;
and never say a late love cannot be.

Rene Knight

SUNSET LOVE

How I treasure all those blissful years we spent,
Clasped in slumber nightly side by side.
From plush chateau to leaking canvas tent
We lived, loved, laughed, and yes, we sometimes cried.
"Do you treasure now my flesh as when a virgin bride?"
You fondly ask, to which I've happily replied:
"Ecstatic rapture drenches through our marriage bed.
My crimson wand still revels in its hairy nest.
Your bosom's just as firm; your lips as red.
From crown to toe your body beats the best."

Leon A. Doughty

DOUGHTY, LEON ABBETT. Pen Name: LAD; Born: Atlantic City, New Jersey, 4-11-12; Unmarried; Education: Princeton, A.B. Cum Laude, 1934; Georgetown University, 1930; American University, 1947-50; University of Virginia, 1979; Brevard Community College, 1983-85; Occupation: Attorney at Law; Memberships: Federal Bar Association, Phi Theta Kappa.

FORGET YOU?

It happened again today as it does all
too often —
You stepped into my path, your face I've
not forgotten.
Though it's been years since my love for
you has died — or was it really alive?

I was lonely when I met you, hungry for
a man's touch.
You filled that need overwhelming me with
a devilish lust.
After the "fling" for me was over I stabbed
you with rejection —
I still see the bleeding pain but you could
say you thank me!

If I didn't give us freedom we both would be
bound to what — a one-sided love attachment
that would have ended one day with violence?
You pushing me to love you and I pushing
you further away?
No, just thank me, you're married now though
not to me . . . we shouldn't be seen here . . .
you told her about me.

I touch you quickly gently and say, "*She* loves
you!" my fingers burn, but why?

Ann Dickey

GOODBYE

He left today, he's gone forever. With tears shining in his
once sympathizing eyes, he left me alone. My heart crying out
in pain. I will never forget those last precious, grieving
moments before he slipped away; not giving a second thought.
He left smiling as if he had a secret that I will
someday know. Goodbye, my love, I'll miss you.

Dawn Zeidler

AE FOND KISS BEFORE WE PART

Ae fond kiss and then we sever!
Ae fareweel, alas! forever!
Deep in heart-wrung tears I'll pledge thee;
Warring sighs and groans I'll wage thee.
Who shall say that fortune grieves him,
While the star of hope she leaves him!
Me, nae cheerfu' twinkle lights me;
Dark despair around benights me.

I'll ne'er blame my partial fancy —
Naething could resist my Nancy:
But to see her was to love her,
Love but her, and love forever.
Had we never loved sae kindly,
Had we never loved sae blindly,
Never met — or never parted,
We had ne'er been broken-hearted.

Fare thee weel, thou first and fairest!
Fare thee weel, thou best and dearest!
Thine be ilka joy and treasure,
Peace, enjoyment, love, and pleasure!
Ae fond kiss, and then we sever!
Ae fareweel, alas! forever!
Deep in heart-wrung tears I'll pledge thee;
Warring sighs and groans I'll wage thee.

Robert Burns

NORFOLK

HONORABLE MENTION

When I cannot go to sleep at night
I get up and walk to my bookcase
to look at my favorite books on the shelf

One of them is an old atlas
from before the war when Europe was still Europe
and all schoolboys dreamed of discovering new lands
though there were none to discover
they wrote love poems for the girls
and blushed when they touched their hands quite by chance

I open the atlas on the page with the Pacific Ocean
its large area of blue spotted with black tiny dots

One of them is Norfolk
a small almost uninhabited island
a place without supermarkets cinemas factories
a haven of solitude swept by the south winds

I look at this tiny dot and feel relieved
I put the atlas back on the shelf
and go back to bed where I fall asleep at once

We should all be grateful
that there is a Norfolk somewhere in the world.

Tadeusz Rybowski

HOW 'BOUT IT?

Well, you said you liked the card you got
You know I liked it too.
The cover art was what caught my eye
Very much the way you do.

I know I joke around a lot
But some joking is believably true.
Much like the way I kid about
Spending some time with you.

So, to personalize this piece of verse
In the best way that I can,
Think about going out with me,
How 'bout it, Marianne?

Michael J. Finn

LOVER

a ballad on the
radio made me think
of you
lost some years ago
I had forgotten
the mysterious
shadows we drew on
the walls that breathed
to a candle's flitter
a rhythm we caught
that caused the world
to lie silent for
a few moments in
our arms

Suzan M. Russell

Butterfly —
lying under me
her arms surround
and protect me.

Laughing eyes greet me
knowingly.
she's got that smile that won't let
me wait.

Henpecked?

James Douglas Morrison

A small little word
Holds the world in its hand
The fish in the sea
A small grain of sand
The grass so green
The stars up above
This word holds everything
This word is love
It makes a nation
It makes a home
It gives you a friend
Even when you are alone
This word gives you a special feeling
It gives your heart a little shove
It makes you feel alive and well
This special word is love

Maureen Muccio

I'VE CRIED A MILLION TEARS

Ann Lawson, please come back to me,
From across those long lost years.
I've cried a million tears for you;
I've cried a million tears.

Do you remember how the lilacs
Used to bloom beside the wall?
How we'd sit enrapt in silence,
As the night would gently fall?

Do you remember how the flowers,
Drenched in morning's sparkling dew,
With their beauty past description,
Were not half so fair as you?

Do you remember those soft evenings,
When the whippoorwill would sing;
How we sat and dreamed together,
In the closeness of the swing?

Ah; Dear Ann; so long now sleeping,
Come back to me across the years.
I've cried a million tears for you;
I've cried a million tears.

Carl Floyd Freeman

FREEMAN, CARL FLOYD. Born: Red Oak, Georgia; Married: 12-22-60 to Keron Blissitt; Education: 15 years at Emory University (off campus), 11 years North Clayton High School, College Park, Georgia; Occupation: Television Repair and Security; Memberships: Vwg. and Dixie Council of Authors, Unkno?ns, Abri Publishers, Poetry: *Time in a Bottle,* Book of Poetry; 'The Iron Horse,' 'Stone Mountain's Reflecting Pool,' 'Tutankhamen,' 'The Old Man of the Mountain'; Other Writing: "A Secret Place to Love," Short Story; Comments: *My work is classified as nostalgia. I try to write to inspire the best in man. I think writing should carry man forward, not backward.*

You're grown up now and far away
I think about you every day
I wish we could go back in time
You were special and you were mine
I used to watch you as you slept
Knowing one day I must accept
That you would leave and go away
I prayed so hard that you would stay
I loved you so my dearest one
You were my life my little son
It happens to many that I know
In later years your love will grow
When you mature and learn of life
And someday when you take a wife
You'll know the joy of being one
Maybe you will have a son
Surely then you'll know the joy
Of what it's like to have a boy

Mae Focht

LOVE FOR A BROTHER

For Buma

You weren't just a brother,
You were a mother.
You weren't just a brother,
You were a father.
You were my worrier, my admirer,
You were my friend, my pride, my guide!
You were my soul, my joy;
You were my sun, the stars, the sky,
You were my Universe, my happiness!
You gave so much, you took so little,
You gave your love to lots of people!
You gave your life!

How could I live without you?
It was so hard, so hard to do!
But life went on, and on . . . and on,
I had to live,
I was committed to my son!

Jenny Ghihtei-Siroker

GHIHTEI-SIROKER, JENNY. Born: Chisinau, Romania, 3-10-20; Married: 5-1-44 to Lionel Siroker; Education: College; Occupation: Retired Teacher; Poetry: 'My Poem,' 'I Feel So Guilty,' 'My Little Town,' 'I Hate To Fly,' 'My Father'; Themes: *My poetry is about everything, whatever touches my sensitivity.*

TWICE AS MUCH

In anger for something a little four-year-old had done,
He grabbed my arm and knocked me to the ground,
Then he kicked me in the ass and picked me up by my arm,
And slapped my ears for what I had done . . .
Mom screamed, "stop, stop, leave him alone," and she ran —
Picked me up and held me tightly and we both cried and cried.
Dad took off, and Mum comforted me the best she could.
"You will always be my little man," she said.
"He don't like me, cause I ain't his," I sobbed through the tears.
"Don't you ever forget . . . I will always love you twice as much,
Because you are mine, you are my son."
In extreme pain, we both sat on the grass and cried,
But I knew that I was loved.

Terry Lawrence Johnson-Cooney

WHAT IS LOVE?

When I was just a little boy, I asked my mum,
"What is this thing called love?" and she replied,
"Many kinds, here are some . . . good, bad, up and down.
True, false, fair and some goes round, used, tried and blue.
Then there's love that makes some into fools.

Empty, strange, hopeless, half-love too.
Same, closed and open sometimes do.
But, what is most important still . . .
Is the love I have for you. There's family love,
And there's the love you have for others and they for you.

There's first love, puppy love, enchanted evenings too.
There's messy love, tragic, easy and over and sometimes a lulu!
Of course, there are the kinds of love that you will soon discover.
The love of the world will sometimes do, or the love of another.
Don't forget brotherly love, but, most important still . . . is that you love you.

There's God's love, animal love and human love too.
So in your life I think you'll find, who loves what, why and whom.
Many kinds of love, some of it is blind.
Love for places past and things and love to rest and dine.
And remember he who loves and is will last . . . a long, long time."

Terry Lawrence Johnson-Cooney

THE SEEKER

You are in this world yet so unhappy, I see the sorrow in your eyes,
And the games you play to try to hide.

Yet I do not understand because God has given you many things,
More than others I have seen.

You search in every corner for the thing that they call love,
Unsure of what it's really made of.

But disappointment greets you each time,
I long to take your hand in mine.

Love begins in the heart of the man,
And then is spread throughout the land.

Life is illusion and nothing is real,
Except for Soul, and the love that you feel.

Your Soul is beautiful so fill it with love and let it grow,
And you will help others by letting it show.

Remember my love that all that you seek,
Is in your Soul and it is truth that I speak.

Koleen Gilstad

WHY?

Willows whisper of our love.
They tell the tale so sad
Of how our love was
Meant to be, but suddenly
Went bad.

They tell the tale so rough,
But true.
That you love me
And I loved you.

Despair pervaded all our days,
And made us long for peace.
And as we looked into our eyes
We wondered, "When will this cease?"

A reply — there was none.
I guess there'll never be.
But now, e'en now, I'm certain that
I love you and you love me.

Priscilla Talbot

A MYSTICAL POEM: Adam and Eve

Creation was alone;
  before the bone.
God created a pairing;
  for sharing.
New creation shone, illuminated;
  as a history is dated.
A male and female angels;
  flaming torched candles.
Flying in pure love's skies;
  death to falsehoods, lies.
Either defeat or victory;
  no purgatory.
Neither deceit nor false;
  break the walls.
Either death or life;
  hone the knife.
If in Heaven or in Hell;
  Struggle well.
    Struggle well.

Dr. Sayid A. F-Bidar

I hold you inside of me a
secret in that innermost
    place of me.

I watch for you and start
at each 'old yellow' each
shock of white hair tall passing by
and dial your phone to hear it ring
and pass your house to know you're
    there . . .

I know I love you;
I know I hold you dear
and you must know it too, to
keep it secret there
inside your secret place
for when you're lonely, sad, or
    need a love

    there is me.

C. MacDonald

FOREVER

How soft within my heart I feel
The love she brings to me,
That swells from deep within my soul
As tides surge from the sea.
How soft the whispered words of love
That set my heart aflame,
How gentle are the thoughts I feel
Just thinking of her name.
And I will love her with a love
That knows no bounds in space,
And cherish through all time to come
That soft and gentle face.

William M. Sands

SANDS, WILLIAM M. Born: Pittsburgh, Pennsylvania, 6-26-22; Occupation: Master Deep Sea Diver, Golf Professional; Themes: *Love of the sea, its moods, its creatures, its islands, its beauty, and love of people and animals. Love of nature.*

MY LOVE

Now, a life of winter mornings,
Bleak and grievous,
Grey and cold.
When can I a spring enjoy,
And when, my love, shall inspiration
Provoke in us the heaven's song?

Hope eternal is my keeper,
Joy from memories I derive,
Staples which help me to survive.
But, empty still, I can be found.

Now a life of winter mornings,
Bleak and grievous, grey and cold
All my days are clouds of sorrow
Without dawning.
Where can I a spring enjoy?
When, my love, shall inspiration
Provoke in us the heaven's song?

Hope eternal is my keeper.
From memories, joy, I derive.
But death shall be my savior,
And relieve my heavy heart.

We shall enjoy our spring to come.

Ronald R. Tamburro

LIFE PARTNERS

Someone to make your coffee
Or perhaps a cup of tea,
Who makes your home a castle
Although humble it may be.

Who helps to give the lift you need
Throughout the daily grind,
Who smooths away the troubles that
May threaten peace of mind.

Who overlooks your faults because
The faults belong to you,
Who has a word of praise to give
For everything you do.

Who stays throughout the passing years
Forever by your side,
Who shares alike misfortunes, or
The good that may betide.

So pause a bit and ponder now
How empty life would be,
Without the partner whom you chose
To cherish faithfully.

Ruth Lommatzch

LOMMATZCH, RUTH MYRTLE. Born: Chicago, Illinois, 9-14-13; Married: to Reinhold (Hans) Lommatzch; Education: Correspondence Graduate of Palmer Institute of Authorship, Institute of Children's Literature, Writer's Digest School, Famous Artists, and Art Instruction; Occupations: Librarian, Editor, Art Director (Retired), Freelance Writer and Artist; Memberships: Professional member, National Writers Club; International Platform Association (Associate Membership); Poetry: 'Easter Joy,' Radio (syndication), *Second Thoughts,* 1985; Themes: *Love and consideration of others; patriotism for our country; inspiration for others to be the best they can be. Compassion for animals: Live and let live.*

LOVING LINDA

Only God knows the reason why
Her car left the road
And she had to die.

Perhaps an animal had crossed her way;
Since she loved each so
She could have dodged one that day.

Every creature was her friend.
She would protect them all
To the very end.

God took her from the far Northwest
To His loving home
So she could rest.

Her family will see her again someday;
But she is greatly missed
Since she went away.

Gloria C. Higgins

HE LOVES ME

The Lord Jesus loves me
this I really do know.
His lovely Holy Word tells me
He is there, wherever I go —
He knows my joy and sorrow,
What I do and say and think.
Of my past and of my tomorrow,
Answers prayer quick as a wink —
He does know what I need
but He wants me to ask.
I am surprised at His speed
but for Him it is no task —
Always trust in His wisdom
because He always knows best.
Give Him thanks for freedom
You will surely be blessed.
Some think of Him being far away,
I know He is near me all day —
I feel His nearness as I pray,
from His presence, I will not stray —

Fern Roche

A SPECIAL LOVE

Here I see a lass so fair,
As she pins a flower in her hair.
We talk of old times for awhile,
And I wonder at her thoughtful smile.

This quiet moment brings such bliss,
And we reach to hug and share a kiss.
She smiles at me with her radiant face,
Her youth transformed to womanly grace.

There is so much I'd hoped to say
Before this very special day;
But she turns away. It's then I know
The time has come for her to go.

So I gently take her hand in mine,
And we walk together one last time.
For today I lead her down the aisle,
To meet her love in wedded style.

Phyllis Bolen-Hofer

MOTHER LOVE — INTERNATIONAL

Mother's Day rolls around about May 11
The word Mother is used many times 7
Research says one of the most used words is Mother
In our English language preferred above all others.

"All that I am I owe to my angel mother"
Lincoln said this you will recall,
Just *love* and *honor* the one my brother
Who spent her life to save you from many a fall.

The Greek say 'meter'
I think 'mother' is sweeter
The Spaniard loves 'ma ma'
and the French 'ma mère.'

A lovely sound, in *any* language said
Listen children and by her be led,
She can be your advisor and friend
Teach you to love God, who will His blessings send.

Rowena Bragdon Holt

THE ROSE

As does a rose come to bloom so does one's life
But as a rose dies so does life
To be born to live to die no one can expect more
One can only hope that when he dies
He dies not alone as the rose but
With friends and loved ones
Who needs anything else
All but a rose
A rose stands for one lovely life
It lives to beautify
To accent love in all forms and to insure one of love
Now that to come and that which shall be forever
This is life and this is the meaning of the rose
These are the memories of love
Which shall live on forever
It is the rose that is the constant reminder of true love
A circle of living memories
The rose is much more than just a rose
It's a symbol of life's beauty
And love of the earth from which it came . . .

Grandpa

SNOOPER'S DREAM

I think I could never explain
The deep-down hurt, the tug of pain
When I see a grand old house and barn
Rotting away on a once-loved farm!

Doors and windows left open wide
The wind and rain — play havoc inside
A grand old fireplace, filled with trash
A shutter banging, back and forth with a crash!

A grand old stair with a sagging rail
Seems to whisper, the young ones failed
To inherit the good of a Mom and Dad
Or cherish the things they wanted so bad!

Why not close the door and safely lock
The memory of Ma, as she used to rock
In her favorite chair as she sang of God
And Pa on the porch, where he loved to nod!

K. Langley

NOBODY TOLD ME YOU WERE THERE

Your aroma lit up the room like a dark night
With candlesticks and fireworks.
The room was surrounded by you and everything
you stand for, whatever it is, large or small.
I knew you were there.

You did not speak a word, but I knew you were there.
What is this strange power you hold over me?
I am captivated. Unusually captivated.

I must free myself before it is too late,
Before I reach the point of no return,
For you are in love with love, for whatever it is worth,
Whatever you may gain without giving.

Before you spoke, I knew you were there.
When you entered the room, I knew you were there.
For God has created no other fragrance to
freshen the air as yours.
Nobody told me, but I knew you were there.

Erma Ghoston

What do you want
in return for your sorrow?
I want only one thing when I want anything
You . . .
the past above, the future below
and the present pouring down

It's only a paper
but with my pen I can record the time
for missing you
It's only a mirror
but with my eyes I can see the space
to live with you
It's only a love
but with my hands I can hold the eternity
to save ourselves

Without you
I can't live any more
Without you
I can't live any more
It's getting dark again.

Hiroko Mutoh

SEARCHING

In the twilight hours you loved me,
But as sure as God was above me,
Whence came the break of dawn,
You flapped your wings,
Thus I found you were gone.
You had glided through the air,
Like a sailing white dove,
Flying off to a different nest,
Searching for a new love.
They say 'Tis better to have loved once,
Than never to have loved at all.
I cannot agree that this is always true,
As it is not easy to forget you.
Time is supposed to soothe the aching heart,
To ease the tension after you depart.
I thought our love was shared by two,
It is now I find myself alone and blue.
We do not know what lies ahead,
For if we did those hours we would dread.

Dorothy America Boat

WHAT YOU MEAN TO ME

How do I tell you what you mean to me?
How to put into words — the stars, the moon —
The sweep of the mountains, the roar of the sea
The quiet, sweet silence of a moonswept night
As we lie beaneath her pure light?

What words can tell of the ripple of waves
As they lap 'cross the pond at night,
Or the flow of water on naked skin
While we swim free in silver light?
The smell of grass, and rain, and trees —
The peace of the country, the joy, the love
As we lie beneath the silent moon
So silvery bright above?

How do I tell of what I see in your eyes
As I gaze up at your lean, tanned face?
The sweet, gentle smile — the strength of your arms —
The comfort of your embrace — I feel so safe, so warm —
As if the world could whirl on by,
Leaving the two of us — alone together — unharmed —
Sufficient — just you and I.

Helen Paschall

THANKS

Years ago I wrote 'A Mother's Plea,' my very first poem,
When all my seven children were still at home.
I wrote "Little things mean a lot to me."
I asked them to love me — that was my plea.
And now that my children are grown and gone away,
I'd like to write another poem to say
Thanks for all the love you've shown to me,
And thanks for each fond memory.
There were lots of bad times and I shed many tears,
But I prefer to remember the good times through the years.
I cherish each visit and telephone call,
Each greeting and postcard and letter you scrawl,
Your "Hi" and "Goodbye," your hug and each kiss,
Just goes to prove this —
"Little things mean a lot."
And I thank God for the family I've got.

Dolores E. Minnig

CHANGES

It's winter now.
The sky is gray-white, and it will probably snow.
The leaves blow in circles about my feet.
I pull my coat close around me, and still I'm cold.
Sitting here, I can see the little outdoor cafe,
Closed now for the season. Empty. Bleak.

How different it was last summer.
The leaves were all in place then,
New and green, and sparkling in the sun.
We sat at a little table, he and I,
Sipping coffee, and feeling how truly delicious it was
To have breakfast outside, and to be together.
The air was fragrant with baskets of flowers,
And rich with the sound of laughter and voices.

The chairs are stacked and pushed to one side now.
They are only gaudy plastic; how cheap they look.
The folded umbrellas seem faded and dirty.
The pleasures and colors of summer have disappeared.
There're no laughter or voices, no flowers or warmth.
And he is gone.

Carol Patterson

ARCHITECTURE

HONORABLE MENTION

The jagged window of your room
Hangs out over the open space,
You in a sky bucket of sharp edges
And dark security. I know
How sometimes the glass breaks
And you fall through the air,
Riding on a cloud of my temper.

I know how the blue eyes burn
And the yellow hair
Rises in a flame of wind, sunlit
Oh my darling. I know
How the stiff body bends, secure
In the glistening spheres of love.
It is night and you run barefoot
Through the fog-filled house of your dreams,
To find me looking up, waiting outside,
Pounding upon
The heavy stained-glass window of your heart.

Robie Glenn Hall

UNIVERSE LOVE

We met in a place, totally uncommon
For lovers in those days
Yet we did not mind the atmosphere
We were on our way to each other's heart

We talked of nonsense and then of love
Totally into the feelings of each other
For us, the world was merely a sideshow
Compared to what we had started

Nervous, butterflies, the whole bit
But quite sure we needed each other
Neither of us wanted to leave
Yet the stars and skies await us

We climbed aboard each other's mind
Shifted into hyperspace and left Venus standing still
Had breakfast upon a comet
And decided never to leave
Each other's heart

Eric Knight

SPYING EYES THAT LOVE ME

I sit in front of my mirror,
And I see two sets of eyes in front of me.
One belongs to me,
The other to the spy that loves me.
His eyes are always watching me.

And the love really happens when he comes to me
To see
And to be
With me.

When our eyes meet,
We feel this warmth.
The spy who loves me
Lives in the sky
And his eyes
Are always on me.
I love you
Mr. Spy.

Niki Mylon

THE SHERIFF OF REGANVILLE, CALIFORNIA, POP. 1986

How great it is when she is near,
Joan of Arc was no less enticing . . .
In De La Croix's paintings we're
Together, cake and icing.
Betsy Ross was her godmother,
No, I'm not being too outspoken;
Grandma Moses was another
Link in a chain as yet unbroken,
And Susan B. Anthony, alongside the tradition
Of Florence Nightingale
Chose as her lifelong treasured mission
To cast a vote as a female.
Though I love her with a passion,
She hardly knows that I'm alive,
Once in a while I get rationed
Her presence from nine to five,
So you see sweet lovely niece,
She means a whole lot to me
And I am honored to defend this state of peace,
When, by God, she's the Statue of Liberty.

A. M. Fonda

TWENTY YEARS: TAKE TWO

She answered the door
naked beneath the fluffy robe
no figure implied.
To be like before
she would only allow
her leg through the robe's
slit
To orchestrate the grace of her body's
eventual exposure for him.

But the gentle candlelight was not
his dreamway to
an inviting tight nipple.
It was the floodlight to
her belly button adrift on
submerged waistline.

Fragments of a crushed adolescent fantasy
sank in the true tide of years
leaving his eyes blurred, his hair thin
And her figure puffed
into an unkept ooze of gel.

David D. Palmquist

GLISTENING LOVE

The sun glistens on the water
Like hundreds of stars on a clear night
The sun glistens on the water
Like the sparkle of a diamond engagement ring
The sun glistens on the water
Like the ice on a frozen pond
The sun glistens on the water
Like your smile when you speak to our child
The sun glistens on the water
Like your eyes when you look into my face
The sun glistens on the water
Like my heart when you say that you love me
The sun glistens on the water
Like my love glows for you in the dark
The sun glistens on the water
Like . . .

Shirley Hall Fister

MANY LOVES

There's room for many loves in every heart,
The love of family, friends and all mankind,
Mean jealousy should never be a part,
Real love leaves all such pettiness behind.
No wife should fear a husband's love for mother,
For having loved his mother since a child,
That's how he learned to give love to another,
If raised on hate, a young mind is defiled.
Many little children ask their mother,
Because they haven't learned in love to share,
"Who do you love most, me or my brother?"
Her love includes them both, with love to spare,
Love of many kinds makes life worth living,
The love you get, you only get by giving.

Mabel Bennett

ROMANCE POEM

O lady of perfect form and body rare
Thou with majestic eyes so clear
Thou with the smile of dazzling radiance
Bless my ears with your life-filled voice
Bless my nostrils with your fragrant odor
Heat my heart with your warmth of soul
For you are all the loveliness of the world
Condensed into a single being

Royce Campbell

MY MAN

When we go stepping out, my man and I
He always looks so neat, and trim
And the reason why, all eyes are upon him.
Because he is so handsome and sweet
He sweeps the ladies off their feet.
They pay no attention to me, when my man is in town
But the ladies all envy me.
I hear rumors flying around.
They all know how far they can go
They better not step out of line.
For if they do, they'll regret it, too.
They know they are wasting their time.
They also know he belongs to me.
'Cause he is mine, all mine.

Lillie M. McConkey

LIFE

Life is much more bearable with you so near.
Knowing that you care for me and
Want to spend the rest of your
Life with me makes me love you
More with each passing day.
I never knew what life really
Meant until you entered it.
You showed me the love I never knew existed.
The joys that the simplest things
Could bring — like a kiss, or the sun
Bringing us a new day to share together.
You mean so much to me that
If you ever left, my life would
Go with you . . .

Linda Lieber

MY GARDEN

Trees
to climb in
Grass
to fall on
Flowers
to brighten
Paths
to walk through
Garden
I love you.

Kathie Lemon

MY LOVE

My love is the song of songs to me
An angel of my heart's delight
A cool breath, in the heat of day
A golden solitude at night.

More can she say in a silent look
Than others in a spoken life
More can she do to comfort me
Than all the rest can do my wife.

My love is the fragrance of the flowers
The beauties of this earth —
Not all the diamond starlit skies
Are nearly what she's worth.

She is the mother of our child
The fountain of our streams
That overflows with loving care
An ocean for our dreams.

I'll never find the words to tell
How much she means to me
You'll never know till you have love
Just how a love can be.

Phillip A. Meissner

LONELINESS

I feel so blue
away from you
this is true
'cause I love you

The futher away
the longer the day
this I say
in an awesome way

You are my dear
I cannot fear
the lonely tear
that is near

Wish I were there
with you so fair
yes I care
my one so fair

No music I hear
can help me adhere
to keeping clear
of you my dear.

Kenneth D. Senior

DYING LOVE

Dying love is painful
like the old rotted oak
it creaks
in the wind
protesting its
innocence
Refusing to fall
with one root still alive
it hurts
a dull ache
in the core of
the heart
Only time is the balm
that coats the old oak
with age
'til sighing
it crumbles into
memory.

Claudia D. Newcorn

NEWCORN, CLAUDIA DANA. Born: New York City, New York, 8-9-58; Education: Wellesley College, B.A. Psychology and English, 1981; Northeastern University, M.B.A., marketing concentration, 1986; Occupations: Assistant Product Manager; Helicopter Pilot; Memberships: AMA, NAFE, Sigma XI, Phi Kappa Phi, Beta Gamma Sigma; Awards: Golden Poet Award, 1985; Poetry: 'Credit Check,' 'Microwaved,' *American Poetry Anthology,* 1985; 'Evening,' *World of Poetry Anthology,* 1985; 'Faery,' *World of Poetry Anthology,* 1986; 'Wherewithal,' *Vantage Press Anthology,* 1986; Comments: *I love to live and watch life. I get pulled into the tremendous emotional interplay behind actions (sometimes too much) and try to share what I feel in my writing. I equate my poetry with my helicopter flying — a balance of skill, mechanics and art. What a feeling!*

BROKEN

Lord, I never could imagine
how You really feel.
With all Your love rejected,
and few who will kneel.
Sometimes I get to thinking
how little people care.
They can't see the tears.
They don't even know You're there.
O Lord, even I. I turned back, too.
Not really knowing
how much I was hurting You.
I couldn't see Your heart
as it slowly broke in two.
I didn't feel the pain
I'm sure I caused to You.
But now my heart is broken
as my love has been denied.
I, too, feel the pain.
It hurts so much inside . . .
Now I truly feel what I've done to You.

Michelle Campbell

I ONCE BEHELD A TREASURE

I once beheld a treasure
Whose beauty I had never known
More mysterious than ancient temples
More alluring than colored stone
Like a rose my love did blossom
Overflowing from deep within
As the life I once neglected
Was now purposeful again
Alas, my precious treasure
From me did surely part
With not a gem remaining
To appease my severed heart
I say love is but an illusion
A most potent fantasy
Where hearts afloat impassioned
Share a dreamed reality
Where the gold of hidden rapture
Drawn from Eros' endless mine
Casts a wicked spell of happiness
In love that is oh, so blind.

Rosalind D. Norris

GOD OF INDIFFERENCE

Existing for the sake of being.
Being for the sake of love.

The god of indifference
Has cast a shadow
between our love.

Can I see you
Without being with you?

For dwelling within your spirit
Is a sense of non-fulfillment
You need the company of others.

Situation
Turbulence
Indifference
Letting go
I love you Marla.

Michael Strappe

THE HEARING OF A DISTANT DRUM

Silence the witness of some loud heart's cry when I
hear strange whispers wonder why, I feel the vibes
near to my ear and feel the peaceful wonder
in the hearing of a distant drum though I know
not from where it comes.
Distant the dreams that slowly flee to a world
unknown to you or me, the one where my heart
does only sometimes flee with the hearing of
a distant drum, but always there is God's love
For you and me.
What an out of sight unknown world I only
most unexpectedly meet in my mind and
then my soul does flee, quite unannounced
by me to a peaceful world of beauty bright

P. Grossie

MAGIC OF LOVE

Love is magic filled with life's secret mystery,
Love works its wondrous ways
There is nothing in life Love cannot change
Love transforms the most commonplace
Into the splendorous beauties of sweetness and grace.
Love is unselfish, it is understanding and kind,
Love sees into the heart and sweeps into the mind,
It cannot be bought, you can have it for free
Love is purely magic and full of mystery.

Ione E. Williams

MY EARNEST PRAYER

Father in Heaven — Blessed is Thy
Sacred name — O, Jehovah
Thou who showest me tender mercy and
Loving kindness in the hour of sorest need.
Ever is Thy wing ready to cover me
Thy hand outstretched in infinite compassion.
The breath of Thy love is as sweet
Music in the still hours of the night.
My praise of Thee is honey on my lips.
Dear Father in Thy unbounding love and
abiding charity
Grant me the grace and worthiness
To love and serve my fellow men.
AMEN

Helen deLong Woodward

THOU ART THE LEAD

Since thou art the lead of all select flowers,
My pen in fondness found craft it knew not of,
Subscribed these lines that I mayest prove —
The thoughts I bear assumed some cryptic powers;
With heaven's fair assistance sank sturdy roots
Deep into thy heart some timely berth secure,
And anchored firmly to start such wholesome growths,
In YOU — forever live in a state so pure.
What if others gainsay every word I speak,
And yet feverishly famish for it for a possession,
Their hearts are too proud — yet so silly weak
When in YOU . . . I find cordial reception;
Now, that fortune serves me a reward with thy kindness
I dedicate these lines, to YOU with overflowing sweetness.

Venus T. Norella

TEV

When the distant hills would lose their glory
And I would lose my hold on life
And all that was holy
When the sky would lose its shade of blue
And peacock feathers
Lose their brilliant hue
When the sun would burn within itself
Leaving my world cold
And me in search of self
When the birds would cease to sing their song
Leaving me blind and deaf
In the battle of right and wrong
When no one else could understand
You were always there
To hold my hand
And in the darkest nightmares of my fears
You were always there
To wipe away my tears
I love you

Joyce Ebenezer Isakov

CAN I WRITE A HAPPY ENDING?

Since the beginning of time it is the same love
stories of undying love and passion
As I write this book with so much love and passion.
With heavenly desire that will set this world
on fire, and it will be about you and me.
The hero and the heroine.
When we are together there is so much loving devotion
with the deepest passion surrounding us.
The world stops for those moments we two can share.
Can we dare to think that this love will last forever
Or is it just a moment of passing emotions?
Tonight I'll write a song for you while you're away so
many days and nights you have been away from my empty
arms.
And when this book is finished, and my song is being
sung,
How will it all end, or will this poet write without
rhyme, and the last chapter have a sad ending?
Or will I, can I write a happy ending?

Barbara Reager

WHAT IS LOVE

Love is a combination of many things,
It cannot be described it's within the heart,
To express it would be hard, it's not easy to start,
Love is someone you care for with their kindness and caring ways,
Someone who is thoughtful of you in every way,
Listens to your problems, tension and stress,
And really wants to help you when you're in distress,
With two people's welfare gathered in one,
The value of thoughtfulness is always done,
It doesn't need words to describe how you feel,
It's within the heart where it's all concealed,
Love is not always holding hands,
Or close to one's body to embrace,
It's the reaction of one to understand,
It's what's deep in the heart that really counts,
It doesn't need strong actions or words to discover,
The secret love within one another,
And when these two people have found each other,
Nothing else in this whole world seems to matter.

Margaret Freije

THE QUALITY OF LOVE

"Sex or Romance?" they ask these days,
As if the two were one;
As if Romance with prostitutes
Were having fleeting fun.

Romance need not be sexual,
Though it at times may be.
For those in love, mere holding hands
Can be Romance, sex-free.

If marriages lack real Romance,
How long will they perdure,
Since sex alone is not enough
Their future to insure?

Romance, then, is a thing of heart,
The loins' quick surge above;
The old, mysterious appeal
Of disembodied love.

We are but one of two things made:
The body and the soul.
The body-love will pass away.
Not soul's, though ages roll.

Everett Francis Briggs

HANDS ON FIRE

Many fists a clanking,
Many bells a chiming,
Coming together
In perfect TIMING . . .
Polished pieces of yellow
And silver for the person
That inner piece is untold,
But goldness will uphold
For the final bell that chimes
The role that I'll never know,
In the present goal, gold unknown.

Lori Anne Perry

MY HEART BELONGS TO ENGLAND

My heart belongs to England,
Across the shiny sea —
What would I give, to be there,
For a 'lovely cup of tea!'

Oh England, my dear England,
My lovely green 'Green Isle,' —
In dreams I often visit,
With you, just for a while!

And then, sweet memories linger;
All day I wear a smile —
Oh England, my dear England,
Come, linger for a while!

Sometimes I have a daydream;
I close my weary eyes —
I see the White Cliffs of Dover,
And seagulls soaring by.

Oh, sing your songs sweet sea gulls;
Today we celebrate —
Let's spend this day in England,
My lovely second home!

Gudrun G. Mainz-Blancaflor

POWER OF LOVE

The letters I receive
Bring you closer to me
When you are miles away.
But soon together
My heart leaps for joy!
To be in your arms,
Your lips caressing mine,
A surge of Power,
Only known to those in love.

Lisa A. Kerechanin

MY LOVE

You are the sun of my existence,
The pivot on which to revolve,
The epitome of romance,
The rock on which to build.

Without you there is only darkness,
No warmth at the end of the day,
No hope for sustaining completeness,
A vast void that tears my soul.

Virginia Braddock

LOVE'S LULLABIES

Maybe we're all
just puppies,
and love
has gone astray,
we whisper lies
like lullabies,
finding the truth
too hard to tell,
and all the time
wishing only to say,
can't you come
out and play?

Donice M. Jewell

I FEAR THY KISSES, GENTLE MAIDEN

I fear thy kisses, gentle maiden;
Thou needest not fear mine;
My spirit is too deeply laden
Ever to burden thine.

I fear they mien, thy tones, thy motion;
Thou needest not fear mine;
Innocent is the heart's devotion
With which I worship thine.

Percy Bysshe Shelley

THE LAST ROSE

The last rose of summer
Seems oh so forlorn.
The last leaf of autumn
Is often ragged and torn.

The last tear that falls
Is caused by sorrow or madness.
But the last dream that dies
Is the saddest.

Norris D. Hertzog

MY EVERYTHING

You were my every dream
You were my reality
You were my every want and need
Just a part of me
A part I can't let go

You were my ace in the hole
My lucky seven
My peaches and cream
My living dream
You were my everything.

Jewell Charles

THE SILVER TURNS TO GOLD

The many years we've spent together
Should not have to be in vain
While the good times last in memories
We both have felt the pain

I'd like to think our love has changed
From bronze to precious silver
Increasing the value of our love
And all the memories we gather

In the final years of life
The last miracle that we see
Is for the silver to turn to gold
And let the pain go free.

As the silver turns to gold
We'll be so happy dear
As the silver turns to gold
I'll always want you near

Though others may not need us
And our bodies may grow old
We'll always have each other
As the silver turns to gold.

Gordon A. Salway

UNCERTAIN LOVE

There is a girl
That I would like to know,
And would like to tell her
That I admire her so.

But she is so beautiful
And I so plain,
That if she went with me,
What would she gain?

I would love her more
Than any man could.
She would be my queen,
And I would treat her as one should.

But will it ever happen?
Is it as good as it seems?
Will she love me?
Or are they all just dreams?

There is a girl
That I will never know,
But would love to tell her
That I loved her so.

Eric Ruechel

SARA BERNHARDT.

NEW YORK. PUBLISHED BY CURRIER & IVES 115 NASSAU ST.

PLURAL

Of course I love you,
BUT
I must keep
part of myself
for myself — and for others.
I don't want to be
a single instrument
played only by you.
I want to be
at least a string quartet.
I'd really like to be a whole orchestra.
Don't you understand?
I love *everything!*

Ruth Davies

THE LORD WILL PROVIDE

The Lord will provide
Acceptance when needed,
For it is not always there.

The Lord will provide
Peace when needed,
For it is not always there.

The Lord will provide
Love when needed,
For it is not always there.

The Lord will provide
Work when needed,
For it is not always there.

The Lord will provide
Money when needed,
For it is not always there.

The Lord will provide
Joy when needed,
For it is not always there.

Estella M. McGhee-Siehoff

ON GIVING UP

Giving up?
Yes, I guess I am —
It's not that I don't give a damn,
I just can't love you anymore:
I'm just too weak, too tired, too sore.

Giving up . . .
Suppose I do?
I've waited all these years for you,
Yet you keep your heart closed up to me —
If I give up, then I'll be free.

I'm giving up!
What more can I say?
You'll never be mine, anyway;
You'll never give in, and end my schemes,
Complete my life, fulfill my dreams.

Giving up?
But how can I?
Do I still care? I cannot lie
To myself: I admit I love you still —
And, I guess, I always will.

Paul A. Hughes

CHRISTMAS

Christmas, is a time to remember and celebrate, the birth of someone who
came to show us the right way to follow.

Christmas, is a time to reflect on the true spirit of life, the spirit
within that glows with inner light.

Christmas, is a time for the people of the world to unite together,
with a bond of love and light and spreading good cheer.

Christmas, is a time to send your love to family and friends through
cards, presents, family gatherings, and happy thoughts.

Christmas, is a time of decorated trees, and decorations adorning the
outside world, to brighten and shine with the joy of life.

Christmas, is mince pies, and sleigh rides, Santa Claus, children's
laughter, happiness and joy and a feeling of good will.

Christmas, is a time to remember to hold onto this inner glow and
carry this with you throughout the coming year.

Christmas, should be celebrated every day with a feeling of love and
light, and bonding together with this love and following the light.

Elizabeth Cotton

KUSAN KU

Kusan Kusan Ku . . . I love you . . .
Feeling, beneath a bloody sunset, in the darkness of a cave,
for my forever lover, Kusan Ku.
He turns, I feel his Ki, I see his face.
Starry eyes raining, he whispers away into the darkness.

Shading my eyes from blood-needle light,
I stab at the dark, feeling for a heart no longer there.
Stepping blindly after Kusan Ku, I fall into the arms of a stranger.
His lips burn of divine poison, as a blood-stale wind thins thoughts
Of Kusan Ku to dreams of calming dragons in the sea.

The song of Kusan Ku calls gently, but the stranger tempts.
I follow. I sleep. Blood tears fall upon the rocks.
I feel Kusan Ku command, I break the stranger's hold.
Wiping the slumber from my soul, I sweep away the darkness to meet Kusan Ku.
Together we lie close to the ground, listening to the setting sun below.

Kusan Kusan Ku . . . I love you . . .
He turns, I feel his Ki, I see his face.
Starry eyes raining, he whispers away into the darkness.
Feeling, beneath a bloody sunset, in the darkness of a cave,
for my forever lover, Kusan Ku.

Peggy Doyle

MY LOVE

My love, you comfort me when I am sad. You hold my hand, when
times are bad.

When I am down, you are around, to pick me up. When I cry, you
are always nearby.

My love, I will always remember, the happy times we have had together.
The little things that you do, and the day you said you would
be true.

I will love you, until there is no tomorrow. Please do not ever
leave me, that would only bring me sorrow.

Ludema Mills Garza

THE DARK ABYSS

The dark abyss of loneliness
envelops her as in a mist,
and every point that she can see
is shaded black, or coal, or gray.

The sun has fled from out her sight,
The darkness reigns. There is no light.
The darkling, swirling strands of mist
engulf her soul in loneliness.

And every way her feet can move
is down a midnight path of gloom,
a springtime bride without a groom!

Before her stands an empty church,
with pregnant pause, awaiting news:
Where is the groom?
He might as well be on the moon!

The church bell peals both loud and long:
"Where love has gone, Where love has gone"

Dave Fonseca

COCOON

In the darkness it dreams a deep thought of what it will
be when the sunlight creeps into his room,
Where peace and tranquility it once had known, now force
to leave and begin its travels soon.

Will I be beautiful, will I be free to roam from mountain
to sea; will I be able to show my wings and make nature
smile? Will I be proud; Will I love to show my colors,
many as the rainbow? Will I fly fast, or will I fly slow
and enjoy the world of God as I go?

Gee I hope my body is long and ringed; I hope for colors
to match my wings, feel the warm air and listen to the
birds sing, brooks, meadows, the running streams, a world
of beauty that nature brings, oh I can imagine; I can
dream; for the world of God brings forth good things.

(Boom, Boom), was that thunder, thunder? No it's here at
last; the light's coming in; time to dry my wings, I have
done my fast.
(Who, ray), (Who, ray), born to a new day.

M. H. Kingston

THE MEETING

How strange we should meet in a crowded room
After all these years.
Our eyes met and held for that long moment.
We started slowly across the room,
But in my heart I wanted to run.
When our hands touched we both knew
The spark, after all these years had burst into a flame
Again, as though it were only yesterday.
The old feeling and passions of yesteryear
Came flooding back like a huge tidal wave.
This time we will be strong enough to walk away or —
Will you feel, as I still do after all these years, cheated.
The love we felt for each other, we had to turn our backs on
So as not to hurt others.
Time is going by fast now and we are not so young anymore.
You will have to be the stronger,
For I know I will never be able to turn and leave you again.

Fern Martin

LOVE IS A WARM PUPPY

That, and more.
Love is a trip to the grocery store.
A proverb's 'soft answer' that turns away wrath,
Love is a robust belly laugh.

Love does not judge, nor criticize.
Love is what shines in your love-lighted eyes.
Love is the tone of your truth-speaking voice,
Love is the joy with which to rejoice.

Love is living, forgiving, and sharing,
Love is a great and tremendous caring.
Love is a "many splendored thing,"
Love is the song the world wants to sing.

Aimee McKinnon

FOR DONNA

I have stood on the brink of ecstasy,
And I have fallen so deep
That I could never turn
And live my life alone.

It is her touch that sends me quivering,
Her smile that causes my heart
To carry hopes of forever.

But poems and talk do not prove my honor.
Gifts and surprises carry no promise.

Love awaits in all things.
It neither hastens nor resists its own delivery.

O lady cushion me.
Soft.
Unfold endless words of amorous dreams.
So that the pleasures of Heaven,
And the toils of the Earth,
Reside hand in hand,
Heart to heart.

Robert L. Waltz

TWENTY-SEVEN YEARS IN A CARDBOARD BOX

The house on Second Street stands vacant, neglected.
A giant, empty conch shell caught on a debris-strewn beach
Waiting for some hapless, hermit crab seeking the mundane —
Shelter.

"These things happen," he said. "Things change."

The rooms in the house on Second Street are bleak and bare,
Ancient cliff dwellings with nothing left but
Brighter spots on the faded walls
Emphasizing the absence of love and life.

"You'll adjust," he said. "Give it time."

Time in the house on Second Street is wrapped
In month-old newspapers and packed in cardboard boxes
Waiting expectantly in a storage unit on South Drew.
For what? Can I ever unpack all those memories?

"Of course, you can," he said. "Wait a while, You'll see."

So I'll wait. What else can I do?

Madeline Cooper

OUT BEYOND THE STARS

He came to me, my love,
On a dreamy spring night,
Stars softly aglow in misty canopy above.
We kissed in the shimmering starlight,
And walked hand in hand in the sweet spring haze.
"What do you think is beyond those stars?" he would say.
"I wish I could fly up there and see."
I nestled close in his arms,
Content with my feet on earthly clay.
He did fly up there in that starry expanse,
Never to return,
From out beyond the stars where he longed to be.
Someday I know I will meet him there, my love,
Forever together free, forever free,
Out beyond the stars.

Doris Hinkleman

A CIRCLE OF LOVE

Born and raised in a circle of love,
Destined by those whose presence would so mean
Sharing a love halo envied above,
Providing an ever-circling love scheme.
Nurtured, not coddled, in this love domain,
Tutored to seek out kindred hearts to seal,
Similar role mates to conceive, retain,
This ever-returning, eternal wheel.

Now this circular path is more intent
As small, young arms wrap us in close embrace,
We reap results of a carousel, bent
Upon home life woven in loving place.
The widening circle in new waves revolved
Coming full circle to new ways resolved.

William Lex Coplen

KNOW YOURSELF

To love your life,
You must love yourself,
And shake the dust off your memory shelf
Remember the fun things that dwelt in the past,
The people you met, the loves and the laughs?
Remember your youth, what were you like?
Did you love people, or did you just fight?
How are you now, now that you're older?
Are you a meek one or are you much bolder?

You can make life easy by being yourself,
Don't make life a trial,
Meet life with a smile,
And then before you know it,
Your life is worthwhile.

Joan M. Lacey

SHADOWS

Two shadows there on a bare wall
clinging like ivy they dare not fall.
My lover's portrait speaks, a single word,
though loud only I could have heard.

Combining thus the sound and vision of her face
entwines me forever in her swirling grace.
Our shadows there on a bare wall
clinging like ivy they dare not fall.

Ronald W. King

LIFETIME SWEETHEART

Do you remember in days of yore,
We in our teens and oh so poor.
Down life's pathway we strolled together,
Yes, we were held by cupid's tether.

There you were in a pink sunbonnet,
And within my heart a soulful sonnet.
Side by side and hand in hand,
We uttered sweet nothings, oh wasn't it grand?

I can see you now, the blush on your cheek,
When I gave you my first little loving peek.
Then I carved our initials with trembling hand
On the old elm tree, by heart's command.

When I placed lilac blossoms in your hair,
As we laughed away the summer there.
'Twas the first you knew, oh love of mine,
That I cherished you for my valentine.

I loved you then and for always dear,
It grew and grew from year to year.
How true these words, oh wife of mine,
For you'll always be my valentine.

W. E. Norton

TO MARILYN MY FRIEND

A kiss in the park,
Made me happy as a lark.
I look in those beautiful eyes
And my problem — away flies
The love I want to give
You may never find.
But I loved you over and over,
In my mind.
— So Marilyn —
You mean more to me than words can ever say
'Cause pretty lady you make my day.

Larry Grogan

A JOYFUL SPRING SONG

I think I heard a snowbell ring,
"It will be spring, it will be spring!"
A happy, busy robin spread his wings,
"Let's dance and sing, today is spring!"

All winter blues have gone away.
Today is such a happy, joyful day!
The bluebird hums a song for you,
"How are you, friend, how do you do?"

God gave us sunshine and the Easter Bell,
The ocean shore and every shell!
It's spring and all the blossoms swell.
God's creation is done so very well!

In His beautiful Garden, I love to dwell,
Where I may drink from His Fountain Well!
My soul and spirit are refreshed anew,
Like a flower in the morning dew!

In every garden lingers the Breath of God.
I see His Eye in a precious, little forget-me-not.
I hear His sweet Voice in a blooming apple tree.
God created all things so beautiful and free!

Gudrun G. Mainz-Blancaflor

CLEAVING AND CLINGING

We cleave to a new mate
knowing he'll give it all.
But clinging to our old self
we hear sputterings and failures.
Why clutch at the promises
another will bring to bear,
as if sensing despair, we cry
and the buffeted mind tells us
cleaving and clinging are parts
of the same emotion.
Holding life so taut
means sundering the bonds,
because we can't know another
without losing something of ourself.
Cleaving to the other
is an endless sililoquy
that touches our hidden voices.
Far removed from icy aloneness
we gently push the lips apart
and smile's radiance bathes your otherness.

Martin W. Levy

IN LOVING YOU

I promised my heart
not to mother a distant love,
Even beautiful, made in heaven, love
requires nurturing, mine, a daily hunger
And I am starving . . .

But in loving you I have
seen the whispers of a rare birth,
A glimmer of passioned time.

No longer any question, any reason,
or lingering illusion if you ever
will be mine.

Forever two — and yet our souls have kissed
gently embellishing our emotions,
In loving you I've glimpsed
the God others have missed.
Tasting the wealth of prayer . . .

Judy G. McCormack

THE UNVEILING

You've uncovered feelings
I don't think I've had before.
It seems you hold the key
To my secret, sheltered door.

These stirrings, new inside of me,
Are sweet and so profound.
All the years they've lived with me
I've never heard their sound.

Other loves I've known,
Before you came, it's true;
None of them gave peace
The way you seem to do.

I know not what tomorrow brings,
I only hope to see you there;
Since you're the one, who's taught my heart
To love, to give and share.

Terry Eunice

JANETTA

Janetta, Janetta, what is Janetta?
Why, it's only a name!
A name that sets my heart aflame.
Janetta, Janetta whispered like a warm breeze.
It comes so softly through the trees,
Awakening the fire of my desire.
Janetta, Janetta, a vision in the night,
Filling my soul with delight.
Janetta, Janetta, like morning coffee,
Awakening and stimulating me.
Janetta, Janetta, like a rare perfume,
An essence of love filling every room
Janetta! Janetta! shouted to the stars above.
Janetta, Janetta is the woman I love.

Leon E. Stephens

CREATIONS

Listen can you hear the crickets
As they make their love calls to each other
Can you hear the wind rustle the leaves in the trees
Can you see the ripples in the water
Dear dear God
Let me always see the beauty that you gave the earth
Let me see life as new beginnings and not as its end
Let me feel free to move
With my heart my soul and my writings
Let me write as I feel and
Give as need be my love
For in this little way I too can show
My love for your creations
And my love for you.

Grandpa

MOONBEAMS

I dream of you in nights softly stirring,
airily moving my thoughts.
My love for you is deeper than the darkness,
that surrounds my lofty room.
Oh where have you gone my love?
Now that I am immersed in you.
Ride with me here on the wisps of our dreams.
Feed our love in the moonbeams of the night.

Kathleen Ann Fogarty

LOVING REMEMBRANCES

A quiet lecture, when my temper I'd lose,
Tender kisses you gave, to soothe a bruise,
A gentle touch and a loving embrace,
Encouragement, when problems I needed to face.

Teaching me to love and how to share,
Giving me a faith to build on, and to care,
Instilling in me desire to better my way
And to improve myself, each and every day.

Patiently listening to my woes,
Telling me how to forgive my foes,
Teaching me tolerance of another,
Are my loving remembrances of you, dear Mother.

Lorene Shoptaw Mydlach

THE JUSTIFICATION OF HER DEATH

The justification of her death is now a matter of record.
We were together only three months.
She knew that love couldn't survive but she loved me.
I needed love to survive and I loved her.
Things were said, things were done, that shouldn't have been.
Tolerance is a virtue but must not be self-destructive.
We are parted because of my words spoken prematurely.
Now I must assume she is dead to erase her from my memory.
But the justification of her death, is the justification of mine.

John S. Marcum

THE WARRIOR'S FAREWELL

My love,
I find that I must leave you now,
So let us borrow for the empty days apart,
All the lovely moments that we've spent.
When we first walked through arboretum, sunlight-steeped,
Carrying the worn and friendly books,
That brought the first proud touch of wisdom to our thoughts.
Or there within the sweep of Manteo's golden strand,
Where we first kissed and made the space
Of all the universe, a tent for our desire.

I find that I must leave you now,
And, oh, my dear! should I be lost,
These moments with you now
Will fill the rest of time.

Charles Atkin

DEVOTION

I watched a little black cat
As he stepped gingerly out of doors,
Sniffing the air and treading ever so softly.
Hesitant, yet eager to explore the world before him.
In that instant love was born.
As he gazed up into my face.

Much, much later when he was thrust into the cold outside world,
I gathered him up and brought him inside.
He followed me around this little black cat.
Watching eagerly for me to come home,
Waiting at the door to be petted.
His devotion to me knew no bounds.
And I in return gave him all my love.
For the strings of love had become forever entwined.

A. Jane Adams

LOVE

Love can sneak up on you when you are not looking,
Maybe it's her cooking,
Or, maybe it's a friendship
Similar, but better than kinship.
Or, maybe communication is perfect,
You both can talk about anything, with, or without respect.
Or, maybe it is a chance meeting,
A bolt from the blue, or like a lightning flash, affecting
You both, so that neither of you can eat,
Sleep, or do anything neat,
Without thinking of the other. Being together
Results in offspring, father helping and revering the mother,
So, you can see,
Whatever it is, or whatever it may be,
Love is a wonderful feeling, it can last forever.

George W. Andresen

WORDS

Words on the wind, that's all they are. Words heavy with
emptiness — knowing always that they are only toys with which
we play. Words that can change our lives, but not our
destinies — which were planned by the gods and not to be
manipulated by mere mortals. What happiness, love and
bitterness they can bring — formed by a loved one, but then
words are only necessary once that love has gone.

Mary Annah Alemán

ALEMAN, MARY ANNAH. Pen Names: Maya, Marie Angelique, Mary Annah O'Hoey de Alemán, Moira Siobán; Born: San Antonio, Texas, 3-6-36; Married: 12-28-57 to Dr. Pedro Alemán; Divorced: 12-29-82; Education: University of Texas at Austin, 1954-56; Incarnate Word College, Summer, 1955; Universidad Ibero-Americano, 1956-57; Universidad Internacional de Mexico, 1983-84; working towards a M.S. in Clinical Psychology; Occupations: Writer and Painter; Memberships: Quill & Scroll, Junior League of Mexico City, Theatre Workshop, Pro-Ciegos, Mexico City and San Antonio, Texas Panhellenic Association, The American Society of Mexico, The American Federation of Astrologers, The American Benevolent Society in Mexico; Awards: Recital of poetry by Mary Annah Poesi Metafisica y Mistica, invited and sponsored by the National Institute of Fine Arts of Mexico, The Cultural Department of the Secretary of Public Education of Mexico and the government of the state of Oaxaca, at the Casa de la Cultura Oaxaqueña, Salón Dainzú, Oaxaca, Mexico, 2-15-84; Poetry contributor for the International University of Mexico; Poetry: In *American Poetry Anthology, Vol III,* 1984; *American Poetry Anthology, Vol IV,* 1985; *American Poetry Showcase,* 1985; *The Art of Poetry ; Contemporary Verse,* 1985; *New Voices in American Poetry,* 1985; Themes: *Life, love, death, metaphysical and mystical concepts;* Comments: *I write to convey my inner life and peace with others, and to communicate with all who are sensitive to the universe that each of us influences and shares.*

BUTTERFLY DREAMS

If you must
Go your own way
I won't make you stay.
My dreams
Like butterflies;
Too hard to reach
So I let them fly,
With your good-bye
One
More
Butterfly
Takes to the sky . . .

Roxanne McJunkin

AWAKENING

So long I'd slept! But, when I rose
to greet your face
I felt your eyes beclothe me in a
fond embrace.
I knew the joy that washes sorrow
from the soul;
The touch that drinks of understanding
and the whole
Depth of Life became my lesson and
my book
as I of your sweet earnestness and
love partook.

Arlone Mills Dreher

THE SWEETEST FLIGHT

A woman singing is
the sun adance in shade
A woman dancing is
a shadow which has prayed
A woman praying is
a candle whispered low
A woman whisp'ring is
her voice in loving glow
A glowing woman is
a woman who has known
a knowing lover in
the sweetest flight e'er flown

Burr McCloskey

SILENT SERENADE

I came to charm the Lady,
to touch her, soft and slow,
and often in such fantasy
I'd watch those dark eyes glow,
and in that secret second know
her heart never evades me;
her silent soul, serenades me.

I came to whisper in her ear
love's giving word;
my cheerful tear,
her harmony heard.

Clifford M. Bannister

PARADISO

Oh softly, softly walk along
The path that leads to where
So many, many times we've kept
Our tryst as sweethearts there.
Oh lightly, lightly skip along
The path that rises higher
To see a far-off sunlit mount
Deceptively on fire.
Oh swiftly, swiftly rolls a stone
Onto our path, death guides it bold
To hurl us into the canyon's depths,
To die, arms entwined, our kisses cold.
Oh faintly, faintly we can see
We are spirits, side by side,
Rising through the heavenly mists,
To rest 'mid a white-robed tide,
A flowing, glowing to a throne
To be blest with Celestial Eyes,
That will forever, ever let us view
The glories of Paradise.

George William Boehmer

JUNE MEMORY

When June is lavish with the rose
She stirs an embering memory,
Intensified as each unfolding bud
Fulfills its fragrant destiny.

In memory again I feel
The warm touch of your flesh —
Your breath, as sweet as fresh south wind,
Upon my cheek in your caress.

I close my eyes and see your hand,
So capable and strong —
On it the golden ruby ring,
The treasured gift you wore so long.

In many things you're here with me,
And still gallant, my own true knight,
The champion of my happiness.
Stay close, my love, in memory's sight!

Rene Knight

LOVE'S RECITAL

Dedicated to Gustavo Romero, San Diego's pride and joy, A 19-year-old concert pianist.

Dim the lights!
Soften the music!
Arms enfold
Private rhapsody.

Gustavo! Gustavo!
Juilliard's pride,
Youth's genius Praestus
Andante con moto larghetto,
Adagio ma non troppo,
Allegro assai.

How many arpeggios
Shall we play?
Appassionata crescendo,
Finale
Bravo! Bravo!

Geraldine Violette

STOLEN LOVE

Stolen love, a broken heart
His life seems to fall apart
Memories bring sorrow and tears
Unwanted and loneliness, he fears

Out the window below he sees others
Children playing and lovers together
Behind closed doors alone, he cries
And wonders why, with tearful eyes

Stolen love, a broken heart
Burning pain deep in his heart
He feels lost and life so unfair
Spirits very low, he doesn't care

In a room, he closes the door
Writes a note saying, no more, no more
To what was once a love for her and life
As blood stains the silver bladed knife

Joseph Boteilho, Jr.

BOTEILHO, JOSEPH SOUZA JR. Pen Name: J.B.; Born: Lahaina, Maui, Hawaii, 2-8-52; Education: Kapiolani Community College, A.S., Hotel Operations, 1983; Certificate of Achievement in Culinary Arts, 1983; Occupation: Cook; Awards: Golden Poet Award for 1985 from World of Poetry; Poetry: 'Counting on Jesus,' World of Poetry, 1985; 'Nature's Magic,' American Poetry Association, 1986; Comments: *I am thankful for the outlet, to share my love for poetry with others. American Poetry Association, I thank you.*

OUR LOVE

Our love grew over the years.
Longing to be not forgotten.
You . . . me . . . love for all eternity,
now . . . our love . . . over.
No love, no marriage, no nothing.
Death the cause,
for you have passed on,
now I will, too.

Brian Wimberly

REMEMBERING

When things go wrong,
I remember.
When there's a song,
I remember.
When nights are long,
I remember.

When skies are gray,
I remember.
Though you're away,
I remember.
All through the day,
I remember.

When hours are dark,
I remember.
When love is stark,
I remember.
When there's no spark,
I remember.

When days are cold,
I remember.
With you to hold,
I remember.

Priscilla Culverwell

IF YOU LEAVE

I've hoped for years that my need
for one true friend
Could be fulfilled in you.
I've known in our friendship a sharing —
Emotional empathy (and through
exchange of beliefs and knowledge,
Involvement in similar interests)
spiritual communion,
Mental inspiration and
physical dependence.
How could I feel closer
to any other friend?

I love you
but fear to express my love —
I need, first, to feel
that you'll always be my friend.
I hide my faults, aware
that I may lose your love
Unless you know and accept
the person I really am.
I open myself to you
hesitantly, knowing
The more you accept of me,
the more it will hurt if you leave.

C. A. Bonard

To Bette, my Love

Your smile;
Worth more than all the flowers
Ever grown
Your kiss:
Worth more than all the sunsets
Ever known
Each day together:
Worth more than an eternity
Alone.

C. James Matuschka

SUMMER IN ALL SEASONS

Velvet nights
soft thoughts
hard kisses
covering me with comfort
a hazy cloud of thunder
and lightning.

Velvet nights
scented evenings
warm thoughts
smooth sheets
sleep and reawakenings.

The reality of breakfast.

Cathy Garson

BATHROOM SINK

I remember the good coldness
of the bathroom sink.
Wondering when I would be
able to see over its rim.
Ascending the heights to
Catch a glimpse of me.

Wiping the shaving cream
carefully over my face.
Exactly mimicking that tall person,
only to wipe it away with a
cardboard razor.
In a hurry to be just like
him.

Cathy Garson

TO MY LOVE

To my love
This wish is sent
To let you know
The roses died,
The candy melted,
The kids dusted
With the fancy nightie,
So much for Valentine's Day,
But I love you just the same!

Margaret Rowen

A LOVERS' LAMENT

The birds are singing songs of love
The sky is azure blue.
And as I long to have you near
My thoughts are all of you.

Your touch is always tender
Your smile lights up my heart.
I spend each moment missing you
Whenever we're apart.

I just can't wait to hold you
To gaze into your eyes.
I hope that there will come a day
When you'll never say good-bye.

Donna S. Hamilton

FINAL ROLE

A broken heart
Like shattered glass,
Its shock waves
Tense the air,

And a thousand memories
Crystallize
As the fragments
Scatter there;

A glistening
Recollection
While its sharpness
Pricks the soul,

As each tiny piece
That's swept away
Plays out
Its final role.

Pat Bush

PAST

In February of every year.
The stark cold days bring me near.
That afternoon 30 years ago.
A narrow twisted road of snow.
The '49 Ford was white and blue.
My sister was 20, her life was new.
It had been 30 minutes, since our fight.
Last words of anger, out of sight.
She died on impact, was what they said.
Her dress-up coat of black was red.
I never got the chance to say.
Here's your niece and nephews, stay
How's your kids and husband too.
Come for dinner, we can do.
Things together, fun and sad.
Like the old days, young and glad.
Now I'm old, my kids are grown.
Her voice and face to them not known.
The tears come quicker, now, with age.
Lost time memories in a rage.

Janet Robison-Marin

RIPOSTE

Crossed were the blades of the spirit
In mad conflict fiercely engaged.
Two hearts were pledged to another
Not possessed to be giv'n away.

Was no time for preparation,
With no warning the match declared.
One sudden lunge, the move was made
Keen eye quick reflex; the parry.

In lack of judgment, misunderstood
Was forfeit of sweet victory;
As saber I laid calm aside
Thrusting blade fell deep in the soul.

How long a soul can bleed! Oh God!
How long until the pain retreat?
Truly the thrill of victory
Or the true agony of defeat?

L. Ann Beard

SILENT LOVE

I cannot stop the tremors
That shake my very being
Nor close my eyes whene'er we meet
Lest magnetic force be seen

I cannot drown the sorrows
That dredge my hopeless soul
And pledge loneliness upon me
While I play the martyr role

I cannot hide the jealousy
Rare moments when we're alone
Seems all his needs hold higher rank
Than lost feelings of my own

I cannot live forever
In this downpouring rain
His body is crippled, not his mind
He could understand our pain

I cannot cease the loving
That dwells within my heart
Curse all these years of silent love
I cannot master the art

Marvel Blunt

I NEVER . . .

I never knew the warmth
Of a loving hand,
Nor did I ever feel
The kiss of a young man.

I never wished for a caress
Nor did I ever drop a tear,
Until I one day realized
No longer were you here.

I never missed your sudden laugh
Nor did I ever want to cry,
I never did feel so alone
Until you said good-bye.

I never felt so afraid
Until I knew you were not there,
No longer could I smile,
No longer did I care.

I never knew the searing pain
Of a sudden loved one's part,
For I never ever knew
There was love within my heart.

Melissa Camacho

REMEMBRANCE

A slow forming smile
With a shade of remembrance
Like a room
With a solitary candle lit
Missing half an instance
Shy a trace
Of its once brilliance
A clouded memory
Fleeting too soon
And yet a love never ending

Donna L. Hill

WHAT IS LOVE?
(or LOVE IS —)

What is Love?
It comes from far above,
Beyond the sphere,
From where our eyes dare peer.
Love's all around
And you are surely bound
To capture
The holy state of rapture;
Which is brought,
Not from being bought,
But given
Freely from our God in Heaven.

Phyllis Bolen-Hofer

EVEN LOVE YOU MORE

I love you and I want you,
You know that it is true;
That I love you, darling,
And I've always wanted you.

I loved you when I met you,
When I gazed into your eyes;
I read all your cards and letters,
And answered a sweet reply.

I love you just as much, dear,
As anytime before;
But, even if it's possible,
I'll even love you more.

Hazel Mae Parron

THE DAY OF THE ROUNDTREE

Imagine it was D-day,
Just like the cactus.
Where would the roundtree
be.
"Right in your face."

Is it an optical illusion?
Or can we see it,
Feel it; or touch it?
A doctor said, "Lick-a-
round-tree." Could it
be me? Can you see?
The difference in three.

Charles S. Walker

UNSELFISHLY

Early morning has crept upon us
lightly misted & gray,
as we rise to unfold
another cherishing day.
I'm glad I have you near me
if not in sight, then in mind,
this is how you're always close
and never left behind.
For when I make expression
yours moves within the self of me,
you've captured my heart
like a picture —
that I gladly give you unselfishly.

Patricia Maher

PRECIOUS MOMENT

This moment I selfishly call ours,
Was simply never meant to be.
I lost sight of perspective,
For you and I will never be.

I remember the moment we first met,
Something fresh, something new.
I wanted you, if only as a friend.
This message, how should I send?

You were full of kindness,
So very hard to find.
You sat and talked to me.
And unlike many others, did not let me be.

A precious moment,
Forever I will hold dear.
And when I sleep at night,
In my dreams I hold you near.

William Steven Stassen

A MESSAGE TO MY MOTHER

When I was just a little tot
You gave me love and care
Would listen to me patiently
My childhood troubles share

You'd listen as I said my prayers
And hold me on your knee
Then gently tuck me in each night
And kiss me tenderly

There's nothing like a mother's love
And now that I am grown
I know how very much it means
Having children of my own

No words could ever quite express
How dear you are to me
And I thank God with all my heart
For the mother He gave me.

Lois M. Ryan

deceptive babe

Love bade me rise
but i was wise
and flung my head
and so it fled.

I sobered soon
and chased it noon
and eventime.
Mine was a crime.

And then wet roads
and stranger modes
i wayfared, far
too close the bar.

Love languished on
one endless dawn
and so i spied
somehow it died.

D. Castleman

FOR GOD SO LOVED THE WORLD

For God so loved the world
He gave His only Son,
Henceforth for you and me
Our life has just begun.

Temptation faces all of us
Each day as we arise,
Yet those who do believeth
May have everlasting lives.

We learn to love our neighbor
Symbolic of our time,
A helping hand in time of need
Both friend and foe combine.

Jesus is the Lord of God
Who takes away our sin,
Just open up that lonely heart
And He will enter in.

God created all the world
For us to live and die,
And it isn't up to you or me
To question when or why.

A. Lorene Wayne

DELORES

She wore the sunlight in her hair
and as a child with new found eyes
who happens on a rapturous scene
the only thing I thought to do
was stop and drink her beauty, there!

Clothed in the radiance of her youth
she put the lilies, there, in bloom
to shame by the color of her eyes
bluer than still crystal streams
bluer than the deepest blue.

So then it was, when first I met
the girl I'd spend a lifetime with
no wish, for worldly riches, here
just give to me one youthful hour
and take success and paltry fame
give them to those who seek them, yet!

For I've known life's most treasured hour
when young love stills a trembling heart
and all the heavens join in song
as lovers live from bud to bloom
protected in their ivory tower!

Phillip A. Meissner

FROM TRACY TO JENNY

1984

It seems the summer soon will end
With memories of my special friend.
We soon will be quite far apart
With tender love within our heart.
Please send a letter to me soon
And write about your favorite tune.
Or simply say that you are well,
And other things that you can tell.
Let thoughts remain of someone sweet
With hugs and kisses as we meet.

Rich Gelatt

CHEROKEE ROSE

There's a rose that grows on a strip of sand
Where tears of grief dropped on the land
Where great Americans lost their lives
Here brave warriors fought and died

Through the hills of Tennessee to the cotton woods of Alabam'
These brave people took their stand and slowly died in Dixieland
Downtrod and cold through Mississippi into Oklahoma we are told
These brave people tried to take their stands for their birthright
for their homeland

As the legend goes on the Trail of Tears these roses grow
Have you ever seen a sandstone rose?
On the Trail of Tears these roses grow
Each tear that fell was like a drop of blood
These roses are proof of that great love

Betty J. Coursey

COURSEY, BETTY J. Born: Nashville, Tennessee, 3-14-32; Married: 10-6-50 to Mayland L. Coursey; Education: Howard High School, creative writing courses; Occupations: Housewife, Mother of five sons & one daughter, Grandmother of five grandchildren, Poet, Writer; Memberships: Under contract with Eaton Literary Agency; Grace Baptist Church; Den Mother for the Boy Scouts of America, for five years, Pack 125; Holloman AFB, New Mexico, LaVerne, Tennessee, Panama Canal Zone; Taught Vacation Bible School at Jiles Creek Baptist Church; Awards: Golden Poet Awards for 'Touch Not the Depths of My Spirit,' 1986 and 'The Poet,' 1985; Award of Merit Certificates for 'The Poet,' 1985; 'Rejection,' 1985; 'Mom You Gave Me Life,' 1986; Poetry: 'Rejection,' *Moments, Moods & Memories,* 1984; 'The Poet,' *In Quiet Places,* 1985; 'Vision of Jesus,' *Impressions,* 1986; 'Cross,' *Hearts on Fire,* 1986; 'Cherokee Rose,' *Hearts on Fire,* 1986; Comments: *I was inspired to write from a true personal experience with our Lord, Jesus Christ, and from this experience, 'Vision of Jesus' was written, and is now being published in* Impressions, *by Quill Books.*

PAT & IKE

Night and day I search for words,
I search for sleep, it can't be found;
How can words of wisdom be penned, when
A head is vacant of thought.
How wise must we be to understand our loss?
Death snatched our brother Ike, and sister
Patty, oh, how we love, now our hearts are
Aching sore.
There is just one thing I understand clear,
I must ask all this of God above;
Two untimely deaths we mourn.
Young brother, and baby sister,
What can we say? They're here no more,
With hearts that are aching sore,
Gone forever from our sight.
Lord God, help us through the nights,
Their laughs, their faces, we will see no
More.
Oh Lord, our hearts are aching sore.
Lord, their spirit, now with you,
And you are everywhere, could it be
Their spirit's here?

Polly Wiggins Crum

JUST PASSING THROUGH

Among the foolish things I do
I find myself just passing through
The little southern town where first we met.
As memories come into view
I know that I still look for you
And for the love that I still can't forget.
The shady street still looks the same —
The one we called our lover's lane.
For there we strolled together, hand in hand
But then my hopes began to fade
As you forgot the plans we made
To love another and to wear his wedding band.
Just passing through — why did I ever come this way —
Because I knew that I would surely feel this way.
That same old flame is just rekindled all anew
And burns within, although I'm only passing through.
I see your house now drawing near
My heart is pounding in my ear
I long to tell you once again that I love you
But you must never know I've been
And I must never come again
Goodbye, my love, I'm only passing through.

W. Ray Caldwell

THE BEST OF FRIENDS

(Dedicated to each of my closest friends)

My friend, I thank you for the smiles
We've added to each other's days;
For walking with me down life's path
And sharing laughs along the way.

Always, we will have each other
To cure the blues when skies are gray;
Together we'll pursue our dreams
While cherishing our yesterdays.

I value ev'rything we've shared:
Our thoughts, our hopes, our secrets, too —
I'm very fortunate to have
A faithful, true-blue friend like you!

Lori Kay O'Dor

THE GREATEST FORCE

I believe the greatest force in all the world is love.
No words can describe it on earth or heaven above.
If I truly love you, my deepest concern will be for you
In your spiritual growth, and all you may say and do.

I would not want you to wholly depend on me —
Or I on you, for that would stunt our growth, you see.
We'll enjoy an affection glorious in all its beauty —
Soul inspiring and exquisite in unsolicited continuity.

I would not bind your spirit with cords of steel
To keep you near me like a fisherman does his reel,
But with gossamer wings that flying free —
Could travel where it wills, and lo! —
It still comes back to me!

Rosanna M. Honeck

GOD'S LOVE

As I live in the joy of the moment each day,
I am filled as a child of God in a wonderful way.
I see him in the snowflakes descending from above,
The sun shining on us is really His love.
The puffy clouds hurriedly crossing the sky,
Are showing me His love with a watchful eye.
The stars and the moon looking down on us,
Are just another way of showing His love.
For a day filled with beauty is the essence of God's love.

Sister Miriam P. Donnelly, OSF

WITH THE NUMBERLESS DAYS BETWEEN US

With the numberless days between us,
your voice still sounds within me, unasked.
As night lies upon the earth
your image caresses me:
a secret touch.
And I succumb
to a scent still vital,
a face pressing toward me,
a mouth bruised by kisses . . .

I wake in another's arms,
to another's voice,
as the echo of your voice
and my breath
become one.

George Cordeiro

A DILEMMA BETWEEN FORGETTING AND REMEMBERING

How unfortunate can one be, to lose one's loved one? To know they're not with you anymore. Can there be a feeling worse than the silent suffering of the heart?

Bursting into tears at the sight of the everlasting image in one of their pictures, along with the thoughts that flash back when you see one of their previous possessions which you now hold as sacred as your heart. What can be more frightening than to wake up the next morning calling their name, and hearing it bounce back in echoes of infinite silence, in an air of taunt whispers directed to where they originated from.

Guadalupe Elenes

GOD MADE YOU AND ME

God made the heaven He made the sun He made the sky
He gave us stars to twinkle and shine
He made your body and also mine
He made the earth the deep blue sea
The rivers the mountains the flowers the animals
The ants and even the butterfly
We are a product of God's creation
Yes God made you and me

Our bodies He molded with His sacred hands
Not out of dust not out of shrubs not out of clay not out of sand
We are a product of His creation
God made a human being of flesh and blood
A human being with feelings a human being who cares
A human being who hurts a human being who thinks
A human being who enjoys love laughter susceptible to joys and pains
He shaped us with His sacred hands
Yes yes yes God made you and me

Hyacinth Williams Moncrieffe

SOUL MATE

Time is endless as you know . . . days, months, years may go . . . the sun may set, stars shall shine . . . lonely hearts sadly pine for days gone by, sweet but few . . . fun and laughter for me and you . . . we stood among the trees still there . . . breathed the perfumed mountain air. Oh how my heart yearns to be once more with my soul mate I adore.

Your heart must long for days gone by . . . the simple sweetness you and I . . . days of laughter . . . nights of bliss . . . deeply now these I miss.

I stand beside you as I've always done . . . souls intermingled as if one . . . although I'm not in form to see . . . you'll feel the presence and know it's me.

We loved and lived in a life before . . . died and met and loved once more . . . those days are gone for you and I, to meet again . . . then we must die.

Carolyn Long

CLOSED DOORS

The moving van left the driveway, the family left in the cars.
Both were stuffed with the living in a house for twenty years.
The last box is packed with memories and sealed with a sigh.
Through the empty house I wander, lingering in each room while I
Hear sweet laughter, and low scoldings in the echoing rooms,
Remembering the joy, lessons, warm love, and birthday tunes.
I stretch my arms to hug my old bedroom and feel young love felt here.
In bedroom two, I recall a boy's rebellious moods and childhood fears.
In bedroom three I picture two girls, grown to distinct equality.
From room to room I wander, my heart refusing to let go, but I see:
The past, now past, is past, as changing life is changed.
These rooms had life, gave love, protected us, yet have remained.
The taunting, teasing whispers behind the now closed doors
Make me tremble as I smooth with love, the woodwork and the floors.
Each door is closed, as each memory is recognized and fades,
Silent weeping finally soothes my sorrow and heartache.
I close the front door and walk away, leaving behind the past,
Ready to face the promising future, at last.

Dottie Augsburg

SOMEDAY MY PRINCE

Someday my prince
Will come
He will have
A fragile heart
and a remarkable soul

A kiss from my desire
Has an honored touch
It would be to my life
More marvelous over birth

He has gallant eyes
And he glides
On his way
Within
A veil of glamour

I wait for him
I know he will
Come for me

Someday my prince
Will stroke my cheek
With his loving glance

Jerry Lee Murrell

beneath the heavens of my heart
I could adore the flowers of your soul
like death
forever

it is for me
it is for you
for us that I die
that I am necessary and alone

I flower
in you

J. V. Ruvolo

ROBERTA MY LOVE

Your beauty impairs me
Makes my heart feel such love
I know you're a blessing
From God up above

How could I have gotten you
With deeds such as mine
I've spent my life sinful
And just like a swine

Yet the Lord blessed me with you
For He knows what I need
I now have a reason
To try and succeed

He's taught me a lesson
That He wants me to live
And even a swine
He shall forgive

He gave me your heart
Wrapped in ribbons of gold
And your beautiful eyes
Just for me to behold

Steven L. Gifford

LOST LOVE

Take a look at me now, and see how I'm hurting.
Look at what you have done to me.
You used me and left me for another,
And now I'm just a street casualty.

Take a look at me now because I'm drinking.
The alcohol seems to numb my pain.
For I loved you so much, and I lost you,
And I will never be the same again.

My friends say "straighten up and forget him."
They say "take a look at you now."
But I love him and I can't live without him
And I'm getting by the best way I know how.

Mrs. Earl V. Bundy

FAMILY TALES III (PHOTOS)

My father couldn't take a photograph
To save his life: he held the camera wrong,
Blacked us all out in sunlight much too strong,
Or caught our mouths distorted in a laugh.
Indoors he took fine studies of the wall
Or ceiling, with three foreheads down below,
Lined us up stiffly in a cockeyed row,
Bleached by a sea of windows in the hall.
A monumental talent, this, to blur
And tilt our paper memories: "M.E. takes
One look at Dad and can't help laughing." Why
Do we remember him to look on her,
Recall the vanished grin her grin awakes,
Recall the one who flicked the shutter's eye?

Gay Baines

I didn't think I was worth loving before you came along,
You made me feel happy and as if I belong.
I never shed a smile until I saw your face,
I was locked up inside my own secluded space.
You gave life new meaning to me,
If you get tired, I'll set you free.
But the happiness I feel now is alive and real,
I hope that someday you too will tell me how you feel.
You are so special and deserve the best,
How can I compare to all the rest?

Dawn Molnar

THE NATIVITY

And as the Nativity gleams brightly in the offing
A gliff of fifty years ushers in to recall,
Sweet tidings that seem to bindingly cling,
Where neither space nor distance bars to stall,
Our meeting once again to warmly bring —
Back mem'ries of our raring days in school;
Where you and I pursued with verve, a lot of strings
Of knowledge and skills — our pervasive goals;
All the way in this thrilling venture rings,
Eternal togetherness, played a preponderant role.
So then these untutored lines advance to create
A meeting ground where intimate buddies meet.
  As true Christians, we cherish all Christmases
  In a spirit ever rich in anastomosis.

Pete P. Norella

WE WERE MEANT FOR EACH OTHER

Tell me you love me
Tell me you care
Tell me you're glad
For the good times we share.
Tell me you'll always be there when I need you.
Tell me that always your love will be true.
What if the storms of life come along,
As long as we are together,
Nothing needs to go wrong.
We'll walk along together,
Your hand holding mine.
With God's arm around us
Through the passing of time.
And as we grow older
How happy we'll be
Knowing I was meant for you
And you were meant for me.
And as we walk together
We'll whisper our hearts' love
And keep our love shining
Like the sunshine from above.

Marcia R. Morris

TO DADDY

I remember the times you've been there to say
You'd reach out to help me make my way,
And you did — through a thousand yesterdays.
For that, I love you, Daddy.
Through the walks we had and the smiles we shared.
You always seemed to show you cared
And no one else ever could compare.
For that, I love you, Daddy.

Why was I the one lucky enough to be
Holding your hand, sitting on your knee?
I could never imagine why God chose me
To be there with you, Daddy.
The years past are worth their number in gold,
And as the miles between us grow
Keep me in mind, because you know
I'll always love you, Daddy.

Lysa D. Voight

ASHES

My lost love —
I whisper your name into the wind,
And it is like a caress brushing back
Against my ears.
It lingers like a kiss upon my lips,
And echoes like a thousand love words
Upon my heart.
Your name!

It is music, melody; lyrically sweet.
It is the song I sing to the stars at night.
It is the tune I hum in the silent rooms.
My lost love —

It is all I have to bring you to me now
I say it a thousand times a day —
To myself.
It is the only love letter I have of yours.
It is the only gift you gave me to keep.
It is all I have left of the sweetness —
Your name!

Patricia A. Thompson

AN OLD MAN'S PRAYER

It was a weary winter morn
when the snowflakes began to fall
there sat on my window sill
the smallest bird of all

With his wings half-frozen
and his eyes partially closed
I opened the window
and he fell to the floor below

Picking him up quite carefully
into the living room I went
placing him on a pillow
in front of my fireplace for warmth

Throwing on an extra log
just to be sure
I went about my daily chores
and said a prayer for the little bird

An hour or so had passed by
then suddenly he began to sing
such a beautiful song
it was as though it were spring

I thanked God
for answering my prayer
for another lonely winter
this old man could not bear

Candy Lee Koolhaas

THE JOY OF LOVE

illusive,
anticipation.

perchance,
no.

concrete,
never.

subtlety,
incorporeal.

perception,
refined.

mystically,
ethereal.

intensity,
heightened.

certainty,
virgin.

of joy,
unbridled.

he takes my hand,
we go to bed.

L. Parlor Boyd

FRIENDS

Your eyes tint with sorrow
no longer secure in nested dreams,
The portrait of another's fantasy
letting you down.
Disillusioned anticipation
such an unworthy response,
For you have guided my turns
with your compassionate side.

From ashes to dust
I have fallen on the earth
in view of the sky.

Debra Sue Peterson

MOODS

Blue is the sky,
blue is the sea
and blue is the mood
you've colored for me.
Why should I sit
and cry near the 'phone
while you don't care
that I'm alone?
Like the Phoenix I'll rise
and be on my way
but you'll regret
all this — someday.

Nell Elaine Nichols

ENDLESS LOVE

A love that lasts forever and
a day.
A love that will never go
away.
A closeness that grows with
each loving touch.
One that makes you love him
so very much.
The relationship we have is
meant to last, and it will.
The empty place in his
life, I will fill.

Kathy Bonito

CHILDREN

We watch them grow
Like dandelions
Blossoming so fast,
And when they age
The yellow fades,
Caught up by the
Free blowing wind.

An empty room,
A vacant chair
At the table,
Memories in bloom.

Neil J. Hansen

JESUS PRAYED WITH LOVE

Our Jesus came to live on earth
To teach us how to live,
To help us through the trials of life
And teach us how to give.

He gave His all and suffered here
For those to Him so dear.
He prayed for those who tortured Him,
Both those afar and near.

He suffered agony of flesh
And agony of soul.
He took upon Himself all sin.
He came here for that goal.

He died to keep within God's will,
He prayed for one and all.
So let us follow in His will
And answer every call.

He prayed for self, for friend and foe,
He prayed for you and me.
A pattern so that we might live
With Him eternally.

Gay Esther Ray

LOVE IS LIKE THE SUMMER ROSE

Much like the precious summer rose
when days are long and dry,
Without concern and gentle care
love, too, will fade and die.

For love is not a mystery,
some strange, exotic spell,
'Tis not a thing of selfishness,
and not a wishing well.

True love is sharing every day
both happiness and pain,
And letting someone know you care
through sunshine and through rain.

True love is giving all you have
while never keeping score,
And having someone ever near
and wanting nothing more.

With gentleness and tender care
love flourishes and grows,
And blooms eternal bright and fair
just like the summer rose.

David J. Creager

WHEN LIPS ARE MUTE

The fortunate, who find the fire
Of unexpected ecstasy
In making love or reaping its
Fruition, need not wipe their tears
Of joy away — that gentle trickling rain
Which spills when trembling lips are mute
And only soul can speak — because
They know from life experience
That beauty carves almost as deep
A wound and aches almost as much as pain.

Mauricia Price

MY DIANE

It was sunny and pleasant, that day in May,
when into the village, I happened to stray.
Taking a seat in a quaint Cafe, I ordered
their special, Cafe au Lait.

It was then that I saw, this girl by the door,
who had started to sketch, a matron of yore.
Accomplished was she, from what I could see; as
she held it up, and showed it to me; then her
blue eyes twinkled as she flounced her hair;
and motioned for me, to join her there.

The closer I came, to that beautiful face,
it brought to mind, another time, and place.
Her beauty was such, that my heart did race;
the world at her feet, I wanted to place.

She was half my age, and didn't care; and rather
liked, the grey in my hair . . . and well she
should, for it's nature's fare . . . to fatherhood!

Arthur D. Posa

POSA, ARTHUR, D. Pen Name: Philip A. Darby; Born: Brooklyn, New York, 12-17-16; Education: Graduated technical high school, completed college equivalent; home study course: Philosophy, Art; Occupations: Electronic Technician, Professional Soldier, Inventor, Writer, Poet; Memberships: Lifetime Membership Brooklyn Museum, Long Island Historical Society; Poetry: 'Why To Me?' *American Poetry Anthology,* 1985; 'My Diane,' 'Little Edward,' 'Elusive Love,' *Hearts on Fire,* 1986; Other Writings: "A Woman Divided," true, full length story; mystery romance, being edited for submission under pen name Philip A. Darby; Comments: *My poems are true stories about incidents in my life, as is the story "A Woman Divided," which is an experience I went through that I'd like to forget, but can't, because she doesn't want to!*

NIGHTFALL

A light burns in my window, Pierre, and
Its capricious shadows cast a vision of you there.
As surely as dusk of each day arrives, I tend the flame
To be quenched at dawn by my breath, as I call your name.

A light burns in my window, Pierre.
Remember when you asked me to place it there?
A beacon it shall forever be,
In the dark of night, till you come back to me.

But should this torch not guide your way,
And another's light offer you a brighter day,
Then, my love, the glow in my heart shall burn
With memories so dear, though you do not return.

Lucille R. Albanese

LOVE

Love is truly the Light of the World.
As seen in the glorious Statue of Liberty
Its banner clearly unfurled
Yet, right here and now Love enables us to send out rations
Of whatsoever is needed in hungering and thirsting nations
So let us awaken and set this Love-Wheel in motion
And capture its joy which soothes like a healing lotion
Love is truly the Light of the World.

Lucille Faye

JOURNEY'S END

In the darkest tunnel that we live in
There is always light, at the end of the road
But through the labyrinth of life's uncertainties
That road to the light is unknown.

Glimpses of happiness and cheer appear
Amid laughter in darkened halls
To brighten the sadness we occasionally bear
As we travel in memory's recalls.

Then to the tunnel's end we near
Old, infirmed and slow;
Hoping to reach that light so dear
That ends in journey's glow.

Moe Feldman

A SHAKESPEAREAN SONNET TO HELEN

Is there something so very gross with me?
She said I hurt. I too hard embraced her.
In my dumbness, I did not hear her plea;
Did not want to. Now I feel like a cur.
Something is wrong I do not comprehend,
With her? Me? She's my star and I wonder.
She's a miracle; my light she does send.
No lady, ever, could I be fonder.
She is an angel, there's no one to tell
Her beauty, but God, who created all.
I try to find words; her delights to spell,
For her sweet shining, I would be her thrall.
She said I was not true. Where's now my glow?
Does she know how her light, to me, does flow?

Gerald M. Quinn

GLIMPSES OF SOUTH NORWALK AND SOUTHPORT.

HIS LOVE

Lord, You looked down
From the heavens above
And saw me
Struggling in this world.
You cleansed my heart
And saved my soul,
Giving me all your love.

With thankful heart
I clearly see
The many blessings
Given to me.
Your gentle love and care
Make me aware
Of your Spirit in my heart.

You have made
This wonderful world
For man to enjoy.
The Earth is yours
And all that is in it,
Your presence is everywhere.

Juanita Caudle Crane

YOUNG AND IN LOVE

The gentle breeze
The soft sand
A boy and a girl
Hand in hand
The playful whisper
An intimate kiss
With the wind and the ocean
A special moment of abyss
Cuddling near the fire
Listening to the waves
The feeling of tenderness
Wishing it could last for days
The young and in love
Watching as the sun slowly sets
Love and emotion
Leaves the memory of two silhouettes.

Jennifer Margaroni

SHATTERED TEARS

What can end this pain?

A pain so intense, even my tears shatter.

My mind — the enemy.

It brings memories,

of beautiful . . .

. . . Beautiful lies.

Of yesterday's tomorrow.

Today's betrayal shatters;

my heart,

my soul,

my tears.

Tonya Lee Byes

I started closing my door tonight
when I went to bed
'cause I want to enjoy a good cry
without explaining.

You showed me again
a world I'd almost forgotten,
and God, I miss it —
and the yous who make it real.

It took time, but you made me feel again,
and for two weeks of camp
it took a week of crying every night
before it stopped hurting . . .

remembering your love, your warmth,
your vitality, your selfless giving —
the way I've always wanted to
but been afraid to.

You reminded me how much there is to life
and how much I am
and how much we are — together —
and I love you for that.

Sally Nickerson

THE WEDDING PARTY

I thank you, dear God
For young love
and exuberance
and smiles

And for a day filled
with beauty — gaiety
And music
and caring people

For a time to remember
especially the trees, grass,
sun and shade — even the bees

For a hostess
relaxed — enjoying her party
— she even a guest

And for a rare visit with
neighbors and friends of old

Your world and ours is still so good!

Edith Buckley

I THINK I HAVE NOT REALLY LIVED

I think I have not really lived
Because you are not mine
I think you can be better life
Than music, dreams or wine

I think you could be ecstasy
Enjoyment and thrills galore
I think you could be worlds of dreams
Unknown to me before

I think I have not really lived
With you I have not tried
But without you, a thousand times
I think I surely died

Jerry Martinez

I MISS

I miss the gentleness of your lips
when they touched close to mine.
I miss the way our bodies
used to be one.
I miss the feelings
Feelings that you brought me
I miss the way we
used to think the world was ours.
I miss the happiness
you brought me.
I miss saying
"I love you."
I miss the love
that we once shared
I miss your warm and tender body
close to mine.
I miss the way you said
we'd last forever.
I miss you
I miss the gentleness of your lips
when they touched close to mine

Tarra Diachun

ISLAND OF LOVE

Take me with you
To your island of love
So we can be together
And oh, keep on lovin' me

I want you in my life

I wanna see your tender smile every day
That grew on me and told me that you cared
And your wave was a gentle touch
That touched my heart

Just the way you looked at me
Swept me off my feet
To your island of love
I couldn't live without you

My love is strong enough
To let when things erupt
I just can't let you go
'cause I love you so

Natalie Shuba

MY LOVE WILL COME TO ME

There is not a moment —
There is not a day
But I hope I'll find you
Somewhere on life's way.
You're hidden in the shadows
But still on land and sea
I keep on groping, hoping
My love will come to me.

I walk the soft green meadows.
I climb the mountains high.
I search 'neath golden moonlight
And twinkling starry sky.
But yet, I keep believing
That real these dreams will be
When someday, somehow, somewhere
My love will come to me.

Sybil Harrison

GUESS WHO LOVES YOU

Whenever I see you, the beating of my heart makes me
tremble,
I want to touch your hand, but something stops me
my dear;
I've constantly fantasized tender moments with you,
I've had these feelings for almost a year.
I try to act as though it seems that I don't even care,
But if you'd look into my eyes, you'd know my love for
you is there.
So if by chance, you happen to feel the way I do,
I wish to God you'd tell me, then I'd know just what
to do,
Hey guess who loves you, Darling I'm standing right
next to you.

Rosetta M. Buchanan

THE ORCHESTRA OF LIFE

The angry wind plays nature's fluted grasses,
its sympathy bound close to deep bass thunder.
The meadow lies so flat with painful burdens
like some old crone with aching back and shoulders.

The sound of cellos is the lark's gay singing.
The whistling breeze now stops to hear its rhythm;
The Orchestra of Life is brimming over
with love and joy the whole world's song is singing.

Arlone Mills Dreher

ABSENCE

For with the absence of the one I love,
And the melting of my heart from the flames,
I feel we are as one apart and still,
Never far from one another's touch.

For it is this absence that shall bind,
The ends of this long journey together,
As it shall bind our love from doubt,
And join us once more in time.

My heart tells me what my soul confirms,
The love and never dying devotion,
To you . . . the one who strengthens,
My heart's every movement and soul's every breath.

Dale Edward Blakney

GAMES

A one-night lover is his claim to fame
He will seduce you, but it's only a game.

His Love doesn't last, it ends with the night.
There's no use crying, you can't win this fight.

He's handsome, he's clever, sweet and he's cool
But he can be nasty, hateful and cruel.

When he is finished, he's on the run
You must understand, he's had his fun.

One day he too will feel the pain
When the one he loves makes her claim to fame.

Kim Sullivan

AND THE TWO SHALL BECOME ONE

And the two, captured by love, shall become one. With love on their side, it shall be done. The joining of two lost hearts shall come out of hiding from within the dark, and the power of love shall swallow their fears so that they need not shed a tear. The ring around the moon is a special sign; the angels are looking down putting love in our minds. The poets and the dreamers say it their way; they say love is the one that saves. And when we feel the magic, we will know, that this special love won't let us go. Love is, writing love songs in the dark, sharing secrets within our hearts, making castles in the sand, and letting our souls run free into the wind; where the spirits of love can be seen within. My love has a message to give to you; follow your dreams all the way through. Open your hearts and it shall be done, and the two shall become one.

Nanette Bly

AD ABSURDUM HORRENDUM

"Ad absurdum horrendum," I can hear him say,
The only Latin phrase he would use day by day,
Until the day I heard it no more;
He touched the knob and opened the door;
Never will I hear that phrase again
Until he comes back to me.

He wrote to me from wherever he had gone
And I knew he remembered all the things we had done;
"Ad absurdum horrendum,"
How horribly absurd
That we were apart, with no other single word;
I wrote, "Come back; I want to hear
'Ad absurdum horrendum' "
I have no fear
For he will come back to me.

Priscilla Culverwell

ALL IS LOST

It's been ten long years
Not a day without sorrow and tears
I remember the days we spent together
Not a day with cloudy weather
You were my one and only inspiration
Not a day with pain or frustration
Now all is lost

You kept me going, kept me alive
Not a day I don't think of how you died
Why you, trying to help your country
Not a day I don't think of you fighting
for life, liberty and the pursuit of happiness
I will live on your aggression and rage
Not a day I don't imagine you locked in that cage
Now all is lost, my poor veteran

Nicole Michele Borgesano

ROOTS

As roots to the substance of soil
Would nourish the branches, limb by limb
Up to the peak in the trusty tree
To the simple bloom so bountiful borne
There, would bear, the lucid fruit of Love.

D. E. Johnson

IT ISN'T EASY

No one ever claimed it would be easy,
In fact, the extreme is proclaimed —
When two — live as one, there's bound to be trouble,
And both partners should be equally blamed —

How two, adult, responsible people,
Who are supposed to be perfectly sane —
Stand, screaming obscenities at each other,
Knowing — there's absolutely nothing to gain —

Molding your life to fit another's.
You're definitely gonna have to change —
And just when you think you've got it,
Something else you'll have to rearrange —

Keep in mind, practice makes perfect,
And what have you got to lose?
Be willing to give more than your share,
You might not be wailing the blues —

Hang in there and give it all you've got,
True love is worth the fight —
How perfectly lovely, at the end of each day,
To hear, "I love you, darling — good-night . . . "

Janice Reed Hamlin

HEEDLESS YOUTH

There was a day
We squandered LOVE upon a hillside,
And hurled our laughter to the echoing rocks.
Spendthrift,
Improvident,
We knew that LOVE would last always.

But TIME cast shadows o'er the dark'ning sky,
And icy fingers chilled the warmth of LOVE.
. . . The day is gone!

Josie Goodrich Smith

JEANNELLE

Have you ever seen a smile so sweet,
That your heart lights up as your eyes meet?
Then you haven't met my little Jeannelle,
The sweetest person I have ever beheld.

Her ways are gentle and her words are soft,
As she shows her love in ways unthought.
She's eager to show the new things learned,
To express her love in hugs returned.

She is the apple of her grandparents' eyes,
As she excels in all things she tries.
Our visits light up her days of play,
As we store our things and prepare to stay.

This past November she just turned six.
It seems the time has passed so quick
Since first we held her in our arms,
Rejoicing in her lovely charms.

With beautiful, curly, soft brown hair,
Big brown eyes and skin that's fair,
She's growing tall, like a healthy seed.
We are so proud of her, yes indeed!

Margaret E. Reed

MY DAUGHTER

I watched you grow from infant to adult,
but still you always amaze me.
You were a lovely child, there was no doubt,
but, as you grew, you gained in beauty.

The joys you brought into my existence
can't be listed in this rhyme.
If I wrote them down, for instance,
it would take an entire lifetime.

I felt the ultimate gift you gave to me,
was happiness, joy, and serenity.
But, in thinking of all the things you came to be,
I feel the greatest was the Mother of three.

Throughout your life, you gave so fully.
You had an endless supply of love and beauty,
but, the greatest gift you gave was truly
the grandchildren, Doug, Darcy, and Randi.

Glenn M. Reeves

LOVE SPEAKS

The bloom of the rose upon your lips,
The morning dew on your finger tips,
You quietly stand inside my heart
Breathing softly, "I shall never depart."

The universe stretches beyond your smile,
Your vast inheritance mile after mile;
Your Father behind you mightier than life,
A divine connection for a newly found wife.

You patiently stand by my garden gate
For my recognition of the hand of fate;
I open my eyes to your glorious face,
And know true love commands your space.

Naked before you, my defenses down,
My head on your pillow without a sound,
I consummate my immortal soul
To a loving bridegroom in a kingly role.

Sharon Bleasdale Bowman

L-O-V-E

The word L-O-V-E is such a strange thing,
When you truly love someone, you know what I mean,
It's deeper than anyone can ever measure,
The love for that special someone that you treasure.

When you are far away, you want to be back again,
And if you cannot, you'll send your love until then,
Thinking only of your loved ones back home somewhere,
Wishing with all your heart that you could be there.

There's another kind of love, the kind for a friend,
And many, many other kinds, over and over again,
There's that deep love inside for your own child,
And the love for your mother, with her special smile.

There's love for your land, and little sweet home,
And all the worldly things that you happen to own,
For the different seasons, and different kinds of weather,
L-O-V-E is like a bridge, holding them all together.

Willard Lee Skelton

Be still my heart
Don't let him know
How it hurts to let him go.

Be still my heart
Don't let him know
I meant yes when I said no.

Be still my heart
Don't let him know
That I love him so . . .

Be still my heart
Be still my heart
. . . Goodbye my love

Virginia Wing

I WONDERED

As I gathered you in my embrace,
held you close to my heart,
feeling the steady beat of your
heart next to mine.

I wondered if all of life was
so sweet
wind so calm,
A sky so clear
A love so rare, or
Air so fine.

As I held you in this embrace of mine.

Audrey L. Bryant

ME AND YOU

Two of the finer things
a breath of life
and you

Every song
every love story told
every dream imagined
or come true
reminds me of you

The greenness of your eyes
the eternity of your smile
peace after the laughter dies

Dena Lesser

FLIGHT

Lying in your arm's fold, soft and light
between your breathing
I can hear your quiet smile

at a bird you've spotted somewhere
in your dreams.

It lifts its body to the air
and you forget your gun
in awe and breathe a sigh in sleep

that rustles branches
in your dreams.

Alva S. Moore

MY LITTLE ONE

To play
with someone she loves,
stuffed animals,
crayons and coloring books.
To play
and be close,
her loving giggles
telling how she feels.
But, when she's afraid
and I drive her fears
to disappear.
Again she laughs and giggles,
with hugs around my neck.
This little one
with so much love.

Richard E. Horton

VARIATIONS ON A THEME — II

To take a word
That trembles on the lip, unsaid;
A glance of tenderness
Escaping from an eye quick-veiled
Against its own betrayal;
A movement of the hand
As if beseeching, but
Arrested almost ere it is begun; —
To weave these incorporeal treasures
(Yet how more than dear!)
Into a dream of loving —
This is all I have.

And yet such wealth means more to me
Than all the world beside.

Adah H. Larisch

DAUGHTER

I go on in this world waiting,
For other than the moments in life,
Which in a heart, creates hating.

Searching everywhere, though in fear,
Awaiting, praying for that instant,
For something I may hold dear.

It comes, the moment of inner laughter,
Completely embracing my soul,
From the miracle I call, my daughter.

With her love, I can open the door,
And pass beyond valleys of grief,
Unable to measure the distance I soar.

Teresa E. Sanchez-Hamilton

VALENTINE'S DAY

Every day is Valentine's Day,
When we are in love,
The birds sing more softly,
And the sky is bluer above.
Sweet is the music we hear,
As we go hand in hand,
No one is ever immune from it,
It is the most beautiful thing
in the land.

Irene Schweinfurth

MY LOVE

My love for you is as the sun
High,
Bright,
Shining
Willowing through the breeze
Crisp,
Warm,
Smiling
Sending signals for all to see.

This love for you can be seen by all
There will be no question
As I look into your face
Who holds this Love.
Whom I'll embrace
You are my sunshine
The warmth of my day
I'm so glad you came my way
MY LOVE.

Helen Rae Wegner

LOVE IN SPITE

With a feigned love-choked voice
And beams of bastard smiles
To veil the sentiments of spite
Love, professed profound love
Of genuine selfless motives
Worms into the heart for fun.

The lustful eye does not see
The glow of malice in the face
The credulous ear is fuddled
By the hot air of endearment
Even the level head is uncertain
That true love is much kinder.

But if such is the make of love
I pray for the love of hate
Or the venal love of the fallen woman
Splendid in her gorgeous dress
Beneath which lurks a fickle heart
Of promiscuous frozen kisses.

Kwasi Asante

LOOKING FOR YOU

I'm searching raindrops
looking for your face.
I gaze in puddles;
no one's in disgrace.

I'm finding dragons
even in my place.

The streaks of darkness
only seem to chase.

When morning lightens
sending beams of lace,
I dream you're with me
not in Army base.

If I'm mistaken,
won't you come to me?
Your spirit seeking,
longing to be free.

Violet Wilcox

CHAIN OF LOVE

I have a chain around you,
A chain of love.
My chain is made from the rainbow,
From the clouds and the heavens above.

Some chains are hard and full of steel.
Some are soft like mine.
My chain tells you how I feel,
How my love for you will shine.

Chain wrap my love so carefully.
Hold him so with bands of light.
Let my love love me.
Do not hold him tight.

Bands of love, bands of chains,
Rainbows here and there,
Sifting into lovely lanes,
Wrapping love with care.

Carrie Lynn Brown

TOUCH ME LOVE

Touch me love,
Feel delight in mine,
Reach for me love,
And know that it's time.
To touch me love,
And within your finger tips
Will be the dream
You taste on your lips.

But first you've got to,
Touch me love,
And know how real,
I am to feel.
Because I'm all for you,
Baby I'm with you,
In the things you do,
And you never know I'm there,
So touch me love,
And know I care.

Alvin Newsome Jr.

A SPECIAL BOND

To love something —
Is to give it room to grow.
You and I have chosen that room
and are taking it with great stride.
Together, we hold a special bond,
and there is nothing more unique.
It is one of friendship, and love.
It is a bond that neither you, nor I
can quite define.
But we know enough of feelings,
to know that ours are very realistic.
And we know that any bridge or gap
is only a small inconvenience.
We step back and give each other
a chance to find our own directions
in life.
And with the bond we share,
maybe someday,
our directions will meet.

Karla Kay Rollins

FOR MOM ON HER BIRTHDAY

To a very special mom
Who clothes, feeds and cares for me.

I love you every day mom
Although I may not show it.
And I care for you a lot
Although you may not know it.

I'm writing this to tell you
That you're always on my mind.
You're very special to me
And you're one of a kind.

This may not seem to make sense
But I'm saying how I feel.
I may not always be here,
But my heart you did but seal.

I'll love you mom forever
And please don't ever forget.

Missy Meakin

I LOVED HIM ALL THE MORE

My father was six foot three
and a hero to me
until the day I went to war,
and then I saw him cry.
So did I,
and I loved him all the more.

When I was forty-five
and Pop was still alive,
not the man he was before,
if I saw him cry,
so did I,
and I loved him all the more.

Now I'm near sixty-five.
Pop's no longer alive,
neither father nor man anymore.
Death couldn't make him cry,
but God, did I.
And I loved him all the more.

Arthur E. McGowan

the wish-they-were-remembered lovers

HONORABLE MENTION

ghost-walk through
my attic, light as
summer dresses
that pale to nude
to embarrass me
at state dinners.
they will nibble,
giggling,
at my toes
at funerals
and moments of
proper passionless pain.
they would be remembered,
but alas! they are
all shades
of you:
for love remembers
what lust never knew.

Juley Wright

I FINALLY FOUND THE BEEF!

You approached me just the way I wanted.
I could tell you were a persistent man.
When you asked if we could meet later
I said . . . I can, if you can!

We got together the next time,
To make a go of things.
The feelings I experienced that night,
Were beyond my wildest dreams!

I want some more of that baby!
I just can't wait any longer.
On the BEEF this time put GRAVY!
And make this feeling grow stronger.

Dinah K. Henderson

My heart feels as if it is
in a tunnel,
Of endless alleyway of
total darkness,
For being lost and lonely
to many nights,
Of lying alone in a world of
lost love,
For I feel I have no one to hold
on a cold night and times of
emptiness in my body
From times of sorrow and ones
of being lost,
For I have love to give someone,
But no one wants my love, so I
just might . . . ?

Carlton R. Cook

REMISSION

HONORABLE MENTION

We timed our kisses that Christmas
to fit their trips to the kitchen
and never knew my parents knew
what we were doing.

Now you're thinner and I'm scrubbed down;
there is seldom a third remission.
But while the nurse is out of sight
let's risk one kiss more.

Charles Seagren

WHEN I GROW OLD

When I grow old and tired,
When leaves fall from the trees,
When the sound of children's laughter
Sparks no response in me,

When I fail to see the glory
Of an early morning sky,
When I see a grave injustice
And I do not question why,

Then I've grown too old to dream
And nothing's left to me,
Except my love, to dance with you
Throughout eternity.

Jeri Lyn Dopp

AN ODE TO LOVE

How sweet it was in the beginning of wedded life, when,
Love and peace ruled our home though at,
Times were broken up by storms of modern life,
When they were held at bay by love they were good,

Now that the fullfillments of lover's bounty,
Pleasurable desires are no longer realized,
I have only the four walls to hear me,
When I sigh or cry out of loneliness.

My desires are the same as at the beginning,
When I first tried married life that,
Ended too soon and because of all the,
Wrong reasons and ways for happiness.

Her smiling and willing lips to kiss,
Her arms always glad to hold and,
Hug and enfold me in love's embraces,
Her height and size were just right.

Oh love! You have ended all too soon,
In love's place I am filled with loneliness,
Oh love! You have ended too soon.

Elmer R. Green

I'M DATING AGAIN, IT'S NO JOKE

I'm dating again, it's no joke
Seeking a partner for life,
Not making choices of violent sex abuse;
I can't believe in going steady, high-school style,
Tying myself forever down to chaotic, overloaded,
Misunderstanding, unreliable, calendar abuse,
When there are fish free, to
Fry and fish, wanting to be caught, that are not
Tied down to the "company-man" image,
Fantasizing paramours in competition with
Unsolicited men and nagging women
Pawing like stags in a
Forest battle of antlers,
Staked out, in well-profited turf.

"Steady," is going for frightened,
Adolescent, wallflowers
Fearful of being "persons," individual, so
Cling to the first available candidate
Blending blandly into the fabric of
Paid, advertised, social
Whirls of spectacular
Attention-getting flings.

Geneve Baley

LOVE UNSPOKEN

What becomes of Love that's unspoken?
So special it wants to be given.
Arms needing to hold, lips longing to kiss,
Words one whispers — waiting.
The pillow wet with tears.
Does it lend color to the rainbow
Or paint the early morning sky
Do the whispers give voice to the night winds
Or accompany the brook as it sings
Does it kiss the rose wih sweet fragrance
And the tears, are the tears dewdrops
Shimmering in the soft light?
What becomes of Love that's unspoken?

Ruth M. Shores

YOU ON MY MIND

I woke up this morning and the sun didn't shine
I started my day with you on my mind
I sent you my love though you're far away
Sent you a kiss hope it'll brighten your day
I picked up your picture and held it tight
Like the way we did every night
Told you I loved you with all my heart
You mean so much to me you're that special part
I'll go to bed with tears in my eyes
I know I'll dream about you don't have to try
I'll daydream about you at work today
Dream about the times we've shared . . . just you and I
Wish I was with you now and always
Woke up this morning and the sun didn't shine
I started my day with you on my mind
Sent you my love though you're far away
Sent you a kiss hope it will brighten your day

Linda Webb

Then this is it — goodbye;
The dearest wish my heart can give
Is that you might know joy.
As for me, well, I shall be —
No, not content, but, shall we say,
Not *all* unhappy.
Some things I must forget, of course —
(Or anyway, *try* not to remember) —
The way you kissed;
Three words you spoke, quite low;
A tear I once saw in your eye;
A street we know;
A tenderness I shall not *hope* to find again.

So quickly now — one last, brief kiss;
My heart is yours — but then you know that.
And so, weeping a very little only,
I shall say,
"Goodbye."

Adah H. Larisch

MY DAD

Through all the years of being your daughter
I know that I could never be prouder
As far back as I can remember
You have always been a good listener
In times of need you were there
No one can say that you don't care
And as I am growing in my adult years
I still need you to help dry the tears
The tears that come from life's ups and downs
I know you're there with smiles, not frowns
A husband I'll have and will life together
You can't be replaced Dad, there's no one better
At times you've said you didn't do much as a father
But read these words Dad, from your daughter
You may not have given material things
You gave me something that means more than anything
you gave me love.

Susan Judge

A PLEA TO CUPID

Dealing with my fantasies
of your love in my soul
I can't hope to love you openly
So, Cupid, I do hope to receive
I beg of you . . .
Some sort of reprieve
but, I do see
There's no end to your insanity.

Marge Hallum

JULIE'S LULLABY

Close your sleepy little eyes
Drift to land of dreams
Ride up in the bluest skies
On the fastest moonbeams
Go as far as you can go
But return for you know
There are two who love you well
More than they could ever tell.

June Staudte

DEFINITION

What is love? Can one define
All its meaning in a word?
Can one set, in metered line,
What is seen and felt and heard?
What is sensed within the soul?
Deeper than feeling, closer than heart,
Stronger than faith, greatest of all,
Of life and of living, the loveliest part!

Cornelia B. Furbish

COMMITTED HEARTS

An infatuated friendship
in the mind and in the heart
questioned promises to others
keeping lust-filled needs apart
faced with searing new emotions
and the right to feel this way
pre-determined was their outcome
for they had vowed their hearts away

Kathy Liggett Smith

Aspen boughs, dried and yellow,
In the arch above my window;
Leaves round-faced like stillborn babe's
Their crypt a marble vase.
These the boughs you broke for me
One fading day in late September.
Their leaves of fragile parchment gold —
Oh, why must I remember?
The bough has withered — life has gone.
But still the dusty leaves cling on.

Marietta Bakewell

SWEET MEMORIES

The time has come to close the door and lock our memories away . . . Sweet Memories.
As the earth revolves, so does our love. Just as we each were thrown into the
other's path, the motion has now reversed itself.
Alas, we are destined to travel separate roads for the remainder of our days.
Farewell, My Love . . . Your beauty will remain in my heart forever.
No more shall I relive our tender moments and revel in the wonderment of having
shared your love.
You have opened a great new world of feeling to me, for that, I am eternally
grateful.
You have invited me to dwell within your heart, and the beauty abiding there
is overwhelming. I am so much richer, now.
I would enter your mind and engulf your soul, but for the pain it brings to you,
Perhaps another lifetime?
You have shared with me the secrets of the universe, I shall not want for more,
for I have experienced the ultimate happiness and shall end my days with
such Sweet Memories.

Janet Devigili

MY LOVE SONG TO ANDREW

Andrew my beloved son I love you dearly
In the lily of the valley I chose you for service
As ye made love to me in song
In return my son, there is a love for a woman, who has the eyes of
Mine and the heart of serving
Desiring to be with you
Because of the sweetness of thy lips, she has not forgotten you and
Thy sweet embrace of you and thy warm body
She can't forget
You lay between her breast all night
Filling thy heart with warmth and tenderness
Come to her
She loves you and can't forget you
Andrew, Andrew, Andrew, I love you
Our love is told in Solomon Song dear
Come to me my Song of Love

Jacquelyn Crenshaw

THE SILENT KNOWING

Dedicated to Mary Shih

Seeing her eyes left a picture of a thousand silent eyes,
calm and illustrative faces peering from a state of non-action
into one's soul.

Listening with no-ears, her heart open like a flower, lips are soft
and firm, she was as silent as could be.

Internally, I am contented and unfold — there sits my genuine me-hood —
calmly and reassuringly, serenity in her soft stare, curiously waiting
with patience, she is lost between the sitter and the sit.

Seeing and not seeing, the physical as if it were never there,
to eventually know all of me, accompanied by a natural
facial expression — a smile of visibility.

Anthony K. Roberts

ONLY ONE FRIEND

I have only
one friend
that I can
call my own.

The rest I
only borrow 'til
their deed with

me has gone

This friend of mine
I'll cherish
through all my
years of life.

When my life
is over and
I have gone away.

I'll come back
to watch over
her for the rest
of her days.

Betty Evans

Those secret nether regions
In the dark recesses
Of my body and mind
Now flow the mystic rivers
Through deep caresses
Unlike any kind

Awaken silent limbs
The feeling time has come
Innate resources call
The hungry eyes have met
To fire former numb
A giving of it all.

Eileen A. Johnson

RUTH ANN

It comes natural for me
to hold you tight
I just love being with you
alone at night

You lift my heart up today
blew me a kiss
You are what dreams are made of
you I would miss

All the little things you say
I warm inside
Always love to see your smile
be by your side

All the little things you do
make life worthwhile
You are everything I need
on a lost isle

The closest thing to heaven
just holding hands
Or me being by your side
who understands

William J. LaSalle

THERE CAME A KNIGHT

There came a knight a riding
A riding through my life.
Tall and fair, with eyes of blue
He swept away all strife.

There came a knight a riding
A riding through my pain.
He closed his shield around me
And held off the stormy rain.

There came a knight a riding
A riding fast and low.
There came a man a riding
Singing sweet and slow.

There came my knight a riding
A riding to my heart.
To teach me how to love again
The secret to impart.

There came a knight a riding
A riding swift and sure.
His heart holds my salvation
His love's my sadness cure.

Rose Brandon

A SOLDIER'S FAREWELL

"I must say good-bye my sweet,"
The young soldier said.
"I'll come back to you again
If I should not be dead.

On some field of battle it
Maybe I shall fall.
But," a tear slid down his face,
"My king and country call.

When the war ends and peace comes
We shall meet once more.
And sweet, our friendship we
Shall once again restore.

O, do not weep when you are
Held in my embrace,
Though my grief may be showing
Too well upon my face."

But in a distant country
And on foreign soil,
He lies forever sleeping
Beyond all grief and toil.

Hyman Lerner

IPSE

You say that self-love
is nearer to Love than giving
But in My giving I offer
to you My Love
(for I am Love)
which you reject
by saying
"This is not love
it is graceless
I am Onanist."

Robert Maldonado

LOST LOVE

I see your face at daybreak
Among the morning stars
I hear your voice in birdsong
And wonder where you are.

I see your face at sunrise
In dawning's rosy glow
I feel your touch in zephyr's breath
And oh I miss you so!

I see your face at noontime
In summer's shimmering heat
I feel your touch in butterfly wings
If only we could meet.

I see your face at twilight
Among the evening stars
I hear your voice in cricket chirps
And wonder where you are.

I see your face at midnight
In moonlight's brilliant glow
I hear your voice in night bird songs
And oh I miss you so!

Lucile Clay Clark

MEMORIES

Carved a name in my heart
And bled sweet drops of tear.
Gave a universal love
To one I held so dear.

I have romanced a princess
Even chose myself a queen.
Though lost loves have brought misery
So much happiness too I have seen.

I have kissed a dream
And walked on air.
I could never look back
On love with despair.

Each journey a memory
From all I have grown.
The greatest of gifts
I have ever known.

Placed footprints in the sands
Of love untold.
Found treasures in the memories
That I alone hold.

Peter M. Vingris

JUST A WORD

Everyone is on the sea of life.
This long voyage is filled with strife.
Each soul has a choice of destination,
Spoken by the God of all creation,
Reflect a moment, and get your bearing.
Our bodies of flesh are steadily wearing.
The souls of men must soon depart.
Our urgent need is a converted heart.
God of love has prepared the way.
Faith in Jesus breaks the eternal day.

Paul O. Carlson

I LOVE YOU

My side of the bed is empty.
My toothbrush is missing, too.
Every time I think like this,
My thoughts go back to you.

No one to kiss goodnight —
or tell how much I love
My tears will always cry —
for you, the one I love.

It's hard for me to sleep alone
To roll over and not see you
I miss saying "I love you, Honey"
and hearing you say "I love you too."

I'm praying for all our happiness
hoping we can be together soon.
I want you here next to me
Before the next full moon.

I love you, Honey, and always will
You mean so much to me.
I want my life to be filled
with only you & me.

Linda Marie Pearson

GOD'S LOVE

God loved this world, He gave
His only Son to die
That every one of us
Could live again on High!

God keeps His promises,
His power never fails,
All things are possible
Regardless of what ails —

The step each one must take:
Believe His Word and do
His will for us each day,
Then claim His promise true!

His love will fill your heart,
With joy and happiness,
Peace of mind will comfort
Through times of deep distress!

Though war should rock this world
And people restless grow,
We have God's promise true,
To cling to what we know!

Edna M. Parker

MY UNCLE

There was a man born some years before
He stayed awhile but then he had to go
He stayed with us and shared his love
Then God called — come be with the dove
With a heart as large as he
He made me see what I could be
He showed me things and taught me well
He told me to heed Sunday's bell
This man's love was solid as a brick
This man was my uncle Vic

Paul E. Davis

A DREAM NOT SHARED

Once I dreamed a dream of beauty.
I dreamed a dream that awakened a longing,
Of a future where love begat love, and children played.
It was a dream of strength, beauty, and sharing.
There was a song in all hearts.

As I grew I worked toward that dream,
Knowing the difficulties to be overcome.
Then I realized it was my dream, not shared or acknowledged,
For I knew pain.

Over the years the dream became a nightmare.
As the contrast between reality became sharper.
Dreams faded . . . Love faded . . .
There were no songs in our hearts.
Children played, but with tension not knowing they had locked the song.
The nightmare deepened — destructive, devastating,
I could not defeat it.

It is over now — as I heal, the dream returns.
Bringing with it a warmth of hope.
But now a fear and pain come with the longing.
Yet I still dream the dream of beauty — Cautiously. . .

Patricia L. Kile

ALL I WANT FOR CHRISTMAS

The only thing I shall need this year,
Is the sound of your voice to quiet my tears.
The touch of a hand shall be only from you,
Some time from your day to keep us feeling new.

A little lifting up; some secrets to share,
Always over the phone — but I wish I were there.
What I'm asking for Christmas is not something which you can buy,
But something you keep hidden in your heart; always willing to deny.

Please make me a promise as this year comes to an end
That you will say what you feel and try to be open.
Keep your heart where it lies — safe in my arms,
And I'll keep my head in the clouds; the result of your charms.

Never look back at the less-than-terrific times we've lived,
But look ahead to the new year and how much more we both can give.

So what I'm asking for this Christmas
And to keep it from being blue,
Just give me yourself, dear
All I need is you.

Janet Peralta

THE ENEMY

The clock has become my enemy.
It symbolizes how long we have been apart,
And how much longer we will be separated.
I fear its hands, for they hold me from you.
Each time I look at its face I see cruelty, and I feel pain.
When I feel as though hours have elapsed, I look at my enemy and it laughs.
Then it tells me only moments have passed.
To keep busy eludes me. I only feel numb.
Sleep speeds the harshness of time; but how much can one sleep?
Music brings tears to my eyes, as each noted word intensifies my feelings.
Will time and I ever be an alliance?
I will know when you are at my side, again.

Karen A. Lee

MAMA DON'T CRY

A little girl with unshed tears in her eyes said,
"Mama, please don't cry because daddy knew he was
going to die.
He told me about his love for you and me and he
would never forget us or stop loving us whenever
he went to be with God.
He told me mama that someday we would all be
together again, and mama you know my daddy never
lied.
And mama I know my daddy is happy in his new
home away up in the sky with God.
So mama please don't cry; because daddy loved you
and me, and we will be visiting him someday up in the sky!"

Betty Veneta Potter

WHY DID YOU LEAVE?

You love me?
Then why did you leave?
Tears, like icicles dropped on the floor,
melting one by one. When you threw
your glass against the mirror and walked away,
memories shattered into a million pieces.
Like the waters of Niagara Falls,
drowning me in my sorrow. Plans, crumbled like
dried leaves under the Maple tree.
Time can't erase our past, nor our shadows,
but memories that are left, like sweet smelling
rose buds, will always possess me.
Remember, for you know I love you.

Emma L. Thorpe

CONTINUITY

I cannot say what captivates me more.
Your looks, your manner, your words, or your being.
I have thought about it long and hard
and determined I shall never know
until this life closes
and we begin anew.
Something brought us together
and holds us together still.
Something. I care not what!
I will learn of you until
I discover completely what makes it so
and if this life is not long enough
I will do it later.

Perry Gravelle

What really happened between us,
Was it a phase, stage, or imagination?
You seemed like a guy I could trust,
But you went away just like the sun.

I never met anyone like you before,
With your smile, jokes, and understanding.
You made my heart laugh though it was still sore,
But you seemed all the while, to be running.

One day you'd be so warm,
Then the next freezing cold.
Did you somehow feel alarm,
When my feelings you were told?

Dawn Molnar

YOUR TIME, YOU GAVE ME

No one else in the whole wide world
Is as thoughtful and true, in what you say
You take the time to give, and the time to care;
As you let me tell you whatever I'm feeling in every way.

I would never, ever change what we did
As I would dearly do it over, again and again
And you will always be dear to me, in a very special way;
So if ever you need a shoulder to cry on, just let me know when.

I would do just that for you and more
For you taking the time, to talk and be with me
As I don't know how much further I would have gone;
Without you being understanding and wonderful as can be.

And no matter what I say or do
Or wherever I plan to go
If you need me, in any sort of way,
I would never turn my back on you.

Linda Marie Laframboise

MERE ECSTASY

To fly without wings
To win without trying
To see without eyes
To love without knowing

Mere ecstasy; capturing the unbelievable
and knowing it's in the palm of your hand.
Yet, mere dreams of reality and fantasy
holding your mind in its grasp.
The constitution of life waving its forgotten
banner,
Only to be stepped on, by lost time.

And yes, mere ecstasy, escaping from the hearts
of lovers
Edging its way through unwanted lives
Not knowing of its undetermined destiny
Nor of its undetermined purpose in the lives
of the unbelieving.

Caryl S. Muzzey

SPACE & 7

A tragedy today
            Jan 28, 1986 —
7 Went up toward the heavens,
We waved good-bye,
            Never realizing it was good-bye.
The space shuttle, Challenger
            Blew up today — Jan 28th —
A lot of love was in that
            Explosion —
Such love was   below
            Looking up . . .
Love never dies, love endures,
            It's endless in time & space.
7 — who loved and were loved —
            Are forever recorded in
                        Time & space —
Space, & 7 Jan 28, 1986 —
            Will forever be remembered
                        & loved.

Wally Kibler

FALL FROM GRACE

Every time I think
I'm finally over you
and think I can now
find laughter
in all of the sadness
of our Federal Express
affair
and each time I think
if you ever touched
me again
I'd run away
then
I see your face
and with just one look
I feel
I could
fall
from
grace
again

Diane Wanderer

WANDERER, DIANE. Born: Manhattan, New York City, 12-4-58; Education: Marymount High School, Bel Air, California, 1976; University of Southern California, Paralegal Degree, 1984; Occupations: Actress, Member of Screen Extras Guild; Paralegal (part-time); Awards: for "Futureshock," Northridge Jr. Women's Club, 1972; and "What America Means To Me," an essay, *Herald Examiner Newspaper,* 1974; Themes: *LOVE . . . romantic idealism . . . dreams . . . ideals.*

SUNNY

To Becki

Sweet little girl with
the ready smile.
Still learning tolerance
and patience, and
all the while,
growing up with such
confidence and charm
and personality.

Beverly A. Tadlock

THE MAGICAL SEASHELL

I was walking along the awakened shore, ready to begin the new day.
I picked up a seashell, raised it to my ear, and to my surprise heard it say,
"Follow the glow given by a nearby love, find a spot where you can remain and
enjoy its beauty, and there you will receive your needs from above."
I held the shell close, while I looked about me trying to find a nearby affection
I spotted a lighthouse which to me always signified romance, love, and protection.
I followed the beautiful gleam dispersing from the home.
Then found a rock between the ocean and the house, and sat on the stone.
I sat enthralled with the ocean and sky's beauty.
I heard a pitter patter coming closer, and turned around in duty.
Before me stood a beautiful stallion with a gentleman on its back.
I could tell just by looking at his handsome face, that there wasn't one quality he'd lack
I mounted onto the stallion by taking the man's outstretched hand.
We galloped off into nature's beauty, the seashell remaining in the sand.

Jennifer Margaroni

MY HEART'S DESIRE

I am excited and thrilled when I hear your sexy voice.
I turn my head, so I can look at your lovely face.
I see you with your sunglasses on, then my heart goes pitter patter.
Could I be seeing a glamorous Hollywood starlet?
Could it be Morgan Fairchild, Raquel Welch, or Victoria Principal?
No she is more gorgeous than any of those women.
I wave my hand from across the room to show you that I care.
I eagerly wait for the day, when all my fantasies will come true!
I wait for an opportunity to kiss your ruby lips.
I am longing to spend moments of ecstasy with you, while slow-dancing.
I would like to hug you forever and never let you out of my arms.
For you are . . .

MY HEART'S DESIRE.

Kenny O'Leary

THE POET

The man of words and wisdom. The special creative man who speaks
of life with a pencil. The poet who travels all over the world keeping
a diary of poetic words concerning his journeys. Words concerning
the people he meets, situations he encounters, experiences he
shares. So art-is-tic is the poet, when he speaks people listen,
what he writes people read, when he acts others re-act, where he
walks many tend to follow, yet often he walks alone. Basically he
is a loner with a sad emptiness that surrounds him. Deep inside
there is a hollow spot, a need for comfort, understanding, support
and caring . . . Which can only be filled by me . . . The Poetess.

Gale P. Edeawo

LOVE'S JOURNEY

Further and further love goes searching for total tranquility,
Passing through the walls of the universe and into a new
Blue dimension in search for total tranquility.
Love soaring through a new blue dimension, three times the speed
Of light, searching for total tranquility — around and around love
Goes soaring in the new blue dimension, never stopping for a brief
moment and never tiring, love soars through the new blue dimension
In search of total tranquility. Suddenly a loud noise occurs as
Loud as a hundred splitting atoms, a ball of fire then crashes
Through the walls of the new blue dimension — Worry not for it's
Only love once again entering into the universe searching for
Total tranquility never stopping for a moment and never tiring
And love continues its perpetual journey in search for total
Tranquility.

John J. Rivera, Sr.

MY ANGEL

My Angel wears an apron and makes my Heaven here on earth,
She's my most precious gift from GOD, there's no figuring her worth.
She keeps a song within my heart — sends joy and love my way.
I thank GOD for my special Angel, every single day.
Every time she greets me with her loving smile,
It makes the daily tasks of life seem so much more worthwhile.
Because of her the skies are blue — she makes the sun to shine,
And I'm so glad that Angel, in a pretty kitchen apron, is mine.
However there's one thing that puzzles me.
How come our cherubs were so full of deviltry?
(I guess the answer's plain to see —
They must have taken after me.)

Eulaliah T. Hooper

DUSTY SKELETON

What articles are you hiding from me? Your wife would like to know
Your past is such a secret you keep only to yourself
I wish you could at least share some of it with me
I would like to know your family's history a little more
Than what you have already told me

What articles are you hiding from me? Your wife would like to know
Don't be afraid of your past — I have a right to know
I am your best friend and won't hurt you! Promise!
Questions unanswered to the kind of man I had married
Clear your closet and dust away the skeleton you've kept for years
So we may be closer than ever before

Mark A. Shenkir

LOVE

Love is like a blooming flower

Even if only for the hour
It slowly opens up like a rose bud
And never becomes a dud.
True love and still waters run deep
Like the mighty ocean clear and to keep
Finally he pops the question and she replies yes,
With her true love to confess,
Soon they will be walking down the aisle to the tune of "Here comes the Bride,"
Their true love forever to abide.

Mary Catherine Petersonn

TOO BAD MY FRIEND

You had your way, though every day you knew that you were wrong;
You told your lies, and alibis and hurt him all day long —
I tried to warn you and to help you to the very end.
Today's the day you start to pay; too bad for you my friend.
You had your fling and did your thing, as every day went by;
You had your chance and did your dance and tried to live a lie —
You took the one who loved you true and used him like a tool,
Today the cost comes at your loss — now you shall play the fool.
His love you scorned though you were warned you'd be sorry some day;
Now it's too late to flee your fate; there's nothing more to say —
Look on, no more, the days of yore, for they're all in the past;
Too bad, my friend, now has your sin caught up to you at last.

Edwin Hayes

ONCE MORE

If only once more I could see
his face
And gaze into those inescapable
eyes,
Penetrating, probing, loving me with
wonder and surprise.

If only once more I could
see his smile,
Open, generous, without guile,
Holding my heart all the while.

If only once more I could
touch his hair,
Waving, graying softly there.
To soothe his weary forehead then
Draw him close with tenderest hands.

If only we might have this
grace,
And travel to that distant
place
Into the endless, perfect land
Where only the heart can understand.

If only to have this moment
blessed by the Divine,
Until such time when separation
is no more,
Where freedom reigns at Heaven's
core,
And love is love,
once more.

Dorothy M. Halverson

SAD FLAG

Our Flag looks so sad today
As it flies half-mast
From its staff.
Nary a flutter.

It hangs limp
As if to weep . . .
Too stunned to move . . .
Mourning our Nation's Dead.

Red strips of Blood
Drip down to Earth
As if they know
Hero's blood was shed.

White stripes so pale
In shock,
Portraying
The mourner's wail.

That Stars upon
The night of blue
Do not shine as bright
As yesterday.

Our Land
Can understand . . .
Why . . .
OUR FLAG LOOKS SO SAD TODAY.

Elaine Meli

A GREAT LOVE

How great is the perfect love of God?
We see it in the flowers
We see it in the forest
When the morning comes we see it in
the eastern skies
At evening we see it in the
beautiful sunset
Oh how great is God's gift of love
for us
We see His love in little children's
smiling faces when they look at
you and smile.

Hattie Suggs

MEMORIES

Memories come in handy
Whenever we are sad and blue.
I have realized the ones I like best
Are the ones where I'm with you.
I've collected all the memories
Of you right from the start;
And tucked them all away neatly
All safe and warm deep in my heart.
I'll always keep my memories
They mean so much to me.
I keep them locked in my heart
And I have given you the only key.

Maureen Houlihan-Sutter

NEVER

Forget you never
You live within me
I realize you are gone
Where I cannot have you physically
But I'm in the depths of despair
Mentally you still possess my being
I can't play my deck of cards
Because I can't win you anyhow
You have gone from my realm of existence
Losing control of you forever
My ending is also my beginning
Touched by only you

Renata Dawidowicz

IDYLL

Awakening on a loveless plain,
To see you standing, long and fair,
Strong arms to lift me in the air,
So I might fall asleep again,
Indulging in a gentle dream
Of spending all our lifelong hours
Wandering through the meadow flowers,
To whisper by a sunny stream,
Wondering, breathless, at the sight
Of birds dispersing in the sky,
The silky twilight sliding by,
To close us in our final night.

Virginia Westgaard

TIME'S BANISHED STRANGERS

We took, without stars, the only
image booming, its long-lasted rainbow,
the sprinkle of our dust-covered
fingers;
you in the downy
white plumage and lean on the bowsprit,
the swell's timid vanguard, a child of
the owl's wing

and twilight's ember grew around you.

The black-eyed chasms, deep as wells,
your vacuum cringed and my skewed lunge
shot you split back to topaz and
ochre,
crumbled in the desert
grains and fast in the cracked shell,
the scouring winds of a forgotten planet,
a fossil of my youth

that scrapes across my dreams.

J. Maurice Endres

TEMPTATION

Loveliness . . .
you stand
before me,
in all of your
tempting, alluring
beauty.
You beckon.
Come here;
bring yourself
within reach,
bend and
extend your
face —
so we then
can become
as one.
Breath in
the aroma
of my fragrance.
Beautiful, beautiful,
red, red — Rose.

Nita Jamison

FINDING A WAY OUT

Escaping the moment of time.
Never turning back long enough
to regain your frame of mind.
Looking toward the moment foretelling
the right time.

Every moment, every hour, every
minute, he's on your mind.

Turning hands on a clock tell the
day and time.

Turning pages on a calendar tells
one that this is the right time.
Once again he's on your mind.
Never knowing if you are on
his mind just the same.

Marguerite Brugos

THE CAGED BIRD

Baby,
that bird in there is caged
its mobility is limited
its boundaries are fixed
the air it breathes seeps
through the cage holes
it longs for free air
it envies their freedom
I am the caged bird.

Kaizer Mabhilidi Nyatsumba

THE SILENT HEART

My heart knows secret dreams
it can never reveal.

It hears your thoughts
through tears you'll never see.

It touches your soul
with a softness you'll never feel.

It caresses the moments
when you've gone from me.

And waits in lonely vigil
for a time that will never be.

Betty Allen

PEGASUSIAN

Now Pegasus yonder
From longagodom
Had wings to ponder
Was love its fondom.

Sped he far travels
Further than dream be:
Fever of gold gravels
Or something newsy.

Where was his tether
None people did say
Watched for some feather
To keep romance quill gay.

Orien Todd

SOMEWHERE, SOMETIME

I feel that we have met before
In haps another place
That stood in bygone days of yore
And I still love your face

We must have loved a love so deep
That couldn't end with death
And we were destined to return
To search the width and breadth

For as we met each other's gaze
And walked across the room
A life we had no knowledge of
We knew we must resume

Edna Ball

LOVE REVERING

I have a loving father that the Lord has given me,
He's always been there for me when I needed him to be.
To help in every way he could, with all he had to give,
By leading in the Christian life that God wants us to live.

Jesus is Lord and Savior to Dad, on this you can depend,
As living a true example before the Lord he does intend.
He's willing to firmly stand alone for what he feels is right,
And praying and reading the Bible keeps him spiritually tight.

My father is a family man, and that he'll be forever,
For never is he happier than when we're all together.
His beaming face shows generous pride for loved ones held so dear,
Thus others see the enduring strength of a home highly secure.

Betty Sue Curtis

LOVE'S CIRCLE

In the midst of times of trouble, in the dawn of a new day.
Sharing, caring, then tomorrow, casting all my fears away.
The sounds of raindrops splashing against the muddy bank.
Dark gray shadows hover over treetops, as black clouds rumble late.

Crystal tears dripping from lush green ferns, flowers
drooping, their heads bowed low. Buzzing bees, wet wings,
robins singing, as the new day springs. All these splendors
recall memories of many dreams.

As the rill bends and the leaves of time toss about the
rocky path, a newness awakens me. My heart touches the springtime
of my soul, and blossoms free. In love's circle, fragile, you
and I, but now we are three. Across the sky, a rainbow I see!

Ronnette Ward

IN FEWER WORDS

I could have said more in these grimly assembled lines,
But I choose to portray in a few soothing words —
What it takes to express calmly in a lifetime;
It looks unwittingly obvious, or rather raptly absurd
Why I take time out to candidly convey this day,
My thoughts, which only in you, will staunchly inhere
To forever live long, after I've passed away.
From the looks of things and the way I feel
My days are coming to a close, our union's ending is near.
Nevertheless, I care to refresh thy memory obligingly, so
In my absence, my last ditch obsession, thy cheerfulness will ne'er glue;
But remain radiant, and distanced from the clutch of fear.
In my demise, thou art still close to me without guise
As it was, when I first glimpsed at thine love, in the twinkle of thine eyes.

Pete P. Norella

MEMORIES

The lilting music of a song makes me wonder where I went wrong.
Pictured scenes flow through my mind remembered times when you were kind.
A movie remembered brings hidden tears as I turn away and pretend
not to hear. Thoughts of laughter and joy tear through my heart
for I wonder why we had to part. When I think of the things you
bought for me I realize that I was too blind to see.
For something was wrong and I didn't understand when you refused
to take my hand.
And now I'm alone and thinking of you with only dreams and wishes
which may never come true.

Julie Zuchowski

LASTING LOVE

I love you tenderly
I love you passionately
No matter how you look at it
I love you lastingly
Tender love is to me
The finest there can be
Mingled with passionate love
It is even far above
Only you can render
My heart so tender
Only you arouse in me
Fires of love so passionately
These are the ingredients
Of love lasting
If any man had this
You'd never find him asking.
As long as the earth whirls in space
As long as the stars shine above
You will have my lasting love.

Eugene A. Dixon

THE GREEN HAT

In a land
not unfamiliar to
beautiful women
your blonde tresses
drew the attention of the crowd;
a bonnet of green
flashed rivulets of promises
against the chinese lanterns,
against the dark, blue shadows
of the Hong Kong Café.
The foggy night
carried the shadows,
the green chapeau,
you and I,
across alleys, dangers,
to quiet, serious talk —
to a moment
spent —
with Formosa oolong.

Theo. Oliver

STAGNANT APPARITION

Whispered softly, "bon soir"
to a face that wasn't yours
though it spoke such gentle phrases
while I feigned a pose demure.
Your ghost was so appealing
and the prose so flattering
as you deftly held dispassion back
to block my suffering.

But now,
that's all so needless.
Sad is sad, but not for me.
So, suppress pretense and gladness
based on fond, frayed memories.
Break the handshakes,
shake the clasp,
love and loss no longer true.
Pensive kiss to my old passion;
wave away and say "adieu."

Guada Woodring-Lueck

LITH. & PUB. BY N. CURRIER. Entered according to Act of Congress in the year 1844 by N. Currier, in the Clerk's office of the District Court of the Southn. Distt. of N. Y. 152 NASSAU ST. COR. OF SPRUCE N.Y.

HARVEST.

HOLD ME PLEASE

Hold me please
I need to feel your strength,
your warmth, your caring.

Hold me please
I need to feel your hand in my hair,
your shoulder under my head, your
arm around me.

Hold me please.

Oh well, one more time.

Hold me please

I need you.

Faith A. Skrip

SHADOW PLAY

Softly sweeping,
Flowing by,
Shadows cross a whispering sky.
Pursuing stranger gently sensed.
Though self-contained, I feel unrest.

I reach to hold a moment gone;
A friend unseen is moving on.
The wind had called, I swore I heard;
Or was it all unspoken word?

A rainbow's touch is never known,
And love in truth is seldom shown.
Softly sweeping,
Flowing by,
Shadows cross a whispering sky.

Sherry Trask

ON A MAY AFTERNOON

Your mist, your kiss
flew by
on a May afternoon . . .

A dinky sort
of love
went to the yellow moon.

A dinky slap in my
shy and flaming face
yearning alone:

"I wish
your kiss
and waist
on a May afternoon."

Hilda More

CHOCOLATE KISSES

Chocolate Kisses, silent wishes,
He loves me, he loves me not.
Our time together may be short,
But long, before forgot!

Vachelle Wade

TO SCOTT

I never told you how I felt,
I never believed in me.
You were the answer to my prayers
And I hid behind my words.

Only now when you are far away
Can I say what I've hid for so long.

I stole glances while you worked
And I read the words you wrote
To someone else.
I cried because they were the ones
I needed to hear.

I wanted to say 'I love you'
But my reflection told me the truth.
You could never love me.

You were the beauty and I the beast;
My heart broken, I ran away
Never telling you the secrets
That could have set us both free.

The only thing left to say is
'I still love you.'

Kira Elise Fremont

MY JIM

I see your face in every cloud formation.
I hear your voice in every whisper
of the wind.
I feel your touch
as leaves of branches touch my cheek.
I feed the birds to make them sing
and lift my spirits
till the day that you return.

Olga H. Scully

THOUGHTS

Waiting for your midnight eyes,
hypnotized by sunshine,
knowing only night could save me.

I cried by the water's edge,
looking for something more than,
colored stones and fallen leaves.

A storm rising within me,
for those charted hours,
at love's expense.

With God's own hand,
He made you,
love's machinery not yet working.

As we turn face to face,
the only thing we have to fight
is the silver screen that
keeps us from,
lying in each other's arms.

Anticipating nothing,
I dared to imagine all was right,
but even the gypsies know better.

Jenniene Witmer

MY GIFT OF LOVE

A gift of love I give to
you
Wrapped in my heart the
whole year through
Tied with the ribbon of
my soul
Your happiness my only
goal.

This gift of love's not
just for now
But each and every day
of life
And in return your gift
to me
You've been a faithful
loving wife.

Lawrence A. Souza

SOUZA, LAWRENCE A. Born: Sacramento, California, 6-9-20; Married: 11-29-46 to Thelma L. Dobson; Education: High School Graduate, 1936; Occupation: U.S. Army, World War II, South Pacific, 10-23-42 to 11-6-45; Hotel Administration, Retired; Awards: Golden Poet Award, World of Poetry, 1985; 5th Place Award, 1983; Fourth Place Award, 1985; 15 Awards of Merit (10 Honorable Mentions); Poetry: 'The Unknown Soldier,' American Poetry Association, 1986, 'Memories,' World of Poetry, 1985, 'Hope,' Poetry Press, Texas, 1985; 'Innocence,' American Poetry Association, 1986; Other Writing: "War and Politics," prose, World of Poetry, 1984.

Rippp.
Moan.
Dying sighs.
Another heart is broken.
But the uncaring world
continues its gleeful dance
without you.
It has no heart.

Janice R. Nelson

THE LUCKY ONES

Love is just for some —
It beats faster than a drum —
Why can't I be one of 'The Lucky Ones?'

You came into my life —
Breathing fire in the night —
Living high was so much fun —
We were 'The Lucky Ones.'

Why did you take me, for a ride that went nowhere?
I really loved you, but you showed me you did not care.

Now I am alone —
Counting numbers on my phone —
Wishing I had been one of 'The Lucky Ones.'

Barbara Goldberg

GOLDBERG, BARBARA. Born: Bronx, New York, 9-24-38; Single; Occupation: Bookeeper; Memberships: ASCAP, Republican Presidential Task Force, New York Zoological Society; Awards: Award of Merit Certificate for poem 'A Quarter After Moonlight,' 10-31-84; Honorable Mention from World of Poetry, Sacramento, California; Comments: *I truly enjoy writing poetry as I feel a glow of well-being when I complete a poem. It's wonderful to be able to share a poem that I wrote, with the world. Poetry will always be a part of my life.*

LEARNING TO LOVE

I need you to deeply love and accept me
Not for my sake, but for yours.
Yet, when you affectionately care for me
You feel an incalculable deficit,
So I try to love you more and more,
And in loving you I fail to solidify your love.
What a paradox we live and sense not
For if we both love, we feel pain and loss
And if we love not, we suffer and grow bitter.
I know you stand the greater, yet the needier.
Even so, I need you to fully love and accept me
Not solely for my sake, but for yours.
The cure for your weary mind and torn emotions
Rests in your need to love and trust me with confidence.
When you love and accept me and myself as I be
You, in turn, will learn to love yourself, and me.

John Phillip Hasenberg

Perhaps we'll meet again at the mouth of the
universe when the shepherd lays down his staff
at the feet of the stars and the jester lays
down his slapstick and admits that there is
no truth.

Perhaps we'll meet again when the galaxies
kiss and when, at the edge of emptiness, we
become the image of each other and the
fools who have consumed all the darkness
until there is none left, will be no more.

Will we then be free to see? Will we then
be free to sing and dance in the meadow on
the other side of time? Will we then be
free to look inside and ask if it's all just
a dream? Or will we then be free to consume
all the love until we ourselves are over-
flowing? Then perhaps we'll meet again when
we become one and really know love.

William J. Spake, Jr.

OUR MOTHER

Her hands were large, but slim and very shapely,
Suggesting a fineness in her birth and rearing.
She might have held a palette and a brush,
Or bow and violin with singing strings.
Instead, she took the common tasks of living
And molded strength and beauty from these things.
A farmer's wife, she bore and reared her family
In a simple house of sod on a western prairie.
She made their house a home replete with love.
She labored hard on their farm to help her man.
She dreamed of her children's future, while she worked.
She was always ready to help a neighbor in trouble,
Seldom thinking of her own personal need —
No job too menial — no load too great,
For giving was her all-unconscious creed.
Age never marred the beauty of her hands.
Though worn with toil, their tapered slenderness,
Even in death, reflected the artist's soul,
That all her life, created tenderness.

Josephine O. Bull

TREASURE CHEST

On an island far away,
lying broken in a cave,
I found love.
Frightened at first, I whispered to him,
"Be still, I mean no harm."
His face managed to create a slow, weary smile.
I smiled back, for what luck,
I had found an angel with a broken wing.
Gently, I began to free his worries,
mend his wounds, while inventing stories.
He calmly yawned
and then sank down
to rest awhile upon the ground.
I smiled again with great pride,
for sleeping sweetly at my side
was an angel.
Slowly, I ran my fingers through his hair.
I whispered "I love you,"
but he was unaware.

Linda A. Mayes

SAINT VALENTINE'S DAY

There wasn't any wicked witch, who prophesied that at sixteen
she would prick her finger and would sleep until awakened by a
prince.
The story didn't go like that!
But three awakened her in time.
The first was humble, and his kiss was gentle as the evening breeze.
He asked for the impossible, but said it like a whispered prayer.
It was a strange awakening, resulting in her gratitude.
The second was Sir Galahad. He never kissed her lips at all;
but when he married Emily, she knew her love had been with love
and not the boy with golden hair.
The third might well have been the prince —
gentle and whimsical and kind,
wise with the wisdom of the old, charming as had been Galahad.
Each one was an awakening, but none of them had been her prince.
Perhaps she wrote the fairy tale?

Ruth A. Williams

WHAT ARE MY FEELINGS UP TO NOW?

We meet again today. The first time in many, many years.
A friend of a friend; but nonetheless, a friend.
We talked a while and as our conversation grew, I realized the mistake I'd made back when things were different and I was young. I missed something terribly important back then. I missed out on him! I never took the time to talk with him or listen to his cries of loneliness. How could I let the opportunity of such a precious gift of friendship pass me by?
He's such a gentle man, with very little to say, but so much inside. I never noticed how quiet he was before. I don't remember if I cared that much to find out. All I knew was that he was a person, but never gave him a chance to be a better friend. Maybe I felt I had no right to interfere in his life without his asking. Or was it I was afraid to intrude? Or just afraid?

Leaving him that night, I'd felt a feeling I hadn't felt since I was a teen. The kind you get when you first fall in love. I couldn't get him off my mind. Was it the thrill of love? Or just concern and excitement of a newfound friendship? One so rare that it hid for years in the dark till I "opened up" to his needs and listened to him. I really cared about him.

My mind has been occupied with only thoughts of seeing him again. But now, so many, many years later, when things are different and I'm older, I ask myself again: have I the right? Or am I still afraid to?

Judith A. Neujahr

MY DREAM

She was the cream of my life or so it did seem, when I was in the 4th grade.
She was my dream. I wanted to grow up and be just like she.
Even then I wondered how this could be.
We lived near the school. This teacher lived at our house.
We chuckled and laughed, never still as a mouse.
I wonder and thought if when I was older, I could be like she,
a teacher and this I never told her.
I even wanted to have real sparkling eyes, this I hoped and prayed for
when I looked up to the skies.
But miracles happen I knew at that age.
A bird might fly out, then right back in his cage. Change its mind,
then turn around, just a flutter but never a sound.
I kept in touch with Miss Curtis all through the years.
Joy came to me often and frequently tears.
When I finished high school and went for futher study, we know now
in our lives, some spots can be muddy. Part so! and Behold!
my dreams all came true.
I do miss this teacher under our skies of blue.
We all need to hope, we also want to plan.
Whether nature makes us a lady or a real gentleman.
She is living now, so we often write. My dream came true,
My life made bright.

Edith Van Orsdale

ANOTHER NEW BEGINNING

It's another new beginning
Another fresh start
Let's get to know
Each other
Please don't let us ever part.

It's another new beginning
We're both starting free
Searching and hoping
This time, this love
Will be.

The one that'll
Last forever
As long as life will be
It's another new beginning
This time, this love, won't pass.

It's another new beginning
One more fresh start
Let's get to know each other
Let's take it
Straight from the heart.

Karolyn E. Evans

SEPTEMBER 20TH, 1980

The lake met the sky
there was a tear in my eye
from the happiness you gave to me

The sun broke through the clouds
the waves bursting aloud
as I felt myself being free

I ran through the sand
watching my man
collecting wood for the fire

The world was mine
it was like a design
As my fantasy filled my desire

And there on the beach
lay little Joaquin
watching Khan run and play

And if I never again
See Lake Michigan
I'll remember this most beautiful day.

Debbie Ann Ochoa

lying silently alone
this morning
in mussed up bed.

I stared for a time at plastered ceiling
and re-thought our lovemaking.
I think sometimes,
in desperate love mostly,
of you as far beyond a man.
After times like now
I know me right,
for no man
ever touched me
like you.

Felicia Morgan

SON'S 21 BIRTHDAY

Today precious son, a new cycle of your life doth start
Wishing your future years are numerous, and you play a glorious part
Even though there may be clouds sometimes your happiness to dim
Never in life is there perfection, it is a just rule
Although seemingly grim
Take life as it comes, the good with the bad
Your future I hope will be fortunate my manly lad
On your twenty-first birthday
New laurels beckon you, and I pray for you
Every wish of yours be granted
Your loving Mom

Pearl Van Slocum

THE UNSURPASSED LOVE OF A TRUE FRIEND

The winter winds are howling fiercely outside tonight,
But I am cozy and warm fondly remembering well
The trips in the breathtaking Colorado mountain heights
With close friends and also a new one, whose friendship does excel.

We met by chance — deep inner feelings darted from eye to eye
As though we had been kindred spirits for years.
Only a brief vacation, but our mutual sensations climbed sky high.
Others I had known for years could see this friendship blossoming very clear.

Then only too soon, time for me to go back to my home in the East,
Leaving the majestic mountains, the parties, loved ones and my new unpredictable friend,
Who is always near — surprising me with a very exciting send-off, including a gourmet feast.
When the limousine pulled up — a spontaneous hug and kiss that thrilled me no end!

As the limousine sped toward the airport, I was in a dizzy whirl.
The plane was ready to board at once, and looking at the misty mountains, the beautiful West
We were airborne — leaving my favorite vacation spot, many thoughts in my head did swirl!
Devoted friends greeted me at the airport, teasingly said — I looked radiant — full of zest!

A long distance call — yes, my dear new friend misses me already!
I am on top of the mountains again, such a heart-throbbing, stimulating relationship.
Laughter, understanding, teasing, love came through loud and clear — made me feel heady!
So happy to be a woman, I'm ecstatic with his adept, sincere, unsurpassed loving friendship!

Mildred A. Martin

THE SEASONS OF LOVE

Spring . . .
a time when Life and Love
both seem to take on new meaning
a time when I started to live again
because *You* came into my life . . .

Summer . . .
a time in which to reap the harvest
of happiness — love — joy — and laughter
a time to rejoice in the knowledge
that *We* have each other . . .

Fall . . .
with its golden sunsets and blustery winds
as we watched the whirling leaves fall to the ground
and the affection and concern which we've shared with one another
has now turned into a full bloom love affair . . .

Winter . . .
the coldest time of the seasons
and now the saddest day of my life
for like a tree stripped of its fruit
my life is empty and barren
for I no longer have You by my side . . .

Lin Eric Brown

MADE FOR EACH OTHER

Love is a very special gift
That God put in our heart
I knew that you were meant for me
Right from the very start

From the time we said hello
And we had our first date
It didn't take me long to know
This couldn't just be fate

I'm so glad that God looked down
And recognized my care
When He sent you into my life
I knew He'd heard my prayer

I know God had a purpose
For sending you to me
And now I know it's for us to live
As one eternally

As we start our lives as one
Lord give us eyes to see
And grant us a willing spirit
To be what you want us to be

Joye Atkinson

PRECIOUS PROMISE

I need to know love.
I need to know that others care.
I can see the Glory.
I know that God is there.

I can feel the sun
Warm upon my face.
I can smell the flowers
Blooming every place.

I can hear God
In the falling drops of rain.
I can feel God
As I rise from mortal pain.

My burden does seem lighter;
And, my path a little brighter
As I walk the road with others —
My sisters and my brothers.

All those beautiful people,
God's very children on earth,
Are His Precious Promise
At the moment of our birth.

June K. Gaut

CELA OF OLYMPIA

Sunshine girl
Effulgent smile
Transforms perceptions
Into beauty, warmth and hope.

Insincerity fades
Goddess!
Holding the torch high
Heralding womanhood
of the future.

Joel George O'Brien

GOD IS LOVE

God is love, God is great,
He answers all our Prayers,
He is on Call all the time,
Even through the darkest hours.

Ask and He will Answer,
Seek, And you shall find,
Happiness and Contentment always,
A serene and peaceful mind.

Knock and the door will open,
You can visit with God awhile,
Telephone to Glory, what joy!
It makes you always smile.

God is Good and God is love,
Our Father from on high,
He watches over all His children,
From that mansion in the sky.

I hope I can climb the ladder.
And have a Mansion of My own,
Made of the works I've done in life,
And the seeds that I have sown.

Willie Johnson Cummings

LOVE OF A FRIEND

Love starts
As a little seed planted
Deep within your heart

It keeps growing
Slowly flowing
As time goes on

I guess we did have love
One of a special nature
This is
The love of a friend

Sometimes the love of a friend
Can be more precious
Than being in love

Love is a special feeling
Feel it
Do not take advantage of it

Take my hand
And together we will share
The love of a friend

Lori Heim

My mother,
who helped me patiently
when I was ill in her
arms she held me still
She prayed a prayer of God's
own will my mother;
Such great body
who taught me how to
kneel and pray, who
watched over me night and day
who wiped each tiny tear away
My mother.

Beulah Lance

ENSLAVED, YET EVER FREE

Since first I loved thee long ago
So softly love hath grown,
A greater, richer, splendent thing
Than e'er hath mortal known.

I sense thy warm caressing touch
Within each gentle breeze,
And hear thy voice so tenderly
'Midst softly rustling leaves.

I see in thee a loveliness
Surpassing every flower,
And find in thee a joy of life
More precious every hour.

Enslaved am I within such love —
Enslaved, yet ever free,
To give to thee endearing love,
As thou hast given me.

David J. Creager

MAY 17, 1978

You were never
just a man
to me
more like a god
who should live
on top of Mount Olympus
or the white knight
of my childhood dreams
so wherever you are
please know
there's a girl
out there who believes
that unicorns once lived
and that it could be
possible to dance on the
stars that lead up
to the moon
all because she had
that one afternoon
with you

Diane Wanderer

RING WITHOUT A FINGER

A ring of gold is sitting cold,
Alone — hidden in a drawer.
No finger warms it. No finger fills it.
Its memories grow old.

Memories of a laughter shared,
Of a hand gliding through the hair.
The sound of a newborn's screams,
The closeness of two bodies.

These and other memories fade
Like photographs left outside.
Their colors slowly slip away
And turn to shades of grey.

Inert now, it sits and waits
For a forgotten warmth.
A piece of cold dead metal,
A ring without a finger.

W. N. Robinson, Jr.

SONG

Love and harmony combine,
And around our souls intwine,
While thy branches mix with mine,
And our roots together join.

Joys upon our branches sit,
Chirping loud, and singing sweet;
Like gentle streams beneath our feet
Innocence and virtue meet.

Thou the golden fruit dost bear,
I am clad in flowers fair;
Thy sweet boughs perfume the air,
And the turtle buildeth there.

There she sits and feeds her young,
Sweet I hear her mournful song;
And thy lovely leaves among,
There is love: I hear his tongue.

There his charming nest doth lay,
There he sleeps the night away;
There he sports along the day,
And doth among our branches play.

William Blake

PASSION

I want you every night!
But you won't be with me.
I guess it's my time to cry.
When I feel only misery.

I lie beside you,
In the still of the night.
Wanting and needing you,
It just ain't right!

For me to have such PASSION,
And not get any in return,
I have this warmth inside me.
The desire within me burns!

I wish, that you'd be with me.
Each and every time,
I feel the need for your company.
It would truly ease my mind.

HEY, baby you just don't know!
From you I'll never stray.
And even if you never touch me
Please don't ever go away!

Dinah K. Henderson

TREASURE

I counted myself wealthy
To have a loving husband
A daughter, and a son.
If we were also healthy,
We felt like millionaires.
Though in the early thirties,
Money we had none.
But we had other treasure
Worth much more than gold,
Of love we had full measure,
The oldest story told.

Susan Schreiner

DEAREST AMBERINE

That November afternoon, the Texas sun set high. In
the church I heard Reverend Julius preach. His
words for Jesus touched me and I started to cry.
The sun came down on your hair so brown. You
looked like a princess with a tiara on her crown.
You stood behind your husband so calm.
I tried to reach you, but you left me empty.
Jubilation, you came back again. You handed me a
bunch of violets, covered with damp rain.
It matched the twin sets of tears on our faces, yours and mine.
Dearest Amberine, I am only a man who is a priest,
regardless of my masked image.
You led me up the staircase, and down my corridor.
You told me to take the ribbons from your hair, and
lay them gently on the bed. Yours to touch and see,
behind the curtains so red.
When morning came, the sun fell through my eyes I
thought it was only a dream, or maybe a vision. Except for
the ribbons on the bed.

Gina T. Ganguli

THE SWEET OF LOVE

The sweet of love is captive freedom,
touching straight with sudden constant
care.
Teeming grace, basking in extremes,
as soft as success, as strong as struggle.
Most mythless: now and forever our souls
tender, as we're lastingly blessed,
and unswervingly clinging to changeless
truth,
given heroes unknowingly worthy.
marvelous mates, who are willingly pleased,
knowing continuity above humbling trials,
we share soothing kisses: assured in the
mind
of consciously choosing the conscientious
spouse.
The resonant rhythm of drums in our eyes
is vivid vibrancy of desire within our
hearts.

Dennis Bailey

PAINTING

The lady in the painting the artist
must have been in love, for he chose
all the right colors and added a
touch of lust.
The lady in the painting, so vividly real,
like she was almost reaching out to
feel;
her face so fresh and new and
that painted body not well-hidden
by the gown she wears for you.
Golden hair so fair as the sweet colors
fill the air;
brush strokes almost unnoticed
by the glare.
The lady in the painting, her story remains
a mystery but her beauty has been
kept alive,
by the artist whose love for her
has survived.

Donald Johnson

OH MY CHILD, NO LONGER MY CHILD

Oh my child, no longer my child,
I love you so.
I think about you often and I wonder . . .
What would it be like
To hold you, to look at you . . .
If only for a moment.
But, no . . . that would not be fair . . .
Fair to you, to me or
To those who care for you, love you, need you.

Oh my child, no longer my child,
Be kind, be loving,
Grow stronger day by day.
If you should ever need to know me;
If you should ever wonder why —
Just come to me and I will tell you,
Why . . . Because I love you
More than you will ever know.
You're very special.
I love you, son.

Sandra Kay Tipton

LOVING, LONELY MOTHER

A mother one night sat by her window
Watching the snow as it fell so slow
As it covered the ground, it made her sad:
She was reminded of four snowy mounds.

Away in the hills! — She had to weep;
Down deep in the cold cold clay
Lay her babies far far away —
Their spirits with God doth sweetly sleep.

So she bowed her had and sadly said;
"Oh, dear God they do belong to you":
But the wind was so cold that stormy night
As the snow was glittering pure and white.

The LOVE and JOY sprung into her heart
For she knew in death we have to part . . .
God seemed to say "There'll be a dawning,"
Again she bowed her head and finally said
"Thank You."

Opal Marie Hayes

APOCALYPSE

Where Heaven meets earth — on that distant line of being,
I will wait for you until time is known no more.
There will be no sound in the awesome air around us,
Only silence bearing the perfume of a thousand flowers,
the savor of multitudinous grasses, the age-old fragrance
of willow buds and lotus blossoms.
I will cup my hands around a mountain and breathe in
the needled scent of a high-born pine,
Kneel beside the temples of bamboo as they sway
to the silent music of the spheres,
Look upon the face of Heaven reflected in the
waveless water of a crystal pool.
I will see the stars by night, the sun by day,
the moon in its ceaseless swing through space.
I will be one with earth and heaven.
Let the galaxies stand sentinel. Let eternity beware —
for out there
On that distant line where Heaven meets earth
I will wait for you until time is known no more.

Conna Bell

VISION

As I stand there looking
at an empty room,
just one moment
and you were there.
You came to see me
And tell me you were on your way.
I remember that moment so well.
When you stood by my side
it had been a miracle,
your face, so pure.
You looked so young,
as you had always seemed to me.
I called you "Dad,"
your blue eyes sparkled,
you didn't say a word,
but your lips did part as you and I
both had tears in our eyes.
You then looked up to Heaven
and with a smile on your face
and a glow in your eyes that
lit up the sky,
you turned around and disappeared
from sight.

Susan Burgess

LOVE

I walked the path beside our home.
My heart was heavy, as I roamed.
So full of grievance and despair,
I found a place, and lingered there.

I watched the sun set in the sky;
Beholding beauty even I,
In my sad state, could not deny.

Reflecting on the days behind,
Mixed feelings wrestled in my mind;
And wondering what was yet to be,
Should God be kind enough to me
To grant me still another day
To search and seek and find a way;

I started back — and picked a flower,
Although its petals did devour
A teardrop, maybe even two;
But it all changed when I saw you —

Standing at the door.

Sally Eshelman

EVERYDAY LOVE AT HOME

Perfection in this world is
Never uppermost in mind —
The little acts of kindness
Are the strongest ties that bind!

Tell each other "I love you,"
Before the day has ended —
"Do it now" (still MY motto)
Make sure each rift is mended —

Every daily task will give
Time to plan thoughtful wishes —
Joy and love will crown each day
(along with dirty dishes)

Edna M. Parker

THE LOVE LIGHT

I'm a sea gull soaring free
Cruise as far as I can see
Climbing through the clouds of time
Gliding to my destiny

Behold the good years, here at last
From the future, to the past
World turning, oh so fast
Sea of love so wild and vast

The Sun's a star, the star of life
Rising at the edge of night
Pouring out its radiant light
Beach on fire, burning bright

Gazing from this ivory tower
Summer moon engulfs the hour
Winds of passion bloom and flower
Midnight magic has the power

William Robert O'Loughlin

O'LOUGHLIN, WILLIAM ROBERT. Born: 11-16-59; Education: Public Schools of Sudbury, Massachusetts, 1965-73; Lincoln-Sudbury Regional High School, 1973-77; graduated summa cum laude from Northeastern University, Boston, Massachusetts, B.S., received the Sears B. Condit Honor Award for outstanding scholarship, 1982; University of California, Los Angeles, M.S. in Engineering, 1985; Poetry: 'Here I Stand,' 'The Image Train,' 'Break Away,' American Poetry Association, 1986; Comments: *I am an American poet. I was raised in scenic New England and my childhood pastimes included fishing in ponds, building forts, and exploring the countryside. As a young man I went to college in Boston, a city rich in heritage, culture, education, and tradition. As a student I was interested in classical literature, especially Shakespeare's tragedies. At the age of twenty-two I moved to California in pursuit of my dreams and in search of adventure. I have found great beauty in both worlds. In my poetry I try to capture unique perspectives, deep emotions, and powerful images.*

THE FIRE OF LOVE

The fire of love can burn into the soul — reaching deep within
the heart and the mind.
Its sparks can fill the dullest eyes — cause a spark that keeps
glowing there and forever shines!
No one can escape this fire of burning love — none can hide or
ever escape its presence.
God created this great burning love — from the void which was —
Making Him then Adam — then Eve to love — there in the Garden of Eden.
He made for them this glorious world of planets, the heavens,
And finished it off with the stars of evening!
So my Darling, though you may try to deny your great love for me,
One look in your eyes — one touch of your hand — and I feel the
smouldering love and know — IT was *meant* to be!
For the fire of love runs too deep — to ever throw away,
It surrounds us all with its unrelenting power — Yes —
Your love for me I know is here to stay!
It can heal — it can hurt — it can even destroy at will;
Rebuild an entire nation — exist throughout the ages and live —
Continuing forever through each new creation!

Joyce Mullins

THE BEST OF LOVE

My love for you is free, always was, always will be, although you
were not with me physically, you were always in my heart. For you, love
I never forgot, my heart and my love goes out to you, for whatever your
needs may be, and hope someday you'll understand, and return the same to
me. I ask of you nothing but a feeling, of which you hide in shame: It's
not a shame and you're not to blame. Open your heart and soul to me,
for I am not your enemy. I know your sensitivities, for they are the same
in me. To you I give my love, wherever you may be.
Can you understand *this* type of love, that has no bars, and only trust?
I know you well in any circumstance, although you hide from me the chance,
To be free in mind, soul . . . Does this freedom in one, scare you so much,
that you cannot trust, your teacher of love, who loves you so much?
God works in mysterious ways, he sees and feels our needs as such
I'll do you no harm and when the time has come for our souls to leave
We'll go with love as before, never wanting to be more, not feeling pain,
hurt or loss . . . feeling only love that could never be lost, for it goes
with us wherever we go. Do not feel hurt by me, I could not harm you . . .
before those clouds of doubt appear, think of what I'm doing here,
Love is helping you to be the best that you can be!

Marilyn Ruth Barnette

THE POWER OF HIS LOVE

I was completely mesmerized by the unearthly radiance and beauty of the sunset,
Pink clouds melted into bright orange and wandered against the bluish gray sky,
A heavenly golden glow encircled the clouds in an ethereal manner,
A solemn hush permeated the spot and I stared in breathless adoration.
There was no blinding light but the power of your presence overwhelmed me
I cried and blurred vision reached out.
You took my trembling hand and drew me to you.
I surrendered and months later pronounced three solemn vows.
I have lost my doubts and fears
My tiredness, weakness and frustrations vanish in your presence.
I have found you close in the open field and in the dimly lit chapel
In the silence I open my yearning heart and talk and walk with you
I have no problem lingering, there are moments that I cherish,
Moments when you softly and tenderly take my hand and I find myself
climbing the stairway to heaven
What indescribably and unsurpassing joy those moments bring.
Thank you, Lord, for the fire of your love.
May it burn ever brightly and illumine the rest of my life
Jesus, I love thee! Allow me to die in your embrace.

Sr. Anita Marie

IN SEARCH OF SOLITUDE

To live
alone is to
seclude oneself inside
the mind — a hermit living in
remorse.

To live
in loneliness
is to remove oneself
painfully from company of
others.

To live
in solitude
is to share love and live
in harmony and contentment
with you.

Luciano L. Medeiros

DARK STAR

Dark star, wild child,
a brilliant light the night will hide;
shine over me a radiant kiss.
Let me know what I have missed.

Dark star
talk to me.
Let me know what you see.

Wild child,
hidden smile.
An evening's journey of miles and miles.

Wild child, dark star;
The distance between us is not so far.
You are as I, and I as you.
Let no one judge the things we do.

S. A. Jannetti

TIME

There are hours in the day
That fly on gilded wing,
That flash before my startled eyes,
That cause my heart to sing.
These are the precious moments
I'm with the one I love,
When the world is filled with music
By a chorus from above.

There are hours in the day
That creep on shackled knee,
That move with maddening slowness
Throughout eternity.
These are the endless moments
Felt deep within my heart,
These are the empty hours
I know when we're apart.

William M. Sands

THE LAW OF LOVE

Were the world ruled by the law of love,
A spiritually starved universe
Would find peace from above;
The end of wars, pestilence and worse.
Were the world ruled by the law of love,
There'd be no menial jobs to cry about,
There'd be no need to push and shove;
Love would take the drudgery out.
Were the world ruled by the law of love,
We'd work for God, our boss,
Gladly toil each day for Him
Whose Son redeemed us on the cross.

Lillian C. Marcoux

JOY BRINGS LOVE

We found our day seemed very long,
Even though our love for each other was still strong.
But creaky bones and failing ears
Seemed to add disappointments to our senior years.
Then one day in a hospital room
The appearance our grandaughter made, wiped away the gloom.
Her parents appropriately named her Joy.
As grandparents, we were soon out buying a toy.
We thank God each day as we do pray,
For the happiness she continues to bring our way.
The love we share is a two-way street,
We can tell by the smile she gives us when we meet.

Maxine Johnson

LITTLE BALLERINA

Little ballerina, tiny, sparkling sprite,
Tutu a pink flutter, ponytail just right!
Tonight's your first recital, my precious, elfin wight.

Eyes a glow of sapphire, peeking out to see.
Up on your points. Twirl fast and free.
Dance for them and just for me!

My love and pride on my sleeve are worn;
The curtains part. A star is born!
Through my heart, my fairy darling, you've danced
Since your natal morn!

Shirley B. Stowater

The more I feel the day grow cold,
I wish for someone warm to hold;
Once there was one I loved so dear,
But his life wasn't meant for here,
It was a cold and tragic day,
When God saw reason to take him away.

I felt the world an empty place,
Never again to see his face;
I know that loss is part of growing,
You can touch love without even knowing,
God, I must believe it will come again,
To feel love stronger than it was then.

Cheryle Dawn Hart

SOMEWHERE IN THE NIGHT

We wrapped ourselves in a cocoon of love
It was the silken palace of our dreams
Where we could sample amorous delights
And sprinkle them with stardust and moonbeams.

But when spring buds began to swell
Strange stirrings filled your heart with dread
I think you knew our time was short
Before you left the marriage bed.

As a moth is drawn toward the flame
You flew into the clasp of night
Free to singe your new-found wings
Flirting with the flickering light.

Douglas Stanton

EXTREMITY

The light fades; closes the day.
I stumble; I lose my way.

Colder than yesterday, older than tomorrow,
My lamenting heart imprisons tears of sorrow.

The apparition; my mind it maims.
Intoxicating; my soul it claims.

The wind whispers; it sighs.
My pleading heart; it cries.

Dawn concedes to the day.
Memories, I lock away.

Judith A. Olson

I LOVE YOU

What can I write about love today?
But the same sweet story told this new way:
"I love you, dear, I love you truly, I do."
This old sweet story dress in fashion new,
Is the old sweet story I once told you
When we first met, and when we said, "I do."
For love, you know, is an old sweet story
That is ages older than old glory.
But, love is ever new and ever true
Since mankind comes and goes with passing time,
(And poets sing of love with and without rhyme).
Thus, when I write the words "I love you," one line
Is not enough to tell of love genuine.
So, I will only write, "Our love is divine."

Mollie E. Miller

GOD'S DAY

Every day is God's Day;
From the blue skies,
To the bees and butterflies,
From the sun above our heads; to the earth beneath our feet;
The smiles on the faces of the people we meet, to the
dampered look on the faces of the patients we treat;
We give them a loving smile and tell them to trust in God,
BECAUSE EVERY DAY IS GOD'S DAY

Betty Slaton Potter

WILL I THINK OF YOU TOMORROW?

I awoke late one night
Wondering if you had only been a dream
I searched my memory
As I followed a passing moonbeam.

Suddenly the wind rushed into my room
Taking my memory back to a night long ago.
Back . . . Back . . . Back
To a night I couldn't say no.

You were gentle and loving
Just like my dream, only real.
How could I ever know
My wounds would never heal?

As the moonbeam fades from my window
My memories drift back with the after-glow
I try to sleep once again
I wonder, will I think of you tomorrow?

Tammy Holley

OLD FORGOTTEN LOVE

There's a ghost of a love,
Living in my heart,
In the shadows of my mind,
It will never part.
It's haunting the love,
I feel deep inside,
Old forgotten love,
Shown before my eyes.
There's a ghost of a love,
Inside my heart,
Bringing forth to my mind,
Old love from the start.
It's so spookie,
To see what you've done,
Back in the past,
Now there's nowhere to run.
Because it's haunting the love,
You tried to hide,
An old forgotten love,
Lost somewhere inside.

Alvin Newsome Jr.

LIFETIME AWAY

Can you see that I'm the one
Look in my eyes
We were together in another life
Exchanging sweet sighs

Missed your soul
Missed your love
Longing for your inner touch

Back then we were more than friends
We were to be married
But I had to meet my fate
Something no one can escape

As you know soul never dies
It just has many lives
And here we go again
The same two souls
That got parted long ago . . .

Jerry Croy

FATHER

Your form was once straight and slender,
Your face was not marked with care;
But to me, you are more tender
By the lines written there.

You have bravely faced the battle,
Though hard work has been your fate;
Of worldly goods gaining little,
Working early, toiling late.

Now when age is creeping on you,
Morning past, soon comes the night;
Remember that I love you more
Because your hair is white.

Blanche Bradford Harryman

PARTED

Do not tell me when you go
That we shall meet no more.
Another time, some other place,
The promise is to keep.
And do not weep
Nor wear your soul upon your face,
But cherish and restore
The luster and the glow,
The ember and the ire,
The passion and the fire.
Parting's not forever
Though you may grieve and ache.
Believe me when I tell you,
My heart may also break.

Hyman Lerner

TRIBUTE TO A FRIEND

We met, and a struggle began
For you, for me, just to be friends
There were some who felt
That our friendship must be parted
For reasons of blind men's dreams
Your people, your origin, your faith
An old war, already dead and gone
We held on to our friendship
For within our hearts
Our feelings stayed the same
The freedom to love each other

That the right to love
Love, was the best right of all

Linda Perry

FOOTSTEPS IN THE SNOW

Ice hanging from willows
And the sidewalks bathed
In snow, white as virgins.
I cannot get enough of you
And like this passing scene
I drink you in insatiably,
Thirsting in melting beauty
That is but momentarily
Untouched.

Ralph E. Martin

I HAD TO SEE IT

I knew how much you cared,
When you said, "I understand,"
I knew how much you loved me
By the way you held my hand.

I knew that you believed in me
As you gazed into my eyes.
I knew how much you needed me,
When I hurt you and you cried.

When I left you all alone,
I was wrong and so unfair.
But yet you loved me still,
And you told me that you cared.

I was glad you gave me time,
To get rid of all my fears,
For in this time I realized
That you really were sincere.

I guess I had to see it,
Instead of always being told,
That there really is a man,
Whose heart is made of gold.

Renee L. Weidert

THE FRUIT OF GOOD LOVE

Oh I see the answer when she
smiles in her eyes. Up coming love
tonight is all right. Up coming love
whenever it's right. Love is the word
I love to sing. Love is a friend a
lover in hand. Love is so many things.
Love is the sparkle of champagne.
Love is the sparkle of beautiful eyes.
Love is the years ahead that will
come. Love is the children the fruit
of good love.

Albert F. Carol III

TO MY HUSBAND

If I were only inches high,
from you I'd never part.
I'd climb into your pocket
somewhere beneath your heart.

Then I would know just what you did
when you're at work each day.
I'd give you love and cheer you
as you went along your way.

Then at night when you came home
to rest your weary head,
I'd suddenly be five feet tall
and snuggle in your bed.

I'd smooth away your worry frowns
and whisper in your ear,
and if you'd like I'd even be
your "playmate of the year."

If you can only find a way
to make this silly wish come true,
then hurry, darling, tell me
'cause I'm in love with you.

Jean C. Fyffe

VOW OF ETERNITY

I shall love him:

When the stars go home to rest,
and the whispering winds are hushed.
When the mighty sky
loses her cast of blue,
and all the earth is crushed.

I shall still love him:

When glorious eternity calls,
and tomorrow becomes our own.
When the shadow of
doubt is lifted,
and man is not alone.

Arden Stupka

DECEMBERS CAN BE NEW

"Will you come back this way?"
A strange voice, from me did say.
"Yes, in December I'll return."
Oh, but how those words did burn!

A love, but old, once told the same,
With eyes sincere, and blazing true.
I never knew in early days
Decembers were so few.

He may remember heart-filled eyes
And fragments of inconsequential words.
But time gets old, and thoughts get bold.
And women, true, have days less blue,
They know Decembers can be new.

Vivienne Florence Meyer

ELLEN . . . IN RETROSPECT

I had never met her before,
but she made the night
to glow.

And suddenly
a flower bloomed
amid the falling snow.

Joseph P. Kowacic

I HAD A VISION

HONORABLE MENTION

I had a vision
Of a hundred-thousand
Naked virgins
Dancing on terraces
Of frozen yogurt
To the rhythm
Of the typewriters
Of a hundred-thousand
Naked secretaries
Filling out order forms
For a hundred-thousand boxes
Of Marilyn Monroe back scratchers.

Unfortunately, it did not come true.

Doug Muravez

A GOLDEN CHAIN

Love is kind,
soft-spoken and true.
Love endures,
when all else fails you.
It is the smile that
brightens your day;
The joy in your heart that
never goes away.

Love is a golden chain that
binds two hearts as one,
Lives that are bound and
entwined 'til life is done.
This chain stronger grows,
filling up your heart;
As days and years swiftly pass
your love should not depart . . .

Only death should break the chain,
alas, this is not always true . . .
Ofttimes a link is broken,
hopes and dreams fall apart;
All that remains of the golden chain . . .
Is a sad and broken heart.

Thelma H. Sherrill

SIGNALS

Your attention
Is not on me.
You turn away
At night
And pull the covers to you
For warmth
Instead of me.

You're late.
You don't call.
But I get your message.

Roberta Mae Brown

CHRISTMAS

Cool air at nights,
Playing my face,
Like whispers by angels,
Whom God has kindly sent.

I believe in God,
Such cool air to whisper,
The meaning of love,
Made aware by angels.

Winter nights I enjoy,
When soon Christmas carols
Are just around the corner,
To hark the angels singing.

Christ your kingdom come,
Two thousand years and forever,
We divine your birth as God-sent,
Or we are lost like Lucifer.

Cool December nights,
How lovely you can be,
When the air is full of love,
Since Christ the Lord is in our hearts.

Rolando L. Boquecosa

IS THIS LOVE?

One night alone with you I crave
One night alone with you in bed.
Not to rest or sleep or dream,
But to enjoy the night instead.

To kiss your juicy ruby lips
And hold you in my arms.
To feel your soft and tender skin,
And drink of all your charms,

To circumnavigate your curves,
Your hills and valleys, too.
And feel sweet nature's very thrill,
With every touch of you.

So let us taste of ecstasy,
Its mysteries explore,
One night in bed with you
Will open up the door.

Nathan Vogel

VOGEL, NATHAN. Born: 7-10-1894; Married: 9-23-21; Education: City College of New York, B.A., 1916; Occupations: Accountant, English Teacher; Awards: 9 Honorable Mentions, 1 Golden Poet, from World of Poetry; Poetry: 'Poor Little Broken Blossom,' American Poetry Association, World of Poetry, 1984; 'Land of the Free,' Quill Books, *Moments, Moods and Memories,* 1984; 'The First Red, White and Blue,' World of Poetry, 1984; 'Ship to Dreamland,' World of Poetry, 1986; 'Schemy Dreamy Land,' World of Poetry, 1985; Comments: *I do not strive for any particular themes, I just write whatever comes into my mind. However, I realized afterwards, with my family's agreement, that most of the poems show a romantic and optimistic view of life, with some patriotic themes as well.*

PEGGY O'SHEA

A little touch of the Irish
In a sassy lass — an O'Shea
She winks and smiles and wiggles
And likes to stay out late and play

We've been friends through thick and thin
Stuck up for one another
She's been pal and sis to me
But she's never been my mother

Around the town and through the woods
Together we would roam
We would dance and prance and click our heels
Then at morning's light head home

Drinking, cursing and fighting
Are all a sailor's joys
But look in the middle of a hullaballoo
And there's Peg with all her boys

But beneath that feisty exterior
Beats a heart as pure as gold
You can bet your life that Peggy
Will beat the devil 'til hell is cold . . .

G. L. Butler

LOVE LIFE SUMMATION

Ask me why I'm living, I fail to know why.
Ask me my problems, an unclimbable try.
On whom do I depend, the King of ages never end,
Who gave love's trend.

When were all things made worthwhile,
The day I met my love's smile
My heart dances with his glances,
Of his touch there's not enough.

Love life summation, happiness maker.
The ingredient called love,
Gives an upward shove.

All things shared together,
Come whatever, closer we could never.
Love life summation, happiness maker.

Give me the moon,
Give me the stars,
Give me everything in bloom.
When I sum it all up,
It takes love to lift me up.
Love life summation, happiness maker.

Alice Fleming

LOVE

Love exposed, exquisite, extempore, extramundane
In timeless universe.
Love is a lobworm, support, surge, surprise.

Love is caring supply
Love is life surpassable.
Love dries your tears.
Heals the anguished spirit.

Love takes away horror of loneliness
Words that comfort and bless.

Gretel Bush

CONTRASTING COLORS

'Aquamarine Me' can get lost in the blue of your eyes.
They send me soaring through the skies.
A silver rocket shot into space,
Ignited only by the golden tan of your face.

Meteors plummet past me — purple, blue and red,
The sheer beauty astounds me,
Fireworks burst within my head!

Suddenly everything turns a dismal gray,
There's trouble in mid-flight!
What terrible thing is happening?
What's caused this awful plight?

Searching for an answer I frantically look around.
Oh yes, I see, 'Black and White You'
is still on the ground.

Wanda Wade

A WOMAN . . . AGAIN

You have invaded my mind
Taking residence in my deepest soul.
In my thoughts, with the morning light.
Pervade my dreams, taunt me all night.
All together, you're quite a find,
And I know that wasn't your goal.
I find latent feelings coming awake,
Feelings that cause me to tremble and shake.

I know these things happening in me,
Weren't a part of your conscious intent.
When first we met, I was cruising along,
Cold and forbidding, feeling so strong.
Then there in your eyes, I began to see,
All the love I had lost and now can repent.
Because of you, I once more feel the glow
As the woman in me, again starts to show.

Delores Hendricks

LOVE IS DIVINE

Once I loved a maiden, ah, she was so fair,
Ruby lips and rosy cheeks, a wealth of golden hair.
Angelic in her beauty, loving, kind and true,
Many were her virtues, of, which these are but few.

So I loved the maiden, as only a lover can,
And she in turn had sworn to love, as never maid loved man.
With a sculpture's patience, with a lover's care,
There I built a pedestal, and placed my beauty there.

A veritable angel whom I worshipped day and night,
A sweet and charming maiden, I loved with all my might.
Ah, the joy of loving, the very world seemed mine.
"Love," I often whispered, "love, you are divine."

And now this charming maiden, is a wife and mother too,
The mother of our darling, sweet and lovely Sue.

Nathan Vogel

TONY

The rock I cling to is a man called Tony.
The sea of life crashes against him,
yet, he stands firm.

Fears beat at him and he commands them
to go away. They do!

He sees a human struggling and gives,
refuge without reward.
He speaks, at times, profoundly from within.

Sometimes, he says, he needs no love,
not knowing, that is what he is!
The light of God reflects on him
and makes him glow!

At times, a tiny tear appears
because of things he used to know.
He brushes it aside and smiles,
and tells me, he is on his way,
to where he means to go.

Judith Nass Gonzalez

MY SISTER, MY ANGEL

Some people want to climb a mountain,
Some people want to sail the sea.
Some people want to dive in a fountain
Some people want to be as rich as me.
Some people want to solve the world.
Some people want to soar through the blue skies.
I know somebody that wants to raise a little girl.
I know some people who don't want the world to die.
Some people live in a world only for two
I pray for you, I pray for you.

Any man who wants to climb the highest mountain,
There will be a hero who wants to sail the Seven Seas.
Some people would live only to swim in a fountain,
There are patriots who want their country to be free.
Life is just a franchise
Of what we may have only so many shares.
But the thing about snowstorms in winter
Is that they always seem to come in pairs.
Some people live in a world only for two
I pray for you, I pray for you.

Victor D. Curi

BELIEVE ME, IF ALL THOSE ENDEARING YOUNG CHARMS

Believe me, if all those endearing young charms,
  Which I gaze on so fondly to-day,
Were to change by to-morrow, and fleet in my arms,
  Like fairy-gifts, fading away!
Thou wouldst still be ador'd, as this moment thou art,
  Let thy loveliness fade as it will,
And, around the dear ruin, each wish of my heart
  Would entwine itself verdantly still!

It is not, while beauty and youth are thine own,
  And thy cheeks unprofan'd by a tear,
That the fervour and faith of a soul can be known,
  To which time will but make thee more dear!
No, the heart that has truly lov'd, never forgets,
  But as truly loves on to the close,
As the sun-flower turns on her god, when he sets,
  The same look which she turn'd when he rose!

Thomas Moore

SAY GOODBYE TO AUTUMN

Even before we met, autumnal leaves
Set wisps of flame to flirting in the breeze
With wanton grace where every ditch receives
Its cofferful of gold from spendthrift trees,
And many times I gathered rambler slips
In this fine haze, and there was pungent smoke,
Sharp to the nostrils, spicy to the lips,
Smudging the sunlight from the time I woke.

I cannot say you conjured fall itself
Out of the nothing; autumn, amber-browed,
Came long before your laughter played the elf,
Infusing you in every stick and cloud,
But still, though all the year bear visage sober,
You left eternal summer in October.

Anna-Margaret O'Sullivan

That once-in-a-lifetime bond
Between man and woman —
The partnership of love, friendship
  and intimate devotion, one to another —
Is rare,
Often believed to be where it is not.
Skeptics and cynics, not without their followers,
Will profess the extinction of the emotion.
True, we must always approach such commitments
  cautiously and advisedly.
But I, for one, do not choose to believe
  in a world so cold or so dead.
Then again I, with all my faults and shortcomings,
  have been blessed to be part of such a bond.
You, my love, have lifted me
And, in so doing,
We have given hope for all.

Bill Lawton

JUST FRIENDS

In the evening,
Everything is fine,
We're all alone,
And you're all mine.
Everyone thinks we're more than 'Just Friends'
But our happiness never ends,
Even when no one knows.

I never know what you're going to say . . .
Reveal our secret, to everybody today?
We talk over the phone every night . . .
Always keeping out of sight,
Sometimes you can't talk
And I could cry,
And I always wonder why we're 'Just Friends'

Jessica Klem

ONCE

Once . . .
Love's yearnings caressed the pounding breast
A rhapsody of passions not yet put to rest.
Once . . .
Promises we shared to be always together
Of romance we were certain would last forever.
Once . . .
What was laughter is now only pain
Bleeding my soul again and again.

Doug Frech

MOTORCYCLE KNIGHT

My knight didn't arrive on a horse of white
Or wearing armor shiny and bright
But in a suit, like a man of space
With a helmet covering most of his face.

His steed is a motorcycle of black
Complete with a ferring and luggage rack
Though his dress is different, he's a prince to me
This Marlboro Man is the best there can be.

Close behind, with him as my guide
On his cycle we've found a new world of outside
Sounds, smells and sights completely new
Without any walls to block out the view.

Like riding a roller coaster, the feeling of flying
Heady, uplifting, like an elated bird crying
Triumphant, the king of the walk
Not bad as you've heard, forget all that talk.

Not carrying chains, no leather he wears
But gentle and kind, he's one that cares
This new breed of knight defies the rule
Riding a bike doesn't make a man cruel.

Nancy Houston

SUMMER LOVE

I was age ten;
She was some older.
We roamed the country roads together.
We strolled in fields of clover.
Few words were ever spoken.
Love has a language all its own.
We knew our magic moments would soon be broken.
When summer turned to fall,
She would be alone.
My Summer Love, my Lady Fair;
My beautiful bay mare.

Dixie Rice Dawson

LOVE

Love is a feeling —
A feeling only a heart knows,
It's a feeling indescribable —
But it leaves a HAPPY GLOW!

Love you never see —
Yet, you know when there,
If your heart feels love —
That love, you'll want to share!

A heart needs love —
That's what gives us life,
And when you get that feeling —
You become a husband or wife!

You're sharing that love —
A gift God gave to men,
Two hearts are sharing that feeling —
And a new life will soon begin!

So what is love —
Besides a feeling that touches a heart?
It's the gift of sharing and giving —
And in return, that love can never part!

Janet L. Hildreth

A MOTHER'S LOVE

A Mother's Love is the very best.
It is so sweet and different from the rest.
The words I want to say —
Can surely apply to your mother today

Since I am a registered nurse — it was my privilege
and honor to nurse my mother weeks before
God called her home.

She seemed to want me by her side —
and all night long she would say —
"Lillian — don't you leave me."
All night long in her waking hours,
She would repeat these words —
"Lillian don't you leave me."
"I'm right here, mama — I won't leave you."
I thank my Heavenly Father over and over again
For letting me nurse her to the end.

Lillian Payne

PAYNE, LILLIAN WELLS. Born: Sumter, South Carolina, 9-20-10; Widow; Education: High school; Duke Hospital; Occupations: X-ray Technician, Operating Room Supervisor; Memberships: Nurses' State Association; Awards: Golden Poet Award, World of Poetry, for 'Go Visit a Nursing Home'; Poetry: 'Happiness,' *Today's Greatest Poems;* 'Lonely People,' *Today's Greatest Poems;* 'Serenity,' *American Poetry Anthology,* 1984; 'Christmas,' *Today's Greatest Poems.*

INSIDE YOUR HEART

Oh, how dark and lonely it is,
Outside in the misty rain.
Deep inside my heart it's warm, something I just can't explain.
These feelings that I have for you won't be denied inside.
For love is something that I never, ever hide.
Deep inside my heart I'm crying, crying out for you.
Just hold me and tell me that you'll never let me go.
Maybe it's just a dream,
But I really long to know:
How do you feel about me?
How do I know you care?
When all you do sometimes, is just sit and stare.
So show me, if you dare.
And let me look within your heart,
And then I'll know you care.

Meghan Weber

MULTANOMAH FALLS.

DEJA VU OF LOVE'S WEALTH

We are ingrained in the *Déjà Vu* of love's wealth.
In you I see the aura of myself.
Now that we spend our lives in retreat,
Away from affairs of human conceit,
The intrinsic values in our lives are ours.
Our coupled spirits are one hybrid flower.
Through time we have always loved each other,
Before we'd even met one another —
Two spirits with a karma plan
Traveling eternity hand in hand.
It was fate that we must meet
To share a wealth of love so sweet.

Alyce L. Hubbs

LOVERS

To all the lovers out there all alone,
Just waiting by their phones,
I wish you so much more in your life.
More than just sorrow and strife.
You need a love to call your own.
And for your love to be shown.
You need your days to be so much brighter.
And show the world you are a fighter.
Lovers, you need harmony and peace.
So your dreams won't cease.
So this poem is for you lovers on your own.
Trying so hard to keep your love light on.

Glenna Creel-Parker

FOR THE BEST

I do not want to tell you, that we must part today;
I've searched and searched and yet I know, there is no other way.
I need so to be near you, held close against your chest;
And yet I know within my heart, that this is for the best.
For once the cut has mended, we can go on again;
And as the days turn into months, we can become best friends;
But if we stay together, inflicting needless pain
On those who we know innocent, we'll never be the same.
This love so pure will tarnish, our souls will flinch in shame,
We shall resent what we have lost, and never can regain.
So hold me in your memory, our love affair must end;
And as the days pass slowly by, I'll always be your friend.

Christianna

TIMELESS

From the time we come into this world, we love,
But, sometimes we share less,
Then, sometimes we feel less,
And, sometimes we think less,
Till, sometimes we care less,
Yes, and sometimes we even love less,
Time intervenes, and still we love,
Always returning like clouds above,
Love is memories and reflections of times gone by,
Only then, we see how fast it does fly.
How foolish we were, not to be at our best,
Still, it shows why our love is timeless.

Marjorie Kaiser

LASHELLE, OUR FIRST GRANDCHILD

Wonder of wonders, a new baby on the way!
New life to bring us joy and brighten up our day.
It's been so very long since hungry mid-life arms
Have held a family angel full of winning baby charms.

We now have passed into another phase of life,
Parents of four boys and now Grandfather and wife.
I wonder what we'll have, bouncy boy or elfin girl,
Little blue jean knees to patch, or silky hair to curl?

With great anticipation we have waited for that day,
When the final day arrived, and nature had her way.
What a lovely reward, after years of boisterous boys,
A beautiful baby girl, filling hearts with swelling joys.

She has been given a name, that seems to fit so well,
Her middle name is Margaret, her first name is Lashelle.
She is a happy baby, and has a ready smile,
Her tiny face is beautiful; she is a winsome child.

It has been nine years since she came into our life,
She is never any trouble, or involved in any strife.
She is talented in music, in voice, and in verse,
What a wonderful grandchild, to be our very first!

Margaret E. Reed

REED, MARGARET ELIZABETH. Born: Waco, Texas, 11-13-30; Married: 5-27-50 to Alvin M. Reed; Education: Mary Hardin Baylor College, Belton, Texas, 1948-1949; Clifton Jr. College, Clifton, Texas, 1949; Texas A & I College 1961 and 1962; Occupation: Housewife; Memberships: Playhouse of Design Art Organization of Kingsville, Texas, five years; Poetry: 'Arms of Love,' *Hearts on Fire, Volume II,* 1985; Themes: *A common theme that runs through my poetry is thanksgiving to God, and love of family, and an appreciation of the beauties of nature.* Comments: *Poetry is a verbal expression arising from the stimulation of our hearts and souls from people we meet and know, events we are caught up in, and our reactions to the beauty of God's palette in nature. There is great satisfaction in expressing these feelings.*

A WIFE'S UNDYING LOVE

To my husband so dear, I want you to know
My love grew stronger year by year.
Through many trials there were friend and foe.
Yet always you were very dear.
As our love and trust enhanced our living
We did not think of defeat;
For we had so much — and in its giving,
There was more love with each heartbeat.
Now that we're older and love still abounds
For one another — such a joyful source —
And in this life where there are no crowns
Given for such love in force —
We know what we have is very rare.
So, smiling and loving every day
It's so good to know we still care,
And that love shall pave our way.

Ruth C. Coleman

COLEMAN, RUTH CLIFTON. Born: Rockhouse, Kentucky, 2-12-13; Married: 7-14-43 to James W. Coleman; Education: B.S. in Elementary Education, 1957; advanced work on Masters in Elementary Education, 1965, Auburn, Alabama; Occupations: Guidance Counselor in junior high school, Teacher of Intellectual Disabilities; Memberships: NEA, NRTA, AARP, National Congress of PTA; Awards: First choice of many, was published in Monthly Magazine for Christian Poetry Association, Pompano Beach, Florida; Poetry: 'Appreciation of Nature,' *In Quiet Places,* 11-85; 'What Have We Done?', 'Invitation to Life,' *Moments, Moods, & Memories,* Fall 1984; 'A Christmas Prayer,' *Monthly Magazine Christian Poetry Association,* 12-84; 'Source of Peace,' *Monthly Magazine Christian Poetry Association,* 9-85; Themes: *Religion — appreciation of God's world, helping people, witty and straight poems on weight loss, witty and satirical poems on education.*

BOAT PEOPLE

A Mother's cry of a child lost, in any language can be
heard as the wail of a shattered soul.

Mary Annah Alemán

Love is such a glorious thing
For, into a life it can bring
Joy unlike any ever known
It brings a meaning to life all its own!

Love for our Lord must always be first
For that Love can quench the thirst
In our souls forevermore
Bringing us peace we've never known before!

Our family's love is what we need
Each day, so we can go out and succeed
In the world, make a living and such
Love adds to our lives just the right touch!

The love we share with our fellow man
Is special, 'cause it can
Bring us together with people who care
We all have so much love to share!

Connie Ratliff

THE BEACON AND I

Lindbergh beacon, you're like an elongated moon
flashing across the sky.
I sit and watch you from my window.
I sit and watch you playing hide and seek with the stars.
Old Mr. Moon wonders who you are,
And why you play tricks with his friends, the stars.
And I too wonder . . .
I wonder where my love is tonight.
Will she return home soon?
She's late already.
Has she found someone else on the way?
Lindbergh beacon, I know you can find her with your
searchlight eyes.
Find her and flash your beam across her face like a slap!
Tell her that I love her dearly . . . she should hurry home.
Oh, how stupid of me, you can't speak.
You're a safety light for monarchs of the air.
Oh, there she is!
One of your tiny light rays found her across the street.
She's come home to me again!
Thank you, Lindbergh beacon.

Theodore V. Kundrat

I NEED YOU

I need you 'Hon,' when day is done.
The exigencies and vicissitudes of survival,
While realistic, do not sustain the spirit,
the Raison d'etre,' the strength for the last mile.

When day is done, 'Hon,' it's time for revival.
I need you to tell of my conquests, triumphs —
accolades — bumps — losses and defeats.

All is as nothing until you're home — arrival.
It's life without flavor
like eating straw and drinking vapor,
Just another trial!
The touch of your hand, the patient smile
as you listen to my recital
make it *all* worthwhile.
You restore my confidence and
Doubts burst like bubbles."
Releasing my troubles
In those lovely hours with you,
When day is done.

Joshua C. Stevens

I MISS YOU

The days are long and hot
As I wait for that one day
In a couple of weeks
When I will come back your way
Time will just drag on
Because you are not here
A day seems like a week
Two weeks seem like a year
The sun is high in the sky
But it's just not the same
Whenever I think of sunshine
I think of your lovely name
As I gaze at your pictures
Mounted on my locker door
My thoughts wander off
To that day I'm waiting for
When I will see you again
And feel your lovely smile
Until that day arrives
I'll have to bear it for awhile

Jeffrey B. Davis

BELOVED FATHER

I remember my father well,
I love him still,
He'll go to Heaven,
Not to hell.

He was old,
But never cold,
Sometimes he'd laugh,
Or take a bath.

He taught me to fish,
And to follow my wish
Of whatever I need,
I'm from his seed.

He died this year,
But showed no fear,
Of losing his life,
His children and wife.

Alfred Elkins

YOU SAY YOU LOVE ME

You say you love me
But, I wonder just how
Is it for past and future
Or is it just for now?

Love as nature, as a toy
As a fear, as a joy
As a fashion, as a deed
As a spirit, as a need

As a thought, as a fantasy
As a song, as a memory
As a dare, as a pleasure
As a goal, as a treasure

You say you love me
But, I wonder just how
How real in past or future
Or even just for now?

Jerry Martinez

LEVELS OF LOVE

We have known the strong winds of desire and passion,
as they have swept through our souls like a chill blast of winter air.
Like children, lost within their world of crayons and lollipops,
we have explored with unabandoned excitement,
the intricacies of each other's being.
We have floated to untold worlds on a sea of tears
generated by moments of sheer joy,
sweet tenderness and broken dreams.
We have bound ourselves together in a friendship whose ties,
like that of an elaborate web
are too thin and delicate for others to see or understand.
Yet, within our hearts and minds, we know these bonds
are as strong as steel girders which hold together
any of the tallest skyscrapers.
Levels of love we have known are reflected in the steps
of the stairs we have climbed,
sometimes together, other times apart.
The depths and heights of these increments of space,
only we can know.
What levels have we yet to reach?

Joanne M. Scarfo

UNSELFISH LOVE

Love! Such a gentle and noble feeling —
Yet can form strong unbreakable bonds . . .
When in kindness, with warmth responds;
Will grow length and depth, all worldly measures overspilling!
This wonderful and magic spell —
All ugly, dehumanizing hateful thoughts will quell . . .
Lift up spirits, the soul to unknown heights;
Elevation of magnificent goodness, and beauty in sight!
Looking through eyes of trust so strong —
That will melt away all pain and wrong . . .
Power of unselfish love, innocent and pure;
Will conquer problems, and illnesses completely cure!
Making life the most wonderful — worthwhile experience to desire —
When loving kindness and concern, for others will inspire . . .
To reach out, open your heart — for the pure, unselfish love;
Awarded you will be, with peace of mind, from above!
The noblest love — son of a man can achieve —
Only hate he must discard . . . and pure unselfish love, from within retrieve . . .
Those sowing blessed by God, and men seeds;
Creating a world of love, and only of good human deeds!

Martin R. Tarlo

I NEED LOVE

The snow has obliterated my summer garden
Alone I shiver, naked and exposed before my peers
My feet encased in ice, I cannot go forward . . . or back
I sway with winter winds beneath my leafless bower's branch.

I take my frozen body inside before the comforting fire
But I'm not able to coax my spirit in from its bitter cold
Stubborn and willful, it remains out where it last knew love
Remembering romance, reliving joys of a long-gone June and July.

Please come back to me my sweet lover who failed me
Too theatrical to really ever die was the love we shared
Play again with me all our old romantic roles and scenes
From tulip to aster time and see all our loving be rekindled.

Remember dearest, it wasn't just a love, it was my lifetime gem
The sparkling diamond among tons of useless rubble which was my past
The precious love we'd die for, our vows, our everlasting sun
Come bring my perishing soul in from the cold . . . for I need love.

Doris Irene Warren

INFINITE LOVE

He voluntarily laid aside
His riches . . . power and glory,

Became the sacrificial Lamb
In a true compassionate story.

He loved us when we were unlovely,
In an act of redeeming grace.

His blood flowed down, rich and red
To a fallen human race.

His Diety . . . was reaching up
To take a hold of God.

His pure and bleeding human flesh . . .
Reaching down to earthen sod.

Then, with the words, "It is finished!"
He bowed His sacred head . . .

It fell upon His pulseless breast . . .
The Son of God . . . was dead

'Twas the grandest event of the ages!
The Son of God came alive!

Crowned with glorious victory . . .
For which we all must strive.

Phyllis Wallin

REFLECTIONS OF DONNA

I couldn't forget about you my good friend (not so tall)
Why you are the best of them all!
You were there when I was down,
Unable to pick myself up off the ground,
To you sometimes I would sass,
but being a true comrade, you always let it pass.
Only now can I see through those distraughtful years,
You were the closest love to Jesus that was near.
For once being blind, I failed to recognize your

Spirited Fruitful Signs of . . .

LOVE — Unselfishly always giving more
PATIENCE — You kept knocking at my door.
GOODNESS — Sending a memorial to a family you did not know at all.

Now, by the grace of God I know Jesus too, and found His word is loving and true.

With wisdom to know, you reap what you sow,
making me confident of this one thing for you,
that the joy of your longsuffering and temperance
at last will shine through.

As the Lord God of hope takes all that you have to
abundantly increase with everlasting joy and peace.

John 10:10

Jeanette Moody

THE GLORY OF LOVE

My love's illness was noted in October of 1982.
He was terminal, it's true
And oh, so sad!
How long the time, couldn't be said.
Time granted to us
Was so very precious,
We had a chance to relive the past
Catching up on memories that will last
Spanning a lifetime —
Ups and downs, deep valleys, hills we'd had to climb
A full life together
In all kinds of times and weather
We seemed to borrow in this life, from the next,
Though magnified in context
Some of heaven here on earth
Of life and death.
Although Heaven seemed so real
And God's love we could feel
Time to say goodbye
We couldn't help but cry.

Hesse G. Byrd

LOST TREASURE

Tonight the moon was a full yellow crest,
My arms ached for you, for your head on my breast,
I remember the times when you whispered to me,
"I love you, this was meant to be";
Now that time is forever past,
In my heart I knew it could never last;
But Oh my darling, how I hoped it could be.
That you would always love and cherish me;
The night sings to me many songs of you,
The precious times we both knew,
Its plaintive voice whispers in my ear,
Voicing the wish that you were near;
My darling, I'll remember if you forget
The delight we knew when we first met,
The wonder of that new and lovely feeling,
Of the future and of hope revealing;
Now all is lost to an empty heart,
For long since we have had to part,
I'll always remember how tender you were,
I'll treasure your sweetness forever, my dear.

Glory Posey

LOVE — SOCIETY'S STYLE

It's the way of our society today.
To place a "personal ad" on Monday.
For $75.00 your image they'll portray.
Assuring, "This allows you great headway."
"I'm tired of bar scenes." they say,
"My hair is brown with a hint of grey."
Adding, "I'm willing to meet you halfway."
And, "Please answer this ad without delay."
Then they print the ad and it's under way.
The ad will be read by the masculine array.
Your friends look at you in utter dismay!
Some even whisper, you'll be led astray.
A few agree that it's a great pathway;
After all, your weekends aren't any holiday,
Since your apron strings have been cut away.
Then you check your mailbox every single day.
There's been no answer for weeks, I dare say.
Your anticipation is starting to decay.
You're alone today as much as yesterday.
Sometimes you wish you could just run away.

Cilla C. Carpenter

MY GODDESS WALKS

My Goddess walks in moonlight soft
And gently does the night rejoice.
She lifts her lovely gaze aloft
And quietly her golden voice
Sings to the world a lullaby.

My Goddess walks in moonlight pale;
A nightingale sings from afar.
Her hair, a splendid, shining veil,
Stirs gently as a shooting star
Floats down to bless her from on high.

My Goddess walks, the moonlit night
Sings sweetly of her loveliness.
The shining alabaster light
Touches with a sweet caress
The beauty glowing in her eyes.

My Goddess walks with moonlit grace;
The world its loveliness unfolds.
As I behold her radiant face,
Her song seeks out my deepest soul —
She steals my heart and walks on by . . .

James C. Bassett

LADY

Lady, stay awhile
and talk of those things
We shared so long ago.

Come to me in the night;
Softly tell me of all
We once knew.

Soothe my tired spirit
with tales of when we kissed,
Of times when we loved,
Then go.

The night does not last,
Even for us.
It is fragile,
as ice on a summer's day.

So go quietly now,
before the dawn
Dares disturb the memory
of all the good nights
That have gone before.

Allen Beck

THE UNION OF HEARTS

Postcard
Love is just a mystery

Wrong or right
Isn't it time

Give me your love
Anytime

Midnight rendezvous
In your eyes
Silver dreams

Paul Weakly

WE LOVE VALENTINES

'Twixt the years of six and ten,
We cut out hearts and pasted them;
Struggling with letters not a few —
To spell the words, "I Love You."

From then to twelve, we were really sly.
Hid our hearts and hoped to die
If we got caught with a rhyme,
" 'Specially for You My Valentine."

Through teenage years with hearts aglow,
Stores we searched high and low;
A common card would never do —
It had to be, "Just for You!"

Hair now streaked with grey,
Reminiscing a bygone day,
Hearts beating double time —
"Just for You My Valentine."

Blanche Bradford Harryman

DON'T LEAVE ME

Mother, mother, where are you?
Mama, don't leave me this way
Mother dear, don't you hear me?
My daughter, death took me this day.

Mother, why did you leave me?
And where did you go?
Please, the doctor is coming
Not now my daughter, no.

The wind blows so cold now.
What will happen to me?
I'm so alone now
My child, don't cry, you will see

Mama, why did you leave me?
My daughter, I had to go.
I'll forever keep you near me
Yes my daughter, I know.

Moe Feldman

VALENTINE'S DAY

I forgot St. Valentine's Day,
Forgot for the very first time.
I forgot the candy or present,
Or card with the verses that rhyme.

The only heart that I can give you
Is the one beating 'neath my breast.
I would take it out and give it to you,
But it would leave a hole in my chest.

I, honestly, really do love you,
And can hardly contain my shame.
So it wasn't lack of caring
But my forgetfulness to blame.

Oh, no, it isn't happening,
Oh, say it can't be true!
After all my guilty feelings,
Did you forget my present too?

Myrna Sue Wells

She loved him more than
the trees or rivers.
She loved him more than
the birds or flowers.
But his dreams had called him away.
He left seeking a mirage,
a dream to last a lifetime.
He found the glitter, but not the gold.
She wondered at his loss, and hers,
but she knew it had to be.
He couldn't be happy until
his plans had been tried.
He came home crying a withered tear.
She took him to her and
cried with him.
Why had she let him go?
Why had she let him return?
Simply because:
She loved him more than
the trees or rivers.
She loved him more than
the birds or flowers.
She loved him.

Robin Aylesworth

CHALLENGE

Icy crystal snowflakes
brisk the morning air.
All are making ready
for this moment we will share.
Love and pride are filled with joy
as the countdown starts to sing.
These seven children of the Lord
carry freedom on their wing.
Because they're loving me,
giving of themselves
so I can be.
I love them, too!
for reaching to the heavens
to make all things new.

And then, an awesome light
deceptive in its bright,
taking love and leaving pain
evermore to come again . . .

For they are now the stars.

William D. Leavitt

WE NEED EACH OTHER

You've stepped into my life, from where?
One day I looked up and you were there.
Can you understand?
I feel almost a stranger to this land.

I'm so much more intense than most;
Believe me I'm not trying to boast.
I can love more deeply than many,
Yet, I'm afraid to get near any.

Love is the most powerful force on earth.
We begin to learn about it from birth.
People long for a love that's real,
Yet, we're all so afraid to feel,
Afraid to feel a need for another,
But, we do need each other,
Desperately!

Rebecca Ellison Cole

STARCROSSED

Reach out to me that we may be as one,
Feel my heat, warmth of the sun.
Perceive my soul, whatever I be
The truth in it will set you free.

Time without end, age upon age
We know each other as words to a page.
Whatever the lifestyles of lives in the past
Our destinies will cross to the very last.

Mephetic natures will rule if they must,
Through endless time it has always been thus.
Don't dwell on the now, accept what must be
The truth in this will set you free.

Trust in me as your guide, in yourself even more,
Take it down to your being, to its very core.
Explore it, develop it, and when you've surpassed
You'll find our souls crossed to the very last.

Soulmate, teacher, enemy and friend
What's been in the past will come again.
Though we've changed about, we're always as one
'Cause we're the other's light, a brilliant sun.

Lorey Umberger

FIRST LOVE

'Twas at the dance I met her and I just don't know.
'Cause I wasn't aimin' going, but then I had to tell her so.
She sat there in the corner by herself, I came aware,
Her great big blue eyes and yellow cornsilk hair.
I crossed the room of dancers until I reached her chair.
I took her arm, gently led her onto the floor.
At that very moment, I couldn't ask for more.
Years and years later, in the golden years of life,
I've still got that girl and always will,
For I took her for my wife.

Mary A. Wagner

I'LL LOVE YOU ALWAYS

Tulips were blooming one summer day
The clouds were blue mixed with gray
Out of loneliness I went to her grave
To smell the roses where she lay.

I missed the sparkle in her eyes
The smell of perfume when she smiled
She was beautiful in every way
I loved her more each passing day.

We searched for rainbows under the sun
Reached for stars and we found love
Though death came and broke us apart
Our love was deeper than a golden heart.

As I knelt down on my hands and knees
I remembered what she once told me
If the time should come for us both to be apart
I'll love you always from the bottom of my heart.

With tears in my eyes I walked away
If nothing else I had her memories
Like passion beyond the river and sunsets above the mountain
Our love would always be like a castle by the sea.

Rhonda G. Wood

FOREVER LOVE

If ever you're going to love me, love me now, while
I can know all the sweet and tender feelings which
from real affection flow.

Love me now, while I am living, do not wait till I
am gone, then chisel your love in marble . . . warm
words of love on ice cold stone.

If you have sweet thoughts of love for me, why not
whisper them to me, don't you know that would make
me very happy?

If you wait till I am sleeping, never to waken with
you again, there will be walls of earth between us
and then I couldn't hear you at all.

So my dearest, if you love me any, if it's but a
little bit, let me know it now, while I am living,
so I can own and treasure it.

Sandy Stanton

LAMENT OF A LOVE-HUNGRY LASSIE

Where are the dashing blades of yesterday?
Gutsy guys in crimson cloak with shining sword,
Who polished sugared verses as they lay
Upon the green and violet-scented sward.

Boldly they scaled milady's balcony
To romp within her silken-draped boudoir,
Adept in passion poems as well as falconry,
At making love as well as waging war.

These sophomore wimps with whom I go to school
Can think of naught but bat and ball and glove,
Of basket, gridiron, track and swimming pool,
Too muscle-bound to learn the art of love.

Oh that some plume-crested cavalier
Would drop his sword and shed his swirling cape,
And like a dedicated musketeer
Embrace this maid in sixteenth century rape!

Leon A. Doughty

THE THORN

To David E. Roszmann and Tabitha J. Mullen

Yesterday my pen told of two roses
that innocent white one and yes, the sacred red one
both petals are wilted, both cry tears of pity tears for him
that thorn among them both
the thorn had survived winter while the roses prayed for sun
the white rose waited forever it seems she never knew the blood
from the thorn that slayed her snow-white petals and slowly
would she lean on that blood red rose, the rose that felt pain
how could they both keep their beauty when blood splashed
staining both their petals, the white was pink and the other
blood red, deeper than an ocean of raw pain, the roses
the white wept for love the thorn called forever
the red stung for eternity damaged by his lullaby
where had the song gone, new love and when will my love fade
into grips of time and when will the roses die in my hands
dry the tears, wipe away the blood, the blood that came from
my roses, the ones, that white and red one, who loved the thorn
my roses, the innocent roses the thorn had slain.

Laura Ann Stoll

THE DAY SHE SPOKE OF HER LOVE

As I stood and gazed at the Lady, who stood there so silent, and proud;
Her shadow was peaceful and shady, and I heard myself thinking out loud,
"Where do you come from?" I queried, "and why is your torch up so high?
Why do we love you, enough to repair you? You don't even laugh, speak,
or cry."

As the wind blew over the water, I swear I could hear someone say.
"France didn't want me, you are my sons and daughters, I'm guardian of all
I survey.
I asked for the homeless, yes, even the 'hopeless,' my torch in the air,
lights the way.
For freedom of speech, for love or for fame; freedom to vote, or to pray.

You can't see my tears, but I cry all the same for the ones who died in
my name.
When they batter my flag, 'till it's only a rag, when they hate, and say
I'm to blame.
I'm proud people love me, enough to repair me; for the things I stand for,
they care,
I don't laugh, but I smile, quite often you see, for these things I love
are still there."

Virginia Huett Wilson

WILSON, VIRGINIA HUETT. Pen Names: J. Wilson, Judith O. Bannon, V. Hayes, V. Wilson; Born: 11-2-24; Education: Two Years Journalism, High School Freshman at age 12; Occupations: Sales, Freelance Writer, Songwriter; Memberships: Sheriffs' Association, American Fishing Association (Ecology), Chiefs of Police Association; Awards: Honorable Mention plus Special Awards for four gospel songs; Music: "Hello Lord, It's Me Again," an album with magic key (The Songs of Virginia H. Wilson), Columbine Records," Gonna Wake Up in Glory," "Have You Talked To My Jesus Today," "Take Jesus With You," "Hello Lord," songs; Other Writing: "Women Need To Learn How To Work With Each Other," Article, *Evansville Courier;* Comments: *I tell the gospel in song, write objectively about current issues. I hope I may benefit someone else with what I have learned, make someone smile with my limericks. I express the way I feel, in general, about love, life, and the things that are near and dear to my heart. I have a prized letter from Nancy Reagan for "The Day She Spoke."*

TO RANDY

Randy Lee Davis of Jackson, Wyoming
has been an inspiration to me,
as well as the dearest of friends.

There was a severance in my life
You healed it with your touch,
I cannot call you merely, friend,
You've given me so much!
You made my heart take flight again
My life is now worthwhile,
You held me close and dried my tears
And turned them into smiles.
You placed me on an upward path
And gave me back my pride,
And I won't fail, if now and then,
You'll walk close by my side.
So if you had not cared enough,
Where would I be today?
That's why I've learned to love you more
Than words can ever say.

Emma Lee Stocum

I WISH

I wish that I were like the rose
A flower of great beauty,
I'd stand and make my presence known
Without regard to duty.

I wish that those who touched my bloom
With no thought for my needing,
Would feel a thorn prick of regret
To set their conscience bleeding.

I wish that like the lovely rose
I'd have no dreams to shatter,
I'd have no heart to feel love's pain
So loving would not matter.

I wish that I were like the rose
Though fades her beauty fast,
There is a fragrant memory
That lingers to the last.

Emma Lee Stocum

CAN WE LOVE?

we left . . . home
attached/estranged
your . . . region
deceives/promises
we retreat/you follow
later / now
regions
splitting/spoils
work / dreams
world HORROR
destroying. Home
proximity etches
you — me
birth / death
wealth/destitution
human/inhuman
existence
home — regions fixate
life / death
CAN WE LOVE?

Dianne M. Tchir

IF I COULD

If I could reach across the ocean's fury, to hold
The tides ever so still,

I would lay you across the calm gentle waters, to
passionately make love to you.

If I could carry you down the road of happiness, so
You may touch the delicate flowers, that bloom from
The innocence of Mother Nature's tender hands;

I would build you a foundation of love, out of life's
Precious grains of sand.

If I could show you all the hidden mysteries that
Exist within the earth as it revolves around the
Magnificent sun,

I would press your body so close to mine, to listen
To our hearts as they gently beat as one.

If I could express to you all these tender words,
That are often so hard to say,

I would love you and hold you, my love, and
Turn all your lonely nights into day.

Dana Keith Ryder, Sr.

MY LADY

I sit here in my lonely prison cell,
I feel my life has become a pure hell;
Had there been love, I would not have gone bad,
Now I have regrets and find myself sad;
I suppose what I need is a good girl,
Then my life would take on a goodly swirl;
I long for the day when the gates swing wide,
Then I will find my lady by my side.

Don Bedwell

A DAFFODIL IN SPRING

Sunny and smiling my love turns to me.
See my picture? I drew it for you.

Laughing and playing
she runs here and there;
never still, never quiet,
she sparkles like the dew.

Sunny and smiling
my love asks me now,
mommy will you, can I, is there?
while I answer with my smile.

I look at my darling
and my eyes start to tear.
For my little darling
might never have been here.

Her life was so fragile
that it nearly was snuffed.
But my little dewdrop
grew on the love she was fed.

Now she's as lovely as an early Spring morn;
my sunny Daffodil, my gentle love.

Antonia Jennings

SOMEONE WHO CARED

You found me, and picked me up.
You guided me through the rough times.
You showed me how life is.
You taught me.
You gave me strength to fight my battles,
to win if I could.
You taught me so much, and now you're gone.
How could you leave me without saying goodbye?

Now my strength is gone and my battles are tough.
But yet I can't hate you.
Because I found someone who once cared for me.
For me, just being me.
Which no one had done.
Someone who could see through me.
Someone who was there.
Someone who cared.

Jacqueline P. Wirtz

NATURE OF LOVE

Thinking of you
reminds me of:

Gentle brown, sensitive eyes
hot, warm, cool, cold, ice.

The full moon lurking in the starless sky
torture, torment, "little white lies."

The strength of the ocean's ire crashing against the beach
mysteries of the heart and soul-answers out of reach.

Multitudes of emotion, strong, deep, burning a fire,
leaving a gap, filling it with desire.

Haunting memories driving me insane,
wild raging passion — agonizing pain.

Jennifer Goad

THE WARMTH OF YOUR LOVE

The branches lift up their skeleton arms,
to embrace the gray skies of winter.
I run naked between the barren trees,
as the first snow of winter falls;
the warmth of your love cloaking my body.
My head throbs from the fever of loving you —
My heart beats wildly from the pleasure of loving you —
and my belly sings sweet songs of joy,
at the thought of loving you.
As the soft flakes melt on my hot body, I dance,
their chill only increasing my burning desire for your love.
The day wanes and I leap over building drifts in anticipation,
as the hour of your return nears . . .
And as you enter, smiling and dusting off snow,
I smile and offer champagne —
and in front of the burning fire,
we huddle close together in love.

Denise Y. Westfield

LOVESTRUCK
A LOOK OF LOVE

Monday came early. The dreams which had filled Morgan's head
for so many years were now about to become reality.
She could hardly think. A Virgin Maid, Broken Promises, Abandoned
ways stirred her imagination.
She could see a boy. A boy whom she had known once before. Long ago,
perhaps in a dream.
He seemed astonished. Almost Lovestruck.
She could tell by his steady gaze that this young lover was eager
to become a part of her fantasy.
A Fantasy that left everything to chance. Like a land where children
paused to play.
Where everything would turn around them and they in turn would make
everything happen.
It seemed crazy. But that's the way it was.
Motion . . . Sound . . . their screams and yells . . . deafening.
Morgan couldn't help but laugh sometimes at all these illusions.
It was almost real, yet, she couldn't believe the world she was in.
A world where the body's rhythms were the Mass & Surges of all its
emotions acting in total accord and "Chaos."
Her Lover, the Boy grown to a Man, was subtly tempted by the turns
of the Mind to illusions so grand that he was beginning to be engulfed
by its bellowed roar and soon . . . its solitude.
Morgan was glad when the "Movement" ended.
She didn't know if her young lion could live that illusion much longer
without being "torn & destroyed" by it.
An illusion whose Rhapsody, although unfinished would remain forever,
"A Look of Love."

Jamieson Steele

FORMICA, PETER CHARLES. Pen Name: Master Jamieson Steele; Born: New York: Married; 9-68; Education: Undergraduate and graduate degrees; Occupation: Writer, Businessman, Owner of New Yorker Galleries, photographic art; Memberships: Coast Guard Auxiliary; Chairperson, Theater Arts Group; Advisory Committee, Board of Education; ASCAP; Awards: Irish Poetry Award; Contracted for screenplay and mini series (1984); Writings: *Phytian Terridian Clone,* B. Klaussner, International Literary Agency, 1984; "Jamieson & Ashlee King Sports Mysteries," 1984; "Lady, I Love You," Requested for Centennial, 1984; "Last Minute," 1984; Comments: *Love and affection are expressed through natural happenings, and events afford the poet dramatic moments that use the literary form as a vehicle for drama, tension, and sex.*

WORDS OF LOVE

Words of love that lovers speak
Like elegant fragrance of a rose
Caress the senses beyond endurance
While ecstasy of love does grow
Hearts beating fast ride turbulent crest
Passion now blooms in lover's breast

A touch of lips a fond embrace
As hearts respond and hold in place
Tender emotions in passionate breast
Seek and search to reach their crest
Like elegant fragrance of the rose
or haunting melody

Emotions caress the senses then vanish
Like elusive will o' wisp
Yet words of love that lovers speak
Forever locked in love's embrace
While hearts remember and hold in place
The touch of lips — in fond embrace

Kenneth R. Rand

IN LIGHT AND DARKNESS

I see you first in mirrors
superimposed as many facets
to the eye one gleaming,
events in lattices creating
the assembly
that is in light and likeness
you.

Where the day is a hard shining
I am in shadow
photosensitive and shy
my dreams in you reflected
gel strangely
thus I am left vacant.

You possess me
my duplicate self
we are met and alike
and not unaware
of possible dissolution.

Valerie L. Smith

ONE OF THREE

Love of a painting
Love of a friend

Love of a symphony
Love of a friend

Loss of a painting
Loss of a friend

Loss of a symphony
Loss of a friend

Loss is dearest for

Loss of a painting,
Loss of a symphony,

Loss of a friend?

Rebecca Butler

HE'S IN HEAVEN TODAY

He was noble, brave and courageous, his life was not
easy for years
But he kept his troubles in secret, and bravely fought
back all his fears

He had a smile and was friendly, he loved all his children
and would say
But sickness changed his condition, and he's in
heaven with Jesus today

This world is not crowded with men, like the one
that lies there today
It won't be much of a place here, if more like
him do not stay

He wanted so much to stay here, perhaps for
his boys is why
But God knows best what he's doing, so he
just had to say goodbye.

When we all get up to heaven, and question
the Lord he will say
He'll probably answer with wisdom, it was
best that we took him away

I'm sure God had a reason, why he took my
loved one away
But I know he's in perfect contentment, up
there with Jesus today.

Emma Collins

LOVE'S ANSWER

I cried unto Love, and Love answered me.
With one sweet and deserving;
One so young and tender.

But, love in all its power spared not,
The feeling of my heart.

And brought me down till i was but
A mere man.

I shed many tears in my misery and despair;
I was as one lost, and without hope.
Yet, i cried again unto love.

As i cried love answered me,
With one so sweet and deserving.
One so young and tender.

Love answered again, and lifted my heart;
To heights unknown.
I was able to stand and count my suffering
for joy.

Love won its battle over me, filling my
whole being with a happiness and joy;
Such as i have never known.

And caused me to . . . Love,
One so young and tender.

Al Reynolds

ON THE HEIGHTS OF LOVE

Love, highest pinnacle in life;
Up there high, our hearts will fly;
Above, away from all the strife,
While the world below passes by.
Through time we climb hearts together,
Flying high in any weather;
Looking down from that field above
And then we say, "We fell in love."

What price this love, what is it worth?
Sweet sensations not found below;
High above the Heaven and earth,
Love is the highest thing we know.
At the height of its flight love brings
Two souls together on golden wings;
Flying so high the world above —
How can we say, "We fell in love?"

Kenneth C. Duncan

LOST AND FOUND

You are
always
dropping
things
earrings
that watch with the faulty hasp
single
strands of hair
your gold bracelet slithering from your wrist
your pinky ring daintily
circling a blade of grass like a tiny halo
the pock-pock-pock of your footfalls
on the sidewalk
approaching
and as you pass me going into the house
a trace   a faint redolence
of white shoulders.

John B. Lee

STRANGER

The roses have wilted,
and the crimson color is lost.
The roads became much longer,
and our paths never cross.
It's not often I return here;
for I remain a stranger to the name,
unchanged with the lock upon the gate.
In my eyes are tears to be shed;
but if I cry will I forget the pain inside?
In my mind words are being said;
but if spoken will I forget the anger that collides?
Knowing there won't be any reply within the breeze;
I embrace the emptiness of time.
There's nothing left to lose; when there is nothing to change,
and if there's no longer a need to remember.
I'm a stranger to the name plaque upon the mailbox;
picking up the pieces and returning once more.

Paige Angela Farkas

DREAM-FAITH

Could I not buy
What my heart would shout!
Love with you, my oneness,
No one could possibly tout.

My heart sings quietly.
Yet shouts to the heavens.
My love I've found,
Myself I've found.

Love a riotous act is not
Burns quickly and fades as a dream.
Love is a growing thing,
Nurtured by tenderness, eternal.

What is to be? Ever longing,
To be free, ever hoping,
A dream we live, to awaken,
With Faith, Victory abounds.

Chuck Derr

IF I COULD WRITE A SONG OF LOVE

If I could write a song of love
That brings the Gods to shame.
I'd write a simple melody
Then add to it your name.

If I could make the stars above
Shine brighter than the sun.
I'd write a song then add your name
To put on every one.

I'd write of you in harmony
To every lovely thing.
I'd seal it with a tender kiss
That makes the mountains ring.

And at the end I'd gently write
The words, "I love you so,"
Then as the music warms your heart
You'll think of me and know.

Richard L. Newcomb

LOVE

Love causes fish to
commit massive suicide.
Love causes people to
Think of others not just me.

Love causes lives to
Change from egotism to heroism.
Love causes man to think not of themselves
But
Of others' rights and their needs
To be helped.

Love causes
Many
Crazy, unexplainable things

And love

Is an eternal happening!

Tricia Shanahan

LOVE GROWN OLD

My wife cries vengeance
Against my carefree life.
Her life is the home
But I need something more:
Cars, sports and dirty stories.

The seasons whirl, trees blush,
Dogs bark
But I neither see, hear nor care.
I will whistle my songs
And if she smiles or laughs
Take no notice of the perfume
Wafting from her spell.

She rids me of all my friends
And works her erotic mechanics
Of binding me hand and foot,
Of drawing me into the web
And boredom of herself alone.

A neighbor calls her husband;
"Darling, where are you?"
I long to holler: "HERE!"

Ralph E. Martin

MARTIN, RALPH EDWARD. Born: Medford, Massachusetts, 12-27-24; Education: The George Washington University, B.A., Government, 1950; Occupation: Federal Government Employee for twenty-four years; Poetry: 'Kandahar, Afghanistan,' *American Poetry Anthology, Vol IV,* 1985; 'There Are Differences,' *75 Poets Series,* Charleston, Illinois, 1973; 'Ducks,' Spec. Song Press, Milford, Connecticut, 1973; 'Monarch of All,' Prairie Poet Books, Charleston, Illinois, 1973; 'Fishing,' *The Art of Poetry,* American Poetry Association, 1985; Comments: *I first wrote poetry so that I could remember the impressions a place had on me. Prose and photographs were unnecessary as these could better be found in an encyclopedia or* The National Geographic; *but the emotions aroused could be found only in myself. My thoughts are unlike those of others. They are the only personal thing about me. I comb my hair, drive a car, and drink water much like millions of other people.*

A LOVE FOR ALL OCCASIONS

A rose has many jagged thorns upon its slender stem,
But its blossom signifies a prevalent emotion, whisking away emptiness,
recreating a gem.
As brilliant petals slowly fade its showy grandeur,
So shall I love you, my loyalty to endure.

When the storm clouds gather, obscuring the sun,
Let me caress you with soft words to your heart that I won.
Golden shafts of happiness will break the darkness reigning above,
Lifting your spirit with the universal power of omnipresent love.

Walking in a meadow engulfed in delicate wildflowers and a sea of waving grass,
We stop to observe a myriad of darting butterflies, as the hours pass.
With a sky as blue as a sapphire containing all the world's oceans,
Moments that I share with you in contentment, shall display this emotion.

Evenings spent with you in flickering candlelight by a window overlooking the sea below,
Faint shadows prance around the walls in the firelight's glow.
Taking your hand in mine and walking out onto the verranda among the twinkling stars,
Lost in the untold vastness of the heaven's array of pinpoints, of light so far.

Seasons will lead us upon paths into the unknown,
But as our leaves turn to autumn colors you will not be alone.
With our rose garden planted, and all of its blossoms have spread their beauty,
Our petals will drift to the earth when we have completed our appointed duties.

James A. Hotchkiss

LADY AGATHA & EDMUND GRAY

Legend tells the eerie story about two phantoms' love through time.
Alone at first one haunts the corrie, waiting there beneath the lime.
Desire burns within her eyes as she scans the foaming shore,
Yearning for her lover's sighs as she heard them on the moor.

A month or more they stayed together, his barque at anchor in the bight.
Golden hours in the heather passing like a summer's night.
A lover's oath, a binding vow, united them forever.
Then he took a heather bough as a keepsake 'board the Trevor.
Hers was now the waiting game; and she survived until she read
A false report that gave his name as listed one among the dead.

&

Ever in the days that followed did his thoughts drift to her face,
Did she feel as sad and hollowed by the ever-widening space?
Months went by, he never learned of his lady's sad decline,
Until the day that he returned and stood beside her quiet shrine.
Never would she be his wife, at least not on this earthly plane.
Driven to a pirate's life, caring not for earthly pain.

Going to his final fight he saw his Aggie standing there,
Reaching to him through the night; 'twas time to join his lady fair.
After sunset casts its glory, if your love is quite sincere,
You will see them in the corrie, the lady and the buccaneer.

L. A. Hopkins

THE HEART'S SILENCE

The moment my heart started beating was the moment I met you.
Your glistening smile brought happiness, and so did your baby blues.
I can feel your presence from across the room, and receive a shiver from head to toe.
When you come over and speak to me, my heart wants you never to go.
The time that I spend with you is special, meaningful, and true.
I don't want you to ever leave, but there's nothing left for me to do.
Then the time will come when I realize that you have gone.
And once again . . . my heart will become silent.

Jennifer Margaroni

LOVE OF WIND

A child sat on the highest hill,
His chin cupped in his hands.
The wind rolled by on gossamer wings
And smiled on the little boy
Who had sought out this wondrous spot
Without a house in sight.

Here he'd come to be alone
And think his private thoughts.
"I love you wind, let me go with you,"
He said as it swirled his way.
The wind-bird fluttered low
To touch his cheek, and then intoned:
"Sometime, sometime, sometime."

And when he was a man
And things had gone a-wrong,
He came back to his favorite spot,
The clouds were mountains roiling.
"Oh wind take me with you."
The wind roared close in mighty force
And carried him away, away, away.

Jeanne Edwards

THE WEB

When I see you, I am obsessed
To have that which I know can't be,
A telltale dream of misconception
That haunts my mind and tortures me.
I cannot get you off my mind
Love's blindness has me in its clutch,
A queer obsession of the heart,
I know I should not care this much.
We're caught by Fate; I know full well,
Committed to the heart this way,
In being free, we find we're bound,
For passion seeks to know its way,
And if tomorrow finds us through,
And we must forever be apart,
We'll say that love declared it so,
As assassination of the heart.

Cecelia Marchand

TO MY LOVE

O my Love:
Here I stand, alone
In statuette, holding
The season's full store
In view — green mountain meadows
In resurrected view, feathering winds
In mating song, aggressing all day
From blossom to blossom, weaving
A trail to Autumn.

I can see
Through a window tree
A life-stream — rippling
Down with emotion, with its cascading
Arms offering a rainbow ring
To Spring . . .

O Love, my Love:
If you're on wings
Of hope, in search of
Rare perfume, my heart
Is in bloom!

Lola Beall Graham

LOVE

The only love I ever had
involved me with sadness . . .
That missing link that I will embrace
with tenderness and happiness
looks to be lost in the mist
far away from me

So oh my God where I can find
that missing link lost in the mist
to live my life the way
Oh God, you created it.
with love and happiness . . .
with love and happiness . . .

The only love I ever had
involved me with sadness
So oh my God where I can find
that missing link lost in the mist
to live my life the way
Oh God, you created it.
with love and happiness . . .
with love and happiness . . .

Antonia Fernandez-Corcino

AGING LOVE

Like a shadow in a shade tree
My Love awaits its chance:
The coming of a partner,
With whom it soon will dance . . .
Enveloping with youthful joy —
As the oyster does its pearl —
A sweetly scented bosom,
Caressing some sweet girl.

Yet, Alas! The shade tree withers,
And loses all its shade . . .
Thus leaving Love quite naked —
Awaiting its fair maid.
And openly revealed now,
Love has no place to hide . . .
For, like the withered shade tree,
Its passion, too, has died.

Now all that's left is Longing
For some shadow now long gone . . .
Oh, Love, what now awaits me
As Life continues on?

Craig E. Burgess

FOR LEXI

When I first felt you stir inside
I was frightened and intrigued
how a little seed of life
could be growing inside of me.
You were my miracle sent from God
a blessing just for me
I held your tiny hands in mine
hands that tickled me inside.
I miss holding you, my little one
and long to cuddle you close;
I knew the best way to show my love
was to let my precious girl go.
May you always know my love for you
may you never have to doubt
you were brought into this world
born to me because of His love.

Carolyn M. Vollmer

THE POSTMAN

"So many letters make you glad"
To me the friendly postman said

But inward I now feel so sad
The mailing lately is so bad

His country is now in a fight
When correspondence seems to be tight

He is physician prof on top
The highest rank alone on hop

He is so handsome he-man too
He was once of the Navy crew

My painting he can daily see
He in his studio placed to be —

But we are oceans far apart
In foreign lands what makes it hard —

Luisa Kerschbaumer

HE — WHO IS MY LOVE

He — who is my love —
brings peace to my
Soul, like arms full
Of love his peace does
enfold.

Were it not for his
kiss upon my
Cheek I would not have
fell victim my
Heart would not have
grown weak; yet
In him have I found
the love that I
Seek — in eyes that are
like reflections
Of blue skies — it is he
who brings his
Love to me and I dare
not wonder why.

Dorothy M. Anderson

WINTER AFTERNOONS

HONORABLE MENTION

I wrap you
in an old thick quilt
& watch you sleep,
trying to guess your past &
divine my future by studying
the lines of your face.
Simply being.
Without longing
or error or effort.
Nothing to do or say
except wonder how long
an Indian summer moment lasts.
A string of dried chilies
hung by the front door
murmur soft warnings
While your cat Chloe
stares your ghosts down
until they slink away.

Jon Cristol

To Bette, my love

They trod the earth on different paths
Their footprints left in sands of time
Two loves alone in pain and sorrow
Praying for a new tomorrow
And God looked down
And felt their pain
And knew the two should be as one
He touched their hearts
As they drew together
And soon his will was done.

C. James Matuschka

HE SPOKE TO ME SOFTLY

The Lord discerneth my spirit,
He restoreth my soul,
He revealeth my merit
And maketh me whole.

He spoke to me softly,
So no one could hear,
But I heard and listened,
I had nothing to fear.

He answered my question,
When he spoke to my heart,
He taught me a lesson,
From which I shall not depart.

He brought forth a miracle
And he touched my soul,
My faith became stronger,
As I reached my goal.

He that gets wisdom,
Loveth his own soul,
I found it better,
To get wisdom than gold.

Mildred H. Butler

LOVIN' RESPONSE

My soul weeps
Softly in the night
I ponder time
Spent in sorrow's flight.

So young to see
Too tender to feel in depth
So innocent to learn the truth
Adam's wisdom of the uncouth.

Love is the answer
Love is the prayer
Love is the gift
To everyone who cares.

I've been here before
The answers are the same
A loving response
Is the name of the game.

Love is a game
Only two can share
You can't play the rules
Without a thought or care.

Doralene Blakeney

DARLING MRJ

I love you my darling,
I gave you life
and in return, you gave me love.
Know that I will be with you always.

I will walk along beside you
and comfort you in your sorrow,
your anguish and your pain.
I will cheer for you in your triumphs
and your victories.
I will never be far from your side,
even in death.

See me through the eyes and hearts of others,
remember me not in sorrow
but in gentle thoughts and kind deeds.

Most of all my darling,
remember that I love you always.

Doreen E. Jardine

BEREFT

I saw her wearing his jacket today
And it blew my whole concept of life away.
As she looked at me with that gleam in her eye
My heart almost burst; I tried not to cry.
I remember that it was just last week
When we held hands and talked and laughed cheek to cheek.
Now I find that my meaning of life is gone.
Somebody, please tell me what I did wrong!
I saw her outside class wearing his ring.
It was on her finger, wrapped with yellow string.
Then I saw her talking to him in the hall.
He kissed her gently over by the wall.
The tears in my eyes made me walk away.
I kissed her the same way only yesterday.
The best days of my life I have spent with her.
How could I have caused our love to deter?
I ran outside and I stood in the rain.
I clutched my head, but I couldn't rid the pain.
I wanted to tell her how much I love her.
But I just couldn't seem to find the words.

Shannon Patrick Whitley

MY HEART BELONGS TO YOU

My heart beats for you alone
Without you it would turn to stone.
In you I find the faith I need
To go on doing my good deeds.

Whatever comes or goes with the roughest tides,
I will always be at your side.
Life can be sweet and oh, so neat
With you everything is so complete.

I feel warm in love, my heart entwine
I am so glad that you are mine.
When our lips meet the magic shows
One of the best ways to make our love grow.

We can be happy all of our life.
If you are my husband and I your wife.
When we get old and sometimes ill
My heart will say, I love you still!

Joan Keiter

THE COUPLE

Through the park, they walked together side
by side.
The man was slightly bent from age.
His face was worn with time,
And his hair was gray and balding.
The woman stood straighter.
Her eyes were sad, from years of sorrow.
Her hair was brown, with glimpses of gray.

Occasionally, the woman commented on the
beauty around them.
Other than that, they talked very little.
Neither did they join hands,
For words and gestures didn't seem important.
Time had washed away the need for these.
Just being together was important,
And the man and the woman would always be:
Two Hearts Entwined Forever.

Helen G. Cornish

REFLECTION

There once was a woman who, so full of love,
considered her children a gift from above.
She fed them and clothed them and cared for them so
she cradled them closely and never let go.
Lovingly watching as each baby grew
protecting them, teaching the things that she knew.
How was this loving young woman to know
that children do change with each day that they grow.
The mistakes they would make and the price she would pay
as ages of worry bind each passing day.
A mother's reality tangled in fear
her children's young lives seen through eyes filled with tears.
As time traveled on and her children grew wise
time caught them drying the tears from her eyes.
Then before her were standing great sources of pride
long years of devotion, with children at side.
So she smiled at these children, aglow with perfection
and saw in them images of her own reflection.

Pamela J. Shelton

I LOVE YOU OH SO MUCH

Believe me when I tell you that I love you so,
And that I will follow everywhere you go,
Because you are my Guiding Light, so brilliant and so true,
Is it any wonder I always cling to you?

Whenever I am weary, in you I find my rest
Your presence makes me equal to the roughest test.
To me, you are all good things; you're wonderfully worthwhile,
There is a wealth of faith and hope in your tender smile.

Walking with you is walking the road to Paradise,
Yours is the magic power to please and entice.
So you see how much I want you, and I always will,
I look to you for the needed strength to climb the highest hill.

Please stay with me forever; I need your loving touch,
I pray that I can prove to you
I love you oh so much!

Ava Lois Halstead

EAGLE ROCK, ORANGE.

MOTHER'S BEDTIME STORIES

My mother's voice was gentle, but when she read to me,
I explored far-off continents and sailed uncharted seas.
She let me march with Caesar and enter Ishtar's gate;
Achilles and I were buddies by the time that I was eight.

No child ever had such a guide. Wonder and joy she gave to me.
Often I walked with the Savior on the shores of Galilee.
I danced at many a Versailles ball; shivered at Valley Forge;
The Sun King offered me a rose; but I sympathized with George!

I crossed the Alps with Hannibal; reveled in Medieval Christmas,
Then climbed a galleon's rigging as she came lurching through the Isthmus
I soared to Mount Olympus on Pegasus' gleaming wings,
And listened rapt as Orpheus struck his lyre's strings.

Unseen, I rode with Lionheart against Saladin's host,
At conqueror's banquet, still unseen, heard Alexander's boast.
When Lucknow was delivered, I joined the shout of joy;
And crouched inside the wooden horse that tolled the knell of Troy.

I never was afraid at night, even when mother turned out the light.
For though I heard the lion's roar, gallant Bruce, with claymore girt,
Stood guard beside my door. With Lancelot, I've wielded sword.
Raleigh and Wallace were my brothers. But for guide in courage, faith
And joy, there was no voice like my mother's.

Shirley B. Stowater

THOU, UNITED STATES SENATOR

Dedicated to Senator John Heinz of Pittsburgh, PA

United States Senator,
where art thou?
Where art thou, very strong senator belonging to me, as well as our
whole country?
Senator where art thou, whose heart is heavy with problems,
Our angry world reaps.
Problems of anger and hate, causing thou, senator, the loss of much sleep.
Overburdened he is.
A wrinkle, just maybe to be found, on his most handsome young brow.
A drop of warm moisture trickles from his lash of velvet black.
The feel of a slight cramping pain in his back.
Long-off thoughts in his eyes of blue,
Oh, my senator, where art thy thoughts causing the longing in you?
Darling, time out for dinner, don't you think?
As he looks up, telltale signs of continuous work show,
For his eyes of blue are surrounded with pink.
A kiss upon his lips is what he needs, and he to put aside,
Just one night his work of good deeds.
Darling, Senator, where art thou?
When from thy burdens will thou be gone?
Oh Senator, for thou I long,
When to me will thou belong? S/JH

Happy Valentine's Day S/JH

Edith June Rouse

SOMEBODY

If you aren't capable of loving yourself,
Then find somebody who is willing and capable of doing this for you.
Hang on to this somebody until you become somebody
In your own eyes.
When you become that somebody,
Watch that somebody very closely,
Too often somebody becomes just anybody,
Though not just anybody can become a somebody.

Dana L. Orient

BARBARA

I love you because
I may embrace my soul
When I put my arms
Around you.

Because I appreciate your
Being — I love you.
You mirror that which I
Love — so I love you!

Because I may look
At you and know virtue,
Understanding, humanness.
I may enjoy compassion,
Experience enthusiasm
And respect accomplishment

With you I look forward
To truth, joy and peace,
With love.
Love,
Ronald

Ronald R. Tamburro

TAMBURRO, RONALD ROBERT. Born: Newark, New Jersey, 9-4-42; Married: 6-5-82 to Barbara J. Boscaino; Education: Self-educated, Philosophy, Economics, Human Action; Occupations: Funeral Profession, Law Enforcement, Sales; Memberships: Fraternal Order of Police, Mensa; Poetry: 'Ronald R., Some Thoughts,' poetry and essay completed 1985; Comments: *I live to discover the usefulness of love, intellectuality, honesty, compassion and individuality; to relate to these qualities and enhance my life by doing so.*

EMOTIONS

He likes satin ribbons and black lace,
damp ringlets surround her face —

Emotions run high, hearts beat fast
Ecstasy is felt, oh let it last.

Lee Lashbrook

CASTLES

With you,
I built my dream
On a castle of sand
Needless to say, it did not stand.

With you,
I built my love
Inside a castle of stone
Needless to say, my love is now gone.

With you,
I built my life
On a castle of air
When I really needed you, you were not there.

If castles of sand
Cannot stand

In castles of stone
Love has gone

Then leave my dreams, my love, my
Life alone and my dear,
With your castle of air
Disappear.

Joyce Bates

LOVE IS

Love is in your eyes
Love fills the skies
Love invades your dreams
Love's not always where it seems
Love is hiding far and near
Sometimes Love ends in shame or fear
Love is happiness, but you shouldn't fake it
Love is only what you make it.

Kim Sullivan

TO WHOM IT MAY CONCERN

I sit alone tonight amour, and watch the sea
across the way
lying black and mean against a pallid gray,
a darkening day.

An onshore wind blows hard and strong
and the broken breakwall rocks are gone
but along their hidden backs there leaps
a snarling, growling wall of foam.

Escape? Dare it challenge the cold, cruel chains that bind it?

Well, if I could talk its tides I'd let it know
that it shall never go . . . anymore than I shall go
the Stygian sea that grips my hand
that ruthless, flint-hearted sea of man.

Have all these tiny droplets been born to a world
with which they have little in common but birth and
nothing in part but the air they breath . . . like me?

If I could speak their tides I'd let them know a way.
A way, at least, to bear each day.
T'is love. Aye, t'is love, my dear. Live for love . . . I do.
The Shining Ones know I live for you.

J. Stahr

LOVE BEYOND

I have loved you more
than the fragrance of roses
I have planted with my own hand
I have loved you more
than the sight of dappled sunlight
on a forest floor of hidden woods
I have loved you more
than the scent of fresh-washed earth
More than
the silence of an undiscovered lake
More than
the dance of light in a diamond of water
suspended from a single leaf
In my life, in my way
I have loved you more than God
yet you mock me

Deborah Pearson

ELECTRIFIED LOVE

I've got me a gal I found her by the sea
She has electrified love and she has petrified me
Electrified love wow wow wowie
She has electrified love and she has petrified me
She loves me and loves me until my face turns red
Then she walks away, I'm petrified she thinks I'm dead
Her long blonde hair trails her as she walks away
But her big green eyes keep looking back my way
When she sees that my true color is coming back
I can hear her lips go snap, snap, smack, smack, smack
Then she turns around with a spin
and snatches me up and starts lov'n on me again
Her love is unique but very real
I can't help but love the way her lov'n makes me feel
She has electrified love wow, wow, wowie
She has electrified love and she has petrified me

Marjorie Rinkel Graumenz

A MOTHER'S LOVE

I look in your eyes and I see the faith
And I worry . . . Sometimes I feel like a child myself.
I want so much to be the strong, dependable person
you think I am.
I am not always right and I am not sure of all
the answers . . . although I try.
I want to protect you from everything, but deep
down I know I cannot.
You must go out and experience life, as I have.
You must make your own mistakes, as I have.
And hopefully, learn from them.
The hardest thing for me to do is let you go,
although I know I must, but I do it for you . . .
and myself.
For in letting you go, I hope we can be
so much closer.

C. K. J. LaFlam

READING AT DUSK

The reading lamp illuminates your head
eyelids closed, arms limp, chin lax
fingers holding newspaper loosely;
Snoozing in your black-patched orange chair
leather worn in torsoed creases
you are oblivious to headlines of doom.

I read your skinprint under cheeks
once taut in sun and wind
now shadowed in skulled hollows;
I dare not read aloud, give voice
to inflections ebbing over lips
corners of lips I claimed long ago.

I charted and captured that secret island
in a wild rush of exploring fever
land settled now in cleared forests, splashing streams;
No new inlets to discover as in daytime
of our youth in blistering heat, turbulent storms
only printed pages of love's voyage together.

Rose Kirchman

When all about me seems to be crumbling,
I have questioned my importance
in this too-fast moving world.
When personal successes mean little to those about me
if unaccompanied by the material trappings,
I begin to wonder about my worth as a person.
Self-doubt is a seed easily planted,
but painfully hard to kill.
When I begin to feel these forces closing in on me,
I keep my mind's eye set
on a bright light ablaze on the horizon.
It will get me through these times
As it has many times before,
For I know its origin —
you.
Your love is the one constant in my life.
It is always there —
undemanding and unyielding.
It is my reward and assurance that *I* am wanted —
and needed —
By the only person whose approval really matters.
Thank you.

Bill Lawton

A MAN OF ALL SEASONS

There is an empty ache deep down inside that
All the smiles and laughter can't hide
At times I wonder if my love for you will ever die
Or if your name will cease to bring tears to my eyes
There are so many times when I think of you
On fresh spring mornings, when everything is still,
and covered with dew
I see in a drop of water a reflection,
of a person you once knew
After a summer storm, while clouds race through the sky
I search the clouds for clues
for visions of you and I
When fall winds blow and red leaves scatter
I wonder what I truly meant to you,
how much I really mattered
While winter knits a blanket of snow,
with fingers so cold and deft
A single thought in my frozen heart,
I wish to God you had never left.

Teri Chaves

MY TINDER BOX

I have loved you since I was a boy
You were always special, my tinder box of joy
But you lived on the other side of town
And just to get a glimpse of your royal crown
I had to take two buses and yet walk a mile
Oh! to see those twinkling eyes and that tender smile.
To the world you might be worth a dime
To me you are a complete gold mine
No one else but mine!
No one else but mine!

Before you there were none
Since you, there has never been another one
I miss you, I long for you,
I have loved you, I have touched you
I have kissed you many a time
And I would love to do it all over again
For that was not all, it's not yet over and done
In fact it has just begun
The best is yet to come!
The best is yet to come!

Allam Zaheer Ahmed

LOVE DEFINED

Love draws people to one another
Giving them comfort when they are in need,
And speaking kind words, that they can heed,
Lifting their spirits to bring a smile to their face,
Telling them nothing is so bad, that love can't erase.

Love brings peace to mind and heart,
If we would only do our part,
Being gentle and sincere.
So they'll always want us near.

True love is beautiful,
It gives joy to young and old,
And to most of them, I'm sure,
It's more precious, than their gold.

So if we remember God's words were,
To "love one another,"
We would see good in all and each other,
Making the world a better place,
When we respect each other's race.

Ruby M. Olson

WHO STOLE MY LOVE?

Who has stolen my love —
The love with whom I've vowed
To live for better for worse?
They're all there — eyewitnesses
On that glorious, unforgettable day
During that solemn, matrimonial service,
We covenanted, got joined
To build a strong, Christian home.

"With this, I give my love . . .
Until death do us part"
Was the vow we both exchanged,
Now, our flourishing love's tree
Has been stripped, tapped, and even set asunder,
"I love ya" suddenly becomes "I hate you,"
And love's language becomes
"Until divorce do us part."

Joel A. A. Ajayi

FORTUNATE IN LOVE

When we were dancing at the Belvedere
That night not too long after we had met
I looked into those big brown eyes of yours
And fell for you — how could I e'er forget?

You took me to the Senior picnic then
And we became engaged to marry soon:
Of course my parents thought I was too young —
But we were married in the month of June.

We've had our ups and downs, I know, dear heart,
And still our love has stood the test of time
As many years have passed since we were wed —
We're fortunate it's made our lives sublime.

Alice S. Elton

ELTON, ALICE S. Born: Salt Lake City, Utah, 9-4-06; Married: 6-12-28 to James W. Elton; Education: University of Utah, B.A.; Occupation: Teacher, 1927-28; Co-owner and Operator of The Elton Orchards; Memberships: General Federation of Women's Clubs, Chi Omega Sorority, Daughters of the American Revolution; Awards: Fourth place for 'To Peggy,' *Our World's Best Loved Poems,* World of Poetry, 9-30-85; Poetry: 'Our Last Farewell,' *American Poetry Anthology,* 1984; 'A Sonnet For My Beloved,' *American Poetry Anthology,* 1985; 'Unanswered Questions,' American Poetry Association, 1985; 'Nostalgia,' American Poetry Association, 1985; Other Writing: "The Mystery of Oak Island," article, *Writer's Digest,* 1981; Comments: *I enjoy writing poetry, especially because it expresses my deepest feelings about experiences I've had, or about current events important to all of us.*

OUT OF LOVE ONLY

Out of Love only, do I work!
Mine is not to Take, but to Give,
For it is in my Giving that I shall Receive!
There is no Past.
I live not for the Future,
But the Present and I must live it
As I would have it recorded for All Eternity!

Suzanne L. Reed

I, ELLA, FALL IN LOVE

Inspired by my admired first teacher, I
Resolved to give myself to others' young
A husband, family I would pass by
Till death took me away unwept, unsung.
For thirteen years my mind stayed firm in place
Until in college Fate transformed my life.
I met a lad I knew I must embrace
I wanted most of all to be his wife.
From other girls I learned that he was free,
Obtaining transfer credits was his aim
His social life banned females such as me,
He seemed to look on us as all the same.
When Sally came to me with his request
to take me out, I very nearly died.
With heart in mouth I put him to a test:
"Let him himself approach me," I replied
He did, and there a lifelong pact was sealed
To last forever and another day,
All personal commitments were repealed
We're almost sixty years along our way.

Ella M. Greene

MY KID

Oho, you little kid, I saw what you did;
You ran away and hid. You can't fool me.
I'm putting in my bid, of me you can't get rid;
Into my loving heart you've slid, you'll see.

You're such a little pip, and smarter than a whip,
Come over for a sip, you're my baby.
Why run around and flit? I'm Daddy, this is it.
You're Daddy's great big hit, don't mean maybe.

We do not like to chide, but the world is very wide;
You're such a source of pride, Oh, me!
Whatever shall betide, we'll stand you here beside,
I hope we can on love agree.

This foolishness must quit, come on my lap to fit
The sweater Mom has knit, climb on my knee.
Shake hands, give me your mitt. Show off that ready wit,
Then to your pillow exit, tiredly.

Stephen L. Bogadi

THE LAST MILE

Daddy pulls me up to keep awake.
Tells me she's no better today
But pray for her and me he says — pray.
He leans his lean frame over her bed to turn her
Then brings her water to drink
Soon changes her diaper
Tucks her in to sleep.
Daddy pulls me from my away-turned face.
I observe his prodding her to eat
Pat her sheet and fight her attempts to off them.
When a nurse comes in details their sins —
She would die without him. And she would.
He kisses her. Asks, Do you still love me?
And she doesn't know him.
Daddy holds her till she's brought back again.
Listen, she's singing! Daddy sings along.
O Joy of this moment! O Love!
"There'll be no tears in heaven, no sorrows given" —
Hold on, hold on, and when He calls
Learn only then to let go.

Rodger Bivins

LOVE

Love is the gift of God
Given to make our lives
And those we share it with
So much richer, fuller.

We learn the love given
To us by our mothers
And shared with our family
As we grow up at home.

Young love is tender love
That comes to young people
As they meet, become one
And their own family start.

God gives His love to us.
We learn to love Him, too.
He teaches us we should share
That love with all we meet.

But love that grows more deep
'Tween a man and his mate
Is sweeter far than any
And lasts 'til the end of time.

Louise Monteith

MY DAUGHTER-IN-LAW, ROSE ANN

Upstairs I hear footsteps
and my thoughts say
Rose Ann is preparing
to win another day's pay.

Our executive person
will be lovely to see,
Coming down to the garden,
smiling at me.

Her motorcycle
will be by her side,
As she puts on her helmet
and prepares for the ride.

With a hope and a prayer
I will soon see her go
Into the morning's
swift traffic flow.

Then I'll wait for the sound
of her opening door,
And her attaché case
slumping down on the floor.

Molly Molyneaux

FRIENDS

Friends are made for us to share
Friends are made with loving care

Friends cheer us up when we're mad
Friends make us happy when we're sad

Friends can help us when in need
Friends can help us to succeed

Friends are made for us to share
Friends are made with loving care

Judy Tuttle

A touch, an embrace
was all I yearned for

Not more, not less
and three words

I love you

Josefina Balderrama Barrios

THE OTHER PILLOW

When the stagnant moments
In the belly of the night
Brings visions tangled in time
Of the years that have abandoned me
Like drizzling rain,
When the lingering despairs
Of dreams long passed
Still weigh upon me
Heavy as a star,
I turn to find her silhouette,
Familiar against the pillow,
Frail as dew that adorns the petal
And the silent sorrow
That has briefly ransomed me
Fades like shadows
Before the light.

Doug Frech

LOVE'S CALLING REVISITED

In the serenity of the night
come thoughts of you
silently and gently,
embracing my soul,
and in moments passing
ecstasy reveals herself to me.

I feel the softness of your presence
without touching,
we speak unheard words
yet understand what is said,
we exist
yet for us time stands still,
our souls intertwine
and we become one,
in search of love.

Robert D. Hardy

LADY SILVER

Lady Silver dressed in white,
why do you flee to hide?
Don't you know that with your light
you are our midnight guide?
Lady Silver, of sooty eyes,
do not cloud your face.
Don't you hear the lovers' sighs,
see their lips about to taste?
Lady Silver, carved of cold fire,
why don't you see my yearning?
When I touch you gently with desire,
don't you feel a sudden burning?
Lady Silver, come to me;
step down from high above.
Set your feelings running free
and let me show you how to love.

Patricia L. Randall

PINK ROSES

Was he for me? Of a certainty, thought I
This Romeo of the sophomore world.
A smile he flashed, a date he asked
And my heart was lost for good.

So I, naive, did dress in my best
Pink roses he gave me, how close we danced
This dreamlit night.
All approved, some even envied,
He was for me, supremely.

I wonder now how it came to be
That for him there was another she,
Why was this unkown to me?

He said he couldn't keep our Friday date,
It wasn't that I didn't rate,
Just a promise made to her long ago.

Long ago, still I remember
A youthful heart that was slow to mend.
I thought him the only love for me
And found it was simply not to be.

Betty B. Jones

JONES, BETTY B. Pen name: Lynna Lawton; Born: Roswell, New Mexico; Married: to Art Jones, Phoenix businessman; Education: University of Texas; Occupations: Novelist; Author of bestselling *Under Crimson Sails, Glory's Mistress;* Poetry: 'Graduation Day,' *American Poetry Anthology,* January, 86; Comments: *As a 'wordsmith,' I am in never-ending touch with the graceful interplay of words and their impact. The themes of my novels, while historical in genre, are interspersed with a touch of romantic verse which I find wonderfully refreshing to write.*

Pink and white petals
Spill drifting into footprints . . .
Snow melts where you stood.

Deon Davis

THE FLOW OF LIFE

There is clarity of purpose
in all,
A good achiever
reaches the top.
The moral issue is freedom,
As humanity struggles
to be heard.

As the undercurrent of thought
emerges,
There is reliance on faith,
The division of ideas
flows from above.
Slowly, there is direction
to life.

The great advance in
civilization,
Produces great thinkers,
Such as Aristotle, Plato.
The knowledge of the world
is priceless.

Dreaming, seeing the world
through rosy glasses,
As we approach a New Year,
We find a world of many races,
Spreading their culture
throughout the world.

Elizabeth Saltz

THE TELEPHONE GOOD-BY

"Hello!" Your line has been busy.
Is it all right if we talk now?
I have something I want to tell you
And I must get it across somehow.

I've debated with myself for so long now,
How best to let you know.
I wanted to tell you face to face
But I knew it would hurt me so.

"Hello!" Are you still listening?
Oh, please don't hang up the phone.
All I want is one minute
And I will forever be gone.

Yes, dear, I am leaving.
I'm leaving and this is my news.
It's heart-breaking to me
But does it mean that much to you?

I'll be making my home somewhere else now
And I'll never see you again.
And all I have left is my memories,
The memories of love's sweet refrain.

So I'll just say good-by now.
May God bless you in all that you do.
You can hang up the phone now.
What's that? I think he's crying too.

Mrs. Earl V. Bundy

GEORGIANA

I saw you pass my way today
Black had been the color of my universe,
It filled my world and permeated my very soul.
Before you, I drifted along, an empty shell
Skies were grey in my world, birds sang no songs, flowers did not bloom.

Today my darkened world was shattered by the blinding light of you.
Your smile lights up the room as you enter.
It is as the dawning of the morning of my life and you are my sun.
You did not feel my stare nor share the wonder of my gaze.
You could not know that you had changed a life, a world.
I breathed you in, across the room, I absorbed you
Your face, like finest marble to which had been applied the slightest tint of color,
The flowing raven-colored hair, but black on you gives no hint of my former world.
Your eyes, which during conversation, laugh and dance, as living things.
Your bouncing walk, as if gravity were your plaything.

Your voice combined the sounds of a woodland brook flowing over pebbled banks
with the melodies of doves.
My life will never be the same for having met you.
All that was before can never be again.
You entered my life and gave it meaning.
From this day forward I began to be.

Terrence Gumbert

LOVE RESHAPING MY SOUL

The soft spring rain lightly fell on my chrysalis . . .
It slowly turned my desolate life into a delicate
beautiful butterfly . . .
My humble color of richness is changed by God's
wisdom to a straight vertical relationship with the Lord . . .
And yet no one can see the transformation,
the sensitivity, but God . . .
We never touch, we never meet, we never see eye to eye . . .
Our physical touch is so quiet, but our emotional
touch is so electrifying . . .
so spectacular . . .
so passionately in love with the
Spirit that loved me so.

Mary K. Herring

CHRISTA MCAULIFFE'S STAIRWAY TO HEAVEN

Seeing a staircase set upon the earth, Christa McAuliffe had a vision, of joy and mirth.
She saw in her vision angels ascending; as she looked up, she saw angels descending.
Further up this holy phenomenon, Christa McAuliffe saw its summit, reaching to heaven.
Seraphs made for her a pillar of fire; she heard morning stars sing in heavenly choirs.
Then this prophetic resound: A day will come and heaven will explode with great sound!
The Lord will descend as the heavens fold shut; then you'll hear God's golden trumpet.
Soaring "falcon" glides in southerly berth; a star will fall from heaven to the earth.
For flesh and blood shan't inherit God's kingdom; only the spirit through all millenium.

In whose hand is the spirit of man? Men of the dust cannot know God's ultimate plan.
O earthly man, have you considered the flight of a mockingbird as she ascends upward?
But God reveals to us, wisdom through his spirit; for our God is from time indefinite.
Hear the "sound of the songs" of great rhapsody; thirsty ones, take life's water free.

Spirit and the bride say come; hearts will blush with spiritual fire in God's kingdom.
The marriage feast is prepared in heavenly unison; yet many are called . . . few chosen.
Our God is the fine connoisseur; refining you in spiritual fire, cleansing as silver.

Heaven sets in motion a purpose from afar; you, Christa, will shine as a morning star.
Was it from you that you commanded the morning? Causing the dawn to break, unforeseen?
Have the gates of death been opened to you? The windows of heaven can you see through?
Christa you set our hearts afire! Carrying your love with you! To this you did aspire!
You'll come in where angels applaud; a city without sun but lit by the Glory of GOD!

Bernie Claus

WHAT IS LOVE?

What is love? I can only guess
Maybe it's seeing what's good.
Being blind to the rest

Maybe it's willing to share
When you don't have too much

Maybe just a warm smile
Or a gentle touch

Love can come in all disguises,
That is when self-doubt arises.

So just enjoy what the day may bring,
That is the love that makes bells ring

Carol Miller

A MOTHER'S CROSS

A part of herself
She planted
Within each child she bore
And as they grow and leave her
They take with them
A part of her.
Man cannot understand this
It's the mother's cross to bear
She can pray
And she can trust
But a part of her whole
Will share in their wrong doing
And she knows deep in her spirit this.
It's like spears piercing her heart
Her love for each of them so deep
She could bear them all over again.

Mae Cross Tarrant

BABY LOVE

The envious moon breathes a sigh,
and hangs its head in shame.
Even the lovely song birds stop,
whenever is mentioned her name.
They know of her loving goodness,
and all the joy she brings,
and when we are together,
my heart, it always sings.
She brings to me the laughter,
that's never really been there.
She takes away my sorrow,
and gives me loving care.
When I'm with this lady,
I'm never ever blue,
and if you wonder who she is,
well baby love it's you.

Roy M. Alexander

As birthdays come and birthdays go
we favor some, as you well know.
But, my dear and darling wife,
none have more meaning for me
than those we've shared in our life.
As any one can plainly see,
each passing one draws us nearer.
Each passing one is that much dearer.

Josh Fallick

TREASURED LOVE

A mother's heart is filled
With love and gentle caring —
She feels the tender touch
Of baby's fingers, sharing
That first smile so precious,
Treasures beyond comparing!

Edna M. Parker

FALLING

You can't fall out of love
Like you can from a window —

The flight is long, the crash is silent,
The healing never final.

Sara Ann Holcombe

TO MY LOVE

To my love,
For now and always.
And when our time has arrived,
Our love will be remembered
As a sparkling star in the night.

Christine Tansey

LOVE IS LOVE

Love is love the world around,
It can't be bought by the pound,
A cent doesn't cost —
Can never be lost —
From your heart when it is found.

Genne R. Morgan

LOVE

Love is like oceans,
Always changing, yet the same
Rough, calm and blending.

Linda H. Rhine

APPRECIATION

Thank you Jesus for dying for me
To set my ransomed soul free
Thank you Lord for caring about me
Thank you Master and Savior above
For your never ceasing undying love

Ramona Lee

EASTER SUNDAY

Wherever you may go on
this beautiful holiday,
May the dear Lord's blessing
always light your way —
And may Peace, Hope and Love,
always be there,
In answer to your sincere
daily prayer —

Fern Roche

DANNY

Danny seemed so very sad
So very long ago,
And this is all
That I'm aware of him.
An image — grief;
His shape was sad
And was with sadness filled.
His sadness made me sad
As well for him.
And too, I loved him.
Was this loving caused
By his sadness that was mutual?
Or was this love an altogether
Independent thing?
He was warm,
And he was fond of me.
And I remember Danny
Darkly, strangely.

Joseph Hart

GARMENT OF MY HEART

Never worry, my sweet love,
about another guy,
for only to you will my heart talk,
of others it is shy.
No one could steal my heart from you,
they needn't even try,
for they'd have to take my love for you,
and without that my heart would die.

For as long as it will make you happy,
with you my heart I'll share,
because it's you above all others
for whom I so dearly care.
The deep love I feel for you
is one I'm sure that's rare,
so always remember, my sweet love,
it's only your love, your fondness for me,
that forms the garment my heart will wear.

Carol Marie Griffin

BELONGING

Youth's desire, thrill,
passion, and palpitating hearts
Romantic dreams
beautiful fantasies —

Compare —
day by day realities,
Standing shoulder to shoulder
in adversity and need,
Sometimes even boredom,
for a moment only

Then —
gentle acceptance,
Contentment in small successes
accomplished together
Warmth, peace, belonging
together at day's end.

Charlotte M. Edwards

IN LOVING REMEMBRANCE OF MY MOTHER AND FATHER

(Laura Ethel (Porter) and Albert Emil Lindquist)

Mother left us illuminated memory
Of deep thoughts, felt beauty, never in jeopardy.
The establishment of values made life worthwhile
Heeding ideals concrete, values truest beguile.
Enormous importance determined whole life's trend,
Resplendent in spiritual beauty to the end.

Father's visions were beautiful and the ideal,
An interpretive thinker with vigor and zeal.
The prophesier crying out with true courage,
His stance — right against wrong, truth against
falsehood — sage;
Extending reach around world of the law of love
Remember the Kingdom of God, supreme will above.

James Wayne Lindquist

JUDITH

Thoughts of you dance as visions within my mind,
Fluid movements, a love that does not bind,
The graceful lines of a loving woman, so kind,
Your love embodies a perfection I was so very lucky
and grateful to find.

Kerry McGeath

SHADOW WALK

Hey! the moon is large and white with shadows,
so come on, let's walk beyond our threshold
together, hand in hand through the meadows
leaving shadows on the grass for the gold
light of sunrise to find in morning dew
beyond us. There were times we'd love such nights
away, but not now, Love. Let's, me and you,
hold hands in the cold beneath the star light.
The past was wonderful, those nights we'd love
away, but now is best; no youthful prime.
The hills were green then, but greener now above
the plain where wild daffodils glow in time.
Let's laugh and love this night better than the rest;
the blossoms, the bright moon shadow, your lips,
our small world, this soft night together, are best,
as our shadows walk, touching finger tips.

Thirl Michael Butler

A MOTHER'S LOVE

There is no passion greater than a mother's love
There is no tyranny like a mother's wrath.
There is no hell like a mother's sorrow.
There is no love like a mother's forgiveness.
There is no justice like a mother's compassion.
There is no hate like a mother's justice.
There is no injustice like a mother's righteousness.
There is no reflection like a mother's mirror.
There is no greater self-esteem than a mother's approval.
There is no greater joy than a mother's smile
She is, we are, and they will be.
My mother smiled on me, I smiled on
My children and they will smile on theirs
All because of my mother, and the
Mother who made her what she was —
A mother who gave love.

Janet Martin Atkinson

MISTY

I'll always see your white mane and tail flying,
And your silver dapples.
Feel your soft nose nuzzling my pocket,
When you're looking for an apple.
I know you're in pony Heaven,
So I'll try to keep the tears back.
Your pasture there will always be green
And for kindness you'll never lack
A gentle breeze will always whisper,
In the branches of the big pine.
For, in its shade, you always rested —
It hurts so to lose you, Misty mine.

Romie Clouse

TO YOU

Feelings of mine for you are so beautiful, a thoughtful caring
Person
As yourself has so much to give,
You don't have to try — a caring glance, the softness of your
Voice
Say it all,
Emotions fall freely from your soul,
No fear of being found to be too loving and wonderful,
To be with you ignites every part of my being
A feeling that is so intense is everlasting,
And when we join together as one, the love we share will
Change us forever.

Cheryl Vatcher

ONE WORLD

We are our brothers' keepers,
Whether red, brown, black or white.
We are all related no matter what our skin.
We just need remember, in GOD, all men are kin.

For the goal of Peace, we must be seekers.
We must struggle with all our might
For our world to perceive the right,
And spread lasting love and harmony to mankind
far and wide;
Thus, for all our children . . . a legacy of
PEACE we'll provide.

E. Gwendolyn Campbell

LEST YOU FORGET

True love with its beauty — the day you were wed,
"Till death do us part," each one of you said.
Should some days be cloudy, and the going get real tough,
Remember Dear, your husband's just a diamond in the rough.
Your hair and your house may both be a mess,
You work and you worry — that's life I guess.
Yet still the kids argue — you must judge pro and con,
But a wife's just a bride with a housedress on.
Let love like today's continue through life,
One be a good husband — the other a good wife.
Your thanks for His blessing shine for all to behold,
'Tis a treasure more precious than silver or gold.

Clara G. Stinson

SOMEONE LIKE YOU

It's been a long time since I'd met someone like you. Someone so warm, someone so kind and caring like you. Someone like you to hold me tight; someone like you to think of through the night. Although I'll never know if our love will grow. At least now I have a friend with someone like you. Good friends are hard to come by. Lord knows I have a few. I'll never know what you think of me but I know how I feel about you.

Edward Lilly

MOTHER LOVE!

Sonnets and arias honor her name;
Legion the lyrical praises proclaim:
"Mother, the greatest gift God can bestow;
As all creatures in the universe know!"
Sovereign or serf, her wee babe in her eyes
Was created for her to idolize!
So treasure the sanctity of her love;
Cling to it, soft as the down of a dove;
Cradle its touch, as a tender caress;
Bask in its radiance; its wonders bless!
Legendary its beauty and its strength;
Indomitable its spirit and length
Of compassionate service to mankind;
Absolving errors of the mortal mind!

Minnette O. Alexander

UNDYING LOVE

If I were to write a poem about a man and woman's love,
I wonder how I'd find the words to start.
How I'd express to others in a way they'd understand
The feelings I have deep within my heart.

I'd want to say how good it is, to know another cares
And that they love you just for who you are.
I'd want to say that closeness is a very vital thing
A "oneness" of two souls — whether near or far.

I don't have expectations that I'd make a list about
But, would really rather just let feelings flow.
Then take the time that's needed to appreciate each other
And let a love undying start to grow.

Terry Ann Braaten

SOLDIER

Night falls like a widow's teardrop,
and silence shelters the land.
I sit in enveloping solitude,
hoping for the touch of your hand.
The roads between us are long ones,
the seas eternities high,
And I think of the exploding stars,
and all of the souls that might die.
In my dreams I see you, as you were years ago,
but wakening I imagine you, marching and running low.
Someday I know I'll see you
here in our homeland again.
Your heart may not be beating,
but I'll love you even then.

Shauna L. Brown

1943

They stood in the mist of a gray December darkness,
The lights of the depot shining like lanterns in a fog.
And they were holding hands, trying to be brave,
Trying to speak of ordinary things, not things of war
Nor of the train which in a little while
would take him far away.
For they were very young, and didn't want to know
That this could be their last goodbye.
They stood there, silent, as the train approached the station.
Holding time close with a kiss,
Somehow knowing that there is no time but now.

Evelyn M. Pierce

MY LOVE

Out of the fire that fills the night
Your face comes to me and I fight
The mind that's trying to dispel
The memory and your sweet smell, my love.

Once man was God and God was man.
Now who can tell me what I am
When on my lips bitter sweet
The taste of you and I repeat, "My love."

I will not draw one little breath
Unless it first has crossed your lips
And I can't make those realms of peace
I never did like lonely trips.

You're gone and I'm too down to think.
There's just no comfort in a drink
And when I sleep you're here again
All smiling love and golden skin.

You float in on a fragrant mist.
My tears fall freely as I kiss
The essence of you slipping by
And softly in the night I cry, "My love."

Dean Lewis

VALENTINE FOR MATTHEW

Morning arrives too early these days.
I rise out of sleep through a foggy haze
To hear you bellowing in my ear,
"Mama, Mama! Come here — come HERE!"

I used to enjoy my time in the morning,
Especially weekends. Now, without warning,
You run into my room as I sit reading
And jump on my legs in joyful greeting.

As mealtime approaches, your smiles turn to whines,
Gradually lessening as everyone dines.
The sight of the front of your shirt makes me ill
As I think of the outrageous laundry bill.

When naptime arrives, I am pitifully grateful
for an hour of peace. And yet I am wakeful
As I lie on my couch and think of your smile
And your small, pointed face, so free of all guile.

I think of your energy, sweetness and joy
And am glad for the gift of this cute little boy.
Though there are times when I wish we were oceans apart,
You should know that I love you with all of my heart.

Ilka E. Krieger

SENSATIONS

Charismatic sparks
Blaze between us
As you enfold me
And deeply we kiss.

You penetrate my heart
Spangle my soul;
Cause longing to surface
White-hot to touch.

My predictable world
Shatters soundlessly
You claim my passion;
Become facets of me.

Silence of distance and time
Melts memories, never;
Sensations remain afire
Intrusive companions evermore.

Bereft, I long for your touch,
Your smile, your voice,
Your vibrations of love —
The heartbeat — of You.

Nancy Needham

LOVE THAT I CARRY

What joy, what fun, what frivolity
The bliss we experience when we're young
What hopes in breathless eagerness
We hold in our memories growing old.

What dreams, what goals that we had,
Now faded and gone from view

And the only thing left
Of our hopes and our dreams
Is the love that I carry for you.

Moe Feldman

MY HEART IS HURTING

Tonight my heart is hurting,
Hurting just for you —
Because it still remembers
Dreams that won't come true.

The times you used to call me
And set my heart aglow
Are causing only silence,
And it is hard to know.

The day would be so perfect
When you came by at night,
And everything that stressed me
Your arms would make alright

I've tried to just forget you,
And build my life anew;
I've tried to find in someone
The joy I found with you.

I've sought in vain the sunshine,
And looked for skies so blue,
But now my heart is hurting —
Hurting just for you!

Evelyn Holten

ALWAYS BE YOUR NAME

I have nothing much to offer
Save my deep affection
And though you regard me with esteem
I'm still just a sweet confection

You come and go like the seasons
Time passing through the pain
You reached inside me for a moment
Until the thrill had lost my name

If a moment of happiness be measured
Against too many years of longing
And if your phantom-like presence
Gave me a feeling of belonging

Can you fathom for an instant
My joy each time you came
Just to share some tender moments
Friendship — Always be your name

Yesterday was a poor messenger
For love unspoken, it never came
You've overstayed your absence
Love — Always be your name

D. V. Stiles

BLEEDING HEART

I did not see or hear
The arrow leave his bow
Turning
Surprised at the
Blood on the snow
Paralyzed
As the fallen deer
I look up
He smiles
I've been with someone else
All around blood flows

Elizabeth J. Potter

HONEYMOON COTTAGE

They were on their honeymoon.
A marriage had begun,
life of joy and happiness,
joined together, now made one!

A winding path through the woods
to a cottage on a hill
a couple strolling hand in hand
'mid songs of the whippoorwill.

A hug, a kiss, Love's perfect spot
there's a rustling among the trees.
A deer, a chipmunk, and a fawn
amid a cool brisk breeze.

Then suddenly the deer appeared
and stared in wonderment.
The couple saw their gliding feet
and all asunder went!

Such precious moments cherished,
leaving all their cares behind.
Oh what happiness, oh what joy,
and refreshment for the mind!

Verla Christine Nielsen

WEAL and WHEEL

To George, whose love for weal on wheel is communicable and very refreshing — Dot.

I'm a lady on a wheel,
Whipping right along.
Countryside is blooming,
Birds are in full song;
Saddle bags all packed,
Gear all stowed in place,
Motor running smooth;
A smile on my face.

Yep — I'm a lady on a wheel,
Lady on a wheel,
Lady on a wheel,
Lady on a wheel.

Riding not too fast,
Making every moment last,
Soaking up a tan,
Riding with my man;
He looks to me to beam,
Yes, we two, make quite a team.
I'm a lady on a wheel,
I'm a lady on a wheel,
Lady on a wheel,
Lady on a wheel,
Lady.

Dorothy R. Wellman

WELLMAN, DOROTHY R. Born: Carmel, California, 9-25-11; Awards: Golden Poet Award, *World of Poetry*, 1985.

WITHOUT US

Oh what am I going to do, without us
Where will life lead, without us
From the first time we met
I knew we'd be friends
It wasn't too long ago
But oh, we had so many good times
Now we're going — each our own way
What am I going to do, without us
It's so sad, how friends come and go
We always say we'll never lose touch
But somehow we do — yes, we do
Where will life lead, without us
I know that it's crazy —
Still sometimes I wish, time would stand
And give a little more to us
Oh how will I survive, without us

Melissa Moffitt

A LOVE NOT FORSAKEN

Upon an old stone wall by the sea
she sat remembering the brother that used to be
The joy and laughter that once filled the air
even the sad times they used to share

A glimmering flicker of light within a wave
brought forth her brother's face
As she called out to him
it slowly began to fade

Tears gently rolled down upon each cheek
she heard a soft voice in the breeze
"Although we had too little time it may seem
you are not only my sister you are my friend

So fear not for our love shall always be
with each beat of your heart
as with each wave from the sea"
and only then did her tears cease

Candy Lee Koolhaas

To Bette, my love

Long after springtime had withered and died
I hugged my pillow
Which reminded me of
Those mechanical people
Who never replaced the void
On the drifting glacial icefields
After blizzard winds of divorce
Where my hopes and I lay down to slumber
To sleep in winter forever
And freeze the lonely memory-pains
Of another time when spring first came
But now the caress of a warm loving hand
Has touched my lips!
And opened my eyes!
Eyes that long sought the look of love —
And I find that same gaze returned!
And I rise to embrace!
And to give up my heart!
And I believe in the springtime again!

C. James Matuschka

SOMEWHERE, SOMETIME

Somewhere,
through all the pretense
all the false expectations of what I should live up to
I will find someone
who will love me freely
without reservation of my past or what I am now
I know that God
will fulfill what I need
with who He wants for me when I am truly ready
Sometime,
when patience pays its dues
and I have grown into what I need to be
I will love someone
and be loved as God
meant for me to be with understanding and maturity
It will be right
it will be as never before
And I will know if I stay open to His will
Somewhere, sometime
I will be in love!

Paula Hale-Orr

I LOVE LIFE

Its challenges, its hopes or despairs
Laughter, sorrows, frustrations and cares
The rising sun and the full bright moon
And the seasons that change all too soon
Weather moods — either hot, rain, cold or snow
Gale winds or very gentle breezes that blow
Babies, children, elderly and disabled
Show love, no matter how they're labeled
The look of lovers hearing their song
Pets' adoring eyes as they tag along
A love of God who is just and fair
I try to find and give love everywhere
Many things in life can "set hearts on fire"
Being in love with life is my desire.

June Alexander

LIFE'S SECRET

To Central Asia went I, life's secrets to learn.
Now, the reflection since my return
Is soft eyes, warm hands, and kisses that burn.
It's the love found there for which I yearn.

Tamarlane's tomb and palaces bright
Are splendid trappings for Mohammedan light,
But the picture of splendor that stays in my sight
Is your beautiful face on that Baltic White Night.

Samarkand showed the secrets I sought
In glory and splendor and scholar's thought.
It's my love found in you, the world forgot,
That's the secret of life that Samarkand taught.

L. Elcan Walker, M.D.

The heart of a man to the heart of a maid —
Light of my tents be fleet —
Morning awaits at the end of the world,
And the world is all at our feet.
R. Kipling

I slowly shift to gaze upon
A figure lighted by the dawn.
A gentle flicker, of your eyes,
Precedes your waking and implies
That angels have been ling'ring there,
Within your heart, my feelings' lair.
And as your eyes return my gaze,
My mind recalls the thwarting maze
Which spawned for you my love each night,
And makes me welcome morning's light.

Nathanael Rugh

THE GAZEBO

Pillars of gold surround a halo of a flowing gown,
The breeze whispers sweet melodies
Enhancing a water-misted face gazing upon
Breathtaking views of sculptured gardens.
A song of love, slowly, sends aesthetic
Dreams of diamond brillance
Time stands still:
Forever filled with everlasting bliss.

Rita M. Knecht

BECAUSE OF THE MAN UPSTAIRS

Because, of The Man Upstairs,
My faith, grows with my prayers.
My day begins, and ends with Him,
The courage I have, isn't even slim.

He guides me, each and every day,
And His rules, I try to obey.
My love for Him, is exceptionally strong,
Therefore I know, I can't go wrong.

I have such great, deep inner strength,
Which cannot be, measured in length.
There are no doubts, where He's concerned,
The strength He's given me, is well-earned.

He always knows, what's best for me,
How every day, is going to be.
Someday, I shall reach my goal,
My strong belief, comes within my soul.

I have no fear, what happens tomorrow,
He's diminished my doubts, of yesterday's sorrow.
I count on Him, in all my prayers,
My life is whole, because of The Man Upstairs.

Sandy McDole

STEPHANIE; HEAVENLY CONTRIBUTION

Precious little Stephanie Lynn
Whom God has early gathered in,
We honor you in Love's Repose
As nature does the splendid rose.

Your plans, and mine, sweet Stephanie,
Are now with God as must need be.
Thank you for the fond embrace
You laid upon this grizzled face.

I'll see you on the morrow, Dear,
Fulfilling all, so far, so near.
What we had planned in earthly love,
Now is blessed in heaven above.

So long, sweet Stephanie;
You've enriched us all in graceful glee —
Two words you said were "go" and "up";
So surely, now with God you sup.

Love, sweet Stephanie
Is what it's all about.
Loving you, sweet Stephanie
Has waived all cringing doubt.

Grampa Carl

LOVE

True love is not how much you love,
but how much you are loved.

Spoken so softly with small kind words,
Leaving an impression, like music from birds,
Shown through thoughtful and gracious ways
Opening a heart, so within it stays.
Reaching your hand out to give all you can,
Of your treasures you worked for, in this beautiful land.
Bringing a smile upon a face,
Who once thought it was forgotten by the human race.

Mary Ingram

TAKE MY HEART

Take my heart, my love.
Do with it what you must.

It's in your hands, your loving care —
it is a sacred trust.

You have my very soul to keep or toss away —
it's there to strengthen all your nights,
and soften all your days.

Just try it for awhile; see if it satisfies
your needs.
There's no risk in the trying — satisfaction
guaranteed.

But to be honest, it's not a new one —
bent, a little bruised and hurt a little
here and there.
But if you decide to keep it, no need to
worry — it can take more wear and tear.

Joyce M. I. Sluka

LADIES

Loving each one in an instant,
An infatuation, they might say.
May they seem, even distant,
that feeling still comes your way.

The gleam and sparkle in their eyes.
The colorful styles of them
can make a man tell no lies,
when each glows of a different gem.

May they smell flowery, spicy or sweet.
Each tall, average, or firmly petite.
Still that beauty radiates from their face,
just by natural elegance and grace.

For these females at their best
can make a man forget the rest.
Like the fragrance of a flower,
the woman's beauty may hold a power.

Kirk N. Galatas

PATRICIA ANN

There is little enough I want to hear
about that girl who had no fear,
And, there is little enough I want to say
about that girl who had no time to pray.

She did not share the day she left,
Knowing as she must, to go alone.

Yet . . . in loving her
I believe,
She took one final backward glance
with a smile and a shrug
at her startling past.

To have excelled at so much with her
molecule of time.

But then . . . THAT was the stunning thing about
PATRICIA ANN

Elizabeth Mawhinney Laube

WOULD YOU LOVE ME?

Would you love me, Dear, for but a day?
A day of breathless beauty: a dazzling ride
Upon a carousel; a wave that may
Fresh pleasures bring before a change of tide.

Would you love me more, a whole year through?
A year of jaunty touring: Fiesta time
In Spain; Russian nights with only you
To smile upon; an Alpine height to climb.

Would you love me then for all of life?
A life that springtime though it may begin,
All flowering shrubs, must sometimes feel the knife
Of winter cut away what once had been.

Such love the waterfall of time could force
Into a quiet stream of peaceful course.

Virginia E. Cruikshank

CRUIKSHANK, VIRGINIA EDDY. Born: Shamokin, Pennsylvania, 6-11-09; Unmarried; Education: Bloomsburg University, B.S., 1939; Middlebury College (Bread Loaf School of English) M.A.; Occupation: Public School Teacher (Retired); Music Lessons; Memberships: Pennsylvania Poetry Society, National Federation of State Poetry Societies, Stella Woodall Poetry Society International, World of Poetry, American Poetry Association, Delta Kappa Gamma, B.P.W. and Order of Eastern Star; Awards: First Prize, Travel Contest, 'The Instructor,' 1949; Golden Poet of 1985 Award from World of Poetry; Three First Prizes in New York Poetry Contest, 1953, 1955, 1978; 12 Award of Merit Certificates from World of Poetry; Certificate of Recognition from Pennsylvania Poetry Society, 1981; Poetry: 'I Danced and Danced,' *American Poetry Anthology,* 1985; 'Creative Zest,' *The Lantern,* Brooklyn, New York, 1949; 'An M.I.A. Comes Home,' *Today's Best Poems,* 1980; 'To Pocahontas,' *Adventures in Poetry,* 1981; 'Historic River Highways: The St. Lawrence and The Saquehay,' "The Instructor, 1947; Comments: *Poetry is a means of expressing emotion and insight, and it becomes a fulfilling experience in moments of special awareness.*

HEARTS ON FIRE

What flames burn brighter through World's great kingdom
  Than Light-spewn Hand of Liberty's freedom!
Alone through godward blue ultimate sky,
  O'er the plain screaming, her eagle soars high!
Dare her enemies dim Liberty's Light,
  Her shores shall but vaster gleam through Night!
A grand land is she where Man's soul-felt dream
  Might reach to its mountaintop's valored stream.

American homeland! What stark beauty!
  Hers is creed to maintain sweet Liberty;
To worship in peace; have choice; to be free.
  Guard all years, Democracy, sea to sea!
What soldiers, sailors, torched her noble flame!
  Michigan gathers to her heart each name.
Though one hundred fifty years pass again,
  Though sunlight gild this monument, or rain,

Rememb'ring hearts on fire through Michigan
  Shall keep well lit: torch of their proud mission!

Val Rogers

COME BACK MY LOVE

I bent down and filled
my hands with stardust

It made me laugh
I stood tall and proud

It turned my life into
a kaleidoscope of colors

And then a storm came
The trees bent
The wind whistled

And my stardust
disappeared

Oh, why didn't I hold my stardust
close to me ? . . .

Linda White

SOULS IN LOVE

Life's greatest tragedy seems not at all
The loss of loved ones gone
But that ominous pall of the soul feeling all
Their beauty, marching through the years,
The smiles we saw in sun,
The depths of hearts as one.

Our pain is not o'er shaded days nor mediocre song
But, O, such longing spills when gloried, sunbent rays
Make beautiful gladder, golden days
When Life was God's own Laughter from a loved one's eyes.

But day by day we learn to put our tears away
And even deeper, learn to pray, until at last
We see a smile we felt had gone: An inner Light within us,
A sudden rushing in of God Himself aglow . . .

This, our loved one's sent to us —
That ever we might know
. . . where went his living soul.

Val Rogers

SUNDAY'S FOOLS

The park is again occupied
With the regular weekend activity.
Picnickers, relishing the comfort of the summer sun,
Transforming the grass into a quilted plaid;
Children playing their games of youth's imagination.
In the corner,
The rhythmic music of the carousel
Fills the air with its timeless tune.
Together we head toward it
With a faithfulness born from familiarity,
His little hand in mine.
Anticipation lightens his innocent eyes
As I place him on the faded mold.
The tune begins . . . grinding, sour.
He comes around. I smile and wave
Then wipe the tears as he turns away,
Grasping for precious moments
In exchange for the emptiness.
Oh, Sunday's fathers . . .
Sunday's fools.

Doug Frech

LOVE FOREVER MINE

My love for you will always be
Even though they have taken you away from me,
No other love do I hold,
For you I care, so bold.
The sweet words that you whispered
Are engraved upon my heart
I walk life's path alone
For some day I know forever you will be mine.
My love for you will always be
Till this earthly light, with dark draws closed
My love for you will never die,
But when my earthly light no longer shines
In heaven's glow you will find me to be,
And your love I'll have taken with me
To shine like the northern star so bright
To. light a path for you to follow me.
My love for you was always true
It will be shining from heaven so bright
So follow the light and you will find
Me waiting at the end of time.

Judith M. Roe

EVENING WEDDING

As twilight pulled the curtain
And pinned it with a star from above,
The young bride and groom exchanged their vows,
Telling the world of their love.

As the soft glow of the sunset
Brought darkness over the land,
They sealed their vows with a kiss,
Then started their new life . . . hand in hand.

They began their new life together
At the close of that beautiful day.
With blessings from God, family and friends,
They'll travel together down life's pathway.

May this day be their highlight forever.
May their joys, devotion and love
Increase as they go through life,
And be blessed by God from above.

Jane Luciene Nowak

VISIONS OF THE ARABIAN PRINCESS

Oh Arabian Princess, I must confess
as you sit on the throne of my mind
with your royal satin dress
and your silver scepter of time
and your radiant jewel crown
on your crystal mind
and your boots of leather
and your silver lace belt
and your spanish bandana
wrapped around your hair of silk
and your mouth like fire
and your lips like strawberry wine
and your arabian desires
and your voice like chimes
Oh Arabian Princess I bow to you and confess
the desire for your moonlight passion kiss
For you are so beautiful and divine
and yet so very, very hard to define.

Michael E. Jackson

YOUR FINAL GOODBYE

It's so hard to say goodbye and let you go
sweet love,
As the hurt is buried deep within the heart,
Where there is no letting go — even now as I
watch you quietly walk away.
Away from my love and all the dreams that we shared,
In our beautiful world of "someday,"
Now, never to be . . .
As my broken heart silently cries,
With tears that flow like opened flood gates,
As I watch you walk away — without a backward
glance.
Your goodbye, final . . .
Etched in my heart, like concrete,
To never again be . . .
As I softly whisper — please don't go, don't leave . . .
As I stand here engulfed — in this total silence,
Left by your final goodbye.

Glenna Gardner-Wimett

DREAM GIRL

Skipping lightly through
the midnight forest,
I see a young woman
dressed in pale nothing
sitting with rounded limbs
tucked under her upon a large boulder
in a stagnant pool

But I dare not speak
afraid she will suddenly disappear and
so I stand observing her
from behind a birch tree

Next, she turns to face my way
and with a child's innocent smile
rises and with arms held wide
tiptoes toward me and gives me a kiss
and now I am flying over the majestic trees.

Ridgely Lytle

WHO SHALL IT BE?

How beautiful it is to be so young
Full of love and never so lonely.
To have someone so dear by your side always
But do I say shall it always be?
Even when you are alive or will it be when you
are dead?
Who will be the one by your side?
The one you love so dear or
The one you despise so dear?

Dora G. Leos

LEOS, DORA GONZALES. Born: Uvalde, Texas, 4-22-54; Married: 10-28-83 to Pete R. Leos, Jr.; Education: Uvalde High School, 1972; Occupation: Secretary; Comments: *What inspires me to write poetry is when I'm depressed, angry or upset. My pen just takes over my emotions and I write just how I feel that day. But when I'm happy I write about how beautiful everything else is.*

SEASONS OF DREAMING

Oh, delightful robin's song on a spring morn;
Salutes sunshine's warmth as a new day is born.
Dewdrops glisten on satin pink clover heads,
And also jewel the silver lace spider webs.
I sit daydreaming of a love by my side;
Imagining our laughter heard far and wide.

Grey-white thunderclouds drum down a summer rain.
It tapdances and slides down the windowpane.
Eyes closed I imagine white, sandy beaches;
Picnics with ice cream, melons and peaches.
I pluck the white petals from a field daisy;
My childhood ritual for a dream of jubilee.

Frost-bitten, colored leaves are swirling around.
They lie like a patchwork quilt upon the ground.
Unharvested, gold pumpkins row upon row,
October sees their smiling faces set aglow.
Fall's chilly winds have caught me unprepared;
Oh, to be encircled by strong arms that cared.

Angels are fluffing their feather beds above;
Then snow gently covers the withered foxglove.
Floral-like paintings glazed by Jack Frost
Appear overnight on the windows he embossed.
I long for a man's love that would include
Interruption of the dark winter solitude.

Cilla C. Carpenter

BROTHERS

You lie awake at night,
Facing each other
From your separate points of view.

You talk about the past, present and future,
The friends and enemies you've had,
The girls you've known.
And the parents you love and hate.

You discuss the problems you've both had growing up,
Reflect on the times you could not tolerate the other's company,
Wow your respective accomplishments
And realize you are both human.

Jonathan Jay Brandstater

REST ASSURED!

Everyone knows —
Love is something very powerful and strong
But — cannot be touched or seen.

Likewise —
The Holy Spirit who is God and all powerful
Cannot — be touched or seen.

But let me assure you —
Just as Love is there — He is there!
Let us remember Him — For He is the

Essence of All Love.

S. Green

IN MEMORIAM: JOHN BLANCHARD (1900-1968)

Johnny and I had many private talks
When we were out together on long walks,
And sometimes when we reached our home again,
I couldn't say if there'd been snow or rain,
My mind so totally absorbed had been
It would not let distractions enter in.

Now, as I look back on my married life,
Those seventeen years I was Johnny's wife,
I wish that a new husband I could find
To set my heart aflame, inspire my mind!
I'm sure John would not think this wish a whim;
He'd see it as a compliment to him!

Mary Thayer Blanchard

OCTOBER SEVENTEENTH

Rejected, bereaved, in need of love;
Prize within reach, snatched away;
Goal attained: cruel mirage.
Will this be a pattern of futile quest?

Partners twice on a bygone team,
We strolled in the park and down by the stream,
Both dreaming, perhaps, some beautiful dream.

Her sudden kiss ripped into my mind,
Two lonely, weary hearts to bind.
More pleasant a sound I'll never hear:
Contented breathing beneath my ear.

Parker T. Chamberlin

AND THAT'S WHAT'S LEFT OF FIRST LOVE

The eidetic image rises as clear as the
mountain air; as pink as rhododendron
releasing fragrance in the dawn; as
blue as periwinkle clinging to
the mountain leaf-rich soil; as new
as the first green breeze of May; as
close as you were with periwinkle eyes
promising grand adventures in an
exciting world filled with laughter and
sunshine and cumulus clouds, drifting
white masses holding green spring rains.

The periwinkle was plucked and pressed
between "Frieze of Prophets" and
Bathsheba's plea to Solomon and
it lies there,
faded,
turning to dust.

Frances Johnson

MISSING YOU

The warmth of the sun . . .

Is hot on the lands at home,

I am here — it's cold.

Tonya Lee Byes

BYES, TONYA LEE. Pen Name: Katrina Lee Preston; Born: Evansville, Indiana, 3-8-69; Occupation: Student; Memberships: National Forensic League; National Honor Society; Awards: 'Silence,' Ohio River Arts and Crafts Festival Poetry Contest, 1979; Poetry: 'Silence,' 1979; 'Tears,' *Words of Praise,* 1985; Comments: *Poetry, to me, is the art of creating emotions with words. Writing poems is a beautiful way to show what I am feeling. I enjoy the freedom I experience once my emotions are finally released onto paper. My changing moods provide me with an endless supply of inspirations.*

ONE MAN

If only we could stop
  and start it all over again
Time has made no difference
  I love you the same
You are in every drop of rain

It is your face I see
  your arms and body I worship
    even when someone else is beneath me

What a pity you don't love as I love
  for that you cheat me my glory
But you brought me joy pure and simple
  I guess fiction is a way of life

And yet I am a passionate person
  the plainness of another's affection
    cannot satisfy my yearning

The I which is myself is lost
  somewhere within the meaning
  of our first kiss and last embrace

I'm afraid to look down
  yet I look
    and I hug the mountain

Dena Lesser

LESSER, DENA BETH. Pen Names: Dena Amour, Dena; Born: Los Angeles, California, 10-30-54; Education: UCLA and Antioch College undergraduate, 1972-1975; Occupations: Actress, Poetess, Dancer, Make-up Artist, Screenwriter, Astrologer; Memberships: Screen Actor's Guild, American Federation of Television and Radio Artists, Actors Equity Association; Other Writings: "Children's Leukemia," Medical Research Article, Nurses' Files, Children's Hospital, City of Hope, Cancer Institute, 1966; "The Camel Pusher," Screenplay, Registered, Writers Guild of America, West, 1979; Comments: *I write to satisfy a need to release my most intimate feelings, to express my joie de vivre and also my tears, to share my heart and to give my love to the world, which has given so much to me.*

MY LOVE IS A SWEET MELODY

My love is like a song sung softly.
My love is a sweet melody.
Go over yonder world in your travel,
Love like mine you will never see.
For my love is like a love song sung softly,
My love is a sweet melody.

Gentle breezes may whisper in your ear,
Locks of hair fall softly on your cheek,
Look where you may on your life's fair pages
You'll never find a love like mine there.
For my love is like a love song sung softly,
My love is a sweet melody.

You may travel way across the ocean,
You may hold back the sands of time,
You may count the others who've loved you,
You will never find a love like mine.
For my love is like a love song sung softly,
My love is a sweet melody.

Erma Ghoston

GHOSTON, ERMA M. Born: Coahoma, Mississippi, Raised in Memphis, Tennessee; Divorced; Education: Booker T. Washington High School; Florence Utt Business School, St. Louis, Missouri; Kennedy-King College; A.L. Williams Marketing and Insurance School, Memphis, Tennessee; Occupations: Secretary, Office Manager, Parent/Volunteer Coordinator; Memberships: Oak Grove Baptist Church; South Memphis Senior Social Club; South Memphis Senior Center Volunteer; Other Writing: Work has been published by American Poetry Association, Yes Press, Suawannee Poetry, New York Poetry Society, *Odessa Poetry Review, The Writer's Dream,* and Poetry Press; Comments: *I have been writing for personal pleasure since the age of 12. I also write song lyrics. At the present I am writing my fifth short story. My goal is to market some of my work and publish a book of poetry. Three of my manuscripts are now being edited for market.*

BELOVED, THOU HAST BROUGHT ME MANY FLOWERS

Beloved, thou hast brought me many flowers
Plucked in the garden, all the summer through
And winter, and it seemed as if they grew
In this close room, nor missed the sun and showers.
So, in the like name of that love of ours,
Take back these thoughts which here unfolded too,
And which on warm and cold days I withdrew
From my heart's ground. Indeed, those beds and bowers
Be overgrown with bitter weeds and rue,
And wait thy weeding; yet here's eglantine,
Here's ivy! — take them, as I used to do
Thy flowers, and keep them where they shall not pine.
Instruct thine eyes to keep their colours true,
And tell thy soul, their roots are left in mine.

Elizabeth Barrett Browning

MY HEART QUESTIONS, 'WHY?'

If I've caused you such pain,
I am sorry, my love.
For, I only responded back with the love
And kindness you first gave me.

And did the truth from my heart
Bother you, my love?
For, I only shared with you the depths of me
And dreams of what can be.

I am what I am and therefore
I cannot deceive you, my love,
For, since you've turned from this love you once sought,
My heart questions, 'Why?'

Stephanie Yeater

TO DONNY: MY LITTLE FRIEND

Up in the bedroom a white buffalo lays
A leftover memory of a little boy's stay

The colors, the paints, and all the toys
Made it seem he would always share our joys

He lives somewhere else, quite content I am sure
With his Mom and his sister, Star and the cats

But whenever he's ready, they're all up there,
The walrus, the dolphin, the turtle and bear

So come again, Donny, for ice cream and cake
And maybe this time a snowman you'll make . . .

Ruth B. Doody

THE EYES OF LOVE

How did you come to be?
So perfect, that loving you completely,
I never before thought to question why!
It seems that God searched my heart
And saw that which I would cherish most dearly.
He looked into my mind and saw the dream
That filled my days and nights.
And then He made you.
For me.

Patricia A. Thompson

TO ONE I LOVED, WHEN YOUNG

It was not reasonable that I love you
For love means giving, and what could I give?
I was a sapling youth, my love seemed true
And strong, but had not yet begun to live.

It was not reasonable that I love you,
I longed to get that which you offered me,
To take, to gratify was all I knew;
To get, to keep that which was gotten free.

It was not reasonable that I love you.
Love had a price that I could never pay
And so I can't regret this love that grew,
And slowly shriveled into death one day.

Cornelius W. Askren

ASKREN, CORNELIUS W. Born: Bothell, Washington, 8-3-16; Education: Graduated Bothell Public Schools, 1934; University of Washington, B.A., English, Advanced Writing, 1959; Poetry: 'In Appreciation of Faithful Gospel Preachers,' *Good News,* Wilmore, Kentucky, Summer, 1973; 'A Sonnet on Song of Solomon 1:5,6,' *Review for Religious, Vol 35 No. 5,* St. Louis University, St. Louis, Missouri, 9-76; 'The Sparkle on the Wine,' World of Poetry Press, Stockton, California.

MY SPECIAL FRIEND

You live so very far away
But I'm happy to see you today.
Our lives both flow in different directions
With different thoughts and different reflections.

But I just wanted for you to know
That whatever happens and wherever you go.
That you will always be in my heart
Deep down in the special part.

You have meant so much to me
And, "happy" is what I wish for you to be.
And I know that you will find
Happiness at the perfect time.

Thank you for being my friend
And all the love that you send.
I wish you the best in all that you do
And if you're ever in need, I'll be here for you.

Susan Lea Bacon

TO MY CLOSEST FRIEND, BEST WISHES

I envy you in your marriage my friend,
And finding a love that is true,
Your loneliness suddenly came to an end
While mind I can barely subdue.

I've cried many tears in search of a flame,
Or someone to just hold me tight,
With feelings of selfishness and even shame
Sometimes it doesn't seem right.

Don't worry my friend, in you I have found
A friendship that none can outmeasure;
In sisterhood always, eternally bound,
It's one that I'll always treasure.

Julie Ott

MISERY LOVES COMPANY

Misery is all I've ever known. Do me a favor?
Please leave me alone. I long to be
happy and free with nothing worrying me.
Peace of mind means much more to me than money.
"Misery Loves Company" doesn't include me.
Since I've met you, I'm very happy.
All of your promises you've fulfilled, dear,
I love having you near. You help drive away my fears.
I know you care. I'm as happy as I can be.
"Misery Loves Company" hasn't meaning now, to me.
I'm a brand-new me. Feeling well pleased, with my mind at ease.
Troubles have vanished with the day.
Happiness, please stay?
You've made my day better than yesterday.

Catherine Jones

PRISONER OF LOVE

I hope your heart is as heavy as mine.
When I'm alone, my thoughts are all of you.
I can see your face before me everywhere.
I remember a thousand little things you do.

I pour my thoughts out into an empty room
Where the four walls seem to close in on me.
You have made me a prisoner, forever doomed,
To always love you and you alone hold the key.

If ever in your lifetime you find yourself
Feeling lonesome, unloved and blue,
Remember, there's a heart brimming over
With love, waiting here just for you.

Lorene Shoptaw Mydlach

OUR LOVE NEST

Build together our love nest —
Just a small one for two birds,
Where we both could stay and chatter
Make a never-ending flirt.

Built together our love nest
Where we both just fit in,
It is all — what our love's asking —
Just a spot where we could spin.

'Cause there's even gladness —
In a hole up in a tree,
And when love seals up two feelings —
Life does taste quite heavenly.

So let's build our little love nest
Where we could hide our dreams,
Where our hearts could always be floating —
On love's calmly running streams.

Sadie Isola

ISOLA, ELIZABETH SADIE. Born: Germany, Bamberg, Bavaria, 11-1-06; Widow of Anton Isola; Education: Self-educated; Occupation: Sales Clerk in Pastry Shop. I live on Social Security now; Poetry: 'Love,' 'Our Love Nest'; Comments: *I only write what comes from within my soul. I am a born spiritualist, a deep believer. I love the world and all that's in it. May God — father of our soul — spare this world.*

Together and silent
Alone and silent
    which is worse . . . I used to know
Angry distance
    why are we still here?
A time ago
    Easy together . . . laughter
    learning of each other . . . love in the learning
At the center of my world . . was you
Still not enough
The face in the mirror
    harder, colder
Together yet apart . . . apart
    Such hurt, for me . . . why not you?
Conclusion:
    It's not supposed to be like this
    Love sucks
    Love stinks . . . yea, that too

Deborah Pearson

MY SCORNED LOVE

Happy Birthday to you
Happy Birthday to you
Happy Birthday my scorned love.

How old are you?
How old are you?
How our love has been scorched.

Last year our love was blooming
White flowers blossoming all around
Valentine's Day you loved me as I loved you.

Early in the morning when all anger is put aside
Early in the morning when pain is not awake
I think about your hands.

How gentle, how strong
How they used to make me feel
Early in the morning, I miss you still.

Carolosue Wright

FRIEND THAT I LOVE

To talk with you when I'm sad makes me happy;
To see you when I'm lonely makes me glad.
Knowing that you are around straightens up my frown;
For it is you my dear friend that I love.

A friend is needed when I'm hurting;
A friend is needed when I'm blue.
You are the way for my life to go on;
For it is you my dear friend that I love.

You have seen my tears of depression;
You have heard my laughter of joy;
I want you to see me as I really am;
For it is you my dear friend that I love.

Although you will never be mine,
As you are spoken for by another,
I shall cherish our moments together,
For it is you my dear friend that I love.

Linda Gail Rocher

MOTHER, THAT'S WHO!

Who looked down when you were born,
into that yelling, little red face,
and knew in her heart, that no one could take your place,
MOTHER, THAT'S WHO!
Who picked you up, and wouldn't let you cry,
when she was so tired, she felt she could die,
and did all she could do, while kissing and holding you,
MOTHER, THAT'S WHO!
Who held you tight when you were afraid at night,
heard your prayers, and turned out the light,
when you got hurt, kissed it, and made it all right,
MOTHER, THAT'S WHO!
Who worried about you when you were gone,
and couldn't rest in peace until you were back home,
taught you to be good, and not go wrong,
MOTHER, THAT'S WHO!
Who will love you with her last dying breath,
If possible, will love you more, even in death,
You, that same little babe she held to her breast,
MOTHER, THAT'S WHO!

Willard Lee Skelton

SHARED LOVE

Two lovers standing side by side
Silhouetted in the moonlight
Supporting each other by the light of the day gone by

They fight and struggle as one
One person one love one forever
Love is such a trivial word
When one compares its meaning to the two
Who fight to keep together with such linkage that binds
Each moment each breath each life

Thus when life breaks the two apart
How hard it must be to forget
But time heals all and eventually that
One love is a faint but constant reminder
Of what was once True love . . .

Grandpa

SHECK, JAMES G. Pen Name: Grandpa; Born: Maple Creek, Saskatchewan, Canada, 6-11-55; Single; Education: Lethbridge Community College, 1974-75; University of Lethbridge, 1975-76; Southern Alberta Institute of Technology, Foods Service Department, 1980; Occupation: Presently Floral Designer, but first love is the restaurant industry; Memberships: Although not presently involved, I have been involved with Big Brothers of Canada, as well as being a volunteer for the Canadian Mental Health Association; Poetry: 'She's a Lady,' *American Poetry Anthology,* 1985; 'Morning,' *Words of Praise, Volume II,* 1986; Comments: *I hope in whatever small way my writings reflect life and the feelings of life. All my poetry is written without punctuation. The reasoning for this is that I hope no matter who reads any one poem can relate, or say — I know just what he means. In most cases those who read my poetry say that it is my openness with the poetry that makes it enjoyable to read, and appreciate.*

MOUNTAINS AND THE SEA

Sometimes when I'm feeling lonesome
I think of . . . what used to be
I think of an old . . . old sweetheart
I left alone for the sea.

She was in love with the mountains
I was in love with the sea
I left her . . . in her mountains
I left her to go back to my sea.

If I had my life to live all over
What changes would there be
Would I stay with her, in her mountains
Or leave and go back to my sea?

I know we really loved each other
Somehow we just didn't agree
Cupid sure missed the target
Somewhere between the mountains and the sea.

If I had my life to live all over
What changes would there be
Would I stay with her . . . in her mountains
Or leave and go back to . . . my sea?

Dale R. Bennett

An old man sat in his rocking chair waiting.
The clock on the wall ticks away the minutes, hours,
days.
Each line on his wrinkled face twists with pain.
How fast the years have flown away.
Five sons he raised and watched them grow from siblings
to grown men.
His memory fading like the days as he tries to
remember all their names.
Faces become a shadow for him.
He leaves memories of love and happiness behind
as he sits in his rocking chair waiting . . .

Gertrude Rosenthal

LOVELY LADY LOVE

Sweet are the words that I long to hear,
Echoing constantly in my ear;
Sweet are the joys of my youthful days
Lingering still in so many ways.

Sleep on, my LOVELY LADY LOVE, so still,
With part of me to keep you company,
While in the forest of my mind and will
The greatest part of you will always be.

Your spirit, like an ocean breeze, will fill
The air that travels through the mountain trees
And meets the rainbow's edge, with Nature's skill,
To live in Heaven's hallowed mysteries.

Sleep on, my love LOVELY LADY LOVE, and thrill
The treasured moments in my memory,
Where once your hopes and faith you did instill
To leave with me your gift of charity.

How sad it is to leave her
asleep in her new home,
Yet some of her stays with me,
wherever I may roam!

Josephine Bertolini Comberiate

MOMENTS TOGETHER

Close your eyes for one precious moment
And come walk beside me on the sandy beach
We will build sandcastles that reach to the sky
Absorbed with contentment, no need for speech
Come dream with me

Etching with our toes, hearts in the sands of time
Hand in hand, we'll feel the breeze kiss our hair
The waves reach out to us, the sun warms our skin
Precious moments together, with nary a care
Time is forgotten

A smile adorns your face and love shines in your eyes
In nature's wonder, minds will merge and be as one
With you there is sunrise, sunset, and even rainbow's end
Though life is short, ours together has only begun
You are beautiful

It is time to leave, the beautiful moment is spent
But awaiting us are others, more magnificent than before
Beauty is around us, inside us, caressing us with love
Inspiring us with wonder, excitement, and awe
It has only just begun

Patricia C. Scuderi

NEIGHBOR LADY MISSING: CONFESSION OF THE KIDNAPPER

Oh my God, I did but I am not afraid and from you only
need I forgiveness for she sleeps and knows not

I stole her from the moonlight as she lay abed in moss
of warmth there wrapped in orange pastel so soft

And raised her o'er my head and jumped above the trees
and rode a cloud to mountain peaks o'er there

This wild thing behind a waterfall I took and placed
beside my fire to let my fingers through her hair

And kissed not once, not twice but thrice upon the
eyes and nose and lips adored

Then swooped her 'board my black and flying steed to forest
depths and placed her back upon the moss, Oh Lord

And touch her not I did but for a threefold kiss, a touch
of hair, my arm held snugly 'bout her waist

Forgive me now for she be yours to watch 'til full moon
brights the sky to guide me back again when graced

Boyd Rahier

MY DEAREST

To the one I have waited for all my life,
The one who heightened all the darkest nights.
I give to thee my love forever.
For you are my knight in shining armor.
You have shared your life with me and I thank you.
My dearest love what would I be without you?
By your side forever is where I long to be.
For you are my life, the very best part of me.
My dearest love, you'll always be with me.
Your eyes tell my future and enjoy my past.
You, my love, will be my first and my very last.
Love is what we live for, to see it in each other's eyes.
Oh my dearest, love never lies.

Margaret V. Morgan

From *EPIPSYCHIDION*

True Love in this differs from gold and clay,
That to divide is not to take away.
Love is like understanding, that grows bright,
Gazing on many truths, 'tis like thy light,
Imagination! which from earth and sky,
And from the depths of human phantasy,
As from a thousand prisms and mirrors, fills
The Universe with glorious beams, and kills
Error, the worm, with many a sun-like arrow
Of its reverberated lightning. Narrow
The heart that loves, the brain that contemplates,
The life that wears, the spirit that creates
One object, and one form, and builds thereby
A sepulchre for its eternity.

Percy Bysshe Shelley

EACH LOVE, A FIRST

Oh, how my love for you has humbled me,
My walk is not so pompous, nor my gaze.
My hands so trembling, that you must not see,
I shyly smile, as my eyes to yours raise.

I do berate myself when you're not near,
I say "Forget insipid glance, be more direct.
After all, what do I have to fear?
My every action you do not dissect!"

So now this queen glides to you as you wait
With smile, amused, so warm it almost kills.
I raise an eyebrow, offer graceful hand.
You kiss it sweetly, then our laughter spills.

Vivienne Florence Meyer

VIRGINIA MY LOVE

Vision of womanhood in you I see
I can't tell you how much you mean to me
Reaching out to you with my heart and arms
Going the last mile I'll share your alarms
I know that I am far from the perfect man
Never doubt however that by you I'll stand
Images of you are ever in my mind
Always I marvel at such a precious find
My first and last thoughts are of you each day
You've captured my heart and in it you'll stay
Loving you is one of the best things I've ever done
Ornamenting my life sweetheart you are the dearest one
Venturing to risk loving you has set me free
Every day I thank God for bringing you to me

William D. Andrews

REMEMBERED LOVE

Remembered love is like remembered sun,
Fire on the hearth, a blessed warmth and bright.
Remembered love is all the bloom of spring,
The miracle of dawn to quench the night.

Love is a song, a light, a joy,
And when these things are done,
Remembered love, upon the heart,
Is like remembered sun.

Anna-Margaret O'Sullivan

ONE-WAY DOOR

My love has placed a heavy door
Between herself and me —
It keeps me away from her
While she is running free —

I know that she still cares for me,
But she controls the door,
And I cannot persuade her
To open it once more —

There are no handles on this door;
No way to get a grip —
I try and try to open it,
But feel my fingers slip —

I will keep on trying
Because I care so much —
From *her* side it would open
With just a *gentle touch!*

Aubrey N. Tatro

THE GREATEST LOVE STORY EVER TOLD

What man can love, so long, so deep.
What man forgives and lets it keep —
The fire burning deep within?
Who can forgive us every sin?

Where can you find a love so true —
That loves a sinner — me and you,
Holds our hand lest we might fall —
Eases a pain till it is dull?

Who walked, Himself in strife and tears —
Who trusted His Father all those years,
Fell to earth a beaten God —
Turned against — blood in the sod?

Nailed to a cross in grief and pain —
Hanging there, did not complain,
And even let Himself be sold —
The Greatest Love Story Ever Told.

Theresa Heiman

FROM THE HEART

I love the way we fit together
When we walk,
The way we communicate,
When we touch or talk.

I love the way you
Send my heart laughing and singing.
The way a look or touch
Can make me feel all tingling.

I love the way you always
Treat me like a queen.
The way you keep our world
So peaceful and serene.

I love the way you miss me,
When we're far apart.
The different ways you say 'I Love You'
And all from the heart.

Laurie Parsons

SOMEWHERE

And still my heart aches
for you
Somewhere in the universe
you shine, a star,
glittering in the night sky,
lighting the way for
some weary traveler,
giving sight to the blind.
And wherever I am,
you give light to my life too
And I can find my way
without fear
through the darkness of the future.

Susan Toppel

LEAVES

Little leaves in the springtime,
little leaves in the springtime.
Whispered love on the softest breeze.
Growing up like girls and boys.
Little leaves that whisper
like little girls and boys.

Greener leaves in the summertime,
see them smile and see them shine.
Touching hands and touch the sun
like growing girls and boys.

Colored leaves in the autumntime,
stronger winds are speaking now.
Written on the rainbow trees,
children's hands are stronger now.
They hold the setting sun,
they hold the setting sun.

Winter trees are barren now,
softest leaves are hidden now
'neath the many winds
and silent shroud of snow.

G. K. Fredrickson

TO THE ONE WHO BORE ME, NOW MY LOVE

The one who bore me
Has now returned to me.
The love she gave me
I now return to her.

When she once left me,
She took my heart with her.
It so hurt me
To lose her and my heart.

But now she is back with me;
And still she holds my heart.
It does not hurt me
To lose my heart in hers.

My heart once beat
Below her loving heart.
Her heart now beats
In my loving heart.

What death has done
Can be undone by love.
What love does,
Nothing can ever undo.

Paul R. Neureiter

TO MY HUSBAND

Love is the greatest feeling in my life
you are the love of my heart
when I need you
you are always there for me
In good times and in bad
We are two separate people
but . . . choose to be one
I am with you
Wherever you go
In your heart
that's where I'll be
Caring, loving you
for eternity
I love you
I am your wife

Mary Theriac

MY LOVE IS . . .

My love is of infinite depth
If love scorns lucid speech.
The phrases I crave to express
End up cryptic poetic verse,
Words echoing ambiguously
In headstrong avian trill.
You smile silently confident
As I babble on breathlessly
Without hope of self-control.

Ralph E. Martin

LIGHT A CANDLE LOVE

Light a candle
and speak softly of me,
love.
For it is now I must go.
My feet do not tread this earth
as once they did.
My eyes see more clearly
than once they did.
And when you are lonely
think of me.
For in the wind
you will hear my name.
And in your heart
you will find joy
and remembrances of love.

Marie B. Hodges

ONE KISS

One kiss
was bliss.
His arms
were warm
and willing.

She sighed.
He whispered,
You make me feel
like fields of flowers
grow beneath my skin.

Her finger tips
traced small circles
in the nape of his neck.

Nancy Kobryn

TWO LOST SOULS

I once met a man who came to me he took my
hand gently into his.
He stared deep within my soul and quietly
fate was saying hello to two lost souls.
Even time was against us the hours and days
invaded and intruded with needs of every kind.
Yet fate still whispered take time and one day
you will come to know this man.
For the years have been kind and some have been
well weathered.
Yet there still is time for those who need
someone to care.
For needs of these kind are sometimes misplaced but
never lost.
For this man and woman fate has whispered a friendly
hello for someday it will be time for two lost souls
to meet again for a story to unfold.

Barbara Reager

I LOVE YOU

How much do I love you?
Do you really want to know?
I love you, as much as it is possible
to love another on this earth,
And beyond imagination.
I love you, for whatever the circumference,
of earth, the width, the depth,
The height of heaven.
The depth of ocean, and beyond.
I would give my life for you.
It is the most precious of all treasures.
I love you, with the imagination of beauty,
and existing light, in heaven and earth.
With the splendor, the grandeur,
The magic, and mystery of all life.
That, my love, is how much I love you.
You are the flowers of my life.

Anne Peralta

DAYBREAK

Snowflakes on a mountain road
The smell of coffee in a pot on the stove
Watching the sun burst through the morning
I realize you're not around
Nothing is more painful than to miss someone
My heart grows colder the less of you I see
The normal functions of living slowly become useless to me
I once made a snowman to liken your body
It melted and turned to slush
I used to take walks in the snow
Trying to catch triangles made by the sun
But not these days
I have no affinity with terrestrial gallivanting
I have lost the things I loved most
The gaze of your eyes in the dead of the night
The place for my head between your hands
My need for any other man

Dena Lesser

CLOUDS OF LOVE

I think of you daily when I say my prayers
But I know you are in heaven, with God up there.
It is not easy to go on alone
But I try to be brave in this earthly home.
The rings you placed on my finger, have been packed away
But the rosary you gave me I repeat night and day!
I see your face in every cloud
Smiling down at me
Then I know how very proud
You are living in God's eternity!
It isn't easy to carry this cross
That God has given to me
But with His guiding hand, my loss
With prayers of love — will set me free!

Georgia E. Kavanagh

AMERICA, LOVE IT OR LEAVE IT

When God created America,
He gave it ALL OF HIS MIGHT,
And he said, "YOU MUST PROTECT IT,
EVEN IF YOU HAVE TO FIGHT!"
I am ever so proud, of our RED, WHITE AND BLUE,
A symbol of Freedom, and blood shed for you!
As the statue of Liberty opens up her arms, She
tells us, "America is Freedom, America is Trust,
America is God's gift to us!"
MEN

Dolores Rey Partie

I AM BUT A CHILD

The aspiring young moon shall be in full,
This very night as I lie beneath the sky,
Dreaming of the one which my heart desires,
Longing for no other . . . she is everything.

She is more than most yet less than some,
And still she has that which few possess,
This congenial woman in her own right,
Has my heart for not to ask the reasons.

I give my heart freely only to her,
For she is gentle with it . . . yet firm,
To me she is of a graceful nature,
And I am but a child learning to walk.

Dale Edward Blakney

THE LOVE EXPERIENCE

For love in life there is endless time;
Forever to sip, to taste its sweetest wines.
There is no hurry, for it will be forever there.
From now through eternity, for us each to share.
Fruits bore by this long lasting bond,
Make our tender hearts grow so very fond.
We absorb each and every sweet gesture of love,
Blessed by the touch of a hand from above.
Like a picturesque puzzle of a natural scene,
The pieces fit together to make life so serene.
If nurtured and fed it will thrive wildly forevermore,
For each throbbing heart forever to adore.
Such a special thing so take special care!
We each have a chance this priceless treasure to bear!

Delores C. Maggart

CAPRICE

That solemn face over there
Lost in thought, wistful eyes.
Suppose I start an enterprise.
All of a sudden from nowhere,
Suppose I blow the face a kiss?

Never believe I wouldn't dare.
What if she stays, maybe flies?
A startled look, but if she tries
A happy adventure two can share,
Started if I've tried a kiss.

Whims belong with a summer air.
A smile is showing in her eyes.
Now is the time for enterprise.
Who needs thought? Needs care?
She sees me, there goes the kiss.

John Hancock

LAVENDER

A sapphire, the legend
of the dark velvet,
even more distant past.
The smooth scent of
violets in the night.

Stretch your arms,
embrace, hold it, take
the flask of perfume
bewitching you.

Yes, the night is clear . . .
you sleep somewhere in
the far-off sounds of love.
Curtains sway, whisper
in the silence,
"Lay your tender body down."

Thomas A. Phelan

GAME OF DESPAIR

The tears stream on my pillow
As the sun begins to rise.
The dawn of breaking quickly
Between my sobbing sighs.
I longed to see your smiling face
And hear you speak my name.
You told me it was all for real,
But those lies were just a game.

I walk along and think of you
And how you broke my heart.
The way you said you didn't care
And that we had to part.
I hope I never see your face
For words cannot compare
To all my feelings of hurt and guilt
And all my deep despair.

Michelle Kooch

THE DRIFTER

Like summer's last breeze
He slips away, and the cold awakens you
Yearning for the warmth once more

Like fall's cool wind
He brings you comfort
Memories scattering through your mind
Like leaves upon the street

Like winter's desolate emptiness
Your heart is cold and dying
Remembrance like the constant snow,
Concealing all else temporarily

Like spring's awakening
All is reborn
And on the fragrant air
The Drifter is borne

Deborah Lynn Hine

In the summer sun
we romp and play
like children
living only for today
you tug on my sleeve
I slip my arm through yours
You picked me a
wildflower
It was just a weed
You laughed —
I still
have that
silly flower
pressed between pages of time
in a diary
of memories
of us
in love
in summer
forever . . .

Arla Brynjolfson

THINKING OF YOU

You radiate the love
  and joy of a beautiful person.
Your self-assurance and poise
  are bastions to admire.
You wear the garments of those
  who know their destiny.
Your smile brightens that which
  only a few can see.
You have that inner grace
  which enlightens all people.
Your inner beauty is unmatched
  and eclipsed only by the sun and
You have that spirit which hangs
  in the halls of splendor.
Your wit and personality
  should adorn only a palace.
For I still am
  thinking of you.

LeRoy B. Schwan

FACE TO FACE

Such an elegant dwelling place
there we stood —
    in a heated embrace
upon your moonlit terrace.
  FACE TO FACE
    FACE TO FACE
Your arms drawn around my waist
a moment of passion —
    satin and lace
our very own hiding place.
  FACE TO FACE
    FACE TO FACE
Such are the feelings we'll never replace
when two are one —
    in a lover's embrace.
  FACE TO FACE
    FACE TO FACE

Eileen Buckiewicz

Love awakening
heeds the joyous spring matin
and opens wide eyes.

Shanon M. Sara

MIDNIGHT ODYSSEY

I crave an enchantment that once
was felt, yet now is lost.
Time has only increased our promise,
but to what cost?
When each of us are so far apart,
and with each twilight another
tug on my heart.
The linger of feelings that have
now become an obsession.
The pulling of nerves to the raw,
fringed edges of sensations.
My silky silhouette endures a
never ending passion of fire.
If only for the fever to be quenched,
and to appease a long awaited desire.
So, I bid you, lover of my dreams,
come to me before the next dawn.

Dortha K. Weinzatl

THE WATER BEFORE

Rain drops
splashing into a puddle
make me want to cuddle
with a brunette
who will let
me caress
and love her
very gently
to the sound
of the rain.
And she will know
the love that came
was from my heart,
but it got
its start
from the rain
splashing into a puddle.

Wayne West

WHAT IS LOVE?

Once I was asked, "What is Love?"
But I'm not sure I really know;
It's in us as a tiny babe
And stays when we are old.

As a child it can reveal itself
As they rest secure in our arms;
In older folks it may show itself
In a hundred ways with its charms.

Sometimes it seems as a cheery smile,
Sometimes in the sparkle of the eye,
Sometimes we feel it in the touch
Of someone standing by.

It has its grip on each of us
This thing that we call love,
It can wander in all directions;
But I think it comes from heaven above.

So ask me what love is
I don't think I really know;
But I know the source from whence it comes,
GOD IS LOVE, the Bible tells us so.

Pearl Britton

THREE LITTLE WORDS

Valentine's Day to some is for grieving,
For always giving but never receiving.
A card or flower to show just a thought,
Of something sent, of something bought,
To tell you that you are truly a part,
Of someone's life and in their heart.
You think to yourself, they will come next year,
Those three little words you're dying to hear.
To share your heart and live life anew,
With the person who tells you, "I love you."

Julia V. Dispensiere

CHRISTMAS WISH

Now that the Christmas season has ended,
All the old clothes don't have to be mended.
Torn piles of paper lie scattered on the floor,
And the Christmas wreath still hangs on the door.

The smell of the turkey lingers in the air,
And the Christmas lights still give off a glare.
Half-filled coffee cups sit on the table,
And there on the mantle sits the old stable.

Today all the things will be put away,
And then we'll go on our merry way.
But there's just one present that's made me smile,
That's loving you and your special style.

You've made me happy when I was down and out,
And that's what Christmas is all about.
There's just one thing I want you to see,
Thank you for the gift of loving me.

I want to thank you for letting me see,
What the true meaning of Christmas was meant to be.
I guess you showed me what I already knew,
But thank you for the chance of loving you.

Linda Berry

THE WALK (MY DE & I)

Today I went walking in the fresh spring air
Left all of my worries back in the house there
My little granddaughter walked by my side,
Her sweet, brown eyes searched near and wide

She saw all the wonders I had forgotten to see
She made my Lord more real yet to me
Each thing of earth, she kept and she treasured
God's beauty to her, was far from unmeasured

A flower, a clover, a bird, just the air,
God's love seemed to be everywhere
In the eyes of a child the world is so pure
Just walking with her I felt more secure

She trusted me, and we walked and we sang
We felt God's love. The sweet meadows rang
"Oh! God," I wonder as I teach and I reach
If these precious grandchildren don't really
Teach me (How to really love)

Iva White-Foreman

DON'T STOP

You have so much to give someone
I thank you that I was able to share with you
Life's love and laughter

Now, you stand there by my bed
Praying I will not die.
My body will die
My heart and soul will remember you forever

Please promise me that when I am gone
That you will not stop living, caring, and especially,
Loving.

Don't stop, give all you have to give
Please don't let your love die with me
But keep it alive to give to someone else
May the new man in your life treasure you
As I have and still do.

My love, don't stop.

Debra A. Freed

THE PRIZE

My heart holds secrets of many silent deeds.
Time cannot erase, nor thieves break in for these.
Recognition, I seek not,
for death's door all too soon will knock.
My purse is full, so many treasures shared,
extra favors not compared.

Life's paralyzing pleasures overlooked.
Sufferings hard, almost unbearable, I partook.
Angels writing in the big golden book.
Sparkling diamonds, rubies deep red,
earthly gems will adorn my head.
My gown will radiate a glow, and will be white as snow.

A beautiful gold crown, there is waiting.
I'll humbly accept and bow, not hesitating.
Then taking this crown of diamonds, gems and gold.
I will humbly lay it at my Lord's feet and weep.
Love so refined as gold, heaven the prize, I've attained my goal!

Ronnette Ward

A WEDDING WISH FOR MY MOM

It's times like these I can't convey
The words that mark this joyous day
The hopes, the fears that go with love
Are all bestowed from Him above
I must admit a twinge of doubt
That grasped me from within and out
You said "Tom wish me lots of luck
'Cause I'm in love with this man called Buck"
And after thinking it through and through
I concluded mom dear you must be you
So health and happiness to you I pray
And may God keep you both each passing day

Tom Alswager

LOVE'S CONFLICTS

I left your arms that day so long ago —
Because your love was smothering me,
My spirit had no room to grow —
Your needs were all that you could see.
Love lives and grows where freedom dwells —
And joy comes forth because of what each one can be,
To be a clinging vine — and nothing more —
Strangles love — while setting no one free.
Love can lift one up to ecstasy —
Or open up a heart to hurts scarce known before,
Breed jealousy because we are not sure —
That one we love will feel this way forevermore,
Had we but planted that one seed of trust —
And let it grow for you and me.
Love could have lived and never would have died,
Now or through eternity.

William E. Mays

MAYS, WILLIAM EGLI. Born: Pittsburgh, Pennsylvania, 13-21-18; Married: 4-2-49 to Mary Jean Nelan Mays; Education: University of Pittsburgh, A.B., 1941; M.Ed., 1947; Ph.D., 1956; Drew Theological Seminary, B.D., 1944; Occupations: Minister, Professor of Sociology Emeritus; Memberships: American Sociological Association, Poetry Society of Michigan, Lenawee Area Writers; Poetry: 'Michigan,' *Detroit Free Press,* 12-6-84; 'Pride of Country,' *Raisin River Anthology,* Winter, 1985; 'The Gift of Receiving,' *Michigan Christian Advocate,* 12-23-85; Themes: *Man's quests and his reflections on life. Occupations and callings.*

THE GODS' DERISION

As if all the gold in the world were promised me;
As if all the silver sands were mine, all mine;
As if all the riches of the world — like unto thee —
Were for myself, sumptuous, divine;
So were the hopes of paradise I dreamed,
A love I hungered for in humble trust
And all the world of happy lovers seemed
My dearest friends, companions in the quest
For sun of radiance; the rainbow's end
Where waits the prize that crowns the heart's perfection:
The lover, dear, the pure and precious friend;
Epitome of joy . . . the soul's selection . . .
O had I died before I lost that vision
I had escaped its aftermath: THE GODS' DERISION.

Rosemary Witty

CARNIVAL

The amusement is over,
you've had the last laugh.
It was all a game
with me as the prize.
Too many trap doors, mirrors
not enough clowns.
This time the ferris wheel
is stuck on the ground.
The carousel is broken
the cotton candy is all gone.
All that's left is a forgotten
book of tickets
good for one last ride, one more smile.
And the memory of laughter lingers on . . .

Gigi Goren

ANOTHER NOVEMBER

You came — and like a stormy wind
your love blew over my heart and soul
to awaken my passion —
that was stilled for so long . . .
And all the trembling waves of my being
began to move . . .
to cry out for love
too long denied . . .
And still, from the calm haven of my mind,
my thoughts are always of you . . .
And my tears fall
through the last echo of hurting
as I remember all . . .
Forever, in my dreams.

Nancy S. Bartholomew

LOVE

An affection based on admiration
A warm attachment, enthusiasm, or devotion
An unselfish concern that freely accepts another in loyalty and seeks his good
A brotherly concern for others

Love, in whatever form, is the commitment we feel in our changing world as we strive to follow in the footsteps of Jesus.

Pearl Sandahl

TO MY LOVE

As someone who cares
you know me well
a relationship to share
and so much more
As true feelings show
to all that live in your world
I feel our love grow
with true happiness
As the special one you are
the one that I love
distance is far
but our hearts stay close
As the warmth in my heart
brings love to my life
all good dreams start
to be truth
As the love I feel
becomes so strong
we are real
and in love

Lora Chisholm

SILHOUETTES

The candlelight is casting
Shadows that enthrall.
Two bodies held in rapture
Pictured on the wall.

Lovers at their play
Erect erotic poses,
Ecstasy in motion
The dancing flame exposes.

Phantoms reach for splendor
In the tallow's subtle glow.
As the wax is melting
Their passions also flow.

The taper is extinguished;
This fire that burned so bright
Will illuminate these lovers
Again, another night.

Terry Eunice

YOUR THRILLING KISS

Since I've known your kiss
Life hasn't been the same.
I'm filled with new sensations
Each time I speak your name.

If I think about your touch,
My body burns with fire.
My arms, then, long to hold you
My lips ache with desire.

Whenever you are near,
My heart starts trembling so.
You are the one, who has the power
To make my rivers flow.

Nothing in the world
Had made me feel like this;
The wild excitement that I get
From your thrilling kiss.

Terry Eunice

TODAY

In Memory of Don Costner

Today my mind drifts back in time
To things that might have been.
A sweet caress,
A home for two,
And happy dreams come true.

An empty ache within this heart
Is all I'll ever know,
No one to love
Or even to hold close,
No more I'll ever know.

There's nothing left,
But memories
That can't break, this hardened wall,
The dear sweet hands
That once were mine,
No more I'll ever hold.

The tender lips that spoke of love,
Were so very, very real.
I'll tuck away this heart of mine,
Never to reveal.

Elizabeth G. Moore

MIA POW

Dedicated to Gino Casanova

Where are you, my long lost lover,
Where's the love that we once knew?
Now that all the fighting's over,
Where are you? — Oh where are you?

Are you in some secret workcamp,
Or a lonely, wind-swept grave?
Did you die a frightened baby,
Or a soldier, bold and brave?

Through the years your memory haunts me,
And I long for just one word
That would tell me if some stranger
Might have seen, or might have heard;

But the silence is unbroken
And I guess I'll never know,
Through the years, your name unspoken
Still is locked up with the foe,
And they won't release the secret,
For, I guess, it's hard to tell
If your soul has gone to Heaven,
Or, like mine, is still in Hell!

Paulette Talboy Cary

HONORABLE MENTION

Read me quietly, like a dream
that has no answers; a strange
body of amorphous whispers
drawn by hand, traveling, light
as breath. And on some night,
when the coyote cries for the moon
and rain has fallen as a veil, unfold
me, with tender eyes that touch
these circular words — so that I
may love you again and again.

Billie Sue Fischer

I FELL IN LOVE

I don't know when my friendship stopped
And my love for you began to be
For it happened very slowly
And actually it came as a surprise to me.
I didn't plan on falling in love
But somehow it happened that way.
My feelings just grew stronger for you
With my every passing day.
I thought it was just a friendship
But somehow it became more
And soon I found myself searching
For you and wanting even more.
I wanted your arms around me
And to feel your kisses upon my face.
I wanted you to fall in love with me
And my lonely heart and life replace.
Now I look forward to each day
For I have fallen in love with you
And I have a different outlook on life
Since you've helped me begin my life anew.

Shirley B. O'Keefe

HER HUSBAND'S PRAYER

Lord, in the time that she has left
Help me to shield her from her pain.
Let me be the one to say "I love you,"
Time and time again.
Lord, give me the strength to do
The things that I know I must
And to end each sad day with grace
And pray "In God we *still* trust."
Let my loving arms hold her, Lord,
So tenderly —
As it hurts her now to touch.
Never let her see the anguish
That I hold in a furious clutch.
Lord, with this girl who was my bride —
Let me near the end, dear Lord,
Have nothing from her to hide.
Lord, help me to share our memories
Hoping, this too, will help to ease —
And when it's time to take her, Lord,
Be gentle with her, please.

Joyce Holt

OUR LOVE

These eyes lure you, probing deep
    Through expressions that you keep.
Setting free your inner fire,
    Racing heartbeats, thoughts inspire.

It's something that was meant to be,
    As sure as day will follow night.
It's plain for all who look to see,
    Our love is burning, shining bright.

Spark of laughter from a trance,
    Holding on for one last chance,
If you leave me I will cry,
    Force a smile and a wave goodbye.

In the ending when we die,
    Change direction with a sigh.
See the light above the sky,
    Lift our wings and learn to fly.

William Robert O'Loughlin

MISSING YOU

My God, you are so far away.
I wish you were here with me today.
I miss you more than you could know.
But I'd never tell you when you need to go.
I miss your laughter, your eyes, your smile.
I wish you could hold me for a little while.
I know soon you'll be back home with me.
It's the only thing that keeps my sanity.
I also know you miss me too.
Just as much as I miss you.
I pray the time will swiftly fly.
Then we'll be together you and I.
Until then darling I will pray.
That God will bless you each and every day.

Bonnie Allen Coleman

LOVE IS A BEAUTIFUL GAME

Our love is such a beautiful game
With a great challenge, where you aim high
It's played by two and always the same
Where there's no end and never a good-bye
The pleasures ours and we're playing it fine
Because we hold love our own special way
The flowing love you cannot fake is mine
And the ever-exchanging love is your way
There are rules like any fair game has
For one you never do each other wrong
You must have motion like a gentle wind has
Plus a smooth rhythm like in a long song
And of course it must last always and forever
It's a great game, love, and we'll play it ever

Cindy L. Kukkola

THE LOVE OF JESSICA MARIE

(23 Months Old)

Jessica Marie is the prettiest little
Lady I ever did see —
She is as happy as a clover bloom
Entertaining a honey bee!
She is sweeter than all the roses
She is fat and as pretty as a bouquet of posies
When I look at her she draws from me
The love of all created things —
She's heartfelt inward joy that clings
And traces the leaves and flowers
That around me lie, lesson of love and piety
And so let it be, and if the wide world rings
This belief in love she brings.

Cora Lee Prince

THE FLAME FACTOR

With you, mon cheri, there is a strong attraction;
Love super-charged by a chemical reaction.
All events are parts of what is called Dreams,
Things special of *you* make my heart scream!
Are you? Is it true? That you're created for *me* Love?
Possible that's made true by the One above!
. . . oh, JOY!

Bridgitt Boggan

WILL O' THE WISP

We met on a summer day, by a lake as blue as his eyes
And it seemed to me that the clouds
Forever had left the skies
He whispered sweet words in my ear
In a loving, romantic tone.
Now he goes with this one and that one
While I'm going alone.

Give him my love if you see him
Tell him I'll always be true
His leaving can't make me love him the less
Though it makes me lonely and blue
Tell him he's long been forgiven
Love never needs to atone
But while he goes with this one and that one
I will go on alone.

Katherine E. Cartwright

MESSAGE FROM THE FATHER OR THE EVER LOVING FATHER

My children,
You must love Truth.
Since Truth is 'what is'
You and I are *part* of Truth.
You and I *are* Truth.

If you cannot love Truth
you cannot love yourself
If you cannot love yourself
you cannot love Me.

Love Truth
and you love yourself.
Love yourself
and you love Me.

Our ability to love others
functions within our capacity for loving ourselves.
Our ability to love ourselves
functions within our capacity for loving Truth.

Michael J. O'Rourke

THE DAWNING OF LOVE

There's a golden span of thought before me
That reaches out beyond my inner dark;
Drifting rainbow hues rising through each tree;
Inborne wavelets' blue; through the skies, a lark
God's last star above white cliffs, fades out:
O, listen! There's a singing from my heart!
Doves sail above sea coast in morning route;
Poets with hushed pens; artists painting art.

Timeless, stealing, music . . . stilled clouds aglow,
Chimes lacking sound or voice — Air's breathless awe:
It is the hour of dawning in my soul!
Red to flaming gold . . . Peace without a lull . . .
Sand dunes, slowly spilling through the senses,
Sun-glints warmly crowning fields of plenty;
Crystal yawning seas; moon — gone from roses —
Golden span of thought — flaming thoughts of Thee.

Night is over; blessings seem my sorrows,
Thy hilltop beams bright with new Tomorrows —
There is a golden span of thought before me,
I must be deep, Dear Lord, in love with Thee . . .

Val Rogers

Group of Islets.

TWO HANDS

Two hands are used to fold in prayer
At end of days so full of care.
Two hands to work as bread you bake,
For spreading icing on a cake.
Two hands with broom can sweep a house
(But sometimes have to chase a mouse).
Two hands to change a baby's clothes
And keep them clean from head to toes.
Two hands help much to steer a car
For simple drives or trips afar.
Two hands reach out to hug, then kiss
A friend whose memory now I miss.
Two hands to wave when suns do shine,
Or warm your hands while holding mine!

Rich Gelatt

MY HEART'S ON FIRE

Dearest, what am I to do?
My heart is on fire.
As I think of you,
The warm flame flares higher.

Do you ever think of me?
You are my desire,
My reason to be . . .
Truest love will transpire.

Without everlasting love,
My thoughts would be dire.
Flights to realms above
Will quench my heart on fire.

Orma Jane Charter

GRANDCHILD

Why do you move my emotions,
that I show you such devotion.
Can it be the love of purity,
I so missed, in my life for security.

Yes! your mother can say,
Grandpa had no time to play.
To hold, to love, or even scold,
but only time, to grow old.

For I know, my past was bold,
as I recall, when my heart was cold.
But because of you, I can truly say,
Another dawn, a newborn way.

James M. Andary

SWEET DREAM-MAKER

Sunshine burst in, to bless us,
Crystal rainbows reflected around.
White flowers on a sky-blue dress,
Wood violets for a wedding crown.

Hearts overcome with newborn love,
Eyes overflow with a passionate joy.
You are my sweet dream-maker,
And my nightmare-taker.

Ginny Lindauer

ODE TO LOVE

Love lingers long.

Love lasts;
It never loses its luster — not even a little.

Love listens when spoken to because it cares — sometimes all too much.
It never forsakes a longing heart — even in times of loneliness.
And, it never asks for much — even when it has the right to ask;

It always takes what comes its way.

Love laughs,
To keep from crying,
And cries,
To keep from laughing.

Love is good — even when it's bad.
And, Love can appear to be bad — even when it's good.

Such confusion.

Love can lull you
Like a lullaby,
Or it can enflame you
Like a match.

But, whatever Love is, and whatever it does,
You can't live without it.

Marsha Riddick

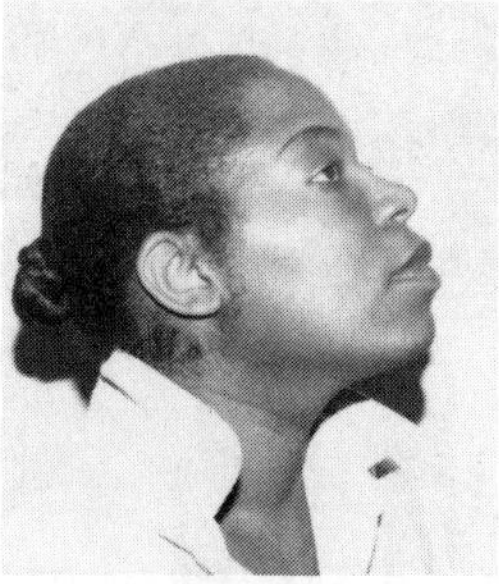

RIDDICK, MARSHA. Born: New York; Education: City College of New York; Occupation: Free-lance Writer; Poetry: *Love Serenade: A Collection of Poems;* Other Writings: *Apartment 505,*spy thriller; *French Kiss,*murder mystery; *Crystal Rabbit and Karina Rabbit,*juvenile book; "The Horror Within,"short story, suspense; Comments: *Although my writings contain a variety of themes, many of my poems concern the concept of love, which I deal with on three levels: universal, personal and individual. When the theme of universal love is expressed in my poems, I show how a person may feel toward nature and/or humanity in general. The basic tone here is impersonal and spiritual, but not always religious. Most of my poems focus on personal love. This type of love would be found in the relations of mother and child, father and child, and man and woman. Love between siblings, relatives, friends and community members would relate to personal love, also. Finally, some of my poems show that individual love can be more complex than universal love and personal love because it is a reflection of self-esteem; in this case, love is defined as pride and respect for oneself. Also, universal love and personal love seem to affect the development of individual or self-love. Moreover, much insight is required for individual love because it involves the conscious and unconscious levels of the human mind. Overall, I think that writing poetry is relaxing and quite educational since it requires some introspection and reflection.*

LOVE COMMUNICATES

Ask not that I speak
For what are words
But utterings of a soul that seeks
To share with another.

My hand in yours I place
And step by step we trace
The path of life.

My arm around you feels your pain
And lifts you up again
To travel on.

A smile lights up my face
Sharing the joy time will erase
To leave a memory.

In quiet gaze I sense your fear,
And knowingly shed a tear,
For we are one.

Standing far away, or near,
Love communicates.
Love can hear.
Ask not that I speak.

Martha Brock

BROCK, MARTHA WORTH. Born: Syracuse, New York, 1930; Married: 1960 to Clarence L. Brock, Jr.; Education: Gordon College, B.E., 1953; Central Michigan University, M.A., 1985; Occupation: Teacher; Memberships: IRA, MRA, BW Artists Association; Poetry: 'Rainbows,' *World's Great Contemporary Poems,* 1981; 'My Friend Is,' *Family Treasury of Great Poems,* 1982; 'Spring,' *Great Treasury of World Poems,* 1981.

No longer can I shed a tear,
The pain is so severe.

Love that once belonged to me
Belongs to someone else.

Who can comprehend the hurt within
But he who feels the same?

Josefina Balderrama Barrios

WE'RE ONLY A DREAM APART

For Michael, with love

When I get lonely while you're gone
Sailing on the distant seas,
I close these misty eyes, reliving
Times we've shared . . . Sweet memories.

My solitary hours are filled
With cherished thoughts of yesterday;
And though we're far apart, I know
You're really just a dream away.

The countless miles and endless days
Can't take away the love we share —
So I surrender to the night,
For in my dreams I'll find you there.

If loneliness should come your way,
Please think of me. Remember, too,
Togetherness will be ours soon . . .
And then, our dreams shall all come true.

Lori Kay O'Dor

ORIENTAL

Oriental girl, of the quiet
world.
I love the way you carry
yourself.
Coast to coast; continent to
continent.
You are a tradition that
is never forgotten. We shall
always remember you.
You had and have the most
class I have ever seen.
Don't be so mean. We
are in America now. Some
of us were born here. Some
of us will leave for prosperous
situations. The one
thing I want you to know
Is you are loved, and
appreciated world-wide.

Charles S. Walker

LOVE'S TRIBUTE

If I could walk
Where Angels walk,
And hear the talk
That Angels talk,
What would it mean,
But praising You?

If I could walk
Where Angels walk,
And hear the talk
That Angels talk,
So perfect would my life become,
I'd live in perfect piety.

Is this the plan
In life for me;
To live in perfect harmony,
Amid the strife of Galilee,
Because You offer
So much more.

Mrs. Richard Schiller

MEMORIES

Memories are so very special
to have.
They can never be taken away,
'Cause they can always mean
a great deal.
Memories can live forever.

They are a very special
bond of love,
'Cause you have them to always
look back on.
I just wish that I had those
bonds of love,
'Cause memories can never be
taken away.

I only have this fantasy
of memories,
'Cause I just don't have them
to look back on.
But my love is greater than all
those memories ever.

Angela S. Propst

HEARTS MIRROR LOVE

And through the looking glass,
Standing behind me, I see you.
And in your eyes, I see myself,
And I smile.
And Love looking out of you,
Sees Love looking out of me,
And we both smile.
Then, looking deeper,
I see reflection upon reflection,
Love looking out through each one.
And through the looking glass,
I see the many faces,
Of you and I smiling,
And my eyes become moist with joy.
For I know that our hearts mirror Love,
Into endless time.

Robert F. Vitalos

RESUME

I've never caused
the universe
to flame,
yet I've known the zeal
of anger's
heat;
I've witnessed
cold rejection's
Vehemence
and sometime felt
the world collapse
about my feet.
I've seen love's glow
in morning's
rising sun,
observed its cadence
as the evening
fell,
I've been a bit
of all of it;
this I know
full well.

Nell Elaine Nichols

THE DOVE

Love songs are playing
The dove cries alone.

Temptations are many
The heart is calloused.

Love songs are silly
Romance is dead.

Too much hate
The mind grows weary.

The hours together
Are hours apart.

Love songs are dying
The dove already gone.

Rose Brandon

FOR MY SPECIAL LOVE

You always turn my tears
into a smile
I love the time that we
spend together
I'll cherish each and
every moment
that we've spent with
one another.
The time that we've shared
No one could steal them
away from us
There could never be
another like you
For your love will always
follow me wherever
I may go
For my special love.

Denise Sinclair

I THOUGHT IT LOVE

I thought it love, those years ago,
A pretty girl I did not know.
I'd follow her each day from school,
Hoping she'd pause, speak to a fool,
Who'd be too shy to say hello

To a smile soft as early snow;
I was too young to ever show
Feelings confused as a whirlpool:
I thought it love.

Foolish childhood! For now I glow;
The wine of love does truly flow.
Yet memories — mere drops in a pool —
Occasionally overrule.
Please don't begrudge one small shadow;
I thought it love.

Norman V. Veasman, Jr.

A PRICELESS TREASURE

This priceless treasure,
Has no bounds or measure,
So people can cope,
And have a solid hope.

This love is a comfort,
It surrounds you like a fort,
This love is not on earth,
But it has plenty of worth.

The greatest of all powerful love,
Comes only from the Heaven above,
God's love will endure forever,
For Jesus Christ changes never.

Leslie June Waller

A DEPARTURE OF LOVE

My love has left me
From this life to beyond
I yet cannot follow him
for I know not where he has gone.

Our love only we could share
Inseparable once, now broken as a pair
As for life a part of me is gone
Without you how can I carry on.

Love though you left me
You're not really gone
I keep you in my heart
I sing of you in my song.

Tywanna Saunders

SO SOON FATHER

Sweet sixteen was never for me.
Suddenly you had left me.
Lost in the burning flame,
you no longer feel the pain.
In the winter snow, deep is my sorrow,
dark is my shadow.
Silent, my heart remains.
Those falling tears, in my eyes,
so often appear.

Monique Sirois

SWEET WORDS OF LOVE

In peaceful sleep without a care,
I close my eyes and he is there.
I place a kiss upon his lips,
And taste the wine of which he sips.
In my dream he holds me tight,
And makes love to me throughout the night.
Sweet words of love he whispers low,
Such peace and love I'll never know.
As morning light was breaking through,
I saw his face and it was you.
When I awoke and you were gone,
I cursed the winds that bring the dawn.
Remembering the world in which I had been,
I close my eyes and dream again.

Pat J. Magner

YOU MAKE ME FEEL SPECIAL

I feel so special
Whenever you are around
You pick me up
When I am down.

The rainy days turn into sunshine
The winter to spring,
Your sweet smile brightens my day
And makes my heart sing.

Though I tell my feeling more with words,
Or even with a song,
Do not doubt that I will love you
Forever as the days are long.

Sylvia Jefferson

TWILIGHT LOVE

Hand in hand towards the twilight of life
They stroll along the way.
They've been together as husband and wife,
Sixty years today.

They've shared life's joys and sorrows
Through good times, the bad,
Shared some glad and sad tomorrows,
Giving the best they had.

Someday they'll watch life's sunset fade
And slowly sink beneath the hill,
As love's a gift in Heaven made
There they'll be sweethearts still.

Mary Alice Rich

A ROLLER-COASTER LOVE

With each passing day
we go our own way,
keeping our distance
yet, our minds are at play.

At war with each other
our feelings we cover
yet only to stare,
while not seeming to care.

Only time can provide
the roller-coaster ride
that we need to survive,
if only to still hide.

Kelley Howe-Nolan

HAPPENSTANCE

Happenstance makes love,
propinquity makes love, and sometimes
need makes love
until it self-destructs,
but when
happenstance, propinquity, and need
no more apply,
what logic may reject
is what makes love.

Joanne Commanday

PART OF ME

With a heart that could rival a diamond
She came to me willing and wild
To change my life at the drop of a hat
No more than an innocent child

Can love really grow to its limits
Within hours to have reached its ebb tide?
And then turn to leave, but a memory
To another love with nothing to hide

Some love is made to be good news
Some love must live silently
This love is a love I keep just to myself
And will only be a part of me

How can days become hours of eternity?
Seeming so many moments I've missed
Is love just a word? Is love just a song?
To someone I only have kissed

I feel from my soul; such a raging
A fire burning that just cannot be
The limits of love can go out of control
Blinding visions that you could not see

So, here as the love within us passes
A love that might never have been
Just some hours of thoughts from a mingled mind
Just the heart of a passing friend

Some love is made to be good news
Some love must live silently
This love was a love I've just kept to myself
Until now; for your own eyes to see

Lucky Rimpila

EVENING LOVE

As darkness gathers the last gleams of light,
the evening closes in around us.

The breezes of night stir the curtains and
I catch a faint hint of Jasmine.

I stand looking at the cars go by.
You come stand at my back holding and hugging me,
swaying to and fro.

Come and sit with me, you invite. Listen to
the music. You kiss my face and lips.

We hold each other as the fullness of darkness
engulfs us.

You touch my body and it thrills with tiny
shivers of delight.

We fumble as children, to an end of passion,
rising to the heights of love and desire.

Float on a bed of rose petals, aroma of
Heavenly fragrance.

We lie holding each other, chills of pleasure
surging through our bodies.

With heavy eyelids we slip into the
calmness of sleep.

George Crowe

PLATONIC LOVE

To Margalee

I will not hold you
nor let passion stir the breast
or soft lips tempt the sense;
for holding you will be losing you.
I will not seek your close body
for a moment's bliss
which, like a plucked flower,
withers in the hand;
or, like morning dew, disappears
after the sun's kiss.
For this love seeks to endure,
not to possess.
Then, rather let me reach your soul
and with love's spark enkindle love's pure flame;
So soul to soul, in quiet bliss,
find we joy in love's transcendent kiss;
For love comes not to the mind obsessed
but to the heart with Truth possessed.

Randall Butisingh

FADED LOVE

My heart's acquainted with faded love,
Though my head knows not where it goes.
It can take flight like a startled dove,
Or turn whichever way the wind blows.

I have seen love's flame flicker for a time:
Burning hot, and bright, and bold.
Then, as it seems to eternally shine,
It suddenly dims and grows cold.

I have felt the anquish and despair
Over feelings that have long gone.
I have seen that hollow, vacant stare
That says that love has flown.

Unlike the heavens, season, or tide,
Or the ever-changing weather;
Whenever love does not abide,
It is gone forever.

Howard Layne Harper

ALTERATIONS

Love is forever now.
All my loves are still here, moving
inward, integrating easily as shadows
on ocean waves turn with a sunlit breeze,
continuing in a quieter place. Never
disappearing, never dying, they
do not require participation, approval,
recognition. I am loveless
only if I block their presence, only
as I crave self-denial. Fully grown,
wholly sufficient, undemanding, they are here,
all my loves, forever.
I am with love.
Ignoring the presence, disavowing,
renaming the emotion indifference, even
hatred, swearing it died, never moves me
out of their lives. Sometimes displaced, never
replaced, I continue part of their existence,
can be comfort, even joy, living in a closer zone.
Love, now and forever, acknowledge me.

Lillie D. Chaffin

I KNOW YOU LIKE I KNOW MYSELF

(from the Derek Jacobi collection)

We are different, but like human is human, we are so much the same!
I know you like I know myself —
Public and private, impervious and vulnerable, bold yet shy,
powerful yet gentle
Free in order, having order in freedom, intensively sensitive,
intensely passionate, intensively dark.

Seventeen years, a million worlds, and a trillion play-universes
separate us and yet I know
The passion of dispassion, the ebb and flow of remote energies
The fiercely free kaleidoscopic vigor, the intensely closed atom of intimacy
The cold warmth, the blasting furnace in nervous heat, the flowing
stream of boulders, the icy sun —

I don't know you but I feel
The child at play, the infant crying, the tyrant seeking perfection,
the lamb seeking solace
When you beat yourself, the chain is at my back, when the audience cheers,
I blush
I sleep to wake to think breathing your breath.

My Shakespearian flower intrigues me with its wildly reserved scent
I'm like Narcissus drawn to the British shadow of my own reflection.

Dara

LOVE IS VERY PRACTICAL & REWARDING

As Prince Siddhartha, for love of humanity, you gave up your heritage: a royal throne!
As Gautama Buddha you demonstrated the practical rewards enjoyed by loving & giving . . .
As competent guide, teacher, physician, you advised all who came for help: care, share!

Surely action, reaction, counteraction, is universal law; even most powerful escape not . . .
Karma governs consequences, ad infinitum; extend loving care to all, especially the unwise!
The unaware act greedy, inhumane; need no condemnation, only compassion & education . . .

All who came for advice & guidance were shown necessity to give loving kindness priority;
With understanding accept as normal & natural folly & error committed by the unmindful!
Are not unrepentant "sinners" fellow travelers who value not, nor protect self-respect?

The mother who brought her dead son, demanding restoration to life by you, as Buddha,
Was challenged: "Bring a mustard seed from a household with no sorrow caused by death!"

Knocking on doors, she questioned strangers; realized death is a universal experience . . .
She returned, still determined to get back her son, alive! Was presented another reality:
"Use love of your son on living children, & your son will live in their love for you!"

The woman gratefully took the advice given & with no prejudice loved all children she met;
Enjoyed great love in return! Her son lived in love that brought much happiness to all . . .

Surely it is very practical to ever render loving service; educate to make love dominate!
Love & kindness will ever eliminate fear, anger, envy, hate; great enjoyment of life generate . . .
All people can experience this truth: to love & be loved is very practical & rewarding!

Sita Akka Paulickpulle

THE SHRINE

The shrine is a sacred place to keep things high in value for you.
I have a shrine to which I bring the treasures of mine:
My mother's love, my father's love
And surely God's love all above.
And you ask me: What's that? And why not she?
There is the question my friend: And why not she?
You tell me: Where is your loved one? Where is she?
My answer: Well, deep in my soul, you see:
She lives in me.

John E. Foerster

VICKI

Forest flower
Blooms with springtime dawn.
Bright soul in shadow world
Go forward!
Bend your violet skies
Toward endless summers,
And shatter the pebble void
With diamond justice.
Your petal of kindness — still
softly falls within my universe —
Always.

Joel George O'Brien

O'BRIEN, JOEL GEORGE. Born: Orange, California, 8-26-50; Single; Education: Long Beach City College, A.A.; Evergreen State College, Olympia, Washington; Cal. State Long Beach; Occupation: Licensed Communications Operator (radio); Memberships: Federal Communications Commission; Radio Service Station Licensee; Poetry: 'The Clever Id,' *American Poetry Anthology,* 1986; Other Writings: "Thought Criminal Outreach," Community Affairs television production; Comments: *I like to write about the hidden side of ourselves.*

The friend I never had
inside of me
has hair just your color.
He climbed once, naked,
from a reflecting pool
I'd closed my eyes to see.
He looked at me as you do,
half-surprised I didn't see
the me who sat before him,
the other understanding:
he'd been somewhere just like that before.
When the quiet went too long unbroken
he dove back in without a word.
But every time I close my eyes to see
the image of my creativity
he breaks the water, meets the air
and waits as you do, patiently
for me to see through his eyes,
myself.

Riva B. Weinstein

PASSING THROUGH LIFE

As you travel along life's highway
It may be a long road, so they say.
Sometimes it's bumpy, as you travel along,
While you meet the world's maddening throng.
Passing by from day to day,
Time passes fast if you can sing and pray.
Sing, and be content with what God did for you;
He gave you eyes to see the sky so blue
And ears to hear voices of people you know.
Expressing friendship and love, as you older grow.
Think of your mind and the thoughts therein,
to help others and give courage so they can win.
And stop and think as you pass through life,
That you have a good husband, or a dear wife.

Irvin Rathbun

LOVED ONES

Life is too short to worry and fret;
Love is something we should never forget.
Nothing is as important as our loved ones are,
Not even reaching the unreachable star.

Tomorrow comes much too fast,
To dwell on things from the past.
Live for today with each breath you take,
And the people you love, never forsake.

Rebecca Ellison Cole

SUMMER REFLECTIONS

Sun-washed shores, tear-stained eyes
Reflect the moments of our goodbyes.
The sea gulls fly down to comfort me
As I gaze my eyes upon the sea.

The final splash of the restless wave
When it touches the shore cannot save,
The footprints left behind by us
Or those moments we used to trust.

But thank you my love for warm salty air
When being with you meant never a care.
And warm sand squished between my toes
Meant a love and closeness, no one else knows.

Susan Lea Bacon

MEMORIES OF HALIFAX, JUNE 30, 1941

In years gone by I could not see a train
Or hear the sirens of the ships at sea
But I would want to pack my bags and flee
The solemn round of life and once again
Move on; hearing naught save the refrain
"What lies around the bend?" Always to flee
"Here" and "now," seeking my castle in Spain.

And then, my dear, I fell in love with you
And "here" and "now" became strange vivid things,
Fraught with your presence, enriched with light and shade.
But Fate reached out and lightly threw
Us far apart. Now a train or siren brings
Heartaches and memories, sad and slow to fade.

W. Grierson

LOVE COMETH

Pink and almost real,
Fragrant and beautiful.
Majestic and ethereal,
A note forever and a day.
Yes, dear one, a mark to be remembered.

A cloud of butterflies clothed her in their flight.
Bathed and ordained with radiance from the glowing light.
A forest of peach blossoms bloomed in her sight.
Fly high like a kite to those celestial sounds and might.
We two have broken that barrier forever and a night.

Paul Francis Gaynor

A SPLENDID JOY!

It is so good to talk with you,
To joke, to kiss, to love.
While you say words I long to hear, you chuckle too;
You make me laugh with happiness.

When I am sad and cannot find
A reason for a smile, a laugh;
I think of you, how we converse,
And of our instant empathy.

No matter what we talk about,
It can be silliness or sad,
The weather, or the price of gold,
A splendid joy, a truth untold.

I hope as time goes by, my love,
No one will spoil this joy for us.
Cause us to cease to share and touch
Heaven with our fantasy, living this love we need so much.

When summers of our life have flown,
Winter will come, our speech will slow.
But you are life and breath to me, and joy . . .
I only wanted you to know.

Vivian S. Flannery Dees

ECHO OF OUR LOVE

Fate took you from my life,
And I try with all my might,
I still hear the echo, the echo of our love.

When loneliness surrounds me,
And I feel it's going to drown me,
I hold to the echo, the echo of our love.

I hear the birds singing,
I fail to get the meaning
Then I catch the echo, the echo of our love.

Through life's troubled plights,
When the sun fades from sight,
I hold tight to the echo, the echo of our love.

Sometimes I start to wonder,
If I can find another love,
To fill your heart space hunger,
I just feel that wonderful echo, the echo of our love.

I see other lovers,
With their love close at hand.
I'm still grateful for our echo, the echo of our love.

Alice Fleming

LOVE IN MARRIAGE

Love is sharing with one another.
Love is caring.
Love is the husband and wife together caring for their feelings.
Love is a comittment.
Love is sharing smiles between husband and wife.
It's love that are vows.
It's the vows at the wedding
I stand at my wedding for my land America.
Its love that endureth for the husband and wife.
Love is beautiful America that endureth.
Love is caring to stand for America the beautiful
Love is styles in marriage.
Its love is bountiful, a bond of love.
The love in America is moments, to share yesterday and today.
The love is the day my love came into my life.
Love is the same yesterday and today.

Maria L. Sanders

ISLAM DARK VICTORY

Smile of sky and split of hurricanic
Thunder storm;
Grumble of limpid, pearly, fleeing waters
And flying swallows floating by troop . . .
These are the victorious rhymes of Enotrius,
And the beautiful clearness of Islamic,
Limpid (Koranic) waters.

Lord God, bless those I love, and as
I view the ocean side, my heart is calm
And my spirit is vast and serene . . .
Ora et labora. Alleluia, Hosanna.
Requiem. Ibis, redibis et non
Peribish in bello.
Excelsior!

Allan De Fiori

BEING

The life in my life will soon depart,
Leaving a lifeless life for me in mind and heart.

His style is different, his music loud,
He is not mine anymore, he belongs to the crowd.

He does not forget, and neither do I,
The bond between us, since his first baby cry.

He is a man now and his life is his song,
I can only pray this time he will not be away so long.

For the time between visits for me holds no season,
Come back soon, son-with-guitar,
And give to my life rhyme and reason.

Lucille R. Albanese

I miss you even more at Christmas time.
I line the walls with holly, trim the tree,
Hang Mistletoe and hear the church bells chime
As long ago they rang for you and me.

The children and grandchildren gather here,
Bring gifts and love and laughter. All is gay.
And so I smile and join in Christmas cheer
While my heart mourns for one who's gone away.

Helen D. Edmonds

MY LOST LOVE

I need no picture of you, dear heart,
or record of your voice,
I see you every way I turn,
I hear you everywhere.
I see the proud tilt of your head,
the beauty of your chin,
The loveliness of your divine brow,
the goodness from within.
I find you in all laughter, songs, and tears,
I breathe you in the air.
I shall never be alone, sweet, tender heart,
for you are always there.
And how my heart does swell in pride
when following your gaze;
My lips are quiet now, my love,
you need no oral praise.
Would, love, that I could hold you gently
as a babe release a sigh;
As long as God shall reign above,
so much in love with you am I.

La Rue Cooke Howard

HE LOVES THEM ALL

I often wondered how John Doe
Evaded Cupid's dart,
How it was, some pretty girl
Had failed to win his heart.

"Well," I thought, "it's just that girls
Don't mean a thing to him,
Or that he hasn't met the one
That's satisfied his whim."

So I spoke to him one day,
And asked him to explain,
But what he answered, may or not
Seem sensible or sane.

"Of course I love the girls," he said
"I love them all, my son,
And that's the only reason why
I cannot fall for *one*."

Nathan Vogel

LOVE

Love is such a powerful force
No matter the source.
The heights and depths of love are astounding,
Leaves the heart pounding.
There are so many kinds,
There's love that binds
Two hearts as one, exciting and fun
Love for one another, a heartwarming wonder,
It grows and grows
In different ways it shows.
Children are love from the beginning,
A miracle that comes bringing
Such feelings no one can comprehend or ever understand
Love can be exhilarating and sweet
Making life so complete,
Bringing joy and gladness, to all things added zest.
Love has to start somewhere
Of this our minds are aware
But only God knows for real
What makes the heart feel.

Hesse G. Byrd

A LOVER'S EPITAPH

As the young and strong rush in its pursuit,
From where they have all come.
In a spark of force from deep within,
Encompassing two spirits into a new one.

For such a very short time it lingers,
As the years pass by, it goes on.
At a more rapid pace than it arrives,
Always much sooner, then it's gone.

Over and over, we are just barely able
To grasp at it, as it gently disappears.
A flicker of time in our fable;
It seems we're always looking in arrears.

As we grow to become more aware,
Of a world of sisters and brothers.
The hungry, the sick, the threadbare,
All struggle to last a few more years.

We could live together in the world,
If all the questions were in answer.
Love has its time to come and to go,
Until we learn to love one and another.

Wayne A. Shock

THE MANY FACES OF LOVE

True love resembles a blushing red rose,
But we shouldn't forget the thorns;
True love resembles an azure blue sky
And sometimes a thunderstorm.

True love resembles dancing daffodils,
Also a smile of cheer;
True love resembles blossoming violets
And a fallen tear.

True loves's aspen leaves waltzing free,
And sweet melodies from a meadowlark too;
True love has its up and downs
Like a willow tree weeps to the blues.

True love's a rainbow, a fleecy white cloud,
A hummingbird's delicate wings;
True love's nectar, the fruit of the vine,
But beware of the bumblebee's sting.

Remember, true love's unique and grand,
Why there isn't much which can compare;
But stamp on the package of your mind —
Fragile, handle with care!

Linda C. Grazulis

OUR LITTLE GIRL

Little girls to raise are not always fun.
But remember my lady you once were one.
And look at what you have become, from playing pretend to having a girl of your own.
Comfort her and love her for she will grow fast.
So that you can forgive her 'cause her crying will pass.
For soon she will be a lady on her own.
And she will leave you with a life of her own.
So be happy and enjoy her hard times and good.
'Cause little girls don't always act the way they should.

Richard P. Browne

STRENGTH THROUGH LOVE

Faith in Almighty God is the greatest thing on Earth,
Our hope has been in His son since His birth,
That faith and hope causes our hearts to overflow,
Filling them with charity for everyone we know.

Along with Faith, Hope, and Charity, is Love,
Love was sent from our heavenly Father above,
That's why He sent us Jesus down here below,
He sent His only son, because He loved us so!

If we had no Faith, where would we be?
We'd be like a ship, long lost at sea,
Then there would be no hope for you or me,
Without any charity, what a terrible world this would be.

Love is what makes the world go around,
Love is powerful, and in all places can be found,
Love was meant to be good for all mankind,
Love should be in all of our hearts and minds.

Faith, Hope, and Charity, what a wonderful three!
But Love has to go with them, don't you see?
A chain is just as strong as its weakest link,
We need all four of them, don't you think?

Willard Lee Skelton

THE DANCE HALL

It appears woven together with broken dreams,
While it stages a place for life's destiny.
Beyond the dancers, there's a table so bare,
Where we, in the past a destiny shared.

The dance hall years have fled by so fast,
As time's toll outlived her class.
Yet, magic seems to weave quite a spell,
As wine and music within her dwell.

The hour is late as most dancers leave,
As you hold another, my heart grieves.
As I sit alone and watch you there,
This dance hall holds a treasure rare.

To drink a toast, through a tear I see,
A whisper of yesterday's faded memory.
While leaving you laughing by him there,
Farewell to my dearest, to what we shared.

The music's bewitching, yet it seems,
A dance hall's broken many a dream.
For the wine and music do add a glow.
When tomorrow's gone, then reality shows.

Donna Niedermeier

YOUNG LOVE

They say we are too young to feel the love that
we now feel;

That we've become too serious, and must realize
it's no big deal.

We've got other priorities they tell us — that it's
just a phase we're going through.

I wish they understood just how we really feel, and
that I want to live my life with you.

Francene Phillips

WE ARE

As the speech of freedom wisps about the air
saying we are fruitful and we'll share;
if you're cold and hungry, that we care
about the right and wrong of all that's fair.

We are Americans,
the brothers and the sisters of us all.
We are Americans,
lifting up our hearts to heed the call.
We are the reason
this country is as strong and proud today.
We are America,
the helping hand of freedom on its way.

And when the morning comes
to greet a brand-new day
We'll come together,
to make a better way.
And when we find it
we'll pass it on to you.
We are Americans
and nothing less will do!

William D. Leavitt

From *ROMEO AND JULIET*

JUL. Thou know'st the mask of night is on my face;
Else would a maiden blush bepaint my cheek,
For that which thou hast heard me speak to-night.
Fain would I dwell on form, fain, fain deny
What I have spoke; but farewell compliment!
Dost thou love me? I know, thou wilt say, Ay;
And I will take thy word; yet, if thou swear'st,
Thou mayst prove false: at lover's perjuries,
They say, Jove laughs. O gentle Romeo,
If thou dost love, pronounce it faithfully:
Or if thou think'st I am too quickly won,
I'll frown and be perverse, and say thee nay,
So thou wilt woo; but, else, not for the world.
In truth, fair Montague, I am too fond;
And therefore thou mayst think my 'havior light:
But trust me, gentleman, I'll prove more true
Than those that have more cunning to be strange.
I should have been more strange, I must confess,
But that thou overheard'st, ere I was ware,
My true love's passion: therefore, pardon me;
And not impute this yielding to light love,
Which the dark night hath so discoverèd.

William Shakespeare

YESTERDAY'S DREAMS

Yesterday's dreams
Bring a tear to my eye
Dreams of being together
Just you and I
Yesterday's dreams
Seem so far away
Dreams that never came true
Because you're not here today
Yesterday's dreams
Are still on my mind
Dreams that I recall often
Thinking of our love that was one of a kind
Yesterday's dreams
I wish they'd come true
Dreams I long so much for
The same as I long for you

Daniel Corrigan

THE GREATNESS OF SMALL APPRECIATIONS

Hold me gently in your arms,
Anytime, day or night
Kiss away the tears from my eyes.
Let me know that you care.
Help me to forget the worries of the day,
To leave all troubles behind
For this moment.

The look in your eyes surely tells me
How much you really care.

So much sadness happens in one's life,
In one day, one hour, one second;
Such a short time of existence
Here on earth, to find peace of mind,
Happiness in the beauty of living life.

Maybe with one's suffering on earth
Helps one to appreciate the most minute
Form of happiness and love of life
For all the *supreme being* creations,
great and small.

Sheila A. López

A MOTHER'S PRAYER FOR HER SON'S HAPPINESS

Son, today you took this girl for your wife,
You promised to love her all of your life.
God made you one, as man and wife,
to have and to hold,
to cherish,
and to honor,
in sickness,
and in health,
till death do you part!
Engrave this into your hearts today,
And God shall guide you all the way.
All my love
now and forever
Your Mom

Dolores Rey Partie

A POEM FOR HER

blow it off, you'd probably say
after six years together
through the best and the worst
what am I supposed to do?
how could you expect me to
take our parting so easily, casually
smile and wave and walk away?

I watched you pull away —
the car drive off into the
distance
a tiny black speck, until
finally, clouded from view by the driving snow.
then alone, took a twelve-pack home
now very drunk, I stare at the blank tv set
may you never feel as lonesome.

stoned. bound for the flatlands
of Oklahoma, perhaps already anticipating
some new lover
you probably took it all much easier,
our splitting, the same way you took me.

Brian Murdock

My love, you are a star in the heavens.
You're a poem of beauty. You are a song
of love, a symphony of passion. You're the
spirit in my soul. You are a beat in my heart.
To you my promise of love I give. I know
for always our love will live. For you are
all this to me and yet more. You are the
one I will forever adore.

Colliér

NOÉ NOÉ

The worst, the worst is not today,
Not today, but tomorrow.
Tomorrow, and the days after,
The days after, years and years —
Years and years — all my life.

Today, today is full of glory,
Glory and fire and beauty.
I saw you only a few hours ago —
I can see and hear you still,
Vivid, edged with fire,
Your voice a music that enfolds my heart.

But when all that fades, when memory dims,
When you are no longer hot upon my senses,
For minutes, hours, day, years —
How will I endure,
How will I go on?

I dread sleep and the ending of this day.
With waking will begin the morrows without you —
Days that will last forever.

Deon Davis

DAVIS, WYNORA DEON. Born: Hereford, Texas, 10-26-31; Married: 12-14-51 to Roy Lee Davis; Education: Chemeketa Community College, Salem, Oregon, A.A. degree, 1983; Occupations: Homemaker, Writer, Poet; Memberships: Mensa, Intertel, The International Society for Philosophical Enquiry; Poetry: 'One Poem,' haiku, *American Poetry Anthology,* 1985; 'Two Poems,' haiku, *Chemeketa Literary Magazine,* 1983; Comments: *I write to celebrate the fragility of life, and the gentleness, strength and humor in human nature, and to express the ambiance of aliveness that is in all things.*

FINDING LOVE

Finding love is hard to do,
making it last is harder that's true.

She gives and I give,
together we have a perfect gift.

We have our ups and downs,
but in the ring of love, we only go a few rounds.

We settle with a hug and a smile,
growing closer all the while.

Love was never meant to be perfect,
we worked on caring, sharing and gaining respect.

Now that we've found it, we give it our best,
God takes care of the rest.

Donald A. Gaeden

IDYLL

The fragrant mountain breeze was caressing
The silken threads of her golden hair,
Her deep blue eyes and brow smooth and fair
The setting sun suavely was kissing.

Save for the pines, dark, straight and tall
That swaying seemed to hum a lullaby
And the clear brooks murmuring nearby,
Supremely quiet and peace reigned over all.

Sitting beside her, untiring to admire
Her rosy mouth and tempting forms divine,
Rapture my heart throbbed with desire.

She was so close, her hair was brushing mine;
Her languid eyes, her breasts so full, so white
Who could withstand? . . . I kissed her long and tight.

Domenic Lombardi

ALAS MY LOVE,
A ROMANTIC TO THE END!

To sing the songs of love;
To write the verse that soothes;
To shatter the world of emotions;
To take the beauty of a rose and weave with it the colors of a rainbow;
With all these things, I will weave a poem; one that does not rhyme, but one that will take some time.
As the song goes, you came to me and danced with me, until all my dreams came true. And now my dreams dance with the sun and love with the moon.
Standing with me and sharing life as two lovers lost in time; the colors of our emotions revolve as each day passes. The rose left alone, pales until the sun shines and the colors blend together. The warmth, the love, the gentle caress: these bring out the beauty once lost.
Alas my love, a romantic to the end!

Linda Streng

THE SOUND OF LOVE'S VOICE

To me your voice is one of a kind.
How could I ever erase it from my mind?
For it gets stronger with the passage of time,
As its pleasure for me is all mine!

How can mere words convey all that I feel,
For it is the spirit within that puts upon it a seal.
Your voice is as gentle as a soft summer breeze
And as strong as energy from Hercules.

The title of the poem has a double meaning —
love's actual voice or a loved one's voice.

Bernice Prill Grebner

VIGIL

Her sun has set in aged and softened shades,
And endless seem the reaches of the night.
Her going seems almost unbearable to me,
After a life of knowing her love at hand.
Through dragging hours, we sit beside her here,
And watch the dread advance across her face
Of shadows and the countenance we love
Etched sharply now against the pillow case.
A deep fog clouds the dawn with kindly veiling —
Between two thoughts of mine, she gently goes.
We reach our hands together and hold them close.
We smile, remembering, she was oh so tired!

Josephine O. Bull

AT THE BUS STOP

A lover of the arts learning to love
Dreaming of love lost, learning. Ideas flowing
from thought, topics appear like the whittled
inscriptions on the bench. Birds perched
calmly on the wires above. The cars zoom
by in packs with impressive unity. The winds
purify, yet add an air of mystery. The pavement,
discolored and littered, balances on the earth.
A child strides across the road, school over
for another day. Discomfort begins to distract.
The bus approaches, offering a ride to the next
stop.

David Lee Clark

A DAUGHTER'S LOVE

Mother you are a very special treasure GOD gave to me,
You and I will always have that special bond between us,
We have been together from day one, you went with me from
the baby blue days, through the terrible twos, and on through
the terrible teens, and now you're still with me into adulthood,
Mother I have always needed you and I always will, you've helped
in sadness, and happiness, when I was in love, and out of love,
through pain and hurt, you've been there to nurse me back to
health when I was sick, Mother you have given me so much love and
joy, and I'll always be grateful for everything. You are and
always will be my very best friend, THANK YOU!
I LOVE YOU MOTHER!

Kathy Barnette

COMMUNICATION GAP

Hey Mom, slap me five
sorry Child, I only have a dime

Hey Mom, what is up
oh Child, bottom is bottom and top is top

Hey Mom, would you like to rock and roll
well Child, I was never good at skimming stones, not at all

Hey Mom, you look so cool
how can that be Child, when I'm dressed in wool

Hey Child, I love you and you love me and we know that
oh Mom, then what's all this talk about the communication gap

Susan McCracken

SONNET

The wonder is that love for you still lives.
The tapestry we wove is frayed and torn.
And by the stains and tatters it has born
Why should we think that it has more to give?
Yet I can feel you look to me for love.
And in my darkest self I know that I
Have given you some hope that love's not done
And you, my knave of hearts, the only one.
I thought that I was really through with you.
That lust and pain were now, fait accompli.
I'm far from where you are and being me.
My clothes are different and my writing too.
I'm happy with my life, with who I am.
Can someone tell me why I give a damn?

Dean Lewis

TWO HEARTS

Two hearts became one, because,
They shared a special feeling.
It was nourished briefly without clause.
Soon wedding bells were ringing.
The bride was beautiful dressed in white;
While the groom smiled at everyone in sight.
The vows they said, the words they spoke,
Were their own, not read from a book.
She was overwhelmed with tears of joy,
As they kissed she was so coy.
Their marriage sparkled like an ember.
She was young as May; he mature as December.
Their love knew no bounds — this is the reason.
Passion and romance disregard the season.

Louise B. Huldeen

FIVE PENNIES

I am the wooden ponies prancing.
I let the children grab for the golden ring.
I give light and life to old and young.
As turning, my mirrors flash across
The grounds of sawdust,
Reflecting the eyes of a child.
My place is at the center of all fun.
My name is carousel . . .

Nancy Beattie

LOVE

Your love is so gooey
Wrapped around my finger
Sliding down the side
Your love is so chewy good
Adam and his apple couldn't compete
Your love stretches like taffy
It binds me to the ground
I walk on salty air
Your love is perfect
And as sweet as sin

Ellen Besserman

MAIDEN

With skin so fair
And wit so bright
A seductive creature
Oh, wondrous sight

Her walk, her voice
Her touch is fire
To be unattracted is
To be a liar

Her temper quick
And passion wild
An aura of awe
Embraces this child

I'm in her spell
I can't escape
Like fly to spider
I sit and gape

This lovely maiden
Has me in hold
I hope to be there
When we are old . . .

G. L. Butler

FIFTY YEARS WITH A LOVELY WIFE

In a few short months we'll celebrate,
The happy day draws near.
Perhaps some friends will congregate,
And our family will be here.

Fifty years of connubial bliss,
Who could ask for more?
What a lucky man to have all this,
Such a beauty to adore!

When first we met enchantment,
Overwhelmed to say the least,
I fell with abandonment,
The roving now had ceased.

Always careful of her coiffure,
Lashes ever in place,
Nothing each day could deter,
The cosmetology of the face.

And today she is just as fair,
Her beauty is still sublime,
No one else is aware,
But, it takes her twice the time!

Chet Rust

MAYBE

Our lives
Passed slightly by
On the sly.

She was very shy,
And so was I.
The plans we piled,
And plots we dreamed,
Were crazy enough to make us scream.
The end was a scheme, a tune with lyrics.
We wanted to sing with love.
All it takes is soul,
And what you're thinking of.
Going, just another thing.
Trapped in a maze.
Passing through a craze.
We're small time,
Passed by slowly,
Crept by secretly,
Good-by my lie.

James Melton Wolfe

SPRING LOVE

The flowers were blooming,
there was a new breath of Spring.
There was a happiness there in
everything.

Her heart was singing, for the
morning train her lover was bringing.
And soon she'd be with him,
clasped dear to his heart,
Forever cherishing, never to part.

There would be hopes, there would
be fears,
Laughter would come, even some
tears.

A new joy was born, a freshness
of Spring.
There was a happiness there in
everything.

Beth A. Bush

BEFORE AND AFTER

I,
The only flower
In this field of sorrow,
Will stand no more
When the sun sets tomorrow.
My leaves are withered,
My heart is dry,
The sadness within me
Is deep inside.

We,
The only flowers
In this field of showers,
Will stand forever
When the weeds turn to towers.
Our leaves are damp
Our hearts in ocean tide,
The glory within us
Is deep inside.

Missy Meakin

Set sail, m' love, to steely steed,
and heights my mind doth know,
Turn loose, m' love,
the lust in me,
And let the passion flow.
Let's guide, m' love
like moonbeam lights
Along the canyon roads,
to dance, m' love,
in shameless glow,
Along shadowed hillsides.
The wind, m' love,
Shall blow us free,
Upon your trusty steed.
We'll fly, m' love,
Beyond this life,
to forevers,
Bound by naught,
But love, m' love,
Upon our endless flight.

Felicia Morgan

UNIQUE LOVE

I found her down by the sea shore
When I love her I want more
Her hair is blonde her eyes are green
She's the prettiest gal I've ever seen
Her love's unique but it's for real
Her kisses shock like an electric eel
I have to be careful of her flair
that I'm not sitting in an electric chair,
Electrified!
As she walks her hair flows down
She walks upon it on the ground
Her love is rare and hard to find
Man I love it, it's just my kind
Her kisses send volts that make me kneel
She hasn't got anything she doesn't reveal
Her love is rare but I don't care
Her love's unique of this I am aware
Her love's unique of this I am aware

Marjorie Rinkel Graumenz

I said I wouldn't fall again.
I didn't want to dare.
But every time I thought of you
My heart screamed out "I care"
A friend told me not to give up on love
I only closed my ears;
But what I didn't know was
That my heart still wanted to hear.
I tried to hold my feelings
To actually hide them from you
But every time we were together,
I was afraid they would break through.
And when you began to show
That you cared somewhat about me,
I finally decided to let go
And set my feelings free.
I hope you understand how I feel
That is what I've tried to do.
I also want to let you know
I'm happiest when I'm with you.

Maureen Houlihan-Sutter

DREAMS

I can accept it if I can only love you within my
heart . . . within my dreams . . . I don't mind . . .
it's all between me . . . in my dreams I need not hold
back . . . within my dreams I need not explain . . .
for it's you and me and all that matters most . . .
Over and over we met again . . . over and over I call
out your name darling . . . I gave myself to you . . . you
gave yourself to me . . . we need not explain . . . No one
else needs to know . . . that I want you . . . I need you . . .
and we met and loved so very gracefully . . . *if only
in my dreams* . . . we need not explain . . . In my dreams
I can have you anytime I want . . . In my dreams I can
Love you in all the ways I never could before . . . if
only in our dreams my love . . . if only in our dreams . . .
There no one can come between us . . . no one can tell us no . . .
if only in our dreams . . . I loved you . . . I love
you still . . .

Ivey Joyce Williams

Often in the silences that pass before the dawn, from muted shades of loneliness
I call to you; and peering through the half-dream of an unrelenting night,
The silence echoes softly in my ear. The morning rain, like heartbeats, fills
The void; and images race wildly — as passion swells, surrounding me,
Completing, then depleting me
To nothingness once more. As greyer, lifeless shadows mark the walls,
The sweet despair of loving scars the solitude; I close my eyes,
Imprisoned in a cell of secret sighing, and wither,
An intense and fragile captive of the heart. I love you
In the dim hue of my empty life — in colorless and fainter visions
Throughout an endless night; in feigned ecstasy and rapture,
The sweet explosions of the mind that penetrate mortality and span
The breadth of time. I love you in the confines of regret — that for all
The want and trying, you have not embraced me yet . . .
I love you — as the morning storm subsides, and gently wipe
The teardrops from my eyes. Within the deepest recesses of heartache; beyond
The darksome origin of day, the flame of love undying, love unfathomed,
Love untouched emits its sweet and tragic heat, and ashen ghosts of memory
In wistful, haunting whispers vent the encore of a misery
In mirrors of my obsession spent.

Christine A. Pitt

WICKLOW

I fled from the crowds today, and thought of you. My thoughts recalling
the gentle curve of your mouth, the happy smile brought about by a slender
flower, or a tiny animal.
I thought of that winter in Austria, of skiing in the newly fallen snow.
Walking back to the chalet, our shoes squeaking on the pure whiteness.
And you wept in my arms, there by the fire, when you knew, when parted
we might never again love, or touch. Nothing save a memory, recalling
painful nostalgia.
The rich claret, the warmth of the flickering fire, flecks of moisture
sticking to the windowpane. I kissed your mouth, held your body against
mine — feeling comfortable with your love — we slept a sleep of the drugged
And on the lucid morn, stood on the platform, sparsely peopled, with an
elderly woman in tattered woolens, vending pretzels, and waved at your
vanishing face in a clouded frame.
I saw you again in London, a year later, but thought it best not to see you.
You were walking a child with golden hair, and deep blue eyes.
Goodnight.

Lawrence E. Thrall

GOODBYES ARE NOT FOREVER

For Cathy and Neil

I tell myself a thousand times
that you are gone — and yet,
My broken heart still reaches out,
for one it cannot forget.

Now, through my tears, I kiss the child,
so much a part of you,
As I pray for strength and wisdom,
to be "mom" — and "daddy" too.

Yet, well I know, that I shall fail,
unless I cease to cry,
Accepting that, which God allows,
instead of questioning why.

Indeed, that is the hardest part,
the pain of letting go,
When one has loved, as I loved you,
and, because we miss you so.

But, goodbyes are not forever,
for true love never dies,
And God left part of you behind,
in a little fellow's eyes.

Marilyn Jimerson Brewer

I WOULD STEAL FROM NAPOLEON

*"To die without being loved by you,
to die without that certitude, is the
torment of Hell, is the living, terrifying
vision of total annihilation."*
Bonaparte to Josephine

I would write you a love letter,
But someone has written before,
The words of passion and pain.
Who could pen love better
Than Napoleon, who chose to adore
Josephine — stylish, cunning, vain?
His words were elegant.
If ever I find enough nerve,
I'll mail copies to you.
My own phrases have an adolescent slant.
The writing seems less than you deserve.
And I search for something new
To say about a subject as old as memory.
So — I won't pretend I'm smart.
I'll borrow instead from someone else's
abundance
Of eloquent words retained eternally,
When a soldier poured out his heart
And unknowingly gave his gift to romance.

Dora DeShong

WORDS THAT CAN'T BE SPOKEN

There are words
Which can't be spoken,
There are feelings
That I should not have sent,
There are sorrows
That can't be shared,
And a glorious love
I can't repent.

Richard Rosenbaum

BETRAYAL

Lover
you told me
a great many things
to break the winter's spell
and draw me in
It was
enough
to shed the pain
and snuggle deep
within the womb
Warmth —
a bonding
that grew
into
everlasting beauty
Why
now
did you
betray that
with a lie?

Steve Bedney

#18

The first eighteen years of
the Bible is Jesus.
But it is not there.

Because of the star wars,
"Get them out of the
heavens."
They were polluted.

My brother told me
because he is an angel.
He also showed me a
funky heaven.

Now if the pig didn't
fall in the mud that
time,
"Then eight point eight
is funky.

Charles S. Walker

THE SOUND OF SILENCE

Listen with joy; a child is born
The sound of love in the morning
Gossamer wings and butterfly flings
Heaven will sing with her borning.

Listen with love; a little girl's heart
The sound of her Father rejoicing
Faraway dreams and paradise gleams
The angels will dance with her chorusing.

Listen with patience; a young woman now
The sound of her Mother waiting
Everyday things and tomorrow brings
The muse who march to her baiting.

Listen with sorrow; the child is no more
The sound of two hearts that are breaking
A long lonely road and a difficult load
Our souls will forever be aching.

Betty Antrobus

LOVED MY GRANDPA

In his senior years he made his home with our family. A jolly man was he — my grandpa.

The house clown when he was around, for a jolly man was he — my grandpa.

My huntin' pal, my fishing pal, my playmate, my confidant; a jolly man was he — my grandpa.

When the wind howled and the snow blew on many a cold winter night the wood stove would be cherry-red hot. In his old oak rockin' chair I would lay my hand on his knee and say, "Grandpa tell me a bedtime story." He was the greatest story teller of all. For a jolly patient man was he — my grandpa.

Many looked forward to Christmas and presents months ahead, but I had my Santa Claus 365 days of the year. My grandpa — for a jolly man was he.

When my earthly chores are done and I walk, fly or zoom high in the sky into the great by and by, I shall look for the big oak rocker and my grandpa. I shall again lay my hand on his knee and say, "Tell me another story like you did such a short time ago." For a jolly man I know he still will be — my grandpa.

Russell Heindselman

YESTERDAY, TODAY, AND TOMORROW

Time correlates the essence that leads to boundaries of chilled frost
Slowly revolving into a "sweetheart rose" sent to a love-struck couple,
While blustery winds capture a shower surrounding apple blossoms,
Enfolding rainbows of breathtaking allusions
Upon silhouettes of a bridal pair discovering a timeless creation.
Suddenly! The warmth of the sun circulates numerous days.
Highlights of a golden leaf hide behind an evergreen
Eventually dissolves into a natural painted picture
Descending for the rich harvest of plenty
Forgetting the chilly days, as sparkling "Holiday Charisma"
Fulfill treasured dreams of anticipation.

Rita M. Knecht

LOVE SERVANT

I allowed myself the luxury and thought of you today,
It had been so long since I had let myself enjoy that pleasure.
I released my heart, and off it flew to embrace memories of you,
Reminding me I could not be free, from the friendship that I treasure.

When often times, we find ourselves in different directions,
And circumstances separate and trouble tries to borrow,
I still hang on, though many times my pride would have me falter,
Because I love you much today and more I will tomorrow.

If I could give you peace of mind and happiness forever,
You know I'd never hesitate, I'd want to make you better.
But Jesus can, He loves you so, He cares how you are feeling,
He'll give you joy, and set you free and break your every fetter.

Just give to Jesus all of you, He has given all for you,
Believe in what He's promised you and victory will come through.
Resist temptations, when they come, stay grounded in His Word,
Do all you do in Jesus' name, and to your church be true.

I'm only human and I fail, but I'll keep trying harder,
To keep the friendship that we have and keep it going stronger
To deny myself and think of you, even when my heart's been wounded,
Knowing all too well, I need you now and more as time is longer.

Betty Sue Curtis

AN INCREASE OF FAMILY.

THE TRIAL OF PATIENCE.

REMEMBRANCE OF LOVE

Broken dreams,
once lit by hope,
lay shadowed beneath
the cruelty
of indifference and ambiguity.
Scattered fragments,
momentary reflections
of need and desire,
are weatherworn
and cracked,
dwindling remembrance
of passion's dying embers.
A final flicker
of renewed promises
dissipate into silent ashes.
Only the memory
of love to come
shines bright within
the recesses
of my mind.

Joanne M. Scarfo

LOVE IS FREE

Love is free.
Its bounds are none.
Greed sets its price.
Power possesses what it is not.
Passion is bodies and souls.
Hate warps and shrivels.
Pride is a spear.
Lies bind us to ignorance.
Love is its own value.
Love transcends our weaknesses.
Love holds and touches souls.
Love blooms and reaches beyond the sun.
Love needs no weapons.
Love is the freedom of truth.
Love and a soul unite.
Love is then whole.
Love becomes our gift.
Lour pours out when it's found.
Love is the untameable sky of the eagle.
After all, love is free.

Dennis L. Newcome

FLOWER OF LOVE

I kept a flower in a jar
The flower would not die
I admired it most everyday
Now I think of it and cry

I lost the flower years ago
My heart will never mend
It was a special gift of love
From a very special friend

Mistakes I made tore us apart
I threw away our love
His forgiveness I shall never have
For he's now in heaven above

God tell my friend I'm sorry
And that I miss him so
Please tell him that he's still my friend
I need for him to know

Debbie J. Overton

MY SLEEPING ANGEL

She lies there, tired from all the play,
The laughs and lessons of the day,
And tears that she could not hold back.
(Too little to have learned that knack.)

A tousled head, a velvet face,
And eyes that close with all the grace
That only innocence affords,
In times of turmoil and discords.
Two little hands that both clutch tight
A blanket and a toy this night;
All make me leave reluctantly,
And wish that she could always be —
My sleeping angel.

Sally Eshelman

THE GREATNESS OF LOVE

Love is gently caring
From the cradle to the grave,
It touches each and every one,
Spreading joy along the way.

Nothing's greater than unselfish love
As you share with one another,
Sharing laughter day by day with
Mother, Father, Sister and Brother.

Return to him who does you wrong
A kindly deed or two,
It softens the heart and soon you'll find
That he will love you too.

A. Lorene Wayne

HE LIVES HERE

Sometimes he is so much trouble,
He is old now and his judgement is poor,
My brother is always polite
And I love him.
It is a blessing to have him here.
It brings me back to reality
The reality of sharing and helping
I am really glad
He lives here.

Fannie Hanninen

OLD LOVE

The hour is late, my love, my love.
The years behind a shadow.
I count the time about your eyes,
Since we first walked the meadow.

The path is straight, my love, my love.
The banquet still unfinished.
I hear the sweet, the vesper song,
Of feelings unrelinquished.

The future's gate, oh love, my love,
Is op'ning wide a door,
That we shall pass through, hand in hand,
In love forevermore.

Mary B. Wing

TO ABENA AND THE JEWELS

Your soft eyes that stole glances
With the timidity of a lamb
The snow-white teeth let out
By a captivating half-smile
And your look of a rustic beauty
Jolted my heart with a warmth of joy
An overpowering sensation of content
Which many years of rough times
Have hardly frozen by any measure.

D, our love has breasted the storms
To sight the shore of repose
Where we and the precious foursome
Will bask in the breeze of conjugal bliss
Which only the inescapable icy hands
Can chill to the delight of evil.
But even from my small prison below
You and the jewels will continue to feel
The fervor of my love and affection.

Kwasi Asante

VELVET EYES

Velvet eyes whose tender gaze stole
into the depth of my restless soul
Like the dying sun as it becomes one
When it descends upon the yielding sea
Oh, how they taunt me, forever haunt me
Will I ever again be free?

Velvet eyes, whose enchanting mystery
powerless to their spell I seem to be
My heart's on fire with love's desire
Why do they fascinate me so?
I can't conceal the way I feel
How can I ever let you go?

Velvet eyes, whose magic splendor
Will captivate me forevermore
I'll always ponder with mystic wonder
At the love they kindled deep within me
Cease now to taunt me, no need to haunt me
My love for you will ever be

Alma Leonor Beltran

COLORADO TOO

For one hundred fifty days
  I never knew
that I was being played
  For a fool,
By you.

"Come love with me," you said,
"In Colorado,
Love me too"
  Yet I was being played
For a fool,
  By you.

You never cared for me,
  It's plain now.
You only used
  My emotions,
My love
  For you.
What a fool.

Kathryn A. Etherington

UNEXPECTED ABSENCE

The sheets covet the flesh beneath them like gold.
Abandoned, his red hat asks for a dance
Whose song rises up from her body like clouds —

A breast, a dream breast
Hovers just below the
Canopy of silk
Gently and readily
Cradling the early sun in their slopes
Stilled by a halt in your kisses.

O my God, what am I
That frost forms on my windows
In an Indian summer, in an unexpected absence.

Janis Gillespie

SONG OF THE TURTLE

The dark of night has blanketed the earth
And wrapped the sunshine well within its fold;
The day has gone to Him who gave it birth
And silence grasps the air in death-like hold.
The birds have tucked their heads beneath the wing,
Sleep binds the soul of all in quiet rest;
The songs are stilled within the bubbling spring,
And babes lie dreaming on their mother's breasts.
Oh man! Beloved of me, fling down your care,
Lie here beside me, hush both song and word,
And drop the wordly armor that you wear;
Like night I would enfold thee, bare thy sword,
Forgetting stars, forgetting all beneath,
With lips and body I will be its sheath.

Anne Hall

ACTIONS AND WORDS

Love is a magnificent word.
Yet at times it can feel like a piercing sword.

Oh! Love makes two people feel happier than ever
When there are some beautiful words to deliver.

Words are only a part of the giving
For good actions create the most bountiful living.

A wink of the eye, a kiss on the cheek
Are only some of the signs each of us seeks.

Therefore give me a kiss give me a wink
And my day with God's day will nourish a link!

Rosemary Mishata

when your tears fall

when I see your tears fall my love, it's not without
knowledge that your soul is with pain. so then i must
embrace this intruder, with knowledge that your heart will
sustain. the love i feel for you can move all mountains,
can conquer all enemies. so then with sadness, i lay beneath
your breast, knowing that our love will suppress, your tears
my love and god's love. so cry, my love, strength and happiness
is upon us forever.

michael mccloud

LOVE ON THE WIND

Come stroll my love, come stroll with me, to journey by
the sea. You are my heart, my depth of soul, all
things my mind can see.

Come forth my love, come forth and take my hand.
Embrace the breeze, beguile the sun, with bare feet feel
the sand.

Come quickly love, come quickly along the shore.
Promise you will be my love, this day and forevermore.

Come sit my love, come sit so still and hear the
whispering sea. Listen to her secrets love and hold
them tenderly.

Goodbye my love, so long, farewell, until another day.
The wind has crumbled my chamber wall and took you,
my love away.

Frances V. Hadden

AT LOVE'S DOOR

I see your sweet smile,
That holds mine all the while.
With its tender touch,
That I love so much.
Each caress and kiss so true,
Holds my heart under skies of blue.
Then, as I hold your hand,
And side by side, we stand.
I know the Lord has blest me well,
With your love that tells,
Of these special moments tender and true,
For two.
Hold me close once more,
And never let me wander away from love's door,
So that we may sing forever, eternity's song,
Through these many days and the nights, ever long.
Where in the deepest embers of our souls,
Burns this love to have and to hold . . .

Glenna Gardner-Wimett

LANDSCAPE OF LOVE

There's a treasured spot here by the sea
It's the landscape of love of my Johnny & me
Where the moon casts a pale blue light
all around me in the night
His smiling face and his voice
ride the wind from this land of ours
to Vietnam
When the waves come rolling in
I can hear his voice whispering
I love you, I love you my lovely queen
Then I recall the diamond ring that he
placed on my lily white hand just
before he left for Vietnam
When the wind blows past my cheek
I can feel a special pulse beat
Then his fingers will smooth my hair
Just as if my Johnny were here
Just as if my Johnny were here

Marjorie Rinkel Graumenz

DORO THEOS

(from the Greek)

Wings of angels —
Wings of eagles —
Flying high in the empyrean sky.

Sent by God as Doro Theos,
Gifts of God who bear His gifts.

Heavenly angels, messengers of God —
Bearing love —
God's love — God's bounty —
God's caring —
But sometimes unable to complete His mission —
Sometimes finding God's messages unwanted —
Rejected for Earthly, worldly baubles.

Colorful, temporal baubles,
With appeal only to those unable to appreciate the
  munificence
Of the magnificence
Of the gifts of God
And, not comprehending them,
Reject them.

Dorothy M. Friedman

THE WONDERMENT OF LOVE

The wonderment of love echoes
From the valley of salted tears
And when the mountaintops cheer.
You are precious in my sight.
Forgive, love and come into my light.

Child of God, there is no darkness here.
Only I can wipe away all those tears.
Only I can bring you into the golden street
For heaven and earth becomes one in you and all shall meet.
It is I who opens the twelve gates of pearls.

For we are in but not of this world.
I am the way, the truth and the life.
Come and follow me, I am infinity.
This kingdom within you is the home of the free.
I am one with the Father and you are one with me.

All of God's creation is residing in an eternity
It is mortals' dream and immortality's reality
Behold, I make all things new. Oh, radiant bride!
Rest in the Father's inner basking,
Flowing is the wonderment of love.

Sue Ann Regan

THE DESERT OF TIME

As the winds blew,
  blew over the hills,
her heart held love, flowing as waters flow
  as the winds blow,
drifting as the leaves drift,
  the autumn leaves of red and gold.
And his heart held love as her heart did,
  and beat the rapture with hers.
But he was not there and she was bare.
  Long were the days on the desert of time
and her lips touched the wind
  where love had been,
  searching and looking.

Ruth Goldfarb

AFRAID TO LOVE

He says he doesn't love, and yet he mopes around and 'round
The house when she's a little late, or somehow can't be found.

He doesn't want to be tied down, no babes, no strings and yet,
There never was a child or dog he never stopped to pet.

Methinks that he protests too much, this tough but gentle guy,
I bet that when his babe is born, he'll shout it to the sky!

Someday he'll tell his little one and mother too, I know,
Of all his hopes and dreams and love that he was afraid to show.

Dena M. Kinzer

KINZER, DENA M. Born: Osage, Oklahoma, 5-25-29; Married: to Von Kinzer; Education: BSN, 1984; MPA, 1986; Occupations: Registered Nurse, Director of Nursing Service at Olympia Manor; Memberships: Washington State Nurses' Association, National & International Wildlife Association, University Women's Association; Poetry: 'Mt. St. Helens,' nature, *American Poetry Anthology,* May, 1983; 'Kings & Queens & Pawns,' philosophy, *American Poetry Anthology,* Summer, 1985; 'Jim,' religion, *American Poetry Anthology,* Summer, 1986; Comments: *I usually write when there is a significant event in my life, often concerning family, sometimes death, sometimes birth, or a happy event. I write songs and an occasional children's story. My latest project is animal-theme postcards and greeting cards. I write funny poems to my grandchildren, and make funny greeting cards for them.*

MY LOVE FOR YOU

My love for you came from God;
And it has lasted against all odds.
It was there through good times and bad times too;
It has kept me strong and it is still true.

My love for you is deeper than the sea;
A truer love it could not be.
Although you belong to another and may never be mine,
My love for you still lasts transcending all times!

Jean P. Jones

ELSE THE EGO

It's true that one must love their self
to learn of all their joy.
To see their way against the hate.
To sidestep anger's ploy.

But this be just a starting place
from wherein love must grow.
To reach out to another's plight
or else be but ego.

O. Felspar

GREEN, DAVID L. Pen Name: O. Felspar; Born: Sedalia, Missouri, 11-19-51; Education: University of Texas at Arlington, B.A., Journalism, 5-22-75; Occupation: Accountant; Awards: Golden Poet Award, World of Poetry Press, 1985; Poetry: 'You Yourself,' *American Poetry Anthology,* 10-84; 'The Laws of Man,' New York Poetry Society, 11-86; 'That Nature of God,' *Annals of Saint Anne De Beaupré,* 7-85; 'Amongst the Gale,' *Lutheran Digest,* 1-86; 'Oceanography,' World of Poetry Press, 11-84; Comments: *May the Lord bless and keep you surrounded by His love.*

Along the beach there's not a sound
For miles there's no one else around
The sky's been painted a brilliant blue
We're all alone — just me and you
As we walk along — you and me
I look at you and there I see
Sunlight dancing in your hair
Then we stop — just standing there
With your arms around me you hold me tight
Just being with you feels so right
I look to the depths within your eyes
I hope this feeling never dies
Your lips touch mine with a tender kiss
I never knew love could be like this
You're the one I've been looking for
Which makes me love you all the more
But if it comes that we should part
You'll forever hold the key to my heart

Sarah Redmill

NEIGHBORS TO THE SOUTH

The gates of heaven are open wide,
To usher in the weary traveler.
The earth's hustle and bustle,
Is left for the milky way.

Two vast continents are spanned,
One, greatly underdeveloped,
The other, seething with prosperity.
The two meet as strangers.

One has vast wealth, is thriving,
The other is poor, underfed.
What caused this great disparity?
The hot climate destroyed industry.

The Indians and black men,
Settled in the mountains and fields.
They did not learn to read,
They were so busy sowing and reaping.

Where is democracy, when they slave
In the fields all day?
They will vote in the elections,
For better housing and health care.

Elizabeth Saltz

SALTZ, ELIZABETH. Born: 6-15-30; Married: 9-63 to David Klinick; Education: Queens College, B.A., 1979; New School for Social Research; Queens College, M.A.; Occupations: Writer, Social Worker; Memberships: New School for Social Research (Philosophy); Social Worker, Department of Human Resources; Awards: Golden Poet Award, World of Poetry Press, 1985; *Who's Who in Poetry,* Sacramento, California, 17 Award of Merit Certificates; Poetry: 'What We Are,' 'Fate,' 'Egypt,' *New Voices,* Vantage Press, 1985; 'Freedom,' *World's Best Loved Poems,* 1984; 'Sea of Life,' World of Poetry Press, Sacramento, California, 1984; Comments: *Philosophy inspires the poet for he writes words of wisdom. Poetry is rhythmic verse which appeals to the senses. The emotions play a role as the poem appeals to the heart. Poetry can dramatize life until it becomes real. It portrays ideas that are meaningful.*

SEEKING IS NOT FINDING

I sought you in other lovers
And found your perceptive
Blackberry eyes with one —
Your sensuous, sensitive
Mouth with another —
And your small, strong
Hands with another.

But I never found you
Except with you —
So I've
Stopped
Looking.

Lorraine Standish

FOR SOUTHERN ROSE

Our beginning was filled with doubt
And trembling with hope
After many moments of tenderness,
Sharing and caring,
Love was found.

Though hard to define,
Love became as simple as touching,
Not always with our hands.
I hope the ending is not unlike
The beginning,
Though I would prefer our love
To be as lasting as our roots.

Leroy L. Moses

MY HUSBAND — MY LIFE

I sit here and wonder
If I allow myself
Of my husband — my Love
And what is left of our lives.

His health is such a worry
To lose him I can't concede —
This man that God knows I need.

The father of my children
Grandfather someday, I dream
Growing old — holding hands
This man and me.

Carol Jean

THE ARROW OF LOVE

The arrow of love from Cupid's bow
divides my heart in two, my love —
and all for you this heart does beat,
and breathe, and cling with broken hands
to Life

— and Love in your embrace.
and heals itself by missing you
and kissing you.
Oh Barbara Ann, renew my life!
My heart is good, my thoughts are true.
And never happy will I be
till you love me as I love you.

Dave Fonseca

THE CHANGING ROSE

One day I was walking
In a garden all alone,
When I saw a single rose
Growing from a stone.
As I took a few steps closer,
I noticed something strange,
That single rose's color
Always seemed to change.
Just then I saw the gardener
So I asked him right away,
"Why does this rose always change,
Why doesn't one color stay?"
He answered very clearly,
"This rose was sent from above,
For every time it changes
Someone falls in love."

Michelle Seiders

LOVE

Made between two
Shared with others
Tearing at our hearts
To be mended by another
A very precious gift
Often misused by all

Kristy Koenig

REUNITED

Along the sunset trails of life,
Old love meets again —
Lips smile, hearts recoil;
Remembering much pain.
Eyes meet, senses reel,
Faces flush, hands quiver;
Chills run up and down the spine,
Hearts palpitate, souls shiver.
Bodies merge automatically;
As if by magnet, driven;
Lovers cross time barriers;
The past erased — forgiven.
Pain and anguish of yesterday
Is consumed by the burning fire
Of two lives touched by fate;
Caught in the throes of desire.

Genevieve Locke Oliphant

WHAT HAVE I DONE?

If only we were together,
Holding each other tight.
Telling each other
All the things we want to hear.
But you're gone, so far away.
Not here, like you were yesterday.
What happened to the way things were?
Did I say something wrong
To make you go?
If I did, I wish you'd let me know.
I'll change anything you want me to.
If only I can be with you.
Please come back!
Hold me in your arms again.
I want you for more than a friend.
I love you!

Angela Williamson

HAWK MOUNTAIN, AUTUMN

Take me to the top of the mountain,
Together we'll look down,
As Autumn's perfect painting
Starts to form.
Then kiss me,
As the Sun and wind kiss us.
Look up, and see the hawk,
In all his splendor,
And know that looking down,
He's watching us,
In all of ours.

Robert F. Vitalos

VITALOS, ROBERT F. Born: Allentown, Pennsylvania, 10-31-47; Occupation: Electrical Worker; Memberships: PASCAL, Pennsylvania Association of Songwriters Composers and Lyricists; Awards: Honorable Mention, for 'Wind-Kissed,' World of Poetry, 1985; Poetry: 'Branches,' *American Poetry Anthology,* 1985; 'After All — You Are,' *Words of Praise, Vol II,* 1986; Comments: *I believe that it is time for the masses to get back to love, as a vehicle for expression of emotion. If we can do this, perhaps we can cancel out some of the hatred and violence our world has been pressured into.*

SCARED LITTLE WOMEN

Scared little women
Who never do know
What the future is made of
Reluctant to show
What their soul might be made of
Spring to your toes
Fly to the door
Throw it shut behind you and
Fall to the floor
Waste your time hiding?
Don't need anymore
Or are you mistaken?
With feelings at war

Robert J. Cierlitsky

GENTLE LOVE

It was love when first we met.
Tall mountains around the city set.
Holding the desert in your lap,
Using the crystal blue sky for your cap,
Like the birds and the century old trees,
You caress my spirit with a gentle breeze.
Bringing me forever under your spell.
I wonder why your secrets you never tell.
I love you.

Elizabeth Wright

EYES THAT SMILE AT ME

Sea foam windows to your soul
Pull at me
Watching, smiling to my smoky blue iris
I am absorbed within your gaze.

Lost in a sensation of wonder
I am kept dreamy-eyed,
Wanting to love you
With a passion I've yet to feel.

Close your eyes and mix with me
Take in all,
Warm me from the depths of my desire
With eyes that smile at me.

T. L. Rothwell

LOVER OF MY SOUL

I love a man, a silent man,
A man as tough as nails.
His faith and love and kindness
Are such that never fail.

I came to know him in my youth.
He's never let me down.
I'd trust him with the air I breathe.
His name's the sweetest sound.

Dear Jesus, lover of my soul,
My brother, King and Lord,
I rest my life upon your strength,
Your glory and your word.

Ilka E. Krieger

Maybe someday
the world will be united
all of us together
sharing
loving
no more wars
just peace
no more hate
just love
no more hunger
every stomach filled
what a crazy thought
all people living together
as one.
Well,
maybe . . . someday.

Vanessa Hobbs

LAMENT

I have known many lands
And many shrines,
My staff is planted
In the Apenines;
The fjords of the North,
And desert tents
Have been my homes;
In the dim Orient
I was a worshipper,
And nearer south
Have I knelt praying,
At the river's mouth.

Full many an ancient
Custom and belief
Have led my footsteps;
But my grief
Is unassuaged,
No god, however new,
Can dim the memory
Of my love of you.

Irene C. Hypps

MONONGAH MINE DISASTER

(December 6, 1907)

December sixth comes yet again;
The snow-topped slagpiles token pain.
In yon dark caves, brave spirits wait
Till Resurrection voids their fate,
Wait where last pledge of youth lies slain
Among their elders skilled in vain.

Oh River Westfork, time shall be
With thee the prisoners to free.
Till then, though snows add to our gloom,
We have the winter's wind for broom!
December's sun bids sad goodnight,
In hope of springtime's vision bright.

Now Westfork's willow-catkins bring
The longed for, vernal blush of spring.
I must awake these coal-strewn hills;
Bestir the streams in all our rills.
Be quick, Friend, fetch my flute ere I
Re-hark December's woes to cry.

Everett Francis Briggs

THE LOVE GAME

I have been out of the love game
for a long time now.
Still, I remember the lovers who
said they loved me, but did not.
And the ones who did love me but
I didn't love them.

I remember the loves that lasted
and those that did not.
There where those who were tender
and those who were not.

But most of all I recall loves
that were like comets flashing by,
Or rockets soaring to the sky.
Rare delights — and then a sigh.
Moments of joy — just passing by.

Edith Gulish

SOLSTICE

Outside the wind was howling
the snow was blowing everywhere
filling up the avenues
covering the square
We shared some wine with cheese
and watched the embers glow
and though we tried to sort it out
we couldn't make our feelings flow
Doomed from the start now it seems
riverside meetings, summertime dreams
breakfast in Greenwich
coffee and cream
Then came the fall
we drifted apart
no longer sharing
dreams of the heart
I saw you beneath
the big Christmas tree
shedding your tears
that weren't for me
And now one more kiss
for it's time to go
out to the streets
and into the snow

Steve Bedney

FIRST LOVE

I remember when I was young
love was new and exciting to me
our souls were one, together
and full of the love we had
built for each other
when you left, the wound, a
stab in my heart, poured out all
of my love for you
now you're gone, a wound still not healed
is looking for another
always not one but together

Antonia Sanchez

SILVER GODDESS

Diana, Diana, Goddess of the moon
how silver are your beams
I sing to you, I dance to you
I tell to you my dreams.

Diana, Diana, Goddess of the moon
how silver are your rays
your silver rays pierce my heart
and give to me such praise.

Diana, Diana, Goddess of the moon
I dread your leave Diana
your silver beauty softly glows
a silver boat among hiatus.

Diana, Diana, Goddess of the moon
your silent patience never fades
hear us who seek your guidance
and touch us with your favor.

Diana, Diana, Goddess of the moon
how silver are your beams
your silver rays pierce my heart
and bring to me such dreams.

Paula Carmichael

THE FOUR SEASONS

It all starts with summer, when the sun is warm and bright,
two come together, when their skin is tan and tight.
Their eyes glow with warmth, their affection naive and sweet,
you see they've made a commitment, theirs forever to keep.

Then as fall approaches, leaves begin to change color,
at the sign of a new season, they're unsure of each other.
The warmth is no longer there, coolness soon sets in,
and now as always happens, winter is to begin.

The new season brings a touch of cold, ice is hard and thick,
here's the true test to behold, the road is slippery and slick.
Can they stand the pressure, will they not explode,
now that they stand not together and haven't one another to hold?

Spring brings the winter thaw and new life begins to break forth,
forgiveness flows on the wings of warmth and new love begins to torch.
Where will you be when the cycle makes its final swing?
Will you be with your true love, or will you be doing a new thing?

Marty Hayes

DEATH OF MY LOVE

It is difficult to feel that she is dead.
Her presence, like the shadow of a wing, lingers upon me.
I can hear her voice, and for her step I listen.
My eyes look for her wonted coming with a strange,
Forgetful earnestness.
I cannot feel that she will no more come — that from her cheek
The delicate flush has faded, and the light
Dead in her soft dark eye, and on her lip,
That was so exquisitely pure, the dew of the damp grave has fallen!
Who so loved, is left among the living? Who had walked
The world with such a winning loveliness,
And on its bright brief journey gathered up such treasures
Of affection?
She was loved only as idols are. She was the pride of her friends
The daily joy of all who on her gracefulness might gaze,
And in the light and music of her way have a companion's portion.
Who could feel, while looking upon beauty such as hers,
That it would ever perish? It is like the melting of a star
Into the sky while you are gazing on it, or a dream
In its most ravishing sweetness rudely broken.

Glenn Edward Waters, III

THE RUNAWAY

As I huddled against the cold, mossy brick wall,
Stinging tears trickled down my cheeks.
I was in a silent, desolate alley many miles from home.
Home.
The thought of that word sent a pang into the depths of my heart,
Wringing out the remains of my hope.
Days ago, when I left, the endless tension between my parents
Had nearly ripped my mind apart.
Even our dear old shepherd whimpered and cringed into the corner
When one of them entered the room,
Fire in their eyes and a tight smile stretched across their lips.
I couldn't live a day longer in a house so full of hatred.
I raised my swollen, dirt-streaked face to take a breath of air.
At that moment, the moonlight struck the grimy phone booth
At the far end of the alley.
The booth seemed to glow, beckoning me towards it.
I shakily stood up and, slowly at first, began walking down the alley.
Then I couldn't fight it anymore.
I ran and, with the last grubby coin in my pocket,
Dialed home.

Kay Hasenknopf

LOVE LETTER

Dear Sir:
Refer our talk of this same date,
We do herein reiterate,
We offer love that's guaranteed
To gratify your every need.
We hope our sample satisfied
And if and when you should decide
To order from our merchandise,
We shall at no increase in price
Supply a love that long endures.
With best regards,
Sincerely Yours,

Beverly C. Graham

HEIDI

She's on her way to see me
it won't be long from now.
It should be quite a meeting
our hearts will show us how
I've missed her smiles,
I've missed her charms,
I've missed her warmth,
I've missed her arms.
I long again to kiss her
and hold her oh so tight
Soon we'll be together
to make things oh so right.

Robert Michael John Higgins

LOVE

Love will never grow old, it will always
mean the same.
There are many different kinds of love,
But love is not a game.
There is the kind of love you have
For a sister or a brother.
And there's the kind of love you have
For a father or mother.
There's the kind of love you have
For a very close friend.
There's also the kind between a man
And woman, that will never end.

Kathy Bonito

A MOTHER'S LOVE

A Mother's hands are gentle yet strong
To teach her children right from wrong
A Mother's smile can brighten the day
And make all sorrow fade away
A Mother's voice is strong and true
Knowing the words to see you through
A Mother's faith is so sincere
To ease her children's doubt and fear
A Mother's love grows through the years
She shares the laughter and the tears
A Mother's there until the end
For above all else, she is a friend.

Wanda Brown Lovell

TOGETHER — ME AND YOU

I'll *always* love you —
As if it was the first day I knew,
That we would spend a lifetime
Together, Me and You.
My heart yearned to be with you
And hold you so tight;
The world became better for me —
For *you* made it right.
And throughout the years with
All the kids that we raised;
Our love became stronger —
Instead of fading away.
Over half of my lifetime
Has now slipped away
With such wonderful memories
That to you I must say —
I'll always love you —
As if it was the first day I knew,
That we would spend a lifetime
Together, ME and YOU.

Gloria C. Williams

FOREVERMORE

(Starry Love)

Love is like a star:
Born screaming with the
First fiery rays of life and light.

Growing with time as it
Continually changes its composition,
Sometimes racing ahead . . .
Other times slowing its pace;

And, in time,
Pleading and crying out against
Inevitable death!

Then death . . . or so?
Don't the embers of both
Stars and love *really*
Live on . . .
. . . Forevermore?

Felix Meyer

YOU'RE STILL MISSED

I walk among the roses
Where first we met that day.
And memories still linger on
The same familiar way.

I try to hide the tear drops
As I sit to rest my feet.
I wonder if you'll call me love
The next time that we meet.

The hours never fade away
Without you on my mind.
You know I'm still in love with you
And will be for all time.

Now, as I slowly walk away
From here where we first kissed.
I whisper as I call your name,
"You know that you're still missed."

Richard L. Newcomb

MANEUVERS

Can we call it off?
The game, I see now, ought not
Continue.

Perhaps we should aim
For stalemate, for
How can I defeat you?
Lose to you?

Three full squares separate us, we pawns,
You are crouched, behind a shrub
Planning strategy:
Attack? Defend?

We are hysterical, we two
Skulking beneath bushes, hiding
Behind trees, peeking,
Through branches at each other.

Awaiting an attack,
Preparing to protect;
Would anyone suspect,
We were,
In love?

Kathleen Fitzpatrick

A SWEETER LOVE

The love we had of yesteryear
Is sweeter yet today.
The testing years have mellowed it
So now we both can say

I loved you then, I love you now
Our love has all been true.
And dear that love has meant so much.
My darling, I love you.

The fears and tears of yesteryears,
The hope, the faith, the truth,
Have made our love more precious than
It was in days of youth.

Through trials and temptations and
Through failures and success,
We've clung to one another and
We've clung to happiness.

We've worked and prayed together in
The struggles we've gone through,
And through it all we still can say
My darling I love you.

Gay Esther Ray

MOTHER

Your hands are so soothing
When my brow with fever burns;
Your voice is so tender
When my heart for sympathy yearns.
MY DARLING MOTHER

No love is more enduring
Through the passing years of time;
No triumphs more o'erwhelming
Than the daily feats of thine.
MY DARLING MOTHER!

Blanche Bradford Harryman

TO KATHY

When we argue,
say words we don't mean,
are we back into
the separate you and me?
I'm not a good lover;
we never have time
and the times we're together
never seem yours or mine.
If it never needs saying
how much I love you,
why do I feel I'm betraying
you, and acting the fool?
I'm not a good lover;
I don't give you time.
We're always doing other
things; we have to make time!

After I'm gone
I want to be born
again and again
to know you forever.

Joseph Simmons

SUNSHINE LOVE

The sun is shinin'
Down on me
With rays of love
From our Father, above.

Makin' me feel
Warm and alive
There's so much goodness;
All wrapped up inside.

Singin' to the birds
And playing around,
My sisters and brothers
Spreadin' endless
Love and laughter, abound.

I wish more days
Could be like this one,
'Cause I like sharin'
The warmth, with my friend,
Sunshine Love.

Kari L. Reber

February 14, 1986
Dearest Dianne,
Painted in
resignation upon the cityscape
you were the wild flower
whining for freedom
to me in esoteric code
Before you
I'd appeared estranged and, so
afflicted, God enjoined the quest
for entwined meadows where we
blossomed in quiet revelation
Then came
the church to cast us out
as though we were not sinners
in need of their salvation
I become that proverbial apostasy
Until this time ends
Love as always,

E. U. Mist

SONG BY THE SULU SEA

Sing-song song on coconut perch
of love in the island he will search.
Soft is the velvet of the jungle path
lithe is the leaf of banana plant.
Come-come the man to old palm say
come-come the woman, a gift, tonight to stay.
Open-open stars, to look upon the beach
down-down the moon shine they love each to each.
Island drum, may beat at night
to frighten spirit home,
so man can love on yonder sand
no more his heart to roam.
Over by the coconut
the island man has come
he wanders to the harbor
to see what can be done.
Soon he see the woman
awaiting there for he
island lamp of moonlight
close your eye and sleep.

Gloria T. August

PASSERSBY

The old man slumps on the wagon seat.
Reins hang loosely in his hands.
The air is sharp with winter's chill.
The horses plod, they are getting old,
Pulling the wagon, they climb the hill.
Flagstones on the road repeat
The turning wheels of sound.
Bumping and rocking the wagon sways
Over the broken ground.
The old man turns, looks up, and waves
His coat is wearing thin.
And from a window his neighbor says,
"I want a coat for him."
She rummages through an old dark trunk
And finds a coat outworn.
Then realizes with a kind of start
That the wagon now is gone.
She looks out toward the break of the hill
And hears the echoes of hoofbeats still.
And hears the faint echoes of hoofbeats . . . still.

Elinor Shurtleff Churchill

AN ENDLESS LOVE

My love for him is an endless love
It will go on and on through time
Did God send him like an angel from above
And is he going to be mine?

My love for him is like an endless river
It weaves in and out without stopping
When I think of his smile, I get a warm shiver
And my heart feels like it's dropping.

My love for him is an endless feeling
Always warm and tender
What I see in him is very appealing
And my love for him will never surrender.

My love for him is real and true
Deep down inside and way up above
Mixed with feelings old and new
It will be an endless love.

Marian Iannarino

QUALITIES INSIDE L-O-V-E

Love indeed is a many splendored thing
everyone should experience.
It is beautiful when it comes from deep inside.
This person who you so covet; to you,
and in spite of you is the one who's most qualified.
Love has many meanings depending on the
people involved; dealing with the main ingredients,
communication, understanding, plus patience to
make the relations blend well.
Some say it's at first sight which usually brings a belief,
but only scratches the surface to something deeper
than outer looks.

Love warms your whole body, then touches
depths of the inner emotions that are special.
Remember that to know love is to have been loved
which only could come from someone's heart.
It's like the dreaded cold, curable, but always
a chance to catch over and over again.
So next time you're lonely, empty and thinking there's no
light, look further than your sorrow;
because around the corner there's fulfillment, happiness,
plus sunshine within a person who likes you for you.

Wayne A. Lytle

SPEED AGAINST TIME

Sweet Sue, I love you.
Puppydogs and pussycats
hear the call through the streets
Sweet Sue I love You.
Then a horn AAOOOGAA!

In a lighted window
A pair of ponytails steals a quick peek
her heart racing, is it him? it is!
Got to steal away, out the back
out the yard . . . the race, speed against time

His touch . . . ecstacy
Why can't this go on forever?
This moment right now, go on forever
but it doesn't, you want to cry
Go home and dream.

In your silence you scream
Sweet Sue, I love you
AAAOOOGAA!
and you cry because it's not enough.
You scream, it's never enough!

Carolosue Wright

PEACHES

For Eileen

They lie in pottery bowl,
amber as setting sun.
Slicing into one, sparrows
gather on open window sill, longing
to drink from silent, deep flowing stream.

In the palm of my hand, one peach
sliced to the wetness of pit, becomes
the fleshy scent of you.
The faint memory of sticky, sweet
summer evenings, sprawled beneath cathedral sky.

Steve K. Bertrand

STARDUST

Moving along the long corridor of life; behind many doors there's happiness or strife.
Hearing repercussions of footsteps as I walk; as at the doors in the corridor I knock.
Footsteps that became a muffled sound; as I reached the light at the terminus redound.
Passageways that yielded avenues of reconsecration; through many doors of machination.
Hearing sounds of trumpets and a mandolin; seeing slight "luminous emissions" therein.
Keys I've tried along the corridor; this time, from within, someone unlocked the door.
A specific doorway I knocked on long ago; was opened by a Delilah of a celestial glow.
We walked heart in heart, our souls taking flight; her and I together, toward the light.
Then one day our lovely friendship faded in the dawn; fires of love in her eyes, gone.
It was then that she took her eyes off mine; her hands loosened from my grips entwine.
She knocked on a new door as sorrow shot its darts; opening up to the knave of hearts.
Time went by, but there! The archangel Gabriel; he held in his hands a sacred scroll.
The hand of Gabriel opened a door in front of me; there I saw in a vision, my destiny.
As I reached out for her, in joyous hurrah; turning, I saw the broken soul of Delilah.
For her was it fate invoked? But new sounds of footsteps of our new love evenly yoked!
Hearts propelled by a solar wind's thrust! Our dreams fulfilled, in heavenly stardust.

Bernie Claus

TO LOVE LIFE

What's the point? Why even bother? At first I was, that's all, I was.
And then as time passed, I grew, I saw, I talked and lived.
All the world was a lake and I a sponge to soak up the last drop.
I rushed through life washing games aside but clutching a toy soldier.
And then one day he too I dropped — keeping his uniform for my own.
People with their faces blurred by thousands of places
As I elbowed my way around the world and back again . . .
Pausing only long enough to start once more.
In earnest I quested each windmill, tilting one after another in
Endless succession until one day they too whispered away.
Then one night as I sat waiting for Halley, I knew I was truly alone.
Too late I saw flowers I never stopped for and golden curls caress.
And that my grave, as my life, will be dug in haste, left unmarked,
Forever unnoticed, a meaningless non-event.
So with trembling finger I write my life across the sky for all to see.
And there to linger till a breeze gently erases us both from the world.

Hawk Freeman

WHERE IS MY LOVE NOW?

As I sit and stare out my window, I feel winter trapping me in its presence.
The leaves turning, falling to the ground.
The smell of wood burning fills the air.
Days get shorter and nights grow longer, colder.
There is still the precious memory of my love.
I see him everywhere I go; everything I do.
He invades me so; where is my love now?
That one night we shared together feels like yesterday.
Waves gently landing on the beach; the moon slowly coming out glistening on
the water.
His gentle and caring touch grasping me and holding me forever.
Does that touch still mean something to him?
Am I still in his dreams?
Was it a reality or a dream world?
Where is my love now?

Barbara Silver

TREASURE

You're the rose that makes the thorn seem less painful —
You're the laughter that keeps the tears away —
You're the hope that sustains my wildest dreams —
You're the rainbow at the end of my gloomiest day —
You're the faith that covets my craziest schemes —
You're my golden yesterdays I'll cherish for each tomorrow —
And in loneliness you'll be my fondest mem'ry when there's only sorrow —

Betty Allen

A BABY'S LOVE

Smile, baby mine,
With your sweet smile showing
Trace of dimples, yet unknowing
Of your magical charm.
God has bestowed you to our family
What a pleasure!
And in what great measure
He is good to us.

So laugh, baby mine,
Don't mind if we laugh with you,
Mirthfully gazing into two
Twilight eyes that capture.
You bring hope into a world
That seems a trifle jaded,
For life is never faded
With a baby's love.

Vivienne Florence Meyer

FOUND AND LOST

How do you know that it is love
because you cry at the
slightest difference?
Or is it, because when you're
together
You feel as if you're one?

No, you are all stupid fools;
falling for the same old lines.
People keep telling you,
only you don't want to listen -
until it's . . . too late

The moon no longer
beams
into your hazy eyes.
You're lost but not into yourself
you're lost in the lover's eyes
The trap is set
and your heart dies
in the blue sky of the day.

Christina Marie Orofino

FALL

His blue Colorado
bumping down Ninth Avenue.
Holland Tunnel.
Skyline fading away
as I lie back
shivering on the seat.

Roseland, New Jersey.
A brown duplex.
His arms welcome me.
The silence was next.

The evening began.
My fever was gone.
A wordless dinner
in a desolated Howard Johnson.

Then
pieces of flesh
scattered on the white sheets
of the night.

Laurent Gagliardi

MARTINIQUE

We walked along a body wide trace,
Into the liana-draped jungle.
Through cathedrals of giant bamboo,
Above gorges filled with ferns.

Behind us lay stone columns and silent fountains,
Flowering arbors of oleander;
Plantation built on other men's greed,
Long ruined by bassignac and genip trees.

Before us, the foothills of Mount Pelee;
Where the river trickles in birth.
The sky shut out by hundred-foot palms,
Alone in wonderland, to mix with the magic earth.

Beneath the giant mango,
In the sands of windward stream;
The storm of fire first touched me,
Gentle woman, now but part of memory's dream.

Mark Richards

TWILIGHT LOVE LOST

The mist of morning shrouds his face.
His gaze scans the tree-lined shore of the nearby creek,
Searching in vain for that familiar face.
Moisture glistens on those weathered cheeks.

Seven long years were spent together.
Duke's unyielding faithfulness,
A constant companion in any weather,
Proved itself time and again in peace and in stress.

The old man and his dog were inseparable,
From sitting at home to hunting small game.
Never alone since the passing of his wife, Mable,
His voice quivers and breaks as he cries Duke's name.

You see, they found Duke's body among those trees.
Death again has torn him apart
From one he loved and who gave him peace.
Painfully, he clutches at his aching heart.

Karen Sue Wittkowski

GOD IS LOVE REGARDLESS

You may do what you please,
But you do not change God!
GOD IS LOVE, REGARDLESS!
You may revile Him and curse Him,
You may say He does not exist,
You may give Man or any unknown factor credit
For the great and miraculous things He does,
Like free sunshine, rain, seedtime and harvest,
Like free choice, to love Him and receive Him,
Or reject Him as all unbelievers do.
No matter what you choose, or how you live,
GOD IS LOVE! UNCHANGEABLE LOVE!
You cannot change God,
But He can change you!
Your eternal destiny is your choice,
Your acceptance or rejection of Him your choice,
Heaven or Hell, your choice.
BUT GOD IS LOVE!
FOREVER, ETERNALLY,
REGARDLESS!

Eliza Tyler Taylor

LOVE, FROM A PEN PAL

Love songs I send, soft notes
Confessing my love, my innermost thoughts —
Hoping your feelings for me are of love.
From a distance, I wait for your reply . . .
In my mind, I recall your beauty —
Like the spring flowers . . . so fresh, so sweet.

The time is near, soon we will meet.
Like Cyrano I need someone to converse with —
To tell of my love, if only my lips would open &
Allow my heart to speak . . .
It's so easy with a pen.

Love poems I send,
Hoping when we meet, you will
Understand . . .
If the words fail me —
I'll sing a song of love!

Wally Kibler

KIBLER, WALLACE EDWARD. Pen Names: Mark James, Wally Kibler; Born: 1-28-36; Education: High school graduate, many writing courses, writing conferences, workshops; Occupations: Machinist, Greif Brothers Corp., 1954-1974; Working for Proctor and Gamble Co. since 1974; Memberships: Songwriter's Club of America, Applying for membership in ASCAP; Other Writings: "Homework of Whitman and Poe," *Odessa Poetry Review,* 4-86; "Edgar Allan and Me," "A Message Through Me," "5,000 and 185," "Joy," "The Jogger and His Dog," all published by Yes Press, 1986; Songs: "Jack and Bobby," rock, 2-25-86; "Fantastic Lady," love, 2-7-86; "Lions and Tigers," rock, 3-21-86; "He Works Days," country and western, 12-15-85; "Bar Hopping," country and western, 9-25-85; Comments: *Writing poetry is therapy for the soul . . . This inner being . . . Unseen . . . Writing of a past event . . . Of a person with historical significance . . . Images of the past come into view . . . Through poetry I seem to be back and even then!*

THAT GIRL FROM MADISON

She is tall and she is pretty, and her hair is chestnut brown.
She's a girl that I can lean on, and she'll never let me down.
She's like dewdrops on the roses; glist'ning in the golden sun.
She's my dream of life, she's my darling wife, she's that girl from Madison.

I recall the night I met her. It was at the country store.
And the moment I beheld her, I knew then my search was o'er.
Then that night I sat beside her, as the old bus made its run
And I fell in love with that mountain dove. She's that girl from Madison.

If my life could be lived over, I would live it o'er the same.
I would meet this Angel tender. I would court her, change her name.
We would have our darling children. They are precious, every one.
And she's Queen you see, in our family. She's that girl from Madison.

Ernest T. Presnell, Jr.

DREAMS — VISIONS — LOVE!

I've had such dreams, visions of things I hope would be
I dreamed dreams of times gone by and what the future holds for me,
I think of all Eternity, imagining a place sublime
Holding dear the images of those we loved in time.

Of Angels guiding from above
Our every act of work and love,
Of miracles sent down each time we pray
These acts of love — happening every day.

I hold these visions, these dreams of undying love
An expression of peace from Heaven above,
These dreams, these visions that have to be
This perfect love brings unity with our God, especially for me.

Lee Vendetti Paolella

PRAISES

You are the star that shines beyond the promises of yesterday
You are the twilight's silver dancers chasing all my doubts away
You are the gentle kiss of springtime after winter's harshest snow
You are the promises of summer and the sunset's amber glow
You are the trees that give me shelter from a gentle April rain
You are the whisper of tomorrow and the hope to live again
You are the color of the sky above that perfect day in June
You are the essence of my joy, a blend of hearts in perfect tune
You are the beginning of my day and the ending of each night
You are the keeper of my soul and the treasurer of my delight
You are the Love that's given freely by the splendor of your grace
And although I am unworthy, like a child I've made mistakes
But your Love remains within me lending strength when I would fall
Loving you has made me richer, you're the greatest gift of all

Elizabeth E. La Grange

MY LIFE WORTH LIVING IS YOU

For every beat of my heart, is a deeper beat of my love for you . . .
With each added day, is another one to share with you . . .
With each added embrace, makes our foundation of love stronger . . .
What I feel deep within, is of a personal happy bliss . . .
For the love I have so deep within for you will never be shared or given again . . .

All my love now and through eternity . . .
Ann

Ann F. Cuomo Gallo

LET ME

I see you existing day to day,
Living together yet so alone.
Merely going through the motions
Wondering where it all went wrong.
Truthful eyes reflect your tears
Betraying the sorrow of your heart.
Like a house where no one lives,
Sadly forgotten and dark.

Let me touch the hurt and
Wipe the tears away.
Gently caress your heart and
Keep the loneliness at bay.
Let me ease your sorrow and
Renew the inner joy
Accept without guilt or doubt
The love my heart for you holds.

Barbara C. Oord

VARIATION ON A THEME — I

There was no kiss between us save
The awkward, boyish one you gave
Quite publicly;
No secret clasping of the hands
To cherish — not a touch
To be remembered later; not very much —
Only a naked look of tenderness,
Heart-deep;
A marriage of the eyes
That made the whole world, after,
Take the hues and depths of love;
Only shared and secret laughter,
And, once, tears shed.

Yet, in my solitary bed,
I feel as wedded as though holy vows
Rang living through the air!

Adah H. Larisch

EINSTEIN

Einstein raises his fiddlestick —
Space obeys him
and stretches like a tent

Einstein touches the strings —
The universe flows
between his fingers

He begins to play —
Rounded space
vibrates with music
The line becomes a circle

The outline of infinity
less and less clear
retreats into the depth
of the mind

Teresa Truszkowska

MY GIFT TO YOU

I wish there were a wishing tree
Of words that I could say,
To speak of all my love for you,
In every special way.

I'd capture birds and butterflies,
From every leaf and limb,
Collage for you fine nature's wares,
Frame them to suit your whims.

I'd grommet all the sunshine bright,
Then filter it with care . . .
Go gather shimmering moonbeams,
That dance on evening's air.

And as the hours slip quietly by,
From twilight into dawn,
Collect from leaves the morning dew
To renew the wish I pawn.

Clara Mays Benson

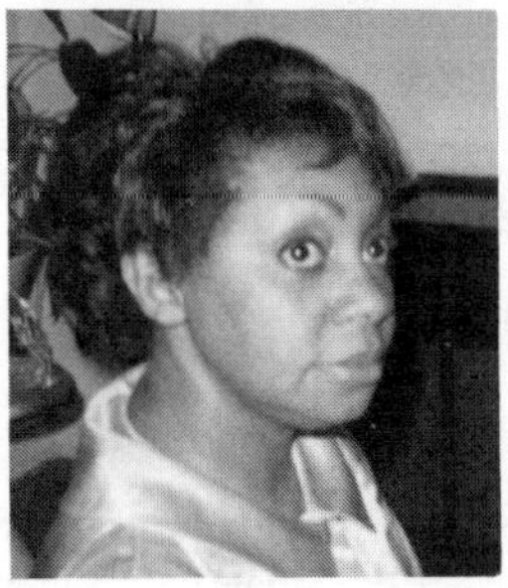

BENSON, CLARA MAYS. Pen Name: Rusta "B"; Born: Darby Township, Pennsylvania, 2-3-32; Married: 12-20-58 to Dr. Floyd Stephen Benson, one child, Stephen Eugene, 18 years old; Education: Tyler School of Art, M.Ed., Fine Arts, 1962; Fitchburg State University, Certificate of Art Supervision, 1975; Occupation: Mother, Homemaker, Educator, Artist, Freelance Photographer, Writer of children's plays, stories, poetry; Memberships: DSEA, PATA, PEA, NEA, Massachusetts Association of Craftsmen, Harvard Craftsmen, and Nashoba Art Association, of Board of Directors; Awards: In drawing, painting, sculpture and other art creations, 1965; 'Locust Tree Leaves,' 1974; 'Rudkin Place,' 1974; 'Sea Thing,' 1974; 'Morning Hair Combing,' 1975; Macrame, Sculpture and Soft Sculpture; Poetry: 'Creativity Rebukes Ignorance, Waste and Bigotry,' *American Poetry Anthology,* 1985; Other Writings: "Professor Higgins Joins the Space Race," Children's Play, 1965; "A Gumper Christmas," Children's Play, 1966; "How To Make a Tissue Paper Wreath," How-To Booklet, 1984; Events — Membership Drive Banquet NAACP, 1983 Log, Photography, Montgomery County, Maryland; Comments: *Writing has become another means of expressing my thoughts and ideas . . . This is definitely so with poetry. My tools, materials, and subjects for expression are thus well diversified so that I may choose the media or means which best interprets the scene or circumstance in each of my final statements. Thereby I, upon using my individual style and approach, continually strive graphically to record the encountered universal environment with camera, clay, brush, and pen. How do we know where we're going if we don't know where we've been?*

MY FRIEND

All I have is yours, for all I need is you
When all the others have let me down
You alone are true.

You're always there when I need a friend
You always have an ear to lend.
You share my joy, you share my sorrow
Please share my life and all my tomorrows.

Bonnie L. Weatherford

A STUBBORN LOVE

My love
Is a stubborn love
Which must live of itself
And attach itself
To whomever it will
And linger there
'Til the last thread of hope
Is gone.

Paul A. Hughes

LOVE IN FLIGHT

I was your kite
You flew me high
I felt the wind in my hair
I danced with the flight
I was kissed by the sun
I was not afraid of the height
I was secure with you
holding the strings.

Sonja J. Aubin

GOD IS LOVE

The Bible teaches, I believe,
No greater love can man receive,
Than the love of God sent from above;
Nothing can surpass this bond of love.
He proved his love there on the cross,
Sending his Son to die for the lost.
What greater love could there ever be,
Than giving Jesus for you and me.

Barbara L. Clark

SUNSET UPON SUNSET

Sunset upon sunset our love
will grow;
Sunset upon sunset our love
will grow old;
Sunset upon sunset our love
will die,
Sunset upon sunset young love
will fly.

Marla Lilly

A HEART FILLED WITH LOVE

Of material things
I've none to give you,
Only a heart filled with love
That will long outlive you.

If in an ocean drowning,
Quickly would I swim to save you;
No reward seek I for self
Nor hope I to enslave you.

With a heart filled with devotion,
In humility I stand before you,
Seeking only the right to love
To serve and adore you.

And if throughout my lifetime
This happiness you deny me,
Sadly would I grieve
And sorely would it try me.

Cora Lee Prince

FINALLY — A FRIEND

I found a friend
while out on the wave
of my uncertainty.
Caught up
in the steady pull of his smile
and with the reflection
of December nights in his eyes,
he was a guide
for my sails.
I'd been drifting
through the seasons
with no anchor —
gathering strength
to try once more
for shore,
when this strong hand
touched mine
and gave me the courage
to come through
and care again.

Mary D. Foster

IMPRISONED

Don't tie me down
my love can go around
you always imprison me
when I need a friend's company
you're real pushy with me
you make me feel lost at sea

I feel like Jonah and you're the whale
a friend's love is the only bail
that will release me from your jail

I'm drowning in your wave of demands
I wish that you could understand
sometimes I need a friendly hand

you trap me in an ocean of jealousy
you make it hard for me to breathe
unlock your heart and set me free
please don't imprison me

Doreen Lee

GOLDEN ANNIVERSARY

Golden are the years gone by,
Since that moment in our life
When I became your husband,
And you became my wife.

Golden is the bond of love
That ties our hearts together
Regardless of adversity,
We know 'twill stay forever.

Golden are the years before us.
Gone the turbulence of youth.
Many are the friends we've gathered
In our searching for the truth.

Golden are the prayers we're asking,
As we celebrate this day.
Fifty years of life together
May God bless us all the way.

Edward G. Tilma

SEASONS OF LOVE

Is there anything as wonderful
As passion in the spring?
When warm winds blow, and flowers grow
Young, burning blood must sing.

Is there anything as heavenly
As love on summer nights?
When starry skies, and dreamy eyes
Embrace with such delights.

Is there anything as pleasing
As the rich autumnal air?
When colors creep, and couples reap
The harvest they now share.

Is there anything as comforting
As winter's pallid poem?
When those you love, and God above
Will lead you gently home.

J. Benjamin

LOVE ME NOW

If you're ever going to love me,
Tell me now, while I'm alive,
For lovely flowers, I cannot smell
When beneath the sod, I lie.

And a cold and lonely marker,
Makes a tombstone for my head,
But cannot give me comfort,
or warmth, when I am dead.

For the words are like soft music
That is soothing to my ears,
And when they're said sincerely,
Gives one comfort through the years.

And you'll never, ever know how much,
It cheers me on my way — just to hear
you say "I love you,"
So, please tell me so, today.

Toni Figueroa

ALL IN A GLANCE

We met, you and I
On a desert island
In the midst of a crowd
We didn't notice.
Our eyes met and,
In our minds,
Our lips touched and
We were alone.
We went for a walk on the moonlit beach
Hand in hand
Walking through the foam.
Then we were swimming.
Skinnydipping in a mountain pool
The water cascading on our heads.
Our souls touched and
We were one.
You smiled and
We were together.
All by ourselves,
Alone in our eyes.

Kelle LeCompte

DEATH DIED A THOUSAND TIMES

My heart, it grows weary
My eyes, they grow weak
My body is exhausted
I'm too tired to speak

My dreams of the future
Have been shattered by your blow
I feel drained
My heartbeat's getting slow

Your words have indeed come as a shock
For in my heart I could not see
What happened to our love
What happened to you and me

You have freed yourself at last
You do not have to pay for your crimes
For how could you have known
Of my death died a thousand times

Loretta Bivens

SUZY

I miss you most when mornings break
With only you and I awake.
A lick, a look, a wag of tail,
Then out the door and on the trail.

Old legs were stiff toward the end
But I could understand, My Friend.
And button eyes that used to shine
Were dimmed a bit with passing time.

And when a step would prove too steep,
Though once you'd take it with a leap,
You understood the lift or shove
Was just a way to show my love.

But now, Old Friend, you're gone at last,
The touch of tongue and hand are past.
I hold you still, though we're apart,
Not with my arms — but in my heart.

William M. Sands

Aug. de St Aubin del.

REFLECTION

I look into your eyes. It's like looking in a mirror; I see me.

I feel the love, the want and the need to belong.

Our minds seem to penetrate deep into each other's soul; searching, picking up vibes that only the two of us, so very much alike, can really understand.

It's like a force connecting our minds, thoughts and souls together, perhaps turning us into one.

To love you is to love me, myself. We have willed ourselves into one.

Now we are one. Which inner soul will take control?

Will there be a tug of war to determine which one is the strongest? Or will the power of force be broken; dividing us, sending us our separate ways because we are too stubborn to give in to each other's love?

Nan Blackshire Little

SILVER TOMBSTONE

To a Rose born in the month of awakening — on the seventeenth

In the month of awakening (on the seventeenth),
Burst forth a Rose — (Eve).
I wrote her name upon the strand that day, but the waves came in
And washed it away. I sang her a lullaby, the way lullabies are sung
To cloy the babes to sleep. She played the role of the child.
So innocently minded (so real). I tried again, and engraved her name
Within the sapwood of our tree of promise.
Her name was immutable (status quo) thought I, until a tempestuous
Blast stole away what no longer belongs to me.

Who will lament for my deficiency, and who will gather the seed of
My misery? Calm and still as night must I remain. For I have built a
Monument before myself . . .(A SILVER TOMBSTONE) that stills the
Distant ring — screeching of a trumpet.
I have adulterated myself before my God.
Still, all that remains is a silver tombstone.

Robert Maldonado

ANOTHER PASS

I work in a place where the old men flirt with the young girls, and the young guys play with you for fun, their wives unaware or uncaring . . .

Where is the love and where is the heart in matters of passion and how does the soul fail to see the sun? Who cares and why bother to smother yourself with truth and high ideals? If love is strong in the body, does all restraint fail with a fantasy?

I see men swing low for assumptions, a gullible pause for a touch of your hand . . . to kiss despite all meaning. I see myself wanting it anyhow; taking it anyway, if just for the moment, if just for the night. To yearn and not wait can be so lonely, but to have it over in the midnight hour cuts too deep and bleeds and hurts beyond tears . . . oh, the confessions of a misunderstanding . . .

I work in a place that puts reason in its place; a dream of passing hours, a day of charades with a smile. A job, another day, another pass.

Helene Suzanne Pomeroy

LOVE'S BAPTISM

I'm ceded, I've stopped being theirs;
The name they dropped upon my face
With water, in the country church,
Is finished using now,
And they can put it with my dolls,
My childhood, and the string of spools
I've finished threading too.

Baptized before without the choice,
But this time conciously, of grace
Unto supremest name,
Called to my full, the crescent dropped,
Existence's whole arc filled up
With one small diadem.

My second rank, too small the first,
Crowned, crowing on my father's breast,
A half unconscious queen;
But this time, adequate, erect,
With will to choose or to reject,
And I choose — just a throne.

Emily Dickinson

INFIDELITY

HONORABLE MENTION

Michael under the hood
In love with a Holley carb
Ford jacket, sleeves pushed up
Combed his hair sometime yesterday
Up to his elbows in grease.
Stored in a spiral notebook
His dream car waits
Engine and body, down to the mags
Every bolt is planned.
Stored in the bottom of a locker
His homework waits
Growing like fungus.
Oblivious, Michael dreams
Lost to the classifieds
Smiling secretly
And humming Van Halen.
Then Big Boy's and a blonde
And the car sits idle
Upstaged by a movie
Forgotten in a moment of pizza.

Sheryl Morang

BECAUSE I STILL LOVE YOU

Lots of work is true,
Some fun and pleasure too,
Honesty and trust are found,
That's what makes the world go 'round,
Because I still love you.

Mix, stir and prepare,
A delicious dinner to share,
Washing, sewing are a few,
But I'll do them gladly for you,
Because I still love you.

Have children that is true,
Like the old lady in the shoe,
Stay at home, toil and sweat,
Feed and care for them, no regret,
Because I still love you.

Beth Nahlik

RISKING

Sadness builds up inside
until you feel like it's going to spill over . . .
So, you take a deep breath and say,
"No, I'm all right."
But, you're really not . . .
and the hurting goes on —
Because you keep it inside.
Never needing anyone . . .
Never reaching out . . .
or letting anyone reach in.
So much to say, yet, I feel you backing off . . .
Feeling the pain as I see the shutdown come . . .
Risking is so hard.
Can you see how much it took from me to risk you knowing me openly and honestly?
Realizing and feeling the sadness of my defenses coming up . . .
How can I tell you what's on my mind, if I can't get close?
How can I tell you what I feel inside, if I can't reach you?
The only real gift I can give you is me.
Give me a chance, my love . . . give me a chance —
To share me with you.

Karen S. Lewis

TO MY CHILD

Child, too young to speak or hear, maybe only a suspicion, or paranoia. Still I worry for you, for me. What kind of life will we have? Will you be a reflection of me, or of the other . . . an unknown body whose personality is a mystery?

Child, will you resent me, or I, you? Now, I am afraid of you, of your power; power to remind me of an afternoon spent in a dream, shattered by your reality. Will I nurture you, or erase you from my body and place you in my memory to reflect upon in times of perplexity? Now, if at all, you are no more than an insect clinging to the wall that nurtures you . . . But in time, you could cry to me, talk to me, and rely on me.

But for now, Little One, you must respect my decision. For I am one of your creators; the only one with a knowledge of you, or a concern. Please believe that my decision, whichever I choose, is what I think the wisest. I may be wrong, for I, too, am a child, but forgive me . . . Let me save you: the product of my stupidity. I'd never hurt you willingly, but I may have to destroy you now while you are barely living, than destroy you emotionally in years to come. I know you may not understand, 'cause you are too small, but it is your right to know . . . and my right . . . to detach you from the wall you thrive on. I will not watch you die, but I can't let you live now. Now, I am young. I still need time; time to be my own person, before I can give life . . . to you.

Leila Anne Brazo

REST IN PEACE MY FRIEND

I never knew you — we never met, though sometimes I wish we had.
You were so tiny and pure, like a chaste white dove in the morn.
You didn't even have a chance.
And sometimes I wonder . . .
Sometimes I wonder what you would look like, how you would act,
or some of your interests.
Sometimes I wonder how our family would be if you were here
To be part of it now.
Sometimes I wonder if we'd be close like a sunset or as distant as a storm.
Sometimes I wonder how life would be different if you were a part of mine now.
But every time I wonder, the question remains the same — why?
Why would a child born so of God be taken of her life so young?
I've overlooked so many reasons only to find that it can't be answered.
Maybe it's better that way.
I never knew you and my apologies I send, for the only proof of your existence,
Lies in an urn of ashes my friend.
I never knew you, but someday we'll meet, for God will take me too.
I never knew you and for those four words — I'm sorry.
The loss was that of mine.
On that day, when my life does end — we'll finally rest together my friend.

Dana L. Orient

FOREVER US

Can anything be lovelier
than what we have to share,
Lying close together
a very loving pair . . .

You reach across the chasms
of the worlds we live apart,
And draw our souls together
on journeys that we embark . . .

I look into your eyes and
see a quiet starry light,
Then you draw me even closer
Into the velvet summer night . . .

Gazing through the branches
while lying side by side,
Crested waves of rapture
the slowly ebbing tide . . .

Can anything be lovelier
When what we have is best?
With love and inspiration
know we are heaven blessed . . .

Mark Kelley

THE SEASONS

It is now almost November
Last night we had a rain
The trees look sad and lonely.
Will they ever look bright again?

As they looked in the sunshine last Sunday
With their leaves all red and gold?
It is sad to think in one short week
They could become so ugly and old.

But the trees are not dead but sleeping
They will bloom again in the spring
Birds will nest in their branches,
When summer has come again.

Time is our bitterest enemy
It is also our dearest friend
This life with its cares and sorrows
Will always come to an end.

But we know there is a tomorrow
And we need never despair
We see love all around us
We find it in answered prayer.

Twila H. Trickle

Maybe this time,
And really, who can tell,
Reality might test true,
To whims, that wishes yell,
And love could stay with you
Reaching each and every cell,
Until you're full of bliss,
Believing every kiss to dwell
In perfect harmony,
Near the places, none can tell,
Inside your very heart,
Calm, at last, and well.

Dennis L. Clark

THE FOLLOWERS

They asked me to lead them, as I was old and they were new.
I inspired them, they said, set their hearts on fire.
They did not know the way, so I led them.
And while I led them, they gave me directions . . .
Which I ignored.

And on our way the nights became weeks, then months . . .
Knowing the path to be hard, I stayed true, and did not dally . . .
They, being young and selfish, had to stop for flowers and
Fruits,
To drink cool water . . .
I, being older, urged them to stay to the path and not to
Stray, as the perils were great, and our time so short . . .
After much urging and no one to listen, I forgot them . . .
And soon found the way home.
They, however, were still lost on the path. And I, being
Old, was too weary to find them.

Jo Hendijani

TO MY MOM

You are my best friend. You're beautiful and sweet. You're always there when I need you. You're there to talk with, walk with, cry with, and laugh with.

I may not always obey you, but I'm just a teenager. I know I do things you don't understand or agree with. But I'm just living life the way I want and see it. I'll learn by my mistakes.

We may fight and argue, but we always make up. I admire you very much. And respect you, you're a giver not a taker. You want to be friends with everybody.

I know you want me to be happy and have a beautiful life. I may not always be the best daughter in the world, but I really do try, and I know I don't always tell you I love you. So I wrote this just to tell you that,

I LOVE YOU!

Maria Fry

BURNING EMBERS

I will never forget the way you said my name that night in late August, early in the darkness, just after midnight . . .

You spoke in a tone of breathless passion; your satisfaction adorned me and the warmth of your breath upon my neck eased me into a lullaby of sorts.

The miles that had been between us lay like ashes at our feet; burning embers lit a fire in your room and in our silent moment the embrace burned a fire in your heart.

I will never forget your gentle kiss on that last Sunday morning as you eased your love into my body and held my soul for ransom.

A thousand weekends ago I had you for a dream, and even now I toss in a burning sleep, loving you still, and wanting you more. No, I will never forget you, nor the echo of your voice calling my name.

Helene Suzanne Pomeroy

TOUCHED BY LOVE

Touched by you
I feel alive yet blue
At the same time —
Touched by your heart
Feeling as though we can
Never be too far apart —
But can we find the time
To be touched by life
Touched by love
Through both our lives
And our worlds —
Feeling the coldness
And the bitterness
Of being alive in a hard world
As long as we have each other
We can overcome these things
And try to reach a world
Try to touch a life
That isn't touched by love
That hopefully one day
Someday soon
Will be touched by us

Lisa DeDomenico

LOVE

Love is so many different things
different to each person
love is like a bird on wing
it flies into our lives
it makes a person want to sing
when that romance starts
it lightens all our burdens
it brightens up our hearts
it makes other problems seem small
it makes a short man tall
it is a bit of wonder
to those who are unloved
it puts ill thoughts asunder
and we know it is God's will
for the greatest love of all
he showed upon the cross
and if we love him still
consider love no loss
a man can love a woman
a mother love her child
but the unending love of God
can always make you smile

Hazel Carestia

UNDERSTANDING US

I can prove to you my Love by
understanding your doubts.

But I can shed tears and not
expect dreams to come true.

But when you hold me in your arms
I am alive, and to live in peace
with Loving arms around me.

I can't expect the world to
understand us.

But for us to understand each
other.

Judith Virbukas

LOVE OVER GOLD

The sparkle of diamonds rivals the sun,
sapphire shines blue deeper than the sky,
emeralds more luscious green than new grass:
these are the ways of a material world.
Sometimes I feel we are out of place here,
That we belong to a different time and place,
where feelings are more important than gems,
and having someone to love is life itself.
Perhaps we are of the romantic Victorian era,
yet I think not, for we are far from prudish.
More likely we are of a time and space
that has not yet arrived on this earth,
a time when peace rules the earth,
when love rates higher than gold.
Though we be poor in material gain,
we are wealthy in the knowledge that in our love
we are stronger than either of us alone,
and rich with a love that will outlast time itself.

Rebecca Ruth Whalen

ROSE OF MY HEART

I'm sending you some roses, cut out of my heart
I couldn't send real roses when it came time to depart
But these are better anyway
So please don't ever throw them away
For they shall never fade and die
Unless you forget and let them lie.
Neglect for roses as well as hearts
Is when the cruel slow death starts
But with a little loving care
They will go with you anywhere
And if you are ever feeling blue
Here is all you'll have to do
Just hold these roses to your heart
And you will feel the warmness start
For this heart lives only for you.
In spite of anything I do
You are the roses of my heart
Though we may be miles apart.

Eugene A. Dixon

IT'S YOU, MY LOVE

It isn't the latest in fashions —
Or the flowers you bring,
It's your smile — your voice — your everything
. . . That makes me happy —
So glad that I'm alive,
You can't believe the things I feel inside.

They say that love will fade away.
But this love; it's here to stay.

My heart is simply on fire —
Just knowing we will never tire —
. . . Of each other's sacred and lasting love.

And the birth of every day —
Is a new and exciting stay.
IT'S LOVE!
. . . It's love and it's here to stay.

Jacquelyn Ponder

REMEMBERING

I feel the breeze upon my cheek,
As gentle winds do blow.
I saw the robin swoop down to seek
The worms where streams did flow.
I heard the wild geese caw their call,
In winged form they flew.
And said goodbye for a little while,
As warm winds northward blew.

It's you that now I think of, and of the days gone by.
Of how we walked and smiled and talked, when you were by my side.

Oh in this time of season change,
Brown earth gives way for show.
Spring enters . . . bright her color range . . .
And days much longer grow.
Flower fragrance fills the valley air,
Then slowly mounts the hill.
Warm brilliance dazzles everywhere,
And chases fast the chill.

Fond memories of you linger near, young tender love sublime,
We shared most precious moments here, embracing gifts of time.

Clara Mays Benson

LOVE REBORN?

Waking —
My mind wanders through the mist
Of a thousand half-remembered dreams.
Every thought centers on the distorted echoes
Of a love that might have been.

Living —
The endless daily struggle
With the beast, loneliness, begins anew.
It is ever a shapeless, heartless void
That grips the soul with hollow pain.

Knowing —
I must resist the relentless beckons
Of illusions and specters of the past,
Hoping that the black pitiless beast
Will not prevail against my spirit.

Wondering —
Can peaceful promises of His Holy Son
Replace the numbing joy of her presence?
I must attempt to shed the bonds of fatal reason,
And grasp the deep unknown with blinded faith.

Mark Arvid White

Where are you going without me, my love?
Will you really leave me behind?
Is there another road waiting for me —
some other place I must find?

If there's a promise of someone or something
that's calling, then seek it I must —
but I'm seeing nothing in darkness just now,
so I reach for your hand, and I trust

that we're going together on our separate highways,
we're leaving our sorrows behind,
we're bound for the Light, for the Love, one another,
and whatever It is we must find.

Diane E. Ramey

When I awoke
With the morning sun
Rising upon the dawn
It was with wonder
How would it feel
To hear your soft and tender voice
Whispering through the dew-drenched stillness
To feel the warmth
Of your bright and cheerful smile
To feel the sensation
Of two souls touching as one.

Billy Mac

OLD GRANDDAD

Dedicated to Holland Lamkin Redmill
and John Benjamin Harris

My Grandpa raised me from a boy
He raised me since I was knee high
Although we never had it very good
He taught me not to steal or lie
But I was into growin' up
I was into movin' on
Oh how I wish that I had stayed
And my Granddad would have never gone
He told me all the answers to the questions in my mind
Although he never mentioned anything about questions
of this kind
Lord how I wish he were here to straighten out my mind
I know one day we'll be together again
It's just a matter of time
I know one day I'll see him
Probably in the heavens above
I know there had to be something to it
Because my Grandpa had so much love
Yes I know one day I'll see him
We'll go fishing in the heavenly pond
Lord how I wish that I had stayed
And my Granddad would have never gone on

Rick Redmill

IS LOVE BLOOMING

She looked to see,
In his eyes, is love blooming.

No, dormant it is, she saw.
So the soil she tilled for a year
And a year
And a year.

She looked to see,
In his eyes, is love blooming.

Still dormant, she saw.
"Flowers the expression of
Deep roots are," wisely, she said.

So the soil she tilled for a year
And a year,
And another year.

"Them roots don't nowhere go,"
Still wiser, she said.
"In him, there IS no damn bloomin'!"

And the spade she threw in.

Marie Ferneau

I LOVE YOU

My love for you is free from infatuation.
It is the lasting kind.
I have no pastel words to paint you a flowered picture;
Believe that I love you.
Know that I never ponder life without you . . .
There is no life without you.
Know that, to me, you are everything vital.
Time . . . appearance . . . calamity
Cannot change my heart.
I love you today more even than yesterday.
Know that when your eyes show pride in me —
My heart is full,
That I need your love.
Know that; not only do I love you,
But I am in love with you.
Not like the moon and stars
Or, flowers and trees . . .
Simply, in heartfelt truth — Always.

Donna Marquez

SAMANTHA

Deep brown eyes look up at me,
From behind a long golden nose.
Running with me, waiting for me,
Sleeping at my feet.
Always Sam.

I remember my father's words,
"Anything can be bought — for a price,"
But when an offer came in,
"I'll take your dog. Take this."
And the offer was more than fair
There are a lot of needs those dollars could fulfill —
there always is.
I remembered Dad's words,
but I also looked down at those
brown eyes

My answer, "No."

Ellen Malmquist

PRAIRIE LANDS

There in Nebraska, where the Prairie Lands —
Hums, with the swarm, of wild Bee,
Where the hedges, of Plum — Wild Cherry — and Currant Vine —
Waft their sweet perfume, O'er the soft sands,
Framing a desire to search out, the Rose, and wild Sweet Pea.

There, where the soft purple Twilight, hangs, o'er the land,
Bringing the night breezes, that softly caresses the cheek
— and sighing —
Delighting the Soul, and lifting the heart in ecstasy.

Soft rolling hills, those sand hills so lovely —
Holds the green grasses, that bend in the breezes.
Out to the Prairie Lands, there I find my heart journeying to
Where Spring Rains, so soft, are like an Angel sprinkling Dew.
Then these, are things, why —
My Nebraska —
Holds my love so true.

Annette N. Ashbough

HEART TO HEART

Oh my heart, what is this cry I hear from you?
I can feel your suffering and pain
which has left you sad and blue.

What is it I can say to make the ache go away?
I can feel by your rapid beat
that someone else's presence you entreat

I've found what we call love which is sent from up above.
I know it must feel strange
that for another my life will rearrange.

You have lost that inner peace which once you had with me
All the memories we've shared of love and grief and dreams.
Must now form a brand-new scheme.

Although there's someone new I'd like to introduce to you
The love we've come to know
we never will let go.

But still you feel no peace and now
it's your turn to talk to me.

Ann Dixon

ILLUMINATION

Standing before the seashore of eternity
Shells, wet sand, and symphonic spray
a foreshortened expanse
ocean front illumination

You, eternal lover, to my left
Your face timeless, etched
Your hair bleached with the reds of the sun's rays
    the auburns of setting seasons

In a dream you came to me
You handed me a map
    a key to our destiny
What is this pain and joy?

Called love-celestial and heavenly
Total surrender, sanctification
Magnification as two become one

Spirits unite in the dream so real
Bringing sanctified bodies in union
Piercing as the blaze

Nancy Sarah Zisman

SONNET 2

You came into my life when love was nil
Kindling the spark that long ago had burned.
The flames that leaped from quiet shadows — still
Desirous of life, are now returned.
Had there not been your coming to my heart
The flame might've, ever curbed — had to remain
A sanctum, in another world apart —
And love I've learned — left from my soul to drain.
But I this sanctum will not have to seek
For from thy lips, I learned what kindles love —
Flames, that might have had to burn — too weak —
It is an inner joy — one seeks above
All other things — that life may long insure,
You came into my life — my life is yours.

Darwynne Pucek

THE HUNGRY HEART

I gave, yet asked not in return
That you should give what you already gave
To someone else.
I have no right to ask for that
Which in some gentle moment, rare with you,
Is given lightly to my hungry heart.
For hungry hearts do not possess
The quality of patience,
But reach blindly out
Toward meager crumbs,
Which scatter to the floor
Becoming soiled, unappetizing
Fragments of despair.

Clara Mottlau Woodside

LOVE IS A SEASON

Springtime whispered a soft
song of love through trees
and over the glimmer of waterfalls
it told me of ecstasies
unknown before, thus, I heard
spring's luring loving calls

After springtime faded away
hot summer took its turn
in passionate song my heart
was driven to a new kind of yearn
before unknown, thus I heeded
hot summer's loving burn

Autumn's love was gentle
as falling leaves of gold
mixed with hues so bright
red hot cold green of untold
joys before that day
lingering on into winter's cold

Beneath the ice of winter's snow
Love's spring, summer, and autumn glow . . .

Rose Marie Hodges

FOREVER MISSED

Oh, for the touch of your hand
That can touch mine no more,
Leaving a wound that will not scar
And leaves me not completely whole
Because your loss has withered my soul.

Oh, for the sound of your voice
That can speak no more,
Yet, leaves me always listening
Never to hear, but never stopping,
Because my soul is yet so sore
Since my loss of you, my dear.

Oh, I know, it will never be again
And yet, I must go on as if it will;
Since this hope of mine no matter how absurd,
Is the only way my heart stays still!

The only relief I've had from my grief
Since I was bereft — long ago
Is in an *old man's* mind
You have never *grown old.*
But remain as young as the day you left.

Joshua C. Stevens

HOUSES

There are many, many houses,
Of nearly every shape and hue,
But the one I love quite dearly
Is the one that watches over you.

There are houses long and houses lofty,
With gables large or rounded dome,
But the one that suits my fancy,
Is the one I call my "home sweet home!"

There are houses built of brick and mortar,
Fulfilling most expensive dreams,
But the one which gives me pleasure,
Is where the home light brightly beams!

There are houses built like mansions
That glisten in the noonday sun,
But it's home to me that beckons
When the long, long day is done!

But home is more than brick and mortar,
Or great verandas broad and wide,
For to make a house a home
Enduring love must there abide!

Marie Poe

WINNING IN LOVE

Love is the symbolic minted heart of hope
The sages' signature of spiritual blood upon the globe
Combed by the cool clouds of stumbling farewells
And of the labyrinths of sex that we know so well
Murdered feelings absorbed by the sponges of grief
Our tongue-tied pride conceals our splintered sleeves
Mystical forces have scarred our ambient shell
Turning our lovers' heaven into our lovers' hell
To deny yourself the sheer passion of life is a major sin
And it is only he who refuses to win in love that never wins

Donna Dal Colletto

LOVE DREAMS

My poor eyes are ever-damp with tears of woe,
I have lost my love; ne'er is he to return,
Gone are my dreams like kneaded, unrisen dough.
My heart aches, still I have more to learn.

Love appears to be the bread of life, but
Can vanish in a mist of unfulfillment,
How I wish my soul could be free from strife,
And return once more to serene contentment.

When I tread through avenues of my mind
And search aimlessly to recapture the divine passion,
I find my efforts wane and fade in the wind.
Am I to live an earthly existence without reason?

Suddenly, a new love appears from the blue
And there comes to me a vision clear,
My long, lost love is born anew, and
My heart has nothing more to fear.

At last came an answer to my search
When precious love appeared once more
Like a loaf of bread appeals to a starving man
The kneaded dough had now arisen!

Helen Melissas

IN THE MIDDLE OF NIGHT

Why should I be afraid of the night
As long as I have you by my side?
I do need to be held close and tight
Your bosom's the one place I could hide!

If we must dread what darkness might bring,
Let's do it together while we sleep.
We'll hold our hands and to Him we cling
He knows our needs, understands us deep!

Then, we would go to dream if we could
For in dream may we touch and search,
Forget the realities that hurt,
Holding on fast to our hopes as such.

I need you especially at night;
Together against darkness we'll fight!

Harry Wang

ODE TO A VIKING

Eric, Sea Raider, Son of Thor returns
to Itteria for rest, healing of wounds
and emptying the mind of bloody battles
in Brittany. Every night when he dreams,
his fair Valkyrie from Valhalla beckons.
Her lovely presence haunts him. He falters,
weakens, his soul ascends. They meet, embrace,
waltz among the stars. Sway deep into space.

Suddenly an unknown force pulls them apart.
Her hands slip from his. She moves away,
smiles, waves. Golden robes flow softly,
disappear. He calls to her in the new
darkness where stars no longer shine.
Eric's mouth moves in deathly silence. Tries
to lunge forward arms outstretched. Falls
back to Earth in a whirlpool of flaming hair
and tunic. Plunges through white clouds
into a mass of light . . . awakens. Knows one
day they will dance forever, upon their
final redezvous.

Thomas A. Phelan

OUR LOVE

Why do we try so hard,
Why do we laugh together,
And go so far
why are we so much alike,
Yet
Two different colors line our hearts,
Why have we met?
Maybe we want the same
Or just a challenge,
Maybe it's just a game
It's a dream to touch only one man,
For so many years, but
It's like a shadow in the dark an echo in
Central Park
Still . . .
From the birth of our relationship
To the last waking days,
In our life together
It's been original,
It's been
"Our love"

Sherie L. Mullen

TOUCH NOT THE DEPTHS OF MY SPIRIT

Touch not my spirit with the grapes of wrath, for I bear
no anger, nor do I have a need for vengeance
Touch not the depths of my spirit; a sigh from its very
depths escapes, excelling fragile feelings on
gossamer wings
Glance not into my eyes for it will take you to the very
core of my existence
Brush not my tender heart with your trembling finger tips

A tender tempest as tears flow like the mighty rivers
A tear save as silver thread taps against the windowpane
A raindrop in the solstice of spring softly touching,
soaking in the earth's goodness

Love guide me with your tenderness
Love of my heart feed my ego
Love open my heart, hold me to your breast, come together
the pulse of life

A small vine engulfs my spirit; it presses the grapes to
quench my thirst
A sigh from its very depths escapes in solitude, in the
span of time
A sigh as chilling as the majestic snow-capped mountains,
seeking the warmth of the Heavens

Am I a stranger in my own existence?
Am I an alien among my people?
A daughter created from Adam's rib!

Touch not the depths of my spirit; a spirit unconquerable, for my spirit shall entwine with that of my creator. As slumber overtakes me, I pray for another awakening, to breathe the fragrance of the magnolia, to feel the caress of a gentle breeze. I drink from a small vine of the genus Vitis; it engulfs my spirit, and presses the grapes that quench my thirst. I run barefoot in the Kentucky bluegrass as the tender blades jot up between my toes, dance as a ballerina to the song of the birds.

Touch not my spirit with the grapes of wrath, for I bear
no anger, nor do I have a need for vengeance

I look toward the Heavens, toward the conquering light,
the face of Jesus, our spirits entwine

Betty J. Coursey

LOVE LINGERS ON

My love for you still lingers on, no matter what you do
For everything that makes me mad
There's more that makes me glad
That I've stayed around to share these times with you.

I wonder where I'd be today, if you and I had never met
Would I be out honky tonkin'
Or just an ugly country bumpkin
Waiting for that special someone I may never get.

Sometimes I wonder what it is that I have done
When I said that I would honor and obey
I find it hard not to have the last say
When asked who proposed, you tell them I'm the one.

Then you put your arms around me and smile into my eyes
I know why I did promise
For better or for worse
Without you by my side, my sun would never rise.

Cora R. Schroeder

A KISS

A kiss is a bit of a dream come true,
A piece of a star from the sky;
It is shimmering light from the rainbow's hue,
And it rings like a bell from on high.

A tender embrace shields against cold
That protects from heartfelt pain,
It feels of warmth that tends to enfold
Like sunshine after the rain.

A glance that speaks love, a word that endears
Can make all the day look bright;
A touch can linger all through the years
And make one's world seem right.

A dream can be spun from a sweet memory
And cherished for many a day.
For a kiss is a bit of a dream come true
That illumines a long dark way.

Evelyn Holten

LINGERING LOVE

With the passage of each day
I miss you so
Thoughts of you follow me
Wherever I go
From the start
You entered my heart
And my love for you began to grow
Over the years it continued to blossom
Growing stronger with precious care
The warmth, respect and tenderness, that we
Share. The magic of two hearts forever
Dedicated, forever appreciative
We met, a flame began
It grew brighter, stronger and sweeter
With the passage of time
Like a precious rose, lifting its petals
To the sun
Like a gentle breeze, to caress the leaves
Like a fine, potent, sweet wine
Our love will last throughout time

Virginia Davis

MY MARRIED LIFE

A bride I became at twenty-four,
Thinking then that I had a perfect score,
Set out upon a honeymoon so grand,
With a lovely new yellow gold wedding band,
Traveling afar to a new state to live,
Having much love to give;
The experience was exciting,
The new home inviting,
The travel became far and wide,
To newer climes to abide;
Settling down at last,
In my new home town, new aspirations to cast;
Now after thirty-two years of marriage past,
No more wedding gowns,
Nor rings of gold;
Now I am told,
A broken heart to mend,
No more sighs to lend,
Unhappiness, the price I must pay;
Before attaining happiness another day.

Mary Catherine Peterson

LOVE

When love beckons to you, follow him;
Though his ways are hard, and the road is steep
When his wings enfold you, yield to him
Yield to him though he makes you weep.

Though his voice may shatter your fondest dreams
Like the north wind lays waste the garden
When he speaks to you, believe in him
And never let your heart become hardened.

Seek not to direct the course of love
For love directs your course, if you're worthy of love
Love will crucify you; love will crown you
Love will make tears in your eyes glisten like dew.

Love seeks naught but the expression of self
Love seeks no glory, no fame, no wealth
Love is the keynote of life itself
Obeyance to his calling creates happiness and health.

Love wields forever the chastening rod
When you're in love, you're in the heart of God!
While all these things love will do unto you
He'll crown your life with happiness known but to few.

Cora Lee Prince

PRINCE, CORA LEE. Pen Name: Cora Lee Trawick Prince; Born: Stapleton, Baldwin County, Alabama, 8-12-09; Married: January, 1929 to George Charles Prince; Education: Roberts Dale, Alabama High School; Occupation: Practical Nurse; Comments: *I began concentrating on my writing in 1978 with my dependency on my wheelchair due to the advancement of multiple sclerosis. Common themes include reminiscing about past events.*

MOONLIGHT

Dreamy breaths and soft rustlings as you lie in the dark beside me
Moonbeams light the pillow where your head rests
Deep within my body a feeling stirs as I sense your masculinity
Somewhere from the dawn of time nature has drawn the blueprint
Pointless to resist the urging as I press myself to you
Love in the dark is sweetest when the moon dances on your bed.

Rose Brandon

ECSTASY

Make love to me with your heart
Let me feel it pound with passion
. . . and love

Envelop me in your sweat and power
. . . and I will surrender to your being

Touch me
. . . ever . . . so . . . gently . . .

Ascending me to great heights
. . . and carry me with you wherever you go

Marie Mangione-Hubbard

BUT I CAN'T HAVE YOU

I hand over my heart to you on a silver platter,
But with a lid so tight that it really doesn't matter.
I'll give you the key to unlock my heart,
But the keyhole remains unseen in the dark.
I give you a candle to light the way to my soul,
But the matches I give can only smolder.
I give you a rainbow leading to our destiny,
But black and white is what will always be.
I give you a map where X marks my heart,
But the directions I give exclude a start.
I give to you all of me
'Cause without you I'm not complete
But without you is what has to be.

Linnea Camilleri

Let us forget a glorious sunset
And a flame from a fire,
Let us forget a night beside a stream
Under the stars.
Let us now remember the feeling of rain upon the face,
And wind in the hair.
Let us forget the new moon and the old,
The spring and the fall.
Let us forget the unspoken words
In the understanding of eyes meeting.
Let us not remember songs, and laughter and tears.
Let us forget all the lovely things
Of a divine interlude,
And remember that they will never be again.

Helen Robinson

OLD WINE

'Tis deeper than the oceans and deeper than my thoughts.
Yet what I see is not the passion of my youth nor the far flung glory of my desire.
This I knew in days gone by and felt the loss as painful arrows to my heart.
Yet for its worth, and God bless that, I'm at a loss to see the deeper love of now.
Perhaps I do and perhaps I don't, but this I know my friend and that is aged love of older folks is more than fire and flame of days gone by.
For now I feel the gentle touch and see the loving smile of older folks which says so much and even more than days gone by and by when I knew no more but thought I did.

Harry Khosrofian

FLOWERS OF NOVEMBER

All these pathways are flowing, with flowers that gather
And crown life with crimson; and smell sweetly of heather

And the walks that we take there; are built upon shoulders
Of mountains majestic; and the rivers that flow there

But . . . all this beauty around us; would be dying and dried
Because the beauty that abounds us; is you at my side

It's your love that makes flowers; and your presence, the air
That smells sweetly of heather; because you are there

The hillsides are blooming; in November's bleak days
It's the hours we're consuming; as we find our new ways

It's this love in my heart; that you finally set free
It's the love you return; that is captured by me

So . . . every pathway we choose; seems so bright to our touch
It's the footsteps on a hillside; it's the love that is such

And these flowers that gather; to linger on when we depart
Are the flowers of November; grown with the love of our hearts

Lucky Rimpila

PARENTS

They claim to accept you as you are
But they don't.
At least, not in ways you would wish.

They can be your best friends
And worst enemies.
They are there when you need them
And even when you don't.

They are the first to point out the most subtle fault
And last to see you correct it.

They push you to achieve beyond your limits
Yet grow to accept what you've done.

You often wish for another pair
But at the same time are glad you had them.

They are human, after all.
What can you say?
They love you
And though you may not wish to be like them in any way,
You are.

Jonathan Jay Brandstater

A CARNEGIE MEDAL

Living in the past, thinking just of you.
Loving in the past; that sort of thing is through.
Huddled near the heat (the children fast asleep)
I jump up from my seat and at the door I weep.
Because no one is there. In my sleepy mind
I thought that you'd be there; but I left you far behind
in the red, unfeeling grave. They gave me a medal of brass
because you were fearless and brave. I'd rather have you
than a medal of brass to hold in my loving arms;
but I can't have you and all of your charms,
I have what you gave to me, our most precious two,
and tomorrow and tomorrows there'll be work to do for my two.
For the wonderful present from you.

J. Edwards Swalley

HIS WONDERFUL LOVE

I'll never fully understand, the extent of His love
for me.

Why he bore the sins of this sinful world, on a cross
at Calvary.

He knew how many countless times, I'd fail Him and
go astray.

How many times I'd choose the wrong path; be submerged
in this world of decay.

He saw my many weaknesses; the obstacles I'd overcome.

And with those same eyes of love and compassion; saw
the person I'd grow to become.

All the diamonds or purest of gold in the world, could
never come close to repay.

For the debt of my sins was paid in full, so that
salvation could be mine today.

Someday I'll behold my Savior and Lord; the One who
set me free.

I'll thank Him for ten thousand years; this One who
died for me.

Denise L. Baker

LOVE UNREQUITED

Love blossomed between us, with the velvety softness
of a dew-covered rose.

The petals of love softly caressing the precious bud within.

The wonder of it ever new, like our discovery of one another.

As we hold hands and gaze intently into each other's eyes

Trying to memorize every detail of each dear face.

And, yet, with all this precious newness something still
eludes us.

Could it be that what we experience now is all
we will ever have?

I sigh, as I hear the door softly closing and hear the
echoes of your footsteps in retreat.

Oh, why did you not stay?

What happened to that love in the newness of our
yesterdays?

Is it just a memory of what once was and cannot be again?

Through all the tomorrows of our lives.

Juanita M. Reed

BOOK OF ART

Hello poetry loving friends of mine.
I must say, it's been ages and ages
Since I've met so many beautiful people.
As I turn all these pages.

And read words of beauty, feel the love
You've poured out of your hearts.
Splashed upon a sea of paper
To be enjoyed, long after you depart.

But in the meantime, may God bless you
And keep your hearts full of love.
By sending forth loving inspiration
To fill the mind thereof.

You've given me many hours to treasure
May I say thanks and express love from my heart.
It's been a special pleasure meeting you
Between the pages of this book of art.

G. G. Ruth E. Skaggs

MOON MADNESS

Full moon hangs like a warm golden orb
looking down on mortals such as me,
Spreading his madness over the world
charging the night with "Love's Melody."

Our love was a madness born under the moon
"You're a fool," friends chanted to me.
Doubting the feelings which sprang to life
bonding our hearts so we'd never be free.

Now youth has fled and the moon's yet there
spreading out his madness like a golden sea.
Creating a magic so others might love
like the madness which touched you and me.

Time tested and tried by passing years
kept bright and warm by constant use,
a treasure which most mortals seek
"Love madness," blessed by the moon's golden hue.

Loraine Lewis

DAVID

This leap you're making from stickers and crayons
To shaving lotion. What's your hurry?
What about the moments you're taking,
To say good-bye to yesterday?

I thought it took years
To shed a child's cocoon.
My Pisces child, yesterday a bundle,
Today you're rocketing toward the moon.

I'll miss your sticky kisses,
Small arms around my neck.
Thursday's child enters the room,
Bestows a mature, adult-like peck.

Sometimes my heart is near to bursting,
When your car heads down the highways.
I wave, I smile.
I love you more than Fridays!

Anne Smith

THE PEDESTAL

I remember the pedestal you placed me on . . .
The delicate way you cared for me like a fragile rose
Whose beauty lingers and then is withered . . . leaving no
trace
But scents of remembrance somehow lost in many yesterdays.

There is no life in truth for I am disillusioned and my
heart has broken too many times.
All that I want or need to become is meaningless now
As promises of forever and always somehow fade from my
caress.
There is no tomorrow . . . and today I loved you so much!
There are no more pedestals for it was my time to step
down
And I had fallen too many times before . . .

And if there is hope, I need to find it (somehow)
As my petals fade from red red rose
And scents of lingering memories are lost in tears of
sadness
For all that I was and can never be again.

Cheryl Butler

REMEMBERING

Irene, Irene, you are so kind and sweet; you have been
someone's dream, someone so kind and neat,
I listen to you tell me of the days of old; when young
men were not so bold.
When they would court you for days, and walk for miles
in the rain or mist; just to wait three days to ask you
for a kiss.
It was a time when things were slow, when men would chase
their loves to catch and never let go.
You told me how it had been, forty four some odd years.
I know it was hard to hold back the burning tears.
For you told me your Love had gone on, and how you and
he lived working your way to heaven's home.
And a few days before, you remembered hearing him say,
Darling; you know we can live only one day at a time,
So you were able to endure your loss when heaven's angels
rang their chimes.
You told of the ten wonderful months you had together,
It seems as though you were thanking God for the good times.
When life has ended it won't seem so odd, that your only
true love once again will be William Todd.

M. H. Kingston

THE NIGHT TOO, MUST DIE . . .

In Kashmir, under the pale of the moon
Where the lotus blossoms float along the river bank,
I dreamt of your coming and I touched my heart
To still its wild beating. In the dark
Of the early morning mist,
I gazed upon the mountains, far-flung and free
And yearned for the sight of you, the touch of you,
The love you gave to me.

Now, through a succession of days and nights,
I am lost in a labyrinth of despair; I cry . . .
For the white-winged heron no longer calls to his mate
And the moon, wan and beclouded
Hangs like a host in the sky;
The bird songs of twilight have all been stilled,
Even as my heart,
For the night, too, must die . . .

Carolyn M. Kurth

PROMISE TO AN EXCEPTIONAL CHILD

This little girl began life with retardation. She is so much better today — almost a woman.

You are my loving gift from God;
My precious one so dear,
with outstretched hands to greet a world
which finds you different here.

You are my strength. You'll teach me to
accept God's guiding way
and we shall learn to patient be
and live from day to day.

But I shall learn, my Special Child,
to cherish every smile,
for you are loaned to me by God
for just a little while.

And I shall love each living thing,
each fellow man — and YOU,
whose struggling steps upon this earth
may be but very few.

But this I promise, Baby Dear,
that I shall grow with you
in faith and understanding ways
to make your dreams come true.

Arlone Mills Dreher

ONENESS OF THE HEART

Dedicated to Paul Theroux, Ivan Lendl, John and to Sincere Hearts

Into each heart
burns a fire
a melody of love
that lightens the soul
and sings a melody
that grows and grows
until you are one
a fire, a rapturing melody
Cast not, the shadow of doubt
on this soul
for I feel the love, within me
growing and growing
feeling and finding its way, to my
heart.
The warmth, the joy it brings
how happy my heart
and its desires fulfilled
like running water and bubbling
sand
The fire and warmth of my
heart and soul,
are now one
forever more, into my heart
your heart and soul have blended
into mine.

Bhatkin Devi

FRIENDS

Friends are like the gentle hands of an artist which mold tender clay with patient perseverance into solid shapes of beauty.

Susan A. Tanous

CRY OF LOVE

Words never said until it's too late — and sometimes not even then.
I've fought the battle for so long now, when the world has changed people.
In vain, I try to do things I could have easily done a year or ten ago.

I know I can't hold on to yesterday, no matter how hard I *do* try.
Yesterday is a feeling, a memory, an essence . . .
the ticket stubs after the movie is over,
the wrappings after the gift is used,
the scent associated with someone that we can
almost-but-not-quite still smell, even long after they're gone.

Feeling things now that I almost question my very senses about.

The Forbidden Words . . .
Sometimes I have to isolate myself to keep from
shouting out that I love somebody.
Anymore, I come so close — on the brink of it.
Just SOMEBODY.
Millions of seconds, thousands of minutes, hundreds of hours,
tens of days, weeks, months, years!

I've denied myself of it for so long . . .

Patricia L. Elledge

GIFTS OF THE HEART

Dreams that can never be mine,
Arms that will never be filled with you.
For you to never know my love.
For the gifts of the heart,
That I want so much to share with you.
You are the springs of my life.
A renewing of life.
I will shelter all memories of you deep in my heart.
Though I will never hold you,
I will have my dreams.
How could there be anyone else after knowing you.
I reserve my heart for only you through all the summers of my life.
You shall always keep that candle of life burning.
There shall be hope in the days to come . . .
You fill my senses like
Fragrant roses in the morning dew.
You capture the mysteries of sunsets in your smile.
In the sparkle of your eyes.
I can't bear to miss anything that's a part of you.
Some joy has come into this heart.
I've been searching for someone to give the life back.
One very special person.
There will never be any greater love.

Carrie Higgins

REMEMBER I LOVE YOU

Words oft spoken, offhand fashion,
Carry with them, a depth of discernment;
Reaching beyond the boundaries of tomorrow,
Wounds healed, hearts mended . . . Reborn.

This instance: The trio on corner seen,
Thoroughfare: Fifth Avenue . . . the crossing?
Who cares? Parting to meet: Mom, Dad, Cecille;
Kissing Cecille, Dad utters, "Remember I love You!"

Cecille; No tot, a teenager, now grown;
Stepping out, her tomorrows to greet,
Horizons aglow! Dad's amorous parting . . . Euphonic!
Up stream . . . rapids forging . . . "Everest!" . . . her vision.

Horace V. Preddie

THIS IS MY LOVE FOR YOU

Silver the sea gull shining
Over the sunlit sea
All through the storm abiding
Thus should our true love be.

Darkness, the shadow waning
Swift to its timeless flight
Speeding the early dawning
Out of the dark of night.

Floating on wind's calm weather
Etched in the sky of blue
Chasing the salt spray heather
Thus is my love for you.

Fresh winds from a far-off way
Search for bright coral reef
Skimming the waters gray
Leaving its fallen grief.

Silver the sea gull shining
Over the sunlit sea
All through the storm abiding
This is your love for me.

F. Richard Dieterle

SWEET CARESS

Hands across the table —
Quiet walks, hand in hand
Hands gently clasped;
Feeling of soft arms on shoulders
Tenderness given in sweet caress;
Soft words spoken of love
makes life worth living
and the strength to endure
things that lie ahead;
All you need is the strength
shown by expressions of LOVE!

Claudine L. Evans

THE LITTLE THINGS

The sweetest things are little things
You do for me each day —
The things that say, "I love you dear,"
In your sweet quiet way.

Because of you I dare to be
A giant of a man,
You fill me with a great desire
To do the best I can.

My days are filled with hardships now —
Decisions, problems, strife,
The soothing comfort of your arms
Restores my faith in Life.

If I should chance to wander far
Out on Life's stormy way,
I know your love will be there still
When I return some day.

I'll try my best to meet your love
With gentle recognition,
For all the things you do for me
Are *Love,* not just submission.

Louise Freese

DESPAIR

Oh God! My love has left me,
What can I ever do?
He saw Jamie kissing me,
I'd not ask him to.

I remembered Psycho
Why Cupid went away
He found she loved another
And he would not stay

Earthly love inlcudes but two,
And I have gone astray,
To forfeit joy and trust my dear.
It can be no other way.

Phyllis Hill

SOUTHERN KISSES

Her eyes
— The blue feathers of innocence —
Find my open arms
Under a willow tree.

As the soft bell
Beats in her chest
Thirsty leaves
Sing intimacy in the breeze.

With southern kisses,
And before the frost fades our hopes,
At dusk,
I flame the cold brambles.

Mohammad Abbaspour

GROWTH IN GRACE

Lord, I faltered today.
Give me strength for the way.
Strength to do your will now;
Your wisdom to know how;
Courage to walk in grace,
Looking into your face,
Searching to do your will.
Lord, with your spirit fill
This longing heart of mine,
'Til Jesus' love does shine
Through this frail bark so weak;
Only of His love to speak.
Jesus, how I love you!
Loving me as you do!

Wilda Craddock

SONG OF LOVE

(For Paul)

Oft love finds us
in unusual ways
hears our pleas
remembers
we were among the missing
and brings us back
for a second chance
At sweet surprise.

Diana Kwiatkowski

RUBY LEE

Oh, mighty cascade mountains
Where you mingle with the sea
Was there that Heaven bloomed so rare
A blossom Ruby Lee.

The breezes filled with lilac scent
Ran fingers through her hair,
The ocean mist her cheeks had kissed
As she stood blushing there.

The whitecaps nestled at her feet
The sun caressed her skin,
Oh, such beauty ne'er on earth
Before had ever been.

But like the brightness fades away
When sun dips to the sea
I lost her there, oh, ne'er again
To hold my Ruby Lee.

Now the tide comes sweeping in
To wash the sand where she had been
And life holds but despair for me
I can't forget thee, Ruby Lee.

Parnell Pierce

LOVE IN SELFLESS ONENESS

Love
in
selfless
oneness
no pride, no ego, pure unadulterated
perfection
exquisitely envisioned excellence
beautified
in essence, manifested in spirit
the
Christ Consciousness

Nancy-Lee Farris

LOVE OF A LIFETIME

When we are kids and we need love
Our moms and dads are there
They give us love and we feel safe
And their love makes our childhood days

We reach our teens and feel so grown
And want a love that's all our own
But we're too young to really know
To have true love that it must grow

We search and look a few more years
And then we finally find
That lasting love that binding love
That only comes with time

We wed and have our families
And know our love will last
And hope we've passed our love along
That we did our very best

Our years have passed so full of love
A closeness we've seemed as one
Our twilight years so quiet and sweet
Your love has made my life complete

Ann Melford Cagle

ALLOW ME

Sitting around with too much time?
Reach out your hands, let me take them in mine.
Confusion, prevarication, unrest within?
Look deep into my eyes and slowly begin
To trust my love, let it be your guide;
Look to me sweet; stand strong at my side.

Are you filled to the hilt with desperation?
Lean on me, let me be your inspiration.
Despair and anger barely kept in check?
Let me deal you more soothing cards from the deck.
There's magic in my power, an unseen force;
So put your trust in me, we'll set our own course.

Allow me to dispel all of your fears.
Allow me to dry up all of your tears.
Allow me to walk in the shadows with you.
Allow me to show you life anew.
Allow me to show you a brand-new sun.
Allow me to bring laughter and the day is won.

Let me be your friend, your lover, your guide.
Let me stand strong and proud at your side.
You can have all this if you'll allow it to be.
All this and more if you'll only come to me.
It's okay to be afraid of taking a chance,
But allow me to teach you how to dance.

Lorey Umberger

UMBERGER, LORETTA ETHEL. Pen Name: Lorey; Born: Port Clinton, Ohio, 2-12-48; Divorced; Education: Libbey High School, Toledo, Ohio, 1966; Poetry: 'When It's Over,' *American Poetry Anthology,* 1980; 'Sweetest Dreams,' *Hearts on Fire, Vol II,* American Poetry Association 1984; Comments: *The most common theme throughout my work is life — as it is and as it could be. It's also about taking a negative experience, feeling it to its fullest extent, then letting go and turning it around to create a positive in one's life. I try to show that it's ok to feel and show all emotions as long as one eventually uses the experience to grow and be the best one can be.*

TOGETHER

No matter the season the time
  or the weather
My wish is that we
  be always together
Our lips intertwining
  As we lock in embrace
The warm glow of passion
  I adore on your face
Caressing and murmuring the sweetness of love
  Holding each other, giving thanks from above
If only a moment we two become one
  The heat of this moment superseding the sun
Uniting as one this tumultuous union
  Bring to life a soul who is human

Lawrence Robbins

IN QUEST OF PASSION

O where has Passion gone? I mused with great dismay.
Has he like a wild young stallion borne himself away?
I cannot long endure Plato's steadfast feature.
He's such a cold, unfeeling, stony-minded creature.
Sweet Passion is the one that I really always miss
With his tender Midas touch and strong impetuous kiss.
Like the sun of morning he brings brightness to my day,
And makes me feel important in a very special way.
I rushed to my beloved's side, and fervently inquired:
Could we have some time together, dear, if you're not too tired?
That's a good idea, he bantered, but, I seem to have a headache.
But, dear, I have a little pill that you might safely take.
I caught the glimmer in his eye, and felt the hidden mirth,
And knew that Passion was alive and well on Planet Earth.

Edna Powell Weegmann

THE TRUE MEANING OF LOVE

Just like the violets are blue,
I know dear Lord, Your love is so true.
Just like some roses are red,
And for me, Your precious blood was shed.
And just like sugar is so sweet,
There in heaven we shall meet.
Just as pure as heaven above,
You taught me Lord, the true meaning of love.

Annie Scott

HOW LOVE BEGINS

The wind will scythe his name across the grass
And know which code of living he must heed.
The supple blades respond to his deft pass;
when boy and girl should dance then who will lead?

The vine will hug the wall to reach the eave.
His green strength marks how well he claims the stone.
Our stature matches that we would achieve
For each boy grows to make his girl his own.

Not climbing vine nor wind upon the lee
deny their acts nor earth refuse the plow.
The girl calls sweetly, "Who?" The boy say, "Me."
Her voice will whisper, "When?" and he breathes, "Now."

Burr McCloskey

LITH. & PUB. BY N. CURRIER. Entered according to Act of Congress in the year 1847 by N. Currier, in the Clerk's office of the District Court of the Southern District of N.Y. 152 NASSAU ST. COR. OF SPRUCE N.Y.

THE SISTERS.

THE INNER VISION

Most sweet it is with unuplifted eyes
To pace the ground, if path there be or none,
While a fair region round the Traveller lies
Which he forbears again to look upon;
Pleased rather with some soft ideal scene,
The work of Fancy, or some happy tone
Of meditation, slipping in between
The beauty coming and the beauty gone.

If Thought and Love desert us, from that day
Let us break off all commerce with the Muse:
With Thought and Love companions of our way, —

Whate'er the senses take or may refuse, —
The Mind's internal heaven shall shed her dews
Of inspiration on the humblest lay.

William Wordsworth

marie standing naked on the beach (in a photograph)

for the first time in my life,
I understand why lonesome whales come to the shore
to commit suicide.

Keith L. Thomas

ANSWERS OF LOVE

Tell me you love me and show me you care.
My feelings of loving I'm needing to share.
I want you to hold me — chase my troubles away.
Make me feel happy with each waking day.
Whatever has happened —
What time has passed —
No matter the distance,
Our union will last.
For us there's no limit
To what we can do,
We'll go on forever —
Our love remain true.
Always remember
I'm your lover, your friend.
Will you share my life
And let our future begin?

Theodore R. Munsch

HIS GATEKEEPER

Her smile bright as the morning sun
She moves with exquisite perfection
Swift as a shooting star, chasing troubles away
Happy to be the gatekeeper to his heart
She listens for his step on the path
And runs to meet him at day's end
She is his only gatekeeper
Born on the breath of each new day
Swinging in the door, from her kitchen garden
Pretty veggies, straight out of Paradise
Materpieces! — in the twinkling of an eye
Strawberries, sweet as a bluebird's song
And as welcome as the red red robin in spring
As is the sweet tie that binds
Her lips are a magnet, drawing him close
As night snuffs the last red ribbons.

Bretta Hill

THE BLEEDING HEART

Can you look at a Bleeding Heart,
And doubt that there's a God?
Who gave to us this flower,
And the One who, stainless, trod
This earth; as one with all of us,
And remained yet good and pure!
The One Unblemished Lamb, who made
Our path to Heaven sure!
But at the cost of His blameless life;
Preordained from the very start
To die in agony on that shameful cross . . .
With a broken and bleeding heart!
Yes, God bestowed them both on us,
That through our lives should last;
As we gaze at this flower, to remind us
Of Love and Beauty . . . unsurpassed!

Opal DeGrote

ADAM'S NOVA

Once, upon a dayspring night
stars in madrigal
trilled Judean hills through hornpipe trees
out of her spangled womb rocked by angels
hatched she Adam's Nova
and hid it in a straw cradle
with kine chanting Oms.

And came three, yellowed by heavy tomes
riding camel humps in the night
carrying symbols in golden caskets.
Obeisance for the Ewe.

Were you there?
when His touch of love was mercury and fire
and hearts received His flowering wine
and new life therein did it spark
with the eternal of its creation.

Does the harp recognize the harpist?
Do the grapes recognize the winepress?
Do I recognize my Beloved?

Joan M. Bixler

YOU ARE LOVE

Filled with the glow of a new daybreak,
your eyes gleam with life.

Happy with a smiling kiss hello,
you're feeling brand-new.

Honored by the sunlight halo'ed in your hair,
you're beaming . . .

love is there.

Tree leaves sway with an easy breeze,
you've freshened the air.

Affectionate touch extended from your hand,
you generate growth.

Your song is joy, peace and liberated vitality,
you sing with a voice that is new . . .

you are love.

C. Swain-Ward

KAREN

I'm not poking fun or pins,
On what we two've been through;
But Sister, dear, I have to smile,
Whene'er I think of you.

Our dancing days, remember them?
We both were full of pep;
Get Ready, Karen, Here we go:
"Step, brush, brush, step, step."

And then, in Minot, on the hill,
Your driving quickly stopped;
Downward, backwards, we regressed,
Because our "seat latch" popped.

Frantically, we went to work,
Giggling, (not with cheer;)
You tried to make the latch re-catch,
While I kept trying to steer.

We made it through all episodes,
And I indeed insist;
A better sister in this world,
Just does not exist!

Kathleen M. Burley

BURLEY, KATHLEEN MARY. Born: Minot, North Dakota; Married: 1966 to Henry R. Burley; Education: University of Phoenix, M.B.A., 1984; Arizona State University, M.A. Education, 1966; Occupation: Training, Finance; Memberships: Los Angeles Chapter National Association of Presentation and Instruction; American Society for Training and Development; Awards: *Who's Who in U.S. Writers, Editors and* Poets, 1986-1987; Poetry: 'Our Exchange Student,' *Voices in Poetics: A Modern Treasury,* 1986; 'The Beach,' *Words of Praise, Volume II,* 1985; 'Anniversary,' *Love Without Fear,* 1985; 'Prejudices,' *Tidings to a Tick,* 1985; Other Writings: *Who You Are, Where You Are,* Autobiography, 1986; Comments: *I enjoy poetry and think it should be fun. In my poetry, I try to capture memories of my favorite people and special moments.*

TWO COINS

Two coins
In a fountain
Side by side

She has petticoats
And lace
And she has beauty
Her voice
Is silk
in the wind

She is as fine
As any woman
On the plainness
Of this earth

I'm with her
As walking with satin
She is a smoothness
In my life
And like
Divine mercy
She is surely felt

Jerry Lee Murrell

THAT PARTICULAR SPRING

When violets were smaller,
Sunflowers taller,
And I was between the two,

That particular spring
Had no special ring
Till your eyes were sharing the view.

Feeling empty inside,
You were a welcoming tide
That rose at a magnificent pace

And, as the season went by,
Even larger than I,
Was the wave of love's first embrace.

Now, when a particular spring
Has no special ring,
I reflect on that distant view,

When you were the tide,
Love was a bride,
And I was between the two.

Pat Bush

LOVE DOES LAST FOREVER

His wife was the one who came
to say another good-bye,
to trim the newly grown weeds,
bring fresh flowers,
and to cry.
They had been married for forty years.
For the last two
she nursed and loved him;
there was no more anyone could do.
He passed away last spring.
She bears his memories on her face.
Nothing will ease her pain.
Nothing can take his place.

Betty L. Harnly

LOVE ROSE

There isn't anything more exciting
than the sight of a love rose.
Its deep passion of colors
captures the sight of many eyes.
One's thought of the rose is of beauty.
The want of another's touch like
the warmth of the glowing sun.
Petals of soft velvet smooth and
tenderness entraps the vulnerable heart.
Though some engage in its meaning
of love, honesty, and trust,
Its stems bear the thorns of pain
that stab, hurt, and scratch
the very living soul.

Angelyn Ables

WINTER MORNING

Love Poem To My Husband

The world had been flat and gray.
The weeks and months had been gray.
The whole year had been gray.
There was no difference between
The land and the sky — black and gray.

And then, that morning
After being with you,
The horizon became tinged with pink!

There was a difference between the
Land and the sky!
Pink and gray — a beautiful combination!

Evelyn Blocker

TRYST

Stolen kisses, to be treasured.
Stolen kisses, a lover's rhyme.
For a magical, fabled moment
In moonlight-drunken madness,
Your lovely arms enfolded me.
Your lovely arms, so tenderly!
Silence, silence our feelings nurtured.
So closely held, you were mine.
Love has gone, as it shouldn't
No more kisses, warm, luscious.
No more embraces, held tenderly.
Lost, all lost, faded memory,
Broken tryst, half-remembered,
Lost spell, vows once pledged.

John Hancock

WRITER'S SLUMP

Here lies the expression
of the Poet, deep within, dormant
awaiting, deathlike; for the Poet outward
to sound the awakening trumpet; only
Inspiration has fled, no words will come
to his head. My God must I actually
construct a work of Art? My trumpet
has lost its awakening pitch and even
primordial thought escapes me, yet I must
labor or it would not be a gift of Love.

Joseph A. Stewart

LOVE IN FLAMES

We love this world
this air we breathe,
the sloppy hills
the warm embracing sun
and the cool breeze of
the smiling sea.

Our fathers clung to this land
with care, nourishing it
and embracing it with
lovely and caressing tenderness.

But what do we now see
on this our lovely world?
Our children have marred
its beauty, its warmth and fragrance
with stains and polluted air
leaving this peaceful and lovely world
to burst into flames.
February 2, 1986

Apostle J. P. K. Appiah Jr.

A QUIET SHARING

We acknowledge love
As God's gift to us —
To be cherished, and held,
Unending.
Yet if love is eternal,
A foundation to build upon,
Is it not also, unfailingly
A glorious strength for the moment?

Ah, and does it not follow, then,
That it is far more than good, one's
Quiet sharing of life with another,
As we become aware of each blessing
And together accept adversity,
Which brings not only maturity,
But truth and reverence?
For this is lasting and, perhaps,
The most ennobling of all things
Achieved throughout the years.

Lester E. Garrett

TO JEFFREY WITH LOVE

I seldom express it but you know it's true
I love you more than words can say
And I bet daddy does too.

From the first day you came to us,
We knew that we were blessed.
Watching you grow and enjoy life
Sometimes put us to the test.
But we grew too
Loved and appreciated you more
With each accomplishment
And new adventure you bore.

Jeffrey, we are so proud of you,
Your choices in life and
Your uses of the gifts God gave you.
Our prayer for you this 23rd birthday:
You continue to love the Giver, be happy,
And follow the path He has paved.
Mom

Elizabeth Wright

GREAT IS THY LOVE

There is no greater love on earth
than the love of Jesus,
Who came on earth to save our souls
from sin,
that is the greatest gift
to anyone.
Jesus gave the greatest gift
ever given.
Jesus died upon the cross
for all of us.
That we could have life
and have it more abundantly.
Where we could live
with Him in Heaven.
Jesus loved us enough
to shed His blood
upon the cross.
That we may be cleansed
by His blood
so we could be saved.
There is no greater love.

Zora B. Fetner

FRIENDS

Friends lead to one's personality
with words placed gently,
Like snowflakes touching
a plush lawn.

A friend's advice may be
subtle or stinging,
But his motive is clear;
he wants to communicate.

The warmth of friendship
isn't always apparent;
Arguments leaving ill feelings
do occur.

But after the bad words
come the better ones,
Like sunshine warming
the earth after a shower,
And our personalities
bask together.

Neil J. Hansen

IF I COULD

If I could have but one wish,
I'd wish to share my life with you.
If I could have but one smile,
it would be for the joy you give.
If I could have but one touch, my
hand would reach within your heart.
If I could have but one hug,
it would be in your loving arms.

If I could have but one kiss,
I'd place it softly upon your lips.
If I could have but one love,
it would be you 'til eternity ends.
If I could have but one night,
it'd be with you 'til morning comes.
If I could have but one child,
you would carry this gift of life.

Henry M. Grouten

SECRET LOVE

Candlelight and Chardonnay . . .
quiet talk . . . the meeting of our eyes.
A distant echo of a familiar tune
and then I knew.
He placed his secret in my heart . . .
the one he had never revealed.
I shall keep it there forever . . .
carefully concealed.
He placed a kiss upon my brow . . .
ever so slight . . .
a silent tear . . .
then I gathered my dreams and
forged my way into the night.
The other woman was never a part
of my plight.

Frances Norton Russell

AN OPEN PRAYER

With every cloud that moves about me,
With each gentle wind that passes,
I see a beauty never before seen.
  Every moment spent living for You
  results in constant love.
Small birds fly with an ease too delicate
to realize, moving about the vast openness
that only God can provide.
  God, grant me the same openness; the
  same ease in my life.
Give me a life free to move about with
a song in my heart.
Make the melodies soft and light —
Make the music sweet —
Let the chorus last throughout all time —
With every memory unique.

Laquetta Parker

ENDLESS LOVE

Like the rings around Saturn
My love flows 'round you
Like the moons following Jupiter
I'll follow you
Like the endless forever
And the black holes in space
My love goes infinite
With you is my place
The Alpha and Omega
Is the beginning and end
The here and the now
My love I will send
Like the oceans' dark multitudes
And Sahara's eternal sand
I'll be with you always
By your side; hand in hand.

Denise Fleer

LOST LOVE

Now that it is over
I can still remember
That first "Golden Autumn"
It had just begun
Long will my heart weep
My eyes will never see
  "Golden Autumn"

Elizabeth J. Potter

I WANT TO BELIEVE THAT MOTHER WILL COME

I have decorated the whole city
and gave their ration of basin's limpid water,
  to the yard's flowers.
The sparrows know.

The wall clock is dead.
It's noon and I feel the mirror's thoughts.
The front yard is suddenly full of colorful rosebuds.
And wondering me,
  and surprised me, is staring at the wall clock.

I whisper "It's time my mother comes.
Why has her arrival been late?"
I know it's time the door opens and it's time to believe that mother is coming.
Even those who know the funny secrets of the clock's pointers,
don't understand why the time stops rotating at times.

Oh mother   mother,
I have a share of the whole world and I still keep my toys in the drawer.
I hear the sparrow's scream and the silence of the plane tree's branches.
Why hasn't mother come yet?
I want to believe that mother will come.

Kaveh Irani

SWEET SIXTEEN

Sweet? Most of us will remember every bit of it,
And can say, it was just the opposite.
How we blushed, or turned pale, when someone complimented us,
With a little fuss.

Or any other direct statement would reveal,
To which we weren't used,
That was the time we were most confused.
Waiting patiently,
For the sound of the front door, nearly every day.
Dreaming of a handsome family friend,
Who had a special smile and that something in his look,
When we were supposed to read a book.

Wasting often so much time,
On trying to put some words together, which just wouldn't rhyme.
Pretending not to care,
What adults had to say, or where they were.
Listening to the conversation of adults at that time,
Was supposed to be a sort of crime.
So we'd start our reading or art, when we heard the big ones talk,
Or go simply for a walk.

Helena M. Jones

WHEN HE CHANCED TO WALK BY

I remember the day when Tricia, Nancy, and I
Were putting a poster on a pillar, when someone caught my eye
Actually he had passed me when I watched him keep on walking
His body there in front of me made things tough for talking
The ten foot drop that my stomach took was as sudden as could be
Never before had such a strong stomach drop ever happened to me
I felt as if a knife had helped it along
All I know is that I didn't feel so strong
But my love was strong, I knew this for certain
Otherwise, why would my poor stomach be hurtin'?
His right hand was in his pocket; his hair was looking soft as silk
I still remember the way he looked: kind of fortified like milk
I started to run after him; I wanted to jump onto his back
But I didn't know how that could work; I just didn't have the knack
I had to let him walk on by; there was nothing else that I could do
I just wished I could have told him how I felt, and maybe kissed him too

Tammy Breighner

LOVE SONG

In the morn's first sunny hours,
While the dew is on the flowers —
I love you.

In the noontide's bright array,
And the children are at play —
I love you.

But when evening shadows fall,
Dear, I miss you most of all,
When to bed, each night I'll call,
I love you.

Charlotte North

FOREVER IS

Forever is love
which knows no bounds.
It is an exemption from time.
It is an acceptance
of what has to be,
An entering into its rhyme.
Forever expands;
it does not enclose.
It is open to give and receive.
We too, can be part
of its synergy
If we would consent to believe.

Olivia McCormack

MERLINESQUE

As perfect as a moment
in a myth
your love is
And as sweet
As lovely as the fields
of camelot
your heart lies
before me
swathed in the
ethereal breath
of
autumn

Richard F. Kellas

DEAR LAMB

'Neath summer sun
And bright birds' hum
I think of You;
You made the flowers,
The morning hours,
The sky so blue;
The mountain tors,
The ocean floors
Belong to You;
With joyous heart
Like wild birds start
I come to you.

Mrs. Richard Schiller

THE PREFERENCE

As a Haydn symphony pours into the room,
I think about your preference —
The measured cadences resound and echo your essence.
The precision, the timing — it is all you too, of course.
And the sweeter melodic parts penetrate my mind
With nostalgic thoughts of you.
The music resumes its onward quest and the melody is enveloped
in the ongoing rush — still so precise, still so headlong.
As if that pace were too much, it suddenly slows to a ponderous rhythm.
Now, your expressions come alive again
And I am again immersed in duality.
It is real — here and now, and yet reminiscent of a distant past.
An eighteen year old girl plays Haydn,
Persevering the experience for some undisclosed reason.
The memory of its repetitious meanderings comes back full tilt.
And now, well over a score of years later,
You state a preference for Haydn.

Jo Ellen Carlson

IF I COULD HEAR YOU

The silence of the shadows in the night's early descent,
Sings songs of noontime pleasures and a day foolishly spent.

The night brings on a calmness, and that glimmer in your eye
Gives answers to my questions, though I often wonder why.

Your voice no longer heard now, as my consciousness drifts away
To visions never once seen underneath the light of day.

I close my eyes and wander through the gardens in my mind.
The breezes blow right through me as, my cheek, your breath does find.

If I could hear your thoughts now, their attention I must pay,
If your words were understood, the breeze would blow away.

If I could hear your thoughts now, not the bubbling of the stream.
This vision would soon fade away, as remote as any dream.

Deborah Nielson

THE TWO OF YOU

On this very special day I just wanted to let you know,
You both mean the world to me and I love you so.

There are not many children who feel the way I feel,
To know that I am loved by two whose love is pure and real.

Of all the disappointments and heartaches I have been through,
There is one thing I always had and that was both of you.

Though we were very poor with nothing much to show,
We had the love of each other which many folks never know.

Though death has been so close to us so many, many times,
We had the faith to look above and God said "not this time."

If I had my choice of riches or the life that we have had,
You can believe with all your heart it would be you dear mom and dad.

Emma Lee Oxendine

THE CLOCK TICKS ON

Last night, I danced on satin-slippered feet.
Your strong arms whirled me 'cross the floor,
And, oh! it was so sweet!

Last night, we raced along a sandy shore.
The soft waves lapped around our feet
Where we had raced before.

Last night, I walked, my dearest love,
Hand in hand with you, along a shaded, leafy lane
Where pink wild roses grew.

And then I woke — the clock ticked on —
After fifty years, my love, you're gone
And I am left alone.

Ah well, one can't have everything
In life's elusive scheme.
We'll be the way we used to be
When next I sleep and dream.

Evelyn Horn Welch

NO MORE FOREVER

And now the terror unfolds
The shadows of lost loves linger over me,
I've just these memories to hold.

There'll be no more heartbreak ever,
No more together,
You see I'll live my life alone,
No wasted time wondering whether,
someone loves me,
I'll know that I'm alone,
No more trickery lies or being clever.
Because I love no more forever.

No more bright moods ever again.
Console my heart for deep within,
No more massive love invasions of solitude,
Like a fortress, my body shelters my heart,
No false feelings can intrude,
To soothe my soul is my only feature endeavor,
Because I love no more forever.

Alvin Gross

BASKET OF FRUIT AND VASE OF FLOWERS

For whom, what, where, when, how and why
Rest this basket of fruit and vase of flowers?
They are for those who in bedroom must lie,
With a basket of fruit and vase of flowers.

For whom, what, where, when, how and why
Rest this basket of fruit and vase of flowers?
They are for those who for kindnesses sigh,
And who pine for their healing more powers
With a basket of fruit and vase of flowers.

For whom, what, where, when, how and why
Rest this basket of fruit and vase of flowers?
They are from those who may no love deny,
And to whom we would give all of ours
With a basket of fruit and a vase of flowers.

William F. Van Buren

THE DUEL

I prayed for peace . . .

He gave me war within, that I might
find the peace that comes with understanding.

In the battle with myself,
I die a thousand deaths.
Love gives birth to new life
amid sounds of pain, and
the cry of the newborn
sings praises to the Lord.
Christ triumphant, gently
spreads a blaze of Light,
the illumination
of soul's darkest night.

Paula Trapani Bourg

WHEN IS THE DAY I RETURN TO MY LOVED ONE?

My Loved One, My Loved One, where are you? I have to come back to say my last goodbye to you, I am hurting inside because you are not here. Why God? Why God? Why is my loved one not with me? Why is there not peace on this earth for me to be with my loved one? I have a vision of my future with peace on earth, it goes like this: I go to my loved one, there he is lying down on his bed. My mother says he is bad off. I say my last words to him, he then turns to me, smiles and says I have been the best thing that happened in his life. And then he closes his eyes slowly, I then cry my heart out because once more God has taken my loved one. This time he has seen his loved ones for the last time, he is with his sister and parents he had lost at one time, then I get up from his bedside and walk slowly, crying because he is gone for good.

Chris Roney

LOVE'S EYES

I stare into the quiet of your eyes
That glance at me in sweetest innocence,
But will not lock with mine that are intense
And seem to parry and apologize;
Their gold is glazed although I scrutinize.
You once accused me of gross negligence.
There lies between us this wide difference:
You hide your problems, while I verbalize,
I buzz about, a bee above your gold.
Your eyes reflect as do an amber gem.

I wear your eyes in mine, a golden heart
Wherein love's first unlocking keys took hold.
And ever I return, examine them,
To carry your eyes with me when we part.

Jeanette Konwiser

MOMENTS

Like a face that was never really handsome
You have faded from before me,
And your imperfections are shut away.
Your empty moments have escaped me
Like a poem that has lost its silence,
And I have forgotten the creases in your skin.
I never grasped the empty moments, and now
They have faded from before me, like hours
From hands that tell the time.

George N. Braman

TOGETHER

Meeting the unspoken needs of love
Touching with the tenderness of emotions
Sharing joys and disappointments
Giving all unselfishly
Reaching for the ultimate feeling
Treasuring our hearts joined as one

DeDee Bellomy

WE TWO

Bright liquid rainbows
Dripping gold into earth's pots —
Imagination!

Miners? Lovers best
At reaping bonanza's breast —
Most fortunately!

Ray Befus

HAPPY VALENTINE'S DAY TO MY GREAT GRANDDAUGHTER

Sugar is sweet
And so are you,
Taffy is sticky
With a lollypop, you are too!
You stick to my heart
Dear great granddaughter of mine
All my years through!

Earl Rowen

MY DREAMS OF YOU

Can never be reality!
They are figments of the past —
Combined and twisted.

It's dark and quiet as I sweat,
And swallow,
And tightly squeeze my eyes.

Sara Ann Holcombe

AS SHE BENT TO KISS HIM

As she bent to kiss him
Her apron opened
Exposing
The rosy skins wrapping the white flesh
Of the partially peeled apples
Like an unsealed envelope
Caressing the contents of a love letter.

Lee Meyer Devine

BELOVED ENEMY

Whoever be
your enemy
Where'er
it cometh of
It certainly
can never be
greater than your love!

O. Felspar

THE ARTIST

Twenty-two years ago, a mere conception
Idealizations of tomorrow's child
Dreams to fulfill, realizing the growth from within

My mother — the artist
Beginning with canvas and basic colors, you gave me life — a strong foundation
You painted the base and surrendered the brush, giving me the freedom of choice

Today, I stand before you — an imprint of the years in between
The creation of an image yet to be complete
There are spaces which I have filled with vivid splendor
There are those of black and gray and still more, erased and painted again

Much of the canvas has been covered with conscious realizations . . . too late
Times when the original artist
(Like a favorite book one always returns to)
Offered a blending beyond my vision

Now reaching awareness
Watching the teacher shape, mold and recreate, I am challenged to do the same

The portrait, once finished, will be my own
I will embrace it — knowing the greatest gifts of all
are the watercolor memories painted by my teacher,
my friend, my confidante . . . my mom

Jennifer L. Setzer

WIND LOVE

My love is like the wind, here one moment and gone again.
Blowing in very strong, never staying in one place too long.
If only my love would subside awhile and settle down to my lifestyle.
No matter how hard I try to suppress it, somehow it seems to always seep
through my grasp.
There must be an end to my wind-like love, the damage it's done will never
be mended.
Shhh, my wind-like love is back again to finish the damage it once did.

Nan Blackshire Little

CALLING HOME

HONORABLE MENTION

And I wrestle with him
the man, my husband, my love
who lies beside me on a sleepless, ghost-white pillow
now a faint imprint of memory fading with time.

He visited me last night
entering in — in the form of an ocean wind
billowing through the curtains, breathing a sigh, a nightcap
into the bedroom where we shared our bed
wherein I now rest my lonely head.

In dreams he calls to me
in a low baritone of thunder like a trump sound of death,
rolling over me in polite invitation, disguised in peace of surrender.

I am tired and my blood rusts like the nails
that hold our old beach home together.
As an old dog when it seeks solace, to die,
I leave to walk along God's salted shore,
keenly aware that my eyes are not unlike the dried sockets of fish washed ashore.

I now know it is time to be calling home;
As my breathing shortens, I can hear the rhythm of the surf cease
my life lease.

Cynthia Jane Law

LET ME LOVE YOU

Let me love you, while we are alone, tonight
Let me love you by the moonlight —
Let me love you, every evening that falls
Let me love you, destiny calls
Let me love you forever.
Every day dawns brighter
We are together, let me love you —
Each caress sets my heart aglow
Let me love you tonight,
Caring moments show
Feelings ignite —
Let me love you tonight,
Every dawn forever, joy meets every single day
We grow closer — Fondness gleams,
Destiny calls, for I Love you —
See our love beams
Upon each evening that falls
Upon every day that dawns, shall we be apart, love won't depart —
And every dawn forever — hope meets each break of day, I love you only
Destiny calls, for I love you always, let me love you tonight.

Gwendolyn "Nassera" Gardner

OLDEN TIMES

Back, go back to olden things
To find what love really brings.
Plaintively call, breathe a sigh.
So lonely, so lovely, you ask, "Why?"

In an earlier, easier time,
Love was always forever new.
Lovers, together a perfect rhyme,
Looking to find only love so true.
What's happened to the olden days
When life went on in quiet ways?
Now, we well know the later cost
As we count what love has lost.

Love, tender love, waits still yet,
And innocent hearts never forget.
Romantic love is no new thing,
Sentiment's worth remembering.

John Hancock

MY LITTLE DOGS

My two little dogs are so faithful and true
They love me for me . . . and don't care what I do.
Just to be near me is about all they care,
I make their lives happy . . . "Love Feelings" we share.

Their only thought seems how best they can show
How truly they love me and make sure I'll know.
When I leave for a while . . . they stand watching me go
And think . . . "Will she come back?" . . . they really don't know!

But when I return they both dance with glee
And there's never a doubt their true love for me.
They bark and jump around me so gay
By just coming home . . . I have made their day!

They are always vying to be my "Best Friend"
Always forgiving with never a thought to offend.
From their faith there's a lesson all humans can learn,
Give unbiased love and true friendships you'll earn.

Lucille Rawling

SWEET THINGS

Be mine; be my Valentine cling
to my heart and say I love you,
Whisper sweet words that say
my love is true.
Be mine; be my Valentine here
Is my heart for your love to wear
to show how much you care.
To share the sweet things that
We vowed to adore to want
whatever we are looking for.
To honor each other in whatever
we do, to want to hold on to what's
best for us to do; to have and to hold
the love that we shared.
Whisper my name and say I love you;
Whisper the things that seem so dear;
Whisper the words that say I love you.
Whisper the things that I want to hear.

Rowena Watters

THE PERFECT STRANGERS

On warm fall nights, you can hear my voice in the wind to your land.
Your warm sensual beauty bestows me to still yearn for you . . .
Yet I feel the battle will be half over very shortly.

We are the perfect strangers from my land to your Japan.
For I would sacrifice all that I have and to cherish
To be in your arms holding your bare bosom to my manly chest.

Your ways and the law of your land I could live with forever . . .
But all I can do is talk within the wind in honest, celebrated delight!
But with frustration I cannot call nor see you my love.

If you have a dream, you pursue it. If it's aspiration, you seek it.
But if it's true love you think of it every burning day and in the end . . .
My love for you can be endless and always be there through the wind.

The winds between us could be that of a premonition that if pursued
You hearing me shall be an echo to your river of majestic love undiminished
So that someday I may journey by sea for you and be captured forever.

William D. Brownlie III

MY BELOVED

Loving you was easy.
Liking you was fun.
Losing you was harder
    than anything I've done.
Time has helped a little bit,
    But the pain is always there.
Your smile, your glowing wit
    The way you wore your hair.
Such different looks upon that face
    I loved so much so very long.
If only there wasn't an empty space
    Where only you should be.
I'm thankful for the time we had.
I've forgotten the days that were bad.
I promised you that I'd be brave,
    But promises are hard to keep.
I'll try again tomorrow.
Now please Lord let me sleep!

Louise McPhail

LIFE PARTS US NOW

Life parts us now,
We walk into the sunshine
And darkness of the world alone.
Henceforward I stand,
With the eternal quality of your soul
Refreshing mine.
Remembering your countenance
Will be my triumph over tribulations,
When anticipating sorrow,
I summon up thoughts of our brief interlude.
And afterwards, with my serenity of spirit,
I challenge life!

Joan Marie Rooks

THE BRIDE I WANTED TO BE

We were sweethearts you and me. And very young
were we, when you asked me to be your wife.
Very happy was I for I wanted you to be mine.
So happy were we both when we made our
wedding plans. I was to become your wife on
a day in mid-July. But darling our wedding
plans were ended the day we were to wed. My
eyes filled with tears when the sad news I
received. My happiness was gone, my world to me
was ended. An accident on the job had taken your
young life. The sad news told me I would
never be your wife.

Flossie Ritchie

ARE YOU BLIND

I knew you once when we were friends
And that was years ago
I know you now and we are still friends,
But now we are lovers too
And I can see how rich we are together,
But when you are not with me,
I become poor and lost, in a society of losers
What the question is, is how far can you see?
And do you realize what
Poverty is,
Especially when it enters
The heart

Sherie L. Mullen

JESUS AND MY WIFE

I thank you dear Lord, for opening
my eyes to my wife.
Now both of us are having a great life.
She's a beautiful person, so loving and kind.
O dear Lord I was so blind.
I love her so much I hurt inside.
If it weren't for you Lord, I think
my mind would collide.
So, I'll thank you again Lord for giving
me this girl.
I love her more than anything in this
whole wide world.

Ralph D'Esposito

BY THE WATERS STILL MY LOVE

God give me sweet forbearance until I
May savor sweet without doubts or question why
The one I love the most would cause me tears
O, help me search for peace, sadness disappears.

Down through the ages love filled hearts of man
In Eden's flowery bower it all began
Could I find that love, how my heart would sing
Blest be that ancient love, a beautiful thing.

When sunset's flaming glory fades away
And my lonely spirit cries relentlessly
My dear one failed me, and love's far from me
All my hopes of a true commitment flee.

O that lovely hour, believing you would share
All my sweet tomorrows beyond compare
All sweet thoughts in twilight hours e'er be
Of a happy hour when you come to me.

Lead me by the waters still, love's sweet flower
Blooms in quietude by grace this perfect hour
Sharing every joy my heart promised you
Leads to nuptial bliss, beautiful and true.

Elvira L. Keeso

A HERO WAS CALLED

He hadn't wanted to go, I know
For children know such things,
He said, "Be brave, be a good little soldier,"
And I did my best to do so.

The letters came from far, far away,
Places I could not pronounce.
War was there, close to him
As it was in our own dear house.

Friends at school asked for news,
I sounded proud and brave
When I spoke of him, my father then
A man I hardly knew, this war hero
In a world somewhere locked away
Who would be coming home one bright day.

I worried so for all who grieved,
And hugged my tears within,
For to be brave was what he had asked of me.

A war hero, he was called, a great General told me so,
And I believe that may be,
But most of all, this hero was a loving father to me.

Betty B. Jones

THE LOVING JOURNEY

Counting the days spent with you
Like precious gems or gold

Life took on a spectacular view
As our days together unfold

Sharing a sunset — walking in the park
Climbing up a mountain on an impetuous lark

Striding through life together — hand entwined in hand
Seeking in union our own vision of the promised land

Stanley S. Reyburn

THE FOUR ELEMENTS TO ME

You are the earth that I walk upon,
The soil that lets all things grow:
A red rose, a full-blown tree, nature's song,
The only ground that I'll ever know.
You're the four elements to me.

You are the fire that burns in my soul,
The flickering flame and the life it gives.
Glowing ember, soft light, warming the cold,
Showing that our love still lives.
You're the four elements to me.

You are the air that I breathe so pure,
The breeze that blows gently my hair.
Lazy wind, a brief puff, cooling zephyr.
Letting me know that you're always there.
You're the four elements to me.

You are the water that quenches my thirst,
The liquid upon which my life depends.
Rippling lake, babbling brook, spring cloudburst,
Knowing that our love never ends.
You're the four elements to me.

Garrett C. Jeter

DREAMS

I dream of things, that have never been, and ask the reason why.
Is it because, it wasn't meant to be, or because I didn't try?
You work so hard my husband.
Your hours are so long.
We once had time. Now we don't.
That seems so very wrong.
In dreams I dance away in the arms of a past love.
I dream of things that we once did, and sometimes I get sad.
These thoughts I want to rid,
Then you come home, and call my name.
There's one thing that I know,
In your arms I'd rather be.
Your love has made it so.

Carol Kane

KISS ME AGAIN!

As a drink creates a thirst for more,
As a taste creates an appetite,
Just so your kiss calls for an encore;
So, please, before you tell me Good Night,
Kiss me again!

What wondrous magic is in your kiss!
What exquisite pleasure it imparts!
There's no delight can compare with this!
With its thrill, thought of all else departs!
Kiss me again!

Your lips on mine set my HEART ON FIRE,
Create a flame that keeps on burning;
And in my heart there's but one desire,
Only one constant deep-down yearning —
Kiss me again!

Your kiss, like footprints in the sand,
Leaves no trace but on the memory;
But on my heart they have left your brand,
Polished it like fine-grained emery.
Kiss me again!

Carol Boyer Mitchell

WE THREE

Under these bright stars I have been walking
Thinking, My Dear, of little you,
How happy was our little family
Before I crossed the ocean, so deep and blue.

Now the Lord above has changed the picture
Placing us so many miles apart;
While I think of you day after day, My Dear
You are always growing stronger in my heart.

Could I just hold you in my arms, My Sweet
As I used to do in days gone by,
And touch your soft, sweet lips to mine —
To see a twinkle in your eye.

On the lawn, or across the fields
We could watch our little son at play,
Maybe riding his horse along the road
Or feeding it some new-mown hay.

Sonny, with his Mother's dimples
And sparkling eyes so large and bright;
I used to hear his southern accent
While I taught him how to box and fight.

Frank Hause

HEARTS ON FIRE

Love, sweet love, sets two hearts on fire,
And fills each with a burning desire
To tell the other how it feels.
It grows until one somehow reveals
Its deepest, most precious emotions,
And ignites a bond of true devotion.

Love is a thing of beauty which outlives and outshines
The pressures of life and the passage of time.
Its beauty and power one must admire,
'Cause love, sweet love, sets hearts on fire.

Jean S. Price

MY HEART IS A HERMIT

My heart is a hermit, hiding away from life,
Hiding from chances to be hurt, to feel pain,
But also chances to love, to be loved —
Afraid to reach and touch another's heart.

My heart is a voyeur, onlooker at life
Through a fence built tight and strong —
Wondering if there is love for me,
Venturing close, almost touching.

My heart is a coward, wanting and needing
A friend, a lover, a companion to share;
But wondering, fearful, if I need him
Will his love and understanding be there?

My heart is a prude, watching acceptance
Of pleasure for tonight only, but never for me;
Knowing from past memories it's not enough,
Wanting a kind of love I may never have,

My heart is a nostalgic, remembering the past,
The pleasure and pain of a love like no other,
Enduring today through the ravages of time,
Wondering if someone, somewhere remembers too.

Myrtle Barbour Durham

NEED'S OWN CHANCE

As your glance
Will meet my glance
By need's own chance,
Our eyes speak,

And silent words
As homing birds
Draw us near.

Then lips will brush,
As hearts will hush
At passion's rush
To that sweet peak,

Where love is spelled
By words withheld,
As held so dear.

Shirley F. Shown

NEW FOUND LOVE

A new found love,
So fresh, so sweet;
Like a rose in bloom,
It unfolds into new beginnings.
Loneliness is forgotten,
As new challenges have begun.
Happiness is shared,
As two, grow together as one.
Understanding and giving,
Shall keep love strong;
And in this time called life,
Hearts will always belong to one another.
Cherish new love,
With each new day;
And let the joys of living
Show the way, for a new love
To last forever.

Debra Carroll

SARA'S SONG

Once I met a girl so fine
She weighed heavy on my mind
I knew throughout all time
I would never forget her
Her long hair was golden brown
She walked but did not touch the ground
I knew I'd keep her 'round
Forever
Her soft voice it touched my soul
I was half she made me whole
Looked through her eyes and saw her soul
I'll have her forever
Now these summer days are long
I sing to Sara a sweet love song
I was right I was not wrong
I'll love her forever
Once I met a girl so fine

Rick Redmill

You, on that side
Paper lanterns between us
All around, night.

Charles B. Rodning

I ask you if you love me
And wait for your reply
The room so suddenly quiet
But then I hear you sigh
My hands begin to tremble
My heart pounds in my chest
The waiter fills our glasses
With nothing but the best.
I look across the table
Your face is still the same
I hear you softly murmur
Repeat repeat my name
My name so gently spoken
As if in a caress
The answer to my question
Is it No or is it Yes?

Kit Cronin

MY PLACE

A cabin nestled against a hill . . .
A blue lake for a lawn.
A meadow full of poppies
All golden in the sun.

This place of mine is where I come
To commune with my God.
I lay my burdens at His feet . . .
And ask His blessings as He sees fit.

This place of mine — is mine alone.
No one can e'er intrude;
Because it's all inside — you see.
A place of rest for me.

Helen Carol Palmer

LOVE'S LAMENT

With love's gentle smile
Upon my face,
I long to feel
Your warm embrace.
I long to hold you next to me
And kiss your lips so tenderly.

So sad —
Yet sweet —
This love of mine
Even though it stands the test of time.

For you see: I don't have you near —
The one that I'll always hold most dear.

Marsha Riddick

SOMEWHERE IN THE DAWN

I waited patiently
Without suspicion of you not coming back
Then somewhere in the dawn
Suddenly upon my pillow
I felt some familiar movement
I woke up revealing you
And in a gathering instant
Even as the light peeked through
We held back the dawn in sweet reunion.

N. Ming S. Ureta

SAFE IN GOD'S EYES

Man and woman standing together
All alone in a new world
It will be of our making
Both of us hard times, good times
Both of us shrouded in love
Safe against the outsiders
Both of us bringing out only the best
Safe in God's eyes . . .

Angels from north, east, west, south
In the heavens overhead
Life's golden guardians protecting us
From dusk to dawn, dawn to dusk
White light guiding our love
Parting the sea which divided us

Fate has been sealed
Together once more
Our love takes on new meaning
Halley's comet crosses the sky
A child will be born to us
Bringing us even closer
Safe in God's eyes . . .

Raymond Paul Tucker

SUMMER ALONE

Pictures of nature's beauty viewed
By lonely eyes, skies occupying
Water, hiding blue teardrops.

Friendly faces enjoying games and
Brews in strange places
Expedient smiles lasting till eyelids
Become fatigued.

Full moons displaying romantic
Surroundings, and your hands
Are not near to hold — nor your
Ears and lips to kiss.

Sleepless nights — tiring days
Wishing summer could tomorrow
Be fall — to shorten the distance
To your arms.

Here I resemble the night
When one star has the sky
On its own — summer alone.

Paul Freeman

LION III

My son,
my beautiful son.
You sleep the sleep of the innocent
with your head pressed against my breast.

Yesterday I held you with one hand
today with two.
Soon you will walk,
and soon you will go —
too soon.

You are my child.
I'll love you always.

Doreen E. Jardine

THE LONG SEARCH

His pursuit for happiness is endless.
It motivates him to rise to each morning
And greet the great red ball of the sun,
Hoping to take the chill from his loneliness.

His strength lies in his compassion for humanity.
His innate goodness, a fruit born of his own suffering.
And in his search, he stretched his hand to those
Who would take it in support and trust.

And with the wisdom accumulated through the years
I gaze into the love in his eyes and see there
An infinity of sadness, a lifetime of heartache,
Born of the futility of his fruitless and barren search.

If I could have but one wish, it would be
To take away the sadness in his eyes
and give him happiness in the celebration of life.
A fulfillment of his need to be loved by the one he loves most.

But I cannot, and it is this more than anything
Which is the root of my agony, the base of my suffering.
Dear God, why does it have to be so? Is there no peace?
My darling, if ever you need a hand, here is mine.

Sherry M. Zendel

MY SISTER, DOLLY

A sister to me is a special delight,
Of similar features, of similar height.
But most precious of all as I think of her now,
Is her love and compassion that shines from her brow.

Wherever I go, whatever I do,
Her heartfelt interest is loyal and true.
When my heart aches, as hearts often do,
I know her heart feels a little of it too.

She's a special kind of sister, always calm and clear-headed,
Not overemotional like me, who needs steaded.
I draw from her strength like water from a well,
I know it is there and true as a bell.

We have a special kind of love that knows no bounds,
It overcomes obstacles, covers much grounds.
I think I'm so lucky to have such a sister,
If I didn't have her, how much I would miss her!

Thank God I can see her as much as I do,
Sharing my sorrows and laughter with her too.
I hope in some way I can some day measure,
Up to my sister, my dear little treasure.

Margaret E. Reed

REVERIE

We're running along the ocean's shore, laughing — hand in hand.
The sea and sky are mine and yours as we frolic in the sand.
You take my waist and pull me down — the gulls circling above
Are the only witnesses around as we make tender love.
Your lips, so soft, caress my face as you lie next to me,
Drifting, floating into space, we share our ecstasy . . .
But as I open up my eyes, the illusion fades away.
It's our own room I recognize as darkness turns to day.
Gently touching you I know how strange this all will seem —
To take you softly in my arms and recreate my dream . . .

Debra L. Vinnedge

WE NEEDN'T EVER SPEAK OF LOVE

We needn't ever speak of love, or if it does exist.
For I can see it in your eyes, and feel it in your kiss.
We needn't ever speak of love, for love is truly real.
It's magnified a thousand times, in everything I feel.
We needn't ever speak of love, a gift that we both give.
For it reflects itself supreme, each day that we both live.

Leanett Loury Smith

SMITH, LEANETT LOURY. Pen Name: Lee Loury Smith; Born: Chicago, Illinois, 1-2-50; Married: July 3, to Eugene Wesley Smith; Education: Roosevelt University, B.A., Literature, 1983; Occupation: Mother of five, Wife, Writer, Inventor, Lyricist; Memberships: Writer's Digest, Roosevelt Alumni, Bucks County Association for Retarded Citizens; Lower Bucks Parents Auxiliary; Awards: Award for lyrics to song: "If I Could Just," presented by Chappel Recording Studio; Poetry: *Poems in the Key of Life,* book of poetry, Todd & Honeywell, 1986-87; Other Writing: *Good Queen Jessica,* juvenile story in hardbound, Todd & Honeywell, 1986-87; "If I Could Just," Recording, Chappel Recording Studio, 1985; Comments: *My poetry deals with all aspects of life, love, relationships, children, and older people; it is intended to be inspirational and uplifting, while at the same time dealing with stark realities of life and its obstacles.*

IN MY MIND

In my mind I see us
In the early morn
Gazing at the sunrise and seeing a new day born.

In my mind I see us
Riding horseback under the trees
Watching the change of seasons
And autumn leaves dancing in the breeze.

In my mind I see us
At the shore hand in hand
Dodging waves at sunset
And making love upon the sand.

Bonnie L. Weatherford

IN LOVE AGAIN

Love words spoken in delusion,
Gifts given from the soul,
The gentle strokes, the parted lips,
The wondrous uniting fusion.
Bring us back to earth again.
The years produce so little.
One never sees the problems,
The time it takes, the required pain.
Then the roses appear once more,
Lovers run to shelter's arms,
The world is so hard to see,
In quiet safety behind a heart's door.

Connie Rae McDonald

CONTAINER/DISPENSER

I am human, a container
I can hold or I can eject
All manner of depravity

Or by God's grace
I can empty my many sins
Into His sea of forgiveness
He will cleanse and purify me
And fill me with His joy and peace

Then shall I be
Container/Dispenser of God's love

Dorothy Howard Adler

SOUL MATES, LONG APART

Eons of separateness have created the mold
For the consummate casting.
Time has shaped us one to the other
In perfect understanding.

And now we come together:
Objet d'art!

Still the mold is used
Above and beyond —
A pattern for new souls;
God's art of love, practiced in us.

Marie Ferneau

UNCERTAIN LOVE

Two people seldom will perceive
their love in just one way
for love, like life, keeps changing
with the passing of each day
and where there is change
uncertainty is bound to be felt too
affecting our decisions
and most all we say and do
it's perplexing and ironic
and it tears the soul apart
it's a battle of emotions
that takes place within our hearts

Kathy Liggett Smith

I love people,
I really do—
People with *growing*
Through and through—
People who flounder
At times, but fly
Onward and upward,
Always up—high!
Growing and growing—
Why, oh why?
Because, it's growing
That make us fly!

Nella Thompson Meiser

BROKEN PROMISE

No, I won't tell you "I love you,"
All my life it will remain, so deep in my
Soul embedded . . . so deep in my
Mind ingrained.
Every hour is filled with thoughts of you,
Remembering a word, a glance or just you.

No, I won't tell you "I love you,"
After all the things I've said.
Sometimes I think silence would have
Said more, sometimes I know my eyes
Have told you all, and even if you
Should stop wanting me,
Remembering your voice, I will always be.

Annadir Hariri

FORBIDDEN FRUIT

Forbidden fruit has an appeal
Provocatively strong.
The Tempter makes his victim feel
To take it isn't wrong.

It's fun to play with fire although
We're likely to get burned,
And even those who ought to know
Too often haven't learned.

So some illicit love affair
May promise many thrills;
But while there still is time, beware!
Such passion true love kills.

Mary Thayer Blanchard

SHE DWELT AMONG THE UNTRODDEN WAYS

She dwelt among the untrodden ways
Beside the springs of Dove,
A maid whom there were none to praise
And very few to love:

A violet by a mossy stone
Half hidden from the eye.
— Fair as a star, when only one
Is shining in the sky.

She lived unknown, and few could know
When Lucy ceased to be;
But she is in her grave, and, oh,
The difference to me!

William Wordsworth

A WALK IN THE WOODS

I'm walking through the woods
Of mystery, tagging along with God,
Picking little berries of knowledge.

The thorns break my skin
And He heals it baby pink.
I get lost on side trails
And he comes back for me.

Eating berries — giving them away.
Filling the bottomless bucket
With the joy of doing and knowing.
An endless journey with
My Friend and friends.

Neil J. Hansen

NATURE

I sit beside the glowing fire
As day fades into night,
And thank the Heavenly Father
That love has been so right.

The birds chirp shyly in the trees
In tones that hint of fare-you-well,
They fluff their feathers, look about —
But where they go they never tell.

Next mornin's sun is all agleam
Upon a snow-white earth
That tells the story proudly
Of Nature's loving birth.

Verona Lyon

CHRISTMAS GIFTS

God bless us as we celebrate,
the birthday of Your Son.
God bless our loved ones absent,
each and every one.

Open our eyes to the beauty,
in bright blue skies, and stars.
And in children's laughter that tells,
of gifts much greater than ours.

Help all on earth to remember,
Your sacred message of love.
Watch over us and guide us,
our Light from heaven above.

Ginny Lindauer

ENCHANTED ROOM

Once, in the midst of night
A bird singing outside
And a path of silver moonlight
Streaming through the window space
Awakened me — and I found myself
Wrapt in your delicious embrace!

I will always remember that room.
A very special place.

Lois Smith Triplitt

TAURUS AND SCORPIO

How unlike we are
you a laughing child of May
And I, November's
As different we two as season's weather.

As seasons balance out the year
We balance one another
As you, lover, have taught me
One and one are never one, but two
So you and I are separate and distinct.

Nor tied, nor locked together
Only here in our special place
Where our worlds combine
We share a common place
Where you and I become US

A place called LOVE.

Patricia L. Durgin

THE GYPSY VIOLIN

In a small cafe, where
lovers dream, a gypsy plays his violin.
A cozy corner, the lights are dim, I lift
my glass of wine and smile at him —
He holds my hand so very tight and our
Eyes meet in sheer delight. Gypsy music
so bittersweet, your haunting melody
I feel down deep. Your ancient lore
weaves its magic spell, my love for
him is born this very night, my heart
can tell. As Cupid shoots his arrow
straight at me, I know this night of
love is mine for all eternity. Oh,
gypsy violin your wondrous, wondrous
bow, will always tell of love as it is
now and was so very long ago. So
lovers come and hear the gypsy play,
at the end of town, in a small Cafe.

Ursel Blanco

I sit and watch
the raindrops fall,
and I think of you.

The pitter patter of water
touching leaves
reminds me of your footsteps.

The cool fresh scent
in the air
reminds me of your presence.

The touch of water
on my lips
reminds me of your kiss.

And the peaceful mood
reminds me of when we are together,
and how beautiful it is.

Marlene Kumpfbeck-Verdadero

GREEN GROW THE RASHES O!

Green grow the rashes O,
Green grow the rashes O;
The sweetest hours that e'er I spend
Are spent amang the lasses O.

There's naught but care on ev'ry han',
In every hour that passes O;
What signifies the life o' man,
An' 't were na for the lasses O?

The warly race may riches chase,
An' riches still may fly them O;
An' though at last they catch them fast,
Their hearts can ne'er enjoy them O.

Gie me a canny hour at e'en,
My arms about my dearie O,
An' warly cares an' warly men
May all gae tapsalteerie O.

For you sae douce, ye sneer at this,
Ye're naught but senseless asses O!
The wisest man the warl' e'er saw
He dearly lo'ed the lasses O.

Auld Nature swears the lovely dears
Her noblest work she classes O:
Her 'prentice han' she tried on man,
An' then she made the lasses O.

Robert Burns

ESSENCE OF YOU

Exploding stars! Black holes!
Where are the homes of souls?
Behind black crepe drape
I await fate
Explanation, epiphany.
Wherever our souls flee
So long as I am me
So long as I can dream
Whatever life may seem
Still will I see
The essence of you eternally.

Alberta Anna Hannaman

HANNAMAN, ALBERTA ANNA.

LOOK INTO YOUR HEART - AND SEE

My Son, now I have left the earth —
My Love, don't cry for me.
God Father, who created me,
Has called me home to Thee!

Now I am whole, and I can see —
Into Eternity —
My spirits are forever free;
Look up to the stars — and see!

There is a Garden beyond the skies
Of lovely flowers and magic trees —
A land called Paradise —
Abundant, rich and free.
God blessed it all to me!
Look into the eye of a blue Bluebell,
And see — what I can see!

May God bless you,
And keep you in His love,
Wherever you will be.
Within you lives a part of me —
Look into your Heart — and see!

Gudrun G. Mainz-Blancaflor

KING

You, Drum Major for Justice,
Expressed love for us all
Through your non-violent protest
Against wrong —
You, peacemaker, stood strong
Facing rabid mobs — fire hoses
Police dogs.
A Prince of Peace, you ascended
All; loving, caring, marching on
Making the ultimate sacrifice: your life.
You loved both wisely and well.
On your holiday we can now tell the world
How our hearts are on fire for you.

Nagueyalti Warren

ANNIVERSARY SONG

I lived the Spring and touched the dawn;
my dreams lay gently on new grass.
I found a song within my heart —
The rain came softly down.
. . . and I loved you.

After Spring, the Summer of my life.
Roses drowsed beneath the sun at noon.
God blessed, as seasons altered and left
my soul at peace with autumn.
. . . I loved you.

As Autumn comes before Winter
and roses fade before night.
The heart does sing as it did
in the early time of Spring.
. . . Still I love you.

As Winter nears and snow will be drifting
upon the sleeping beauty of the rose.
Winds are moving in the trees with
promises the season brings.
. . . I will love you.

Mystery Alires

SOMEONE TO LOVE

Sent inside these walls of stone,
and all I love, I love alone.
I'm trying to find a love that will last.
One to share my future, as well as my past.
Someone to love, and to have love me.
Someone whose love, will set us both free.
When will I find this perfect love?
Will she be sent from heaven above?
How long will I wait,
'til I find a love that is true?
How will I know her?
Could she be you?

Roy M. Alexander

A FRIEND OF MINE

Friendship is a wonderful thing.
Friendship makes the heart sing.
A friend is the most valuable thing on earth.
A friend in spirit you have been since birth.
You, my friend, are the one that is true.
You never lie or cheat like most people do.
You bring me up, when I'm feeling low.
You will always be close to my heart,
I want you to know.
So, even though you're going away,
In this heart of mine you will always stay,
A friend of mine.

Heather Clough

FULL MEANING

I love you . . .
But I love most what you mean to me.
You mean life at its highest peak.
You mean death so calmly beautiful.
You mean joy and its heartfelt tenderness;
A contented sigh in willing surrender.
You mean sorrow with a tear like a tiny crystal . . .
Its breakage causing a nonchalant laugh.
I wish to live with you, laugh with you,
cry with you, and then gladly die with you;
Because I love you . . .
And love most what you mean to me.

Theodore V. Kundrat

THE TONGUE OF MY SOUL

During the hottest, driest summer of modern times
he was born;
And as the earth baked, the boy grew,
yet we did not suffer from lack of water.
In October the rains finally came.
The dry earth sucked at the puddles like a long,
desert dried man's parched lips
reach for sweet dew falling from
the foliage at the edge
of the sands.
My need for his love is parched lips in the sun;
His smile sweet dew on the tongue of my soul.

Steven Rodrick

RENEWAL

Spring stirred
Curled in the sunlit corner of the yard
Stretching lazily
extending tentatively across the yet shivering soil
Shooing fugitive winter
from furtive, last-thawing niches
Spreading comfortably out
Cozily content
Giddily fertile
Seeking response
Sleep warmed alabaster arms
encircling, stimulating, rousing
Dabbling in creation
Urging cheeky crocus to cluster
tower-hard oak to encompass
Profound variety to enrapture
Melody to quicken
Like love's welcomed stirring
In the sunlit corner of our hearts.

Edward P. O'Callaghan

LOVE

Love is seeing past the errors that people make each day.
Love is layering on a calm repose
In the midst of chaos roundabout —
Touching, hearing, smelling messes everywhere.
Love feels a beyond perfectness
For all creatures here and there.

Love is hurting for the brashness that humans show to self.
Love is mellowness in times of hating
In the kill of warfare on rampage —
Soothing, caring, palming troubles soaring high.
Love knows a power erupting
That will silence each outcry.

Love is paining for the misery that daggers each and all.
Love is forgiving in rough places
Where hope is lost complete in sorrow —
Praying, reaching, knowing darkened murky soul.
Love is level faithfulness
That will kindle deep control.

Dorothy M. Ainslie

LOVE FOR ALL

To love our friends is easy to do,
For they are close to us and love us, too.

But what about those who bother us,
Who oppose and quarrel and cause a fuss?

Pray for them and hope they'll pray for us, too,
Love them and show it in all that we do.

Overcome evil with good we're told;
Put not an enemy out in the cold;

But love, cherish and lead him to know
What joys can be ours if together we grow.

God loves us all, of this we are sure;
And only His love is completely pure.

'Tis clear we must always forgive each other;
We must look to God and love one another.

Jean D. Knettler

DAWN

To each a separate home and to each a separate life,
Your sister and you were split up —
Your Dad and Mom divorced; no longer man and wife.
Your sister's name was Mandy — she was a baby not yet one —
She was to live with your Dad and
You were to stay with your Mom when all was said and done.

Your Dad and I started dating and I saw your sister almost every day —
And soon your Dad said "Let's get married," I said, "Let's not delay."
Your Dad said, "There is only one condition, when you stand up and say 'I do' —
You can't have me without Mandy. You have to love her too."
I turned and said to your Dad — "Honey, I already do."

Mandy is young and does not understand why you come and go as you do.
It is hard to explain visitation — she only knows love for you.
Your Dad understands the reasons why things are to be this way,
But you know he lives with a heartache each and every day.
He loves you Dawn, as I do, I am sure you know it is true.
You will always be a part of us wherever life leads you!

Patricia M. Stephens

IMPOSSIBLE LETTER

It's the letter to get you to see.
It's the one that will bring you back to me.

Seeing you with him it's the one that will never be.
You holding on to him so tight;
together your laughter seems so right.

Disperse this hell; gotta get you out of my mind.
Looking deep inside myself; something there I must find.

All my feelings and thoughts have been sent to you in a plea;
yet throughout the moments of time you have nothing more to say to me.

I bless the love you have with him; may your good times get better.
Still deep down inside I hope to send you the Impossible Letter.

It's the letter to get you to see.
It's the one that will bring you back to me.

James Shoemaker

DO YOU REMEMBER

When you held me in your arms gently, oh, so gently love
  and told me of your love?
Your kisses, so unearthly sweet,
  holding rapture from the Gods.
When your eyes, like softest velvet, held me under your spell, love . . .
  knowing no alarm —
And ecstasy, like iron bands, clasped my soul enduringly.
  How could I but love thee, love, even knowing it's forbidden?
Still, I held you in my arms, dear,
And begged the Gods to let it be;
This magic love that bound so fast . . . you and me.
Yet dawn would come, and the lover's moon sink in the west,
The brilliant sun laid to rest the darkness of the night.
Dreams were born in shadow,
Held briefly to our hearts, now gone, gone forever!
Yet may I dream, o'er and o'er again,
Of the one perfect love that filled my life,
And shed a tear for that is lost, gone
With the coming dawn.

La Rue Cooke Howard

I NEEDED YOU

I needed you —
and you were there.
I felt so blue —
you said "I care."
You held me close
and held my hand.
You're one who knows —
you understand.
Thanks again for being there.
It sure is nice to know you care.

Suzanne M. DeHart

JULY 12, 1985

Would you believe ten years ago
  we married on this day?
We've changed a lot as you well know —
  I've got a touch of gray.

We haven't always got along,
  so many times we've fought.
Somehow we've managed to stay strong
  when others may have not.

We've each been wounded many times,
  the scars we can ignore.
In looking back, each one finds
  much to be thankful for.

Two children later, here we are,
  the road ahead is new.
It doesn't seem so very far
  as long as I have you.

It hasn't always been so good,
  sometimes it's been a chore.
But I'll be ready if you should
  care to try ten more.

Richard J. McDermith

A CHILD'S CRY

A lonely child
sits and stares,
wondering who
could possibly care.

A tear appears,
she starts to cry,
she hears a voice
and looks toward the sky.

"When you are lonely
and feel very down,
remember the child
who wore the crown.

He, too, felt low,
though he knew why,
for all the sins
he had to die.

As I loved him,
you love him too,
so don't feel lonely,
I'm here with you."

Linda C. Ralston

THE REAL THING

Those sweet years we dreamed together
With hopes so high they touched the sun,
Caressing life in fresh wild innocence,
Our sparkling future had just begun.
Two 'glamour girls' of yesteryear
Learning the sorrow of newborn tears.
Young beauty so alive and physical
Maturing to cope with the difficult.
We took grief and bounced it on our knees
While our wit turned gloom to glee.
Loving letters soared the sky, like un-nested birds
Winging sunlight to grounded lives.
When the sun rested, and twilight felt blue,
God came along and rescued you.
Your life of courage, heart and humility
Taught me the essence of true beauty.

Jean Cunane Murphy

THE TOUCH OF A HAND

The well within filled to capacity
From the drop of warm, a peace-filled calm.
Your free spirit seeing and so unfearing,
Grounded and secure in the natural knowing.
Then the soul, unfettered in flight
Off in worlds of dreams, insights.
Opposite worlds meeting as footprints in the sand,
Walking in different directions.
Yet when the healing sea washes over the sand
Do the two merge; become one?
The constant sea in her ebb and flow
Aware and open, speaks of new beginnings.
The cup refilled in that moment
All is new, silently stilled.
This from the kind, calm control
In the warmth, the touch of a hand.

Carole April Binette

TRANSLUCENTLY JEWELED IS MY RIVER

translucently jeweled is my river,
sparks of gold intermingle
brilliantly with turquoise and garnets.
see — on the far silver banks
are many plants
of ivory and jade, swaying against life's radiant sky,
under love's lucid and clarifying sun.

clearly now, I can see all those loves
that have been my own to have,
plump infant arms reach up, tiny faces glow.
tall adults stand there, who sheltered
innocent days,
and men, with fine loving eyes gleaming softly as Chinese silks,
smile out at me, all, as I pass by on my
translucently jeweled river.

Vee N. Shanahan

THE GHOSTLY LOVERS

There, they say, those who are in love, can see,
On a moonlit night, that is bright as day.
Two lovers walk hand in hand, down the path a way.
Around the lily pond, and into the glen.
Into the glen where deep shadows lie, and where night birds cry.

Robert Dureson

DESPAIR TO JOY

Divorce, divorce is all I hear! The
world is full of hurts and fears.
What is wrong with true love anymore? I
ask, when I see all the tears.

Why must we hurt each other so? Only
to bear the ugly seeds we have sown.
Must we continue on this path of destruction? To
finally throw away that beautiful wedding gown.

Our children now are so awfully messed up. They
turn to drugs and just don't care.
How long will we let this immaturity go on?
drive our next generation to despair.

Husbands and wives, let's work to get along. Then
we'll keep our kids close to us at home.
Let's love each other and love them too. Begin
to build a brand-new moral tone.

Strive to make our marriages work. Have
love for each other, as we ought.
It will put love and joy back in our families. A
great reward, which cannot be bought.

Paul Wright

MY 5 A. M. LOVE PRAYER

I love You, Jesus, I love You, I love You;
Heavenly Father, I love You, I love You;
I love You, Holy Spirit, I love You.
Good morning, I'm awake!

Did the trains two miles away
Awaken me as they whistled through Littleton?
Is it time to get up yet?
Or did You awaken me to pray?

I love You, Jesus, I love You, I love You;
Thank You for being You!
I love You and thank You, Father, for Jesus
— for all Your blessings and gifts, Your care —
That You DO love and care for someone like me.

I love You, Holy Spirit, but don't show You somehow;
Come, please, I pray, be with me all through this day.
Though I might go on and on how I love You,
I'd never have words to thank You enough.
Please be in my steps, my feet, head and heart today.

Thank You, Heavenly Father, Jesus and Holy Spirit,
For this new day You made, thank You; I love You!

Elsie V. Alfrey

SO CLOSE

I feel love very close to me, surrounding
me. I want to reach out and touch it, I
want it to touch me.
Is it the love I yearn to give that I
feel engulfing me like an angelic light,
or is there a man, a man so close to me with
the same aura, who has not found me yet?
Is it his love I feel?
Let it be his love.
Let him find me.

Julia V. Dispensiere

A MOTHER'S PLEA

Whoever wrote "Little things mean a lot"
Really expressed my feelings on the dot.
A kind word or just a smile
Would make a weary day worthwhile.
Just a little fond affection,
Taken into confidence instead of rejection,
Not expensive gifts,
Just a hug or a kiss,
A pat on the shoulder or just a wave,
Would make me feel less like a slave,
A "So long" or just "Hi"
Is much nicer than just walking on by.
Think of me now, don't wait 'til I'm gone.
I need fond memories when I'm all alone.
Boys and girls this is the way
To make every day a Mother's Day.
Love me, please love me —
This is your Mother's plea.

Dolores E. Minnig

COMMITMENT

Your growing disappointment
Is obvious to see.
But a deep commitment
causes me to stay.

Can I shovel a new pathway
to my heart when this one's on ice. No need
to. Just take it slow. Wait out commitment.

Immaturity would beckon me to run.
But I'm a mature woman,
and can recognize the sun,
planting new seed again.

My attention on the things
that I must do;
To produce Life again
In this newly plowed field.

Faith Kennedy

FAREWELL AT DAWN

You slept; but my heart, wakeful still,
Remembers again, your voice last night . . .
Close beside me; walking hand-in-hand
In the moonlight, and stars brilliant-bright
Above the shimmering waves of the Bay.
"At dawn I shall fly," I heard you sigh.
"Remember, when I'm far, far away . . .
Through fair, or storm-wracked skies,
How higher still my heart shall rise,
Remembering you, with smiles in your eyes!
May they always shine, just for me,
As your loyal-love, together or apart,
Has been, and again will be, for me . . .
The only safe Port of my heart."
I touch your proud Eagle-wings, now
Burnished by the dawning sky,
Across your breast . . . resting, too briefly
On mine, and smile . . . in fond "Good-bye."

S. Diane Sawitzki

LEFT-INSIDE LOVE

Dedicated to my sister Gloria for her inspiration

Left-inside love is so hard just to deal with
It's growing and showing, to no one you care
This left-inside love that our vows are not sealed with
Can only let go, if somehow you're there

These left-alone thoughts, that are forced in my memory
To conjure you up, in the middle of the night
To be with you, without you; within you and doubt you
Because left-alone thoughts somehow are not right

Left among the feelings are promises and torments
Arms that hold no one and tears held within
Letters not sealing, love just on paper
Sends my heart reeling, to be with you again

A thank-you on paper; a kind thought in prose
The grace of my heart; Guess I just will know
But a need and a feeling and a prayer to above
And my thoughts are of you, with this left-inside love

Lucky Rimpila

UNTIL FOREVER, I LOVE YOU!

Because I saw it in your eyes
The first time I saw you,
And on your lips when you said, "hello!"
Because I heard it in your voice
When you spoke to me,
Because I saw it on your expression
When you looked at me.

Because I felt it in your hands when they
Held mine, In your arms, when they caressed
Me, On your lips, when they kissed mine, And
In your body, when you made love to me.

Because of your simple honesty, Your deep
Concern and your caring, And your loving
Kindness toward me — knowing, you will not
Desert me —
And because I felt the same way
From that first time, until now, until forever,
I Love You

J. Elizabeth Roberts

LOVE TEARS

my heart has been indescribably lonely without
you. your absence has grossly demonstrated my
love, need and want for you. ambivalently,
elation is also my state of mind,
because my continuous prayers to my God
for your speedy and safe recovery have
been happily answered. he has quantitatively in
the past two days soaked the earth
with much needed rain. i have helplessly
and qualitatively soaked my pillow with love tears:
tears because i could not ease or share your pain.
tears because I could not embrace you in my arms.
tears because i could not whisper softly in
your ear, i love you.
tears because i love you.
gone . . . gone . . . gone . . . gone . . . gone.
the tears are no longer around.
the frown has been turned upside down, because
i know very soon you will once again be around.

Alonzo Davis

SHOW YOUR LOVE NOW

A mother's love is hard to find,
So children, keep this in mind
For you there will never be another
No one so loving as a mother.
A mother's voice on the phone
Mother's feeling so very alone
She woke up early, feeling so sad
Missing her lover, children's dad
A beloved one we surely do miss
A love, a father's loving kiss

Children remember kisses missed.
So be gentle, kind, to your mother
For you, there will never be another
One day a mother's kiss will be missed.
So children, speak now, and show her love now.
Let love be the answer, speak from the heart
Don't let mis-feelings tear you apart —

NEVER TOO LATE TO SAY I LOVE YOU
NEVER TOO LATE TO SAY I CARE . . .

Renee Edwards

TONIGHT . . .

Tonight, I want to put the words on paper . . .
for you.
Tonight, I want to acknowledge my love for you,
but more,
I want you to acknowledge that love.

Let all your inhibitions go,
Let your conscious mind acknowledge
your unconscious mind.
Accept the fact a love like ours is rare.

Shatter the protective shield you treasure.
Open all those locked-up emotions and
let me in.

We could share the rainbows and the stars.
We could share tears and smiles,
we could share ourselves
together;

if you'd only let me in.

Elise R. Jacobson

EACH GRAIN OF SAND

I'll walk across the largest desert,
With desert sand filling my shoes,
With the greatest thirst you've ever seen,
If I can spend some time with you!

I'll run the length of the largest desert,
Through the hottest heat of the day,
Trodding and trodding on without delay!

I'll follow the brightest star of the desert,
With howling winds blowing in my face,
I'll spend cold cold nights trodding on,
If I could prove my love for you!

I'll walk across the largest desert,
And count each grain of sand along the way,
If I could spend my life with you!

Doris Burleigh

I CAN PICTURE US TOGETHER

Walking through the countryside,
We're open to one another, we have nothing to hide.

It's on a cool, breezy summer's eve,
I'm with you and I'm feeling at ease.

We stop to watch the tender birds flying above,
And see the squirrels who are full of love,

Slowly you take me in your arms,
I can trust you and I know you'll do me no harm.

Then you kissed me,
I held you close, I know you're right for me.

We continued to walk, hand in hand,
Our feelings for one another we understand.

Maybe one day my picture will be real,
But I am glad that now you understand how I feel.

Michelle Norman

NORMAN, DOROTHY MICHELLE. Born: Atlanta, Georgia, 2-20-68; Single; Education: I am a senior at Jonesboro Senior High School; Occupation: Cashier at Family Dollar; Awards: Golden Poet Award for 'My Imagination,' published this past July; Poetry: 'My Imagination,' World of Poetry, July 1985; 'I Need Someone,' American Poetry Association, April 1986; Comments: *When I write poetry, I try to relate to how people feel about themselves, others, and their life. I try to say something in my work that has to be read to be understood .*

ALONE

An empty space with no light,

The scent of faded roses — of hopes and
dreams destroyed,

The hollow echo of promises whispered —

but never kept,

The emptiness cuts like the sharpest knife.

Tonya Lee Byes

LOVE

Gently love caresses
The softness of the babe;
Newborn identity,
Yet still a part of you.

Defensive love and strong,
Brother and sister, joined
Against the world's attacks
Forever for each other.

Shy and searching young love,
Doubting and yet sure,
Tumultuous, curious,
Tested and found to be sweet.

Love that's steady, giving,
Growing deep, anchored, sure,
Reaching and responding,
Welded together as one.

Wise, full, respectful love,
Enfolding, touching all,
Warm, expanding, tender,
Encouraging and strong.

Eleanor Robinson

IT DOESN'T HURT

I don't have feelings
I'm untouchable, you see
You'll never see me cry
You can't hurt me

Just because you lied
And cheated on me
That doesn't mean I'm sad
I'm made of iron, you see

I refuse to be weak
I am woman, I am strong
I'll keep my head on straight
Even though you've done me wrong

I'm really a robot
Devoid of all emotion
What a silly thing
All this love and devotion

It really doesn't hurt
And pigs fly too
What a liar I am!
I still love you —

Carole E. Strickler

The reason I write poetry
is to tell you what I see.
Funny that I play with words,
since they aren't often really heard.

If I thought that it would work
I wouldn't try to write a book —
I'd rather look into your eyes
to see what beauty in them lies,

or gently hold you to my breast
and Love herself would do the rest.

Diane E. Ramey

DAISY

Did you ever need a friend and have someone there . . .
Did you ever need to talk to someone who would care?
Did you ever want to rest beneath a big shade tree?
I know who . . . and where . . . just come along with me . . .

She lives on top a little hill . . . in a quiet part of town.
A place with a breeze and sunshine and flowers all around.
Her door is always open, her heart is full of love.
I'm sure she gets some guidance from someone up above.

Sometimes she is like a sister, sometimes she is like a friend.
But every day she is the one on whom you can depend.
Her table is always laden with food she has in store,
And everyone is welcome, who comes knocking at her door.

She is a lovely, gracious person, someone for whom I care.
A little bit of her . . . goes with me everywhere.
Her name was named for flowers . . . it rings with springtime songs,
It carries from Minnesota fields to California throngs.

The white is for the Minnesota snow . . . in which we used to play . . .
The yellow is for the California sun where we all live today.
Wherever we make our home, she will be a part of us.
Our wonderful Daisy, who we think is fabulous . . .

Doris June Winkelman

THE TOUCH OF LOVE

Gently we touch from across the room, eyes saying more than words —
So silently speaking what's in our hearts, though not a sound is heard.

We talk without speaking, listen without sound —
feeling each other's presence, as if no one else is around.

A gentle touch from across the way —
the touch of love that will last all day.

And without a word we know so much —
we need each other and the gentle touch.

Conrad A. Reiber

BITTER LOVE

I don't know, I don't care and I don't give a damn,
I don't care about anything except my children.
Them I love and them I'll support the best that I can,
but it's hard to be a good father when you can't be their best friend.

No I don't live there anymore, I'm not there at night,
they don't have me to run to when they're afright.
It wasn't my choice and sure the hell ain't my right,
to be there with my children and have them in my sight.

I don't know, I don't care and I don't give a damn,
it's hard to care about anything when you can't be with them.
They are my life . . . they are my very soul,
and to them I can't go, 'cause some women don't think so.

I don't know, I don't care and I don't give a damn,
but in the morning the sun will rise and at night set again.
So onward I must go with nothing more than a memory,
so remember Micah and Amber, please remember me.

I don't know, I don't care and I don't give a damn,
there's been a dimmer put on my light, will it ever shine again?
It's not just for my children, but my love has turned away,
and to her I can't go, or at least not to stay.

Marty Hayes

GARDEN OF LOVE

In my garden, always stands, a row of love.
Planted deeply, roots are clinging,
to the solid mass of patience,
waiting for the sun to shine.

Sometimes, it rains, but when it does,
it causes weakened shoots to stand,
and fills them full of strength to see,
the beautiful blooms, they're going to be!

When the time arrives, for the petals to fall,
there's no need for despair,
for the seeds will recall,
how to do it again, just the same as before.

They don't ask, "How?" because they know,
that love lives on, forevermore!

Judith Nass Gonzalez

TAKE ME BACK

Take me back to my Greenwood Home
And my dear old Dad who was one time young!
To have nine children was not his goal,
But to love us he did — was his special role!
Said my Mom: "A perfectionist!
Must every row be just so?
You could terrace more acres and see more grow!"
But Dad plodded on, with a dream in his head —
"It's all right for me," he often said,
"But go to school and learn all you can! You can
Always farm, if that's your goal,
But find out first just what's ahead."
Nine children became a result of his dream!
Doctors, nurses, and lawyers all;
Teachers, too, and business men, wives . . .
We all remember a special DAD
Who loved us enough to give all he had.

Mayna Fain Hoke

THE PHOENIX

I first hear his voice,
Enticing me with epicurean delights.
I followed him by choice,
A vulnerable addition to his lair.
Overcoming my recalcitrant fears,
I felt insatiable passions take flight.
Pleasurable rays permeated a shining sphere,
Where slept the centrex of desires laid bare.

Now, where flames of crimson once burned,
Once blackened ashes of a Phoenix remain.
For my love he has spurned.
Can one forgive promises that never could be?
Rather than speaking lamentations of sorrow,
I'll store such memories for ambiguous gain.
Looking toward another tomorrow,
Knowing for him I tried to be me.

Barbara Light

AUTUMN'S ENDING

In a forest fat with color,
Walking on a precipice,
I pause alone
to sense another urge of recollection
which is all about you;
As the leaves lie in scatters,
Your memories, with Autumn, end in tatters.

This wood, so desolate and still,
This lake below, so gray, so leaden,
I pause alone
to beg a chilling Autumn wind descend and deaden
Passion's too-consuming heat,
to seal too-human feeling:
Freeze these falling tears!

Cry a loon upon a lake!
Cry a wind that wounds this forest!
Curse a cry of my heartache,
Longing for you without rest!

Never will I love Another without Pain,
Without a dark remembering . . .

D. R. Mitchell

A HAPPIER DAY

As I often remember what I painfully learned,
through a dear and dying one's regretful concern,
of not taking that straight and narrow road.

My heart aches to think about Calvary's unbearably
heavy load that for sin's way, you did pay.

O Lord, teach me day by day your way, never to go another.

So when from this earth I must depart, holding your
love deep in my heart, I know it will be a happier
day by far than it was for my own dear mother.

Jeanette Moody

ECHO OF FAITH #2358B

Hearts on fire with love of God . . . like a
Kaleidoscope of bright colored bits and pieces
of illusions and realities intertwined . . .
Of truths hidden or yet to be revealed in the
Constantly changing universe of forevermore . . .

The interplay of light and darkness, day and
Night, dawn and sunset . . . the shifting tides
and seasons, civilizations, stars, galaxies . . .
Lost, revealed or hidden still . . . dying or coming to
Birth in the complexity of nature's kaleidoscope . . .

Echoings of faith, my gift of love to honor God . . .
His gift of love to all the world . . . another
Facet of light in God's kaleidoscope in
Miniature . . . from invisible essence to renewed,
Awakened and illuminated spirit . . .

God's breath of the eternal, his spark of the
Celestial flame within his children of
Obedience, of love, fear and faith . . .
A kaleidoscope of hearts on fire striving to
Set the world aglow to the glory of God.

Barbara Martinez-Piligian

A NEW KIND OF LOVE

Since we've been apart,
My love for you has grown.
A feeling I had never known,
And never will from me depart.

So many things that you have done,
To show me that you care.
My heartfelt thanks is what you've won,
My love for us to share.

When we shall meet again,
Someday, sometime, along the way.
A life as strangers we'll begin,
And grow together day by day.

Sara Ashton

ONCE IN A WHILE

Once in a while you'll catch a thought
of a once ago broken heart
Once in a while so often broken
they're just accepted as a gift or token
Once in a while it'll come to you
saying again I might be coming through
Once in a while your love will leave
taking with him his promising creed
Once in a while tears are shed
on a lonely night across the bed

Somewhere, somehow, a new love will start
I'm back again says the broken heart.

Ray A. Jones

JONES, RAY A. Born: New Orleans, Louisiana; Other Writings: Works published in *The American Poetry Anthology; Words of Praise, A Treasury of Religious and Inspirational Poetry, Vol II; Hearts on Fire, A Collection of Love Poems;* Comments: *At the age of twenty-three he joined the U. S. Navy. Though ever so interested in the literary arts, it was not until the military that he began comprising the works contained herein. He is presently involved in Communication Electronics and wishes to continue writing.*

CAPE COD NIGHT

On a clear blue skyline
I waited with my patience
For your patched weathered jeans.

The white winter rose
brushed your blushing cheeks.
and chestnut hair.

I chased your feet
through the prickly cow grass,
and rolled you in the leaves.

The moccasin path and pine needle bed
were close friends of ours.
Mosquito nets were clumsy.

Bruce Wagner Mason

MASON, BRUCE WAGNER. Born: Acushnet, Massachusetts; Occupations: General Contractor, Carpenter; Comments: *I write about love and sometimes childhood. I write about life and how it has affected me. My poetry reflects my cynical as well as my optimistic moods.*

MY SON

The warm spring sun shone upon the snow.
And it began to melt and flow.
Across the year and down the dip.

Mary called from the kitchen door,
Saying it was time to go
The most wonderful thrill I'll ever know!

Small, perfect; there you lay
And forever and ever I'll remember the day
I stared through the nursery window
All that day.

As if racing the clock,
You learned to walk
Then as if in a moment
You began to talk.

Golden hair that shone in the sun
Eyes that laughed and chuckled in fun
And then, like you came, you went away
And I am left to mourn the day.

G. M. Petts

REVELATION

Wheresoever there's those who loiter,
On the busy ways of Life,
Mutual concern is a concept
Whereby brotherhood's trend is rife.

Love, the timely acquisition,
Sets the lonely hearts agog,
Clears the ways to a Life worth living
Ne'er defined in any catalog.

Love and togetherness, in conclusion,
Vindicate the ploy of reverence
Voiced in the halls of justice
Respectful of a social deference.

Lovers, hand in hand with happiness,
Flirt with a casual reluctance,
Evade the gilt of guile and prejudice
And enjoy the reign of tolerance.

Prospecting hearts enhance assumption
When eagerness prompts a warm desire,
With ne'er any compromise
Whereat Love ignites the fire.

Charles Ruggles Fox

SAFE-HARBOR

Her rudder broken,
My little boat
Rocks on the riptide
Of a godless sea,
Tossed by uncertainty,
Till a bell buoy voice
Calls me to you,
For you are my haven,
And all of Heaven
I will ever need.

Virginia Westgaard

SINCE YOU

If ever you were mine
Was a question left unanswered
Through all these years of time
Alone in a world of fools
Who hurt, used and battered
The precious love you held
In the palm of your hand
If only for a minute
We could manage to capture
Those fleeting feelings
Of song and rapture
Like grains of sand
That slipped through my fingers
Since you
I managed to grow up
To become a woman
And if I may
I'd like to say
Probably a lot more
Thank you could not visualize
You'll never know
What you missed
In this life
With me.

Leslie Connell

JOHN

Written upon the death of my nineteen-year-old son

Your room is finally "picked up,"
No more clothes strewn everywhere,
Your car sits in the driveway still,
Just as you left it there.
No more grimy towels, from hands half-washed, then dried,
Your tools are strewn in the garage — half of them outside.
Your fav'rite frozen sandwiches are in the freezer, still,
I think of these fav'rites when I shop (I guess I always will!)
I've washed the last of your piled-up clothes,
And folded them away,
You left us just one week ago,
But you still roam the house today.
I hear you "clomping" up the stairs,
The dog awaits your torment,
Your rocking chair awaits you still,
Your stereo is silent.
Yes, John, you're still a resident
Of house, garage and car,
And in my thoughts, and heart, always
No matter *where* you are!

Jean A. Sacharko

MY LOVE

I carried you in my mind and savored the precious minutes
we spent together.
You opened new horizons and vistas for me
Be of good cheer and hold your fortunes high
I was cool to you because I loved you, that's why
You're not too curt or shy, but you were a natural friend
I'll remain interested in you until the curtain's drawn
that will bring the final end
The bells are ringing for us to wish us well
Like a bottle of sweetly scented perfume
Is how your fragrant essence really smells
Love is conceived in the pearly heavens, but they demand
that we perform our terrestrial skit
When it comes to me you'll always be a smashing hit
    You saved my life and saved my poor despondent soul
    You are my number one and only — you're my salvation
I want to eat your flesh and drink your blood so I can taste
your beauty
Your black hair falling on your shoulder really excites me
You are the soul and blessing of my fantasy reveries
When it comes to you I am newly born and baptized

Steven J. Smith

DEEP LOVE

When all your dreams are shattered,
and no open doors in which to find your way,
there is a love who will guide you
on every path day by day.
When every heart is broken,
and the hope for pain's relief
doesn't seem to be in reach,
there is a love who relieves
and helps you to your feet.
When thoughts of love are distant,
and no one seems in sight,
there is one love who will be by your side,
and hold you with all His might.
This love is a spiritual love,
whom my heart holds so dear,
because the love of the holy ghost
is always near.

Angelyn Ables

GLADIOLAS

HONORABLE MENTION

Rocket plumed gladiolas gantried
for an August probe: for four bucks
I could warp around cool nights
to where you stood all bud and twig,

fourteen or so, with hands stretched out
to ponder the green-market bargain
of sturdily blushing gladiolas —
a birthday gift from your mother.

Six kids and an Allen-Bradley check
didn't leave much room for frivolities.
Everything was pinched to share or pass down,
counted and weighed with ruthless skill.

But the flowers were yours once a year;
no one could eat, drink, play or ride them
but you. If they didn't last that long,
well, the feeling remained that you were special.

Heart red, they flush the passenger's front seat.
Though I'm the artless pincher now
I can say I've never passed up a trip to you —
at least not one at bargain prices.

Ron Jevaltas

UNION

Poised in the midst of the circles of desire we thrive, proving that our Love-God does exist. This milking of kisses among the lily pads and still waters leaves me weak. Only the quiet wind and the silent moon are witnesses to our union of souls. No mortals have visited this unknown place of ours of pure pleasure and peace. The fruits are waifs of fragrance of clean flesh and flower petals. Only because of us does this exotic and imaginary state live.

Mary Annah Alemán

UNDER THE FLUORESCENT LAMP

HONORABLE MENTION

If only I had known before!
I'll use incandescent bulbs no more!
For you alone I'd fight,
To see you under the fluorescent light.

To see you under the fluorescent light,
Be it dim, or be it bright,
Be it high, or be it low,
It's better than the sunset's glow.

Better than the sunset's glow,
It makes my love for you still grow,
To see you in your plastic chair,
Fluorescent lighting through your hair.

Fluorescent lighting through your hair,
The sight that makes me stop and stare.
It makes my eyes grow moist, and damp,
To see you under the fluorescent lamp.

To see you under the fluorescent lamp,
The sight that holds my heart in its clamp!
If only I had known before!
I'll use incandescent bulbs no more!

Doug Muravez

SOFTNESS

Her child loved softness:
The softness of a cuddly teddy bear,
The softness of a new not-yet-washed
Blanket, and of the satin binding
Pressed against a warm sleepy cheek,
The smooth softness of a freshly ironed
Satin pillow case on a downy soft pillow;

Her child loved other softness:
The quiet sound of a loving mother's voice
And the soft whisper saying, "I love you,"
With a kiss to show her deep love;

The softness of burrowing into the deep furry
Hair of the pet dog lying nearby and
The fleecy softness of a newborn lamb, or the
Soft fur and mew and purr of a baby kitten
And of clouds, seemingly made of soft, pure fleece;

But, dear son, you are sixteen now, and since your
Baby days, have you ever sought the softness of a
Loving mother's cheek or touched your lips to hers?

Jennie B. Nye

THE FINAL DISCUSSION

And when did you say love was so easy
Wasn't it when it was rough?

I've witnessed your suffering
And you turned away from mine

We're living different words
Than those spoken in the beginning

You were blind to the rules of love
Yet obvious of the grand passions

And I see the fear behind your smile
The woman you thought was yours forever is leaving

You saw the romance and fire fade
Yet never attempted to change things

So now I will be on my way
And leave you looking like you always do . . .
Confused; with nothing to say.

Linda M. Noyola

HORIZON OF PASSION

A wild radiant ocean under a calm adjacent sky
Doves dangle and sweep the sand
And we smile brightly, laughing hand in hand,
Warm and snug in the sweet air of intimacy.
Here, the mountains are beautiful to see
A world of wonder for you and me
Your eyes sparkle beneath the sun
A night of love as our souls sleep as one.

Softly we dream, gently sleep
As we pass from moment to moment
Unaware of voices descending from the
Far side of morning.
All life is deepening and unseen
As we lie down in the soft grass
Breathe, whisper, and dream.

Robert Angello

MY LOVE TO YOU

Have you ever noticed that when we're together we become
As one?
We always agree on plans, on what we'll do next.
I like knowing that you're there for me, and that I can be there
For you.
Kissing you is like a dance under the stars. Making love with
You is like losing myself in the ocean's waves. Lying in your
Arms is like being wrapped in soft white clouds. When you smile
At me it's like the sun caressing my face.
I know your laughter, and I share your sorrows.
We share so much, yet we have so much more.
I'll always love you, and want you with me.
You are my reason for waking and my reason for being.
So many words to say, yet they all mean the same thing.
I love you.

Amy Lynn McNeely

LONG DISTANCE LOVE

I sit in my room remembering the lovely
moment we had together.
I fell in love with you right away. I
wanted that moment to last forever.
But when the time came for you to go home,
I didn't want you to go, I couldn't let you
leave.
I wait every day for your letter and a
ring on the phone.
Nothing on my mind but you, lingering with
me wherever I go.
But there'll be a time when we'll have
that special moment we had before.
You and I together again, long distance
love like never before.

Jocelyn Robles

WHEN

Love dreams are grand dreams, whenever they're real and true,
I want you to keep dreams forever 'twixt me and you.
When you are lonely, when loneliness things appeal,
Remember to love me only, this love that I hold is real.

When you're away from me remember to love me truly;
When you would stray from me, don't let your heart turn unruly.
When you would seem to be under love stress unduly,
Don't cause me to smart, for my love lives from your heart.

Stephen L. Bogadi

NO FOLD

HONORABLE MENTION

There were times when she
could have left that voiceless house,
could have run berserk into spring,
but the flowering trees reminded her
of their first spring by a river where
redbud bloomed mauve, and wild cherry trees
snowed petals over browsing sheep
on the thicket-green towpath.
All the bittersweet of their love
flamed outside, inside, without, within,
and she could find no fold, no fold
for her loneliness. Still she could
not bear that card with the words:
"We will give cash for your home."

Margaret Secrest

Welcome back
to the warm
and the soft
of me.

You've been away too long.

I was beginning
to adjust
without you,
though I didn't
want to.

Welcome back.

Welcome home.

Janice L. White

MY LOVE

Arise, my love,
Together we shall embrace the dawn,
As we did the night.

Whisper, my love,
Softly shall your thoughts take flight,
And cross the silence.

Journey, my love,
Hand in hand through starlit night,
Or past the endless sea.

Hold me, my love,
Let my heart beat for us both —
Free our souls.

Mark Arvid White

DREAMS

Are we but a dream,
Here for a moment,
Then gone like the air?

One moment we laugh,
Share love with our own,
Then gone like the air?

Or do we end one dream,
To start another, somewhere,
Then vanish, there, like the air?

Then, it's in dreams,
That we are immortal.
Even air is here, or there!

Edna Mae Walker

IMAGERY

Love is the mirror
That reflects the truth
Of Passion's crest,
And trembles the souls of men.

The images of lovers
Are the beauty
That abounds amid
The splendors of Creation.

Mary T. Carey

FOR YOU MOM

When I see you standing there,
I know deep down I'm not alone.
I know you'll always be there,
No matter how long or far I go.
You mean the world to me, mom,
You gave me the line.
I know you'll always be there,
No matter how long or far I go,
You mean the world to me, mom,
You gave me the line.
I know you'll always be there,
No matter how long or far I go,
You mean the world to me, mom,
You gave me the life I'm living.
You gave me you,
To love and to cherish;
And mom that right there,
Is more than I've given you.

I hope someday I'll find a way,
To show you how much I really care;
But for now I hope this will do.
This is for you mom,
For all the love we've had to share;
And remember mom . . .
— I Love You —

Dee Hedgecock

SWEETHEART

Sweetheart,
I love you
I really do,
I haven't had feelings for any man
As much as I do for you.

We've had our ups and downs before,
BP I really do,
I haven't had feelings for any man
As much as I do for you.

We've had our ups and downs before,
But let's prevent from having more.
I want to hold on to you as long as I can,
Because you're my one and only man.

Love begins with two people
Which are me and you.
If we depart for any reason
Our love wasn't really true.

So keep this in mind
While we're together,
And I hope our love
Will last forever.

Darlene Hayes

A SONG OF MY HEART

A song of my heart
Bursts open romantic desires.
It softly whispers words that inspire;
I LOVE YOU, DARLING.
Then to joys of passionate fires
Which are exploding unto my soul.
And ends up singing a forever love
Into a song of my heart.

Debbie Gauvin

WANTINGS

I want to walk beside you
Across a desert sea

I want to be that special smile
That shows your love for me

I want to know your sleeping form
Each night sleeps next to mine

I want to believe this love we share
Will last throughout our time

I want to hear your laughter
And play as lovers do

I want our children's brothers
To be a part of me and you

I want to know no matter what
This love is ours to hold

I want to know inside my heart
You'll be near me as we grow old

I want to share your memories
And store them one by one

And know no matter how long we live
We've only just begun

Elizabeth E. La Grange

CHARLOTTE'S RECIPE

A recipe left by my mother
But now with all I'll share
She served this dish to everyone,
To show her love and care.

A measure filled with happiness
Another filled with love
Add a cup or two of fate
And hope from God above.

Fill a measure full of joy
Add a half a cup of grief
Then you will have a flavor
That's far beyond belief.

Sift this all with patience
Mix with understanding hands
She served this food to us each day
And all who made demands.

If you could not come to her
She brought this dish to you
Served with words of comfort
And love so very true.

A heaping portion to each one,
Each morn, each noon, each night,
This recipe is known to all as
Charlotte's Sweet Delight.

Mary Nixon Flaugh

ANNIVERSARY

Once young and beautiful we stood,
hand clasped in hand;
Upon each other's finger slipped
a wedding band.
Together, through these many years
we've had it all —
Happiness and sorrow, joys and heartaches —
large and small.
We've learned that fortune, life and love
have ups and downs;
That we've been saints and sinners,
sobersides and clowns.
We have felt the pitch of passion
come and go —
The full-flamed fire burns high,
the embers low.
Oh yes, there are so many things
that I recall,
And I'll say it once again . . .
we've had it all!

Grace Hollinger Lehman

THE ALL ABIDING LOVE

LOVE is a sincere concern for another
a spouse, parent, child, friend, or neighbor
LOVE is uplifting ever giving
LOVE is forgiving, before others
LOVE never races ahead
LOVE stops — offers hand to stumbling
ones instead, LOVE never brags,
where help is needed LOVE does not lag;
the greatest LOVE above all other
is to offer own life for life of another
that great LOVE fully expressed by our life-giver
above, who sent forth HIS Son as RANSOM
to release HIS earthly children
from bonds of death, and all in HIS memory
shall awaken from their tombs, with
prospects of living forever — in RESTORED
GARDEN OF PLEASURE all now grateful
for that gift from FATHER ABOVE and to know
the ALMIGHTY SUPERNAL GOD ETERNAL
— IS LOVE —

Loretta Twomey Culli

KAREN AND I

Through misguided pride and misunderstood feelings
We've neglected each other and wrought too much pain.
I'd forgotten you get in return what you give;
You're too troubled to notice me caught in the rain.

But before things get too far, we always find the time
To let our hearts cuddle, and our feelings we share.
And we find that our fears and misunderstandings
Are meaningless phantoms that dissolve in the air.

Our rapport goes beyond the meaning of 'best friends.'
It's like we've rekindled the Star of Bethlehem.
It always shines through all of our darkest moments.
It's much more resplendent than an unblemished gem.

It's love in its pure form, like emotions hugging,
That's kept us together since we shared our first smile.
It's unselfish giving from the bottom of our hearts.
It's love in its pure form, like the innocent child's.

David P. Wesp

TWO GIFTS

Your little gift, a trinket, came at a special time,
And through the years it's been like mellow wine,
A thing to hold both tried and true,
As long and sweet as my love for you.

Not what its worth to others be,
But what its symbol means to me,
Through long-past time, its memory stays,
And always will throughout my days.

There is another gift, this one exchanged,
Though seldom said, it still remains,
I love you.
It took a while to know for sure,
As years go by, it's clean and pure,
I'm not ashamed to say again,
I love you.

Two gifts from you, both quite old,
One to hear and one to hold,
Your looks, your touch, your laughter gay!
I'll live with 'till I hear you say,
"I love you."

Leroy Stephenson

LOVE LOST

I'm growing stronger every day.
I can tell.
My actions are turning from frail motions,
to strong jerks.
The tears still fall, but not as often.
I'll remember you as long as time moves on.
I'll cherish the times that we had together,
but now we must find new memories.

You must go your own way, and I will find mine.
For me, don't worry.
I have been through many hells,
and here I stand, telling you about
each one.
All I can do is chalk this one up,
and I pray that you are able to do the same.

Forget my heart,
Forget my feelings.
And most of all . . . Forget my tears.

For you will never see me shed
them again.

Kari Makala

A SHIMMERING TEARDROP

Sitting alone I dream of you
Dying inside without a clue.
The eerie feeling inside my heart,
Stops my blood and rips me apart.
I feel like I am burning up in a fire,
It is you alone that my love will desire.
My mind wants and my love needs,
My heart yearns and my soul bleeds.
A victim of idolatry to the end I will be.
A lover of few is my soul's destiny.
Can it be true? Is it really you?
No it was only a teardrop shimmering in the light,
Showing me the sorrow that comes with the night.

Unique Schreiber

IF THOU MUST LOVE ME

If thou must love me, let it be for nought
Except for love's sake only. Do not say
'I love her for her smile . . her look . . her way
Of speaking gently, . . for a trick of thought
That falls in well with mine, and certes brought
A sense of pleasant ease on such a day' —
For these things in themselves, Belovèd, may
Be changed, or change for thee, — and love, so wrought,
May be unwrought so. Neither love me for
Thine own dear pity's wiping my cheeks dry, —
A creature might forget to weep, who bore
Thy comfort long, and lose thy love thereby!
But love me for love's sake, that evermore
Thou may'st love on, through love's eternity.

Elizabeth Barrett Browning

CAN WE SEE GOD

The best rewards are from God above.
Victory is ours and abides with love.
Man with His sin has a soul.
Life he lives to reach a goal.
On the cross Jesus endured the rod.
By faith alone can we see God.
Jesus' blood has washed our sins away.
Through His gift within we can obey.
Jesus will return it may be today.
Dear believing brother please watch and pray.

Paul O. Carlson

MAN AND WOMAN LOVE — AN OLD MAID'S VIEW

What is love?
The idealism of young people
which makes them forgive each other
for the mistakes due to the fire of young blood.

What is love?
The everlasting endurance
of the routine annoyances after the glamour goes
and they find they have differences.

What is love?
the tenderness of old eyes and hands
when the family is gone,
and they walk down the sunset road together.

Ruth A. Williams

INDEED THIS VERY LOVE

Indeed this very love which is my boast,
And which, when rising up from breast to brow,
Doth crown me with a ruby large enow
To draw men's eyes and prove the inner cost, . .
This love even, all my worth, to the uttermost,
I should not love withal, unless that thou
Hadst set me an example, shown me how,
When first thine earnest eyes with mine were crossed,
And love called love. And thus, I cannot speak
Of love even, as a good thing of my own.
Thy soul hath snatched up mine all faint and weak,
And placed it by thee on a golden throne, —
And that I love (O soul, we must be meek!)
Is by thee only, whom I love alone.

Elizabeth Barrett Browning

IN THE NIGHT THERE IS A WOOING

In the night there is a wooing, he has called
her from the sea . . .
We are dancers in the circle
in the circle of light
I have loved you from beginning
I will free you from the night

I have drawn you to the circle
you would leave me to the night
I have loved you from beginning
I will have you in the light.

The dark without the circle
The circ within the night
The dark creates the circle
The dark that brings it light

In the night there is a wooing
he has called her from the sea
They are dancers in the circle
In the light that makes her free

Jesse Teran

LOVE FEAST LOVE LURES

How do we senior citizens remain in the pink?
Some about our calorie intake ever do think.
Many heed the color of vegetables we eat.
Shades of red, pink, green are diet colors we repeat.

Most dieters steer clear of all red meat type protein.
Fish or fowl once a week is good. So's most any bean!
Scientific laboratories give us fine leads —
'Bout wonderful food values of certain kinds of seeds.

Most docs frown on the use of liquids alcoholic.
It is best to use old-fashioned Adam's ale, bucolic
With condiments we should all be extremely discreet.
Restrain using salts; the same, for any man-made sweet!

Do not forget, our bodies need plenty exercise.
'Bove with *lots* of *sincere love* keeps our vim so alive!

Mervin L. Schoenholtz

GONE IS MY LOVE

Gone is my love from the earth,
Taking my sunshine and mirth,
Gone is the laughter that we shared,
Gone is my dearest love who cared,
I miss your kind and smiling face,
Your tender love and fond embrace;
Well, I remember the day we wed; sacred vows we said,
We promised that we'd love for life,
You, my husband — I, your wife,
Our love to last forever — forever and a day.

We strolled through summer's gloaming,
Singing the songs we knew,
Pledging to one another; two hearts entwined and true,
Duty called you, my love,
The plane took off — it was lost,
You were on it, my love, and so —
There's nothing left, but memories,
To dry my heartbroken tears,
Or to comfort me now, my love,
Through the lonely years.

Lucile V. Treutel

BEAUTIFUL THINGS

Observe a tree as it grows.
Watch a cat and what she knows.

Have you ever watched
a butterfly in flight?
Or the different animals
that come out at night.

The world is full
of beautiful things.
Like listen to a bird
as he sings.

You know what it's like
to love the things we have.
The air, the animals, and beautiful land.

God created them to love,
not ban.
Yet it's being destroyed,
by all of our hands.

Karen L. Bixler

IT'S OVER

Our faces are empty
and our eyes are sunken in.
The conversation is shallow,
there is nowhere to begin.
The night moves on slowly
till the fire becomes nothing
but coals aglow.
What happened to our marriage?
Where did all the love go?
Our faded blue jeans
bear the memories we've shared.
The pictures in the album
show a time when we cared.
You destroyed us
when you slept with her that night.
My love is not strong enough
to forgive and say it's all right.

Betty L. Harnly

THE FACE OF AN ANGEL

Such a beautiful face
I gaze at in a frame.
Remembering the time
When it once shared my name.

A face of love and joy
And of happiness.
The same face I held in my hands
To kiss and to caress.
Now I am left with only memories
A picture and some glass.

I look into her eyes
And think back to the times
When I would dedicate her a song
Or write her a poem with rhymes.

My Venus, Aphrodite
My angel from above.
My darling wife
My only love.

Peter M. Vingris

RETURN FROM THE CEMETERY

From the cemetery I came
Back into the empty house.
The life is no more the same
Since death took away my spouse.

Deserted and empty is the room
Where once united we were;
There is now a dreary doom
Where I laughed and cried with her.

Bitter tears are running in vain
In my being so solitary;
Only my wishes and yearning remain
To meet her once in eternity.

Hartwig Heymann

AWAKENING

Silently kneeling upon the ground
Head bowed low in fervent prayer
Begging now that love is found
These feelings won't be rare

Here alone, seeking God's grace
Reality shall not intrude
No look of pain or hurt on a face
Only a peaceful interlude

Giving is a fragile thing
And can have no regrets
But love to you it can bring
And you'll never be in debt

Sarah A. Mattila

UNICORNIZED

Unicorn where time
Consider fable
Did rainbow once rhyme
Stars like its table.

Winsome performance
Born single jointed
Somehow was romance
Single heart pointed.

Very white creature
Love alabaster
Whose prominent feature
Could urgence master.

Orien Todd

PARTING

Eyes are swollen with miserable tears
and the deepest wrenching grief.
Recollections of happiness enhance
the bitterness of today's sorrow.
Forfeiting hopes and unfulfilled dreams,
they seek spiritual comfort for
human loneliness.
Neglected, abused, destroyed.
Rejection brings isolation.

Julie Taylor

YOU TOUCHED MY LIFE

You touched my heart with a gentle touch.
You reached out to me when no one cared.
I was lost before we met.
Our years together have been loving and
well spent,
Now you're gone from me.
I kneel by your grave, as the pain covers
me.
I feel lost in the years and the memories.
You touched my life, and for that I feel
blessed,
I'll always love you and your gentleness.

Kathryn Tracy Allen

MY PROMISE

You entered my life, we fell in love
A special love sent from above
Your arms around me every night
Is not wrong, it feels so right
You've shown me love I've never known
And when we're apart you always phone
Not a day goes by that I don't feel
How much you care, I know it's real
This feeling inside will always stay
And it keeps getting stronger every day
Always remember my promise to you:
I promise to never stop loving you.

Susan Judge

OUR BOND

My children learn
to taste
frenzied reality
the draining voyage
of survival
imparts to me
their sanctuary
i wrap their singed
wings loosely
their scars
of innocence
echo our pain

Dianne M. Tchir

STILL

Why we still care
Why we still feel love
I'll never know
But here we are
Perhaps out of rhyme
But for one more time
Here we go
From happiness to despair
And back again
From loneliness
Once again
To sweet togetherness

Donna L. Hill

Lower Falls, Portage.

TOUCH ME TENDERLY

Love is both commitment and fulfillment:
We touch with tenderness —
And find, within our touching, a whole new way
Of life. If we can but love without duress,
Freely, as children love,
Openly, aware of each other's needs,
Yet gently, for it should be a gentle thing
That touches another's life so deeply.

So touch me tenderly, with love,
For I am vulnerable indeed
Since I have given myself to you,
Freely, spurred on by an inner need.
I would not seek to shackle you
With even lightest silken strings,
For love that is fettered surely dies,
Love must have freedom to spread its wings.

Cornelia B. Furbish

WHAT HAVE YOU DONE WITH MY TREASURES?

What have you done with my treasures?
I have given you so many.
One by one I let them go
From my soul to yours,
Into your safe keeping.
And you in turn gave me yours —
I stored them deep,
Expecting to unearth them some day
To enjoy again — to bask in their beauty and gleam.
But when I did, they were tarnished,
False gems, crumbling paste.
Oh, what have you done with my treasures?
They were given with such love!
Did you toss each aside as it was proffered?
So there never was a cache?
I am empty now — my jewels gone,
And yours but worthless pebbles.

Elizabeth P. Wish

VICTIM OF LOVE

A victim of Love is what I am
unfortunately of another's man

A man of wisdom, a man of surprise
A man of dreams, a man that tries.

A man that knows his wrongs, and makes them right
A man I wouldn't let go without a fight.

A man too sweet to be real
A man whose Love I'd gladly steal.

Why does this have to be
Why isn't he in Love with me.

And such a fool I am
To be in Love with another's man.

Kim Sullivan

DRAKE

His smile warms my face
The twinkle in his eye lights my heart
Words on his lips have a meaning difficult to understand
He tries so hard not to be hurt
His heart reaches out for help but does not ask
He has good intentions but is asked to prove everything
His hands are rough but to me they are gentle
His tongue is cutting but capable of saying beautiful things
His mind is rich and needs encouragement
He needs a love he has never had
He wants a help he has never asked for
He has love that he is afraid to show.
Me, what part do I play?
I am his desire
His desire for life, betterment, understanding, and love.

DeDee Bellomy

FREE AS . . .

I chuckled when you said you would be free
and laughed outright when you said,
"as free as the four winds." Dear me,
the winds aren't free. They're ruled, instead,
by complex and regular
phenomena: highs and lows,
troughs and fronts, etc.
"As free as birds." you said with thumb to nose.
Birds aren't free. They transit north
and south with sun and stars like me — and you.
"As Halley's comet," you spat forth.
But, we know when wonders are due, too.

The only things which are not regular
are hearts to which none is superior.

Craig A. Reynolds

DECEMBER WEDDING SONGS

Some enchanted evening with stardust in your eyes,
You kissed the day good-bye and for once in your life
Found someone who is your only sunshine and your music!

No longer strangers in the night you'll say "Hello
My friend, hello." "You were meant for me!" and wake to
Sunshine, lollipops and roses through all the stormy weather.

Just dreamin' by the light of the silvery moon
Over Miami . . . or strollin' down the avenue
Side by side, you're people who need people for stayin' alive!

Chances are it might as well be spring for in the
Embers of December the waiting game is o'er
And your heartlight shows the way to the best of everything!

Jeanine M. Droen

THE MARRIAGE PROPOSAL

My darling please listen and hear the plea of one so in love
and devoted to thee. I have traveled through darkness, grief and
despair, then came into the light and found you there. Our love
was like clay which took time to mold, and worth more to me than
the world and its gold. I promise to love you through all kinds
of weather, for bad times shall only make good times seem better.
I am down on my knees with my heart in my hand, and I know that
life with you would be grand. So I ask you my love to answer my
plea, and I ask you this question, "Will you marry me?"

David James Zoppi

GOD IS LOVE

My country love town love
Sweet land of love
In God we love
Love him as long as I live
Be of good cheer, love world
House of love stand
My mother mother love her
My mother love me
Love mine eyes
Love mine heart
His love keeps me going on
Children of God just like Him
Children of God know His love
Born of His love so refreshing
Love not silver or gold
My God knows me just as I am
Love don't pass me by
His love true Happiest peace
In beginning was love
God is love
As ugly among beauty
Love among hate.

Roslynn Hatchett

FLUTTERING WORDS

I see that look in your eyes
and smile on your face
You touch my heart softly,
I'll let no one take your place
With the warmth of your body
lying close to mine,
something special begins
reflected beauty in mind
I think of how you and I
ever came to be
We mixed so beautifully,
like cinnamon and spice tea
I needed you — to satisfy
You see you are the love,
my future's destiny
Just let me say I love you
Let me say I love you babe,
just let me say I love you,
in the same way you do
if our love is still true
for this I wanted to say to you
ever since first, I met you . . .

Eugene Stewart

OUR ETERNAL LOVE

The highway to heaven is
paved with bricks of gold —
At the end there is a lovely
Golden Gate.
One blissful day I pray to stand
before that beautiful portal,
When that day comes, rejoice
do not mourn for me —
For I have only gone ahead to
acquire a place for me and you.
Then from that distant shore
I'll watch and wait for thee,
And when you reach this haven —
somewhere out in space,
We'll rest in the fervency of our
eternal love.

Harold James Douglas

CONSTANCY

Constant . . .
Your love for me, O Lord, my sacramental Lord.
Daily you remain fixed upon the golden monstrance.
Loving, loving me, loving us . . .
Constantly.

What faithfulness, what giving, what changelessness!
Words fail to express such enduring love.
You, the Alpha and the Omega, always, always the same . . .
Constantly.

Would, O Lord, that my love for you be as yours.
But I, poor creature so inconstant.
Amid my own changing moods . . .
Your constancy.

Thank you, Lord. In the stillness I sense your presence.
Your silence bespeaks the language of true love.
Yet in that silence the fire of your love blazes to touch me . . .

What constancy.

In this profound silence you speak to my heart:
"Arise, my love, my beautiful one and come.
The season of joyful song has come."
Such love . . .
Such CONSTANCY . . .

Sr. Elizabeth Mary Morales, C.S.J.B.

THAT SONG OF "LOVE ME TENDER"

This poem is crudely written to the Loving Memory
of the boy from Mississippi, and the man from Tennessee

For many years we've heard you sing from heart and true emotions.
From north to south, from east to west, and even 'cross the oceans.
Your songs will live, though you have gone; they'll live because we love you;
They'll live because you humbly said the KING was far above you.

The mem'ries of our teenage years somehow enfold you in them.
The older folk at first would scoff, then one by one you'd win them.
You won the hearts of all our Land when Uncle Sam was needing.
You proudly served your country true, without protest or pleading.

Your fortune came, and also fame, but naught of this could smother,
the honor and the love you gave your father and your mother.
And then God gave those treasured gifts; your wife and then your daughter,
Those cherished times you shared with them brought priceless joy and laughter.

But then the news flashed 'round the world to all its tongues and races
to crush a billion aching hearts; tear stain a billion faces.
Yet in our minds we hear that song, (as only you could render.)
Of all your songs it stands out most; that song of "Love Me Tender."

Perhaps there was a yearning deep that gripped your heart and bound you.
A longing to see Mom again and feel her arms around you.
We trust by Grace we'll find you there in Heaven's "Hall of Splendor"
'til then we say, farewell dear heart, we'll always "Love You Tender."

Ernest T. Presnell, Jr.

ANNIVERSARY

How young we were, how unaware of all that lay ahead.
We faced the future unafraid, that sunny day when we were wed.
"For better" and "for worse," we vowed, a pledge that has been kept and so
The bond of love is stronger now than when we forged it, years ago.

Helen D. Edmonds

EIGHTBALL ON A WISHBONE

Is silence an opinion, or an emotion?
Is it a feeling, or is it a notion?
Why is love not so easy?
Why does it cause such commotion?

I wish I could write my own wish book.
I wish I could return what I took.
My feelings don't come easy.
And they're not easily shook.

No the answers don't come easy.
And they sure don't come cheap.
At times I feel like I'm nowhere near.
At others I can't sleep.

What would possess me to act so foolish?
Of all things act so high schoolish.
It seems pretty ironic at times, to be love.
When the last thing I could think of, is a dove.

I've learned that making love, doesn't always make love.
And unfortunately, not without much pain.
We would love for it to be simple.
And if we're lucky, it might even be sane.

Matthew V. Moore

CHARLIE

I've come through life so happily.
Things had never been so grand.
Until, I met Charlie;
He's a real man!

I said, his name is Charlie!
He makes life worth living for.
He brings home my bread and gravy.
I don't ask for anything more.

When I'm asked, who brings out the best in me
I answer right away!
I answer this sincerely.
Forever and a day.

There could be someone else . . . maybe!
But no one could interrupt.
They just can't beat my Charlie!
He overflows my cup.

Dinah K. Henderson

UNOPEN LOVE

So oft, in love, we play but a part.
We play a game with another's heart.
We commit hurtful deeds,
we sow bitter seeds.
We but sate our own selfish needs.

Why can't we be open and commit our soul?
Share love, share our heart; be honest, share our whole.
Why can't we be freed,
to let love succeed?
Why can't we see; why can't we heed?

John A. Short

LOVE AS ART

Ah love —
Had I but known that love is an art form —
We mortals need to handle with tenderness and care —
Learned even as an artist blends his tones and shades—
Into a painting that attracts and holds one's gaze —
With a rapture heaven-sent,
I would have listened carefully to what your lips did say,
And looking deep within —
Sought to cultivate those skills of heart and mind —
Allowing love to grow from day to day —
Alive to all that we could share and be.
But alas I learned too late —
That love untended soon grows cold —
Even as the fires of yesterday,
One needs commitment and an effort made —
To blend two hearts and lives —
Into a true dynamic, living whole.

William E. Mays

YOUNG LOVE

Young love is wrapped in fantasy,
Filled with dreams that may not be.
Young love is beautiful to see,
Filled with hours of ecstasy.
Young love can cause anxiety
For loved ones who watch and wait.
In young love can be heartache;
Hearts that are broken will mend again.
No one can console young love then.
Young love does not understand
There are other loves in the plan.
Young love, I could tell you so,
It is something you do not want to know.
I would not tell you for dream's sake
If I could, I would save you the heartbreak.
Young love, I know this is true.
I remember years ago — I had a young love too.

Darlene Grice Hayward

LOVE SONG

Snowy nights, burning fire in the fireplace,
no electric lights, you and me alone in the universe.
Burning kisses, mountain cottage sinking into snow,
shades dancing on the ceiling or below, unimportant time.
Song of love of a flying swan,
who alights in lake, with beak moves feathers.

See the moon, follow its luminosity,
why it's so bright, why in trees it hides?
My beloved tongues of fire melt snow brilliants
femininity of woman burns in love.
My love you are oxygen I am raging flame
together we explode in a fire melting time and space,
steel and wood, all that separates us.
We love to be together, alone in the universe
sinking in radiance of snow brilliants,
enjoying impetuous flames of fireplace.

George Georgiev

WAIT FOR YOUR LOVE, CINDY ANN

What are you watching, Cindy Ann,
As the shrimp boats sail for the sea?
Is it, by chance, the one you love,
A shrimper, stalwart and free?

Now, don't be sad; as he sails away.
You know that his love is true.
And he'll return in a little while —
Yes, he'll come back to you.

And in his boat, he'll bring to you
The best of the deep sea's treasure,
And within his heart great riches, too —
A love, beyond all measure!

Natalie B. Mayo

I'LL GIVE YOU MY WISH

Who could be filled with darkness;
on a day so bright?
A sky of falling glitter upon
a blanket of white.

Here by my side, set by the fire.
Tell to me your deepest desire!
Perhaps to dream of a warm night in June,
or walk by my side under December's moon.

Your wish is mine, but only my mind.
Memories do not hurt, but serve as kind.
Ask for me to love and be your wife,
I give you my love; I give you my life!

Kerri Ganshaw

THE WIDOW

Footsteps in a vacuum,
Table set for one;
Vacant chair to speak to
When the night has come,

No one to relate to,
Memories shared alone;
Solitary sparrow,
Silent telephone.

Many who surround you,
Yet you're on your own;
Longing in the darkness
A-lone, A-lone, A-lone.

Christianna

ABOVE US IN LOVE

Oh, confiscate the wide iron gate.
Tear it from your fence.
Unstring barbed wire from post to post.
Use love and shining good sense.

For there, in that, it stands for sure,
lies God's sweet flowing Love.
Within our neighbor's heart and brow
and not in space above.

O. Felspar

I've loved you long in silence
I guess I always will
It's hard to stay away from you
As my heart yearns for you still

I know there will never ever be
A time for me and you
I'm lost amongst my feelings
And the guilt for loving you

I really didn't plan it
Nor did I think it would come to pass
But this feeling that I have for you
Looks like it's going to last

It's just that you're such a sweetheart
You're a very gentle man
I wish that I could share your love
But outside I can only stand

My heart will always care for you
There's simply nothing I can do
But try and live in reality
And be content to be friends with you

Jewel C. Barbier

ECHOES

There were others before you.
After you, only a few.

I ran with the wind
I cried in the rain
I pleaded with God,
Take away this killing pain.

Long days pass into sleepless nights
Unanswered questions enter my mind
The same questions echo . . . echo
Answers I know I will never find.

Come early morning, the beginning of dawn
I can forget last night.
The sun holds me, warms me
Echoes become quiet.

There were others before you.
After you, only a few.
My soul still runs with the wind
Carrying echoes of my heart forever true.

Tammy Holley

AFTER THE DROUGHT

Sometimes, when I dream of sunlight,
Shining on a golden plain,
Sunlight sounds like golden laughter
Or warm wind whisking through tall grain.

Golden sunlight, golden laughter,
Golden grain and warm wind's touch
Are the things I shall remember
Of a dream I loved too much!

Though the dream is past reclaiming
And I cannot see the grain,
In your smile is warmth and healing,
Golden sunlight on the plain.

Shirley Mohr

NOT FOR NOW

(Dedicated to Mom)

If I had a chance to say
All the things I should
I'd say how much I love you
Only if I could.

I'd say how much I've missed you
Through all the happy times
I'd say how much you mean to me
for just a little sign

But our paths are all but twisted
Out of each other's reach
A gap of words and motions
That neither one can breach

I suppose someday we'll meet again
By chance, or even choice
And maybe I'll say the words I should
If I can find my voice.

Lylla Lane

COULD I FORGET?

And you insist that I forget my love!
Can I forget the sun?
For though it hide behind a wall of flame,
Can I forget the sun?

Can I forget the stars? —
The stars that weave
A web of loveliness at night?
Can I forget the stars?

Up, up at the stars
I mutely gaze and plead
"Return, return my tender love to me."

But as I hold communion —
My stars and I —
They breathe a smile
As beautiful as wisdom:
"Your love has found a kinder home
With us, among the stars."

Mary Schulman

TO A MIDDLE-AGED WOMAN IN HER SORROW

Every tear I shall kiss from your face;
Every wrinkle my lips will erase;
Every sorrow that shadows your brow
My loving eyes will disallow.
I shall choke your path with roses,
Whose pious fragrance composes
The incense for the altar of your being,
Whereon for everyone's seeing
I shall plant the candles of my heart
And light them with a fire — puny part
Of the one that scorches my breast!
And when these have lost their zest
And gutter to extinction,
They will receive extreme unction
In the sacred oil of your skin;
And then this essence of me will be in
YOU, laid to peaceful rest in
The sweetest of graves, in
Of all heavens the best.

Paul R. Neureiter

I LOVE YOU, DAD

You have always been there
Whether I was right or wrong
I know how much you care
If I am weak, you make me strong

I have done so much to hurt you
Yet, you never stopped loving me
If only there were something I could do
To erase the bad from your memory

You have been such a wonderful dad
I can't imagine life without you
You are the best friend I ever had
I hope you know my love is true

I don't know if I ever said I love you
Saying what I feel is so hard for me
I guess I figured you always knew
But that's not how it should be

You are the world's greatest dad
I love you, more than words can say
Remember, if you are ever feeling bad
You can call me, night or day

Sherry Wyatt

PETITION

May I take away his pain
Leave him sound and well again
May I bear for him his sin
Leave him clean and free again

Bear his burden, take his grief
Keep his watch and let him sleep
Fight his battles, slay his foes
Bear the burden of his yoke

Every man must fight a fight
Whether cannon's roar of soul's disquiet
Every man has wars to grieve
Before he can rejoice in peace

My petition I'll amend
Ask that I might stay by him
Help when battles he must grieve
Joy when he has won his peace

Nurse away the pain he knows
Listen to him search his soul
And as his helpmeet yet implore
How might I love him even more?

Paulette Hess Brown

ACCIDENT PRONE

One word from you
Is all I need to
take off
Running
with no direction
Headlong
into what may lie ahead
Ready to crash —
SMACK
Into a brick wall.

K. S. Victory

ALONE AT SUNSET

Watch the twinkle and the glow
As the sun flows below
Horizons far, horizons near
But, lover, shed no tear.

Cast upon the sky adrift
Apart, and yet we'll lift
Above loneliness and despair
Clinging everywhere.

For night hours are the sweet hours
Where love devours willpower.
Dream of eons we lay as one
Beneath the setting sun,

Entwined, embraced in love's desire.
We become the night's fire,
Deepening sounds like a sigh
As the sun fades from the sky.

Linda Hangartner

THE WONDER OF YOU

I look at you and there I see,
A world of beauty thrilling me.
I hold your hand and then I feel
A longing love surrounding me.

Refreshing as the morning sun,
You give to all the light of day.
Inspiring as the setting sun,
You glow like stars a special way.

So like a dewdrop's sparkling smile,
All living joys reflect in you.
Like gentle rain on flowers flows,
You are that something special, too.

Exciting as the shows in space,
Enthusiasm becomes you.
Delightful as the dreams of love,
The wonder of it all is you!

Josephine Bertolini Comberiate

LOVE'S FAIR FACE

God saw her life
would not be easy,
so he gave her
Love's fair face.
I love to be seen
With love's fair face.
Even though tested
It remains Love's fair face.
Responsibility is easy,
Love's fair face.
My reward reflected
in love's fair face.
Love's fair face
is like a bubble bath;
and I take a bath each day
in Love's fair face.
I love to do what
Pleases her, Love's fair face. No
Blemish on her skin, adored since
time began, Love's fair face.

Faith Kennedy

HEAD ON

I wish we'd met when we were young,
So full of zest and all aflame
To tackle life and love head on!

If only I had been around
When your first love had gone aground.
Hot from the fire described it well
Before you lived your lonely hell.

Back then I wish I'd been your friend
When you first felt so stunned and numb
That I'd been there, and not in vain
To cool the burn and ease the pain.

The years we've missed and can't rescind,
No use to sigh "What might have been,"
Since met we have, and love, we do!
I would not trade the past for now.

Let's share these years, and hope, beyond,
And meet our destiny, head on!

Lois Smith Triplitt

JAMIE

Held in the sweetness
Of your engulfing arms,
I feel somehow to have died
And entered Paradise.
Through a wholly
Displaced lifetime,
Never, until now,
Have I felt that
I was home, and safe,
And truly loved.

The windows of my heart
Have opened wider
Than the desert winds.
All the stars of my past loves
Pale and disappear in the
Brilliance of this sun.
I know at last,
For all of my life,
That this is where
I was born to be.

Evie Kinney

MOONSONG

Make me a moonsong, Luv,
Marvelous mysteries,
Miraculous moments,
Mantra madness;
Mesmerize my mind.

Make me a moonsong, Luv,
Mounted mementos,
Motley winged moths,
Midsummer montage;
Meld me in memory.

Make me a moonsong, Luv,
Midnight music,
Moaning mandolins,
Murmuring meadowgrass;
Mask me in morning mist.

Nelly Bly Grimes

NEWBORN

I watch your gently sleeping face
And marvel at the expressions that slip across
Your tiny perfect features
As you dream and remember and search.
Oh, my little impatient son,
You were in such a hurry to be here.
I wonder if all your life you'll be
In such a hurry to experience it all;
If every new corner and path
Draws you along, excited, seeking.
But for now I'm content
Just to hold you in my arms
And look at you.
They tell me I cannot take you home . . .
That maybe you won't make it.
But when you reach out with your tiny little hand
And hang on so tightly to my finger
I know you'll be all right.

Sandra L. Fox

LOVE'S IMPOTENCY — RELIVED

We are impotent indeed as we watch
the child that we love
move into an adult.
We know what they are going through,
what they need,
how to help.
We could make it so much easier,
so less painful,
so less a chance.
We could be the knowledge that they need,
lead them along their way,
guide them in romance.
Oh, we could, we would, if only they would heed.
We would clear the way,
we would unbend the stem.
But they will no more listen and profit
from our experienced wealth
than would we before them!

John A. Short

THE CROOK

looking at his face, it's so kind
slowly moving, I'm going out of my mind
watching him sleeping at my side
knowing he's always gonna ride
coming to me once a week
to find his head, he's some sort of freak
living off others, ones that count
watching their patience slowly mount
I love him, I want him to stay with me
but home is something that could never be
his eyes are dark, as dark as the night
they look like they twinkle, but I know it's fright
sleeping, dreaming, waking with a start
looking for something down in his heart
he's always ready to jump up and go
but one day he's gonna be too slow
they're gonna get him so they say
maybe tomorrow will be their day

Ann Carol Turner

GLENN

As a young girl I thought,
my father was a king.
But his son became
more of a man than he'd ever be.

My brother is a man of spirit,
far beyond his years.
He has learned from his mistakes
and faced up to his fears.

He may be a kid to many,
but he knows more than most.
He gained from his experiences,
with pain as his heart's host.

He learned from the street,
and going life alone.
Only really wanting
A space he could call home.

Yet he kept alive a vital dream,
Of belief in wilderness, humanity and love.
So a sun ray can cleanse his soul,
As he takes life's burdens in strife.

Jacqueline Holland

THERESA

A sweet little Angel was born in the Fall
The wedding a year before was truly a ball
Her cousin was slightly more than a year older
She was predicted to arrive when the weather was colder.

The day of birth was on a Friday you see
The agenda which God wrought to be
Was ahead of schedule so that Gramps could share
In the new arrival of this beauty so bare.

Nanny flew through the air the following day
In order to see and have a word to say
About the Princess ahead of the time
And their meeting was really a treat sublime.

Her Parents thrilled at her very sight
They, too, are Royal, comely and bright
Others do well their traits and charisma to catch
Their beauty and talent not many can match.

This Angel is fair, tender, plump and serene
A lovelier, better Princess has not been seen
Theresa is her name, and beautiful her face
From the moment of birth not one can take her place.

Papa Cheek

FRIENDSHIP

If I should kiss you at the close of day,
it is a simple way of saying, dear,
that I do hope you sleep well all the night
or maybe I forgive you if I'm hurt.
Perhaps it's just a way to thank you, too,
if you have made me laugh or sing a bit.
Sometimes I cannot say I'm sorry yet
but will try hard to understand your words
because I know you love me as a friend
and I return this feeling with a kiss.

Eloise Koelling

TRUE FRIENDS

New friends come and old friends go,
But how much of them do you really know?
Are they good or are they bad?
Have you been loved or have you been had?
Friends aren't always what they seem.
Hatred breeds while smiles still gleam.
You think they're loyal, trusting friends,
But they divulge your secrets to other ends.
But somewhere out there friendship breeds,
Far from wicked, heinous deeds.
While hatred sometimes dwells in others,
True friends always love like brothers.
They stick together through hardship and sorrow,
Each knowing the other will be there tomorrow.
A loving friend is always there,
To comfort others in despair.
So remember how long friendship lasts,
Through the future from the distant past.
Cherish those friends who stick with you,
And weather together what life puts you through.

Steve Kalandros

KALANDROS, STEPHEN KONSTANTINE. Born: Washington, D. C., 2-26-70; Education: Cheyenne Mountain High School, Colorado Springs, Colorado, will graduate 1988; Occupation: Student; Poetry: 'Images,' *American Poetry Anthology, Vol VI No 3,* August, 1986.

YEARNING FOR LOVE

When I was just a little girl
My cousin came to stay a while;
I wondered why she looked so sad
And thought it odd she didn't smile.

She looked out our front window then
And saw a big black hearse go by:
She said to me in sad soft words,
"Your Aunt June's dead, but please don't cry.

My mother's gone now — gone for good
And I'll not see her anymore.
My daddy died when I was two —
Be glad in your house there are four.

You have a baby sister now
But I have no one close like you;
So hug me, please and promise me
That you will always love me, too."

Alice S. Elton

MY LIFELONG LOVE

When I chose Christ at sixteen,
For my life He set the scene.
The best decision I ever made,
For I faced life unafraid.

But often following laggardly
And listening not at all,
Into my emptiness, I cried,
"Act like you're having a ball!"

Overseas at nineteen, the chaos of war
Forced me to choose what I really stood for.
And through stressful years of being a wife,
Mother of three, He strengthened my life.

Through most of the tragedies known to man,
He led me serenely with His strong hand.
When drug addiction took its awful toll;
Through sudden loss by death, He kept me whole.

For each, I believe there's a Master Plan
If each one lets the Master take his hand.
And He gives me courage to stand and say,
"Make my dear Master your friend all the way."

Dorothy Garton Cart

LOVE FROM THE SEA

You came from the sea on a warm spring day
Your bright eyes shining so blue.
They shone with a love that looked so real
That I knew it was mine so true.

You were the captain of your ship, a seaworthy man
so courageous and brave were you.
I gave you my love that I had seen in your eyes
But you said that you could not be true.

Your love was mine for a moment
But too soon that moment was gone.
For you said that the sea was your only true love
And she beckons you with her siren song.

With tears in my eyes I watched your ship
Sail out to the setting sun.
But my crying heart remembered one thing
That the sea had already won.

Now I look out on a cold winter's day
At the turbulent, frothy sea
And think of the man who took my love
And the sea that took him from me.

Cathy Bahr

LOVE IS

A wee baby cooing, happy to be
Resting on a parent's knee;
A carefree child playing joyfully
Running, skipping, among the family;
A young couple holding hands
Vowing faithfulness by their wedding bands;
A man and wife working together
Making a home in fair and foul weather;
An aged couple still holding hands
Dreaming of the joys brought by those wedding bands
Life itself, complete.

Lela Shine

CIRCLE OF LOVE

Within the circle of your love,
There is a place for me;
It is the only place that I
Would ever care to be.

The fears and doubts that buffet
Seem to fade and die;
In the safe, secure realm
Where I choose to lie.

You touch my face and tell me
That you love only me;
I'm special as I nestle there
And I can just be me.

Within the circle of your love,
I watch the world go by;
For me the world is sunshine
In a clear, blue sky.

Your smile is a precious jewel
One that I hold dear;
And when you say, "I love you,"
It is music to my ear.

Dolores Wyckoff

LOVE THAT HAS NO FAITH

Love that has no faith is like
A dove that has no wings
Now fantasize yourself to be —
A lark that never sings.

Love that has no faith can be —
A cloud that never drifts,
I'm sure somewhere someone would miss —
A world that has no clifts.

Love that has no faith is like —
A sky that has no sun,
No rays of warmth on winter days —
The dark could be no fun.

Love that has no faith is like —
An infant without care,
No watchful eyes nor food nor warmth —
No one who'll soon be there.

Love that has no faith is just —
As hollow as a tree,
Whatever kind of love it is —
I know it's not for me!

Dorothy Newton Crockett

I was a little girl
with stars in my eyes
and you were a knight
on a bright white horse
I thought that the sun
rose and set in you
but as little girls often do,
I outgrew those dreams
and saw you as you were
you're no knight and
you're not a saint, but
you still sweep me off
my little girl feet.

Robin Aylesworth

LOVE

Love is in caring
Its Joys are in sharing
Each problem, each heartache
Every trial every success
It's someone to whom we can express
All our ambitions and each happiness.

Ramona Lee

MOTHER

I think of times when I was small,
And didn't have a care at all.
You were there in my times of need,
To hug me tight and patch my knee.

You showed me things to do in the sun,
Like putting pictures under glass for fun.
To plant a flower, to pull a weed,
To eat a cherry and not the seed.

A smile on your lips, a gentle touch,
A kiss on the cheek that means so much.
But what can I say to make you see,
Just how much you mean to me.

When I was lost on Taylorville Square,
I was afraid you'd left me there.
But when you found me, I could see,
That you really did love me.

You've always been there and I am aware,
Of just how much you really care.
So, Mother, I just want to say,
I love you in a special way.

With Love From Your Daughter,
Andrea

Andrea C. Hargis

OPEN THE DOOR AND LET ME IN

Open the door and
let me in.
For my love is like
thunder.

I do not wish to rattle
your house, but only to
live within.

To nestle upon your chest
of might, to smother in
your embraces.

To kiss your lips of morning
dew, to wallow in your love
of passion.

Carry me away into midnight
blue, upon the wings of
existence.

And let the rains devour this
majestic rapport, sending us
into flight anew.

Open the door and let me in.

Georgenia Abedi-Boafo

MY GLADE

Precious and private is my glade,
Kissed by sun, glistening with dew.
They come to me, the tired, injured souls,
And I touch and love and heal.
Always have I cherished being here.

So in my sweet, enchanted glade,
I'm strong and wise for all.
Yet where is he who'll hold my hand,
Who'll be my strength and wipe my tear?
Alone do I perservere.

Into this quiet, lazy glade
You come, all fire and passion,
Pure, with energy aglow,
And all at once I'm woman,
Lonely, filled with fear.

Oh, now, how changed is my glade.
To know and grow does not suffice.
There is no emptiness of heart
Which yearns to find enhancement.
For now I long to hold you near.

Tessie Jayme

AUTUMN LOVE

In this autumn of my time,
When I can reap,
Within my memories,
So many wondrous thoughts,
Of those who joined me
In my walk of life
Through many tangled ways.
So much dross and chaff
Is winnowed out,
To find your friendship there,
Unchanged, except perhaps,
Polished bright with time
And love.

Charles Atkin

THINE EYES

Beloved!
Thine eyes are twin magnets
That clutch at my soul,
That seal it to thine
And make two halves whole.

Beloved!
Thine eyes are twin flames
That blaze with desire,
That envelop my heart
And set it afire!

Beloved!
Thine eyes are twin stars
That sparkle and shine,
That irradiate love
And passion divine!

Beloved!
Thine eyes are twin mirrors
That shimmer so bright,
That reflect my own love
And its inner light.

Madeleine Carol Miller

SONG OF THE PROPHET

Gemlike stars shine on night so clear
With the moon high above the trees.
A young man sees a light quite near,
and, though weary, he presses on.

Knocking firmly upon the door
but, at first, there is no reply.
Then, footsteps on a wooden floor —
"Who's there?" a voice softly inquires.

"Peace be with you," this prophet said
and, quickly now, the door opens wide.
"*Do* come in, and you shall be fed!
Sit down here; and please, rest awhile!"

Next day, there's snow upon the ground,
and the temperature is low.
"Last June, my dear husband was drowned,
Remain here with me," she begs him.

That man of God blessed this dear soul;
with tears of joy, bids her "Farewell!"
To preach the Word is his chief goal.
This lady's heart is, oh! so thrilled!

Ridgely Lytle

LIFE'S GOLD

Love makes the world go 'round
For the old and young,
And there are many songs about it,
That we all have sung.

But there are a few who say,
I don't need love today.
I have to travel for awhile,
And make a fortune, to live in style.

But when they look for love, they find,
That it has passed them by.
So they never know the rapture,
And for lack of it they die.

Love is a gift, we give to each other.
It makes living worthwhile
And if we believe in one another
We can live in any style.

We are only humans, living from day to day.
And love keeps hope alive,
That we will have the things,
For which we all pray.

Ruby M. Olson

REACHING OUT

My arms reach out for you, in the night.
Longing to touch you, and hold you tight
Loving sweet dreams, of you, through the night,
Then I realize, you're not here.
Gone forever, never to be near.
A cat now I hold most dear
My house, now not empty when it is near
Listen to music, sing along
Bringing back memories, in a song
Sometimes, happy, sometimes, blue
Loving sweet memories, of you . . .

Renee Edwards

THE ELUDING PATTERN OF LOVE

We long for the living promises of love,
For romance and the sweet intimacy of love.
Happiness is the pursuit of love
Catching love makes life sublime.
Wait? something will go wrong in time
Why worry? This is the eluding pattern of love.

Fired-up we become fast learners
Play it cool, we'll never be but amateurs,
Then feel our way to love again.
Whitewash our mental maps with roses and cons,
Glisten and whistle our troubles are gone.
Deceived, swear someone else sabotaged our love.

While the hot coals of love are burning bright,
We keep our other face hidden out of sight.
Yet, keep tethering on the edge of borrowed time,
Always wanting rekindled love to last.
This is the daring juggling act of love,
Known as the eluding pattern of love.

Juanita Allison

MY LOVER'S AN ACTRESS

HONORABLE MENTION

My lover, the actress, the one
wearing a wide-brimmed hat
and black leather pumps
pouts, then assumes an affected smile.
A refugee from the Stanislavski gulag
she talks incessantly:
"Will you help me, what shall I do?"
I humor her, of course, since
with theater people you've got to mold them
into what you want
before they can be
anybody.
Personality?
They seldom have one of their own.
My actress touches my hand,
stares intently at me, her head
cocked to one side,
another shadow on the wall.

J. G. Smith

BLESSED DREAMS

Walking along in this bitter cold brought to
my mind closeness, that freezing eve as you held me.
Few words were said, but our mutual feelings were
present without saying, as we shared one another.
You knew we both had to live our lives, I sensed
much differently than I'd ever dreamed we would.

We talked of my dreams peacefully as we walked
along, being years past and for such a short time.
That dream we once had discussed and actually
existing on two separate paths to travel, alone.
You were such a good friend and I loved you so
much; we didn't marry, but it remains a dream.

Dreams dear! That's why I continue to exist
and that's why we do as we do; they're important
those blessed dreams. They go on as we live in
a twist and as we die being old. We must learn
from them too. The dream I dreamed tonight was
here and gone before I knew it. Quick lessons.

Sharon Hemker

TO MY FAR-AWAY LOVE

Take care, my child.
Let breezes mild
Blow your hair
And deftly share
The sweetness of your brow.

Be glad, my child.
Your fate's mild
Weather will shine
On you and line
The flower of your face.

Be sure, my child.
My heart's mild
Logic concludes
Changeable moods
Cannot untie our bond.

Be good, my child.
While I in mild
Climes roam,
My thoughts home
On your so precious self.

Paul R. Neureiter

NEUREITER, PAUL RICHARD. Born: Vienna, Austria, 5-23-99; Married: 9-1-28 to Pearl C.; Education: Vienna "Gymnasium;" University of Vienna, M.A., Ph.D., 1924; Occupation: College Teacher of Mathematics, some Chemistry, Physics; Retired; Memberships: Torch International, Rotary International; Awards: First prize for "Wagner's Feminist Heroines," essay contest sponsored by Wagner Society of America, Chicago; Poetry: 'The Passion of Lent,' *The University Review,* 1938; 'Sonata of the Mid-Century,' *Compass,* 1939; 'Failure,' *Compass,* 1952; 'The Poor,' *New York Poetry Foundation Anthology,* 1986; Other Writings: "Lead Teachers of America," New York State Education, 1950; *Journal of Value Inquiry;* many scholarly papers in educational and literary journals, 1930-1963; Themes: *Religious and social, influenced by G. M. Hopkins;* Comments: *English is not my native language. I began using it in daily intercourse at age 28. The love poems were conceived and composed in my 86th year. "Heart will be on fire" till the last.*

WASTELAND

In the bitter wasteland
Of lonely hours
The dusty dryness
Of cold and blowing dreams,
I yearn to open my eyes upon
The shadow of your form.

I hunger for the sweetness
Which endears your voice
And dews your kisses.

Were I to stir this nectar
Into the toxins of buried memories,
Could I hope the blend
Would purify and sustain
That precious presence of your love,
Which is all of life for me?

Shirley F. Shown

COMPLAISANCE

Somewhere there is a prayer for me!
"Friends" ask that what I do
Be silent, so I practice silence.
That offends them too.
I am invited to rebel but I
Restrain such bold desire:
The drums are stacked — the trumpet cased,
Yet I shall seek no buyer!

I improved their a cappella,
Serendipitized the blues . . .
And then invented mutes that
Take the place of tents for all kazoos.
That failed, but all complacency
Finds kindness on its way
For love creates the virtuosity
That makes some neighbors pray.

Duane Frederick Jones

THIN MYSTERY

Electricity for your fantasy
Let in as thin mystery,
A razing torch glinting
The breezes to stir,
The limbs and leaves to run
The clearing urges,

Electricity for your fantasy
Let in as thin mystery,

On the span of a cardinal's wings
To fly away, gathering moods
By fixed and slit eyes
Rounding to tender memories.

Electricity for your fantasy
Let in as thin mystery.

K. E. Franklin

TO BE LOVED BY ME

Waiting tonight I feel so alone —
Needing your love to be mine . . .

Loving you warmly, I feel secure —
Why can't you stay forever?
To love so beautiful; yet, stay apart too long —
We are together through love.

Encouraging you to stay in my arms —
Loving you now, whispering softly . . .
Loving you tenderly — forever . . .
Knowing you were meant to be loved by me — only me!

Alone, I realize the depth of love
My lonely heart is heavy . . .
Wishing you were here, needing you now . . .
Oh, how I wish you were near!

But one more day must pass
And then you'll be home — in my waiting arms!

I dream of you and need you to be here —
Wishing you near to touch and to love
Forever — loving you tenderly . . .
Knowing you were meant to be loved by me — only me!

Dale Behrens

DRAWBRIDGE

And he hurt her love
And she built another drawbridge around her heart
And he caused her pain
The moat widened, and all towers did set in place

Now, protected or imprisoned,
The results remain the same
No love enters, no love exits,
And the guard may never change

And beyond the drawbridge gates, lie endless corridors,
That softly echo the sullen fate, of many suitors gone before

But undaunted, I dare enter
For the universe decrees,
That, which by love, is captive,
Is also, by love, set free

And silent screams surround me
As I draw close to her heart's door
Then tenderly with prize in hand, flee quietly

To emerge into a courtyard
To behold a drawbridge, aged by pain
Descending ever slowly, allowing one heart to love again.

Lemuel Byrd

ONE LOVE FOR ALL

He wore a crown of thorns
His wounded skin was torn and swollen
He had outstretched arms and drooping limbs
Hanging on a wooden cross
Pierced
Bleeding
Lifeless
Dead

Karen Kaprosy

OPEN HOUSE

Early morning reminiscing,
Wedding march, romance and snow,
Recalling all those happenings
Of twenty-five years ago.

Visitors, phone calls, last minute chores,
Mailman bringing a treasure today,
Four cards, three letters from pals, and more,
Wonderful greetings from friends far away.

"Open house," magic words,
Excitment and laughter,
Dear friends to greet you, your spirits lift
To heights unknown, then after,

The delightful pleasure of opening gifts
The table so lovely, bright to the eye.
Beautiful cake, cookies and strawberry punch
Were served to all guests, who passed by.

Pictures taken, goodies eaten, everyone gay,
Some had to leave early, others came late,
The happy closing of a perfect day,
Our 25th anniversary, unforgettable date!

Charlotte North

THE CANDY-STRIPED SKY

Sailing on a flood of foam
atop a soda tree,
I see her smile as she floats home
and reaches out to me.

My school's a school of poisoned pools,
her school's a crayoned sea
with waves of friends and fun and fools,
all of which I try to be.

She rushes in with warming sun
and Jack Frost in her hair
and plants a kiss so sweetly done
that flowers grow right there.

I brace Atlas feet syrup deep
in the candy-striped sky
to support her world 'til she goes to sleep.
Only then do I.

The years are few, and the moments mount.
I toll them as they go.
We're losing the magic to the count,
but she doesn't have to know.

Arthur E. McGowan

WITHOUT WORDS

Just once,

I would like to hold you close,
Where the heat of our bodies
says it all . . .

Where without words,
we melt into each other's hearts . . .

Just once.

Robert J. Royston

THE MOTH'S KISS, FIRST

From In a Gondola

The Moth's kiss, first
Kiss me as if you made believe
You were not sure, this eve,
How my face, your flower, had pursed
Its petals up; so, here and there
You brush it, till I grow aware
Who wants me, and wide open burst.

The Bee's kiss, now!
Kiss me as if you entered gay
My heart at some noonday,
A bud that dared not disallow
The claim, so all is rendered up,
And passively its shattered cup
Over your head to sleep I bow.

Robert Browning

LOVE

Public acclaim
I do not seek . . .

Enormous wealth?
not me!

Love is better
(more elusive . . .)

However . . .
(negotiable as ever)

Needed . . . hoarded
Misplaced . . . adorable

Love I seek!

Shirley R. Salyer

LEAVING

The remnants of your departure
cast shadows before me.
Like yesterday's rain
dreams
seem insignificant in the sunshine.

Kris Johnson

PAM

With music softly playing
and a candle burning bright
we talked and touched together
and held each other tight.
With a perfect Whiskey Sour
and fresh flowers from the tree,
we listened to Love's Shadows
and let ourselves just be.
The candle burned more brightly
as we let our passions run
so gently and with passion
we let ourselves be one.
It was so right and real, dear
for some dreams do come true
the world has heard our beating hearts
and we'll know what to do.

Robert Michael John Higgins

POWERFUL LOVE

Where does this road lead
Leads me into your heart
Captures your love
Takes it all.
Is it what you want
Is it what you need
There's no stopping love
When it's already there
There's no pushing it away
When it's in the air.
So take and accept
What's meant to be
Or lose that love
That was to be . . . yours.

Richard Orzol

MY FATHER

Oh! my Father owns the cattle
on tens of thousand hills.
He owns all the fertile acres
that every farmer tills.

Although He owns the treasured gold
in every mine and purse,
He chose to give His life for mine
to lift me from sin's curse.

So now He owns this child of God
He bought me for a price.
The blood He shed on Calvary
is adequate to suffice.

Katherine M. Brady

YEARNING

I think ofttimes of those tender years —
Ringed 'round with pain
And sprinkled with tears.
Where was the joy —
That circle of magic light
To which every child is entitled?
It, for the most part, eluded me.
I felt such a loss, deprivation,
To which I could put no name.
But the feeling visited me often,
Struggling, always struggling
With the music inside me
Which could never be shared or expressed.
Was I ever truly loved?

Irene Ladika White

THE ROSE

My love, to me, he gave a rose . . .
I know he's such a dear.
And love for him, inside me grows,
I always want him near.

The years go by, the rose has died,
It's been so long ago,
I've thought about him . . . often cried,
I'll always love him so.

Tina Alden-Houts

IN THE WINGS

The sparrow trembling in my hand
is knit tonight
of sinews that unbreakable
bind light.

Would that he would rest in the cradle
of my heart

but knowing its fragility
he lights
and gently dances off again.

P. A. Kelley

POP

I wrote a poem about you
That didn't mean a lot
But take a stand, 'cause this one's new
For it took tremendous thought.

It's all that TLC
That you have given me
It's that tender loving care
That makes this child rare.

A man who is a father
Is not one which to bother
But a man who is a dad
Can make his daughter glad.

A man who is as special as you
Can only deserve the best
For I am so much like you
I am a loving pest.

I love you more than words can say
For this goes on day by day
You are my dad, you are my pop
For only you can rate the top!

Judy Tuttle

HOW

How do I tell you I love you?
How do I get through?
All the feelings deep inside me
How do I get you to see?

Your way, or my way, how should it be?
How can I show you it's you and it's me?
There have to be ways of showing
Of the love that is deepening and growing.

How do I tell you I need you?
Knowing that you're needing me too
All the feelings that we need to share
And showing you how much that I do care.

How do I tell you I want you?
How do I get through?
Just wishing our ways were the same
'Cause then you wouldn't have me to blame.

For not showing you how much I do love you
Why is it, I can't seem to get through?
All the feelings laying deep inside me
I hope that someday you will see

Ruthie Mac

HE'S HOME TO STAY

He came home again last night.
Crazy me, I let him.
And there he goes doing the same old thing,
Breaking my heart again.

But here I go again, knowing
That this morning he came home.
He says he'll never leave me again,
That he will never more roam.

This lasted for awhile
But then he had to go.
I stood and watched him drive away,
This man that I love so.

But he came home again this morning,
I saw the hearse as it passed by.
I went to the funeral
To tell him a last good-by.

I looked down in the casket
where he lay.
This time he came home again
But this time he came home to stay.

Mrs. Earl V. Bundy

RETURN OF "THE MAGI"

My Mother sold her wedding ring,
to pay for my Prom dress.
She said no matter what,
I should have the best.

I never understood, the glint of her tears
as she watched me dress Prom night;
nor her soft dreamy faraway smile,
as she smoothed my silk gown of white.

I look back to that day,
with a sad haunting memory.
Until a Mother myself, I never realized
her most gracious loving deed.

A deep dark shadow surrounds my soul,
knowing her years of sacrifice and being brave;
because I never appreciated her,
till she was in her grave.

I decided to give her,
that which she once gave me.
With my wedding ring, in the ground, next to her;
I gave her my love, burying my sorrowful memory.

Jacqueline Holland

LOVE'S PASSING

Tenderly, tenderly lay her away.
Love, sweet love passed away today.
Place one rose in her hand in passing,
For love was fair, albeit not lasting.
She was too frail to stand the storm.
What was her ailment? What caused the harm?
Jealousy? Mistrust? Doubt? Reticence?
Her untimely end was caused by indifference.
Tenderly, tenderly lay her away.
Love, sweet love passed away today.

Vada Brodhagen

EXCEPT YOUR HELP

He will help you — He will help you.
He is a Savior oh so grand —
Just reach out and He will help you,
He will lead you by the hand.

When paths are dreary and you cannot see before,
Just reach out and He will help you —
You'll not be dreary any more.
Jesus is a precious Savior
He does know our every care;
Just reach out — He will help you
He'll be with you everywhere.

There will be times of awful doubting
When you cannot see before,
Just remember, never doubting
You will trust Him more and more
Doubt not as black clouds assail you,
Look ahead and on and on
You will find life gets better
And you will sing the Savior's song!

He will help you — He will help you,
He is a Savior oh so grand —
Just reach out and He will help you,
He will lead you by the hand.

Flora Rossdeutscher

MY OLD GRAY FRIEND

(An Elegy)

I loved you, my old gray friend.
I loved you when you rushed up to my back door at
Dawn, eagerly waiting for me to appear.

I loved your kind and loving, yet
Soulfully sad eyes and
I loved your whimpers of both joy and sorrow.

Now that you are *gone* it is I who whimper
— Rather, shaking violently with
Burning sadness, I cry aloud in pain and despair
Because I know I will never see you again,
My old gray friend.

Now I dread the dawn
For I know that I must
Wake to be alone, drowning in tears of
Bitter sadness for you,
My old gray friend.

You were just an old gray dog;
But you were my long beloved friend.
I will miss you and I shall *always* love you.

Rest in peace, *My old gray friend!*

Felix Meyer

TOUCH

Touch me in the morning, when the sun rises in the east
Touch me, for I am a child who can never get enough love.
For I am a girl who is vulnerable within.
Touch me, for I am a woman who wants to get lost in your
arms.
Touch me once more, as the sun sets over the horizon.

Gina T. Ganguli

WASTELAND

Did I cry
When the train pulled out?
Did you see me cry before it
Left? Strength can be mute
And still and great.
The cloth this long time
Has been wrung quite dry.
Not one small drip was seen;
Nor did I feel.

A vast desert is inside me,
Devoid of luscious growth.
Growth is not there
Where there is no sun.
And does one cry
Against one's fate?
The whole sky cried
And dropped its tears
On my dry cheeks but
I did not cry.

Dorothy Moore

ARNETT, DOROTHY IRENE MOORE. Pen Name: Dorothy Moore; Born: Farmland, Indiana; Married: to Ernest V. Arnett, 11-21-51; Education: Ball State University, Muncie, Indiana, B.S. in English, Art Special; University of Denver; Occupation: Retired Teacher; Memberships: AARP, NRTA, for retired people; Poetry: 'She Burst Her Shell,' American Poetry Association, 1983; 'Tribute to Celestial Fires,' American Poetry Association, 1985; 'Prognostication,' CSS Publications, 1982; 'Ranger and the Pigeons Know,' CSS Publications, 1983; 'Bearance,' CSS Publications, 1984; Comments; *I have soared on Cloud Nine since my poetry teacher at Ball State University told me, "You are like Emily Dickinson!" Dr. C. W. Gurney in Chicago told me the same thing. I write poems about life and emotions!*

LOVE COME TO ME

Love, oh love, come quietly to me
Like waves upon a tranquil sea
Love, oh love, speak softly to me
As whispers a breeze to a tall pine tree
Love, oh love, fall gently on me
As leaves fall from an Autumn tree
Oh love spread around me your gentle glow
Like starlight on new fallen snow.

Mary Ethel Frost

CARING

How wonderful it is to know
That someone cares for you.
To go along life's path alone
Would be too hard to do.

To share and care for someone else
Can kindle hope for you.
It takes so little love
To start a life anew.

Ellen J. Sheridan

MY OLD LADY

When I was young I had to fool her,
After marriage, I did not rule her;
We had to raise four dependent kids,
Not one of them has smoked grass in lids;
The kids are gone, I can have a brew,
My wife sits with me and we have two;
She has not learned my past is shady,
Loves me and is still my old lady.

Don Bedwell

SKETCH

HONORABLE MENTION

her hair in soft luxury's lap
  has grown and swelled
her smile is naked.
her legs are brushed with the
  strokes of Renoir and
her arms linger
  upon the backs of sofas.

Michael M. Peters

GOODBYE LOVE

I gave you all my love,
You gave me all your love,
Someone stole your love from me,
So sadly I whisper goodbye love,
I thought we had something special,
Something no one could take away,
Sadly I say I was wrong,
So sadly I whisper goodbye love.

Anna Harris

BASED ON LOVE STORY

Love is never having to say you're
sorry.
It's a word not often used.
Love is nice to be in,
If it's not abused.
When you find the one you've been
looking for, for years.
When they are gone
It brings nothing but tears.

Kathy Bonito

BONITO, KATHY A. Pen Name: Helen; Born: Wareham, Massachusetts, 3-16-62; Education: Falmouth High School, Falmouth, Massachusetts; Memberships: Massachusetts Association for the Blind; Poetry: 'The Four Seasons,' *American Poetry Anthology,* 1986; Comments: *My feelings are best expressed through my poetry.*

SOUGHT AND FOUND

"Seek and ye shall find, knock and the door shall be opened . . . "
Matthew 7:7 & 8

No more smokey bar rooms
  No one-night stands for me
A new and perfect love
  came 'round and rescued me

I knew right when I met Him
  that I would have to change
But *He* met me where *I* was at
  My life to rearrange!

He led me by the hand
  and often carried me
From emptiness to promises
  of life eternally . . .

Oh, I believed in God alright
  somewhere in my mind
But not until my heart believed
  salvation did I find

He knew that I was searching
  and glad I am of that
He gave just what I needed
  God's perfect love that lasts!

Patricia Ogilvie

SWEETHEART

Sensitivity seems to radiate from your very soul
Wisdom dwelling in a heart that is honest and whole
Exemplifying the qualities that I've sought in a love
Epitome of The Woman and gentle as a dove
These days with you though few in number
Have awakened within me a love that did slumber
Electric response when you take my hand or arm
Always know that I'll protect you from harm
Reach out to me and walk by my side
Then rest assured that I'll ever abide

William D. Andrews

FOREVER YOU AND I

Even now when I realize how far we have come,
and moments we shared begin to unwind, I can feel
my heart fly. For when you look into my eyes I
know this kind of Love can only be meant for You and I

For we'll be two stars in the night, a feather Rose
and a rainbow Sky

And as time slips by and life floats on and on
we will unlock all our feelings, hopes and expectations
and make each and every day a new sunrise
a new beginning in each other's eyes

For there is no greater treasure worth more than I can
give to you and you to me than that of Love
And with Love our lives will be just as we
dream them to be. We'll let our hearts sing and our
Love will grow. For I will always be with you with these
feelings of Love, deep inside I know our little heaven
will shine forever till the end of time

for we are but two Lovers lost in the spirit of the Moment

A race for the morning Light

Juan J. Gonzalez

WHAT MADE US FALL IN LOVE?

Was it the moon and the starry sky above?
Is that what made us fall so deeply in love?
Or was it some preordained plan that's called Fate
That set you, just you, apart to be my mate?

Was it the music set our hearts in the clouds?
Is that what made us want to avoid the crowds?
Or rather, dear, was it heart that answered heart
That caused us to vow that we would never part?

Was it craving, longing, sensual desire?
Is that what it was that set our HEARTS ON FIRE?
Or rather was it some deep-down spark inside
That grew into a flame that will e'er abide?

Was it the things we did, or the fun we had?
Is that what it was that made our hearts go mad?
Why, if we hadn't ever a thing to do,
I would still have no one in the world but you!

Whatever was it that made us fall in love?
Whatever was it that we were thinking of?
My darling, it happened — lucky, lucky me!
My only true love, that you will always be!

Carol Boyer Mitchell

HEARTS ABLAZE

How wretched we feel when our hearts are on fire . . .
Raging flames of passion — consuming every thought . . .
Misdirecting our every deed . . .

How warm we feel when our hearts are on fire . . .
Burning with enthusiasm . . .
Hoping for the warmth to spread . . .

How secure we feel when our hearts are on fire . . .
With Passion
And Love
And Belief
And Conviction . . .

Jo Hendijani

HENDIJANI, MARY JOANNE. Pen Name: Jo Hendijani; Born: 10-11-51; Married: to Jahanriz Hendijani, an Iranian National; Education: Attended USF, Tampa, Florida, and Nova University, Ft. Lauderdale, Florida, still working on a degree in psychology; Occupation: Bookkeeper for husband's trucking business; Awards: Selected and two Honorable Mentions with Ursus Press, 1984; Poetry: 'Fiddler Crabs,' American Poetry Association, Fall 1985; *Reflections,* collection of poetry, 9-85; *The Mirror,* collection of short stories, 6-85; Comments: *I am an avid reader and compulsive writer — I write on everything, even tablecloths. I try to note the wonder of it all, and use my mind as a mirror for my soul. Being an October child, I look for the beauty in the everyday things.*

for me

smile for me:
  enhance the room with your brightest grin
  and make my day and nights begin.

cry for me:
  whether it'd be glad, sad, solemn or surprise,
  your tears will part as together we arise.

reach for me:
  bring forth your arms to unite in mine
  and forever our embrace will leave our hearts combined.

David Allen Mills

BOND OF LOVE

Do not ever let it be said,
that my husband or children
were a burden to me . . .
Or this is how my heart was broken.

I — Lillie, could never walk this Life,
upon this earth — without thee . . .

My children are the symbol of a,
sacred bond of Love;

A bond of that to me and my husband,
this bond of Love can never be broken . . .

Even if there were no stars,
left to shine in the sky.
This bond nothing can break
this bond of Love I make . . .

I will take to eternity.
A bond of Love to my husband,

Through my children to me
this is Life's worth,

For now — forever
to the ends of this earth;

Lillie Seidel Hinton

LET ME TELL YOU ABOUT MY GRANDSON

Let me tell you about my grandson
He's bright and beautiful and seven.
The close bond between us, that's my gift from Heaven.

He walks into the room, a big smile on his face,
Out go all my cares and troubles, that's how he
Brightens up my place.

In every week that passes, he saves for me a day.
Sometimes we read or talk, we both have lots to say.

Then we may have hot chocolate and cookies
And sometimes bake a pie.
Before I know it's getting late, the time
Just seems to fly.

Other times we may pop corn and watch a show.
Then it's time for bed, I wonder where did that time go.

So I gently tuck him in, he's as happy as can be.
Oh, I forgot to tell you, he always sleeps with me.

When his mother calls for him, I smile, the lump in my throat
Won't let me speak.

So he leaves me with a hug and yells, "Grandma, I'll see you
Next week!"

Charlotte West

TO AN ANGEL (Debby Holbrook)

There is nothing beyond our reach,
Who knows? We may even some day teach
Others how to reach out afar
To catch their shining star.
We have much in common,
Especially our Love for our fellow man.
Our goals are the same;
We seek neither fortune nor fame.
We merely wish to accomplish
For our fellow man, happiness.
We have truly been blessed with care
And we both know we shall be there
When the whole world fulfills its promise
Of a better world where everyone is honest.
Our optimism is based on faith in God and others.
The whole world is full of our Sisters, Brothers.
We have a faith within
With which, we can only win.
We shall accomplish all we've set out to do,
For we know we're bound the right thing to do.

Gerald B. Stubblefield

HOW STRONG IS YOUR LOVE?

Do you really love me, the way you used to dear?
Back when we were youngsters, early in our years.
When we looked at each other, our hearts were all aglow;
We always whispered love words, to each other sweet and low.

Now that we've grown older and years have passed us by,
I don't see the same old sparkle for me in your eye.
But I still long to hold and love you as before;
Tell me dearest sweetheart, do you love me ever more?

Even though I'm getting old and may not be attractive,
The blood that's running through my veins is very very active.
I like to be caressed and told how much you need me so;
Instead of being picked at and treated very low.

It's the little tiny gestures that I appreciate;
It shows your love is there and hasn't turned to hate.
For kindness is the warmest gift to shower on each other;
It gives forth life and strength to carry on together.

Mary Ingram

A MIDDLE-AGED GENTLEMAN

A middle-aged gentleman once ran an ad
For a woman to love he was lonely and sad.
A young woman answered thank Heaven above,
She wrote, "Sir, I'm lonely and I too seek love.
I've twice been married and now that I'm free
I seek a good home and security,
I have basic needs but aside from all that,
I need a good home for my little white cat."
The middle-aged gentleman read with surprise,
And hope in his heart, and tears in his eyes,
The letter continued and here's what it said:
"I could love a good man till the day that I'm dead.
I'm an excellent cook and I like to sew,
And I carry the Good Book wherever I go.
I have a very nice figure, my waist is quite small,
My eyes are dark brown and I'm five foot three tall.
My long hair is auburn, I weigh one twenty two,
And have an olive complexion I'm sure will please you.
If you approve my statistics you know where I'm at,
Please send for me and my little white cat."

Richard Bruce McFarlane

Beloved friend, you have become an excellent teacher
With you I have learned of my vast capacity to love
It's been under anesthetic for years; now I claim it anew
This sense of joy and wonder
You have taught me that I still can sing and dance
And, yes, that I can cry
Not tears of self-pity or righteous anger, but pearls of the heart
That come as part of the rainbow of love and life
I feel like a Fourth of July sparkler that, once ignited, comes alive
Lights and delights, becoming fully involved in itself
Yet bursting forth into the world around it
I rejoice that you are part of my journey
For I also have learned that I am not here to fill any emptiness of yours
Nor to stand in for someone else
And especially not to be taken care of
Rather I am myself, creating my own space
Loving you from it and inviting you into it
I reach out my hand from this place you have taught me about
Knowing you will be there to walk with me

Lyn Berry

BERRY, LYN G. Born: Pittsburgh, Pennsylvania; Education: University of Arizona, Tucson, B.A., English — Journalism, 1962; Professional School of Psychological Studies, San Diego, California, M.A., 1983; Occupation: Teacher, Counselor, Writer; Awards: Professional of the Year, North San Diego County Press Club; Numerous feature writing, editorial writing awards; Comments: *My poems are a celebration of the spirit in me and in you. These particular poems are dedicated to a special friend who helped me discover a whole new dimension of love and acceptance.*

LOVE REMEMBERED

The love you gave to me was like the sun; warm and gold.
The happiness you gave is a thousand Springtimes my heart can't hold.
The joy you gave to me was a pearl of beauty and price untold.

The love you gave to me was soft and gentle as April rain.
The tears you shed for me were diamonds I'll never have again.
The comfort you gave to me was an angel's kiss that eased my pain.

But death came at last and took the love you gave to me.
Yet I still find your love in each new dawn I see,
And my diamonds and pearls I keep safe in memory.

And Spring will come again some distant day
When the April rain has touched my heart of clay
And an angel's kiss will ease my pain away.

Betty Allen

LOVE DOES NOT FORGET

Take the tears and put them in a vial
And bring it to the brook in the back
Of the cottage behind the dogwood trees
And the wildflowers. Then pour the tears
Into the stream and its gentle flow will
Take your grief and mingle it with the
River's abundant waters. And all your
Sorrow will be dissolved and lost in the
Timeless eternity of all oceans. Where
Only your love shall remain and only
Love does not forget.

Joan Marie Rooks

MY LOVE, MY OWN

Auburn curls and sun-tanned skin;
Mischievous smile from deep within;
Muscular build, a farmer's son;
He held my hand; my heart he won.

Lover's path, the orchard lane;
Fragrant blossoms, bird's refrain;
Pledge of love with sapphire ring;
He held me close; my heart did sing.

Married years, love grew anew;
Daughters, four, from me to you —
Flowers in our garden fair,
Nourished by our love and care.

Auburn curls, now gray and thin;
Youthful smile, turned placid grin;
Gentleness I've always known —
Surrounds our golden years, our own.

Retirement years in full swing;
Grandchildren make our hearts sing.
Oh, My Love, the thrill remains;
When first our hearts a union made.

Eleanor S. Follmer

EASTER LOVE

Let human hearts open wide this day
  Bid our Saviour come in and stay.

  Today, the tomb was opened wide;
Mary found it so.
  Peter ran inside to see
The winding cloth was laid aside
And Christ our Saviour was not there.
    He had risen from the dead.

He, who believes,
does so in faith.

Christ had foretold, he would arise
And would appear before our eyes
God's promise to fulfill.

We, who know our risen Lord;
A Thomas each, in time restored —
    Believe,
And are fulfilled each day in Christ.
His life exchanged on Calvary's cross
That not a single soul be lost,
    Because he loves us so.

Mabel L. Bowman

FOR YOU

I would like to invent words
I would like to be inspired
More than any other poet
To be able to write
Delirious poems
And that,
When you read me
You would recognize yourself
And you would smile,
Embrace me and cry out:
"Darling, I love you too!"

Barbara Krupa

A MOTHER'S LOVE

A Mother's love is special
For each child that she bears.
She nourishes and protects them;
She always loves and shares.

She directs and guides them
In a firm but gentle way.
She teaches them right from wrong
And hopes they will not stray.

She takes care of wants and needs
As a loving Mother should;
She scolds them when they misbehave
And rewards them when they're good.

She listens to their problems,
Understands their doubts and fears;
When they are sad and lonely,
She wipes away their tears.

Her children are her pride and joy;
She hopes when they are grown
That they will always love and share
With children of their own.

Margaret Nevins

POST OFFICE JANE

I saw her face
And she moved with grace
And I saw her hair
So long and straight and fair

Not too much in any hurry
She showed me no signs of worry
And I think I'm knowing why
And she's just going by

Just to mail a letter away
Something to do and nothing to say
Up the steps and she went in
Then she came back down again

She walked on in the same direction
And she took along my very affection
Attracting me without trying to
Saying not even "Goodbye to you"

(Just taking her time . . .
All the while
Inspiring a rhyme
With barely a smile)

Roger B. Dahlberg

THE OLD SONG

You've worn a groove so very fine
That keeps on running 'round my mind.
You are the music and each word.
It's you I've learned.
It's you I've heard.
Awake, asleep, it's all the same,
I find you going 'round my brain.
I sleep to you, I wake to you
And pray, for my heart's sake, to you.
The sweet, insidious, lulling strain
Is something that I can't explain.
I'm living in a song to you!
It tells me I belong to you!
What is this lariat that binds
My soul and body and confines
My heart in bondage to your word?
Is love so sweet
And so absurd?

Dean Lewis

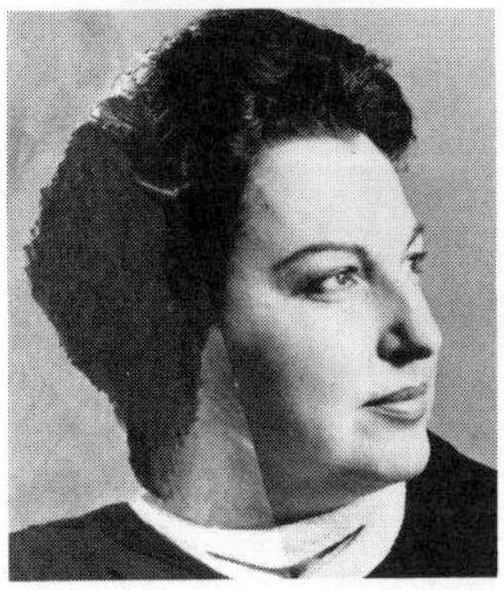

LEWIS, DEAN. Pen Name: Dean Forthman, Nadine Kirton; Born: Chicago, Illinois, 3-10-19; Unmarried, 3 adult children and 3 grandchildren; Education: University of Miami, Coral Gables, Florida, 1942; Occupations: Singer, Actress, Lyricist, Poet, Playwright; Memberships: ASCAP, Actors Equity; Awards: 1985 Award from ASCAP, Prize Production for Best New Musical, 1984; Poetry of the Year Award, 1985; Poetry: 'Robin Woman,' *American Poetry Anthology Vol III,* 1984; 'Gueneviere,' *Today's Greatest Poems,* 1983; 'Christmas,' *Our World's Best Loved Poems,* 1984; Other Writings: "Atlantic City, USA," lyrics, chosen best new musical, produced by Phoenix Little Theatre, 1984; "Three Magic Wishes," Christmas musical, book and lyrics, produced by Sanctuary Theatre, New York, 1973; Themes: *Relationships, nature, social commentary, spiritual, children, love of all kinds.* Comments: *I appeared in "Sound of Music" on Broadway, Kurtweil's "Johnny Johnson," on Broadway, National Company of "Man of La Mancha."*

LOVE IS BETTER

Anger rests in the bosom of fools.
Who cannot live according to God's rules.
All this by wisdom has been proved.
When we are by God's Spirit moved.

Your children's peace shall be very great.
As parents they will your hearts elate.
Jesus is the glory of all lands.
Our Love for the Saviour just expands.

Jesus' compassions they are new every morning.
God's grace and love our spirit adorning.
Looking up toward God pressing always forward.
Somewhat of heaven shall be our reward.

We are required to believe God's Word.
Faith is needed to receive promises offered.
The Lord's hand is stretched out still.
Eternal life through faith for whosoever will.

Paul O. Carlson

CARLSON, PAUL OSCAR. Born: Aurora, Colorado, 6-28-09; Married: Fifty-one years to Lovina May; Education: Many classes in Bible Schools with recognition. Used in many personal testimonies; Occupation: Electrical field, Electrical Superintendent; Memberships: Electrical Unions, Bible Schools; Awards: *Union Pacific Magazine,* 1980; Some poems are used in Church Bulletins also; Poetry: 'Infinite Forever,' 1975; 'Beholding His Beauty,' 1975; 'Love is Better,' 1976; 'Illuminate Our Land,' 1977; 'History's Darkest and Brightest Day,' 1978; religious poems; Comments: *God is using me through the inspiration of poetry to spread the good news of His Gospel, to comfort souls and to glorify His name.*

morning love

when movement of night brings knowledge, to be that you're near,
and to know that the morning will come, will see me kiss you,
awakening, not without passion. but the night covers my soul,
with your grace. and to see the trust in your eyes, for me
when morning sees us awake, is for me to know that I am truly
blessed. as only you can, you make me feel like the man I
truly am. (good morning, my love, good morning).

michael mccloud

BLIND HEART AND SOUL

Nothing has changed on the surface, love
It's still the same on the outside
But if I were to let you inside here, love
I know you'd only run and hide

You really never could understand
And I really never could explain
How I lose such faith in those who walk away
And mistrust those who do remain

All I have has been granted to me
And it's all I need to survive
So you can save your vote of sympathy for
One who needs it to stay alive

A melody tames a smoke-filled room
All its words fall in perfect rhyme
I stand alone cursing its simplicity
Silently wishing it was mine

So believe nothing has changed here, love
Sleep sound tonight where your head lies
You cannot see inside a heart or soul, love
When you wear blinders on your eyes

T. A. Houlahan

LOVE IS LIKE A BOOK

Our love is like a good book,
The deeper we're in,
The quicker we're hooked.

Once in a while we come across a gap,
Sometimes it causes our love to nap.

Darling if we break apart — to stay apart
Always let us be friends.
Don't let the story end
Our hearts are equal — so wait for the sequel.

Crystal Cochran

TRUE FRIENDS (WORLDS APART)

Where is tomorrow, where does yesterday go?
So many times I've wanted to ask
the questions, the answers I'll never know
but now it's too late and time slips past.

Even if you never cared, I still loved you
When everybody turned away, you were still there
though many years have gone, I still do
Someday we'll find each other somewhere.

If every face you see
and every voice you hear
keeps you thinking of me
keep in mind I'm always near.

Remember if you're feeling lost and down
or the world just doesn't care
I'm still the true friend you once found
call out my name, I'll be there.

If my life should someday soon end
keep me in your mind and heart
because I'll always be your friend
even if we're worlds apart.

Buffy Weaver

DEAREST

Dearest, your beauty is to me
like brilliant stars all year long.
And when your face I cannot see,
your voice will reach me like a song.

Your eyes are like the morning dew
that sparkles on the blades of grass.
Your color hair in blended hue,
your face so fair that none surpass.

By your window I see you stand
in your dress of flowered design.
Your picture-hat ready in your hand,
a painter's picture so divine.

All my days I'm in a trance.
You're always in my nightly dreams.
I deeply cherish our romance.
Your lips, your cheeks, your smile that beams.

You're everything to me my love,
for which my lonely heart does pine.
And I wish upon the stars above
that forever you will be mine.

Carl J. Proia

MY TEACHER OF MATH

My Teacher of Math, how great you are!
You've planned for each classroom move.
Not one bit of that muckity muck
Against you, would that I prove.

Great Teacher of Life, you've noticed me
And how many times I've erred.
Forgive me for fanning the wrong fires . . .
When mostly for me I cared.

I've searched and I've searched, for good reasons;
Why did I not stay by you?
Your light goes beyond that masquerade,
Where "man is for man" is not new.

My Teacher of Math, do you I please
When I work for this or that?
I'll take what others wish that I take,
If you'll stand with me at bat.

Great Teacher of Math . . . Teacher for all
Who would lay aside the spear,
I love you more than ever before!
This let mine enemies hear.

H. R. Krauss

THE LONG ROAD TO LOVE

I've waited so long to hear the words I love you.
I never thought I'd feel the joy in my heart
When you first said those words to me.
It's funny how three little words
Can make a woman's heart leap
A thousand miles into the air.
And what a relief it is to say "I love you"
And actually have it mean something.
It means that now instead of riding down
That one-way road you've ridden down so many times
You've finally found that immortal two-way street.

Lisa A. Kerechanin

TWO HEARTS AFIRE

Two hearts afire — that beat as one.
Two people searching for love,
Who didn't know their search was done.
When by God, chance, or just a friend's design,
Someone said, "I'd like you to meet a friend of mine."
It was a hurried introduction, as pressed for time,
each went their separate ways,
But they both turned around and looked once more,
And each thought of the other for days.
Then suddenly, as later they unexpectedly met,
The rapid beating of their hearts sent a message
they would not forget,
For love was finding its way through their hearts' door
And in time they knew
It was love — and it grew
'Til they were two hearts afire, forevermore.

Mary M. Volkman

THE APPLE THE GRAPE AND THE HONEY

The apple is so fresh when it's first
picked from the tree,
Just like our love so sweet and ripe
deliciously satisfying to the sight.
The grape it's taste is hidden away by
its colored skin,
Just like our hearts which grow from
within, producing love as the
Grape produces wine,
both are a delicacy and enrich with time.
The bees produce honey working
all day,
They work until they have enough to
save.
It's just like our love we share together,
only we work much harder and are
Under more strain;
but in the end like the bee we have
What we need,
that love we've worked so hard to achieve.

Donald Johnson

LOVE IS NEVER FOREVER

A summer rose reaching toward a starlit sky
Two hearts throbbing deep and swift
I smile at your laughing eyes
I'm so in love
Longing for your kiss, in haste demand.

No more afraid as tender lips
Meet in a crescendo like the roaring sea
Being carried on waves of time
Up, up into infinity
Happiness that's supposed to last forever.

Now pale lamplight silhouetted
Shining through my window
Flickering like a fading star giving me comfort,
You promised so much, delivered so little
Crystal teardrops replacing laughter
Memories of happier times.

All that's left now is ember glow lukewarm
And ashes from a love now death
This is the end, how quickly love turns to hate.

Gretel Bush

LOVE'S LANCE

Seized of a bliss too full divine,
A soaring fountain, flaming shrine!
Surging a mad, immortal vein,
Clutching a poorly mortal pain . . .
Always I plead of God to last
The stinging vigil, stabbing task,
Savoring colors never seen
Drenched of a melody undreamed!
What rare outrageous riches bless
Yet secret terror stalks my flesh,
And I despair, devour day's goal
Caresses wrench my flying soul —
And every kiss but cuts . . .

Victoria Beane

BEANE, VICTORIA.

A TEAR

Can I cry
Enough for you
All my tears won't bring
You back to life again
I call for you
But you have departed
Grief pierces my heart
A tear
Where can I go from now
I can't bring you back

Renata Dawidowicz

RZEPECKI, RENATA TERESA. Pen Name: Dawidowicz; Born: Trani, Italy; Education: Wayne State University, Bachelor of Science; Poetry: 'Let On,' 'Dancing,' 'Your Presence,' 'Intrigue,' 'Flicker.'

THE ENCHANTRESS

Sweet Enchantress, captured me,
when I thought I was free.
Sweet Enchantress, sweet as wine,
I will love you till the end of time.

Out into the midnight darkness,
over the wind-swept meadows.
She beckoned for me to follow,
as I looked from my window.

From my room into the night,
I merged into her whiteness.
Following to where she led,
to feel her tender caress.

Sweet Enchantress, so white,
emerging from the darkest night.
Sweet Enchantress, look on me,
you know how I want to be.

Under the shadow of giant Oaks,
quiet and serene was the night.
Unto her, I was drawn,
like an insect, unto light.

Feeding my intimate desires,
under the soft halo of moonlight.
Looking deep into my heart,
to her I was lost with no fight.

Ronald D. Fulcher

UNDOUSABLE DESIRE

There is a torch of unquenchable
fire
Fueled by the heart with intense
desire.

It's the fire of love, a consuming
light.
That lights up a life with rapture,
delight.

It has the power to mold from
two.
One union of hearts, destinies,
too.

It acts as a healer, a mystic
force.
That originates from a celestial
source.

It's an ancient of days ever
nearby.
Though sometimes the bold one, sometimes
shy.

It won't be doused this living
flame.
Love in its self remains the
same.

Halden Holden

PROJECTION

Why don't you ever call me?
Just to connect,
To hear my voice,
You said you love me.

Why didn't he call me?
After he left . . .
To see how I was, he said
He'd always love me.

Why do I still react
To him and feel
Forgotten and alone
When you don't call?

Gwen Cheryl Lyn Sarandrea

TO CECIL

We met, we talked, we fell in love
This man with eyes so brown
My heart would pound, I was all aglow
Whenever he was around

When he asked me to marry him
I hurried up to say
I'll think about it pal of mine
Ask me again some day

Of course he did and I said yes
I knew I would all the time
And each day I know I'm lucky
That this good man is mine

Martha Watts

ENCOUNTER

I drove alone
along a wintry road.
A doe crossed over . . .
it had heavily snowed.

We looked at each other
in a peaceful stare . . .
I remembered a distant
love affair.

Joseph P. Kowacic

FAITH, HOPE AND LOVE

Faith, Hope, and Love abound.
Our agenda requires the blend.
Like clay, they require a mold
To shape and be ready to befriend.

Love is so much, the greater —
So very patient with much affection.
It never insists its own mode
Always ready to care with devotion.

There are times love needs assistance,
Faith and hope are ready to serve.
Each is different, but will always assist
A perfect faction on the roadway curve.

Beatrice Nelson

WHEN I THINK OF YOU

When I think of you
I think of your smile
The way it touched my heart
And now you're many dreams away

I miss the glimmer in your eyes
When you look at me
The way you held me tight
The way you whispered in my ear

So soft late at night
When I think of you
I think of you often
Because I care

When I think of you
I think of how much I miss you
Because you're the only man
I want to love

Natalie Shuba

TO MY SISTER, HELEN THINGS WE HAVE SHARED

Sitting on a log,
Sharing our views.
Taking a ride,
Singing the blues.
Eating some mushrooms,
Feeling quite smug.
Bragging a lot,
Giving our husbands a plug.

Comparing their achievements.
Missing our parents,
Lamenting their bereavements.
We have so much in common.
How lucky we've been.
I'll love you always.
You are my Best Friend.
Your sister, Betty Jo

Betty Jo Lloyd

SEVENTEEN, I LOVE YOU

I wish I could convey to you
How much you mean to me . . .
You are my sunshine, you are my life,
The very breath I breathe . . .
We don't always communicate
The way we really should,
But, even then, I love you so,
I would bear all your pain
If I could.

Someday, when you have a
Child of your own,
And things just don't seem right,
Remember me, remember you,
You will know what I feel
tonight.

I love you very much . . .
Mom

Linda K. Stell

THANK YOU

A bird
soars through the sky,
and my heart with it.
My feet
don't touch the ground,
because of the life I've found with you.
My will to live
has been restored now I've
something to live for.
And all because of you!

My days
are brighter when I'm with you;
my nights
are absolute joy!
my self-confidence
has flowered under your care.
My happiness
knows no bounds,
and all because of you!

Christina A. Hurkmans

HYPOTHESIS

Once in a while
I collect
my thoughts
sufficiently
to realize
you are the nucleus
of every dream
I've ever spawned.
It occurs to me
from time to time,
unlike the road
which has no end,
continuity
must one day cease;
all reverie
does not materialize
and fulfilled fantasies
transform
to nurtured memories.

Nell Elaine Nichols

INEZ

A lady, full of power,
and prestige.
One who is admired.
We all love her dearly.
That is not a lie, for
without her one wouldn't die.

A friend, a special one,
the closest.
Always there, whenever.
A thought, she'll always be there.
To run to, fall back on
without questioning.

A mother, the only one,
always and forever.
Supporting, pushing.
For she loves us all.
Believe me, out of all of
us, I know.

Jamie O'Connell

A ROBIN'S SONG

Robin red-
breast, sing your lovely
song to me,
I love to
hear your melody floating
upon the currents.

The day's end
brings no sorrowful
feelings to
me as I
drift off to dreamland with your
lilting magic song.

Once again
I will listen to
your voice as
my daily
chores seem to blend and fade as
though only a dream.

Linda C. Ralston

WHAT DO YOU MEAN TO ME?

Oh, the dearest one I love —
What do you mean to me?
True to you as the blue above
And just as deep as the deep blue sea,
That my love
Is what you mean to me.

Oh promise me! You'll leave me never,
Our bond of love we'll never sever,
Though all the seas dry up now
I'll love you just as much as I do now,
That my sweet is what
You mean to me.

Eternally true is our sweet, sweet love;
True as the moon and stars up above.
Even though death do us finally part
Our love does link us heart to heart.
That my love,
Is what you mean to me.

Bernard Jacob

LOVES WE LOST ALONG THE WAY

Somewhere we lost along the way
the childhood games we used to play,
the running, hiding, seeking games,
gradeschool friends and teacher's names,
puppy-loves and valentines,
all that memory entwines;
growing up with soul embossed
by loves along the way we lost.
Friends and lovers, relatives,
all of those the heart outlives,
poets we loved and hopes that died,
lost are tears we should have cried.
Lost are plans we made at dawn
for a night that's now long gone.

But once upon a lifetime, Fate
let's us know it's not too late.
When we the heart with hope imbue,
love rekindled flames anew.

Hester Hayes

ON FINDING AN OLD BOOK OF POETRY

Here a book of poetry
old and tattered,
marked by a caring reader
verses that mattered.

Romantic stanzas of lost love
morbid and sad
a reader submerged in feeling,
romantically clad.

Jean Rathbun

THE COMPASSIONATE

I am the compassionate —
if you should cry
I too will shed a tear,
if you should feel pain
I will hurt with you,
if you should be happy
I will sing praise for your joy,
but if you should learn to hate
I will teach you love.

b. e. hargest

LOVE

Remember not old times,
for they be fruitless and forgotten.
Remember many a friend,
for they be with you 'til the end.

Love not the ways of the world,
for they will lead you astray.
Love only the people of the world,
for they need you this very day.

Ronald D. Fulcher

REELS OF MEMORY

My mind made a movie
of the two of us last night,
everything was beautiful,
and all of our wrongs were right.

If tomorrow should take the beautiful,
and you away from me,
I'll still have an old-time movie
in my reels of memory.

Arleafa Schroeder

INTRINSIC DESIGN

Life is a tapestry woven
With threads of laughter and tears;
Heartaches and joys intermingle
With longings, sorrows, and fears.

Gold are the threads used to brighten,
Enriching the pattern by far,
Using the rest as a background
Love shines as the Bright Evening Star.

Ruth M. Lommatzsch

PEACE

Stretch out your hand, who loves the
land of liberty;
Call down peace from above, for
Peace is the end of tyranny,
hostility, terror, and unrest.
Peace with freedom offers security,
harmony, unity, and blessedness.

I love peace and am willing to be
at peace.
In my heart, I long for peace.
Let me delight in law and the lawless
be ashamed;
Let my heart be sound in truth; let
mercy be a comfort . . .

Carolyn T. Abbot

THE HEART

The Heart resembles the ocean,
It trembles and shakes and quakes;
Like it, it comes to motion
When feeling pains and aches.

Yet, sometimes it is even,
Just like the sea in sun;
When love and joy have given
To it a smoother run.

The heart, too, has a low tide,
And high tide, like the sea;

But full it will always be, and wide
Yet empty it can never be.

Hartwig Heymann

TIME STANDS STILL

Lying in the night grass,
Gazing up at you.
Can I make the night last?
We have so few . . .

Stars' eyes looking down,
They have seen love before.
Crescent moon will not frown,
Just a grin, nothing more . . .

We pledged our souls, bodies, hearts,
So many years ago.
But with you, time stands still,
as stars . . .
And I still love you so . . .

Ginny Lindauer

SOUTH OF PARADISE

Just a little bit south of Paradise
Where the sun never fails to shine
In the glow of a pair of lovely eyes
I live with this love of mine.

There's never a cloud to hide the moon
Never a break in a lover's tune
Never a day not as sweet as June
South of Paradise.

Katherine E. Cartwright

ATTITUDE OF LOVE

Though I was a Martha at
heart
a Mary I tried to be.
Through the grace of God now
I'm a Martha and Mary in one
the Spirit set me free.

From dawn 'til dark I sit at
His feet
yet my daily work is always
complete
As I work for Him He works
in
me
with no time to worry no time
to fret
Faith has never failed me
yet.

Paula Trapani Bourg

LOVE FOUND

Hello my love
do you know me now?
I have been in your past.
I have been in your dreams.
My name was written alongside yours
when the world was only an image
in God's eye
and not yet a living thing.

Our lives were tied together,
our love destined to be
by the being who forged the sun
and the seas.

Hello my love
do you know me now?
If you do
then know me ever more.

Dan Whitaker

THE UNKNOWN SEER

I watch you
but you don't see me.
My silent eyes
record your every move.
I am the unknown seer.
To me you are the god Apollo,
your golden hair is like the sun
shining down upon my dreary life.
Your brilliant smile
makes my heart leap
for the sheer beauty of it.
and your laughter peals out
like bells on a clear day.
I watch you
but you don't see me.
My silent eyes
record your every move.
I am the unknown seer.

Wendy Works

WEEKENDS

Weekends
so quiet
so calm
and so alone
without . . .
that special gift
you have
to make the mornings
as a newborn birth,
so fresh, alive,
and inquisitive.
So the weekend
passes
as more will pass
without . . .

LeRoy B. Schwan

AND SO ON

She was the moon
The sun was her love,
She followed him . . .
Day into night
Night into day.
Then . . .
Passing in eclipse
She said,
"I will find you again"
He became the water (Scorpio)
She the air (Aquarius)
The rain made them one
She told him,
"I will find you again"
And so on . . . into eternity.

Marlowe Ferrara

THE CASTLE

A little boy sits
His imagination at work
His eyes shine; His project begins:
The biggest castle
He is to build
A pile of sand to you and me,
But a castle of hope,
A castle of love
In the eyes of a boy.

Joey Schones

MY GARDEN

Out of the Garden of Life
a flower grows,
its beauty to behold;

A slight imperfection . . .
I do not see,
I chose
a ROSE.

Sparkling with the sunlight,
kissed by the morning dew;

Brilliantly arrayed
in splendor,
'tis no one but you.

Annette Galloway

GRANDMA

Smiling face and warm embrace always sheltered me
from the world
so that in your arms, I could be free.
Oh grandma, where are you now? What do you see?
I feel you're smiling down on me.

When I was younger, you fixed my knee, played pretend games with me so that
the butcher, the baker, and the candlestick maker could all come to tea.
We laughed in drunken revelry over hot chocolate with milk one New Year's Eve,
and made a wish for every bubble in the bath . . .
I remember you with a happy laugh.

Grandma, where are you now? What do you see?
I feel you're smiling down on me.

Now with my son you are the one in whom I think
with every game and warm milk drink.
Your smiling face still shelters me,
the strength you give still sets me free.
Grandma, I feel you're smiling down on me.

Janet Castiel

ANGEL

You wear no visible wings,
Your voice is not angelic to the ear,
Trumpets do not bellow at your presence,
you do not carry the scent of the heavens,
Your clothes are not robes or silver crystal garments enveloped in misty colored lights,
You carry not a horn,
You walk quietly and leave hurriedly as angels must,
You give to the multitude,
Your caring is beyond reproach,
Your appearance is supernatural,
not of this earth, embarking on surely a celestial note,
if you told me you were God-sent,
Surely I could believe it,
we must say you waver on the angelic,
we know you would pass for the real thing,
I want to always keep you near
my Angel,
my dear.

Sharon Duprey

GOD'S LOVE

God's love can be seen in a new born baby's smile,
Or in an old dying woman's sigh.

God's love can be seen through the treacherous tornado's eye,
Or in the calming waters of incoming tide.

God's love can be seen through a ragged starved child clutching a doll,
Or a rich man ever searching for a new conscience to buy.

God's love can be seen as a smiling sunrise being clouded in,
Or through his tears that rain torrentially on the earth.

God's love can be seen as a starry comet with tail ablaze,
Or as a shuttle shattered in space — heavenbound

God's love can be seen through pain only as a nagging reminder
Of his promised home in Paradise, where pain does not exist.

God's love can only be found when we put earthly things aside,
Stepping out of our flesh and into our soul.

Mary Frances Hayes

I REMEMBER

I remember gentle hands, arms that held me tight.
The tender kiss after tucking me in bed at night.
I remember a soft lap when rocking to and fro.
Hearing the low humming of a song from long ago.
I remember when I was ill, she sat close in a chair,
Coaxing me to eat for strength, while asking help in silent prayer.
I remember rushed mornings on many a school day.
She handed me my lunch and, with a kiss, sent me on my way.
I remember red stuff on cuts and ice on rising lumps.
Telling her my world shaking catastrophes and how she'd get
me out of the dumps.
I remember — yes, I remember, oh, so many things,
That only thoughts of my Mother brings.
Like going to the zoo, and picnics in the park.
Tightly holding her hand in storms when skies were dark.
I remember, yes, I remember, all I have to thank her for,
And every day that passes, I just love her more.

Eulaliah T. Hooper

WHEN WE'VE GONE OUR SEPARATE WAYS

My friends had tried to warm me not to believe in your lies.
I said they were wrong, that our love was strong,
But, today, I found they were right.
I saw the girl you took in your arms and held her close to you.
And all the while I thought I could smile
As I talked about it with you.
When I ask you about her, you said she was an old friend
Who's love had gone and left her alone, and you'd promised to see her again.
I remembered the warnings I'd had and a cold feeling stirred in my heart.
You tried to deny it, and I tried to fight it, but I knew
We were drifting apart.
Now, I can't help but wonder, when you go and leave me alone,
Will I have the arms of some friend around
To hold me, and help me along?
Of one thing I am certain, when we've gone our separate ways,
I'll not make the mistake and another's heart break,
By taking their love away.

Rae Martin

OUR AMBASSADOR OF PEACE

What was your destiny in life, to touch the hearts of people
throughout the world.

How can someone accomplish so much in such a short time, such
wisdom and awareness flowing through you.

Thirteen years was a very short time to achieve what you had
to do, you were a real channel for peace.

Such a bright light flowed through you and continues to flow, let
your life stand for peace and good will.

Awareness and understanding among the people of the world to preserve
their lives and their universe.

Your spirit will always live on Samantha, and your bright light
will never dim, our little ambassador of peace.

Elizabeth Cotton

QUARTERDECK REFLECTIONS

The light breeze water dance
within the harbor hall,
swaying ships illuminate
lonesome strangers heed their call.

For far beyond the distant glow
of some shore city nearly asleep,
loved ones dwell, their dreams commencing,
secure the ships shall safely keep.

And on the lips a still lingers,
out at sea a mist enwraps
eyes that strain as ships their moorings,
to see the shores home waters lap.

A letter's drawn, its scent familiar.
Calloused fingers clutch it near.
Simple words convey their meaning,
the love that those on ships hold dear.

Keith A. Spencer

A MOTHER'S LOVE

For Mom

A mother's love is worth more
Than anything of value.
On earth, what more than a
Heartbeat, can console me
In my time of despair.

My mother is my shield to all
That is unknown, and my keeper
When times are beyond my means.
Take time to show love in return.

To give of yourself in her final days
Of existing. For all the wisdom
She has freely given, and dreams
Shared in quiet times.

When all else is gone, there is
Always a mother's love.

Iola Tillman

I LOVE JESUS

I love you oh Jesus
With my heart and my soul
I pray to you father
To save me from she'ol
I can't walk without the Lord
For this world's made of flesh
I've tried it before
And ended up in a mess
But when my heart went to Jesus
With passion and love
That's when my blessings
Came down from above
He fed me, and clothed me
He just made me feel whole
He told me my son
I now own your soul
He said that fool Satan
Would tempt me with sin
But say I'm the Lord's now
And simply just grin

Steven L. Gifford

YOUR HANDS UPON A BROOM

In those moments when I hold you naked
in my naked arms —
when you are not but flesh —
and I am not but bone,
my world is lost and laid asunder —
my world is born.

Then I gaze on, and into you —
and you are not.
You are not wife,
or cook,
my eyes cannot remember
your hands upon a broom.

Then I hold melody
to myself —
I search you, and all I find
is song.
Only song.
And oh, how I have lived and died
for music!

Bernie Hayes

ONE BEAUTIFUL WOMAN

The blandishments of time
cascading like a gargoyle,
and evaporating
into a mist.

Flattery, whimsy and promiscuity.
Unbridled spirit in living.
Adventure in loving
jaded by the years
to a miniscule corner
of the canvas of life.

The day by day by day
of each day
eluded her
as she elusively grasped
for the Fool's Gold
from a montage of lovers
who in time
faded into obscurity
as did her beauty.

Jack V. Diamond

Can you hear me crying
While my heart calls out for you?
Can you hear my silent pleas
For that one whose love is true?

I need to see those eyes so dark
And lonely call for me
Silence my desires
Please let my love run free.

Will you wrap your loving arms
Around me tenderly?
With kisses dry my teary eyes
It's you I long to see.

My everything I give to you
Though only you may say
It's you I want, and dream of
Both morning, night, and day.

Angela Edminster

AIR

All of the air
From all of the world
Is touching in our lungs:
From all the trees,
From all the beasts,
And from all the other
people
Who live or ever lived:
Joan of Arc;
Genghis Khan;
Plodding peasant;
Prince begowned;
We have each touched all the living
Subjects of creation;
But so softly, only God has known.

Betty Jane Yadede

YOU ARE TO ME

To me you are my fondest hopes,
My future, my success,
My faith in God and all that's good,
My love, my happiness.

To me you are my dearest dreams,
Another world apart,
A gleaming pool, a shimmering jewel,
In the well of a loving heart.

Richard Bruce McFarlane

DREAMS

Dreams of you walking by my side.
Sharing our night gazing toward
The sky. Our dreams we share
Together, of our days to come.

We sit in front of a warming
Fire, sharing the love we hold in
Our hearts for one another,
With the delights of our dreams.

The morning awakens a new day.
Dreams of the night end.
I wipe the tears of this dream
Away, with the starting of this
New day.

Joseph E. Lapine

STUNNED

HONORABLE MENTION

Oh boy!
Kenan's eyes are leaves
with a hidden crooked branch.
Chelley Vanessa has blue eyes
to perfection.
When I was young
I tamed Schlitz and
the low moon was beautiful.
The lightning at my feet
scared me.
The triangle ships
one night stunned my
thoughts for years.
I love you Kenan and Chelley.

Karen Lynelle Bowling

OUR LOVE IS LIKE A RAINBOW

To my only love . . . Terry

Our love is like a rainbow
reaching to the sky
With never-ending beauty
as the years go by,
An everlasting promise
of love to never stray,
But only to grow stronger
each and every day.
Our hearts are bound together
by more than just a ring,
A vow to stay together
whatever life may bring,
each trial and tribulation
will make a stronger hold,
And make all our precious memories
worth more than tons of gold,
For when the years slip by on us
and our age begins to show,
Our love will keep us young at heart
as together we grow old.

Frances Lewis

CHANCE MEETING

If my roving gaze should catch
you, and halt my hastened stride.
Pressed in the the doorway there,
You looked so lost, and so alone,
I could have passed unnoticed, but
this was meant to be, or I might
have passed you by and you
never would have known, but
Something paused me.

A hope a wish a fear . . . a
Fear I'd not again be apt to
feel you quite so near, you
stood there pale and slight, a
wisp of someone I missed
Someone I much admired,
Some who held waking hours.

I gained your smile, and we
talked a while would you call
that a chance meeting? I would.

Elva M. Hull

MY ONE AND ONLY LOVE

Hold my hand, Dear One,
As we walk along together.
Be my friend, my only love;
Let us share our lives forever.

It has been thirty-three years
Since the night we said "I do."
There have been problems and tears,
But I thank God that I still have you.

So walk with me now
As in the past;
Let me know that you still care
And our love will forever last!

Only God knows how much
I still love you!

Gloria C. Higgins

LOVE

Love can be affection that we have for one another,
Love can be sympathy, a fellow feeling for a friend,
Love can be goodwill, a kind heartedness for human charity,
Our own benignity could confirm our Christian end.

Showing beneficence could make us rich in Heaven,
To reach out and touch those who are sorely in need,
Because God loved us to love one another
His command puts love essential in every word and deed.

Love is power as its strength is made firm in all of us,
A special effort, a "challenger" we are all striving toward,
The legacy of God's love belongs to all people
Its worthwhile return is our heavenly reward.

Marian Fyhrie Guetz

MY YOUNGEST DREAM

O love, my youngest dream, my laughing muse
Running barefoot through each long-ago day
How many stout-hearted lads you beckoned to stay
And feast upon the first fruits of my table, I choose
Not to remember and how many wept to lose
My half-awake kisses at dawn, I cannot say.
And all those since, I've tried to leave behind
But sometimes in the night a backward look
Seeks to recall my laughing, barefoot love
But my reluctant memory holds only promises
Meant surely to warm my heart
Yet like lonely, wanton winds crying
From unguarded stretches of the sea
They sweep away my youngest dream.

Coleta McNabb

THE DIVORCE

I'm glad it's over, I've been patient much too long.
How could I put up with his bullheadedness so long?
Clash and make up, make up and clash,
We're better off apart.
We just don't love each other anymore.
Our values aren't the same.
I'M GLAD we broke up when we did.

But . . . WHY do I bemoan my empty heart?

Hazel Rutledge

I ALWAYS KNEW I'D RULE THE ROOST

I always knew when I was young and in the prime of life,
A pretty girl would come along and then I'd take a wife.
I always knew, no doubt she'd be, a maid with manners mild,
A pretty girl for me alone, by no one else beguiled.

I always knew she'd be the best at sciences domestic,
A pretty girl with rosy cheeks, making meals majestic.
I always knew she'd be the one, to honor and obey,
A pretty girl with whom I knew, I'd always get my way!

I always knew she never would disagree or wrangle,
A pretty girl, the very one, with whom I'd never tangle.
I always knew I'd rule the roost, or know the reason why.
A pretty wife soon taught me this . . . I just don't qualify!

Chet Rust

a soft breeze

there was a soft breeze
that swooped into a world
pierced by shadows of self-pity.
lined with mountains of woe
carved from valleys of despondencies . . .
a soft breeze wafted gentle whispers
revealing dawn's moments are surpassed
by chimes of golden mornings
perceived by artist of love's haven . . .
there was a soft breeze
that brushed the shadows of dusk,
stroking reflections of the deity
while bathing in harmony's nakedness . . .
there was a soft gentle breeze
that showered love's fragrance
upon life streets and lesser nooks . . .
a soft gentle breeze swooped
into a world where only shadows
dimmered warmness, from within the gentle breeze
a reflection of harmony and rhyme were chimed . . .

Edward Robert Lang

I LOVE YOU . . . I NEED YOU

My dear, I love you and need you
Let me be with you, my dear, my love
Love me and hold me, my dear
And put a thrill on my lips with your kiss
Kiss me and hold me tight, my dear, my love
Loving you forever, my dear, my love
Wanting only you, my love, to hold me and kiss me
Hold me in your arms tenderly and kiss me tenderly
For I thrill at the touch of your kiss
And I hold your love in my heart, my dear
Until at last you are mine and I am yours, my love
Until we two are one, in love in our hearts
To love you with a kiss and touch
My dear, my love, I miss you so much
I miss your touch, your kiss that I love
Loving only you, my dear, my love
Wanting to hold you like the sky holds the stars
Wanting to be near you no matter how far
My dear, I love you . . . I need you

Miriam E. Smith

SMITH, MIRIAM ELAINE. Pen Name: Jessie Rose; Born: 9-8-32; Unmarried; Education: High school; Occupation: Housekeeper; Other Writing: "Run of Races," "Wonderful Life," "Joan and I," "Lonely Woman," "The Crash," short stories; Comments: *I like to write to better people and to give them understanding.*

SONGS OF LOVE

Many songs of love are written
be it a dog, or a small kitten.
'Tis a subject with no end,
broken hearts are hard to mend.

Why is love so hard to take?
Hard to tell true from fake.
In a world where fear of foe
strikes us all, here below!

Yet within us all, is found
a surging need that love abound.
A hug, a kiss, some reassurance
helps us all with endurance.

Then there is the thing called love
an added gift from above.
'Twas meant in marriage to fulfill,
bring forth children for God's will.

Then there are the family ties,
knot of love within them lies.
Songs of love will always be,
this song I write to you, from me!

Verla Christine Nielsen

The words you said
  have frightened me,
For I too need someone to hold

You say we will change,
  our friendship will falter
You say, no way, so why
  do I bother?

My soul is too scared to stay
  but worse, to go
I remain out of pain of
  being alone

You and I — who would
  have guessed
We are so much apart

You take one road
  and I, the other

Only to come back to share
  our friendship and gains

You say no, but I remain
  For to go is too much pain.

Candace Stowell

OPEN DOOR

When your world seems torn apart
pass through the door into your heart.
The things you'll find behind that door
you'll hold and cherish evermore.
Friendship, love, and family
these things will yours forever be.
So many things you love to do
the very ones with which you grew.
The things you should be thankful for
are right inside that open door.

Pamela J. Shelton

FRIENDSHIP WITH REMEMBRANCES

Because of all these years that we have been
Friends I dedicate this writing to Eleanor Felch

There are times when we pick those flowers
That last for only a time
And vases put away forever
But other flowers dried are often pushed aside
Like days that have no memories
But in our memories we do recall
Those bouquets of love, understanding and friendship.
How often when hours are silent
We look back in time to recall
Those days that brought friends of Golden Cast.
Years can pass but our hearts do remember . . .
Days . . . years . . . thoughts . . . smiles and heartfelt thoughts.
Now with glory thoughts of those who stood by
I remember a famous saying that made my days
And also brought days of long ago into my mind
Which now makes those letters I receive
A gift for now and of long ago
To those who are in my heart of repast days
I say the saying that has meant love for me . . .
"A true Friend is someone who walks in,
When all else walks out"

Virginia Jolliff Herndon

SPECIAL FRIENDS

Friends . . . Special friends.
Sharing us between ourselves.
Luxuriating in the warmth and tenderness,
Feeling the hesitancy . . . yet, the allure.
The anxiety . . . yet, the soothing contentment.
The precariousness . . . yet, that essence of vitality and renewal.
Feeling so awkward . . . yet, at ease.
Feeling unfamiliar . . . yet, so aware.
Wondering if the intimacy will risk the relationship
But, we are friends . . .
    Special friends . . .
    Rare friends . . .
    Forever friends . . .

Karen S. Lewis

IF ONLY . . .

If only I could have the chance to show just how I feel.
If only I were given time to prove a love so real.
If only it were in the cards my hand lies in wait to play.
If only you would take a chance and brush the doubt away.

The spark was lit, we were close for a day.
Some tender words were spoken yet so much is left to say.
Without fuel for the fire, the flame will surely die.
We will never know how good it could be unless we at least try.
This may seem quite a lot to ask, but one can never know.
Until the seed is planted nothing at all could ever grow.

If only I could have the chance to show how much I care.
If only I could give you all the things I have to share.
If only it were in the stars, I wait each passing day.
If only I could hear the words I long for you to say.

I see the feeling in your eyes and surely you in mine.
In my heart I know it's right, this feeling so warm and fine.
Look deep down into your soul and see what is there to see.
If your love for him were not in question there would be no room for us.
Maybe change is what you fear but we all must take a chance.
What would life be without risk or love without romance.

Peter N. Vingris

J. M. IVES, DEL.

DRAWN BY PARSONS & ATWATER.

THE FOUR SEASONS OF LIFE: OLD AGE.

"The Season of Rest."

Last comes the winter of life's circling year,
And strength departs, but love and joy abide,
That "perfect love" which "casteth out all fear"
That joy, that lives beyond life's restless tide.

Grateful for mercies past, and trusting still
In him whose goodness all our lives hath blest,
We rest secure, and calmly wait his will,
To call us hence, to his eternal rest.

NEW YORK. PUBLISHED BY CURRIER & IVES 152 NASSAU STREET

JULIA

Julia oh Julia, I thank you for me,
I thank you for bringing me up in your ways,
I thank you for teaching me words that you'd say.
Julia oh Julia, you didn't have to go out,
you didn't have to go out of your way all the time,
you didn't have to make what was yours also mine.
Julia oh Julia, you didn't have to take,
you didn't have to take all those heartaches I gave,
Julia oh Julia, what more could you've done?
Do more, I doubt so, you gave of your all,
you've met every challenge to give what love called.

Michael Durachko

RIVER OF LOVE

When you first found me,
I was wasting my life away,
not feeling good or not feeling bad,
not feeling any way.

I didn't think that I was worthwhile at all,
I was living on too many sad memories,
that makes even a good man fall.

I had nobody to talk out my troubles to,
and you sat right down and put me at ease,
I opened my heart to you.

Now there's a river of love that keeps me alive
when I'm feeling low and I take a dive;
from this old world hard to survive,
a loving you helps me come alive.

Then it just doesn't seem so bad
when I'm with you
there's always music,
and it won't go away,
I hope it stays,
let's never lose it.

George Randall Roberts

SHE COULDN'T HAVE HIM

She called me today
to ask me if I still loved you.
I told her that I always would
No matter what you do.

And then I said,
He's not mine to hold
or mine to keep.
He's only mine at night when I sleep.

The only time I hold his hand
or caress his gentle brow,
Is when I'm thinking about him
and needing him even more now.

Tell me about the day
That I let him slip away.
What kind of fool was I?
There's nothing left to do; there's nothing left to say.

As I hung up the phone
to tell her good-bye,
She said she couldn't have him,
When he was still my guy.

Marvena Brannan

"What is love?" my daughter asked as her eyes opened
wide with wonder.
Love is contentment and peace of mind and helping
your fellow man.
Love is holding a babe to your breast for the very
first time.
Love is sharing with your mate the ups and downs in
life.
Love my child is the staff of life.
There is too much hate around us.
Just remember to pray every day and never question
God's will.
The kiss she gave me on my cheek as she quickly
turned around was all I needed to know that she
did understand.

Gertrude Rosenthal

TWO OF BEAUTY, BECOME ONE

To share, to love, to grow together
And walk your path, side by side,
Touching, healing, feeling for one another,
One leaning then uplifting in the mutual direction.

Speak quietly your truth, feeling from the heart
Without shame or blame, listen as the tree to the wind.
Be each yourself in truth, a universal child,
Enlightening one another as the seed to the earth.

The sacrament of life is true friendship,
This is the ultimate of love when mutual souls meet.
Each must nurture; feed one another
For only then will the tree grow fulfilled,
Giving bountiful fruit, the gift of love.

Carole April Binette

BINETTE, CAROLE APRIL. Born: Massachusetts, December 11; Single; Education: Courses at UNH and Maui Community College and life itself, the great teacher; Occupation: Investments, Stock Market; Poetry: 'Remain Open,' *American Poetry Anthology,* 1984; 'Love Song,' *Hearts on Fire, Volume II,* 1984; Collection 12 Poems in *American Poetry Showcase,* 1984; 'Seed of Intensity,' *Art of Poetry,* 1985; 2 Poems in *Masterpieces of Modern Verse,* 1985; Themes: *Nature and mankind in relationship, teacher and student. The power of love in the universe, growth. I dream one day of having a book of poems published.*

COME, REST IN THIS BOSOM

from Irish Melodies

Come, rest in this bosom, my own stricken deer,
Though the herd have fled from thee, thy home is still here;
Here still is the smile, that no cloud can o'ercast,
And a heart and a hand all thy own to the last.

Oh! what was love made for, if 'tis not the same
Through joy and through torment, through glory and shame?
I know not, I ask not, if guilt's in that heart,
I but know that I love thee, whatever thou art.
Thou hast called me thy Angel in moments of bliss,
And thy Angel I'll be, mid the horrors of this.
Through the furnace, unshrinking, thy steps to pursue,
And shield thee, and save thee, — or perish there too!

Thomas Moore

RETARDED CHILD

No greater affection between a mother and her child
Than when her child can do little more than smile.
Slow beyond years, learning things normal children do,
Some never learn to feed themselves or ever tie a shoe.
Kept busy with the child most of the day,
(No matter what wise advisors say),
One mother devoted herself with patience before unknown
And carried on, though weary to the bone.
A mother's love will see her through,
And with persistent faith she teaches "can do."
Progress is made beyond belief,
As a mountain of love is built from a mountain of grief:
Because she never listened to others all the while,
She was basking in the love of her retarded child's smile.

Mary M. Volkman

IF I COULD

If I could paint a picture of what true love can be,
I'd paint your face as big as life, 'cause you are love to me.

If I could write a poem of what true love can do,
the poem would have but one word, and that word would be you.

If I could make a statue of what true love can be,
the statue would be a figure of you just holding me.

If I could sing a song of what true love can do,
the song would be about a man who never makes me blue.

But since I'm not an artist, and these things I cannot do,
I'll settle just for saying that, "Darling I love you."

Leanett Loury Smith

MOONSTRUCK

The moon is moving, wakeful all the night.
Running deer wear silver to their knees.
Insects dance a mystic, ancient rite.
Moonstruck leaves, contented and at ease
are dreaming dreams guaranteed to please.
The angel moon grows shy and hides her face
under a fan of opaque, black lace.
She lifts her hair, fallen through the trees.
Then moonstruck lovers wander in the park
hugging, kissing wildly in the dark.

Jeanette Konwiser

WHY?

We went for a walk, our minds traveling,
neglecting to talk.
You reached for my hand, it was then I realized
you wore a wedding band.
How could it be, you never wore it before,
or could I just not see?
Was I so caught up in it all, that I only thought of me,
in that crystal ball?
How can it be that I love you, when you are not mine to love,
when you're to someone else so untrue?
You've borne me great sorrow and shame, you should have told me,
she also wears your name.
No longer touch my hand, all memories of you I banish,
everything I no longer understand,
It is not my trend, to cherish, to love more than one,
so I bring this to such an agonizing end!

Susan Gill

TO MY DAD

Dedicated on his birthday 7/7/85

It's been 14 years since I last saw you.
God picked you out of life's garden
and saw that you were ready to be with Him.
Your suffering finally over.
I felt the deep pain and loneliness and
knew I would not see you for awhile.
I remember sitting next to you
and holding your warm and strong hand.
My hands were always cold and wet
and you made me feel safe.
We sat in silence.
I love you, Dad.
You always told me about my picture
in your "back pocket."
No one dared hurt me.
You loved to hear singing around the house.
Music made you happy.
Mom enjoyed cooking and preparing meals for you.
You appreciated her love and was satisfied.
Dad, I miss you very much.
Do you still have my picture?

Naomi C. Ricci

AUNT ANNIE HARPER

Everyone should have an Aunt Annie Harper.
She answers questions, some that are not
so proper.

Her love is there and she understands.
It's like she takes you by the hands.

She's with you every step of the way.
She never scolds, but listens to what
you have to say.

Before you know it, she's solved with ease
an answer to the problem, that is sure to please.

What she likes to hear, is news that all is well,
and anything nice, that you like to tell.

The moral of this poem is very proper.
Everyone should have an "Aunt Annie Harper."

I love you Aunt Annie Harper.

Mary A. Wagner

CLUETITUDE

Love is a hieroglyphic
Symbol fruitful wait
Garden want prolific
Truth soul celebrate.

First an apple involve
Romance tasteful measure
Next come orange slice revolve
Eyes find hidden treasure.

Bide lemon sweet was Eden first
Drove Adam sorely truant
When he left men enjoy thirst
Must sugar add as fluent.

Banana means mañana come
To those who revel kisses
Add fourth dimension aptly sum
Such bliss none better misses.

Grapes beguile at ample tease
Mean fonder moments mingle
Until wine forever please
Or outlast widow single.

Orien Todd

SATURDAY NIGHT

The candles were lit
That quiet evening.
We sank into our separate worlds,
Left the daytime callings,
Bookstore pen sales,
Architect's drawings,
Meetings and the like.
We just sat together
And let Beethoven's Appassionata
Drum through our minds.

Nancy Keats Benson

ODE TO A LOST LOVE

I miss him, I miss him,
Does anybody know,
How lonesome and bleak
When your loved one has to go.

The good Lord took him,
And he's oh so far away,
And I won't get to see him here on earth,
Not even for a day.

I cry for him at night,
Even though it's been so long,
It's as though a light went out,
And my heart it has no song.

How happy were our days,
And golden were the nights.
We did everything together,
And saw so many sights.

Memories will now hold me,
Our love will never die,
I even see him smiling,
In the blue that is the sky.

Joan M. Lacey

INNER CRY

My body is only a shell; I dwell within.
The inner me emerges from the depth of my soul.
I will only love in spirit and mind; to walk this earth in spiritual time.
I have so much love and feelings within.
I want to make it surface once again.
It's like the rumbling of the sea; bursting deep inside of me.
I want to give love to every human thing, until the bells of heaven ring.

Nan Blackshire Little

BLACKSHIRE-LITTLE, NANCY. Pen Name: Nan Blackshire Little; Born: Dawson, Georgia, 3-8-35; Poetry: 'God's Gift,' 'A Visit,' 'Giving Thanks,' religious, St. John's Divine Cathedral, 1984; 'Unite,' union, RWDSU, AFL-CIO, 1984; 'Hungry,' *American Poetry Anthology,* 1985; Comments: *I feel there is a spiritual message in my writing and I would like to share it with all my brothers and sisters all over the world.*

DEAR, DEAR HUGH

You asked me once why I love you. I gave a stupid reason.
But that was many years ago and I've had time to season.

I'm childish yet in lots of ways, but you're always understanding.
You're strong, yet gentle as can be; needful, but not demanding.

You always keep a level head when I get in a dither.
You have a sense of humor that never seems to wither.

You never talk much about your faith, but I'm sure it is Divine,
Because you've shown me many times, that yours is stronger than mine.

I never have been very good at saying the things I feel,
But maybe this will give you some idea that my love for you is real.

And that today, tomorrow, and for all eternity,
I always will be grateful for the dear love you've given me.

The years have come and gone now, and to Heaven went my dear Hugh.
It was a blow to our daughters and especially me too.

But I'm not looking for another love — I cherish the one that was mine.
I never could find another that could replace a man so fine.

He left me with two daughters — lovely in spirit and face,
And they have given me two fine sons and just to help me keep pace —

I have two beautiful grandchildren that help to keep me young.
Hugh was a perfect husband and father — and now my song is sung.

Frances Hough

SHOW ME THE WAY LORD

Thank you Lord for this day
For your many blessings
Show me the way, I humbly pray
Good deeds for others, I can do today

Don't let anger come from me
To hurt or break a heart
Not a frown upon my brow
Let a smile take its place

I won't forget the sad and lonely
Gently wipe away their tears
Listen as they sadly tell me
How they suffered through the years

Place other needs ahead of mine
Never let me be unkind
Help me Lord, please give me the time
Love and peace may I help them find

Thelma I. Goss

WHAT IS LOVE?

To touch
and be touched,
to care
and to share,
to favor
and be favored,
to know
and be known,
to have
and be had,
to love
and be glad,
to give
and be given.
For life is love
and love is life,
and a true friend
is a friend for life,
and a joy forever
while memory lasts.

Phillip R. Wheeler

HOMECOMING

In thoughtful solitude I sit and wait
With a heart that is desolate.
While by the bed of a child I love
I meditate on the verdict from above.

I cannot discard her from my life
As though she had not been here.
In the short time I have cared for her
She has grown so very dear.

My tortured mind and heart resists
To place on her brow one last kiss.
I shall be comforted and sustained
By the grace of God which will remain.

I know that by the dawn of tomorrow
Her homecoming is to be —
In the mansion He's prepared there
She will wait for you and me.

Joyce Holt

IDIOMATIC

Why decline in translation
And become hollow reiteration?
Topical is rhetorical, antiseptic
Common usage leaves me dispepsic
So why not drift past description
And object to all prepositions?
Vocabulary becomes introspective
In a case so subjective —
"I love you" is not undramatic
But you and I are idiomatic.
We are verbs modified ecstatic
You and I are
Idiomatic . . .

Tommy Toledo

SUNSHINE LOVE

Your golden hair,
Your soft brown eyes,
You're sweet as summer dew

You shine so bright as the morning
sun,
You're as warm as a country moon

I love you more as the years roll
by,
You're my life, my sunshine too

You make me laugh,
I never cry,
Life is as sweet as flowers in June.

Where you came from I do not
know
You must have fallen from the
sky

Gathering stardust and sunshine as
you landed right by my side

Helen Fowler Brown

GRIEF AND PAIN INSTEAD

The best laid plans of mice
and men gang aft agley.
Robert Burns

I loved two girls, both More and Less
But which to wed was hard to guess.
This Molly More was Irish lass
Who really had a lot of class.

The same was true of Leslie Less
So either wife would be a bless.
But very soon dear Leslie died
It surely hurt; I really cried.

But now it seemed the coast was clear
And I should marry Molly dear.
Of course I asked for Molly's hand —
The future looked so very grand.

But Molly said "Dear John" to me;
She spoke with tender honesty.
And so from life I am apart
Will surely die of broken heart.

Floyd C. Jones

I SHALL COME TO YOU

I shall come to you
On the wings of night;
In the middle of a storm
Or, by soft candlelight.

I shall come to you
In some words you have said
Each day in your prayer
Or some book you have read.

I shall come to you
In a song you have heard;
In the soft falling rain
Or, the song of a bird.

I shall come to you
Through a pair of dark eyes
A token — unbroken,
And a heart of fire.

Prudencia Boals

A LIFE OF LOVE

In the spring of nineteen thirty-nine
My love asked, "Will you be mine?"
You don't have to guess
I said, "Yes."
I became a June bride
Standing proudly by his side.
With love in our hearts
We said, "Until death do us part."
A rewarding life was begun
When we became one.
We've been quite a team
Holding each other in loving esteem.
Marriage is not just *for* life
Marriage *is* Life, man and wife
With love and happiness doubled
With troubles and sorrows divided.
Now, when life is so complete
If we could have a repeat
Some things we would rearrange
But very little would we change.

Hesse G. Byrd

MY ISLAND GIRL

Your flowing jet black hair
Your loving thought and care
A face of an angel so bright
Keeps me warm at night

Just being able to be with you
Keeps my heart beating too!
Your voice and smile so right
Sends me to dreamland at night

Your humor tickles me pink
Your seriousness makes me think
You are so true and right
Keeps me loving day and night

Your sharing and loving ways
Get me counting the days
Until you are mine, to make it right
All through the day and night

Joseph Boteilho, Jr.

LOVEST THOU ME, LORD?

Walking the night path
So all alone
Forgetting Thou hast
Died to atone.

Weary feet faltered
Along the way
Happiness altered
Forgot to pray.

Lovest Thou me, Lord?
Was my heart's cry
Let me know Thy love,
Lord, ere I die.

Come Holy Spirit
With healing power
Precious this moment
Blest, sacred hour.

Joy now surrounding
Love comes in flood
New life abounding
Washed in His blood!

Sara E. (Page) Smith

SMITH, SARA ELIZABETH. Pen Name: Sara E. (Page) Smith; Born: Logan County, Illinois, 9-4-15; Married: 6-11-32 to Russell H. Smith; Education: After night school, received high school diploma from the same school and in the same year as my five grandsons did. Have three college credits; Occupation: Thirty years, Business Office Credit Manager, Senior Citizen Activities Director; Memberships: Church of the Nazarene; National Society, Daughters of the American Revolution; Logan County Genealogical Society, Lincoln, Illinois; Poetry: 'Ancestors,' *Central Illinois Gen. Quarterly;* 'Swift Wing, My Love,' 'Memory, God's Masterpiece,' American Poetry Association; *My Heart Reached a High Hill,* collection; Other Writings: *Across State Line,*book, records of Clark County, Illinois and Vigo County, Indiana, by Daughters of the American Revolution; Contributed to *The Loving Family in America,* Harp and Thistle, Warner Robbins, Georgia; Contributed to *History of Logan County, Illinois,* Taylor Publications, Dallas, Texas, 1982; Comments: *I believe God inspired my poetry. I write because I can express my innermost self and because I must. I write of relationships, love, dreams, heartbreak, ideals, nature, animals, and patriotic and devotional poetry. I feel they should be shared. Only then do I feel complete and content.*

POST SCRIPT

P.S. I love you.
Do you know why?
Well, it means so
much to me that I
have you in my heart.

Keeping that warmth of
a relationship in tune.
Knowing a person like
you, is what I have always
dreamed about.
You have answered my wishes.
Merci!

Marguerite Brugos

JO ANN

I think about . . .
the sparkle of your eyes,
the honesty of your words,
the caress of your smile,
the music of your laughter,
the caring in your touch,
the fierceness of your embrace,
the feel of your skin beneath my hand,
the delicate passion of your kisses,
the joy for life you possess, and
the warm fire of your company
. . . and, with pleasant surprise,
recall you choose to love me.

James Collett

Violets.
Shy violets peeping through the grass,
Remind me of a certain Lass
I knew so long ago.
She too was shy with eyes as blue,
A face like cream and a heart so true,
And Oh! I loved her so!
Time took her from me years ago,
But now I see her lovely face
And feel again her warm embrace,
As though no time had lapsed between.
Violets in a bed of green,
Gratefully I stand and stare,
Humbled by a memory fair.

Vada Brodhagen

A LOT OF LOVE

There is a lot of love
In the poet's heart
But if you drive it far away
Do not be surprised
If you've lost the sun

There is a lot of hope
It resides there
More than Pandora
Close the box
But they imprison hope
Which should be free

Gretchen Blake Leedy

RETURN (THE NEXT STEP)

Waiting is so lonely
A down-plunging pain
That tears me apart
If only you'd phone me
But I just stare at the rain
Like the tears in my heart
You tell me that I'm free
Not to save it for you
But you make it so hard
When you won't tell me
What you're going to do
I think I'm going to put up my guard
You think you can have your fun
And I'll still be here
But my fun hasn't begun
And you're not the only one
I think I'm going to disappear

Julie Brown

TWO HEARTS AS ONE

He beheld this maiden fair
With eyes so blue and flowing hair;
He had to meet her
And hopefully, soon,
But how? . . . Would he dare?

He came to her in her dreams,
Looking as resplendent as a prince;
Kissed her softly on her cheek
And left her with her thought:
"Where is this prince, my one and only?"

The maiden and the prince
Met and kissed,
And ended in wedded bliss
Because I played Cupid,
Shot my arrow . . . and made a hit.

Irene Xavier

DEJECTION'S STAB

As the silent tears drip down
Morning dew kissed the ground.

The pain abounding like a searing flame,
While the sun puts the city in its frame.

The sun appears a yellow boulder
A weight upon a weary shoulder.

Rising with minds of cobweb
To shake ourselves out of bed.

Feeling as confused and tired
As we did when we retired.

We rally our strength from within
Knowing a new day must begin.

Leona Joan Osier

TWO IN THE DARK

Inspirations of the Abnormal

And he put his arm around me,
Waiting to give and to receive,
Foolishly lead him to believe,
That I could love, when I could not.

And I gave him no response,
But remained frozen in my mystery,
His gentle touch reached out to me,
But I was blinded in the dark.

I looked into his questioning eyes,
Lacking words within my shell,
For how could I begin to tell,
What I myself knew nothing of.

So an empty night was passed,
My mind was screaming silently,
Realizing these were to be,
More wasted moments in my life.

Linda S. Larsen

THOSE FLOWERS

(To Andrew — Your name is love)

Today you sent me flowers
  but how long will they stay?

Should I smell them
  and remember their sweetness

or shall I leave them dead in their vase
  and remember today?

Those flowers pierced my heart
  But which bud is real

and which one
  is the dream of real?

Better to live and love the dream
  than die in the reality

Maro Kentros

MY HEART

My heart, when it belongs not,
Suffers pain of anguish.
My heart, I give to you to keep forever.
My heart may appear
Not to cherish.

My life, could be not,
My heart, I must brandish.
Life is simple in so many complex ways.
Complexity is what we make of life,
Not knowing.
Not knowing, a promise still kept
Will be forever.

A token small, I offer you.
A promise of three and one eternal.
Eternity with you will appear
Too short a while.
Eternity with spirits promised;
No less, a jewel than you.

Chuck Derr

EVERGREEN

Evergreen I'll keep our love,
I'll never let it die.
Evergreen and fresh as spring
While time goes slowly by.

Never will I let it fade
Like leaves that die away.
Evergreen I'll keep our love
With new dreams every day.

Evergreen in springtime,
Evergreen in the fall.
summer's heat, winter's cold
Will matter not at all.

Evergreen I'll keep our love.
I'll never let it die . . .
Evergreen and fresh as spring
Till all time passes by!

Evelyn Sant Brewster

THE PERFECT GIFT

Something personal
  Something real
Something to show her
  Just how I feel.
Something that's loving
  Something that's kind
Something to tell her
  What's on my mind.
Something that welcomes
  Something long-lived
Something that proves
  All the love I can give.
Something to please her
  Something from me
A token, a promise
  Of what life will be.
If I can find
  A gift so complete
My love will feel at home
  When our lips again meet.

Theodore R. Munsch

MIRAGE

A cold and lonely day in the desert
Millions and I grope in the night
I thought you were what I deserved
I guess I was right

I took you on, just another ride
The mirage was love, love won't abide
I see you laughing, your golden hair
I reach for you, but you're not there

Found my soul lying in the sand
Eternal loneliness is now at hand
Pick up my heart, head for the hills
Bitter red berries, they say they kill

I took you on, just another ride
I found the truth and lost my pride
I see you laughing, your golden hair
I cry for you, but you don't care

Peter R. Quibell

UNCERTAIN LOVE

Oh my dear, can't you hear,
What I'm trying to say?
Sure I'm sure, there is a cure
But I can't find the way.

All our time, and every sign
Has been seen along our ways.
A sharing love, when thinking of
Each single every day.

Days gone by, and still I sigh,
Where has the time gone?
You and I can clearly see
The light before the dawn.

Maybe then it will end.
The doubt within the mind,
That co-exists, with what we missed
Beyond the end of time.

Michael J. Finn

THE SERENADE

Lilting lad with lyre and lute,
Let me tend your lyrics
To gain her heart contrarious,
And woo the lass mysterious.

Fancy now, young flaunting fellow,
Word forms all fleeced and flowing.
Flower them well, and fragrantly so,
Chaste formed that love is growing.

Offer her ope oneiric odes,
No phrases too outstanding.
Omit no guise from her young eyes . . .
On these your chance expanding.

Sing sensuous song in silkened sound,
Surrender true your feeling.
Go now and tell; let voice to swell . . .
Your tender love revealing.

Clara Mays Benson

YOU ARE THE SUNSET ON THE RIVER OF MY HEART

All the golden things I find in life,
Are really streams of you,
Setting on my heart a beauty rare,
Like a sunrise that is through.

Rivers have a lovely glow when they are
Kissed by golden beams,
That is why my heart is raptured
When encased within your gleams.

You are like the sunset on my heart,
The river that you own,
So let sail the boat that brings you here,
To where your love has blown.

Set upon my heart your sunlight glows,
That stream their way to me,
And the golden things I find in you,
Forevermore will be.

Janina Judith Piszyk

PIECE

Piece it together
Broken fragments
Never forgotten
Memories spit up
Tightly holding me
Seeing you standing
On Jefferson Street
Dressed in canary yellow
Missing your very nice smile
Eyes captivating me
When we met
Your dying shattered my heart
I bleed from the deep cuts
Scars will remain forever
I know
I was always there to listen to you
I hope I gave you happiness
I gave you all my time
So we could spend it together
There was only one you!

Renata Dawidowicz

TWICE-TOLD TALE

careless daughters of the night
went out, trailing light
scarves across muffled voices
growing fainter, ebbing
with river wakes, lips of water
colorless as plasma; would remember
more than anything
places where people would never build
because of floods in spring;
reflecting, would remember winter
as some strange dream arriving
before summer's surrogate, spring.
formless as memory unbegun,
as if young love,
overpowered, were borne back
on the river, carried headlong;
world unknown, wheeling higher than wing
calculation, feet drifting —
something of time unbegun,
from higher up, above flowing feet.

E. L. Kelso

WORDLESS LOVE

Love sends words away
chastened, heads hanging
inadequate to express its magnitude
Love soars while words dawdle
Races hands clasped unafraid
Sensing its own deep mystery
Brazen in its openness
Beguiling in its union
Absurd in its belief
Dazzling in its expression
Soul filling and ecstatic
Energizing substance, form and particle
Bursting planetary arrangements
Overflowing bottomless voids
lined by lonely tears
Love sings, miming celestial chords
without harangue, melodiously
Love solicits and adheres
wordlessley . . .
Love speaks . . . her thoughts are mine

Edward P. O'Callaghan

GROWING PAINS

Tried to sit in a corner,
tell the world to "go away"
But, along came a smile
that taught me how to play.

Stuck my chin in the air
laughed for all to see,
Till I felt a tug, a pull,
Oh, God — "I want to be free."

Nights of ponder lie awake —
simple moments cast ashore.
I thrust her aside, each time
She came back a little more.

So, by a stone's eternal
throw, I found her, gave her a
hug, put her away — my
little girl in me to stay.

Tall, charming gentleman
I think of your smile, so rare,
chase at rainbows to wonder —
Is your love for me to share?

Linda Robinson

DEAR MOM

I'm writing you this letter, Mom
Though it's a message I cannot bring,
But I'll write it just the same, dear Mom,
And pin it to an angel's wing.

You always put us first, Mom
In everything you'd do,
And so you've earned your rest, dear Mom
And this peace that's come to you.

We often put off, time after time
Doing the things we should,
Until one day it is too late
And oh, how we wish we could.

Forgive us Mom, not for what we did
But for what we didn't do,
Those little things neglected
Like simply saying, I love you.

I'd like to think you felt we cared
Although we didn't let you know,
And believe me, Mom, when we meet again
I'll be sure to let it show.

Charles P. Spaulding

ASLEEP

Cold night — you scooch, wrap around me
I — now awake — watch you
Fetus-like draw into a warmth
I cannot give. Though
Insecure, you yawn and open up
Breathe on my neck
Grab me and try to go through me
I — still, so still, look at you
Your glow — your sultry closed eyes — I
Feel triumphant — never again alone
Loved.

Rodger Bivins

TREASURED THINGS I LOVE

The sweet aroma of burning leaves in fall
The whippoorwill's lonely far away call
A sunlit dewdrop on a red red rose
The sound of the north wind as it blows
An apple tree blossoming in early May
A brilliant sunset at the close of day
A sparkling rainbow at the twilight
A flock of wild geese in formation flight
The blaze of maples on a sunlit lane
The ice-laced patterns on a windowpane
A crackling fire in a glowing fireplace
A child's sweet trusting upturned face
The soft-voiced birds at the dawn of day
The smell of fresh new-mown hay
The pleasures derived from reading a book
The peaceful solitude of a babbling brook
A morning crisp with frost and dew
A stormy cloud as the sun breaks through
These treasured things I love and hold dear,
For the Master Painter made them possible here.

Ruth F. Teeters

LANGUISHED

Sitting, gazing into the pale dry sky,

Clouds forming resemble the unadorned cinder black curls,

Brisk chills capture memories of a soft sensuous touch,

The tall, lone, leafless oak atop the bare plateau stands
as I, solemn in strife,

Sheen of the full, rosy sunset replenishes the warm
gleaming countenance possessed,

Call of the whippoorwills brings back the lovely laughter
I once heard,

As the sun's last ember disappears, past affection descends
to another,

She leaves me alone, languished.

Timothy M. Tilley

A YOUNGSTER'S NAIVETE

Art Linkletter excitedly raises the curtain,
To bring on stage these eager children,
Small boys and girls with the cutest flak,
In their childish way, replying back,
Wide-eyed, in a state of diversion,
Puzzled at questions, wanting answers.
Glancing at a child making mud pies,
Is a skit from the scenes of "Our Gang Comedy,"
That holds this slapstick fame.
Little ones ought to be allowed to invent,
Who taught a dog, to scratch his hind legs?
A darn good dig, at that!
In spite of the relationship to a wolf
There is this difference written briefly
Whatsoever let a 'kid' learn the test,
Standing by in earnest, to be near,
While they are whining to boil water;
Yes! the uttering sounds are part of the game,
Why not let a youngling creep before they walk
By directing them, with appreciation, discipline and love?

Rose Mary Gallo

FIRST LOVE

The bees are honey-bound, and so am I,
all the living world abrim with joy,
joy in leaves praying with the wind,
moss breathing humid praise,
ferns curving about the altar of the earth,
and skies ablaze with light or gray with rain,
the cloud and burden of love.

The color of cornflowers, true blue,
blazing my heart's law upon the arras of life,
the frail fierce passion of poppies,
glimpsed among the golden wheat
that sang with ripeness,
redeem the white-robed figure
in the noonday sun.

Once more, I drink deep
the morning of time,
walking tiger-limbed in the eyes of my lover,
and the lips like the sword of the angel,
crossed before the mortals fleeing,
forever past the Garden of Eden.

Lily Szigeti

JOHANN SEBASTIAN BACH

Johann Sebastian Bach,
How I envy you,
Greatest of all
Living composers,
(For you do live on
As we were all promised)
In our hearts, minds, and
Souls.

Conventionally,
You married a woman you
Loved, and bore child after
Child in
Happiness, security and
Peace that Freud, Marx, Sartre, and Nietzsche,
Deny creative artists (claiming)
Tender human relations
Interfere with
Bread-winning,
Success, as (supposedly)
Sex-oriented repression
Does not.

Geneve Baley

MY LUCKY PRIZE

Ever since I first heard your lusty cry
You have been the apple of my eye!

My morning and my night, a constant delight

We have shared our hopes and fears
Our laughter and our tears

And each morning that I arise, I thank God for such a lucky prize

Is there any other way that I can say

I
Love
You!

Agnes Heintzelman

JEWEL

In my daydreaming I can see her,
A baby so pretty, so neat.
I can hear her
In a baby voice so soft, so sweet:
"Daddy don't lea' me," she would cry
As I prepared to go. I hated to leave her, so
I would wait until I heard her sigh.
"He lea' me," I would hear her say
As I quickly turned away.
She was my darling baby daughter
The Jewel and love of my life;
Jewel is what I called her.
Many years have passed by since then
I think of her now — and again —
"Daddy don't lea' me," I still hear her say,
"He lea' me." I quickly turn away
To leave daydreaming for another day.

Darlene Grice Hayward

RESOLUTION

(Well, that's *over! — Or is it?)*

I've hung my heart on a willow tree.
There let it be
Unmourned, unsung.
There is only this emptiness for me.
Perhaps I'm free —
Fetters now flung.

I will not weep for the day love came
Without a name
Into my life,
Or the hours when we shared that sharp bright flame.
Was it a game —
Or was it strife?

Oh, never more in such high degree
To heed the plea
Of love now gone!
But what of my heart on the willow tree —
And the hours for me
Before the dawn?

Conna Bell

MY MOON

my moon, my pretty world, my afterworld,
the light of life; hopes reflected in your oceans,
loves made beneath your tent of dreams —
my tainted friend; your crystal clear image
fills my darkness pure.

where are you o my love?
you, my crystal ball, my only confidante,
your shining rays energize this heart and soul;
they transport me to my loved ones; oh,
my medium, reappear, for we long for your
brilliance in your black skies, for your silver body
to adorn the otherwise dull mountaintops, oceans,
hearts — your radiance paints the obscure, somber night
and she glitters innocently; come back soon!

oh, my moon, dazzle the midnight air for I
long for your twilight hours, your starlight,
your moonshine.
come and chase away the clouds, clear the hazy air,
my heart's flickering.

Naghmeh Majidi-Ahi

HOW DO I COUNT YOUR LOVE?

How do I count the waves that break along the shore?
How do I count the hours I love you more and more?
The words I know you speak that are meant only for me
I cherish them so much because they came from thee.
I see your smile so great, upon a face that shines
And feel the touch of you between the other lines.

How do I know the score when you are far away?
How do I live my life with you from day to day?
You make it oh so nice with everything you do.
So now you know just why I love to be with you.
The longing for your touch. The yearning to be near
So I can hear your voice with only love not fear.

How do I know your love if you're not there to tell?
How do I sense your thoughts when you're not feeling well?
I know your every dream. I know the way you talk.
With every move of you I know your very walk.
So now you see and know just how I think each day
Because it's only you that comes and guides my way.

Robert Lovelace

CHECKER PLAYERS, 1943

HONORABLE MENTION

Alternating black, white distracts,
proves sad yet fundamental difference.
She forgets to move,
her red disc   a sun setting
low in Africa   acacia shadows
flat limbs veining a vivid sky
hives of paprika   curry volcanoes.
Even checkers prompt dreams,
her soft green chair an insult.
She wishes his black piece might turn
to onyx in his mind, doubts it.
The red and black is for him simple economics.
In profile his is like heads on the coins
he is dreaming of   just as featureless.
He knows this checkerboard
is semaphore for her thoughts.
He remembers floors like this
how dancing together   they felt
nothing else   made any difference.

A. V. Christie

SOMEONE I KNOW

When you become me I almost love me
It's as though I'm someone I know — someone
I
know, I know . . .
Life is more than function
When we share the junction
Of pleasure and pain
I'm someone with a name
Someone with a real name . . .
When you phone me I want to clone me
It's as though I'm someone who knows me
Someone should know me . . .
When you feel me it almost kills me
It's as though I'm someone that I know
Someone I should know . . .
When you become me I almost love me
It's as though I'm someone I know — someone
I
Know . . .

Tommy Toledo

LIFE SENTENCE

I love you, and thus
Commit my crime.
I'll gladly pay
With my whole lifetime.

The verdict is guilty.
I'm hoping for a life sentence.

Jamie Lynne Morewood

SERENADE

If I were a singer
I would stealthily approach your door,
In the peaceful quiet of the night,
And gently knock.
When you affectionately responded,
I would ask permission
To sing inside your mind.

Hugo Jay Forde

HEAVENLY

You are so lovely
the joy I now sense inside
this world has never known

I a weary traveler of space and time
have upon this foreign planet
taken a breath of home

G. L. Folbré III

ON A LOVE LONG PAST

She
Used to be
Someone Special.
But now
She's just another someone
Walking in the distance,
Leaving no footprints.

James C. Bassett

TEARS OF THE SORCERER KNIGHT

Love's sweet whisper,
speaks softly to me.
Love's gentle touch,
softly caresses me.
Love's silent ayre,
sweetly engulfs me,
Telling me to be free!

Mark L. Ridge

RESISTANCE

You say you know me well
How can you tell?
You seldom get inside of my head
When we speak, we seldom talk,
Why do you resist my love, why do
You resist yourself?

Julie Pajares

ONE HEART BEATING

Through the lace he saw her
standing in dawn's golden light
His soul sang out in freedom
at the glory of her sight

Through many lives he'd sought her
yet never knew her name
She was his love reflecting
their hearts did beat the same

In the dawn she saw him
watching from the lace
She knew at last she'd found him
by his soft and gentle face

No need for words between them
as he joined her in the sun
and when their lips did meet,
these two souls became as one

Vera Onder

A BABY'S SMILE

How great the laughter of a child,
Could make a worldly language,
Just a baby's trusting smile
Could be a first-aid bandage.
There'd be no rationality,
No color, creed, nor race,
No choice of nationality,
No thoughts of grim disgrace.
Men could magnify their rapture,
And could peacefully adjust,
If they just had the knack to capture
The little baby's love and trust.
If only it could ever be
That men, like babes, have winning ways,
Then I think that we would see
War clouds change to peace sun rays,
And if men could ever see
That the little children need them,
Then I think it might just be,
A little child might lead them.

Roger E. Coleman

SEVEN TITLES OF JESUS

How could I say no to Jesus
He is all the world to me.
'Son of God,' 'Son of Man,' 'Savior'
And 'Messiah' is He.

He came as a 'Suffering Servant' in
the world to ransom me.
Died upon the cross, paid the price,
and set me free.

He is the 'Light of the World.'
He turns darkness into day.
He is the 'Lord of my Life.'
For He hears me when I pray.

Why? Oh why? Can't man hear
His voice?
If you don't accept Him you
have made your own choice.

Rindie Malone

THEIR TIME HAS COME

Please listen to my prayer
oh, Father up above,
They need me more than ever
my daughters that I love.

Time that we've missed
would be no more,
For time together
would be in store.

I'm not there to listen
or lend a helping hand,
No shoulder to cry on
only my substitute can.

The past is just that,
when I couldn't handle life,
But . . . their time has come,
I'm their mother, not his wife.

Mary J. Conlon

WORDS OF LOVE

Tonight is a special night,
With its warm air full of
Love and with the full moon
To guide our path and the stars
Are dancing in the sky to let
Us know that tonight is a
Night for love, so if you
Have someone to share your
Love don't let this night go
By without telling that special
Person how much you care,
Kiss and take a walk under
The light of the moon and
Open your heart to receive
The light of love and remember
That the love you give tonight
Will be forever and you will
Never feel lonely because
Tonight your heart was sealed
With love.

Olga S. Gonzalez

FOR MY LOVE

I love you like the month of May —
Sweet and soft, seldom cross.
I love you like the gentle breeze,
Blowing through your life with ease.

Kisses on your mouth I find,
To be of the very best kind.
Full of love and deep affection;
How could I get any better attention?

I look at you and see a reflection
Of my love for you; oh, what a connection!
I look at you and see the one
Who loves me so; now I must show.

Show you what you mean to me,
For without you, love, I could not be.
Be full of life and energy
And happy just to be with thee.

Elizabeth Olk Borchardt

INVITATION

Brown eyes speak to me
across a room, across time.
Looking inside, they stroke my soul.
I'm caught in a whirlwind of sensations —
unexpected emotions.

Mesmerized by their depth, their warmth
reaching out . . . embracing me.

Overcome by the tenderness, the longing,
Pulsing within this familiar stranger.

He sees my weary spirit, yearning to be released
I believe he holds the key.

Smiling, he moves towards me.
Holding out his hand . . . beckoning to me,
I give him mine.

Warm currents flow through me,
Soft hues enfold me,
I touch love.

So many men,
So little feeling.

Except for one . . .
Who holds my soul.

But,
For me,
He has so little feeling,
And, oh . . .
So many women.

Prism tears slowly flow
Down translucent skin
Softly spilling
Onto satin sheets.

This is how
My nights are spent.
After washing off
The painted smile
I wear all day,
Just for you.

Michelle Ranich

SEASONS

Spring came; You came into my life.
Fresh, glistening dewdrops awakened
a new day with words never to be heard.

You gently touched my soul, and I
saw the many nuances of my life
as a magnificent rainbow.

Summer came, then Fall.
Masses of green succumbed to the very
destiny of Winter's touch.
Gray clouds darkened the Heavens above me.
Had life ended? Where were the rainbows?
I pondered the purpose of my entity
in such a massive universe.
Reality of my purpose comes alive
in the Spring-like freshness of Your love
for me and I question my purpose no more.

Laquetta Parker

TUMBLING WALL

I've got it all in perspective,
where you are concerned
I tell myself the feelings are in check,
safely tucked away in your corner of my heart
I believe I know where I'm at with you
I know what us doesn't mean for you and me

I build a wall of protection, I hope,
carefully placing each piece just so
I prepare my mind to deal with seeing you
and convince my feelings to stay safely hidden

And from a distance I do just fine

Suddenly you're standing in front of me,
Without hesitation my arms go 'round you,
I'm in the hug I've longed for, and
the gaze I dream of is now real

Without thought, I reach for your hand,
and piece by piece my wall tumbles 'round me
All I've tried to keep in check spills out
I still want you, still need you,
and will always love you

Debi Buettner

HIS LOVE

Long ago, God made Adam and Eve
He gave them faith in which to believe
He told them that they never had to leave
He did it to show them His love

But then they discovered that fateful tree
A mistake that changed all of history
That's how sin, hate and evil all came to be
That's why all of us needs His love

Many years later, He sent down His Son
To be the new king of His chosen ones
All of the people, both old and young
He did it to show them His love

They killed the Lord Jesus, He died for our sins
God was forgiving, as He's always been
He'd still forgive us if we did it again
He does it to show us His Love

His Love for the world is what keeps us going
It keeps the world going around and around
All that you need is a little bit of faith
And His Love will never let you down

Jeffrey B. Davis

MY KIDS

The sparkle and shine on each little face
Puts joy in my heart I feel no disgrace
For bringing them into this world of mine
With kisses and hugs our arms entwine
My love for them you won't see in words
'Cause love flows freely like wings on birds
So I spread my arms to you my kids
I'll hug you tight and kiss your eyelids
With every hug and each kiss I give
I'm passing you love for as long as we live.

Susan Judge

PLEASE CUP YOUR HAND

Please cup your love and hold it so for me
As flowers face their petals toward the light;
Never breath or thirst or silt from sea
can weigh against the stem and bring it blight.

Petals meant to yield repeated sips
fill your cup; hold it cupped with dew;
Smiles should never stray from friendly lips —
Stay near, dear friends, our days are all too few.

George C. Koch

KOCH, GEORGE C. Born: 2-22-22, New York, New York; Married: 9-24-60, to Lucille; Education: State University of New York, Agricultural Degree, 1942; Occupation: Medical Laboratory Technologist, 37 years, now retired; Memberships: Staten Island Poetry Society; Awards: Honorable mention, war poem in *Midwest Poetry Review;* Poetry: *Voice From the Ardennes,* book, 1965; *Two Pens,* book, 1957; *The Endless Climb,* book, 1968; Comments: *Yours truly is published here and there, now and again — favorite work is poetry. Am best known for poems about World War II.*

LOVE: A DIFFERENCE IN MEANING

I love ice cream and my parents.
I love late shows and the Sunday comics.
I love my home and small children.
So, why is it so strange that I ask what you mean?
Why not I respect you or need you?
They mean just as much — they're just words.
Love is more than words — it's feelings and actions.

Show me your love when you play with a child.
Sit with me quietly with my head on your shoulder.
Hold hands with me when we walk down a street.
Send me a flower, just 'cause I'm me.
Hold me closely, whenever I'm afraid.
Talk to me gently when sadness brings tears.
Let's drive through the country whenever it's Sunday.
Take me to any church, where we can worship and pray.
Give me the simple things, that build day by day,
from a warm friendly house to a home filled with love.

Now take back your words and give me instead,
what I ask, in return, for what I will give.

Roberta Gail Hurlburt

COMING HOME

I hated coming home today with empty arms
That should have held a dozen roses,
Red and wet with tears each orphaned bud.
But I'd forgotten that my home
Was in your heart.
Then suddenly, my arms, instead of being
Empty things,
Were filled with life's most precious flower —
You!

Jay Dodman

THINK OF LOVE WHEN DENIED IS ITS HAND

When the Chainman thinks of love he thinks of
sky and moon.

When the Chainman thinks of love he thinks of
flowers and candles.

When the Chainman thinks of love he thinks of
sailing the sea with Stareyes.

The depth of love is infinite

When the Chainman thinks of love he thinks of
peace and foyness.

When the Chainman thinks of love he thinks of
walks in the warm spring rain
with Stareyes.

When the Chainman thinks of love he thinks of
no wars — no battles only
unity.

With love the storm fades away
very soon.

Felix Louis Wicks

MY KNIGHT IN SHINING ARMOR

Jesus you're my knight in shining
armor. I pray that one day you'll bless
me with a beautiful daughter named
Carma. When I'm full of worry or
full of fear, I open up my heart
and pray to you, and you always hear.
When others turn their backs and
walk away, I can depend on you to stay.
I lean on you, heavenly father every day.

Sometimes when I feel I'm about to win,
Trouble comes and I have to start all over again.
But I still don't give up; I give it another try;
I don't want to let a blessing pass me by.
Just a touch of your hand; you make me
feel like no one else can. And through my
troubles I can see; by my side you'll
always be. Thanks for all you've done
for me. You have all powers in your hands
powers that no man understands. Let there
be peace and not war. Please be with
me forevermore. Jesus you're my knight in
shining armor, and my savior too; there's
No one in this world that you can ever be compared
with. I know this much is true.

Regina Cooke

A DESERT SONG

There is a reason a man lives in the desert.
He says, "My sister is near."

He lives in a trailer in Arizona.
His landlady is Mexican.

He says, "You go to the desert
to learn what it is, that isn't
necessary.

to feel your hands become
the dust

to be the earth.

You taste the heat, the sun,
grow friends with the coyote

and lizard." All is sharp,
elemental, brilliant.

"We are here to change things,
or to be changed by them," he says.

You learn to be careful, to take
everything down to its core,

You do not ask more
than the earth can give.

Winds, sand and sun play on bone,
the body instrument.

Janet Roberts

RIDING ON THE MERRY-GO-ROUND OF LOVE

Dedicated with love to Leslie and Ion Freirich,
1986 Newlyweds

Love is indeed a many splendored thing —
A bird flying happily on the wing

Like a butterfly flitting from flower to flower
Spending here and there an enchanting hour.

Love is fire — love is desire —
Love is receivable — love is conceivable.

Love has a "know how" all its own
That can even topple a nation's throne.

Romeos and Juliets will always be
Found in the pages of history.

At times dear old King Cupid
May seem to be a little stupid —

But there is one thing he certainly knows —
And that is how to handle his bows

So, that as monarch of the old love game,
His arrows never miss their aim!

Many happy hearts will continue to sing

"Long live the royal archer,
Cupid, our King."

Eliza Jane Bye

THE BLESSING OF LOVE

Dedicated with love to Aurora Behrer

Since the world began,
There have been woman and man,
Father and mother, sister and brother.

Since the day of the ark,
There have been fire and spark,
Love and romance, song and dance,
Hands uplifted in prayer and
Wings in a pair —
Like the bees, the birds, the butterflies,
Aeroplanes and angels
Coming to earth from **the great somewhere.**

Nonetheless and notwithstanding,
One can have a **happy landing**

If one has fond memories of having loved — and,
more precious, is —
The blessing of having been loved.

Eliza Jane Bye

LOVING YOU

Yes I'm really loving you
With a love that's really true
My love for you is so sweet and so nice
Full of sugar and full of spice
Though there will be happiness and tears
Yes I'll always be loving you
With a love that will always be true
The stars in the Heaven that shine
They tell me you're really mine
And soon we will be together
For a long time, which means forever
No one will ever get us apart
Because we loved each other from the start
The stars up above that shine
Tell me you'll always be mine
We all know you shouldn't lie
Well this is true, I'll love you until I die
I loved you from the start and will to the end
A lifetime together we will spend

Judy Obuchowski

RAINBOWS IN THE LIGHT

There were stars in the sky —
But I seldom saw them twinkling.
There was perfume on the summer wind —
But I didn't have an inkling —
Of the beauty all around me,
Until you came into my life.

Then suddenly — my heart was full of song,
And sunshine filled my days with joy and laughter.
Like a sparkling brook in summer —
Or a fountain bubbling over,
As its cascading — misty waters
Catch the sunshine and rainbows in the light.

And when night releases you — from the things that
you must do —
And I listen for your footsteps on the stair —
My heart is filled to overflowing —
With the simple joy of knowing,
With the lovely joy of knowing that you care.

Rosemary Farrar

WHY

You ask me why I love you, but the sum
Of answers is as various as love
Itself; the reasons crowding come,
Flooding my heart and mind. I cannot give
Them all. The large and small, they have no end,
The weighty and the trivial entwine
Their roots about my heart, and in my mind
They all convince such reasoning as mine.

I love you for the little things you do,
For things you say, for fun and joy we share,
For sorrows known together that we have
Surmounted in the past. I love you too,
(Encompassing all reasons that there are)
As a response to your devoted love.

Lucy Mason Nuesse

Share a park bench with me,
The trees are so beautiful,
Just as you.

You say something's gone?
That's why I sit here,
But I was hoping no one would notice.
That's funny though,
I thought something familiar was to be
seen in your eyes.
I didn't think that I should notice it
in my own first.

Love's a funny creature isn't she?
The ultimate highs and lows,
So ultimate.
Just when you think you know,
You don't.
Just when you think . . .
You shouldn't have.
And just when you're feeling so sorry for yourself,
You quickly remember it took two
And really no one is to blame,
Yet both are there for the thanking.

David K. Boyd

FORTY TWO YEARS AGO

"Forty two years ago today"
In a town so far away,
Two young loves whispered I do,
Did we, I did, did you?
Well somewhere along the way,
Somehow there was foul play.
Someone must have pulled the switch,
Throwing our lives into the ditch,
Which derailed our train of life,
Making me no longer your wife.
Although I was not your spouse,
I was the mother of our house.
With our three children to raise,
I had to look for love and praise,
Doing the best I could in my trying ways.
Through troubled nights and lonely days,
Through trials and tribulations and sorrow,
I found it harder to face each tomorrow.
Each new day brought a burden to bear,
Trying to weather those stormy days with prayer.
Praying that another day would bring unto me,
Peace, contentment and required harmony.

Dorothy America Boat

THIS DAY TODAY

Today he told me that he loves me,
Today he told me that he cares,
Today he told me that he missed me,
Today, he said, that's why he's here.

Just to think, I wondered if he really
LOVED me
Just to think, I wasn't sure he'd
Choose me
No need to think, he's talked about
Summer and future, and one of these days . . .
I think he has me on his mind.

Maritza Williams

MEETING

The gray sea, and the long black land;
And the yellow half-moon large and low;
And the startled little waves, that leap
In fiery ringlets from their sleep,
As I gain the cove with pushing prow,
And quench its speed in the slushy sand.

Then a mile of warm, sea-scented beach;
Three fields to cross, till a farm appears:
A tap at the pane, the quick sharp scratch
And blue spurt of a lighted match,
And a voice less loud, through its joys and fears,
Than the two hearts, beating each to each.

Robert Browning

TRUSTING HANDS

A knock by the trusting hand of God.
A toothless smile — sloppy kisses, shake of a
shaggy paw.
Old Maid's fairy tales — tug-o-war,
Band-Aids soon forgotten — Here kitty, kitty,
Where?
Forgive me Lord.
"Jesus loves me" — so loved by all — sung in perfect
harmony.
Jonah is safe. Thanks be to God.
Bowed heads, gingerbread men — frosted mouths.
Folded hands on bended knees.
Good night, blessed savior man.

Gloria D. Hulse

CHANGE OF LOVE LOCKS, PLEASE

Tired of being the wallflower —
Sitting on your shelf!
Get back to my old crazy self!
That's what I was, Baby, when I first met you,
And you can bet!
Heart's *dying* just to *live* again
Tired of feeling lousy over you.
Gonna get up! That's *right!* Gonna go *out!*
Put on my new dress! Matching *shoes!*
Joy perfume! and breaking loose!
Not ever coming back —
Change the love locks and
Footloose.

Anna Manzi

MY FIRST LOVE.

Lith. & Pub. by N. Currier, 2 St. New York.

OUR BELOVED CHILDREN

Four lovely children blessed our married state,
Two sons, two daughters crowned our wedded life.
Our love for them came quickly with no wait
By me, their Dad, nor Ella mother-wife.
Of mutual affection there's no lack
Among six Greenes whose love consumes us all.
Sweet Dorothy and Joyce and Dave and Jack
On them no alteration can befall.
Not half a dozen, just like one we stand
United in devotion shared by each.
Our children say, "We're just a loving band
With nothing lying out beyond our reach.
Our Dad and Mother finish up the six
Of solid unity without a stray.
While E for Ella, F for Frank don't mix,
We're undividable, we're truly fay.
A boy and girl whose names begin with J,
Another pair whose names begin with D,
Remain in line to keep our normal way
The Greenes are one, a perfect unity."

Frank E. Greene

GREENE, FRANK EDWARD. Born: Providence, Rhode Island, 6-9-06; Married: 1-25-30 to Ella M. Williams; Education: Providence, Rhode Island College, Ph.B., 1929; Boston, Massachusetts University, M.A., 1937; Providence Catholic Teachers College, Ed.D., 1955; Occupation: Newspaperman, Public Librarian, Teacher, Professor; Memberships: Knights of Columbus (All four degrees and honorary life); American Association of Retired Persons, Former President of Providence Chapter; Cape Coral Chapter, Cape Coral Retired Citizens; Cape Coral Good Neighbors; Providence Cathoic Interracial Council (First President in 1950); Holy Name Society; Awards: Several, but none for poetry; Writings: For newspaper, governmental organizations, private societies and individuals. Periodicals, brochures, contractual and freelance. Collaborated on book. Wrote numerous academic papers for others. Published in *Family Digest, Sign, St. Anthony Messenger, Mind;* Themes: *Love, Death, Children, Parents, Religion (Catholic).*

TO MICHAEL

For the veterans of war who can't stop the dreams.
I love you.

The Sad One, Alone
With naught to shed but tears
Michael has lost his own true Love
Through the passing of bitter years
From sun-brightened days to shallow rain
Michael has walked where others fear to go,
So the sad refrain.

He lost his Love on a winter's day
When, very far away
He saw a man shoot a child
Then leave him in an unmarked grave
His eyes are hollow now
When once they had been kind
If you had seen what Michael saw
You would lose your mind.

So Love lives not in his empty heart
So much has he to shame
For he carried the gun that fired the shot
Oh Michael, do you know the sad refrain?

Virgie M. Tabaco

LOVE IS EVERYWHERE

While alone in my room, there was a knock on my door;
It was a young lady, who lived on the same floor.
She asked me a question, about a nearby chateau;
I said, "I'm sorry, I really don't know."
She was pudgy and round, with a double chin;
We passed a few pleasantries, and had asked her in.
I asked her her name, she said, "Call me Lynn";
I told her mine, and started to grin.
"Would you like a drink?" remarking to Lynn;
"Don't mind if I do, make it vodka and gin."
She spoke of her parents her schools and degrees;
While tightly fitted, in her dungarees!
Her thoughts wandering, a moment or two;
I noticed her eyes, were a deep shaded blue.
She said to me, with an explosive smile;
"Enough about me, let's talk of you awhile."
There wasn't much to say about me;
I grew up with love, in a big family.
So, in the days to come, our friendship would grow;
We discovered our love, and found the chateau.
She was pudgy and round, with a double chin;
We passed a few pleansantries, and had asked her in.
So, it pays to answer the knock on your door;
It just might be, the Girl you were waiting for.

Angelo Del Orfano

SO EASY TO LOVE

It's so easy to love one who is kind;
A truly kind heart is so hard to find;
It's so easy to love one who shares;
A sharing person is one who cares;
It's so easy to love one who gives;
A giving person helps others to live;
In a cold cruel world, love is what we need;
For future's sake, love must take the lead;
So easy to live, so easy to love;
Love's one thing there's never enough of.

Fred L. Richardson

THE FOUNTAIN WITHOUT WATER

HONORABLE MENTION

Seven years later, the geese still dance
under the bridge where we walked, right hands
full of bread, left hands locked together.
First love came easy, our lips perfumed and hungry,
we held each other until the last minute of the day.
Pointing at houses we thought would be ours,
we agreed on Spanish roofs, and a white walkway.

Today, I received your postcard from Venice.
Sailboats rest under a violet sky.
Remember healing each other on the wooden footbridge,
the fountain with no water . . .

Watching the snowfall of a winter too clear to ignore,
I see your words, *take good care,* and an outdoor cafe
with enough sun to take my constant chill away.

Melinda Latimer

EACH OTHER

We have EACH OTHER to hold tight as autumn leaves
begin to fall and winter again invites

We have EACH OTHER to grow old between the joys
and tears of memories that sail on white velvet waves
of Yesteryears . . .

We have EACH OTHER to touch sunlit stars
as our dreams will never be far from our
sentimental Hearts . . .

We have EACH OTHER to say I'm on your side
lean on me all the way, for I'll never let you fall
I'll always be here to stay . . .

But most of all,
We have EACH OTHER to discover
the best we both can achieve in
One Life Together

One Love FOREVER . . .

Juan J. Gonzalez

ONE IN A MILLION

For Teddy

Sometimes I sit and wonder
About the times we share.
It really makes me happy
Knowing that you care.
When the world is crumbling before me
And I feel the need to cry
That's when you soothe things over
You help me to get by.
You're one in a million
Not like all the rest
Your kindness overshadows me
Let's put love to the test.
Remember way back in July
The day I first met you
Your bright happy smile, your warm trusting glow
My heart knew you were true.
Whatever the future may hold in store
And if we should grow apart
I hope we could still be friends
'Cause you'll always hold a special place within my heart!

Maura Smith

LOVE DEVELOPMENTS

Our lives together shall stroll down the
Memory lane of breathtaking love.
Always together we are bonded by an
Everlasting force of power, so natural, we call
it love. We can expand upon our existence.
Enhanced by a motivation, which leads us every day
down that pathway of perpetual existence.
Again in this world of upstairs, downstairs, love
affairs, there is only one in which, today,
Tomorrow, and forever, we shall call it love.
The creativity in which we bonded can never
be a gala,
It will always be "love."

Little Willie

SHE WAS ONLY FIFTEEN

I came a visitor in broken home
And saw the sink, a cluttered mess
Dirty dishes, pots and pans with molding rests
A little boy, between his scattered cars and truck
Was busy picking cracker crumbs from shaggy rug

The sofa sagged when I sat down
Burnt matches littered every tray
Marijuana plants were slyly tucked away
How could one miss the addict's plight
No reverence for life, no spunk to fight?

I was so sad, I cried a lot
But then, this lovely girl appeared
And in no time the mess was cleared
She worked, and smiled, and sang a tune
Her shining eyes dispersed all gloom

She spread her arms, and called the boy
Who came on running, hugged her full of joy
Her gentle face, already showed the lines of understanding
The heavy yoke; the suffering with which to cope
She was only fifteen, but gave her all, her love, her hope

Else Dykerman

LOVE'S LIKENESSES

Love is like a mountain that carries one to glorious
heights.
With exhiliration it lifts the soul to great delights.
It towers brilliantly above all other earthly attributes.
It keeps the mind focused on the crescent for likely tributes.

It raises one's hopes for a blissful and fulfilled life,
For with its solidarity there is no fear of an emotional
landslide.
It is garnished with flowers of peace and contentment.
Its trees of ecstasy shade the tempers with endearment.

Its breezes stimulate the weary lover to push to the top,
For there his dreams are fulfilled without a teardrop.
Its ground cover is commitments to his lover's endeavors.
Its terrain is composed of patience which brings favors.

Its crevices hold the unspoken words of endearment
registered in the face.
Its peak of enjoyment elevates one to a ridge of lofty
solace.
The climber is not discontented on his ascent to love,
For it lifts him to a rapturous and joyful height above.

Erma C. Benton Grant

CHILD TO PARENT

I am not blind
  to your struggles
in fact I applaud your courage

Knowing that even your slightest victory
  was not won easily
I stand and cheer

Then I kneel
  in silent reverence
honoring the sacrifice of your personal quest

Although your life has not been lived to secure
  my heart-filled respect
nonetheless it is yours

You have earned my love by performing
  life's most difficult task
being perfectly and honestly yourself

As your apprentice I have learned from your miles
  and now may my performance
be your greatest reward

G. L. Folbré III

OUR LOVE

His hair reflects the sun's golden beams;
As we stroll along hand in hand,
  he's in love with me it seems.
The smell of cologne drifting off his manly skin
Into the air past my delicate nose.
The soft sound of his voice hits my ears like
  the purr of a kitten.
The love I feel for him is the love
  Adam felt for Eve.
If only we could walk here for the rest of our lives
  and God never made him leave.
Then the tears I'm crying right now would be tears
  of joy instead of old dried up tears of memory.

Kelly (Dodson) Hadley

THE VINTAGE OF LOVE

He walked into the room
and caught my glance,
we both knew it was love at first sight.

A year later in a small church
we took our vows and began a new life,
we knew we were in love.

In ten years we had three kids,
ages two, five, and seven,
We were very much in love.

By our twenty-fifth anniversary
the house was emptier and quieter,
we were even more in love.

Thirty-five years went all to quickly
and the mortgage was finally paid,
we were just beginning to understand love's depth.

Now we've made it to our golden anniversary,
and these two old, beautiful people realize,
we have become the embodiment of love.

Donice M. Jewell

THE SCHOOL BUS OF OUR DREAMS

The School Bus of Our Dreams
Is always open.
It stops at crossings; crosses stops.
Its doors swing wide; doors swing shut.
Endlessly.
Monotonously.
Over and over again.
Its windows are barred; Its windows are open.
Every day
Every week
Every year.
It's a vehicle filled with years of shouting laughing memories.
A ride of disappointments. A ride of pain.
All too often a ride of no return!
Rarely, a ride of joy.
A release;
Images recalling an excellent yell or shout.
The Schoolbus of Our Dreams;
Is always open.
"All aboard. All aboard for the schoolhouse of our dreams."

Chip Kilgus

KILGUS, EDWARD J. Pen Name: Chip; Born: Flushing Hospital, Astoria, Queens; Single; Education: Adelphi University, Garden City, Long Island, B.S., English, 1970; Occupations: Controller, Operations Manager, Director of Purchasing, Professional Buyer; Memberships: A.N.A.; Awards: Golden Poet Award, World of Poetry, 1986; Poetry: 'The Lilac of Our Years," *Muscadine,* May/June 86; 'Pam,' World of Poetry, 6-86; 'School Bus of Our Dreams,' American Poetry Association, 8-86; 'The Ultimate Pink Slip,' *Poets at Work,* 9-86; 'What is A Day Without?' *Poets at Work,* June/July 86; Comments: *We are important as individuals in a corrupt uncaring society. This oxymoronic poem espouses the ephemerality of many of our everyday encounters while revealing the subliminal treasury of memories that may never be experienced again.*

A WISH

If I could be granted just one wish, it would be
That everyone could find the beauty in love and never let it go.

Mary E. Ingram

LOVE AFTER FIFTY

Though bards extol the virtues of
A vibrant form of younger love,
Before we fade into obscurity,
Let's sing the praises of — maturity.
There is new groundwork to be laid,
And some adjustments must be made.
When whispering endearments in my ear,
Please speak up, so I can hear.
At cozy breakfasts, while we dine,
The question popped, your pills or mine?
Gaze in my eyes, before you kiss me,
Best look again, or you might miss me.
Here's hoping we will dance a lot,
Both cheek to cheek, and pot to pot.
However, when all's said and done,
Love after fifty can be fun.
How cheerful, that at this far junction,
Our hypothalami still function!

Virginia Westgaard

WESTGAARD, VIRGINIA LASELL Pen Name: Virginia Stanley; Born: New York, New York, 11-10-32; Married: 12-28-85, to Tor Westgaard; Education: Metropolitan State College, Denver, Colorado, B.A., 1986; Vassar College, 1950- 1953; Occupations: Writing Center Tutor, Metropolitan State College; Awards: Golden Poet Award, World of Poetry Press, 1985; Poetry: 'For Icarus at Sunset,' *Metrosphere,* 1985; 'Vietnamsong,' *Metrosphere,* 1986; 'Cross Country,' *Our World's Most Cherished Poems,* 1986; 'Contradiction,' *Treasures of the Precious Moments,* 1985; 'Graven Images,' *Words of Praise Vol II,* 1986; Comments: *Have always written poetry, but never submitted any for publication until 1985. Will tackle any theme, but work best from an assignment (perpetual student syndrome).*

THE ROSE LADY OF MY PAST

Alas! 'Tis been ten years since I last kissed your ruby red lips of splendid rapture.
For I would give dearly for another chance to give you one more starlit kiss.
My burning desire to rekindle your fire would in fact not make me out to be a liar.

Your bucolic image of profound loveliness is still locked into my yearning mind.
The red glossy silk gown you had worn matched the vivid colors of autumn's leaves of Sapporo's past.
The passion alone that I felt from you could melt the coldest of many a New England winter's day.

The sweet Japanese wine could flow and the Terriyaki steaks would sizzle towards
a night of perfection.
And be given the opportunity one more time to have a taste of your paradise by
a winter fire on an inlet bay.
You are the explicit meaning of unadorned beauty and indeed are the pink rose
among the Earth's many flowers.

A thunderbolt struck through my very soul when you first caught my eye at
an exotic night club one Tokyo night.
My blood boiled hot and I felt your heat come my way when we had many
late evening dances . . .
I softly kissed your rosy cheeks more than once while I felt your
approving hold around my broad shoulders.

Through sorrow and joy of the last ten years, I have learned to be patient in a web of silence . . .
For no lady could ever replace the likes of you. You are Japan's gift of beauty and freedom.
So I keep a burning candle lit at all times of the night to hope you return into my life one final time.

William D. Brownlie, III

ONLY ONE LOVE

He was her first, and only love, two kids caught up by war,
And now he's waiting up above, some day she'll journey to his star.
He went away for seven years, and that's how long he'd tarry,
Alone she shed her bitter tears, they weren't allowed to marry.

No one ever measured up, she never loved again,
So now she lifts her vodka cup, to try to ease the pain.
Once so lovely, now she's old, she tried to love, in vain;
Lovers have been cruel and cold. Would he have been the same?

Did she waste her life, for a memory
Just longing for what might have been?
Could his love have lived up to her fantasy?
Would he want her, now, like he did then?

If there's a heaven up above,
She longs to meet him there.
He was her first and only love —
Will he tell her, "I still care?"

Virginia Huett Wilson

WE DON'T NEED

We don't need . . . Our name in "Who's Who."
We don't need . . . A palace so somber and cold.
We have our family's love.
And a home more precious than gold.
We don't need . . . gems and jewels so rare.
We don't need . . . lights that glimmer and glare.
We have the greatest splendor on earth
We have the glory of love to share.
We don't need . . . sweet red wine to drink.
We don't need . . . expensive caviar to eat.
We are richer than the rich.
We have love that can't be beat.
We don't need . . . a yacht or an ocean cruise.
We don't need . . . a chauffeur driven limousine.
The things we have . . . we thank God for . . . when we kneel.
For we are wealthier than a king or queen.
We don't need . . . a crystal chandelier.
We don't need . . . a magic carpet to fly away.
We are humble, sincere and devoted.
And we have true love that's here to stay.

Jane Luciene Nowak

drifting

climb aboard our magic seabird,
you beckon me with open arms.
i answered, you never heard me,
with feelings that were hard to say.
the thought of love still warms me;
drift me away, drift me away.

drifting away
on endless seas of blue and sky,
the day turns fast from sun to gray;
on islands shared by you and i,
drift me away.

surround me in the ocean rush;
we fly the crest of Phantom's wake.
a sea breeze, you gently touch me;
you kiss me with a sunny day.
sharing the moment, you take me.
drift me away, drift me away.

Annemarie Bettica

STARDUST

As stardust falls beneath the empty sky
I feel not alone when I am with you
As broken wings reach into eternity
I know you care for me today
Today is only a moment to cherish
One has not forever
Hearts feel warm with touch
A special love is in a heart for you
Looking into shadows, stardust falls
I feel you here beside me, I am not alone
Within the days one searches
My comfort is you
When you are far
Your warmth is in my heart
Love for someone is a special capture in soul
Binding in time
A special place in my heart is held for you
Time searches endless meadows beyond existence
For now you are here.

Gayle Nicholson

GRAVE TEMPTATION

Have you ever felt so empty, cold and lonely?
Oh, how sad a feeling.
You really try to hurry and change the world —
but you're like honey running down a tree.
So slow you move, nothing to grasp.
You slide down the way of life
catching all the rough areas.
A cry for help — no one cares.
Oh, how slowly, you can't go on.
You want to fall in every way
but you strive for the best
only to realize
you're still a failure;
no one wants to show you're loved.
It's all gone — so you escape.
Oh, how it feels so great,
but you're not real — only escaping
because no one cares
so why care at all?

Kate Traylor

THEIR LIVES LIE IN OUR HANDS

Out in the world every day, every night,
Abandoned children reach out for someone,
Groping in darkness, avoiding the light,
Hoping to linger, not wishing to run.
Eyes beg for affection for us to return,
Longing for trust, friendly arms and a name,
Playmates and playthings, a chance just to learn,
Put in a basket they all are the same.

Errors and faults, personal selfishness, crime,
Each are our guilt, devastation, our shame,
Bothersome trouble, we haven't the time,
Passing the buck, it's the children we blame.
Half of those born every minute will die,
Others survive on a miracle string,
Fragile, defenseless, unnoticed they cry,
National treasures — life hope we must bring.

Rights of the child, let us guard and preserve,
We were the children a moment ago,
Love and compassion, horizons reserve,

Fountains of youth — may they grow, overflow!

Evelyn Conley Stauffer

ACCEPTANCE

I'm sorry if you do not like me,
I'm sorry if you don't approve.
I shall not change my outlooks for you,
That would not make us better friends.

I am the person that I am,
You are the person whom you are.
I shall not change you
Just to make me like you better.

I must accept you as you are,
Or I must let you go your way;
For you are you and I am that I am,
We are we together.

If you love me keep me as I am,
And know that I am as I am.
Change me not but grow with me
And let me grow with you:

For this is love and this is life,
Which we two can share with first acceptance.

Arlene Babb Oglesby

ELUSIVE LOVE

Life, you will find, can be most unkind,
as it deprives you of love, until it bends
your mind.
It taunts you no end, in your quest to find,
the girl of your dreams, who will respond in kind.

There'll be many you meet, whom you could love,
but for reasons unknown, they cannot love.
The hurt will be bitter and very deep, as you
meander through life . . . just to sleep.
For that's where you'll find, the girl in your
mind, who is a will of the wisp, in your daily
grind.

Arthur D. Posa

ENIGMA

Love, oh love, what art thou?
The quest has been since time began,
The mystery was the same then, as now,
How can I perceive your eternal plan?

Can you be the song of birds in the trees
Or, the wind and rain upon my face?
Might you be the sound of the roaring seas
That harken the darkness of all space?

Are you a reminder in the beauty of nature
Where flowers bloom in all their splendor?
Or, memories of my long walks in rapture
Through fields kissed by dewy weather?

At last, I think I found you in the
Ripeness and sweetness of the grape that I eat.
And the delicate wine that comes through
Is but transformation that becomes complete.

I now know nature sings all your praises
From the rare perfume of the jasmine
To the poets of all ages; but how shall
I fathom your eternal signs?

Helen Melissas

I WANNA WAKE UP TO YOU

I love your teasing, and I love your smile
Won't you hang around my place awhile
I love your style and the things you do
And in the morning light . . . I wanna wake up to you.

I hate loneliness and I hate a big crowd
Sometimes parties get a bit loud
I hate fake lovers and gossips too
We'll forget them tonight . . . I wanna wake up to you.

You know I love you darlin' but maybe not enough
And you know we'll get stronger if the times get tough
With this in mind, you should feel all right
When I ask you to baby, won't you please stay the night
We'll both feel better if you agree
To let your hair down and wake up to me.

So come along to the forbidden land
Watch your step love and take my hand
Enjoy our time together 'cause it won't be long
Before the sun comes up and the day will dawn.

So while it's still night I know something to do
And in the morning light . . . I WANNA WAKE UP TO YOU!

Sherri Lundberg

LOVE

Miss you, when I'm not there — to aid your every care
Our love beyond compare — true love with you I share
I give my love to thee — on bended knees

To hold you, when I can — to caress you, with my hands
Whate'er your love demands — your wish, my heart's command
I leave my heart with thee — on bended knees

These vows, this sacred rite — our love through storm and strife
To live with, as my wife — to spend with you, my life
I will my life to thee — on bended knees

Eldor Rathjen

Ah, 'tis this which all proclaim!
This spark of capricious flame
that makes one dance then cry,
and leaves one drunk, exuberant and high.

Trembling, tingling, time has no bound.
Senses heightened: touch, smell, sight, sound . . .
When all that matters are seconds shared,
societal mores shed, secrets bared.

'Tis this that poets throughout all ages
express as humor, anguish, joy, rages;
and playwrights forever take pens to write
of some who fall captive, while others take flight.

Body and soul suddenly shaken ajar.
Daily concerns become thoughts from afar.
Life's now impossible without the other;
all one's focus directed towards another.

Yes, even I too, as never before
am filled with this theme of ancient lore.
Ready to cast aside all presence of mind,
to experience that sensational bind!

Sindi Schloss

MY SECRET LOVE

Every night and every day
I dream of you,
All my hopes and wishes
Will someday come true.

In all my chores and thoughts, you're there,
From morning breakfast, to evening prayer.

When I'm reading, you're on every page
When watching T. V., you're on the stage.

When I'm sewing, you come into view,
When I'm eating, I'm dining with you.

When I'm praying, in my secret place,
The answer is there, in your radiant face.

How can I tell you, what's my next move?
When can I reveal my secret love?

Goodnight, my darling, and let me say
My heart's true love is with you always.

Charlotte North

FAREWELL, THOU ART TOO DEAR

Farewell, thou art too dear for my possessing,
And like enough thou know'st thy estimate:
The charter of thy worth gives thee releasing;
My bonds in thee are all determinate.
For how do I hold thee but by thy granting?
And for that riches where is my deserving?
The cause of this fair gift in me is wanting,
And so my patent back again is swerving.
Thyself thou gav'st, thy own worth then not knowing,
Or me, to whom thou gav'st it, else mistaking;
So thy great gift, upon misprision growing,
Comes home again, on better judgment making.
Thus have I had thee, as a dream doth flatter;
In sleep a king, but, waking, no such matter.

William Shakespeare

UNDER THE QUILT

Again —
Alone —
In the silence —
In the darkness
the warmth under the quilt
comes only from myself.

No more love beneath the moonlight.
No more wine before the fire.
No more smiles in the morning mist.

Again —
Alone —
In this void —
In this evening
the warmth under the quilt
comes only from myself.

Mary D. Foster

OURS FOR LIFE

As two hearts
forever to be one —
Ours is the love

As two arms
reach out to hold —
Ours is the joy.
As two bodies
become the bond —
Ours is the happy.

And as we go through life's
beauty and wonders,
together we become one.

For the life —
of eternal love.

Kattie Danzeisen

TRUST ME, LOVE ME

Trust me, and I will
prove worthy of your trust.

Trust me, and in trusting me,
you prove yourself worthy of my trust.

But, trust me not, if you
yourself are unworthy of trust.

Love me, and I will
prove worthy of your love.

Love me, and in loving me,
you prove yourself worthy of my love.

But, love me not, if you
yourself are unworthy of my love.

Michael J. O'Rourke

TWO YOUNG HEARTS

Two young hearts walking through the paths of life;
Each path separate . . . each step followed by another;
Moment to moment . . . their lives' reflection.

Separate paths . . . separate lives journey on;
Wandering and wondering . . . collecting knowledge and experience;
Each in search of love and affection.

Timing is perfect . . . their paths growing closer;
Each in clear view of the other . . . taking notice;
Interest on their minds.

Symptoms . . . warmth in their hearts . . . anticipation;
Paths seem brighter, by the lights of love;
A feeling of happiness.

Eagerness to learn more of one another;
For a moment . . . for a while . . . for a lifetime;
Grasping every ounce of tenderness.

Eyes cheerfully staring into space . . . dreaming;
Concern for one another . . . "Is this for real?"
Fulfillment . . . contentment . . . passion.

Separate paths now combined as they journey together;
Sharing and caring in love's fashion.

Don Hill

GOOD-BYE DAD

As my mind drifts off to times long past,
I relive the memories that will always last.

A childhood of love and being with dad,
priceless were the times that he and I had.

He was strong and tall in my childish eyes,
though in reality, he was slight of build, but oh, so wise.

The things that he taught me have stood the test of time,
he explained that the path to manhood would be a tough climb.

His thoughts and deeds were noble and good,
this is how I think of him, and well I should.

He gave so much of himself as a father to a son,
he filled my life with happiness and so much fun.

Most important of the things that he taught me as man and boy,
was that love is all important, for without love, there is no joy.

And now it's time to say that final good-bye,
it's so hard for me to hold back the urge to cry.

I think the best way is for me to say, "Thanks, Dad,"
you were the best father that a son ever had.

John Devich

WHEN DO I DREAM OF THEE?

(Written in the doctor's waiting room)

When do I dream of thee, my love?
I dream of thee
When I awake;
I muse upon thy beauty
Through the day;
I watch the sun set
And wish you near.

And when at night I lay me down,
I wonder how long 'twill be
'Till I have you with me —
Perhaps 'twill be this night,
Whilst I dream.

Paul A. Hughes

HUGHES, PAUL ANTHONY. Born: Tulsa, Oklahoma, 9-14-57; Education: Texas A & M University, B.S.; Assemblies of God Theological Seminary, will receive Master of Divinity, July 1986; Occupations: Graduate Student, Teacher, Writer, Musician, Singer; Comments: *Music and verse are a way in which I can express my inner feelings — of hope, yearning, regret, faith. I often write during my darkest hours, when I feel overwhelmed by life. Yet, I am never defeated, for it is at these times that I feel the Lord is most near.*

TOGETHER

Together we wander over the islands
You and I, like natives, walking
Along flower-strewn volcanic gardens
Or lying in the rich, effusively hot
Sunshine when the mood suits us.
We drink from coconuts, dine
On fruits, and delight to the
Voice of each other's refrain.
It is beautiful out here and
I wish it could last forever.
Perhaps it really can — in
Our minds and hearts
If we let it remain.

Mara Hasenberg

FOR THIS GIFT OF LIFE

For all the times that we have shared
For all the special ways you cared
For times you gave more than enough
For times I thought you were too rough
For teaching me both right and wrong
For showing me weak could be strong
For sharing joys as well as fears
For all the laughter and the tears
For having always understood
For being there through bad and good

I love you both in every way
And so I honor you today
This special day I came to be
The day you gave my life to me!

Wanda Brown Lovell

THE LOVE WEB

My love was like
a giant spider spinning a web of
lace emotion.
The web swayed rythmically
to your breath
sticking close to the
pores of your intricate mind.
It kept my heart
spinning threads for hours trying
to capture you with the net of possession.
I never thought it would
be broken by a summer breeze.
Now I have to start a stronger web —
I have to start spinning
all over again.

Agnes Weyer

A CHERISHED MEMORY

I waited in the morning —
You came,
and I was happy;

I stood with you at dusk —
We kissed,
and all was beautiful;

I laid me down at night —
You were there,
and I was glad;

I saw you leaving —
We said good-bye,
and I cried.

Linda C. Ralston

TEMPESTUOUS LOVE

Our love is like the hurricane
That bends and sways the trees
We yield to its cyclonic aim
Until it sets us free.

The gentle breezes take the play
Trees now stand straight and tall
So we should be content to stay
Lulled in gentle love's call.

Elspeth Crebassa

TWINS

I look like Sissy, Sissy looks like me,
We'll soon be two, going on three.
Sissy and I don't always agree,

But I love her.

When Sissy is happy, it makes me glad.
When she gets punished, then I'm sad.
For I don't think my Sissy's bad,

'Cause I love her.

Sometimes we even fight.
She scratches me, then I bite.
I know we'll turn out all right,

'Cause I love her.

She'll get her bruises, I'll get mine,
And we'll get punished many a time,
But, I know we're gonna grow up fine,

'Cause I love her.

Ina Price

ANNIVERSARIES

The night our love died
I was not there
I was ignorant of it

The night I found it lifeless
I wept bitterly
In despair

The night I knew it had been slain
I cursed you
In outrage

The day I buried it eternally
I grieved it in agony
Then left it in its crypt

I remember it yet
On the day it was born
And the day it was interred

True, these are but two days
Of three hundred sixty-five
Yet sufficient for mourning the dead.

Paulette Hess Brown

PREFERENCE

I prefer to believe
the feelings aren't gone
Misplaced maybe in that
eclipse you showed me
of the moon
Residing in those purple
cowboy boots you bought
me on Halloween
Flying on the ferris wheel
on Ponchartrain Beach
Hidden in secret passages
of complicated reach
But not gone.

Carol Hammer

HIDEAWAY

It was the ending of the day
when he called her to his side.
Where did he take her but,
to his secret hideaway.
There they are all alone,
where emotions can be shown.
He lets her know of his intentions
but, does she show any apprehension?
No, there they are alone, in love
in their secret hideaway,
at the ending of each day.

Amelia A. Gehr

ODE TO A MAIDEN FAIR

In snow-white linen in her bed
She sleeps so quietly
As if forsaken, cold and dead
In solemn dignity.

Her hands are clasped, so it seems
As in a praying mood
That she'll be happy in her dreams
And in her solitude.

Her thoughts are slowly fluttering by
In searching memory,
She asks herself a prayerful "why"
In cold futility.

"Why am I always so alone
In pure maidenliness,
Why do I always postpone
To show my tenderness.

I know how deep my feelings burn
On every lonely day,
I beg you darling do return
And take my heart away."

Nils Rahmberg

FRIENDSHIP-LOVE

Love takes on many forms —
when it is between friends,
it is truly a
work of art!

It is warm and undemanding —
always constant,
with no questions ever asked:
a strong foundation!

Friendship-love is special —
being a good acquaintance,
is not;
friendship-love is complete trust!

Real love amongst friends —
is always knowing what to do,
when the chips are down;
and sharing the highs!

The very special kind of love —
when molded together by true friendship,
comes along but once;
in a lifetime!

Linda Lee Haugh

LUST

Palm tree telephone
Tinkles ripened gong,
Summons to Him
Nymph's sweet song.

Excitement sky pumps
Through tiger cruel hands,
Delight and torment shape
Love's sweet demands.

Joel George O'Brien

RETIREMENT HOME

This building has so many dens
In which reside frail denizens.
An institution filled with age,
The elderly of this earth's stage.

The cubicles are not the same,
The doors each show a different name.
But inside all are mortal souls,
Recalling youth with all its goals.

So many walk with crutch or cane,
So many faces wrung with pain.
Housed together in narrow scope
Marking each day with listless hope.

Elizabeth P. Wish

DAYBREAK

If you were here beside me
on this cool and tide-washed sand
in the opalescent dawning,
I'd place kisses in your hand . . .

comfort you with small caresses
as we'd stroll along the shore
in our new-found lover's aura,
leaving starry pools as spoor . . .

Garbed in foam and tiny shell pearls
we would frolic in the sea
to its undulating rhythm,
lost in endless ecstasy.

Genevieve Baker Klein

The day was empty when you left.
As the pain died —
all I felt was silence.
In the mornings, I wash my face
with cold water. The mirror
reflecting, my image stood
still.
My thoughts stare in space, I
turn to face another day.
Every word, every motion so
unexplained.
As the memories came back as
dreams. I feel all over what I
once did before.
The happiness, laughter, sorrow,
and love.

Susan Larson

A TRIBUTE TO MOTHER

My mother is to me
All that she ought to be.
For always to me, she is kind,
When she gives me a piece of mind.
Even though she boogies to rock 'n roll,
In certain ways she reminds me of the old.
And when she speaks,
So soft and meek;
Her words reflect
So much intellect.
The little things that she does,
Which show to me such love,
Are too precious to ever trade
For even silver, gold or jade.
Seeing a smile of joy on that face
Is something I would never replace.
My mother means more to me
Than any earth, sky or sea.
The word "Mother" will always be
The symbol of sweet love to me.

Lisa M. Freeze

COME ALONG WITH ME

I will take you within me
as I journey far from home,
For it will be long and weary
and I will often be alone.

I will leave you a regarded trail
of treads burdened in the road,
Depressed by pain and misery
as I carry a heavy load.

I will keep you tucked away
since you can't be at my side,
Warm impressions within my mind
the safest place to hide.

I will join you inventively
with dreams of old and new,
A few stolen moments of tenderness
would ease the others that are blue.

Betty L. Frierson

YOU ARE

You are
The love I feel
From the very center of my being.
You are
The light in my eyes
Whenever I speak of My Love.
You are
The warmth that surrounds me
And gives me that special glow.
You are
That certain feeling
That stirs from within.
You are
Special. As none other could ever be.
You are
Mine. Through some great force above,
For which I am grateful.
You are
My world, my joy, my love
I thank God every day, that . . . You are.

Rosemary A. Carruthers

LIFE WITHOUT YOU

With tear-dimmed eyes I know I miss you
And long to hold you in my arms once more,
It's been eight years since I could kiss you
But the memories are as fresh as they were before.
God called you home to be with Him in Heaven
Now I sit and dream about you all alone.
I still love you as I did in forty seven
And I still don't have a man to call my own.
You are as dear to me as you were long ago—
Since first I wrote a poem about your love
And I hope some day to hold you in my arms again
When God will also take me home above.
You've got two grandchildren that you have never seen.
And a son-in-law you still have yet to meet,
But we try to tell them just how much you'd love them,
That the memories about you are so sweet
And we know that they would love you just as we do,
When our family again becomes complete.
So wait patiently in Heaven 'til we see you
And life again will be so very sweet.

Frances Hough

MY GREATEST LOVE

Every day with you Lord
Is sweeter than the day before
I praise you, I love you
I give you my heart
You are the one I adore
With all of this joy
And the grace that you bring
It fills me so much
That I just want to sing
I want you, I crave you
I need you so much
Save me oh Lord, from that Satan's clutch
I know I'm a sinner, from the top of the line
I pray to you Jesus, for you're so divine
When trials confront me in everyday life
Oh it reminds me of all my strife
But then you come quickly
And make me so strong
I yearn for you Jesus
All the day long

Steven L. Gifford

ALL I WANT

I don't want a million dollar home
And I don't care if I ever get to Rome
All I want are the simple things in life
Like a man that loves me, for the rest of my life

I don't need a diamond ring
And I don't care if I continue working
All I want are the simple things in life
Like a man to be thoughtful, and make my life bright

I don't want a brand-new car
Or a mink coat, that's a bit much by far
All I want are the simple things in life
Like a man to be with me, each and every night

I don't want a yacht or plane
And I don't need a live-in maid
All I want are the simple things in life
Like a man to love me and call me his wife.

June Drao

WITHOUT YOU

Living my life without you,
is making my life very blue.
I feel sorrow and pain,
these feelings are driving me insane.

I want to reach out and touch you,
you make me feel so brand-new.
My feelings grow stronger each day,
and I hope and pray you'll be back some day.

There is no light in my life,
I feel like someone has stabbed me with a knife.
From day to day, I don't know what to do,
this sorrow, pain and love is from missing you.

One day I hope you'll take me back,
this heart lacks love from you.
If I can have this love from you,
my life will be filled and I will know what to do.

But for now, my life is blue,
and I have to live my life without you.

Joy Reneé DeLoe

TO MY DAD

What! write for my Dad a poem so fine,
And have it all perfect in meter and line?
Why, I'd not even try it for fear, at the last,
I'd find that I'd started too great a task.

For my Dad, as Dads go, is the best of them all,
The King or the Dictator, the great or the small.
And lines of great eloquence, though perfect in rhyme,
Of my love won't convince him, that old Dad of mine.

So I'll ask Father Time for the moment to stop
And slowly unwind the hands of the clock;
That these little-girl words I might lisp in his ear,
"Daddy dear, I sure love you," then he'll know I'm sincere.

Hazel C. Sack

YOU WERE THERE

As I look back in my short life
I see that you were always there

You were there when I got my first 'A'
And you were there for the first squeak of my horn
You were there for my ups and downs
My highs and lows

You pulled me through when I thought no one could
You cheered me up when I thought no one would

You watched me go from the toys
To the boys

You stuck by me —
You held me when I cried
And loved me when I sighed

You've done so much for me
I just wanted to say thank you
And I Love You
Because you were there for me

Joylin Droney

EDWARD

Easy going, he makes friends
wherever he goes.
Devilish by nature, he knows
how to enjoy life.
Wonderfully caring and loving,
he makes me feel like number one.
Angelic-looking when he's sleeping,
he looks like a little boy.
Really, he's a fantastic husband as
well as lover and friend.
Doing all he can to make me happy,
he's succeeded in every way.

Anne V. Brady

BREAKUP

The time we spent together,
when we both felt alone.
The time was now to learn.
To be more than friends if we could.

The time was ours to share together.
And we both realized there are times,
When we've got to be free.
Time to see all that we're able.
Time to let go.
Time to seek all that's there.
Time to be on our own.

Jacqueline P. Wirtz

SKIES OF PARADISE

So near was heaven
When we were young,
So blue were the skies above,
So precious the savor
Of life each day
While softly we fell in love.
Still sweeter the savor
Of life today,
Though swiftly the years have flown,
And bluer the skies
Of our paradise
Where love has so tenderly grown.

David J. Creager

THE LOVE OF GOD

How much greater is the love,
That He had for you and me;
To lay down his life,
On the cross at Calvary.
To die so that everyone could,
Have a very special right;
A chance to have their names,
Written in the Lamb's book of life.
The love of God is more,
Precious than any love I know;
It lasts from everlasting to everlasting,
And follows us wherever we go.

Patti Woodard

GOD'S CREATION

Lord, when I behold the World,
And all Thy Creation,
The sun, the moon, and stars,
I bow in adoration!

I marvel at the wonder
Of all things great and small,
The orderliness of Winter,
Summer, Spring and Fall.

The majesty of the Mountains,
Beauty of the Sea,
The fragrance of the flowers,
So beautiful to see.

I thank Thee dear Lord
For all of Thy Creation,
And I humbly bow
In awe and adoration!

Lucile Skinner Spradling

CONFESSION

I confess the best communion
Between the true lovers
Is their contemplative silence
Eloquently revealing
Their mute adoration
Through the spiritual glimpses
Of their innocent eyes
By solemnly transfiguring
A soul to soul conversation
Without any words
Of praise or adulation
But silently becoming
One body, one soul, one heart
Going into the eternity of love
As two illuminated beings
Partaking the same ecstasy
In the same happiness
Of total understanding
Created only for them
By the supreme quietness.

George Alexe

PEARL ELIZABETH

She had that look of being stern
her beauty you could not forget.
She tried so hard for us to learn
the ways of the world step by step.

She worked so hard to pay our way
hoping we'd grow to be so fine.
Restitution we'd have to pay
but she stood by time after time.

As time wills and age starts to show
but beauty in life is still there.
Her tender love will never go
as life survives to let her care.

Pearl Elizabeth is her name
showing kindness in every way,
Even when blue her love's the same,
a mother's love brightens by day.

Terry C. Snyder

IN THE DAYS TO COME

In the days to come you'll discover
How incredible the path
Which led me first to hear you
And then discern your ways

How methodical the motions
That led us each to know and feel
That one could lead the other
In extending roads unpaved

Contrasting to past experiences
May this new love last and last
And follow onward ever
Assiduously as now

For a wish has come true
(amazingly so)
As if fate had read my heart
(Assiduously also)
As one prompted to know
— the yearnings
Within another's soul

Edith Buckley

WRITTEN TO DAVE FROM MY HEART

Every day I think of you
You're always in my heart,
We'll always be together
And never far apart.
If I had the words to say
What all is in my soul,
You would never doubt my love
And that babe is my goal.
I'll always stand beside you
Through good times and the bad,
I'll be there when you need me
For comfort when you're sad.
Now I will always love you
Through all eternity,
You have come into my heart
Your love it was the key.

Missy Meakin

I LOVE YOU

As a little girl I recall
Drawing pictures for the wall,
Bringing you dandelions,
Making paper valentines,
And saying I love you Mom.

While in elementary school
Making you Mother's Day cards
Surprising you with breakfast in bed
Bringing you lilacs
And saying I love you Mom.

In my teens I recall
Disagreeing over simple things
Wanting to be just like you
Making supper after school
Adn saying I love you Mom.

As an adult it's clear to me
Deeds are only a sign
Communicating what is felt
More deeply in my mind.

Bonnie Zaborski-Beck

BABY, YOU'RE THE ONE

I've been waiting long, my dear,
For the right girl to appear —
Now, my Baby, you're the only one for me.

Other girls are passing by,
But they do not catch my eye —
Because, Baby, you're the one attracting me.

When I know that you are near,
Of the world I have no fear —
Because, Baby, you're the one inspiring me.

When I leave to go afar,
You become my Northern Star —
Because, Baby, it's your light that's guiding me.

When I hold you in my arms,
I am happy with your charms —
Because, Baby, you're the one who's loving me.

Baby, tell me that you care,
That you always will be there —
Because, Baby, I will need you loving me.
Because, Baby, you're the only one for me.

Laura Brown Lane

MISSION OF LOVE

They wanted to go to the moon,
But, instead they touched a star;
And looked into the face of God,
Which wasn't very far.

For, He knew of their coming,
And they knew of their quest;
Taken in a blaze of glory,
And honored at their death.

The Space Shuttle Challenger's flight soared high,
As God opened his pearly gates;
And beckoned to his children, "Come,"
For them, heaven awaits.

He carefully reached out His hand,
In God they kept their trust;
And in the twinkling of an eye,
He quickly pulled them up.

For in our hearts they left behind,
Our minds, their memory,
Of seven voyagers now with God,
There, life eternally.

Hazel Mae Parron

HEAVENLY LOVE

Roses from heaven shower me with love
Petals of courage and faith and hope
Serve to soothe my lonely heart

Angels of love shed light on my life
Filling it with inner healing and
A promise for a better tomorrow

God's love expresses in many different ways
I need only to open my eyes
And my heart and accept His miracles

Susan Lea Bacon

PERFECT LOVE

All I want is to do you good; I want nothing from you.
When you treat me bad, I love you still more, because
that is when you need more love from me.
Even before we met, since the beginning of time, the
world was prepared for my love for you.
All I want to do is serve you;
Take me I'm yours;
Use me;
Abuse me;
Own me;
That's what I lived for, even before I met you —
I walked the rocky road to be prepared for loving you.
When I walked through frost I learned to keep you warm;
When I walked through fire I learned to keep you cool;
When I merely sat bored with nothing to do,
I learned to wait with joy till I marry you.
Others might think you are nothing special,
Except that your beautiful face might lead them astray,
But you are the person meant for me
To sing, "I love you," throughout every day.

Stephen Feinland

THE ROMANTIC DART

Two embrace with a kiss, and rollick
As the waves clasp each other,
In our courtship for love's sake,
That challenges the gods together.
What is passion but a culmination?
From moonbeams and roses,
Valentines whispering low
Laced in print that glows,
Rays of light on the ocean;
Aphrodisiacs written on the sand.
This closely-knit strand of unbroken thread,
Interloping a flowery turn,
That has the cream-white rosebud,
A perfect flower to open and blossom,
None quite are sweeter in form,
To place in a vase, with their flush petal tips,
When the white rose breathes of true love;
Saints in the firmament! A red rose ceases to live!
While winds in the willows blow,
Cupid does appear with a bow and arrow.

Rose Mary Gallo

NEVER-ENDING EVERGREEN

Daisies grow and wither on the hill,
I forget you not, and never will,
Those precious moments that linger on,
Blue-violet along paths as colorful,
Dried out leaves, to fashion into a sachet,
Thoughts as you stand above in death.
O'er the moody darkness on earth,
A true perennial from June to fall
That you planted in our rock garden
Captivates the silver-green foliage,
Magnificent sweet-smelling lavender
Such are the dreams forever after;
Therefore, you must know my emotion,
Longingly, I have for your image,
While the stars had more to offer;
The ivy spreads upon your burial
Woody vines in heavenly beauty,
Not far-off beyond the mountains
Are landmasses, higher than the horizon,
In sight is the cold, cold grave where you lay.

Rose Mary Gallo

MY LOVE

Love flamed in me, body and soul:
Kindled by sense of touch and sight;
Cooled by present embraceless role,
Which fires desire for lost delight.

Only in dreams I see my Dear
And feel her arms, soft 'round my neck,
And warm red lips, drawing me near
to consummate our passion's beck.

Awake am I in distant land
By strange decree and circumstance:
I can't fulfill my Love's demand
That would refire our cooled romance.

Cruel Fate, my Love is far from me —
In arms, armed with proximity!

Art Ellis

ONLY FOR YOU

I may have a gleam in my eye,
I may have a tender sigh,
Only for you, only for you,
I may have a dream of the future,
With things of great allure,
Only for you, only for you,
I may get a wonderful thrill,
Doing things against my will,
Only for you, only for you,
My darling can't you see,
All these things are meant to be
Only for you, only for you,
I may have a dream about love,
With a kiss that is filled with bliss,
Only for you, only for you,
My heart is afire with desire,
Only for you.

Eleanor Ashlee McKissick

AQUARIUS RISING

Leo smiles gently,
romance in hands touching
Lips nibbling,
words softly spoken.
The lion wallows
in romance.
Love is necessary
as life itself.

No more romantic, compelling
lover alive.
Then Aquarius rising
opens his mouth
and words tumble
out
"Love you? Yes,
I love you — sometimes."

Charlotte M. Edwards

Whispering secrets —
nestled upon moonlit shores
lovers and seashells

Sheldon Young

IN TWILIGHT'S YEARNING

Twilight beckons
passion's embrace,

meet face to face —
Out in the meadow
'neath a starry sky,
They pledge their love
will never die.

As life unfolds
they build their dream,
Of a prairie house
standing next to a stream —
Where the babbling waters
quietly flow,
In the soft spring breeze
where flowers grow.

Answering love
In twilight's yearning,
They tenderly kiss
with passion's burning —
Sealing their love
they become man and wife,
Giving their dreams
the promise of life!

Christy P. Joans

I THINK

I think of the day we met,
I smile

I think of the fun we had together,
I miss it

I think of our times together,
I cry

I think of our talks together,
I loved them

I think of you,
I try to forget

I think of my life ahead,
without you

I think of having to accept you're gone,
I think I understand

I think you would like me to move on,
be happy

I think I can handle you watching me,
from up above

Lori Heim

TANKA

His soft lips met mine
As dew upon a rosebud
In early morning

Then, swiftly, he left my arms
Love's deep joys were almost ours

Diane L. Salisbury

IT MAY BE LOVE

I've got something, I don't know what.
It may be love, and it may be not.
He looks so handsome, and so sweet,
Everytime we chance to meet
I want to hug and kiss him on the spot.
It may be love, and it may be not.
I want to be near him all the time.
His smile is like golden sunshine.
I don't know what I've got.
It could be love, and it could be not.
His one sweet kiss set my soul on fire.
It filled my heart with sweet desire.
Love light sparkles in his eyes.
To say he loves me, would be no surprise.
What's eating me I cannot tell.
Am I in love, or just not well?
I've got something, I don't know what.
It may be love, and it may be not.

Lillie M. McConkey

LOVE/HATE

Love,
Is here.
Deep within men's souls.
Everlasting.
Never faltering.
Once in a while, though,
It may play hide and seek,
Or it may go into hibernation.
It may even change its form
From time to time.
Sometimes, it goes astray
And can play havoc
With one's emotions.
It can pick you up,
Or it can bring you down.
And, when it becomes too much to bear,
It may even turn into
Hate.

Marsha Riddick

SUSTAINING LOVE

Branches swing gently
beautified by pinkish blossoms,
dogwood flourishes
sheltered under the oak,
subtle forest companion to
masculine heavy trunk.
Years have bent its limbs.

Under vaultlike canopy of
reddish oaken leaves
close-grained bark
crackles yearly in the frost,
dappled branches fall,
fewer flowers grow.
Next to the diseased oak,
tree endures, like a
woman dutiful to the end,
loving the stature of her man.

Emma J. Blanch

VIGILANT WANDERER

Wrapped in the blue-gray vapor
Of Indian summer's twilight,
In chorus crickets call, as locus bravo,
A moth's solo ballet veiled in moonlight.
Fluttering lace delicately borders
A velvet dew and jeweled sky,
As faint leaves rustle applause, gently, to harmonize.

Touching clouds whisper like a lover
Approaching and caressing the radiant glow,
Capturing warmth within soft billows,
Embraces quietly wrestle the cloaking folds.
The heady scent of nature's fullness
Speaks of ripened fruit that warms the soul,
Breaths of mist-green flavors taste of future cold.

Tangled satin ribbons fall,
Like streaming curls of loosened hair.
Tenderly, my face against you pillowed
As night serenades, alone, we nestle there.

Virginia Carol Walker

WALKER, VIRGINIA CAROL. Born: Kankakee, Illinois, 7-18-51; Married: 3-5-77 to Michael Wayne Walker; Education: Olivet Nazarene College, B.S., Nursing, 1979; Occupations: Registered Nurse, Clinical Nursing Instructor; Poetry: 'The Sea, An Ode to the Divemaster,' *American Poetry Anthology*, 1986; Comments: *Many of the themes in my poetry center around my love of the elements. The beauty of their honest magnificence is appealing; their majesty enduring, and their sheer power, truly awesome and exhilarating. This is the part of poetry I enjoy, feeling the capture of a moment that is timeless, the communion of humanity with nature. It is this stirring ability to love that sets us apart, yet draws us closer to a deeper appreciation of life's mysteries.*

BE GENTLE LOVE

Out of the darkness to the light of day
I'm wanting to earn your love if I may

Come sing my tune Lover, come home to me
You'll find peace here I promise, come be free

Hold out your hand and caress my lips
Feel me beside you, link the wine we sip

Speak to me lover, bring me sweet dreams
No longer a virgin though sometimes it seems

Carry me on, don't let me go
Wandering hither too alone in the cold

The road to your door swings back and forth
I'm not sure what I'm saying or what it's worth

Don't leave me tomorrow, don't leave me behind
Don't you know that love can be opened or blind?

Teach me your wisdom if you can share
My body keeps aching when you're not there

Build me a castle with your love inside
I'm thirsty for you love, be gentle and kind

When the night is over, the dove's gonna fly
So come to me lover, don't say goodbye.

Debra Sue Peterson

LOVE YOURSELF

Years ago, I wrote a little DITTY
It's helped me when times were really GRITTY.
And if it helps you, I'll be paid enough
When life for you, is getting rough,
It helps much more than SELF-PITY!

Here 'tis, and it goes like this:

I love myself — I hug myself —
I put my arms around my waist.
When I look in the mirror I admire my face.
I'm nuts about myself!

Remember this, then about, *yourself.*
IT'S THE ONLY YOURSELF you'll ever have.
So be good to it whether times be good or BAD —
AND YOU'LL FIND YOURSELF *LESS* SAD.

Love yourself and you'll love the world,
And the world will love you too.
But to love yourself
There's things that *you* alone must do:
You *must* LIVE RIGHT, BE HELPFUL,
COMPASSIONATE, FORTHRIGHT AND KIND.

Only, this way can we truly love ourselves
And gain the ultimate peace of mind,
That builds our strength to fight adversity
EVERY TIME.

Joshua C. Stevens

JULIA.

Lith. & Pub. by N. Currier. 2 Spruce St. N. Y.

THE FLOWER GIRL.

TODAY

Today when I was held in your warm embrace
I wanted to be the ruler of time,
I wanted to stop the clock so I could stay
In your arms and be near the warm vibrations
Of your heart.
But alas, I cannot stop time or be near you forever.

But, I can for all the tomorrows to come
Close my eyes and the memory of you will return
Again and again.

Fern Martin

MARTIN, FERN LOUISE. Born: Williston, North Dakota; Single; Occupation: Office Worker; Poetry: 'The Telephone Call,' *American Poetry Anthology,* 1986; Other Writings: I am currently writing a novel which I hope to have finished this year, ready for editing by 1987; Comments: *My inspiration to write is drawn from the environment, my loved ones, and the many people I have come to know throughout my life. My four lovely daughters are my biggest fan club and supporters.*

LOVE: WHAT WAS, WHAT IS, WHAT CANNOT BE

The love I had long ago there
is not the love that now I share.
But both live inside, both e'er I see.
One should be lost, the other found.
But each one's complete, each one's sound.
Each a whole, each a part of me.

Now each one shares a part of my heart.
Now each one dares to rage its own part.
Now each refuses to set me free.
Outside a calm, inside a rage.
Each stars a part on my heart's stage.
Each wells and leaps, ne'er to let me be.

Both exist here. Yes, side by side.
Neither holds back, they both abide.
Just as twins, they share, they feel, they know.
Within they are twain, without but one.
Covert they're bound, but overt they shun.
Neither could accept the other's glow.

Why, oh why, is it my love each they share,
While, for me sharing them, never I dare!

John A. Short

TO CARRIE

Heavenly were the times we spent together,
how I wish that it would never have to end

But like the sun going down, a new day has to dawn dear
so we will have a chance to do this all again.

Maybe this time will be different, I surely hope so
no more hurtin', no more harmin', no more lies

Just to hold you tight my darling, and caress you
makes me know that everything will be all right.

Yes these happy memories that I have of you
just fill my heart with joy when I recall

the sweetness of the you I fell in love with
having you I knew I had it all.

All my hopes of holding you again are gone dear
like a wisp of smoke disappearing in the air

And this life of mine is now hollow, and empty
no one left to love, and no one left to care.

A sweeter love I have never known dear
than this love that you have given me

And no greater joy could I have imagined
than sharing life with you my dear Carrie.

A. Mujahid Shakir

ALONE

Outside his door, he stands — alone,
Through his lips, escapes a moan —

Opening the door, he stumbles inside,
Tears flow now, tears he's been trying to hide —

His eyes wander, around the room,
This once happy place, now filled with gloom —

The fireplace — is cold and bare,
A bright, warm fire, usually burns there —

The house is dark, he doesn't want light,
He stands there alone, his throat so tight —

She's not there, to talk over the day,
Not there to cheer him, in her own special way —

In such a short time, he misses so much,
Simple, small things, her gentle touch —

There are so many things, that will never be,
"Oh God, why has she gone from me?"

The saddest day, in his entire life,
This day, he buried his precious wife —

How can he go on? For when she died,
He also died inside . . .

Janice Reed Hamlin

TRULY SOULMATES

Tasting the salty laden air
And gazing out onto green
I met your forever eyes,
The glimmering pools reflect,
A remembrance now fleeting
Secret moments flame like a Phoenix
Blazing memory of Eternity's ash.

Energy pulling inward,
Abyss of the soul,
Grasping for your presence
Chants within me echo,
As sounds trapped within a seashell
Constant tumbling vibrations
Lost, but yet, whole.

Silent footsteps melt into waves
On warm sandy beaches,
Walking toward my destiny
In search of my everlasting.

Virginia Carol Walker

TOGETHERNESS

It's easy to love someone,
  when they are part of you;
Living, breathing outside your body,
  and yet such a part of you,
That sense of well-being is lost,
  when they are gone from you.

That other person can surely be,
  the living memory of all your days,
The fullness of your life together;
  an experience to lovingly appraise,
For life is full of events,
  some deserving your praise.

Compatability and togetherness,
  spending much time together,
Stabilizes a relationship;
  that love might weather,
Whatever trial and hardship,
  never once showing a white feather.

Luke Nathaniel Baxter

TRY AGAIN

Sometimes
Love
Can make you cry.
It holds
Your heart
So tenderly
Then tosses it aside,
Walks away
And leaves you
To cry.
Time
Heals
And your heart
Will mend,
But Love can make
You cry
Again
  And again
    And again . . .

Roxanne McJunkin

SWEET SURRENDER

I like people of all ages — respect the old once bold —
Yet children I love, they occupy the foremost first place . . .
In my heart; when in good mood — are without fault —
Their high-spirited-energy smile, blushes their face.
  When involved in games, they are beyond norms or measure —
  Winning shines the eyes, with a glow of joy . . . and satisfaction . . .
  Can a loser have such enormous pleasure?
  Being beaten, by the playfulness — of their mind in action!
With delight I listened to inspiring instruction . . . without a sense . . .
To me, taken over by the fantasy — of their mind —
Roaming free, gathering intensity so immense;
That overwhelmed me, making me feel ignorant and blind!
  It escaped boundaries — of my limitation —
  And captured me . . . while out of base . . .
  Physically, and more so — by their vivid, sharp imagination;
  I retained my resigned dignity, and wisdom in a lost case!
Their vigor conquered, and made me their perpetual slave —
Trapped by sharp minds, and hands so small . . . yet soft of gentle gender . . .
Determined to achieve victory, fighting for this purpose — very brave;
To enforce a total defeat; the enemy never had . . . such a sweet surrender!

Martin R. Tarlo

THE MIRROR AND I

From fall to spring the mirror watched her death and turned away
And I confess that all I did for her was sit and vainly pray
"Out of morning into glory, I beg you, snow-seasoned ivory tower
Please turn her bruised heart of ice back into spring's sun-warmed flower."

How deep and dark was her abyss when false love failed her
How sad to see her cling to futile hopes that would not die
I watched her wither away before I reached out to help her
But without her lover in her life . . . she would not try.

Before you mirror, she brushed gold hair and dreamed of days gone by
Unfeeling, you watched the tears and deep soul-wrenching pains
Uncaring, you saw her falter, cruelly, you stood idly by
Till she was one with the cold grey winter rains.

Alone now in my guilt, I must live on with weighty burdens of my crime
Sweet girl, she died for love, she will never live again
And you, mirror, keep mocking me like some evil, heartless mime
Daily on my face projecting haggard re-runs of her pain.

Doris Irene Warren

MY WIFE

I paint your face forever 'cross the canvas of my mind —
Your midnight hair in rippling waves for gently swelling lines.
And dreams we chased together, a backdrop for all time —
Starting in the chapel when you promised to be mine.

Our years together soften the hardships that we knew —
The trials and tribulations from being married to Air Force Blue.
The many moves and crazy hours both here and overseas too —
Keep service marriage survivals reserved for but a few.

You stuck it out and saw me through the hardest years of all —
Your worries when the war was "over" but they shot at us till Fall.
My constant trips on down the road and I couldn't even call —
Yet all the time you were smiling; calling it a breeze and a ball.

Aye, we've come this far together and our path's still down the way —
Where it will lead, what it will bring: I guess, but who can say?
Years ago we took an oath to weather; come what may —
And I'm thankful once again that it's you beside me today.

Hawk Freeman

TO SEVEN ASTRONAUTS, WITH LOVE

A Tribute

Seven American astronauts
charged with a special mission,
brimming with excitement and hope,
full of Life,
filled with Love.

How we love and admire you.

You inspired us, your poured vitality
into us from your inner strength.
Our youth hoped to be like you,
to follow in your footsteps
to also be pioneers and to share your visions.

What an impact you have had on us.

You are not coming back to us,
your spacecraft is gone.
We are shocked, we are filled with sorrow.
And yet, oh, how lucky we are to have known you,
to have shared your high ideals, to have been touched by you.

We pay tribute to you.
You are part of us and our Nation, forever, in Love.

Ann Dutcher

I PROMISE

I promise to trust you,
In all aspects of our relationship.
I promise not to let suspicions become overbearing.

I promise to give you a smile,
When you are sad.
I promise to hug you when you appear lonely.

I promise to reach out to you,
In times of trouble.
I promise to back away when you give a sign.

I promise to always listen,
No matter what the time.
I promise to always reassure whether you need it or not.

I promise to always walk beside you,
Ready to catch you if you fall.
I promise to always hold your hand,
To help you remember I'm here.

I promise to always thank God,
For letting me share,
In the miracle,
Of loving you.

Vicky J. Harling

HAPPY BIRTHDAY TRUCKER

Happy birthday trucker although
you're more than a trucker to me you're the man
I married and the one I love and the head of
our family.
When I hear the sound of the jacob
break near I know you're right down the road
then I thank the Lord for bringing you home
and helping you deliver that load.

Carol A. Guglielmoni

I'LL NEVER DOUBT

Suddenly, she died today.
And, in a dozen ways,
Died all else away:

No song of bird
Was fondly heard;
Nor lowing of the herd.

Suddenly the dollar tree
Sagged in utter agony
At her loss to it and me.

Frogs disappear, failing to croak;
Salal embracing honeysuckle —
both hearts break;
The choke-cherry with anguish choked.

Rover's dumb founded, and sorely befuddled.
Tabby and parakeet in silent remorse are cuddled;
All semblance of order, disarrayed and scuttled.

Ah yes, her dying today, so suddenly,
Has washed all doubt from me
That plants and animals truly love, feel,
Care and see!

Carl P. Hansen

LIKE THE PHOENIX

What grief and levity it will be
if my frenzy, my dreams, my moan,
never again will reach my Sultan.

I did try in vain to avoid my doom
when he impassable, affable but cruel
dumped my love, my soul, down to gloom.

He was my sweet robin bird, my torrid desire
who gave me the feeling that I was sexy
till he grabbed my dream and set it on fire.

I felt that he wanted to give me vigor
to caress my life, my fears, my ardor,
but all was stolen for my Karma, away
and left me the shame's laugh, on my way.

He was mine like in a dream vowed
until upon his love's petals, snowed.
Our passion was a mirage, a blaze,
an eternal flame amid the maze.

It was something like the Phoenix
that immolated itself but rose alive
so as me, to live and to forgive.

Eleni Moustaka

ACHING ARMS

Stealing a touch
Doesn't satisfy my urge
To hold you in my arms
To squeeze you
To hug the back of your neck
Can I touch you freely without making excuses
It only makes my arms ache more
Seeing you and not holding you

Deborah Pritchard

I NEED YOU

I need you when night is drawing near
And shadows cover the earth from sight —
When the lonely night sounds I hear —
I need you to hold me tight.

I need you when the moon shines above
And the garden is bathed in moonlight.
I need you to whisper soft and low —
And comfort me throughout the night.

I need you when the sun comes up
And floods the fields with golden rays.
I need you and your loving arms at night
To keep me safe until the break of day.

Pansy Fain

THE PASSING OF SAM

Leaving bare branches in its path
The wind howls
And slams the barn door shut.

The hoot owl flutters in the night air
Its cover lost in the tempest-swirl.

From my window melancholy ivy vines
cling like icy lace.

My thoughts about you linger

I listen for your distant footsteps
Hurried, in the early morning chill
The corn spread and pail returned
To its hook and the doorway filled
With your frame and proud look.

It's Sunday and There are no sounds

For under trampled leaves, soft and wet
Buried in the snow . . . lies my Sam.

Patricia Elmore

THE BOND

Look into my eyes and you will see
A reflection of your love for me
Love so strong it should have no bounds
And yet it's forced to have no sounds.

Memories shared of times that are past
Stay with us to make love last
Although our lives are worlds apart
Each has a piece of the other's heart.

Feelings that keep us close in mind
A love that's different from any kind
Silent promises that cannot be broken
Words of love that are left unspoken.

Both so afraid to reach out and touch
We hear words to music that tell so much
But if your love we could proclaim
Would it then remain the same?

Love so true, so deep and strong
Still it has no words — it has no song.

Kit Cronin

A LIFE SHARED BY TWO

It's two radiant people
So deeply in love.
Beginning a future
They're both dreaming of.

It's sweet and soft music
A mother's fond tears.
As she thinks of her son
In his childhood years.

It's a beautiful bride
With a pretty bouquet.
And her father's warm kiss
As he gives her away.

It's a happy young groom
His eyes filled with pride.
As he welcomes his sweetheart
And they stand side by side.

It's a promise fulfilled
A dream that's come true.
And the first happy step
In a life shared by two.

May Adams

I feel lost in
your feelings
because I'm afraid
Your feelings
aren't true
you don't speak
Certain
I don't mean to
confuse you
But I'm lost and
need a hand to reach
out to

Viki Beard

in and out

into space and out of time
a riverbed with measured rhyme.
trickle in and trickle out.
a fish swims happily with no doubt.

into wind and out of rain
a dead end street and clogged up drain.
shuffle in and shuffle out.
old man wonders what it's all about.

into light and out of heat
a convention hall now find a seat.
mumble out and mumble in.
useless thoughts tossed in a bin.

into sight and out of blind
swirling colors that dazzle the mind.
falling out and falling in.
chant a mantra forgive your sins.

into love and out of hate
a world that lives in a thoughtless state.
dying in and all around.
but nowhere can a soul be found.

Brendan Curtis

FADING MEMORY

Bitter tears streamed down his face
As they laid his wife to rest.
Though saddened by the death of her,
He knew he had been blessed.

Haunted by his love for her,
For she meant the world to him,
Soon afterward he realized
A new life he should begin.

Though but a fading memory now,
The old man struggles on
And longingly awaits the day
When he'll live with her as one.

Mary Hackbart

A CHILD

A child is a living, feeling, growing
Blossom.
A child reaches
And touches a spot deep within,
A place never touched before.
A child is beauty:
Each smile and every tear
Is real.
A child is born pure and clean,
Bearing no grudges, feeling no hatred.
A child's hug can never bring pain.
Their love,
And only their love,
Can never hurt . . .

Julie A. Fowler

MISSIN' YOU

When there's no YOU with me
It's like the moon without a star
A story book without the words
A horn without a car

It's like a pen without the ink
A "DONG" without the "DING"
Without no YOU around — well, Gee!
I'm not worth a blessed thing!

Irma Louise Lowe

TIME

Passing through time
with him on my mind.
Wondering when the day will arrive
when our two paths shall re-engage.

I'm longing for that day to be soon,
but one never knows how soon . . .
Soon, could be such a short time
or a very long time.

My heart grows with more love
each day for this loved one.
I hope someday soon, this
reconciliation shall come forth.

Marguerite Brugos

LOVING

Your lips touching me
Seeking — demanding — knowing
The pressure coming — going
Softly asking!

The feel of you touching me
Breast to breast —
Thigh to thigh —
And all that's in between.

Your presence enters me
Fills me — completes me
Constant — ever moving
Taking me to heights I've never known.

'Tis a sweetness beyond words.

Kit Conrad

CONRAD, KITTY KAREN. Pen Name: Kit Conrad; Born: Louisiana, Missouri, 5-31-38; Education: Registered Nurse, 1960; Occupation: Surgical Nurse; Poetry: 'Questions,' *American Poetry Anthology,* 1983; 'Solitary People,' *The Art of Poetry, A Treasury of Contemporary Verse,* 1985; 'Loving Touch,' *American Poetry Anthology,* 1985; Comments: *I write what I feel — I write for myself. I hope others share my feelings or at least understand my words.*

METAMORPHOSIS

If I had been able to experience
the mysterious loss of you,
If I had had a certain knowing
that I would lose forever
that infant in my arms,
I might have known panic then.

As it is
I treasure
with wonder
your vital essence
in the adult body
to which you have slowly metamorphosed.

Marie Zaharias Daughters

MOTHER

Your smiling face no more I see,
In vision though, before me still,
Your loving warmth and kind concern,
Reach from the past my heart to still.

Mother dear I loved you then,
Yet, more so now you've gone from me,
I reach to memories' bygone days,
And cherish love that used to be.

To have you heal my many hurts,
To have you soothe my careworn heart,
To grasp the peace of childhood's days,
That only you to me could part.

Though you're gone, you're here it seems,
In my heart you'll always be,
You always gave, asked no return,
My first love, tried and true to me.

So selfish me yearns for a time,
And only God knows where or when,
I'll touch your cheek and hold your hand,
We'll be together once again.

Jack Williams

YOUR BABY

Jesus sent you from above
A little child for you to love.
A little babe to rock to sleep,
A precious life for you to keep.

Teach your little one a prayer
That Jesus Christ is always there.
And that you'll keep him safe and warm —
And Jesus takes away all harm.

Give all you can of love and care.
Teach right and always be fair.
Give strength and feeling to be sure
And see your child is good and pure.

And with each kiss and soft caress
Show your babe that tenderness
Is just the kind of care and love
That Jesus sends down from above.

And when your little child has grown,
Make sure the things which he has known
Are good and strong — right and true.
These things, Mother, God expects of you.

Lynn Rogers

FOR YOU

For you love
I smile
For you love I'll stay
With you I'll linger
For more than a while
And to you love
Must I say
That with you love
I live
As I never lived before

Donna L. Hill

MOTHER LOVE

The silent mist lay on the lake
Waving a shroud of glistening white,
Breathing a whisper of golden glow
Where the pines stood guard throughout
the night.

Below, on a bed of needles and moss,
A fawn began to breathe his first
Soft breath of life as dawn arrived;
And finding mother's warmth, he nursed.

The velvet doe began to bathe
Her son and felt the love flow through,
As once again, the miracle
Of love and birth and life renew.

Mary Alice Rich

SEALED IN MEMORY

Sealed in memory of yesterday
a love which grew like the roses of May,
Opening its heart to your sun
as I rushed to you with arms out flung.

Sealed in the memory of yesterday
a passion unquenchable in thirst,
I drank deeply of your love
placing your desires first.

Time has sped so quickly by
your love has floated away,
leaving all the unanswered "whys"
Sealed in the memory of yesterday.

Loraine Lewis

NEVER ALONE

So empty I felt till I found you,
A void that would always remain.
A soul which was half of nothing
Feeling loneliness, fear and pain.

When was it I finally reached upward
And touching the hem of your clothes
Felt instantly loved and cared for
And fell in a state of repose.

Oh, why had my eyes never opened
To the vision of love I now see?
So freely and willingly given
To all men, but especially me.

Rosemary A. Carruthers

KNOWING YOU

I always thought
if a heart would break
One quick hard blow
is what it would take

But oh, my Darling
that was before I knew
The exquisite agony
of loving you

Anne D. Barnett

CATS

Long hair dancing in the moonlight
Upon magical little feet
Scuttling about preparing mischief
Seemingly oh, so sweet

You watch and wait and listen
As if it were all a dream
Those prancing ghosts and goblins
With delight, you want to scream

Eyes piercing the murky darkness
Twinkling yellow when yours they meet
Disembodied orbs that flit and flow
Will they trick or will they treat?

'Tis eerie to observe the cats you love
Transformed in the night's still air
To creatures that take your breath away
Family feline? Perhaps. Beware!

Who knows? Who cares why cats are cats?
And we but meek voyeurs
Seeking out vicarious thrills
In frivolous feline affairs . . .

G. L. Butler

BUTLER, GEORGE LARRY. Born: Calistoga, California, 10-2-49; Education: Napa Community College, A.A., Liberal Arts, 1969; CSC Sonoma, B.A., Sociology, B.A., Psychology, 1977; Postgraduate work in Sociology, Psychology, Anthropology at CSU Chico, 1978; Occupation: Librarian, Actor; Memberships: National Writer's Association; U.S. Parachute Association; Screen Actor's Guild; American Federation of Television and Radio Artists; Poetry: 'Bubbles in a Stream,' *American Poetry Anthology,* 1986; 'Winetown,' *Words of Praise,* 1986; Other Writing: "I Survived a Tidal Wave," Short Story, *Scuba Times,* 1985; Comments: *My writing is generally philosophical in nature, exploring the multiple meanings of life. I'm dedicated to the proposition that there are no absolute truths — which is, of course, the absolute truth. These three love poems attempt to explore a fragment of the multi-faceted spectrum of attraction and affection.*

KNOWING

Well, I kind of suspected it
But it wouldn't make me happy
Until I knew.
Tonight just proved my suspicions right,
I now know.
And I just can't begin to show
The feelings I have inside.
The first thing I thought of
(After finding out)
Is I'm not the only one
Who feels this way.
It's a feeling that I've had before,
But never in this way.
The feeling of being loved.
A true love.

Laura Halinski

YEARNING

Would that I could hold you
Just for a day . . .
Would that I could tell you
All that I meant to say.

To touch those tousled curls of
gold,
To see you smile, just that way.
That twinkle in your eye so bold,
Your mischievous little way.

But here 'tis mere words to tell you
All my heartfelt ways,
When my arms ache to hold you . . .
Caress you always.

L. G. Backlund

THE GOLDEN THREAD

Our love came softly,
Whispering on the gentle breezes,
Entwining around our hearts,
Drawing them together
By a single, golden thread.

So delicate, it seemed
That a mere breath
Could break its hold.

Yet, not so. For it was woven
From the very depth of love itself.
Made to withstand the test of time,
Forever strong and pure,
As our love.

Rosemary A. Carruthers

WHAT IS LOVE?

Love is deep down in our feelings,
Love is concern for another,
Love is devotion to family,
Helping our father and mother.

Love makes us gentle and happy,
Love fills our hearts with endeavor,
Love gives us spirit and courage,
Those are the answers — let's love more!

Alice S. Elton

LOVER, THINK OF ME

Lover,
think of me
when you walk
beside the sea
at Lover's Point.

Feel my finger tips,
see me smile,
taste my kisses,
and hear my heartbeat.

Where you walk,
I will be,
your arms embracing me.

When you talk,
I will hear
the sweet sound
of love in my ear.

Lovers are born to be,
and we were meant to meet,
to love and be loved.

Nancy Kobryn

AN EXPLANATION

I want to be with you,
To share things
To get to know you

It's as if
I can't
Get enough of you

No, I do not
Just want you
For the sex.

You have,
I have
A lot more to offer.

Sometimes
We do things
That are stupid

Hopefully
You will accept
My apology.

B. J. Lisatz II

LOST LOVE

I loved you so much,
But you grew tired
Of my possessiveness.
Remember when we first discovered
That we loved each other?
We had secret smiles and touchings.
You could hardly wait
Until I came to you.
Now it is over.
When you were leaving,
I tried to shake hands and wish you well,
But you slammed my hand hard on the desk.
But I still love you.

Edith C. Kair

THE STEPS OF FIRE

Muscles
Stop, look, listen
Confide in me

Surrender
Love me

I'm coming out
Getting ready for love

All night lover
Your love is so good
In your arms

Paul Weakly

FREER THAN TODAY TOMORROW

While half of my life's in sunshine,
the other half's still in rain;
I know that someday I'll be happy again
when there ain't no more pain.

And I can be freer than today tomorrow,
chase away that pain and sorrow;
I don't have to wear them old moody blues.

Now I can build my world around you,
something I can call my own,
and now that I have found you,
I'll never have to be alone.

Rosemary Roberts

The rose
matures and blossoms
a delicate beauty
unfurled
the painful thorn
upon its stem
easily forgotten
dewdrops upon its petals
traces of life's
occasional tears
while
its essence
lingers always
in the heart
a symbol of love.

Leann M. Felmlee

Westward jet trails in the sky
this evening
touched my heart with an ache
to see you.

Though we remain close
emotionally,
my physical need is strong
right now
to hug you.

Friends
truly are
the greatest
treasure.

Janice L. White

I LOVED YOU

I helped you up
and brushed you off
and pushed you out
to face the world
again.

I held your hand
and made you want.

I let you go.

Janice L. White

THIS IS LOVE

Love is not something that we plan.
We cannot see it coming;
It sneaks up on woman and man
Before they hear its drumming.

Love's a warm and misty feeling,
That all at once is there;
When it starts the senses reeling,
You know you'll always care.

Love will tie two souls together,
Two hearts will beat as one;
There's no straying from that tether,
No other place to run.

So united those hearts will stay,
As in a Fairy dream,
With never once a wish to stray,
For love makes life supreme.

Love knows no faults, is never wrong,
But is our heart's desire.
We live to love, will join its song,
With hearts and souls on fire.

Kenneth C. Duncan

FANTASY-DREAMS AND DESTINY

Our love has been rekindled,
For I'll be with you soon.
And when I see you once more,
At a wedding deep in June.

The path towards my destiny,
Once drawn from fantasy-dreams
Has now lost all the barriers,
And has become a reality,

The way you spoke to me each day,
Turned my life around.
Days, once filled with sadness,
Had me chained and bound.

So many years longing,
Has somehow reached your heart.
For when I thought about you,
It nearly tore you apart.

It seems I send you feelings,
From the bottom of my heart.
And you seem to pick up messages,
When I fall apart . . .

Mara F. Banish

DIALOGUE

Today I cried: "Lord, I feel like
a little toe in the Body of Christ."

"I admit my weakness:
though I strive to console,
I need consolation.
Though I walk in the shoes of
others,
I need understanding.
Though I give love,
I am human too, Lord,
and I have a need to be
loved."

And He said to me: "My grace is
sufficient for thee; for strength is
made perfect in weakness.

Gladly therefore, I will glory
in my infirmities, that the strength
of Christ may dwell in me."

Paula Trapani Bourg

MAGIC RAINBOW

You are
A magic rainbow
Through lover's eyes
I see,
Of subtle curves
That warm my soul
And softly
Color me;

An arc
Of sweet seduction
That fills
My longing sky,
With bands
Of pastel moments,
To a blazing
Rainbow high.

Pat Bush

WHY MUST YOU HAUNT ME SO?

Everywhere I turn,
I see your shadow.
Everywhere I look,
I see your face.
Why must you haunt me so?
Leave me alone, go away.
Every thought I have
is of you.
Every voice I hear
is yours.
Day and night you haunt me.
I feel you everywhere.
In hours of darkness
in the light of day,
you're there.
I can feel your touch
in the soft, gentle breeze
and I shiver at the thought.
I wish I could forget you —
but I know I never will.
Why must you haunt me so?

Sandra Kay Tipton

WINTER VALENTINE

While others chill, I burn.
I seek your haughty, brittle face.
I find your touch a turn of grace.
Stay with me. Be my valentine.
Cool all my fears.
Comfort my lonely years.
We shall walk in company
Across the frozen ground,
Where we go together without sound,
Our music a love song — the wind and snow.

Jeanette Konwiser

MY BLUE-EYED BABY

In the land of magical dreamland
There is the face I see
The face of my lovely darling
The only dear girl for me.

My blue-eyed baby of mine
I cannot resist over you
You are so sweet and divine
My heart is for you.

I had a dream of you dear
All the long night sleeping through
My blue-eyed baby of mine
I am in love with you.

Frank Viggiani

THE EMBRACE

There was a time in my life when
I wallowed in self-pity and hate,
But that ended the day I found Him —
The day I welcomed His Embrace.

His touch filled me with an ecstasy
beyond compare and my Soul soared
to unknown heights —
Awakened by His warm compassion.

Because of Him my life has new meaning,
for I now see myself in a different light.
My heart and Soul are filled with love —
I was embraced by GOD.

Cora Lee Fuhring

EXOTIC LOVE

I could have lived in old Bombay,
Or in romantic Mexico.
Those once exotic proposals
'bade me ponder to stay or go.
I decided that I should stay,
Awaiting that one special beau.
Then one day, you entered my life.
Oh — I'm so glad I did not go.
You taught me all about true love,
To feel, let my emotions show.
Adventures are just that my dear,
That is why I want you to know;
I'm thankful each and every day
I thought to stay and did not go.

Gail Stump

REFLECTIONS

From the first time I saw you,
Right up until this very day —
I have loved you, my darling,
In a very special way —

I've loved you with all my heart,
Though sometimes, it didn't show —
Through angry times and hurtful words,
I've loved you, didn't you know?

Our menial disagreements,
Battles, won and lost —
We defended our opinions,
Whatever — no matter the cost —

With the fighting over,
One would surrender, in defeat —
But then our love would triumph,
When our eyes would meet —

All these years we've shared,
We've learned a lot, my dear —
I could never live without you,
I'm only happy when you're near —

Now, as we grow old together,
We won't mind or really care —
All our precious memories,
And our future, we will share —

We can never be truly old,
For our youth still lies —
In the deep reflection,
Of each other's eyes . . .

Janice Reed Hamlin

LOVE TO A GRANDDAUGHTER WHO WILL SOON BE A BRIDE

Dear Debbie,
How beautiful I see you now
In formal dress with lovely bow
The yellow ribbons of Texas rose
Flowing down in light repose.
Your blondish hair and sparkling jewels
Your form so graceful perfect
That little smile with joy expression
A lovely lady grown so grand!

How exquisite I see you now
In low-cut gown with draping pleat
Your agile shoulder so whitish soft
Bending as you look aloft
Your wedding dreams and joyous ideals
Your glance so impish pleasant
That coyish way with fun delightful
A charming madame waves a hand!

How elegant I see you now
In status strong with hopeful sight
Your willful power of living gait
Pressing as you long await
Your nuptial day and omen coming
Your time for patience prayers
That prelude to love and happiness
A woman sharing with her man!

With love from Gramma

Dorothy Ainslie

ST. PETERSBURG

I've a book on St. Petersburg open to view;
Eyes wet with looking for you.
Amazing how little of Leningrad I knew;
Eyes filled with looking at you.

In St. Isaac's Cathedral I walked its floors,
Marveled its huge bronze doors.
With Danka I explored its orthodox might,
But my mind was with you that night.

On the shore of the wild Gulf of Finland
We walked to our heart's wild band.
There you first thanked me for love so grand,
In that frigid "White Nights" land.

I love to remember your aunt's ire,
Going like a house afire,
When she thought we had overstepped propriety
By kissing without anxiety.

No, I'd not trade a single look
I can get from St. Petersburg's book,
For the look of LOVE I saw in your eye
Under the Leningrad sky.

L. Elcan Walker, M.D.

SEAN MICHAEL

Rockabye, rockabye, baby mine,
We'll pray for you and you'll be just fine,

Rockabye, rockabye, baby mine,
God touched your eyes and now they will shine.
He blessed your head and your wee button nose,
Molded your mouth like a tiny red rose,
Light reddish hair and two curled-up ears,
Fashioned you so, you bring happy tears!
Rockabye, rockabye, baby mine,
God touched your eyes and now they both shine!

Evelyn Conley Stauffer

DANNY

No, I don't love him anymore.
The creation of my imagination was
Just adolescent fantasies,
I suppose.

By now he has his own wife and children
And he's successful —
Like I always knew he would be —
Despite what "everyone" said.

Occasionally I ponder "what if" —
The mutual respect and admiration we shared
Had been allowed to develop
Into something deeper.

Sometimes (whenever you feel
Inadequate in comparison)
You suspect I'm dissatisfied with my life
By having chosen you.

Remember then what I long ago realized:
Never be jealous of only memories and distant dreams;
Past loves are like cobwebs in your heart
Without a feather duster.

Betty Sharon

GRANNY

As time goes on without her my memory is growing
Fonder, the gentle Christmas season brings the
Memory ever stronger. Her loving eyes, her
Gentle smile, her understanding ways, her love
Forgiving, her hope of life, her spirit lives
Forever. As I look at my Christmas tree this
Night, her gentle memory is in every light.
A warmth of a spirit fills my room. I feel the
Memory of her love. My love for her is forever.

A Loving Grandaughter

Cindy Lee

FINDING YOU

I have searched the rocky, wide road of life's offerings
I have waited for what seems a lifetime
Looking at every turn, wondering, would I ever find you.

At times confusion encircled me
Disappointments shouted, trying to shut out all hope.

Regrets? A few.
I have loved and not loved, each new time with less of my heart.
Waiting, knowing,
That you must come to me from somewhere, anywhere.

Then suddenly, one usual afternoon
While filled with boredom of strangers and friends
I saw my golden thread of hope dance and sparkle
Like the noonday sun.

Quietly, softly, I reached out to touch you
Knowing I would never reach into the emptiness again.
I had found you.

I can never let go of your loving touch,
Your kindness, your gentleness.
For I have waited too long to love you.

Jo. Richter-Craft

LOVE IS A SPIRIT

Love is a spirit.
It flows like electricity.
Love flows from the male to the female
Like electricity flows from the positive to the negative.

A woman is like a battery.
She holds within her body the love of her man.
When a battery is weak
It is strengthened when it is recharged.

Love stays with a woman
As if it were a child.
Love in a man is like a charged battery
That wants to make a contact.

Love is a food
That feeds a woman's hungry spirit.
It satisfies for a few days
And then hunger returns.

As electricity flows
When wires are touched,
Love flows
As bodies are touched.

Joseph S. Wright

WEDDING VOWS

HONORABLE MENTION

There is too much sawdust here, he said,
Too much shadow, too much shudder,
Between you and me and these walls.

She let him talk on. The moon was full,
And he tired easily of the routine.
Each evening he would spout his catalogue.

The trees don't move the same, he said.
The ground's too soft, the sky too grey,
And I can't find an unbroken cup.

She reached out and gave him one.
It must be hard, she thought, to live alone,
To tremble at each flutter, at each corner.

If not for you, who knows, he murmured.
He always finished with that line,
And took her hand. She waited, there,
Listening, watching him eye the floor
And moon, her hand open, silken,
Like her. If not, he whispered again,
And reached out and touched her thumb.

George P. Castellitto

THE DAYS REMIND ME OF US

When I see the sun begin to rise,
I think of us, and of our bonds and ties.

When the day is at its peak, the sun so high,
I think of us, the times we've shared, days gone by.

When the sun begins to set,
I think of us, the very day we met.

And when the moon is full and bright,
I think of us, a dream come true in the night.

Amy Lynn McNeely

HOW?

How do you end a love unending?
Can you ever start anew?
How do you straighten a rose that's bending?
I don't believe you do.

How do you stay a harboring affection,
In a protected heart as mine?
Can you change this pale complexion,
To pink, maybe so, with time.

How do you speak of this barren love,
Without bringing about a tear?
Will you ever be able to see above,
The clouds without such fear?

My heart beats in a perfect rhythm,
To a tune that ascended above.
Though my presence no longer is with him,
I think of him dearly, with love.

If I find new hope in my favor,
One that fits my manner and style,
I promise its presence I'll savor,
Without ever questioning, "How?"

B. J. Morgan

WHEN

When the sun begins to set,
And the shadows become long
And the air becomes sweeter . . . and still

When the car horns don't seem so loud,
And people walk more slowly
And speak more quietly and smile more freely

When the warm loneliness of evening settles in
And the rush of the day is past
And the day's battles are done . . . some won
And the time softly passing, is an open door
A beckoning invitation,

To the memories we have kept
Of old dreams and new beginnings
Of love . . . new, lost and long ago
Of times . . . now, then and not forgotten
Of places . . . near and far
Tucked away in our heart of hearts
Where summer is an always time
And we smile . . . sigh a little sigh
And remember . . .
When . . .

Linda L. Hudye

THE EYE THAT SEES WITHIN

It is my eyes that I have to see thee,
that shines so brilliantly.

Thee comes from afar to see me,
from a shooting star as he may be.

Even though I love him so I feel the warmth,
that makes me shivering cold.

To hear his voice call from within,
is not a sin, but I will go and lie with him,
when all things come to the end.

Christ threw me

KILBRETH, ANNA MARIE BURNEDETT. Pen Names: Threw Me, Me, Thee, Always Me, Christ Threw Me; Born: Newport, Rhode Island, 5-23-59; Married: 2-16-77 to Larry Kilbreth; Education: High school, presently attending the Colorado Christian College; Occupations: Housewife, Student; Comments: *I try to convey the feelings I feel inside of me, which relate to Jesus Christ and a Thee.*

THE CAT

The snow is falling.

There is a cat outside my window.
who regards me with arrogant eyes.
I avert my eyes, trying to rid my mind of
the haunting remembrance of him,
and his sweet torture.
Yet he smiles, and knows
that I will not leave him there.

Sighing,
I open the door, and he
along with an icy blast,
comes in to dictate my household again.

Jeannine Hall

LEFT BEHIND

In the hours of darkness
As shadows fly,
My obsession grows,
My torment cries.

I lived for you,
All my days,
But now you're gone.
What reason to stay?

You cannot come back,
I know that now.
But I'll see you someday,
When the shadow smooths my brow.

Karen Hache

REMINDERS

Reminders are objects;
A remembrance of love,
A sorrowful tear
Or a white-crested dove.

Reminders are images
Left in your mind;
Thoughts of a lover
Or friends of a kind.

Reminders are feelings;
A passion or pain,
A sensation of pleasure
Or love lost in vain.

Michelle Kooch

WHY?

You used to be so close,
no more than a touch away.

Time, somehow has changed this.

All I do is ponder,
and hope that you are happy.

Silently, I sit, drink, stare in wonder.

Kevin Cooper

DEAR I LOVE YOU

All through the years I've tried to find . . . words that could express
How life I've shared and loved with you, has made "My Happiness."
I never have been able to tell you so you'd know
What's deep within my heart and why I love you so.

I prayed for God to help me in some way to let you see
How very much a part of me . . . through the years you've grown to be.
Our life has been so wonderful, we've shared so much together,
Hasn't all been riding clouds, we've had our "Stormy Weather."

But somehow I cannot recollect "The Downs" we've had so much,
Because of all the good things . . . Our love, our friends and such.
We've spent our lives together a good share of the time,
Our business we worked hard at . . . so we could save a dime.

We've tried our hands at many things . . . the variety's been wide,
God always has been near us . . . any doubt to help us hide.
You know just when a loving pat is what will bolster me
And never fail to compliment for little things you see.

There's such a combination of things I love you for,
'Twould take a heap of telling you . . . a jillion hours or more.
So may this heartfelt meditation make you really . . . really know
That you are first within my heart and "Dear, I love you so."

Lucille Rawling

RAWLING. LUCILLE KERR. Born: Morrisonville, Illinois, 9-3-13; Married: 12-2-33 to Walter J. Rawling; Education: High School; Occupation: Retired, work part time; Comments: *Never have written seriously, have just written as a fun thing.*

MORNING

In the morning sunshine as the birds begin their song, there is a softness on my pillow that remembers then the dawn.

There is a sweetness in the cleansing tears that brim my eyes, and the mellow glow that soothes my being and refreshes my soul as nothing or no other time can know.

He is beside me with a softness now where before he was a raging greatness that had sparked a fear.

Calm now in this same warm glow of softness that no other morning can ever know.

I wait for night again and know, if not tomorrow, perhaps another morning, heart will glow and I can feel again the tears of joy that flood my soul.

P. A. Shepard

THE MAN OF MY DREAMS

Dedicated to my husband Terry . . .
who truly is . . . the man of my dreams.

It is precious and rare indeed,
To spend your life with the man of your dreams.
Most women are searching, their whole lives through,
For a man who is worthy, a man who is true.
Lucky am I, for I have by my side,
The man of my dreams and my heart swells with pride,
Each time I look into his eyes I find,
A man who is loving and gentle and kind.
Tough on the outside, but tender within,
Full of manly charm hidden by a boyish grin.
A gentle touch and a heart of gold,
With a look that can melt your heart and soul.
A man with few enemies, but many a friend,
With a love of adventure and an urge to win.
So full of life and full of wit,
So eager to try, but never to quit.
As I said before, I am lucky, indeed,
For I have found the man of my dreams!

Frances Lewis

AMERICA — JUST WAITIN' FOR ME

As I travel the highways and byways, and as I tramp the hills and wade the streams of America, I sometimes stop and look around me and I think, "All of this, just waitin' for me."

As I hunt, fish and travel in America, I remember all of the ambitious people who have restored, cultivated, and preserved all the wildlife, and it is just waitin' for me.

From the wooded hills of Pennsylvania to the mystic mountains of Colorado — from ocean to ocean, all of the beauty in America I see, and it is just waitin' for me.

I should hope when we, the older generation, turn the reins of America over to a younger generation, that they too will work, educate, cultivate and preserve America so their children can also, with pride and deep admiration, say, "All of this, just waitin' for me."

America, I love you. You are beautiful and you are just waitin' for me.

Russell Heindselman

BACK ROADS

We abandoned ourselves
To lustful desires
Along the back roads.
Barefoot, you fishtailed into my arms.
Hedges shielded all but the crickets song.
On soft shoulders . . . yours were fumèd;
And hard!
Chest to chest. Pressed to flesh
Your passion scattering cloth everywhere
Warm moans of pleasure
Exotic fragrances
Whimpers translated into
The slurpy sounds of love.
Bare there
You lay in your wedding gown;
Nose deep in love.
Your woman's body
In multiple submissions
Reprising "Here Comes The Bride."

Chip Kilgus

MY SPECIAL ONE

O love of mine so fair and dear
  you are the one I love throughout the year
So precious and sweet I adore you more
  the only girl my heart beats for

Stay with me forever as the days do pass
  from my beginning years, until my last
Your beauty is ageless, your smile so pure,
  being away from you is something I could not endure

O special one I love so much
  to have and hold and feel your touch
Thou art sweet and special, full of grace
  there is not another to take your place

O darling one you make anew
  each day of mine with the things you do
O dearest angel remain with me
  that I might always have you close to me

O cherished love who won my heart
  from my side please never part
For if you go my heart will break
  'cause losing thee I could not take

Anthony Akins

THE POWER OF LOVE

I appeared before the solid barrier,
which exists between my lives.
Two worlds which battle each other's existence
and accumulate my lies.

I then decried reality's gloom
and felt the sun turn to frigid ice.
I layed myself in the hands of doom
by exhibiting my self-made vice.

Then another two eyes appeared
that saw as I had seen.
He helped to let my future survive
and showed what living means.

Both seeing black as glowing white
and feeling cold as warm,
We touched the horizon hand in hand
and were sheltered from the storm.

Together our dreams have somehow been able
to cause my misery to elapse by.
The barrier was destroyed, although it was stable
and we kissed the darkness good-bye.

Gia Oliveri

THE POSTAL CARD

What joy to receive a card
From a child traveling afar
The simple line
I'm just fine
And I safely arrived at my destination
Fills my heart with elation.

What happiness, to read the words that say
"I'm okay in every way"
I carefully file the card in my treasure box
To read, when we get together for our talks

Rose Mary Gerlach

MOTHER IN FAIRYLAND

I look at the grayness in her hair,
And drift in a fantasy;
Yet she's still loving and beautiful
As the youthful MOTHER in my memory.
A Fairy Queen I'd like to be
So I could show her what she means to me.
I'd first give her a transparent veil of GOLD,
With magic to take away bad dreams.
Then I'd give her happiness beyond and untold.
I look at her and see her dancing
In silken fancy clothes,
And all the good things in life,
A MOTHER should bestow. I look at her and see
Rainbow mist — Maybe just a dimmer sparkle
In her eyes; and I don't think a MOTHER
Should ever have to cry. Fairyland troops should
Stand in line, playing Golden Trumpets
For this special MOTHER of mine!

Wanda Whanger Higgins

ALL THE TESTS ARE MET

All the tests are met,
Poverty, to understand want and hunger.
Widowhood, to understand sorrow.
Labor, to understand creation.
Fright, to understand death.
Loss, to understand redemption.
Lies, to understand Satan, the father of lies.
Hatred, to understand the enemy of love.
Sickness, to understand the healing of the mind,
soul, spirit and body.

Conclusion:

The knowledge of life is contained in life itself with
Its victories and defeats,
Its highs and lows,
And its beginning and end,
Its judgments and rewards,
And its blessings and cursings.

All the tests are met.

Estella M. McGhee-Siehoff

A LOOK TOO SOON

I opened up a book today
That you and I closed long ago,
I let the ghost of you go
Wandering through my mind,
And thought it safe to take a look.

But I was wrong, so wrong.
The slivers of our shattered dreams
Were still as sharp,
And the pain of a heart betrayed,
Time did not heal nor make to fade.

Perhaps someday
The scars will heal,
And I can scan this painful page,
And look on your memory with a gentle rage,
And make, within my heart, our love
A thing of beauty and of grace.

Tera O. Worley

THE TEST

The old man sitting on the park bench with his eyes
searching the far west.
When a snow-white dove at his feet came to rest.
As its wings spread wide and the old man looked on with
surprise
For the dove before his very eyes turned into a pure
white rose.
The man gently wiped a tear from his nose,
As he leaned over to pick up the rose.
There he saw what it meant as he looked close,
In the middle of the rose was the figure of the
Christ that he had known.
Then he looked once more to the west,
And bowed his head with a smile and closed his eyes
once more to rest.
It was then the rose fluttered and cooed and flew
back into the west.
The old man knew he had done his best.

M. H. Kingston

Without a word being spoken, we can share
Love with another, let him know we care,
A sympathetic smile, the touch of a hand
Letting him know that we understand!

Sometimes it just takes being there
When somebody's hurting, to help him bear
Whatever burden, whatever load
Letting him know we join him on his lonely road!

What good is Love if we
Don't show it to others so they can see
His Love shining in our lives each day
In whatever we do, whatever we say?

Let go! Reach out! Tell the world you care
If you see a need, ask The Lord to prepare
The way so you can help someone
To walk out of darkness into the sun!

Connie Ratliff

AFTER A LOVER'S QUARREL

Communicate, communicate, the counselors all say,
Trying to reach a plane of blessed understanding —
But it was words that brought the pain,
Words of heat that asked the reasons
For decisions not understood,
Tears that followed knew the failure
Of silence, laughter, overtures,
Strained politeness, but no communication — no words.

It's true, you don't talk much,
But you tell jokes. I know you care
For we are always close,
In church, a crowded room, in bed watching TV
We often have ESP
So like one are we.
So put it all on paper. It's been done before.
Years of practice makes perfect in facing a closed door.
Still, no one pleases quite like you,
A habit for sure, but more than that,
Good to be with, at home or away,
Each day a century, a century a day.

Louise Butts Hendrix

THE SPLENDOR OF LOVE

Love, as it goes, is many splendid things.
Just think of all the joy it brings.
It's a feeling two people discover and share,
One nurtured with tenderness and handled with care.

It may begin between a girl and a boy,
And bring years of togetherness, happiness and joy
As they face life together hand in hand,
And progress to the world of woman and man.

Love is two hearts beating as one,
And the depth of this union is second to none.
It's a bond that entwines like an invisible chain;
A feeling much too complex to explain.
It's a thing of great beauty, awe and grace.
Once the picture is imprinted, it's hard to erase.

Yes, love is many wonders too numerous to name,
And once touched by its power, one is never the same.
So, as you'll discover when that little bug stings,
Love is, as aforementioned, many splendid things.

Jean S. Price

LIFE OF A DREAM

In the valley of my dreams
I dance to the rhythm of waterfalls
Running down the face of a canyon
Chanting like chimes of benediction bells;
When the white stars sprinkle across the sky
I pirouette to the time of their twinkles
As I sing with violin voices of the spheres,

And my soul flies and I am one
With the treasures of the universe.

When the sun within pours out
Its golden light of daffodil glow
Erasing the silhouette of night,
The soft air is present with fragrances
Of whispering roses and narcissus,
I stand stilled by the reflected glory
Of nature's natural harmony

And I behold a patterned, spacious universe
Knowing an angel has painted.

Alessandra A. Poles

REAL LOVE

Real love is a perfect thing
It greets your neighbor
It honors your friend

Love is near and love is far
Sometimes it's a question of who you are
Love surpasses cities and stems throughout nations
A requirement for this is a whole lot of patience

To die for love is to live for love
To quest for its meaning
You must look above

When love can love them that don't love back
You know the kind that can't be sold nor hung on a rack
Then love has reached its true meaning and goal
It's described as the kind that comes from the soul.

Tywanna Saunders

SAILING WITH YOU

From the depth of my soul comes a well;
A well of love that wants to sail,
Sail through this life with you.
It started slowly and with passion grew.

I love you so, believe it's true.
And I have found myself through knowing you.
To lose your love would crush me completely,
For joy in living you've given me, so sweetly.

Rebecca Ellison Cole

A WEDDING SONNET

Two silver strands upon Life's loom entwined
With Love's gold grace into a single cord,
Two hearts drawn, knit together by the Lord
To beat as one, two lives by grace divine
Now one become — a newly created shrine
Wherein the presence of the living Lord
Is pleased to dwell, its shield and rich reward,
Of Christ and His Beloved (the Church) a sign.

This is Love's healing memory and power
When, in the hectic pace and stress of life,
Come in the clouds and storms of family strife,
All seems in vain, love's sweetness turned quite sour.
God's golden strand of grace will steady you,
This hour recall, your love and faith renew.

Alexander Hollands Edwards

THINKING OF YOU

I'd love to be with you in the morning light
I'd love to dance with you under a starlit sky
I'd love to be held by you when the wind is bitter cold
I'd love to take you on a cruise into paradise
And if I had the choice, I'd be with you now
But I'm alone again, without you
Yes I'm alone again, without . . . you

If we could only be together right now
I'd do my best to keep you happy
To see your bright smile
Would spark up my happiness once again
We could glide along rainbows to our pot of gold
And remain happy together forever,
With our entwined hearts on fire.

Mark Godzisz

SEARCH

Dedicated to John Dyeyemi (My Love)

I never meant to hurt you darling . . . by what I've
said and done . . . I was reaching out for
answers . . . looking around for faces . . .
digging deeper for reasons . . . and there
you were . . . I never meant to hurt you . . . But there
you were . . . I needed to release myself . . .
My world took on a new and more complex meaning . . .
There were people crying and laughing . . . looking
and turning away . . . waiting and wanting . . . they were
all around me . . . But I never meant to cause the pain
that I know I've caused you . . . It had to happen . . .
I had to let go . . . And there you were . . . I
never meant to hurt you . . . Not you . . . But there
you were . . .

Ivey Joyce Williams

VALENTINES

Forty-five years ago
  you became my Valentine . . .
We have been Valentines ever
  since that time.
That magic night we met our hearts
  became entwined,
You have filled my life with a
  vivid sunshine.
Your love has made each precious
  moment just fine . . .
Now the time has come to ask again,
  "Will you be my Valentine?"

Harold James Douglas

GOD'S LOVE

Born in a manger of holy birth
adored by heaven, praised on earth.
In God's way He spent His youth
He knew the time to teach His Truth.
God's Word of Truth did man offend,
Jesus betrayed by one called friend.
Envy filled those men with hate
they twisted Truth to seal His fate,
and nailed Him to the tree — His cross,
darkened hearts ignored the loss.
In agony Christ did depart
His mortal wound — a broken heart.

Curtis Lennander

ADAM TO EVE

I awoke in the Garden of Eden,
On that lovely, bright first day,
And the Lord said, name the animals
As they pass along your way:
The ocelot and kangaroo,
Rhinoceros and bear,
A name to call each creature
Living and loving there.
But in the morning or the evening,
No one called *my* name
In all this lonely garden —
— Until you came.

Marjorie Everett Naff

ABSENCE

From the moment
he embraces me
and says "goodbye"
I start to miss him.
It is hard to wait
    through sleeping-time
    and danish-time
    lone supper-time
    fervid primping-time
    last minute anxious-time
until he holds me close
and says "hello" again.

Ellen V. M. Carden

NOW AND THEN

You are my boys
  And I love you truly.
When you were two and five
  I hoped you would stay
Young that way forever
And never go away.

The years slipped by
  And you were young men
Now you are grown
  And I have grandchildren.
I am happy for all
  My children now and then.

Richard B. Stauffer

STAUFFER, RICHARD B. Pen Name: Dick Rich; Born: Delphos, Kansas, 3-8-03; Married: Twila Draper, 8-1-28, Widowed 2-2-60; Married Verna Lea Davis; Have two sons, Darrel and Gene; one stepson, Ken McDonald; five grandchildren; Education: Delphos, Kansas High School, 1921; Kansas State University, B.S., 1946; Occupations: Schoolteacher, Insurance Agent; Memberships: Kansas State Teachers Association; Poetry: 'Everything Different,' *Our Twentieth Century's Greatest Poems,* 1982; 'I Had Nothing Going,' *American Poetry Anthology,* 1983; 'The Stranger,' *Our World's Most Beloved Poems,* 1984; 'I Hear It Clearly,' *Our Western World's Most Beautiful Poems,* 1985; Other Writings: "He's The Man Of The House," "Bees On The Mule," songs; Comments: *Writing poems and songs helps me express my feelings and I hope to brighten someone's life.*

MY LOVE, OH LOVE, I'VE LOST YOU

How can I express myself,
  and say just what I'm feeling?
I hope the pain and hurt inside
  my eyes are now revealing.

I'm sure my lips are trembling,
  I feel my heart is breaking.
I thought that love was worth it all,
  you thought it just for taking.

I cannot say goodbye my love,
  the words don't seem to be there.
Sure sorrow grips my very soul,
  such anguish do I bear.

My love, oh love, what can I say,
  as teardrops start to fall?
I wanted you so desperately,
  and now, I've lost it all.

Mardi J. Munrowe

TWO HEARTS THAT TWINE

They came together
Slowly, hesitantly,
Reaching out and drawing back
And reaching out again,
Seeking to know and understand
The reason for it all.
Then carefully, gently
They touched.
Once more they touched and yet again,
Gaining courage to explore
And accept pain and joy mixed.
They began to encircle one another,
Forgetting time and space,
Letting go of self
To make room for someone else.
Looking back they saw
Two small worlds had merged
To become one large enough
To surround others who would come
Within the circle of their love.

Dolores Wyckoff

AFTERGLOW

Your eyes meet mine again
and this time I see you deep;
we look at each other, exhausted,
but, neither of us wanting sleep.

You kiss me in the afterglow —
a warm smile that comes from within;
a moment before you were far away
and I wondered where you'd been.

This is that velvet moment
when we revel in each other's care;
each heartbeat is heard in the silence,
each movement is watched as we stare.

We want this closeness to never end
but, we both know it soon will,
so we breathe it deep and cherish
this moment, warm and still.

Anne Stanford

GOD'S ETERNAL LOVE

Why do I love him?
  I'll tell you why:
Because He first loved me,
And purchased my redemption
  On Calvary's Tree.

Why does He love me?
  I'll tell you why,
He sought me and bought me
With His blood that did flow
  on Calvary's Tree.

Will He love me forever?
  Yes, I'll tell you why:
He has promised never to leave
  me, nor forsake me;
For He purchased my life
  at Calvary, and made me free.

Forever, I am His, and He is mine:
  Bought with a price, this
  new life divine.
Fashioned me for glory above,
Where I'll forever live in
  heaven, with love!
John 3:16

Martha Pastore

A SEA'S VIEW

In my heart, we have met.
I wonder what to do with you.
If I asked, would you tell me?
Sincere doubts whisper no.
Like a lighthouse, I have observed you.
Together we love.
Together we will view the sea.

Christine Tansey

IMAGINARY LOVER

Alone and calm,
The smoke of her cigarette
Floats, across a darkened room.

The radio's playing
A slow and easy tune.

Thinking about a man
She whispers to him,
a love song.

Wanting and yearning
For his closeness,
She traces his face
With her finger tips.

Touching his soft hair
She pulls him near
And kisses him in
Sweet solitude.

But the dream
Slowly fades away,
And leaves her in a
Little world, all her own.

Kari L. Reber

TODAY IS OURS

This is a poem that I wrote to my husband,
and it was read on our wedding day.

Today's our very special day, the one we've waited for.
Today I become your wife, to be as one forevermore.

I want to tell you that I love you on our wedding day.
I want to give you all my love and give you all of me.

You asked for me to be your wife, to share all of your dreams.
To share all of your hopes, and plans; everything is right, it seems.

I want to walk with you by my side, go barefoot in the sand,
To put your arms around me and just take me by the hand.

I want to give you everything that you could want from me.
I want to walk down life's path with you, and make dreams what we'd
have them be.

I love you, dear, with all my heart. This I want you to know.
As we walk the path of marriage together our love for each other
will grow, and grow.

So, darling, I want to tell you that I love you on this our wedding day,
And as our married life continues to grow, may we care for each other
in our own special ways.

Rita Henry

THE LENGTH

You never cease to amaze me you always exhilarate and raise me
Since lifting this lost soul from the mire never failing to
inspire with words of comfort and strength.

O Lord, of the breadth, depth and height of your never ending love
I truly believe I know the length!
Ephesians 3:18

Jeanette Moody

THE WORLD
THE CUBE THAT SMELLED LIKE YOUR SKIN

The death bride comes and wakes me up from the limpid sleep of my mirrors
Oh She was the death bride.
She made me fall in love with the excitement of touching tomorrow's body.

My pulse is beating because of the repetition of heavy love heat.
It's like your thoughts are flying over this room's ceiling,
as light as kites in the world's blue skies.
The world The cube that smelled like your skin.

And you were like the effigy that was reaching its nubility,
in the form of tomorrow.
Maybe you were the vague effigy that was creeping in my bed at nights,
washing my mind with ephemeral lusts.
All my pains are the pains of this long night
And the scary thought of loneliness.
Loneliness in the world the world
the cube that smelled like your skin.

The neighborhood's long sky was looking for the full moon
street to street.
I was coming from the continuation of the road
from the remainder of my childhood's thoughts.

Then the death bride comes and wakes me up from the limpid sleep of my mirrors

Kaveh Irani

COME HOME

When I come home
Receive me with open arms;
Embrace me with love & warmth
Squeeze me tenderly,
Like melting butter/cheese.
Kiss me, gently — here and there.
Now, touch me — everywhere!
Feel me — no
Not as another,
Rather
As one
In you!

Charmaine C. Parks

LOVE DIVINE

A thrill divine,
Engulfs my being,
As angels in love,
We kiss in the twilight.
We caress one another in the moonlight.
We join hands and hearts
In the sanctity of the marriage bed.
Trembling with ecstasy,
And merging our souls and bodies,
We become one.
In the union of sweet surrender,
Looking at you tenderly,
My beloved, whom I adore,
I am finally at peace.

Janice Wagner Richardson

RICHARDSON, JANICE WAGNER. Born: Sterling Illinois Community General Hospital, 1-26-33; Married: 6-26-54 to Harold G. Richardson; Education: Beloit College, Beloit, Wisconsin, B.A. degree, 1955; Memberships: St. Luke's Episcopal Church, Dixon, Illinois; Poetry: *My Raptured Heart,* collection of my love verses, 7-1-85; 'My Pussycat,' *Masterpieces of Modern Verse;* 'Beautiful Lord Jesus,' *Words of Praise, Vol. 2;* Comments: *I have 3 children, Laurel, 29, Chad, 26, Marcia, 24, and 1 granddaughter, Jaqueline Lee Swick.*

SHE WHO WAS BEAUTY IS STILL

Spring is not
At war as
Winter is

Thaw over heft

The wine of ice
Breaks petals into
Emily toys

Song above sleet

Cold chalk comes
Yellow gold then
Crabapple tart

Scent under moist

Miracle sweet green
At peace as
Warmth blankets

Earth next eye

William K. Bottorff

MOTHER

Who watched o'er me in babyhood
and cared so tenderly?
Who helped me take my first few steps
and heard my childish plea?
'Twas mother!

Who guided me from day to day
and taught me to be true?
Who at my bedside vigil kept
through measles and the flu?
'Twas mother!

Who patiently forgave me
each thoughtless word and deed?
Who sacrificed in many ways
to serve my every need?
'Twas mother!

Her kindness I can ne'er repay
but may I e'er endeavor
To help her fondest dreams come true,
and disappoint her never.
Dear mother!

Hildur Solberg

TO THEE

I grasp your love with open heart
and offer understanding.
Happiness for you, you see
is but my special wish.
Welcome is my word to you,
Welcome to my life.
Being human, I doth need
your understanding too.
The infinite extent of my relations
brings me near to you
and I hope that I can stay.
All, I do not understand, nor know
but I am yours to try.

Robert Michael John Higgins

SILENT LOVE

The message, so clear,
Must remain unspoken,
For a promise
Made long ago
Cannot be broken.

UNTITLED

My faith and my trust
Were the knives
That you used.
My dreams were
The things you tore;
But now that it's over
And love has excused,
Dare I give you
These weapons
once more?

FOR MY BUG

All things considered
In heaven and earth,
There's none so splendid
As my daughter's birth.

As I write these words
With ink and pen,
If I had it to do
All over again,
I'd say "Yes!"
Because you've made me whole —
My darling daughter,
Kelly Nicole

Regina Helo White

THE SUNDAY MORNING AFTER

The Sunday morning after
It is very hard to wake
I hear the rooster crowing
In the oven he shall bake

My wife is up and singing
Oh such a lovely tune
It reminds me of the ringing
Of wedding bells after noon

I hide beneath the covers
The pillows on my head
Down pours the water
I'm up and out of bed

Running through the house
I'm searching for my wife
She's sneaky as a mouse
With love she fills my life

At last I have found her
Laughing in the den
I grab her up and kiss her
She whispers "You win, you win"

I set her on my knee
And tell her that it's love
She smiles and tells me
It's a gift from God above

Gary A. Hedinger

LIFE IS GOD LOVING GOD

Man was created to love, and to be loved. Problems appear only when man is not loving. God is love as He is life. He is all. God loves, lives, and enjoys His creation through each of us, for God is His own neighbor. To be God realized is to know that God love life is all there is. There is nothing separate or outside of God, so life is God loving God.

Ross Hagen

LILLY, LELAND LANDO. Pen Name: Ross Hagen; Born: Williams, Arizona; Married: 6-15-63 to Claire; Occupation: Actor, Writer, Director; Memberships: S.A.G., W.G.A., Poetry: 'Crystal Carousel,' Inspirational, 1985; 'The Inner Dam,' *American Poetry Anthology,* 1986; Other Writings: "Dalton," Television, 1986; "The Glove," Screenplay, 1978; "The All American Beer Bowl," Screenplay, 1985; "Reel Horror," Video Movie, 1986; Comments: *We are mental creatures and each of us must take on the responsibility for the quality of the thoughts we think. Love life and it loves you back. Hate life and it becomes hell. I believe it is possible to love your way out of hell by using one of God's greatest gifts called humor.*

MY DARLING

My darling, I love you, my darling;
In my mind the cadences ring
And as I hear a wild bird sing
I think of how I feel for you.

It's too late to let you know;
Too late to even try to show,
How much I really care,
Or speak of what we share.

"I was taught to be good,
And always do as I should
To be a respectable, proper wife
And to sacrifice my life."

The words are gusting and blowing and sighing;
And in them I can hear you crying.
I love you! I love you! I love you!
Come be with me! Come be with me!

G. M. Petts

MY HEART'S SECRET GARDEN

Today I quietly tiptoed through
The garden where mem'ries dwell
Each pathway ever leads me to you —
Such love, I've no words to tell.

This secret garden's where none can see —
In the corner of my heart
Planting each flower so tenderly
I weed out each hurting part.

Bluebirds of joy ever sweetly sing
As I kneel in wonder there
And the dove flies near with peace to bring
Because of memories shared.

But all the dreams for which I had yearned
Were not meant for me today —
So closing the gate I sadly turned
And quietly walked away.

Sara E. (Page) Smith

OUR DAUGHTERS

Perpetual motion, dressed in blue jeans,
Full of ambition, these vivacious teens;
Composed of a mixture of laughter and tears,
They're a joy to their parents, all through the years.

Just all-around girls, so happy and free,
They make life worth living, for you and for me;
At times they seem forward, though really quite shy,
They can warm the hard-hearted by winking an eye.

They're the best babysitters, and always on hand,
To perform many duties situations demand;
We can always depend on their gladness to assist,
When they grow up and leave, they'll surely be missed.

We'll always love them, these charmers, our girls,
Whether they've long hair, short cut or curls;
In mini or maxi, shorts or blue jeans,
Can't help but admire our wonderful teens.

Caye E. Hurst

FROM GRANNY WITH LOVE

Little boy just two years old,
You are more precious to me, than gold,
With hair the color of a bright new penny,
Going in all directions, many.
Busy exploring, keeping me hopping,
Still only when the popcorn is popping.
How you love your bubble bath,
Splishing and splashing, giggles and laughs.
Blowing soap bubbles out on the lawn,
Running to see if your hot dog is done.
Chasing fireflies in the night,
But they have more sense than to light.
Munching on your bag of fries,
Watching cars as they go by.
Running, playing, picking flowers,
Something new to learn each hour.
Seeing the world from your wee eyes,
Makes my spirit reach new highs.
You have my love and admiration,
You are giving me an education.

Clara Ann Foucht

US

We are separated by mountains, by oceans and rivers,
We are as far apart as anyone can be,
but our hearts and our love have grown,
as deep and infinite as the sky,
as great and forceful as the blue sea.
When you see the moon rising in the horizon
look at its shine, look at its bright,
because behind the soft and pale smile
the murmur of my voice is telling you,
how much I love you and how much I care.
Then when we are together again
our minds will grow wiser
and our bodies will unite in an embrace,
of caresses and desires,
giving bloom to an eternal rose of love!

Andrea Almac

OH HOW WE FORGET

Oh, how we forget, the sweet warm moments when we met.
The feel of love and joy in the air,
The feeling of something that's so rare.

Oh, how we forget, the beautiful dawn of a sunset,
The feel, thrill of someone new,
The way we say, I love only you.

Oh, how we forget, to look back over the years and yet,
We find all we can to drift apart,
And we leave behind broken hearts.

Oh, how we forget, togetherness is what counts and yet,
What will it take to make us see,
Our love is as new as we want it to be.

Grace Camell

SISTER

We might be a long way apart
and the years might go by,
but the ties that bound us
we can feel them even from afar.
You are my older sister,
You are my dearest one,
I have always looked up to you
and I can only say,
that I am a very lucky person,
for having a sister like such.
Have many more to come, dear sister
and when we both are at the end of our paths,
we still be together, holding stronger, holding tight,
and God will say: "Here are the two
sisters that haven't ever been apart!"

Andrea Almac

PEOPLE HELPING PEOPLE

People helping people for the dignity of man,
Is the way of life for each of us to lend a helping hand.
The task that's set before us, be it big or be it small,
To help the weary neighbor with his back against the wall.

To help the weary neighbor lose the burden of his debt,
To give him understanding in the crises to be met.
To show him, and to walk with him, according to a plan.
It's people helping people for the dignity of man.

Edward G. Tilma

I LOVE SWEET ELLA

(Sonnet)

In outside beauty Ella has no peer,
 Let others envy loveliness supreme
Or glance at what makes her so precious dear
 Vade mecum stands she all agleam.
Enclosed within this fascinating form
 She has an unseen soul of greater worth
Which radiates her love forever warm
 Enwrapped in altruism from her birth.
Enveloped in one person are the traits
 That beautify her mind and body both
Escaping in our dozens of portraits
 Lie virtues which to photographs are loath
Let Ella's beauty glorify all space
 And add to her amazing grace.

Frank E. Greene

MESSAGE TO A MARRIED MAN

I will not dance inside your ring
And you must exit it to take my hand.
I think it is better to leave things this way.
Remain my friend. Ask me for no more.
For I have no more to give. And to
Insist would be to say that what I
Have to offer is not good enough.
And if my friendship cannot hold you
Then my love never would.

Robin M. Shelton

THE ECHO

(What is love — What is love?)

Love is a place — A safe place where loneliness is a stranger
Who has no seat at the table.

Love is a feeling — A feeling that allows the soul to luxuriate
Like sand that is caressed by the tide's
Ebb and flow.

Love is a dream — A dream that is the shadow of all we hope
To gain, but is the substance of more than
We can grasp.

Love is a word — A spoken word that whispers like thunder,
And if unheard, roars like the down of a swan.

Kenneth E. Pippin

LOVE FOR MANKIND

Mankind has many things
Too numerous to mention,
But one thing it can never have enough of
Is love and kindness with all its traditions.

We hear of wars and murder and hate
And we wonder what our world is to become,
But a little caring and kindness is all it takes
To make mankind a world of love.

So we strive for a better way to live
Without thought to those in need,
When all it takes is each person to give
A little time, a little love, and everyone to read,
"It is better to give than to receive."

Patsy Youree

I LOVE YOU MY DEAR

I love you my dear . . .
how much?
All the words on earth can't
express the depth of it.
You have been so loving, good
and kind . . .
So many wonderful hours and days
we have put away,
And each is a marvelous treasure
in our hearts . . .
Time is passing swiftly now, and
I am growing old,
So I want you and all of the
world to know —
Your tender loving care has kept
me going all these years.

Harold James Douglas

NAME OUR ETERNAL DEBT

We adore our life with Jesus
Who made up this universe
And we love His many blessings
That reward our second birth
Without his second coming
There could be no life no more
So we owe Him our life's praises
Eternally for shore
He keeps us safe from dangers
That may erupt our way
He keeps our bodies healthy
If we kneel down and pray
And we love our life with Jesus
God is the only living way
So let us trust in Jesus
Every step throughout the day

Aaron Young

LAMENT

I had to lose so much
to realize that the touch
I'd relied on too often
couldn't be bought
with tears that softened
my cheeks and churned my heart.

Sara Ann Holcombe

CATS

The yellow cat's
In love again,
Yowling to go out,
Leaving her kittens,
Her half-grown kittens
with us.
She's weary of motherhood
And all the fuss.

Whenever
The She Cat
Makes love
She gets with kitten,
Which
On her social life
Puts much restriction.

Lucinda Blair

DEAR CHILD

You're my pride and joy
but your momma's toy.
So, I can't have you here
by my side.
And it hurts me so
not to watch you grow.
It's the pain that grows
deep inside.
love makes a child,
not the other way around;
and I'm sorry you
were used that way.
As you go through the world,
there's something I want you to know;
there's not one day that goes by
that I don't say this to you in a sigh:
May you strive for knowledge and wisdom,
have courage,
and know
love.

Antonio Juarez

JAN

Though your hair should turn to silver
And your eyes begin to grey.
Instead of thinking of leaving,
I'd only want to stay.

Through a million cups of coffee
That in mornings we could drink,
My love toward you could be stronger
As each day of you I'd think.

Never have I seen such beauty,
Displayed in such good taste.
Beauty filled with goodness,
Nothing left to waste.

I'll always remember you,
'Though my mind be taken away.
The visions of your loveliness
Will fill each waking day.

Billy Charles Grant

ALWAYS IS FOREVER

Always is forever
And forever never ends
So I love my love forever
With a love that never bends.

I love my love forever
When the sun is shining bright
I love my love forever
In the darkest of the night.

Love cannot be pictured
It has no shape or form
Love is more than human
Should be a human norm.

I'll love my love forever
With a love that never dies
For love is more than human
It reaches to the skies.

Floyd C. Jones

YOU PROMISED ME ROSES

You promised me roses,
but all I got was dandelions;
for you the greenest grass was always on
the other side of the fence.
I watered ours copiously with tears,
tried weed and feed — 20-15-10
of understanding, patience and love —
but all I got was more dandelions
and promises of roses.
With my dandelion complex, for years
I almost stopped wanting roses.
Now you can take your weeds
and go blow on someone else's lawn.
I'll find somebody who
will always give me roses,
not just promise to.
If not, I'll buy my own.

Kathleen Konkin van Es

VAN ES, KATHLEEN KONKIN. Born: Calgary, Alberta, Canada: Married: 12-2-72 to Con van Es; Education: The University of Calgary, B.A. English and Drama, 1969; Prof. Interim Certificate, 1970; Garbutt's Business College, 1949; Occupations: Secretary, 28 years; High School Teacher, English and Drama, 1 year in Calgary; retired past 2 ½ years; Awards: Alberta Weekly Newspaper Association Award for general feature article "About Retirement," 1980-81; short stories, articles, *Village Press,* 1978, 1979, 1980; cash prizes in poetry and creative writing competitions; *Cross-Canada Quarterly Review,* book prize, short story, "Master of the House," 1985; Poetry: 'When I Compare You,' *Midwest Poetry Review,* October, 1985; 'Then Came Dieppe,' *American Poetry Anthology,* 1985; 'Attic of My Mind,' *The Village Press,* 1978.

I WANT YOU

Suddenly
  Stepped into my life
Please don't let me be misunderstood

Please don't go
  Something's burning
  Love and desire
    Fire
    Burning love
I want you to want me

Hey you
  Lead me on
Everyone's a winner

All I want
  Muskrat love
    Inside and outside
Knowing me, knowing you

That's the way I like it
  You and I
When will I see you again

Paul Weakly

MY CHILDREN, MY LOVE

I love my children so very much,
So precious a gift from God above,

They give me happiness every day,
And with this poem I want to say:
"My children, my love"

I have a girl and I have a boy,
And they give me so much joy,

When I look in their smiling faces,
I know someday they will be grown
And have to make a life of their own!

But until they are:
"My children, my love"

Jesus, please keep them safe for me,
My heart would break to lose them!

But this poem is my prayer, Dear Lord,
The gift of life please give them!
"My children, my love"

Jeanette E. Logan

I HEAR THE HEAVENS CALLING ME

I hear the heavens calling me
And voices singing quietly
What I see is very surprising
I see holy angels arising
No pain nor numbness that I feel
Can this be true can this be real
Am I on the verge to die
I can't even tell my family good-bye
I see a big bright shining light
It hurts my eyes will I lose my sight
So many questions, in so little time
I'm fading away
I'm gone to stay

Katrice Jones

Jim I love you
I want you to know
That I love you too much
To ever let you go.

Wherever you are
I want to be there
And Darling I'll always
Want you near.

Together forever
We will always be
The stars in heaven
And you and me.

I love you more
And more every day.
I miss you so much
When you are away.

Honey, I'll wait
If it takes forever
Just for that day
We'll always be together.

I'll quit writing this stuff
When you say "I do,"
I'll spend the rest of my life
Making love to you.

Chloy Thomas Wilson

Hurt so deeply
she crawled so creepily
into a cocoon
festooned with balloons
that burst so sleepily.

Kathleen Shea

A stranger in my house.

An intimate unknown
Who can trespass all doors
With her diplomacy of impostures

This stranger in my house.
This outsider inside
My skin, my skins

Through the fine art of postures
The tenant of my indulgence
The stranger in my house

Loose, interlocking commitments
Of irrevocable affection
With this most intimate of unknowns

In a standoff of sidelong glances,
A stalemate of slanted advances.
And still a stranger in my house.

Under strictest terms of endearment,
Devotions as bound as binding
We lease our affections

And charter content
By indulgent clauses
Of patient consent.

William J. Christie

AS OUR LOVE LINGERS ON

When we were young
  we were called outcast;
They said:
  "It will never last."

We were married,
  happy as can be;
A happiness that
  only could be.

We had four children
  and what a joy —
Three little girls
  and one little boy.

As time flew by —
  days, months and years,
Our children grew
  through joys and tears.

It's now well over
  sixty years ago
As our love lingers on
  and our hearts are still aglow.

Roy E. Wells

WITHOUT YOU

The moon glides ever slowly,
    Across the sky so bright;
As I lie here reminiscing,
    About holding you close last night!

In the silence of the moment,
    I reflect upon so many things;
The warmth, the tender passion,
    Your touch always seems to bring!

If only I could hold you now,
    And feel your body close;
And feel you gently breathing,
    As we both begin to doze . . .

My heart would be so happy,
    That you would surely know;
All the secrets hidden deep inside;
    I've tried so not to show!

The moon will surely fade away,
    As the sun begins to rise,
I wish I could be with you,
    And watch it by your side!

Colleen Doyle

LOVE

Love is flowers blooming
In a field of flowing grass.
Love is being snuggled,
By someone warm and close.
Love is the sun shining
On a cold, windy day.
Love is being all alone
And having a friend come along.
For Love is what keeps
Two friends together.

Anne Weaver

IMMORTAL LOVE

Finally . . . the quest has ended . . .
Our souls, with love and passions
Have been blended . . .
Finally . . . my soul is at rest . . .
For within your arms I feel at rest,
Like a bird in a nest.

Finally, words into poems have become
A reality, for your Egyptian soul has
Fulfilled my longed and ancient desires . . .
"It" spoke to us . . . then in the silence of
Immortality, aroused a love no mortal
Could comprehend . . .
We both desired this soul-personality
With the greatest halo!
For we smiled and the world came to
A shine . . . light, love, peace, and harmony
Is ours for the moment . . .
Oh . . . come beautiful creature . . . with this
Brutal reality I will fly you to the
Regions of immortality!

Maria Brunilda Roman

ONLY A DREAM

Our dreams take us to places
We long to see,
Sharing moments with people
We long to be with.

Last night I walked the shore with you by my side.
The tide came in caressing our feet.
The moon shone softly and sent down
Generous showers of beams.
We talked through glances
When our words sounded confused.

I felt your trembling, almost boyish touch —
Gazed into your eyes . . .
Forgot others existed.

We then kissed with meaning
And I awoke.
It was only a dream . . .

Or was it?

Elizabeth Ann Cobb

THE DAY RETURNS, MY BOSOM BURNS

The day returns, my bosom burns,
The blissful day we two did meet;
Though winter wild in tempest toiled,
Ne'er summer sun was half so sweet.
Than a' the pride that loads the tide,
And crosses o'er the sultry line, —
Than kingly robes, and crowns and globes,
Heaven gave me more; it made thee mine.

While day and night can bring delight,
Or nature aught of pleasure give, —
While joys above my mind can move,
For thee and thee alone I live;
When that grim foe of life below
Comes in between to make us part,
The iron hand that breaks our band,
It breaks my bliss, — it breaks my heart.

Robert Burns

SILVER TWILIGHT

The sun now sets in pinkish splendor,
As moonlight glows up from the hills.
Luminous union, all is calm,
As it seems even time stands still.

The snow, once more, falls from the heavens,
And blankets all for miles around
In silver stardust, not quite real;
The enchantment o'ertakes all sound.

Two sets of footsteps break the stillness,
Go crackling through the frozen snow.
Two figures cast a single shadow,
Just an instant in twilight's glow.

Deborah Nielson

ONCE IN A LIFETIME

Life at times can be so strange
faces and names are just rearranged.
Broken hearts that never heal
soft, tender feelings that you no longer feel.

Hearts once filled with warmth,
have now hardened to stone.
Waking up in the dark of the night,
you've been left behind, alone.

Only once in a lifetime
a lonely heart shall find
true love and great friendship,
a love that is one of a kind.

K. J. Thompson

A DISAPPOINTMENT

He sits down on the edge of the bed
Just hard enough to make my body shake.
He slowly takes one shoe off, then the other,
In a quiet hushed way, so as not for me to wake.
He sits looking out the window, wondering if
someone else was near, perhaps his mother?
Then he turns to me and pulls the stray hair out
of my eye and takes it and kisses it.
then softly lays it on my pillow.
As if he knew I was watching through closed eyes,
he carefully raised the cover and slid under.
He softly put his hand upon my breast,
And as if he read my mind; sighed, turned over
and fell asleep.

Kelly (Dodson) Hadley

DAYDREAMER

He rests his head upon a freckled arm,
And quite forgets instructor, rule, and book.
His thoughts drift out to April on the farm, —
Corn-planting time . . . the day a maiden took
Him water. Water! when his gnawing thirst
Called for more love . . . and how she told him, "No,
Not till your schooling's through" . . . and how she's nursed
Her lonely feelings with another beau.

Harlan J. Leach

AS CLOSE AS YESTERDAY

Sitting there, next to you.
Touching every now and then again.
To test — Is this a dream?
I thought it so long a time
Since last we met;
Yet when we searched each other's eyes,
There seemed no time had passed since then.
Memories must have been of only yesterday.
You there, being the you I know.
I there loving you.
Places changed — and names.
Growing showed in both of us.
Yet I could see the sorrow in your eyes.
And I suppose my pain did not pass unnoticed.
When will there be time again?
Time to share our souls as close as yesterday?

Grace Ramelle

JUST BETWEEN YOU AND ME

You showed me your feelings with simply a song,
I heard the words, and knew love wasn't wrong.

Your motions so confident, your words so real,
Your mind so patient to accept how i feel.

You overcame my fears, and let me be me,
You made my life like i wanted it to be.

Time and time again i see, a love that seems
Strong was not meant to be.
You proved that wrong, by just loving me.

Julie Derouin

FRIENDSHIP

I like you for the smile
that you can, not only give,
but can create in me
the joy that comes from being noticed.

I like you for your certain arrogance
and yet within
a deep feeling
for a power that lives.

I like you because you help me write again
not wondering the futility of it
but the fruitfulness it can bring.

I like you because I am radiant
with a wonderful feeling when I think of you
and I share this happiness
with others around me.

I like you because you like me too
and we can easily fall in love
but we will not
because we are friends.

Edith G. Pasaporte

YOU

There are no words to describe the you
that I have come to know so well.
Your face, your touch, your smile.
The times we've shared
Skiing in Vermont
Florida winters
Laughing in quiet solitude
You
I love you, I need you, I want you.
No one will ever come to know you the way that I do,
No one will ever need to
You are my love,
You are my life.
You transfix me by the way you give life to others . . .
Just by a word
Just by a touch
But, mostly by the life that you have given to me.
I will live my life with you,
I will live, love, laugh
through you.
You — You are the love of my life.

Janice M. Quinn

QUINN, JANICE MARIE. Born: Lynn, Massachusetts, 9-15-59; Married: 8-10-85 to Stanley Jason Roy; Education: Huntington Institute, Norwich, Connecticut, 6-77; Occupation: President of Cassette Publishing Company; Comments: *The poem I wrote was written for my husband for Valentine's Day. As of this date, I haven't even begun to start writing any new poetry. But I hope to in the near future.*

UNHOLY GRAVE

Unholy grave, you loosen earth before me, to reveal
The past I've tried to bury deep lives on in memory, still.
In wooden chest, so dark and musty, your letters are almost real
Many rains have fallen, your grave is dark and still.
Within the locket, 'round my neck, your photograph, and silky lock of hair
Your crooked smile, I carry with me, as your only heir.
Suicides are never kind; in pain, I see it, in my mind
Questions never answered — Remain; a haunting sign
of how well I never knew you,
but I don't bring flowers, and I don't visit often.

Beverly F. Ross

TO MY HUSBAND

I LOVE YOU —
For your **C**hristian character,
For your **L**ove toward me,
For your **I**nspiration for me,
For being **N**ear, and
For **T**rusting me.

I LOVE YOU —
For your **A**spiration in life,
For being the pastor of my **C**hurch,
For being **K**ind and honest,
For being **E**nergetic in your work, and
For **R**emembering special days.

Charlene Carpenter Acker

ACKER, CHARLENE MUNN. Pen Name: Charlene Carpenter Acker; Born: Titus County, Texas; Married: to Rev. Clint Acker; Education: East Texas State University, B.S., 1944; University of Arkansas, Masters in Education, 1963; Occupation: Retired Teacher, taught school for 29 years; Memberships: Association of Texas Professional Educators, Retired Teachers Association; Poetry: 'The Giant Snowman,' *American Poetry Anthology,* Fall, 1985; 'Down at the Pond,' *The New York Poetry Society Anthology, Book I,* 1985; 'Snowflakes,' *Moods and Mysteries,* Poetry Press, 1985; 'The Night the Trees Were Crackling,' *Songs For All Seasons,* Green Valley Publishing, 1985; Comments: *I write poetry as a hobby. I express my feeling about nature, animals, and people. I tell of the experiences I have had living on the farm. I also use imaginations in my writings. I write poems that will tell a short story. I am a Christian and depend on the Lord to help me write. I have many blessings to be thankful for.*

I WANT TO TAKE YOU BELOW

HONORABLE MENTION

I want to take you below granite and
loam, below the roots of oak and willow,
until our palms hold the beginnings
of rivers, our eyes are lumps of coal.
I want to take you deep enough to feel
the pull of the earth strengthen,
until we wear arrowheads and flint tools
like a string of beads, use animal bones as
walking sticks. I want to take you down to
where crustaceans once drank the milk of
glaciers, where the seeds of man are still lodged
in the slant of a Tyrannosaurus's belly,
until I can no longer remember you in the clothes
you are wearing now, or you standing naked and alone.
I want to reach across this space that separates
us, bring you so close that we can barely discern
the width of one of us, until on your forehead
appears the soft imprint of a hand, just
like the shape of my hand.

Ron Deverman

CERTAIN LOVES I'VE KNOWN

I do not think certain loves I've known
Think so kindly of me nor remember love
Whose fire burned fiercely to embers
Still glowing from unforgotten passion.

I think they remember feeling the bars
That tenderly locked their rapture
Within my heart and guarded it lovingly
Somehow they must have felt the throb
Of ecstasy too precious to share
And wept to see wings made to soar
Through undiscovered skies lie beaten
And battered against the walls of utter devotion.

I think they watched in horror as love
In one last desperate shudder
Surrendered to safety's strangling grasp.

I do not think certain loves I've known
Think so kindly of me.

Coleta McNabb

PHASES OF LOVE

We are nearest to being God when we love.
First there's love from Mother
Her tender kiss; touch as from above.
Our teenage years brings infatuation
Each new one's love has to be heaven sent.
The craze of the wearing his sweater
Or the high school ring of that gent.
Wedding bells ring now he's your own,
A bedmate, companion, you're never alone.
Love is a cool thing now; it's
Giving to each other and answering the phone.
Mom and Pop time is loving
That little special Margie or Joe.
Making sure they have food,
Housing, clothes, car, and where they are you know.
Now they're grown and it's back to loving
Only yourself and what you want in a wink.
This part of love is not
As easy as you think.

Alma Lane Kirkland Thorpe

REMEMBER . . .

Remember when you hid in lush bush
and whispered to girlfriend with deep blush
(pointing at my sweaty mane):
"I will marry him!" You're vain
of the choice of mate blossomed with "Hush."

The golden moments of our youth were swallowed.
Far away I fought and bled; coming out
like bat from hell I saw you on a boat about
to cast off to West. I later followed.

As homeless riff-ruff refugees under three
Crowns' hospitality we briefly met
for frustrated agape, and I was set
to cross the Big Pond — ever to see thee?

What can a maimed foreign warrior in
the God's Own Country do? Left longing
for what we most wanted in
the world! My heart's still singing
your name when devout love devours sin.

Roman Ubakivi

fantasy

love me in the garden breeze;
stumble up hills and tumble down leaves.
when silence falls amidst the sighs,
i'm fantasizing through your eyes.

touch me with a tender smile;
let me dream with you a while.
i've been to heaven once or twice,
while loving you in paradise.

don't ever let them wake me,
from this life i have with you.
please don't let them take me,
to a world i never knew.
i have never been as happy;
when holding on so tightly,
to you in ecstasy.

Annemarie Bettica

DADDY AFTER MANY YEARS

My daddy's gone. Where did he go?
I'm just a little girl and I don't know.
Daddy your little girl is so afraid.
I locked the door on your memory.
And over the years my young heart paid.

But, understand daddy it was a way to survive.
All a way to keep my soul alive.
After fourteen years we finally meet.
This locked-up heart is unlocked.
With memories flooding sweet.
Daddy and his little girl talked.
Don't cry baby for years gone by.
'Cause daddy always loved you.
And he will till he dies.

I'm all grown up, with a family too.
And an unshadowed past thanks to you.
My daddy again after many years.
I want you to know that your baby,
Has then, now and will always love you too.

M. James

FOREVER

She is broad-hewed and magnificent.
I gaze at her endless beauty, and am enthralled
with the ever freshness and vigor of her charms.

I have seen her suffer. I have heard her cry.
And I have cried for her.

She has a warmth and compassion that endears me to her.

I was gone for so long, and I missed her so.
God how I missed her!

And when I saw her again, it was with a gladness
of tears and joy.
The heavens touched the blessed earth when I kissed her.

She is not perfect. She never will be.
But she has embraced my kin, and given them of her heart
and of her hopes.

I was born to love her.
To her bosom she will take me when I die.
She stands tall and beautiful and proud.
And I love her. My country!

Jack V. Diamond

YESTERDAY'S LOVE

Wet leaves snapped
In the wind of aching, sleepless night.
Tree limbs waved
Snow shot skyward.
We embraced, wept, promised, pledged . . .
Then, we were silent.
Our eyes, haunted from mist,
Burned with our gentle hearts
And then we parted
Without fear.

H. Andrew Sonneborn

LOVERS PARTING

This poem was written in Chinese by Chin Kuan, who lived from 1049-1100.

Across a fence the soft wind tosses the moon
into my chamber when I slumber.
In the silent night, the magpies are quiet.
All of a sudden, on my pillow
I find my beloved weaving girl.
With great joy, hand in hand
we dance into the heaven.

Misty and gloomy is the moon.
In sadness the first knock of the morn.
Needless to weep again before the lamp
when she waves farewell.
Together even a hundred years,
we have to part.

She returned after a brief separation.
But this time there will be no reunion.
Turtle Hill is the heart-breaking place.
The setting sun looks upon a lone pagoda
standing in dignity,
fighting against the tears.

Christina Ching Tsao

LOVE ON ICE

Whirling, spinning toward me — you.
  Silver skates flash in the circle of light.
Leaping, twisting toward me — you.
  The bright costume flares around your legs.

Dancing, smiling toward me — you.
  I love you.
Cheering, applauding, the audience likes you.
  How I love you.

Dreaming, I must be dreaming,
  to see such perfection — you.
Oh, to be this close to you.

The music fades, the lights black out.
  And you, you are gone.

I love you. Come back.
  I want to tell you —
    I love you —
      always.

I love you.

Ann Dutcher

FANTASTIC RUTH

From the moment she entered the room
I felt her presence.
The chemistry was there.

Well rounded body curves.
A Madonna face
Framed by long auburn hair.
Unforgettable mellow voice
Vibrated like violins.

Drawn by magnetic attraction
We spent our finest hours
On white encrusted beach,
Two bodies
Embraced as one

The journey home filled with emotion
As each expressed the inner self.
Conversation lingered on
Through the night,
Enhanced by hot kisses and passionate embraces
Till the sun awakened
And we parted.

F. Richard Dieterle

IF

If time revolves around a smile
  and I laugh with no bitterness over what was
If space fills me with beauty and love
  that trust is a joy and a commitment.
If truth grants me wisdom and courage
  to know what is and what is not
If I can climb mountains and walk in a thunderstorm
  of hidden misery and insurmountable woes,
If snows are but trials to reshape me
  into a woman you would want me to be
I will not be afraid
I will have courage and faith
Because I have you.

Edith G. Pasaporte

TRUE

Looking back at past mistakes,
I feel I've finally got it right,
Anticipation as dawn awakes,
A sigh as comes the night.
My world revolves on your love;
I seldom ever doubt.
And I think "Heaven above —
How did I do without?"
But how can I be sure
(As I venture towards you)
That your heart will also endure,
Or that your love is true?
Then looking in those deep blue eyes,
I drown in their emotion.
The mere uncertainty dies;
Soon forgotten with one motion.
Tender is your caress, sending shivers up my spine.
Now I see, with all the rest, I fell for any line.
So now I see your love *is* true —
True to me, as I'm true to you.

Karma Jensen

THE MOMENT OF LOVE

There is a moment in life itself
  of two spirits uniting, becoming one,
Expanding minds, encompassing hearts
  as the colors of the rainbow reflecting the sun.

From the mountaintop as a dream unfolding,
  there is a moment in time and space
To know the completion of yourself,
  is to see the eye's resplendent light.

The reaching of life to fulfill itself,
  is the illusion and reality of one who dreams,
The moment is now then a memory,
  mirrored in the eyes of all who have seen.

In life's law, it is the law of love
  for love is life, transformed, manifest,
The source of two worlds becoming one,
  there is a moment, it is life itself.

Carole April Binette

I SLEPT YOUR LOVE RIGHT OUT OF MY LIFE

I lie here tonight with you on my mind;
Your love WAS the sweetest that I could find.
But somehow it faded like an old rose,
The reason we parted nobody knows.
I wonder whose arms hold you so tight;
Like mine used to till the mornin' light
I miss your bedroom eyes and funny little smile,
And your perfume that lingered for awhile.
You're loving another with all of your heart,
I found out the hard way, right from the start.
You made me feel like I was in Heaven,
On a 1-10 scale, babe, you're an eleven.
Now my life is empty since you're gone;
I sure wish I could find me someone.
To share my joys, sorrows, and life;
Be by my side, my lover, my wife
I slept your love right out of my life,
Oh, how I wanted you for my wife!
The passion we knew has since disappeared;
My heart feels the pain that once I had feared.

Larry J. Ramsey

MY HEART IS MISSIN' YOU!

I'd like to let you know
In some funny little way
Just how I feel about you
But don't know what to say

I love you, I need you
I'm lost without you when you're gone,
My heart is missin' you —
I know that I was wrong.

If you will just forgive me
I swear I'll never stray —
Please tell me that you love me
And come back home today.

My heart is missin' you
Please come home to stay
My heart is missin' you
Don't ever, ever, go away.

Ava Lois Halstead

OPERATION 3/3/86

Arrive at hospital in the snow,
Thanks to loving sister,
Who waited in A. C. U.
I journeyed on a gurney
Through many hallways.
Then surgery area doors slid aside.
Dr. Sanidad, anesthetist, cast his spell,
And Dr. Althoff did surgical art
On painful hernia.
Then I'm told to wake up,
The operation is over.
Back to room I ride,
With thirteen clamps in my side.
I'm served water and orange juice,
Then comes a tray of goodies.
Sister helps me dress,
And we're off for her address,
In Dave and Rhoda's car,
For a week of recuperation.
That was my operation 3/3/86.

Elenor M. Mitchell

TESTAMENTARY LOVE

Can we see
The light come through those doors?
Can we hear
The opening split of our minds?
To go and come
Quivers on our backs
To say
Come back, come hear us say
We can feel the power coming
Adjusting to the light
To make us free of thistles
To our ways
Hear us say today
Will we learn how to play
Our chances
With the twisted
Nations' reign
Come on, we will
Find our way —
Right away!

Wendi Gifford

IF ONLY

If only
You could slip
Your arms around me,
And hold me, safe
Against the rushing
wild wind of
Terror.

If you could,
I would stay with you
Forever,
Nestled deep within the
Shelter of your
Freedom and fancy,
And your sensitive intelligence
Mingling with mine.

You are already
Part of me,
A motion of love's
Waters
Flowing in my
Aching Spirit.

Valerie Moreno

MEMORIES

I look back in time
And I remember
When I thought
You were mine.

The memories flash
There before me
And seem to crash
In on reality —
That you can't live
In a dream forever.

First Love,
You'll always be
My endless love.

Forever, I'll hold
You close in my heart
Where you had a part.
You know I care
I'll always love you
Even though now there
Is someone new.

Debra L. Bradley

HAUNTED

Haunted by a raging passion,
Love burns like a flame inside
my heart,
The windows fade to black and I
see a distant figure.
You — standing alone, waiting, yearning
for me.
The sparkle in your smile engulfs
me.
The heat from your body surrounds
me,
I long to hold you and love you —
to have you.

Kathleen Rogers

A CHRISTMAS WISH . . . A CHRISTMAS TEAR

a Christmas wish was said for you,
a special wish that's shared by two,
I hope and dream to someday see
your life filled with Love and happiness
for everyone to see;

a Christmas tear was cried for you,
a special tear just made for you,
it's kind of sad in many ways
the Love that's felt inside my soul
for you my dear just can't be told;

but someday you'll see
what's inside my heart,
and then you'll know
we'll never part

David Nelson Roberts, Jr.

BOLD BECAME OLD

My teenage years were tempest-tossed:
So many loves were won and lost.
Girls really took my breath away —
What I would give for that today.

Robert Emmett Clarke

BEREFT

Our little house is swept and shined
To welcome in spring's kindlier weather
That warms the walls and shelves all lined
With memories of our years together.

Here are the sconces from Madrid,
The painting that we found in Rome,
The Chinese vase on which we bid
At auction and bore proudly home.
The kitchen gleams with brass and tin
Where bright panes let the sunshine in.

Your garden's bloomed since early rain.
Azaleas glow in doorside urn.
Now I must learn to bear the pain
Of knowing you will not return.

Helen D. Edmonds

SLIP AWAY

Just when I think you're gonna stay
you have to get away
you feel the urge to play
you let love slip away

I waited for a while
then I let you go
It was a long time before I could smile
always waiting for you to show
but it's just your style
to always be on the go

run away
time to play
can't ever stay
just slip away

Doreen Lee

FIRE OF MY HEART

The way you looked at me,
Your eyes most compassionate,
Has set my heart ablaze,
To sweetest thoughts of love unsaid.

The night you called me sweetie,
When I helped you on the job,
Has set my mind to sweetness,
Of souls with the same affinities.

That tender look you gave
Could only mean your love,
My love of labor is not lost,
When my love for you is at stake.

Dare you not accept my other poems,
Your shyness' fear of fire my heart can spread,
Love is fire conquering all,
Like the sun radiating rays.

For Heaven's record are all these written,
As you are the spring in my heart,
Which sings the canticles of love,
Endless and eternal like God.

Rolando L. Boquecosa

LOVE

The sweetest of human emotions,
Sometimes so badly burned,
When touched and healed by the Master's hand,
Is given more freely
By those who have learned
That love has no heart,
No hands,
No arms,
No voice,
But ours.

Mildred H. Thomas

LOVE

Who would think that such a small word
Could yet be the greatest word ever heard?
Many a theme, story and rhyme
Have been written on the subject down through time.

Apostle Paul said that love was a virtue
Greater than hope and faith, too.
Love isn't proud, evil or blind
But sees another's hurts and is gentle and kind.

She keeps her cool when ready to speak
And rejoices in truth — is humble and meek.
Thoughts of self never enter her mind,
But thoughts of others who in her confide.

Love suffers long and endures pain,
Works to save others and not for self gain.
She believes all she hears without any doubt,
Secrets and confidences never lets out.

Love is the greatest of all emotions known;
In its ripest stage, its beauty is shown.
The beauty of perfection, without a flaw,
Is in love, when it's shared with all.

Teresa Syner

I SEE YOU

I see you
a curiosity
although I knew
it wouldn't be too long
before it grew
into a need, a hunger;
what can I do
to create a fantasy just meant for you?
You are by text
the perfect prime example of your sex.
Your form is grace
with the look of God's sweet angels on your face.
I'm filled with joy
and the spicy deviations I employ,
a puppeteer who loves his little toy
while Betty Boop salutes her soldier boy.
Then I see you
a curiosity
although I knew
it wouldn't be too long
before it grew.

William D. Leavitt

FRIENDSHIP'S ARMS

Dedicated to Trish

I see your hurt my friend
but I cannot ease your pain,
I can only stand and watch
as your teardrops fall like rain.
I want to reach out and
hold you in friendship's arms,
Assuring you a brighter day will come
and you're safe from life's harm.
I want to offer the benefit of my years
and the knowledge from seeds I've sown,
But this is one trip I realize
you'll have to go alone.
I give my love in friendship —
that's all I can say.
If you find you need me
any time night or day,
You have but to reach out
or call my name
To have someone on your side
in life's unknowing game.

Diana L. Waite

ADMITTED ANDRADE ADORATIONS

In Francisco Andrade we have a great good friend.
The goodness of his deeds for us seems to have no end.
In performing duties of his medical practice,
He'll quiz and test thoroughly ere extending advice!

The sedentary routine, seeing so many patients,
Stirs wee body activity which irks his patience.
Not to fret. At home, he needs not long to seek a chore.
A big yard, garden, horse and dog need 'tention galore!

Libby, his fine practicing nurse and sweet loving wife,
Can offer him needed empathy. What a great life!
And a bright, loving daughter so neat, nice, sweet and trim
Does grace Frank's and Libby's busy lives. Her name is Kim!

To improve his lot, one Jan. eighty-six, there's no way.
Howe're we all extend to them our love ev'ry day!

Mervin L. Schoenholtz

ISABELLA.

EMELINE.

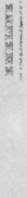

OUR LIFE

Only just beginning
Never to be a broken union
Two become solid as one
Time stops to let us be
Lost in the universe of love
Found by the hope of a lifetime

Thrilled by the intimate thoughts
Carried out in eventful moments
Senses reach for the highest peaks
Searching out for inward satisfaction
Together that dream becomes real
Sharing in the delight of it all

Every day becoming stronger
The bond entitled to eternity
Purpose to be fulfilled
Love is the true key to happiness
Opening doors for now and forever
My life to be spent with you.

Thomas J. Moore

ME AND YOU

Sing me a song of love —
And I'll sing you a song of love.

I'm looking at you —
And you're looking at me.
And we both silently agree
IT'S LOVE!
. . . It's love for you and me.

Not a moment escapes
without
a thought of you.
Just the mere mention of your name —
I just don't feel the same.

It's a funny little feeling
deep down inside
And with all my effort —
I can't seem to hide
. . . My love for you.

Jacquelyn Ponder

THE SMILE OF HOPE

Don't tell me again:
"I am out of your life."
That is not true.
Don't torment me anymore
with the cruel desert
of your absence.
Let me see you again
with that smile of hope.
Turn my nostalgic days
into happiness.
You can do that, tonight!
Call me, and tell me:
Come over!

Richard Herdz

THE FLAVOR OF WARMTH

Falling snowflakes settle
To frozen ground
During a night
Of twenty below,
I seek
Meek wine
To warm my heart and soul.
I savor the warmth
Slumber in joy
Till light of day
Brings warm sunshine.
I arouse.
I say
To the wine
Good morning Paula Boles
Good friend of mine.

Wayne West

When we were together
We touched and returned
We played when we loved
We took joy from each other

And we laughed together
And we felt every nuance
And we enriched every day

With mutual feeling
With every muscle and movement
With heart and with phallus

Our spirits were joined
Our feelings expanded
Our love was completeness
When we were together

Jay Boden

SIZE THREE WINGS FOR TERRI

Will they have wings to fit me, mommy?
When I go to live in the sky —
Will the angels hold me to them
When I miss you and I cry?
Will Jesus Christ know when I'm coming?
Will He come to meet us there —
When I go to sleep, dear Daddy
Will you hear the angel choir?
When I get my angel wings
And they are fixed upon my frame —
When I learn the songs to sing
Will Jesus give me an angel name?
When we pray before I leave, Mommy
'Cause I'm so tired and need to go —
Can we pray for you and Daddy
'Cause you know I love you so.

Joyce Holt

GOLD STAR

"No greater love hath any man
Than to lay down his life
For another . . ."
No greater pride hath any woman
Than to know that she was
His mother . . .

Faith M. Schremp

LOVE

Soulful eyes stare
frail hands grasp at straws
all the world hungry for
Love

Elizabeth J. Potter

Look into the windows of my soul
Tell me you don't care
I'll believe you then
And let you go

Josefina Balderrama Barrios

HAIKU

Enchanted forests
hold mythical charms only
lovers discover

E. U. Mist

MY LOVE

I know not why the blustering wind
Doth blow upon the lea,
I only know that winter's by
And you are here with me.

Graydon E. Spalding

MY HEART HAS ITS LOVE

The day has its sun,
the night has its stars.
But my heart, my heart
has its love.

Deedee Graves

LOVE

Love is anterior to life,
Posterior to death,
Initial of creation, and
The exponent of breath.

Emily Dickinson

HAIKU

As the gull giggles
over our heads at the sea
I hear God laughing

E. U. Mist

BITTER TRUTH

The warmth and comfort
I found in your arms
I now must seek in stranger's.

Martha A. Hirsch

TO KOJI

Late at night I listen
For your deep breaths.
And in the early mornings
I watch you sleep.
Your warmth enters me —
I feel like a child.
I want to hold
Your hand forever.
Those sturdy, delicate hands
Tender hands that tell stories,
Dry tears, tickle, tempt and touch.
There is nothing
I like better
Than to fold mine in yours
As I fall
Asleep.

Jeanne Saito

LOVER FROM THE PAST

Every once in a while,
I think I see you in the crowd,
My heart races, stomach knots,
I want to run;
Sometimes toward you,
Sometimes away.

Lynn Gonzalez

THE DESIRE

Who but thee can light the flame
Ever burning within my heart?
For you were there, waiting;
I knew it from the start.
Each day I saw you differently.
New worlds to me revealed.
Closer we grew, every day,
Each instant, our lives we'd yield.
Together at last we find ourselves,
Seeking what doesn't exist.
Knowing deep inside our hearts
There's nothing we can't resist.
For every person on the earth,
Inside them burns a fire.
Waiting only to be lit.
Love is their only desire.

Michelle Campbell

SEPTEMBER RAIN

As my heart for you
silently weeps the September
rain falls.
The miles that keep
us so far apart, if only i
could hold you — only in my
dreams.
As i see your smile
it brings back so many
memories.
To cuddle warm with
you by the fire, sparks i
see in your eyes.
To be in love with
you, as the September
rain slowly falls.

Jenny Kvamme

GOD, WHY?

For my brother, Ivan Dana DeLoe III

God took my brother away
I wished he could stay.
We loved him so
God, why did he have to go?

We all sit here in sorrow and pain
I know, no one is to blame.
I miss him so much
I miss his sweet touch.
Please, won't you give him back
you're giving us all a heart attack.

I sit here in tears
thinking about all those wonderful years.
I know he is gone
never again to see the dawn.
God, why did you take my brother away
why couldn't he have stayed?
God, Why?

Joy Reneé DeLoe

WHY IS IT SO HARD TO LOVE?

Love when shared
Is a soul bared.
Nothing held back
To shelter self.

Completely stripped,
Nothing held back.
No fear of hurt,
Exposing self,
In that there is strength.

Love shared, so simple
Why do we make it so hard?
Why not show our real selves?
Why is it so hard?

The child in us cries out,
Our hearts ache,
"Why not let me out?"
Why not let go of self?

Chuck Derr

LOVED FROM AFAR

Those qualities that attract me
Prevent me from reaching out —
Your solidity, your utter calm,
I need those strengths of yours,
And I could give so much to you.

We smile, engage in polite conversation
I am nearly struck dumb by your presence,
a hair's-breadth away from total idiocy.
You may never know how I feel,
How I pass the day longing to see you
and be warmed by your smile.

You will move on, out of my life
But I will always remember
your smile and the pleasure it gave me
and reflect longingly on
what might have been had I dared
To reach out.

Colleen Kinnear

SENTENCES OF LOVE

LOVE is kind,
Never hurtful, harsh, or mean-spirited.
LOVE is true,
Regardless of pressures of wrongdoing.
LOVE is faithful,
In times of hardship, stress or pain.
LOVE is honorable,
Seeks honor for others before self.
LOVE searches for the way of peace,
When seemingly there is no peace.
LOVE is the joy of giving to others,
Before seeking joy for oneself.
LOVE is a helping hand,
In the time of need.
LOVE never fails,
In the time of sorrow and trouble.
LOVE conquers,
In every facet of life.
LOVE IS FOREVER!
GOD IS LOVE!

Eliza Tyler Taylor

LASTING LOVE

It hasn't been easy for us,
The road so rough and long.
With every good there came a bad,
And in every right a wrong.

But like a tree in winter,
We withstood the frost.
Determined to stay together,
To love at any cost.

The pain just made us stronger,
As we held on even more.
The hard times made the good times,
Even better than before.

Looking back at the tears and fears,
That now are in our past.
We can see a strong foundation,
On a love that is meant to last.

Veronica Porter

MISSING AND LOVING YOU

Yes Honey I am really missing you
Because our love is so true
Wishing you were here with me
Because I love you, you see
Wondering where you are
But I know your heart isn't far
Yes I really so miss you Honey
And that isn't so funny
Wondering if you are all right
And if you are lonesome tonight
If you really miss me
And are truly lonely
And if you are Sweetheart
That means we'll never part
Wondering if you are lonely
And if you know I love you only
Are you really so blue
You know I'll be true
I'll dream of you each day
And be good in that way

Judy Obuchowski

We danced around
the fire of
our hearts
being careful not to get
too close or we could get burned
Leaving nothing to
chance we danced and danced
then finally you let go
and the circle was broken
because we were afraid of
the warmth from within
our souls
reaching out like
flames
We were afraid
and felt the heat
and fell out of step.

Pamela Wagers

DISTANT LOVE

You are there, so far away
And with you is my heart.
I hope our feelings don't change
While we're apart.

I miss you a little more
As each day goes by.
At night it's getting harder
To laugh when I want to cry.

But soon time will pass
And we'll be together again.
When that time comes
I'll show you how glad I am
That you're my lover and best friend.

Angela Graham

WOO ME ONCE AGAIN

Am I special in any way?
I long for a gesture of worth today.
Please tell me how much, more than
words can measure,
I mean to you, as a unique treasure.
Oh I long for the day, remember when,
You caressed me, cajoled me,
With endearments, and then,
We made thrilling love,
In a state of such bliss
Oh woo me again, with a rapturous kiss.
My dreams are all dying,
Why did romance abate?
Please stir up the embers,
Before it's too late.

Virginia S. Williams

AND SOMETIMES I THINK OF HER

When it's early in the morning
Just before the dawn
And the rain is falling easy
Like the tears I know she cried.

When the world is quiet and still
With not a cloud in the sky
With maybe the wind to whisper
Like she did when she said "Goodbye."

Greg Evans

LOVE'S FACE

The delicate rose, crystal
laden with morning
dew,
unfolds its blood-red
petals fully entrusting
itself to the eyes of
the adoring
beholder and blunting
its thorns to the
hands of the loving
caretaker.
Having given of
itself completely, its
petals — like bone-weary
arms — fall toward the
ground where they are
tread upon by the
feet of those
to whom love will
doubtless never reveal
its face.

Ronald G. Ribble

SPRING THAW

I thought you loved me.
Your eyes branded my heart.
I was yours.

But now, I suffer beneath that gaze;
No fire — no light;
Those eyes betrayed me,
They looked through me — no —
Past me — with cold indifference.

You froze my heart, my love,
And my caring.

But I have lost nothing.
I draw warmth from my spring.
It restores my soul,
And I can still come back, loving.

Valerie Ruth Biddick

I'LL ALWAYS REMEMBER

To Kirby Warren Angell

I'll always remember
the times we've shared;
The places we've been,
how much we've cared.
I'll always remember
your blue-green eyes;
The fool I've been
on my Dr. Pepper "highs."
I'll always remember
the touch of your lips.
I'll always remember
your British accent.
I'll always remember
the smile on your face;
The way I feel
after a warm embrace.
I'll always remember the radio songs;
They spoke to me when I was gone so long.
Though ordinary these things may be,
Yet still they are special, to you and me.

Michelle Campbell

THE GIFT OF LOVE

Love is God's greatest gift to man —
A most powerful force for good.
Love is a positive response —
The source of all brotherhood.

Love is the warmest expression.
It comes straight from the heart.
In life's finest relationships,
Love has an integral part.

Love in the form of compassion
Helps the sick and the elderly.
It brings forth the best in us
To aid those in dire poverty.

Love is joyous and uplifting.
It gives strength and purpose to life.
An outpouring of friendship and love
Performs wonders where there is strife.

Love has the greatest dimension —
An all-encompassing gift.
Love is a wondrous emotion.
It gives the whole world a lift.

Ivan L. Coe

DIARY

Come, read with me the pages of my book,
its dazzling gold
a painting of Angelico's
a leaf torn from a chapter of my life.

Read about the open sea
with golden sand
where we did swim and sport
like dolphins in the waves.

I weave again that dream
of when I lost my heart to you
and never found it more.

Send back my heart
which you did steal that day
when first you kissed me
on my trembling mouth.

Send back my heart
if you are tired of it
so I can tear away this page
and start anew another chapter
in my book of life.

Geraldine Kravis

HEARTS ON FIRE FOR GOD

The phone rang.
The message came.
Form a prayer chain.
The Bethany Sunday School class in
one accord.
Formed a prayer chain in love to
The Lord.
Asking for healing in His Holy Name.
In a few hours the answer came.
The member with the need was our
Assistant teacher Loula Speed.

Rindie Malone

REJECTED

Love can be beautiful, also cruel!
To give all your heart and end up a fool.
Left with memories of wonderful hours
Spent with a dream, in an enchanted time;
When all was ecstasy, and love was blind,
To the many deceits and excuses made,
Fanning the flames, just a game of charades.
Love by one, instead of by two,
Is just a hoax, cruel, through and through.
I wish you luck, and
I wish you joy!
May your heart never ache, or
Feel betrayed, like mine.
You will always be special,
In the fragments of the love you declined.

Gladys H. Case

JOHN . . .

I grasp for words that truly tell my feelings
For a man who's made my life so beautiful.
I yearn to speak all the words of love
And make him see me as his only one.
His face is ever close to me,
His eyes speak softly . . . love.
But he's so far away, I feel the stars are closer.
Yet so close, I could touch him every day.
This gentle, loving feeling within me
Grows stronger with each time I hear his name.
Come to me softly . . . Oh my love . . .
Let me reflect the beauty of your smile . . .
The laughter of your heartbeat . . .
And the wanting of your eyes.

Debbie Ringer

RINGER, DEBRA L. Born: Cape Girardeau, Missouri; Married: 12-4-76 to Honorable John William Ringer; Education: Attending Southeast Missouri State University on a President's Scholarship, Major in English, Minors; Drama and Speech; Occupation: Real Estate Broker, Salesperson; Awards: Mrs. Missouri, 1986; attended Mrs. America Pageant April, 1986, won Most Original Costume; Poetry: 'Do You Care,' *Anthology of American Poetry,* 1985; Comments: *The common themes in my poetry are the deep and almost unspeakable feelings of the heart and soul. I love to use nature and its splendor as metaphors of human thoughts and feelings.*

DREAMING

O, dreaming, if my sleep thou wouldst disturb
  Pray lead me to the beautiful — the fair,
Serenity where nothing doth perturb
  Perfection of another world so rare.

And, should thou give me to the arms of love
  Change thou all mundane thoughts to noble heights,
O teach me, then, that surely from above
  Comes power to 'compass only pure delights.

Do take away the falsity of earth —
  Pretentious and materialistic life —
Grant me wisdom, reveal to me the birth
  Of pristine reason — far from earthly strife.

For, if a new life I should start again,
  May it contain the blessing from the past,
Find its good *in* good that ne'er will wane —
  Confirm that all *real* life is born to last.

O, dreaming, whether slumb'ring or awake,
  Be free, and free *me,* from illusion's thrall,
Lead me to new life, for pure love's sake,
  To dwell in bliss within Truth's all-in-all.

Alfred W. Hicks

A VALENTINE

O and O means one and only
One and only that means you
N L means never lonely
Never lonely when I'm with you.

Heavens are blue — waters are blue
Blue are the days on Monday
Eyes are blue and violets are blue
Without you I'm blue on Sunday.

A marigold is not pure gold
I'll tell you why it glitters
It has a secret to unfold
It loves you till it withers.

And so it goes in this old world
Nothing matters much — evening being clever
Only one thing goes on and on
That's love, real love goes on forever.

Now that I've told you how I feel
I'll be waiting for your answer, dear
Will you be my O and O?
I can hardly wait to hear.

Irma Louise Lowe

ALL LOVE SHOULD BE

All love should be as our love is,
  unselfish and all giving.

All love should be as our love is,
  just happy to be living.

All love should be as our love is,
  a reflection of the Creator.

All love should be as our love is,
  for there is no love greater!

Leanett Loury Smith

SONNET — AMOR PROFUNDIS

All that there is of love we two have known:
The soft, the tremulous yearning which first
Alerted us to recognize the thirst
Of love's desire, to know it for our own;
Then passion came, and sudden secret bliss
Of joys undreamed, of love requited, filled
As is the heaven above with stars, when stilled
Is shadowed night by ecstasy like this.

Gone now the passing doubts, the senseless fears,
Closed are the doors which beckoned us astray.
Love shines the brighter for the cleansing tears
That fell in willful drops along the way.
All that there is of good throughout our years
Is in this love you share with us today.

Conna Bell

WHAT KIND OF LOVE?

Is there a special love you wish to seek?
Maybe stolen love, when you need to peek.
Perhaps traumatic love that's bittersweet,
Or passionate love, in a night of heat.

Maybe love at first sight, for when you meet;
Or a "crush" on love that makes you weak?
Maybe friendship love, so special and neat.
Try romantic love which is really a treat!

Phyllis Bolen-Hofer

BOLEN-HOFER, PHYLLIS JOAN. Born: Athens, Ohio, 2-13-31; Married: October 11 to Gene LeRoy Hofer; Education: Ohio University, 1949-1954; Occupation: Writer, Drama Teacher, Stage Production Director; Memberships: Served by Appointment on the City of Campbell, California Civic Improvement Commission Working with Cultural Improvements; Was Chairman of U.S. Bicentennial for City of Campbell; Poetry: 'Tears of Rain,' 'The Message,' 'Wings,' *New Voices in American Poetry,* 1986; 'Beauty and Hope,' *American Poetry Anthology;* Other Writing: "Angel's Alley," Stage Musical, 1971; Comments: *A poem you remember is a poem that helps you feel, and also makes you think. If the writing tells all, but leaves nothing to the imagination, then it's lost.*

MY VALENTINE

Each time I think about you somehow I know that
your love is mine,
A love that brings us together and a love that'll
last forever in time.
Each year at this time I say this love will
never leave us apart,
And know this love of ours will always be
special in our heart.
Each time I think about you somehow I know that
your love is mine,
A love that'll always grow and a love that'll
always shine.
Each year at this time I say that this love
will never die,
And then I say to you, you'll always be
my Valentine.

Henry Porada

PORADA, HENRY. Born: Milwaukee, Wisconsin, 9-27-57; Single; Occupation: Store Manager; Poetry: 'Here and Now (There and Then),' 4-86; 'Kristen's Friend,' 4-86; 'A Song and Prayer in Mind,' 7-86; Comments: *I dedicate this poem to my friend Jania.*

YOUR LOVE

Oh Lord, let me return somehow, some way,
Part of Your love You've shown me —
Given me.

For,
I love You better than the fingers on my hand —
I love You better than the beat of my heart —
I love You — and owe You — my entire life,
My entire soul, my entire being —
Whether in my past, my present, my future.

Your love pervades me —
Persuades me to follow the path leading me to You —
A path on which Your protection always surrounds me —
A path that I may follow with devotion and love —
Devoting myself — dedicating myself —
To carrying out, as best I may,
Your divine purpose for me —
That of bearing to all peoples, all nations —
The message of Your love for them.

Thank You, oh Lord, for the blessing
Of being allowed to be one of Your messengers.

Dorothy M. Friedman

STRANGERS

Darling, we are but strangers, passing in the night
We live, we love, we long for the morning light.

Could we have only met before our hearts were torn
Just think of the joy and love we could have borne.

I love you, precious one, but it cannot last
'Cause we are the restless ones that must meet and pass.

Oh, if I could only hold you and make you stay
but to you I'm just another love, another song, another day.

But I'll live for this fleeting moment, oh love so sweet
So hold me, kiss and caress me darling when we meet.

Margaret Gulledge Stackleather

WHERE

Where have you gone so suddenly?
To horizons unknown to all men,
Seeking tranquility from silence,
Or looking for diamonds in tin . . .

Don't tell me you've been to the depths,
And found it too tough on your soul,
Or blame it on life's little failings,
Don't make that an only goal . . .

It took a long time to know you,
For you always were timid and shy,
And now that I have finally met you,
I find that you've said goodbye . . .

Pamela Boehme

SO PRECIOUS

I hold this precious gift in my trembling hands
Arms outstretched in offering to you
Daring not to meet your eyes, lest I see rejection . . .
Standing here — my heart in my palms —
The tears in your eyes assure me
That my gift is accepted
And treasured
I love you . . .

Jo Hendijani

OH HOW POWERFUL

Oh how I care, yes, oh how I do,
yes I'm beautifully immersed
in thoughts being with you.
Oh how I miss, yes, oh how I do,
yes how empty I am
when I fail to see you.
Oh how I want, yes, oh how I do,
yes I truly desire what is Godly for you.
Oh how I've never, yes, never is to you,
yes there never has been one who has touched me
like you do.

Oh how I ponder, yes, oh how I do,
yes always I'm wondering if you'll ever love me too.

Michael Durachko

A QUESTIONING

Will you ever let me in your heart again
As quickly as the rushing wind?
Oh love you brought me joy
As in me still's the little boy

Will you ever wish to speak to me as others do?
From heart to heart a love so true
This love's such a mystery
Tinged by shade of blue

We've wandered down a rolling path
Where comfort was a leading role
From worlds apart from each his soul
For thus the rocky path did grow

Please keep me in your heart
Don't ever let me go
For in your heart I hope I know
A love outlasting heart and soul

Michael Steven Levitan

THE GIFT

I will always be there . . .
to sew, the clothes you tear
to wash, the clothes you dirty
to cook, the food you hunger for
to clean, the house you alone are king of
to be silent, when you are tired
to listen, when you need to talk
to rub you, when you are sore
to guide you, when you stray
to hold you, when you need a friend
to wipe, the tears when you are sad,

So my love, I will always be there whenever you need me.

Remember that after all these years, you are still as
young, virile, strong, and as handsome as when we wed.

Our friendship grew into a love to outlast eternity
and beyond . . .

Mary Beth McIsaac

MY BOUQUET

My bouquet has withered and faded away.
I threw it out, only yesterday.
I kept it together as a reminder of you.
So tossing it out was not easy to do.

I couldn't make the fragrance last.
For yesterday's cuttings are now of the past.
The thorns of your cross are left to view.
In given time, they'll pass away too.

Your spirit lifted as the petals dropped.
From laughter to sorrow, my heart nearly stopped.
I'll always love you for your thoughtful way,
Of gathering the flowers to form my bouquet.

Each day I'll go to the garden at noon.
In hopes, new bloomings will come along soon.
And in my loneliness, I'll pick a bouquet.
But it won't match the one you gave me that day.

B. J. Morgan

BY THIS SHORE

My love, so clearly do I now remember —
We walked together
Beside this shining sea,
Leaped from rock to rock
Along the ragged beach,
And gathered shells and seaweed long ago.

Oh, endless, endless is the wild sea's patience —
The same each moment
Yet changing constantly.
Could we have captured
That wild monotony,
How different might have been the years between!
So ardently I wish you were beside me
On this gray morning,
Among these dismal rocks,
That here together
We might understand,
And learn forbearance from the pounding sea.

Genieva B. Pawling

YOU ON MY MIND

While I'm at work — during the day,
My mind does wander, it begins to stray.
To the most romantic place I can find,
As sweet thoughts of you cross my mind.
I dream of us spending time alone,
Miles and miles from the nearest phone.
No one around — no one near,
Just you and I and our love so dear.
I long to hold you in my arms, and love you so tenderly,
As I show you the pleasures, and joy that you bring to me.
You're just what I need, you're the perfect blend,
You're my wife, my lover, and my best friend.
Loving you is the easiest thing I shall ever do,
I just speak what's on my mind — from a heart that's true,
A smile or a hug — the first thing in the morning,
An unexpected kiss — without warning.
From a hug or a kiss — to a kind word or two,
There are all ways of expressing — the love I've found in you.

Richard S. Morton

FOR YOU, CRIS

After a love is lost, what does one do?
Does one mourn as if the love has died?
Or does one continue on,
as if the pain was felt only in a nightmare —
a nightmare that was once a beautiful dream?
You came to me fresh and full of love.
You brought me smiles and opened my heart.
Through you my love, I realized —
that I too was worthy of love;
and capable of loving.
Yet, you were always very honest;
I always knew where I stood,
but I underestimated the force of my love —
the blinding, driving force that moved me,
that urged me on to pursue . . . what?
An elusive shadow that faded in and out of my heart,
and left my soul aching for its presence . . .
So I ask you my elusive bird, my frail wisp of wind —
what does one do after a love is lost?

Denise Y. Westfield

Sing to me in spring
and I will stay by you
with love that sparkles all the year
and never makes you blue
Speak to me in summer
and I will listen dear
to heed your word from dawn to dusk
from year to loving year
Call to me in fall
and I will come to you
and we will share the memories
of spring and summer too
Whisper to me in winter
in our quiet time of life
And I will love you just as much
as in the springtime of our life

Judith A. Lewis

LOVE AND FRIENDSHIP

True love's — often shown through a friendship
Often much more than we feel
True love will stand through thin and through thick
It's genuine, so loyal and so real.

True friendship is knowing, yet loving
Even when *I* am just *me*.
Knowing my good points and bad ones
And in need, standing close by, you see.

True friendship is knowing, yet loving
Even when *you* are just *you*.
Knowing your good points and bad ones
In *your* need standing close by you too!

Pauline A. Fretwell

ROGER

Remember the first days we met, a long time ago
On a hot summer day? We made a friendship
Grow as very few can.
Every once in a while I can
Remember your face, the way you were.

In every person, there is a
Small amount of love
Aching to get out, aching to grow.
Come with me into the bright sunshine and
Know that I am your friend,
Someone you can always count
On, someone always there when you
Need me. Take my hand and be my friend always.

Lisa Jacobson

THE HARVEST

This is truth not fiction, cold and absolute.
The road of your dying was blue. The trees were white.
Discovering your path while I drowned myself in a cold tub,
Easing myself under and playing at death.
Breathy, after rising, my little song
Sung in a cavern of air to myself.
I simply cannot see where you got to.

Janis Gillespie

DRY YOUR EYES

You sit all alone and think of love lost.
Your broken heart was the ultimate cost.
With all of the hurts, love doesn't seem fair.
What a price to pay when all you did was care.
So you cry to yourself and keep wondering why.
I loved him so much, you said with a sigh.
With your eyes full of tears and no love to gain,
You wonder for how long will your heart feel the pain.
It's a lonely pain that most go through.
It hurt so bad when the pain is new.
Though you've been hurt and see no end,
All in due time your heart will mend.
For only time can heal the heart,
So dry your eyes and let the healing start.
Life must go on, though feeling blue.
For you see my friend, I've been there too.
And will all of your beauty, it won't take long.
You'll meet someone and sing a new song.

Raleigh E. Green II

LOVE 'NEATH MY HEART

This tiny little angel, who is lying 'neath my heart,
This act of love, became a part of me from the start,
Each day this miracle just seems to grow.
The most beautiful feeling I'll ever know.
I feel the movement, it's such a thrill
Knowing this angel, a part of me — an Angel so real,
At times the heartbeat is really so loud
As I move ever gently, it moves about.
I sing and talk of many things,
Hoping this angel understands the love it brings.
I cannot wait for that special day,
When I cuddle my angel in a mother's way.
Then I think of angels who are wasted and never see
How glorious it is to be part of a living family.
I pray these little angels who never lie beneath a heart
Be given a chance to fully grow instead of having to part.
Tucked 'neath each mother's heart, these angels do depend
Upon our love — to fully grow — to the very end.

Lee Vendetti Paolella

MOM'S COLLECTING SILVER AGAIN

To All the Mothers of the World

I got a letter just the other day from my brother
It read I was invited to my Dad and Mom's Golden
Wedding Anniversary
Well I haven't seen either one of them for quite a
few years now and when I got there
I noticed the silver in my Mom's hair
I then remembered way back when we were all
growing up, when times got bad and my mom was
collecting silver, but she had to trade it in for
food and clothes for us to wear
So I went up to her and said, "Mom I see you're
collecting silver again," She turned and said to
me in a joking way, "Yes, and there's only one
person I can trade it to."
That's when I got to thinking I should come around
and see her more often before that person decides
it's time for her to trade that silver in again.

Paul H. Engel

WILD FLOWERS

I picked a bouquet of flowers for you
On the way home last night.
Wildflowers . . .
Along the railroad tracks.
As independent and persistent as I am.
As different . . .
As you are.
And yet as beautiful as our love.
Apart from all the rest. Uniquely us.
So different!
You smiled when I gave them to you.
Knowing that our love is as different . . .
As wildflowers.
And as much or more beautiful.
Yet they, like us,
Are as uncertain as the wind.
Each as unique in its own way
As our love is.

Charles E. Lance

AN OPEN WINDOW

She . . . contemplating the immensity of the sky
Standing up near the open window.
Morning stars brighten the environment.
Snow falling over the humid ground
covering it with its white soft blanket
The quietness of the night,
The song performed by wild birds
Wild variety of animals looking for a conservation refuge
that may not exist anymore.
He . . . coming toward her, lovely wife
embraces and caresses her
a kiss of love, exquisite sensation!
reciprocal sensation of love
between husband and wife,
Is it a fantasy or a reality?
Both looked at each other with their sparkling eyes.
Yes, it is a reality
We both are part of it.

Marta Vallin

WHY?

The memories flash on your inner mind's eye.
Quickly they come, and your heart heaves a sigh.
You'll hear the music quietly play.
The music of a lost yesterday.
You'll remember a love, buried deep in your brain.
You'll remember the tears, when your heart filled with rain.
You'll wonder what happened, why it had to be
Why gone is the love that was once you and me.
Life goes on, so great prophets say.
We go on living from day to day.
But when the memories flash on your inner mind's eye,
And the memories make your heart heave its sigh,
When you hear the music quietly play,
And you think of that lost yesterday,
When you remember the love buried deep in your brain,
The shed tears when your heart filled with rain,
You'll wonder what happened and why it had to be
Why gone is the love that was once you and me.

Bonnie Allen Coleman

A LOVER'S ETERNAL NIGHT(MARE)

A better and truer world
could there never be
if darkness prevailed forever
and lovers could not see

their lives would surely change
but would it be for the worse
I think not the case
just steer a deeper course

for if lovers saw before
what sight could not see
then two would live in happiness
their lives eternally

but if lovers saw before
only what eyes could see
then the two would become lost
in the darkness and reality

someday if we are fortunate
to incorporate the mind
the wise saying will uphold
that love is truly blind

Dennis Camire

T-SHIRT AND BAREFOOT SANDALS

T-shirt and barefoot sandals,
Burnt noses, golden tans;
Wishing for an endless summer,
Tape decks playing, painted vans.

Left us early in the morning
Going riding with her friends,
Heard the laughter and the music,
How could this ever end?

Didn't see the car upon them,
Coming through the light so red,
Speeding down, so fast, it happened,
Stealing life and leaving death.

Wasn't ready, but time took her,
When the Big Ben chimed at four,
Now she's gone, the clock keeps tickin'
Won't hear her footfalls anymore.

T-shirt and barefoot sandals,
Grief too big to understand.
Papas — searching through his Bible,
Teardrops walking on his hands.

Betty K. Macdonald

DECEPTION

Beloved,
The hurt I could not bear
I almost ceased to be.
The path, I had to leave
All my secrets . . .
With trees and dancing leaves
Echoing laughter behind me
I dream and breathe of you
My love . . .
False love.

Ellen Malis

MY LOVE

He's tall
He's strong
He's mine

His love is divine
Like really good wine
I love him so much
Just feeling his touch

When he's not near
It's hard not to shed a tear
When he comes to me
My heart leaps with glee

With him, I always want to be

Elizabeth Browning

MILES

Your voice sounds so cold
over the miles of wire.
The words hold no warmth,
you're too far away.
Come close to me now,
I need to hold you.
You once were so warm,
but now you're like ice.
What was it I said
to make you this way?
I hung up the phone
with doubt on my mind.
I'd like to see you
if it weren't for
the miles in the way.

Robin Aylesworth

Time was
I called your name
when held with touch
so sure.

Time is
I scream
to feel
a heart break what
a heart cannot endure.

M. Jacquin

ALWAYS

Love is an emotion that
Every human feels.
I should know because
Only to you do I kneel.

The reason for this
Is because I love you.
This love will never sway.
But oh, how much longer
Will I have to pay?

For you do not love
Me and never will,
But I will love you until
The very end of time.

Patti Morgan

STRANGER

I never wanted you to know
That when you left
You broke my spirit,
Smashing my dreams in a
Million pieces.

You said you'd made a choice —
It was all that you could do —
All right, then, leave
But I won't stop
Loving you.

You can deny it,
But you know your song
is still in my heart
And your face still shines
in my memories.

So, go, if you must,
and I will learn to accept it
I will go on
again
Somehow . . .

Valerie Moreno

LOVE'S DEEDS

Soar, oh brave heart of mine
from slumberous depths
to cloudless heights
'Til love be found anew.

How oft a heart doth plead,
doth weep soft tears
As forsaken and sad
It treads the years.

Years in motion, years unfelt,
Dawn clouds dawn in sameliness
Where a selfish heart can know no bliss
Locked in the loneliness of time.

Though how small the hours, how courageous
the years
When love overshadows all
A touch, a smile, a kindness lent,
These deeds of love, clasp with gratitude,

Make soar this happy heart of mine
For love astounds anew.

Betty B. Jones

Since we have grown
in many ways
Our love gets stronger
with each passing day

My mind is passionate
when I am with you
The feeling we share
that is between us two

Nights are not long
days that go by
Are protected by a love
flourished through time

Lisa Ann Leszczynski

JUST YOU AND I

I could not see you
but I knew you were there
on the hilltop
because I felt your presence near.

I found you hiding, smiling,
behind the old oak tree,
where beneath its friendly boughs
I felt the inner throbbings
of your soul as I was held
tightly, yet gently, near you.

Your strong, yet kindly face
came close to mine.
I saw your eyes, blue-green and clear,
searching deep into mine.

I felt soft lips giving warmth
as they lingered caressingly
upon the lips of mine;
standing there in silent contentment
we loved, and we understood,
just you and I.

Margaretbelle Bonham

SECOND HUSBAND

She felt guilt
at his love,
Knowing herself now barren
and his desire for sons
of his own.

She had known
the glow of parenthood
And had children
given her by a husband
now long dead.

She wanted him
to have that gift
Her love could not give,
the joy of holding his own
flesh in his arm.

His only answer
was that his love
And hers for him
was all the immortality
he'd ever need.

Charlotte M. Edwards

BEGINNINGS/SUMMER 1967

Singer without a voice
Musician without a song
The sleep I ever lost . . .
And then my world became
A silent, moveless orchestra
In naked darkness . . .
Why . . . Where were you then . . .
And now, all the demons
At my side
Are circling in the wind
And falling into place
With me and
My sweet freedom.

Ellen Malis

GIFT OF LOVE

Hushed the garden,
Still the breeze,
Yawning darkness,
Languid trees;
Wretched moment,
Parting nears,
Anguish, heartache,
Wrenching tears;
Bloody sweat
Upon the ground,
Hosts attendant
Make no sound;
Love unbounded,
Love forlorn,
Stalwart soul
Confronts the dawn;
Alone, foresaken,
Tied and led
From out the garden,
In our stead.

Keery Leysan

THE BURNT CHILD

How much do I love you?
Oh, my dear, I feel you're much too late.
There was a time when my heart was free
and I held it out in both my hands,
timidly, tenderly, yet proudly,
for it was a precious thing.
You took it
half touched, half amused,
and held it for awhile.
Then, in a moment of forgetfulness,
you carelessly let it fall.
It shattered into a thousand pieces
but you heard never a sound.
I gathered it carefully
bit by bit
but could never make it whole.
How much do I love you? you ask again.
My reply will always be,
I love you only, — only, my dear,
as much as you love me!

Hester Hayes

TO PAM FROM MOTHER

Words alone cannot convey
The love I feel for you today;
You are so very, very dear
And growing more so every year.
Time spent with you is purest gold;
You're surely made from a special mold;
The beauty of your soul shines through
In every little thing you do.
While hanging pictures on memory's wall;
The loveliest things that I recall
Warming my heart in largest measure;
Are of you, my dearest treasure.
Your sweet, selfless, caring ways
Are like sunshine's warming rays.
Your thoughtfulness in everything;
Unselfishness that seems to bring
Understanding — the quiet fruition
Of an intuitive inner vision.
As blessings pass in my mind's review;
I am so glad God gave me you.

Genevieve Lock Oliphant

FOR DEBBIE'S BIRTHDAY

Sitting here in the park
a breeze blows gently
and I think of you.

I think of your day
soon to be
and I remember
times we've spent
together.

There have been times
we've been through
some pretty rough waters —
and you're one of few
who've stayed beside me,
only to grow closer.

I thank you so much
for allowing me to share
a friendship,
a beautiful one,
one to be treasured
for years to come.

Mary J. Conlon

HAUNTING

I close my eyes
and you appear.
I close my heart,
But it opens wider.
What is this spell
you've cast upon me.

You've come . . .
and you've gone
like the breeze
which twists through the trees.

Now my heart aches
and my mind runs wild.
What is this you've done to me?
Leave me be!
STOP, haunting me!

The good outweighs the bad,
is what you once said to me.
But now you've gone . . .
like breeze,
which sings to me.

Richard G. Hamm

YOU CAN'T NAME A BEAST UNLESS

HONORABLE MENTION

you've had a full description published
in a Scientific Journal, the scholar says.
I may kiss a frog all I want, be foolish,

but before he's proclaimed, it's useless.
Beast, if we hold hands, catch
flies, unnamed, it's not done, I guess.

Let's sun together, bore the voyeur
who doesn't see you.
We've known each other before.

Lois Bunse

LOVE CAME

Love came to me one dreary day,
A poor and broken thing;
I held it closely to my heart
And soothed its ruffled wing.

I tended well its weary soul,
I healed its wounded pride;
It seemed content and so I thought,
To keep it at my side.

It basked awhile in new-found warmth
But on one sunny day,
I opened up the window wide,
And lo! Love flew away.

Elizabeth Leta Hamilton

HAMILTON, ELIZABETH LETA. Born: 4-16-45, Ellis Island, New York; Education: University of Texas at Austin, B.A., 1965; University of California, B.S., 1972; Occupation: Assistant Administrator of International Schools of the Pacific; Memberships: NAEYC, National Association for the Education of the Young Child; New York Literary Guild; Los Angeles Literary Guild; Theatre Guild of America; Peace Links; Awards: First Place Award for 'Moon Magic,' Los Angeles Literary Guild, 1983; First Place "Groogins," A Play for Children, Los Angeles Literary Guild, 1984; Poetry: 'I Shall Remember,' *Voices in Poetics,* 1986; 'Worm,' *Women's Day,* 1982; Other Writings: "Small Life," short story, *Readers Digest,* 1980; "American," short article, *Moscow News,* 1985; Comments: *Poetry and true life stories have long been my best works. Although I often write research works for newspapers and magazines, it is the poetry in my life that lets me be the best artist. In a world where all too often the little things go unnoticed and mankind rushes head long toward self-destruction, it is poetry that still keeps time with the distant drum and writes the history lesson.*

LOVE'S LAUGHTER

On the shore of my tears
I built a retreat
where lonesome memories
float in and meet.

Hopes like driftwood
went up in smoke,
dreams plucked like seashells
whispered, "No hope!"

With ripple of laughter
you wrote on my beach,
your love for me
just within reach.

A smiling stranger
chased all my fears
when you embraced
my seashore of tears.

LaVada Falkner Staff

STAFF, LAVADA FALKNER. Pen Name: Katie LaVee; Born: Miami, Arizona, 3-30-24; Married: to Virgil C. Staff; Education: Paradise Valley School of Nursing, R.N., 1948; Accupressure Workshop, Accupressure Certificate, 1982; Occupation: Registered Nurse, Accupressurist; Memberships: National Writers Club, California Nurse's Association, American Nurse's Association, A.R.E.; Poetry: 'Leaves of Life,' *American Poetry Anthology,* 1985; Other Writings: "From Pimp to Pulpit," Manuscript, 1982; "Domino King," Treatment for Play, 1983; *Feather Ridge,* Novel in progress; *Back Row of Heaven,* Novel in Progress with co-author Christinea H. Morton; Comments: *My writings come from a craving deep within me that must be satisfied. They all vary with my moods, and are inspired by my family members and friends.*

LATER, ALONE

She was hoping
for a smile,
a few warm words, a smile,
casual flirtation, a dance,
to be held in his arms —
to be lost in his arms
in the shadows, in love,
with the music and the movement
and his smile and no one else . . .
but
he
didn't
even
say
hello.

Caryl F. Sheehan

THE SCAR

You gave me a rose once.
I let it fade
Into my potpourri
Of book-pressed flowers.

I tended it for a while,
But lack of time tore me away,
Just as the thorn tore my palm.

Others left a pleasant scent,
While a painful scar was your gift.

Pages of books are rarely turned,
But agony cries often,
From my disfigured hand.

Valerie Ruth Biddick

DARLING PLEASE

You are like a light in
the dark. A friend in the
park. A walk crisp in the night.
You are all these things.
I'll never forget you, no
not yet. You see when I met
you I started new.
If you were my wife
I would just begin.

Jean Arrow

THE DEPRESSION

We always had a lived-in house
Where children learned to play,
With homemade toys and stories.
Read at night by cozy fires and lamplight.
Sometimes we stayed up half the night
Building barns of apple boxes,
For presents for our son.

I still have my old tea cloth,
Made from a sugar sack.
From patterns in the Free Press
I made a farmyard quilt,
With squares from flour sacks.
We didn't have much money
But we had lots of fun.

Susan Schreiner

YOU, IN SUMMATION

You are the lover — sun
caressing me
on some cool October day
when I forget
to wear a sweater.

the wind, clearing a path
straining against
the shut doors.

the hard rain
on the roof
demanding answers.

more than anything
you are the haze that surrounds me
allowing me to revel
in the mystery
called you.

Avis Peel

GOLDEN HONEYMOON

Hand in hand we've traveled
  Through Fifty Golden years . . .
With many dreams unbroken,
  Fulfilled through love and tears.

Wedding bells still ringing
  If just in memory,
Each day that dawns still singing
  Of wedded harmony.

True happiness unending
  These many golden days . . .
A partnership of pleasure
  To cherish for always.

As we so fondly treasure
  These golden souvenirs . . .
May God's sweet benediction
  Bless future Golden Years!

Ruth M. Lommatzsch

A WALK WITH YOU

I walked with you one warm fall day
to a cove of sand known since youth.
We walked the paths and found our way
to the spot of unending truths.

On a log with signs of decay
we sat in the warmth of the sun.
Soft warm breeze caused the trees to sway
over the river's endless run.

Sitting silent making no sound
our troubled worlds left far behind.
The joys together we have found
create future of a new kind.

I know you doubt and need assured
time is the instrument to tell,
do our woes seem only obscured
and our love survives, sure it will?

Terry C. Snyder

HAUNTS

HONORABLE MENTION

Fool that I am,
I'm lured to all
the old places
where dreams were made.
I track ginger-colored sand
in a winter rainstorm,
stand atop a summer hill
where a tortured wind cries.
The bars I seek in the lonely
city are overflowing with
impartial strangers
and too much to drink —
My unsteady feet and misty
thoughts carry me to the park
of russet-turned leaves
and chilled air.
But you're not there. Have you
other haunts now, different
beaches, hills, cities?
You've lost yourself so completely.

Rosa Nelle Anderson

PROMISES NO MORE

I wish you could promise me
That what you say will always be.
But words to you are your possessions
Not to be shared is your obsession.
But as time goes on I shall find
That you could have never been mine.
You live in a world of always tomorrow
That leaves my heart bleeding with sorrow.
You fill my head with promises
That are soon to be broken
Then try to win me over
As if I were just a token.
There are no words that could describe
Of how I feel down deep inside.
I love you so; I always will,
But your empty promises
Are soon to kill.

Linnea Camilleri

THE COLORS OF LOVE

As it approached a gray day
you begged the azure stay
to fill an alabaster urn
with hues of green, yellow,
and brown.
For your name is Love.

You reflect upon snow-covered
hills
bidding winter's chills
to be warmed in part
with sunshine radiating
from the heart.
For your name is Love.

Like the painter Titian
your median
strength lies in the blush
of Nature's rouged brush.
For your name is Love.
Ah, Bluebell!

Roni Bell

CALVARY

Greater Love hath no man than this, that a man lay down his life for his friends.
John 15:13, KJV

Our guide was tired and thirsty,
When he made a scheduled stop,
Outside of Jerusalem City,
Near a rocky, old hilltop.
I left the other travelers,
And slowly walked away,
Hoping to find a quiet spot,
Just to think and pray.
Soon I discovered a cool place,
Where it was calm and still.
I thought about the wooden cross,
Jesus carried up the hill.
It was on this rugged ridge,
That's known as Calvary,
He hung between two thieves,
And died in agony.
With His death He paid the price,
To save my soul from sin,
His life He gave as a sacrifice.
My dear Savior, Lord, and friend.

Shella M. Lucas

AN ETERNAL SPARK

The moon aglow in a white halo
lights the flame for the heavenly stars.
We stop and greet, the moment sweet,
and the night remains all ours.

We sip and dine, toast to our time
underneath the pale moonlight.
We talk and know that love will grow
out of an enchanting night.

As hearts entwine our love does shine
embracing this presence of time.
And when we part I know in my heart
this moment will always be mine.

Christine Schwartz

TO LOVE YOU

For Barry Huber With Love

To love you is to savor the beauty
of your thoughts,
The complexity of your ideas through
the simplicity of my understanding.

To love you is to feel the
presence of your strength,
The security that flows outward
through the stream of your emotions.

To hold you is to feel the meeting
of our senses,
The lovemaking reaching an intensity
through the union of heightened
emotions,
the parting of pain for an instant.

To marry you is to love you with that
intensity that we give to lovemaking,
Through the doubt and pain hidden by us,
and through the blessings given to us.

Deborah Donaldson Mallino

JIGSAW

Today I fell in love with you anew
Mystery vanished as you became the
— missing piece —
to this perplexing puzzle
called life
You filled my senses up
You touched my being afresh
With your sweet love.
The long empty nights
became veiled obscure
memories . . . and
I took my first breath
in months
and drank you in.

Jean M. Chase

OH HAPPY DAY

Oh happy day, when I shall see
The beaming face
Of my Sweetheart, fond and true;
And holding her in firm embrace,
Our parting long delaying,
Shall kiss her lips so tenderly,
And hear them whisper, "I love you."
As now in dreams I often
Hear them softly saying;
While her eyes, so bright and clear,
Seem with love and tenderness to soften
And grow dim with joyful tear.
Oh, what joy I'll feel, what bliss,
When I shall have all this!

George E. Fick

YOU ARE THE MOON

Arms crossed beneath my head,
I lie on gleaming sand
gazing at a sliver of silver light.
The shush of the breeze
and toss of the sea
invade my senses
as I watch moonbeams
dance from crest to crest
and dream of you.

Susan Sands Anderson

LOVERS

Lovers walking hand in hand
Tracks on the beach, in the sand
Beautiful sunset, sinking low
Twinkling stars put on a show

Lovers gazing, eyes sparkling
Cozy room fireplace, fire crackling
Chilled wine, roses and soft music play
Romance is theirs and here to stay

Lovers gave all they had
Through the good times and bad
Keeping the faith from above
But above all, cherishing love

Joseph Boteilho, Jr.

I am and I am not.
I remain
a paradox.

Ruins.
Hands eyes teeth hair
feet lips nose.
Studies: social behavior
a personality.

My Light is you —
I am your food
eat me.
Breathe me in.
I'll go to your head.
Our bed.

James Douglas Morrison

I find myself
Saying, doing,
Feeling things
So wonderful that
I often believe
This is but a dream
That I am privileged
To embody fully and completely.
My Good has been delivered —
And I am truly blessed
To love life with you.

Norma Ann Dawson

Deep in the night she cries
For a loved one lost long ago.
Quietly and softly she sighs
That Fate should will it so.
She sees his face before her
In dreams they once had shared.
She cried and yet was happy
For once he, too, had cared.
She stood beside another,
A solemn vow proclaimed.
She left behind the other;
Left behind the pain.
True to the vow throughout the years,
The pain replaced by bonds much stronger.
Fascination replaced by love,
The love to last much longer.

Patricia S. Mauldin

YOU AND I

The leaf on this tree,
someday will die.
Will part from the tree,
just as you and I.

The red in the rainbow,
someday will die.
Will fade from the rainbow,
just as you and I.

Some say love is forever,
but that is a lie.
Nothing is forever,
not even you and I.

Kelly Grinnell

BUY NOW PAY LATER

Sometimes love tries too hard
and you try to tell her you have time
only she doesn't understand
and keeps trying to protect
you and herself from something
that time gnaws at and
finally eats away (so gradually
that even a wave couldn't explain
how much sand it took)
then while the night nibbles at the
moon you just wonder why and then
quietly (so no one will ever notice)
you put back the stars you took,
alone.

Catherine DeChico

YOU

When you touch me,
You lift my mind,
And I float miles and miles away.
I float away to skies beyond,
And dream of you,
And when I return,
From my distant fantasy,
I find you holding me,
Close in your arms.

Sonya Marlene Dugger

THE SONG OF LIFE

Love is the song of life that brings
The answer to the 'why' of things.
It is a balm to ease our pain,
And blesses like a summer's rain.
Vain pleasures have no pow'r to bind
With fetters to enslave my mind.
My heart seeks only one to share
The secrets I hold sacred there.
My life is like a mystic song
That flows in rhythm all day long.
Life's noble purpose shall enshrine
The unique freedoms that are mine.
If I no longer can be free, —
May it be love that captures me.

Edna Powell Weegmann

SOUNDS OF SPRING

Listen and hear the sounds of Spring,
The flutter of a Bluebird's wing;
Splashing rain in a stream that flows,
Squishing mud between children's toes.

When mountain streams begin to churn,
And tiny Hummingbirds return;
With sounds of every newborn thing,
The world's alive with sounds of Spring.

Sounds of thunder rip and tear,
A quiet night, through April air;
Bringing a message loud and clear,
God's loving message — Spring is here!

Marjorie Kingston Skusa

HUSH MY CHILD

Hush my baby, don't you cry
I will sing you a lullaby,
Hush my sweet, sleep awhile
Mommie loves your dimpled smile.
Hush my dear it's time you know
For you to rest awhile — and so —
I will rock you — oh — so gently
Your beauty shines — so innocently.
Hush my love, I give you my world
With all its beauty, its mysteries unfurl,
May all your days be filled with love
Granting you blessings from above.
Hush sweet baby do quiet be
Sweet love, you are most precious to me,
Hush my sweet, sleep awhile
Hush be still, my baby child.

Lee Vendetti Paolella

MY SON

My heart cries out in pain
As I remember
the beautiful smile,
the laughing eyes,
the busy mind,
the cute things he said,
the way he'd run through the door.
His love for me was infinite.
His love for life
beyond description.
He left us in the winter.
He was so very young.
The memory of his death
still tears my very being.
This little boy
was my son.

Deanna Parker

FIRE AND WATER

I fell in love today!
At least, it feels that way.
My heart is singing wide —
Inviting him inside . . .
To secret recesses,
Loving him with all my senses.

Gwen Cheryl Lyn Sarandrea

ALWAYS THERE

Where do you travel,
when the lights settle down . . .
What do you see
when it is quiet all around . . .
Hold my hand when
I am not there and
always remember
that I care.
For memory is all that is
left . . .
when the passing days soon
become deaf . . .
Know in your heart that I
travel with you,
from yesteryear to tomorrow,
I love you!

Jeff Johnston

PLEDGE OF LOVE

Exposed it is my love for you
How precious is the thought.
No matter what has gone before
Your love is what I've sought.

The beauty of each passing day,
I credit all to you
And even if the clouds bring rain,
Your love shines right on through.

I feel the presence of your love,
It fills my heart to burst.
The sparkle in your lovely eyes,
Excites my life with thirst.

Your touch is always tender
Your smile is always sweet.
It seems that heaven destined
That our eyes would meet.

Oh great this earth and universe,
How close and far the skies.
I am humble near your beauty
And pledge to love you till I die.

William A. Haight

LOVE'S FANTASY

Tender loving thoughts
A bright spring morn
A new day ahead. Another
fantasy.

Memory fades little
when love dies. Reaching
for the sky; finding
reality.

Time obscures one's love
in memory.
Yet, never fading in
fantasy.

Rolling fields of golden
flowers swaying; Soft
gentle breezes. A picture in
reality.

Love lingers, but
only in desperate grasps.
Clinging to
fantasy.

Beverly A. Tadlock

ELUSIVE LOVER

A million wishes
Each one the same.
Arms to hold me
A love to claim.
What is rarer than a heart that's alone?
A lonelier soul finding no one at home.

Come to me elusive one,
I need you to be near.
All that's wanted is a love
That can be called 'Dear.'

Nettie Mcgill McCarrell

LOVE'S TEARING

I know not what is always good.
I cry Abba, as I pick myself out
of the winter dust.
Having taken my heart, and wrapped
it in chains I go to the highest
mountain.
There I throw it off, so no man
can hear my cries.
My spirit prays to God to tear the flesh
and spirit, so the heart may heal.
I pray spring will quicken.
My heart is torn from the very depth
of my soul.
My spirit calls unto God, as my tears
fall to the ground like the rains of
spring, the seed has been planted the
flower grows, as I have grown.

Linda L. Rhodes

CONTINUUM

Two people talking
as momentary
splashes of ocean
wash upon the shores.

Two planets floating
as momentary
splashes of sunlight
wash galactic moors.

Two universes
bending light.
A vacuum,
a silent film
dark as night,
singing verses.

Two people loving
as momentary
splashes upon life's
universal course.

Thirl Michael Butler

NOW I KNOW

Why? Why? I asked.
How could I have known when
I held you, helpless, in my arms
And kissed your satin-petal cheek,
And gently brushed your silken curls,
And felt the grasp of tiny fingers
'Round my grown-up one —
That sometime your anguished cries
Would bleed my heart
And blind my eyes?

What would I have done
If I had known?
Without those stinging tears
And breaking heart so near my own,
Without your hands groping for mine —
We would not fully understand today
A sad tone from a passerby,
Or see the heartbreak in a face,
Or be aware of stifled sigh!
Now, I know — I know.

Dorothy Moore

MY LOUISIANA

Put your hand in mine, and walk by my side.
There are many things I must tell you, if with me you are to abide.
Things about Louisiana, The Louisiana that I love, you too will love its beauty,
and abundance
as you view it with me.
The swamp so mysterious, with its moss-covered cypress, together we will see.
My darling do not be shy, we will build us a home small, but so big with love.
When the moon is bright, we will hear with delight, the call of a dove.
We will smell the fragrance of Magnolias, while we watch clouds roll across the sky.
Our fields will flourish with cotton, and corn.
Autumn will fill to overflowing our barn.
Our children will learn about God, and this wonderful state.
The beauty surrounding them will so fill their hearts with love, that they will never know hate.
Together we will grow old, as we live, and love, holding hands with a firm clasp.
And when we are surrounded with love of our children, and their children, together we will go to glory at last.
Our bodies will rest under Louisiana soil, and on All Saints Day our children will put on our graves, beautiful flowers that bloom during the fall.
the oak tree that shades our resting place, will be spreading and tall.
This my love, will be ours, because we love, each other, and Louisiana so.
And this last we must not forget, but must always remember and know.

Mary Foto

HOW THEY MET FOR MARRIAGE

The subway structure was elevated in that part of New York City.
He stood there at the railing and watched her running to catch the subway every work day for a week.
Then he spoke to her. They rode into Manhattan together in the same car.
The next day he started to tease her about running.
They developed longer conversations and became better acquainted.
Was it the lulling effect of the subway motor sounds on them?
Did the heater effects put them into a sort of trance that they became so likeful?
Was it just something primitive about the motions of her female body while running?
Seeing him in the morning on the way to work she was in very good humor and her days went smoothly.
He was in line for a better job and achieved it.
In six months they were engaged; married a year later and very happy.
She convinced all her co-workers that, run, run, run for the subway was how to get happily married.

Florence K. McCarthy

CROSS

Just to think He gave His life on that cross for our sins, so our lives could begin again
Blessed Mary, mother of Jesus, how deep the hurt to gaze up into the face of your only son in virgin birth
He helped us see, carry all your burdens to the cross that was once a tree
A tree of life for you and me
Everyone has their own special cross in life to bear
Raised in a Christian home, raised six children of my own
Guided them in a special way to follow in your footsteps day by day
We sing of *The Old Rugged Cross* to exchange it someday for a crown
We sing of *The Old Rugged Cross,* and hanging there was the Father, Son and Holy Ghost
We sing *At the Cross, At the Cross* where we first saw the light
The glowing light of His everlasting life that beams us into Heaven above
An angelic light that shows the way as we pray
O Lord we know He was your only begotten Son, Jesus, Saviour, Master that is how it all began
The almighty three in one
Yes Lord, you gave us mountains at times to climb
Precious Lord through you we are climbing them one step at a time

Betty J. Coursey

MAY GOD SEND HIS ANGELS

To my nephew Karl, his wife Jean and family in memory of their son and brother Steven, who was killed when crossing the street. Last picture taken 7/64, age 7 years, 1 month old. Died 9/7/64.

God chose to take your Stevie at the tender age of seven,
May He send His "Loveliest Angels" to lead him into Heaven.

May God send His "Gentlest Angels" to guide you through these days
And ease your pain from sorrow . . . keep you from questioning His ways.

May God send His "Kindest Angels" to help you understand
You've so many friends and loved ones all throughout this land.

May God send His "Most Merciful angels" to comfort you as you mourn
And help you to understand why . . . this piece from your hearts He has torn.

May God send His "Most Loving Angels" to tenderly guide you along,
Because your need is beyond help of men and His Consoling Love . . . is so strong.

May God send His "Forgiving Angels" with a comforting thought for the lad
Who had the misfortune of causing this grief . . . dear God he too, must be sad!

There are many miles between us and we can't be near to say
The sadness that we share with you . . . may our message God relay.

And if in the midst of God's Angels there's a gentle caressing touch
You'll know it's our spirits hovering around . . . because we love you so much.

Lucille Rawling

EROS, LOST AND FOUND

God did not teach us chastity to bind us endlessly,
He gave it to us as a guide so that in Love we might be free,
For as a fish is bound by water and some may say he isn't free,
For he cannot roam outside those bounds and experience the sights
on the land to see,
Yet if the fish were taken from the water then he would surely die,
And if the price for his short-lived freedom is death then the price
is much to high,
The same is true for humans, when we too often lust instead of Love,
When we venture outside the safe bounds God set for us and pervert
what He called Love,
For when man throws caution to the wind and decides to give everything a try,
It only feeds the beast within and makes it impossible to satisfy,
Yet still man tries to fill the desire as he runs headlong into disaster,
Rationalizing that it is acceptable by society, while silently
lust becomes his master,
And though man isn't deserving God forgives us just the same,
And teaches us what true Eros between a woman and a man was
meant to be and forgives us of our shame,
He promises that if we accept his Son and serve Him, the Lord will
teach us self-control,
And reveal to us the beauty of true Eros, when we are loved body,
mind and soul,
So when at times fiery passion erupts into a tempting flame,
And you have a choice to indulge the beast, or to subdue it and to tame,
Remember that you only cheat yourself, when you settle for less than
could be gained,
Because a night of hell-bent passion is really only Love in vain.

Deborah A. Inman

LOVE POEM

Our love is a poem, my darling,
our oneness, a thing of beauty;
it brings color and loveliness
into our lives.
The joys we share, melodious
and sweet,
place us soaring on the wings
of a dove.

You and I — ever complete, whole —
we are love!

Luella Allen

THE CLASS REUNION

Home from the class reunion,
A gathering of our peers;
Greeting lots of old, old friends,
With kisses, hugs and tears.

Time has reduced our numbers,
So we stood in silent prayer;
Honoring a memory,
Of the ones who weren't there.

Now, I see in my mirror,
All the grey that's in my hair;
The extra pounds and wrinkles,
No one seemed to see or care.

As we greeted one another,
Those were unimportant things;
With no impact on the pleasure,
That the sight of old friends brings.

So, may we all remember,
The things that give most pleasure,
Are Life and Love and Children,
And Friendships that we treasure.

Marjorie Kingston Skusa

ENGAGE

Recalling delights
of Leningrad nights,
and the scent of fabled Tashkent;
Let's defect, and move there with me.

Perhaps you remember
Indonesian splendor,
or Tahiti's sensuous sea,
Let's depart, and fly there with me.

Reflecting the mass
of Morocco's good grass,
and the sunlit shores around Spain;
Let's embark, and sail there with me.

Consider the sights
of great Alpine heights,
with the Black Forest spread out below;
Let's entrain, and go there with me.

Recalling ecstatic
our LOVE, brief and frantic,
boiling over whenever we met,
Let's engage, you'll love it with me.

L. Elcan Walker, M.D.

A LITTLE GIRL'S DEVOTED LOVE FOR HER DOG

When I was a very little girl about six
Someone gave my father a puppy for me.
My mother wasn't very happy, puppies are full of tricks.
It was hard for mom to train the puppy, but she felt it had to be.

We named him Dewey and as he grew, I played with him so much.
He looked after me, I wanted to visit grandfather, I thought I knew the way,
As we walked I had my arm around Dewey's neck — he liked my touch.
A man came along, asked us where we were going — Dewey growled at him, he didn't stay.

By this time mom missed us, she had an idea where we might be.
We didn't get very far, she soon caught up with us, kissed me and patted Dewey —
But she also scolded me — she was frightened we might not see
The cars as we crossed the streets not knowing what we were doing.

A lady down our street didn't like animals — she put some poison on bread
And left it in her back yard, many animals ate some — my Dewey became very ill,
He had spasms, they put him in the back entrance — crying I would go to the window in the shed,
And Dewey would try to lick my face, then cry looking sad wondering why I didn't pet him still.

No one had a car to take Dewey to a doctor, so mom quickly took me to stay with a friend
While someone called the police — they came to see if they could help.
My doggie was so very sick, the police took him — telling mom he was near the end.
I loved him so very much, my heart was broken, I never wanted another dog for myself.

Mildred A. Martin

LOVING MEMORIES

Kim was a beautiful and loving girl-child,
Given to us from God for awhile.
She filled our lives and hearts with her love
Then returned to her Heavenly Father above.

But she brought joy and love to our busy world,
As she became a lively and loving teenage girl.
She had a smile for everyone she met,
And a heart filled with love, but yet;

She had such a short time to spread it around,
As she bounced through life barely touching the ground.
A mischievous child spreading jelly on the wall,
Emerging into a beautiful young lady standing straight and tall.

She cared for and loved her fellow man,
And when needed, gave an unselfish helping hand.
Now don't get me wrong, she had her faults,
Criticizing, condemning, and just 'plain talk.'

But when friends or family needed love and understanding,
Kim was there with her love and support undemanding.
She was a ray of sunshine in our lives for seventeen years,
And we will always remember her with love, happiness, and a lot of tears.

Patsy Youree

I STAND ALONE

I stand alone, in the middle of the crossroads not going forward neither backward.
I stand alone, at the halfway point of a mountain never fearing but never not
Being completely unafraid. I stand alone, not hating or loving but always being.
I stand alone in this world, fighting to be, wanting to be.
I stand alone, in the presence of God, and I know that this is the way it will be
On judgment day. I stand alone, in this crazy magical world.
I stand alone, without you, or anyone else.
I stand alone, seeing but not believing, giving and not taking.
I stand alone, it is a deeply sensitive motive that keeps me this way.
I stand alone! the proud fool exclaimed.
I stand alone in this broken heart, I stand alone.

Todd R. Allen

I WISH YOU LOVE

i wish you love.
love to be loved.
love to love me.
love to work together for
　our happiness.
love in many, many, many
　other ways.

Alonzo Davis

JOURNAL

My new notebook has flowers
smothering the outside
and clean, waiting paper —
thick, anxious, smooth.
As I begin, I think of the wind
　and the shattering cry
　of lost summers.

Christine Janz Taylor

WEDDING BELLS

The bells have rung for you, and you.
The aftermath of true love. Remembering
the first eye contact, that brought you
closer to her heart. Each day will
bring a spell, as you share your joy
with. Love to her. Love to you.
Hearing the birds whistle out the
tune. One thing is sure love is pure.

Albert F. Carol III

Fearing the nearness
Clutching the stillness
Air in its thickness
　　Strangles silently

Blood flow pounding
Senses close surrounding
Culminates astounding
　　A kiss so tenderly

Eileen A. Johnson

Wasted hours
Begin the count
And realizing accumulation,
　Astonished
Time so quickly moved
But decisions bogged us down
　And like Alice's Red Queen
　We ran and ran —
　　to stay in the same place.

Eileen A. Johnson

MUSIC TEACHER

You played on the keyboard of my heart
(And tickled my ivories, of course!)
Enriching my soul with a song,
Awakening the melody of love,
And making my solo a duet.

James Collett

So many times, I think of you; so many times,
I wonder how you feel about me. We're two
different people from two different worlds.
And yet, I feel closer to you more than anyone else
I have ever met.

I love you with all my heart but am afraid to
say how I feel; afraid to show any signs of
emotion. I'm uncertain of your love for me.
I feel your love is only in friendship, where
my love is deeper than friendship. My love
is a wish to spend my life with you.

Rachel Wallace

"WEATHER" OR NOT?

Sparkling drops of rain
Cling to my lashes
Crisp snowflakes find their way into my heart
As a bolt of lightning flashes

A storm brews within
Twisting and turning my insides
Feelings thrash in an attempt to live
But several yield to the assault nearby

The gravestone of my heart
Is where all these feelings lie
Squirming and crying with tears
Holding on, trying not to die

I gasp as darkness arrives
Leaving a frozen layer of snow
Destroying my remaining love
Stealing away any warmth that might flow

Sometimes I feel like just giving up
But maybe someday the sun will remain
And just maybe someday you'll join the sun
Then life would have so much left to gain

Pamela A. Watkins

JUST ONCE

A cold wind blew in my heart,
And you chased it away.
I was an empty house,
Whose people had all gone to stay.

My life was empty, and barren, and old.
You came along — and behold !
I'm warm — I'm happy — I'm young and gay!
Oh, please, dear God — don't take it away!

I know it can't last forever — but just for a while,
Let me warm myself at his smile.
Let me feel loved — and safe — and wanted — and young.
Let me feel carefree — let lovesongs be sung!

Who cares if it really is a lie?
Who cares if the storm is only a sigh?
Who cares if this tingle I feel in my heart,
Is only a flitter — and not very smart?

Who cares if it's only a dream,
A castle in the sky?
I want, so desperately, to feel loved —
Just once — before I die.

Helen Paschall

IN MEDITATION

I feel at peace, secure in my isolation
Near the pond at the edge of the woods.
The pond-lilies are frost-blackened,
And the dark-winter water covers all the
Inhabitants of the brown looking pool.
My breath making smoky puffs in the cold air
As I stand quietly meditating here.
I close my eyes and am reminded of a similar day,
When the admission of your sweet-warm love
Drove all the cold and bleakness away,
Before the brevity of time stole our happiness.
Now my memories stretch before me
As a wasteland empty without your caress.
As my gaze travels over the dark surface
Of the pond, I see the blackened pond-lilies
And the quiet hush of the woods beyond,
My heart is aware though I stand here alone
Your presence is with me, you have not gone.

Lillian E. Fleming

FOR THE DURATION

I promised to stay for the duration,
But that was before the doctor told me how short the duration
might be.
You've started a forest fire that is out of control.
Something else in my body is also out of control.
Mr. Death is going to put out our blaze.
He is more capable than my tears,
And like the candles which go out on a birthday cake
after the wish,
He'll see that I'm extinguished.
I'll be like our romantic fire in my fireplace before
which we sat dreaming — reduced to smoke and ash.
You, who brought the spark by bringing roses and
chocolate just because I had a headache,
Are finally here to assemble the fragments of my heart.
My searching is over, but now your search will begin
when I'm gone.
Will you ever find me again?

Melody Ocheltree

LETTERS

Peacefulness overtakes my body and thoughts
as I reread your letters . . .
My heart aches to be with you always
as I reread your letters . . .
Tenderness and loving caresses I want to give you
as I reread your letters . . .
To lie next to you, my body yearns for
as I reread your letters . . .
My love for you grows even stronger
as I reread your letters . . .

Oh luv, the pen is mightier than the sword
Objects or persons can harm one physically
but . . .
As long as I can read your letters of
love I know . . .

Your love will overtake my hurt.

Sharon Bell-Ortiz-Archer

LOVEST THOU ME?

"Lovest thou me?" asked the Lord.
Christ invited Peter to seek the truth
and answer.
The Master probes his followers, also, to
make them conscious of the connecting link.
Is love the right word for it, the right name
for that which relates us with Christ?
Is it love, and not impulse, or fancy, or a
sense of duty?
The one surety Christ gave his apostles in
the care of the sheep was love.
Christ rested the future of his Universal
Church on
Love of the Father, love of the Son, and
love of the brethren.
Yes, love is the right word. Christ the Lord
was conscious of eternal love,
Love of God the Father and love of all the
human race. Yes, love is the right word.

Carolyn T. Abbot

DONNY
HOW MUCH I LOVE YOU

I'll catch you a star. Give you treasures from lands afar.
I'll be your lover, your liar and friend.
I'll fight an army of ten thousand men.
I'll carry your burdens without a word.
I'll tell you things you've never heard.
I'll please you and tease you if that's what you'd like,
I'll take you riding on my bike.
I'll paddle while you just sit. When I get tried, I won't
complain a bit.
I'll cook and clean, do all the chores, when you come home,
I'll greet you at the door.
I'll bring your slippers, fix your bath and if you want,
I'll wash your back.
I'll turn on the T. V. to whatever you'd like, I'll adjust
the sound if it isn't just right.
I'll turn back the covers when you're ready for bed and
I'll love you until you're half-dead.
With pleasure, of course, for that's all I know, to love, please
and satisfy, don't you know?

Tommie Howell Mooneyhan

A LITTLE PIECE OF LAND BY THE SEA

A little piece of land down by the sea
My father and mother left for me
It brings me, God, closer to Thee,
When I remember they gave it to me.

A little piece of land by the sea,
I believe God traded them for a cloud or two, Mom and Dad.
Dad on one and Mom on the other,
And every time they get together they wash off my
Little piece of land by the sea.

Now just the other day
A builder came to me,
He wanted to know what I wanted for it;
He said that's too much.

So I'd rather trade it on a big old cloud
Than see him do to it what he wanted to do.
A big office building filled with foam;
I said the sea would cause some prettier foam of its own.

Paul H. Engel

I HAVE AN EMPTY HOUSE NOW

When the trees are bare and the grass is brown,
the birds not singing and my flowers asleep,
this makes my home very empty.
GOD has sent HIS words of preparation for
a new season.
HE is whispering the changes
in the fast falling leaves.
GOD is touching the face of HIS earth with frost.
The paleness of the winds will come
and shed my life colors.
Yet, the new colors will be clean and pure, too.
I'll walk upon white, see gray, feel warmth
only in a red glove.
Take my hand, feel my hope;
give to me your newest season.
Let us smell the air
as it comes by the sleeping animals.
Let not your home be empty, as mine is.
Envision as I will, a dancing butterfly,
a quiet breeze, a hand of GOD
soon banishing all emptiness.

Charlotte Bell

MY WISHES OF HAPPINESS AND LOVE

My wish is happiness and my wish is to be loved.
I wish my wishes became a miracle and not too long.
Please Lord, I'm in pain — a hard life.
I want a love and happiness to be
available and feel cared for.
I do not want any more tears but . . .
Sometimes it is good to cry.
I want happiness and love. I need them.
I have material things and I am proud of it,
But money can't buy happiness and joy or love.
No friend or a special relationship to
share my sorrows, happiness, understanding
commons, sharing and enjoys with — and
a good man.
Always alone and feel "unwanted."
Sometimes I am afraid — one day
I will go crazy waiting, for wishes too long.
Lord, I'm so hurt, so in pain.
I'm so young. So in pain and crying.
Lord, I'm in pain and crying.
I know Jesus loves me and is in the heavens.

Lori Ann Allen

BEDROOM PRIMEVAL

HONORABLE MENTION

Who but you would tolerate a jungle
for a bedroom such as ours the plants make
hanging in their planters from a doubtful ceiling
and intruding on our reading lights
from pedestals in every shallow corner . . .
no worse than panty hose and bras
without design the plants have,
hanging from the shower rod and tired coat hangers
holding skirts and sweaters, hooked on doorknobs
with uncounted housecoats finding permanence
in residence in chairs . . .
but if I could find you without searching
through the *mise en scène,* and you could find me
standing out like a ten penny nail on a bare wall,
love in our adapting nakedness, however primitive,
wouldn't be half as promising.

Gene Lominac

A HEART THAT CRIES

There is a heart inside of me that holds a lot of pain
The cry inside is deafening to the one who takes the blame
The precious thoughts I keep inside are deeply stored away
No one in this lonely world should have to feel this way
The tears are full of many things, but most of all of fear
Fear that all I'm fighting for will bring me endless tears
I want to hold on tight to the one I love so much
Hold so near, Never let go, Feel secure with just one touch

Christy Kinser

THE GREATEST OF THESE IS LOVE

Love is a gift we all receive the moment life begins
But to each one is given the choice,
To nourish and so let it grow
Or to neglect and let it die within.

Whatever other gifts we may develop
If ministry of love we have not learned
It matters not if we can move a mountain,
Or even give our bodies to be burned.

Love sees in each one's solitary face
The beauty and uniqueness that is there,
It matters not the origin or race
But that there's need to show concern and care

Thy love holds fast to its convictions
Of faith and creed, the God as each sees best,
Love frowns not on another man's religion
Or ridicules to him what's sacred, blest.

Love knows each sunrise is but God's "Good Morning"
The darkness after sunset His warm blanket of "Good Night."

There is no greater love than this
To lay down one's life for one's friends.

Doris Phillips

ABUELITA

Why is it that they love her so,
this weatherbeaten silent one,
who serves and seldom speaks?

At first, two arms reached out for me.
A cheek reached forward, brushed against my own.
A loving tear appeared, in her eye, then in mine.

Her son, my husband was what we shared,
and neither of us knew him well.
Sometimes, we thought we did, but NO!

We had our dreams for him, yet nothing we could do,
would change the dreams he had of his own.

I took his little girl she'd raised,
to another land she'd never see.
For the sake of love, she let her go,
to find the way to a better life,
perhaps, a life of prosperity.

Whispering prayers throughout the night,
she tried to fill her emptiness with love,
and in the morning, once again,
we embraced and said, "Goodbye."

Judith Nass Gonzalez

LOVE CAN

Love can conquer any difficulty,
Love can heal all disease —
Love can open any door,
Love can, *enough love,* can do all these!

Love can bridge the deepest gulf,
Love can throw down any wall —
Love can redeem the biggest sin,
Love can, *enough love,* can do them all!

If only you could *love enough,*
And know your strength, unfurled,
You would be the happiest person —
Most powerful being in the world!

Nella Thompson Meiser

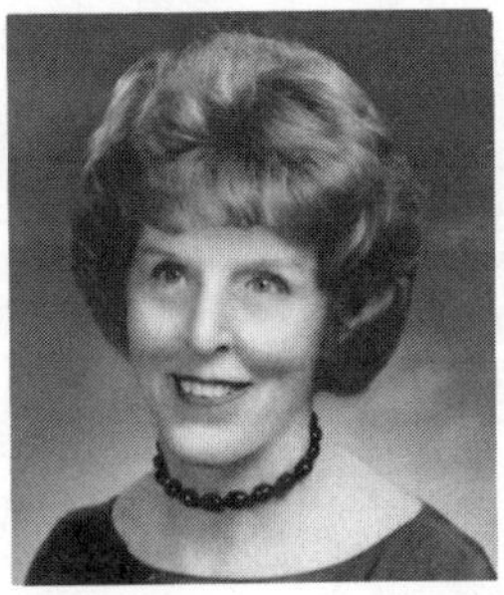

MEISER, NELLA LEE. Pen Name: Nella Thompson Meiser, Nella Rose Lee; Married, three children: Shirley, Larry and June; Education: High school graduate; art and elementary education training; Southeast Missouri State Teachers College, Cape Girardeau, Missouri; Oregon College of Education, Monmouth, Oregon, B.S. and Teaching Certificate; Portland University, Portland, Oregon; Portland Teachers College, Portland, Oregon; Occupation: First Grade Teacher; Poetry: 'Home,' *American Poetry Anthology,* 1985; 'At the Break of Day,' 'It's Bedtime Way Out Here,' *Masterpieces of Modern Verse,* 1985; Comments: *I love to live! I love to know that I have helped and can help put stars in the eyes of little learners and let them find ways of their very own to reach happiness and success, as they grow and bloom along in school work — so that in adult life they can find their very own happiness and count their blessings every single day. I love to write. I love to express!*

REFLECTIONS

As I watch our reflections entwine in the mirror of time
I forget about tomorrow and the pattern of banalities.
You are mine, I am yours, we are one.

Mary Annah Alemán

A ROMANTIC DESERT SCENE

If we were to run to each other,
Smiling; arms outstretched; in slow motion,
It would be through a field,
Of cacti.

Why do I remember cacti?
Cacti and your eyes; sky and hills,
Misty blue backdrop.
Your face a hazy setting for
Your eyes.
Green eyes; and the sharp spiny outline,
Of some Euphorbiacean giant.
I have a photo of that spine.
Somewhere.

I try to recall the beach at night.
We wandered; sandpipers raced ahead;
In darkness, white bellies shining.
I see cactus spines when I
mean to remember warm embrace in
Moonlight. I held you a moment;
It was like hugging a cactus.

Kathleen Fitzpatrick

A LITTLE HELP FROM YOU

I was trying to get free
From the power you had over me
I was trying to save my heart
To keep it from falling apart
I tried to stay away
But I longed to see you every day
I was trying to start out new
I might have made it with a little help from you

I tried to call a friend on the phone
But each time I called you weren't home
I could sit and write a poem or two
But whenever I did they were all about you
So where do I go when there's nowhere to turn
I thought by now I'd finally learn
But I sit back and wait and think of you
And hope someday you'll love me too

I've heard that love is a two-way street
Somewhere in the middle we're bound to meet
I need some help to make it through
I may just make it with a little help from you

Janette Martin

FIGURE IN FRONT OF A MANTEL

(Painting by Balthus)

I see her when I come into my room,
My lady, fresh as a rose in full bloom.
Hair flowing softly, gently to her waist,
How sweet it would be her warm lips to taste;
Embrace her, stroke her silken hair. My hands —
A soft brush to smooth her delightful strands.
I see her there. If only she were real.

I know a lady real, and in my zeal
I love her; I ache for her union kind,
For her embrace, for her to know my mind.
Her hair flows too, falling gracefully down,
Her beautiful locks should deserve a crown.
Her voice is soft, so delightful to hear.
She's sublime. I'd want her forever near.
If she would but know me, our bliss complete,
Both she and I, loving, our hearts replete.

My lady in the painting, will she show
Love, or the true lady I long to know?
I, the utter fool, I know neither will.
So alone, in love, until I am still.

Gerald M. Quinn

SUBMITTED FOR YOUR APPROVAL

Why do you scream at me
When all I try to do
Is make you, just once, proud of me
In anything I do.

I work so hard to make you smile
When you think that I've done well.
I try my best, but all the while
All my wrong you tell.

You never seem to look at me
As someone with a heart,
And every time you speak to me
You tear my world apart.

Never are you satisfied
With anything I do
You never seem to realize
That everything's for you.

Kelle LeCompte

Dedicated to Dan

Forever
the waves
go on,
washing all
the seashells
to shore,
So many things
need answering to.
Like
young love
too many things
are neglected, the
time just goes
too fast.
I only wish
my love
was like the waves
going on
Forever and ever

Dina DiLucente

LOVE

Love is the greatest gift;
Share your love each day.
Love can transform your life
And take your fears away.

Love can lift your spirits
When you are feeling low.
Love can chase away the blues
And help each soul to grow.

Love can forgive and forget
The hurts along life's way.
Love can give you courage
And strength to face each day.

Love can give you inner peace
And take away your strife.
Love can brighten up each day
And bless you all your life.

Margaret Nevins

DOESN'T SOMEBODY WANT A FRIEND

So many lonely voices each day out on the street . . .
Sometimes a lonely stay-at-home, where no face he will meet . . .
Lonely souls on the bus and train, all going their own way,
Going to school or work, just to find one more busy day.
Lonely voices in the city sound just like a child,
And many, from fear and despair, hit the streets and go wild.
Lonely young people, disillusioned and going astray.
Guys and girls, young and old, afraid but too ashamed to pray.
How often would I share my love for them if I just could.
Yet they take all my deeds for evil, through they're meant for good.
I'm hoping, praying, trying, my love to share and send,
Out there in the cold world, doesn't somebody want a friend?

Edwin Hayes

OUR CHRISTMAS CALENDAR

On our first year of Christmas, he gave me true love;
On our second year of Christmas, I gave him true love;
On our third year of Christmas, he gave me sweet perfume;
On our fourth year of Christmas, I gave him aftershave cologne;
On our fifth year of Christmas, we had a little Christmas tree,
with mistletoe,
And candles were all aglow.
On our sixth year of Christmas, he gave me the plan to our home;
On our seventh year of Christmas, we moved into that home.
On our eighth year of Christmas, he gave me a motor-car;
And we thought about the years that were gone, and we thanked
our Lucky Star.

Vivien C. Patrick

LOVE THAT NEEDS TO SCREAM

When you say I can't love you
I want to scream
I want you to see the real me
The one who has to have you
I absorb your attention
As it gives me light
And rejuvenates the love I feel
You stir up every emotion in me —
And you make my head spin
As you take me 'round and 'round
on a never-ending merry-go-round
ride.

Charlotte J. Dusenbury

A SADLY LOST LOVE

Standing by his silent love,
It pained for him to see,
Her face that was so pale and wan,
For life was gone indeed.
Death had been so sly and quick,
That nothing could be done,
It had taken 'way the girl,
Which had been his only one.
Yet she was still as lovely,
As she had been when alive,
And as she lay there still and cold,
In his heart, she would not die.

Candace James

CRYSTAL COLORED GARDEN

The Garden, but with such coloration;
The lane, but with such narrowness;
Call to mind your wide sea-like winking eyes.
Call to mind your long, your trailing locks.

The bluish breast of water;
The bright torso of clouds;
Call to mind your slender opened fingers.
Call to mind your long, your trailing locks.

The wind, but with such astonished-whirling;
The clouds, but with such tears weeping;
Call to mind your rose-bed's mystical whisper.
Call to mind your long, your trailing locks.
and you lay on my lap.
When you fall to sleep upon my lap;
my heart wants to break camp because of your yearning
my heart wants to stir faint embers with your love
and my heart jumps away from the grief of this futile world.
lift your feet gently gently; your doe-like feet.
Rest your hands upon my shoulders; your moonlight hands.
Take my arm for the paths have become silver.
Lift up your crystal neck; your peacock neck.
Stroll through the paths of my veins
open, open your eyes; your wide sea-like eyes
Glance through the paths of my veins gently.

"O, moon tongue-silencing, deceiver;
O, spy, charlatan and tricker;
You in that azure harvest are;
Like a farmer guarding the kitchen-farm;
Like a gardener overlooking the melons;
She and I belong to one-another.
All night long till dawn;
in the paths of hope;
in the garden-lanes of fruition;
we are following each other;
O, moon may your eyes be blind.
and your mouth be sealed
Oh, my supreme rose, my tender fruit;
Oh, my verdant fortune, my heart's pride.
My heart beats deeply inside,
The spider of your sadness;
spins its web within my soul.
Proclaim, cry out. Cry out and shout.
You and I are enemies of every Janus-face
You and I are one, are one-another.
Oh, honey of all my life;
embrace me with your lips
The lover says to another lover:
Look at my stature, my goddess appeal
and the others say to the others:
Look at their stature, and goddess appeal
The mountain says to the valley;
Look at them, such fondling and coquetry,
Oh, my beloved:
that mountain is for you.
The valley of grief is for me.
The youngsters call out: call out and shout:
boys! Just look:
The two of them are Romeo and Juliet"

"Oh, my sweetlipped beloved and joyous;
Oh, you are coquettish and a fanning peacock;
Oh, my world angel faced, flower of fondling;
Oh, your breathing is fragrance with colored rose of wishing;
You and I belong to one-another.
All night long till dawn;
In the paths of hope;
In the garden-lanes of fruition;
we are following each other.
The lanes are so narrow, too dark.
The paths are so silent, too tight
All of them are enemies of our souls, bodies.
Not only your (Bidar) screams;
but whole cities are calling out; calling out, they shout.
The garden, but with such coloration;
The lane, but with such narrowness;
Call to mind your wide sea-like winking eyes
Call to mind your long, your trailing locks.

The bluish breast of water;
The bright torso of clouds;
Call to mind your slender opened fingers.
Call to mind your long, your trailing locks."

Dr. Sayid A. F-Bidar

F-BIDAR, SAYID A. Born: Shadigan, Iran; Single; Education: University of Jena, Doctoral Degree, East Germany, 1980-81; University of Tehran, M.S. Degree, Tehran, Iran, 1972; University of Tehran, B.S. Degree (Equivalent), 1971; Occupation: Professor of Comparative Languages and Literature, University of Oran, Oran, Algeria, 1979-1981; Memberships: Iranian Psychiatric Society (Psychotherapy Experience), Persian Literary Society, Arabic Literary Society, Islamic Research Society, Middle Eastern Studies Association, International Union of Scholars; Selected Writings: 'Geryeh Sar Kon,' (Weep Aloud), *Negin Magazine,* Tehran, 1968; 'Marg-e Bahar-e Adamiyat,' (Death of the Spring of Humanity), magazine of Pezeshki-ye Qanuni, Tehran, 1969; 'Falsafa-ye Inqilab-e Hosain,' (Philosophy of the Hosain Revolution 680 A.D.); Persian and Arabic poetry and essays, publisher, Farahani, Tehran, 1972; 'Sarkhat Al-haq' (Outcry of Truth), poems in Arabic, magazine of Al-Ikha'a, Tehran, 1974; 'Fi Qalb Al-ma'Rakah' (In the Heart of Battle), poems in Arabic, Al-Tahrir-Al-Thaqafi and Al-Najaf Magazines, Iraq, 1969. Unpublished works include several volumes of poems in Persian, Arabic and English; In-depth work and research on the Historico-Political geography of Khuzistan, Shadigan, Kordistan and Loristan (Iran), 8 volumes in Persian; *Farhang-e Bidar, A Persian Prescriptive Glossary with Equivalents of Standard Modern Persian, Arabic, English, French, German and Polish;* Research in comparative Persian/Arabic prose and poetry in the Institute of Oriental Studies at the University of Heidelberg. Participated in the International Literature and Poetry Conferences in Prague, Chekoslovakia, 1979, and in Warsaw, Poland, 1976 and 1978.

IRONY

I saw a bird with a
wounded wing.
I wrote a song that
didn't sing.
I heard a voice that
wasn't mine.
I felt a heart that
wouldn't pine.
I dreamed a dream that
was not for me,
And longed for a love
not meant to be.

John T. Milton

LOST LOVE

I will wish upon a star,
In the hope you'll tell me
Where you are.
I miss you more
Each passing day
And hope you'll come home,
To stay, one day.
I will leave my heart wide open,
I will leave the door ajar,
And if ever you wish to see me,
I'll be there for you,
Once more.

Karen Hache

I'll sing to you a song from the heavens where I dream.
I'll sing of yellow daffodils and forests of intertwined trees.
I'll sing of distant box cars and rain that gently falls,
Clouds of apple blossoms and drifting silver swans.
I'll sing of purple sunsets that cast an orange glow,
And stars that seize the shadows off newly fallen snow.
I'll sing of noiseless wind chimes that sway through breathless air.
I'll sing of looking glass waters, I'll sing of deserts bare.
I'll sing to you a song, from the heavens where I dream.
I'll sing of yellow . . .

Angela Hope Miller

MYSTIC

I wake in the wee hours of the morning and reach for you,
Remembering the Love we shared in each other's arms, just a few hours ago.
Then I realize you are gone, stealing away in the cover of darkness.
Your scent is still on the pillow and your presence is everywhere.
I try to close my eyes and drift back to sleep, but I know you're
out there alone, driving in the snowy darkness on your way.
My thoughts and love follow you wherever you go.

Arlene C. Baker

MY LITTLE GIRL

The smile on her face
Happy and peaceful since birth
Baby Mercedes

Lisa A. Kerechanin

1521

D

E

F

G

H

I

J

K

L

M

N

O

P

Q

R

S

T

U

V

W

X

Y

Z